**The 1979
Dow Jones-Irwin
BUSINESS ALMANAC**

The 1979 Dow Jones-Irwin BUSINESS ALMANAC

Edited by
SUMNER N. LEVINE
State University of New York
at Stony Brook
and Editor
Financial Analyst's Handbook

Executive Editor
Caroline Levine

DJ-I **DOW JONES-IRWIN** Homewood, Illinois 60430

ISBN 0-87094-179-8
Library of Congress Catalog Card No. 76–53629

Printed in the United States of America

1 2 3 4 5 6 7 8 9 0 K 6 5 4 3 2 1 0 9

Preface

This edition of the *Dow Jones-Irwin Business Almanac*, like its predecessors, provides a handy source of useful but widely scattered information on business, economics, and investments. Included in this edition is a comprehensive summary of the 1978 Energy and Tax Legislation. The section on "Doing Business in the Near East" has been extensively revised. Many of the tables, addresses, and phone numbers have also been brought up to date.

We wish to express our appreciation for the many helpful comments received from our readers. We welcome further suggestions. Please write:

> Business Almanac
> P.O. Box 116
> Setauket, NY 11733

We acknowledge the splendid cooperation of the many organizations which provided the material contained herein.

January 1979   SUMNER N. LEVINE

Contents

Contents

Business in Review

Mary McNierney Grant

January 1978

3 Leading indicators fell 0.2 percent in November, but government economists continue to express tempered optimism about the economy in 1978. Many see moderate increases in economic growth and inflation but little change in joblessness or the foreign trade gap.

Eastman Kodak will boost prices 3–7 percent this month on a broad range of photographic films and some photographic equipment. Fuji Photo Film's U.S. unit also announced price rises of 4–7 percent on films and cameras.

Coal contract talks between the United Mine Workers (UMW) and industry operators broke off on December 30, 1977, almost assuring that the 29-day-old walkout will last at least through mid-January.

Treasury notes and bonds are trading at about seven points less than their prices at the beginning of 1977. For 8 percent notes of 1986, the paper loss has been about $532 million on the issue's $7.6 billion outstanding.

4 Steel price "triggers" to detect cut-rate foreign dumping in the United States were partially listed by the Treasury Department. Still unclear is the list's effectiveness, which depends partly on additional trigger prices, and partly on importers' ability to circumvent the system and on U.S. steelmakers' acceptance of the system. U.S. trade negotiator Robert Strauss will go to Japan next week for another round of trade talks. This announcement was seen as a sign that the Japanese are ready to make further concessions to correct their large trade imbalance.

The value of the U.S. dollar resumed its slump by hitting record lows against the West German Mark and Swiss franc and the lowest levels in almost 22 months against the British pound and French franc. Gold's price jumped $4.25 an ounce to $169.20 in London.

The stock market got off to a bad start for 1978 as the Dow Jones Industrial Average dropped 13.43 points to 817.74, its second sharpest decline since July 1977. Trading was sluggish. The American Stock Exchange's (AMEX) options trade-reporting scandal is expected to lead to indictments of as many as 20 of the exchange's floor members. AMEX officials protest it as unfair because of penalties already meted out by the exchange and the Securities and Exchange Commission (SEC).

Big oil companies' heavy diversification into the mining industry is running into problems of profitability and other difficulties. But the companies do not seem to be losing interest in such investments. Union Oil's Molycorp plans to develop an underground molybdenum mine at Questa, New Mexico, and has paid its partner, Kennecott, to terminate its interest there.

5 Foreign exchange intervention was started by U.S. officials to bolster the long-declining value of the dollar. They plan heavy use of the Treasury's $4.6 billion Exchange Stabilization Fund and the Federal Reserve's $20 billion swap network "to check speculation and reestablish order" in currency markets. The value of the U.S. dollar soared in New York in response to the announcement after earlier general weakness abroad. But although the plan was welcomed for going beyond Washington's previous statements supporting the dollar, there is doubt that it will have much long-term effect on the currency. Market reaction was mixed. Stock prices recovered part of an early decline, while hopes of renewed interest from foreign investors strengthened the bond market. But commodity futures markets, including those for gold and other metals, were knocked into a tailspin.

Large-screen, projection television systems for the home may be catching on. But at current prices of up to $4,000, mass marketing of the big screens (some range up to nearly 4½ feet by 6 feet) is not likely soon. Matsushita, which makes Panasonic products, and Mitsubishi, two big Japanese companies, will introduce color projection television systems at a consumer electronics trade show that opens in Las Vegas today. Sony, which has been in the business in a small way, says it

1

plans to bring out an improved system in May. General Electric later this year will become the first major U.S. manufacturer of television sets to offer a system.

Companies planning new offices should avoid Los Angeles and locate in either Chicago or New York, says Eva Maddox Associates, an office-planning firm. The cost of office space in Los Angeles is about $9.80 a square foot this year compared with $8.99 in Chicago and $8.11 in New York.

The FDA proposed a labeling requirement for many permanent hair dyes to warn consumers that they contain a chemical that causes cancer in test animals. The chemical is said to be found in some dyes made by Alberto-Culver, Bristol-Myers' Clairol unit, Cosmair, and Revlon.

Japan, a heavy international borrower in the past, is emerging as a source of capital for foreign governments and corporations. But sudden reverses in the world economy could halt the trend.

6   Carter's tax proposals this month are expected to contain more revenue-raising revisions than previously reported. The President's changes will probably affect institutions' bad-debt reserves, borrowings for tax "shelters," accelerated depreciation of real estate, and political contribution benefits.

Eastern railroads plan an "interim emergency" freight-rate rise of 6 percent on May 1. Separately, the chairman of the Interstate Commerce Commission (ICC) warned that the Milwaukee Road will have trouble keeping its trains running through this year without further government or other outside aid.

The central market pronouncement due this month from the SEC may do little more than set rather lenient deadlines for developing the national quotation-execution system. There also are indications the commission will not alter remaining exchange curbs against members trading listed securities in the over-the-counter (OTC) market.

The U.S. Postal Service had a $687 million deficit in fiscal 1977, narrower than the $1.1 billion deficit originally expected but wider than the $400 million deficit forecast at midyear.

9   Economic growth in the United States will slow to 4–5 percent this year after growing at a little less than 6 percent in 1977, the Commerce Department estimated, excluding any tax cuts or

energy laws that Congress may pass. The study roughly matches forecasts of private and government economists.

Cowles Communications' board voted to liquidate Cowles as a closed-end management investment firm. The company also operates television stations.

Satellite Business Systems, a partnership of units of Comsat, Aetna Life, and IBM, awarded Hughes Aircraft a $50 million contract for three communications satellites.

10   The Federal Reserve, escalating its efforts to bolster the value of the U.S. dollar, tightened up on credit. The Fed indicated it had raised to at least 6¾ percent from 6½ percent its target for the key federal funds rate, and some said the rate could soon hit 7 percent. Market reaction was severe—sharply lower prices and higher yields for bonds and short-term money instruments. Stock prices tumbled broadly, dropping the Dow Jones Industrial Average 8.93 points to 784.56, its lowest in more than two years. The value of the U.S. dollar was narrowly mixed, holding most of last week's gains with only little intervention by the Fed. The currency's recovery is expected to take months if not years, and nervous foreign exchange trading indicates growing concern that monetary action alone will not overcome economic factors weakening the dollar's value.

Robert Strauss, President Carter's special trade representative, returns to Tokyo under growing clouds of protectionism. The Japanese are expected to reduce trade barriers further and to outline steps to stimulate their economy. Failure to offer convincing concessions or a symbolic change in direction could worsen the serious trade dispute with the United States. The Treasury ruled that five Japanese companies sold carbon- steel plate in the United States at less than fair value. But it said dumping margins were narrower than previously calculated, reducing the possibility that the case will conflict with the Treasury's trigger-price system.

Nigeria's 55 percent take-over of Texaco and California Standard oil operations there in 1975 was settled by agreement on $71.6 million in payments to the companies.

Xerox announced lower sale-price options for two copier models—the 660 and 4000—but higher rental prices for five —the 660, 720, 813, 914, and 1000.

Pork belly futures prices closed higher and those for hogs ended mixed after profit-taking trimmed initial strong advances. At one point pork belly prices rose their daily two-cent-a-pound limit, while hog prices advanced to new life-of-contract highs. Lighter marketings of hogs and higher cash market quotations fueled the price advances, brokers said. Cattle futures prices closed mixed in less-active trading.

Interest rate futures prices plummeted after the announcement on January 6 by the Federal Reserve Board of higher interest rates on its loans to member banks, brokers said. Nearby delivery futures in long-term U.S. Treasury bonds and Government National Mortgage Association (GNMA) certificates fell their allowable daily limits of 24/32 or $750 a contract, while 90-day U.S. Treasury bill futures prices were sharply lower. It was the first limit move for the four-month-old bond contract and the first since late summer in GNMA futures, traders noted. When interest rates rise, the value of fixed-income securities drop.

11 The Federal Reserve intervened actively in foreign exchange markets, and the value of dollar moved only fractionally lower. Economists and analysts are coming to believe that the Carter administration's fight to bolster the value of the dollar could drastically alter the flow of funds in domestic money markets.

An 8 percent prime rate became industry-wide as dozens of big banks followed the ¼-point boost. Meanwhile, Mellon National posted a 9 percent rise in fourth-quarter operating earnings to $19.1 million.

IBM introduced a small business computer selling for as little as $10,000. It also cut prices on some electric memory typewriters and copiers, added to its line of electronic typing systems, and said it created a new French unit.

U.S. antitrust tactics are changing under the Carter administration to smaller and swifter attacks against more targets. Time and money saved on leaner major cases could permit more innovative actions.

Litton's Ingalls Shipbuilding division got a $64 million Navy contract to overhaul, repair, and refuel the nuclear-powered submarine Sunfish.

12 Economic growth in the fourth quarter was at a 4 percent annual rate or a bit less, according to the Commerce Department's chief economist. She predicted real GNP growth this year of 4.5 percent or a little higher, compared with slightly less than 5 percent in 1977.

Saudi Arabia's oil minister ruled out any boost in 1978 oil prices and suggested that discounting is likely by some other Organization of Petroleum Exporting Countries (OPEC) members.

Farrell Lines bid $33.7 million for American Export Lines in a bankruptcy court; it was the only bid and was accepted.

The Supreme Court held that foreign governments may sue American companies for treble damages based on U.S. antitrust charges. The case involved tetracycline prices of six U.S. drugmakers.

13 Wholesale prices slowed their climb last month with an adjusted 0.5 percent gain after November's 0.7 percent gain. Food price performance improved, but the advance in prices of finished goods accelerated.

Capital spending by business is planned to rise only 4.5 percent this year after adjustment for inflation. That is less than 1977's estimated 8 percent advance and the 9–10 percent administration goal.

The U.S. dollar's recent weakness is again worrying Saudi Arabian officials and is sure to be a topic during Energy Secretary Schlesinger's visit. Some Saudis even suggest abandoning the dollar for OPEC's oil pricing.

American Motors will close its U.S. auto assembly operations because of a parts shortage caused by a Canadian strike.

A variety of mortgages with terms tied to the borrower's particular situation may be available from federally chartered savings and loans (S&Ls) by the end of the year if the Federal Home Loan Bank Board gets congressional encouragement to authorize alternative mortgages.

16 The United States and Japan reached agreement in Tokyo that will avert a trade war, but the truce is temporary. The U.S. negotiators got more than they expected from the Japanese. Major problems remain, chief among them the ability of each government to persuade potential protectionist forces that the pact will be more than a stopgap measure.

The dollar eventually may be linked with the West German Mark in order to bolster confidence in the U.S. currency. Separately, the U.S. government's efforts to aid the dollar are likely to cause heated debate at the Federal Open Market Committee meeting and possibly split the panel into two factions.

The Federal National Mortgage Association (FNMA) plans to buy up to $200 million in urban home mortgages starting February 1 to stimulate inner-city home buying and rehabilitation.

Sun Life Assurance delayed for three months a policyholders' vote on its planned move to Quebec. The firm had said that it could not comply with the province's law enforcing the primacy of the French language.

17 A monopoly complaint by Greyhound Corp.'s computer unit against IBM was left standing by the Supreme Court, which refused to interfere with an appeals court ruling that the case should go to the jury. IBM contended the appeals court decision would affect other private antitrust suits pending in trial courts. IBM's net profits rose about 18 percent in the fourth period to a record $797 million, and revenue was up 12 percent to $5 billion, also a high. Data processing equipment sales were cited as a cause.

American Telephone lost its bid to have the Supreme Court review a lower court finding that the Federal Communications Commission (FCC) acted improperly when it barred MCI Telecommunications from competing with AT&T in long-distance phone service.

Conrail is expected to seek massive increases in federal financial aid, possibly as much as $2 billion, because of lagging revenue and continuing rehabilitation problems.

18 Industrial output rose a slim 0.2 percent last month, seasonally adjusted, as the coal strike cut sharply into production. The three previous gains were revised downward.

Budd directors approved Thyssen AG's tentative $272 million bid, clearing the way for merger talks.

The National Urban League said the economic outlook of blacks and cities is unlikely to be helped by the broad tax cut the President is planning. Restating the league's cautious view of the administration, its president, Vernon Jordan, said lowering federal revenues would create an excuse to ignore essential urban and social programs.

Outside directors of corporations have an obligation to check the accuracy of information their companies provide investors, the SEC has warned. The SEC position—regarded by agency officials as the commission's strongest statement thus far on responsibilities of directors who are not company officers —was asserted in a report issued earlier this week on former outside directors of National Telephone Co., currently in bankruptcy proceedings. The report concluded that the six outside directors on the telephone equipment company's seven-member board "failed in their obligation" to assure that National was making full disclosure of its financial condition.

The value of the U.S. dollar generally firmed against other major currencies, despite some late-afternoon weakness in New York market. Trading was once again quiet, both in New York and overseas, leading some dealers to express "cautious optimism" that the recent U.S. efforts may have succeeded in restoring order to foreign exchange markets, at least for the short term. "If participants in the market can see only a one-way trend without any end in sight, they will all jump on the bandwagon and only sell dollars," commented one London dealer. But "they are very, very wary of taking large positions" against the dollar currently, added another. This is because some moves by the Federal Reserve System last week boosted the value of the dollar late in the New York day, after many Europeans had gone home.

19 The Federal Reserve Board has started a broad study of bank holding companies that could lead to changes in its policy toward them.

U.S. savings banks had a $75 million net deposit outflow last month, a sign of possible trouble ahead for the housing industry.

Toyota and Nissan posted record vehicle exports for 1977. Domestic sales eased.

Coal-slurry pipelines would be the cheapest way to ship coal in some instances, posing a competitive threat to railroads, Congress's technology office said.

20 President Carter told Congress it has "failed the American people" by stalemating his energy bill, and he warned that economic recovery and foreign policy depend on its passage. He also proposed a $25-billion-a-year tax cut, linked that to undisclosed tax revisions, and called for a voluntary anti-inflation program to hold 1978 wage-price boosts below 1976–77 averages.

Economic growth slowed further to a 4.2 percent annual rate in 1977's fourth quarter as sharp cutbacks in inventory accumulation offset strong gains in consumer spending. The full year's real growth averaged 4.9 percent, trailing the administration's 5.1 percent target.

Labor law revision supporters announced major concessions to aid Senate passage of the Carter proposal. The bill would streamline procedures governing union organizing efforts and stiffen penalties against employers who illegally stifle organizing.

Initial resale trading in the bond market brought a price markup for the Treasury's recent 7½ percent note issued but a sharp drop for Municipal Assistance Corp's 8 percent bonds.

23 The tax package proposed by the President will be overhauled by Congress, many tax experts and politicians believe. The $24.5 billion tax-cut plan includes tax reductions for individuals and businesses next year and a score of offsetting revenue-raising revisions. Observers see a package with bigger cuts and fewer revisions.

An inflation rate of 6–6½ percent is expected to persist throughout 1978, government economists say, although consumer prices in December rose at a moderate 4.8 percent annual rate. Separately, both business and labor expressed displeasure with Carter's voluntary program to curb inflation.

G. William Miller, Carter's nominee as Fed chairman, supports U.S. intervention on behalf of the dollar. He also believes the value of the dollar is low in relation to the West German Mark and Swiss franc.

Oil and gas firms won two court cases that challenged the Energy Department's power to regulate the production and sale of oil and gas.

New York City is still in deep financial trouble, municipal officials say, and its recovery date was pushed back to 1982 from mid-1978.

The Agriculture Department will publish the names of "chronic problem" meat and poultry companies and will make changes intended to improve its meat grading and labeling system.

24 Fiscal 1979 spending of $500.2 billion, up 8 percent from 1978, was outlined by President Carter in a budget that projects a $60.6 billion deficit. That deficit, which Congress is likely to widen, undermines Carter's goal of a balanced budget by 1981. Pentagon outlays of $115.2 billion would be up 9.4 percent from fiscal 1978. The budget emphasizes strengthening conventional forces in Europe.

The Senate hearings today on G. William Miller's nomination to head the Federal Reserve Board are expected to feature a previously undisclosed $2.9 million in Iran by a unit of his company, Textron. The company has prepared a briefing paper aimed at satisfying suspicions.

The Federal Reserve Board has solved a tax problem that last year halted its open-market repurchase agreements for central banks. It now will act as a principal instead of as an agent.

Offshore oil-leasing rules would be rewritten under a bill that the House Rules Committee cleared for floor consideration. Oil-state legislators had sidetracked the measure.

The number of part-time jobs could increase in federal agencies under a proposed experiment. The idea is to test the feasibility of expanding the number of permanent part-time workers in the federal bureaucracy from the current 38,000. President Carter wants such an expansion to enhance job prospects for homemakers, students, and disabled persons who need work but can not adjust to full-time schedules. The program is outlined in the President's fiscal 1979 budget. The year-long experiment will be conducted by five agencies: the Veterans Administration, Federal Trade Commission, Environmental Protection Agency, Export-Import Bank, and General Services Administration. Federal officials maintain that while the program might boost the total number of federal workers, it will not mean the bureaucracy itself will be enlarged.

The transitional arrangements aimed at de-emphasizing the monetary role of gold agreed to in August 1975 by the group of ten major industrialized countries and Switzerland will not be extended, the Paris office of the International Monetary Fund announced. The agreement will lapse. Under the accord, the 11 countries agreed that they would not peg the price of gold on the free market or increase their stocks of monetary gold by buying the metal on the open market. They were allowed, however, to sell gold.

Control Data Corp. said it formed a division to make computer terminals and peripheral products for large users of IBM Series/1 minicomputer systems. Philip W. Arneson, vice president of the new division, said Control Data entered this market because of IBM's practice of attaching non-IBM peripheral products to the Series/1 and Control Data's success in making peripherals for other manufacturers' computers. The new division, based in Roseville, Minnesota, employs more than 700 people.

26 Stock options traders who manipulate markets in options or their underlying securities face harsher penalties, the SEC warned in an order against J. Newman & Co.

The Treasury Department said it will raise $1.7 billion of fresh cash through sales of bonds and notes next week. At the quarterly refinancing, the Treasury will sell about $6.75 billion in debt to help redeem $5.03 billion in securities maturing February 15 and to raise the $1.7 billion of fresh cash.

27 The SEC gave the securities industry until September 30 to come up with key elements of a national market system. The commission put off any action to remove remaining bars against offboard trading by exchange members in stocks listed on the exchange.

Tax-revision plans of President Carter to curb the "three-martini" lunch, the DISC tax break, and tax deferral on foreign subsidiaries' earnings drew a skeptical reaction from Senate Finance Chairman Russell Long.

The Federal Reserve got its requested introduction of legislation to bar the immediate release of the monetary policy directives of its Open Market Committee, as a court has ruled.

30 Coal strike talks broke off yesterday after industry bargainers refused to increase their latest money offer. Sources said the package exceeded slightly the 30 percent increase in wages and fringe benefits won by steelworkers last year.

Top accounting leaders will go before a House unit this week to argue that they can regulate themselves without further government help. The committee's chair is considering a bill creating a self-regulatory group that all accounting firms practicing before the SEC would have to join.

31 A trade deficit of an adjusted $2.03 billion last month boosted the 1977 total to a record $26.72 billion. The widening from 1976's $5.88 billion deficit was fueled by another surge in oil imports, which are expected to cause a large deficit again this year.

Weeden Holding listed a $6.1 million loss for its December 31 first quarter, in contrast to a year-earlier profit. It blamed reverses in over-the-counter

trading in exchange-listed stocks and said its securities dealer unit would end such dealings.

An oil-gas lease-sale of offshore New England tracts will not take place as a federal appeals court upheld a ban on the Interior Department's acceptance of bids.

Sears will market and install National Subscription Television pay-television service in the Los Angeles area. It is the first national department store chain to offer subscription pay-television.

February 1978

1 Building awards last year climbed 26 percent to $139.21 billion, the biggest gain in nearly three decades. McGraw-Hill's F. W. Dodge division put the December rise at 48 percent to $10.44 billion.

The oil industry won a key victory as the House voted to limit the Interior Department's ability to change bidding procedures for offshore oil leases. Later actions could undo the victory.

The Labor Department is said to be planning to sue some former trustees of the Teamsters' Central States Pension Fund over allegedly poor asset-management practices.

3 The coal strike, although apparently on the verge of settlement, may cause electric power cutbacks as some utilities in key industrial states run low on coal. Even after a tentative settlement, it will take several weeks to get supplies flowing to utilities.

IBM said the FTC has ended its investigation of the company's position in the electric typewriter market.

6 The decline in the jobless rate in January 1978 to 6.3 percent of the work force, its lowest level since October 1974, confirms a return to stronger growth, the Carter administration said. The White House maintained, however, that its proposed tax cuts are needed to keep the economy growing at a healthy pace.

The New York Stock Exchange board decided against extending trading hours but also ordered its staff to continue studying the subject.

Feedgrain farmers would be urged to plant fewer acres and would receive higher storage fees under Agriculture Secretary Bergland's proposal to bolster grain prices.

7 The Social Security payroll tax rate would be cut almost one-third under a bill introduced by five members of Congress and two Senators. The change would result in higher income taxes or more Treasury borrowing.

New auditing rules for privately held companies were proposed by the American Institute for Certified Public Accountants.

The New York and American Stock Exchanges closed early because of a snowstorm in New York City. Commodity exchanges in the city also closed early.

8 The FCC granted increases in depreciation rates that will allow 11 telephone companies a total of $213 million in additional write-offs for last year. The boosts will reduce their reported profit and allow them to request rate increases sooner. The bulk of the increases went to units of AT&T and General Telephone.

Newport News Shipbuilding's illegal refusal to bargain caused the ten-month strike by most of its 1,200 marine draftsmen, an NLRB administrative law judge ruled. The decision could force the Tenneco unit to rehire all the striking designers.

9 Bankers are studying the establishment of a private telephone network, an ambitious system that could mean substantial savings for ABA members and a revenue loss for AT&T. The banking industry spends $500 million a year on phone bills, 20–40 percent of that for interbank calls.

Kodak reduced the price of its least expensive instant camera and disclosed plans to replace its other two instant models with improved, lower-priced cameras. It also plans a similar replacement of its line of pocket-sized traditional cameras and a new low-light, color-slide film.

Brokerage commissions for institutional securities trades will be raised by Shearson Hayden Stone, narrowing its average 47 percent discount to no more than 40 percent.

Only 19 percent of farmers surveyed in ten grain-producing states plan to participate in the administration's set-aside program, but the White House is going ahead with it anyway.

10 The coal strike is beginning to pinch more electricity users in the Midwest and Appalachia, leading to cutbacks and actual or requested declarations of emergency. The union's Bargaining Council is reviewing a tentative accord.

Iran joined Saudi Arabia in maintaining that OPEC's benchmark price for oil will remain frozen all this year. Iran's prime minister added that gradual annual price rises should be expected to resume next year.

Penn Central wants court permission to sell three real estate holdings in New York City for $40.3 million to an affiliate of Olympia & York Developments of Toronto.

Oil companies criticized an Energy Department suggestion that the data they provide for statistical purposes might be passed on to regulators and other agencies.

13 Top financial officials of the United States, Japan, West Germany, France, and Britain are meeting in Europe apparently to cope with intensifying strains over currency, growth, and trade protection policies.

Bert Lance told Financial General Bankshares he represents a London bank, which manages Arab funds, that may seek control of the company, Financial General said.

14 The SEC is planning to ask Congress to delay for a year the May 1 effective date of a law severing brokerage activities from investment adviser activities. Proposed SEC rules to carry out the law have run into heavy criticism, and the securities industry has changed since the law was passed.

Kuwait again invited foreign oil companies, including several from the United States, for "final negotiations" on buying about $550 million a year of liquefied petroleum gas.

15 Coal industry and union bargainers were called to the White House for negotiations, and President Carter warned that he might seek a court order forcing miners back to work if the new talks fail. The 71-day strike 's causing power cutbacks and threatening wide layoffs, including production cutbacks and some plant closings in the automobile industry. Schools and residential users also will be affected.

The HUD-FNMA dispute may come to a head after months of quarreling over policy. At issue is how much influence the United States should exert in the operation of the mortgage corporation.

16 Pacific Gas's electricity rates will be cut at least $400 million annually because heavy rains and snow have made hydroelectricity more available.

17 The IRS said corporations will not have to list the total amount of deductions claimed for entertainment, gifts, travel, and similar expenses on 1977 tax forms. Companies have complained that they did not know the information would be requested.

The money supply rose $900 million on the M1 basis and $2.4 billion on the broader M2 basis—lesser gains than had been expected. Meanwhile, officials at a Conference Board session forecast higher interest rates this year as credit demand continues to surge, but they said heavy Treasury financings appear increasingly unlikely to trigger a credit crunch.

21   The AFL-CIO's plan to stimulate the economy and cut taxes differs sharply from President Carter's proposals. It calls for a $13.25 billion boost in direct spending programs, eliminating a proposed $8.4 billion business tax cut and rolling back the Social Security payroll tax.

22   The Supreme Court refused to interfere with development of mid-Atlantic offshore oil-gas leases sold in August 1976, apparently removing the bidder's final impediment. Separately, the Interior Department set the date of March 28 to sell oil-gas leases off four southeastern states.

A program to help states calculate taxes owed by multistate companies is constitutional, Supreme Court Justices affirmed as they rejected a challenge by some big concerns. They left standing a lower court's contempt finding against J. P. Stevens for violating union activity.

Economic growth in the final quarter of 1977 was revised downward to an estimated 4 percent annual pace from 4.2 percent. That was a further slowing from 5.1, 6.2, and 7.5 percent gains previously.

23   The SEC reluctantly moved to make it more likely that controversial shareholder proposals get in proxy materials. It limited the circumstances in which its staff will tell companies that they can exclude a proposal without fear of an enforcement action.

G. William Miller was delayed further in his nomination as Federal Reserve Board chairman as the Senate Banking Committee voted to fully investigate how much he knew about a questionable corporate payment in Iran.

IBM is trying to correct problems with its top-of-the-line office copiers, the Series III. A survey found that 89 percent of users had some trouble.

24   AT&T won a major victory in its fight to keep a monopoly over long-distance phone service as the FCC ruled it does not have to make additional connections of competitors' nonprivate lines to its own system.

IBM filed suit charging that Xerox's electronic typing systems infringe on seven of IBM's U.S. patents.

Textron auditors have discovered that at least four divisions funneled kickbacks to foreign customers. The finding, which could involve millions of dollars, will likely lead to a new line of questioning at Senate Banking Committee hearings on Textron Chairman G. William Miller's nomination to head the Fed.

Fannie Mae lending practices and financial reporting obligations would be subject to new regulatory authority under an administration proposal, the latest move in a long-running policy dispute.

28   The U.S.-Japan trade announcement last month has "global application," a Japanese minister said in apparent response to Common Market pressure for Japan to reduce its trade surplus. He ruled out special concessions to the European Community.

Representatives of industrialized nations at an OECD meeting seemed cheerful about stimulating world economic recovery by five or six countries doing all they can to spur domestic demand. The previous notion of West Germany and Japan expanding their economies to boost nations with payments deficits has come under increasing fire.

March 1978

1   Leading indicators dropped 1.9 percent in January, the steepest decline in three years. It was considered more a result of bad weather than a sign of economic weakness. Separately, the fourth quarter's productivity gain was revised to an 0.5 percent annual rate, even more sluggish than the 1.4 percent pace reported earlier.

Industrialized nations ended an OECD strategy meeting with agreement on a general program to spread the burden of economic stimulation among more countries.

Robert P. Beasley, Firestone's former vice chairman, pleaded guilty to five counts of a 40-count indictment charging he stole $1 million from a company fund for illegal political contributions.

2 Building awards surged 39 percent in January to $9.39 billion, according to McGraw-Hill's F. W. Dodge division. But that included $1 billion for a Seabrook, New Hampshire, nuclear power plant that faces further delays.

3 Textron chief G. William Miller was overwhelmingly approved by the Senate Banking Committee to head the Federal Reserve Board. Separately, the SEC took Textron to court to enforce a subpoena in an inquiry into its overseas practices.

United Technologies agreed to acquire Ambac Industries for cash or stock valued at $210 million. Ambac shares could be swapped for $48 each.

6 Coal miners rejected a proposed new contract, and President Carter prepared to take strong action to end the strike. But UMW leaders warned that if the government goes to court for an 80-day back-to-work order under the Taft-Hartley Act, most of the 160,000 strikers are likely to defy it.

Factory orders in January fell 3.6 percent to an adjusted $17.22 billion, the steepest drop in more than three years. A major factor was a 59 percent decrease in spending for defense aircraft and parts after a big rise in December.

Jamaica, seeking to bolster its dwindling cash and reserves, proposed that five North American aluminum firms issue it notes to cover an estimated $180 million of their future bauxite levy payments.

Privileges for "insiders," such as letting them overdraw checking accounts without paying interest, are granted by many banks, according to a federal study stemming from the Bert Lance affair.

7 Accounting leaders, responding to SEC and congressional criticism, plan to recommend changes in the structure of the American Institute of Certified Public Accountants' new section for firms that audit publicly held corporations.

8 Seizure of coal mines by the government as a way to end the miners strike is under serious consideration by President Carter, Special Trade Representative Strauss said. Other U.S. officials, however, emphasized that seizure is only one possibility. Peabody Coal, the nation's largest producer, meanwhile seems to be studying trying to negotiate a separate pact with miners. The coal strike, besides hurting the nation's economy, may harm prospects for organized labor's bid to revise labor laws.

Wages and salaries in the United States rose an average 1.7 percent in the fourth quarter of 1977, the Labor Department said, trailing the increases of 1.8 percent in the previous period and 1.9 percent in the fourth period of 1976.

9 The price of gold surged $3.75 an ounce to a near record $190. Analysts said the underlying reason for the bullion's rise is the decline in the value of the dollar and worry over the U.S. economy. The Fed separately reported that it and the Treasury had intervened aggressively in January to calm disorderly foreign exchange trading. The dollar's weakness is causing more OPEC members to become disenchanted with using dollars for oil pricing. Pressures are building for a switch to a new pricing mechanism or currency, or for an increase in the dollar price.

Ghaith Pharaon, a Saudi businessman, is seeking to delay a deadline on his proposed tender offer for part of the shares of the National Bank of Georgia, once headed by former Budget Director Bert Lance.

A securities group criticized Carter's proposal for a taxable bond option in local government financings, charging that the President and Congress had a distorted view of the market's capital-raising efficiency.

10 Pan American Airways' president, F. C. Wiser, is leaving after an apparent high-level clash. Recommended as his successor will be Dan Colussy, an executive vice president.

Penn Central's plan for paying off creditors and claimants will be approved after minor changes, a federal judge said. The company should emerge solvent in a few months.

13 The United States and Bonn are expected to announce a joint action program to defend the dollar. Sources said the plan will describe an expanded currency "swap network" that includes a $2 billion credit line between the Fed and the West German central bank and links between the U.S. Treasury and the Bonn bank.

The FTC subpoenaed documents of company operations from General Motors, Ford, Chrysler, and AMC, but the agency's staff is still uncertain where the auto industry probe will lead. Separately, the Department of Transportation is investigating possible gear changing and steering problems on three Ford car models.

The National Association of Securities Dealers (NASD) took initial steps toward linking the over-the-counter securities market to the proposed national stock market system.

U.S. businesses expect an 11 percent rise in 1978 pretax profits compared with a 9.5 percent gain last year, a McGraw-Hill unit's survey said.

14 Most coal miners defied a back-to-work order, but the administration is hopeful that the Taft-Hartley injunction would spur coal production anyway. Contract talks showed signs of continued progress.

15 Coal negotiators tentatively agreed on a contract to be submitted to the union's bargaining council today. The revised settlement would boost wages and fringe benefits 39 percent instead of 37 percent as in a rejected pact; it includes concessions on health and pension benefits and labor stability language.

An air-fare accord opening a number of U.S. cities to discount service on London flights appeared close as British bargainers seemed about ready to drop their opposition.

16 Coal union leaders approved a sweetened tentative contract by a vote of 22 to 17. While the margin of approval was narrower than some had expected, the vote cleared the way for submission of the pact to a rank-and-file ratification vote.

Fuel economy rules for 1980 and 1981 model light trucks and vans were eased by the Transportation Department after industry protests. The standards call for gasoline mileage increases of up to 24 percent instead of 42 percent.

17 The natural gas impasse came a step closer to settlement as House Democratic energy conferees accepted in principle much of a Senate proposal to deregulate the price of newly discovered gas over some years. But the offer would make changes that could disturb the delicate Senate majority.

20 The SEC's suit against Bert Lance and ten others involved in a battle for control of Financial General Bankshares shows once again that the agency will be tough on untraditional take-over bids. The suit was settled Saturday when a judge approved an order barring the defendants from violating stock-ownership reporting rules.

The nuclear power plant licensing bill is being criticized by environmentalist who doubt it will adequately protect public health and the environment. Industrial proponents are concerned that the bill will not cut as much time from the process of plant completion as they would like and that it may prove needlessly complicated.

The U.S. Metric Board, a new agency whose members have not yet been confirmed by the Senate, must decide in the months ahead whether the government will actively promote a national switch to the metric system or just be neutral about it.

23 Continued high inflation will force the Federal Reserve to tighten monetary policy to head off serious recession, Fed Chairman Miller warned. He said President Carter is considering ways to bolster the anti-inflation program with harsh steps if the private sector will not cooperate.

Damages against Kodak of $37.6 million were voted by a jury in Berkey Photo's antitrust suit. That would be tripled by the court; more damaging to Kodak could be possible steps to end alleged monopoly practices.

Red meat prices this year will climb at least 11 percent instead of the 7.5 percent expected earlier, according to an Agriculture Department economist. The agency's latest hog and pork survey led to maximum daily gains in most meat futures contract prices.

Canada's government has moved "too far, too fast" and will try to restrain its economic intervention, Prime Minister Trudeau said. He promised further curbs on spending and bureaucratic intrusions.

24 Curtiss-Wright proposed a proxy fight to replace Kennecott's board, then selling off Kennecott's big Carborundum unit and distributing proceeds to Kennecott stockholders.

The CAB, instead of just authorizing discount fares, approved 35 percent reductions across the board in normal air fares for National Airlines and Western Air Lines.

27 Coal miners are expected to start returning to work this week under a new contract ratified on March 24, but a normal flow of coal into users' stockpiles is not likely until well into April.

28 A new urban policy seeking better use of current funds was disclosed by the President. Major proposals include: making the present employment tax credits available only for hiring the hardcore jobless; creating a new national development bank that can back up to $11 billion in private loans to induce business investment in distressed areas; and setting a 5 percent tax credit in addition to the current 10 percent credit for firms investing in such areas.

Saudi Arabia apparently is taking a harder line on the U.S. dollar. King Khalid reportedly warned President Carter that the Saudis' moderate position on oil prices might not continue if the value of the dollar keeps declining.

The Supreme Court left standing an appeals court order dismissing a challenge by the New York Stock Exchange and the Investment Company Institute to "automatic investment service" plans offered by banks.

29 Foote, Cone & Belding said it will acquire New York–based Byoir & Associates, one of the nation's oldest and largest public relations firms.

Louisiana Pacific and Arcata say the government's valuation for redwood timberland in California is outdated and too low and that they will seek higher compensation in court. The President authorized $359 million to buy 48,000 more acres for the Redwood National Park.

30 The UMW's Bargaining Council unanimously approved a proposed pact covering striking mine construction employees. The accord will be offered for a ratification vote. However, picketing by the strikers continued to disrupt resumption of normal coal output.

Two commodity options firms based in Chicago and 13 individuals were accused by the Commodity Futures Trading Commission (CFTC) of cheating and defrauding customers.

31 The IMF's new rules to abolish gold's "official" price and permit closer surveillance of the exchange rate practices of 133 member nations take effect on April 1.

Mutual funds' cash and short-term securities holdings totaled $4.26 billion

in February, up sharply from $3.61 billion in January and $2.79 billion a year earlier.

April 1978

3 A trade deficit of $4.52 billion for the United States in February, a record, sent the value of the dollar reeling and left administration officials scrambling for measures to correct the imbalance. The unexpected deficit came on a broad-based rise in imports and was almost twice as deep as January's $2.38 billion deficit. Money market analysts believe the Fed may tighten its credit reins in an attempt to restore confidence in the sagging dollar. Arthur Burns, the former Fed chairman, outlined a controversial plan to help the dollar that included having the United States indicate its willingness to use its gold stock to defend the currency and to issue new bonds denominated in foreign currencies.

A steel price increase of $5.50 a ton appears to have prevailed after government pressure to forgo a larger boost, but the pricing situation for some products remains uncertain.

4 The Supreme Court set back environmentalists' opposition to nuclear power plants with a ruling that lower courts cannot prescribe procedures for regulatory agencies. Justices separately rejected Warner-Lambert's bid for review of a 1975 FTC order to run "corrective advertising" for Listerine mouthwash.

5 Inflation is the nation's biggest problem, say lawmakers after hearing from constituents, and President Carter apparently agrees. That suggests trouble for new spending programs or big deficit budget resolutions. Meanwhile, Reserve Board Chairman Miller forecast inflation of 6.5–7 percent and economic growth of 4–4.75 percent from late 1977 to late 1978, more pessimistic than administration forecasts.

Social Security taxes should be reduced $7.5 billion as part of this year's tax cut, the House Budget Committee agreed.

The Postal Service proposed a 13-cent surcharge on some letters in large or oddly shaped envelopes.

Marine Midland Bank directors approved

an accord under which Hongkong & Shanghai Banking ultimately would acquire 51 percent of the company. The agreement would pump about $200 million of new capital into Marine by year-end 1980.

IBM, in a 10-K filing with the SEC, for the first time indicated revenue from its computer business. It showed higher sales and lower rentals than many analysts had thought.

6 Social Security payroll taxes would be cut and income taxes used to make up the loss to the Social Security trust funds under a plan of House Democrats. But Senate Finance Committee Chairman Long opposed the income tax feature, and President Carter opposed reconsidering Social Security financing this year.

The Postal Service agreed to a $60 million settlement of suits by 80,000 present and former employees charging failure to pay overtime and other violations. Settling a similar Labor Department suit could push total settlement costs close to $1 billion.

Commodity options sales in the United States were suspended as of June 1 by the Commodity Futures Trading Commission. It said that the business has become "fraught with fraud" and that the suspension will be lifted when options buyers can be protected better.

The Tribune, a New York daily newspaper that made its debut on January 9, said it had run out of funds and was ceasing publication.

7 Eastern Airlines contracted to buy 19 Airbus jets in a $778 million package, including leasing costs for the four it has already. The approval of Eastern's lenders is needed.

A retirement-age law ensuring most private-sector employees the right to work at least to age 70 was signed by President Carter. There is some fear that it could complicate operations of pension plans and others benefit programs.

Penn Central asked its bankruptcy court for permission to sell Loews' three New York City hotels for $45 million.

Bringing U.S. branches of foreign banks under some federal regulation was approved by the House, although the bill is not expected to have much effect.

Britain's budget, to be disclosed on April 8, is expected to seek economic growth almost entirely through tax cuts. It is believed between $3.75 billion and $4.70 billion will be put into the economy.

10 A grain-car shortage, the worst in over a decade, has become a problem for railroads, shippers, and the ICC, which are taking steps to alleviate the scarcity. A major cause of the pinch is the intensified desire of farmers and elevator owners to sell grain that was stored last year when prices were low.

Securities scandal lawsuits involving the University of Houston indicate that some brokerage houses believe they sustained millions of dollars of trading losses as a result of the dealings.

11 A second energy plan is being prepared by the President as his original proposal is still held up in Congress. The new plan, called "phase two," will not be ready for a year, but some major elements will be sent to Congress around May 1.

An ITC order for major Japanese trading concerns to halt "unfair" import competition involving stainless steel pipe and tube is expected to be rejected by President Carter.

A securities firms probe by a federal grand jury of suspected antitrust abuses in brokerage rate procedures and other practices is not expected to produce any criminal charges.

The AMEX's chairman may propose key changes in the American Stock Exchange's governing structure, including more seats for floor members on the board of governors.

12 Anti-inflation steps including a 5.5 percent cap on pay boosts for white-collar federal employees and a freeze on top-level Executive Branch salaries were outlined by President Carter. He called for broad public cooperation to limit wage-price increases to less than the past two years' average. Congressional reaction was mixed, but disappointed foreign exchange traders pushed the value of the dollar lower.

American Stock Exchange members elected an insurgent, Allan S. Gordon, Bruan Gordon's managing partner, as a governor, while another independent was defeated. The challenge was said to reflect the discontent of the floor members.

The Portland Cement industry is under FTC investigation for possible antitrust violations.

13 The anti-inflation campaign of President Carter drew some general statements of support but also broad criticism and skepticism from business and union officials surveyed. Many called for

more government restraint, and Carter will also be under heavy pressure from his advisers to limit the federal deficit. Treasury Secretary Blumenthat said the inflation rate could be boosted 0.5 percentage point by the dollar's current depreciation.

A Social Security tax rollback next year was rejected by the Senate Budget Committee.

An investigation of Japanese television exports is being dropped by the Justice Department after the year-long study failed to find anticompetitive practices against U.S. makers.

14 Freight rate rises of 4 percent for eastern and western railroads and 2 percent for southern lines are planned for June 1. Boosts of up to 7 percent on steam coal probably would be passed along by utilities.

Oil-gas lease bids on 14 tracts in last month's federal sale off the southeast coast were rejected as inadequate. They totaled $9 million, but 43 high bids totaling $100.7 million were accepted.

Aerospace companies are pushing a plan for satellites to turn solar energy into electricity that would be beamed to earth as microwaves. The Energy Department is resisting more spending.

17 The stock market exploded in a surge of trading that produced record New York Stock Exchange volume of 52,280,000 shares and a 19.92-point spurt in the Dow Jones Industrial Average, the biggest in over 18 months.

Merrill Lynch acquired White Weld for about $50 million in cash, one of the largest mergers in Wall Street history. Merger pressures are intensifying on Wall Street amid growing industry concern over rapidly increasing competition.

Work on the tax bill for this year will begin in the House, with inflation, workers' gripes about Social Security taxes, and the energy bill clouding the prospects for predicting an outcome.

A new rail merger policy aimed at encouraging consolidations was proposed by the Interstate Commerce Commission.

AT&T cannot withhold certain local telephone connections from specialized carriers competing with its long-distance service, a federal appeals court ruled, opening the way for expansion of MCI Communications' Execunet service.

18 Tax-revision proposals of President Carter to repeal deductions for state or local taxes on retail sales and personal property were rejected by the House Ways and Means Committee. It did approve his plan to repeal the deduction for state or local motor fuel taxes.

Brokerage houses could seek millions of dollars of tax refunds following an appeals court's rejection of New York State's method of taxing some major revenue sources of securities firms. The issue, which may be appealed further, involves unincorporated business taxes and the state's franchise tax.

19 The New Haven Railroad has a plan to end its bankruptcy proceedings of almost 17 years and become an investment company. It would settle senior creditor claims and administrative costs with cash, then swap new securities for outstanding bonds.

Killing the Commodity Futures Trading Commission and replacing it with an agency directly responsible to the President was recommended by the administration.

An SEC rule requiring large institutional investors to make annual reports of all their holdings at year's end was approved in principle. Holdings now must be reported only when an institution acquires 5 percent of a company's stock.

20 Economic activity declined at an 0.6 percent annual rate in the first quarter, the first real drop in GNP since 1975. At fault were the coal strike and the harsh winter. The period's annual inflation rate rose to 7.1 percent from 5.9 percent. Help for the dollar is planned by the Treasury in monthly auctions from the U.S. gold stock—300,000 ounces at each of the first six sales. The dollar generally gained on news of the smaller than expected drop in GNP. Also aiding it was a report of U.S. oil imports' running much below the 1977 level.

Trustees of Teamsters' Central States Pension Fund and Health and Welfare Fund fired the executive director of both funds, apparently escalating the struggle to control the union after President Frank Fitzsimmons's expected resignation.

21 Market makers on the Chicago Board Options Exchange have been hit hard by the stock market's unexpected rally. Because of "short" call positions, many had to raise additional capital and a dozen likely will have to sell their seats.

24 A gas compromise was reached by energy conferees, but they may have a tough time selling it to their colleagues. The proposal would deregulate all newly discovered natural gas by 1985. It would cost $25–$31 billion more over seven years than the bill supported by the House and President Carter, but about $30 billion less than the Senate's plan.

Monetary changes are planned by Western European leaders to bring greater stability for their currencies and to isolate them from the dollar, which shows signs of bottoming out.

25 Output of IBM will increase 60 percent for computer systems, 80 percent for terminals, and 200 percent for office systems this year, its chairman said. IBM is adding 10,000 manufacturing workers in the 1977–78 period.

Brokerage-house customers may sue an accounting firm for preparing allegedly false and misleading audits of the broker, an appeals court ruled. The court also gave Securities Investor Protection Corp. and the defunct broker's trustee the right to prosecute such claims on behalf of customers. The case involved the defunct Weis Securities and its auditor, Touche Ross.

The stock market advanced broadly after overcoming jitters about the Federal Reserve's apparent credit tightening. Trading continued heavy, and the Dow Jones Industrial Average climbed 13.26 points to 826.06.

26 The mortgage market remains in relatively good shape despite rising interest rates, analysts told a home builders' conference. They said home loan commitments are strong, the savings flow seems to be easing, and new home prices may rise less rapidly.

27 Bert Lance, National Bank of Georgia, and Calhoun First National were charged by the SEC and the Comptroller of the Currency with questionable and unsafe practices. They consented to injunctions, and National Bank of Georgia said that removes one of the major barriers to a proposed Saudi bid for 60 percent of its stock.

A fiscal 1979 budget deficit of $55.6 billion was slated in a Senate vote, much the same as President Carter is proposing.

A tax on stevedoring may be imposed by a state without running afoul of the Constitution, the Supreme Court ruled. That reversed a position it had held for more than 40 years.

28 The Federal Reserve tightened credit for the second time in about a week, raising to 7¼ percent from 7 percent its target for the federal funds rate. The move puts pressure on the 8 percent prime rate and makes an increase in the discount rate likely.

The natural gas price compromise is in danger of unraveling in Congress, prompting feverish efforts by President Carter to save the energy bill. Meanwhile, a study found that two more Gulf of Mexico gas fields are producing as rapidly as possible. A fee on imported oil should not be imposed by President Carter, the Senate Finance Committee declared. Its resolution helped depress the value of the U.S. dollar on fears that fuel imports would surge.

De Beers's selling unit will cut its anti-speculation surcharge on rough diamond prices to 25 percent from 40 percent.

May 1978

1 The continuing steep rise in consumer prices could make it even harder for the President to sell the public on his voluntary anti-inflation program, some officials fear. March's prices jumped an adjusted 0.8 percent, equivalent to a 9.6 percent annual pace, and brought the inflation rate to a 9.3 percent annual rate in the first period.

Federal banking agencies are seeking ways to help savings institutions, which have experienced decreased deposits since January. Interest rate moves by the Fed and some banks are likely to accelerate the slump.

The SEC delayed for three months, until August 1, the deadline for start-up of a composite quotation system by the stock exchanges and the National Association of Securities Dealers.

2 Leading indicators declined 0.1 percent in March after February's revised 0.5 percent rebound in the index, which tends to foreshadow economic trends. March's construction spending rose 3.5 percent to a $184.5 billion adjusted annual rate.

Philip Morris offered up to $440 million for Seven-Up, but families controlling much of Seven-Up's stock indicated they would refuse the $41-a-share bid.

The Supreme Court agreed to decide whether findings of securities law violations in a government suit can be used against a company when the same violations are alleged in a private suit. The issue involves Parklane Hosiery.

3 Mortgage bankers would get access to a major new market for their home loans under an agreement presented to Congress this week. The proposed legislation would let them sell mortgages directly to the Federal Home Loan Mortgage Corp.

Saudi Arabia named Ralph M. Parsons Co. management services contractor for the giant Yanbu industrial complex being built over 28 years at an estimated cost of $10 billion.

Henry Ford II made an impassioned and detailed defense against recent charges that he took corporate funds for personal use and awarded company contracts to family members.

Britain's informal 10 percent guideline for wage increases expires on July 31, and debate is mounting over what, if anything, will follow. Limits of 7 percent for total earnings gains and 5 percent for basic pay raises are under discussion.

4 The U.S. dollar will be a main issue at OPEC talks this weekend, but the currency probably will continue to be used for pricing oil despite complaints that the dollar's weakness has cost cartel members dearly. That weakness has also brought calls to boost the dollar price of oil, a worry that yesteryear depressed the value of the currency.

Japanese steps to reduce a huge trade surplus were outlined to President Carter. Prime Minister Fukuda said plans include buying U.S. planes and uranium, paying in advance for services delivered later, increasing stockpiles of oil and nonferrous metals, and hastening aid to less-developed nations.

5 A natural gas pricing compromise is still pending as the administration and House Democratic leaders try to find the votes to get it through a conference committee.

8 The continuing improvement in the jobless rate may signal a stronger-than-expected economic rebound this quarter, according to government economists. They noted the Labor Department's report that business continued to hire large numbers of workers in April and that the jobless rate fell to an adjusted 6 percent of the work force from March's 6.2 percent.

The Fed is being closely watched for any clues that it might be tightening credit again. It is expected to tighten credit throughout the year to combat inflation, but no one is sure how fast or how far it will go.

Saudi Arabia and Iran, meeting informally with other OPEC producers, favored continuing the current oil price freeze for the rest of 1978. Some producers are demanding an increase to make up for losses in purchasing power resulting from the weakness of the dollar, which is used in oil pricing.

9 Energy consumption is slowing in the United States and will likely grow 2–3 percent a year through 1990, according to a federal study. But that slowing is not enough to stem the flow of imported oil.

Truckers and railroads are under investigation by at least six grand juries for possible illegal gifts or other favors to shippers and government employees.

A ruling that AT&T cannot withhold local phone connections from specialized long-distance competitors will not be reconsidered by an appeals court. Separately, the New York Telephone unit asked for rate increases of $80 million a year for some business gear and services.

10 Gulf Oil was charged by the United States with antitrust violations in its participation in a uranium cartel. The charges, though only misdemeanors, could complicate Gulf's defense against civil suits. Gulf protested the charges.

Touche Ross lost a round as a court ruled that the SEC has authority for a public hearing in its action against the firm's accounting practices.

New York City aid legislation faces a close vote in Congress amid heavy White House lobbying but stands a good chance of passage by the June 30 expiration of the current federal loan program, a Treasury official said.

11 Retail sales climbed a strong 2 percent in April to an adjusted $63.56 billion as auto sales accelerated. That reinforced administration optimism about brisk economic growth in the second quarter.

Anti-inflation efforts of President Carter were dealt a setback as the AFL-CIO refused to commit its 105 member unions to seeking wage increases smaller than those of the past two years.

A savings certificate tied to the Treasury bill rates is being planned to bolster the flow of funds into banks and thrift institutions. The new certificates, with a six-month maturity, would have a $10,000 minimum.

Swiss Credit Bank will buy a further 31 percent interest from Merrill Lynch in their Credit Suisse–White Weld joint ventures for a reported $25 million.

12 The Fed raised the discount rate to 7 percent from 6 percent, and fears of a further credit tightening spread on news of a $4 billion surge in the basic money supply in the week of May 3. The fears fueled higher short-term interest rates, while the discount-rate rise boosted the value of the U.S. dollar. Fiscal policy should be tightened and monetary policy relaxed, Federal Reserve Chairman Miller asserted. He called for a smaller deficit in fiscal 1979 and a balanced budget by fiscal 1982.

President Carter decided tentatively to trim his tax-cut proposal to $20 billion from $25 billion and to delay the effective date three months to January 1, 1979.

15 Postal rate increases, which probably will take effect later this month, will include sharper-than-expected boosts for some business and nonprofit mailers and a two-cent rise for most first-class mail to 15 cents.

16 Oil and nuclear fuel companies should not be barred from buying or keeping coal properties, the Justice Department concluded. Such a prohibition could curb new competition, the Antitrust Division said.

Dymo Industries got a surprise take-over bid from Sweden's Esselte AB at $24 a share, or up to $45.3 million. Dymo earlier recovered a 28 percent stake from a French company at $17 a share to prevent a take-over.

17 Price rises are expected to be widespread for the rest of 1978, according to a survey of purchasing managers. For May so far, a steep 67 percent of the managers said they were paying more than they were a month ago.

Social Security tax boosts enacted last year should keep the system solvent into the next century, Cabinet trustees reported. The finding likely will hinder further the congressional moves for a rollback.

18 Steel prices would need to rise 7 percent above cost inflation in order for U.S. producers to recover the $4.2 billion in revenue lost during the past two years to dumped imports, a trade group estimates. The figures could be used to support a bid for increases above anti-inflation targets.

Securities law changes will likely be proposed by the American Law Institute. Its plan would increase director-officer liability for SEC filings, lighten the burden of clearing the new officers, preempt state tender offer laws, redefine such offers, and impose new rules on investment advisers and banks.

19 Corporate profits after taxes in the first quarter took their sharpest fall in over a year, tumbling 2 percent to a $102.9 billion adjusted annual rate after a revised 1.4 percent rise in the prior period. The quarter's real GNP was revised to an 0.4 percent adjusted annual rate of decline from the 0.6 percent reported last month.

Conrail, in a confidential five-year plan, projected that its 1978 net loss would widen to $379 million from $366.6 million in 1977. But it forecast that the loss would shrink to $119 million in 1979 and that profits would follow.

The nuclear power plant licensing speedup the President is seeking ran into Senate opposition at an environment and public works hearing. With up to four more hearings to come, its prospects seem poor.

A Social Security tax rollback is not likely to be pressed by House Democrats, Speaker O'Neill said. Senate Majority Leader Byrd opposed a cut this year.

22 Increased postal rates, including parcel post charges higher than the Postal Service would like, will go into effect next week. The service, fearing it will lose parcel business, is drawing up a proposal to reduce the rates.

Short interest on the New York Stock Exchange in the past month surged to another record, 42,868,973 shares, up 7 percent. The AMEX posted a 4 percent increase to 6,731,861 shares.

GM said it plans to hold salary increases for its top officers this year to less than last year's level in an attempt to help fight inflation, but it was not clear what size pay boosts would be allowed under the policy.

23 Federal funds were allowed to trade at 7½ percent without Fed intervention in a further confirmation that the central bank has lifted its interest target on the reserves from 7¼ percent. House Banking Chairman Reuss meanwhile, urged that the target for money supply growth be raised.

The Supreme Court denied AT&T a stay of a lower court ruling requiring it to make added phone connections for specialized carriers' long-distance service, clearing the way for competition. The justices also refused to interfere with a bid by municipal utilities to invoke antitrust laws against Indiana & Michigan Electric for alleged price squeezing.

Eight building unions and 50 construction companies, under a pact covering 11 southeastern states, will bar most work disruptions in a bid to cut the cost of heavy industrial facilities.

24 Commodities stockpile revisions to conform with newly projected defense needs have reached Congress. A House panel yesterday voted tin sales beyond the White House's aim, signaling a conflict that will also involve silver and copper.

Merrill Lynch will join Bache in switching its main market in dually traded options from the Chicago Board of Trade to the American Stock Exchange because of processing problems.

25 Executive pay curbs are drawing expanding corporate attention in response to the President's anti-inflation pitch. Time joined AT&T, GM, and Ford in planning such restraints.

Gold deposit certificates representing bullion in Zurich have drawn $37 million of purchases since Deak & Co. introduced them last summer as U.S. investors turn to them as an easy means of direct ownership.

International monetary conferees addressed the newly ratified flexible exchange system, which Treasury Secretary Blumenthal hailed as a key move away from externally imposed stability, but indicated basic despair over flow management.

Cocoa futures prices are expected to stay resilient despite a big surplus not significantly diminished by lowered Ghanian output; shipping delays and African political problems have kept available supplies tight.

26 Fed Chief Miller warned Congress that if the government does not move against inflation with spending cuts, the Reserve Board may impose restrictions that could slow expansion or even cause a recession. He urged paring the fiscal 1979 budget to $50 billion from a projected $53 billion.

American Airlines sought CAB authority to fly from Dallas/Fort Worth to Tokyo, Hong Kong, and Seoul in a major move to broaden its mainly domestic service.

An SEC reporting proposal that would have required companies to disclose details when they dismiss outside accountants is being scrapped in favor of a voluntary approach.

Big Board–SEC discord is expected over the agency's plan for electronically pooling and displaying limit orders from all markets under the emerging national system. The Big Board, which handles 90 percent of such business, wants separate files.

30 GM, in its fourth new-car pricing action this year, is raising prices of its Chevette subcompacts between $75 and $95 a unit. AMC is raising its car prices an average of $79 a unit, or 1.4 percent.

The SEC moved closer to publicizing its pending questionable-payment charges against International Telephone & Telegraph, although its right to make the charges public is yet to be decided.

OECD members heard estimates that this year's economic growth among the 24 member nations will be only 3.25 to 3.5 percent, below previous estimates of 4 percent, if new stimulative measures are not taken.

31 Wages in the United States rose an average 1.9 percent in the first quarter, topping the prior quarter's 1.7 percent and the year-earlier 1.5 percent. Nonunion workers' gains outstripped those of unionized employees.

June 1978

1 Consumer prices, fueled by a record 6.6 percent increase in beef prices, spurted an adjusted 0.9 percent in April for a 10.8 percent annual rate. It was the biggest monthly jump since February 1977 and brought inflation back to the double-digit pace for the first time since then. Farm product prices for May meantime posted a 3 percent rise. The eighth consecutive monthly gain, following 4 percent rises for April and March, signaled more increases for consumers.

The Supreme Court ruled that owners of gas-producing properties must continue out-of-state sales if they were conducted while the land was under lease. The decision upheld regulators in a victory for an El Paso Co. unit. Separately, justices overturned a ruling that water is a mineral for which claims to public land may be made.

Long Island Lighting filed a bid to boost electric rates 18.5 percent and gas rates 13.1 percent for total added revenue of $171 million a year.

Eli Lilly sued three New York officials over the state's generic drug substitution law, charging that its patent rights to an antibiotic were being violated.

2 Business loans by leading New York banks spurted a record $1.21 billion this week, the biggest gain since July 1974. The M1 money supply took a surprise drop of $1 billion in the preceding week.

The Wage Price Council blasted West Coast electrical workers' contract settlements, featuring raises of 9.5 to 11 percent the first year, as highly inflationary.

5 Capital gains taxes would be cut substantially under a bill the House Ways and Means Committee is expected to approve. The measure is strongly opposed by President Carter, who wants to raise the taxes.

The first exploratory well drilled off New Jersey's shore is apparently a dry hole, Continental Oil said. Meanwhile, the Interior Department increased its estimate on gas in the area to 13.3 trillion cubic feet and revised its figures for oil to 800 million barrels from between 400 million and 1.4 billion.

Banks and savings and loan associations were disappointed by the slow sales of new high-yielding saving certificates pegged to Treasury bill rates.

Levi Strauss agreed to a $3.5 million settlement of a court action in California alleging illegal price maintenance between 1972 and 1975.

6 Consumer confidence slumped in May, according to two surveys plus individual interviews in a dozen cities. The Conference Board index fell to 88.5 from a restated 96.9 in April, and Citibank found that 60 percent of Americans foresee woes for the economy.

World oil supplies should be adequate for the rest of the century because of lower economic growth and better use, according to a research group. The finding conflicts with the crisis view reiterated by the International Energy Agency.

The stock market moved broadly and sharply higher, buoyed by economic news and technical pressure on institutions. The Dow Jones Industrial Average rose 16.29 points to a near nine-month high.

Ernst & Ernst and two partners were disciplined by the SEC for allegedly improper accounting that the agency said helped drive up prices for Westec stock during the mid-1960s.

7 Inflation worries have prompted the President to approve an effort to trim up to $5 billion more from fiscal 1979 spending, sources said. The President is being urged by the budget director to accept a tax cut narrowed to $15 billion from $19.4 billion.

Alaska-pipeline rates set by the ICC were upheld by the Supreme Court. This was a defeat for the line's oil-company owners, who had challenged the agency's authority. The decision likely will mean refunds of the higher fees charged during a stay of the schedule.

8 Fed Chief William Miller declared the Reserve Board has no agreement with the White House to ease monetary reins in response to tightened fiscal policy. Interest rates can only reflect existing conditions, he said.

Rail freight rate increases of 2–4 percent were granted by the ICC. But it deferred the effective date to July 17 and rejected the roads' bid for a 7 percent higher steam-coal fee.

SEC rules calling for disclosure about director committees and director-management ties were set in motion. But the commission put off decisions on more complicated aspects of how companies are run.

9 Chairman Henry Ford's youngest brother was elevated to a top executive post at Ford Motor. President Lee Iacocca, in a further setback to his aim of running the firm, was made responsible to Vice Chairman Philip Caldwell.

12 A prime-rate boost to 8¾ percent from 8½ percent appears likely, analysts said, due to cost pressures and booming loan demand. Separately, in what may be the precursor of another increase, Citibank raised from 8 percent to 8¼ percent its broker loan rate, the fee charged securities firms on loans backed by stock as collateral.

General Dynamics and the Navy settled their dispute over submarine contracts by agreeing to divide an estimated $843 million company loss on the orders. The Navy hopes the accord will serve as a model in solving its other shipbuilding problems.

The world economy's current slowdown may indicate a basic long-term break in the post–World War II pattern of rapid growth, the Bank for International Settlements cautioned.

13 Bethlehem Steel raised its prices 3 percent effective July 30, and conditionally promised no more increases this year. White House inflation fighters hailed the pledge. But steel buyers were skeptical, and other steelmakers stayed mum.

The Supreme Court upheld FCC rulings that most joint ownerships of newspapers and broadcast stations in the same community need not be disbanded, although the practice will be barred in the future.

Ford Pintos and Bobcats, along with Mustang II's, are being probed anew by the United States, this time for steering defects in 1973–75 models. Granadas and Monarchs also are being studied for fuel leakage problems.

Foreign exchange accounting required by the Financial Accounting Standards Board is being challenged by the Treasury and the New York Federal Reserve Bank as possibly further disturbing currency markets.

14 The value of the dollar stabilized in foreign exchange trading after Federal Reserve Chief Miller's reiteration of the U.S. commitment to keep it steady. He promised steps to stop speculation until economic improvement strengthens the currency.

Accounting firms practicing before the SEC would be required to join a self-regulatory organization under a bill to be introduced by Representative John E. Moss, but prospects for its passage this year are dim.

OECD ministers are expected to endorse freer business policies as a spur to economic growth at a meeting of the 24-nation economic planning group this week.

15 Oil companies were barred from operating filling stations in Maryland as the Supreme Court upheld a state law aimed at protecting dealer-run stations. Under the potentially far-reaching decision, the producers have a year to shed their retail outlets.

GM is recalling 598,000 of its 1977 and 1978 cars and utility trucks to correct potential safety defects.

OECD members are expected to agree on the general principles of government subsidy limits, but it is unlikely that the envoys from the industrialized nations will decide how to remove such measures.

APL Corp. contested the application of take-over laws by Wisconsin and Arkansas on its bid for Milwaukee's Pabst. APL said it will pursue its bid for 52 percent of the brewer in other states.

16 Iowa's taxes on corporate income on the basis of sales there, regardless of property and payroll location, were upheld by the Supreme Court. It rejected arguments of bias against out-of-state firms. Justices also upheld a Massachusetts tax that federal S&Ls contended was discriminatory.

19 The economy is ending the current quarter at a slower and more sustainable growth than the brisk pace at which it began, indicating an end to the sharp rebound from the winter doldrums. Private housing starts dropped 4.9 percent in May following April's 6.5 percent advance, and personal income slowed to a 0.9 percent rise last month after a 1.3 percent gain in April.

The Fed's Open Market Committee favored some moderate credit tightening at its current meeting, despite worries over a slowing in the economy. Separately, most major commercial banks lifted their prime rate to 8¾ percent from 8½ percent.

Eastman Kodak's photofinishing operations may lose access to exclusive data on Kodak's plans for new films, under a proposed ruling by a federal judge in Berkey Photo's antitrust case. Also the judge, in effect, reduced Berkey's expected cash award to $81.5 million from $112.8 million.

The Chicago Options Board and the Midwest Stock Exchange agreed to combine their options trading on the CBOE floor. The action, which was protested by the American Stock Exchange, revived rumors that the two eventually would seek to merge. The SEC asked for more public comment on several key issues in its study of options trading.

New England Petroleum's $1.6 billion breach-of-contract suit against Libya and its National Oil Corp. was dismissed by a federal judge, who based his dismissal on lack of jurisdiction.

20 AT&T said it will not make any more common equity investments in its Pacific Telephone. The company's first such move in 40 years follows rulings on the unit's use of accelerated depreciation by California regulators and the IRS calling for refunds, rate reductions, and back taxes.

Class-action plaintiffs generally must pay the cost of compiling the names and addresses of those in the class, the Supreme Court held. The decision came in a securities fraud case involving Oppenheimer Fund. The IRS can issue a summons for taxpayer records held by a third party even if criminal prosecution follows, the justices ruled in a case involving LaSalle National Bank. A lower court has held the only permissible motive was a civil probe. The high court also ordered an antitrust award that a Trailways Bus operator won from a Greyhound unit partially reconsidered.

Brazil's coffee growers face a possible frost. They likely will not fare as well on prices as after the 1975 freeze, because demand is less strong and Colombia has just harvested a record crop.

21 Antitrust damage suits could be brought by customers against manufacturers even if the purchases were made from a middleman, under a bill cleared by the House Judiciary panel. The measure, similar to one passed by a Senate unit, would reverse a Supreme Court ruling.

The federal budget will not be balanced by 1981 as President Carter has often promised, Budget Chief James McIntyre said. He indicated that the administration hopes to balance the budget by fiscal 1982.

22 Zenith Radio lost its Supreme Court bid to have the United States impose special penalty duties on Japanese television sets and other electronic imports exempted from Japan's commodity tax. The defeat would appear to doom U.S. Steel's appeal of the Treasury's refusal to impose countervailing duties on European steel.

The Fed indicated it raised from 7½ percent to 7¾ percent its target interest rate on the uncommitted reserves banks lend one another. The move could press increases in the Fed's 7 percent discount rate and the 8¾ percent prime rate. Chairman Miller of the Federal Reserve, citing a need for federal regulation of foreign banks, criticized a House bill for failing to prohibit interstate branching by the banks and limiting the Fed's authority over them.

23 President Carter again threatened to raise U.S. oil prices through administrative action, such as import fees, if Congress does not pass his proposed crude oil tax. Energy Secretary Schlesinger refused to set any deadline for White House action, but he said the ad-

ministration probably would give Congress until the end of the year to act.

Stock exchanges and the National Association of Securities Dealers were asked by the SEC to continue a voluntary moratorium on options trading until at least next March.

26 Inflation fears among consumers reached their greatest proportion last month since the 1974–75 recession, according to a University of Michigan survey. The survey said consumers expect inflation to rise an average of 8.2 percent over the next 12 months and it forecast continued brisk consumer spending in the near term.

27 Nuclear plant liability limits in case of a catastrophic accident were upheld by the Supreme Court in a defeat for environmentalists. The decision, in a case involving Duke Power, should help free the industry to develop atomic sources.

28 The trade deficit for the United States shrank in May to an adjusted $2.24 billion, the smallest gap since September. The narrowing, spurred by a 1 percent export expansion to a record $11.75 billion, prompted speculation of further contraction.

Soviet trade with less-developed nations reached a record $12.2 billion last year, giving the nation both a hard-currency trade surplus and increased access to valuable raw materials.

TWA filed for CAB approval to boost transatlantic fares from 5 percent to as high as 15 percent effective November 1, citing increases in costs beyond its control. The proposal includes the first basic coach fare increase since 1974.

Oil companies should be prevented from owning pipelines but not from owning such alternative fuel sources as coal or uranium, according to testimony that U.S. antitrust chief John Shenefield presented to Congress today.

29 The capital gains tax cut proposed by Representative William Steiger was attacked as millionaires' relief by Treasury Secretary Blumenthal. He also warned a Senate unit that it would not boost stock prices.

ABC was sued by Warner Cable in an effort to keep the broadcaster from preventing the cablecasting of certain college games to Warner's pay-television subscribers. The antitrust action is likely to have wide repercussions in the industry.

Women-owned businesses should be encouraged via federal training programs, loans, and enforcement of anti-bias measures, a government task force recommended. The President pledged support for the effort.

30 The value of building contracts awarded in May reached a record $17.79 billion, up 11 percent from the year before. For the first five months, awards were up 19 percent. The biggest gains were in nonresidential contracts.

Coca-Cola is letting bottlers boost the amount of cost-saving corn sweeteners they substitute for sugar in its noncola drinks, a move with broad implications for the sweetener industry.

Federal Reserve chief Miller urged Congress to put off for two years the boost in the federal minimum wage set for January 1 as a brake on inflation. He also encouraged a lower youth wage.

July 1978

3 A prime-rate boost of ¼ percent to 9 percent was touched off by Citibank and was quickly followed by the nation's major banks. Later the Fed, over the objections of Chairman Miller, raised its rate on loans to member banks to 7¼ percent from 7 percent. Although smaller than expected, the increase was seen as a defeat for Miller.

Farm prices rose in June for the ninth consecutive month, the Agriculture Department said. A separate report shows that farmers will plant fewer acres this year, meaning that price-depressing big surpluses are not likely to occur.

A report on pension plans by the federal Pension Benefit Guaranty Corp. estimates that 160 of the nation's 2,000 multi-employer pension plans are so weak financially that they could fail within the next decade.

5 The Conference Board's economic forum predicts slower economic growth in 1979 and faster inflation.

China's new leaders appear to have decided to start seeking direct loans, a policy reversal that has far-reaching implications for its economic growth.

Big gambling concerns are rushing to Atlantic City to buy up land in the wake of the spectacular success of the resort's first gambling casino.

6 Construction spending climbed 2.9 percent in May to an adjusted $198.6 billion annual rate, after a 4.4 percent

rise in April. The biggest gain was in public building.

The accounting sector's efforts at self-regulation drew qualified support from the SEC. In a report to Congress, the agency said the profession's initiatives should be allowed to develop.

Stock exchanges will not generally be able to replace involuntarily delisted options with those already traded elsewhere, under new SEC guidelines.

Mortgage funds apparently will continue to be available in most parts of the United States, despite the savings deposit pinch. With new mechanisms and a pledge of support from the government, the industry is seen as being better equipped to compete for lendable money than it was in the 1973–74 crisis.

Britain renegotiated a $1.5 billion, seven-year syndicated bank loan, obtaining a four-year extension and lower interest charges. The improved terms reflect a liquidity buildup in Europe's dollar market.

7 Real GNP will increase 4.1 percent this year instead of the 4.7 percent projected earlier, primarily because consumer prices will rise 7.2 percent rather than 6.1 percent, the administration predicted. It also shaded its forecast for next year.

The inflation rate will be trimmed 0.2 percent this year and 0.4 percent next year by the effect of California's Proposition 13 on housing costs, the Congressional Budget Office estimated.

Business confidence rose in the second quarter, a Conference Board estimate of 1,500 top executives found. But 36 percent of them saw prices rising faster this year than last.

Kaufman & Broad agreed with the FTC to pay for repairing construction defects in up to 20,000 homes and to refrain from unfair or deceptive practices.

10 Business activity shows early signs of settling into a more moderate pace, according to June data in a survey of the nation's purchasing agents.

Air fares may be cut as much as 70 percent under a plan likely to go into effect on about August 31, the CAB said, further extending airlines' fare-cutting authority. Carriers also would be allowed to raise fares 5–10 percent.

Firestone may be able to avoid much of the financial impact of a government move to force it to recall millions of its "500" radial tires. The National Highway Traffic Safety Administration has found that the tires pose a serious safety risk.

11 Business data-reporting programs that the FTC is conducting in the face of vigorous industry opposition were unanimously upheld by a federal appeals court. The agency wants details of financial and manufacturing activities to spot anticompetitive trends, but business people say the reports are onerous and fear they will be made public.

The Energy Department has begun a probe of how it handles sensitive information in the wake of the embarrassing disclosure that an industry lobbyist got an advance look at agency regulations. An official told a Senate panel that clear guides will be drawn up for the future.

A second exploratory well off the New Jersey shore will be abandoned as a dry hole. Shell Oil drilled to the targeted depth of 14,000 feet without encountering oil or gas accumulations. The rig will be moved to another Baltimore Canyon prospect.

Chicken prices are continuing to rise despite record production, buoyed by the strong demand reflecting unexpectedly high beef and pork prices. Wholesale prices are averaging 7 percent more than a year ago.

12 Economic forecasts by Congressional Budget Director Alice Rivlin indicate little improvement in the inflation rate next year but no recession either, assuming the Federal Reserve Board does not tighten credit further.

Europe's new monetary plan relies chiefly on a revised currency unit to curb speculation. The device increases the participants' ability to stabilize the value of their currencies by effectively creating new funds for intervention.

West Germany proposed a $6 billion, five-year plan aimed at creating 100,-000 jobs and stimulating investments of $13 billion. The plan involves subsidies and investment funds in the areas of conservation and energy.

13 The economy is not headed for a recession, according to the White House. The President said the United States, acting in concert with its trading partners, could stave off such a recurrence, adding that he expected no further economic deterioration. Two top aides echoed the projection in congressional testimony.

The CAB is easing the way for charter carriers to compete with scheduled service, permitting one-way flights, eliminating group size requirements, and scrapping advance-purchase rules.

Hilton Hotels estimated a 124 percent gain in the second quarter per-share earnings to $1.50, citing its Las Vegas casinos. It also disclosed that it may consider an Atlantic City operation.

14 Capital gains tax reduction is expected to be proposed by the administration next week, despite its original opposition. The President and Treasury Secretary are drafting a measure said to be similar in effect to a pending compromise bill that cuts the top rate to 35 percent from 49 percent.

AT&T's proposal that single-line customers be required to use at least one utility-owned phone was rejected by the FCC, and the Justice Department pressed for competition in the long-distance market. But the firm's attempt to enter the data communications area got a boost from the FCC.

17 The economic summit in Bonn is not likely to produce rapid progress in the effort to spur world economic growth, conserve energy, and stabilize currency rates. But there were no signs that the seven-nation meeting would break down in bitter disarray. President Carter was reported to have stated that he expects "positive results" in Congress on a crude oil tax measure.

Datsun and Honda cars sold in the United States will cost about $200 a piece more because of the dollar's decline in value against the Japanese yen. The boost may further dampen faltering import-car sales.

Capital gains could be adjusted to eliminate the effects of inflation before being subject to the 15 percent minimum tax, Senator Russell Long proposed. But there would be no inflation adjustment gains subject to the regular capital gains tax. The Treasury meanwhile is working out details of a proposal for cutting capital gains taxes.

Tire makers will be required to grade their tires for tread wear, traction, and heat resistance under long-delayed rules issued by the Transportation Department.

18 The economic summit ended with pledges from West Germany and Japan for a stronger growth push and from the United States for oil-import reductions amounting to 2.5 million barrels a day by 1985. The outcome exceeded the modest hopes fostered by officials in recent days. The value of

the dollar rose against other major currencies, buoyed by the tone of co-operation that emerged from the Bonn talks.

19 The tax proposal by President Carter was replaced on the House Ways and Means panel agenda with a new bill containing few of his "reforms" and a cut in the top rate on capital gains to 35 percent from 49 percent that he has threatened to veto.

Coal conversion legislation requiring some utilities and factories to switch from oil and gas cleared the Senate by a vote of 92 to 6. But Congress is not expected to enact enough energy measures this year to fulfill the President's import-reduction summit pledge.

Proxy-rule changes proposed by the SEC to give shareholders more information about corporate directors were released for public comment as a first step in the commission's review of how companies are run.

20 Housing starts in June continued at an unexpectedly strong pace, rising to an adjusted annual rate of 2,099,000 units, up a bit from May and 9 percent more than a year earlier. Building permits, an indicator of future construction, rose 13 percent in June after declining in May, amid signs that funds to finance new homes will remain ample.

Hyatt International Corp. said it got an unsolicited proposal to merge with a firm headed by Saudi businessman Ghaith Pharoan. As a result, the Pritzker family, 55 percent owner, will withdraw its offer for the remaining stock.

The American Institute of Certified Public Accountants shelved an auditing proposal eliminating certification of financial reports subject to various uncertainties, a formula used to warn investors after it drew sharp criticism.

21 U.S. productivity may not grow at all this year, Wage-Price Council chief Bosworth told legislators. Calling the trend a major inflation factor, he added that output per hours worked may have slowed to a 1½ percent rise from the 2 percent increase of the past decade.

U.S. coal producers' negotiations with Japanese steelmakers, as expected, have resulted in sharp order cutbacks and smaller price rises than existing contracts called for, because the mills' inventories are up amid sluggish demand.

Continental Oil is under criminal investigation for alleged oil price violations as part of a new government crackdown on industry infractions following the 1973 embargo.

24 Consumer confidence slipped last month from May, but durable goods spending is likely to stay strong for a while, the University of Michigan Survey Research Center said. The center added that consumers are pessimistic on the outlook for business and are buying to avoid future price increases.

The economic growth rate forecast by the Carter administration for the full year, 4.1 percent, may be reduced further because of slower-than-expected growth in the second quarter. A 4.7 percent rate was forecast originally. Separately, Treasury Secretary Blumenthal cautioned that higher interest rates could harm the nation's economy.

The value of the dollar climbed on reports of an oil strike by Texaco in the Atlantic Ocean but then fell sharply after a denial by the company. The prices of gold and some other commodities jumped.

25 The budget surpluses of state and local governments, which the administration had hoped could justify curtailing federal aid, are being revised downward by the Commerce Department to account for pension fund contributions. The new figures will bolster opponents of Proposition 13-type tax cuts.

Japan announced that it has an agreement with Peking for the joint development of oil resources off eastern China in the Pohai Bay.

26 The OECD warned that economic growth in the United States could slow significantly more than the administration envisions if current policies are maintained.

Exports of sugar to the United States by Common Market members are being subsidized under the European Community's agriculture policy, the Treasury said. It set a countervailing duty of 10.8 cents a pound.

27 The trade deficit registered by the United States for June shrank to an adjusted $1.6 billion, its lowest level since May 1977, as exports climbed 3.2 percent to a record $12.13 billion. The improvement was seen to reflect the dollar's decline against trading partners' currencies, though there was little change in the wide gap with Japan.

The SEC will propose expanding disclosure of executive pay to as many as ten top corporate officers as well as to aides of subsidiaries.

Commodity export sales would have to be reported to the CFTC within 48 hours to prevent further injury to U.S. farmers from secretive foreign purchases, under a measure the House passed by a vote of 273 to 125.

The Energy Department will let the price of hard-to-extract oil rise to an uncontrolled $14 a barrel as of September 1 in order to spur production.

28 A safety probe of certain 1977-model GM cars for possible sudden and frequent stalling was announced by the Transportation Department, following customer complaints.

Gulf Oil agreed to settle for $42.2 million government allegations that it overcharged customers as a result of overstated crude oil purchase costs; $79.1 million had originally been sought.

31 The price of gold soared to a record $201.30 an ounce on weakness of the value of the dollar, which tumbled to lows against the Swiss franc and Japanese yen. The dollar's decline is approaching the payoff stage for the United States, an OECD analysis suggested. American exports have become more competitive because the value of the dollar has dropped against other currencies by more than enough to offset U.S. inflation.

August 1978

2 Xerox and IBM settled an eight-year dispute over patents on office copying and electronic typing machines. Under the agreement, IBM will pay Xerox $25 million and each company will be licensed to use, without royalty, all patents held by the other and all patents applied for during the next five years.

Oil imports will increase in the second half and will continue to rise through 1979, a Treasury official predicted. Higher consumption, declining production and imports for the U.S. strategic stockpile will contribute to the rise, he added.

3 The stock market rallied stunningly on hopes of a peak in interest rates. The Dow Jones industrial average rocketed 22.78 points, its sharpest gain since January 1975, on the highest trading volume since early June.

Pacific Northwest Bell's $150 million of 40-year debentures were priced to yield a lower-than-expected 8.75 percent on the strength of a further jump in the bond market.

The SEC will consider a proposal requiring lawyers to disclose client fraud to the agency or the victim. The plan, by a nonprofit law firm, is one outgrowth of the 1972 National Student Marketing case.

John DeLorean will locate his planned automobile plant in Northern Ireland, Ulster officials indicated. The former GM aide also had been negotiating with Puerto Rico.

4 The Stock Market recorded its heaviest trading day ever as New York Stock Exchange volume spurted to 65.4 million shares. European capital, lured by the rally on August 2, led the move, joined by institutional and domestic individual investors. After seesawing, the Dow Jones industrial average finished up 3.38 points.

A sugar-price bill guaranteeing growers 16 cents a pound this year, up from the current 13½ cents, won tentative House Agriculture Committee approval despite White House objections that the level is inflationary.

7 The IMF, using proceeds from gold auctions held since June 1976, distributed more than $1 billion to 104 developing nations.

8 Japanese analysts increasingly believe the nation will need to enact a supplementary budget to meet its 7 percent growth target for the current fiscal year as a result of the expected exports decline stemming from the yen's appreciation.

9 Color TV prices suggested to retailers were raised by RCA $10 to $50 a set, its first such boost in five years. The move, which was expected, follows sharp sales gains amid declining Japanese imports. Zenith said it's studying a similar increase.

10 Xerox was found liable for $11.7 million in damages to SCM for excluding it from the plain paper copier market during 1969–76 and for other losses. The award could be tripled under antitrust law, but Xerox will ask that most of it be set aside.

Fuel-oil entitlements for East Coast users were put at 50 percent of the current level paid to domestic refiners under a compromise measure passed by the Senate. The current subsidy is 30 percent, but the administration wanted it raised to over 60 percent.

11 The Intermarket Trading System was authorized by the SEC to operate for another year, because the small num-

ber of participants hasn't permitted a conclusive evaluation of the experiment.

More tax relief than the $16.3 billion in cuts approved by the House is needed, said Senate Finance Committee Chairman Russell Long, who has mentioned a figure of $20 billion.

The Treasury proposed to tax foreign governments on income earned from operating businesses in the United States.

24 A U.S.-German air pact providing for expanded service through eased restrictions was hailed by CAB chairman Alfred Kahn as an enormous step toward increasing international competition. The proposal will be presented in Bonn September 12.

Fedders accused Chrysler of fraudulently overvaluing the assets of its Airtemp division, which Fedders bought in 1976. The allegations were contained in counterclaims amounting to $525 million that Fedders filed in reply to a Chrysler suit seeking further payment.

25 Pan Am asked the CAB to let it acquire National Airlines and buy up to 25 percent while the request is pending, noting that Texas International, a rival suitor, earlier won permission for such a holding.

Mead told shareholders it opposes Occidental Petroleum's takeover bid because the proposed exchange of stock would be inadequate and problematic and because of doubts concerning Occidental's earnings base and management.

31 Wages and salaries in the United States rose an average 2.1 percent in the second quarter, the biggest such increase ever registered in the employment cost index's three-year existence. Accelerated raises for construction, transportation, and especially for sales workers fueled the spurt.

A wheat cartel modeled on the oil exporters' OPEC is being urged by politicians from U.S. and Canadian growing regions. The contemplated group would also include Australia and Argentina but exclude the Common Market, the world's other major producer.

September 1978

5 Four investment firms were censured by an SEC administrative law judge for their trading actions prior to the uncovering of the Equity Funding scandal in 1973. Their informant, Raymond Dirks, was suspended from the brokerage business for 60 days.

6 Gas-pricing legislation goes before the Senate by next week (September 11–15) with the White House's political prestige at stake. The uneasy compromise has drawn fire from an unusual coalition of interests, but the President's intense lobbying may have given him an edge. Less favorable are prospects for a Senate tax bill that meets his objectives.

The Navy and IBM, prime contractor for the so-called LAMPS submarine-hunting helicopter system, a $3.9 billion program, are drafting $400 million of cost reductions to present to Congress, in hopes of heading off an effort to halt the troubled development.

Hong Kong's real estate boom may be stabilizing after an 18-month explosion that saw prices of residential apartments soar 30 percent. But the market, fueled by rising income's effect on social trends and by speculation, should continue strong.

7 Fed chief Miller told a Senate panel the government can stabilize the dollar if it acts within 60 days to curb inflation and energy imports. Meanwhile, officials at the New York Federal Reserve Bank asserted the currency has been badly undervalued by heavy selling pressure. A tax cut of around $15 billion would be appropriate for 1979, Miller said, but instead of some of the House-passed bill's individual and business cuts, he urged deferring the Social Security tax increase and other revisions.

Alcoa is raising prices 5.5 percent on aluminum sheet used for beverage cans. The boost follows a steel-industry price increase for sheet sold to the drink-can market.

8 Wage-price guides backed by a system of limited sanctions are finding favor with the administration as a way to strengthen the anti-inflation program. The voluntary wage standard would be tied to the cost of living; the price guide would call for increases below the prior year's by 1 to 1.5 percentage points. The plan would be harder to ignore than this year's "deceleration" campaign.

11 Fairchild Industries and its chairman, Edward Uhl, were indicted by a federal grand jury for preparing false tax returns for 1971 and 1972 to hide il-

legal political contributions by Fairchild. The jury probe is continuing.

12 Federal Reserve nominee Nancy Teeters, whose appointment seems headed for quick approval, told Senators at her confirmation hearing she doesn't believe inflation can be fought solely with tighter credit and budget policies and said that interest rates may be approaching their limits.

A report on OSHA by a presidential task force is focusing on how the government can foster workplace safety. Measures would be aimed at helping develop technology, providing more data on hazards, and giving companies incentives for better internal programs.

13 The railroad industry's bids for higher rates should be more generously received by the ICC, the Transportation Department said. The agency argued the roads need higher profits to finance capital spending to improve efficiency.

14 The industrial innovation study seeking to spotlight deterrent government policies and devise ways to foster invention enters its public phase next month with meetings that may provide a clue to the federal panel's recommendations, due by April 1979.

15 A tax exemption boost for individuals and dependents to $1,000 from $750 was approved by the Senate Finance Committee, making the House-passed change almost sure to take effect in 1979. The panel also agreed to lift the maximum earned income credit for the poor to $600 from $400.

Delivery for the Transbus, a commuter vehicle that accommodates the handicapped, was pushed back three years, to 1983, by the Transportation Department in response to complaints by GM and Congress. Design standards were also eased.

18 The CAB was urged by the Justice Department to block further purchases of National Air stock by two competing suitors, Texas International and Pan Am, until the board acts on the proposed merger.

Newport News is fighting for an overhaul of the Navy carrier Saratoga that appears headed for the Philadelphia Naval Shipyard. The work would enhance the Vice President's political image in the city, but the GAO says it might be cheaper to have the Tenneco unit do the work.

19 Wage-price guidelines proposed by White House economic counselors may be too tough, Carter's political

advisers fear. They are considering trying to persuade the President to make the voluntary anti-inflation measures more palatable to business and labor.

Tax cuts of 33 percent over three years sought by Republicans were rejected by the Senate Finance Committee which then squabbled over raising the earned income credit for the poor, possibly delaying completion of work on the bill this week.

20 The gas compromise portion of the energy package survived a recommital move when the Senate rejected an effort to send the bill back to conferees. Senate Energy Chairman Henry Jackson predicted approval when the measure comes up for final action, expected a week from today (September 27).

21 Credit was tightened still further as the Fed, worried about inflation and money growth, indicated it raised to at least 8½ percent from 8⅜ percent its target rate on federal funds. The move, which may augur boosts in the discount and prime rates, was criticized sharply by the Federal Home Loan Bank Board, which saw a threat to the housing industry. Bond prices plunged still lower.

The Treasury's sale of $2.69 billion of two-year notes brought an average yield of 8.65 percent, the highest since the security was first offered in September 1974.

Tougher anti-inflation efforts were promised by the President. Mr. Carter didn't elaborate, but he told steel workers that his program wouldn't penalize labor or any other sector.

22 Capital gains tax cuts moved one step closer to reality as the Senate's Finance Committee voted to exclude 70 percent of long-term capital gains from regular income tax, instead of the current 50 percent. The panel's package would provide a net capital gains tax cut of $3 billion next year.

25 Durable goods orders climbed 7.6 percent in August to $70.13 billion, after falling 5.3 percent in July and 1.7 percent in June, for the steepest rise in almost eight years. The increase, aided by a sharp boost in aircraft orders, gave the Carter administration an indication of moderate economic growth.

Machine tool bookings last month rose 23 percent from July to $391.6 million, making tool builders optimistic about continued strong demand.

An anti-inflation package that is both

tough and balanced is difficult to assemble, the President said. He promised a wage-price plan very quickly, but officials see a mid-October unveiling.

26 The Fed signaled it raised its target rate on federal funds to 8⅝ percent from 8½ percent, and many analysts expect further credit tightening. Even before the action, First National Bank of Chicago and First Pennsylvania raised their prime rates to 9¾ percent from 9½ percent.

Yields on short-term Treasury bills rose to an average 8.106 percent, the highest since the 8.185 percent return of September 16, 1974.

Carrier rejected United Technologies' offer to negotiate a merger and proposed tender bid as inadequate financially. It also filed a suit to keep United from acquiring or attempting to acquire Carrier stock.

27 An export promotion policy was unveiled by Mr. Carter, but it probably will be a long time before it affects the massive trade deficit. It seeks to provide financial help and technical advice to U.S. firms and reduces some export barriers.

The banking bill expanding reserve requirements was shelved by the Senate Banking panel, but the House is pushing ahead with a measure broadening regulatory control over banks and limiting insiders' activities.

28 The natural gas bill was approved by the Senate and sent to the House. It would end federal price controls on newly found gas in 1985 and permit sizable price boosts in the interim. It would also for the first time put federal controls on gas produced and sold in the same state.

The U.S. trade deficit narrowed sharply last month to an adjusted $1.62 billion, continuing a trend and reinforcing Carter's forecasts of shrinking deficits. August exports climbed to a record $12.47 billion and steel import tonnage rose for the second consecutive month.

29 Work on a tax cut of $23 billion for 1979 was completed by the Senate Finance Committee. The panel's reduction, which goes to the Senate next week (October 2–6), will have to be reconciled with the smaller House-passed tax cut bill of $16.3 billion.

France and Britain set an accord for the U.K.'s entry into the Airbus Industrie venture. Britain would finance 25 percent of the wide-bodied A310 jet's development and would promise not to buy the plane's major rival, Boeing's 757, past the 19 it has agreed to purchase.

Acronyms and Abbreviations

ABA	American Bankers Association
ABC	American Broadcasting Corporation
AFL–CIO	American Federation of Labor–Congress of Industrial Organizations
AMC	American Motors Corporation
AMEX	American Stock Exchange
AT&T	American Telephone & Telegraph Company
CAB	Civil Aeronautics Board
CBOE	Chicago Board Options Exchange
CFTC	Commodity Futures Trading Commission
COMSAT	Communications Satellite Corporation
DISC	Domestic International Sales Corporation (U.S.)
FCC	Federal Communications Commission
FDA	Food and Drug Administration
FTC	Federal Trade Commission
GM	General Motors
GNP	Gross National Product
HUD	Housing and Urban Development (Department)
IBM	International Business Machines
ICC	Interstate Commerce Commission
IMF	International Monetary Fund
IRS	Internal Revenue Service
ITC	International Trade Commission
ITS	Intermarket Trading System
NASD	National Association of Securities Dealers
NLRB	National Labor Relations Board
OECD	Organization for Economic Co-operation and Development
OPEC	Organization of Oil Exporting Countries
OSHA	Occupational Safety and Health Administration
S&L	Savings & Loan (Association)
SEC	Securities and Exchange Commission
TWA	Trans World Airlines
UMW	United Mine Workers

Major Legislation Enacted

Major legislation passed by the 95th Congress are listed below in chronological order. Copies of enacted legislation may be obtained by ordering under the appropriate public law number from the Superintendent of Documents, Government Printing Office, Washington, D.C. 20402. Alternatively, call or write the office of your own member of Congress for a copy of the bill.

Public Law Number	Description	Date Signed into Law
PL 95-143 (HR 6415)	Export-Import Bank Act extended from June 30, 1978, to September 30, 1978	Oct. 26, 1977
PL 95-151 (HR 3744)	Minimum levels increased under the Fair Labor Standards Act	Nov. 1, 1977
PL 95-154 (HJ Res 611)	Authority of Federal Reserve banks extended to buy and sell certain obligations	Nov. 7, 1977
PL 95-156 (HR 9090)	Disaster payments in connection with 1977 crops of feed grains, upland cotton, wheat, and rice exempted from payment limitations in the 1949 Agricultural Act	Nov. 8, 1977
PL 95-158 (HJ Res 621)	Presidential decision on Alaskan Natural Gas Transportation System approved	Nov. 8, 1977
PL 95-176 (HR 4458)	Certain provisions of the Internal Revenue Code of 1954 pertaining to distilled spirits amended	Nov. 12, 1977
PL 95-181 (HR 9704)	$50 million added to the capital stock of the Federal Crop Insurance Corporation	Nov. 15, 1977
PL 95-187 (HR 8346)	Program giving federal operating assistance for programs under Urban Mass Transportation Act revised	Nov. 16, 1977
PL 95-188 (HR 9710)	Authority extended for flexible regulation of interest rates on accounts and deposits in depository institutions; promote Federal Reserve System accountability	Nov. 16, 1977
PL 95-194 (S 1184)	Programs authorizing federal government to insure U.S. fishermen from financial loss as a result of the seizure of their boats on the high seas extended	Nov. 18, 1977
PL 95-198 (HR 422)	Duty-free treatment provided for any aircraft engine used as replacement for an engine being repaired in the United States if duty was already paid on replacement during a prior importation	Nov. 23, 1977
PL 95-214 (HR 9378)	Employee Retirement Income Security Act of 1974 amended	Dec. 19, 1977
PL 95-216 (HR 0346)	Social Security Financing Amendments of 1977 enacted	Dec. 20, 1977
PL 95-217 (HR 3199)	Federal Water Pollution Control Act Amendments of 1977 enacted	Dec. 28, 1977
PL 95-219 (HR 9794)	International fisheries agreement with Mexico approved	Dec. 28, 1977
PL 95-220 (S 904)	Federal Program Information Act enacted	Dec. 28, 1977
PL 95-222 (HR 6666)	Legal Services Corporation Amendments Act of 1977 enacted	Dec. 28, 1977
PL 95-227 (HR 5322)	Excise tax imposed on sale of coal by producer; Black Lung Disability Trust Fund established	Feb. 10, 1978

MAJOR LEGISLATION ENACTED (*continued*)

Public Law Number	Description	Date Signed into Law
PL 95–233 (S 1360)........	National Forest Management Act amended with regard to role of Secretary of Agriculture in selecting bidding methods for sales of timber	Feb. 20, 1978
PL 95–234 (HR 7442).......	Those providing communication services are assured that they are allowed to use existing space on poles used by regulated utilities; Federal Communications Commission forfeiture procedures simplified	Feb. 21, 1978
PL 95–241 (HR 10368)......	Clarification that aircraft registered by U.S. citizens do not have to be based primarily in the United States to be eligible for U.S. registry	Mar. 8, 1978
PL 95–245 (HR 9851).......	Permit supplemental air carriers to obtain certificates to provide for scheduled cargo service	Mar. 14, 1978
PL 95–254 (HR 10982)......	Certain budget authorities totaling $55,225,000 in the presidential January 27, 1978, message rescinded	Apr. 4, 1978
PL 95–256 (HR 5385).......	Age limit for retirement under Age Discrimination Act increased from 65 to 70	Apr. 6, 1978
PL 95–257 (HR 9169).......	Allow the guarantee of obligations for the financing of vessels for a sum not exceeding 87.5 percent of the actual of depreciated actual cost of each vessel	Apr. 7, 1978
PL 95–258 (HR 11055)......	Farmers permitted to treat 1977 crop disaster to target price payments made in 1978 which are attributed to 1977 losses	Apr. 7, 1978
PL 95–268 (HR 9179).......	Basic operating authority of Overseas Private Investment Corporation extended until September 30, 1981	Apr. 24, 1978
PL 95–273 (S 1617)........	Ocean Pollution Research Program Act enacted	May 8, 1978
PL 95–279 (HR 6782).......	Emergency Agricultural Act of 1978 enacted	May 15, 1978
PL 95–283 (HR 8331).......	Improved procedures to protect customers from insolvent brokers and dealers provided through the federal courts and the Securities Investor Protection Corporation	May 21, 1978
PL 95–333 (HR 13385)......	Public debt limit set at $798 billion through March 1979	Aug. 3, 1978
PL 95–334 (HR 11504)......	Federal credit assistance programs for ranchers, farmers, rural communities, and businesses improved	Aug. 4, 1978
PL 95–339 (HR 12426)......	Funds for long-term loan guarantees for New York City authorized	Aug. 8, 1978
PL 95–342 (S 920).........	Permitted oil and gas leases within the Lake Murray Recreational Demonstration area	Aug. 11, 1978
PL 95–345 (HR 7581).......	Made clear the income source requirement that a cooperative or mutual telephone company must satisfy to be exempt from federal income taxation	Aug. 15, 1978
PL 95–351 (HR 2777).......	A National Consumer Cooperative Bank to make loan guarantees to eligible consumer cooperatives established	Aug. 20, 1978
PL 95–361 (S 2543)........	Title 29 of U.S. Code amended to improve procedures for preventing fraudulent solicitation through the mail	Sept. 9, 1978
PL 95–369 (HR 10899)......	Federal regulation of participation of foreign banks in domestic financial markets provided for	Sept. 17, 1978
PL 95–372 (S 9)...........	Policy established for oil and natural gas management in the Outer Continental Shelf	Sept. 18, 1978
PL 95–376 (HR 10878)......	Voluntary insurance program provided by the Fisherman's Protective Act extended to October 1, 1981	Sept. 18, 1978
PL 95–378 (HR 8112).......	Federal Records Council abolished	Sept. 22, 1978
PL 95–381 (S 2928)........	Funds for programs under the International Investment Survey Act to collect and disseminate information on foreign investments in the United States and American overseas investments authorized through fiscal 1981	Sept. 22, 1978

MAJOR LEGISLATION ENACTED (*concluded*)

Public Law Number	Description	Date Signed into Law
PL 95–383 (S 3107)........	Uniform control and supervision of employees of referees in bankruptcy provided	Sept. 22, 1978
PL 95–387 (S 1103)........	Several states permitted to sue for taxes in D.C. Superior Court	Sept. 27, 1978
PL 95–390 (HR 7814).......	Federal agencies and employees authorized to experiment with compressed work and flexible schedules	Sept. 29, 1978
PL 95–396 (S 1678)........	Federal Insecticide, Fungicide, and Rodenticide Act amended and extended through 1979	Sept. 30, 1978
PL 95–397 (HR 3702).......	Various changes made in the Retired Servicemen's Family Protection Plan and Survivor Benefit Plan	Sept. 30, 1978
PL 95–402 (S 3468)........	Insure that the interest rates on price support loans for upland cotton are as favorable to producers as are interest rates for such loans on other commodities	Sept. 30, 1978
PL 95–405 (S 2391)........	Commodity Futures Trading Commission extended through fiscal 1984	Sept. 30, 1978
PL 95–409 (S 3272)........	Firms engaged in the sale of livestock permitted to base charges for such sales on a percentage of the gross sale price of the livestock as well as a per-head charge	Oct. 2, 1978
PL–410 (HR 8149)..........	Customs Procedural and Simplification Act of 1978 enacted	Oct. 2, 1978
PL–415 (HJ Res 1088)......	Loan guarantee authority for New York City and appropriations in case of default provided	Oct. 5, 1978
PL 95–421 (S 3040)........	Review of the Amtrak system called for and funds for the National Railroad Passenger Corporation for fiscal 1979 authorized	Oct. 5, 1978
PL 95-427 (HR 12841)	Issuance of regulations on taxation of fringe benefits prohibited	Oct. 7, 1978
PL 95–440 (S 1267).........	Mandatory application of the General Records Schedules to all federal agencies now required	Oct. 10, 1978
PL 95–460 (S 3384).........	Foreign persons acquiring, transferring, or holding interests in agricultural land must report such information to the Secretary of Agriculture	Oct. 14, 1978
PL 95–473 (HR 10965)......	Interstate Commerce Act and related transportation laws revised and codified	Oct. 17, 1978
PL 95–474 (S 682)..........	Regulations concerning vessel safety standards expanded and strengthened	Oct. 17, 1978
PL 95–475 (HR 6503)	Federal Maritime Commission's power changed to suspend general rate increases or decreases in domestic off-shore trade	Oct. 18, 1978
PL 95-598 (HR 8200).......	Federal bankruptcy court system restructured	Nov. 6, 1978
PL 95–600 (HR 13511)......	Revenue Act of 1978	Nov. 6, 1978
PL 95–630 (HR 14270)......	Financial Institution Regulatory Act to protect an individual's financial information when sought by the federal government	Nov. 10, 1978

New Energy Legislation

Albert R. Hunt

Congress, ending one of the longest and most acrimonious legislative battles in years, approved an energy package much sought by President Carter.

The energy legislation, passed earlier by the Senate, cleared the House early yesterday morning on a 231-to-168 vote. But in a crucial procedural vote that preceded final passage, the measure barely squeaked through, 207 to 206, after some tense, last-minute political pressure was applied.

Final House consideration was delayed by a 14-hour Senate filibuster of the energy tax portion of the package, led by Sen. James Abourezk (D., S.D.), who charged the bill was a "giveaway" to oil and gas interests. He finally relented and the Senate approved the tax provisions in a 60-to-17 vote.

House passage thus ended a year-and-a-half struggle, which congressional leaders characterized as one of the most intense ideological and geographical fights in years. Although the final product bears only a faint resemblance to President Carter's initial proposals offered in April 1977, the White House considers the measure—which the President labeled his top domestic priority—an impressive and important political victory.

In a statement issued by the White House shortly after the final vote, the President said, "We have declared to ourselves and the world our intent to control our use of energy, and thereby to control our own destiny as a nation."

COMPLICATED COMPROMISES

The measure is the result of complicated compromises between competing interests and there's little consensus as to what it actually will achieve. The major provisions of the energy package include:

A gradual move toward deregulation of newly discovered natural gas in 1985 and sizable price increases in the interim. It also would put intrastate gas under federal price controls for the first time.

A mild energy tax bill, which taxes gas-guzzling cars, starting in 1980, provides tax credits for homeowners and businesses that install energy-saving weatherization devices, and gives various tax breaks to oil and gas producers.

Requirements that most electric power plants burn coal instead of oil or natural gas

and, where feasible, for industrial plants to do likewise.

Provisions seeking to force state regulatory agencies to consider new rate structures for utilities that would promote energy conservation. The power of the federal government to order power-sharing arrangements also would be expanded.

General conservation measures, including a requirement that utilities offer information and arrange financing for residential users for energy-saving insulation equipment, and the establishment of new efficiency standards for major appliances.

Supporters of the legislation hope it will signal to foreigners that the U.S. is serious about curbing its reliance on oil imports and thereby strengthen the dollar. While the bill isn't all they hoped for, they said during the early-morning debate that it constitutes the first serious effort in the U.S. at a comprehensive national energy policy.

DIFFERING VIEWS

"We're here to stop the downslide of the dollar," proclaimed Rep. Thomas Ashley (D., Ohio), who led the House effort for the measure. "It will reassure our allies and perhaps it will demonstrate to our critics that we are able to move on this all-important energy issue." But some supporters took a more modest view of the legislation in a sparsely populated House chamber. "This is the best thing we could come up with," observed Rep. Harley Staggers (D., W.Va.).

But the opponents—liberals and conservatives alike—hammered away at the measure without making any such apologies. Calling the bill "hopelessly complex and confusing," Rep. Clarence Brown (R., Ohio) suggested, "foreign financiers aren't fools and won't believe the U.S. has solved its trade deficit problems." And Rep. Toby Moffett (D., Conn.) complained that the measure will "put the cost on the back of the American consumer and won't produce the supplies we need."

The key question is how much energy saving will result from the legislation. The Carter administration asserted that its original energy proposals would have saved 4.5 million barrels a day of oil imports by 1985. The administration estimates the final version will save between 2.5 million and three million barrels a day by then. This would meet President Carter's pledge at this summer's economic summit in Bonn.

Source: *The Wall Street Journal*, October 16, 1978, pp. 2, 18. © 1978 by Dow Jones Corporation. Reprinted by permission.

The administration calculates the natural gas provision will save about 900,000 barrels a day by 1985; the tax provisions between 400,000 and 500,000 barrels; and coal conversion, utilities, and general conservation combined more than one million barrels. Additionally, the administration says higher gas prices will pave the way for the proposed Alaskan gas pipeline, which would curb oil imports by a further 300,000 to 400,000 barrels daily.

DON'T BELIEVE ESTIMATES

Critics, representing both consumer and producing interests, don't believe the administration's savings estimates. "Nobody in Washington or in Europe believes those numbers," alleges James Flug, director of Energy Action, a consumer group that waged a fierce campaign against the energy bill. Mr. Flug contends that the higher price of natural gas will make oil more competitive and actually will increase imports.

Alan Cope, an economist for Continental Oil Co., expects the energy package will save only about 750,000 barrels a day of oil imports by 1985, or less than one-third of the official estimates. Administration analysts "take credit for a lot of savings that are going to happen even if they did nothing," he contends.

Currently, the U.S. imports about eight million barrels of oil daily, or more than 40% of the approximately 19 million-barrel-a-day consumption. At present levels, without any legislation, it's estimated these imports would climb to 11 million barrels a day by 1985.

There is a parallel disagreement over how much additional natural gas will be produced as a result of the bill. The administration estimates the additional gas produced will be the equivalent of 3.5 million barrels a day of oil between enactment and 1985; critics say these estimates, too, are vastly inflated.

While there are clear differences of opinion on the bill's merits, there's little argument that its enactment is due chiefly to President Carter's perseverance and flexibility in overcoming a maze of legislative obstacles. Last August, the House passed most of the Carter energy plan, including his proposal to raise natural-gas prices, but stopped short of deregulation. But it then was torn to shreds in the Senate, which killed the original centerpiece of the program—a crude-oil equalization tax—and decided to deregulate the price of new natural gas within two years.

UNEASY ACCORD

A House-Senate conference committee then bickered over the controversial natural-gas measure for more than eight months. Following months of closed-door negotiating sessions, vigorous outside lobbying pressures and a few bitter confrontations, an uneasy accord finally was reached in August. After considerable debate, the Senate passed the nontax pieces of the energy package.

But House Speaker Thomas P. O'Neill (D., Mass.) was determined to have the House take up the legislation on a take-it-or-leave-it basis and thereby avoid a separate vote on the natural-gas bill. His plan was temporarily thwarted Thursday night in the Rules Committee when three Democrats broke ranks and joined the Republicans to require a separate natural-gas vote. But the Democratic leadership and the White House immediately swung into action and pressured one of those Democrats, Rep. B. F. Sisk of California, who is retiring, to switch. The next morning the Rules Committee changed its mind and cleared the package proposal.

Mr. Sisk, who only hours earlier said "in no circumstances" would he change his vote, explained he switched so as not to "be a party to killing the energy bill." But critics said the California Democrat may have been motivated by his desire to head the Immigration and Naturalization Commission, a presidential appointment. In addition, sources report the administration did promise Rep. Sisk a speedup of some water contracts in his congressional district that had been stalled.

Nonetheless, when the measure came to the floor, it produced one of the most tense votes of recent memory on the key procedural question of whether to avoid the separate natural-gas vote. With a minute to go, the vote was tied and the two sides remained even until the end, with the opponents of the Democratic leadership seeming to nudge into a slim 205-to-202 victory. . . .

Here are details of the energy package:

NATURAL GAS

The price controls on newly discovered interstate and intrastate natural gas would be removed Jan. 1, 1985. Controls also would be removed then on hard-to-get gas from wells more than 5,000 feet deep that were drilled after Feb. 19, 1977. On July 1, 1987, price controls would be removed from gas produced by extensions of the reservoirs of wells 5,000 feet or shallower.

After price controls on new gas had been removed for six months—in July 1985—there would be a two-year period in which either the President or both the house and Senate, through a concurrent resolution, could reimpose the controls for up to 18 months if prices were deemed to be rising too quickly. If the President reimposed controls, it would take both the house and Senate to overrule him. By Dec. 31, 1988, all controls would be off unless a new law were passed.

On enactment of the current legislation, the ceiling price of new gas would rise to $2.09 a thousand cubic feet from $1.50. Through April 20, 1981, this price ceiling would climb annually by the rate of inflation plus 3.7%. Thereafter, it would increase by the inflation rate plus 4.2%, until decontrol occurred.

Depending on inflation, this formula is expected to increase gas prices 9% to 12% a year. Assuming an average inflation rate of 6%, the price when decontrol occurs in 1985 would be $3.73; at an average rate of 8%, the price would be $4.26. This contrasts with the $3.44 price that would have been in effect under the original Carter plan.

Gas qualifying for decontrol, or defined as new gas, would include any new onshore gas produced 2.5 miles away from, or 1,000 feet deeper than, an existing well or from a reservoir that hadn't produced in commercial quantities. Basically, if a reservoir didn't have gas that had been sold and delivered to a user, it would qualify as new gas under the definition. The trigger date for qualifying would be April 20, 1977.

Gas found to have been intentionally withheld before April 20, 1977, wouldn't qualify for decontrol, however.

On the Outer Continental Shelf, any gas produced from a lease acquired after April 20, 1977, would be defined as new gas. In the case of a lease that was acquired before that date but on which gas hadn't yet been discovered, any gas eventually discovered would be controlled, but with a more generous price ceiling.

More generous treatment also would apply to special development gas in new wells drilled into an existing reservoir. This price would start at an estimated $1.86 a thousand cubic feet and climb by the inflation rate, plus 0.2% a year. Old gas that wasn't under contract would start at $1.45 and also climb annually at the inflation rate plus 0.2%.

The legislation includes a complicated provision for incremental pricing designed to have large industrial users bear most of the burden of higher prices until controls are removed. The aim is to ease the economic impact on homes, schools, and hospitals and also to force industrial users to convert to other forms of energy. It would be in effect for new gas, special high-cost gas, and liquefied natural gas imports. For gas from Alaska's North Slope, only the amount selling above $1.48 a thousand cubic feet would be incrementally priced.

Within one year after the bill's enactment, the Federal Energy Regulatory Commission would list the large industrial users that would have to shoulder the heaviest burden of the higher costs. Then, within 18 months of enactment, the commission would propose a second group of medium-size users and industries that burn gas in processes, as opposed to fuel, such as the petrochemical, textile, and glass industries, to share in the burden of incremental pricing. This second proposal could be vetoed by either the House or Senate, however.

When an existing contract expired, the measure would treat interstate and intrastate gas differently. For interstate gas, if the contract price were less than 55 cents a thousand cubic feet, the price automatically could be rolled up to 55 cents, plus inflation since April 1977.

Intrastate gas could be rolled up to $1, plus inflation. If it had been selling for more than $1 under the expired contract, however, it could only be adjusted for inflation.

The legislation would authorize the federal government to allocate gas but only in an emergency and only intrastate gas. The first stop would be to allocate away from large industrial users. After that, allocation would be allowed only when several requirements are met, such as the exhaustion of emergency voluntary sales.

Several taxes levied by producing states could be included in the ceiling price and thus passed on to consumers. But any increase in these taxes from Dec. 1, 1977, levels would have to be incrementally priced so industrial users would bear the added costs.

Certain unusual gases would be eligible for deregulation one year after enactment of the legislation. These include such high-cost gas as that derived from Devonian shale, methane, geopressurized brine, and wells deeper than 15,000 feet. But this higher price also would be borne by industrial users.

The bill also would limit the Federal Energy Regulatory Commission's regulatory authority over matters other than price. The commission would lose most of its nonprice powers over interstate gas that isn't currently flowing. For instance, producers no longer would have to file an application before they sold this natural gas or get permission before they abandoned a sale.

Further, the measure seeks to limit a recent Supreme Court decision, the so-called Southland case, which broadened the commission's powers to direct the flow of natural gas from the intrastate market to the interstate market.

COAL CONVERSION

New electric power plants and most new industrial facilities would be required to burn coal as a boiler fuel instead of oil or natural gas. Basically, new plants would be those on which construction began after April 20, 1977, the date President Carter proposed his energy program.

The Energy Secretary could grant exemptions if certain conditions were met, such as proving that coal supplies were unreliable or unavailable. Before granting an exemption, the Energy Secretary would have to find that using a mixture of oil and coal or other fuels wasn't feasible economically or technically.

Existing power plants would have to stop using natural gas by 1990, and the Energy Department could order them to stop using oil. Existing power plants would be barred immediately from burning more gas in the future than they averaged between 1974 and 1976, and if a utility didn't use gas as a primary fuel in 1977, it couldn't switch to gas between now and 1990.

Existing industrial facilities with the capability to burn coal could be ordered to switch. The Energy Department would be authorized to issue such orders on a case-by-case basis or for broad categories of plants, such as all those in one specific industry.

This measure also would aid communities benefiting from an increase in coal or uranium development. Over two years, $180 million was authorized to assist such areas—basically where this development was increasing employment by 8% or more annually—in planning and to build adequate public facilities.

Initially, these regulatory requirements were to have been coupled with a stiff tax on the industrial use of oil and gas, which would have produced considerable conversion to coal. But the tax provision was killed, so the overall conversion will be much more modest.

UTILITIES

State regulatory agencies would be pressured to consider different types of rate structures to force more energy conservation. Although changes wouldn't be required, the state public utility agencies would have two years to hold hearings and consider specified rate-making changes on a utility-by-utility basis.

The types of changes that would have to be weighed include lower rates for off-peak use, senior citizens, and the basic energy needs of most residential users, seasonal rates, and a prohibition against volume discounts. The state agencies would have to make these changes or explain why they shouldn't be made. Although the bill is watered down from the original Carter proposals, consumer groups hope, and utilities fear, it could have a significant impact.

The Department of Energy would be able to intervene in the state deliberations to argue for energy-saving measures. If the department entered such a case, it could participate in any legal appeal of the decision.

The Energy Department also would be empowered to order certain utility power-sharing arrangements, called interconnection and wheeling. This provision could be used to aid any power-short public utilities. But there are severe restrictions on the exercise of this authority, as the department first must show the power-sharing wouldn't impair the reliability of any utility and would significantly increase conservation.

CONSERVATION

Utilities would be required to offer residential users information about and provide some financing for energy-saving devices such as a storm windows and insulation. The utilities would be prohibited from actually entering the home-weatherization business. Grants and subsidized loans would be provided to poor and moderate-income families for weatherization measures, although this too is much milder than the initial Carter proposal.

Schools and hospitals, over a three-year period, would receive $900 million to conduct energy audits and install energy-saving equipment. Another $65 million would go to public buildings for the same purposes and additional money would be given to demonstrate solar energy in federal buildings.

The current civil penalties imposed on automobile manufacturers who don't meet the federal government's mileage efficiency standards would be stiffened. Also, the Energy Department would set new efficiency standards for 13 major appliances, including refrigerators, air conditioners, dishwashers, and furnaces.

Here are the provisions of the energy tax bill as approved by the conferees:

Insulation: Homeowners and renters would get a tax credit when they insulated or installed storm windows or other energy-saving devices. The credit would be 15% of the first $2,000 of outlays, or a maximum credit of $400, which would be subtracted from taxes due. The credit could be spread over several years. To limit paper work, however, credits of less than $10 wouldn't be allowed but could be saved until later years and added to other credits.

To qualify for the credit, the insulation, or other items would have to have been installed between April 20, 1977.

Solar: Homeowners and renters who installed solar, wind, or geothermal energy devices would get a tax break, too. Their credit would be 30% of the first $2,000 of outlays and 20% of the next $8,000, for a maximum of $2,200.

Gas guzzlers: Starting with 1980 models,

low-mileage cars would be taxed on the basis of fuel consumption. The tax would be imposed on the manufacturer, who could be expected to pass it along to customers. The 1980-model cars that get between 14 and 15 miles a gallon would be taxed $200; those that get 13 to 14, $300; and those that get less than 13 would bear a tax of $550. The threshold would rise to 17 miles a gallon in 1981-model cars and, in annual steps, to 22.5 miles a gallon in 1986 and later model years. The tax also would climb, so that by 1986 cars getting less than 12.5 miles a gallon would be taxed $3,850.

The tax would apply to new-car leases as well as new-car sales. It would be imposed on cars weighing less than 6,000 pounds, but wouldn't apply to trucks or vans of any weight. Emergency vehicles would be exempt and companies making fewer than 10,000 cars a year could apply to the Treasury for special treatment.

Although the auto companies still don't like the concept of a gas-guzzler tax, this measure was so watered down at the last minute that it's unlikely to have much bite.

Motorboats: The conferees agreed to repeal the existing two-cent-a-gallon tax break for gasoline and special motor fuel used in motorboats, lawn mowers, snowmobiles, and other off-highway engines. Starting Jan. 1, these fuels would be taxed at the regular gasoline tax rate of four cents a gallon. The change wouldn't affect farmers, commercial fishermen or other businessmen.

Gasohol: Gasoline that contains at least 10% alcohol would be exempt from the four-cent excise tax from Jan. 1, 1979, through Sept. 30, 1984. The Treasury Secretary would be directed to speed issuance of permits to alcohol producers.

Buses: The bill would repeal the 10% excise tax on buses, retroactive to April 20, 1977, and remove a variety of other federal excise taxes on buses, bus parts and tires, fuel, and lubricating oil used by buses, effective Nov. 1 or Dec. 1, depending on when President Carter signs the bill.

Vans: The conferees approved tax breaks for employers who buy vans to carry employes to and from work and for the employes themselves. Employers would get a 10% credit, instead of the existing investment credit, which is usually 3⅓% for vans. The extra credit would be available for vans purchased from the day the bill is signed through 1985. Employes, meanwhile, wouldn't be taxed on the value of any free van transportation received during the same period.

Alternative energy: Businesses would receive a 10% investment credit, in addition to the regular 10% credit, for installing certain equipment that uses something besides oil or natural gas as its fuel or feedstock. The credit would be available for equipment placed in service on Oct. 1, 1978, or later.

Penalties: The 10% investment credit and accelerated depreciation would be denied to businesses that installed oil or gas boilers, except where these were required by air pollution rules. These penalties would apply only to manufacturing, mining, or processing. Other equipment would be exempt, including equipment used in oil and gas production and development and in certain processes where oil or gas is required.

Geothermal: Existing law gives a number of tax breaks to oil and gas producers but doesn't give them to producers of geothermal energy. Oil and gas producers can take a current deduction for labor, fuel, and other "intangible" costs of drilling wells. These intangible deductions are a preference item subject to the individual minimum tax, but independent oil and gas producers have been given temporary relief from the minimum levy. Producers also can take a deduction for depletion of their oil and gas equal to 22% of their income this year on the first 1,400 barrels a day produced. The figures are due to phase down to 15% by 1984 and to 1,000 barrels a day by 1980.

The conference committee agreed to give geothermal producers a current deduction of intangible costs. It agreed to give independent geothermal producers permanent relief from the minimum tax and to give all geothermal producers percentage depletion at 22%, phasing down to 15% by 1984, without any barrel limitation.

Methane: The tax status of geopressurized methane gas currently is uncertain. The bill would permit all producers of this gas to take percentage depletion deductions at the rate of 10%, without any barrel limitation. But this tax break would be available only for methane wells drilled during the next five years.

Oil drilling: The bill would make permanent a tax break for independent oil and gas producers that expired last Jan. 1. Intangible costs of drilling wells wouldn't be subject to the minimum tax unless they exceeded the taxpayer's oil and gas income. Generally, this provision wouldn't benefit doctors, lawyers, corporate executives, and other high-income people whose chief occupation isn't drilling for oil and gas but who invest in oil and gas ventures to "shelter" their regular income.

Boilers: The bill would provide rapid depreciation for oil or gas boilers that are replaced before the end of their useful lives by boilers using other sources of energy.

Regulatory Agencies

The following section provides compact summaries of the functions of the major regulatory agencies together with addresses and phone numbers. This information was abstracted from the latest United States Government Manual.

ANTITRUST DIVISION (DEPARTMENT OF JUSTICE)

CONSTITUTIONAL AVENUE AND TENTH STREET NW, WASHINGTON, DC 20530
INFORMATION: 202-737-8200

The Assistant Attorney General in charge of the Antitrust Division is responsible for enforcement of the federal antitrust laws. Such enforcement, which constitutes the principal function of the division, involves investigating possible antitrust violations, conducting grand jury proceedings, preparing and trying antitrust cases, prosecuting appeals, and negotiating and enforcing final judgments. The antitrust laws are enforced by criminal actions designed to punish violators for restraints on and monopolization of trade and by civil suits for injunctive relief aimed at maintaining or restoring competitive conditions in the system of free enterprise, which the antitrust laws protect.

In addition, the Antitrust Division represents the United States in judicial proceedings to review certain orders of the Interstate Commerce Commission, Federal Maritime Commission, Federal Communications Commission, and Nuclear Regulatory Commission, and directly represents the Secretary of the Treasury and the Civil Aeronautics Board in certain review proceedings. It also participates in cases of the Federal Trade Commission before the Supreme Court.

Other duties assigned to this division include studying, reporting, and advising on the competitive considerations involved in policies of government departments and agencies, and making recommendations with respect to such policies. Specific statutory responsibility to render such advice to other government bodies includes matters involved in NRC licensing of nuclear power reactors; activities connected with the nation's defense program, the Interstate Oil Compact, the development of nuclear energy, disposal of government-owned surplus property; and the filing of reports on the competitive factors involved in proposed bank mergers with the appropriate bank regulatory agencies. The division is also responsible for supporting competitive policies within the federal government. It does this through comment and testimony on pending legislative and other matters, participation in interagency committees (e.g., government patent policy, communications satellite policy, oil import policy, foreign trade policy), and formal intervention in regulatory proceedings (e.g., before the Interstate Commerce Commission, Civil Aeronautics Board, Federal Maritime Board, Federal Communications Commission, Securities and Exchange Commission). It also responds to requests from other agencies for advice respecting competitive aspects of activities within their jurisdiction.

The division represents the United States on the Restrictive Business Practices Committee of the Organization for Economic Cooperation and Development and, through the Department of State, maintains liaison with foreign governments on antimonopoly laws and policies. It also is charged with reporting annually to the President and the Congress on the nature and extent of identical bidding in public procurement.

The Consumer Affairs Section of the Antitrust Division is responsible for the institution of civil and criminal proceedings in cases referred to the Department of Justice by other

FIELD OFFICES (Antitrust Division)

City	Address
Atlanta, GA 30309...............	1776 Peachtree Street NY
Chicago, IL 60604...............	219 S. Dearborn Street
Cleveland, OH 44199.............	New Federal Building
Los Angeles, CA 90012..........	U.S. Courthouse
New York, NY 10007.............	26 Federal Plaza
Philadelphia, PA 19106..........	501 U.S. Customhouse
San Francisco, CA 94102.........	Box 36046, 450 Golden Gate Avenue

agencies, such as the Food and Drug Administration and the Federal Trade Commission, which have primary responsibility for consumer protection activities. Such proceedings generally arise when a person has violated a statute enforced by these agencies or an order or rule issued by these agencies in the course of their consumer protection activities. Many of these proceedings involve acts or practices that are unfair and deceptive to consumers.

CONSUMER PRODUCT SAFETY COMMISSION (CPSC)

1111 18TH STREET NW
WASHINGTON, DC 20207
INFORMATION: 800-638-2666

The commission has primary responsibility for establishing mandatory product safety standards, where appropriate, to reduce the unreasonable risk of injury to consumers from consumer products. In addition it has authority to ban hazardous consumer products. The Consumer Product Safety Act also authorizes the commission to conduct extensive research on consumer product standards, engage in broad consumer and industry information and education programs, and establish a comprehensive Injury Information Clearinghouse.

In addition to the new authority created by the act, the commission assumes responsibility for the Flammable Fabrics Act (67 Stat. 111; 15 U.S.C. 1191), the Poison Prevention Packaging Act (84 Stat. 1670), the Hazardous Substances Act (74 Stat. 372; 15 U.S.C. 1261), and the act of August 2, 1956 (70 Stat. 953; 15 U.S.C. 1211) which prohibits the transportation of refrigerators without door safety devices.

The act also provides for petitioning of the commission by any interested person, including consumers or consumer organizations, to commence proceedings for the issuance, amendment, or revocation of a consumer product safety rule.

ECONOMIC REGULATORY ADMINISTRATION (DEPARTMENT OF ENERGY)

1000 INDEPENDENCE AVENUE, WASHINGTON, DC 20545
INFORMATION: 202-376-4000
202-254-8505

The Economic Regulatory Administration (ERA) administers the department's regulatory programs, other than those assigned to the Federal Energy Regulatory Commission. These functions include the oil pricing, allocation, and import programs designed to ensure price stability and equitable supplies of crude oil, petroleum products, and natural gas liquids among a wide range of domestic users.

The Economic Regulatory Administration ensures compliance with existing regulations and carries out new regulatory programs as assigned. ERA also administers other regulatory programs, including conversion of oil and gas-fired utility and industrial facilities to coal, natural gas import/export controls, natural gas curtailment priorities and emergency allocations, regional coordination of electric power system planning and reliability of bulk power supply, and emergency and contingency planning.

On behalf of the Secretary, ERA organizes and manages an active intervention program before the Federal Energy Regulatory Commission and other federal and state regulatory agencies in support of departmental policy objectives.

AREA OFFICES (Consumer Product Safety Commission)

City	Address
Atlanta, GA 30309	1330 W. Peachtree Street NW
Boston, MA 02110	100 Summer Street
Chicago, IL 60604	230 S. Dearborn Street
Cleveland, OH 44114	55 Erieview Plaza
Dallas, TX 75201	500 South Ervay
Denver, CO 80202	Guaranty Bank Building, 817 17th Street
Kansas City, MO 64106	Traders National Bank Building, 1125 Grand Avenue
Los Angeles, CA 90010	3660 Wilshire Boulevard
Minneapolis, MN 55111	650 Federal Building, Fort Snelling
New York, NY 10048	6 World Trade Center, Vesey Street
Philadelphia, PA 19106	400 Market Street
San Francisco, CA 94111	100 Pine Street
Seattle, WA 98174	3240 Federal Building, 915 Second Avenue

FEDERAL ENERGY REGULATORY COMMISSION (DEPARTMENT OF ENERGY)

1000 INDEPENDENCE AVENUE, WASHINGTON, DC 20545

INFORMATION: 202–376–4000
202–275–4006

An independent, five-member commission within the Department of Energy, the Federal Energy Regulatory Commission has retained many of the functions of the Federal Power Commission, such as the setting of rates and charges for the transportation and sale of natural gas and for the transmission and sale of electricity and the licensing of hydroelectric power projects. In addition, the authority to establish rates or charges for the transportation of oil by pipeline, as well as the valuation of such pipelines, has been assigned to the commission from the Interstate Commerce Commission.

REGIONAL REPRESENTATIVES (DOE)

The Secretary will be represented in each of the ten standard federal regions by regional representatives.

REGIONAL REGULATORY PROGRAMS (DOE)

The Department of Energy's regional allocation and compliance program will be conducted by Directors of Regional Compliance, under the supervision and direction of the Administrator of the Economic Regulatory Administration and with the legal support of the General Counsel's field staff. These programs are separate from the outreach and other activities of the regional representatives.

The field activities of the Federal Energy Regulatory Commission will be separate from other department field activities but will have offices colocated with regional compliance or other department field offices in order to share common administrative support.

ENVIRONMENTAL PROTECTION AGENCY (EPA)

401 M STREET SW, WASHINGTON, DC 20460

INFORMATION: 202–755–0707

AIR AND WASTE MANAGEMENT PROGRAMS

The air activities of the agency include development of national programs, technical policies, and regulations for air pollution control; development of national standards for air quality, emission standards for new stationary sources, and emission standards for hazardous pollutants; technical direction, support, and evaluation of regional air activities; and provision of training in the field of air pollution control. Related activities include study, identification, and regulation of noise sources and control methods; technical assistance to states and agencies having radiation protection programs; and a national surveillance and inspection program for measuring radiation levels in the environment.

WATER AND HAZARDOUS MATERIALS PROGRAMS

EPA's water quality activities represent a coordinated effort to restore the nation's waters. The functions of this program include development of national programs, technical policies, and regulations for water pollution control and water supply; water quality standards and effluent guidelines development; technical direction, support, and evaluation of regional water activities; development of programs for technical assistance and technology transfer; provision of training in the field of water quality; analyses, guidelines, and standards for the land disposal of hazardous wastes; technical assistance in the development, management, and operation of waste management activities; and analyses on the recovery of useful energy from solid waste.

ENFORCEMENT

The Office of the Assistant Administrator for Enforcement provides policy direction to enforcement activities in air, water, pesticides, solid waste management, radiation, and noise control programs; plans and coordinates enforcement conferences, public hearings, and other legal proceedings; and engages in other activities related to enforcement of standards to protect the nation's environment.

RESEARCH AND DEVELOPMENT

The Office of the Assistant Administrator for Research and Development is responsible for a national research program in pursuit of technological controls of all forms of pollution. It directly supervises the research activities of EPA's national laboratories and gives technical policy direction to those laboratories that support the program responsibilities of EPA's regional offices. Close coordination of the various research programs is designed to yield a synthesis of knowledge from the biological, physical, and social sciences which

REGIONAL OFFICES (Environmental Protection Agency)

Region	Address
I	John F. Kennedy Federal Building, Boston, MA 02203
II	26 Federal Plaza, New York, NY 10007
III	Curtis Building, 6th and Walnut Streets, Philadelphia, PA 19106
IV	305 Cortland Street NE, Atlanta, GA 30308
V	230 S. Dearborn Street, Chicago, IL 60604
VI	1201 Elm Street, Dallas, TX 75270
VII	1735 Baltimore Avenue, Kansas City, MO 64108
VIII	1860 Lincoln Street, Denver, CO 80203
IX	215 Fremont, San Francisco, CA 94111
X	1200 6th Avenue, Seattle, WA 98101

can be interpreted in terms of total human and environmental needs. General functions include management of selected demonstration programs, planning for agency environmental quality monitoring programs, coordination of agency monitoring efforts with those of other federal agencies, the states, and other public bodies, and dissemination of agency research, development, and demonstration results.

REGIONAL OFFICES

EPA's ten regional offices represent the agency's commitment to the development of strong local programs for pollution abatement. The regional administrators are the agency's principal representatives in the regions in contacts and relationships with federal, state, interstate, and local agencies, industry, academic institutions, and other public and private groups. They are responsible for accomplishing within their regions the national program objectives established by the agency. They develop, propose, and implement an approved regional program for comprehensive and integrated environmental protection activities.

EQUAL EMPLOYMENT OPPORTUNITY COMMISSION (EEOC)

2401 E STREET NW, WASHINGTON, DC 20506

INFORMATION: 202-634-6930

The commission's field offices receive written charges of discrimination against public and private employers exclusive of the federal government, labor organizations, joint labor-management apprenticeship programs, and public and private employment agencies. Members of the commission also may initiate charges alleging that a violation of Title VII has occurred.

Charges of Title VII violations must be filed

with the commission within 180 days of the alleged violation (or up to 300 days where a state or local fair employment practices agency initially was contacted), and the commission is responsible for notifying persons so charged within 10 days of the receipt of a new charge. Before investigation, a charge must be deferred for 60 days to a local fair employment practices agency in states and municipalities where an enforceable fair employment practices law is in effect. The deferral period is 120 days for an agency that has been operating less than one year. Under a work-sharing agreement, executed between the commission and state and local fair employment practices agencies, the commission routinely will assume jurisdiction over certain charges of discrimination and proceed with its investigation rather than wait for the expiration of the deferral period.

The commission has instituted new procedural regulations that encourage settlement of charges of discrimination prior to a determination of decision by the agency on the merits of the charges. In addition, fact-finding conferences may be required as a part of the investigation and may assist in establishing the framework for a negotiated settlement. After an investigation, if there is reasonable cause to believe the charge is true, the district office attempts to remedy the alleged unlawful practices through the informal methods of conciliation, conference, and persuasion.

Unless an acceptable conciliation agreement has been secured, the commission may, after 30 days from the date the charge was filed, bring suit in an appropriate federal district court. (The Attorney General brings suit when a state government, governmental agency, or political subdivision is involved.) If the commission or the Attorney General does not proceed in this manner, at the conclusion of the administrative procedures, or earlier at the request of the charging party, a Notice of Right to Sue is issued, which allows the charging party to proceed within 90 days in a federal district court. In appropriate cases the commission may intervene in such civil action if the case is of general public interest. The investigation and conciliation of charges having an industrywide or national impact are coordinated or conducted by the Office of Systemic Programs.

Under the provisions of Section 706 (f)(2), as amended by Section 5 of the Equal Employment Opportunity Act of 1972, if it is concluded after a preliminary investigation that prompt judicial action is necessary to carry out the purposes of the act, the commission or the Attorney General, in a case involving a state government, governmental agency, or political subdivision, may bring an action for appropriate temporary or preliminary relief pending final disposition of a charge.

The commission participates in the development of the law of employment discrimination through issuance of guidelines, publication of significant commission decisions, and involvement in litigation brought under Title VII and related statutes.

The commission has direct liaison with state and local governments, employer and union organizations, trade associations, civil rights organizations, and other agencies and organizations concerned with employment of minority group members and women. The commission engages in and contributes to the cost of research and other mutual interest projects with state and local agencies charged with the administration of fair employment practices laws.

Furthermore, the commission enters into work-sharing agreements with the state and local agencies in order to avoid duplication of effort by identifying specific charges to be investigated by the respective agencies.

FEDERAL COMMUNICATIONS COMMISSION (FCC)

1919 M Street NW, Washington, DC
20554
Information: 202–632–7260

BROADCAST

The Broadcast Bureau administers the regulatory program for the following broadcast services: standard (AM), frequency modulation (FM), television (TV), instructional television fixed (ITFS), experimental, international shortwave, and related auxiliary services; issues construction permits, operating licenses, and renewals or transfers of licenses; and oversees compliance by broadcasters with statutes and commission policies.

CABLE TELEVISION

Cable television system operators must obtain a certificate of compliance from the commission before commencing operation or adding additional television broadcast signals to existing operations. The Cable Television Bureau administers the program for cable television and the cable television relay services, including the issuance of certificates of compliance and CAR (Cable Television Relay) authorizations, and maintaining regulatory relationships with state and local jurisdictions who also have responsibility and authority concerning cable television systems.

COMMON CARRIER COMMUNICATIONS

In interstate and international common carrier communications by telephone, telegraph, radio, and satellite, the Common Carrier Bureau administers the program of regulation. Common carriers include companies, organizations, or individuals providing communications services to the public for hire, who must serve all who wish to use them at established rates. In rendering interstate and foreign communications services to the public, common carriers may use landline wire or cable facilities, point-to-point microwave radio (signals relayed by stations spaced at given intervals), land mobile radio (two-way telephone or one-way signaling communications between base and mobile units), or satellite systems. Communications services between the United States and overseas points by common carriers are provided by means of ocean cable, high-frequency radio, and satellite communications.

OTHER RADIO USES

The commission regulates the use of radio

FIELD OFFICES (Federal Communications Commission)

City	Address
Boston, MA 02109	Customhouse
New York, NY 10014	201 Varick Street
Philadelphia, PA 19106	601 Market Street
Baltimore, MD 21201	Federal Building
Norfolk, VA 23502	870 N. Military Highway
Atlanta, GA 30303	1365 Peachtree Street NE
Savannah, GA 31402	125 Bull Street
Miami, FL 33130	51 SW First Avenue
Tampa, FL 33602	Federal Office Building
New Orleans, LA 70130	600 South Street
Mobile, AL 36602	439 U.S. Courthouse and Customhouse
Houston, TX 77002	New Federal Office Building
Beaumont, TX 77701	Federal Building
Dallas, TX 75202	New Federal Courthouse Building
Long Beach, CA 90807	3711 Long Beach Boulevard
San Diego, CA 92101	Fox Theater Building
San Francisco, CA 94111	Customhouse
Portland, OR 97204	120 SW Third Avenue
Seattle, WA 98174	Federal Building
Denver, CO 80202	U.S. Customhouse
St. Paul, MN 55101	U.S. Courthouse
Kansas City, MO 64106	Federal Building
Chicago, IL 60604	220 S. Dearborn Street
Detroit, MI 48226	Federal Building
Buffalo, NY 14202	Federal Building
Honolulu, HI 96808	Federal Building
San Juan, PR 00903	Federal Building
Anchorage, AK 99510	U.S. Post Office
Washington, DC 20554	1919 M Street NW

LICENSING/GRANT RESPONSIBILITY (Federal Communications Commission)

Service	Bureau or Office
All broadcasting (radio and television)	Broadcast Bureau
Common carrier radio	Common Carrier Bureau
Section 214 of FCC Act	
Satellite	
Experimental radio	Office of Chief Engineer
Type equipment	
Equipment certification	
Type approval	
Land mobile radio in Chicago, Ill. area	
Aviation radio	Safety and Special Radio Services Bureau
Amateur radio	
Ship radio	
Industrial radio	
Public safety radio	
Citizens radio	
Amateur radio operator	
Certificates of compliance	Cable Television Bureau
Cable television relay radio	
Commercial radio operators	Field Operations Bureau

for many purposes other than broadcast and common carrier communication. The Safety and Special Radio Services Bureau administers the program of regulating the following radio services: aviation, marine, amateur, public fixed stations in Alaska, public safety (police, fire, etc.), industrial (manufacturers, petroleum, etc.), land transportation (railroad, taxicab, etc.), and citizens (private short-distance radiocommunications, signaling, control of objects, etc.), and of implementing the compulsory provisions of laws and treaties covering the use of radio for the safety of life at sea. The Office of Chief Engineer administers the program of regulating the experimental and low-power equipment.

ENFORCEMENT

Much of the investigative and enforcement work of the commission is carried out by its field staff. The Field Operations Bureau has 3 regional offices, 31 field offices, and 13 monitoring stations, in addition to a mobile network. The field staffs, in effect, are the commission's "eyes and ears" in detecting radio violations and enforcing rules and regulations. Monitoring stations maintain continuous surveillance of the radio spectrum, detecting unlicensed operation and activities or nonconforming transmission, and furnish radio bearings on ships and planes in distress.

RADIO OPERATORS

The commercial radio operator program is administered by the Field Operations Bureau. The Safety and Special Radio Services Bureau administers the amateur operator program.

FEDERAL MARITIME COMMISSION (FMC)

1100 L Street NW, Washington, DC 20573
Information: 202–523–5764

AGREEMENTS

The commission approves or disapproves agreements filed by common carriers, including conference agreements, interconference agreements, and cooperative working agreements between common carriers, terminal operators, freight forwarders, and other persons subject to the shipping laws, and reviews activities under approved agreements for compliance with the provisions of law and the rules, orders, and regulations of the commission.

PRACTICES

The commission regulates the practices of common carriers by water and other persons engaged in the foreign and domestic offshore commerce of the United States, and conferences of such common carriers in accordance with the requirements of the shipping statutes and the rules, orders, and regulations of the commission.

TARIFFS

The commission accepts or rejects tariff filings of domestic offshore carriers and common carriers engaged in the foreign commerce of the United States, or conferences of such carriers, in accordance with the requirements of the shipping statutes and the commission's rules and regulations. In the domes-

tic offshore trade, the commission has the authority to set maximum or minimum rates or suspend rates. It approves or disapproves special permission applications submitted by domestic offshore carriers and carriers in the foreign commerce, or conferences of such carriers, for relief from the statutory and/or commission tariff requirements.

LICENSES

The commission issues or denies the issuance of licenses to persons, partnerships, corporations, or associations desiring to engage in ocean freight forwarding activities.

PASSENGER INDEMNITY

The commission administers the passenger indemnity provisions of the act of November 6, 1966 and issues or denies the issuance of certificates of financial responsibility of shipowners and operators to pay judgments for personal injury or death and to refund fares in the event of nonperformance of voyages.

WATER POLLUTION

The commission administers Section 311(p) of the Federal Water Pollution Control Act Amendments of 1972 (86 Stat. 816; 33 U.S.C. 1151 note) with respect to evidence of financial responsibility by owners and operators of vessels which may be subjected to liability to the United States for the cost of removal of hazardous substances from the navigable waters of the United States, adjoining shorelines, or waters of the contiguous zone.

INFORMAL COMPLAINTS

The commission reviews and determines the validity of alleged or suspected violations of the shipping statutes and rules and regulations of the commission by common carriers by water in the domestic offshore and the foreign commerce of the United States, terminal operators, freight forwarders, and other persons subject to the provisions of the shipping statutes. After investigation, it concludes such complaints by administrative action, formal proceedings, referral to the Department of Justice, or achieving voluntary agreement between the parties.

FORMAL ADJUDICATORY PROCEDURE

The commission conducts formal investigations on its own motion and adjudicates formal complaints pursuant to the Administrative Procedure Act.

FIELD OFFICES (Federal Maritime Commission)

District	Address
Atlantic	6 World Trade Center, Suite 603, New York, NY 10048
Gulf	P.O. Box 30550, 600 South Street, New Orleans, LA 70190
Pacific	625 Market Street, San Francisco, CA 94105
Puerto Rico	U.S. District Courthouse, Federal Office Building, Room 762, Carlos Chardon Street, Hato Rey, PR 00917

RULE-MAKING

The commission promulgates rules and regulations to interpret, enforce, and assure compliance with the shipping statutes of common carriers by water and other persons subject to the statutes.

INVESTIGATION, AUDIT, AND FINANCIAL AND ECONOMIC ANALYSES

The commission prescribes and administers programs to assure compliance with the provisions of the shipping statutes of all persons subject thereto, including without limitation those for: the submission of regular and special reports, information, and data; the conduct of a plan for the field investigation and audit of activities and practices of common carriers by water in the domestic off-shore trade and the foreign commerce of the United States, conferences of such carriers, terminal operators, freight forwarders, and other persons subject to the shipping statutes; and rate and related financial analysis studies, economic studies, and reports reflecting the various trade areas, the extent and nature of competition, commodities carried, and future commodity trends.

INTERNATIONAL AFFAIRS

The commission, in conjunction with the Department of State, conducts activities to effect the elimination of discriminatory practices on the part of foreign governments against United States flag shipping.

FEDERAL TRADE COMMISSION (FTC)

PENNSYLVANIA AVENUE AT SIXTH STREET NW, WASHINGTON, DC 20580
INFORMATION: 202–523–3625

The commission's principal functions are:
To promote free and fair competition in interstate commerce through prevention of general trade restraints such as price-fixing agreements, boycotts, illegal combinations of competitors, and other unfair methods of competition.

To safeguard the public by preventing the dissemination of false or deceptive advertisements of consumer products generally and food, drug, cosmetics, and therapeutic devices particularly, as well as other unfair or deceptive practices.

To prevent discriminations in price; exclusive dealing and tying arrangements; corporate mergers, acquisitions or joint ventures, when such practices or arrangements may substantially lessen competition or tend toward monopoly; interlocking directorates that may restrain competition; the payment or receipt of illegal brokerage; and discrimination among competing customers in the furnishing of or payment for services or facilities used to promote the resale of a product.

To bring about truthful labeling of textile and fur products.

To regulate packaging and labeling of certain consumer commodities within the purview of the Fair Packaging and Labeling Act to prevent consumer deception and to facilitate value comparisons.

To supervise the registration and operation of associations of American exporters engaged in export trade.

To petition for the cancellation of the registration of trademarks that were illegally registered or used for purposes contrary to the intent of the Trade-Mark Act of 1946.

To achieve true credit cost disclosure by consumer creditors (retailers, finance companies, nonfederal credit unions, and other creditors not specifically regulated by another government agency) as called for in the Truth in Lending Act; to assure a meaningful basis for informed credit decisions; and to regulate the issuance and liability of credit cards to prohibit their fraudulent use in interstate or foreign commerce.

To protect consumers against circulation of inaccurate or obsolete credit reports, and to insure that consumer reporting agencies exercise their responsibilities in a manner that is fair and equitable and in conformity with the Fair Credit Reporting Act.

To gather and make available to the Congress, the President, and the public, factual data concerning economic and business conditions.

ENFORCEMENT

The commission's law enforcement work falls into two general categories: actions to foster law observance voluntarily and formal litigation leading to mandatory orders against offenders.

For the most part, law observance is obtained through voluntary and cooperative action by way of staff level advice which is not binding on the commission, advisory opinions by the commission, trade regulation rules, and issuance of guides delineating legal requirements as to particular business practices.

The formal litigative proceedings are similar to those used in courts. Cases are instituted by issuance of a complaint charging a person, partnership, or corporation—the respondent—with violation of one or more of the statutes administered by the commission. Cases may be settled by consent orders or occasionally through informal administrative correction of minor violations. If the charges are not contested, or if in a contested case and after hearing the charges are found to be true, an order to cease and desist is issued requiring discontinuance of the unlawful practices.

LEGAL CASE WORK

Cases before the commission may originate through complaint by a consumer or a competitor; the Congress; or from federal, state, or municipal agencies. Also, the commission itself may initiate an investigation to determine possible violation of the laws administered by it. No formality is required in submitting a complaint. A letter giving the facts in detail is sufficient, but it should be accompanied by all evidence in possession of the complaining party in support of the charges made. It is the policy of the commission not to disclose the identity of any complainant, except as required by law.

Upon receipt of a complaint, various criteria are applied in determining whether the particular matter should be docketed for investigation. Within the limits of its resources, investigations are initiated which are considered to best support the commission's goals of maintaining competition and protecting consumers.

On completion of an investigation, there may be a staff recommendation for informal settlement of the case, issuance of a formal complaint, or closing the matter.

If the commission decides to issue a complaint, the respondent is served with a copy of the complaint and proposed order. Prior to the hearings, respondent and commission counsel may negotiate a cease-and-desist order to which the respondent agrees to consent. If such a consent order is worked out, the respondent does not admit any violation of the law but agrees to discontinue the challenged practice.

If an agreement containing a consent order is not entered into, litigation usually ensues.

The case is heard by an administrative law judge who, after taking testimony at public hearings, issues an initial decision. This becomes the decision of the commission at the end of 30 days unless the respondent or the counsel supporting the complaint appeals the decision to the commission, or the commission by order stays the effective date or places the case on its own docket for review. In the commission's decision on such appeal or review, the initial decision is sustained, modified, or reversed. If it is sustained or modified, a cease-and-desist order is issued.

Under the Federal Trade Commission Act, the Clayton Act, and the Wool, Fur, and Textile Acts, the order to cease and desist, or to take other corrective action such as affirmative disclosure, divestiture, or restitution, becomes final 60 days after date of service upon the respondent, unless within that period the respondent petitions an appropriate United States court of appeals to review the order. In case of review, the order of the commission becomes final after affirmance by the court of appeals or by the Supreme Court of the United States, if taken to that court on certiorari. Violations of an order to cease and desist after it becomes final subject the offender to suit by the government in a United States district court for the recovery of a civil penalty of not more than $10,000 for each violation and, where the violation continues, each day of its continuance is a separate violation.

Under each of these statutes the respondent may apply to a court of appeals for review of an order and the court has power to affirm, modify, or set the order aside. Either party, on writ of certiorari, may apply to the Supreme Court for review of the action of the court of appeals.

In addition to the regular proceeding by complaint and order to cease and desist, the commission, after consultation with the Attorney General, may bring suit in a United States district court to enforce its subpoenas, to obtain preliminary injunctions, and to sue for civil penalties. The commission also has specific authority to enjoin the dissemination of advertisements of food, drugs, cosmetics, and devices intended for use in the diagnosis, prevention, or treatment of disease, whenever it has reason to believe that such a proceeding would be in the public interest. The preliminary injunctions remain in effect until an order to cease and desist is issued and becomes final, or until the complaint is dismissed by the commission or the order is set aside by the court on review.

Further, the dissemination of a false advertisement of a food, drug, device, or cosmetic, where the use of the commodity advertised may be injurious to health or where there is intent to defraud or mislead, constitutes a misdemeanor; and conviction subjects the offender to a fine of not more than $5,000, imprisonment of not more than six months, or both. Succeeding convictions may result in a fine of not more than $10,000, imprisonment of not more than one year, or both. The statute provides that the commission will certify this type of case to the Attorney General for institution of appropriate court proceedings.

COMPLIANCE ACTIVITIES

Through systematic and continuous review, the commission obtains and maintains compliance with its cease-and-desist orders. All respondents against whom such orders have been issued are required to file reports with the commission to substantiate their compliance. In the event compliance is not obtained or if the order is subsequently violated, civil penalty proceedings may be instituted. Violation of a commission order that has been affirmed by a decree of a U.S. court of appeals makes the respondent further subject to contempt proceedings in the court of appeals.

COOPERATIVE PROCEDURES

In carrying out the statutory directive to "prevent" the use in commerce of unfair practices, the commission makes extensive use of voluntary and cooperative procedures. Through these procedures business and industry may obtain authoritative guidance and a substantial measure of certainty as to what they may do under the laws administered by the commission.

Whenever it is practicable to do so, the commission will furnish an advisory opinion as to whether a proposed course of conduct, if pursued, would be likely to result in further action by the commission. Such opinions are binding on the commission but are subject to the right of the commission to reconsider and rescind the opinion should the public interest require. Information submitted will not be used as the basis for a proceeding against the requesting party without prior notice and opportunity to discontinue the course of action pursued in good faith in reliance upon the commission's advice.

Trade regulation rules express the experience and judgment of the commission, based on facts of which it has knowledge, concerning the substantive requirements of the statutes it administers. These rules may cover all applications of a particular statutory provision and may be nationwide in effect, or they may be limited to particular areas or industries or to particular products or geographic markets. Where a rule is related to an issue in an adjudicative proceeding thereafter instituted, the commission may rely upon such rule, provided that a fair hearing is afforded on the legality and propriety of applying the rule to a particular case.

Industry guides are administrative interpretations in laymen's language of laws administered by the commission for the guidance of the public in conducting its affairs in conformity with legal requirements. They provide the basis for voluntary and simultaneous abandonment of unlawful practices by members of a particular industry or industry in general. Failure to comply with the guides may result in corrective action by the commission under applicable statutory provisions.

TRUTH IN LENDING

The purpose of the Truth in Lending Act is to assure that every customer who has need for consumer credit is given meaningful information with respect to the cost of that credit. In most cases the credit cost must be expressed in the dollar amount of finance charges, and as an annual percentage rate computed on the unpaid balance of the amount financed. Other relevant credit information must also be disclosed so that the customer may compare the various credit terms available to him from different sources and avoid the uninformed use of credit. The act further provides a customer the right, in certain circumstances, to cancel a credit transaction that involves a lien on his residence. The Truth in Lending Act was amended in October 1970 to regulate the issuance, holder's liability, and fraudulent use of credit cards. New credit cards may be issued only in response to a request or application by the person who is to receive the card. Also, the liability to the cardholder for unauthorized use of a credit card is specifically limited to $50 if the cardholder has taken reasonable steps to notify the card issuer of the loss or theft. The act also establishes penalties for the fraudulent use of credit cards in interstate or foreign commerce when the aggregate retail value is $5,000 or more. The commission enforces the requirements of the Truth in Lending Act over finance companies, retailers, nonfederal credit unions, and other creditors not specifically regulated by another government agency, and persons or their agents who issue credit cards.

REGIONAL OFFICES (Federal Trade Commission)

Region	Address
Atlanta—Alabama, Florida, Georgia, Kentucky, Mississippi, North Carolina, South Carolina, Tennessee	1718 Peachtree Street NE, Atlanta, GA 30309
Boston—Connecticut, Maine, Massachusetts, New Hampshire, Rhode Island, Vermont	150 Causeway Street, Boston, MA 02114
Chicago—Illinois, Indiana, Iowa, Minnesota, Missouri, Wisconsin	55 E. Monroe Street, Chicago, IL 60603
Cleveland—Michgan, Western New York, Ohio, Western Pennsylvania	118 St. Clair Avenue, Cleveland, OH 44144
Dallas—Arkansas, Louisiana, New Mexico, Oklahoma, Texas	2001 Bryan Street, Dallas, TX 75201
Denver—Colorado, Kansas, Montana, Nebraska, North Dakota, South Dakota, Utah, Wyoming	1405 Curtis Street, Denver, CO 80202
Los Angeles—Arizona, Southern California	11000 Wilshire Boulevard, Los Angeles, CA 90024
New York—New Jersey, Eastern New York	26 Federal Plaza, New York, NY 10007
San Francisco—Northern California, Hawaii, Nevada	450 Golden Gate Avenue, San Francisco, CA 94102
Seattle—Alaska, Idaho, Oregon, Washington	915 Second Avenue, Seattle, WA 98174
Washington, DC—Delaware, District of Columbia, Maryland, Eastern Pennsylvania, Virginia, West Virginia	2120 L Street NW, Washington, DC 20037

FAIR CREDIT REPORTING ACT

This law represents the first federal regulation of the vast consumer reporting industry, covering all credit bureaus, investigative reporting companies, detective and collection agencies, lenders' exchanges, and computerized information reporting companies. The purpose of this act is to insure that consumer reporting activities are conducted in a manner that is fair and equitable to the affected consumer, upholding his right to privacy against the informational demands of others. The consumer is given several important new rights, including the right to notice of reporting activities, the right to access to information contained in consumer reports, and the right to correction of erroneous information that may have been the basis for a denial of credit, insurance, or employment.

TEXTILE AND FUR LABELING

Under the Wool Products Labeling Act, the Textile Fiber Products Identification Act, and the Fur Products Labeling Act, the commission engages in compliance investigations, inspections, and industry counseling; issues registered identification numbers; and records continuing guaranties. The commission has published rules and regulations under these statutes, together with illustrations of acceptable labeling, which supply full information concerning their requirements. In connection with the Fur Act, the commission has issued a register of animal names, known as the *Fur Products Name Guide,* for use in properly describing furs and fur products.

ECONOMIC FACT-FINDING

The commission makes economic and statistical studies of conditions and problems affecting competition in the economy. Reports of this nature may be in support of legislative proposals, in response to requests of the Congress and statutory directions, or for the information and guidance of the commission and the executive branch of the government as well as the public. Not only have the reports provided the basis for significant legislation, but by spotlighting uneconomic or otherwise objectionable trade practices, they have also led in many instances to voluntary changes in the conduct of business, with resulting benefits to both industry and the public.

The commission prepares quarterly reports on the financial position and operating results of the nation's manufacturing industries. These quarterly summaries present a composite income statement and balance sheet for all manufacturing corporations, classified by both industry and asset size.

The commission also prepares annual reports on current trends in merger activity, large mergers in manufacturing and mining, and rates of return for selected manufacturing industries.

FOOD AND DRUG ADMINISTRATION (FDA)
(DEPARTMENT OF HEALTH, EDUCATION, AND WELFARE)

5600 FISHERS LANE, ROCKVILLE, MD 20852
INFORMATION: 301–443–4177

The name "Food and Drug Administration" was first provided by the Agriculture Appropriation Act of 1931, approved May 27, 1930 (46 Stat. 392), although similar law enforcement functions had been carried on under different organizational titles since January 1, 1907, when the Food and Drug Act of 1906 (34 Stat. 768; 21 U.S.C. 1–15) became effective.

The Food and Drug Administration's activities are directed toward protecting the health of the nation against impure and unsafe foods, drugs, and cosmetics, and other potential hazards.

BIOLOGICS

The Bureau of Biologics administers regulation of biological products shipped in interstate and foreign commerce; inspects manufacturers' facilities for compliance with standards; tests products submitted for release; establishes written and physical standards; approves licenses of manufacturers of biological products; conducts research related to the development, manufacture, testing, and use of new and old biological products; and evaluates claims for investigational new drugs that are biological products.

DRUGS

The Bureau of Drugs develops FDA policy with regard to the safety, effectiveness, and labeling of all drugs for human use; evaluates new drug applications and notices of claimed investigational exemption for new drugs; develops standards for the safety and effectiveness of all over-the-counter drugs; monitors the quality of marketed drugs through product testing, surveillance, and compliance programs; develops guidelines on good manufacturing practices; conducts research and develops scientific standards on the composition, quality, safety, and efficacy of human drugs; disseminates toxicity and treatment information on household products and medicines; evaluates applications for operation of activities using methadone or other drugs; directs the FDA antibiotic and insulin certification program.

FOODS

The Bureau of Foods conducts research and develops standards on the composition, quality, nutrition, and safety of foods, food additives, colors, and cosmetics; conducts research designed to improve the detection, prevention, and control of contamination that may be responsible for illness or injury conveyed by foods, colors, and cosmetics; coordinates and evaluates FDA's surveillance and compliance programs relating to foods, color, and cosmetics; reviews industry petitions and develops regulations for food standards to permit the safe use of color additives and food additives; collects and interprets data on nutrition, food additives, and environmental factors affecting the total chemical insult posed by food additives; and maintains a nutritional data bank.

RADIOLOGICAL HEALTH

The Bureau of Radiological Health carries out programs designed to reduce the exposure of man to hazardous ionizing and nonionizing radiation; develops standards for safe limits of radiation exposure; develops methodology for controlling radiation exposures; conducts research on the health effects of radiation exposure; and conducts an electronic product radiation control program to protect public health and safety, including the development and administration of performance standards to control the emission of radiation from electronic products and the undertaking by public and private organizations of research and investigation into the effects and control of such radiation emissions.

VETERINARY MEDICINE

The Bureau of Veterinary Medicine develops and conducts programs with respect to the safety and efficacy of veterinary preparations and devices; evaluates proposed use of veterinary preparations for animal safety and efficacy; and evaluates FDA's surveillance and compliance programs relating to veterinary drugs and other veterinary medical matters.

MEDICAL DEVICES

The Bureau of Medical Devices and Diagnostic Products develops FDA policy regarding the safety, efficacy, and labeling of medical devices and in vitro diagnostic products; collects and evaluates data on significant hazards to the public health which may be caused by the use of medical devices and diagnostic products; evaluates the safety, efficacy, and labeling of medical devices and diagnostic products and recommends their classification into regulatory categories; conducts research and coordinates the develop-

REGIONAL OFFICES (Food and Drug Administration)

Region	Address
I	585 Commercial Street, Boston, MA 02109
II	850 Third Avenue, Brooklyn, NY 11232
III	1204 U.S. Customhouse, 2nd and Chestnut Streets, Philadelphia, PA 19106
IV	880 W. Peachtree Street NW, Atlanta, GA 30309
V	175 W. Jackson Boulevard, Chicago, IL 60604
VI	3032 Bryan Street, Dallas, TX 75204
VII	1009 Cherry Street, Kansas City, MO 64106
VIII	500 U.S. Customhouse, Denver, CO 80202
IX	Federal Office Building, 50 Fulton Street, San Francisco, CA 94102
X	Federal Office Building, 909 First Avenue, Seattle, WA 98174

ment of standards for appropriate categories of medical devices; conducts research and testing activities relating to medical devices; and collects and evaluates data on significant hazards to the public health which may be caused by the use of medical devices.

TOXICOLOGICAL RESEARCH

The National Center for Toxicological Research conducts research programs to study the biological effects of potentially toxic chemical substances found in man's environment, emphasizing the determination of the health effects resulting from long-term low-level exposure to chemical toxicants and the basic biological processes for chemical toxicants in animal organisms, and the development of improved methodologies and test protocols for evaluating the safety of chemical toxicants and the data that will facilitate the extrapolation of toxicological data from laboratory animals to man.

REGIONAL OPERATIONS

The Executive Director of Regional Operations executes direct line authority over FDA field activities; provides a central point to which headquarters officials can turn to for field support services; develops programs and plans for activities between FDA, state, and local agencies; and administers FDA's state-federal program policy.

Field operations necessary for the enforcement of the laws under the jurisdiction of FDA are carried out within the 10 regional offices, 22 district offices, and 121 resident inspection posts throughout the United States and Puerto Rico.

INTERSTATE COMMERCE COMMISSION (ICC)

TWELFTH STREET AND CONSTITUTION AVENUE NW, WASHINGTON, DC 20423
INFORMATION: 202–275–7252

In broad terms and within prescribed legal limits, commission regulation encompasses transportation economics and service.

In the transportation economics area, the commission settles controversies over rates and charges among competing and like modes of transportation, shippers, and receivers of freight, passengers, and others. It rules upon applications for mergers, consolidations, acquisitions of control, and the sale of carriers and issuance of their securities. It prescribes accounting rules, awards reparations, and administers laws relating to railroad bankruptcy. It acts to prevent unlawful discrimination, destructive competition, and rebating. It also has jurisdiction over the use, control, supply, movement, distribution, exchange, interchange, and return of railroad equipment. Under certain conditions, it is authorized to direct the handling and movement of traffic over a railroad and its distribution over other lines of railroads.

In the transportation service area, the commission grants the right to operate to trucking companies, bus lines, freight forwarders, water carriers, and transportation brokers. It approves applications to construct and abandon railroad lines, and it rules upon discontinuances of passenger train service.

Although public hearings on matters before the commission may be held at any point throughout the country, final decisions are made at the Washington, D.C. headquarters in all formal proceedings. These cases include rulings upon rate changes, applications to engage in for-hire transport, carrier mergers, adversary proceedings on complaint actions, and punitive measures taken in enforcement matters.

Consumer protection programs involve assuring that the public obtains full measure of all transportation services to which entitlement is guaranteed by the Interstate Commerce Act. This law ensures that rates will be fair and service will be reasonable. Discrimination, preferential treatment, or prejudicial actions by carriers is illegal and instances of such violations should be brought to the attention of the commission at its headquarters or any field office.

REGIONAL OFFICES (Interstate Commerce Commission)

Region	Address
1. Connecticut, Maine, Massachusetts, New Hampshire, New Jersey, New York, Rhode Island, Vermont	150 Causeway Street, Boston, MA 02114
2. Delaware, District of Columbia, Maryland, Ohio, Pennsylvania, Virginia, West Virginia	600 Arch Street, Philadelphia, PA 19106
3. Alabama, Florida, Georgia, Kentucky, Mississippi, North Carolina, South Carolina, Tennessee	1252 W. Peachtree Street NW, Atlanta, GA 30309
4. Illinois, Indiana, Michigan, Minnesota, North Dakota, South Dakota, Wisconsin	219 S. Dearborn Street, Chicago, IL 60604
5. Arkansas, Iowa, Kansas, Louisiana, Missouri, Nebraska, Oklahoma, Texas	819 Taylor Street, Fort Worth, TX 76102
6. Alaska, Arizona, California, Colorado, Hawaii, Idaho, Montana, Nevada, New Mexico, Oregon, Utah, Washington, Wyoming	450 Golden Gate Avenue, San Francisco, CA 94102

The Regional Rail Reorganization Act of 1973 created in early 1974 a Rail Services Planning Office to assure that public interest is represented in the restructuring and revitalization of railroads in the Northeast and Midwest. The office was given permanent status by the Railroad Revitalization and Regulatory Reform Act of 1976 (90 Stat. 31; 45 U.S.C. 801 note). In addition to its other responsibilities, it provides planning support for the commission.

LABOR-MANAGEMENT SERVICES ADMINISTRATION (LMSA) (DEPARTMENT OF LABOR)

THIRD STREET AND CONSTITUTION AVENUE NW, WASHINGTON, DC 20216
INFORMATION: 202–523–7408

The Assistant Secretary for Labor-Management Relations has responsibility for the department's labor-management relations activities and serves as administrator of the Labor-Management Services Administration.

The Labor-Management Services Administration administers three laws and major parts of a presidential executive order. It also provides assistance to collective bargaining negotiators and keeps the Secretary posted on development in labor-management disputes of national scope.

LMSA provides technical assistance to state and local governments in matters concerning public employee labor relations and pursues research and policy development in the overall labor-management relations field.

VETERANS REEMPLOYMENT

Veterans reemployment rights are provided for in Title 38, Chapter 43 of the United States Code. LMSA helps veterans, reservists, national guardsmen, and rejectees exercise their reemployment rights pertaining to the job, seniority, status, and rate of pay they would have achieved had they not been away.

General information is provided to veterans and their preservice employers at the time the veteran is released from the armed forces.

Technical assistance and more specific information are provided to veterans and employers, aimed at voluntary resolution of reemployment problems. When such efforts are not successful, cases may be referred to the Department of Justice for legal action.

PENSION AND WELFARE PLANS

The Employee Retirement Income Security Act of 1974 (ERISA), approved September 2, 1974 (88 Stat. 829; 29 U.S.C. 1001 note), requires administrators of private pension and welfare plans to file copies of those plans with LMSA; to provide plan participants with easily understandable summaries of plans; and to report annually on the financial operation of the plans and bonding of persons charged with handling plan funds and assets. Such persons must also meet strict fiduciary responsibility standards administered by LMSA. Vesting, participation, and funding standards are administered by the Internal Revenue Service.

The Welfare and Pension Plans Disclosure Act (WPPDA) was repealed by ERISA on January 1, 1975, except that certain reporting provisions have been carried over by regulation.

REGIONAL OFFICES (Labor-Management Services Administration)

Region	Address
New York—Maine, New Hampshire, Vermont, Rhode Island, Massachusetts, Connecticut, New York, New Jersey, Virgin Islands, Puerto Rico......	1515 Broadway, New York, NY 10036
Philadelphia—Pennsylvania, Maryland, Delaware, Virginia, West Virginia......	3535 Market Street, Philadelphia, PA 19104
Atlanta—Kentucky, Tennessee, North Carolina, South Carolina, Mississippi, Alabama, Florida, Georgia..............	1371 Peachtree Street NE, Atlanta, GA 30309
Chicago—Illinois, Wisconsin, Indiana, Minnesota, Michigan, Ohio.............	230 S. Dearborn Street, Chicago, IL 60604
Kansas City—Montana, Wyoming, Utah, Colorado, New Mexico, North Dakota, South Dakota, Nebraska, Kansas, Oklahoma, Texas, Iowa, Missouri, Arkansas, Louisiana..............	911 Walnut Street, Kansas City, MO 64106
San Francisco—Alaska, Hawaii, Idaho, Washington, Oregon, California, Nevada, Arizona........................	450 Golden Gate Avenue, San Francisco, CA 94102

LABOR ORGANIZATIONS

The Labor Management Reporting and Disclosure Act calls upon labor organizations to file with LMSA copies of their constitutions and bylaws and annual financial reports of their transactions for public view.

The act also prescribes rules for election of union officers, administration of trusteeships by labor organizations, rights of union members, and the handling of union funds.

Through technical assistance in all these areas LMSA seeks to obtain voluntary compliance with provisions of the act. Enforcement through the federal courts also is available under the law.

FEDERAL EMPLOYEE ORGANIZATIONS

Federal labor-management relations are governed by Executive Order 11491, as amended. The Assistant Secretary for Labor-Management Relations, under the order, decides appropriate bargaining units, supervises representation elections, rules on unfair labor practice complaints, and decides questions as to grievability and arbitrability.

As with labor organizations in the private sector, unions of federal employees are required to file annual financial reports for disclosure to the public, and to observe standards of conduct with respect to election of union officers, administration of trusteeships, handling of money, and the rights of union members. LMSA's emphasis in federal labor-management relations matters, as with the laws it administers, is on voluntary compliance through technical assistance.

LABOR-MANAGEMENT RELATIONS SERVICES

Services offered by LMSA cover a broad range. They include assistance to employers and unions in meeting long-range, complicated problems caused by major economic and technological change; reporting on current and potentially critical dispute situations, analyzing data for immediate use in specific collective bargaining situations; providing staff assistance to presidential emergency boards and other ad hoc boards and commissions dealing with major disputes, such as in the transportation industry; making sure under Section 13(c) of the Urban Mass Transportation Act that protective arrangements exist so that the improvement of such systems with federal funds will not worsen the employment conditions of the workers; and exchanging information with, and giving technical assistance to, state and local governments and organizations of their employees to help them achieve sound labor-management relations.

DEVELOPMENT, RESEARCH, AND EVALUATION

Functions of LMSA in labor-management policy development and research include: review of collective bargaining performance and its contribution to meeting economic needs; development of policy for legislation and executive orders; study of impact of private policies affecting collective bargaining; and coordination of labor-management relations research activities. The evaluation function is the review of LMSA programs to assess their effectiveness and efficiency.

REGIONAL OFFICES (Occupational Safety and Health Administration)

Region	Address
I	John F. Kennedy Federal Building, Government Center, Boston, MA 02203
II	1515 Broadway, New York, NY 10036
III	3535 Market Street, Philadelphia, PA 19104
IV	1375 Peachtree Street NE, Atlanta, GA 30309
V	230 S. Dearborn Street, Chicago, IL 60604
VI	555 Griffin Square Building, Dallas, TX 75202
VII	911 Walnut Street, Kansas City, MO 64106
VIII	1961 Stout Street, Denver, CO 80294
IX	450 Golden Gate Avenue, San Francisco, CA 94102
X	909 First Avenue, Seattle, WA 98174

REGIONAL OFFICES (Federal Contract Compliance)

Region	Address
I	John F. Kennedy Federal Building, Boston, MA 02203
II	1515 Broadway, New York, NY 10036
III	3535 Market Street, Philadelphia, PA 19104
IV	1371 Peachtree Street NE, Atlanta, GA 30309
V	230 S. Dearborn Street, Chicago, IL 60604
VI	555 Griffin Square Building, Dallas, TX 75202
VII	911 Walnut Street, Kansas City, MO 64106
VIII	1961 Stout Street, Denver, CO 80294
IX	450 Golden Gate Avenue, San Francisco, CA 94102
X	909 First Avenue, Seattle, WA 98104

OCCUPATIONAL SAFETY AND HEALTH ADMINISTRATION (OSHA) (DEPARTMENT OF LABOR)

200 CONSTITUTION AVENUE NW, WASHINGTON, DC 20210
INFORMATION: 202–523–8151

The Assistant Secretary for Occupational Safety and Health has responsibility for occupational safety and health activities.

The Occupational Safety and Health Administration, established pursuant to the Occupational Safety and Health Act of 1970 (84 Stat. 1590), develops and promulgates occupational safety and health standards; develops and issues regulations; conducts investigations and inspections to determine the status of compliance with safety and health standards and regulations; and issues citations and proposes penalties for noncompliance with safety and health standards and regulations.

FEDERAL CONTRACT COMPLIANCE (FCC) (DEPARTMENT OF LABOR)

THIRD STREET AND CONSTITUTION AVENUE NW, WASHINGTON, DC 20210
INFORMATION: 202–523–8743

The Office of Federal Contract Compliance is responsible for establishing policies and goals and providing leadership and coordination of the government's program to achieve nondiscrimination in employment by government contractors and subcontractors and in federally assisted construction programs; coordinating with the Equal Employment Opportunity Commission and the Department of Justice matters relating to Title VII of the Civil Rights Act of 1964; and maintaining liaison with other agencies having civil rights and equal employment opportunity activities.

SECURITIES AND EXCHANGE COMMISSION (SEC)

500 NORTH CAPITOL STREET, WASHINGTON, DC 20549
INFORMATION: 202–755–4846

FULL AND FAIR DISCLOSURE

The Securities Act of 1933 requires issuers of securities making public offerings of securities in interstate commerce or through the mails, directly or by others on their behalf, to file registration statements containing financial and other pertinent data about the issuer and the securities being offered. A similar requirement applies to such offerings on behalf of a controlling person of the issuer. Unless a registration statement is in effect with respect to such securities, it is unlawful to sell the securities in interstate commerce or through the mails. (There are certain limited exemptions, such as government securities, nonpublic offerings, and intrastate offerings, as well as offerings not exceeding $500,000 in amount, which comply with the commission's Regulation A.) The effectiveness of a registration statement may be refused or suspended after a public hearing, if the statement contains material misstatements or omissions, thus barring sale of the securities until it is appropriately amended. Registration of securities does not imply approval of the issue by the commission or that the commission has found the registration disclosures to be accurate. It does not insure investors against loss in their purchase but serves rather to provide information upon which investors may make an informed and realistic evaluation of the worth of the securities.

Persons responsible for filing false information with the commission subject themselves to the risk of fine or imprisonment or both; and persons connected with the public offering may be liable in damages to purchasers of the securities if the disclosures in the registration statement and prospectus are materially defective. Also, the above act contains antifraud provisions which apply generally to the sale of securities, whether or not registered (48 Stat. 74; 15 U.S.C. 77a et seq.).

REGULATION OF SECURITIES MARKETS, BROKERS, AND DEALERS

The Securities Exchange Act of 1934 requires all national securities exchanges and national securities associations to register with the commission and to adopt rules that are designed, among other things, to promote just and equitable principles of trade. The commission is given broad powers to alter or supplement rules of exchanges if such action appears to be necessary or appropriate for the protection of investors or to insure fair dealing in listed securities or fair administration of exchanges, and to abrogate rules of an association if such action appears to be necessary or appropriate to assure fair dealing by members, to assure fair administration, or otherwise to protect investors.

The Securities Exchange Act also requires the filing of registration applications and annual and other reports with national securities exchanges and the commission by companies whose securities are listed upon the exchanges, by companies that have assets of $1 million or more and 500 or more shareholders of record, and by companies that distributed securities pursuant to a registration statement declared effective by the commission under the Securities Act of 1933. Such applications and reports must contain financial and other data prescribed by the commission as necessary or appropriate for the protection of investors and to insure fair dealing. In addition, the solicitation of proxies, authorizations, or consents from holders of such registered securities must be made in accordance with rules and regulations prescribed by the commission. These rules provide for disclosures to securities holders of information relevant to the subject matter of the solicitation.

Disclosure of the holdings and transactions by officers, directors, and large (10 percent) holders of equity securities of companies is also required, and any and all persons who acquire more than 5 percent of certain equity securities are required to file detailed information with the commission and any exchange upon which such securities may be traded. Moreover, any person making a tender offer for certain classes of equity securities is required to file reports with the commission, if as a result of the tender offer such person would own more than 5 percent of the outstanding shares of the particular class of equity involved. The commission also is authorized to promulgate rules governing the repurchase by a corporate issuer of its own securities.

Brokers and dealers who engage in any over-the-counter securities business must register with the commission. In addition, the commission has broad rule-making authority with respect to, among other things, short sales, the trading of options on national securities exchanges, stabilizing transactions, floor trading, and the activities of specialists and odd-lot dealers. The commission also is authorized to adopt rules concerning the financial responsibility of brokers and dealers, and rules specifying the reports to be made by brokers and dealers. The Securities Exchange Act also empowers the Board of Governors of the Federal Reserve System to prescribe rules relating to the extensions of credit by brokers and dealers for securities transactions. Such rules include the establishment of minimum margin requirements with respect to securities registered on national securities exchanges and certain securities traded over the counter (48 Stat. 881; 15 U.S.C. 78a et seq.).

REGULATION OF MUTUAL FUNDS AND OTHER INVESTMENT COMPANIES

The Investment Company Act of 1940 provides for the registration with the commission of investment companies and subjects their activities to regulation to protect investors. The regulation covers sales and management fees, composition of boards of directors, and capital structure. Also, various transactions of investment companies, including transactions with affiliated interests, are prohibited unless the commission first determines that such transactions are fair. Under the act, the commission may institute court action to enjoin the consummation of mergers and other plans of reorganization of investment companies if such plans are unfair to security holders. It also may impose sanctions by administrative proceedings against investment company managements for violations of the act and other federal securities laws, and file court actions to enjoin acts and practices of management officials involving breaches of fiduciary duty involving personal misconduct and to disqualify such officials from office (54 Stat. 789; 15 U.S.C. 80a–1—80a–52).

REGULATION OF COMPANIES CONTROLLING ELECTRIC OR GAS UTILITIES

The Public Utility Holding Company Act of 1935 provides for regulation by the commission of the purchase and sale of securities and assets by companies in electric and gas utility holding company systems, their intra-system transactions and service and management arrangements. It limits holding companies to a single coordinated utility system and requires simplification of complex corporate and capital structures and elimination of unfair distribution of voting power among holders of system securities.

The issuance and sale of securities by holding companies and their subsidiaries, unless exempt (subject to conditions and terms which the commission is empowered to impose) as an issue expressly authorized by the state commission in the state in which the issuer is incorporated, must be found by the commission to meet statutory standards, namely: that the new security is reasonably adapted to the security structure and earning power of the issuer; that the proposed financing is necessary and appropriate to the economical and efficient operation of the company's business; that the consideration received, and fees, commissions, and other remuneration paid, are fair; and that the terms and conditions of the sale are not detrimental to investors, consumers, or the public.

The purchase and sale of utility properties and other assets may not be made in contravention of rules, regulations, or orders of the commission regarding the consideration to be received, maintenance of competitive conditions, fees and commissions, accounts, disclosure of interest, and similar matters. In passing upon proposals for reorganization, merger, or consolidation, the commission must be satisfied that the objectives of the act generally are complied with and that the terms of the proposal are fair and equitable to all classes of security holders affected (49 Stat. 803; 15 U.S.C. 79–92z–6).

REGULATION OF INVESTMENT COUNSELORS AND ADVISERS

The Investment Advisers Act of 1940 provides that persons who, for compensation, engage in the business of advising others with respect to their security transactions must register with the commission. The act prohibits certain types of fee arrangements, makes unlawful practices of investment advisers involving fraud or deceit, and requires, among other things, disclosure of any adverse interests the advisers may have in transactions executed for clients. The act authorizes the commission to issue rules proscribing acts and practices that may operate as a fraud or deceit upon investors (54 Stat. 847; 15 U.S.C. 80b–1–80b–21).

REHABILITATION OF FAILING CORPORATIONS

Chapter X of the Bankruptcy Act provides for commission participation as adviser to federal courts in proceedings for the reorganization of insolvent corporations. An important aspect of this activity is the advice rendered to the parties and the court with respect to the fairness and feasibility of proposed plans of reorganization (52 Stat. 883; 11 U.S.C. 501–676).

INDEPENDENT REPRESENTATION OF THE INTERESTS OF HOLDERS OF DEBT SECURITIES

The interests of purchasers of publicly offered debt securities issued pursuant to trust indentures are safeguarded under the provisions of the Trust Indenture Act of 1939. This act, among other things, requires the exclusion from such indentures of certain types of exculpatory clauses and the inclusion of certain protective provisions. The independence of the indenture trustee, who is a representative of the debt holder, is assured by proscribing certain relationships that might conflict with the proper exercise of his duties (53 Stat. 1149; 15 U.S.C. 77aaa–77bbbb).

ENFORCEMENT ACTIVITIES

The commission's enforcement activities are designed to secure compliance with the federal securities laws administered by the commission and the rules and regulations adopted thereunder. These activities include measures to compel obedience to the disclosure requirements of the registration and other provisions of the acts; to prevent fraud and deception in the purchase and sale of securities; to obtain court orders enjoining acts and practices that operate as a fraud upon investors or otherwise violate the laws; to revoke the registrations of brokers, dealers, and investment advisers who willfully engage in such acts and practices; to suspend or expel from national securities exchanges or the National Association of Securities Dealers, Inc., any member or officer who has violated any provision of the federal securities laws; and to prosecute persons who have engaged in fraudulent activities or other willful violations of those laws. In addition, attorneys or accountants who violate the securities laws face possible loss of their privilege to practice before the commission. To this end, private investigations are conducted into complaints or other evidences of securities violations. Evidence thus established of law violations in the purchase and sale of securities is used in appropriate administrative proceedings to revoke registration or in actions instituted in federal courts to restrain or enjoin such activities. Where the evidence tends to establish fraud or other willful violation of the securities laws, the facts are referred to the Attorney General for criminal prosecution of the offenders. The commission may assist in such prosecutions.

INVESTOR INFORMATION AND PROTECTION

Complaints and inquiries may be directed to the home office or to any regional office. Registration statements and other public documents filed with the commission are available for public inspection in the public reference room at the home office. Much of the information also is available in its New York, Chicago, and Los Angeles regional offices, and to a lesser extent in the other regional offices of the commission. Reproduction of the public material may be purchased from the commission at prescribed rates.

Executive Liability Under Federal Law

The regulatory agencies have been showing an increasing disposition to hold executives personally accountable for violations. An example of how far the agencies can push matters is provided by a Supreme Court ruling in June 1975 in favor of the Food and Drug Administration (FDA). The case named Acme Markets, Inc. and its president, John R. Park. Park maintained that after receiving a warning from the FDA about rat infestation in Acme warehouses, he designated the job of eliminating the rodents to a qualified subordinate. However, a continuance of the infestation caused the FDA to impose a fine on Park. The Supreme Court, in rejecting Park's argument, affirmed that an executive's liability for criminal conduct ex-

REGIONAL OFFICES (Securities and Exchange Commission)

Region	Address
1. New York, New Jersey	26 Federal Plaza, New York, NY 10007
2. Maine, Vermont, New Hampshire, Massachusetts, Connecticut, Rhode Island	150 Causeway Street, Boston, MA 02114
3. Tennessee, North Carolina, South Carolina, Mississippi, Alabama, Georgia, Florida, Louisiana (southeastern portion only)	1375 Peachtree Street NE, Atlanta, GA 30309
4. Minnesota, Wisconsin, Michigan, Iowa, Missouri, Illinois, Indiana, Ohio, Kentucky	219 S. Dearborn Street, Chicago, IL 60604
5. Kansas, Oklahoma, Texas, Arkansas, Louisiana (except southeastern portion)	10th and Lamar Streets, Fort Worth, TX 76102
6. North Dakota, South Dakota, Colorado, Kansas, Utah, Wyoming, New Mexico	Two Park Central, 1515 Arapahoe Street, Denver, CO 80202
7. California, Nevada, Arizona, Hawaii	10960 Wilshire Boulevard, Los Angeles, CA 90024
8. Washington, Oregon	915 Second Avenue, Seattle, WA 98174
9. Pennsylvania, West Virginia, Virginia, Maryland, Delaware	4015 Wilson Boulevard, Arlington, VA 22203

tends to organizational levels well below that of his immediate responsibility.

Pressures for personal accountability are increasing. Pending before the Senate is a bill (S.1) to codify the concept of "reckless default," by which an executive would be subject to personal prosecution for failure to properly supervise subordinates who violate federal regulations.

Agencies that can name individuals for violations are listed in the accompanying table.

FUTURE CAPITAL NEEDS

The Carter administration's objective is to limit the growth in energy requirements to 2 percent annually over the next ten years. Many private estimates, however, are based on the view that it will be impossible to restrict the annual increase in demand much below 3 percent without seriously impeding the growth of the economy and the nation's ability to reduce unemployment to 4 percent.

A 3 percent growth rate would generate a capital requirement for energy programs of about $750 billion over the next ten years. This represents a rate of between 2 and 2.5 times the annual rate of investment in the past six years. Roughly half of this total must come from external sources.

The capital needs of the U.S. electric utility industry alone for the ten-year period of 1978 to 1987 have been estimated at $450 billion. By comparison, the capital expenditures of the industry in the 1965 to 1974 period were $120 billion. Furthermore, one big utility, Commonwealth Edison, has projected the amount of needed *external* financing for the industry to rise from $75 billion in the 1965 to 1974 period to $300 billion in the period of 1978 to 1987, or two thirds of the total requirement.

In addition to the needs of the electric power industry, which accounts for about one third of all new capital raised externally in the United States, many other energy processes have enormous funding needs. Adding the requirements of coal gasification, shale oil, and many other advanced-technology programs would raise our total energy-financing requirements to unprecedented amounts.

Source: "Financing High-Cost, High-Risk Energy Development" by Franklin A. Lindsay, *Harvard Business Review*, November–December 1978.

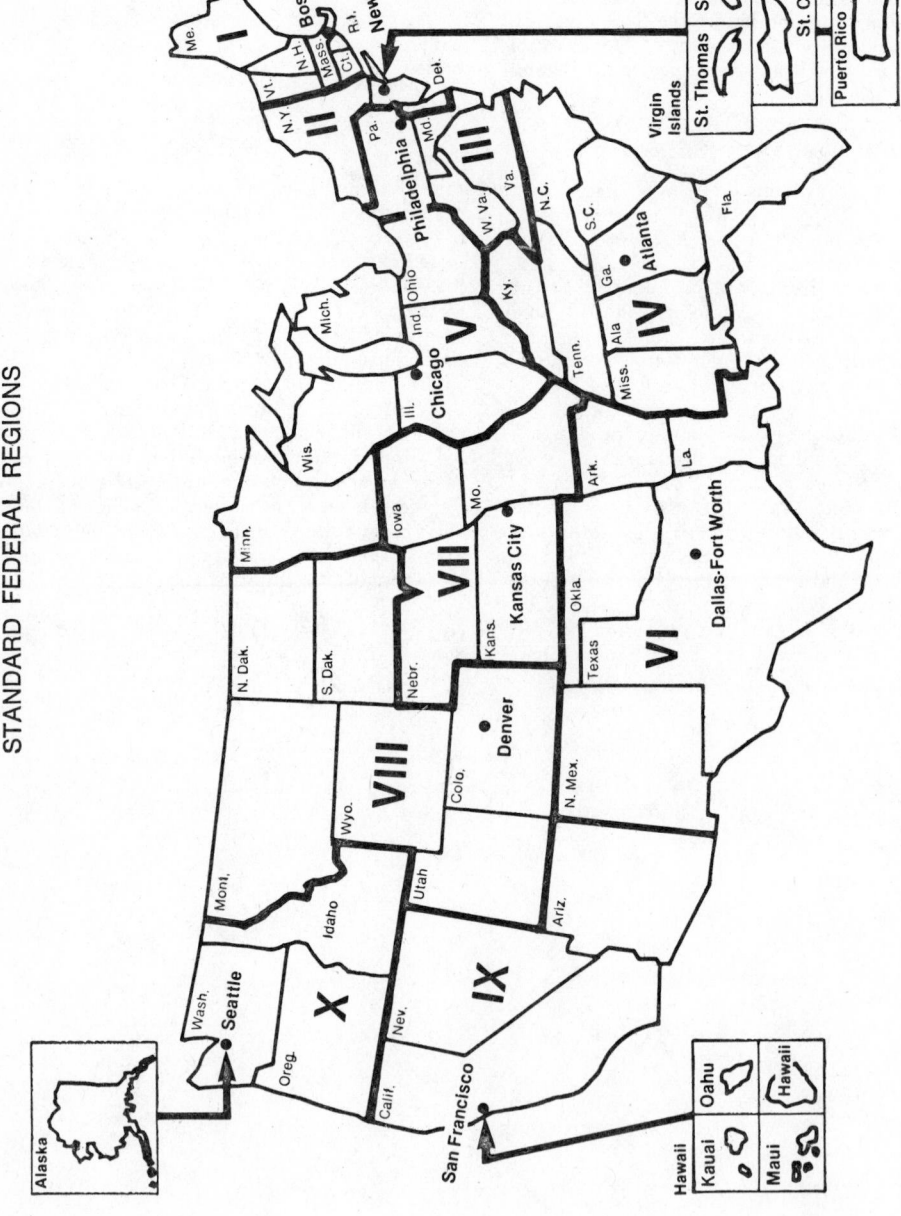

STANDARD FEDERAL REGIONS

THE RISKS EXECUTIVES FACE UNDER FEDERAL LAW

Agency	Year Enforcement Began	Complaint May Name Individual	Maximum Individual Penalty	Maximum Corporate Penalty	Private Suit Allowed under Applicable Statute
Internal Revenue Service..............	1862	Yes	$5,000, three years, or both	$10,000, 50% assessment, prosecution costs	No
Antitrust Division (Justice Department)......	1890	Yes	$100,000, three years, or both	$1 million, injunction, divestiture	Yes
Food and Drug Administration..........	1907	Yes	$1,000, one year, or both for first offense; $10,000, three years, or both thereafter	$1,000 for first offense; $10,000 thereafter; seizure of condemned products	No
Federal Trade Commission.............	1914	Yes	Restitution, injunction	Restitution, injunction, divestiture, $10,000 per day for violation of rules, orders	No
Securities and Exchange Commission.......	1934	Yes	$10,000, two years, or both	$10,000, injunction	Yes
Equal Employment Opportunity Commission............	1965	No		Injunction, back-pay award, reinstatement	Yes
Office of Federal Contract Compliance......	1965	No		Suspension, cancellation of contract	Yes
Environmental Protection Agency...........	1970	Yes	$25,000 per day, one year, or both for first offense; $50,000 per day, two years, or both thereafter	$25,000 per day, first offense; $50,000 per day thereafter; injunction	Yes
Occupational Safety and Health Administration............	1970	No*	$10,000, six months, or both	$10,000	No
Consumer Product Safety Commission......	1972	Yes	$50,000, one year, or both	$500,000	Yes
Office of Employee Benefits Security (Labor Department).............	1975	Yes	$10,000, one year, or both; barring from future employment with plan; reimbursement	$100,000, reimbursement	Yes

* Except sole proprietorship
Source: Reprinted from the May 10, 1976 issue of Business Week by special permission © 1976 by McGraw-Hill, Inc., p. 113.

Finance and Accounting

ACCOUNTING AND ALLIED FINANCIAL ORGANIZATIONS

American Accounting Association (AAA): A private professional organization representing academic accounts. Address: 653 So. Orange Avenue, Sarasota, FL 33577.

American Institute of Certified Public Accountants (AICPA): The largest private association of certified public accountants (CPAs). Address: 1121 Avenue of the Americas, New York, NY 10036.

Cost Accounting Standards Board (CASB): A federal board established in 1970 for promulgating cost accounting standards for use by contractors with the federal government. Address: 441 G Street NW, Washington, DC 20548.

Financial Accounting Standards Board (FASB): The private body created to establish accounting standards. Established in July 1973, it succeeded the earlier Accounting Principles Board (APB). It is jointly sponsored by the AAA, AICPA, FEI, FAF, and NAA. The standards are officially recognized by the Securities and Exchange Commission (SEC). Address: High Ridge Park, Stamford, CT 06905.

Financial Executives Institute (FEI): An organization of corporate financial officers. Address: 633 Third Avenue, New York, NY 10017.

National Organization of State Boards of Accountancy (NOSBA): An organization representing state boards which license CPAs. Address: 1211 Avenue of the Americas, New York, NY 10036.

National Association of Accountants (NAA): An organization of businessmen and accountants. Address: 919 Third Avenue, New York, NY 10022.

The "Big Eight" Accounting Firms: The leading accounting firms within the profession. Clients of the Big Eight include 92 percent of the firms listed on the New York Stock Exchange and 76 percent of those listed on the American Stock Exchange. Listed in alphabetical order, the names and addresses of the Big Eight are:

Arthur Andersen & Co., 69 W. Washington Street, Chicago, IL 60602.

Arthur Young & Co., 277 Park Avenue, New York, NY 10017.

Coopers & Lybrand, 1251 Avenue of the Americas, New York, NY 10020.

Ernst & Ernst, 1300 Union Commerce Building, Cleveland, OH 44115.

Deloitte, 1114 Avenue of the Americas, New York, NY 10036.

Peat, Marwick, Mitchell & Co., 345 Park Avenue, New York, NY 10022.

Price Waterhouse & Co., 1251 Avenue of the Americas, New York, NY 10020.

Touche Ross & Co., 1633 Broadway, New York, NY 10019.

ACCOUNTING STATEMENTS
AND OPINIONS

ACCOUNTING RESEARCH BULLETINS (ARB)

ARB Number and Title	Date
43. Restatement and revisions of accounting research bulletins ...	June 1953
44. Declining balance depreciation	July 1958
45. Long-term construction-type contacts	October 1955
46. Discontinuance for dating earned surplus	February 1956
47. Accounting for cost of pension plans	September 1956
48. Business combinations	January 1957
49. Earnings per share	April 1958
50. Contingencies	October 1958
51. Consolidated financial statements	August 1959

ACCOUNTING PRINCIPLES BOARD (APB) STATEMENTS

APB Statement Number and Title	Date
1. Statement by the Accounting Principles Board	April 13, 1962
2. Disclosure of supplemental financial information by diversified companies	September 1967
3. Financial statements restated for general price-level changes	June 1969
4. Basic concepts and accounting principles underlying financial statements of business enterprises	October 1970

ACCOUNTING PRINCIPLES BOARD (APB) OPINIONS

Opinions	Date Adopted
1. New depreciation guidelines and rules	November 1962
2. Accounting for the "investment credit"	December 1962
3. The statement of source and application of funds	October 1963
4. Accounting for the "investment credit" (amending No. 2)	March 1964
5. Reporting of leases in financial statements of lessee	September 1964
6. Status of Accounting Research Bulletins	October 1965
7. Accounting for leases in financial statements of lessors	May 1966
8. Accounting for the cost of pension plans	November 1966
9. Reporting the results of operations	December 1966
10. Omnibus opinion—1966	December 1966
Consolidated financial statements, poolings of interest—restatement of financial statements, tax allocation accounts—discounting, offsetting securities against taxes payable, convertible debt and debt issued with stock warrants, liquidation preference of preferred stock, installment method of accounting	
11. Accounting for income taxes	December 1967
Timing differences, operating losses, tax allocation within a period, other unused deductions and credits, financial reporting	
12. Omnibus opinion—1967	December 1967
Classification and disclosure of allowances, disclosure of depreciable assets and depreciation, deferred compensation contracts, capital changes, convertible debt and debt issued with stock warrants, amortization of debt discount and expense or premium	
13. Amending paragraph 6 of APB Opinion No. 9 application to commercial banks	March 1969
14. Accounting for convertible debt and debt issued with stock purchase warrants	March 1969
15. Earnings per share	May 1969
16. Business combinations	August 1970
17. Intangible assets	August 1970
18. The equity method of accounting for investments in common stock	March 1971

ACCOUNTING PRINCIPLES BOARD (APB) OPINIONS (*continued*)

Opinions	Date Adopted
19. Reporting changes in financial position	March 1971
20. Accounting changes	July 1971
Change in accounting principle, change in accounting estimate, change in the reporting equity, correction of an error in previously issued financial statements	
21. Interest on receivables and payables	August 1971
22. Disclosure of accounting policies	April 1972
23. Accounting for income taxes—special areas	April 1972
Undistributed earnings of subsidiaries, investments in corporate joint ventures, "bad debt reserves" of savings and loan associations, "policyholders' surplus" of stock life insurance companies	
24. Accounting for income taxes—investments in common	April 1972
Stock accounted for by the equity method (other than subsidiaries and corporate joint ventures)	
25. Accounting for stock issued to employees	October 1972
26. Early extinguishment of debt	October 1972
27. Accounting for lease transactions by manufacturer or dealer lessors	November 1972
28. Interim financial reporting	May 1973
29. Accounting for nonmonetary transactions	May 1973
30. Reporting the results of operations—reporting the effects of disposal of a segment of a business, and extraordinary, unusual and infrequently occuring events and transactions	June 1973
31. Disclosure of lease commitments by lessees	June 1973

FINANCIAL ACCOUNTING STANDARDS BOARD (FASB) STATEMENTS
(FASB succeeded APB in July 1973)

FASB Statement Number and Title	Date Adopted
1. Disclosure of foreign currency translation information	December 1973
2. Accounting for research and development costs	October 1974
3. Reporting accounting changes in interim financial statements (amendment of APB Opinion No. 28)	December 1974
4. Reporting gains and losses from extinguishment of debt (amendment of APB Opinion No. 30)	March 1975
5. Accounting for contingencies	March 1975
6. Classification of short-term obligations expected to be refinanced (amendment of ARB No. 43, Chapter 3A)	May 1975
7. Accounting and reporting by development stage enterprises	June 1975
8. Accounting for the translation of foreign currency transactions and foreign currency financial statements	October 1975
9. Accounting for income taxes—oil and gas producing companies (amendment of APB Opinions No. 11 and 23)	October 1975
10. Extension of "grandfather" provisions for business combinations (amendment of APB Opinion No. 16)	October 1975
11. Accounting for contingencies—transition method (amendment of FASB Statement No. 5)	December 1975
12. Accounting for certain marketable securities	December 1975
13. Accounting for leases	November 1976
14. Financial reporting for segments of a business enterprise	December 1976
15. Accounting by debtors and creditors for troubled debt restructurings	June 1977
16. Prior period adjustments	June 1977
17. Accounting for leases—initial direct costs (amendment of FASB Statement No. 13)	November 1977
18. Financial reporting for segments of a business enterprise—interim financial statements (amendment of FASB Statement No. 14)	November 1977
19. Financial accounting and reporting by oil and gas producing companies	December 1977
20. Forward exchange contracts	December 1977
21. Suspension of the reporting of earnings per share and segment information by nonpublic enterprises (amendment of APB Opinion No. 15 and FASB Statement No. 14)	April 1978
22. Changes in the provision of lease agreements resulting from refundings of tax-exempt debt	June 1978

International Accounting Standards: Problems and Progress

Joseph P. Cummings*

As U.S. business continues its growth in foreign markets and as foreign business in the United States increases, there is a growing awareness of the differences in accounting standards and practices for U.S. and foreign financial statements. Business has found that investing, lending, or operating abroad may prove more costly because of these divergent accounting standards and practices. A lack of understanding of the true foreign financial picture has sometimes led to untimely acquisitions and subsequent excessive parent company supervision.

Governments, as users of financial statements, have also encountered difficulties in working with varying standards. They express fears that nonuniform accounting practices are being used to shift income to those countries with the lowest tax rates. Their resulting actions have often proved costly as they separately attempt to legislate "fairness and comparability" into financial statements.

If accounting is the language of business, then the users of financial statements have found the interpretation and understanding of the divergent languages to be difficult.

DIFFERENCES IN ACCOUNTING STANDARDS AND PRACTICES

Most listings of differences between accounting and reporting in local countries and accounting and reporting in the United States will include the following:

A. Conceptual differences.
1. Consolidated financial statements are not always required for controlled subsidiaries, and the unconsolidated subsidiaries may be carried on the cost basis rather than on the equity basis. The reader of the financial statements is thus left with only a partial view of the total financial position and results of operations. Since income from these unconsolidated subsidiaries is reported on the cost basis, management may greatly influence the

ways in which results of operations are reported.
2. Investments in affiliates (associated companies that are not controlled subsidiaries) may also be reported on the cost basis rather than on the equity basis. Again, as described above, this may allow the reporting group to influence the smoothing or trending of income reported.
3. Reserves may be used to manage the trend of earnings. Where financial statements have traditionally been prepared for closely knit groups of investors, there has been a tendency toward conservatism. To introduce symmetry into reported results of operations, many non-U.S. companies have used reserves for inventory, warranties, unspecified "general business" risks, and other items. Disclosure of such reserves is generally inadequate to permit measurement of their impact.
4. Fixed asset upward revaluations may be allowed or price level accounting partially required. The resulting changes to financial statements previously reported on a historical cost basis are often reported in a number of different ways.

B. Income reporting differences.
1. Unusual income and expense items may be recorded directly to stockholders' equity without being reflected in the income statements, thus causing comparability problems.
2. Inventory may be calculated on a direct cost basis with no inclusion of overhead costs related to manufacturing. Changes in the methods of calculations and/or components of cost may not be disclosed from period to period.
3. Depreciation may be recorded at allowable tax rates rather than on a basis that systematically allocates the asset's cost over its expected useful life. Some assets, principally buildings, are not depreciated.
4. Capitalizable leases are seldom recorded as assets and debt, thus distorting financial position and income charges.

---

* Joseph P. Cummings is Deputy Senior Partner and Vice Chairman of International Relations of Peat, Marwick, Mitchell & Co.; Chairman of the International Accounting Standards Committee; Vice Chairman of the American Institute of Certified Public Accountants; and was the U.S. representative on the United Nations Group of Experts on International Accounting and Reporting.

5. Financial statements may be translated under various methods, and the resulting gains and losses from foreign exchange transactions and operations may be deferred rather than recognized on a current basis.

6. The difference between reporting income and expense for tax purposes and reporting similar items for financial statement purposes is not always tax allocated. Recorded tax expense thus may not recognize any timing differences, and deferred credits or charges for taxes may not be reflected in the balance sheet. Where deferred taxes are recorded, the balance sheet items may be recorded at a present value amount.

7. Provisions for losses expected on long-term contracts may not be recorded until the contract is closed. Thus, unrealized losses can be deferred from period to period.

8. Pension expense may be recorded as it is currently being paid or on the basis of amounts allowed for tax purposes, rather than being recorded on a discounted basis over the period of employees service.

9. The effect of events occurring subsequent to the balance sheet date, but prior to the issuance of financial statements, which may have an effect on the financial statements may not be disclosed or reflected in such financial statements.

10. Goodwill in acquisitions may be measured as the excess of cost over the book values of the acquired net assets rather than as the residual after assigning fair market values to the net assets acquired. Goodwill may not be amortized or may be taken directly into stockholders' equity.

C. Disclosure and presentation differences. The following items are often not disclosed:

1. The effects of changes in accounting estimates or principles.
2. Long-term lease commitments or other contingent liabilities.
3. Methods of inventory costing.
4. Fixed asset revaluations.
5. Methods and policies of amortization and depreciation.
6. Movements in "reserve" accounts.
7. Subsequent events.
8. Methods of foreign exchange translation and treatments of gains and losses.
9. Pledged assets.

10. Maturities, interest rates, or terms of long-term debt.
11. Restrictions on stockholders' equity.

One area in which the accounting recommendations adopted in various countries have resulted in divergent income reporting and disclosure differences is that of reporting for changing prices.

Because of the continuing effects of inflation over many years, changes to the traditional historical cost-basis of financial statements have been proposed throughout the world. The need to make changes has focused attention on three methods: (1) specific price changes (sometimes called *replacement cost accounting*), (2) changes in the general level of prices (sometimes called *general purchasing power accounting*), and (3) a combination of the two approaches.

Since the specific prices of goods and assets held or sold by an enterprise may change even when there is no significant change in the general level of prices, some countries have proposed reflecting changes for the current value of assets held at the balance sheet date and/or those assets sold or consumed during the period. There are a number of proposed ways of measuring this current value (for example, replacement costs, net realizable value, and discounted present value).

Other countries have proposed modifying financial statements expressed in units of money so that relevant information would be expressed in terms of units of general purchasing power. Various indexes (for example, gross national product, deflator index, and consumer price index) are suggested as the means to best modify historical cost statements to reflect changing prices.

Once a method is selected, there are a number of alternative recommendations for applying the method. Some countries (such as the United States under the regulations of the Securities and Exchange Commission) ignore holding gains or losses for the net monetary financial position and reflect only changing prices for inventory and fixed assets. Other countries follow this approach but limit the changing price effect by assets financed from stockholders' equity.

There are also alternative proposals as to whether (1) gains and losses from changing prices should be reflected in the current period's income or through revaluation reserves, (2) the final measured change should reflect deferred tax adjustments, and (3) the changes should be reflected as supplementary information or as adjustments to the basic financial statements.

Faced with all these diverse suggestions, the Financial Accounting Standards Board

(FASB) in the United States is now working toward a new conceptual framework for financial reporting. The American Institute of Certified Public Accountants (AICPA) has formed a task force, and a number of groups are developing accounting and reporting systems based on alternatives other than historical cost. Companies working with the AICPA are now experimenting with these alternative methods and the AICPA will report the results to the FASB.

A final accounting response to changing prices will not be easy; however, it is an area of critical concern. Without a response to this problem, many other actions may be only partial steps toward achieving more effective financial reporting.

ATTEMPTS TO ACHIEVE HARMONIZATION

There are many reasons for the above differences. Local laws (e.g., the British Companies Acts or the U.S. Securities Exchange Acts) have greatly affected accounting standards and practices. The type of financial statement user (for example, the dominance of European banks in European financing as compared to stockholder demands in the United States) has also affected reporting needs. And the size and status of the various professional accounting bodies have influenced their effectiveness.

Accountants have been meeting at international congresses every five years for nearly four decades to talk about the above problems. However, the demands for uniformity in accounting standards were usually biased toward the standards of the countries from which the demands arose. The Americans thought their accounting standards were best and should be applied universally, but so did the English, Canadians, Germans, and others.

A first positive step toward developing uniform accounting standards was taken in 1966 with the formation of the Accountants International Study Group (AISG). This group's major function was to publish comparative studies of standards in the United States, Canada, and the United Kingdom. However, the AISG lacked two ingredients vital to success: worldwide membership and procedures for enforcing its recommendations. But this first effort did prove that nations could work together to achieve a single goal.

The European Economic Community has been attempting to set up uniform standards for its members in both corporate law and financial reporting. The Commission of European Communities has issued for comment a *Fourth* and *Seventh Directive* to try to harmonize the reporting for individual and con-

solidated accounts of companies within its countries. There is also a strong European union of 24 accountancy bodies in 18 countries which is issuing drafts of proposed directives, issuing a quarterly, and beginning to issue formal recommendations. This union appoints the representatives to the Common Market Study Group, which has a consultative status with the Commission of European Communities.

Other international accounting groups include the Inter-American Accounting Conference and the Confederation of Asian and Pacific Accountants. Their objectives are to further the understanding of accounting in various countries through periodic conferences.

Having viewed the problems and the results of the above groups, the International Congress of Accountants, meeting in Sydney in 1972, established ,the International Coordination Committee for the Accounting Profession (ICCAP). ICCAP's objectives were "the development of a coordinated, worldwide accounting profession with uniform standards." Nine months later, the International Accounting Standards Committee (IASC)* was formed as a part of ICCAP but is independent and autonomous with respect to the issuance of accounting standards. The initial members of the IASC were the leading accountancy bodies of Australia, Canada, France, Germany, Japan, Mexico, the Netherlands, the United Kingdom (Britain and Ireland), and the United States.

Once formed, the IASC took steps to achieve worldwide representation. To this end, associate members were admitted, and the IASC in 1977 is composed of 53 accounting groups in 41 countries. These groups have more than 400,000 members.

The objectives of IASC are to formulate in the public interest and to publish basic standards to be observed in the presentation of audited accounts and financial statements and to promote their worldwide acceptance and observance. With so many different accountancy bodies represented, the committee realized that achieving agreement and uniformity would not be easy. Thus, the initial topics addressed by IASC are areas of basic standards of reporting that generally do not go beyond the standards currently existing in the United States. The selection of initial topics, however, does begin to address those areas of standards and reporting where there are the greatest conceptual, income reporting, or disclosure differences.

* For information and publications contact: International Accounting Standards Committee, 3 St. Helen's Place, London, EC3A 6DN, England.

INITIAL IASC STANDARDS, EXPOSURE DRAFTS, AND FUTURE SUBJECTS

The committee has now approved 13 exposure drafts, eight of which have received final approval as international accounting standards, on various dates as listed below:

1. Disclosure of Accounting Policies (January 1975).
2. Valuation and Presentation of Inventories in the Context of the Historical Cost System (October 1975).
3. Consolidated Financial Statements (June 1976).
4. Depreciation Accounting (October 1976).
5. Information to be Disclosed in Financial Statements (October 1976).
6. Accounting Responses to Changing Prices (June 1977).
7. Statement of Changes in Financial Position (October 1977).
8. Unusual and Prior Period Items and Changes in Accounting Policies (February 1978).

"Disclosure of Accounting Policies" requires the disclosure of significant accounting policies and states that, where the effects of accounting changes are material, these changes in policies should be disclosed and quantified. It also states that the concepts of going concern, consistency, and accrual are fundamental accounting assumptions. It requires prudence, substance over form, and materiality as concepts in selecting and applying accounting policies, and states that financial statements should be comparative.

The standard on inventories should have a major impact on many countries because it eliminates inventory reserves (which have been used as income-smoothing devices), requires the systematic allocation of overhead costs to manufacturing inventories, and states that nonallocation of overhead costs should be justified and disclosed. Fifo (first in, first out), weighted average cost and specific identification are established as the basic methods of inventory pricing, but Lifo (last in, first out) and base stock pricing are permitted if disclosure of the difference between the carrying value and the current replacement cost is given.

The standard on consolidated financial statements generally requires a parent company to issue consolidated financial statements, unless the parent's control of the subsidiary is temporary or unless impaired by severe long-term fund restrictions, or the subsidiary's activities are so dissimilar that the presentation of separate financial statements would be more meaningful. The equity method of accounting for associated companies is also required, and rules are stated for appropriate income statement recognition of declines in the value of investments dealt with on the equity method.

Although the standard on depreciation will not affect current U.S. practices, it will have a potential effect on countries where certain types of assets (principally buildings) have not been depreciated in the past. The standard requires that depreciable assets be systematically written off to income over their useful lives, that the method used be consistently applied, and that any changes in method be adequately justified, quantified, and disclosed.

The standard on disclosures in financial statements contains certain minimum disclosure requirements, including: descriptions of contingent assets and liabilities; methods of providing for pension and retirement plans; restrictions on assets, descriptions, and terms for long-term debt; restrictions on stockholders' equity; and certain significant income item disclosures, including descriptions of intercompany transactions. The overall concept outlined is that "all material information should be disclosed that is necessary to make the financial statements clear and understandable."

In the standard on "Accounting Responses to Changing Prices," the disclosure requirements of the first international accounting standard have been extended. The standard requires that all enterprises should present, in their financial statements, information that describes procedures adopted to reflect the impact on the financial statements of specific price changes, changes in the general level of prices, or both. If no such procedures have been adopted, that fact should be disclosed. The standard does not prescribe the appropriate way of responding to changing prices; it requires disclosure to the extent that the effects of inflation are reported in the financial statements. At the time that the standard was approved in March 1977, the committee also issued a discussion paper entitled "Treatment of Changing Prices in Financial Statements: A Summary of Proposals." This paper sets forth some of the proposals discussed earlier in this article. During 1975 and 1976, proposed standards were issued in Australia, Belgium, Canada, France, Germany, Israel, Mexico, the Netherlands, New Zealand, South Africa, the United Kingdom, Ireland, and the United States.

The standard requiring issuance of a statement of changes in financial position, known as a "funds" statement in some countries, was issued in October 1977. The statement of changes in a financial position is an integral part of the basic financial statements of an enterprise and should be presented for each reporting period for which an income statement is shown. The standard sets forth a broad concept of reporting all financial resources and the application of these resources. The latest standard "Unusual and Prior Period Items and Changes in Accounting Policies" did not attempt to mandate specific types of items that may be classified as extraordinary but insisted that unusual items be included in net income and separately disclosed. The standard also states that changes in accounting estimates are to be recognized prospectively. The cumulative adjustment on all prior periods resulting from changes in accounting policies may be disclosed separately as a part of current income or reported by adjusting opening retained earnings and restating prior periods' comparative information.

An exposure draft on "Accounting for Research and Development Costs" was issued in February 1977 and is expected to be issued as a standard in March 1978. It states that research and development costs generally are expenses of the period in which they are incurred. Development costs can be accrued and amortized over future periods only if the costs can be attributed to a specific product or process for which technical feasibility and a future market or internal use have been demonstrated and if management intends to produce and market or use the new product or process. Sufficient revenues must be expected to cover the accrued costs, and adequate resources must be available in order to complete the project.

"Contingencies and Events Occurring After the Balance Sheet Date" was issued as an exposure draft in July 1977. This proposed standard delineates the application of the prudence concept to contingent gains and losses. Contingent losses are to be accrued by a charge in the income statement if it is probable that an asset has been impaired or a liability incurred at the balance sheet date and the amount of the loss can be determined with reasonable accuracy. Contingent gains are not accrued but are disclosed. Financial statements are adjusted for events occurring after the balance sheet date when the events provide further information as to the actual amounts existing on the balance sheet date. The effect of significant events must only be disclosed and need not be adjusted if the event represents changes in subsequent periods that do not affect the assets or liabilities at the balance sheet date.

An exposure draft on "Accounting for Foreign Transactions and Translation of Foreign Financial Statements" was issued in December 1977 for comment. This proposed standard states that the exchange rate existing at the date of the foreign currency transaction is to be used for translation purposes, except that the forward rate specified in a foreign exchange contract may be used if the contract is a hedge of a foreign currency commitment. The draft also states that either the temporal method or the closing rate method should be used in translating the financial statements of foreign-based operations into the operating currency. Translation policy and the treatment of foreign exchange gains and losses are required to be disclosed.

"Accounting for Construction Contracts" was issued for exposure in December 1977 and states that the percentage of completion method of accounting may be adopted only if certain conditions are met: (1) the total contract revenues can be determined, (2) an adequate estimating system exists whereby the costs to complete the contract and the percentage of contract completion as of the reporting date can be reliably estimated, and (3) accurate cost accounting records exist for the accumulation of contact costs and their allocation to contracts so that actual experience can be compared with prior estimates. The completed contract method is allowed under all conditions. Foreseeable losses on a contract are required to be recognized in the period the anticipated loss is estimated. Provision is made for the entire loss on the contract irrespective of the amount of work performed. The draft also states that the accounting policies adopted for revenue recognition on construction contracts should be disclosed and applied consistently. Any change in the accounting policy should be quantified, if practicable, and disclosed together with the reasons for the change in method. In October 1977, the IASC approved for exposure, "Accounting for Taxes on Income." This proposed standard requires separate disclosure of the tax expense related to income from ordinary activities and that related to any unusual items not included in ordinary income. The nature of permanent differences and the affect on the period's tax expense would also be disclosed. Either the deferred or liability methods would be used to determine the tax expense for the period.

Other topics currently on the committee's agenda are "Accounting for Diversified Operations," "Accounting for Leases," "Current Assets and Current Liabilities," "Disclosures in Financial Statements of Banks," and "Accounting for Pension Costs and Commitments."

ENFORCEMENT PROCEDURES FOR IASC STANDARDS

Thus we find at present a number of divergent accounting practices in various countries and a group of international standards that are intended to harmonize divergent practices or at least to require their disclosure so that the user may be able to judge how the use or departure from certain standards has affected the financial statements. However, international standards *do not* override local regulations, and the IASC cannot require that financial statements be prepared in conformity with international accounting standards. Its task is to persuade its member bodies to respond positively and to convince businessmen, stock exchanges, and others that these standards should be followed since they are essential to the users of financial statements.

Let's look first at how the member accountancy bodies of IASC have responded. The American Institute of Certified Public Accountants (AICPA), the group that represents the United States in IASC, has pledged to work toward the enforcement of international accounting standards. But it finds itself faced with the dilemma of supporting accounting principles that may not always constitute generally accepted accounting principles as defined in the United States. To achieve acceptance of IASC standards within the United States, such standards have to be specifically adopted by the Financial Accounting Standards Board (FASB). The AICPA has decided that where there are no significant differences between international standards and generally accepted accounting principles (GAAP), compliance with one would constitute compliance with the other. However, where an international standard differs significantly from GAAP, the AICPA "will urge the FASB to give early consideration to such differences with a view to achieving harmonization of those areas in which differences exist."

The response of Canada's professional accountancy body has been similar to that of the United States. In France, the Ordre des Experts Compatables Agrees has adopted the standards of IASC and has established disciplinary procedures for auditors who do not monitor compliance with the standards. Similarly, the Council of the Netherlands Institute has insisted that its members comply with international standards.

Where professional accountancy bodies do adopt international standards, sanctions may be imposed on members who do not comply with these standards. These sanctions, which may involve disciplinary proceedings for members, are significant in assuring that financial statements are presented in compliance with the standards. However, the organization and standing of the accountancy profession in member countries vary, and in some countries there may have to be changes in laws or constitutions which govern the operations of the accountancy profession in order to make the sanctions effective.

Turning from the responses of accountancy bodies, let's look at the response from business. Discussions with the stock exchanges in the major business centers of the world have resulted in their recognition of international accounting standards. In October 1974, the General Assembly of the Federation Internationale des Bourses de Valeurs (International Federation of Stock Exchanges) recommended that its member exchanges in countries whose professional accountancy bodies are members of IASC should include in their listing requirements reference to compliance with international accounting standards. This recommendation was also positively followed in October 1974 by the Council of The Stock Exchange in the United Kingdom. All companies with a listing on this exchange are expected to prepare their financial statements in accordance with international accounting standards. The French Stock Exchange Commission has also declared its support for IASC and is reminding accountants in France that any departures from IASC standards require disclosure.

Industry groups have also taken a considerable interest in the work of the IASC. Discussions have been held between IASC and the chairman of the International Association of Financial Executives Institutes, and arrangements have been made to maintain relations on activities of mutual interest. A large proportion of the comments received on the exposure drafts issued by IASC come from industry groups. Eugene Minahan, former Vice President and Controller of the Atlantic Richfield Company, is now serving as deputy U.S. representative to IASC.

The need for acceptance and enforcement of standards is clear. International accounting standards will achieve their objectives of harmonizing accounting and reporting differences only if they are of a quality that is acceptable to the users and preparers of financial statements and if they are consistently observed in financial statements. This quality and consistency will come only if IASC's members fulfill their enforcement obligations in their member countries.

THE FUTURE

After discussing the divergent accounting practices of the world and the attempts of various groups to achieve harmonization and enforcement to date, what may we predict for the future? First, I am encouraged by the progress IASC has made; however, we must work to ensure that what we have begun will continue.

If the private sector does not succeed in achieving a workable harmonization of standards, there are government groups beginning a similar task. The United Nations established a Group of Experts on International Standards and Reporting to work toward achieving a more uniform accounting and reporting system for transnational corporations which will meet their definitions of user needs (including governments as well as creditors and stockholders). The group has met twice, in August 1976 and again in July 1977. IASC has worked with this group, and the chairman of IASC was a member of this United Nations group.

The Organization for Economic Cooperation and Development (OECD) is a 24-country group (principally Western Europe, Japan and the United States), which meets periodically to discuss such issues as economic cooperation and trade. In 1976, OECD released guidelines for reporting by multinationals. While these guidelines are not currently enforceable, some observers feel that unless companies begin to comply with the private sector's reporting standards, the OECD "guidelines" may be made law.

To continue the accounting profession's response to such demands, the International Federation of Accountants (IFAC) was established at the 11th International Congress of Accountants in Munich in October 1977. The objectives of the IFAC are to coordinate and guide the international efforts in the following areas: technical standards, uniform code of professional ethics, requirements for education and training, encouragement of the formation and development of regional organizations and arrangement of international congresses of accountancy at five year intervals. IFAC will replace the older ICCAP organization and will broaden the membership base, input, and support. Thus, whereas the United

States was represented on ICCAP only by the AICPA, IFAC has extended membership invitations not only to the AICPA but also to other U.S. groups such as the Financial Executives Institute, National Association of Accountants, Federal Government Accountants Association, the Institute of Internal Auditors, and the Municipal Finance Officers Association of the United States and Canada. The IASC will be related to IFAC and might well serve as its technical arm, though remaining autonomous in operations, financing, and pronouncements. The IASC will continue to be the body having the responsibility and authority to issue in their own name, pronouncements on international accounting standards.

It has been suggested that, during the past several years, the proliferation of accounting standards may have seemed to be too much of a "growth" business for the overworked preparers and users of financial statements. Let me reemphasize that, in formulating international standards, we are not trying to add an additional layer of confusion, but instead we hope to provide a harmonizing influence for those trying to reconcile GAAP, companies' law, and so forth. The efforts and the impact in future years of harmonizing international accounting standards will be great. The expanding needs of our world require a free and efficient exchange of multinational companies' expertise and an efficient flow of capital from country to country. In harmonizing the language of business, we as accountants and businessmen have an opportunity to aid in achieving many international goals. The establishment and acceptance of international accounting standards will be a major part of our contribution to the demands of the future.

Guide to Foreign Financial Statements

George C. Watt

This section is intended to assist a U.S. reader to understand local financial statements prepared in accordance with local accounting principles and practices. It is not intended to apply, for example, to the financial statements of an overseas subsidiary of a U.S. parent company, where the local financial statements have been adjusted to accounting principles generally accepted in the United States for the purpose of preparing consolidated financial statements. The differences listed here result from a comparison of accounting and reporting practices in the United States with those of 24 highly industrialized countries in the 86 countries in which Price Waterhouse International practices.

EFFORTS TO DEVELOP WORLDWIDE ACCOUNTING STANDARDS

Without question, the most important development in the efforts to narrow major differences has been the emergence of the International Accounting Standards Committee (IASC). The IASC was founded in early 1973 by the professional accounting institutes of Australia, Canada, France, Germany, Japan, Mexico, the Netherlands, the United Kingdom, and the United States in response to the expressed desire of the Tenth International Congress of Accountants. In January 1975, the IASC issued its first definitive pronouncement, "International Accounting Standard No. 1—Disclosure of Accounting Policies." In addition, the IASC has issued exposure drafts on "The Valuation and Presentation of Inventory in the Context of the Historical Cost System" and "Consolidated Financial Statements and the Equity Method of Accounting." The degree of authority vested in this group has yet to be determined in many participating countries including the United States. It is too early to say whether the IASC will achieve the level of acceptance necessary to eliminate significant differences between national accounting principles or to cause the disclosure of differences between national and IASC-recommended principles.

Another organization that continues to produce valuable background information regarding differences in accounting principles is the "Accountants International Study Group" (AISG). The AISG, which includes accountants representing the American Institute of Certified Public Accountants, the Canadian Institute of Chartered Accountants, the Institute of Chartered Accountants in England and Wales, the Institute of Chartered Accountants in Ireland, has published ten studies on accounting and reporting practices in Canada, the United Kingdom, and the United States.

The impact of and concern with international accounting standards are also demonstrated by the fact that the United Nations commissioned a study to determine "The Impact of Multinational Corporations on the Development Process and on International Relations." One of the conclusions of the study was that a group of experts on international accounting standards should be convened to develop standards on which multinational corporations should report. This group has expressed its intention of allowing IASC to take the lead for the time being.

READERS OF FOREIGN FINANCIAL STATEMENTS

This article may be of use to:

1. **Companies.**
   a. In evaluating their minority interest in a foreign investment held.
   b. In contemplating an investment in an overseas company.
2. **Educators.**
   a. As an illustration of differences in accounting principles and practices.
   b. As a research springboard to determine reasons for these differences in accounting principles and practices.
3. **Accounting professions.**
   a. In determining how accounting principles and practices in other countries differ from those in the United States.
   b. In narrowing the accounting differences between other countries and the United States and vice versa.
4. **Banks and other credit grantors.**
   a. In adjusting local financial statements of overseas companies to a basis similar to the United States, thereby facilitate the granting, monitoring, and calling of loans.
5. **Investment analysts.**
   a. In evaluating the performance of an overseas company for statistical or investment purposes or comparing

the results of an overseas company to a similar company or industry in the United States.
6. **Others.**
    a. Government agencies.
    b. Insurance companies.
    c. Financial writers.

PRACTICES VARY WITHIN COUNTRIES

It should not be assumed that offices in the countries mentioned accept each one of the practices listed. Our offices do not accept a number of such practices as being in conformity with generally accepted accounting principles. Further, terminology, language, law, and degree of development of the country make this field difficult to research and document. Because many of the practices in some countries are not formalized in law or recommendations of authoritative bodies, we can not be sure that we have listed all significant differences. Notwithstanding this limitation we feel this article will be helpful to many accountants and businessmen.

KNOWING THE DIFFERENCES IS ONLY THE FIRST STEP

A word of warning. Readers of foreign financial statements are generally not equipped to obtain from such statements all the information that is available in financial statements prepared in accordance with accounting principles generally accepted in the United States, because many of the differences listed here arise from the *absence* of information in the foreign financial statements. Further, the monetary effect of using an accounting practice not acceptable in the United States is generally not determinable. For example, where it is not customary to record known liabilities until they are deductible for tax purposes, it is impossible to make the numerous adjustments that may be required to meet U.S. standards. In many countries pension plans and service and severance indemnities are governed by complex statutes. The costs and liabilities resulting from such statutes vary widely and variations from U.S. accounting principles and disclosure practices are not fully described in the very brief comments in this article. These examples demonstrate that this article can most effectively be used only as a guide to develop further specific inquiries regarding specific foreign companies and not as a tool for converting foreign financial statements of a specific company into financial statements that would meet generally accepted standards in the United States.

Further inquiries in the foreign country by accountants familiar with local standards and U.S. standards are essential in specific cases, but this article should provide lines of inquiry for preliminary investigation.

DIFFERENCES IN ACCOUNTING PRINCIPLES AND PRACTICES BETWEEN UNITED STATES AND 24 OTHER COUNTRIES

This article deals with differences in the preparation of financial statements between the United States and 24 other countries arising from (1) the application of accounting concepts, principles, and methods that are not generally accepted in the United States and (2) insufficient disclosure in relation to disclosure standards generally accepted in the United States. The differences are classified below.

CONCEPTUAL DIFFERENCES

Examples of this type of difference are:
Consolidated financial statements: In the case of a parent company having subsidiaries, consolidated (or group) accounts are not included in local statutory financial statements. Further, the parent's equity in subsidiaries carried at cost is not disclosed.

Investments: Investments in affiliates owned, say 30 to 49 percent, are carried on a cost basis. Further, the parent's equity in affiliates carried at cost is not always disclosed.

Price level changes: Partial price level accounting is required by law. An adjustment must be or may be made on the basis of indices for restatement of fixed assets and accumulated depreciation, intangibles and accumulated amortization, certain investments, and foreign currency accounts. The net effect of these adjustments must be recorded in a variety of ways, some as charges to income, reduction of deficits, adjustment of foreign currency liabilities, reduction of accumulated depreciation, and credits to capital surplus accounts.

Appreciation of fixed assets: Revaluations of fixed assets may be made on arbitrary bases.

DIFFERENCES IN INCOME DETERMINATION

Examples of this type of difference are:
Changes in accounting methods: The monetary effect of a change in accounting practice is seldom disclosed.

Profit realization: Profit is sometimes taken up before cash or right to receive cash is definitive and collection is assured.

Contingency reserves: General provisions (and subsequent reversals) are often used to shift income between periods. (For example: excessive write-down of inventories.)

Accounts payable: Known liabilities or losses generally are provided for only when they are deductible for tax purposes.

Inventory: Inventories are carried at cost until disposed of; seldom are they reduced to market.

Income taxes: If accounting per books differs from tax accounting the tax effect of the difference:

a. Is not recorded as a deferred charge or credit.

b. Is not disclosed in footnotes.

DISCLOSURE AND PRESENTATION DIFFERENCES

Examples of this type of difference are:

Historic cost: Variations from the historic cost concept are not always disclosed.

Changes in accounting methods: The monetary effect of a change in accounting practice is seldom disclosed.

Rental commitments: Material rental commitments on long-term leases (say, over one year) are seldom disclosed.

Investments: Even when market quotations of investments are available, the aggregate quoted amounts are seldom disclosed.

Subsequent events: Subsequent events are seldom disclosed.

The differences in each category are listed in what we believe to be their order of importance. Differences that are apparent from the financial statements themselves are not listed in the article. An example of such a difference would be that a statement of changes in financial position is not presented. Another example would be mandatory transfers of unrestricted retained earnings into a statutory (equity) reserve.

Countries Included

Alphabetical	By Location
Argentina	Africa
Australia	South Africa
Belgium	Australasia and the
Brazil	Far East
Canada	Australia
Chile	India
Colombia	Japan
France	New Zealand
Germany	Philippines
India	Europe
Ireland	Belgium
Italy	France
Japan	Germany
Mexico	Ireland
The Netherlands	Italy
New Zealand	The Netherlands
Peru	Spain
Philippines	Sweden

Countries Included (*continued*)

Alphabetical	By Location
South Africa	Switzerland
Spain	United Kingdom
Sweden	North America
Switzerland	Canada
United Kingdom	Mexico
Venezuela	South America
	Argentina
	Brazil
	Chile
	Colombia
	Peru
	Venezuela

Argentina

CONCEPTUAL DIFFERENCES

Consolidated financial statements: In the case of a parent company having subsidiaries, consolidated (or group) accounts are not included in the statutory financial statements. Further, the parent's equity in subsidiaries carried at cost is not disclosed.

Investments: Investments in affiliates are carried on a cost basis plus the par value of stock dividends received. Further, the parent's equity in affiliates carried on such basis is not disclosed.

Price level changes: Fixed assets are generally written up at least annually by applying indices to account for price level changes without full application of price level accounting. This practice is mandatory for entities that meet a sales volume size test and is voluntary for smaller entities. The surplus arising on revaluation is carried to a capital reserve account.

DIFFERENCES IN INCOME DETERMINATION

Investments: Stock dividends (share distributions) received are generally taken into income at par value.

Property, plant, and equipment: Fixed assets are seldom written down (other than by depreciation) if their value to the business is substantially lower than cost or restated cost less accumulated depreciation.

Lease transactions: Lease or rental contracts (leases) are not accounted for by the lessee as an installment purchase (capitalized) although the substance of the arrangement transfers the usual risks and rewards of ownership from the lessor to the lessee.

Inventory: Cost of inventories seldom includes an appropriate portion of variable and fixed manufacturing overheads calculated at a level of normal capacity.

Exchange losses: The cost of fixed assets is generally increased by exchange losses arising on foreign currency liabilities incurred for the purchase of such assets.

Income taxes: If accounting per books differs from tax accounting, the tax effect of the difference:

a. Is not recorded as a deferred charge or credit.

b. Is not disclosed in footnotes.

Debt discount: Discount and expense on an issue of long-term debt are amortized over the term of the debt by other than the interest method, i.e., based on the outstanding principal balance.

Maintenance and repairs: Provision is seldom made for estimated major repair costs that derive from past operations.

Retained earnings: Stock dividends (share distributions) are recorded at par or nominal value by the issuer. Directors' remunerations are generally charged directly to retained earnings without passing through the income statement.

DISCLOSURE AND PRESENTATION DIFFERENCES

Rental commitments: Material rental commitments on long-term leases (say, over one year) are not disclosed.

Lease transactions: The method of accounting for lease transactions is not disclosed.

Capital commitments: Capital commitments are not disclosed.

Receivables: Receivables from directors are seldom shown separately. Receivables from officers are seldom shown separately.

Non-interest-bearing notes: Imputed interest on non-interest-bearing notes receivable or payable is not reported in the balance sheet as a direct deduction from the face amount of the notes.

Insurance coverage: Where material risks are not covered by insurance, the fact is not always disclosed.

Long-term debt: Maturities, interest rates, and terms of debts outstanding are seldom disclosed.

Capital stock: The status of stock options outstanding and changes occurring during the period are not disclosed. However, stock options are rarely granted.

Australia

CONCEPTUAL DIFFERENCES

Investments: Investments in affiliates are usually carried on a cost basis. Further, the parent's equity in affiliates carried at cost is not always disclosed.

Appreciation of fixed assets: Fixed assets are sometimes written up to current values following a revaluation. However, the basis on which fixed assets are stated is disclosed. The offsetting credit is taken to an equity reserve, i.e., capital reserve arising on revaluation of assets.

Contingency reserves: Special charges to income for replacement (equity) reserves in addition to the normal charges for depreciation are allowed. However, they are seldom found in practice.

DIFFERENCES IN INCOME DETERMINATION

Property, plant, and equipment: Depreciation of buildings is generally required. However, property investment companies do not always depreciate buildings. Depreciation charges are sometimes computed for book purposes at the maximum permissible tax rates.

Lease transactions: Lease or rental contracts (leases) are rarely accounted for by the lessee as an installment purchase (capitalized) even where the substance of the arrangement transfers the usual risks and rewards of ownership from the lessor to the lessee.

Goodwill: Goodwill is usually not amortized until it is apparent that it has diminished in value. Goodwill is sometimes written off, upon acquisition, against capital or revenue reserves (capital surplus or retained earnings). If this is done it will be disclosed in the year in which it happens in the table of movements in reserves. Negative goodwill, often called "Capital reserve arising on consolidation," is never amortized into income; but is generally taken direct to a capital reserve (with disclosure) in shareholders' equity. The excess of the cost of acquiring a company over the total of the book amounts of the net assets acquired is not always assigned to the tangible and identifiable intangible assets (e.g., patents) and to liabilities on the basis of their fair values at the date of acquisition and any unassigned amount recorded as goodwill.

Inventory: Although rarely used, direct costing is permissible. Cost of inventories does not always include a portion of fixed manufacturing overheads calculated at a level of normal capacity.

Income taxes: Comprehensive tax allocation is sometimes adopted, but (1) the amount of the tax deferral is sometimes adjusted for changes in the tax rates and (2) tax deferral is sometimes picked up retrospectively when tax allocation is adopted for the first time (by a direct charge to an equity reserve).

Debt discount: Discount and expense on an issue of long-term debt are sometimes amortized over the term of the debt by other than the interest method, i.e., based on the outstanding principal balance.

Non-interest-bearing notes: Interest is seldom imputed on non-interest-bearing notes receivable or payable.

Surplus entries: Unrestricted retained earnings are sometimes increased or decreased directly by gains or losses of an unusual nature or magnitude without passing through income. Capital reserves generally include items constituting capital gains which are carried to equity reserves with or without passing through (crediting) income. Capital reserves, other than stock issue premiums and revaluation reserves, are generally available for cash dividends and stock dividends and are sometimes charged in practice for this purpose.

Retained earnings: Stock dividends (share distributions) are recorded at par or nominal value by the issuer.

DISCLOSURE AND PRESENTATION DIFFERENCES

Rental commitments: Material rental commitments on long-term leases (say, over one year) are seldom disclosed.

Lease transactions: The method of accounting for lease transactions is not disclosed.

Pledged assets: The nature and extent of pledged assets are seldom disclosed.

Property, plant, and equipment. Cost of land is seldom shown separately.

Inventory: The basis of determining the cost of inventory (Fifo, Lifo, Average, etc.) is not always disclosed.

Receivables: Receivables from officers other than directors are not shown separately.

Insurance coverage: Where material risks are not covered by insurance, the fact is seldom disclosed in the financial statements.

Belgium

CONCEPTUAL DIFFERENCES

Consolidated financial statements: In the case of a parent company having subsidiaries, consolidated (or group) accounts are not included in statutory financial statements but they are sometimes published as supplementary information. Further, the parent's equity in subsidiaries carried at cost is not disclosed.

Investments: Investments in affiliates are carried on a cost basis. Further, the parent's equity in affiliates carried at cost is not disclosed.

Contingency reserves: General provisions (and subsequent reversals) are sometimes used to shift income between periods (for example, excessive write-down of inventories).

DIFFERENCES IN INCOME DETERMINATION

Liability for purchase contract losses: Provision is seldom made for anticipated losses on unfulfilled (open) purchase contracts.

Property, plant, and equipment: Fixed assets are seldom written down (other than by depreciation) if their value to the business is substantially lower than cost less accumulated depreciation. Depreciation charges are usually computed for book purposes at the maximum permissible tax rates. Depreciation is sometimes more or less than an amount determined by a rational and systematic method of measuring expiration of service life, depending upon income tax considerations.

Lease transactions: Lease or rental contracts (leases) are not accounted for by the lessee as an installment purchase (capitalized) even where the substance of the arrangement transfers the usual risks and rewards of ownership from the lessor to the lessee.

Goodwill: Goodwill is generally written off, upon acquisition, against capital or revenue reserves (capital surplus or retained earnings). If this is done, it will be disclosed in the year in which it happens in the table of movements in reserves. The excess of the cost of acquiring a company over the total of the book amounts of the net assets acquired is not assigned to the tangible and identifiable intangible assets (e.g., patents) and to liabilities on the basis of their fair values at the date of acquisition and any unassigned amount recorded as goodwill.

Pensions (accrued): Pension accounting is sometimes on a pay-as-you-go basis.

Income taxes: If accounting per books differs from tax accounting, the tax effect of the difference:

a. Is not recorded as a deferred charge or credit.

b. Is not disclosed in footnotes.

Debt discount: Discount and expense on an issue of long-term debt are sometimes amortized over the term of the debt by other than the interest method, i.e., based on the outstanding principal balance.

Non-interest-bearing notes: Interest is not imputed on non-interest-bearing notes receivable or payable.

Maintenance and repairs: Provision is seldom made for estimated major repair costs that derive from past operations.

Surplus entries: Unrestricted retained earnings are often increased or decreased directly by special charges or credits for (a) directors' fees, (b) income tax liability, and (c) sometimes depreciated and amortization without passing through income. Unrestricted retained earnings are often increased or decreased directly by gains or losses of an unusual nature or magnitude without passing through income. Capital reserves generally include items constituting capital gains which are carried to equity reserves without passing through (crediting) income.

Retained earnings: Profits of a company earned prior to its acquisition by another company (accounted for by the purchase method) are sometimes included in the retained earnings of the combined organization. Stock dividends (share distributions) are generally recorded at par or nominal value by the issuer.

DISCLOSURE AND PRESENTATION DIFFERENCES

Changes in accounting methods: The monetary effect of a change in accounting practice is seldom disclosed.

Contingencies: Contingent liabilities are seldom disclosed.

Rental commitments: Material rental commitments on long-term leases (say, over one year) are not disclosed.

Lease transactions: The method of accounting for lease transactions is not disclosed.

Capital commitments: Capital commitments are seldom disclosed.

Pledged assets: The nature and extent of pledged assets are seldom disclosed.

Subsequent events: Subsequent events are seldom disclosed.

Exchange gains and losses: The basis of translating the financial statements of foreign subsidiaries is seldom disclosed.

Sales: Sales are seldom disclosed.

Investments: Investments in affiliates are seldom segregated from other investments but names and percentage interest in affiliates are usually given. Even when market quotations of investments are available, the aggregate quoted amounts are seldom disclosed but a list of investments is usually given.

Property, plant, and equipment: Cost of land is seldom shown separately. The accounting methods for computing depreciation and amortization are not disclosed. Accumulated depreciation is sometimes shown on the liability side of the balance sheet. The basis on which fixed assets are stated is seldom disclosed.

Inventory: The basis of carrying inventories is seldom disclosed. The basis of determining the cost of inventory (Fifo, Lifo, Average, etc.) is seldom disclosed.

Accounts receivable: Receivables from affiliated companies are seldom shown separately. Receivables from directors are not shown separately. Receivables from officers are not shown separately.

Insurance coverage: Where material risks are not covered by insurance, the fact is not disclosed in the financial statements.

Long-term debt: Maturities, interest rates, and terms of debts outstanding are seldom disclosed.

Contingency reserves: Movements in reserves are not always disclosed.

Retained earnings: Restrictions on retained earnings are not disclosed.

Brazil

CONCEPTUAL DIFFERENCES

Investments: Investments in affiliates are carried at cost plus the par value of stock dividends received.

Appreciation of fixed assets: Fixed assets are revalued annually in accordance with official indices. The offsetting credit is taken to an equity reserve arising on revaluation of assets.

Price level changes: Partial price level accounting is required by law. An adjustment must be or may be made on the basis of indices for restatement of fixed assets and accumulated depreciation, intangibles and accumulated amortization, certain investments, and foreign currency accounts. The net effect of these adjustments must be recorded in a variety of ways, some as charges to income, reduction of deficits, adjustment of foreign currency liabilities, reduction of accumulated depreciation, and debits or credits to capital surplus accounts. Tax regulations allow, and accounting practice permits, a provision for maintenance of working capital (limited to recorded income before provision) representing erosion of working capital through inflation. In the case of a negative working capital at the beginning of an accounting period, tax regulations require that a credit to income be made representing inflation gain and the corresponding debit be made to the existing reserve or to a deferred charge account if no reserve exists.

Overconservatism: Overconservatism is often practiced through unwarranted general provisions for doubtful accounts receivable.

Contingency reserves: Reserves are often used to absorb charges that would otherwise be charged against income of current or future years. General provisions (and subsequent reversals) are sometimes used to shift income between periods.

Consistency: Accounting principles not applied on a consistent basis are not always disclosed.

DIFFERENCES IN INCOME DETERMINATION

Long-term contracts: Provision is seldom made for estimated losses on completion when expectation of loss is discovered.

Liability for purchase contract losses: Provision is seldom made for anticipated losses on unfulfilled (open) purchase contracts.

Accounts payable: Known liabilities or losses are generally provided for only when they are deductible for tax purposes.

Investments: Adjustments to the initial valuation of permanent investments are seldom made even though there is evidence of a permanent decline in value. Stock dividends (share distributions) received are generally recorded at par value. Regardless of the source (capitalization of profits or price level restatement of the distributing company's fixed assets) the credit may be taken to income or to a capital surplus account.

Property, plant, and equipment: Fixed assets are not written down (other than by depreciation) if their value to the business is substantially lower than cost or restated cost less accumulated depreciation. Accumulated depreciation is often shown as a separate reserve in the equity section of the balance sheet. Depreciation charges are generally computed for book purposes at the maximum permissible tax rates.

Lease transactions: Lease or rental contracts (leases) are not accounted for by the lessee as an installment purchase (capitalized) although the substance of the arrangement transfers the usual risks and rewards of ownership from the lessor to the lessee.

Goodwill: Goodwill is generally not amortized until it is apparent that it has diminished in value. Negative goodwill, often called "Capital reserve arising on consolidation," is not amortized into income; but is generally taken direct to a capital reserve (with disclosure) in shareholders' equity.

Accounts receivable: Allowance for bad and doubtful accounts receivable is often shown as a separate reserve in the equity section of the balance sheet.

Debt discount: Discount and expense on an issue of long-term debt are amortized over the term of the debt by other than the interest method, i.e., based on the outstanding principal balance.

Maintenance and repairs: Provision is seldom made for estimated major repair costs that derive from past operations.

Surplus entries: Unrestricted retained earnings are often decreased directly by special charges for directors' fees (participations) without passing through income. Unrestricted retained earnings are generally increased or decreased directly by gains or losses of an unusual nature or magnitude without passing through income.

Retained earnings: Profits of a company earned prior to its acquisition by another company (accounted for by the purchase method) are sometimes included in the retained earnings of the combined organization. Stock dividends (share distributions) are generally recorded at par or nominal value by the issuer.

DISCLOSURE AND PRESENTATION DIFFERENCES

Contingencies: Contingent liabilities are seldom disclosed.

Sales: Sales are seldom disclosed.

Investments: Even when market quotations of investments are available, the aggregate quoted amounts are seldom disclosed.

Appreciation of fixed assets: The basis of any voluntary revaluation of fixed assets is not disclosed.

Inventory: The basis of determining the cost of inventory (Fifo, Lifo, Average, etc.) is seldom disclosed. Although company law generally requires inventory to be stated at the lower of cost or market, the average cost method is generally used.

Non-interest-bearing notes: Imputed interest on non-interest-bearing notes receivable or payable is not reported in the balance sheet as a direct deduction from the face amount of the notes.

Capital stock: The number of capital shares outstanding is seldom disclosed. Rights and preferences to dividends or to principal on invested capital are seldom disclosed.

Retained earnings: Restrictions on retained earnings are not disclosed. Cumulative dividends in arrears are not disclosed.

Canada

CONCEPTUAL DIFFERENCES

Investments: Investments in affiliates owned, say 20 to 49 percent, are carried on a cost basis. The parent's equity in affiliates carried at cost is disclosed. The basis for equity accounting is generally "Effective control" and not significant influence.

Appreciation of fixed assets: Fixed assets are sometimes written up on the basis of appraisals.

DIFFERENCES IN INCOME DETERMINATION

Business combinations: In a business combination accounted for as a purchase, deferred taxes previously recorded by the acquired company are carried forward to the consolidated balance sheet.

Property, plant, and equipment: The sinking fund method of depreciation is acceptable under certain circumstances.

Lease transactions: Lease or rental contracts (leases) are not always accounted for by the lessee as an installment purchase (capitalized) although the substance of the arrangement transfers the usual risks and rewards of ownership from the lessor to the lessee.

Debt discount: Discount and expense on an issue of long-term debt are often amortized over the term of the debt by other than the interest method, i.e., based on the outstanding principal balance.

Non-interest-bearing notes: Interest is seldom imputed on non-interest-bearing notes receivable or payable.

Retained earnings: Stock dividends (share distributions) may be recorded at par or nominal value or at any value determined by the directors of the issuer.

DISCLOSURE AND PRESENTATION DIFFERENCES

Lease transactions: The method of accounting for lease transactions is seldom disclosed.

Inventory: The basis of determining the cost of inventory (Fifo, Lifo, Average, etc.) is not always disclosed.

Insurance coverage: Where material risks are not covered by insurance, the fact may not be disclosed in the financial statements.

Chile

CONCEPTUAL DIFFERENCES

Consolidated financial statements: In the case of a parent company having subsidiaries, consolidated (or group) accounts are not included in local statutory financial statements. Further, the parent's equity in subsidiaries carried at cost, as adjusted per the following paragraph, is not disclosed.

Investments: Investments in affiliates are generally carried on a cost basis increased by the par value of stock dividends or when the investee is a partnership, by the investor's proportion of the investee's mandatory equity revaluation.

Price level changes: A company is required to revalue its invested capital by applying the official cost-of-living index to it. The amount is credited to a special (equity) reserve and charged first to net fixed assets as prescribed by the tax laws. If there is a residue it may be charged against taxable income up to 20 percent of such taxable income. Depreciation of fixed assets is computed on the adjusted value. Certain marketable securities are adjusted to market value by debit or credit to an investment fluctuation (equity) reserve. In addition certain other investments are adjusted by the change in the cost-of-living index, independent of the invested capital calculation mentioned above or in the case of other investments, such as a partnership, the adjustment is equivalent to the investor's proportion of the revaluation made by the investee. From time to time the government allows companies to elect to revalue their inventories, by credit to a revaluation (equity) reserve, on payment of a nominal rate of tax on the amount of the revaluation. Such tax is in lieu of subsequent income tax but is not reflected as income tax on the income statement.

Retained earnings: Operating losses are shown on the asset side of the balance sheet and are not offset to appropriated profits of other years which are accumulated on the balance sheet with capital stock and capital surplus.

DIFFERENCES IN INCOME DETERMINATION

Long-term contracts: Provision is not always made for estimated losses on completion when expectation of loss is discovered.

Liability for purchase contract losses: Provision is not always made for anticipated losses on unfulfilled (open) purchase contracts.

Investments: Stock dividends (share distributions) received are taken into income at par value.

Property, plant, and equipment: Fixed assets are not always written down (other than by depreciation) if their value to the business is substantially lower than cost less accumulated depreciation. Depreciation charges are generally computed for book purposes at the maximum permissible tax rates.

Lease transactions: Lease or rental contracts (leases) are not accounted for by the lessee as an installment purchase (capitalized) although the substance of the arrangement transfers the usual risks and rewards of ownership from the lessor to the lessee.

Goodwill: Goodwill is often not amortized until it is apparent that it has diminished in value. The excess of the cost of acquiring a company over the total of the book amounts of the net assets acquired is not always assigned to the tangible and identifiable intangible assets (e.g., patents) and to liabilities on the basis of their fair values at the date of acquisition and any unassigned amount recorded as goodwill.

Inventory: Cost of inventories seldom includes an appropriate portion of variable and fixed manufacturing overheads calculated at a level of normal capacity.

Exchange losses: The cost of fixed assets is increased by exchange losses arising on foreign currency liabilities incurred for the purchase of such assets. However, the revaluation of the fixed assets is limited to the higher of the cost of living or exchange difference adjustments.

Income taxes: If accounting per books differs from tax accounting, the tax effect of the difference:

a. Is not recorded as a deferred charge or credit.

b. Is seldom disclosed in footnotes.

Maintenance and repairs: Provision is seldom made for estimated major repair costs that derive from past operations.

Retained earnings: Stock dividends (share distributions) are recorded at par or nominal value by the issuer. Dividends declared and paid out of current year's income are treated as provisional and shown as assets on the balance sheet, rather than reductions of retained earnings, until approved by shareholders.

Capital stock: As a general rule a company cannot acquire shares of its own stock without specific approval. When such transactions have been approved, however, it is required that the shares be shown as an asset, valued at cost, rather than as a reduction of shareholders' equity since it is assumed that such shares are to be held for a short time.

DISCLOSURE AND PRESENTATION DIFFERENCES

Changes in accounting methods: The monetary effect of a change in accounting practice is not always disclosed.

Contingencies: Contingent liabilities are not always disclosed.

Rental commitments: Material rental commitments on long-term leases (say, over one year) are seldom disclosed.

Lease transactions: The method of accounting for lease transactions is not disclosed.

Capital commitments: Capital commitments are seldom disclosed.

Pledged assets: The nature and extent of pledged assets are not always disclosed.

Subsequent events: Subsequent events are seldom disclosed.

Property, plant, and equipment: The accounting methods for computing depreciation and amortization are seldom disclosed.

Inventory: The basis of determining the cost of inventory (Fifo, Lifo, Average, etc.) is not always disclosed.

Receivables: Receivables from affiliated companies are seldom shown separately.

Non-interest-bearing notes: Imputed interest on non-interest-bearing notes receivable or payable is not reported in the balance sheet as a direct deduction from the face amount of the notes.

Insurance coverage: Where material risks are not covered by insurance, the fact is seldom disclosed.

Long-term debt: Maturities, interest rates, and terms of debts outstanding are not always disclosed.

Contingency reserves: Movements in reserves are not always disclosed.

Capital stock: The status of stock options outstanding and changes occurring during the period are not disclosed. However, stock options are rarely granted. Rights and preferences to dividends or to principal on invested capital are not always disclosed. Such rights and preferences are seldom found in practice.

Retained earnings: Restrictions on retained earnings are not always disclosed.

Colombia

CONCEPTUAL DIFFERENCES

Consolidated financial statements: In the case of a parent company having subsidiaries, consolidated (or group) accounts are not included in local statutory financial statements. Further, the parent's equity in subsidiaries carried at cost is seldom disclosed.

Investments: Investments in affiliates are carried on a cost basis. Further, the parent's equity in affiliates carried at cost is seldom disclosed.

DIFFERENCES IN INCOME DETERMINATION

Long-term contracts: Provision is not always made for estimated losses on completion when expectation of loss is discovered.

Liability for purchase contract losses: Provision is not always made for anticipated losses on unfulfilled (open) purchase contracts.

Property, plant, and equipment: Companies are required to record in contra accounts the differences between cost and official valuations for real estate. Fixed assets are not written down (other than by depreciation) if their value to the business is substantially lower than cost less accumulated depreciation. Depreciation charges are usually computed for book purposes at the maximum permissible tax rates. Items no longer in service are seldom removed from fixed assets and accumulated depreciation accounts.

Lease transactions: Lease or rental contracts (leases) are not accounted for by the lessee as an installment purchase (capitalized) although the substance of the arrangement transfers the usual risks and rewards of ownership from the lessor to the lessee.

Inventory: Inventories are carried at cost until disposed of; seldom are they reduced to market. Cost of inventories seldom includes an appropriate portion of variable and fixed manufacturing overheads calculated at a level of normal capacity.

Accounts receivable: Provisions for doubtful accounts are often based on arbitrary percentages of the receivables, allowed for tax purposes, which may exceed actual needs.

Pensions (accrued): Pensions and pension accounting are regulated by law. In broad terms prior service costs must be amortized over ten years.

Exchange losses: The cost of fixed assets is sometimes increased by exchange losses arising on foreign currency liabilities incurred for the purchase of such assets.

Income taxes: If accounting per books differs from tax accounting, the tax effect of the difference:

a. Is not recorded as a deferred charge or credit.
b. Is not disclosed in footnotes.

Debt discount: Discount and expense on an issue of long-term debt are sometimes amortized over the term of the debt by other than the interest method, i.e., based on the outstanding principal balance.

Non-interest-bearing notes: Interest is not imputed on non-interest-bearing notes receivable or payable.

Maintenance and repairs: Provision is seldom made for esimated major repair costs that derive from past operations.

DISCLOSURE AND PRESENTATION DIFFERENCES

Changes in accounting methods: The monetary effect of a change in accounting practice is seldom disclosed.

Contingencies: Contingent liabilities are seldom disclosed.

Rental commitments: Material rental commitments on long-term leases (say, over one year) are not disclosed.

Lease transactions: The method of accounting for lease transactions is not disclosed.

Capital commitments: Capital commitments are seldom disclosed.

Pledged assets: The nature and extent of pledged assets are seldom disclosed.

Subsequent events: Subsequent events are seldom disclosed.

Sales: Sales are not always disclosed.

Investments: Investments in affiliates are seldom segregated from other investments. Even when market quotations of investments are available, the aggregate quoted amounts are seldom disclosed.

Property, plant, and equipment: Cost of land is not always shown separately. The accounting methods for computing depreciation and amortization are not disclosed in the financial statements. The basis on which fixed assets are stated is seldom disclosed.

Inventory: The basis of carrying inventories is seldom disclosed. The basis of determining the cost of inventory (Fifo, Lifo, Average, etc.) is seldom disclosed.

Directors' interests: Interests of directors in contracts are seldom disclosed in financial statements.

Accounts receivable: Receivables from affiliated companies are seldom shown separately. Receivables from directors are seldom shown separately. Receivables from officers are seldom shown separately.

Insurance coverage: Where material risks are not covered by insurance, the fact is seldom disclosed in the financial statements.

Long-term debt: Maturities, interest rates, and terms of debts outstanding are seldom disclosed.

Capital stock: Rights and preferences to dividends or to principal on invested capital are seldom disclosed.

Retained earnings: Restrictions on retained earnings are seldom disclosed. Cumulative dividends in arrears are not disclosed.

France

CONCEPTUAL DIFFERENCES

Consolidated financial statements: In the case of a parent company having subsidiaries, statutory financial statements must include either:

a. An informational schedule on first-tier subsidiaries only which sets out parent company equity.
b. Consolidated financial statements.

The former is more usual.

Investments: Investments in affiliates are generally carried on a cost basis. Further, the parent's equity in affiliates carried at cost is seldom disclosed.

Appreciation of fixed assets: Fixed assets acquired prior to 1960 were generally written up to current values following a revaluation. Although acquisitions since 1960 may be revalued, this practice is rare. The offsetting credit (after deduction of applicable income taxes) is taken to an equity reserve, i.e., capital reserve arising on revaluation of assets.

Overconservatism: Overconservatism is generally practiced through:

a. Extraordinary charges for depreciation of fixed assets.
b. Special inventory write-downs.
c. Overprovision for contingencies charged to income accounts.

Contingency reserves: General provisions (and subsequent reversals) are often used to shift income between periods.

Consistency: Accounting principles not applied on a consistent basis are not always disclosed.

DIFFERENCES IN INCOME DETERMINATION

Profit realization: Profit is sometimes taken up before cash or right to receive cash is definitive and collection is assured.

Long-term contracts: Provision is not always made for estimated losses on completion when expectation of loss is discovered.

Liability for purchase contract losses: Provision is not made for anticipated losses on unfulfilled (open) purchase contracts.

Accounts payable: Estimates of certain nontrade liabilities that are not definitely determinable are sometimes not recorded.

Property, plant, and equipment: Fixed assets are seldom written down (other than by depreciation) if their value to the business is substantially lower than cost less accumulated depreciation. Depreciation charges are usually computed for book purposes at the maximum permissible tax rates.

Lease transactions: Lease or rental contracts (leases) are not accounted for by the lessee as an installment purchase (capitalized) even where the substance of the arrangement transfers the usual risks and rewards of ownership from the lessor to the lessee.

Goodwill: Goodwill is usually not amortized until it is apparent that it has diminished in value.

Debt discount: Discount and expense on an issue of long-term debt are sometimes amortized over the term of the debt by other than the interest method, i.e., based on the outstanding principal balance.

Non-interest-bearing notes: Interest is seldom imputed on non-interest-bearing notes receivable or payable.

Retained earnings: Profits of a company earned prior to its acquisition by another company (accounted for by the purchase method) are sometimes included in the retained earnings of the combined organization. Stock dividends (share distributions) are sometimes recorded at par or nominal value by the issuer. Directors' fees are not charged to income.

DISCLOSURE AND PRESENTATION DIFFERENCES

Historic cost: Variations from the historic cost concept are seldom disclosed.

Changes in accounting methods: The monetary effect of a change in accounting practice is not always disclosed.

Contingencies: Contingent liabilities are seldom disclosed.

Rental commitments: Material rental commitments on long-term leases (say, over one year) are not disclosed.

Lease transactions: The method of accounting for lease transactions is not disclosed.

Capital commitments: Capital commitments are never disclosed.

Pledged assets: The nature and extent of pledged assets are not disclosed.

Subsequent events: Subsequent events are not disclosed.

Exchange gains and losses: The basis of translating the financial statement of foreign subsidiaries is not disclosed.

Cost of sales: Cost of sales is seldom disclosed.

Investments: Even when market quotations of investments are available, the aggregate quoted amounts are not disclosed.

Appreciation of fixed assets: The basis of revaluation of fixed assets is not disclosed.

Property, plant, and equipment. The accounting methods for computing depreciation and amortization are seldom disclosed in the financial statements.

Inventory: The basis of carrying inventories is seldom disclosed. The basis of determining the cost of inventory (Fifo, Lifo, Average, etc.) is not disclosed. However, tax authorities require that inventory be stated at the lower of average cost or market.

Accounts receivable: Receivables from affiliated companies are not shown separately. Receivables from officers are seldom shown separately.

Insurance coverage: Where material risks are not covered by insurance, the fact is not disclosed in the financial statements.

Long-term debt: Maturities, interest rates, and terms of debts outstanding are not always disclosed.

Contingency reserves: Movements in reserves are not always disclosed.

Retained earnings: Restrictions on retained earnings are not disclosed. Cumulative dividends in arrears are not disclosed.

Germany

CONCEPTUAL DIFFERENCES

(A.G. COMPANIES)

Investments: Investments in affiliates are carried on a cost basis. Further, the parent's equity in affiliates carried at cost is not disclosed.

Overconservatism: Overconservatism is sometimes practiced through income charges permitted by income tax regulations, such as:

a. Additional depreciation for certain categories of fixed assets.
b. Special inventory write-downs under particular conditions.

DIFFERENCES IN INCOME DETERMINATION

(A.G. COMPANIES)

Property, plant, and equipment: Depreciation charges are usually computed for book purposes at the maximum permissible tax rates.

Lease transactions: Lease or rental contracts (leases) are seldom accounted for by the lessee as an installment purchase (capitalized) even where the substance of the arrangement transfers the usual risks and rewards of ownership from the lessor to the lessee.

Goodwill: Goodwill arising on acquisition of the net assets of a business is required to be written off against income over a period not exceeding five years, but goodwill arising on acquisition of subsidiaries is not written off but carried as a "Consolidation adjustment item."

Pensions (accrued): Pension accounting is sometimes on a pay-as-you-go basis.

Exchange gains: Foreign exchange profits on noncurrent balances are not credited to income until realized.

Income taxes: If accounting per books differs from tax accounting, the tax effect of the difference:

a. Is seldom recorded as a referred charge or credit.
b. Is not disclosed in footnotes.

Maintenance and repairs: Provision is not always made for estimated major repair costs that derive from past operations.

Retained earnings: Profits of a company earned prior to its acquisition by another company (accounted for by the purchase method) are generally included in the retained earnings of the combined organization. Stock dividends (share distributions) are recorded at par or nominal value by the issuer.

Capital stock: The unpaid portion of capital stock issued is shown as an asset under the heading "Unpaid capital."

DISCLOSURE AND PRESENTATION DIFFERENCES

(A.G. COMPANIES)

Rental commitments: Material rental commitments on long-term leases (say, over one year) are seldom disclosed.

Lease transactions: The method of accounting for lease transactions is seldom disclosed.

Capital commitments: Capital commitments are never disclosed.

Exchange gains and losses: The basis of translating the financial statements of foreign subsidiaries is not disclosed.

Cash: Cash is not segregated as between restricted and unrestricted items.

Investments: Even when market quotations of investments are available, the aggregate quoted amounts are not disclosed.

Property, plant, and equipment: Accumulated depreciation is not disclosed, fixed assets being stated net after depreciation.

Investment grants: The method of treatment of investment grants is not always disclosed.

Insurance coverage: Where material risks are not covered by insurance, the fact is not disclosed in the financial statement.

Long-term debt: Maturities, interest rates, and terms of debts outstanding are seldom disclosed.

CONCEPTUAL DIFFERENCES

(G.M.B.H. COMPANIES)

Consolidated financial statements: In the case of a parent company having subsidiaries, consolidated (or group) accounts are only sometimes included in local statutory financial statements. Further, the parent's equity in subsidiaries carried at cost is not disclosed.

Investments: Investments in affiliates are carried on a cost basis. Further, the parent's equity in affiliates carried at cost is not disclosed.

Overconservatism: Overconservatism is sometimes practiced through income charges permitted by income tax regulations such as:

a. Additional depreciation for certain categories of fixed assets.

b. Special inventory write-downs under particular conditions.

DIFFERENCES IN INCOME DETERMINATION

(G.M.B.H. COMPANIES)

Property, plant, and equipment: Depreciation charges are usually computed for book purposes at the maximum permissible tax rates.

Lease transactions: Lease or rental contracts (leases) are seldom accounted for by the lessee as an installment purchase (capitalized) even where the substance of the arrangement transfers the usual risks and rewards of ownership from the lessor to the lessee.

Goodwill: Goodwill arising on acquisition of the net assets of a business is required to be written off against income over a period not exceeding five years, but goodwill arising on acquisition of subsidiaries is not written off but carried as a "Consolidation adjustment item."

Pensions (accrued): Pension accounting is sometimes on a pay-as-you-go basis.

Exchange gains: Foreign exchange profits on noncurrent balances are not credited to income until realized.

Income taxes: If accounting per books differs from tax accounting, the tax effect of the difference:

a. Is seldom recorded as a deferred charge or credit.

b. Is not disclosed in footnotes.

Maintenance and repairs: Provision is not always made for estimated major repair costs that derive from past operations.

Retained earnings: Profits of a company earned prior to its acquisition by another company (accounted for by the purchase method) are generally included in the retained earnings of the combined organization.

Capital stock: The unpaid portion of capital stock issued is shown as an asset under the heading "Unpaid capital."

DISCLOSURE AND PRESENTATION DIFFERENCES

(G.M.B.H. COMPANIES)

Changes in accounting methods: The monetary effect of a change in accounting practice is seldom disclosed.

Rental commitments: Material rental commitments on long-term leases (say, over one year) are not disclosed.

Lease transactions: The method of accounting for lease transactions is not disclosed.

Capital commitments: Capital commitments are never disclosed.

Subsequent events: Subsequent events are not disclosed.

Exchange gains and losses: The basis of translating the financial statements of foreign subsidiaries is not disclosed.

Cash: Cash is not segregated as between restricted and unrestricted items.

Investments: Even when market quotations of investments are available, the aggregate quoted amounts are not disclosed.

Property, plant, and equipment: Cost of land is seldom shown separately. Accumulated depreciation is not disclosed, fixed assets being stated net after depreciation.

Investment grants: The method of treatment of investment grants is not disclosed.

Inventory: The basis of carrying inventories is not disclosed. The basis of determining the cost of inventory (Fifo, Lifo, Average, etc.) is not disclosed.

Insurance coverage: Where material risks are not covered by insurance, the fact is not disclosed in the financial statements.

Long-term debt: Maturities, interest rates, and terms of debts outstanding are not disclosed.

India

CONCEPTUAL DIFFERENCES

Consolidated financial statements: In the case of a parent company having subsidiaries, consolidated (or group) accounts are not included in the statutory financial statements. Further, the parent's equity in subsidiaries carried at cost is not disclosed. However, financial statements of subsidiaries must be sent to shareholders of the parent company.

Investments: Investments in affiliates are carried on a cost basis. Further, the parent's equity in affiliates carried at cost is not disclosed.

Appreciation of fixed assets: Fixed assets are sometimes written up to current values following a revaluation or (more rarely) the application of price level indices. However, the basis on which fixed assets are stated is disclosed. The offsetting credit is taken to an equity reserve, i.e., capital reserve arising on revaluation of assets.

DIFFERENCES IN INCOME DETERMINATION

Liability for purchase contract losses: Provision is seldom made for anticipated losses on unfulfilled (open) purchase contracts.

Investments: Adjustments to the initial valuation of permanent investments are not normally made even though there is evidence of a permanent decline in value. However, if the permanent decline in value of the investments is not covered by the existing reserves of a company, disclosure of the fall in value is made in the balance sheet.

Property, plant, and equipment: Fixed assets are not written down (other than by depreciation) if their value to the business is substantially lower than cost less accumulated depreciation. Depreciation charges are usually computed for book purposes at the permissible tax rates.

Goodwill: The excess of the cost of acquiring a company over the total of the book amounts of the net assets acquired is not assigned to the tangible and identifiable assets (e.g., patents) and to liabilities on the basis of their fair values at the date of acquisition and any unassigned amount recorded as goodwill.

Pensions (accrued): Pension accounting is generally on a pay-as-you-go basis.

Exchange losses: The cost of fixed assets is increased by exchange losses arising on foreign currency liabilities incurred for the purchase of such assets.

Income taxes: If accounting per books differs from tax accounting, the tax effect of the difference:

a. Is not recorded as a deferred charge or credit.

b. Is not disclosed in footnotes.

Maintenance and repairs: Provision is not made for estimated major repair costs that derive from past operations.

Surplus entries: Capital reserves sometimes include items constituting capital gains that are carried to equity reserves without passing through (crediting) income. Capital surplus representing realized capital gains carried to equity reserves is distributable as cash dividends or stock dividends. Capital reserves credited by revaluation of fixed assets are not distributable as either cash dividends or stock dividends. Stock issue premiums are only distributable as stock dividends if received in cash.

Retained earnings: Stock dividends (share distributions) are generally recorded at par or nominal value by the issuer. Financial statements generally include charges against (equity) reserves and credits to an account payable for dividends based on the results of the period covered by the financial statements even though the dividends are often proposed after the financial statement date for subsequent declaration by the shareholders.

DISCLOSURE AND PRESENTATION DIFFERENCES

Contingencies: Descriptions of status of law suits, tax controversies, etc. and the opinion of the management or counsel with respect thereto are seldom disclosed in financial statements or in notes thereto.

Rental commitments: Material rental commitments on long-term leases (say, over one year) are seldom disclosed.

Lease transactions: The method of accounting for lease transactions is not disclosed.

Exchange gains and losses: The basis of translating the financial statements of foreign subsidiaries is seldom disclosed.

Cash: Cash is not segregated as between restricted and unrestricted items.

Property, plant, and equipment: The accounting methods for computing depreciation and amortizing are not disclosed in the financial statements. Under statutory requirements some depreciation must be charged in each year, although the amount may be more or less than an amount determined by a rational and systematic method of measuring service life.

Inventory: The basis of determining the cost of inventory (Fifo, Lifo, Average, etc.) is seldom disclosed.

Non-interest-bearing notes: Imputed interest on non-interest-bearing notes receivable or payable is not reported in the balance sheet as a direct deduction from the face amount of the notes.

Insurance coverage: Where material risks are not covered by insurance, the fact is seldom disclosed in the financial statements.

Ireland

CONCEPTUAL DIFFERENCES

Consolidated financial statements: Private companies are not required to prepare consolidated financial statements but subsidiaries are usually accounted for on an equity basis.

Appreciation of fixed assets: Fixed assets are sometimes written up to current values following a revaluation or, more rarely, they are written up by application of price level indices. However, the basis on which fixed assets are stated is disclosed. The offsetting credit is taken directly to an equity reserve, i.e., capital reserve arising on revaluation of assets.

Contingency reserves: Special charges to income for replacement (equity) reserves in addition to the normal charges for depreciation are allowed. However, they are seldom found in practice.

DIFFERENCES IN INCOME DETERMINATION

Property, plant, and equipment: Depreciation of nonindustrial buildings is not always provided.

Lease transactions: Lease or rental contracts (leases) are not accounted for by the lessee as an installment purchase (capitalized) although the substance of the arrangement transfers the usual risks and rewards of ownership from the lessor to the lessee.

Goodwill: Goodwill is usually not amortized until it is apparent that it has diminished in value. Negative goodwill, often called "Capital reserve arising on consolidation," is never amortized into income; but is generally taken direct to a capital reserve (with disclosure) in shareholders' equity. The excess of the cost of acquiring a company over the total of the book amounts of the net assets acquired is seldom assigned to the tangible and identifiable intangible assets (e.g., patents) and to liabilities on the basis of their fair values at the date of acquisition and any unassigned amount recorded as goodwill.

Pensions (accrued): Pension accounting is sometimes on a pay-as-you-go basis.

Exchange losses: The cost of fixed assets is generally increased by exchange losses arising on foreign currency liabilities incurred for the purchase of such assets.

Income taxes: Comprehensive tax allocation is broadly adopted, but (1) the amount of the tax deferral is generally adjusted for changes in the tax rates and (2) tax deferral is picked up retrospectively when tax allocation is adopted for the first time. The related charge is made directly to retained profits/reserve as a prior period adjustment.

Debt discount: Discount and expense on an issue of long-term debt and any premium paid on redemption are written off as far as possible to share premium account through the income statement in the year in which they occur; otherwise, they are written off to income. Discount on redemption of long-term debt is credited through the income statement before the determination of net income to a capital reserve in the year in which it occurs.

Non-interest-bearing notes: Interest is seldom imputed on non-interest-bearing notes receivable or payable.

Surplus entries: Capital reserves created by revaluation of fixed assets are not distributable as cash dividends. However, such reserves are generally available for stock dividends.

Retained earnings: Stock dividends, (i.e., share distributions or capitalization issues) must be recorded at a minimum of par value by the issuer. Financial statements generally include charges against (equity) reserves and credits to an account payable for dividends based on the results of the period covered by the financial statements even though the dividends are often proposed after the financial statement date for subsequent declaration by the shareholders.

DISCLOSURE AND PRESENTATION DIFFERENCES

Rental commitments: Material rental commitments on long-term leases (say, over one year) are seldom disclosed.

Lease transactions: The method of accounting for lease transactions is seldom disclosed.

Pledged assets: The nature and extent of pledged assets are seldom disclosed.

Sales: Sales are not always disclosed.

Appreciation of fixed assets: The basis of revaluation of fixed assets is not always disclosed.

Property, plant, and equipment. Cost of land is seldom shown separately.

Inventory: The basis of determining the cost of inventory (Fifo, Lifo, Avearge, etc.) is not always disclosed.

Receivables: Receivables from affiliates other than subsidiaries are not usually shown separately. Receivables from officers other than directors are not shown separately.

Insurance coverage: Where material risks are not covered by insurance, the fact is seldom disclosed in the financial statements.

Retained earnings: Restrictions on distributions of retained earnings are seldom disclosed.

Italy

CONCEPTUAL DIFFERENCES

Consolidated financial statements: In the case of a parent company having subsidiaries, consolidated (or group) accounts are not included in local statutory financial statements. Further, the parent's equity in subsidiaries carried at cost is not normally disclosed.

Investments: Investments in affiliates are carried on a cost basis. Further, the parent's equity in affiliates carried at cost is not always disclosed.

Overconservatism: Overconservatism is often practiced through:

a. Extraordinary charges for depreciation of fixed assets.
b. Special inventory write-downs.
c. Overprovision for contingencies charged to income accounts.

Contingency reserves: General provisions (and subsequent reversals) are often used to shift income between periods.

Consistency: Accounting principles not applied on a consistent basis are seldom disclosed.

DIFFERENCES IN INCOME DETERMINATION

Liability for purchase contract losses: Provision is seldom made for anticipated losses on unfulfilled (open) purchase contracts.

Property, plant, and equipment: Items of fixed assets are often charged to expense as repairs and maintenance. Depreciation charges are usually computed for book purposes at the maximum permissible tax rates.

Lease transactions: Lease or rental contracts (leases) are not accounted for by the lessee as an installment purchase (capitalized) even where the substance of the arrangement transfers the usual risks and rewards of ownership from the lessor to the lessee.

Goodwill: Negative goodwill, often called "Capital reserve arising on consolidation," is never amortized into income; but is generally taken direct to a capital reserve (with disclosure) in shareholders' equity. The excess of the cost of acquiring a company over the total of the book amounts of the net assets acquired is seldom assigned to the tangible and identifiable intangible assets (e.g., patents) and to liabilities on the basis of their fair values at the date of acquisitions and any unassigned amount recorded as goodwill.

Income taxes: Income taxes are often charged against results of operations only as and when paid (i.e., on a cash basis) rather than being based on the current income (accrual method).

Non-interest-bearing notes: Interest is not imputed on non-interest-bearing notes receivable or payable.

Maintenance and repairs: Provision is not made for estimated major repair costs that derive from past operations.

Surplus entries: Unrestricted retained earnings are generally decreased directly by special charges for directors' fees without passing through income. Unrestricted retained earnings are generally increased or decreased directly by gains or losses of an unusual nature or magnitude without passing through income.

Retained earnings: Profits of a company earned prior to its acquisition by another company (accounted for by the purchase method) are sometimes included in the retained earnings of the combined organization. Stock dividends (share distributions) are generally recorded at par or nominal value by the issuer.

DISCLOSURE AND PRESENTATION DIFFERENCES

Changes in accounting methods: The monetary effect of a change in accounting practice is seldom disclosed.

Contingencies: Contingent liabilities are seldom disclosed.

Rental commitments: Material rental commitments on long-term leases (say, over one year) are not disclosed.

Lease transactions: The method of accounting for lease transactions is not disclosed.

Capital commitments: Capital commitments are never disclosed.

Pledged assets: The nature and extent of pledged assets are not disclosed.

Income taxes: Income taxes are not shown separately, but are generally included in a caption "Taxes" which includes taxes other than on income.

Exchange gains and losses: The basis of translating the financial statements of foreign subsidiaries is not disclosed.

Current assets: Assets and liabilities are seldom classified as current and noncurrent.

Cash: Cash is seldom segregated as between restricted and unrestricted items.

Investments: Even when market quotations of investments are available the aggregate quoted amounts are not disclosed.

Appreciation of fixed assets: The basis of revaluation of fixed assets is not disclosed.

Property, plant, and equipment: Cost of land is not shown separately. Accumulated depreciation is rarely disclosed, fixed assets being normally stated net after depreciation. The accounting methods for computing depreciation and amortization are not disclosed in the financial statements. Accumulated depreciation is generally shown on the liability side of the balance sheet. The basis on which fixed assets are stated is not disclosed.

Inventory: The basis of carrying inventories is not disclosed. The basis of determining the cost of inventory (Fifo, Lifo, Average, etc.) is not disclosed.

Receivables: Receivables from officers are not shown separately. Provisions for bad and doubtful accounts receivable are generally shown on the liability side of the balance sheet.

Insurance coverage: Where material risks are not covered by insurance, the fact is not disclosed in the financial statements.

Long-term debt: Maturities, interest rates, and terms of debts outstanding are not disclosed.

Contingency reserves: Movements in reserves are not disclosed.

Capital stock: The status of stock options outstanding and changes occurring during the period are not disclosed.

Retained earnings: Restrictions on retained earnings are not disclosed. Cumulative dividends in arrears are not disclosed.

Japan

CONCEPTUAL DIFFERENCES

Consolidated financial statements: Even in the case of a parent company having subsidiaries, parent company financial statements, rather than consolidated statements, are regarded as the primary statements for statutory purposes. However, parent company financial statements filed with the Ministry of Finance must include either:

a. Financial statements on individual significant subsidiaries.

b. Consolidated financial statements.

The parent's equity in subsidiaries carried at cost is not disclosed in parent company financial statements. However, transactions with affiliated companies must be disclosed.

Investments: Investments in affiliates owned, say 20 to 49 percent, are carried on a cost basis. Further, the parent's equity in affiliates carried at cost is not always disclosed.

Overconservatism: Overconservatism is often practiced through income charges permitted by income tax regulations, such as:

a. Additional depreciation of certain fixed assets.

b. Provisions for excessive reserves for inventory price fluctuations and for doubtful accounts.

DIFFERENCES IN INCOME DETERMINATION

Profit realization: The profit on certain long-term credit sales is usually recognized in the periods the installments are collected.

Long-term contracts: Provision is not made for estimated losses on completion when expectation of loss is discovered.

Liability for purchase contract losses: Provision is not made for anticipated losses on unfulfilled (open) purchase contracts.

Investments: Stock dividends (share distributions) received are often taken into income at par value.

Property, plant, and equipment: Depreciation charges are usually computed for book purposes at the maximum permissible tax rates.

Pensions (accrued): Retirement allowances to directors are often on a pay-as-you-go basis. Retirement allowances to employees are often accrued only to the extent allowable under the income tax regulations, which is generally 50 percent of the annual increase on a voluntary retirement basis.

Income taxes: If accounting per books differs from tax accounting, the tax effect of the difference:

a. Is not recorded as a deferred charge or credit.

b. Is not disclosed in footnotes.

Stock issue expenses: Stock issue expenses are not permitted to be charged to capital surplus and are, therefore, charged direct to income or deferred for future amortization.

Surplus entries: Unrestricted retained

earnings are often decreased directly by special charges for directors' bonuses without passing through income. A free distribution of stock to existing shareholders is often made by transferring an amount from capital reserve to capital stock account. Such a free distribution is clearly distinguished from a stock dividend paid out of profits which, under the commercial code, must be approved by the shareholders. All stock dividends are recorded at par value by the issuer.

Capital stock: As a general rule a company cannot acquire shares of its own stock except for certain transactions specified in the commercial code. When such transactions have occurred the treasury shares acquired are shown as an asset, valued at cost, rather than as a reduction of shareholders' equity.

DISCLOSURE AND PRESENTATION DIFFERENCES

Restatement of prior years: The restatement of prior period financial statements is not permitted for any reason.

Rental commitments: Material rental commitments on long-term leases (say, over one year) are not disclosed.

Lease transactions: The method of accounting for lease transactions is not disclosed.

Capital commitments: Capital commitments are never disclosed.

Cash: Cash is seldom segregated as between restricted and unrestricted items.

Investments: Even when market quotations of investments are available, the aggregate quoted amounts are seldom disclosed.

Property, plant, and equipment: The basis on which fixed assets are stated is not disclosed.

Inventory (long-term contracts): Payments received on account of work in progress are not deducted from inventories.

Accounts receivable: Excess provisions for doubtful accounts receivable are often shown on the liability side of the balance sheet, as are additional depreciation and other excessive reserves permitted by tax regulations.

Non-interest-bearing notes: Imputed interest on non-interest-bearing notes receivable or payable is not reported in the balance sheet as a direct deduction from the face amount of the notes.

Insurance coverage: Where material risks are not covered by insurance, the fact is not disclosed in the financial statements.

Capital stock: Rights and preferences to dividends or to principal on invested capital are seldom disclosed.

Retained earnings: Cumulative dividends in arrears are not disclosed.

Mexico

CONCEPTUAL DIFFERENCES

Consolidated financial statements:[*] In the case of a parent company having subsidiaries, consolidated (or group) accounts are seldom included in statutory financial statements. Further, the parent's equity in subsidiaries carried at cost is only required to be disclosed when materially under cost.

Investments: If an investment in an affiliate is carried on a cost basis for a valid reason, the parent's equity is seldom disclosed.

Appreciation of fixed assets: Revaluations of fixed assets, not recognized for tax purposes, may be recorded only when:

a. The revaluation is based on appraisals made by qualified independent technicians.
b. Subsequent depreciation is based on the new values and expected asset lives.
c. The basis of the revaluation is disclosed.

The offsetting credit arising on such revaluations is taken to an equity reserve, i.e., capital reserve arising on revaluation of fixed assets.

DIFFERENCES IN INCOME DETERMINATION

Profit realization: Gross profit on installment sales may be recognized either in the period of sale or in the periods the installments are collected.

Property, plant, and equipment: Depreciation charges are usually computed for book purposes at the maximum permissible tax rates.

Intangible assets: Intangible assets are generally amortized against income at the maximum permissible tax rates (5 percent per annum, unless a higher rate is specifically

[*] The Committee on Accounting Principles of the Mexican Institute of Public Accountants is presently engaged in the preparation of bulletins on the following subjects:
1. Accounting for income taxes and employees' obligatory participation in profits. It is expected that at least partial income tax allocation will be required.
2. Consolidation and combination of financial statements, permanent investments in associated companies, accounting for mergers, and disclosures of transactions among associated, affiliated, and holding companies. It is expected that this bulletin will require consolidation of more than 50 percent owned companies when appropriate, and the use of the equity method when unconsolidated statements of a parent are prepared for statutory purposes.

authorized to the taxpayer). As a result of the recognition of five-year loss carry-for-wards, a trend has developed towards immediate write-off of preoperating, organization, research and development, and similar expenses. Goodwill amortization (which is not deductible) is not mandatory and is left to management discretion.

Inventory: Cost of inventories not always includes an appropriate portion of variable and fixed manufacturing overheads calculated at a level of normal capacity. Direct costing is permissible.

Pensions (accrued): [*] Pension accounting is generally on a pay-as-you-go basis unless the plan is funded. Prior service costs and unfunded vested benefits are seldom disclosed. Severance payments, determined in accordance with length of employee service as provided by the Mexican Labor Law, are generally charged to expenses of the period in which they become payable. A note to this effect is usually included in financial statements.

Exchange losses: The cost of fixed assets is increased by exchange losses arising on foreign currency liabilities incurred for the purchase of such assets.

Income taxes: [*] If accounting per books differs from tax accounting, the tax effect of the difference is not recorded as a deferred charge or credit. However, the difference is generally disclosed in footnotes.

Debt discount: Discount and expense on an issue of long-term debt are sometimes amortized over the term of the debt by other than the interest method, i.e., based on the outstanding principal balance.

Non-interest-bearing notes: Interest is not imputed on non-interest-bearing notes receivable or payable.

Maintenance and repairs: Provision is seldom made for estimated major repair costs that derive from past operations.

Retained earnings: Stock dividends (share distributions) are generally recorded at par or nominal value by the issuer.

DISCLOSURE AND PRESENTATION DIFFERENCES

Lease transactions: The method of accounting for lease transactions is seldom disclosed.

Insurance coverage: Where material risks are not covered by insurance, the fact is not disclosed in the financial statements.

---

[*] The Committee on Accounting Principles of the Mexican Institute of Public Accountants has issued a pronouncement on accounting for pension and severance plans similar to Opinion 8 of the Accounting Principles Board. It is expected that differences in this area will gradually disappear.

The Netherlands

CONCEPTUAL DIFFERENCES

Contingency reserves: Special charges to income for replacement (equity) reserves relating to fixed assets and inventories are sometimes found in practice.

DIFFERENCES IN INCOME DETERMINATION

Investments: Stock dividends (share distributions) received are often taken into income at par value.

Property, plant, and equipment: Revaluation reserves are generally charged directly with depreciation on the increment arising as a result of the revaluation (thus not passing through income).

Goodwill: Goodwill is generally written off, upon acquisition, against capital or revenue reserves (capital surplus or retained earnings). If this is done it will be disclosed in the year in which it happens in the table of movements in reserves. Negative goodwill, often called "Capital reserve arising on consolidation," is not usually amortized into income; but is generally taken direct to a capital reserve (with disclosure) in shareholders' equity. The excess of the cost of acquiring a company over the total of the book amounts of the net assets acquired is not always assigned to the tangible and identifiable intangible assets (e.g., patents) and to liabilities on the basis of their fair values at the date of acquisition and any unassigned amount recorded as goodwill.

Income taxes: Comprehensive tax allocation is almost universally adopted but sometimes the amount deferred is a discounted amount.

Debt discount: Discount and expense on an issue of long-term debt are sometimes amortized over the term of the debt by other than the interest method, i.e., based on the outstanding principal balance.

Non-interest-bearing notes: Interest is seldom imputed on non-interest-bearing notes receivable or payable.

Surplus entries: Unrestricted retained earnings are sometimes increased or decreased directly by gains or losses of an unusual nature or magnitude without passing through income.

Retained earnings: Profits of a company earned prior to its acquisition by another company (accounted for by the purchase method) are occasionally included in the retained earnings of the combined organization. Stock dividends (share distributions) are generally recorded at par or nominal value by the issuer.

DISCLOSURE AND PRESENTATION DIFFERENCES

Historic cost: The monetary effects of variations from the historic cost concept are seldom disclosed.

Property, plant, and equipment: Cost of land is seldom shown separately. Accumulated depreciation is rarely disclosed, fixed assets being normally stated net after depreciation.

Inventory: The basis of determining the cost of inventory (Fifo, Lifo, Average, etc.) is not always disclosed.

Receivables: Receivables from directors are not shown separately. Receivables from officers are not shown separately.

Insurance coverage: Where material risks are not covered by insurance, the fact is seldom disclosed in the financial statements.

Capital stock: The status of stock options outstanding and changes occurring during the period may not be disclosed. However, stock options are rarely found in practice.

New Zealand

CONCEPTUAL DIFFERENCES

Investments: Investments in affiliates are usually carried on a cost basis. Further, the parent's equity in affiliates carried at cost is not always disclosed.

Appreciation of fixed assets: Fixed assets are sometimes written up to current values following a revaluation. However, the basis on which fixed assets are stated is disclosed. The offsetting credit is taken to an equity reserve, i.e., capital reserve arising on revaluation of assets.

Contingency reserves: Special charges to income for replacement (equity) reserves in addition to the normal charges for depreciation are allowed. However, they are seldom found in practice.

DIFFERENCES IN INCOME DETERMINATION

Property, plant, and equipment: Depreciation charges are sometimes computed for book purposes at the maximum permissible tax rates.

Lease transactions: Lease or rental contracts (leases) are rarely accounted for by the lessee as an installment purchase (capitalized) even where the substance of the arrangement transfers the usual risks and rewards of ownership from the lessor to the lessee.

Goodwill: Goodwill is usually not amortized until it is apparent that it has diminished in value. Goodwill is sometimes written off, upon acquisition, against capital or revenue reserves (capital surplus or retained earnings). Negative goodwill, often called "Capital reserve arising on consolidation," is never amortized into income; but is generally taken direct to a capital reserve. The excess of the cost of acquiring a company over the total of the book amounts of the net assets acquired is not always assigned to the tangible and identifiable intangible assets (e.g., patents) and to liabilities on the basis of their fair values at the date of acquisition and any unassigned amount recorded as goodwill.

Inventory: Although rarely used, direct costing is permissible. Cost of inventories does not always include a portion of fixed manufacturing overheads calculated at a level of normal capacity.

Income taxes: Comprehensive tax allocation is sometimes adopted, but (1) the amount of the tax deferral is sometimes adjusted for changes in the tax rates and (2) tax deferral is sometimes picked up retrospectively when tax allocation is adopted for the first time (by a direct charge to an equity reserve).

Debt discount: Discount and expense on an issue of long-term debt are sometimes amortized over the term of the debt by other than the interest method, i.e., based on the outstanding principal balance.

Non-interest-bearing notes: Interest is seldom imputed on non-interest-bearing notes receivable or payable.

Surplus entries: Unrestricted retained earnings are sometimes increased or decreased directly by gains or losses of an unusual nature or magnitude without passing through income. Capital reserves generally include items constituting capital gains which are carried to equity reserves with or without passing through (crediting) income.

Retained earnings: Stock dividends (share distributions) are generally recorded at par or nominal value by the issuer.

DISCLOSURE AND PRESENTATION DIFFERENCES

Rental commitments: Material rental commitments on long-term leases (say, over one year) are seldom disclosed.

Lease transactions: The method of accounting for lease transactions is not disclosed.

Pledged assets: The nature and extent of pledged assets are seldom disclosed.

Appreciation of fixed assets: The basis of revaluation of fixed assets is not always disclosed.

Property, plant, and equipment: Cost of land is seldom shown separately. The accounting methods for computing depreciation and amortization are seldom disclosed in the financial statements.

Inventory: The basis of determining the cost of inventory (Fifo, Lifo, Average, etc.) is seldom disclosed.

Receivables: Receivables from officers other than directors are not always shown separately.

Insurance coverage: Where material risks are not covered by insurance, the fact is not usually disclosed in the financial statements.

Peru

CONCEPTUAL DIFFERENCES

Consolidated financial statements: In the case of a parent company having subsidiaries, consolidated (or group) accounts are not included in local statutory financial statements. Further, the parent's equity in subsidiaries carried at cost is seldom disclosed.

Investments: Investments in affiliates are carried on a cost basis plus stock dividends. Further, the parent's equity in affiliates carried on such basis is seldom disclosed.

Appreciation of fixed assets: Revaluations of land and buildings may be made on arbitrary bases. Fixed assets are generally written up by applying indices to account for price level changes without full application of price level accounting. The surplus arising on revaluation is carried to a capital reserve account.

DIFFERENCES IN INCOME DETERMINATION

Long-term contracts: Provision is seldom made for estimated losses on completion when expectation of loss is discovered.

Liability for purchase contract losses: Provision is seldom made for anticipated losses on unfulfilled (open) purchase contracts.

Accounts payable: Known liabilities or losses are seldom provided for when they are not deductible for tax purposes.

Investments: Adjustments to the initial valuation of permanent investments are seldom made even though there is evidence of

a permanent decline in value. Stock dividends (share distributions) received are generally taken into income at par value.

Property, plant, and equipment: Depreciation charges are generally computed for book purposes at the maximum permissible tax rates. Fixed assets are not written down (other than by depreciation) if their value to the business is substantially lower than cost less accumulated depreciation.

Lease transactions: Lease or rental contracts (leases) are not accounted for by the lessee as an installment purchase (capitalized) although the substance of the arrangement transfers the usual risks and rewards of ownership from the lessor to the lessee.

Goodwill: Goodwill is generally not amortized until it is apparent that it has diminished in value.

Pensions (accrued): Pension accounting is generally on a pay-as-you-go basis.

Exchange losses: The cost of fixed assets is increased by exchange losses arising on foreign currency liabilities incurred for the purchase of such assets.

Debt discount: Discount and expense on an issue of long-term debt are sometimes amortized over the term of the debt by other than the interest method, i.e., based on the outstanding principal balance.

Maintenance and repairs: Provision is seldom made for estimated major repair costs that derive from past operations.

Retained earnings: Stock dividends (share distributions) are recorded at par or nominal value by the issuer.

DISCLOSURE AND PRESENTATION DIFFERENCES

Lease transactions: The method of accounting for lease transactions is not disclosed.

Non-interest-bearing notes: Imputed interest on non-interest-bearing notes receivable or payable is not reported in the balance sheet as a direct deduction from the face amount of the notes.

Insurance coverage: Where material risks are not covered by insurance, the fact is not disclosed in the financial statements.

Philippines

CONCEPTUAL DIFFERENCES

Consolidated financial statements: Consolidated financial statements are not required by statute; some companies, however, prepare consolidated financial statements for presentation to stockholders.

DIFFERENCES IN INCOME DETERMINATION

Property, plant, and equipment: Depreciation charges are usually computed for book purposes at the maximum permissible tax rates.

Exchange losses: The cost of fixed assets is sometimes increased by exchange losses arising on foreign currency liabilities incurred for the purchase of such assets.

Income taxes: Income tax deficiencies are often charged against results of operations only as and when paid (i.e., on a cash basis) rather than being based on the current income (accrual method). If accounting per books differs from tax accounting, the tax effect of the difference:

a. Is seldom recorded as a deferred charge or credit.

b. Is not disclosed in footnotes.

Maintenance and repairs: Provision is seldom made for estimated major repair costs that derive from past operations.

Retained earnings: Stock dividends (share distributions) are generally recorded at par or nominal value by the issuer.

DISCLOSURE AND PRESENTATION DIFFERENCES

Non-interest-bearing notes: Imputed interest on non-interest-bearing notes receivable or payable is not reported in the balance sheet as a direct deduction from the face amount of the notes.

Insurance coverage: Where material risks are not covered by insurance, the fact is seldom disclosed in the financial statements.

South Africa

CONCEPTUAL DIFFERENCES

Investments: Investments in affiliates are generally carried on a cost basis.

Contingency reserves: Special charges to income for replacement (equity) reserves in addition to the normal charges for depreciation are encountered in mining and certain other industries.

DIFFERENCES IN INCOME DETERMINATION

Investments: Stock dividends (share distributions) received are occasionally taken

into income at quoted market or par value. However, the general practice is not to attribute a value to stock dividends.

Property, plant, and equipment: Depreciation of buildings is not always provided.

Goodwill: Goodwill is usually not amortized until it is apparent that it has diminished in value. Negative goodwill, often called "Capital reserve arising on consolidation," is never amortized into income; but is generally taken direct to a capital reserve (with disclosure) in shareholders' equity.

Inventory: Cost of inventories not always includes an appropriate portion of variable and fixed manufacturing overheads calculated at a level of normal capacity.

Maintenance and repairs: Provision is not always made for estimated major repair costs that derive from past operations.

Surplus entries: Capital reserves sometimes include items constituting capital gains which are carried to equity reserves without passing through (crediting) income. However, the movements in capital reserves are disclosed.

DISCLOSURE AND PRESENTATION DIFFERENCES

Rental commitments: Material rental commitments on long-term leases (say, over one year) are seldom disclosed.

Lease transactions: The method of accounting for lease transactions is seldom disclosed.

Non-interest-bearing notes: Imputed interest on non-interest-bearing notes receivable or payable is not reported in the balance sheet as a direct deduction from the face amount of the notes.

Insurance coverage: Where material risks are not covered by insurance, the fact is not disclosed in the financial statements.

Spain

CONCEPTUAL DIFFERENCES

Consolidated financial statements: In the case of a parent company having subsidiaries, consolidated (or group) accounts are seldom included in local statutory financial statements. Further, the parent's equity in subsidiaries carried at cost is not disclosed.

Investments: Investments in affiliates are carried on a cost basis. Further, the parent's equity in affiliates carried at cost is not disclosed.

Appreciation of fixed assets: Fixed assets

are sometimes written up to current values following a revaluation. However, the basis on which fixed assets are stated is not disclosed. The offsetting credit is taken to an equity reserve, i.e., capital reserve arising on revaluation of assets.

Overconservatism: Overconservatism is sometimes practiced through special inventory write-downs.

Contingency reserves: General provisions (and subsequent reversals) are sometimes used to shift income between periods.

DIFFERENCES IN INCOME DETERMINATION

Liability for purchase contract losses: Provision is seldom made for anticipated losses on unfulfilled (open) purchase contracts.

Accounts payable: Estimates of liabilities that are not definitely determinable are often not recorded.

Investments: Adjustments to the initial valuation of permanent investments are not always made even though there is evidence of a permanent decline in value.

Property, plant, and equipment: Fixed assets are not written down (other than by depreciation) if their value to the business is substantially lower than cost less accumulated depreciation. Depreciation charges are usually computed for book purposes at the maximum permissible tax rates.

Lease transactions: Lease or rental contracts (leases) are not accounted for by the lessee as an installment purchase (capitalized) even where the substance of the arrangement transfers the usual risks and rewards of ownership from the lessor to the lessee.

Goodwill: Goodwill is usually not amortized until it is apparent that it has diminished in value. The excess of the cost of acquiring a company over the total of the book amounts of the net assets acquired is not assigned to the tangible and identifiable intangible assets (e.g., patents) and to liabilities on the basis of their fair values at the date of acquisition and any unassigned amount recorded as goodwill.

Inventory: Inventories are carried at cost until disposed of; they are not always reduced to market. Cost of inventories generally includes only prime costs (i.e., direct labor and direct materials). Cost of inventories frequently does not include an appropriate portion of variable and fixed manufacturing overheads calculated at a level of normal capacity.

Accounts receivable: Provisions for bad and doubtful accounts receivable are often not made.

Pensions (accrued): Pension accounting is generally on a pay-as-you-go basis.

Exchange losses: The cost of fixed assets is sometimes increased by exchange losses arising on foreign currency liabilities incurred for the purchase of such assets.

Debt discount: Discount and expense on an issue of long-term debt are sometimes amortized over the term of the debt by other than the interest method, i.e., based on the outstanding principal balance.

Non-interest-bearing notes: Interest is not imputed on non-interest-bearing notes receivable or payable.

Maintenance and repairs: Provision is seldom made for estimated major repair costs that derive from past operations.

Surplus entries: Unrestricted retained earnings are generally decreased directly by special charges for (a) directors' fees and (b) income tax liability without passing through income. Unrestricted retained earnings are sometimes increased or decreased directly by material gains or losses of an unusual nature or magnitude without passing through income. Capital reserves often include items constituting capital gains which are carried to equity reserves without passing through (crediting) income.

Retained earnings: Profits of a company earned prior to its acquisition by another company (accounted for by the purchase method) are sometimes included in the retained earnings of the combined organization. Stock dividends (share distributions) are generally recorded at par or nominal value by the issuer.

DISCLOSURE AND PRESENTATION DIFFERENCES

Changes in accounting methods: The monetary effect of a change in accounting practice is not disclosed.

Contingencies: Contingent liabilities are seldom disclosed.

Rental commitments: Material rental commitments on long-term leases (say, over one year) are not disclosed.

Lease transactions: The method of accounting for lease transactions is not disclosed.

Capital commitments: Capital commitments are never disclosed.

Pledged assets: The nature and extent of pledged assets are seldom disclosed.

Subsequent events: Subsequent events are not disclosed.

Income taxes: Income taxes are not shown separately, but are generally included in a caption "Taxes" which includes taxes other than on income.

Exchange gains and losses: The basis of

translating the financial statements of foreign subsidiaries is seldom disclosed.

Sales: Sales are not always disclosed.

Cash: Cash is seldom segregated as between restricted and unrestricted items.

Investments: Investments in affiliates are seldom segregated from other investments. Even when market quotations of investments are available, the aggregate quoted amounts are seldom disclosed.

Property, plant, and equipment: Cost of land is not shown separately. The accounting methods for computing depreciation and amortization are seldom disclosed in the financial statements. Accumulated depreciation is generally shown on the liability side of the balance sheet.

Inventory: The basis of carrying inventories is seldom disclosed. The basis of determining the cost of inventory (Fifo, Lifo, Average, etc.) is seldom disclosed.

Receivables: Receivables from affiliated companies are seldom shown separately. Receivables from directors are not shown separately. Receivables from officers are not shown separately.

Insurance coverage: Where material risks are not covered by insurance, the fact is not disclosed in the financial statements.

Long-term debt: Maturities, interest rates, and terms of debts outstanding are seldom disclosed.

Deferred income: Deferred income is seldom shown separate from other liabilities.

Contingency reserves: Movements in reserves are seldom disclosed.

Capital stock: The status of stock options outstanding and changes occurring during the period are not disclosed.

Retained earnings: Restrictions on retained earnings are not disclosed. Cumulative dividends in arrears are not disclosed.

Sweden

CONCEPTUAL DIFFERENCES

Appreciation of fixed assets: Fixed assets are sometimes written up to current values following a revaluation. However, the basis on which fixed assets are stated is seldom disclosed. The offsetting credit must be used either to provide for required depreciation of the fixed assets or to increase share capital by a stock dividend.

Overconservatism: Overconservatism is generally practiced through:

a. Charges for depreciation of fixed assets at maximum rates allowed for tax purposes which are usually higher than rates based on estimated lives.

b. Special inventory write-downs allowed for tax purposes.

Contingency reserves: General provisions (and subsequent reversals) are often used to shift income between periods. For example, such provisions are made for excessive inventory write-downs and for liability reserves for future investments.

DIFFERENCES IN INCOME DETERMINATION

Property, plant, and equipment: Charges to income are not always made in a systematic and rational manner for depreciation of machinery, equipment, etc.

Goodwill: Goodwill is usually not amortized until it is apparent that it has diminished in value. The excess of the cost of acquiring a company over the total of the book amounts of the net assets acquired is not assigned to the tangible and identifiable intangible assets (e.g., patents) and to liabilities on the basis of their fair values at the date of acquisition and any unassigned amount recorded as goodwill.

Income taxes: Although seldom encountered in practice, if accounting per books differs from tax accounting, the tax effect of the difference:

a. Is not recorded as a deferred charge or credit.

b. Is not disclosed in footnotes.

Debt discount: Discount and expense on an issue of long-term debt are sometimes amortized over the term of the debt by other than the interest method, i.e., based on the outstanding principal balance.

Non-interest-bearing notes: Interest is not imputed on non-interest-bearing notes receivable or payable.

Maintenance and repairs: Provision is seldom made for estimated major repair costs that derive from past operations.

Surplus entries: Unrestricted retained earnings are sometimes increased or decreased directly by gains or losses of an unusual nature or magnitude without passing through income. Capital reserves sometimes include items constituting capital gains which are carried to equity reserves without passing through (crediting) income.

Retained earnings: Profits of a company earned prior to its acquisition by another company (accounted for by the purchase method) are sometimes included in the retained earnings of the combined organization. Stock dividends (share distributions) are generally recorded at par or nominal value by the issuer.

DISCLOSURE AND PRESENTATION DIFFERENCES

Changes in accounting methods: The monetary effect of a change in accounting practice is seldom disclosed.

Rental commitments: Material rental commitments on long-term leases (say, over one year) are not disclosed.

Lease transactions: The method of accounting for lease transactions is seldom disclosed.

Capital commitments: Capital commitments are seldom disclosed.

Income taxes: The realization of a tax loss is not disclosed.

Investments: Except for investment companies, even when market quotations of investments are available, the aggregate quoted amounts are seldom disclosed. However, a list of investments is usually given.

Property, plant, and equipment: Cost of land is seldom shown separately. Accumulated depreciation is not always disclosed, fixed assets being normally stated net after depreciation. The accounting methods for computing depreciation and amortization are not always disclosed in the financial statements.

Inventory: The basis of carrying inventories is not always disclosed. The basis of determining the cost of inventory (Fifo, Lifo, Average, etc.) is seldom disclosed. However, tax authorities require, in principle, that inventories be stated on a Fifo basis.

Receivables: Receivables from officers are seldom shown separately.

Long-term debt: Maturities, interest rates, and terms of debts outstanding are seldom disclosed.

Deferred income: Deferred income is seldom shown separate from other liabilities.

Capital stock: Rights and preferences to dividends or to principal on invested capital are seldom disclosed.

Switzerland

CONCEPTUAL DIFFERENCES

Consolidated financial statements: In the case of a parent company having subsidiaries, consolidated (or group) accounts are not always included in local statutory financial statements. Further, the parent's equity in subsidiaries carried at cost is not disclosed.

Investments: Investments in affiliates are carried on a cost basis. Further, the parent's equity in affiliates carried at cost is seldom disclosed.

Overconservatism: Overconservatism is generally practiced through:

a. Extraordinary charges for depreciation of fixed assets.
b. Special inventory write-downs.
c. Unwarranted general provisions for doubtful accounts receivable.
d. Overprovision for contingencies charged to income accounts.

Contingency reserves: General provisions (and subsequent reversals) are generally used to shift income between periods (for example: excessive write-down of inventories).

Consistency: Accounting principles not applied on a consistent basis are seldom disclosed.

DIFFERENCES IN INCOME DETERMINATION

Property, plant, and equipment: Depreciation charges are usually computed for book purposes at the maximum permissible tax rates.

Lease transactions: Lease or rental contracts (leases) are not accounted for by the lessee as an installment purchase (capitalized) even where the substance of the arrangement transfers the usual risks and rewards of ownership from the lessor to the lessee.

Inventory: Cost of inventories generally includes only prime costs (i.e., direct labor and direct materials). Cost of inventories seldom includes an appropriate portion of variable and fixed manufacturing overheads calculated at a level of normal capacity.

Income taxes: Provision is frequently not made for taxes assessable in future years based on income of current or preceding year. If accounting per books differs from tax accounting, the tax effect of the difference:

a. Is not recorded as a deferred charge or credit.
b. Is not disclosed in footnotes.

Debt discount: Discount and expense on an issue of long-term debt are sometimes amortized over the term of the debt by other than the interest method, i.e., based on the outstanding principal balance.

Non-interest-bearing notes: Interest is not imputed on non-interest-bearing notes receivable or payable.

Retained earnings: Stock dividends (share distributions) are generally recorded at par or nominal value by the issuer. However, they are seldom found in practice.

DISCLOSURE AND PRESENTATION DIFFERENCES

Changes in accounting methods: The monetary effect of a change in accounting practice is seldom disclosed.

Rental commitments: Material rental commitments on long-term leases (say, over one year) are not disclosed.

Lease transactions: The method of accounting for lease transactions is not disclosed.

Capital commitments: Capital commitments are seldom disclosed.

Subsequent events: Subsequent events are seldom disclosed.

Income taxes: Income taxes are seldom shown separately, but are generally included in a caption "Taxes" which includes taxes other than on income.

Cost of sales: Cost of sales is seldom disclosed.

Cash: Cash is seldom segregated as between restricted and unrestricted items.

Investments: Investments in affiliates are seldom segregated from other investments. Even when market quotations of investments are available, the aggregate quoted amounts are not disclosed.

Property, plant, and equipment: Cost of land is seldom shown separately. Accumulated depreciation is not disclosed, fixed assets being normally stated net after depreciation. The accounting methods for computing depreciation and amortization are not disclosed in the financial statements. Accumulated depreciation is sometimes shown on the liability side of the balance sheet. The basis on which fixed assets are stated is seldom disclosed. However, if they are insured, the law requires the insurance value be disclosed in the balance sheet.

Inventory: The basis of carrying inventories is seldom disclosed. The basis of determining the cost of inventory (Fifo, Lifo, Average, etc.) is seldom disclosed.

Receivables: Receivables from directors are seldom shown separately. Receivables from officers are seldom shown separately. Provisions for bad and doubtful accounts receivable are sometimes shown on the liability side of the balance sheet.

Insurance coverage: Where material risks are not covered by insurance, the fact is not disclosed in the financial statements.

Long-term debt: Maturities, interest rates, and terms of debts outstanding are not always disclosed.

Deferred income: Deferred income is seldom shown separate from other liabilities.

Contingency reserves: Movements in reserves are not disclosed.

Retained earnings: Cumulative dividends in arrears are not disclosed.

United Kingdom

CONCEPTUAL DIFFERENCES

Appreciation of fixed assets: Fixed assets are sometimes written up to current values following a revaluation or, more rarely, they are written up by application of price level indices. However, the basis on which fixed assets are stated is disclosed. The offsetting credit is taken to an equity reserve, i.e., capital reserve arising on revaluation of assets.

Contingency reserves: Special charges to income for replacement reserves in addition to the normal charges for depreciation are allowed. However, they are seldom found in practice.

DIFFERENCES IN INCOME DETERMINATION

Property, plant, and equipment: Depreciation of nonindustrial buildings is not always provided.

Goodwill: Goodwill is usually not amortized until it is apparent that it has diminished in value. Goodwill is sometimes written off, upon acquisition, against capital or revenue reserves (capital surplus or retained earnings). If this is done it will be disclosed only in the year in which it happens in the table of movements in reserves. Negative goodwill, often called "Capital reserve arising on consolidation," is never amortized into income; but is generally taken direct to a capital reserve (with disclosure) in shareholders' equity. The excess of the cost of acquiring a company over the total of the book amounts of the net assets acquired is not always assigned to the tangible and identifiable intangible assets (e.g., patents) and to liabilities on the basis of their fair values at the date of acquisition and any unassigned amount recorded as goodwill.

Inventory: Cost of inventories does not always include an appropriate portion of variable and fixed manufacturing overheads calculated at a level of normal capacity.

Pensions (accrued): Pension accounting is sometimes on a pay-as-you-go basis.

Income taxes: Comprehensive tax allocation is broadly, but not invariably, adopted. If it is adopted, either the deferral or the liability method of recording deferred taxes may be found. The related tax deferral is picked up retrospectively when tax allocation is adopted for the first time (by a direct charge to an equity reserve).

Debt discount: Discount and expense on an issue of long-term debt are sometimes amortized over the term of the debt by other than the interest method, i.e., based on the outstanding principal balance.

Non-interest-bearing notes: Interest is seldom imputed on non-interest-bearing notes receivable or payable.

Retained earnings: Stock dividends (share distributions) are generally recorded at par or nominal value by the issuer. Financial statements generally include charges against (equity) reserves and credits to an account payable for dividends based on the results of the period covered by the financial statements even though the dividends are often proposed after the financial statement date for subsequent declaration by the shareholders.

Surplus entries: Capital reserves created by revaluation of fixed assets are not distributable as cash dividends. However, such reserves are generally available for stock dividends.

DISCLOSURE AND PRESENTATION DIFFERENCES

Rental commitments: Material rental commitments on long-term leases (say, over one year) are not always disclosed.

Pledged assets: The nature and extent of pledged assets are not always disclosed.

Cost of sales: Cost of sales is seldom disclosed.

Retained earnings: Restrictions on retained earnings are not disclosed. However, they are rarely found in practice.

Venezuela

CONCEPTUAL DIFFERENCES

Investments: Investments are recorded at market value, when quoted.

Appreciation of fixed assets: Fixed assets are sometimes written up to current values following a revaluation. However, the basis on which fixed assets are stated is disclosed. The offsetting credit is taken to an equity reserve, i.e., capital reserve arising on revaluation of assets.

Contingency reserves: Reserves are often used to absorb charges that would otherwise be charged against income of current or future years.

DIFFERENCES IN INCOME DETERMINATION

Long-term contracts: Provision is seldom made for estimated losses on completion when expectation of loss is discovered.

Liability for purchase contract losses: Provision is seldom made for anticipated losses on unfulfilled (open) purchase contracts.

Investments: Stock dividends (share distributions) received are sometimes taken into income at par value.

Property, plant, and equipment: Fixed assets are not written down (other than by depreciation) if their value to the business is substantially lower than cost less accumulated depreciation. Depreciation charges are usually computed for book purposes at the maximum permissible tax rates.

Lease transactions: Lease or rental contracts (leases) are not accounted for by the lessee as an installment purchase (capitalized) although the substance of the arrangement transfers the usual risks and rewards of ownership from the lessor to the lessee.

Goodwill: Goodwill is usually not amortized until it is apparent that it has diminished in value. The excess of the cost of acquiring a company over the total of the book amounts of the net assets acquired is not assigned to the tangible and identifiable intangible assets (e.g., patents) and to liabilities on the basis of their fair values at the date of acquisition and any unassigned amount recorded as goodwill.

Inventory: Inventories are carried at cost until disposed of; they are not always reduced to market. Cost of inventories not always includes an appropriate portion of variable and fixed manufacturing overheads calculated at a level of normal capacity.

Debt discount: Discount and expense on an issue of long-term debt are sometimes amortized over the term of the debt by other than the interest method, i.e., based on the outstanding principal balance.

Maintenance and repairs: Provision is seldom made for estimated major repair costs which derive from past operations.

Surplus entries: Unrestricted retained earnings may be increased or decreased directly by prior year adjustments without passing through income.

Retained earnings: Stock dividends (share distributions) are generally recorded at par or nominal value by the issuer.

DISCLOSURE AND PRESENTATION DIFFERENCES

Rental commitments: Material rental commitments on long-term leases (say, over one year) are seldom disclosed.

Lease transactions: The method of accounting for lease transactions is seldom disclosed.

Capital commitments: Capital commitments are seldom disclosed.

Non-interest-bearing notes: Imputed interest on non-interest-bearing notes receivable or payable is not reported in the balance sheet as a direct deduction from the face amount of the notes.

Insurance coverage: Where material risks are not covered by insurance, the fact is not disclosed in the financial statements.

Contingency reserves: Movements in reserves are seldom disclosed.

KEY BUSINESS RATIOS

Although terms like *median* and *quartile* are everyday working language to statisticians, their precise meaning may be vague to some businessmen.

In the various ratio tables, three figures appear under each ratio heading. The center figure in bold type is the **median**; the figures immediately above and below the median are, respectively, the **upper** and **lower quartiles**. To understand their use, the reader should also know how they are calculated.

First, year-end financial statements from concerns in the survey (almost exclusively corporations with a tangible net worth over $100,000) are analyzed by Dun & Bradstreet statisticians. Then each of 14 ratios is calculated individually for every concern in the sample.

These individual ratio figures, entered on data processing cards, are segregated by line of business, and then arranged in order of size —the best ratio at the top and the weakest at the bottom. The figure that falls in the middle of this series becomes the **median** for that ratio in that line of business. The figure halfway between the median and the top of the series is the **upper quartile**; the number halfway between the median and the bottom of the series is the **lower quartile**.

In a statistical sense, each median then is the **typical ratio figure** for all concerns studied in a given line. The upper and lower quartile figures typify the experience of firms in the top and bottom halves of the sample, respectively.

CURRENT ASSETS TO CURRENT DEBT

Current assets are divided by total current debt. Current assets are the sum of cash, notes, accounts receivable (less reserves for bad debt), advances on merchandise, merchandise inventories, and listed federal, state, and municipal securities not in excess of market value. Current debt is the total of all liabilities falling due within one year. This is one test of solvency.

NET PROFITS ON NET SALES

This figure is obtained by dividing net earnings of the business, after taxes, by net sales (the dollar volume less returns, al-

"Key Business Ratios" copyright 1977 by the Business Economics Division of Dun & Bradstreet, Inc. Used by permission. Revised ratios are published annually by Dun & Bradstreet.

lowances, and cash discounts). This important yardstick in measuring profitability should be related to the ratio which follows.

NET PROFITS ON TANGIBLE NET WORTH

Tangible net worth is the equity of stockholders in the business, as obtained by subtracting total liabilities from total assets, and then deducting intangibles. The ratio is obtained by dividing net profits after taxes by tangible net worth. The tendency is to look increasingly to this ratio as a final criterion of profitability. Generally, a relationship of at least 10 percent is regarded as a desirable objective for providing dividends plus funds for future growth.

NET PROFITS ON WORKING CAPITAL

Net working capital represents the excess of current assets over current debt. This margin represents the cushion available to the business for carrying inventories and receivables, and for financing day-to-day operations. The ratio is obtained by dividing net profits, after taxes, by net working capital.

NET SALES TO TANGIBLE NET WORTH

Net sales are divided by tangible net worth. This gives a measure of relative turnover of invested capital.

NET SALES TO NET WORKING CAPITAL

Net sales are divided by net working capital. This provides a guide as to the extent the company is turning its working capital and the margin of operating funds.

COLLECTION PERIOD

Annual net sales are divided by 365 days to obtain average daily credit sales, and then the average daily credit sales are divided into notes and accounts receivable, including any discounted. This ratio is helpful in analyzing the collectibility of receivables. Many feel the collection period should not exceed the net maturity indicated by selling terms by more than 10 to 15 days. When comparing the collection period of one concern with that of another, allowances should be made for possible variations in selling terms.

NET SALES TO INVENTORY

Obtained by dividing annual net sales by merchandise inventory as carried on the balance sheet. This quotient does not yield an actual physical turnover. It provides a yard-stick for comparing stock-to-sales ratios of one concern with another or with those for the industry.

FIXED ASSETS TO TANGIBLE NET WORTH

Fixed assets are divided by tangible net worth. Fixed assets represent depreciated book values of building, leasehold improvements, machinery, furniture, fixtures, tools, and other physical equipment, plus land, if any, and valued at cost or appraised market value. Ordinarily, this relationship should not exceed 100 percent for a manufacturer and 75 percent for a wholesaler or retailer.

CURRENT DEBT TO TANGIBLE NET WORTH

Derived by dividing current debt by tangible net worth. Ordinarily, a business begins to pile up trouble when this relationship exceeds 80 percent.

TOTAL DEBT TO TANGIBLE NET WORTH

Obtained by dividing total current plus long-term debts by tangible net worth. When this relationship exceeds 100 percent, the equity of creditors in the assets of the business exceeds that of owners.

INVENTORY TO NET WORKING CAPITAL

Merchandise inventory is divided by net working capital. This is an additional measure of inventory balance. Ordinarily, the relationship should not exceed 80 percent.

CURRENT DEBT TO INVENTORY

Dividing the current debt by inventory yields yet another indication of the extent to which the business relies on funds from disposal of unsold inventories to meet its debts.

FUNDED DEBTS TO NET WORKING CAPITAL

Funded debts are all long-term obligations, as represented by mortgages, bonds, debentures, term loans, serial notes, and other types of liabilities maturing more than one year from statement date. This ratio is obtained by dividing funded debt by net working capital. Analysts tend to compare funded debts with net working capital in determining whether or not long-term debts are in proper proportion. Ordinarily, this relationship should not exceed 100 percent.

RETAILING

Line of Business (and number of concerns reporting)	Current assets to current debt (Times)	Net profits on net sales (Per cent)	Net profits on tangible net worth (Per cent)	Net profits on net working capital (Per cent)	Net sales to tangible net worth (Times)	Net sales to net working capital (Times)	Collection period (Days)	Net sales to inventory (Times)	Fixed assets to tangible net worth (Per cent)	Current debt to tangible net worth (Per cent)	Total debt to tangible net worth (Per cent)	Inventory to net working capital (Per cent)	Current debt to inventory (Per cent)	Funded debt to net working capital (Per cent)
5531 Auto & Home Supply Stores (47)	3.29	4.26	12.96	25.00	6.12	8.48	**	7.5	12.3	28.3	68.2	67.7	49.4	9.8
	1.98	1.54	7.04	12.50	4.01	6.07	**	5.7	29.4	74.3	85.1	93.0	89.7	44.5
	1.48	0.38	2.48	2.84	2.64	3.61	**	4.0	57.4	122.0	184.7	150.4	172.4	92.4
5641 Children's & Infants' Wear Stores (37)	5.22	3.36	14.08	19.25	5.26	6.82	**	6.7	7.4	28.3	72.7	55.7	39.3	17.9
	2.57	1.68	6.67	8.29	4.21	4.40	**	5.4	18.9	51.6	97.1	102.1	67.4	32.1
	2.07	0.32	1.77	1.61	2.92	2.90	**	2.8	31.3	71.7	175.6	127.9	88.6	52.0
5611 Clothing & Furnishings, Men's & Boys' (202)	5.46	4.18	13.50	15.12	4.75	5.68	**	6.6	4.9	21.9	59.0	60.2	37.3	18.2
	3.15	1.72	5.85	7.16	3.26	3.58	**	4.5	13.1	44.6	117.2	89.1	66.3	35.7
	1.85	0.51	1.29	1.52	2.23	2.58	**	3.3	29.5	104.0	216.5	131.9	101.7	53.7
5311 Department Stores (280)	4.31	2.88	9.56	12.91	4.86	6.22	**	6.7	14.1	24.1	54.0	56.8	42.9	19.1
	2.81	1.61	5.47	7.09	3.64	4.42	**	5.7	33.0	45.3	88.9	80.2	69.4	39.1
	2.05	0.36	1.24	1.69	2.58	3.11	**	4.3	60.1	74.9	134.6	110.5	96.7	67.5
Discount Stores (180)	3.00	2.67	14.52	20.87	7.99	11.09	**	7.0	14.2	41.6	71.2	98.4	51.1	19.1
	2.18	1.42	9.04	10.60	5.84	6.76	**	5.3	30.9	70.0	123.1	130.9	62.9	36.5
	1.70	0.35	3.11	4.11	4.23	4.63	**	4.0	57.4	118.0	183.0	186.7	85.6	69.0
Discount Stores, Leased Departments (46)	3.32	3.25	13.81	17.15	8.16	9.35	**	7.0	10.0	42.7	94.3	86.3	53.9	20.4
	2.20	1.17	6.53	7.86	5.88	5.69	**	5.4	25.9	93.7	139.4	121.0	62.3	32.6
	1.84	0.02	0.08	0.06	4.17	4.52	**	3.7	38.0	128.8	187.4	184.5	89.2	55.9
5651 Family Clothing Stores (93)	5.89	4.55	12.60	14.69	4.45	5.40	**	6.8	3.6	18.2	44.6	49.5	41.1	16.9
	3.41	2.06	6.24	8.37	3.01	3.53	**	4.6	11.3	38.5	77.3	76.8	64.2	34.3
	2.20	0.30	0.41	1.24	2.04	2.41	**	3.2	27.9	69.8	98.1	112.8	105.6	52.7
5712 Furniture Stores (149)	5.52	4.46	11.36	11.49	4.78	4.87	29	6.4	5.1	23.3	62.1	33.3	47.2	10.6
	2.82	2.00	5.66	6.00	2.94	2.89	83	4.5	12.0	53.1	111.8	69.5	75.6	25.7
	1.98	0.28	1.41	1.03	1.72	1.75	177	3.5	27.4	99.2	213.2	113.0	114.9	59.9

Line of Business (and number of concerns reporting)	Current assets to current debt (Times)	Net profits on net sales (Per cent)	Net profits on tangible net worth (Per cent)	Net profits on net working capital (Per cent)	Net sales to tangible net worth (Times)	Net sales to net working capital (Times)	Collection period (Days)	Net sales to inventory (Times)	Fixed assets to tangible net worth (Per cent)	Current debt to tangible net worth (Per cent)	Total debt to tangible net worth (Per cent)	Inventory to net working capital (Per cent)	Current debt to inventory (Per cent)	Funded debts to net working capital (Per cent)
5541 Gasoline Service Stations (70)	2.88	8.36	25.51	77.62	5.44	16.10	**	22.7	26.1	25.8	41.1	55.4	91.1	16.3
	1.73	4.97	15.67	44.06	3.72	9.44	**	10.9	38.6	44.1	68.9	88.5	133.9	39.5
	1.41	1.56	7.54	23.31	2.40	5.34	**	6.5	61.4	72.3	103.1	146.1	219.8	92.7
5411 Grocery Stores (114)	2.21	1.49	18.78	41.61	18.60	41.53	**	21.0	50.5	47.7	87.3	98.6	70.6	30.3
	1.63	0.94	12.78	23.27	12.80	21.62	**	16.1	77.2	77.7	117.3	155.9	96.3	68.0
	1.25	0.49	5.21	10.31	8.49	13.82	**	12.3	105.2	120.5	188.0	257.1	123.4	128.6
5251 Hardware Stores (83)	6.25	5.25	16.38	20.45	4.55	5.02	**	5.7	5.2	16.0	41.0	60.1	27.3	9.3
	3.36	3.27	8.41	10.82	3.08	3.74	**	4.7	15.1	36.4	69.4	81.8	55.5	36.7
	2.03	1.49	4.63	5.48	1.97	2.48	**	3.2	33.2	68.3	159.0	114.0	82.2	67.3
5722 Household Appliance Stores (78)	2.97	3.36	12.60	15.08	8.85	9.24	16	7.4	6.4	42.9	108.6	62.8	60.6	10.7
	2.00	1.20	7.26	7.37	5.34	5.74	26	4.7	19.7	88.7	150.7	108.8	83.4	33.6
	1.45	0.29	1.83	1.72	2.77	3.47	57	4.0	50.0	174.3	316.1	185.1	121.1	66.5
5944 Jewelry Stores (78)	4.99	6.23	13.16	13.90	2.84	3.07	**	4.0	2.5	24.0	49.5	56.8	35.1	10.2
	3.46	3.79	7.46	8.19	1.87	2.00	**	3.0	8.0	36.2	81.8	80.3	57.5	17.0
	2.38	1.57	3.36	3.79	1.52	1.63	**	2.2	15.0	65.0	130.6	107.9	85.0	37.9
5211 Lumber & Other Bldg. Mtls. Dealers (145)	4.20	4.01	13.79	17.41	5.08	7.04	30	9.7	14.3	23.6	50.9	54.8	42.8	22.1
	2.86	2.27	7.43	8.75	3.52	4.90	48	5.9	28.1	44.6	93.8	80.7	71.6	32.7
	2.15	0.97	3.48	4.47	2.36	2.97	61	4.0	45.5	69.4	138.2	105.2	121.5	50.6
5399 Miscellaneous General Mdse. Stores (86)	6.68	4.36	14.17	17.95	5.46	6.88	**	6.7	6.6	15.3	47.3	60.2	33.3	9.6
	3.25	2.34	8.70	12.30	3.24	4.05	**	4.1	17.2	42.4	104.5	93.5	46.0	29.4
	2.03	1.30	4.86	4.74	1.98	2.36	**	3.2	33.4	70.6	155.3	148.3	80.9	59.5
5511 Motor Vehicle Dealers (69)	1.79	2.17	17.75	30.04	11.66	17.96	**	7.9	10.4	80.4	127.7	152.2	76.1	10.4
	1.43	1.02	9.09	14.63	8.95	14.13	**	6.6	30.8	126.8	198.3	188.4	95.4	33.0
	1.25	0.42	4.41	6.75	6.52	10.48	**	5.0	60.7	235.5	263.9	275.5	120.3	76.4

** Not computed. Necessary information as to the division between cash sales was available in too few cases to obtain an average collection period usable as a broad guide.

RETAILING (*continued*)

Line of Business (and number of concerns reporting)	Current assets to current debt	Net profits on net sales	Net profits on tangible net worth	Net profits on net working capital	Net sales to tangible net worth	Net sales to net working capital	Collection period	Net sales to inventory	Fixed assets to tangible net worth	Current debt to tangible net worth	Total debt to tangible net worth	Inventory to net working capital	Current debt to inventory	Funded debts to net working capital
	Times	Per cent	Per cent	Per cent	Times	Times	Days	Times	Per cent	Per cent	Per cent	Per cent	Per cent	Per cent
5231 Paint, Glass & Wallpaper Stores (28)	6.17 / 3.70 / 2.10	6.85 / 3.13 / 1.31	17.44 / 8.57 / 4.62	51.47 / 14.29 / 7.86	5.25 / 3.45 / 2.45	6.82 / 4.33 / 3.73	** / ** / **	9.0 / 7.0 / 5.4	11.4 / 30.4 / 74.1	17.9 / 29.2 / 66.1	38.9 / 80.6 / 158.0	47.3 / 71.9 / 117.2	31.3 / 51.7 / 109.3	15.2 / 30.1 / 68.4
5732 Radio & Television Stores (45)	3.45 / 2.28 / 1.61	3.90 / 1.48 / 0.70	23.34 / 10.17 / 5.63	25.35 / 15.88 / 6.95	8.94 / 4.79 / 3.78	11.31 / 5.86 / 4.14	** / ** / **	6.7 / 4.8 / 3.1	10.7 / 22.7 / 36.2	33.6 / 71.7 / 153.8	100.9 / 143.3 / 319.1	96.8 / 126.1 / 187.5	37.5 / 60.0 / 93.4	17.3 / 40.8 / 65.7
5261 Retail Nurseries, Lawn & Garden Supp. Stores (54)	3.41 / 2.00 / 1.40	7.02 / 3.86 / 1.53	24.51 / 12.33 / 6.72	44.10 / 29.34 / 9.00	5.98 / 3.82 / 2.53	12.06 / 6.26 / 4.41	** / ** / **	10.5 / 6.9 / 5.4	16.2 / 36.1 / 54.3	25.4 / 59.8 / 96.9	55.8 / 84.3 / 134.6	58.1 / 89.4 / 145.2	50.7 / 88.4 / 154.4	24.0 / 37.6 / 46.3
5661 Shoe Stores (89)	4.69 / 2.69 / 1.99	3.38 / 1.34 / 0.12	9.26 / 4.45 / 0.56	12.53 / 5.00 / 0.83	5.22 / 3.45 / 2.28	5.97 / 3.98 / 2.68	** / ** / **	4.9 / 3.7 / 2.9	5.6 / 13.2 / 31.6	24.9 / 49.3 / 94.1	64.1 / 106.7 / 201.3	71.5 / 104.1 / 147.2	33.3 / 54.3 / 78.5	12.3 / 24.5 / 60.5
5331 Variety Stores (66)	4.06 / 4.88 / 2.05	3.06 / 2.20 / 1.33	13.61 / 8.80 / 5.13	16.33 / 10.94 / 6.32	6.16 / 3.98 / 3.06	7.52 / 5.13 / 3.52	** / ** / **	5.1 / 4.0 / 3.4	11.4 / 28.4 / 46.2	27.5 / 48.6 / 70.9	65.0 / 89.8 / 129.4	96.0 / 128.9 / 162.3	32.2 / 44.8 / 66.1	17.1 / 30.2 / 63.6
5621 Women's Ready-to-Wear Stores (175)	4.63 / 2.68 / 1.87	3.57 / 1.82 / 0.42	14.18 / 6.68 / 1.45	17.90 / 7.31 / 1.66	5.93 / 3.89 / 2.77	7.55 / 4.62 / 3.19	** / ** / **	9.6 / 7.1 / 5.0	6.8 / 29.4 / 46.1	24.0 / 49.6 / 89.3	61.9 / 109.4 / 172.6	48.1 / 72.5 / 103.5	53.8 / 84.6 / 126.7	13.7 / 32.3 / 72.2

** Not computed. Necessary information as to the division between cash sales was available in too few cases to obtain an average collection period usable as a broad guide.

WHOLESALING

Line of Business (and number of concerns reporting)	Current assets to current debt (Times)	Net profits on net sales (Per cent)	Net profits on tangible net worth (Per cent)	Net profits on net working capital (Per cent)	Net sales to tangible net worth (Times)	Net sales to net working capital (Times)	Collection period (Days)	Net sales to inventory (Times)	Fixed assets to tangible net worth (Per cent)	Current debt to tangible net worth (Per cent)	Total debt to tangible net worth (Per cent)	Inventory to net working capital (Per cent)	Current debt to inventory (Per cent)	Funded debts to net working capital (Per cent)
5075 & 78 Air Condtg. & Refrigtn. Equipt. & Supplies (45)	4.33	3.30	13.40	16.59	6.89	7.65	35	8.9	7.8	28.1	56.5	49.0	41.3	5.2
	2.62	1.70	5.98	6.56	4.72	5.09	49	7.1	12.4	48.7	107.7	80.2	76.2	18.8
	1.87	0.29	2.44	2.87	2.49	2.97	58	4.7	22.7	105.5	169.2	107.2	138.6	34.1
5013 Automotive Parts & Supplies (144)	3.79	4.36	16.67	19.70	5.56	6.44	27	6.8	6.7	28.2	46.9	75.0	43.3	9.9
	2.84	2.78	11.01	13.32	3.91	4.64	34	5.0	15.4	46.7	78.9	93.8	61.6	19.6
	1.97	1.67	7.03	8.31	2.94	3.33	42	3.8	30.2	82.9	120.5	121.6	91.9	45.2
5181 & 82 Beer, Wine & Alcoholic Beverages (99)	3.35	3.14	19.82	28.35	11.15	15.09	8	12.8	10.0	33.0	69.5	78.2	53.1	8.3
	1.96	1.58	11.91	14.65	8.22	10.44	17	8.0	25.1	76.0	167.3	118.4	88.9	33.1
	1.46	0.61	3.88	5.52	4.87	6.87	35	6.0	45.2	162.8	234.2	199.3	122.1	69.6
5161 Chemicals & Allied Products (45)	2.95	4.95	31.07	41.85	8.66	11.13	28	15.7	14.1	33.7	46.9	46.2	94.3	5.2
	1.99	3.35	16.60	23.71	5.94	8.02	36	11.5	29.4	65.9	89.7	75.7	133.3	15.9
	1.75	1.48	6.78	12.80	3.40	4.21	55	6.8	49.5	108.2	207.6	104.0	205.3	44.2
5137 Clothing & Accessories, Women's, Children's & Infants' (60)	4.11	1.88	11.04	14.98	7.99	9.55	25	18.3	1.4	24.8	45.7	38.8	69.4	5.0
	2.44	0.77	4.64	4.95	5.31	6.18	36	9.6	4.5	57.1	69.0	64.6	102.4	37.7
	1.76	0.17	1.57	1.20	3.00	3.80	52	5.6	12.2	104.9	81.0	93.1	179.4	39.5
5136 Clothing & Furnishings, Men's & Boys' (58)	3.48	2.77	13.85	17.23	7.94	8.73	18	8.1	1.4	36.1	69.0	72.5	56.2	6.0
	2.28	1.35	8.04	8.02	4.92	5.67	39	5.5	7.1	69.5	112.5	96.1	73.6	21.2
	1.71	0.48	3.54	3.77	3.19	3.80	53	4.3	19.6	134.8	155.2	126.5	102.1	35.3
5081 Commercial Machines & Equipment (53)	4.06	2.85	11.73	15.45	8.02	8.46	35	10.0	5.3	35.1	78.6	46.8	58.2	6.1
	2.08	1.73	8.89	9.35	5.45	5.62	53	7.7	13.9	75.3	126.9	77.2	131.3	31.5
	1.77	0.97	4.17	4.86	3.14	3.55	66	5.1	34.5	129.7	221.5	108.3	167.8	51.4
5145 Confectionery (34)	4.32	2.55	21.90	29.87	18.94	21.03	11	20.9	6.4	24.3	98.5	59.6	56.5	20.9
	2.33	1.27	14.42	15.18	9.28	11.90	17	14.2	15.6	65.9	166.9	87.3	74.1	34.0
	1.80	0.48	8.05	8.71	5.38	6.93	22	8.0	28.8	96.2	236.0	121.4	112.8	82.8
5143 Dairy Products (46)	2.65	3.01	23.18	57.74	13.51	22.01	25	59.1	15.2	43.1	102.5	21.7	95.1	3.6
	1.65	1.70	11.52	17.77	6.44	13.26	32	22.7	28.8	55.9	137.0	52.7	170.9	22.2
	1.31	0.72	7.58	10.35	4.69	6.80	44	12.0	50.9	125.5	331.4	78.6	350.8	79.4
5122 Drugs, Drug Proprietaries & Sundries (86)	2.67	2.20	14.20	18.19	9.87	11.14	25	8.0	9.0	52.5	84.3	85.3	68.2	15.0
	1.97	1.14	8.29	9.43	6.74	8.18	34	6.7	22.0	91.0	147.4	111.7	92.3	27.0
	1.61	0.66	5.32	5.67	4.83	5.47	47	5.8	38.3	156.9	207.0	147.6	122.7	51.2
5064 Electrical Appliances, TV & Radio Sets (86)	2.49	2.01	11.29	12.94	8.17	9.56	31	7.8	4.6	61.3	96.2	73.3	70.0	10.2
	1.86	1.10	5.92	7.12	5.84	6.56	41	6.3	9.0	95.4	142.0	105.6	95.4	18.4
	1.54	0.26	1.04	1.87	4.38	4.90	54	4.8	23.4	162.5	225.2	161.2	137.0	61.2

WHOLESALING (continued)

Line of Business (and number of concerns reporting)	Current assets to current debt (Times)	Net profits on net sales (Per cent)	Net profits on tangible net worth (Per cent)	Net profits on net working capital (Per cent)	Net sales to tangible net worth (Times)	Net sales to net working capital (Times)	Collection period (Days)	Net sales to inventory (Times)	Fixed assets to tangible net worth (Per cent)	Current debt to tangible net worth (Per cent)	Total debt to tangible net worth (Per cent)	Inventory to net working capital (Per cent)	Current debt to inventory (Per cent)	Funded debts to net working capital (Per cent)
5063 Electrical Apparatus & Equipment (122)	3.20 / 2.17 / 1.75	3.04 / 1.66 / 0.93	16.53 / 9.86 / 5.61	17.82 / 11.45 / 6.31	9.03 / 5.51 / 3.85	9.77 / 6.13 / 4.39	35 / 40 / 50	10.2 / 7.4 / 5.5	7.8 / 16.8 / 29.7	38.5 / 73.0 / 120.3	64.4 / 111.9 / 203.3	65.2 / 82.6 / 104.1	60.4 / 98.3 / 147.0	9.8 / 19.7 / 41.3
5065 Electronic Parts & Equipment (48)	2.81 / 2.26 / 1.63	2.60 / 1.55 / 0.52	14.21 / 9.71 / 2.71	15.47 / 9.02 / 3.17	7.69 / 5.84 / 4.12	7.40 / 5.06 / 3.94	35 / 44 / 54	6.3 / 4.5 / 3.4	8.7 / 14.4 / 25.9	51.4 / 99.3 / 150.4	102.8 / 206.7 / 266.3	78.6 / 107.1 / 155.2	60.9 / 83.6 / 108.7	16.6 / 36.7 / 63.7
5083 Farm & Garden Machinery & Equipment (128)	2.99 / 1.83 / 1.50	5.00 / 2.99 / 1.72	24.50 / 15.25 / 8.52	29.50 / 19.38 / 10.75	6.94 / 5.36 / 3.73	8.31 / 6.29 / 4.50	19 / 33 / 50	7.1 / 4.7 / 3.2	9.7 / 16.9 / 37.1	48.2 / 88.9 / 149.5	78.2 / 123.1 / 202.9	80.9 / 123.8 / 197.5	66.0 / 84.7 / 111.1	8.2 / 23.3 / 39.1
5139 Footwear (56)	3.83 / 2.49 / 2.01	3.14 / 1.63 / 0.34	12.68 / 5.64 / 1.77	12.65 / 6.65 / 1.91	5.02 / 3.59 / 2.47	5.84 / 4.29 / 2.89	34 / 49 / 80	10.3 / 6.9 / 3.8	1.0 / 3.2 / 8.1	35.1 / 59.0 / 94.2	64.0 / 83.6 / 140.3	44.9 / 69.0 / 102.4	61.9 / 84.4 / 136.8	4.7 / 12.7 / 29.9
5148 Fresh Fruits & Vegetables (72)	2.89 / 1.96 / 1.39	2.92 / 1.24 / 0.29	18.75 / 10.81 / 3.47	37.59 / 19.26 / 6.42	14.50 / 7.76 / 4.84	25.17 / 15.95 / 8.54	12 / 18 / 36	70.4 / 32.4 / 15.9	21.4 / 46.6 / 73.9	29.3 / 57.8 / 121.6	73.8 / 120.0 / 245.1	21.2 / 40.5 / 86.8	95.2 / 176.8 / 386.8	7.0 / 16.9 / 104.4
5021 & 23 Furniture & Home Furnishings (70)	3.46 / 2.71 / 1.81	2.67 / 1.61 / 0.73	14.14 / 7.58 / 2.61	16.67 / 7.37 / 3.08	6.78 / 4.97 / 3.32	7.99 / 5.29 / 3.59	24 / 41 / 53	9.1 / 6.3 / 4.3	5.1 / 10.5 / 25.5	37.1 / 52.9 / 117.8	65.0 / 114.5 / 201.6	66.1 / 79.7 / 127.8	48.9 / 81.3 / 121.9	5.2 / 12.6 / 30.5
5141 Groceries, General Line (160)	3.36 / 2.08 / 1.65	1.45 / 0.83 / 0.28	17.12 / 10.26 / 4.89	21.69 / 11.43 / 5.68	19.64 / 12.94 / 7.40	24.37 / 14.50 / 8.41	8 / 11 / 16	17.7 / 13.2 / 9.5	9.4 / 28.2 / 71.3	38.7 / 72.5 / 134.9	88.7 / 138.7 / 224.4	86.9 / 114.8 / 164.8	50.0 / 74.2 / 107.9	22.2 / 43.6 / 89.6
5072 Hardware (150)	4.41 / 2.87 / 1.96	2.98 / 1.77 / 0.92	12.37 / 7.37 / 3.49	14.04 / 8.78 / 4.38	5.56 / 3.84 / 2.86	6.64 / 4.70 / 3.28	30 / 38 / 47	7.3 / 4.9 / 3.8	7.0 / 12.7 / 28.8	26.3 / 46.7 / 95.4	53.1 / 99.2 / 147.9	70.8 / 94.3 / 124.9	38.1 / 61.5 / 93.7	9.9 / 23.7 / 39.9
5084 Industrial Machinery & Equipment (87)	3.53 / 2.45 / 1.86	3.94 / 2.30 / 1.07	19.86 / 11.92 / 6.88	25.41 / 14.34 / 8.33	7.73 / 5.08 / 3.34	9.00 / 6.00 / 3.96	31 / 37 / 51	14.3 / 6.7 / 4.4	7.3 / 19.9 / 44.0	32.1 / 57.8 / 107.9	69.0 / 116.2 / 188.7	60.1 / 82.8 / 120.5	55.3 / 80.9 / 119.7	10.4 / 30.1 / 56.2
5031 & 39 Lumber & Construction Materials (120)	3.79 / 2.55 / 1.88	3.00 / 1.34 / 0.45	13.14 / 7.97 / 2.66	16.67 / 8.77 / 3.21	7.58 / 5.23 / 3.45	9.22 / 5.92 / 4.14	31 / 41 / 54	11.1 / 7.7 / 5.3	9.1 / 17.3 / 40.9	27.1 / 54.5 / 92.1	57.9 / 102.9 / 172.9	52.2 / 77.4 / 102.9	51.4 / 83.3 / 143.3	8.8 / 29.3 / 55.8

5147 Meats & Meat Products (49)	2.51	1.35	15.90	22.09	29.52	33.60	15	78.1	8.1	50.8	76.6	39.2	110.0	14.2
	1.74	0.55	8.93	11.50	17.13	24.35	18	38.0	24.4	91.7	134.6	60.2	167.2	24.1
	1.47	(0.08)	(1.60)	(1.83)	11.39	14.85	29	24.6	42.0	165.6	268.1	84.7	328.5	50.5
5051 Metals Service Centers & Offices (74)	3.73	4.72	21.52	28.83	6.11	7.57	25	8.9	10.4	30.3	65.1	61.9	53.3	8.1
	2.60	2.99	11.59	14.76	4.11	5.05	35	5.5	21.4	53.8	89.8	85.8	78.4	27.3
	1.82	1.09	3.93	5.18	2.99	3.79	43	4.1	41.5	90.4	126.3	125.2	108.6	46.3
5198 Paints, Varnishes, & Supplies (32)	4.03	2.97	15.31	18.87	5.03	7.36	29	8.6	6.4	25.9	52.1	54.2	62.2	9.2
	2.89	2.12	7.68	11.78	4.34	5.18	39	6.5	16.8	44.8	89.7	75.3	76.8	24.5
	1.98	1.28	3.74	5.18	2.95	3.63	50	5.5	35.9	81.1	143.2	100.6	123.4	53.7
5111-12-13 Paper & Paper Products (107)	3.83	2.78	14.59	18.44	8.38	10.41	30	13.9	5.8	30.4	55.6	48.4	57.6	11.4
	2.53	1.86	10.73	12.47	5.72	6.89	38	9.5	12.6	56.1	89.7	66.8	87.0	23.8
	1.91	1.13	6.63	7.65	4.06	4.52	49	6.5	29.6	94.0	157.4	94.9	148.6	54.3
5171 & 72 Petroleum & Petroleum Products (88)	3.17	4.34	20.00	49.02	9.70	21.47	16	28.5	29.1	27.6	43.3	42.6	93.1	13.2
	1.80	1.73	12.49	28.46	6.25	13.29	23	18.0	44.0	57.6	87.7	80.1	131.6	51.2
	1.43	0.84	6.54	13.46	4.04	8.38	34	11.4	75.5	97.1	171.7	120.4	227.1	118.3
5133 Piece Goods (100)	2.97	2.42	12.11	13.29	7.42	8.45	26	9.2	2.1	48.6	74.1	59.6	61.9	12.1
	2.11	1.22	6.30	7.52	5.32	5.68	46	6.6	5.4	84.9	130.2	78.8	103.7	25.6
	1.66	0.01	1.15	1.15	3.74	3.85	61	4.9	19.1	143.3	238.3	125.3	146.9	44.1
5074 Plumbing & Heating Equipment & Supplies (166)	4.50	3.72	14.63	18.02	6.46	7.12	34	8.4	7.6	26.4	56.9	58.4	46.8	7.4
	2.72	2.09	8.63	10.45	4.16	4.92	43	6.2	15.2	48.4	96.0	78.2	75.5	22.2
	2.06	1.05	4.43	5.59	3.01	3.41	52	4.7	32.7	86.5	144.1	101.7	109.8	43.8
5144 Poultry & Poultry Products (44)	3.31	1.18	12.77	25.38	20.38	30.97	14	80.0	12.2	25.2	18.5	23.1	87.0	10.5
	1.82	0.62	7.02	12.10	11.61	20.90	18	52.2	23.5	71.1	81.8	62.5	157.6	35.6
	1.43	0.28	2.91	5.11	5.88	12.20	27	13.0	82.9	118.4	139.6	120.6	360.0	131.5
5093 Scrap & Waste Materials (63)	3.95	5.32	21.12	32.18	6.76	11.23	20	43.0	13.3	16.1	36.4	26.9	73.9	7.5
	2.48	2.37	7.66	17.94	3.16	7.10	29	11.4	33.3	33.3	68.8	51.5	114.6	19.9
	1.64	0.80	2.94	5.05	2.15	3.86	40	6.0	49.8	69.5	141.0	74.3	338.0	37.1
5014 Tires & Tubes (30)	2.50	2.61	11.33	21.45	6.63	9.79	32	8.0	13.5	40.6	83.4	66.5	85.4	10.4
	1.78	1.89	6.49	9.39	4.58	6.95	39	5.8	29.8	96.0	179.1	114.7	105.9	17.4
	1.49	0.38	1.79	2.97	3.24	4.69	53	3.9	53.9	157.4	252.5	165.8	141.1	75.4
5194 Tobacco & Tobacco Products (83)	3.11	1.57	17.75	22.73	19.89	22.78	11	22.2	7.3	41.2	60.4	63.9	59.8	6.2
	2.25	0.93	11.85	13.65	12.00	15.08	16	16.0	14.7	68.6	106.4	91.3	90.0	13.4
	1.66	0.48	5.96	8.24	8.12	10.88	21	12.7	26.1	129.3	186.5	120.9	130.7	40.5

( ) Indicates loss.

MANUFACTURING AND CONSTRUCTION

Line of Business (and number of concerns reporting)	Current assets to current debt (Times)	Net profits on net sales (Per cent)	Net profits on tangible net worth (Per cent)	Net profits on net working capital (Per cent)	Net sales to tangible net worth (Times)	Net sales to net working capital (Times)	Collection period (Days)	Net sales to inventory (Times)	Fixed assets to tangible net worth (Per cent)	Current debt to tangible net worth (Per cent)	Total debt to tangible net worth (Per cent)	Inventory to net working capital (Per cent)	Current debt to inventory (Per cent)	Funded debts to net working capital (Per cent)
2873-74-75-79 Agricultural Chemicals (39)	2.98 / 2.21 / 1.55	10.09 / 6.60 / 4.35	26.16 / 21.59 / 15.41	55.31 / 35.87 / 24.12	4.84 / 3.83 / 2.00	10.53 / 5.89 / 3.94	16 / 38 / 63	10.3 / 7.4 / 4.7	16.3 / 31.6 / 73.6	35.3 / 53.8 / 82.9	51.6 / 97.3 / 166.1	56.2 / 87.0 / 126.2	68.8 / 97.9 / 167.9	10.0 / 34.9 / 88.9
3724-28 Airplane Parts & Accessories (58)	3.84 / 2.63 / 1.96	8.48 / 4.57 / 2.93	18.43 / 13.98 / 10.26	32.22 / 17.71 / 10.63	3.57 / 2.93 / 1.89	4.78 / 3.62 / 2.44	36 / 49 / 68	6.4 / 4.3 / 3.2	21.8 / 37.1 / 58.3	28.2 / 49.0 / 78.7	48.6 / 86.9 / 170.5	60.5 / 81.1 / 106.9	54.2 / 73.2 / 117.5	14.4 / 38.8 / 61.5
2051-52 Bakery Products (55)	2.84 / 2.22 / 1.55	5.66 / 2.95 / 1.78	19.72 / 14.20 / 8.49	63.77 / 35.09 / 21.68	7.58 / 4.99 / 3.99	19.22 / 10.89 / 7.54	17 / 24 / 35	40.2 / 23.8 / 14.6	52.5 / 70.3 / 103.0	23.3 / 34.0 / 58.5	34.8 / 64.5 / 121.2	32.4 / 52.3 / 88.9	112.8 / 209.4 / 324.6	19.5 / 51.8 / 163.0
3312-13-15-16-17 Blast Furnaces, Steel Wks. & Rolling Mills (44)	3.27 / 2.46 / 1.83	6.17 / 4.45 / 2.31	15.68 / 10.31 / 7.57	26.80 / 20.96 / 12.23	3.45 / 2.59 / 2.11	6.28 / 4.69 / 3.60	31 / 36 / 49	5.9 / 4.7 / 4.0	50.0 / 81.6 / 100.9	24.5 / 38.2 / 60.8	52.8 / 78.8 / 115.3	77.5 / 90.9 / 116.0	53.5 / 81.1 / 97.5	31.5 / 72.1 / 111.5
2331 Blouses & Waists, Women's & Misses' (41)	2.53 / 1.79 / 1.43	2.83 / 1.28 / 0.58	20.52 / 10.27 / 4.01	27.23 / 12.35 / 5.22	13.15 / 6.89 / 4.04	14.69 / 8.79 / 5.43	33 / 40 / 53	13.9 / 9.1 / 7.1	2.9 / 10.2 / 24.9	57.2 / 112.5 / 212.8	70.0 / 126.5 / 250.0	63.2 / 91.7 / 132.5	97.3 / 123.6 / 205.1	10.4 / 30.0 / 52.8
2731-32 Books; Publishing, Publishing & Printing (44)	4.77 / 2.92 / 2.23	8.46 / 5.24 / 2.57	16.74 / 11.30 / 7.46	19.94 / 14.59 / 8.06	3.60 / 2.25 / 1.83	4.30 / 2.99 / 2.30	47 / 64 / 86	8.2 / 4.7 / 3.0	10.8 / 31.7 / 49.7	21.7 / 41.9 / 57.5	48.2 / 74.8 / 143.3	51.1 / 65.1 / 88.6	54.9 / 82.7 / 130.7	5.1 / 24.4 / 67.8
2211 Broad Woven Fabrics, Cotton (38)	4.24 / 3.31 / 2.03	2.63 / 1.79 / (1.48)	5.72 / 4.49 / (4.18)	11.78 / 6.49 / (4.81)	3.89 / 2.69 / 2.22	5.14 / 3.77 / 3.25	40 / 58 / 75	9.3 / 6.5 / 4.4	45.7 / 53.9 / 93.2	17.9 / 34.1 / 57.0	40.9 / 67.2 / 135.5	53.0 / 71.7 / 82.4	52.2 / 76.6 / 107.9	15.4 / 39.3 / 90.7
2032-33-34-35-37-38 Canned & Preserved Fruits & Vegbls. (65)	2.36 / 1.75 / 1.32	4.36 / 2.50 / 1.03	15.77 / 9.18 / 4.32	28.27 / 16.99 / 7.14	6.31 / 3.81 / 2.93	10.56 / 6.38 / 4.54	16 / 25 / 34	6.4 / 4.1 / 2.5	34.9 / 58.2 / 83.4	49.5 / 88.1 / 158.6	80.8 / 145.3 / 253.7	80.6 / 150.9 / 227.6	69.3 / 81.7 / 116.6	7.2 / 45.5 / 105.3
2751 Commercial Printing except Lithographic (48)	3.71 / 2.51 / 1.73	5.00 / 2.41 / 1.26	12.46 / 9.32 / 5.27	23.63 / 15.75 / 9.72	4.69 / 2.98 / 2.14	8.48 / 5.06 / 3.71	32 / 42 / 53	** / ** / **	30.1 / 52.6 / 70.5	20.5 / 36.7 / 64.4	39.8 / 60.6 / 104.0	** / ** / **	** / ** / **	9.2 / 23.9 / 67.5
3661-62 Communication Equipment (54)	4.18 / 2.87 / 2.14	7.49 / 4.45 / 2.35	20.28 / 13.20 / 6.08	21.93 / 16.18 / 7.57	3.64 / 2.91 / 1.95	4.54 / 3.11 / 2.37	47 / 61 / 85	7.5 / 4.7 / 3.7	16.5 / 36.3 / 50.7	26.6 / 47.6 / 91.2	40.3 / 94.5 / 135.0	44.4 / 65.6 / 86.1	52.3 / 81.2 / 140.7	5.3 / 27.7 / 58.3
3271-72-73-74-75 Concrete, Gypsum & Plaster Products (60)	3.92 / 2.54 / 1.61	5.79 / 3.74 / 1.92	15.27 / 8.15 / 3.59	45.65 / 15.71 / 8.04	4.29 / 2.60 / 1.82	8.78 / 5.76 / 3.29	33 / 41 / 57	12.7 / 8.9 / 5.3	43.6 / 63.3 / 102.1	20.8 / 28.6 / 72.6	43.0 / 73.0 / 111.2	41.1 / 66.2 / 86.2	63.5 / 104.3 / 262.1	12.1 / 58.1 / 98.7

( ) Indicates loss.

** Not computed. Printers carry only current supplies such as paper, ink, and binding materials rather than merchandise inventories for resale.

Line of Business														
2065-66-67 Confectionery & Related Products (28)	4.89	4.39	19.75	38.64	11.75	4.89	8	15.7	24.5	16.1	38.4	57.7	49.6	10.9
	2.41	**3.24**	**13.41**	**23.16**	**6.64**	**4.15**	**16**	**8.7**	**43.9**	**43.8**	**67.2**	**79.4**	**78.2**	**27.3**
	1.56	(0.13)	0.00	(0.43)	3.18	1.97	29	4.9	62.8	84.1	112.3	160.4	131.1	67.0
3531-32-33-34-35-36-37 Const., Min.& Handling Machy. & Equipt. (78)	3.39	7.93	23.34	27.49	4.98	4.37	34	5.4	25.5	31.7	54.9	61.3	53.6	13.7
	2.54	**4.82**	**13.04**	**17.99**	**3.59**	**2.84**	**60**	**3.1**	**46.9**	**54.5**	**100.2**	**90.6**	**70.1**	**43.3**
	1.87	2.97	6.91	8.76	2.35	1.93	81	2.5	61.4	84.7	138.7	116.2	111.0	63.1
2641-42-43-45-46-47-48-49 Convtd. Paper & Paperboard Prods. (64)	4.71	5.29	16.18	25.39	6.24	4.41	33	10.4	27.4	17.3	40.2	49.1	60.6	7.8
	2.97	**3.25**	**11.47**	**18.31**	**4.94**	**3.24**	**44**	**6.6**	**49.2**	**31.9**	**86.1**	**65.6**	**78.8**	**31.1**
	2.12	1.67	5.92	9.90	3.85	2.42	58	5.2	77.1	51.3	106.0	93.4	111.8	75.4
3421-23-25-29 Cutlery, Hand Tools & General Hardware (76)	4.66	7.01	14.15	21.99	4.70	3.63	36	5.7	25.6	18.7	46.2	58.3	38.9	14.0
	3.19	**3.86**	**10.19**	**13.48**	**3.59**	**2.28**	**45**	**4.2**	**38.5**	**33.8**	**72.0**	**81.3**	**66.5**	**29.2**
	2.21	1.77	5.14	6.45	2.48	1.67	58	3.3	58.1	55.8	118.2	108.5	83.8	60.7
2021-22-23-24-26 Dairy Products (86)	1.98	2.98	18.63	65.32	33.82	10.42	19	40.1	57.9	44.9	76.6	58.2	134.6	14.4
	1.40	**1.59**	**12.54**	**36.24**	**20.89**	**8.03**	**27**	**24.8**	**69.4**	**78.0**	**110.1**	**99.4**	**233.1**	**62.8**
	1.17	0.92	8.72	19.63	12.31	5.19	34	14.5	104.4	122.6	192.8	170.5	345.9	164.2
2335 Dresses: Women's, Misses' and Junior's (76)	2.99	1.67	14.17	14.78	13.77	10.59	34	17.1	2.9	36.7	83.8	41.7	83.9	5.1
	2.06	**0.50**	**2.63**	**3.69**	**7.47**	**5.83**	**51**	**9.9**	**8.2**	**93.3**	**135.5**	**71.9**	**132.0**	**17.9**
	1.54	(0.66)	(2.93)	(4.53)	4.11	3.94	64	6.5	20.9	160.5	188.3	110.4	245.7	50.6
2831-33-34 Drugs (56)	3.15	10.16	18.86	26.90	4.79	3.69	44	5.8	28.9	30.5	46.7	60.0	61.2	8.7
	2.46	**6.15**	**14.37**	**18.48**	**3.37**	**2.19**	**59**	**4.4**	**44.6**	**45.0**	**77.0**	**81.2**	**87.9**	**42.1**
	1.92	3.27	7.46	10.76	2.49	1.71	77	3.8	72.4	59.9	148.7	98.6	114.9	86.0
3641-43-44-45-46-47-48 Electric Lighting & Wiring Equipment (42)	5.45	6.14	15.80	21.26	6.15	3.69	29	6.3	15.5	13.5	27.9	44.2	36.0	11.2
	4.06	**2.79**	**8.61**	**11.64**	**3.18**	**2.54**	**43**	**4.5**	**33.4**	**25.8**	**57.4**	**72.9**	**53.2**	**16.8**
	2.11	0.92	2.08	2.91	2.47	1.83	57	3.3	47.1	72.5	91.5	87.9	87.8	38.9
3612-13 Elec. Trans. & Distribution Equipment (43)	6.10	8.78	17.11	32.27	4.68	3.41	48	6.8	16.2	20.5	34.5	69.2	50.3	13.5
	3.05	**5.39**	**12.90**	**16.26**	**3.79**	**2.65**	**62**	**4.7**	**34.1**	**39.8**	**66.7**	**80.1**	**73.8**	**29.7**
	2.16	1.26	2.27	3.39	2.60	1.56	79	3.0	57.1	84.9	119.8	95.1	110.0	69.2
3621-22-23-24-29 Electrical Industrial Apparatus (59)	4.28	5.07	13.86	19.14	4.76	4.22	48	6.2	23.6	22.6	51.3	62.3	40.6	16.9
	2.59	**3.68**	**9.59**	**12.40**	**3.72**	**3.00**	**57**	**4.3**	**41.6**	**52.3**	**101.5**	**75.2**	**69.9**	**38.7**
	2.09	1.48	3.70	5.13	2.75	2.48	69	3.6	60.2	77.7	194.1	101.1	108.6	86.9
1731 Electrical Work Contractor (97)	3.43	3.81	21.09	28.26	10.36	8.21	**	**	11.2	32.6	59.6	**	**	7.6
	2.14	**2.23**	**11.68**	**14.32**	**7.45**	**5.75**	****	****	**21.3**	**63.4**	**126.9**	****	****	**17.6**
	1.60	0.99	6.07	6.75	4.88	3.65	**	**	41.4	124.0	257.1	**	**	54.8
3671-72-73-74-75-76-77-78-79 Electronic Compnts. & Acces. (81)	4.24	5.98	16.72	18.29	5.62	3.86	47	7.3	28.0	29.5	44.0	54.2	49.8	15.8
	2.79	**3.48**	**9.87**	**10.04**	**3.53**	**2.74**	**56**	**4.9**	**42.7**	**43.7**	**83.7**	**71.5**	**87.3**	**42.6**
	2.04	0.59	1.33	2.40	2.79	2.05	66	3.6	78.5	85.8	147.5	93.6	141.5	76.8
3811 Engineering, Laboratory & Scientific Instruments (47)	5.65	7.21	16.79	16.85	3.87	3.64	57	5.4	18.1	20.9	42.5	52.2	40.7	7.5
	3.39	**3.75**	**8.73**	**10.19**	**2.61**	**2.33**	**72**	**3.5**	**35.0**	**42.0**	**77.6**	**71.1**	**68.2**	**29.3**
	2.16	1.52	4.59	5.46	1.91	1.48	86	2.8	46.6	84.3	140.7	86.9	101.1	53.9

( ) Indicates loss.

** Not computed. Building trades contractors have no inventories in the credit sense of the term. As a general rule, such contractors have no customary selling terms, each contract being a special job for which individual terms are arranged.

MANUFACTURING AND CONSTRUCTION (continued)

Line of Business (and number of concerns reporting)	Current assets to current debt (Times)	Net profits on net sales (Per cent)	Net profits on tangible net worth (Per cent)	Net profits on net working capital (Per cent)	Net sales to tangible net worth (Times)	Net sales to net working capital (Times)	Collection period (Days)	Net sales to inventory (Times)	Fixed assets to tangible net worth (Per cent)	Current debt to tangible net worth (Per cent)	Total debt to tangible net worth (Per cent)	Inventory to net working capital (Per cent)	Current debt to inventory (Per cent)	Funded debts to net working capital (Per cent)
3441-42-43-44-46-48-49 Fabricated Structural Met. Prodts. (142)	4.15 2.55 1.93	6.56 4.23 2.45	25.84 14.39 8.51	35.17 18.96 10.51	4.63 3.46 2.40	6.15 4.76 3.28	35 46 58	11.2 6.2 5.2	25.0 39.3 63.8	24.3 48.1 90.7	50.0 95.0 148.7	47.4 71.7 104.1	56.3 92.0 162.4	19.0 41.8 66.2
3523 Farm Machinery & Equipment (66)	3.68 2.12 1.66	6.03 3.59 2.04	21.60 14.66 6.47	27.24 19.13 7.78	5.67 3.81 2.74	6.88 4.73 3.09	26 37 61	5.6 3.9 2.9	20.5 32.0 54.4	33.6 92.5 157.5	90.8 128.5 188.7	70.1 117.9 156.6	52.2 77.0 101.8	16.4 40.5 59.5
3143-44-49 Footwear (56)	4.16 2.70 1.95	5.18 3.12 1.10	13.54 8.83 2.45	16.64 9.76 2.76	5.94 3.73 2.87	6.87 3.95 2.87	16 49 61	15.1 5.7 3.5	5.4 17.3 29.2	29.6 55.9 90.5	40.3 87.9 124.2	54.7 85.7 107.4	52.5 82.7 118.9	3.5 20.5 36.6
1541-42 General Building Contractors (103)	1.77 1.43 1.23	2.96 1.18 0.44	21.52 11.30 4.07	42.16 16.67 7.07	14.54 7.32 4.43	24.43 15.02 8.19	** ** **	** ** **	11.2 22.9 46.7	73.5 133.8 235.6	123.9 234.0 388.9	** ** **	** ** **	19.0 48.3 120.9
3561-62-63-64-65-66-67-68-69 Gen. Industrl. Machy. & Equipment (101)	4.05 2.61 2.06	7.83 5.16 3.05	18.91 13.63 7.96	27.81 18.95 8.73	4.31 2.91 1.98	5.38 3.78 2.85	41 48 65	6.6 4.2 3.5	28.5 39.1 57.0	23.0 40.9 87.4	44.0 86.3 129.6	59.0 81.5 99.2	45.5 69.6 93.8	11.6 26.7 57.2
2041-43-44-45-46-47-48 Grain Mill Products (67)	3.71 2.20 1.75	4.95 2.59 1.36	26.61 14.52 7.82	45.59 23.40 9.85	8.02 5.85 4.39	16.09 9.74 6.43	15 23 31	19.1 11.6 8.9	30.4 55.5 82.3	23.7 48.5 80.6	65.4 101.6 130.0	47.7 79.8 116.2	61.7 97.3 141.7	26.9 60.4 96.3
3431-32-33 Heating Equipt. & Plmbg. Fixtures (40)	4.74 3.52 2.20	5.85 3.85 1.70	13.07 10.41 5.83	19.94 13.16 7.71	3.53 2.82 1.92	5.27 3.64 2.27	28 48 65	5.7 4.2 3.3	15.8 33.3 56.4	24.0 32.7 56.5	42.7 59.0 94.5	63.8 74.3 117.0	42.6 57.0 82.4	6.8 33.1 61.0
1622-23-29 Hwy. Construction, except Hwy. & Street (79)	3.64 1.89 1.44	5.53 2.69 0.63	21.93 10.60 1.35	34.69 18.26 2.93	5.38 3.85 2.08	11.42 7.02 3.62	** ** **	** ** **	29.9 53.8 71.8	24.1 60.2 108.3	63.7 1u4.0 157.3	** ** **	** ** **	6.5 30.1 73.0
2251-52 Hosiery (40)	4.94 2.58 2.13	3.52 1.41 (1.18)	10.00 6.54 0.00	17.84 8.50 0.20	5.31 3.15 2.13	6.49 4.65 3.81	33 49 67	9.2 6.3 4.4	23.9 40.1 60.1	16.5 41.5 68.3	61.0 95.0 237.4	53.1 87.9 117.8	50.4 72.0 99.8	31.2 48.5 74.2
3631-32-33-34-35-36-39 Household Appliances (39)	4.21 3.03 2.34	6.93 3.92 1.98	14.90 10.43 3.16	20.90 11.31 6.20	4.17 2.90 2.33	4.16 3.68 3.10	42 60 68	6.1 4.5 3.8	22.7 34.4 52.2	20.7 39.1 81.6	42.4 68.5 139.7	56.5 75.0 85.7	52.3 71.8 99.0	14.8 34.8 51.1
2812-13-16-19 Industrial Chemicals (206)	3.49 2.11 1.37	8.01 4.96 1.85	25.26 15.63 7.54	50.35 29.61 14.26	6.80 3.74 2.17	10.64 5.77 3.87	30 43 58	15.6 9.6 5.8	24.8 62.2 105.5	25.5 45.6 113.8	57.7 111.7 205.6	39.9 67.5 100.9	78.8 140.0 229.7	24.3 70.1 134.1
3822-23-24-25-29 Instruments, Measuring & Controlling (65)	3.96 2.88 2.15	5.67 3.28 0.90	15.57 9.95 2.74	16.16 11.09 4.48	3.34 2.64 1.94	3.89 3.19 2.46	50 62 91	5.2 4.1 3.0	24.3 37.8 50.1	28.9 41.4 83.3	52.9 80.9 166.1	65.8 80.0 92.2	46.4 66.7 97.8	19.7 39.4 56.5

( ) Indicates loss.

Industry	1	2	3	4	5	6	7	8	9	10	11	12	13	14
3572-73-74-76-79 Office, Computing & Accounting Machines (57)	3.11	7.33	15.46	20.95	4.66	4.32	60	5.3	21.4	34.6	80.8	62.3	62.1	12.5
	2.31	3.70	9.54	11.77	3.12	2.75	78	3.9	31.4	72.6	126.1	84.5	94.2	43.2
	1.80	0.60	2.55	2.65	2.60	1.96	99	2.9	53.7	108.1	190.5	107.5	111.1	95.4
2361-63-69 Outerwear, Children's & Infants' (43)	3.03	2.36	15.94	17.09	11.72	9.33	28	10.3	5.7	47.4	72.5	60.2	70.2	14.0
	2.13	1.57	9.37	11.97	7.25	5.93	45	7.4	11.4	84.5	138.7	94.4	114.1	33.6
	1.50	0.74	4.72	5.26	5.31	3.89	56	4.6	20.0	171.5	257.5	146.7	150.0	45.3
3321-22-24-25 Iron & Steel Foundries (50)	4.17	9.25	24.82	48.99	9.11	3.98	31	20.0	40.2	19.7	34.3	38.8	72.7	18.2
	2.39	6.16	16.11	29.48	6.10	3.04	43	11.9	58.7	34.2	65.4	56.3	130.2	37.2
	1.79	3.52	10.00	19.87	3.17	2.21	56	7.4	80.9	56.0	107.6	88.1	214.3	86.6
2253 Knit Outerwear Mills (61)	3.98	4.31	14.45	17.95	7.22	6.50	24	12.0	14.5	31.2	41.8	50.1	47.5	8.6
	2.69	1.33	6.77	8.00	4.74	4.22	40	7.4	37.2	49.3	67.6	73.5	86.6	32.0
	1.82	0.30	2.44	3.07	3.54	3.06	49	5.5	79.5	96.9	178.1	91.0	144.8	62.3
2082 Malt Liquors (19)	2.61	4.05	14.15	69.23	25.61	4.59	8	16.4	73.6	25.4	50.7	53.2	91.7	41.1
	1.66	3.23	9.46	30.24	9.28	3.28	12	14.0	85.8	35.2	71.1	106.9	121.6	72.4
	1.32	(1.03)	(6.13)	(10.95)	5.82	2.75	19	9.0	111.6	49.8	101.3	165.2	157.2	265.2
2515 Mattresses & Bedsprings (31)	4.20	3.17	12.87	13.13	9.43	7.30	21	9.3	14.6	28.1	55.1	43.9	59.5	22.6
	3.31	1.98	8.87	9.90	4.63	3.80	34	7.3	28.0	42.3	86.6	61.1	80.1	34.6
	1.92	(0.05)	2.41	5.82	3.54	2.58	52	5.0	59.1	76.6	226.3	87.4	117.7	56.2
2011 Meat Packing Plants (60)	3.67	2.33	18.06	42.42	27.92	17.09	12	36.6	37.9	21.5	45.6	41.8	70.4	13.0
	2.57	1.09	13.29	21.65	18.58	10.61	15	30.7	56.4	42.0	87.3	64.5	134.7	49.8
	1.55	0.40	4.51	10.41	14.15	6.96	18	18.2	84.4	100.0	187.4	97.5	232.9	107.2
3465-66-69 Metal Stampings (75)	4.10	6.45	17.65	30.02	7.06	4.43	33	12.7	31.4	20.0	52.3	43.6	58.0	17.7
	2.53	3.97	10.89	22.32	5.42	3.28	39	8.1	52.6	39.5	88.5	68.4	110.7	44.5
	1.77	1.67	3.87	7.83	3.83	2.11	50	6.3	81.9	81.3	168.9	98.5	160.8	101.5
3541-42-44-45-46-47-49 Metalworking Machy. & Equipment (114)	3.97	5.41	13.99	21.07	6.25	4.13	35	11.0	26.3	22.4	44.6	44.9	52.7	12.3
	2.76	2.93	9.31	12.83	3.85	2.70	48	5.6	42.0	40.6	84.6	80.3	83.5	38.3
	1.86	0.72	2.74	5.18	2.59	1.83	66	3.5	61.5	80.4	162.8	104.0	136.9	72.0
2431 Millwork (52)	4.06	3.51	12.65	14.77	8.73	4.85	25	8.0	21.3	26.5	46.8	49.6	61.0	14.6
	2.69	2.20	6.58	10.15	4.73	3.62	39	6.4	35.0	41.6	80.0	83.6	75.3	45.5
	1.76	0.74	3.27	3.70	3.56	2.46	50	4.9	65.2	92.5	174.7	125.4	111.0	72.2
3592-99 Misc. Machy., except Electrical (72)	4.36	5.56	21.01	36.51	7.01	3.96	32	17.3	33.5	16.6	39.8	31.8	62.9	12.7
	2.68	3.91	12.85	20.86	4.58	3.00	44	7.3	47.8	29.8	81.3	59.9	91.1	31.8
	1.75	2.00	4.32	13.19	3.49	1.62	58	4.4	78.5	73.9	123.5	94.8	167.1	64.4
3714 Motor Vehicle Parts & Accessories (91)	4.15	4.85	15.14	22.67	6.62	4.70	37	7.4	30.8	24.3	44.7	61.5	53.3	11.8
	2.93	3.51	9.82	12.37	4.16	3.07	45	5.2	46.6	41.2	85.0	79.3	70.5	39.7
	2.10	1.55	4.54	5.91	2.98	2.16	60	3.9	70.0	71.1	133.6	98.2	110.2	86.1
3361-62-69 Nonferrous Foundries (51)	4.40	6.97	19.92	34.20	7.91	4.09	35	17.5	27.5	18.3	34.7	34.7	69.8	11.9
	2.91	4.47	11.78	20.51	5.35	3.11	43	8.6	43.6	28.1	55.8	57.5	109.1	28.6
	1.68	2.32	7.87	13.53	3.72	2.37	54	5.7	70.0	55.8	102.8	90.5	125.6	66.3
2541-42 Office & Store Fixtures (42)	5.32	5.05	18.65	25.34	6.59	6.24	30	11.1	11.2	17.4	42.4	46.4	51.2	14.6
	2.94	2.03	8.60	12.28	4.46	3.21	52	8.4	31.8	53.6	93.0	63.5	85.6	43.7
	1.79	0.35	0.86	1.18	2.68	2.12	66	5.5	55.1	91.5	179.3	94.6	143.9	108.3

MANUFACTURING AND CONSTRUCTION (*concluded*)

Line of Business (and number of concerns reporting)	Current assets to current debt (Times)	Net profits on net sales (Per cent)	Net profits on tangible net worth (Per cent)	Net profits on net working capital (Per cent)	Net sales to tangible net worth (Times)	Net sales to net working capital (Times)	Collection period (Days)	Net sales to inventory (Times)	Fixed assets to tangible net worth (Per cent)	Current debt to tangible net worth (Per cent)	Total debt to tangible net worth (Per cent)	Inventory to net working capital (Per cent)	Current debt to inventory (Per cent)	Funded debts to net working capital (Per cent)
2851 Paints, Varnishes, Lacquers & Enamels (87)	3.90 / 2.98 / 2.13	4.66 / 2.71 / 1.46	13.13 / 9.05 / 3.82	19.61 / 11.01 / 5.12	5.26 / 3.26 / 2.48	6.34 / 4.76 / 3.27	31 / 37 / 49	9.2 / 6.1 / 5.2	19.6 / 29.6 / 53.5	22.9 / 38.0 / 68.5	38.5 / 78.1 / 137.2	55.9 / 71.6 / 104.9	53.3 / 75.7 / 106.0	9.2 / 26.6 / 65.3
2621 Paper Mills, except Building Paper (38)	3.12 / 2.55 / 1.85	8.68 / 4.65 / 1.02	14.05 / 10.41 / 10.7	49.77 / 22.78 / 2.05	2.73 / 2.19 / 1.66	8.08 / 4.96 / 3.96	34 / 39 / 53	10.0 / 7.7 / 5.9	56.3 / 90.3 / 111.8	25.2 / 33.5 / 50.4	40.6 / 76.4 / 113.0	54.5 / 75.7 / 103.5	78.8 / 109.2 / 153.0	23.3 / 109.6 / 145.1
2651-52-53-54-55 Paperboard Containers & Boxes (54)	5.38 / 3.52 / 2.35	5.24 / 3.26 / 0.00	13.96 / 7.88 / 3.41	25.94 / 11.83 / 4.05	3.73 / 3.23 / 2.13	6.18 / 4.48 / 3.42	25 / 31 / 37	10.2 / 7.8 / 5.9	29.9 / 45.3 / 91.6	14.2 / 26.4 / 54.3	32.6 / 75.0 / 119.7	39.4 / 53.5 / 81.2	43.5 / 69.1 / 106.7	9.5 / 39.1 / 109.4
3711-13 Passenger Car, Truck & Bus Bodies (52)	3.84 / 2.57 / 1.71	3.61 / 2.37 / 0.71	14.46 / 11.00 / 5.42	21.66 / 13.49 / 5.73	5.73 / 3.63 / 2.54	9.52 / 4.68 / 3.10	20 / 34 / 54	8.0 / 4.7 / 3.7	21.8 / 33.6 / 53.5	35.7 / 46.9 / 118.1	46.8 / 75.7 / 151.0	72.6 / 90.0 / 126.1	50.2 / 79.4 / 127.7	14.3 / 28.1 / 64.4
2911 & 1311 Petroleum Refining (66)	1.86 / 1.38 / 1.19	6.34 / 4.19 / 1.72	23.52 / 15.10 / 9.95	98.27 / 54.49 / 50.52	8.62 / 3.60 / 2.68	24.28 / 14.13 / 7.51	27 / 40 / 57	26.1 / 13.3 / 9.4	58.7 / 96.9 / 136.1	39.1 / 71.8 / 119.1	83.8 / 132.6 / 187.2	53.6 / 84.0 / 234.5	156.9 / 218.9 / 292.2	77.5 / 180.2 / 410.7
2821-22-23-24 Plastics Materials & Synthetics (36)	3.69 / 2.32 / 1.76	4.58 / 2.80 / 1.21	15.60 / 7.81 / 3.64	23.95 / 11.70 / 5.55	4.48 / 2.83 / 1.88	7.46 / 5.04 / 3.06	49 / 55 / 95	10.3 / 7.8 / 5.3	39.5 / 57.0 / 100.5	19.7 / 41.8 / 83.2	38.0 / 96.6 / 169.5	43.4 / 66.4 / 97.4	61.4 / 108.8 / 171.9	19.0 / 50.9 / 143.8
1711 Plumbing, Heating & Air Conditioning (86)	2.97 / 1.76 / 1.34	3.20 / 1.51 / 0.82	14.37 / 10.61 / 6.08	21.15 / 13.49 / 7.23	9.73 / 6.92 / 4.17	14.38 / 8.68 / 5.25	** / ** / **	** / ** / **	11.3 / 18.8 / 34.6	44.1 / 107.9 / 179.3	88.3 / 182.0 / 262.9	** / ** / **	** / ** / **	11.3 / 34.6 / 64.3
2421 Sawmills & Planing Mills (50)	5.11 / 2.76 / 1.73	5.36 / 2.20 / (0.47)	10.34 / 5.42 / (1.71)	34.09 / 9.84 / (4.82)	3.12 / 2.04 / 1.27	6.16 / 3.53 / 2.33	19 / 29 / 44	8.7 / 5.9 / 4.2	22.3 / 36.9 / 70.1	13.0 / 30.2 / 54.0	25.5 / 55.2 / 107.8	41.8 / 71.5 / 101.0	42.8 / 81.8 / 172.4	13.4 / 39.2 / 174.8
3451-52 Screw Machine Products (61)	4.82 / 3.47 / 1.93	6.93 / 4.14 / 1.82	15.60 / 10.90 / 5.33	37.93 / 15.85 / 7.37	4.55 / 2.61 / 1.85	6.77 / 4.81 / 3.19	31 / 38 / 48	11.9 / 6.4 / 4.4	28.0 / 52.8 / 75.9	16.2 / 29.0 / 56.2	42.6 / 66.0 / 124.1	50.1 / 70.3 / 90.5	48.4 / 74.5 / 128.3	23.1 / 57.4 / 87.9
2321-22 Shirts, Underwear & Nightwear, Men's & Boys' (54)	2.75 / 2.21 / 1.57	5.56 / 2.97 / 1.13	20.78 / 13.15 / 6.14	24.31 / 14.98 / 7.03	7.99 / 4.96 / 3.31	9.40 / 5.34 / 3.38	44 / 54 / 61	9.8 / 6.0 / 4.0	5.4 / 13.2 / 25.7	52.5 / 77.0 / 150.9	67.6 / 86.0 / 156.2	66.3 / 86.0 / 131.7	73.9 / 91.7 / 150.7	4.8 / 16.7 / 41.1
2841-42-43-44 Soap, Detergents, Perfumes & Cosmetics (348)	3.88 / 2.40 / 1.60	7.99 / 4.40 / 2.17	31.14 / 17.92 / 8.41	35.60 / 21.79 / 10.67	7.14 / 4.03 / 2.67	8.85 / 5.45 / 3.67	29 / 40 / 55	13.2 / 8.3 / 5.9	17.5 / 35.3 / 65.0	25.6 / 50.6 / 120.7	52.1 / 98.3 / 212.8	43.0 / 64.3 / 95.1	66.3 / 111.1 / 177.7	14.3 / 33.1 / 83.8

Industry														
2086 Soft Drinks, Bottled & Canned (53)	3.55	8.53	29.70	80.50	5.84	15.51	14	26.9	47.8	19.0	35.2	30.4	108.4	10.7
	2.10	6.46	19.05	56.49	3.61	8.53	17	19.5	72.5	31.8	48.1	54.4	154.5	37.3
	1.75	3.62	12.95	33.93	2.72	6.16	22	14.0	105.1	52.9	155.5	82.8	232.2	124.7
3551-52-53-54-55-59 Special Industry Machinery (67)	4.06	6.79	15.72	27.86	3.78	5.46	39	7.2	26.0	27.9	44.9	60.1	53.0	12.5
	2.53	3.82	11.15	14.66	2.85	3.80	61	4.3	35.6	48.0	80.5	80.0	79.1	24.0
	1.90	1.68	5.11	6.08	1.90	2.50	74	3.1	47.5	70.3	100.7	108.9	114.2	49.5
2337 Suits & Coats, Women's & Misses' (54)	2.98	3.57	24.10	33.33	10.79	12.86	27	13.5	3.6	37.0	123.2	51.4	84.8	19.0
	1.96	1.85	12.34	12.63	7.32	8.27	43	10.1	7.4	88.9	174.8	85.1	148.7	28.0
	1.43	1.05	6.41	7.95	3.57	4.57	57	6.0	15.2	187.0	317.6	134.0	200.9	67.7
2311 Suits, Coats & Overcoats, Men's & Boys' (70)	3.89	2.41	10.04	10.26	6.79	6.34	29	11.4	3.3	33.1	68.8	50.5	48.8	10.3
	2.54	1.37	4.18	4.33	4.13	3.56	64	5.5	11.3	65.6	107.6	74.2	69.7	28.5
	1.81	(1.16)	(3.32)	(3.82)	2.90	2.77	90	3.2	31.3	122.2	225.3	107.0	123.1	59.9
3841-42-43 Surgical, Medical & Dental Instruments (50)	4.55	6.65	16.30	22.95	3.19	4.35	43	7.5	13.2	24.5	38.5	54.2	43.5	13.4
	3.22	4.71	12.29	16.36	2.61	3.25	59	4.9	27.8	31.2	60.0	69.0	64.2	25.7
	2.63	3.89	9.49	10.84	2.02	2.43	78	3.8	48.8	42.4	77.4	80.1	96.4	43.4
3942-44-49 Toys, Amusement & Sporting Goods (53)	4.20	5.10	17.23	19.37	3.64	4.65	38	6.9	21.2	28.0	37.7	52.9	51.1	8.1
	2.82	3.27	9.75	11.97	3.03	3.42	58	4.8	38.6	49.9	103.7	80.7	74.0	41.0
	1.99	2.13	6.03	7.09	2.32	2.88	77	3.5	58.1	85.1	127.2	110.1	103.3	78.1
2327 Trousers, Men's & Boys' (43)	3.71	2.44	9.62	10.99	5.88	6.33	40	16.1	4.3	40.6	71.9	35.0	79.4	7.4
	2.29	1.20	5.23	5.31	4.47	4.50	61	7.1	10.2	63.3	80.9	67.9	106.0	18.9
	2.01	0.41	1.61	1.72	3.91	3.55	96	5.3	21.6	86.5	142.6	104.4	147.2	33.3
2341 Underwear & Nightwear, Women's & Children's (45)	3.16	3.65	13.72	18.05	7.46	8.89	25	11.1	4.5	41.1	60.3	59.0	60.6	3.1
	1.96	1.44	7.63	9.06	5.56	6.12	54	7.1	10.4	83.2	119.6	93.1	103.4	19.1
	1.69	0.71	0.52	0.58	3.14	3.51	68	4.8	24.8	143.2	150.8	126.5	180.4	36.1
2511-12 Wood Household Furniture & Upholstered (101)	5.11	3.09	8.87	13.21	4.40	6.28	34	9.2	22.1	18.2	36.1	56.0	42.2	9.4
	3.11	1.74	5.49	7.58	2.79	3.82	46	5.2	37.2	32.1	85.4	79.7	60.0	39.1
	2.01	0.20	0.63	0.65	2.19	3.07	57	3.7	63.3	71.3	138.5	99.4	98.8	81.8
2328 Work Clothing, Men's & Boys' (31)	7.70	5.45	18.81	21.52	6.81	7.15	32	5.5	8.1	16.5	47.2	58.9	25.6	6.6
	3.12	3.37	12.54	13.62	3.14	3.21	42	4.3	16.6	43.7	67.4	76.3	50.4	29.4
	1.78	2.40	7.48	8.28	2.45	2.34	58	3.2	28.3	97.0	117.6	118.0	117.2	44.6

( ) Indicates loss.

** Not computed. Building trades contractors have no inventories in the credit sense of the term. As a general rule, such contractors have no customary selling terms, each contract being a special job for which individual terms are arranged.

FINANCIAL STATEMENT RATIOS BY INDUSTRY

Many quantitative indicators are used to assess the financial strength of an enterprise and the success of its operations. The simplest is to assemble related financial items, such as sales and profits, and express the relationship in the form of a ratio. Using these ratios, various aspects of company operations may be compared with the performance of other companies or groups of companies of similar size or in a similar line of business.

The Quarterly Financial Report's (QFR) ratio formatted income statement and balance sheet tables are expressed as a percent of net sales and total assets, respectively. The operating and financial characteristics of the respective industries and asset size groups are thus reduced to a common denominator to facilitate analysis.

The ratio tables include the following additional basic operating ratios:

1. *Annual rate of profit on stockholders' equity at end of the period* is a ratio obtained by dividing income for the quarter before or after domestic taxes [including branch income (loss) and equity in the earnings of nonconsolidated subsidiaries net of foreign taxes] by stockholders' equity at the end of the quarter; all multiplied by four to put the ratio on annual basis.

2. *Current assets to current liabilities* is a ratio obtained by dividing total current assets by total current liabilities. It is expressed

Source: Quarterly Financial Report, Federal Trade Commission. The exhibits that follow are from the same FTC publication.

as the number of times total current assets cover total current liabilities.

DESCRIPTION OF THE SAMPLE

The sample on which the QFR estimates are based is a composite sample selected from two mutually exclusive sampling frames. The frame from which the major portion of the sample is selected consists of the Internal Revenue Service file of those corporate entities that are required to file form 1120 or 1120-S and that also have as their principal industrial activity manufacturing, mining, retail trade, or wholesale trade. The IRS file is sampled once each year. At the time the sample is selected, the file does not contain those corporate entities whose first income tax return has not been processed. In addition, several months elapse between the selection of this sample and its introduction into the QFR program. To keep the composite QFR sample as up to date as possible, a separate sample is drawn each calendar quarter from a frame comprising all applications for a Federal Social Security Employer's Identification Number filed with the Social Security Administration (SSA) during the previous quarter by new corporations whose principal industrial activity codes fall within the QFR's coverage. In processing the composite list of sample companies, a screening technique is used to insure that corporations drawn from the SSA frame could not have been drawn from the IRS frame.

In sampling from the IRS frame, stratification by industry and size is used, but in sampling from the SSA frame, stratification is by size alone. The measure of size used in the IRS frame is total assets, whereas the measure of size used in the SSA frame is number of employees.

PRESENT VALUE OF $1

Periods until Payment	1%	2%	4%	6%	8%	10%	12%	14%	15%	16%	18%	20%	22%	24%	25%	26%	28%	30%	35%	40%	45%	50%
1	0.990	0.980	0.962	0.943	0.926	0.909	0.893	0.877	0.870	0.862	0.847	0.833	0.820	0.806	0.800	0.794	0.781	0.769	0.741	0.714	0.690	0.667
2	0.980	0.961	0.925	0.890	0.857	0.826	0.797	0.769	0.756	0.743	0.718	0.694	0.672	0.650	0.640	0.630	0.610	0.592	0.549	0.510	0.476	0.444
3	0.971	0.942	0.889	0.840	0.794	0.751	0.712	0.675	0.658	0.641	0.609	0.579	0.551	0.524	0.512	0.500	0.477	0.455	0.406	0.364	0.328	0.296
4	0.961	0.924	0.855	0.792	0.735	0.683	0.636	0.592	0.572	0.552	0.516	0.482	0.451	0.423	0.410	0.397	0.373	0.350	0.301	0.260	0.226	0.198
5	0.951	0.906	0.822	0.747	0.681	0.621	0.567	0.519	0.497	0.476	0.437	0.402	0.370	0.341	0.328	0.315	0.291	0.269	0.223	0.186	0.156	0.132
6	0.942	0.888	0.790	0.705	0.630	0.564	0.507	0.456	0.432	0.410	0.370	0.335	0.303	0.275	0.262	0.250	0.227	0.207	0.165	0.133	0.108	0.088
7	0.933	0.871	0.760	0.665	0.583	0.513	0.452	0.400	0.376	0.354	0.314	0.279	0.249	0.222	0.210	0.198	0.178	0.159	0.122	0.095	0.074	0.059
8	0.923	0.853	0.731	0.627	0.540	0.467	0.404	0.351	0.327	0.305	0.266	0.233	0.204	0.179	0.168	0.157	0.139	0.123	0.091	0.068	0.051	0.039
9	0.914	0.837	0.703	0.592	0.500	0.424	0.361	0.308	0.284	0.263	0.225	0.194	0.167	0.144	0.134	0.125	0.108	0.094	0.067	0.048	0.035	0.026
10	0.905	0.820	0.676	0.558	0.463	0.386	0.322	0.270	0.247	0.227	0.191	0.162	0.137	0.116	0.107	0.099	0.085	0.073	0.050	0.035	0.024	0.017
11	0.896	0.804	0.650	0.527	0.429	0.350	0.287	0.237	0.215	0.195	0.162	0.135	0.112	0.094	0.086	0.079	0.066	0.056	0.037	0.025	0.017	0.012
12	0.887	0.788	0.625	0.497	0.397	0.319	0.257	0.208	0.187	0.168	0.137	0.112	0.092	0.076	0.069	0.062	0.052	0.043	0.027	0.018	0.012	0.008
13	0.879	0.773	0.601	0.469	0.368	0.290	0.229	0.182	0.163	0.145	0.116	0.093	0.075	0.061	0.055	0.050	0.040	0.033	0.020	0.013	0.008	0.005
14	0.870	0.758	0.577	0.442	0.340	0.263	0.205	0.160	0.141	0.125	0.099	0.078	0.062	0.049	0.044	0.039	0.032	0.025	0.015	0.009	0.006	0.003
15	0.861	0.743	0.555	0.417	0.315	0.239	0.183	0.140	0.123	0.108	0.084	0.065	0.051	0.040	0.035	0.031	0.025	0.020	0.011	0.006	0.004	0.002
16	0.853	0.728	0.534	0.394	0.292	0.218	0.163	0.123	0.107	0.093	0.071	0.054	0.042	0.032	0.028	0.025	0.019	0.015	0.008	0.005	0.003	0.002
17	0.844	0.714	0.513	0.371	0.270	0.198	0.146	0.108	0.093	0.080	0.060	0.045	0.034	0.026	0.023	0.020	0.015	0.012	0.006	0.003	0.002	0.001
18	0.836	0.700	0.494	0.350	0.250	0.180	0.130	0.095	0.081	0.069	0.051	0.038	0.028	0.021	0.018	0.016	0.012	0.009	0.005	0.002	0.001	0.001
19	0.828	0.686	0.475	0.331	0.232	0.164	0.116	0.083	0.070	0.060	0.043	0.031	0.023	0.017	0.014	0.012	0.009	0.007	0.003	0.002	0.001	0.001
20	0.820	0.673	0.456	0.312	0.215	0.149	0.104	0.073	0.061	0.051	0.037	0.026	0.019	0.014	0.012	0.010	0.007	0.005	0.002	0.001	0.001	
21	0.811	0.660	0.439	0.294	0.199	0.135	0.093	0.064	0.053	0.044	0.031	0.022	0.015	0.011	0.009	0.008	0.006	0.004	0.002	0.001		
22	0.803	0.647	0.422	0.278	0.184	0.123	0.083	0.056	0.046	0.038	0.026	0.018	0.013	0.009	0.007	0.006	0.004	0.003	0.001			
23	0.795	0.634	0.406	0.262	0.170	0.112	0.074	0.049	0.040	0.033	0.022	0.015	0.010	0.007	0.006	0.004	0.003	0.002	0.001			
24	0.788	0.622	0.390	0.247	0.158	0.102	0.066	0.043	0.035	0.028	0.019	0.013	0.008	0.006	0.005	0.004	0.003	0.002	0.001			
25	0.780	0.610	0.375	0.233	0.146	0.092	0.059	0.038	0.030	0.024	0.016	0.010	0.007	0.005	0.004	0.003	0.002	0.001	0.001			
26	0.772	0.598	0.361	0.220	0.135	0.084	0.053	0.033	0.026	0.021	0.014	0.009	0.006	0.004	0.003	0.002	0.002	0.001				
27	0.764	0.586	0.347	0.207	0.125	0.076	0.047	0.029	0.023	0.018	0.011	0.007	0.005	0.003	0.002	0.002	0.001	0.001				
28	0.757	0.574	0.333	0.196	0.116	0.069	0.042	0.026	0.020	0.016	0.010	0.006	0.004	0.002	0.002	0.001	0.001	0.001				
29	0.749	0.563	0.321	0.185	0.107	0.063	0.037	0.022	0.017	0.014	0.008	0.005	0.003	0.002	0.002	0.001	0.001					
30	0.742	0.552	0.308	0.174	0.099	0.057	0.033	0.020	0.015	0.012	0.007	0.004	0.003	0.002	0.001	0.001	0.001					
40	0.672	0.453	0.208	0.097	0.046	0.022	0.011	0.005	0.004	0.003	0.001	0.001										
50	0.608	0.372	0.141	0.054	0.021	0.009	0.003	0.001	0.001	0.001												

SOURCE: By permission, from Robert N. Anthony, *Management Accounting: Text and Cases*, rev. ed. (Homewood, Ill.: Richard D. Irwin, Inc., 1960), p. 656.

EXHIBIT 1: INCOME STATEMENT FOR CORPORATIONS IN ALL MANUFAC-
TURING, FOOD, TOBACCO, TEXTILE MILL PRODUCTS (ESIC industries 20, 21, 22)

	All Manufacturing*				
	1Q 1976	2Q 1976	3Q 1976†	4Q 1976†	1Q 1977
			($ million)		
Income statement in ratio format					
Net sales, receipts, and operating revenues.............	100.0	100.0	100.0	100.0	100.0
Deduct: Depreciation, depletion, and amortization of property, plant, and equipment.......................	3.0	2.8	2.9	3.0	2.9
Deduct: All other operating costs and expenses (net of purchase discounts)....................................	89.0	88.4	89.0	89.6	89.7
Income (or loss) from operations....................	8.0	8.8	8.1	7.4	7.3
Nonoperating income (expense).........................	−0.3	−0.3	−0.3	−0.3	−0.1
Income (or loss) before income taxes................	7.7	8.5	7.8	7.1	7.2
Net income (loss) of foreign branches and equity in earnings (losses) of nonconsolidated subsidiaries (net of foreign taxes).................................	0.9	1.0	0.8	0.9	1.0
Deduct: Current and deferred domestic income taxes...	3.4	3.6	3.4	3.1	3.2
Income (or loss) after income taxes.................	5.2	5.9	5.3	5.0	5.0
Operating ratios					
Annual rate of profit on stockholders' equity at end o period:			(percent)		
Before income taxes..................................	21.94	25.48	22.33	20.99	21.30
After taxes..	13.30	15.72	13.66	13.11	12.98
Annual rate of profit on total assets:					
Before income taxes..................................	11.79	13.76	12.01	11.29	11.32
After taxes..	7.15	8.49	7.35	7.05	6.92

* During the first quarter of 1977 a considerable number of companies were reclassified by industry. To provide comparability, the four quarters of 1976 have been restated to reflect these reclassifications.
† Revised.

Food and Kindred Products*					Tobacco Manufactures					Textile Mill Products				
1Q 1976	2Q 1976	3Q 1976	4Q 1976	1Q 1977	1Q 1976	2Q 1976	3Q 1976	4Q 1976	1Q 1977	1Q 1976	2Q 1976	3Q 1976	4Q 1976	1Q 1977
($ million)					($ million)					($ million)				
100.0	100.0	100.0	100.0	100.0	100.0	100.0	100.0	100.0	100.0	100.0	100.0	100.0	100.0	100.0
1.6	1.6	1.6	1.7	1.7	1.5	1.9	2.6	2.5	2.2	2.6	2.4	2.5	2.7	2.6
93.1	92.4	92.5	93.2	93.5	82.3	81.8	80.6	81.9	82.1	90.8	91.3	92.5	92.7	92.7
5.4	6.0	5.9	5.1	4.8	16.2	16.3	16.8	15.6	15.6	6.7	6.3	5.0	4.7	4.6
−0.4	−0.3	0.0	−0.5	−0.4	−2.4	−2.8	−2.9	−2.2	−2.6	−1.0	−0.9	−1.2	−2.0	−0.8
4.9	5.7	5.9	4.7	4.4	13.8	13.5	13.9	13.5	13.1	5.7	5.4	3.8	2.6	3.9
0.4	0.5	0.4	0.4	0.3	1.5	2.6	2.6	0.1	2.4	0.1	0.0	0.2	0.2	0.1
2.2	2.5	2.5	2.1	2.0	7.1	7.1	7.4	6.1	6.9	2.7	2.5	1.9	1.3	1.9
3.1	3.7	3.9	3.1	2.7	8.2	9.0	9.2	7.5	8.7	3.0	2.9	2.0	1.6	2.0
(percent)					(percent)					(percent)				
22.88	27.37	27.68	21.71	19.82	28.25	28.50	30.66	27.85	29.52	19.00	18.74	13.17	9.52	13.22
13.33	16.35	16.83	13.06	11.36	15.17	15.98	16.94	15.41	16.47	9.98	10.10	6.60	5.31	6.80
11.53	14.02	14.19	10.97	10.08	14.29	14.43	14.95	13.59	14.46	9.93	9.81	6.77	5.04	6.90
6.71	8.37	8.63	6.60	5.77	7.67	8.09	8.26	7.52	8.07	5.21	5.29	3.40	2.81	3.55

EXHIBIT 2:   BALANCE SHEET IN RATIO FORMAT FOR CORPORATIONS IN ALL
MANUFACTURING, FOOD, TOBACCO, TEXTILE MILL PRODUCTS (ESIC indus-
tries 20, 21, 22)
ITEMS STATED AS A PERCENT OF TOTAL ASSETS

	All Manufacturing*				
	1Q 1976	2Q 1976	3Q 1976†	4Q 1976†	1Q 1977
Assets					
Cash on hand and in banks.............................	3.8	3.9	3.7	4.0	3.6
U.S. government and other securities...................	3.7	3.6	3.5	3.9	3.9
Receivables...	16.3	16.6	16.7	15.7	16.4
Inventories..	21.2	20.9	20.9	21.2	21.0
Current assets not elsewhere specified..................	2.5	2.4	2.4	2.5	2.5
Total current assets.................................	47.4	47.3	47.3	47.2	47.4
Land and depreciable fixed assets......................	65.5	65.2	65.0	65.1	64.9
Deduct: Accumulated depreciation, depletion, and					
amortization.................................	31.0	30.8	30.5	30.3	30.3
Net property, plant, and equipment.................	34.6	34.4	34.5	34.8	34.6
Noncurrent assets not elsewhere specified, including					
investment in nonconsolidated entities, other long-					
term investments, intangibles, etc.....................	18.1	18.2	18.2	18.0	17.9
Total assets..	100.0	100.0	100.0	100.0	100.0
Liabilities and stockholders' equity					
Short-term loans and current installments..............	4.6	4.5	4.3	4.1	4.3
Trade accounts and trade notes payable................	7.9	8.0	8.0	8.4	8.3
Income taxes accrued, prior and current years net of					
payments					
Federal..	2.1	1.9	2.1	2.2	2.3
Other..	0.4	0.4	0.4	0.4	0.4
Other current liabilities..............................	8.4	8.6	8.6	8.4	8.6
Total current liabilities............................	23.4	23.3	23.5	23.5	23.8
Long-term debt due in more than 1 year					
Loans from banks....................................	4.0	3.9	3.7	3.6	3.5
Other long-term debt................................	13.7	13.6	13.7	13.8	14.0
Noncurrent liabilities not elsewhere specified, including					
deferred income taxes...............................	4.8	5.0	5.0	5.1	5.2
Minority stockholders' interest in consolidated domestic					
corporations..	0.3	0.3	0.3	0.3	0.2
Total liabilities.....................................	46.2	46.0	46.2	46.2	46.7
Capital stock and other capital........................	16.6	16.4	16.2	16.0	15.9
Retained earnings......................................	38.2	38.6	38.6	38.7	38.4
Deduct: Treasury stock, at cost........................	1.0	1.0	1.0	1.0	1.0
Stockholders' equity................................	53.8	54.0	53.8	53.8	53.3
Total liabilities and stockholders' equity.............	100.0	100.0	100.0	100.0	100.0
			(times)		
Balance sheet ratios					
Current assets to current liabilities.....................	2.02	2.04	2.02	2.01	1.99
Total cash, U.S. government and other securities to total					
current liabilities......................................	0.32	0.32	0.31	0.33	0.31
Total stockholders' equity to debt......................	2.41	2.47	2.47	2.51	2.46

*During the first quarter of 1977 a considerable number of companies were reclassified by industry.
To provide comparability, the four quarters of 1976 have been restated to reflect these reclassifications.
† Revised.

	Food and Kindred Products*					Tobacco Manufactures					Textile Mill Products				
	1Q 1976	2Q 1976	3Q 1976	4Q 1976	1Q 1977	1Q 1976	2Q 1976	3Q 1976	4Q 1976	1Q 1977	1Q 1976	2Q 1976	3Q 1976	4Q 1976	1Q 1977
	3.9	3.9	3.7	3.9	3.5	1.0	1.5	1.5	1.8	1.9	4.0	4.0	3.6	4.4	3.3
	2.9	2.8	2.8	2.4	2.6	0.8	0.8	0.7	0.2	0.3	1.5	1.7	1.9	1.7	1.5
	16.0	16.2	16.4	15.8	16.1	8.7	8.7	9.6	9.5	10.6	25.6	25.7	25.9	24.6	25.0
	24.2	23.5	23.9	25.2	24.7	39.2	35.7	35.6	37.0	36.1	28.5	28.5	28.8	28.4	29.6
	2.4	2.5	2.5	2.5	2.5	0.9	0.7	0.7	0.7	0.6	1.9	1.8	1.8	1.8	1.9
	49.4	48.9	49.3	49.8	49.4	50.6	47.3	48.1	49.2	49.5	61.5	61.7	62.0	60.8	61.3
	59.8	60.5	60.2	59.4	60.0	28.4	28.7	32.6	32.7	32.8	68.6	69.2	69.0	70.9	69.9
	26.2	26.4	26.3	25.9	26.0	10.8	10.8	10.6	10.5	10.5	38.0	38.7	38.7	39.8	39.2
	33.6	34.1	33.9	33.5	34.0	17.6	17.8	21.9	22.3	22.2	30.6	30.6	30.3	31.1	30.7
	17.0	17.0	16.9	16.7	16.6	31.8	34.8	30.0	28.5	28.3	7.9	7.7	7.7	8.0	8.0
	100.0	100.0	100.0	100.0	100.0	100.0	100.0	100.0	100.0	100.0	100.0	100.0	100.0	100.0	100.0
	8.0	7.0	6.9	7.4	7.4	6.8	9.9	7.7	6.9	5.2	8.3	8.5	8.8	7.5	7.4
	9.2	9.5	9.8	10.3	10.0	3.6	2.9	5.0	4.9	3.7	12.5	12.1	12.5	11.9	13.3
	1.9	1.7	1.7	1.6	1.7	2.8	1.2	1.5	2.1	2.8	1.6	1.6	1.8	1.6	1.2
	0.4	0.4	0.4	0.4	0.4	0.4	0.4	0.4	0.5	0.5	0.3	0.3	0.3	0.3	0.2
	6.8	7.0	6.7	6.6	6.3	4.5	5.0	5.1	6.9	5.0	4.8	5.2	5.0	4.8	5.0
	26.2	25.4	25.5	26.3	25.7	18.2	19.4	19.8	21.3	17.0	27.6	27.7	28.2	26.1	27.2
	4.0	4.2	4.2	4.2	4.1	8.7	8.5	8.3	7.8	7.8	5.2	5.0	4.9	4.9	5.1
	15.1	14.9	14.6	14.6	14.8	18.6	17.7	19.5	18.2	22.6	12.9	13.0	13.3	13.6	13.3
	3.8	3.9	4.0	4.1	4.2	3.8	3.7	3.5	3.7	3.5	1.9	1.9	2.0	2.3	2.0
	0.4	0.4	0.4	0.4	0.4	0.1	0.1	0.1	0.1	0.1	0.1	0.1	0.1	0.2	0.2
	49.6	48.8	48.7	49.5	49.2	49.4	49.4	51.2	51.2	51.0	47.7	47.7	48.6	47.0	47.8
	15.7	15.5	15.2	14.9	15.3	11.9	11.8	11.2	10.8	10.6	14.9	14.9	14.9	15.2	14.3
	35.6	36.7	37.1	36.5	36.4	40.3	40.3	39.1	39.4	39.7	38.9	39.3	38.2	39.3	39.6
	0.9	1.0	0.9	0.9	0.9	1.6	1.5	1.5	1.3	1.3	1.6	1.8	1.6	1.5	1.7
	50.4	51.2	51.3	50.5	50.8	50.6	50.6	48.8	48.8	49.0	52.3	52.3	51.4	53.0	52.2
	100.0	100.0	100.0	100.0	100.0	100.0	100.0	100.0	100.0	100.0	100.0	100.0	100.0	100.0	100.0
	(times)					(times)					(times)				
	1.88	1.92	1.93	1.90	1.92	2.78	2.44	2.43	2.31	2.91	2.23	2.23	2.20	2.33	2.25
	0.26	0.26	0.25	0.24	0.24	0.10	0.12	0.11	0.09	0.13	0.20	0.21	0.20	0.23	0.18
	1.86	1.97	1.99	1.93	1.95	1.48	1.40	1.37	1.48	1.38	1.98	1.98	1.91	2.04	2.02

EXHIBIT 3: INCOME STATEMENT FOR CORPORATIONS IN PRINTING AND PUBLISHING, CHEMICALS, DRUGS (ESIC industries 27, 28, 28.1, 28.3)

	Printing and Publishing				
	1Q 1976	2Q 1976	3Q 1976	4Q 1976	1Q 1977
	($ million)				
Income statement in ratio format					
Net sales, receipts, and operating revenues.............	100.0	100.0	100.0	100.0	100.0
Deduct: Depreciation, depletion, and amortization of property, plant, and equipment..............	2.6	2.5	2.6	2.5	2.5
Deduct: All other operating costs and expenses (net of purchase discounts).........................	89.1	87.0	87.0	87.9	89.5
Income (or loss) from operations...................	8.2	10.4	10.5	9.5	8.0
Nonoperating income (expense)........................	−0.3	−0.5	−0.5	0.0	−0.3
Income (or loss) before income taxes..............	7.9	10.0	10.0	9.5	7.7
Net income (loss) of foreign branches and equity in earnings (losses) of nonconsolidated subsidiaries (net of foreign taxes)................................	0.2	0.1	0.1	−0.1	0.1
Deduct: Current and deferred domestic income taxes...	3.6	4.5	4.6	4.4	3.6
Income (or loss) after income taxes................	4.4	5.6	5.4	5.0	4.2
Operations ratios					
Annual rate of profit on stockholders' equity at end of period:	(percent)				
Before income taxes...................................	22.27	29.44	30.04	29.29	23.63
After taxes..	12.26	16.30	16.31	15.37	12.73
Annual rate of profit on total assets:					
Before income taxes.................................	12.16	16.24	15.67	15.71	11.92
After taxes...	6.69	8.99	8.51	8.24	6.42

* Included in Chemicals and Allied Products.
† During the first quarter of 1977 a considerable number of companies were reclassified by industry. To provide comparability, the four quarters of 1976 have been restated to reflect these reclassifications.

	Chemicals and Allied Products†					Industrial Chemicals and Synthetics*					Drugs*				
	1Q 1976	2Q 1976	3Q 1976	4Q 1976	1Q 1977	1Q 1976	2Q 1976	3Q 1976	4Q 1976	1Q 1977	1Q 1976	2Q 1976	3Q 1976	4Q 1976	1Q 1977
	($ million)					($ million)					($ million)				
	100.0	100.0	100.0	100.0	100.0	100.0	100.0	100.0	100.0	100.0	100.0	100.0	100.0	100.0	100.0
	3.7	3.5	3.6	3.8	3.7	5.1	4.8	5.2	5.3	5.2	2.3	2.5	2.3	2.4	2.3
	83.6	84.4	85.0	87.0	85.4	81.2	82.1	83.7	85.6	84.0	83.0	83.9	83.0	85.2	83.1
	12.7	12.2	11.3	9.2	10.9	13.8	13.1	11.2	9.1	10.8	14.7	13.7	14.8	12.5	14.6
	−0.6	−0.3	−0.1	−0.1	−0.4	−0.9	−0.8	−0.3	−0.6	−0.8	0.5	1.0	−0.1	0.2	0.4
	12.1	11.9	11.2	9.0	10.4	12.8	12.3	10.9	8.6	10.0	15.1	14.7	14.7	12.6	15.0
	1.2	1.1	1.2	1.1	1.2	0.4	0.4	0.2	0.1	0.5	4.3	4.7	5.3	4.4	4.4
	5.4	5.0	4.8	3.7	4.7	5.5	5.1	4.4	3.2	4.0	7.0	6.8	7.4	6.0	7.3
	8.0	8.1	7.5	6.4	7.0	7.8	7.6	6.7	5.5	6.5	12.3	12.7	12.6	11.0	12.1
	(percent)					(percent)					(percent)				
	27.66	27.81	25.30	20.40	24.60	27.38	27.20	22.22	17.32	22.29	29.46	27.90	29.68	25.54	29.54
	16.55	17.21	15.31	12.83	14.86	16.15	16.28	13.47	11.00	13.69	18.78	18.22	18.67	16.52	18.36
	15.35	15.59	14.10	11.29	13.50	14.35	14.42	11.71	8.98	11.46	18.61	17.92	18.97	16.18	18.58
	9.18	9.65	8.53	7.10	8.16	8.46	8.63	7.10	5.70	7.04	11.86	11.70	11.93	10.46	11.55

EXHIBIT 4: BALANCE SHEET IN RATIO FORMAT FOR CORPORATIONS IN PRINTING AND PUBLISHING, CHEMICALS, DRUGS (ESIC industries 27, 28, 28.1, 28.3)

ITEMS STATED AS A PERCENT OF TOTAL ASSETS

	Printing and Publishing				
	1Q 1976	2Q 1976	3Q 1976	4Q 1976	1Q 1977
Assets					
Cash on hand and in banks.............................	8.0	7.6	7.6	7.9	7.9
U.S. government and other securities..................	4.7	5.0	4.5	5.1	4.9
Receivables...	20.9	21.1	22.4	22.2	20.8
Inventories...	12.9	13.0	12.8	12.7	12.5
Current assets not elsewhere specified.................	4.2	3.9	3.9	3.9	4.1
Total current assets.................................	50.7	50.7	51.2	51.6	50.3
Land and depreciable fixed assets.....................	57.8	58.2	55.7	56.2	54.5
Deduct: Accumulated depreciation, depletion, and amortization...	26.3	26.7	25.7	26.1	25.1
Net property, plant, and equipment................	31.4	31.5	30.0	30.1	29.5
Noncurrent assets not elsewhere specified, including investment in nonconsolidated entities, other long-term investments, intangibles, etc....................	17.9	17.9	18.8	18.4	20.3
Total assets..	100.0	100.0	100.0	100.0	100.0
Liabilities and stockholders' equity					
Short-term loans and current installments..............	4.1	4.4	4.8	4.6	5.0
Trade accounts and trade notes payable..............	8.4	8.7	8.5	8.9	9.0
Income taxes accrued, prior and current years, net of payments					
Federal...	2.2	2.1	2.3	2.5	2.2
Other...	0.3	0.2	0.2	0.4	0.3
Other current liabilities.................................	7.2	7.4	7.5	7.5	7.5
Total current liabilities.............................	22.2	22.8	23.3	23.9	23.9
Long-term debt due in more than 1 year					
Loans from banks...................................	5.8	5.3	5.0	4.7	4.9
Other long-term debt................................	9.3	8.9	11.0	9.0	11.0
Noncurrent liabilities not elsewhere specified, including deferred income taxes................................	7.7	7.6	8.2	8.4	9.4
Minority stockholders' interest in consolidated domestic corporations...	0.3	0.3	0.3	0.3	0.3
Total liabilities......................................	45.4	44.8	47.8	46.4	49.6
Capital stock and other capital.........................	14.8	14.2	13.7	13.4	12.9
Retained earnings......................................	41.8	43.0	40.5	42.1	39.3
Deduct: Treasury stock, at cost........................	2.0	2.0	2.0	1.9	1.8
Stockholders' equity................................	54.6	55.2	52.2	53.6	50.4
Total liabilities and stockholders' equity.............	100.0	100.0	100.0	100.0	100.0
			(times)		
Balance sheet ratios					
Current assets to current liabilities......................	2.28	2.22	2.20	2.16	2.10
Total cash, U.S. government and other securities to total current liabilities................................	0.57	0.55	0.52	0.54	0.54
Total stockholders' equity to debt......................	2.84	2.97	2.50	2.93	2.41

* Included in Chemicals and Allied Products.

† During the first quarter of 1977 a considerable number of companies were reclassified by industry. To provide comparability, the four quarters of 1976 have been restated to reflect these reclassifications.

	Chemicals and Allied Products†					Industrial Chemicals and Synthetics*					Drugs*				
	1Q 1976	2Q 1976	3Q 1976	4Q 1976	1Q 1977	1Q 1976	2Q 1976	3Q 1976	4Q 1976	1Q 1977	1Q 1976	2Q 1976	3Q 1976	4Q 1976	1Q 1977
	3.4	3.4	3.5	3.6	3.1	2.5	2.4	2.2	2.7	2.3	5.5	5.0	5.7	4.7	4.8
	3.5	3.4	3.3	3.1	3.1	3.0	2.7	2.5	2.2	2.2	2.0	2.2	1.9	1.9	1.8
	16.2	16.0	16.0	14.9	16.5	16.5	16.6	16.3	15.2	16.8	14.4	13.5	13.0	13.8	14.5
	17.3	17.6	17.4	17.9	17.0	15.0	15.5	15.6	15.9	14.8	17.6	18.1	17.9	17.5	17.0
	2.8	2.6	2.7	2.6	2.7	2.8	2.4	2.5	2.5	2.3	2.8	3.0	3.2	3.4	3.9
	43.2	43.0	42.9	42.0	42.4	39.8	39.7	39.1	38.4	38.4	42.4	41.7	41.7	41.2	42.0
	72.0	72.2	71.8	72.3	71.9	91.6	91.8	91.6	91.8	92.1	43.4	43.6	43.2	42.7	41.7
	33.6	33.4	33.1	32.9	32.7	46.5	46.3	46.0	45.5	45.6	16.4	16.5	16.3	16.2	16.8
	38.5	38.8	38.8	39.4	39.1	45.0	45.4	45.6	46.3	46.5	27.0	27.1	26.9	26.4	25.6
	18.3	18.2	18.3	18.6	18.5	15.2	14.9	15.3	15.2	15.0	30.5	31.2	31.4	32.4	32.4
	100.0	100.0	100.0	100.0	100.0	100.0	100.0	100.0	100.0	100.0	100.0	100.0	100.0	100.0	100.0
	3.4	3.2	3.1	3.0	3.6	3.2	2.7	2.7	2.4	2.8	3.8	3.9	3.7	3.9	4.8
	6.4	6.5	6.2	6.8	6.6	5.9	5.9	5.8	6.6	6.2	3.6	3.6	3.5	4.6	4.0
	2.5	2.0	2.4	2.0	2.4	2.4	2.0	2.2	2.0	2.2	2.8	1.7	1.9	2.0	3.0
	0.5	0.4	0.4	0.4	0.4	0.5	0.4	0.4	0.4	0.4	0.4	0.3	0.4	0.5	0.4
	5.8	5.7	6.0	5.6	5.5	5.7	5.5	5.5	5.1	5.1	6.5	6.6	7.7	7.0	6.7
	18.7	17.7	18.1	17.9	18.5	17.7	16.5	16.7	16.6	16.8	17.2	16.1	17.1	17.9	18.8
	4.1	3.8	3.5	3.0	2.9	4.4	4.0	3.4	2.5	2.6	1.1	1.1	1.3	1.4	1.2
	16.8	17.3	17.3	18.1	18.1	19.2	20.0	20.6	21.9	22.0	15.1	15.0	14.1	13.6	13.4
	4.7	5.0	5.0	5.4	5.3	5.9	6.1	6.3	6.7	6.8	3.4	3.6	3.4	3.7	3.7
	0.2	0.2	0.2	0.2	0.2	0.4	0.4	0.4	0.4	0.4	0.0	0.0	0.0	0.0	0.0
	44.5	43.9	44.3	44.6	45.1	47.6	47.0	47.3	48.1	48.6	36.8	35.8	36.1	36.7	37.1
	16.3	16.2	16.1	15.9	15.7	17.4	17.3	17.3	16.9	16.8	15.4	15.3	15.3	14.9	14.4
	40.1	40.8	40.5	40.3	40.1	36.0	36.8	36.5	35.9	35.7	48.3	49.5	49.1	49.0	49.0
	0.9	0.9	0.9	0.9	1.0	1.0	1.0	1.0	1.0	1.1	0.6	0.6	0.5	0.5	0.5
	55.5	56.1	55.7	55.4	54.9	52.4	43.0	52.7	51.9	51.4	63.2	64.2	63.9	63.3	62.9
	100.0	100.0	100.0	100.0	100.0	100.0	100.0	100.0	100.0	100.0	100.0	100.0	100.0	100.0	100.0
		(times)					(times)					(times)			
	2.31	2.43	2.36	2.34	2.29	2.25	2.40	2.34	2.31	2.28	2.47	2.59	2.43	2.30	2.24
	0.37	0.38	0.38	0.37	0.33	0.31	0.31	0.28	0.29	0.27	0.43	0.45	0.45	0.37	0.35
	2.28	2.31	2.32	2.29	2.23	1.96	1.98	1.98	1.93	1.88	3.16	3.23	3.35	3.35	3.27

EXHIBIT 5: INCOME STATEMENT FOR CORPORATIONS IN PAPER, PETRO-
LEUM, COAL, RUBBER, PLASTICS (ESIC industries 26, 29, 30 and other nondurable manufacturing products)

	Paper and Allied Products				
	1Q 1976	2Q 1976	3Q 1976	4Q 1976	1Q 1977
			($ million)		
Income statement and ratio format					
Net sales, receipts, and operating revenues..............	100.0	100.0	100.0	100.0	100.0
Deduct: Depreciation, depletion, and amortization of property, plant, and equipment..............	3.5	3.6	3.5	3.5	3.6
Deduct: All other operating costs and expenses (net of purchase discounts)..........................	86.3	85.9	87.3	88.4	88.5
Income (or loss) from operations....................	10.2	10.5	9.2	8.1	7.9
Nonoperating income (expense)........................	−1.0	−0.9	−1.0	−1.3	−1.0
Income (or loss) before income taxes................	9.2	9.6	8.3	6.8	6.9
Net income (loss) of foreign branches and equity in earnings (losses) of nonconsolidated subsidiaries (net of foreign taxes).................................	0.7	1.0	0.9	0.8	0.6
Deduct: Current and deferred domestic income taxes...	3.8	3.9	3.4	3.0	2.7
Income (or loss) after income taxes.................	6.1	6.7	5.7	4.7	4.8
Operating ratios (based on preceding industry dollar tables)					
Annual rate of profit on stockholders' equity at end of period:			(percent)		
Before income taxes..................................	23.38	25.77	21.60	17.90	17.40
After taxes..	14.48	16.26	13.55	10.94	11.16
Annual rate of profit on total assets:					
Before income taxes..................................	12.45	13.88	11.70	9.62	9.32
After taxes..	7.71	8.76	7.34	5.88	5.98

* During the first quarter of 1977 a considerable number of companies were reclassified by industry. To
provide comparability, the four quarters of 1976 have been restated to reflect these reclassifications.
† Revised.

	Petroleum and Coal Products*					Rubber and Miscellaneous Plastics Products					Other Nondurable Manufacturing Products*				
	1Q 1976	2Q 1976	3Q 1976	4Q 1976	1Q 1977	1Q 1976	2Q 1976	3Q 1976	4Q 1976	1Q 1977	1Q 1976	2Q 1976	3Q 1976	4Q† 1976	1Q 1977
	($ million)					($ million)					($ million)				
	100.0	100.0	100.0	100.0	100.0	100.0	100.0	100.0	100.0	100.0	100.0	100.0	100.0	100.0	100.0
	4.2	4.2	4.1	4.2	3.9	3.1	2.7	2.9	2.9	2.8	1.0	0.9	1.0	1.1	1.1
	86.0	86.7	85.9	87.3	88.7	89.8	89.5	91.6	89.4	89.7	93.4	93.6	93.3	94.0	93.8
	9.7	9.2	10.0	8.5	7.4	7.2	7.8	5.4	7.8	7.5	5.7	5.4	5.7	4.9	5.1
	1.2	1.4	0.5	0.9	1.7	−0.9	−0.8	−0.9	−0.7	−0.4	−0.5	−0.3	−0.4	−0.6	−0.4
	10.8	10.6	10.5	9.4	9.1	6.3	7.1	4.5	7.1	7.1	5.2	5.1	5.3	4.4	4.7
	1.5	1.9	1.5	1.7	1.8	0.6	0.5	0.2	0.1	0.4	0.1	0.2	0.2	0.1	0.2
	3.8	3.7	3.8	3.3	3.2	3.0	3.0	1.9	3.2	3.1	2.4	2.5	2.5	2.2	2.4
	8.5	8.8	8.1	7.8	7.7	3.9	4.5	2.8	4.0	4.3	2.9	2.8	3.1	2.4	2.4
	(percent)					(percent)					(percent)				
	20.87	20.70	20.20	19.53	19.64	18.77	22.58	12.98	20.52	21.41	24.69	25.11	25.98	21.75	21.01
	14.35	14.55	13.74	13.76	13.87	10.63	13.38	7.61	11.43	12.35	13.49	13.51	14.46	11.35	10.55
	12.81	12.60	12.23	11.76	11.72	9.42	11.61	6.78	10.61	10.79	12.33	12.33	12.96	10.95	10.81
	8.81	8.86	8.31	8.29	8.28	5.33	6.88	3.98	5.91	6.23	6.74	6.64	7.21	5.72	5.43

EXHIBIT 6: BALANCE SHEET IN RATIO FORMAT FOR CORPORATIONS IN PAPER, PETROLEUM, COAL, RUBBER, PLASTICS (ESIC industries 26, 29, 30, and other nondurable manufacturing products)

ITEMS STATED AS A PERCENT OF TOTAL ASSETS

	Paper and Allied Products				
	1Q 1976	2Q 1976	3Q 1976	4Q 1976	1Q 1977
Assets					
Cash on hand and in banks............................	3.9	4.1	4.1	4.0	3.5
U.S. government and other securities...................	2.0	1.9	2.3	2.7	2.3
Receivables...	12.6	13.0	13.2	12.5	12.9
Inventories...	14.7	15.1	14.8	15.2	15.4
Current assets not elsewhere specified.................	2.6	2.5	2.7	2.8	2.6
Total current assets................................	35.9	36.6	37.1	37.2	36.7
Land and depreciable fixed assets......................	84.8	84.6	84.4	85.2	85.3
Deduct: Accumulated depreciation, depletion, and amortization..	36.8	36.6	36.4	36.3	36.5
Net property, plant, and equipment.................	48.0	48.0	48.0	48.9	48.8
Noncurrent assets not elsewhere specified, including investment in nonconsolidated entities, other long-term investments, intangibles, etc.....................	16.1	15.4	14.9	13.9	14.5
Total assets..	100.0	100.0	100.0	100.0	100.0
Liabilities and stockholders' equity					
Short-term loans and current installments..............	4.7	4.0	3.7	3.9	4.0
Trade accounts and trade notes payable................	5.9	6.1	6.2	6.5	6.5
Income taxes accrued, prior and current years, net of payments					
Federal..	1.4	1.2	1.4	1.3	1.3
Other..	0.3	0.2	0.3	0.3	0.3
Other current liabilities...............................	5.3	5.5	5.2	5.0	5.1
Total current liabilities.............................	17.6	17.0	16.7	17.0	17.2
Long-term debt due in more than 1 year					
Loans from banks..................................	3.7	3.8	3.6	3.3	3.5
Other long-term debt...............................	20.5	20.2	20.6	20.6	20.3
Noncurrent liabilities not elsewhere specified, including deferred income taxes................................	4.5	4.6	4.5	4.9	4.9
Minority stockholders' interest in consolidated domestic corporations..	0.4	0.4	0.4	0.5	0.6
Total liabilities.....................................	46.7	46.1	45.8	46.3	46.4
Capital stock and other capital.........................	17.8	17.8	18.3	18.2	18.2
Retained earnings.....................................	36.4	37.0	36.8	36.5	36.3
Deduct: Treasury stock, at cost.......................	0.9	0.9	0.9	0.9	1.0
Stockholders' equity..............................	53.3	53.9	54.2	53.7	53.6
Total liabilities and stockholders' equity.............	100.0	100.0	100.0	100.0	100.0
			(times)		
Balance sheet ratios					
Current assets to current liabilities.....................	2.04	2.15	2.22	2.18	2.14
Total cash, U.S. government and other securities to total current liabilities......................................	0.34	0.35	0.38	0.39	0.34
Total stockholders' equity to debt......................	1.85	1.92	1.94	1.94	1.93

* During the first quarter of 1977 a considerable number of companies were reclassified by industry. To provide comparability, the four quarters of 1976 have been restated to reflect these reclassifications.
† Revised.

Petroleum and Coal Products*					Rubber and Miscellaneous Plastics Products					Other Nondurable Manufacturing Products*				
1Q 1976	2Q 1976	3Q 1976	4Q 1976	1Q 1977	1Q 1976	2Q 1976	3Q 1976	4Q 1976	1Q 1977	1Q 1976	2Q 1976	3Q 1976	4Q† 1976	1Q 1977
2.8	2.7	2.4	2.7	2.6	3.5	3.4	4.2	4.3	3.7	6.5	5.9	5.3	6.8	6.0
5.5	5.0	4.3	4.8	5.1	1.6	2.1	2.7	2.6	1.9	1.8	1.4	1.2	1.7	1.9
10.0	10.4	10.6	10.4	10.1	19.6	20.6	20.1	19.8	22.0	28.6	28.0	30.4	28.7	28.3
7.0	7.0	7.4	7.2	7.2	23.5	21.8	20.7	22.2	22.6	36.8	39.0	37.3	36.7	37.6
1.0	0.8	1.0	1.0	1.0	2.4	2.4	2.4	2.7	2.6	3.2	3.0	3.3	3.2	3.4
26.3	25.9	25.7	26.1	26.1	50.6	50.3	50.1	51.6	52.8	77.0	77.3	77.4	77.0	77.2
82.0	81.3	81.6	81.2	81.7	63.9	64.7	65.7	64.9	62.9	30.1	30.0	30.1	30.4	29.7
36.5	36.0	35.7	35.2	35.3	31.1	31.6	32.3	31.9	31.2	15.0	14.8	15.2	15.3	15.2
45.5	45.3	45.9	46.0	46.4	32.9	33.1	33.3	32.9	31.7	15.1	15.2	14.9	15.1	14.6
28.2	28.8	28.4	27.9	27.5	16.5	16.7	16.5	15.5	15.5	8.0	7.5	7.7	7.8	8.2
100.0	100.0	100.0	100.0	100.0	100.0	100.0	100.0	100.0	100.0	100.0	100.0	100.0	100.0	100.0
2.1	2.1	2.2	1.6	1.6	4.9	4.1	4.0	3.7	6.3	10.1	11.0	11.3	9.7	9.3
7.2	7.5	7.4	8.2	8.2	8.2	8.0	8.3	9.1	8.7	16.8	16.8	15.0	15.3	15.1
2.4	2.1	2.4	2.5	2.4	2.5	2.3	2.2	2.5	2.7	2.0	1.8	1.9	2.1	2.0
0.4	0.4	0.4	0.4	0.4	0.5	0.5	0.5	0.5	0.6	0.3	0.3	0.3	0.4	0.3
3.4	3.4	3.6	3.3	3.5	7.8	8.1	7.9	7.7	7.6	6.3	6.7	6.7	6.7	6.7
15.6	15.3	16.0	16.0	15.9	23.7	23.1	22.8	23.5	26.0	35.5	36.6	35.2	34.2	33.3
1.2	1.3	1.5	1.4	1.2	4.3	4.4	4.2	4.2	4.3	4.2	4.3	4.5	5.3	4.1
12.5	13.0	12.9	13.0	13.6	18.4	17.6	17.2	17.0	15.7	8.2	8.1	8.3	8.1	8.9
8.9	9.1	8.8	9.0	9.4	3.2	3.4	3.4	3.5	3.5	2.0	1.8	2.1	1.9	2.1
0.4	0.4	0.4	0.3	0.2	0.2	0.2	0.2	0.2	0.2	0.2	0.1	0.1	0.1	0.1
38.6	39.1	39.5	39.8	40.3	49.8	48.6	47.8	48.3	49.6	50.0	50.9	50.1	49.6	48.5
16.5	16.4	16.0	15.7	15.7	13.5	13.7	14.1	13.8	13.3	15.4	14.9	15.3	15.5	15.8
45.6	45.1	45.1	45.2	44.6	38.0	39.1	39.4	39.2	38.4	36.3	35.8	36.3	36.6	37.5
0.7	0.7	0.6	0.7	0.7	1.3	1.3	1.3	1.3	1.3	1.8	1.5	1.7	1.7	1.8
61.4	60.9	60.5	60.2	59.7	50.2	51.4	52.2	51.7	50.4	50.0	49.1	49.9	50.4	51.5
100.0	100.0	100.0	100.0	100.0	100.0	100.0	100.0	100.0	100.0	100.0	100.0	100.0	100.0	100.0
		(times)					(times)					(times)		
1.68	1.69	1.61	1.63	1.64	2.13	2.18	2.20	2.20	2.04	2.17	2.11	2.20	2.25	2.32
0.53	0.50	0.42	0.47	0.49	0.21	0.24	0.30	0.30	0.22	0.23	0.20	0.19	0.25	0.24
3.84	3.71	3.67	3.76	3.64	1.82	1.97	2.07	2.08	1.91	2.21	2.10	2.07	2.19	2.31

EXHIBIT 7: INCOME STATEMENT FOR CORPORATIONS IN STONE, CLAY, GLASS, PRIMARY METAL, IRON, STEEL, NONFERROUS METALS (ESIC industries 32, 33, 33.1–2, 33.5–6)

	Stone, Clay, and Glass Products				
	1Q 1976	2Q 1976	3Q 1976	4Q 1976	1Q 1977
			($ million)		
Income statement in ratio format					
Net sales, receipts, and operating revenues.............	100.0	100.0	100.0	100.0	100.0
Deduct: Depreciation, depletion, and amortization of property, plant, and equipment.......................	4.3	3.7	3.5	3.7	4.2
Deduct: All other operating costs and expenses (net of purchase discounts)...........................	90.5	86.1	86.6	88.9	91.2
Income (or loss) from operations....................	5.2	10.2	9.8	7.4	4.6
Nonoperating income (expense).........................	−0.6	−0.7	−0.5	−0.4	−0.2
Income (or loss) before income taxes................	4.6	9.5	9.3	7.0	4.3
Net income (loss) of foreign branches and equity in earnings (losses) of nonconsolidated subsidiaries (net of foreign taxes)..................................	0.3	0.4	0.4	0.2	0.3
Deduct: Current and deferred domestic income taxes...	2.6	3.7	3.4	2.7	2.3
Income (or loss) after income taxes................	2.3	6.2	6.2	4.6	2.4
Operations ratios (based on preceding industry dollar tables)					
Annual rate of profit on stockholders' equity at end of period:			(percent)		
Before income taxes..................................	10.41	24.83	25.02	17.46	10.12
After taxes..	4.82	15.52	16.13	11.14	5.13
Annual rate of profit on total assets:					
Before income taxes..................................	5.71	13.56	13.51	9.47	5.53
After taxes..	2.64	8.48	8.71	6.04	2.80

* Included in Primary Metal Industries.
† During the first quarter of 1977 a considerable number of companies were reclassified by industry. To provide comparability, the four quarters of 1976 have been restated to reflect these reclassifications.

Primary Metal Industries†					Iron and Steel*					Nonferrous Metals*†				
1Q 1976	2Q 1976	3Q 1976	4Q 1976	1Q 1977	1Q 1976	2Q 1976	3Q 1976	4Q 1976	1Q 1977	1Q 1976	2Q 1976	3Q 1976	4Q 1976	1Q 1977
($ million)					($ million)					($ million)				
100.0	100.0	100.0	100.0	100.0	100.0	100.0	100.0	100.0	100.0	100.0	100.0	100.0	100.0	100.0
3.6	3.3	3.5	3.6	3.5	3.5	3.3	3.5	3.5	3.6	3.7	3.2	3.5	3.7	3.4
90.8	89.4	91.0	92.2	93.0	90.5	89.6	91.2	91.9	94.1	91.4	89.1	90.6	92.8	90.6
5.6	7.3	5.5	4.3	3.5	6.0	7.1	5.4	4.6	2.3	4.8	7.7	5.8	3.5	5.9
−0.9	−0.9	−1.1	−1.2	−0.9	−0.7	−0.6	−1.1	−0.8	−0.6	−1.4	−1.6	−1.3	−2.0	−1.2
4.7	6.4	4.4	3.1	2.7	5.3	6.6	4.3	3.8	1.7	3.5	6.0	4.5	1.5	4.6
0.7	0.9	0.8	1.2	0.7	0.3	0.7	0.6	1.0	0.4	1.5	1.4	1.1	1.8	1.2
1.8	2.5	1.2	0.7	0.9	1.9	2.4	0.9	0.9	0.5	1.7	2.7	1.7	0.2	1.9
3.6	4.8	3.9	3.6	2.4	3.8	4.8	3.9	3.8	1.6	3.3	4.8	3.8	3.1	4.0
(percent)					(percent)					(percent)				
11.07	16.55	10.89	8.73	7.20	12.24	17.05	10.89	10.01	4.63	8.95	15.62	10.88	6.31	11.95
7.37	10.87	8.28	7.29	5.11	8.12	11.33	8.74	7.94	3.47	6.01	10.01	7.43	6.07	8.14
5.82	8.68	5.65	4.51	3.64	6.59	9.18	5.76	5.28	2.39	4.51	7.80	5.47	3.14	5.83
3.87	5.70	4.30	3.77	2.58	4.37	6.10	4.62	4.19	1.79	3.03	5.00	3.73	3.02	3.97

EXHIBIT 8: BALANCE SHEET IN RATIO FORMAT FOR CORPORATIONS IN STONE, CLAY, GLASS, PRIMARY METALS, IRON, STEEL, NONFERROUS METALS (ESIC industries 32, 33, 33.1–2, 33.5–6)

ITEMS STATED AS A PERCENT OF TOTAL ASSETS

	Stone, Clay, and Glass Products				
	1Q 1976	2Q 1976	3Q 1976	4Q 1976	1Q 1977
Assets					
Cash on hand and in banks.....................	4.4	4.6	4.6	5.4	4.7
U.S. government and other securities...................	2.8	2.7	3.3	3.6	2.6
Receivables...	16.8	17.8	18.4	16.2	17.4
Inventories...	16.4	16.6	15.6	16.0	16.5
Current assets not elsewhere specified.................	2.0	2.0	2.1	2.2	2.4
Total current assets...............................	42.4	43.7	44.0	43.4	43.6
Land and depreciable fixed assets.....................	90.1	87.5	86.0	86.5	85.6
Deduct: Accumulated depreciation, depletion, and					
amortization.................................	43.9	42.5	41.1	41.1	41.0
Net property, plant, and equipment.................	46.2	44.9	44.9	45.4	44.7
Noncurrent assets not elsewhere specified, including					
investment in nonconsolidated entities, other long-					
term investments, intangibles, etc....................	11.4	11.4	11.1	11.3	11.8
Total assets.......................................	100.0	100.0	100.0	100.0	100.0
Liabilities and stockholders' equity					
Short-term loans and current installments..............	4.5	4.3	4.4	4.5	4.2
Trade accounts and trade notes payable...............	6.7	7.0	7.1	6.9	6.9
Income taxes accrued, prior and current years, net of					
payments					
Federal...	1.5	1.6	2.0	2.1	1.8
Other...	0.2	0.2	0.3	0.3	0.3
Other current liabilities...............................	5.9	6.2	6.1	6.0	6.3
Total current liabilities............................	18.7	19.4	19.8	19.8	19.5
Long-term debt due in more than 1 year					
Loans from banks.................................	5.0	5.2	5.2	4.5	4.6
Other long-term debt..............................	17.1	16.5	16.5	16.9	16.3
Noncurrent liabilities not elsewhere specified, including					
deferred income taxes..............................	4.1	4.1	4.2	4.4	4.7
Minority stockholders' interest in consolidated domestic					
corporations...	0.2	0.2	0.2	0.2	0.2
Total liabilities.....................................	45.1	45.4	46.0	45.8	45.3
Capital stock and other capital.........................	17.4	17.3	16.9	16.6	17.2
Retained earnings.....................................	38.8	38.5	38.3	38.8	38.7
Deduct: Treasury stock, at cost.......................	1.3	1.2	1.2	1.2	1.2
Stockholders' equity...............................	54.8	54.6	54.0	54.2	54.7
Total liabilities and stockholders' equity.............	100.0	100.0	100.0	100.0	100.0
			(times)		
Balance sheet ratios					
Current assets to current liabilities.....................	2.26	2.25	2.22	2.20	2.23
Total cash, U.S. government and other securities to total					
current liabilities......................................	0.38	0.37	0.40	0.46	0.37
Total stockholders' equity to debt.....................	2.07	2.10	2.06	2.10	2.18

* Included in Primary Metal Industries.

† During the first quarter of 1977 a considerable number of companies were reclassified by industry. To provide comparability, the four quarters of 1976 have been restated to reflect these reclassifications.

	Primary Metal Industries†					Iron and Steel*					Nonferrous Metals*†				
	1Q 1976	2Q 1976	3Q 1976	4Q 1976	1Q 1977	1Q 1976	2Q 1976	3Q 1976	4Q 1976	1Q 1977	1Q 1976	2Q 1976	3Q 1976	4Q 1976	1Q 1977
	3.2	3.3	3.2	3.4	2.7	3.6	3.5	3.6	3.8	3.0	2.5	2.8	2.6	2.8	2.2
	1.9	1.5	1.7	1.5	1.6	2.6	2.2	2.2	2.0	2.2	0.8	0.5	0.6	0.4	0.6
	13.2	13.9	13.4	12.2	14.0	14.0	14.4	13.8	12.2	14.3	11.8	13.0	12.5	12.2	13.5
	18.3	18.5	18.8	19.6	19.0	17.8	18.3	18.7	19.9	18.7	19.1	18.7	18.8	19.1	19.4
	1.6	1.6	1.6	1.4	1.7	1.5	1.6	1.5	1.4	1.7	1.7	1.7	1.8	1.5	1.6
	38.1	38.8	38.6	38.1	39.0	39.4	40.0	39.9	39.3	39.9	35.9	36.7	36.3	36.0	37.4
	92.6	92.1	92.1	92.3	91.2	101.6	100.5	99.9	99.9	99.1	77.3	77.5	78.3	78.5	77.3
	45.9	45.6	45.4	45.0	44.5	54.5	53.7	53.1	52.4	52.0	31.1	31.3	31.7	31.7	31.3
	46.8	46.5	46.7	47.3	46.7	47.1	46.8	46.8	47.5	47.1	46.2	46.1	46.6	46.8	46.0
	15.1	14.7	14.7	14.6	14.3	13.4	13.3	13.3	13.2	13.1	17.9	17.2	17.1	17.2	16.6
	100.0	100.0	100.0	100.0	100.0	100.0	100.0	100.0	100.0	100.0	100.0	100.0	100.0	100.0	100.0
	3.3	3.4	3.4	3.4	3.9	2.9	2.7	2.8	2.9	3.4	4.1	4.7	4.1	4.5	4.9
	6.9	7.0	6.8	7.1	7.2	7.3	7.6	7.3	7.4	7.5	6.1	6.1	6.1	6.5	6.5
	1.2	1.1	1.1	1.2	1.1	1.5	1.3	1.0	1.2	1.1	0.9	0.8	1.1	1.2	1.2
	0.3	0.3	0.3	0.4	0.3	0.3	0.2	0.2	0.3	0.2	0.4	0.4	0.3	0.4	0.4
	6.3	6.3	6.1	6.0	6.5	7.3	7.5	6.9	7.0	7.5	4.5	4.3	4.7	4.3	4.8
	18.0	18.2	17.6	18.1	19.0	19.2	19.3	18.3	18.8	19.7	16.0	16.4	16.3	16.8	17.8
	3.4	3.4	3.1	3.3	3.5	2.8	2.6	2.6	2.6	2.8	4.5	4.6	3.9	4.4	4.7
	19.2	19.0	20.3	20.1	20.0	17.5	17.6	19.2	19.1	19.2	22.2	21.4	22.3	21.7	21.5
	6.3	6.5	6.6	6.4	6.4	5.9	5.9	6.4	6.0	6.0	6.8	7.5	7.1	7.2	7.0
	0.5	0.5	0.5	0.5	0.5	0.7	0.7	0.7	0.7	0.7	0.2	0.2	0.2	0.1	0.2
	47.4	47.6	48.1	48.4	49.4	46.1	46.2	47.1	47.2	48.4	49.6	50.1	49.8	50.3	51.2
	16.4	16.2	15.8	15.8	15.4	15.6	15.4	15.1	15.0	14.8	17.8	17.5	17.0	17.2	16.5
	37.0	37.1	37.0	36.7	36.0	39.2	39.5	38.8	38.8	37.8	33.2	33.0	33.9	33.1	32.7
	0.9	0.9	0.9	0.8	0.8	1.0	1.0	1.0	1.0	1.0	0.6	0.6	0.6	0.6	0.5
	52.6	52.4	51.9	51.6	50.6	53.9	53.8	52.9	52.8	51.6	50.4	49.9	50.2	49.7	48.8
	100.0	100.0	100.0	100.0	100.0	100.0	100.0	100.0	100.0	100.0	100.0	100.0	100.0	100.0	100.0
			(times)					(times)					(times)		
	2.12	2.13	2.19	2.11	2.05	2.06	2.08	2.18	2.10	2.03	2.25	2.24	2.23	2.14	2.10
	0.28	0.26	0.28	0.27	0.23	0.32	0.29	0.32	0.31	0.26	0.21	0.20	0.19	0.19	0.16
	2.03	2.03	1.95	1.93	1.85	2.33	2.34	2.15	2.15	2.04	1.64	1.62	1.66	1.62	1.57

EXHIBIT 9: INCOME STATEMENT FOR CORPORATIONS IN FABRICATED METAL, MACHINERY, ELECTRICAL AND ELECTRONIC EQUIPMENT, INSTRUMENTS (ESIC industries 34, 35, 36, and 38)

	Fabricated Metal Products				
	1Q 1976	2Q 1976	3Q 1976*	4Q 1976*	1Q 1977
			($ million)		
Income statement in ratio format					
Net sales, receipts, and operating revenues.............	100.0	100.0	100.0	100.0	100.0
Deduct: Depreciation, depletion, and amortization of property, plant, and equipment..............	2.2	2.1	2.1	2.2	2.2
Deduct: All other operating costs and expenses (net of purchase discounts)...........................	89.2	88.6	89.5	90.7	90.0
Income (or loss) from operations....................	8.5	9.2	8.5	7.1	7.8
Nonoperating income (expense).........................	−0.5	−0.5	−0.3	−0.4	−0.4
Income (or loss) before income taxes................	8.0	8.8	8.2	6.7	7.4
Net income (loss) of foreign branches and equity in earnings (losses) of nonconsolidated subsidiaries (net of foreign taxes).................................	0.3	0.4	0.4	0.5	0.4
Deduct: Current and deferred domestic income taxes...	3.4	3.9	3.7	3.2	3.4
Income (or loss) after income taxes.................	4.8	5.3	4.9	4.1	4.4
Operating ratios (based on preceding industry dollar tables)					
Annual rate of profit on stockholders' equity at end of period:			(percent)		
Before income taxes...................................	25.89	30.59	27.51	22.89	24.26
After taxes...	15.01	17.66	15.77	12.92	13.74
Annual rate of profit on total assets:					
Before income taxes...................................	13.14	15.62	14.14	11.76	12.23
After taxes...	7.62	9.02	8.10	6.63	6.93

* Revised.

† During the first quarter of 1977 a considerable number of companies were reclassified by industry. To provide comparability, the four quarters of 1976 have been restated to reflect these reclassifications.

Machinery, Except Electrical†					Electrical and Electronic Equipment†					Instruments and Related Products				
1Q 1976	2Q 1976	3Q 1976	4Q 1976	1Q 1977	1Q 1976	2Q 1976	3Q 1976*	4Q 1976*	1Q 1977	1Q 1976	2Q 1976	3Q 1976	4Q 1976	1Q 1977
($ million)					($ million)					($ million)				
100.0	100.0	100.0	100.0	100.0	100.0	100.0	100.0	100.0	100.0	100.0	100.0	100.0	100.0	100.0
3.5	3.2	3.4	3.4	3.4	2.6	2.4	2.5	2.4	2.5	4.3	3.8	4.0	4.1	4.1
86.7	85.8	86.3	86.8	86.6	90.8	89.6	89.9	90.0	90.0	85.5	83.8	82.9	85.6	85.2
9.8	11.0	10.3	9.8	9.9	6.6	8.0	7.6	7.7	7.5	10.2	12.4	13.1	10.3	10.7
−0.2	−0.9	−0.1	−0.1	−0.1	−0.3	−0.3	−0.2	0.0	0.0	0.2	0.3	0.5	0.9	1.5
9.6	10.1	10.2	9.8	9.9	6.2	7.7	7.4	7.7	7.5	10.3	12.8	13.6	11.3	12.2
1.7	1.8	1.7	2.0	1.7	0.8	0.5	0.7	0.8	0.8	1.4	1.6	1.3	1.5	1.4
4.2	4.7	4.4	4.2	4.5	3.1	3.5	3.7	3.6	3.8	4.9	5.8	6.2	5.3	5.2
7.1	7.3	7.5	7.5	7.1	3.8	4.8	4.4	4.9	4.5	6.9	8.6	8.6	7.5	8.4
(percent)					(percent)					(percent)				
23.55	26.33	24.41	24.23	24.17	19.07	23.93	22.75	25.27	23.17	21.00	27.16	27.95	23.79	24.31
14.72	16.09	15.35	15.52	14.79	10.47	13.76	12.28	14.54	12.53	12.23	16.28	16.31	13.94	15.01
13.24	14.90	13.94	13.86	13.64	9.33	11.72	11.12	12.46	11.55	13.03	16.93	17.32	14.75	15.16
8.27	9.10	8.77	8.88	8.35	5.12	6.74	6.00	7.17	6.64	7.59	10.15	10.11	8.65	9.36

EXHIBIT 10:   BALANCE SHEET IN RATIO FORMAT FOR CORPORATIONS IN
FABRICATED METAL, MACHINERY, ELECTRICAL AND ELECTRONIC EQUIP-
MENT, INSTRUMENTS (ESIC industries 34, 35, 36, and 38)
ITEMS STATED AS A PERCENT OF TOTAL ASSETS

	Fabricated Metal Products				
	1Q 1976	2Q 1976	3Q 1976*	4Q 1976*	1Q 1977
Assets					
Cash on hand and in banks............................	6.1	6.2	6.1	6.2	5.3
U.S. government and other securities..................	2.5	2.8	3.2	3.3	3.6
Receivables...	22.2	22.3	22.1	21.1	21.8
Inventories...	26.5	26.1	26.4	26.5	26.5
Current assets not elsewhere specified.................	2.6	2.8	2.7	2.6	2.5
Total current assets................................	59.9	60.1	60.5	59.7	59.7
Land and depreciable fixed assets.....................	54.9	54.2	54.1	54.3	54.0
Deduct: Accumulated depreciation, depletion, and amortization..	26.9	26.7	26.7	26.3	26.2
Net property, plant, and equipment.................	28.0	27.5	27.4	27.9	27.8
Noncurrent assets not elsewhere specified, including investment in nonconsolidated entities, other long-term investments, intangibles, etc.....................	12.2	12.4	12.1	12.3	12.6
Total assets..	100.0	100.0	100.0	100.0	100.0
Liabilities and stockholders' equity					
Short-term loans and current installments...............	5.3	5.1	5.2	5.0	5.3
Trade accounts and trade notes payable................	9.2	9.4	9.3	9.3	9.1
Income taxes accrued, prior and current years, net of payments					
Federal...	2.6	2.4	2.7	2.7	2.7
Other...	0.4	0.4	0.4	0.4	0.4
Other current liabilities................................	11.2	11.1	11.2	11.0	11.5
Total current liabilities..............................	28.5	28.4	28.7	28.4	29.1
Long-term debt due in more than 1 year					
Loans from banks....................................	6.0	5.3	4.9	5.0	4.9
Other long-term debt.................................	11.2	11.5	11.3	11.5	11.7
Noncurrent liabilities not elsewhere specified, including deferred income taxes.................................	3.4	3.5	3.5	3.5	3.7
Minority stockholders' interest in consolidated domestic corporations..	0.2	0.3	0.3	0.2	0.2
Total liabilities.....................................	49.2	49.0	48.6	48.6	49.6
Capital stock and other capital.........................	15.7	15.3	15.0	15.2	14.7
Retained earnings......................................	36.4	37.3	37.8	37.6	37.2
Deduct: Treasury stock, at cost........................	1.4	1.5	1.4	1.4	1.4
Stockholders' equity................................	50.8	51.0	51.4	51.4	50.4
Total liabilities and stockholders' equity.............	100.0	100.0	100.0	100.0	100.0
			(times)		
Balance sheet ratios					
Current assets to current liabilities......................	2.10	2.12	2.11	2.10	2.05
Total cash, U.S. Government and other securities to total current liabilities..............................	0.30	0.32	0.32	0.33	0.31
Total stockholders' equity to debt......................	2.27	2.33	2.40	2.40	2.31

* Revised.
† During the first quarter of 1977 a considerable number of companies were reclassified by industry. To provide comparability, the four quarters of 1976 have been restated to reflect these reclassifications.

	Machinery, Except Electrical†					Electrical and Electronic Equipment†					Instruments and Related Products				
	1Q 1976	2Q 1976	3Q 1976	4Q 1976	1Q 1977	1Q 1976	2Q 1976	3Q 1976*	4Q 1976*	1Q 1977	1Q 1976	2Q 1976	3Q 1976	4Q 1976	1Q 1977
	3.7	3.8	3.8	3.9	3.6	3.9	3.8	3.6	4.4	4.4	3.9	4.5	4.1	4.2	4.2
	5.8	5.9	6.5	6.6	5.8	3.1	3.0	3.8	4.0	3.7	5.5	4.4	5.5	6.4	6.4
	17.9	18.4	18.0	17.4	18.2	20.8	21.0	21.4	20.4	20.5	17.0	17.6	18.1	17.7	17.0
	25.2	24.6	24.2	24.3	24.8	29.3	29.8	29.2	28.5	28.7	22.7	22.9	22.4	22.3	23.1
	3.3	3.2	3.1	3.2	3.1	3.1	3.2	3.3	4.0	4.0	4.1	4.2	4.0	3.8	3.8
	55.9	55.9	55.6	55.4	55.6	60.2	60.8	61.2	61.3	61.3	53.2	53.6	54.1	54.5	54.6
	50.7	50.6	50.5	50.6	50.9	46.4	45.5	44.7	44.6	44.6	58.2	57.6	57.4	56.9	56.9
	24.2	24.1	24.1	23.7	23.9	22.4	22.0	21.5	21.5	21.5	27.6	27.4	27.4	27.2	27.5
	26.6	26.5	26.4	26.9	27.0	24.0	23.6	23.2	23.1	23.0	30.5	30.1	30.0	29.7	29.5
	17.5	17.7	18.0	17.7	17.4	15.8	15.7	15.6	15.7	15.7	16.2	16.3	15.9	15.8	15.9
	100.0	100.0	100.0	100.0	100.0	100.0	100.0	100.0	100.0	100.0	100.0	100.0	100.0	100.0	100.0
	5.5	5.5	4.7	4.4	4.9	4.5	4.7	4.6	4.4	4.4	3.8	3.7	3.2	2.7	3.5
	6.6	6.7	6.7	7.3	6.9	8.1	8.3	7.8	8.9	8.5	5.7	5.3	5.6	5.8	5.4
	2.1	1.9	2.2	2.3	2.5	1.7	1.7	2.1	2.6	2.7	2.2	2.2	2.6	2.5	2.7
	0.4	0.4	0.5	0.5	0.5	0.3	0.4	0.4	0.5	0.4	0.4	0.4	0.5	0.5	0.4
	9.7	9.8	10.1	9.7	10.2	16.8	17.3	17.9	16.5	16.6	8.0	8.4	8.4	8.9	8.4
	24.5	24.3	24.1	24.2	24.9	31.4	32.3	32.8	32.8	32.6	20.1	20.0	20.3	20.3	20.4
	4.6	4.4	4.3	4.2	3.9	4.1	3.8	3.4	2.8	2.9	3.1	2.9	3.5	3.6	3.4
	11.2	11.2	10.9	11.1	11.4	11.1	10.6	10.7	10.7	10.4	11.5	11.4	11.0	10.7	10.6
	3.3	3.3	3.3	3.2	3.3	3.9	3.8	3.9	4.0	3.9	3.3	3.3	3.3	3.3	3.3
	0.2	0.2	0.2	0.2	0.1	0.5	0.5	0.3	0.3	0.3	0.0	0.0	0.0	0.0	0.0
	43.8	43.4	42.9	42.8	43.6	51.1	51.0	51.1	50.7	50.2	38.0	37.7	38.0	38.0	37.6
	20.9	20.8	20.8	20.4	20.2	21.3	21.0	20.6	20.4	20.3	18.9	17.9	17.4	17.1	17.0
	36.0	36.5	37.0	37.5	37.0	29.5	29.9	30.1	30.5	31.1	43.7	44.9	45.0	45.3	45.8
	0.6	0.7	0.7	0.7	0.8	1.9	1.9	1.8	1.7	1.6	0.5	0.5	0.5	0.4	0.4
	56.2	56.6	57.1	57.2	56.4	48.9	49.0	48.9	49.3	49.8	62.0	62.3	62.0	62.0	62.4
	100.0	100.0	100.0	100.0	100.0	100.0	100.0	100.0	100.0	100.0	100.0	100.0	100.0	100.0	100.0
			(times)					(times)					(times)		
	2.29	2.30	2.31	2.29	2.23	1.92	1.88	1.87	1.87	1.88	2.65	2.67	2.66	2.68	2.68
	0.39	0.40	0.43	0.43	0.38	0.22	0.21	0.22	0.26	0.25	0.47	0.44	0.47	0.52	0.52
	2.63	2.70	2.86	2.91	2.80	2.48	2.56	2.62	2.74	2.81	3.39	3.45	3.51	3.66	3.59

EXHIBIT 11: INCOME STATEMENT FOR CORPORATIONS IN TRANSPORTA-TION AND MOTOR VEHICLE EQUIPMENT, AIRCRAFT, GUIDED MISSILES (ESIC industries 37, 37.1, 37.7, other durable manufacturing products)

	Transportation Equipment†				
	1Q 1976	2Q 1976	3Q 1976	4Q 1976	1Q 1977
			($ million)		
Income statement in ratio format					
Net sales, receipts, and operating revenues.............	100.0	100.0	100.0	100.0	100.0
Deduct: Depreciation, depletion, and amortization of property, plant, and equipment..............	3.0	2.7	3.2	3.4	2.8
Deduct: All other operating costs and expenses (net of purchase discounts).........................	89.8	88.9	91.4	90.0	89.7
Income (or loss) from operations...................	7.2	8.4	5.4	6.6	7.4
Nonoperating income (expense).........................	−0.3	−0.3	−0.3	−0.3	−0.1
Income (or loss) before income taxes...............	6.9	8.1	5.0	6.3	7.3
Net income (loss) of foreign branches and equity in earnings (losses) of nonconsolidated subsidiaries (net of foreign taxes).................................	1.7	1.8	1.1	1.3	1.7
Deduct: Current and deferred domestic income taxes...	3.4	4.0	2.6	3.0	3.6
Income (or loss) after income taxes................	5.2	5.9	3.5	4.6	5.4
Operating ratios (based on preceding industry dollar tables)					
Annual rate of profit on stockholders' equity at end of period:			(percent)		
Before income taxes..................................	28.38	34.77	18.44	25.32	30.88
After taxes..	17.05	20.94	10.48	15.42	18.64
Annual rate of profit on total assets:					
Before income taxes..................................	13.67	17.00	8.95	12.40	14.89
After taxes..	8.22	10.23	5.08	7.55	8.99

* Included in Transportation Equipment.
† During the first quarter of 1977 a considerable number of companies were reclassified by industry. To provide comparability, the four quarters of 1976 have been restated to reflect these reclassifications.
‡ Revised.

Motor Vehicles and Equipment*†					Aircraft, Guided Missiles, and Parts*†					Other Durable Manufacturing Products†				
1Q 1976	2Q 1976	3Q 1976	4Q 1976	1Q 1977	1Q 1976	2Q 1976	3Q 1976	4Q 1976	1Q 1977	1Q 1976	2Q 1976	3Q 1976	4Q 1976‡	1Q 1977
($ million)					($ million)					($ million)				
100.0	100.0	100.0	100.0	100.0	100.0	100.0	100.0	100.0	100.0	100.0	100.0	100.0	100.0	100.0
3.4	3.1	3.8	4.1	3.2	2.0	1.8	2.0	1.8	2.0	3.0	2.7	2.9	2.8	2.9
88.5	87.5	91.5	88.9	88.8	92.5	92.3	91.6	92.5	91.6	90.9	88.6	89.3	90.1	90.1
8.1	9.4	4.7	7.1	8.0	5.5	5.8	6.5	5.7	6.4	6.1	8.7	7.8	7.0	7.0
0.0	−0.1	0.0	−0.3	0.1	−0.7	−0.6	−1.1	−0.4	−0.3	−0.5	−0.9	−0.8	−0.7	−0.9
8.0	9.3	4.7	6.8	8.1	4.8	5.2	5.4	5.3	6.2	5.6	7.8	7.1	6.3	6.1
2.2	2.3	1.3	1.7	2.1	0.9	0.9	0.9	0.3	0.8	0.2	0.1	0.2	0.3	0.2
4.1	4.6	2.7	3.2	4.0	2.3	2.6	2.6	2.4	2.9	2.5	2.9	2.8	2.7	2.5
6.2	7.1	3.3	5.3	6.2	3.3	3.5	3.7	3.2	4.0	3.3	5.1	4.4	4.0	3.8
(percent)					(percent)					(percent)				
31.80	38.46	16.40	27.28	34.33	20.75	24.20	22.23	21.03	24.42	17.83	27.53	25.06	22.89	20.64
19.19	23.43	9.07	16.90	20.96	12.30	13.82	12.96	12.03	13.95	10.10	17.53	15.23	13.76	12.58
18.56	22.40	9.36	15.84	19.45	7.21	8.78	8.28	7.93	9.20	8.77	13.65	12.22	11.19	10.16
11.20	13.65	5.17	9.81	11.88	4.27	5.01	4.83	4.54	5.26	4.96	8.69	7.43	6.73	6.20

EXHIBIT 12: BALANCE SHEET IN RATIO FORMAT FOR CORPORATIONS IN TRANSPORTATION AND MOTOR VEHICLE EQUIPMENT, AIRCRAFT, GUIDED MISSILES (ESIC industries 37, 37.1, 37.7, other durable manufacturing products)

ITEMS STATED AS A PERCENT OF TOTAL ASSETS

	Transportation Equipment†				
	1Q 1976	2Q 1976	3Q 1976	4Q 1976	1Q 1977
Assets					
Cash on hand and in banks	2.7	3.5	2.8	3.5	3.4
U.S. government and other securities	4.4	5.1	3.7	5.5	6.0
Receivables	15.0	14.9	15.5	12.9	15.2
Inventories	30.1	28.7	29.7	30.6	29.3
Current assets not elsewhere specified	2.8	2.7	2.7	2.7	2.8
Total current assets	54.9	54.9	54.4	55.2	56.7
Land and depreciable fixed assets	56.5	55.6	55.1	54.9	53.4
Deduct: Accumulated depreciation, depletion, and amortization	30.9	30.7	30.5	30.3	29.7
Net property, plant, and equipment	25.6	24.9	24.6	24.6	23.7
Noncurrent assets not elsewhere specified, including investment in nonconsolidated entities, other long-term investments, intangibles, etc.	19.5	20.2	20.9	20.3	19.6
Total assets	100.0	100.0	100.0	100.0	100.0
Liabilities and stockholders' equity					
Short-term loans and current installments	2.9	2.6	2.3	1.9	1.9
Trade accounts and trade notes payable	9.3	9.1	10.0	9.6	10.2
Income taxes accrued, prior and current years, net of payments					
Federal	2.5	2.5	2.8	3.3	3.3
Other	0.4	0.4	0.6	0.5	0.4
Other current liabilities	18.3	18.8	18.5	18.7	19.5
Total current liabilities	33.4	33.5	34.1	33.9	35.4
Long-term debt due in more than 1 year					
Loans from banks	3.8	3.8	3.5	3.1	3.0
Other long-term debt	10.8	9.6	9.7	9.9	9.5
Noncurrent liabilities not elsewhere specified, including deferred income taxes	3.5	4.0	4.0	3.9	3.8
Minority stockholders' interest in consolidated domestic corporations	0.3	0.3	0.3	0.2	0.2
Total liabilities	51.8	51.1	51.5	51.0	51.8
Capital stock and other capital	11.5	11.3	11.1	11.3	10.7
Retained earnings	37.2	38.2	37.9	38.3	38.1
Deduct: Treasury stock, at cost	0.6	0.6	0.5	0.6	0.5
Stockholders' equity	48.2	48.9	48.5	49.0	48.2
Total liabilities and stockholders' equity	100.0	100.0	100.0	100.0	100.0
			(times)		
Balance sheet ratios					
Current assets to current liabilities	1.64	1.64	1.60	1.63	1.60
Total cash, U.S. government and other securities to total current liabilities	0.21	0.26	0.19	0.26	0.27
Total stockholders' equity to debt	2.75	3.07	3.15	3.29	3.34

* Included in Transportation Equipment.
† During the first quarter of 1977 a considerable number of companies were reclassified by industry. To provide comparability, the four quarters of 1976 have been restated to reflect these reclassifications.
‡ Revised.

Motor Vehicles and Equipment*†					Aircraft, Guided Missiles, and Parts*†					Other Durable Manufacturing Products†				
1Q 1976	2Q 1976	3Q 1976	4Q 1976	1Q 1977	1Q 1976	2Q 1976	3Q 1976	4Q 1976	1Q 1977	1Q 1976	2Q 1976	3Q 1976	4Q 1976‡	1Q 1977
2.9	3.9	2.8	3.6	3.0	2.5	2.7	2.7	3.2	4.4	5.0	5.1	4.8	5.4	4.3
6.4	7.4	4.9	7.3	8.3	1.8	2.3	2.3	3.7	3.7	1.6	1.3	1.3	1.8	1.6
15.5	15.4	16.7	13.1	16.3	13.9	14.1	14.1	12.9	13.6	18.3	19.7	20.0	18.9	19.0
21.7	20.3	22.0	23.0	21.6	46.9	45.3	45.1	45.1	44.2	23.7	22.8	23.2	23.8	24.3
3.4	3.1	3.0	3.0	3.2	2.2	2.4	2.6	2.2	2.3	3.4	3.5	3.3	3.3	3.5
49.9	50.1	49.3	50.1	52.4	67.4	66.9	66.9	67.2	68.1	52.0	52.5	52.6	53.1	52.6
63.9	61.9	59.8	61.0	58.5	40.9	41.7	43.8	41.3	41.3	65.6	64.4	64.5	63.9	65.9
36.4	35.6	34.2	35.2	33.9	23.7	24.3	26.2	23.9	24.4	27.0	26.3	26.2	25.9	26.8
27.4	26.2	25.6	25.8	24.6	17.2	17.4	17.6	17.4	17.0	38.7	38.1	38.3	38.0	39.0
22.7	23.7	25.0	24.1	23.0	15.5	15.7	15.5	15.5	15.0	9.3	9.4	9.1	8.9	8.4
100.0	100.0	100.0	100.0	100.0	100.0	100.0	100.0	100.0	100.0	100.0	100.0	100.0	100.0	100.0
2.0	1.5	1.6	1.1	1.2	3.2	3.5	2.3	2.4	2.7	8.3	7.7	8.1	7.6	8.1
10.3	10.1	11.4	10.6	11.7	7.4	7.1	7.8	7.6	7.3	8.7	8.5	8.4	9.4	8.6
2.5	2.6	2.8	3.5	3.5	2.8	2.9	3.1	3.5	3.6	1.4	1.6	2.0	2.1	2.0
0.5	0.5	0.5	0.5	0.5	0.3	0.4	0.9	0.4	0.4	0.3	0.3	0.4	0.4	0.3
11.6	12.5	12.7	11.7	13.1	31.5	31.3	29.4	31.7	32.4	5.4	5.8	5.8	5.7	6.1
26.9	27.1	29.0	27.4	29.8	45.2	45.4	43.6	45.7	46.4	24.1	23.9	24.8	25.1	25.2
2.2	3.0	2.5	2.8	2.6	6.2	5.1	5.2	3.5	3.0	8.1	7.9	7.9	7.8	7.2
8.5	6.9	7.1	7.2	6.6	11.8	11.1	11.2	11.4	11.2	14.8	14.9	14.8	14.3	14.2
3.8	4.5	4.2	4.2	4.0	1.5	1.6	2.1	1.6	1.7	3.8	3.7	3.6	3.8	4.0
0.2	0.2	0.2	0.2	0.2	0.5	0.5	0.6	0.1	0.1	0.1	0.1	0.1	0.1	0.1
41.6	41.7	43.0	41.9	43.3	65.3	63.7	62.8	62.3	62.3	50.8	50.4	51.2	51.1	50.8
10.6	10.1	9.8	10.0	9.3	12.7	13.0	13.5	13.6	13.4	17.8	17.7	17.2	17.4	17.1
48.2	48.5	47.6	48.5	47.7	22.9	24.1	24.6	24.9	25.1	32.7	33.4	32.9	32.9	33.7
0.3	0.4	0.4	0.4	0.3	0.9	0.9	0.9	0.9	0.8	1.3	1.5	1.3	1.5	1.6
58.4	58.3	57.0	58.1	56.7	34.7	36.3	37.2	37.7	37.7	49.2	49.6	48.8	48.9	49.2
100.0	100.0	100.0	100.0	100.0	100.0	100.0	100.0	100.0	100.0	100.0	100.0	100.0	100.0	100.0
		(times)					(times)					(times)		
1.85	1.85	1.70	1.83	1.76	1.49	1.47	1.53	1.47	1.47	2.16	2.20	2.12	2.12	2.09
0.35	0.42	0.27	0.40	0.38	0.10	0.11	0.12	0.15	0.17	0.27	0.27	0.25	0.29	0.23
4.61	5.13	5.10	5.25	5.49	1.64	1.83	1.98	2.18	2.23	1.57	1.63	1.58	1.65	1.66

EXHIBIT 13:   INCOME STATEMENT FOR CORPORATIONS IN MINING, RETAIL, WHOLESALE

	All Mining*				
	1Q 1976	2Q 1976	3Q 1976	4Q 1976†	1Q 1977
			($ million)		
Income statement in ratio format					
Net sales, receipts, and operating revenues	100.0	100.0	100.0	100.0	100.0
Deduct: Depreciation, depletion, and amortization of property, plant, and equipment	7.7	7.4	8.5	8.3	8.4
Deduct: All other operating costs and expenses (net of purchase discounts)	76.8	77.6	75.7	77.9	77.7
Income (or loss) from operations	15.6	15.0	15.8	13.7	13.9
Nonoperating income (expense)	−0.3	−0.4	0.2	0.6	−0.2
Income (or loss) before income taxes	15.3	14.7	16.0	14.3	13.7
Net income (loss) of foreign branches and equity in earnings (losses) of nonconsolidated subsidiaries (net of foreign taxes)	0.6	0.9	1.4	1.0	1.3
Deduct: Current and deferred domestic income taxes	4.9	4.7	5.1	5.4	5.2
Income (or loss) after income taxes	11.0	10.8	12.3	10.0	9.8

Operating ratios (based on preceding industry dollar tables)

			(percent)		
Annual rate of profit on stockholders' equity at end of period:					
Before income taxes	26.21	26.26	27.77	24.23	22.17
After taxes	18.16	18.22	19.65	15.75	14.49
Annual rate of profit on total assets:					
Before income taxes	13.93	14.21	13.98	12.65	11.22
After taxes	9.65	9.86	9.89	8.22	7.34

* During the first quarter of 1977 a considerable number of companies were reclassified by industry. To provide comparability, the four quarters of 1976 have been restated to reflect these reclassifications.
† Revised.

	All Retail Trade*					All Wholesale Trade*				
	1Q 1976	2Q 1976	3Q 1976	4Q 1976	1Q 1977	1Q 1976	2Q 1976	3Q 1976	4Q 1976	1Q 1977
	($ million)					($ million)				
	100.0	100.0	100.0	100.0		100.0	100.0	100.0	100.0	100.0
	1.1	1.2	1.1	1.1		0.8	0.7	0.8	0.8	0.8
	95.8	95.1	95.2	94.1		95.9	95.1	95.9	96.2	96.1
	3.1	3.8	3.6	4.8		3.3	4.2	3.3	3.0	3.1
	−0.4	−0.1	−0.3	−0.3		−0.1	−0.1	−0.1	−0.1	−0.2
	2.8	3.7	3.4	4.5		3.3	4.0	3.2	2.8	2.9
	0.1	0.1	0.1	0.2		0.1	0.1	0.1	0.1	0.1
	1.0	1.2	1.2	1.6		1.2	1.2	1.1	1.0	1.0
	1.8	2.6	2.2	3.1		2.2	2.9	2.2	1.8	1.9
	(percent)					(percent)				
	18.13	26.90	23.99	35.18		26.27	33.47	26.79	23.54	23.67
	11.28	18.41	15.50	23.02		16.92	23.43	17.41	14.90	15.23
	7.95	11.68	10.14	15.08		10.56	13.19	10.83	9.31	9.23
	4.94	7.99	6.55	9.87		6.80	9.23	7.04	5.89	5.94

EXHIBIT 14: BALANCE SHEET FOR CORPORATIONS IN MINING, RETAIL, WHOLESALE (in $ million)

	All Mining*				
	1Q 1976	2Q 1976	3Q 1976	4Q 1976†	1Q 1977
Assets					
Cash and demand deposits in the U.S.	1,349	1,291	1,328	1,428	1,318
Time deposits in the U.S., including negotiable certificates of deposit	1,025	988	758	808	837
Deposits outside the U.S.	13	11	19	17	14
Cash on hand and in banks	2,387	2,290	2,106	2,253	2,170
U.S. Treasury securities					
Subject to agreements to sell	69	139	138	163	229
Other, due in 1 year or less	464	362	209	223	215
Other, due in more than 1 year	25	29	10	11	10
Federal agency securities					
Subject to agreements to sell	5	37	39	1	0
Other, due in 1 year or less	82	110	123	91	47
Other, due in more than 1 year	22	19	36	43	25
Commercial and finance company paper of U.S. issuers	211	212	174	212	266
State and local government securities due in 1 year or less	72	83	38	20	40
Foreign securities due in 1 year or less	2	1	0	4	0
Other short-term financial investments including bankers' acceptances	120	119	175	117	102
Total cash, U.S. government and other securities	3,459	3,402	3,047	3,139	3,103
Trade receivables from U.S. government	56	57	61	62	109
Other trade accounts and trade notes receivable (less allowances for doubtful receivables)	3,822	3,781	4,089	3,836	4,070
Total receivables	3,878	3,837	4,150	3,898	4,179
Inventories	1,726	1,779	1,773	1,790	2,002
Current assets not elsewhere specified	763	742	812	849	751
Total current assets	9,826	9,759	9,782	9,676	10,035
Depreciable and amortizable fixed assets, including construction in progress	23,227	23,448	23,472	23,628	24,312
Land and mineral rights	4,359	4,487	4,287	4,411	4,666
Deduct: Accumulated depreciation, depletion, and amortization	11,309	11,493	10,689	10,737	10,872
Net property, plant, and equipment	16,278	16,442	17,070	17,301	18,107
Noncurrent assets not elsewhere specified, including investment in nonconsolidated entities, other long-term investments, intangibles, etc.	4,943	4,964	5,291	4,705	4,609
Total assets	31,046	31,166	32,143	31,683	32,750
Liabilities and stockholders' equity					
Short-term loans (original maturity of 1 year or less)					
Loans from banks	1,371	806	1,087	512	415
Commercial paper	23	11	5	10	6
Other short-term loans	181	214	495	288	284
Advances and prepayments by U.S. government	0	1	0	0	0
Trade accounts and trade notes payable	2,335	2,355	2,272	2,148	2 632
Income taxes accrued, prior and current years, net of payments					
Federal	533	360	386	460	557
Other	54	38	32	29	45
Installments, due in 1 year or less, on long-term debt					
Loans from banks	591	558	605	624	601
Other long-term debt	450	403	533	344	390
Current liabilities not elsewhere specified, including excise and sales taxes, and accrued expenses	992	1,052	1,307	1,154	1,324
Total current liabilities	6,529	5,799	6,723	5,569	6,254
Long-term debt due in more than 1 year					
Loans from banks	2,704	2,751	2,905	2,954	2,918
Other long-term debt	3,703	4,096	4,485	4,628	4,572
Noncurrent liabilities not elsewhere specified, including deferred income taxes	1,507	1,551	1,722	1,874	2,261
Minority stockholders' interest in consolidated domestic corporations	108	99	124	120	162
Total liabilities	14,552	14,296	15,960	15,145	16,168
Capital stock and other capital	4,845	4,984	5,006	5,036	5,141
Retained earnings	12,030	12,237	11,636	11,916	11,879
Deduct: Treasury stock, at cost	380	351	459	415	437
Stockholders' equity	16,495	16,870	16,183	16,538	16,582
Total liabilities and stockholders' equity	31,046	31,166	32,143	31,683	32,750
Net working capital					
Excess of current assets over current liabilities	3,296	3,961	3,059	4,107	3,781

* During the first quarter of 1977 a considerable number of companies were reclassified by industry. To provide comparability, the four quarters of 1976 have been restated to reflect these reclassifications.
† Revised.

	All Retail Trade*				All Wholesale Trade*			
1Q 1976	2Q 1976	3Q 1976	4Q 1976	1Q 1976	2Q 1976	3Q 1976	4Q 1976	1Q 1977
9,503	9,490	9,926	10,749	9,184	9,255	8,903	9,465	8,832
1,672	1,726	1,656	1,892	1,923	1,917	1,741	1,952	1,802
42	14	21	10	472	441	437	265	178
11,216	11,230	11,604	12,651	11,578	11,613	11,081	11,682	10,812
23	37	19	33	43	38	109	28	92
370	450	464	320	255	355	367	418	231
61	13	6	104	64	110	60	67	55
15	32	1	0	3	1	2	5	1
48	69	91	99	64	16	57	31	14
73	25	15	15	22	15	56	32	18
917	1,025	797	1,102	899	852	879	576	567
111	97	81	74	86	138	132	172	125
0	7	25	34	57	54	87	60	84
491	492	434	521	901	822	880	1,035	1,136
13,326	13,479	13,538	14,952	13,974	14,016	13,711	14,106	13,135
4	3	16	12	224	149	146	259	194
25,630	25,662	26,691	27,801	51,914	53,225	53,260	52,738	52,763
25,634	25,665	26,707	27,813	52,137	53,374	53,406	52,997	52,957
63,330	66,068	70,930	63,654	53,907	57,130	55,840	57,822	58,950
5,137	5,908	5,719	5,727	6,894	6,629	5,874	6,278	5,565
107,426	111,120	116,894	112,147	126,912	131,149	128,831	131,203	130,606
68,202	68,169	70,696	70,425	42,904	44,062	45,473	45,847	47,394
5,182	5,214	5,643	5,171	3,685	3,561	3,714	3,645	3,627
28,953	28,741	30,065	29,200	19,403	19,581	20,801	21,114	21,318
44,431	44,641	46,274	46,396	27,185	28,042	28,387	28,378	29,703
11,866	12,362	12,824	12,667	11,029	11,585	11,941	12,178	12,207
163,723	168,124	175,993	171,209	165,126	170,776	169,159	171,759	172,516
8,692	10,296	12,029	9,093	21,324	21,100	20,926	22,266	22,628
1,814	729	962	306	1,325	1,444	1,436	1,699	1,571
7,852	8,514	8,168	9,139	2,999	3,079	3,052	2,813	3,086
0	3	0	0	6	8	15	1	1
25,699	26,399	29,400	27,581	38,806	42,050	39,570	40,215	40,335
2,651	2,437	2,418	2,787	2,323	1,972	2,256	2,248	2,050
402	386	500	607	344	341	340	385	360
1,716	1,815	1,746	1,812	1,403	1,342	1,477	1,795	1,506
1,823	1,649	1,605	1,308	1,057	1,097	1,212	1,300	1,231
10,111	10,627	11,336	11,548	7,387	8,003	8,393	8,724	8,006
60,761	62,855	68,163	64,181	76,975	80,436	78,677	81,446	80,774
9,885	10,181	10,240	11,017	8,092	7,913	7,708	7,995	8,315
17,245	18,000	18,892	18,075	10,797	12,141	11,209	11,364	12,877
3,764	3,893	4,058	4,397	2,704	2,753	2,888	2,807	2,999
335	222	243	134	168	226	268	213	262
91,990	95,151	101,596	97,804	98,737	103,468	100,750	103,825	105,227
24,747	24,841	24,951	24,352	22,955	21,879	21,693	21,347	22,098
48,714	50,085	51,303	51,082	45,377	47,624	48,851	48,677	47,207
1,727	1,953	1,859	2,029	1,942	2,195	2,136	2,090	2,016
71,734	72,973	74,396	73,405	66,390	67,308	68,408	67,934	67,289
163,723	168,124	175,993	171,209	165,126	170,776	169,159	171,759	172,516
46,666	48,265	48,731	47,965	49,936	50,713	50,154	49,757	49,831

EXHIBIT 15: BALANCE SHEET IN RATIO FORMAT FOR CORPORATIONS IN MINING, RETAIL, WHOLESALE

ITEMS STATED AS A PERCENT OF TOTAL ASSETS

	All Mining*				
	1Q 1976	2Q 1976	3Q 1976	4Q 1976†	1Q 1977
Assets					
Cash on hand and in banks	7.7	7.3	6.6	7.1	6.6
U.S. government and other securities	3.4	3.6	2.9	2.8	2.9
Receivables	12.5	12.3	12.9	12.3	12.8
Inventories	5.6	5.7	5.5	5.6	6.1
Current assets not elsewhere specified	2.5	2.4	2.5	2.7	2.3
Total current assets	31.6	31.3	30.4	30.5	30.6
Land and depreciable fixed assets	88.8	89.6	86.3	88.5	88.4
Deduct: Accumulated depreciation, depletion, and amortization	36.4	36.9	33.3	33.9	33.2
Net property, plant, and equipment	52.4	52.8	53.1	54.6	55.3
Noncurrent assets not elsewhere specified, including investment in nonconsolidated entities, other long-term investments, intangibles, etc.	15.9	15.9	16.5	14.9	14.1
Total assets	100.0	100.0	100.0	100.0	100.0
Liabilities and stockholders' equity					
Short-term loans and current installments	8.4	6.4	8.5	5.6	5.2
Trade accounts and trade notes payable	7.5	7.6	7.1	6.8	8.0
Income taxes accrued, prior and current years, net of payments					
Federal	1.7	1.2	1.2	1.5	1.7
Other	0.2	0.1	0.1	0.1	0.1
Other current liabilities	3.2	3.4	4.1	3.6	4.0
Total current liabilities	21.0	18.6	20.9	17.6	19.1
Long-term debt due in more than 1 year					
Loans from banks	8.7	8.8	9.0	9.3	8.9
Other long-term debt	11.9	13.1	14.0	14.6	14.0
Noncurrent liabilities not elsewhere specified, including deferred incomes taxes	4.9	5.0	5.4	5.9	6.9
Minority stockholders' interest in consolidated domestic corporations	0.3	0.3	0.4	0.4	0.5
Total liabilities	46.9	45.9	49.7	47.8	49.4
Capital stock and other capital	15.6	16.0	15.6	15.9	15.7
Retained earnings	38.7	39.3	36.2	37.6	36.3
Deduct: Treasury stock, at cost	1.2	1.1	1.4	1.3	1.3
Stockholders' equity	53.1	54.1	50.3	52.2	50.6
Total liabilities and stockholders' equity	100.0	100.0	100.0	100.0	100.0
		(times)			
Balance sheet ratios					
Current assets to current liabilities	1.50	1.68	1.46	1.74	1.60
Total cash, U.S. government and other securities to total current liabilities	0.53	0.59	0.45	0.56	0.50
Total stockholders' equity to debt	1.83	1.91	1.60	1.77	1.81

* During the first quarter of 1977 a considerable number of companies were reclassified by industry. To provide comparability, the four quarters of 1976 have been restated to reflect these reclassifications.
† Revised.

Financial Statement Ratios by Industry

All Retail Trade*				All Wholesale Trade*				
1Q 1976	2Q 1976	3Q 1976	4Q 1976†	1Q 1976	2Q 1976	3Q 1976	4Q 1976	1Q 1977
6.9	6.7	6.6	7.4	7.0	6.8	6.6	6.8	6.3
1.2	1.3	1.1	1.3	1.5	1.4	1.5	1.4	1.3
15.7	15.3	15.2	16.2	31.6	31.3	31.6	30.9	30.7
38.7	39.3	40.3	37.2	32.6	33.5	33.0	33.7	34.2
3.1	3.5	3.2	3.3	4.2	3.9	3.5	3.7	3.2
65.6	66.1	66.4	65.5	76.9	76.8	76.2	76.4	75.7
44.9	43.6	43.4	44.1	28.2	27.9	29.1	28.8	29.6
17.7	17.1	17.1	17.1	11.8	11.5	12.3	12.3	12.4
27.1	26.6	26.3	27.1	16.5	16.4	16.8	16.5	17.2
7.2	7.4	7.3	7.4	6.7	6.8	7.1	7.1	7.1
100.0	100.0	100.0	100.0	100.0	100.0	100.0	100.0	100.0
13.3	13.7	13.8	12.7	16.9	16.4	16.6	17.4	17.4
15.7	15.7	16.7	16.1	23.5	24.6	23.4	23.4	23.4
1.6	1.4	1.4	1.6	1.4	1.2	1.3	1.3	1.2
0.2	0.2	0.3	0.4	0.2	0.2	0.2	0.2	0.2
6.2	6.3	6.4	6.7	4.5	4.7	5.0	5.1	4.6
37.1	37.4	38.7	37.5	46.6	47.1	46.5	47.4	46.8
6.0	6.1	5.8	6.4	4.9	4.6	4.6	4.7	4.8
10.5	10.7	10.7	10.6	6.5	7.1	6.6	6.6	7.5
2.3	2.3	2.3	2.6	1.6	1.6	1.7	1.6	1.7
0.2	0.1	0.1	0.1	0.1	0.1	0.2	0.1	0.2
56.2	56.6	57.7	57.1	59.8	60.6	59.6	60.4	61.0
15.1	14.8	14.2	14.2	13.9	12.8	12.8	12.4	12.8
29.8	29.8	29.2	29.8	27.5	27.9	28.9	28.3	27.4
1.1	1.2	1.1	1.2	1.2	1.3	1.3	1.2	1.2
43.8	43.4	42.3	42.9	40.2	39.4	40.4	39.6	39.0
100.0	100.0	100.0	100.0	100.0	100.0	100.0	100.0	100.0
	(times)				(times)			
1.77	1.77	1.71	1.75	1.65	1.63	1.64	1.61	1.62
0.22	0.21	0.20	0.23	0.18	0.17	0.17	0.17	0.16
1.46	1.43	1.39	1.45	1.41	1.40	1.45	1.38	1.31

CORPORATE PROFITS
AND MARGINS

CORPORATE PROFIT MARGINS

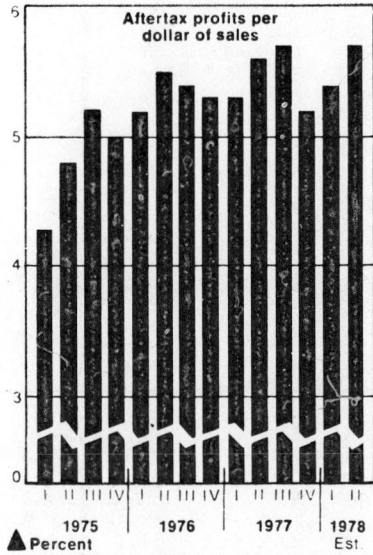

Aftertax profits per dollar of sales

1975   1976   1977   1978 Est.

▲ Percent

CORPORATE PROFITS

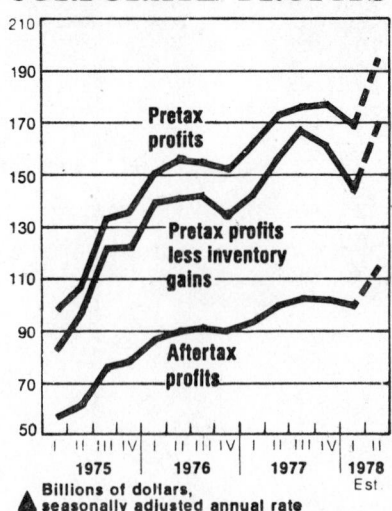

Pretax profits

Pretax profits less inventory gains

Aftertax profits

1975   1976   1977   1978 Est.

▲ Billions of dollars, seasonally adjusted annual rate

Data: Standard & Poor's Compustat Services Inc., Commerce Dept., BW est.

Reprinted from the August 21, 1978 issue of *Business Week* by special permission. © 1978 by McGraw-Hill, Inc.

STANDARD INDUSTRIAL CLASSIFICATION CODES (SIC)

01–09 Agriculture, Forestry, and Fishing
01. Agricultural production—crops
02. Agricultural production—livestock
07. Agricultural services
08. Forestry
09. Fishing, hunting, and trapping

10–14 Mining
10. Metal mining
12. Bituminous coal and lignite mining
13. Oil and gas extraction
14. Mining and quarrying of nonmetallic minerals except fuels

15–17 Construction
15. Building construction—general contractors and operative builders
16. Construction other than building construction—general contractors
17. Construction—special trade contractors

20–39 Manufacturing
20. Food and kindred products
21. Tobacco manufacturers
22. Textile mill products
23. Apparel and other finished products made from fabrics and other similar materials
24. Lumber and wood products except furniture
25. Furniture and fixtures
26. Paper and allied products
27. Printing, publishing, and allied industries
28. Chemicals and allied products
29. Petroleum refining and related industries
30. Rubber and miscellaneous plastic products
31. Leather and leather products
32. Stone, clay, glass, and concrete products
33. Primary metal industries
34. Fabricated metal products, except machinery and transportation equipment
35. Machinery, except electrical
36. Electrical and electronic machinery, equipment, and supplies
37. Transportation equipment
38. Measuring, analyzing and controlling instruments; photographic, medical, and optical goods; watches and clocks
39. Miscellaneous manufacturing industries

40–49 Transportation, communications, Sanitary services, and utilities
40. Railroad transportation
41. Local and suburban transit and interurban highway passenger transportation
42. Motor freight transportation and warehousing
44. Water transportation
45. Transportation by air
46. Pipe lines, except natural gas
47. Transportation services
48. Communications
49. Electric, gas, and sanitary services

50–51 Wholesale trade
50. Wholesale trade—durable goods
51. Wholesale trade—nondurable goods

52–59 Retail trade
52. Building materials, hardware, garden supply, and mobile home dealers
53. General merchandise stores
54. Food stores
55. Automotive dealers and gasoline service stations
56. Apparel and accessory stores
57. Furniture, home furnishings, and equipment stores
58. Eating and drinking places
59. Miscellaneous retail

60–67 Finance, insurance, and real estate
60. Banking
61. Credit agencies other than banks
62. Security and commodity brokers, dealers, exchanges, and services
63. Insurance carriers
64. Insurance agents, brokers, and service
65. Real estate
67. Holding and other investment companies

70–89 Services
70. Hotels, rooming houses, camps, and other lodging places
72. Personal services
73. Business services
75. Automotive repair, services, and garages
76. Miscellaneous repair services
78. Motion pictures
79. Amusement and recreation services except motion pictures
80. Health services
82. Educational services
89. Miscellaneous services

Largest Corporations

100 LARGEST U.S. INDUSTRIAL CORPORATIONS (ranked by sales)

Rank 1976	Rank 1975	Company	Sales ($000)	Assets ($000)	Rank	Net Income ($000)	Rank	Stockholders' Equity ($000)	Rank
1	1	Exxon (New York)	48,630,817*	36,331,346	1	2,640,964	2	18,470,352	1
2	2	General Motors (Detroit)	47,181,000	24,442,400	2	2,902,800	1	14,385,200	2
3	4	Ford Motor (Dearborn, MI)	28,839,600	15,768,100	6	983,100	4	7,107,000	6
4	3	Texaco (New York)	26,451,851	18,193,818	4	869,731	9	9,002,077	4
5	5	Mobil (New York)[1]	26,062,570*	18,767,450	3	942,523	5	7,651,811	5
6	6	Standard Oil of California (San Francisco)	19,434,133	13,765,397	7	880,127	8	7,007,013	7
7	8	Gulf Oil (Pittsburgh)	16,451,000*	13,449,000	8	816,000	10	6,942,000	8
8	7	International Business Machines (Armonk, NY)	16,304,333	17,723,326	5	2,398,093	3	12,749,287	3
9	9	General Electric (Fairfield, CT)[2]	15,697,300	12,049,700	9	930,600	6	5,252,900	10
10	10	Chrysler (Highland Park, MI)	15,537,788	7,074,365	16	422,631*	19	2,815,326	20
11	11	International Telephone and Telegraph (New York)	11,764,106	11,070,078	11	494,467	15	4,574,256	13
12	12	Standard Oil (Indiana) (Chicago)	11,532,048*	11,213,198	10	892,968	7	6,146,705	9
13	14	Shell Oil (Houston)	9,229,950*	7,836,516	14	705,838	11	4,591,182	12
14	13	U.S. Steel (Pittsburgh)	8,604,200	9,167,900	12	410,300	21	5,129,000	11
15	15	Atlantic Richfield (Los Angeles)	8,462,524*	8,853,334	13	575,178	14	4,091,133	14
16	17	E. I. du Pont de Nemours (Wilmington, DE)	8,361,000	7,027,100	17	459,300	17	4,039,200	15
17	16	Continental Oil (Stamford, CT)	7,957,620	6,041,516	21	459,994	16	2,635,444	24
18	18	Western Electric (New York)	6,930,942	5,178,460	24	217,383	40	3,261,615	17
19	19	Procter & Gamble (Cincinnati)[3]	6,512,728	4,102,996	32	401,098	22	2,357,470	26
20	22	Tenneco (Houston)	6,389,236	7,177,100	15	383,500	23	2,651,000	23
21	21	Union Carbide (New York)	6,345,700	6,621,600	19	441,200	18	3,055,100	18
22	20	Westinghouse Electric (Pittsburgh)	6,145,152	5,318,342	23	223,217	39	2,138,435	30
23	23	Goodyear Tire & Rubber (Akron, OH)	5,791,494	4,336,125	29	121,967	88	1,861,911	36
24	26	Phillips Petroleum (Bartlesville, OK)	5,697,516	5,068,463	25	411,656	20	2,720,341	21
25	32	Dow Chemical (Midland, MI)	5,652,070	6,848,664	18	612,767	13	2,865,010	19
26	25	Occidental Petroleum (Los Angeles)	5,525,451	3,904,995	34	183,721	48	1,305,276	52
27	24	International Harvester (Chicago)	5,488,123	3,574,832	42	174,088	51	1,580,781	40
28	30	Eastman Kodak (Rochester, NY)	5,438,170	5,524,416	22	650,618	12	4,026,299	16
29	36	Sun (Radnor, PA)[5]	5,387,064	4,835,573	27	356,182	27	2,555,069	25
30	27	Union Oil of California (Los Angeles)	5,350,693*	4,226,825	31	268,815	33	2,103,815	32
31	34	RCA (New York)	5,328,500	3,837,700	36	177,400	50	1,277,700	54
32	35	Esmark (Chicago)	5,300,566	1,757,480	98	82,550	138	710,588	126
33	28	Bethlehem Steel (Bethlehem, PA)	5,248,000	4,939,100	26	168,000	53	2,692,600	22
34	31	Rockwell International (Pittsburgh)[6]	5,220,100	2,888,600	49	123,400	85	1,178,900	59
35	40	United Technologies (Hartford)	5,166,264	2,626,405	55	157,403	58	1,244,633	56

The definitions and concepts underlying the figures In this listing are explained on page 148.

Employees		Net Income as Percent of				Earnings per Share			Growth Rate 1966–76		Total Return to Investors				Industry Code
		Sales		Stockholders' Equity							1976		1966–76 Average		
Number	Rank	%	Rank	%	Rank	1976($)	1975($)	1966($)	%	Rank	%	Rank	%	Rank	
126,000†	15	5.4	196	14.3	204	5.90	5.60	2.53	8.84	201	26.98	286	11.08	140	29
748,000†	1	6.2	146	20.2	37	10.08	4.32	6.24	4.91	305	45.85	181	8.24	215	40
443,917†	2	3.4	344	13.8	224	10.45	3.46	5.63	6.38	269	46.15	175	10.44	155	40
72,766	33	3.3	352	9.7	377	3.20	3.06	2.62	2.02	363	27.28	283	3.05	368	29
199,500	7	3.6	322	12.3	286	9.08	7.95	3.51	9.97	163	44.96	188	8.70	202	29
38,397	102	4.5	262	12.6	272	5.18	4.55	2.52	7.47	239	46.89	171	9.56	177	29
53,300	57	5.0	227	11.8	316	4.19	3.60	2.44	5.56	284	49.27	159	5.36	298	29
291,977	5	14.7	8	18.8	57	15.94	13.35	3.83	15.33	52	28.04	277	8.67	203	44
380,000†	3	5.9	157	17.7	74	4.12	3.17	1.88	8.16	215	23.64	312	5.25	302	36
244,865†	6	2.7	388	15.0	164	7.02**	(4.33)	4.16	4.37	290	104.17	27	0.50	401	40
375,000	4	4.2	280	10.8	343	4.00	3.20	2.04	6.97	253	57.66	128	2.89	370	36
45,399	83	7.7	80	14.5	193	6.09	5.36	1.81	12.90	94	45.28	187	13.51	90	29
32,227	128	7.6	84	15.4	153	10.11	7.59	4.19	9.21	186	66.70	101	7.40	240	29
166,645†	8	4.8	240	8.0	409	5.03	6.89	3.07	5.06	300	19.70	337	13.35	94	33
26,972	150	6.8	119	14.1	213	5.04	3.08	1.99	9.74	165	30.96	263	12.98	100	29
132,737	13	5.5	192	11.4	333	9.30	5.43	8.23	1.23	379	10.96	389	3.23	366	28
43,899	85	5.8	164	17.5	81	4.38	3.25	1.27	13.18	87	26.98	285	12.17	118	29
151,052	11	3.1	364	6.7	429	n.a.	n.a.	n.a.	—		—		—		36
52,200	63	6.2	144	17.0	89	4.86	4.05	1.74	10.82	143	7.61	400	12.26	115	43
82,074	28	6.0	152	14.5	196	4.33	4.15	1.88	8.70	204	44.18	198	11.38	135	29
113,118	17	7.0	110	14.4	197	7.15	6.23	3.82	6.47	267	5.32	408	7.55	234	28
160,945	9	3.6	320	10.4	357	2.54	1.89	1.59	4.80	313	39.04	217	1.06	394	36
151,263†	10	2.1	419	6.6	431	1.69	2.24	1.66	0.18	389	14.25	374	5.38	297	30
27,797	144	7.2	99	15.1	162	5.39	4.50	2.26	9.08	190	25.12	302	14.12	81	29
53,033	58	10.8	28	21.4	29	3.30	3.33	0.68	17.11	38	(3.36)	435	18.26	35	28
33,600	117	3.3	348	14.1	212	2.77	2.64	0.64	15.78	50	78.58	64	9.33	188	10
97,550†	22	3.2	360	11.0	340	6.02	2.77	3.86	4.54	318	55.10	138	5.46	294	45
127,000	14	12.0	15	16.2	121	4.03	3.80	1.97	7.42	241	(17.02)	467	4.78	318	38
32,499	126	6.6	128	13.9	218	7.33	4.20	2.50	11.36	128	82.97	56	7.26	247	29
15,725	249	5.0	221	12.8	263	7.42	6.81	4.74	4.58	317	49.12	163	5.31	299	29
110,000	20	3.3	346	13.9	222	2.30	1.40	2.20	0.45	387	45.74	182	(0.58)	409	36
47,000†	75	1.6	440	11.6	322	4.49	5.05	1.30	13.20	85	18.03	349	10.35	159	20
105,000†	21	3.2	359	6.2	438	3.85	5.54	3.72	0.34	388	28.90	271	9.44	179	33
119,117	16	2.4	410	10.5	356	3.62	2.96	4.11'	(1.26)	410	40.10	212	5.44	295	41
133,383	12	3.0	371	12.6	269	5.05	3.89	2.02	9.60	172	72.78	79	4.04	340	41

100 LARGEST U.S. INDUSTRIAL CORPORATIONS (continued)

Rank 1976	1975	Company	Sales ($000)	Assets ($000)	Rank	Net Income ($000)	Rank	Stockholders' Equity ($000)	Rank
36	29	Caterpillar Tractor (Peoria, IL)	5,042,300	3,893,900	35	383,200	24	2,027,300	34
37	33	Kraft (Glenview, IL)	4,976,643	1,821,854	91	135,650	76	1,015,906	75
38	38	Beatrice Foods (Chicago)⁸	4,690,569	1,844,434	89	153,107	62	997,934	77
39	37	LTV (Dallas)	4,496,893	2,134,874	72	30,700	300	413,242	207
40	39	Xerox (Stamford, CT)	4,403,897	4,612,382	28	358,906	26	2,178,960	28
41	41	R. J. Reynolds Industries (Winston-Salem, NC)	4,291,149*	4,276,761	30	353,893	28	2,112,817	31
42	46	Monsanto (St. Louis)	4,270,200	3,959,100	33	366,300	25	2,252,500	27
43	45	Ashland Oil (Russell, KY)⁶	4,086,845*	2,104,863	74	135,983	74	808,973	106
44	44	General Foods (White Plains, NY)⁹	3,978,294	2,012,932	78	150,428	65	983,172	79
45	53	Cities Service (Tulsa)	3,964,600	3,614,900	40	217,000	41	1,798,200	38
46	42	Firestone Tire & Rubber (Akron, OH)⁴	3,939,107	3,260,593	46	96,003	120	1,567,950	41
47	43	Boeing (Seattle)	3,918,535	1,918,598	84	102,895	110	1,084,826	71
48	54	Amerada Hess (New York)	3,914,595	2,777,271	53	152,637	63	1,161,843	62
49	41	Greyhound (Phoenix)	3,727,306	1,472,554	123	77,081	146	652,327	143
50	47	W. R. Grace (New York)	3,615,153	2,755,862	54	131,882	81	1,155,342	63
51	52	McDonnell Douglas (St. Louis)	3,543,713	2,129,657	73	108,855	99	945,350	84
52	58	International Paper (New York)	3,540,600	3,639,600	38	253,600	37	1,826,500	37
53	56	Minnesota Mining & Manufacturing (St. Paul)	3,514,259	3,324,135	45	338,520	29	2,045,754	33
54	66	Colgate-Palmolive (New York)¹²	3,511,492	1,790,153	95	149,250	67	960,685	81
55	63	Marathon Oil (Findlay, OH)	3,488,436*	3,043,005	47	195,808	46	1,150,527	64
56	57	Continental Group (New York)¹³	3,458,200	2,189,200	68	118,300	92	933,700	87
57	69	Gulf & Western Industries (New York)¹⁴,¹⁵	3,395,596	3,480,304	44	200,169	45	1,095,988	70
58	55	Ralston Purina (St. Louis)⁶	3,393,800	1,556,300	114	125,900	83	765,500	114
59	51	Borden (New York)	3,381,075	1,808,479	93	112,807	98	938,211	86
60	49	Litton Industries (Beverly Hills)¹⁴	3,365,365	2,057,054	76	28,297**	310	806,158	107
61	50	Lockheed Aircraft (Burbank, CA)	3,202,700	1,585,900	111	38,700	262	166,700	378
62	60	Sperry Rand (New York)⁹	3,202,556	2,581,352	57	145,294	69	1,169,265	61
63	59	Armco Steel (Middletown, OH)	3,150,974	2,833,601	50	123,726	84	1,406,140	46
64	65	American Can (Greenwich, CT)¹⁶	3,142,500	1,956,000	81	100,900	113	870,100	95
65	74	Philip Morris (New York)	3,134,496*	3,582,209	41	265,675	34	1,429,982	45
66	62	Deere (Moline, IL)⁴	3,133,790	2,893,153	48	241,571	38	1,378,844	48
67	61	Getty Oil (Los Angeles)	3,058,670	3,628,865	39	258,475	35	2,157,224	29
68	80	Georgia-Pacific (Portland, OR)	3,038,000	2,584,000	56	215,300	42	1,352,100	50
69	64	Coca-Cola (Atlanta)	3,032,829	1,903,065	86	284,959	31	1,356,516	49
70	70	Bendix (Southfield, MI)⁶	2,947,000	1,653,000	106	104,700	105	760,000	116
71	71	TRW (Cleveland)	2,929,014	1,869,745	87	133,063	80	839,392	100
72	85	Aluminum Co. of America (Pittsburgh)	2,924,400	3,569,500	43	143,800	70	1,689,100	39
73	76	Standard Oil (Ohio) (Cleveland)	2,916,420	6,260,218	20	136,857	72	1,549,302	43
74	79	Champion International (Stamford, CT)	2,910,523	2,180,482	70	103,124	109	938,453	85
75	78	Weyerhaeuser (Tacoma, WA)	2,868,379	3,681,744	37	305,967	30	1,981,886	35
76	91	National Steel (Pittsburgh)	2,840,542	2,798,040	52	85,737	133	1,263,122	55
77	83	PepsiCo (Purchase, NY)	2,727,455	1,541,650	117	136,033	73	752,982	118
78	75	Consolidated Foods (Chicago)³	2,726,458	1,146,544	159	89,453	130	623,633	150
79	68	CPC International (Englewood Cliffs, NJ)	2,695,800	1,459,300	125	122,000	86	722,300	124
80	72	American Brands (New York)	2,671,559*	2,456,241	59	121,992	87	1,171,584	60
81	84	General Mills (Minneapolis)¹⁷	2,644,952	1,328,196	139	100,538	115	640,245	147
82	82	Allied Chemical (Morristown, NJ)	2,629,567	2,439,327	60	116,799	95	1,114,288	66
83	77	Textron (Providence)	2,627,178	1,523,135	118	121,056	90	839,283	101
84	88	Owens-Illinois (Toledo)	2,571,709	2,195,231	67	178,336**	49	1,007,534	76
85	98	General Dynamics (St. Louis)	2,553,481	1,457,190	126	99,578	116	644,237	145
86	81	Republic Steel (Cleveland)	2,545,645	2,333,111	63	65,869	173	1,318,890	51
87	92	Johnson & Johnson (New Brunswick, NJ)	2,522,510	1,730,719	102	205,376	43	1,301,939	53
88	67	Honeywell (Minneapolis)	2,495,295	2,203,728	66	113,053	96	1,128,024	65
89	89	American Home Products (New York)	2,471,727	1,510,862	120	277,931	32	991,482	78
90	90	Raytheon (Lexington, MA)	2,462,770	1,511,257	119	85,242	135	536,188	166
91	97	Signal Companies (Beverly Hills)	2,451,639	1,869,442	88	64,796	176	814,213	104
92	99	Inland Steel (Chicago)	2,388,217	2,068,876	75	104,045	108	1,104,655	68

| Employees | | Net Income as Percent of | | | | Earnings per Share | | | | | Total Return to Investors | | | | Industry Code |
| | | Sales | | Stockholders' Equity | | | | | Growth rate 1966–76 | | 1976 | | 1966–76 Average | | |
Number	Rank	%	Rank	%	Rank	1976($)	1975($)	1966($)	%	Rank	%	Rank	%	Rank	
77,793	31	7.6	87	18.9	56	4.45	4.64	1.76	9.72	168	27.88	278	12.48	109	45
46,790	78	2.7	387	13.4	244	4.86	5.01	2.54	6.70	262	14.40	371	7.55	235	20
67,000†	38	3.3	355	15.3	155	1.86	1.71	0.79	8.94	195	24.15	310	11.44	132	20
56,800	50	0.7	476	7.4	423	2.34	1.02	4.02	(5.27)	435	32.09	255	(11.36)	454	20
97,336	23	8.1	69	16.5	108	4.51	3.07	1.25	13.69	77	17.05	359	(0.17)	406	38
37,296	105	8.2	65	16.7	99	7.48	7.39	3.44	8.08	221	15.05	366	12.31	113	21
61,903	43	8.6	54	16.3	117	10.05	8.63	3.41	11.41	125	18.98	338	12.37	112	28
30,000	137	3.3	347	16.8	97	5.03	4.42	2.43	7.55	233	85.87	49	5.60	290	29
47,000	74	3.8	309	15.3	158	3.02	2.00	1.87	4.91	307	14.93	368	2.74	374	20
17,600	228	5.5	194	12.1	300	7.98	5.12	4.82**	5.17	298	60.25	116	7.36	244	29
113,000	18	2.4	407	6.1	443	1.68	2.36	1.76	(0.46)	400	11.69	386	4.48	328	30
65,400†	41	2.6	391	9.5	382	4.85	3.60	4.13	1.62	372	88.70	45	(0.96)	416	41
6,634†	425	3.9	296	13.1	252	3.90	3.26	1.39[10]	10.87	141	96.60	34	6.13	274	29
51,976†	64	2.1	421	11.8	311	1.76	1.87	1.50	1.61	373	22.60	318	5.73	284	20
59,700	44	3.6	318	11.4	331	3.55	5.31	3.95**	(1.06)	405	26.30	292	(0.09)	403	28
57,867	49	3.1	369	11.5	328	2.85	2.27	1.81[11]	4.64	316	59.89	119	3.51	354	41
52,287	62	7.2	103	13.9	221	5.60	4.93	2.40	8.84	200	22.72	316	14.79	70	26
79,522	30	9.6	41	16.5	105	2.94	2.29	1.29	8.59	208	4.64	412	5.62	289	38
52,625†	60	4.3	278	15.5	145	1.95	1.73	0.67	11.27	130	(1.50)	433	14.11	82	43
12,927	294	5.6	181	17.0	88	6.52	4.28	2.35	10.74	146	40.96	211	10.27	161	29
58,879†	46	3.4	342	12.7	267	4.01	3.64	2.54	4.67	315	29.90	268	6.98	252	34
110,000	19	5.9	159	18.3	67	4.26	3.26	0.94	16.31	43	17.18	357	7.16	248	34
59,000	45	3.7	316	16.4	109	3.53	2.80	1.49	9.01	192	14.86	370	10.49	153	20
40,400†	92	3.3	345	12.0	302	3.64	3.01	2.16	5.36	291	32.76	253	5.64	288	20
92,800	24	0.8	464	3.5	463	0.64**	0.85	1.76	(9.62)	442	121.65	14	(13.52)	456	44
54,600	54	1.2	449	23.2	19	3.10	3.86	5.29	(5.20)	434	21.27	329	(16.39)	457	41
87,090	26	4.5	260	12.4	282	4.19	3.81	1.02	15.18	55	11.06	388	5.27	300	44
48,946†	68	3.9	294	8.8	395	3.93	3.71	2.93	2.98	352	26.08	294	9.41	182	33
47,700†	71	3.2	358	11.6	324	5.10	4.17	4.18	2.01	364	31.48	259	4.22	337	34
51,000	66	8.5	58	18.6	60	4.47	3.62	0.77	19.23	27	18.54	342	24.22	10	21
55,242	52	7.7	82	17.5	79	4.04	3.01	1.37	11.42	124	25.79	295	10.19	165	45
12,187	312	8.4	60	12.0	304	13.81	13.71	4.43	12.04	110	21.93	322	15.09	64	10
34,200	112	7.1	105	15.9	129	2.21	1.60	0.64	13.19	86	42.03	208	18.55	31	26
32,952	121	9.4	43	21.0	34	4.76	4.00	1.56	11.80	113	(0.73)	430	7.99	224	49
79,700	29	3.6	328	13.8	225	4.74	3.66	2.52	6.52	265	44.24	196	10.82	146	40
87,625	25	4.5	259	15.9	134	4.05	3.08	1.87	8.03	222	41.10	210	8.95	196	40
43,300	87	4.9	232	8.5	401	4.14	1.85	3.22	2.54	359	51.78	150	4.02	341	33
21,062	199	4.7	244	8.8	394	3.55	3.42	2.32	4.35	324	13.82	377	12.42	111	29
46,928	76	3.5	332	11.0	342	3.04	1.82	1.87	4.98	303	55.48	136	6.70	260	26
47,211	73	10.7	31	15.4	149	2.32	1.51	0.65	13.57	78	27.41	282	20.86	19	26
36,152†	108	3.0	374	6.8	428	4.53	3.10	4.56	(0.07)	393	25.34	300	7.64	232	33
54,000	56	5.0	224	18.1	70	5.56	4.41	1.83	11.75	115	16.47	360	10.43	157	49
76,600	32	3.3	353	14.3	201	2.99	0.27	1.64	6.19	272	33.23	246	3.43	358	20
42,500	89	4.5	263	16.9	94	5.15	4.62	2.64	6.91	257	17.43	356	5.25	301	20
54,800	53	4.6	257	10.4	361	4.54	5.63	2.95	4.41	320	25.69	297	10.29	160	21
51,778	65	3.8	306	15.7	142	2.04	1.59	0.77	10.23	157	17.48	354	11.14	138	20
33,448	119	4.4	268	10.5	355	4.18	4.17	3.19	2.74	356	25.73	296	6.80	256	28
64,000	42	4.6	248	14.4	198	3.23	2.58	1.87	5.62	282	42.38	206	4.48	329	41
67,056	37	6.9	111	17.7	75	11.58**	6.02	3.52	12.65	95	12.05	385	3.47	357	32
71,600	34	3.9	295	15.5	148	9.11	7.94	5.64	4.91	306	42.86	205	3.29	364	37
39,593†	96	2.6	395	5.0	455	4.07	4.46	5.94	(3.71)	423	26.62	291	5.15	307	33
57,900	48	8.1	70	15.8	138	3.53	3.18	0.67	18.08	32	(11.92)	457	15.95	51	42
70,775	35	4.5	261	10.0	368	5.50	3.96	3.12	5.83	279	49.81	157	(0.95)	415	44
47,570	72	11.2	23	28.0	7	1.75	1.58	0.61	11.11	132	(1.13)	432	11.45	131	42
52,957	59	3.5	339	15.9	131	5.58	4.69	1.62	13.16	89	33.92	241	10.53	152	36
42,300	90	2.6	390	8.0	412	3.14	1.89	2.48	2.39	360	68.96	90	4.72	320	40
34,476†	111	4.4	272	9.4	384	5.20	4.43	3.73	3.38	345	30.98	262	11.77	125	33

100 LARGEST U.S. INDUSTRIAL CORPORATIONS (concluded)

Rank			Sales	Assets		Net Income		Stockholders' Equity	
1976	1975	Company	($000)	($000)	Rank	($000)	Rank	($000)	Rank
93	95	Warner-Lambert (Morris Plains, NJ)	2,349,198	1,929,924	82	159,661	57	1,185,013	58
94	87	American Motors (Southfield, MI)⁶	2,315,470	991,586	182	(46,340)	492	311,373	256
95	93	Uniroyal (Middlebury, CT)	2,314,841	1,633,655	107	20,132	369	628,177	149
96	96	NCR (Dayton, OH)	2,312,713	2,311,795	64	95,644	121	888,848	93
97	86	FMC (Chicago)	2,298,353	1,919,553	83	80,157	141	868,206	97
98	104	Burlington Industries (Greensboro, NC)⁶	2,284,626	1,733,899	100	104,918	103	972,220	80
99	94	United Brands (Boston)	2,276,559	1,085,268	164	16,340**	399	498,968	175
100	109	PPG Industries (Pittsburgh)	2,254,800	2,033,200	77	151,500	64	1,021,600	74

n.a. = Not available.
* Does not include excise taxes; see the explanation of "sales" at the end of the table.
** Reflects an extraordinary credit of at least 10 percent; see the explanations of "net income" and "earnings per share" at the end of the table.
† Average for the year; see the reference to "employees" at the end of the table.
‡ Reflects an extraordinary charge of at least 10 percent; see the explanations of "net income" and "earnings per share" at the end of the table.
¹ A holding company created in 1976 as a successor to Mobil Oil, now a wholly owned subsidiary.
² Figures for 1976 include Utah International (1975 rank: 273), merged in December 1976.
³ Figures are for fiscal year ending June 30, 1976.
⁴ Figures are for fiscal year ending October 31, 1976.
⁵ Name changed from Sun Oil in April 1976.
⁶ Figures are for fiscal year ending September 30, 1976.

Sales include service and rental revenues but exclude dividends, interest, and other nonoperating revenues. All companies on the list must have derived more than 50 percent of their sales from manufacturing and/or mining. Sales of subsidiaries are included when they are consolidated; sales from discontinued operations are included when these figures are published. All figures are for the year ending December 31, 1976, unless otherwise noted. Sales figures do not include excise taxes collected by the manufacturer, and so the figures for some corporations—most of which sell gasoline, liquor, or tobacco—may be lower than those published by the corporations themselves. When they are at least 5 percent lower for this reason, there is an asterisk (*) next to the sales figure.

Assets are those shown at the company's year-end.

Net income is shown after taxes and after extraordinary credits or charges when they are shown on the income statement. A double asterisk (**) signifies an extraordinary credit reflecting at least 10 percent of the net income shown, a double dagger (‡) an extraordinary charge of at least 10 percent.

Stockholders' equity is the sum of capital stock, surplus, and retained earnings at the company's year-end.

Employees: The figure shown is a year-end total except when it is followed by a dagger (†), in which case it is an average for the year.

Earnings per share: For all companies, the figures shown for 1976 and 1975 are the "primary" earnings per share that appear in the company's income statement. These figures are based on a weighted average of the number of common shares and common-stock equivalents outstanding during the year. "Common-stock equivalents" generally include (a) convertible securities whose cash yield is less than two thirds of the prime rate at the time the securities were issued and (b) options and warrants when the effect of their inclusion in the computation would reduce the "primary" earnings per share. Weighted averages are used for 1966 where these are available; where they are not, figures are based on a simple average of 1965 and 1966 year-end shares outstanding. Per-share earnings for 1975 and 1966 are adjusted for stock splits and stock dividends. They are not restated for mergers, acquisitions, or accounting changes made after 1966. A double asterisk (**) signifies an extraordinary credit reflecting at least 10 percent of the net income shown, a double dagger (‡) an extraordinary charge of at least 10 percent. Results are listed as not available (n.a.) where the companies are cooperatives, joint ventures, or wholly owned subsidiaries of other companies. The growth rate is the average annual growth, compounded. No growth rate is given if the company had a loss in either 1966 or 1976.

Total return to investors includes both price appreciation and dividend yield, i.e., to an investor in the company's stock. The figures shown assume sales at the end of 1976 of stock owned at the end of 1966 or 1975. It

Employees		Net Income as Percent of				Earnings per Share					Total Return to Investors				Industry Code
		Sales		Stockholders' Equity					Growth Rate 1966-76		1976		1966-76 Average		
Number	Rank	%	Rank	%	Rank	1976($)	1975($)	1966($)	%	Rank	%	Rank	%	Rank	
58,000	47	6.8	120	13.5	236	2.01	2.08	0.90	8.37	212	(12.43)	460	7.13	249	42
29,524	140	—		—		(1.56)	(0.92)	(0.66**	—		(28.02)	473	(4.10)	438	40
54,020†	55	0.9	462	3.2	467	0.57	0.68	1.63	(9.97)	444	28.55	274	(1.90)	423	30
67,000	39	4.1	282	10.8	346	3.75	2.99	1.55	9.24	184	60.93	112	3.06	367	44
40,247	93	3.5	338	9.2	387	2.36	3.24	2.09	1.22	380	26.72	288	2.00	382	45
70,000	36	4.6	252	10.8	344	3.75	1.43	3.08	1.99	366	6.95	402	4.57	324	22
48,300	69	0.7	472	3.3	466	1.28**	0.80	0.08‡	31.95	4	100.09	29	4.52	325	20
36,300	107	6.7	124	14.8	178	7.28	4.28	2.38	11.83	112	68.20	93	12.50	108	28

7 Figure is for North American Aviation.
8 Figures are for fiscal year ending February 29, 1976.
9 Figures are for fiscal year ending March 31, 1976.
10 Figure is for Hess Oil & Chemical.
11 Figure is for McDonnell Aircraft.
12 Figures for 1976 include Riviana Foods (1975 rank; 366), acquired June 14, 1976.
13 Name changed from Continental Can, April 27, 1976.
14 Figures are for fiscal year ending July 31, 1976.
15 Figures for 1976 include Kayser-Roth (1975 rank; 320), acquired in October 1975.
16 Figures for 1976 include U.S. Reduction (1975 rank; 920), acquired in June 1976.
17 Figures are for fiscal year ending May 31, 1976.
Source: Reprinted from the 1977 Fortune Directory by special permission; © 1977 Time Inc.

has been assumed that any proceeds from cash dividends, the sale of rights and warrant offerings, and stock received in spin-offs were reinvested at the end of the year in which they were received. Returns are adjusted for stock splits, stock dividends, recapitalizations, and corporate reorganizations as they occur; however, no effort has been made to reflect the cost of brokerage commissions or of taxes. Results are listed as not available (n.a.) where shares are not publicly traded or traded on only a limited basis. Where companies have more than one class of shares outstanding, only the more widely held and actively traded has been considered.

Total-return percentages shown are the returns received by the hypothetical investor described above. The ten-year figures are annual averages, compounded. Where corporations were substantially reorganized—e.g., because of mergers—the predecessor companies used in calculating total returns are the same as those cited in the footnotes dropped from the earnings-per-share figures.

Industry code numbers used in the directory indicate which industry represents the greatest volume of industrial sales for each company. The numbers refer to the industry groups below, all of which are based on categories established by the U.S. Office of Management and Budget. They are the same industry groups as those shown in the tables beginning on this page. The median figures in those tables refer only to results of companies among the 100, however, no attempt has been made to calculate medians in groups with less than four companies.

Rankings: These refer to relative position within the Fortune list of 500 Largest U.S. Industrial Corporations.

Code No.	Industry
10......	Mining, crude-oil production
20......	Food
21......	Tobacco
22......	Textiles, vinyl flooring
23......	Apparel
25......	Furniture
26......	Paper, fiber, and wood products
27......	Publishing, printing
28......	Chemicals
29......	Petroleum refining
30......	Rubber, plastic products
31......	Leather
32......	Glass, concrete, abrasives, gypsum
33......	Metal manufacturing
34......	Metal products
36......	Electronics, appliances
37......	Shipbuilding, railroad, and transportation equipment
38......	Measuring, scientific, and photographic equipment
40......	Motor vehicles
41......	Aerospace
42......	Pharmaceuticals
43......	Soaps, cosmetics
44......	Office equipment (includes computers)
45......	Industrial and farm equipment
46......	Jewelry, silverware
47......	Musical instruments, toys, sporting goods
48......	Broadcasting, motion-picture production and distribution
49......	Beverages

100 LARGEST INDUSTRIAL CORPORATIONS OUTSIDE THE UNITED STATES (ranked by sales)

Rank 1976	Company	Country	Industry	Sales[1] ($000)	Assets[2] ($000)	Net Income[3] ($000)	Stockholders' Equity[4] ($000)	Employees
1	Royal Dutch/Shell Group	Neth.-Britain	Petroleum	36,087,130	29,645,758	2,347,766	11,186,285	153,000
2	National Iranian Oil[b]	Iran	Petroleum	19,671,064	6,544,991	17,175,182	4,261,182	57,331
3	British Petroleum	Britain	Petroleum	19,103,330	14,925,935	324,615	4,862,138	78,000
4	Unilever	Britain-Neth.	Food products, detergents	15,762,219	7,793,812	517,614	2,949,024	317,000
5	Philips' Glöeilampenfabrieken	Netherlands	Electronics, appliances	11,521,549[6]	12,245,086	212,940	4,142,039	391,500[6]
6	ENI[5]	Italy	Petroleum	9,983,105*,[6]	12,803,525*,[6]	(37,026)*,[6]	1,561,125*,[6]	100,747*,[6]
7	Française des Pétroles	France	Petroleum	9,927,775[7]	8,946,164[7]	34,731[7]	1,662,038[7]	44,000[7]
8	Renault[5]	France	Motor vehicles	9,352,884	N.A.	N.A.	N.A.	241,259
9	Hoechst	Germany	Chemicals	9,332,979[6]	8,753,727	188,010	1,891,270	182,980[6]
10	BASF	Germany	Chemicals	9,202,592[6]	6,579,049	241,176	2,330,841	112,686[6]
11	Petróleos de Venezuela[5]	Venezuela	Petroleum	9,083,587	4,962,648	876,153	3,357,774	23,000
12	Daimler-Benz	Germany	Motor vehicles	8,938,321[6]	3,566,418	164,182	977,264	160,863[6]
13	Volkswagenwerk	Germany	Motor vehicles	8,513,304	6,144,450	399,164	1,611,331	183,238
14	Bayer[8]	Germany	Chemicals	8,297,808[6]	8,516,779[6]	181,364[6]	1,980,957[6]	171,200[6]
15	Nippon Steel[9]	Japan	Metal refining—steel	8,089,530	11,624,997	38,572	1,466,814	98,746
16	Siemens[10]	Germany	Electronics, appliances	8,060,411	8,229,723	221,969	2,360,882	304,000
17	Thyssen[10,11]	Germany	Metal refining—steel, machinery	7,947,640	5,647,055	105,499	1,269,672	139,440
18	Toyota Motor[12]	Japan	Motor vehicles	7,695,997[6]	4,834,433[6]	345,433[6]	1,802,237[6]	59,479[6]
19	Nestlé	Switzerland	Food products	7,627,869	5,706,916	348,922	3,007,705	137,329
20	ELF-Aquitaine[5]	France	Petroleum	7,536,225	9,770,720	340,108	2,410,557	34,000
21	Imperial Chemical Industries[13]	Britain	Chemicals	7,465,412	7,773,570	442,328	3,116,232	192,000
22	Peugeot-Citroën[14]	France	Motor vehicles	7,346,998[6]	4,823,651[6]	287,426[6]	1,269,079[6]	185,875[6]
23	Petrobrás (Petróleo Brasileiro)[5]	Brazil	Petroleum	7,252,110	8,259,491	934,579	3,779,641	49,435
24	Hitachi[10]	Japan	Electronics, appliances	6,680,423	8,388,765	200,377	1,990,350	143,014
25	BAT Industries[10,15]	Britain	Tobacco, paper products	6,668,743	5,182,520	323,541	2,314,040	148,000
26	Nissan Motor[10]	Japan	Motor vehicles	6,583,517	5,233,182	273,005	1,588,756	76,089
27	Mitsubishi Heavy Industries[10]	Japan	Industrial equipment, motor vehicles	6,137,230	8,917,191	47,711	705,741	109,300
28	Saint-Gobain-Pont-à-Mousson	France	Building materials	5,979,469	5,685,223	98,775	1,413,289	160,075
29	Montedison	Italy	Chemicals	5,826,436[6]	7,221,152[6]	(195,019)[6]	842,090[6]	144,595[6]
30	Matsushita Electric Industrial[16]	Japan	Electronics, appliances	5,736,562	5,101,767	220,641	2,146,643	83,081
31	AEG-Telefunken	Germany	Electronics, appliances	5,351,388	3,693,985	164,134	653,607	161,900
32	General Motors of Canada	Canada	Motor vehicles	5,264,237	1,284,673	162,101	569,358	31,639
33	British Steel[5,9]	Britain	Metal refining—steel	5,203,793	6,247,750	(541,209)	1,805,927	219,000
34	Ruhrkohle	Germany	Mining—coal	4,904,094	4,992,769	14,668	253,162	147,505
35	Ford Motor of Canada	Canada	Motor vehicles	4,837,782	1,651,434	128,010	889,273	36,700
36	Mannesmann	Germany	Metal manufacturing	4,688,566	3,778,677	109,372	883,848	108,684
37	Pechiney Ugine Kuhlmann	France	Metal refining—aluminum, copper, steel	4,662,784	5,478,604	31,994	1,306,059	96,500
38	Fiat	Italy	Motor vehicles	4,668,028[17]	6,159,348[17]	80,412[17]	817,711[17]	143,223[17]
39	Rhône-Poulenc	France	Chemicals	4,554,127	4,938,731	(76,265)	1,378,784	113,500
40	Tokyo Shibaura Electric	Japan	Chemicals, Electric...					

#	Company	Country	Industry	Sales	Assets	Net Income		Employees
41	Idemitsu Kosan[9]	Japan	Petroleum	4,425,749	4,208,787	(3,859)	41,162	11,040
42	Imperial Oil	Canada	Petroleum	4,365,762	3,109,807	267,788	1,719,855	14,753
43	Gutehoffnungshütte[11]	Germany	Industrial equipment	4,306,991[6]	3,317,777	31,241	358,774	84,508[6]
44	National Coal Board[5,9]	Britain	Mining—coal	4,208,618	2,439,458	11,382	57,669	312,000
45	British Leyland[8]	Britain	Motor vehicles	4,177,512*	2,747,819	61,205*	641,490	183,384
46	Dunlop Pirelli Union	Britain-Italy	Rubber products, cables	4,172,326	N.A.	N.A.	N.A.	164,200
47	Denain Nord-Est Longwy	France	Metal refining—steel	4,122,641	6,686,268	(516,843)	610,563	80,000
48	Petrofina	Belgium	Petroleum	4,091,955	4,697,841	156,247	1,383,113	21,000
49	Sumitomo Metal Industries[10]	Japan	Metal refining—steel	4,075,256	6,905,397	23,678	527,408	44,867
50	Akzo Group	Netherlands	Chemicals, synthetic fibers	4,069,438	3,564,574	(57,831)	1,069,378	91,100
51	Mitsubishi Chemical Industries[18]	Japan	Chemicals, aluminum	3,983,086	4,248,604	17,492	363,943	17,194
52	Esso	Germany	Petroleum	3,935,196[6]	1,880,062[6]	86,537[6]	458,429[6]	6,131[6]
53	Nippon Kokan[9]	Japan	Metal refining—steel	3,930,131[17]	6,025,785[17]	16,226[17]	641,602[17]	41,523[17]
54	Fried. Krupp	Germany	Metal refining—steel	3,868,292	2,823,410	10,048	336,775	76,161
55	Ciba-Geigy	Switzerland	Pharmaceuticals	3,796,528	5,882,614	128,045	3,853,098	74,355
56	General Electric[9]	Britain	Electronics, appliances	3,720,731	3,241,320	210,836	1,501,108	206,000
57	Kobe Steel[10]	Japan	Metal refining—steel	3,678,133	5,050,856	20,430	483,745	43,129
58	Volvo	Sweden	Motor vehicles	3,614,727	3,808,463	14,465	1,385,451	62,441
59	Thomson-Brandt	France	Electronics, appliances	3,533,555[6]	3,859,227[6]	43,936[6]	359,760[6]	105,600[6]
60	ESTEL	Netherlands	Metal refining—steel	3,524,337	4,572,173	(26,136)	1,320,602	76,100
61	DSM[5]	Netherlands	Chemicals, fertilizers	3,522,642[6]	2,837,586[6]	49,980[6]	833,708[6]	32,600[6]
62	Ford-Werke	Germany	Motor vehicles	3,440,374	1,511,889	249,505	447,639	52,929
63	Michelin	France	Rubber, plastic products	3,394,224	4,068,280	157,140	966,720	110,000
64	Kawasaki Steel[10]	Japan	Metal refining—steel	3,377,064	5,787,441	23,027	558,478	38,892
65	Brown, Boveri	Switzerland	Industrial and farm equipment	3,373,580	4,732,814	N.A.	N.A.	99,100
66	Veba-Chemie	Germany	Petroleum	3,336,697[6]	1,774,657[6]	(7,359)[6]	310,197[6]	11,427[6]
67	Imperial Group[9]	Britain	Tobacco	3,321,595*,[6]	2,577,797[6]	147,648[6]	1,167,710[6]	96,700[6]
68	Robert Bosch	Germany	Electronics, appliances	3,305,778	2,251,224	86,242	639,127	110,880
69	Générale d'Electricité	France	Electronics, appliances	3,283,178[6]	3,842,309[6]	86,723[6]	509,139[6]	130,200[6]
70	Pemex (Petróleos Mexicanos)[5]	Mexico	Petroleum	3,137,742	3,069,423	22,415	2,010,077	90,090
71	Schneider	France	Industrial equipment, steel	3,040,785[6]	6,732,299[6]	10,706[6]	327,779[6]	94,000[6]
72	Rio Tinto-Zinc	Britain	Mining—aluminum, copper, iron	3,019,565	4,355,751	165,557	1,126,572	46,500
73	Taiyo Fishery	Japan	Food products	2,993,551	1,362,408	2,565	84,895	20,585
74	Chrysler Canada	Canada	Motor vehicles	2,983,257	714,455	43,135	316,867	16,200
75	Esso	France	Petroleum	2,963,095	1,289,262	29,354	235,195	4,813
76	Ford Motor	Britain	Motor vehicles	2,938,321	1,439,726	106,700	452,976	68,000
77	Maruzen Oil[9]	Japan	Petroleum	2,883,791[17]	1,867,408[17]	11,927[17]	46,898[17]	4,603[17]
78	Flick Group	Germany	Paper products and wood products	2,875,078	3,537,120	19,958	419,317	54,547
79	George Weston Holdings[20]	Britain	Food products	2,826,886	1,097,980	51,910	285,699	105,222
80	Massey-Ferguson[19]	Canada	Industrial and farm equipment	2,771,696	2,305,145	117,914	803,021	68,200
81	Guest, Keen & Nettlefolds	Britain	Motor vehicle parts	2,710,315	2,360,001	54,686	1,030,228	107,685
82	Italsider[5]	Italy	Metal refining—steel	2,665,334[17]	5,723,205[17]	(157,609)[17]	318,582[17]	53,524[17]
83	Esso Petroleum	Britain	Petroleum	2,660,424	2,317,783	(22,976)	455,871	10,561
84	Alcan Aluminum	Canada	Metal refining—aluminum	2,656,072	3,090,239	44,007	1,269,604	60,000
85	Salzgitter[5,10]	Germany	Metal refining—steel, shipbuilding	2,580,529	2,914,262	(18,517)	285,670	54,069
86	Tate & Lyle[10]	Britain	Food products	2,558,717	879,715	50,650	301,758	16,291
87	Courtaulds[9]	Britain	Textiles	2,476,311	2,333,566	55,841	834,758	138,770
88	Charbonnages de France[5]	France	Mining—coal	2,475,267[6]	2,607,956[6]	(158,132)[6]	206,647[6]	100,000[6]
89	BSN-Gervais Danone	France	Food products	2,463,100[6]	938,159[6]	9,676[6]	471,653[6]	61,607[6]
90	Honda Motor[21]	Japan	Motor vehicles	2,435,632	1,905,803	60,902	402,270	28,218
91	Metallgesellschaft[10]	Germany	Metal refining—nonferrous	2,427,219	1,457,015	6,534	219,507	26,053
92	VOEST-Alpine[5]	Austria	Metal refining—steel	2,408,400	3,433,735	N.A.	858,340	81,120[6]
93	IBM Deutschland	Germany	Office equipment (includes computers)	2,368,482	1,849,379	305,758	466,070	24,215

100 LARGEST INDUSTRIAL CORPORATIONS OUTSIDE THE UNITED STATES (ranked by sales) (continued)

	Company	Country	Industry	Sales[1] (000)	Assets[2] (000)	Net Income[3] (000)	Stock-holders' Equity[4] (000)	Employees
94	Broken Hill Proprietary[21]	Australia	Metal refining—steel	2,335,042	3,694,205	80,555	2,076,343	61,000
95	Toa Nenryo Kogyo	Japan	Petroleum	2,333,937	1,718,759	82,124	314,740	4,077
96	Solvay	Belgium	Chemicals	2,276,994[6]	2,566,458[6]	105,831[6]	1,039,490[6]	44,109[6]
97	Mitsubishi Electric[10]	Japan	Electronics, appliances	2,273,437	3,055,209	31,111	413,712	66,997
98	Reed International[9]	Britain	Paper and wood products	2,258,257	1,976,251	23,780	689,149	87,000
99	Statsföretag Group[5]	Sweden	Mining—iron, paper products	2,238,078[6]	4,438,284[6]	44,682[6]	1,091,735[6]	47,710[6]
100	Saab-Scania	Sweden	Motor vehicles	2,207,241	2,159,366	24,959	260,130	41,386

N.A. Not available.
* Fortune estimate.

[1] All companies on the list must have derived more than 50 percent of their sales from manufacturing and/or mining. Sales do not include excise taxes or customs duties levied according to either volume or value of sales, and so the figures for some corporations—most of them sell gasoline, liquor, or tobacco—may be lower than those published by the corporations themselves. Unless otherwise noted, figures exclude intracompany transactions and include subsidiaries more than 50 percent owned, either on a fully consolidated or prorata basis. Sales and net income have been converted to dollars, using an exchange rate that consists of the average rate in the official exchange market during the company's fiscal year; total assets and stockholders' equity have been converted at the market rate prevailing at the company's year-end (December 31, 1976, unless otherwise noted).

[2] As shown at the company's year-end.
[3] After taxes and minority interest. Figures In parentheses are losses. Figures in parentheses are losses.
[4] Sum of capital stock, surplus, and retained earnings at the end of the fiscal year. Figures in parentheses are losses.
[5] Government owned.
[6] Also includes certain subsidiaries owned 50 percent or less, either fully or on a prorated basis.
[7] Includes all subsidiaries on a prorated basis.
[8] Includes Agfa-Gevaert (1974 rank: 175), 50 percent owned.
[9] Figures are for fiscal year ending March 31, 1976.
[10] Figures are for fiscal year ending September 30, 1976.
[11] Name changed from August Thyssen-Hütte on April 29, 1977.
[12] Figures are for fiscal year ending June 30, 1976.
[13] Excludes Carrington Viyella (sales rank: 415) 63 percent owned.
[14] Peugeot (1975 rank: 49) and Citroën (1975 rank: 74) merged September 30, 1976.
[15] Company reorganized and name changed from British-American Tobacco in July, 1976.
[16] Figures are for fiscal year ending November 20, 1976.
[17] Parent only.
[18] Figures are for fiscal year ending July 31, 1976.
[19] Figures are for fiscal year ending October 31, 1976.
[20] Figures are for fiscal year ending February 29, 1976.
[21] Figures are for fiscal year ending August 31, 1976.
[22] Figures are for fiscal year ending May 31, 1976.
Source: Reprinted from the 1977 Fortune Directory by special permission © Time Inc.

100 LARGEST FOREIGN-OWNED COMPANIES IN THE UNITED STATES*

U.S. Company	Foreign Owner, Nationality, Percent Owned†	Estimated 1975 Sales of U.S. Company	Industry or Product	Estimated 1975 Employment of U.S. Company
1. Shell Oil	Royal Dutch Petroleum Company, Netherlands, and Shell Transport & Trading Co., U.K. (69%)	$8,876 million	Oil, chemicals	32,496
2. Brown & Williamson Industries	British-American Tobacco, U.K.	2,600	Tobacco, department stores, supermarkets	40,000
3. Joseph E. Seagram & Sons	Seagram Company, Canada	1,630	Liquor, oil	12,500
4. Grand Union	Cavenham Ltd., U.K. (82%)	1,611	Supermarkets	21,000
5. National Tea	George Weston, Ltd., Canada (84%)	1,472	Supermarkets	18,600
6. North American Philips	Philips N. V., Netherlands (60%)‡	1,410	Electrical/electronic products, instruments, chemicals, home furnishings, musical equipment	30,896
7. International Nickel Co. (U.S.) Inc.	International Nickel Co., Canada	1,031	Metals and alloys, batteries	14,103
8. American Petrofina	Petrofina, S. A. Belgium (72%)	986	Oil, chemicals	3,055
9. Ciba-Geigy Corporation	Ciba-Geigy, Switzerland	880	Chemicals, plastics, pharmaceuticals	9,700
10. The Nestlé Company	Nestlé Alimentana, Switzerland	850	Food	6,000
11. Lever Brothers	Unilever, Netherlands and U.K.	747	Detergents, soap, toothpaste, food	6,700
12. Akzona	Akzo N. V., Netherlands (65%)	682	Chemicals, man-made fibers, wire and cable, food, leather	15,791
13. Alcan Aluminum	Alcan Aluminium, Canada	650	Aluminum	4,200
14. American Hoechst	Hoechst A. G., Germany	617	Chemicals, man-made fibers, plastics	8,968
15. Moore Business Forms/F. N. Burt Co.	Moore Corporation, Canada	613	Business forms	12,971

100 LARGEST FOREIGN-OWNED COMPANIES IN THE UNITED STATES (continued)

	U.S. Company	Foreign Owner, Nationality, Percent Owned†	Estimated 1975 Sales of U.S. Company	Industry or Product	Estimated 1975 Employment of U.S. Company
16.	Hoffman-La Roche	F. Hoffman-La Roche & Co., Switzerland	600	Pharmaceuticals	8,200
17.	BASF Wyandotte	BASF, Germany	590	Chemicals	5,665
18.	Massey-Ferguson Inc.	Massey-Ferguson, Ltd., Canada	562	Farm and construction machinery, engines	6,351
19.	Hanson Industries	Hanson Trust, U.K.	559§	Food, textiles	8,500
20.	Certain-Teed Products	St. Gobain Pont-à-Mousson, France, & Turner & Newall, U.K. (51%)	553	Building products	9,136
21.	Burmah Oil‖	Burmah Oil Company, U.K.	515	Oil	3,000
22.	Matsushita Electric Corp. of America/Quasar Electronics Corporation	Matsushita Electric Industrial Company, Japan	500	Consumer electronics	4,250
23.	Loblaw, Inc.	George Weston, Ltd., Canada	481	Supermarkets	4,000
24.	Libby, McNeill & Libby	Nestlé Alimentana, Switzerland	475	Food	6,143
25.	Thomas J. Lipton	Unilever, Netherlands and U.K.	465	Food	5,619
26.	Michelin Tire Corp.	Compagnie Générale des Etablissements Michelin, France	450	Tires	3,000
27.	Mobay Chemical	Bayer A. G., Germany	417	Chemicals	4,360
28.	MacMillan Bloedel	MacMillan Bloedel, Ltd., Canada	415	Forest products	3,506
29.	Indian Head	Thyssen-Bornemisza Groups, Netherlands	413	Glass containers, automotive products, utility products	9,500
30.	Hiram Walker and Sons	Hiram Walker-Gooderham and Worts, Canada	412	Liquor	1,650
31.	Conalco	Alusuisse, Switzerland (60%)	411	Aluminum	5,000
32.	Fiat-Allis	Fiat S.p.A., Italy (65%)	401	Construction machinery	4,818
33.	Timex Corporation	Olsen and Lehmkuhl Families, Norway	400	Watches	21,000
34.	Howmet Corporation	Pechiney Ugine Kuhlmann, France	398	Aluminum, gas turbine components	8,860
35.	Alumax	Mitsui & Co., and Nippon Steel Company, Japan (50%)	384	Aluminum	5,600
36.	Fed-Mart	Hugo Mann, Germany (64%)	381	Retail trade	5,700

#	Company	Parent company, country		Business	
37.	Abitibi Paper Company#	Abitibi Paper Company, Canada	360	Forest products	2,500
38.	Husky Oil Company	Husky Oil, Canada	345	Oil, steel, briquets	2,200
39.	Sony Corporation of America	Sony Corporation, Japan	344	Consumer electronics	2,000
40.	Keebler Company	United Biscuit, U.K.	335	Food	7,514
41.	Bowater, U.S.	Bowater Corporation, U.K.	295	Paper	3,000
42.	Copperweld	Société IMETAL, France (69%)	283	Steel and other metal products	3,567
43.	Dow Badische	BASF, Germany (50%)	277	Chemicals, man-made fibers	5,500
44.	ICI, U.S.	Imperial Chemical Industries, U.K.	276	Pharmaceuticals, chemicals, plastics	6,000
45.	J. Lyons U.S. Holdings Inc.	J. Lyons & Co., U.K.	275	Food	2,000
46.	Kay Corporation	Bowater Corporation, U.K. (72%)	242	Retail jewelry stores, stock-yards, trading	1,310
47.	TOTAL Leonard, Inc.	Total Petroleum (North America) Ltd., Canada	237	Oil	1,164
48.	Davy Powergas	Davy International, U.K.	230	Construction engineering	1,000
49.	Sandoz, Inc.	Sandoz A. G., Switzerland	225	Pharmaceuticals, chemicals, food, seeds	3,200
50.	Liquid Air Corp. of North America	L'Air Liquide, France (67.5%)	215	Industrial gases	2,700
51.	American Chain & Cable Co.	Babcock and Wilcox, U.K.	200	Materials handling equipment, industrial supplies, wire products	5,300
52.	Dunlop Tire & Rubber	Dunlop Holdings, U.K.	200	Tires, sporting goods	3,300
53.	U.S. Borax & Chemical	Rio Tinto Zinc, U.K.	200	Mining, chemicals, consumer products	2,006
54.	Beecham, Inc.	Beecham Group, U.K.	190	Pharmaceuticals, toiletries	1,500
55.	DHJ Industries	Dominion Textile, Canada	182	Apparel	2,250
56.	SKF Industries	A. B. Svenska Kullagerfabriken, Sweden‡	182	Bearings	4,490
57.	Azcon Corporation	Consolidated Gold Fields, U.K. (85%)	181	Drilling equipment, wholesale steel products	1,600
58.	Stouffer Foods	Nestlé Alimentana, Switzerland	180	Food, restaurants, inns	10,000
59.	Gardinier, Inc.	Sopag International, France	177	Chemicals	1,300
60.	Carling National Breweries	Carling O'Keefe, Ltd., Canada	171	Beer	2,000
61.	Cominco American	Cominco, Ltd., Canada	167	Chemicals, metals	931
62.	Soo Line Railroad	Canadian Pacific, Ltd., Canada (56%)	161	Rail transportation	4,470
63.	National Union Electric	A. B. Electrolux, Sweden	160	Electric appliances	3,000
64.	Korf Industries	Coinvest BV, Netherlands	150	Steel	2,348
65.	Ohrbach's	Brenninkmeyer Family, Netherlands	150	Department stores	2,500

100 LARGEST FOREIGN-OWNED COMPANIES IN THE UNITED STATES (concluded)

U.S. Company	Foreign Owner, Nationality, Percent Owned†	Estimated 1975 Sales of U.S. Company	Industry or Product	Estimated 1975 Employment of U.S. Company
66. R. T. French Company............	Reckett & Coleman Holdings, U.K.	150	Food	2,250
67. Plessey North America Corp.......	Plessey Company, Ltd., U.K.	150	Electronics, metals	3,500
68. Olivetti Corporation of America....	Ing. C. Olivetti, Italy	149	Office machines	3,920
69. Grand Trunk Corporation..........	Canadian National Railways, Canada	146	Rail transportation	5,000
70. Burroughs-Wellcome.............	Wellcome Foundation, U.K.	142	Pharmaceuticals	2,220
71. AMCA International...............	Dominion Bridge, Canada	138	Steel products	5,000
72. Siemens Corporation..............	Siemens A. G., Germany	130	Medical equipment, electronics	2,700
73. Cutter Laboratories...............	Bayer A. G., Germany	128	Pharmaceuticals, hospital supplies	3,900
74. Capitol industries-EMI Inc........	EMI, Ltd., U.K.	125	Records and tapes	2,500
75. Coats & Clark....................	Coats Paton, U.K.	125	Textiles	6,300
76. Thomson Newspapers#............	Thomson Newspapers, Canada	123	Newspapers	4,200
77. Stinnes Corporation..............	Veba A. G., Germany	111	Machine tools, machinery reconditioning, trading	775
78. Terra Chemicals International......	Anglo-American, South Africa (51%)	110	Chemical fertilizers	553
79. Noranda Aluminum/Norandex.....	Noranda Mines, Canada	105	Aluminum	2,000
80. Robert Bosch Corporation	Robert Bosch GmbH, Germany	101	Auto parts	1,050
81. Nipro, Inc./Columbia Nitrogen.....	DSM, Netherlands	101	Chemicals	653
82. Sears Industries.................	Sears Holdings, U.K. (69%)	101	Linen supply, laundries, knitwear	5,200
83. Rhodia Inc......................	Rhone Poulenc, France	100	Chemicals	900
84. Cadbury-Schweppes USA..........	Cadbury-Schweppes, U.K.	100	Food	3,000
85. Northern Telecom................	Bell Canada, Canada	100	Communications equipment	1,600
86. Alaska Lumber and Pulp Co./Alaska Pulp America.......	Alaska Pulp Co., Japan	100	Forest products	787
87. Bond Industries.................	Seamar BV, Netherlands (54%)	99	Apparel retailing and manufacturing	3,625
88. American Thread.................	Tootal Ltd. U.K.	98	Thread, yarn	3,350
89. Brooke Bond Foods..............	Brooke Bond Liebig, U.K.	96	Food	450
90. Bic Pen.......................	Société Bic and Bich family, France (67%)	93	Consumer products	1,524
91. Brown Boveri........	Brown Boveri, Switzerland	93	Power equipment	317

	Company	Parent	Product	% Owned	Employment
92.	Theo H. Davies and Company	Jardine Matheson and Co., Hong Kong	Sugar production, heavy equipment distribution	91	1,753
93.	Sandvik Steel	Sandvikens Jernverks AB, Sweden	Steel products	87	1,225
94.	Travelodge International	Trust Houses Forte, U.K.	Motels	80	1,600
95.	Bekaert Steel Wire	N. V. Bekaert, Belgium	Steel products	77	500
96.	Progresso Foods	Imasco Ltd., Canada	Food	75	650
97.	S & W Fine Foods	Imasco Ltd., Canada	Food	75	600
98.	Bantam Books	IFI International, Italy	Publishing	75	600
99.	Bata Shoe	Bata Shoe, Canada	Footwear	70	3,900
100.	CGR Medical Corp.	Compagnie Générale de Radiologie, France	Medical electronics	68	1,321
	Total			$44,739 million	540,911

*This table includes industrial, surface transportation, retail, and service companies at least 50 percent owned by foreign investors. Excluded are foreign-owned banks, insurance companies, wholesale trading firms, airlines, and steamship companies. While most of the companies listed here do not publicly report sales or employment, many of them did provide us with the data listed here. In other cases, sales and employment were estimated.
† If no percentage of ownership is listed, U.S. company is at least 90 perent foreign owned.
‡ Through a U.S. trust.
§ Restated to include 1976 acquisition of Hygrade Food Products Corp.
‖ Principal U.S. subsidiaries divested in 1976.
Numerous U.S. subsidiaries. Sales and employment estimated for all subsidiaries together, even though there is no single U.S. parent firm.
Source: *Across the Board*, The Conference Board.

Executive Recruiting Organizations

With the exception of CPA firms, most of the other firms listed below are members of one or both of the following organizations:

Association of Consulting Management Engineers, Inc.
  347 Madison Avenue
  New York, NY
  212–697–9693

Association of Executive Recruiting Consultants, Inc.
  30 Rockefeller Plaza
  New York, NY 10020
  212–541–7580

Further information regarding complete listings of domestic and foreign branches of the member firms can be obtained from the above organizations or from the main offices of the firms themselves.

Ahrens, Davis & Associates, Inc.
  750 Main Street
  Hartford, CT 06103
  203–247–3241

Amansco Incorporated
  Pittsburgh National Bank Building
  Pittsburgh, PA 15222
  412–765–3710

George V. Anderson and Associates
  500 Fifth Avenue
  New York, NY 10036
  212–LO4–6540

Antell, Wright & Nagel
  230 Park Avenue
  New York, NY 10017
  212–686–4144

Appointments Selection Ltd.
  1 Dover Street
  London W1, England

Aspemar
  Rue Bosquet 44
  1060 Brussels, Belgium

Bacci, Bennett & Gould
  375 Park Avenue
  New York, NY 10022
  212–688–8671

  600 Montgomery Street
  San Francisco, CA 94111

Theodore Barry and Associates
  1151 W. Sixth Street

Los Angeles, CA 90017
  213–481–7371
  245 Park Avenue
  New York, NY 10017

Bartholdi and Company
  45 William Street
  Wellesley Hills, MA 02181
  617–237–3710

  1415 W. 22nd Street
  Oak Brook, IL 60521

Battalia, Lotz and Associates, Inc.
  342 Madison Avenue
  New York, NY 10017
  212–986–4380

Beach & Sill, Inc.
  South Road
  Holmes, NY 12531
  914–855–5800

Billington, Fox & Ellis, Inc.*
  20 N. Wacker Drive
  Chicago, IL 60606
  312–236–5000

  250 Piedmont Avenue NE
  Atlanta, GA 30308

  1100 Superior Avenue NE
  Cleveland, OH 44114

  3701 Wilshire Boulevard
  Los Angeles, CA 90010

  529 Fifth Avenue
  New York, NY 10017

Booz, Allen & Hamilton, Inc.*
  135 South La Salle Street
  Chicago, IL 60603

  229 Peachtree Street NE
  Atlanta, GA 30303

  1100 Chester Avenue
  Cleveland, OH 44115

  2210 Republic Bank Tower
  325 N. St. Paul Street
  Dallas, TX 75201

  245 Park Avenue
  New York, NY 10017

  555 California Street
  San Francisco, CA 94104

  523 W. Sixth Street
  Los Angeles, CA 90014

Boyden Associates, Inc.*
  260 Madison Avenue
  New York, NY 10016
  212–949–7600

---

* A firm with foreign offices or affiliates.
† A CPA firm with executive search divisions.

3390 Peachtree Road NE
Atlanta, GA 30326

10 S. Riverside Plaza
Chicago, IL 60606

River Oaks and Trust Building
2001 Kirby Drive
Houston, TX 77019

5670 Wilshire Boulevard
Los Angeles, CA 90036

625 Stanwix Street
Pittsburgh, PA 15222

1 Maritime Plaza
Golden Gateway Center
San Francisco, CA 94111

606 Madison Avenue
Toledo, OH 43604

2701 Commerce Court North
Commerce Court Postal Station
Toronto, Ontario M5L 1G3, Canada

D. A. K. Brown & Associates
342 Madison Avenue
New York, NY 10017
212–TN7–5530

1179 Pequot Avenue
Southport, CT 06490

Frank C. Brown & Company, Inc.
30 Rockefeller Plaza
New York, NY 10020
212–PL7–5860

Thomas A. Buffum Associates
Two Center Plaza
Boston, MA 02108
617–227–4350

Bureau van de Keft
Hergengracht 414
Amsterdam, The Netherlands

Burke & O'Brien Associates, Inc.
233 Broadway
New York, NY 10007
212–WO2–2811

Burr, Dowd & Associates, Inc.
211 E. 53rd Street
New York, NY 10022
212–371–9785

E. A. Butler Associates, Inc.*
70 Pine Street
New York, NY 10007
212–344–3670

6500 Pearl Street
Cleveland, OH 44130

Exchange Bank Tower
Exchange Park
Dallas, TX 75235

10 Corbin Drive
Darien, CT 06820

33 W. Court Street
Doylestown, PA 18901

10889 Wilshire Boulevard
Los Angeles, CA 90024

2040 W. Wisconsin Avenue
Milwaukee, WI 53233

2820 W. Maple Avenue
Troy, MI 48084

1245 Sherbrooke Street West
Montreal 109, P.Q., Canada

The Caldwell Partners*
50 Prince Arthur Avenue
Toronto, Ontario M5R 1B5 Canada
416–920–7702

1115 Sherbrooke Street West
Montreal, P.Q., H3A 1H3, Canada

Camden and Associates, Inc.
Suite E200
McDonald's Plaza
Oak Brook, IL 60521
312–325–8770

Canny, Bowen, Inc.*
425 Park Avenue
New York, NY 10022
212–758–3400

Case and Company, Inc.*
30 Rockefeller Plaza
New York, NY 10020
212–581–7730

Suite 2109
Prudential Plaza
Chicago, IL 60601

634 Union Commerce Building
Cleveland, OH 44115

4314 Marina City Drive
Marina Del Ray, CA 90291

Russ Building, Suite 965
235 Montgomery Street
San Francisco, CA 94104

Landmark Square, Suite 1720
Stamford, CT 06901

Centre de Promotion et de Selection S.p.r.L.
Avenue Louise 30
1050 Brussels, Belgium

William H. Clark Associates, Inc.
330 Madison Avenue
New York, NY 10017
212–661–8760

200 E. Randolph Drive
Chicago, IL 60601

555 Flower Street
Los Angeles, CA 90071

1 Embarcadero Center
San Francisco, CA 94111

David W. Cogswell and Associates
400 Montgomery Street
San Francisco, CA 94104
415–788–1070

Stephen D. Coiné and Associates
250 Post Road
Westport, CT 06880
203-226-7263

Communications Executive Search
50 Avenue des Arts
1040 Brussels, Belgium

Conley Associates, Inc.
135 S. La Salle Street
Chicago, IL 60603
312-263-4680

Consulting Partners, Inc.*
33 Rue Galilee
Paris 16, France

99 Park Avenue
New York, NY 10016
212-OX7-3730

Herbert Cooke Associates
14908 Piney Grove Court
Gaithersburg, MD 20760
301-424-1343

Coopers & Lybrand†
1251 Avenue of the Americas
New York, NY 10022
212-489-1100

220 First National Bank Tower
Atlanta, GA 30303

222 S. Riverside Plaza
Chicago, IL 60606

5000 First International Building
Dallas, TX 75270

211 W. Fort Street
Detroit, MI 48226

555 S. Flower Street
Los Angeles, CA 90071

1900 3 Girard Plaza
Philadelphia, PA 10102

1 Bush Street
San Francisco, CA 94104

Corporate Growth Assistance Limited
14 Berkindale Drive
Willowsdale, Ontario M2L 1Z5, Canada
416-447-1650

Elmer R. Davis & Associates, Inc.
60 E. 42nd Street
New York, NY 10017
212-682-7717

Charles E. Day & Associates, Inc.
610 S. Forest Avenue
Ann Arbor, MI 48104
313-769-7407

Thorndike Deland Associates
1440 Broadway
New York, NY 10018
212-564-8100

Devine, Baldwin & Associates, Inc.*
250 Park Avenue

New York, NY 10017
212-867-5235

Statler Office Building
Boston, MA 02116

DeVoto, Sullivan & Berry, Ltd.
120 S. Riverside Plaza
Chicago, IL 60606
312-346-8278

Diewald Management
Jiron Camina 370
P.O. Box 4425
Lima, Peru

Eastman & Beaudine, Inc.*
39 S. La Salle Street
Chicago, IL 60603
312-726-8195

437 Madison Avenue
New York, NY 10022

44 Montgomery Street
San Francisco, CA 94104

Ernst & Ernst†
140 Broadway
New York, NY 10005
212-943-7800

1300 Union Commerce Building
Cleveland, OH 44115

333 W. Fort Street
Detroit, MI 48226

3500 One Shell Place
Houston, TX 77002

Eurosearch Consultants, S.A.
Headquarters for Europe:
Avenue Louise 505
1050 Brussels, Belgium

Eurosurvey S.A.
Boulevard du Regent 25
1000 Brussels, Belgium

Walter Evers and Company
13615 Shaker Boulevard
Cleveland, OH 44120
216-861-6353

Executive Appointments, Ltd.
78 Wigmore Street
London W 1, England

Executive Search Limited
45 Brompton Road
London SW 3, England

Fairbanks Associates, Inc.
509 Madison Avenue
New York, NY 10022
212-755-5615

FEM Management Consultants, Inc.
515 Madison Avenue
New York, NY 10022
212-759-2120

Fernow Associates
292 Montgomery Street

Bala-Cynwyd, PA 19004
215-MO7-9391

Foster & Associates, Inc.
One Market Plaza
San Francisco, CA 94105
415-398-8018

Pacific Building
Seattle, WA 98104

Geary Associates, Inc.
230 Park Avenue
New York, NY 10012
212-MU9-3330

N. W. Gibson Associates*
5900 Wilshire Boulevard
Los Angeles, CA 90036
213-939-3126

Golightly & Co. International, Inc.*
Personnel Services Division
One Rockefeller Plaza
New York, NY 10020
212-245-0900

5100 Westheimer
Houston, TX 77056

Gregg Associates, S.A.
Rue du Progres 52
1000 Brussels, Belgium

Halbrecht & Co., Inc.
201 E. 42nd Street
New York, NY 10017
212-682-3333

Haley Associates, Inc.
375 Park Avenue
New York, NY 10022
212-421-7860

Handy Associates*
405 Park Avenue
New York, NY 10022
212-755-1911

Haskell & Stern Associates, Inc.
230 Park Avenue
New York, NY 10017
212-689-3644

Frank W. Hastings Associates
110 Vernon Lane
Morrisville, PA 19067
215-295-4194

Heidrick & Struggles, Inc.*
125 S. Wacker Drive
Chicago, IL 60606
312-372-8811

100 Federal Plaza
Boston, MA 02110

1110 Superior Avenue
Cleveland, OH 44114

2728 Republic National Bank Tower
Dallas, TX 75201

2650 Pennzoil Place, South Tower
Houston, TX 77002

Union Bank Square
5th and Figuerosa Streets
Los Angeles, CA 90071

245 Park Avenue
New York, NY 10017

600 Montgomery Street
San Francisco, CA 94111

Rof Helm
Bad Honnef-Rhondorf
Frankenweg 33, West Germany

Helmich, Miller & Pasek Inc.
5725 E. River Road
Chicago, IL 60631
312-393-6270

1100 Quail Street
Newport Beach, CA 92660

Hergenrather & Company
3435 Wilshire Boulevard
Los Angeles, CA 90010
213-385-0181

Hodge-Cronin and Associates, Inc.
9575 W. Higgins Road
Rosemont, IL 60018
312-692-2041

Hoff Associates
380 Madison Avenue
New York, NY 10017
212-687-6850

Robert Howe & Associates
2971 Flower Road South
Atlanta, GA 30341
404-455-6618

Ward Howell Associates, Inc.
99 Park Avenue
New York, NY 10016
212-697-3730

1 IBM Plaza
Chicago, IL 60611

10100 Santa Monica Boulevard
Los Angeles, CA 90067

3 Embarcadero Center
San Francisco, CA 94111

Hubbard, Buck & Associates, Inc.*
222 Wisconsin Avenue
Lake Forest, IL 60045
312-295-1520

Alexander Hughes
34 Rue de la Loi
1040 Brussels, Belgium

Human Resource Management
Residence Louvois
1 Rue Lulli
75002 Paris, France

Human Resource Services, Inc.
610 Fifth Avenue
New York, NY 10020
212-581-5444

The Hunt Company
274 Madison Avenue
New York, NY 10016
212–889–2020

International Management Advisors, Inc.
485 Lexington Avenue
New York, NY 10017
212–490–3858

Jonas & Associates, Inc.
733 N. Van Buren Street
Milwaukee, WI 53202
414–271–6100

Kahlert Associates, Incorporated
375 Park Avenue
New York, NY 10022
212–759–9090

A. T. Kearney, Inc.
100 S. Wacker Drive
Chicago, IL 60606
312–782–2868

Investment Plaza
Cleveland, OH 44114

One Wilshire Building
Los Angeles, CA 90017

437 Madison Avenue
New York, NY 10022

Keating, Grimm & Leeper, Inc.
445 Park Avenue
New York, NY 10022
212–758–2300

540 Frontage Road
Northfield, IL 60093

Kensington Management Consultants, Inc.
25 Third Street
Stamford, CT 06905
203–327–9860

860 Charleston Road
Palo Alto, CA 94303

Kienbaum Beretungen GmbH
Hindenburgstrasse 4–8
5270 Gummersbach, West Germany

Kiernan & Company*
10 Rockefeller Plaza
New York, NY 10020
212–489–8333

1 Beacon Street
Boston, MA 02108

Korn/Ferry International*
1900 Avenue of the Stars
Los Angeles, CA 90067
213–879–1834

260 Peachtree Street
Atlanta, GA 30303

10 S. Riverside Plaza
Chicago, IL 60606

4803 First International Building
Dallas, TX 75270

1100 Milam Building
Houston, TX 77002

277 Park Avenue
New York, NY 10017

600 Montgomery Street
San Francisco, CA 94111

Krall Management Incorporated
Station One
Paoli, PA 19301
215–647–5445

Kremple & Meade
1900 Avenue of the Stars
Los Angeles, CA 90067
213–456–6451

Krief Consultants for Europe
Rue Gachard 43
1000 Brussels, Belgium

Lamalie Associates
13902 N. Dale Mabry

Tampa, FL 33624
813–961–7494

3340 Peachtree Street NE
Atlanta, GA 30326

120 S. Riverside Plaza
Chicago, IL 60606

Central National Bank Building
Cleveland, OH 44114

Lauer, Kunzer & Associates, Inc.
135 S. La Salle Street
Chicago, IL 60603
312–372–7050

Laugery, de Labrusse & Associates
38 Rue de Lisbonne
Paris 8e, France

Lawrence-Leiter and Company
427 W. 12th Street
Kansas City, MO 64105
816–474–8340

419 N. Harrison Street
Princeton, NJ 08540

Robert Lee & Partners
24 Berkeley Square
London WC 1, England

Locke and Robinson
One NCNB Plaza
Charlotte, NC 28280
704–372–6600

Fred Lustig and Associates, Inc.
405 Lexington Avenue
New York, NY 10017
212–MU7–0427

Robert Madigan Associates, Inc.
60 E. 42nd Street
New York, NY 10017
212–863–6550

Management Selection Group Limited
17 Stratton Street

London W 1, England

Management Woman, Inc.
The Galleria
115 E. 57th Street
New York, NY 10022
212-751-9290

D. McClure & Associates
P.O. Box 38
New Lynn, Auckland, New Zealand

William McCulloch Associates, Inc.
20 E. 46th Street
New York, NY 10017

McFeely, Wackerle Associates, Inc.
20 N. Wacker Drive
Chicago, IL 60606
312-641-2977

Mendheim & Associates, Inc.
6055 N. Lincoln Avenue
Chicago, IL 60659
312-973-6969

Menzel Robinson Baldwin & Hill
800 W. Central Road
Mt. Prospect, IL 60056
312-394-4303

Middle West Service Company
55 E. Monroe Street
Chicago, IL 60603
312-726-8730

Mincher & Associates
Centre International Rogier
1000 Brussels, Belgium

Robert Murphy Associates
708 Third Avenue
New York, NY 10017
212-661-0460

Oliver & Rozner, Inc.
1 E. 53rd Street
New York, NY 10022
212-688-1850

Owen, Webb Associates, Inc.
280 Park Avenue
New York, NY 10017
212-661-3700

P. A. International Management Consultants, Ltd.
Hyde Park House
60-A Knightsbridge
London SW 1X 7LE, England

200 Park Avenue
New York, NY 10017
212-682-1330

P-E Consulting Group
14-20 Headfort Plaza
London ZWIZ 7HN, England

John Paisios & Associates
332 S. Michigan Avenue
Chicago, IL 60604

312-922-8836

109-23 71st Road
Forest Hills, NY 11375

Paris Survey Associates
39 Avenue Hoche
Paris 8, France

Peat Marwick & Mitchell & Co.*†
345 Park Avenue
New York, NY 10022
212-758-9700

225 Peachtree Street NE
Atlanta, GA 30303

1 Boston Place
Boston, MA 02108

2001 Bryan Tower
Dallas, TX 75201

Commerce Tower
Kansas City, MO 64199

555 S. Flower Street
Los Angeles, CA 90024

80 S. 8th Street
Minneapolis, MN 55401

Permark Management Consultants
777 Summer Street
Stamford, CT 06901
203-325-2677

The Personnel Laboratory, Inc.
733 Summer Street
Stamford, CT 06901
203-325-4348

Pierce Sandford & Associates, Inc.
Republic National Bank Tower
Dallas, TX 75201
214-651-0809

Pinsker, Winguth & Shattuck
133 Lawrence Expressway
Santa Clara, CA 95051
408-247-5050

100 Bush Street
San Francisco, CA 94104

Price, Waterhouse & Co.†
153 E. 53rd Street
New York, NY 10022
212-371-2000

3700 First National Bank Tower
Atlanta, GA 30303

200 E. Randolph Street
Chicago, IL 60601

606 S. Olive Street
Los Angeles, CA 90014

555 California Street
San Francisco, CA 94104

Promodag
17 Avenue des Marronniers
94 Nugent-sur-Marne, France

Paul R. Ray & Company*

1208 Ridgeleg State Office Building
Fort Worth, TX 76116
    817-731-4111

1201 Peachtree Street NE
Atlanta, GA 30361

Sears Tower
Chicago, IL 60606

9841 Airport Boulevard
Los Angeles, CA 90045

277 Park Avenue
New York, NY 10017

Russell Reynolds Associates, Inc.*
245 Park Avenue
New York, NY 10017
    212-682-8622

230 W. Monroe Street
Chicago, IL 60606

1100 Milam
Houston, TX 77002

515 S. Flower Street
Los Angeles, CA 90071

Robertson, Farrell & Wengert
300 S. Wacker Drive
Chicago, IL 60606
    312-786-9068

Roche Associates*
65 Prospect Street
Stamford, CT 06902
    203-327-7910

Joseph L. Rodgers & Company
155 E. 38th Street
New York, NY 10016
    212-682-0255

Sampson-Neill Associates, Inc.
543 Valley Road
Upper Montclair, NJ 07043
    201-783-9600

Michael Saunders Management Services, Ltd.
115 Mount Street
Mayfair
London W 1Y 5HD, England

F. R. Schwab & Associates, Inc.
645 Madison Avenue
New York, NY 10022
    212-PL8-6800

5525 Wilshire Boulevard
Los Angeles, CA 90036

The Robert V. Sedwick Company
4850 Bank of America Center
San Francisco, CA 94104
    415-788-7040

Selpe
Via Pozzone 5
Milan, Italy

Roy Shirley and Associates
Avenue Louise 344
1050 Brussels, Belgium

John W. Siler & Associates
5261 N. Port Washington Road
Milwaukee, WI 53217
    414-962-9400

Simmons Associates, Inc.
2550 M Street NW
Washington, DC 20007
    202-333-5000

Skott-Edwards Consultants, Inc.
521 Fifth Avenue
New York, NY 10017
    212-697-7640

Norman Spencer & Company, Ltd.
14 Brandon Street
Wellington C1, New Zealand

Spriggs & Company, Inc.
875 N. Michigan Avenue
Chicago, IL 60611
    312-751-1200

Stack Associates
230 Park Avenue
New York, NY 10017
    212-889-1135

Staff Selection and Services
Avenue Louise 409
1050 Brussels, Belgium

Paul Stafford Associates, Ltd.
45 Rockefeller Plaza
New York, NY 10020
    212-765-7700

222 S. Riverside Plaza
Chicago, IL 60606

888 17th Street
Washington, DC 20006

Staub, Warmbold & Associates, Inc.
919 Third Avenue
New York, NY 10022
    212-758-8200

229 Peachtree Street
Atlanta, GA 30303

200 E. Randolph Street
Chicago, IL 60601

350 California Street
San Francisco, CA 94104

S. K. Stewart & Associates
The Executive Building
P.O. Box 40110
Cincinnati, OH 45240
    513-771-2250

Spencer Stewart & Associates*
437 Madison Avenue
New York, NY 10022
    212-754-1400

500 N. Michigan Avenue
Chicago, IL 60611

Republic National Bank Tower
Dallas, TX 75201

4 Landmark Square
Stamford, CT 06901

George Sullivan Associates, Inc.
P.O. Box 338
Rumson, NJ 07760
201-741-4544

Alexander Tic et Cie.
10 Rue Royale
Paris 8, France

Touche Ross & Co.°†
1633 Broadway
New York, NY 10510
212-489-1600

111 E. Wacker Drive
Chicago, IL 60601

3700 Wilshire Boulevard
Los Angeles, CA 90010

One Maritime Plaza
San Francisco, CA 94111

John Tyzack & Partners, Ltd.
10 Hallam Street
London W 1, England

Vogel & Associates
759 N. Milwaukee Street
Milwaukee, WI 53202
414-273-7111

Nelson Walker Associates, Inc.°
52 Vanderbilt Avenue
New York, NY 10017
212-889-8640

Edward Warren Organization
120 E. 56th Street
New York, NY 10022
212-758-7410

Hilton N. Wasserman & Associates, Inc.
200 Park Avenue
New York, NY 10017
212-661-8840

Westcoff Associates
135 S. La Salle Street
Chicago, IL 60603
312-332-6336

William H. Willis, Inc.
445 Park Avenue
New York, NY 10022
212-752-3456

Witt & Dolan Associates, Inc.
1415 W. 22nd Street
Oak Brook, IL 60521
312-325-5070

Woods, Gordon & Co.
P.O. Box 253
Toronto-Dominion Centre
Toronto, Ontario M5K 1J7, Canada
416-368-4761

WS & Y Consultants
1 California Street
San Francisco, CA 94111
415-981-6060

Wytmar & Co., Inc.°
18 S. Riverside Plaza
Chicago, IL 60606
312-236-1350

Arthur Young & Co.†
277 Park Avenue
New York, NY 10007
212-922-2000

John P. Young & Associates Pty., Ltd.
2 Forholm Road
Hawrthorn, Victoria, Australia 3122

Jorge Zauber Associates
Berliner Allee 48
Dusseldorf, West Germany

Egon Zehnder International
Toblerstrasse 80
CH 8044 Zurich, Switzerland

Stock Market

SECURITIES MARKETS: NOTABLE DATES

1792   Original brokers' agreement subscribed to by 24 brokers (May 17).

1817   Constitution and the name "New York Stock Exchange Board" adopted (March 8).

1830   Dullest day in history of exchange— 31 shares traded (March 16).

1840s   Outdoor trading in unlisted securities begins at Wall and Hanover Streets, moves to Wall and Broad, then shifts south along Broad Street.*

1863   Name changed to "New York Stock Exchange" (NYSE) (January 29).

1867   Stock tickers first introduced (November 15).

1868   Membership made salable (October 23).

1869   Gold speculation resulted in "Black Friday" (September 24).

1871   Continuous markets in stocks established.

1873   NYSE closed September 18–29.
Failure of Jay Cooke & Co. and others (September 18).
Trading hours set at 10 A.M. to 3 P.M.; Saturdays, 10 A.M. to noon (December 1).

1878   First telephones introduced in the exchange (November 13).

1881   Annunciator board installed for paging members (January 29).

1885   Unlisted Securities Department established (March 25).

1886   First million-share day—1,200,000 shares traded (December 15).

1908   E. S. Mendels forms New York Curb Agency in first departure from informal trading.*

1910   Unlisted Securities Department abolished (March 31).

1911   Trading rules established with formation of New York Curb Market Association.*

---

* Refers to American Exchange (AMEX) (formerly Curb Exchange).

† Applies to both the New York Stock Exchange and the American Exchange.

Sources: New York Stock Exchange *FACT BOOK* and American Stock Exchange *DATA BOOK.*

1914   Exchange closed from July 31 through December 11—World War I.

1915   Stock prices quoted in dollars as against percent of par value (October 13).

1919   Separate ticker system installed for bonds (January 2).

1920   Stock Clearing Corporation established (April 26).

1921   New York Curb Market association moves indoors at 86 Trinity Place; name shortened to New York Curb Market and ticker service initiated (June 21).*

1927   Start of 10-share unit of trading for inactive stocks (January 3).

1929   Stock market crash; 16,410,000 shares traded (October 29).
New York Curb Market modifies its name to New York Curb Exchange.*

1930   Faster ticker—500 characters per minute—installed (September 2).

1931   Exchange building expanded; Telephone Quotation Department formed to send stock quotes to member firm offices.*

1933   New York Stock Exchange closed for bank holiday, March 4–14.

1934   Enactment of Securities Exchange Act of 1934 (June 6).

1938   First salaried president elected—Wm. McC. Martin, Jr. (June 30).

1946   Listed stocks outnumber unlisted stocks for first time since the 1934 act imposed restrictions on unlisted trading.*

1952   Trading hours changed: weekdays, 10 A.M. to 3:30 P.M. Closed Saturdays (September 29).*

1953   Name of New York Curb Exchange changed to American Stock Exchange.*

1958   First member corporation—Woodcock, Hess & Co. (June 4).
Mary C. Roebling becomes first woman governor.*

1962   Committee system of administration replaced by expanded paid staff reporting to president. Specialist system strengthened, surveillance of trading increased, listing and delisting standards introduced, and board restructured to give greater representation to commission and out-of-town brokers.*

1964   New member classification—Registered Trader (August 3).

New ticker—900 characters per minute—put into service (December 1).†

Am-Quote computerized telephone-quotation service completed as first step in major automation program.*

1965   Fully automated quotation service introduced (March 8).

Electronic Systems Center created (October 15).

First women, Phyllis S. Peterson and Julia Montgomery Walsh, elected to regular membership.*

1966   New NYSE Stock Price Index inaugurated (July 14).

AMEX Price Change Index System introduced; computer complex installed for ticker, surveillance, and compared-clearance operations.*

1967   First woman member admitted—Muriel F. Siebert (December 28).

1968   Ticker speed increased to maximum 900 characters per minute; transmission begun to six European countries. Trading floor modernized; line capacity for communications doubled. Visitors gallery expanded.*

1969   Central Certificate Service fully activated (February 26).

1970   Public ownership of member firms approved (March 26).

Securities Investor Protection Corporation Act signed (December 30).

1971   First negotiated commission rates effective (April 5).

First member organization listed—Merrill Lynch (July 27).

AMEX incorporates and marks 50th anniversary of move indoors; Listed Company Advisory Committee formed, composed of nine chief executives of AMEX-listed companies.*

1972   NYSE reorganization, based on Martin Report, approved (January 20).

Board of Directors, with 10 public members, replaced Board of Governors (July 13).

Securities Industry Automation Corporation established with AMEX to consolidate facilities of both exchanges (July 17).

First salaried chairman took office—James J. Needham (August 28).

Board of Governors reorganized to include 10 public and 10 industry representatives plus full-time salaried chairman as chief executive officer.*

1973   Depository Trust Company succeeded Central Certificate Service (May 11).

Chicago Board of Options Exchange opened with trading in 16 classes of call options (April 26).

AMEX formally adopts affirmative action employment plan; Market Value Index System introduced to replace Price Change Index.*

1974   Trading hours extended to 4 P.M. (October 1).

Consolidated tape begun; 15 stocks reported (October 18).

1975   Fixed commission system abolished (April 30).

Full consolidated tape begun (June 16).

AMEX trades call options.*

Trading begins in call options and odd lots of U.S. government instruments.*

1976   New data line installed, handling 36,000 characters per minute (January 19).

Specialists began handling odd lots in their stocks (May 24).

Varo, Inc.—first stock traded on both NYSE and AMEX (August 23).

Competition between specialists begun (October 11).

1977   Independent audit committee on listed companies' boards required (January 6).

Competitive Trader category for members approved (January 19).

Foreign broker/dealers permitted to obtain membership (February 3).

Full Automated Bond System in effect (July 27).

1978   First 60 million share day in history (63,493,000 shares) (April 17).

Trading in Ginnie Maes inaugurated on the AMEX Commodities Exchange (ACE)* (September 12).

COMMON STOCK PRICES AND YIELDS

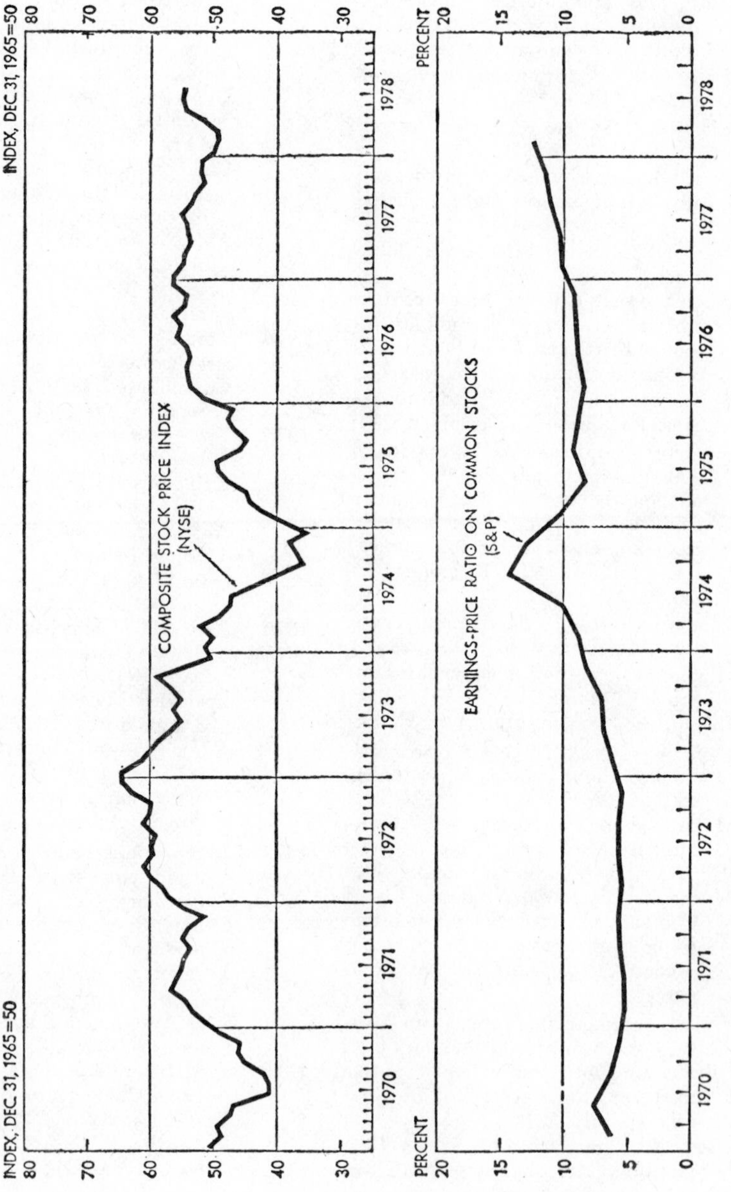

INDEX, DEC. 31, 1965=50

COMPOSITE STOCK PRICE INDEX (NYSE)

EARNINGS-PRICE RATIO ON COMMON STOCKS (S&P)

SOURCES: NEW YORK STOCK EXCHANGE AND STANDARD & POOR'S CORPORATION   COUNCIL OF ECONOMIC ADVISERS

Period	Common stock prices							Common stock yields (percent)[5]	
	New York Stock Exchange indexes (Dec. 31, 1965=50)[2]					Dow-Jones industrial average[3]	Standard & Poor's composite index (1941-43=10)[4]	Dividend-price ratio	Earnings-price ratio
	Composite	Industrial	Transportation	Utility	Finance				
1972	60.29	65.73	50.17	38.48	78.35	950.71	109.20	2.84	5.50
1973	57.42	63.08	37.74	37.69	70.12	923.88	107.43	3.06	7.12
1974	43.84	48.08	31.89	29.79	49.67	759.37	82.85	4.47	11.59
1975	45.73	50.52	31.10	31.50	47.14	802.49	86.16	4.31	9.15
1976	54.46	60.44	39.57	36.97	52.94	974.92	102.01	3.77	8.90
1977	53.69	57.86	41.09	40.92	55.25	894.63	98.20	4.62	10.79
1977: July	54.94	58.90	43.52	42.44	57.29	908.20	100.18	4.59	-----
Aug	53.51	57.30	41.04	41.50	56.52	872.26	97.75	4.72	-----
Sept	52.66	56.41	39.99	40.93	55.33	853.30	96.23	4.82	11.09
Oct	51.37	54.99	38.33	40.38	53.24	823.96	93.74	4.97	-----
Nov	51.87	55.62	39.30	40.33	54.04	828.51	94.28	5.02	-----
Dec	51.83	53.55	39.75	40.36	53.85	818.80	93.82	5.11	11.45
1978: Jan	49.89	53.45	39.15	39.06	50.91	781.09	90.25	5.32	-----
Feb	49.41	52.80	38.90	39.02	50.60	763.57	88.98	5.49	-----
Mar	49.50	52.77	38.95	39.26	51.44	756.37	88.82	5.62	12.31
Apr	51.75	55.48	41.19	39.69	55.04	794.66	92.71	5.42	-----
May	54.49	59.14	44.21	39.47	57.95	838.56	97.41	5.20	-----
June	54.83	59.63	44.19	39.41	58.31	840.26	97.66	5.19	-----
July	54.61	59.35	44.74	39.28	57.97	831.72	97.19	5.25	-----
Week ended:									
1978: July 28	55.57	60.49	46.27	39.60	58.97	845.04	98.96	5.14	-----
Aug 4	57.50	62.82	48.43	40.09	61.36	876.35	102.34	4.98	-----
11	58.46	63.92	49.25	40.34	63.35	888.44	103.94	4.91	-----
18	58.85	64.44	49.55	40.27	63.98	893.40	104.46	4.91	-----
25	58.98	64.63	49.82	40.27	63.94	894.25	104.62	4.90	-----

[1] Averages of daily closing prices.
[2] Includes all the stocks (more than 1,500) listed on the NYSE.
[3] Includes 30 stocks.
[4] Includes 500 stocks.
[5] Standard & Poor's series. Dividend-price ratios based on Wednesday closing prices. Earnings-price ratios based on prices at end of quarter.

Source: *Economic Indicators*, Council of Economic Advisors.

NOTE.—All data relate to stocks listed on the New York Stock Exchange (NYSE).

Sources: New York Stock Exchange, Dow-Jones & Company, Inc., and Standard & Poor's Corporation.

MAJOR MARKET AVERAGES

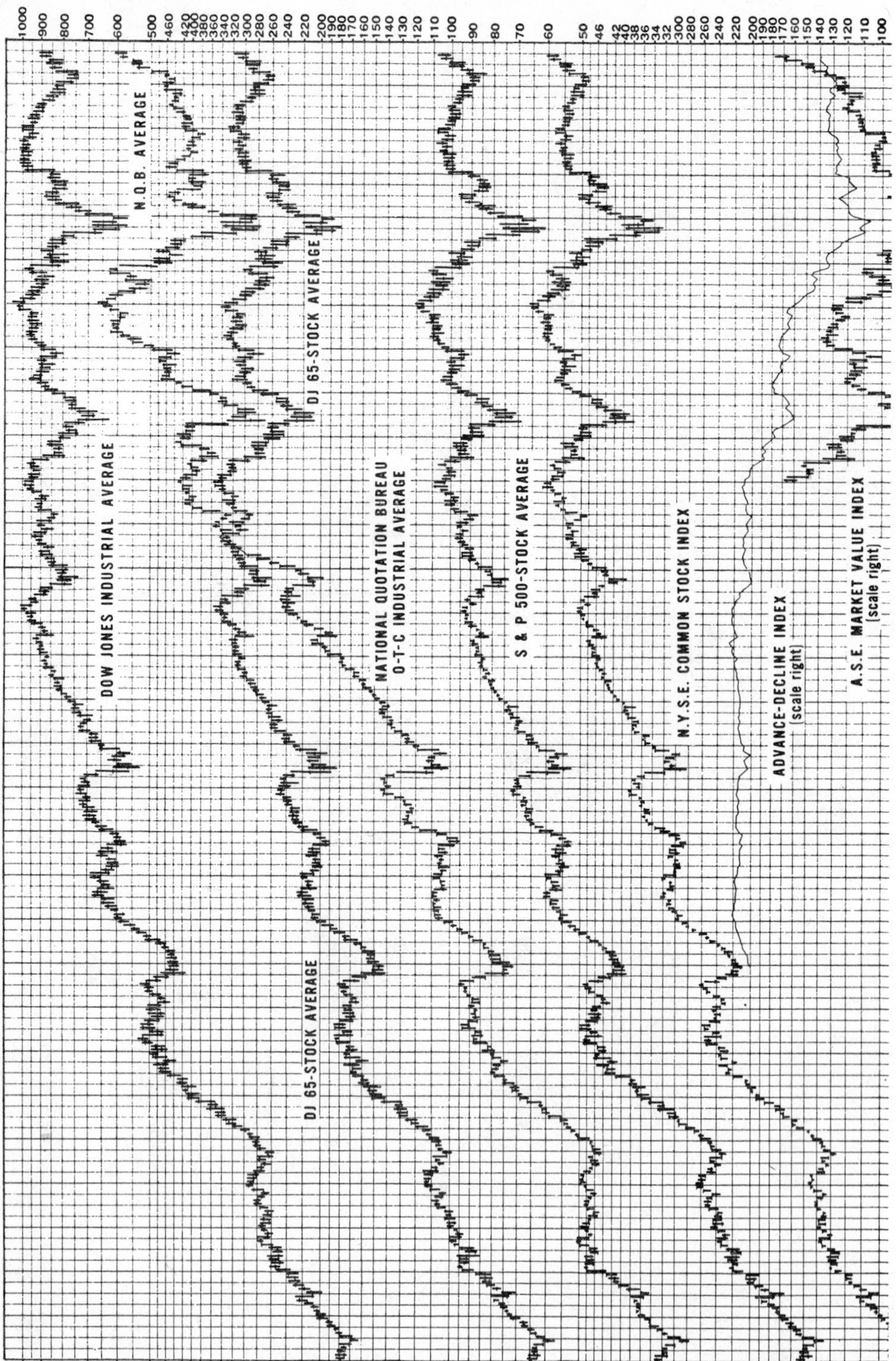

N.Q.B. AVERAGE

DJ 65-STOCK AVERAGE

DOW JONES INDUSTRIAL AVERAGE

NATIONAL QUOTATION BUREAU
O-T-C INDUSTRIAL AVERAGE

S & P 500-STOCK AVERAGE

N.Y.S.E. COMMON STOCK INDEX

DJ 65-STOCK AVERAGE

ADVANCE-DECLINE INDEX
(scale right)

A.S.E. MARKET VALUE INDEX
(scale right)

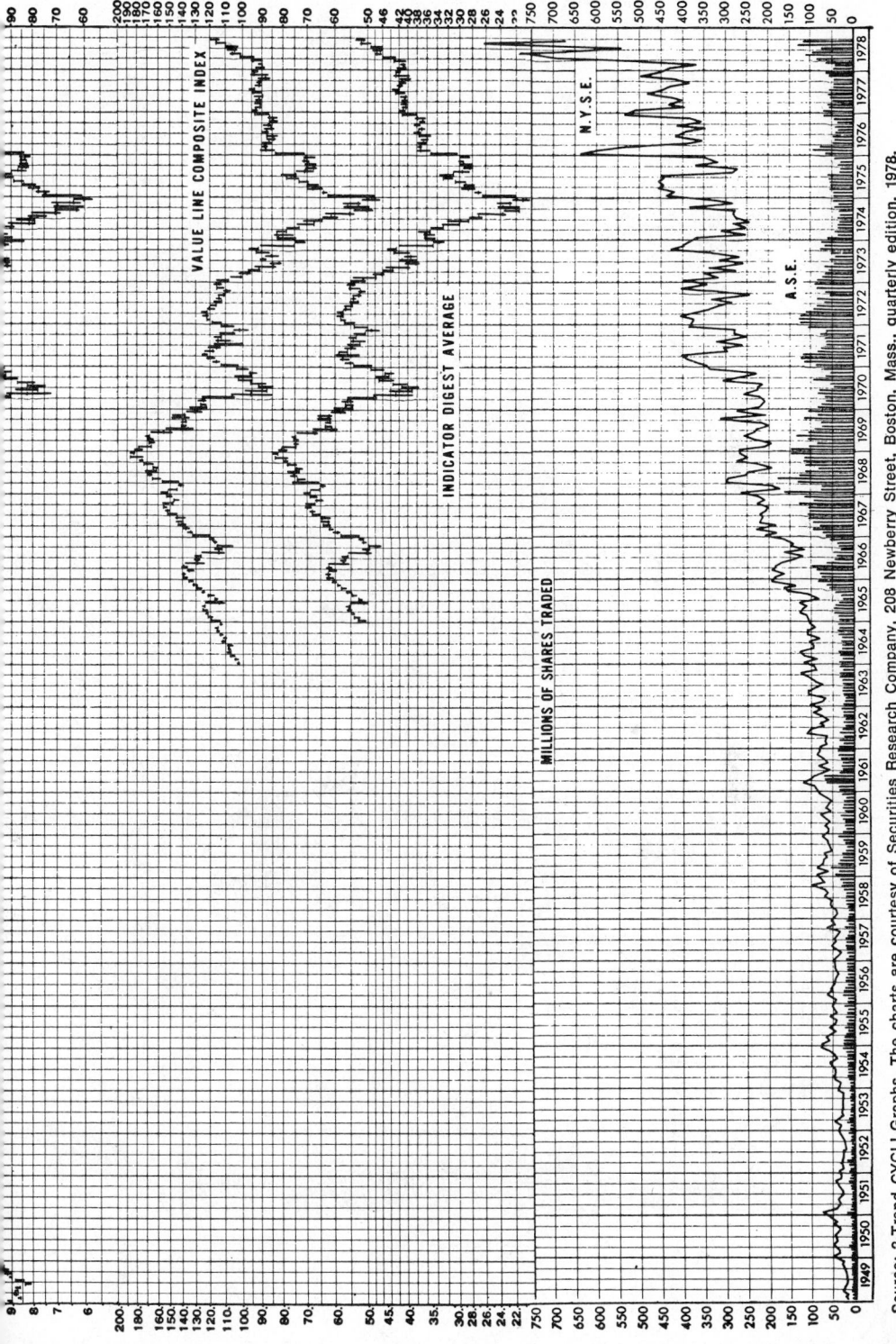

VALUE LINE COMPOSITE INDEX

INDICATOR DIGEST AVERAGE

MILLIONS OF SHARES TRADED

N.Y.S.E.

A.S.E.

Source: 3-Trend CYCLI-Graphs. The charts are courtesy of Securities Research Company, 208 Newberry Street, Boston, Mass., quarterly edition, 1978.

DOW JONES INDUSTRIAL, TRANSPORTATION, AND UTILITY AVERAGES

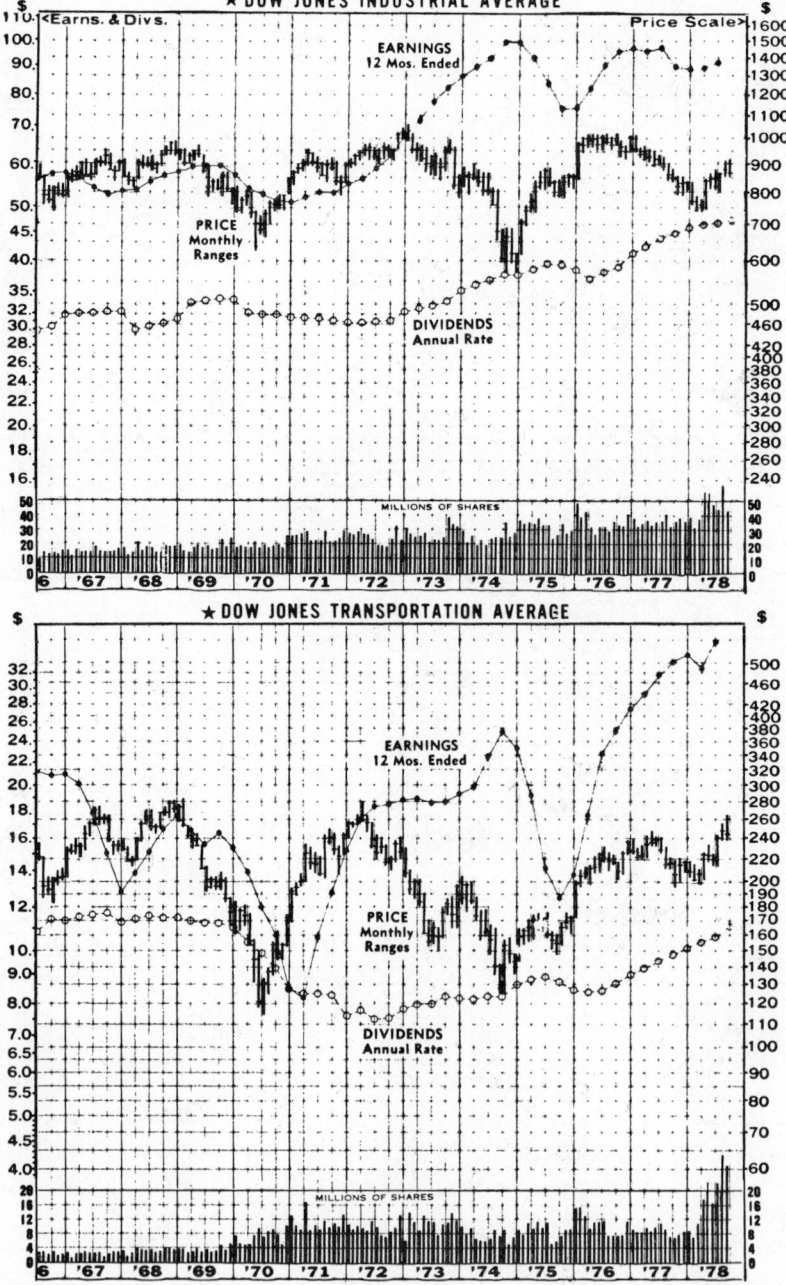

DOW JONES INDUSTRIAL, TRANSPORTATION, AND UTILITY AVERAGES (*continued*)

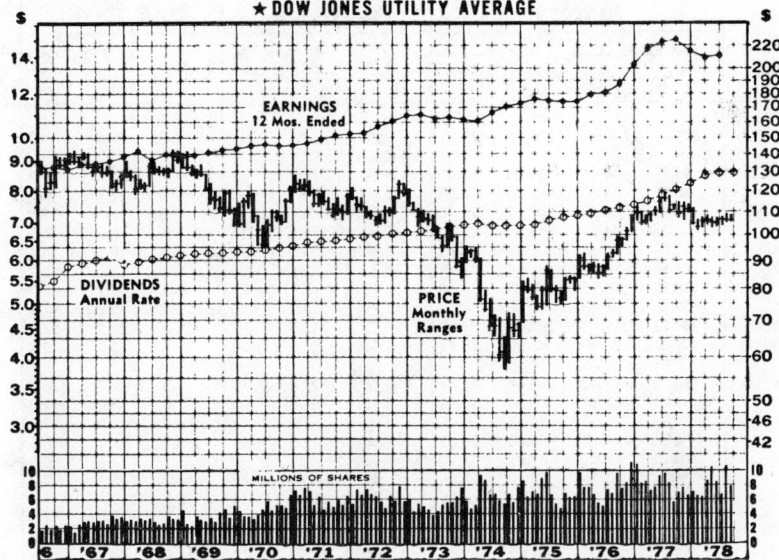

★ DOW JONES UTILITY AVERAGE

Source: 3-Trend CYCLI-Graphs. Charts courtesy of Securities Research Company, 208 Newberry Street, Boston, Mass., quarterly edition, 1978.

DOW JONES INDUSTRIALS

	History				Earnings			P/E Ratio			Dvds	
	52-Week		5-Year		Last	%	5-Yr.		5-Year Avg		Indic.	
	High	Low	High	Low	12Mos	Ch	Growth	Today	High	Low	Amt	Yield
	$	$	$	$	$	%	%	-	-	-	$	%
Dow Jones Ind.	900.12	742.12	1051.70	577.60	89.64	- 5.89		10.0	12.5	7.3	48.51	5.4
Allied Chemical	45.63	34.13	54.25	23.00	4.54	- 7.54	5	8.4	11.2	7.0	2.00	5.3
Alcoa	49.75	38.50	61.25	25.88	5.90	15.46	15	8.1	16.7	9.7	2.00	4.2
Am Brands	53.00	39.38	53.00	27.75	6.25	28.87	7	8.2	9.4	7.0	3.50	6.8
Am Can	43.38	34.63	43.38	22.50	5.72	17.45	11	7.5	8.2	6.3	2.70	6.3
Am Tel & Tel	63.50	56.88	65.63	39.63	7.40	13.85	9	8.3	10.3	8.4	4.60	7.5
Bethlehem Stl	27.13	18.25	48.00	18.25	- 8.52	NE	- 39	NE	8.0	5.3	1.00	4.1
Chrysler Cp	16.88	10.25	44.25	7.00	- 1.95	NE	- 21	NE	7.9	3.7	1.00	8.0
Dupont Corp	130.50	97.63	203.50	84.50	12.70	31.88	5	10.1	18.6	12.1	5.75	4.5
Eastman Kodak	68.13	41.13	151.75	41.13	4.63	20.26	2	14.2	29.7	17.9	2.50	3.8
Esmark	32.63	25.00	42.00	16.41	3.51	- 6.90	2	8.4	8.7	5.8	1.84	6.2
Exxon	50.00	43.00	56.88	27.44	5.78	2.12	- 1	8.3	9.0	6.6	3.40	7.1
Gen Electric	57.63	43.63	75.88	30.00	5.13	15.28	14	11.0	18.0	11.9	2.60	4.6
Gen Foods	35.00	26.50	36.13	16.00	3.52	.00	11	9.7	10.9	7.5	1.64	4.8
Gen Motors	70.88	57.13	84.63	28.88	11.55	4.05	21	5.5	11.1	6.5	6.75	10.7
Goodyear Tire	20.13	15.63	31.88	11.75	2.56	2.81	3	7.2	11.5	6.9	1.30	7.1
Inco Ltd	22.38	13.38	40.13	13.38	.91	- 64.73	- 25	18.0	15.1	8.7	.72	4.4
Intl Harvester	40.13	26.00	40.13	16.75	6.74	15.02	15	5.9	7.2	4.5	2.10	5.3
Intl Paper	48.00	35.13	79.75	31.63	5.37	16.99	5	8.7	13.2	7.9	2.00	4.3
Johns Manville	35.00	28.13	38.25	14.38	5.23	54.73	15	6.5	10.8	6.8	1.80	5.3
Minn Mng Mfg	66.00	43.00	91.63	43.00	3.85	24.60	9	16.9	26.7	18.4	2.00	3.1
Owens-Illinois	25.25	19.50	31.63	13.75	2.92	- 4.89	6	7.9	9.6	6.6	1.16	5.0
Proct & Gambl	92.00	73.38	120.00	67.00	6.19	10.73	12	14.2	22.2	16.4	3.00	3.4
Sears, Roebuck	32.75	22.00	61.63	20.75	2.62	9.62	9	9.4	22.3	14.1	1.27	5.2
Std Oil Cal	45.00	34.25	45.50	20.13	5.88	1.03	3	7.5	7.6	5.1	2.60	5.9
Texaco	28.88	22.88	43.13	20.00	2.93	- 13.82	- 11	8.8	8.5	6.2	2.00	7.7
Union Carbide	47.38	36.00	76.75	29.25	5.98	- 8.42	0	6.9	9.5	6.1	2.80	6.8
US Steel Corp	34.25	24.88	59.38	17.84	1.13	- 67.34	- 28	24.6	12.0	7.3	1.60	5.8
Unit Technols	52.50	32.25	52.50	10.38	4.53	17.05	18	11.2	9.6	5.7	2.00	3.9
Westinghouse	25.00	16.38	47.38	8.00	3.33	20.22	15	7.3	12.9	6.4	.97	4.0
Woolworth FW	21.38	17.50	31.88	8.00	3.02	- 5.92	4	6.9	9.0	4.9	1.40	6.7

Source: *The M/G Financial Weekly,* Media General Financial Services, 301 East Grace Street, Richmond, Virginia 23261, August 21, 1978.

STOCK MARKET AVERAGES BY INDUSTRY GROUP

These definitions apply to the following charts.

Price scale: The price ranges are always read from the scale at the right-hand side of each chart. This scale is equal to 15 times the earnings scale at the left, so when the price range bars and the earnings line coincide, it shows the price is at 15 times earnings. When the price is above the earnings line, the ratio of price to earnings is greater than 15 times earnings; when below, it is less.

Monthly price ranges represented by the solid vertical bars show the highest and lowest point of each month's transactions. Cross-bars indicate the month's closing price.

Monthly ratio-cator: The plottings for this line are obtained by dividing the closing price of the stock by the closing price of the Dow Jones Industrial Average on the same day. The resulting percentage is multiplied by a factor of 7.0 to bring the line closer to the price bars and is read from the right-hand scale. The plotting indicates whether the stock has kept pace, outperformed, or lagged behind the general market as represented by the DJIA.

Source: 3-Trend CYCLI-Graphs. The charts are courtesy of Securities Research Company, 208 Newberry Street, Boston, Mass., quarterly edition, 1977.

INDUSTRY GROUP AVERAGES*

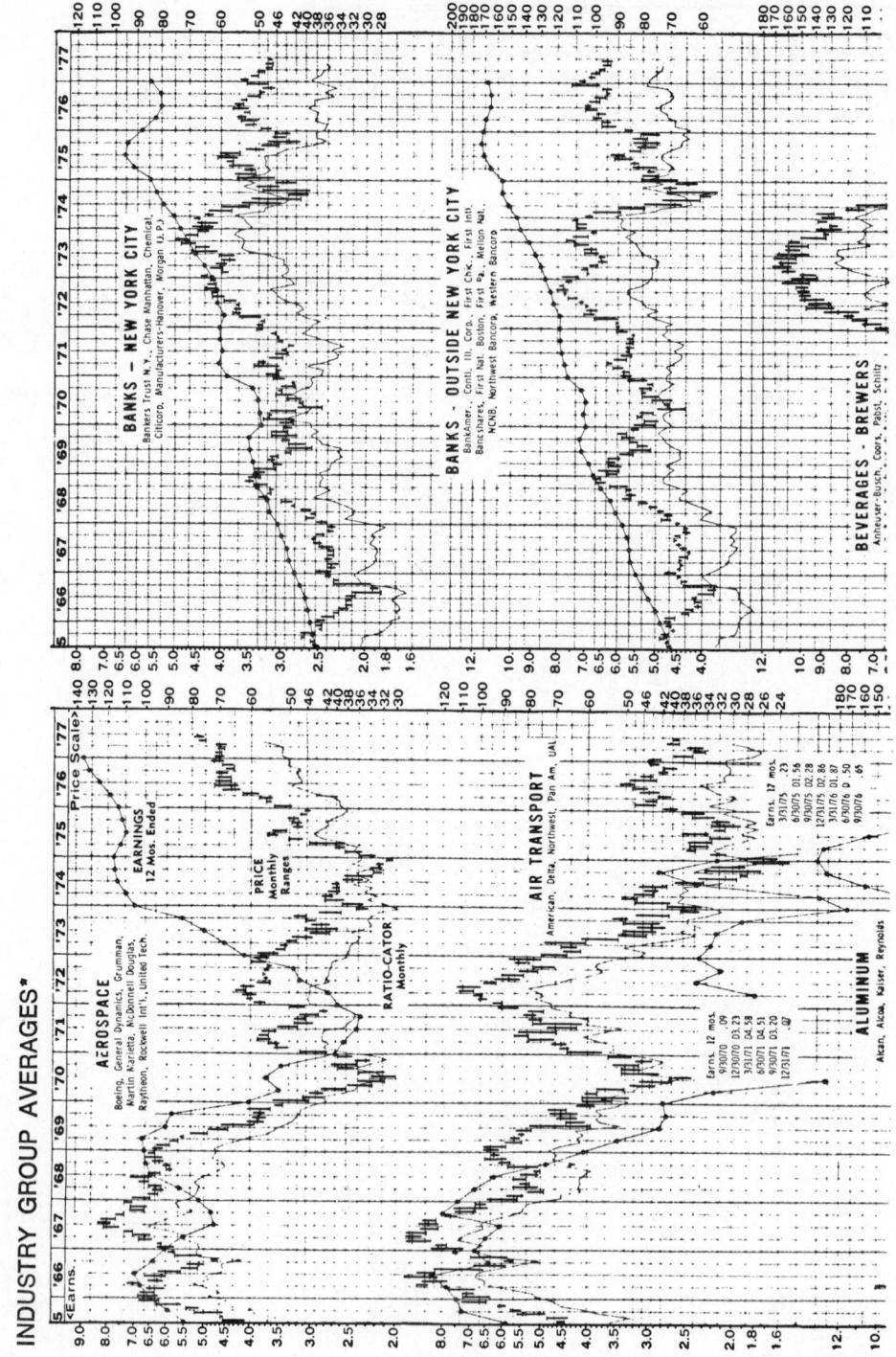

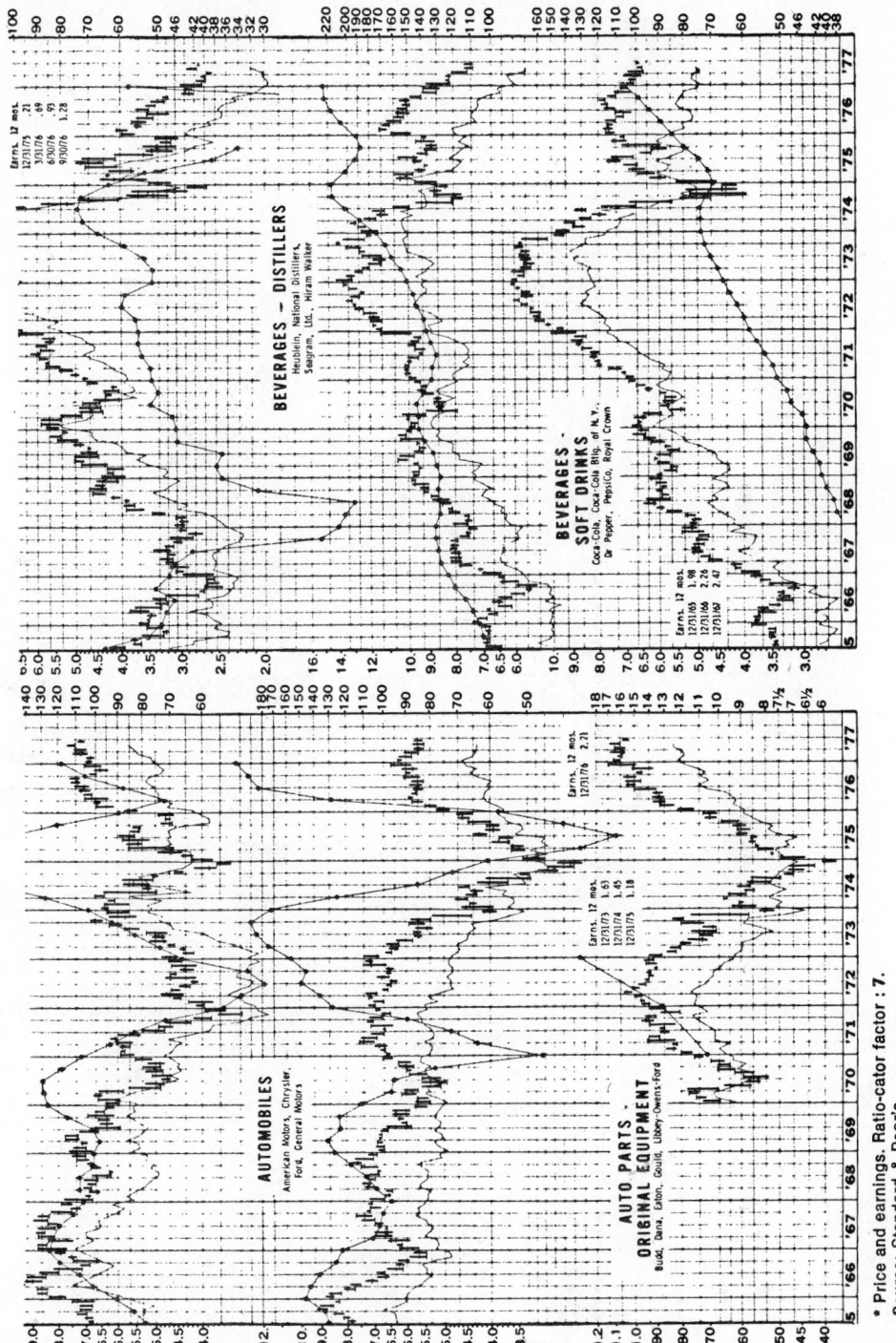

BEVERAGES – DISTILLERS
Heublein, National Distillers,
Seagram, Ltd., Hiram Walker

Earns. 12 mos.	
12/31/75	.21
3/31/76	.69
6/30/76	.93
9/30/6	1.28

BEVERAGES –
SOFT DRINKS
Coca-Cola, Coca-Cola Btlg. of N.Y.
Dr Pepper, PepsiCo, Royal Crown

Earns. 12 mos.	
12/31/65	1.98
12/31/66	2.26
12/31/67	2.47

AUTOMOBILES
American Motors, Chrysler,
Ford, General Motors

AUTO PARTS –
ORIGINAL EQUIPMENT
Budd, Dana, Eaton, Gould, Libbey-Owens-Ford

Earns. 12 mos.	
12/31/73	1.63
12/31/74	1.45
12/31/75	1.18

Earns. 12 mos.	
12/31/76	2.21

* Price and earnings. Ratio-cator factor : 7.
Source: Standard & Poor's.

INDUSTRY GROUP AVERAGES (continued)

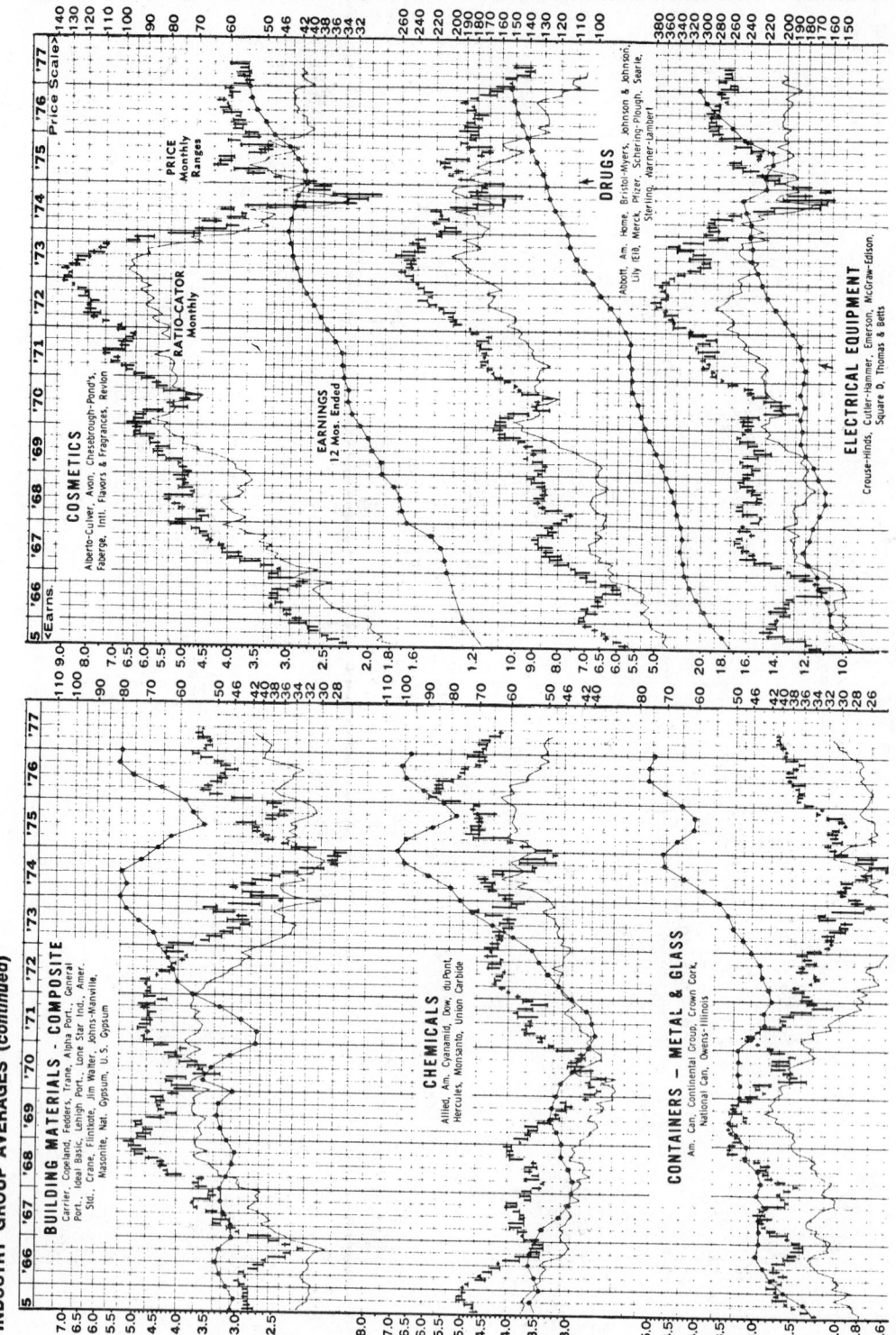

COSMETICS
Alberto-Culver, Avon, Chesebrough-Pond's, Faberge, Intl. Flavors & Fragrances, Revlon

PRICE Monthly Ranges

RATIO-CATOR Monthly

EARNINGS 12 Mos. Ended

DRUGS
Abbott, Am. Home, Bristol-Myers, Johnson & Johnson, Lily (Eli), Merck, Pfizer, Schering-Plough, Searle, Sterling, Warner-Lambert

ELECTRICAL EQUIPMENT
Crouse-Hinds, Cutler-Hammer, Emerson, McGraw-Edison, Square D, Thomas & Betts

BUILDING MATERIALS – COMPOSITE
Carrier, Copeland, Fedders, Trane, Alpha Port., General Port., Ideal Basic, Lehigh Port., Lone Star Ind., Amer. Std. Crane, Flintkote, Jim Walter, Johns-Manville, Masonite, Nat. Gypsum, U.S. Gypsum

CHEMICALS
Allied, Am. Cyanamid, Dow, duPont, Hercules, Monsanto, Union Carbide

CONTAINERS – METAL & GLASS
Am. Can, Continental Group, Crown Cork, National Can, Owens-Illinois

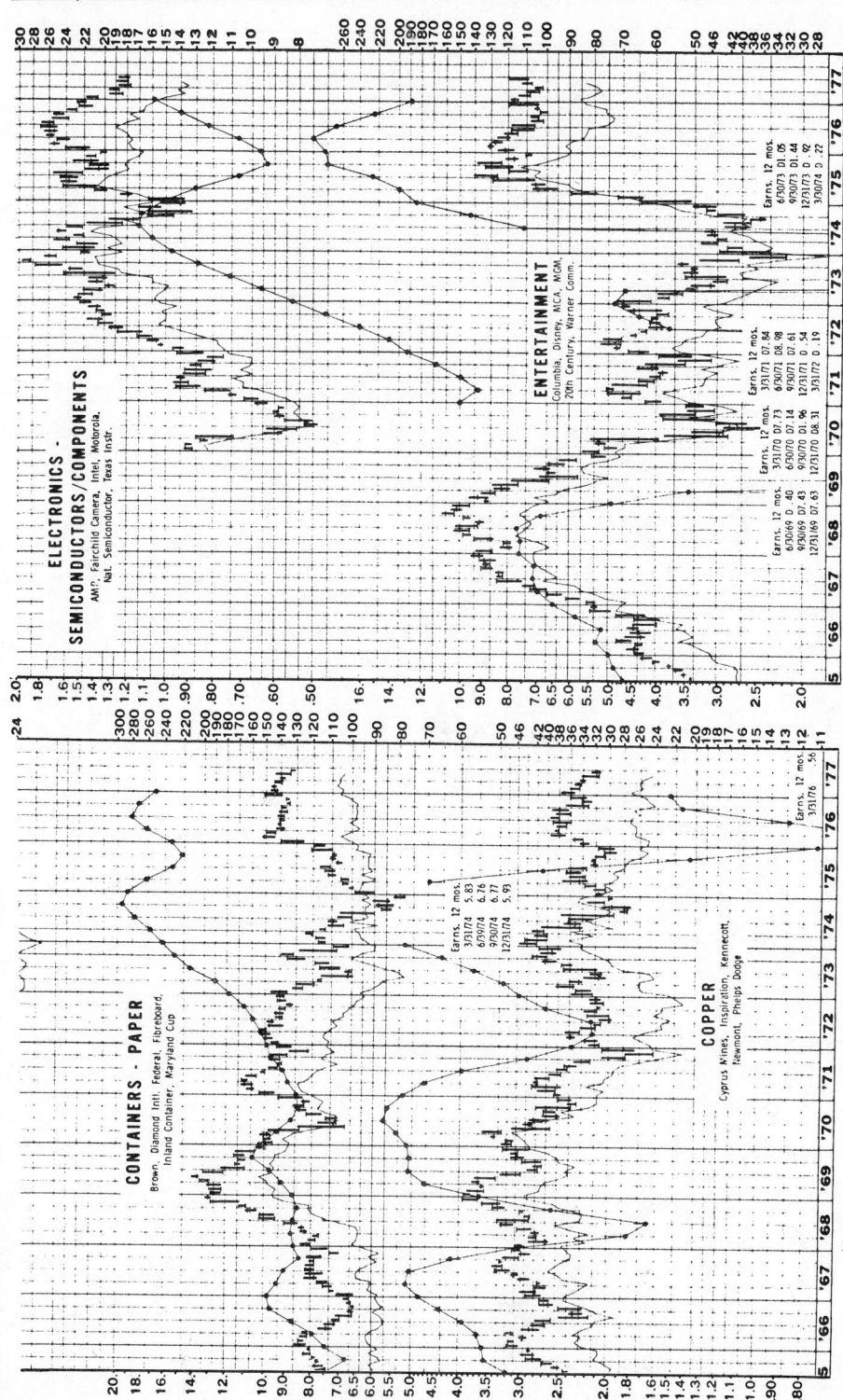

ELECTRONICS -
SEMICONDUCTORS/COMPONENTS
Am't. Fairchild Camera, Intel, Motorola,
Nat. Semiconductor, Texas Instr.

ENTERTAINMENT
Columbia, Disney, MCA, MGM,
20th Century, Warner Comm.

Earns. 12 mos.
3/31/70 D1.73
6/30/70 D1.14
9/30/70 D1.96
12/31/70 D8.31

Earns. 12 mos.
6/30/69 D .40
9/30/69 D .43
12/31/69 D7.63

Earns. 12 mos.
3/31/71 D7.84
6/30/71 D8.98
9/30/71 D7.61
12/31/71 D .54
3/31/72 D .19

Earns. 12 mos.
6/30/73 D1.05
9/30/73 D1.44
12/31/73 D .92
3/30/74 D .22

CONTAINERS - PAPER
Brown, Diamond Int'l, Federal, Fibreboard,
Inland Container, Maryland Cup

COPPER
Cyprus Mines, Inspiration, Kennecott,
Newmont, Phelps Dodge

Earns. 12 mos.
3/31/74 5.83
6/30/74 6.76
9/30/74 6.77
12/31/74 5.93

Earns. 12 mos.
3/31/76 .56

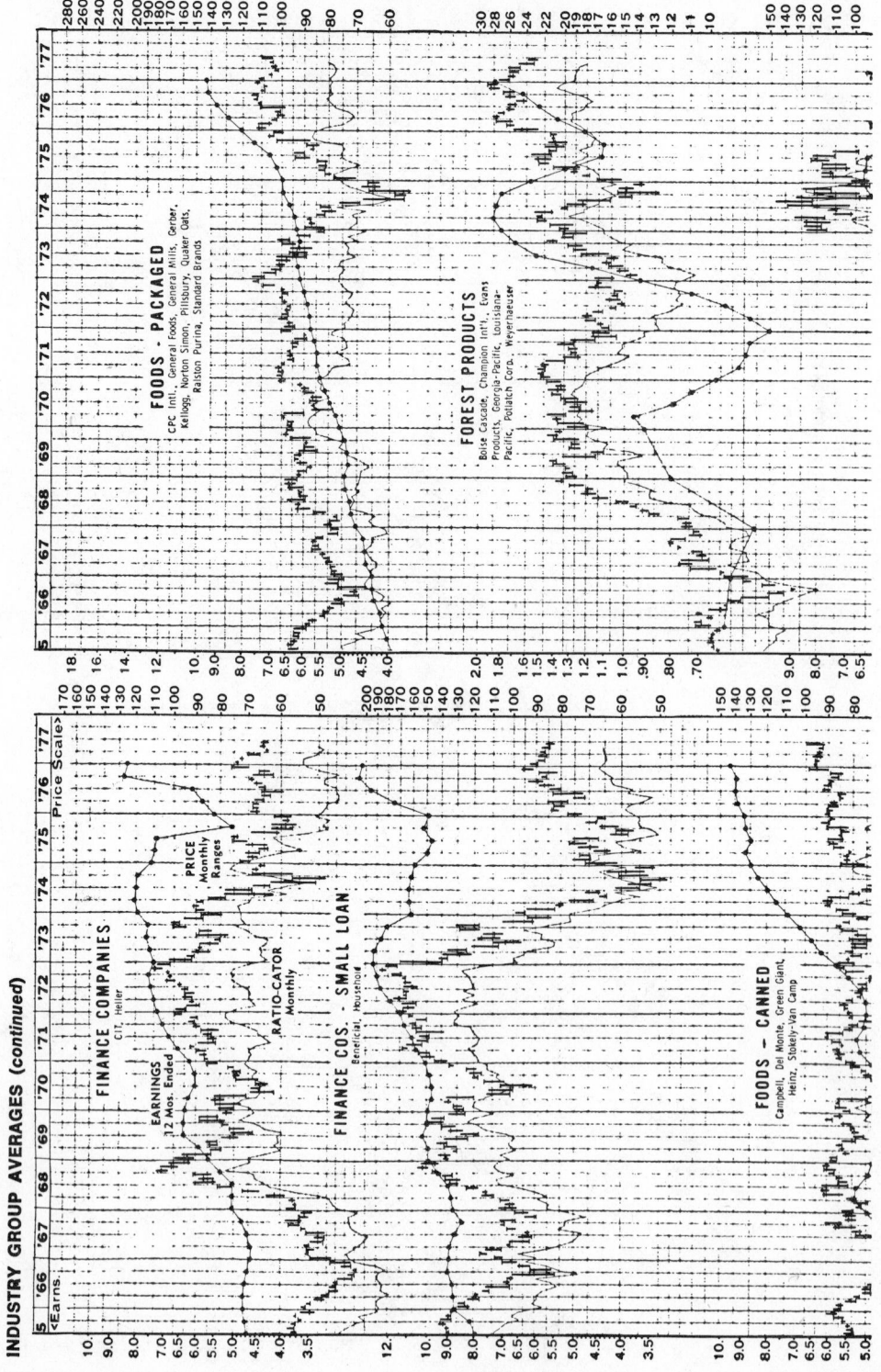

INDUSTRY GROUP AVERAGES (continued)

FINANCE COMPANIES
C.I.T., Heller

FINANCE COS. - SMALL LOAN
Beneficial, Household

FOODS - CANNED
Campbell, Del Monte, Green Giant,
Heinz, Stokely-Van Camp

FOODS - PACKAGED
CPC Int'l., General Foods, General Mills, Gerber,
Kellogg, Norton Simon, Pillsbury, Quaker Oats,
Ralston Purina, Standard Brands

FOREST PRODUCTS
Boise Cascade, Champion Int'l., Evans
Products, Georgia-Pacific, Louisiana-
Pacific, Potlatch Corp., Weyerhaeuser

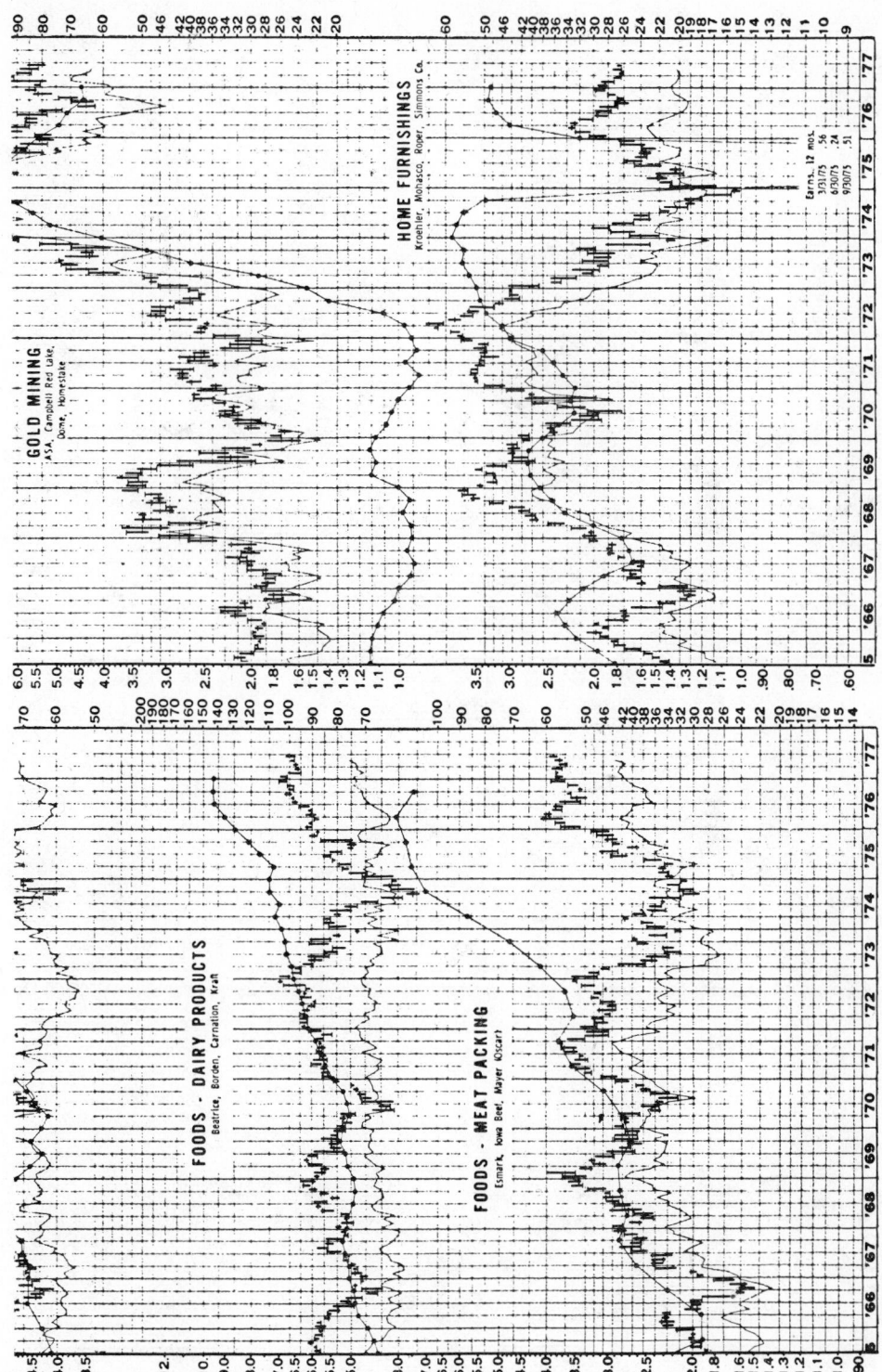

GOLD MINING
ASA, Campbell Red Lake, Dome, Homestake

HOME FURNISHINGS
Kroehler, Mohasco, Roper, Simmons Co.

Earns. 12 mos.	
3/31/75	.56
6/30/75	.24
9/30/75	.51

FOODS - DAIRY PRODUCTS
Beatrice, Borden, Carnation, Kraft

FOODS - MEAT PACKING
Esmark, Iowa Beef, Mayer (Oscar)

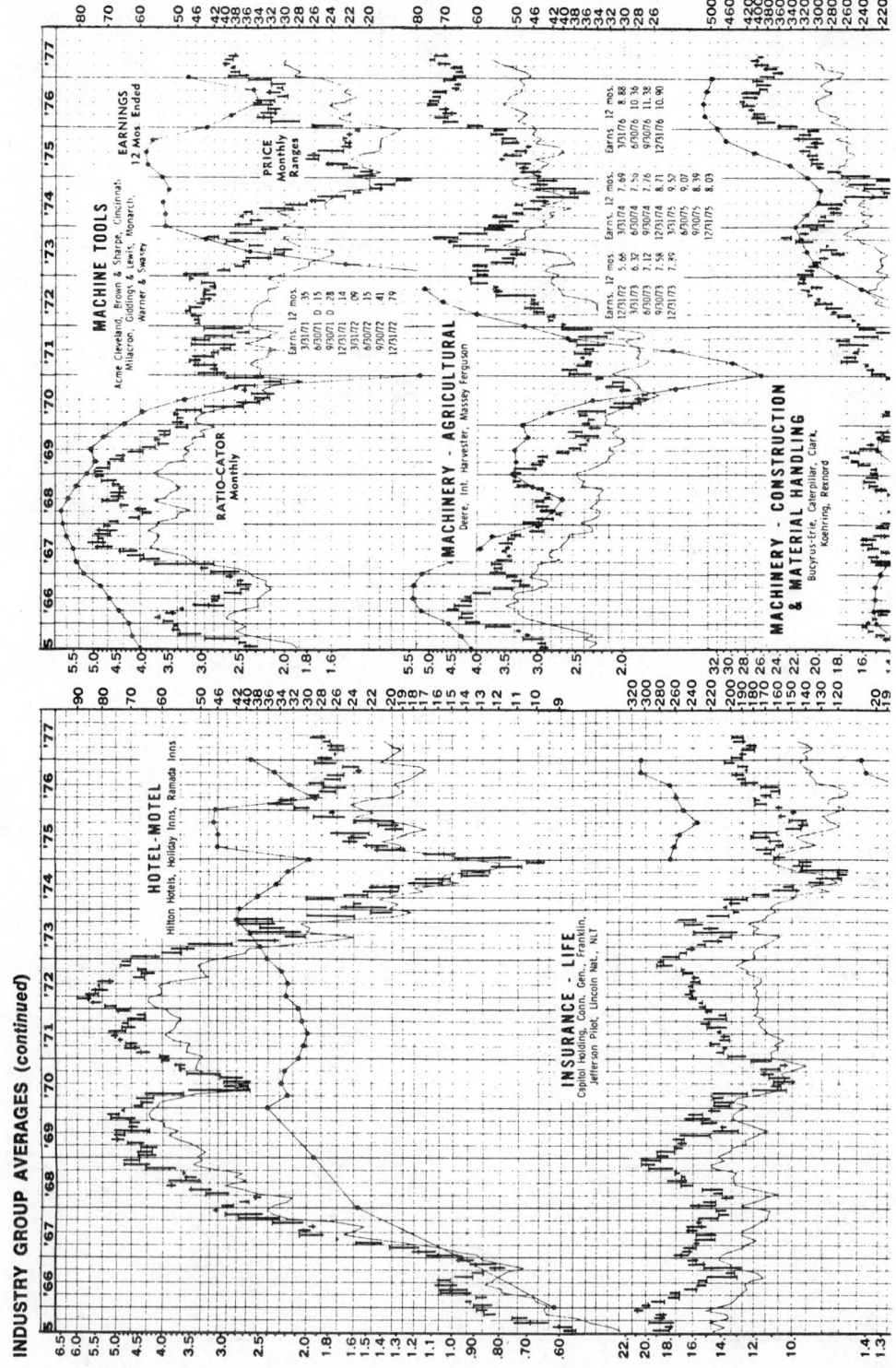

INDUSTRY GROUP AVERAGES *(continued)*

MACHINE TOOLS

Acme Cleveland, Brown & Sharpe, Cincinnati, Milacron, Giddings & Lewis, Monarch, Warner & Swasey

EARNINGS
12 Mos. Ended

PRICE
Monthly
Ranges

RATIO-CATOR
Monthly

MACHINERY - AGRICULTURAL

Deere, Int. Harvester, Massey Ferguson

MACHINERY - CONSTRUCTION
& MATERIAL HANDLING

Bucyrus-Erie, Caterpillar, Clark, Koehring, Rexnord

HOTEL-MOTEL

Hilton Hotels, Holiday Inns, Ramada Inns

INSURANCE - LIFE

Capitol Holding, Conn. Gen., Franklin, Jefferson Pilot, Lincoln Nat., NLT

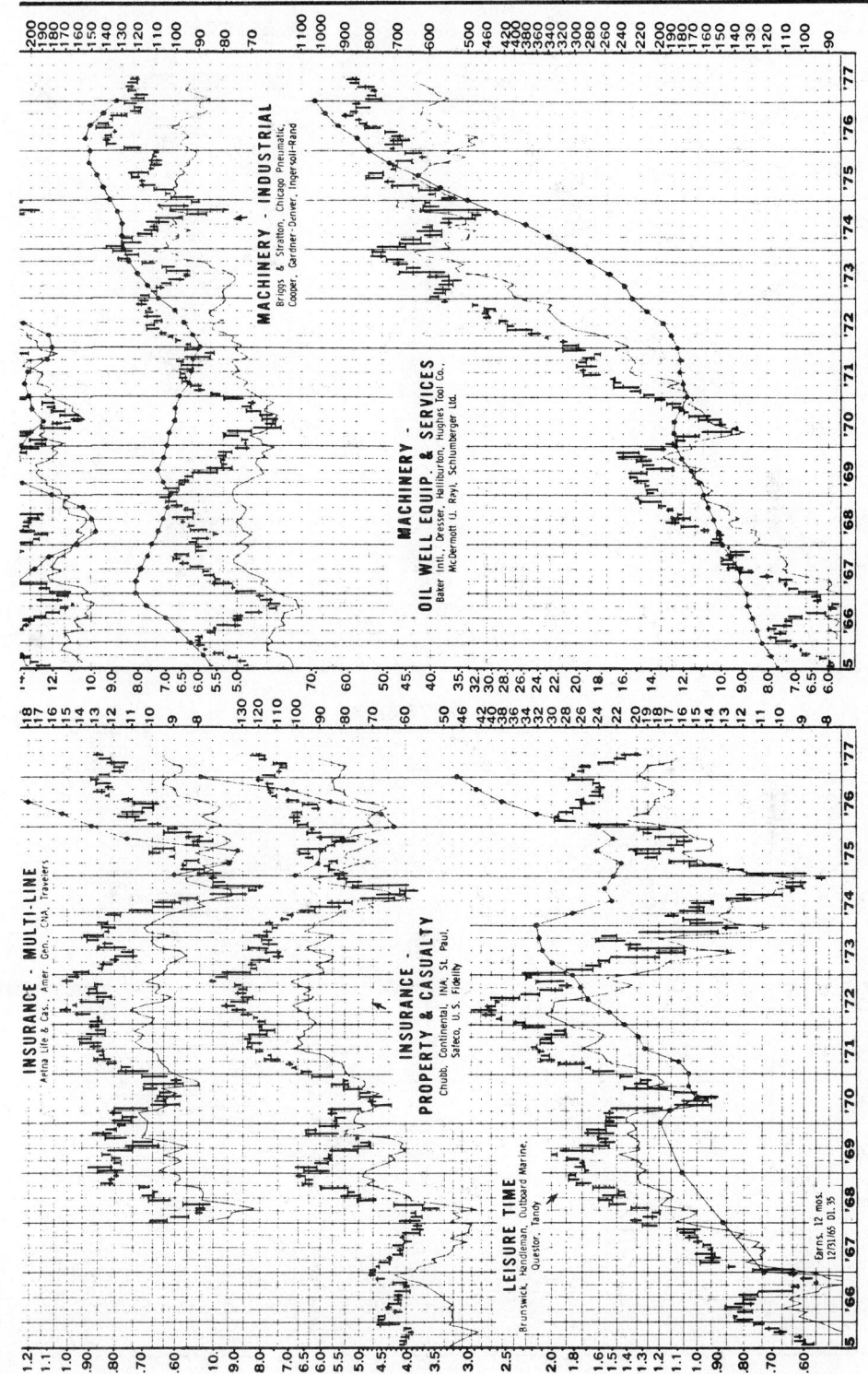

MACHINERY - INDUSTRIAL
Briggs & Stratton, Chicago Pneumatic,
Cooper, Gardner-Denver, Ingersoll-Rand

MACHINERY -
OIL WELL EQUIP. & SERVICES
Baker Intl., Dresser, Halliburton, Hughes Tool Co.,
McDermott (J. Ray), Schlumberger Ltd.

INSURANCE - MULTI-LINE
Aetna Life & Cas., Amer. Gen., CNA, Travelers

INSURANCE -
PROPERTY & CASUALTY
Chubb, Continental, INA, St. Paul,
Safeco, U.S. Fidelity

LEISURE TIME
Brunswick, Handleman, Outboard Marine,
Questor, Tandy

Earns. 12 mos.
12/31/65 D1.35

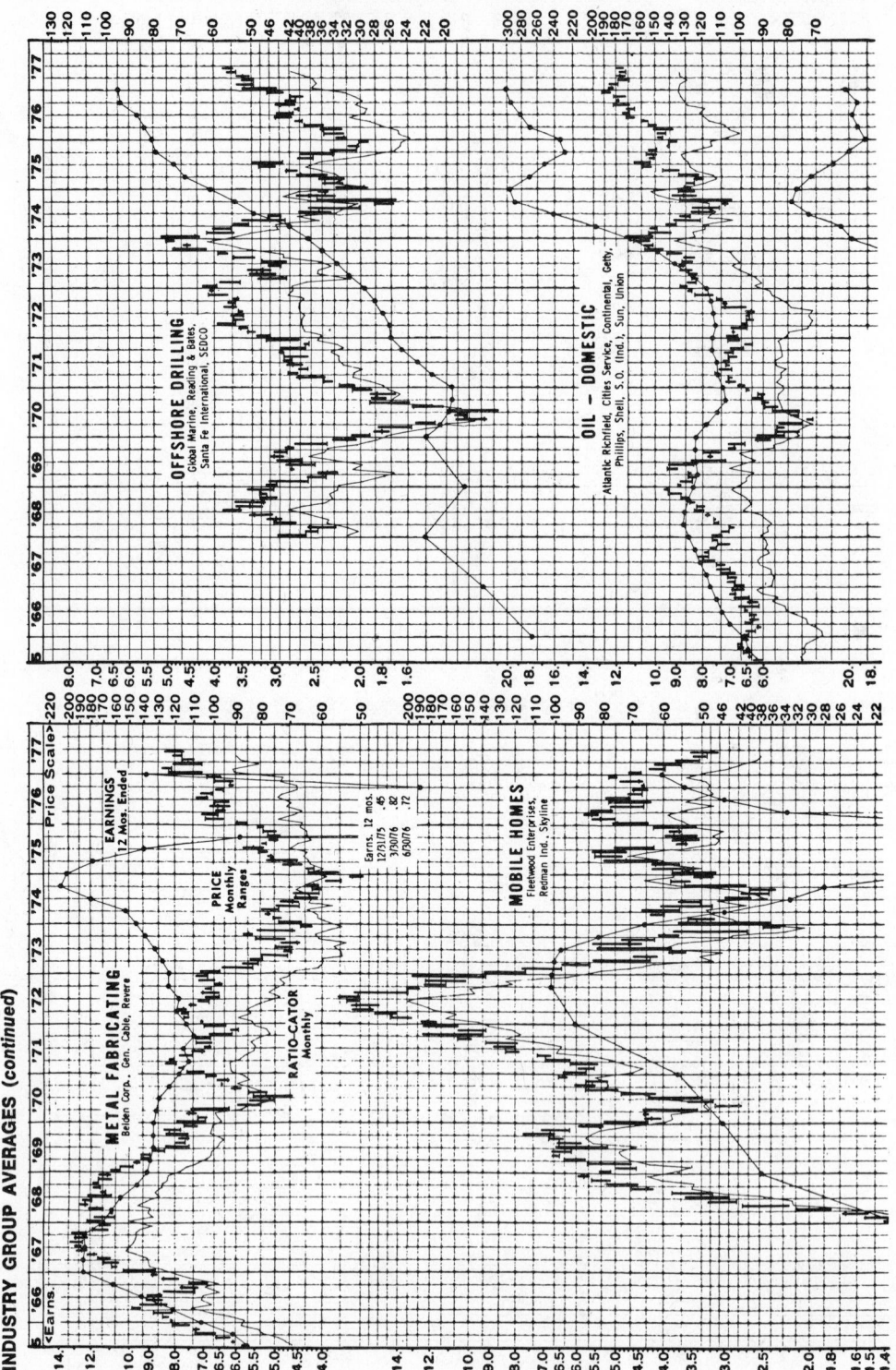

INDUSTRY GROUP AVERAGES *(continued)*

OFFSHORE DRILLING
Global Marine, Reading & Bates,
Santa Fe International, SEDCO

OIL — DOMESTIC
Atlantic Richfield, Cities Service, Continental, Getty,
Phillips, Shell, S.O. Ind. I., Sun, Union

METAL FABRICATING
Belden Corp., Gen. Cable, Revere

EARNINGS
12 Mos. Ended

PRICE
Monthly
Ranges

RATIO-CATOR
Monthly

Earns. 12 mos.
12/31/75   .45
3/30/76   .82
6/30/76   .72

MOBILE HOMES
Fleetwood Enterprises,
Redman Ind., Skyline

<Earns.
<Price Scale>

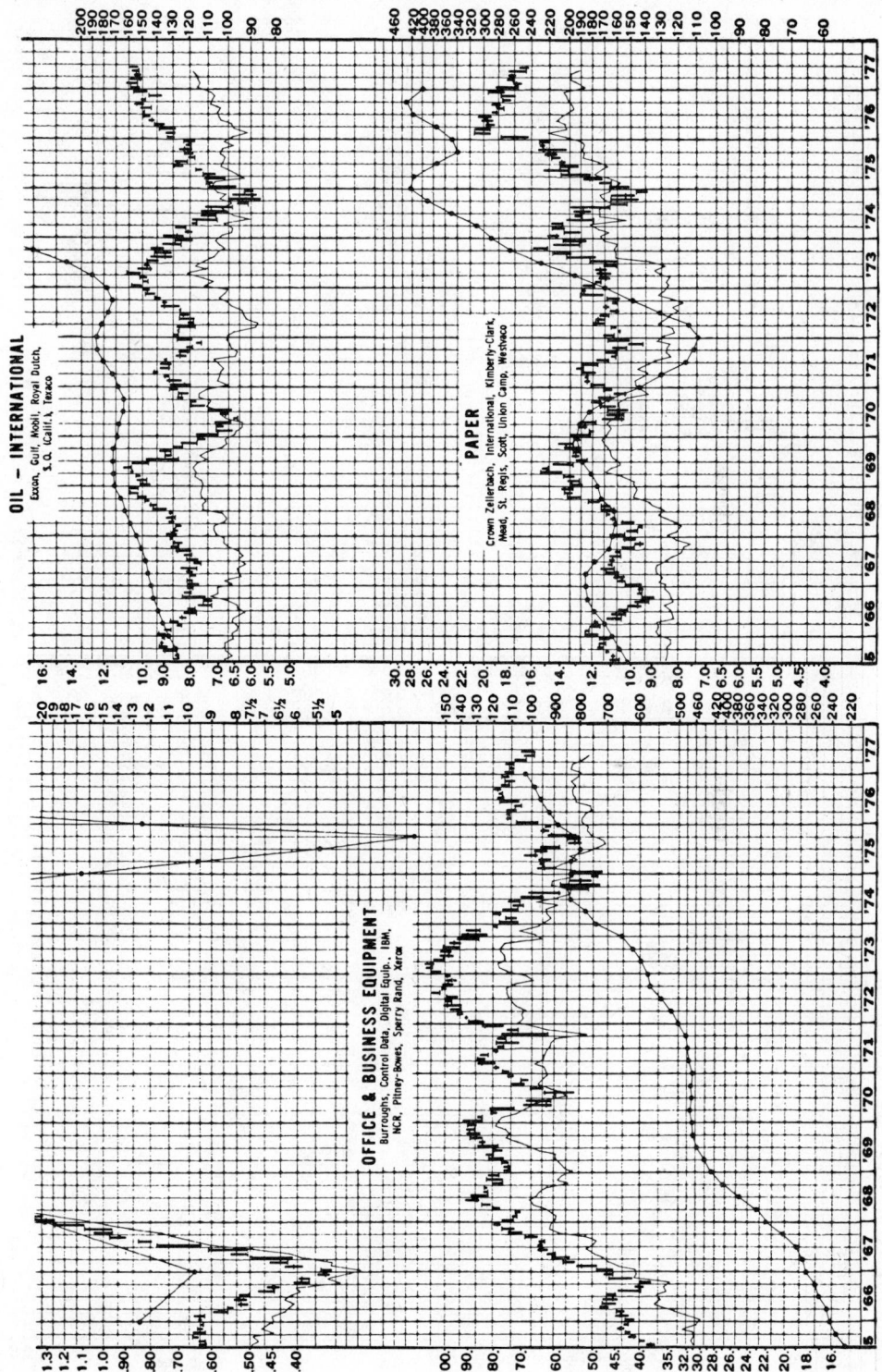

OIL — INTERNATIONAL
Exxon, Gulf, Mobil, Royal Dutch,
S.O. (Calif.), Texaco

PAPER
Crown Zellerbach, International, Kimberly-Clark,
Mead, St. Regis, Scott, Union Camp, Westvaco

OFFICE & BUSINESS EQUIPMENT
Burroughs, Control Data, Digital Equip., IBM,
NCR, Pitney-Bowes, Sperry Rand, Xerox

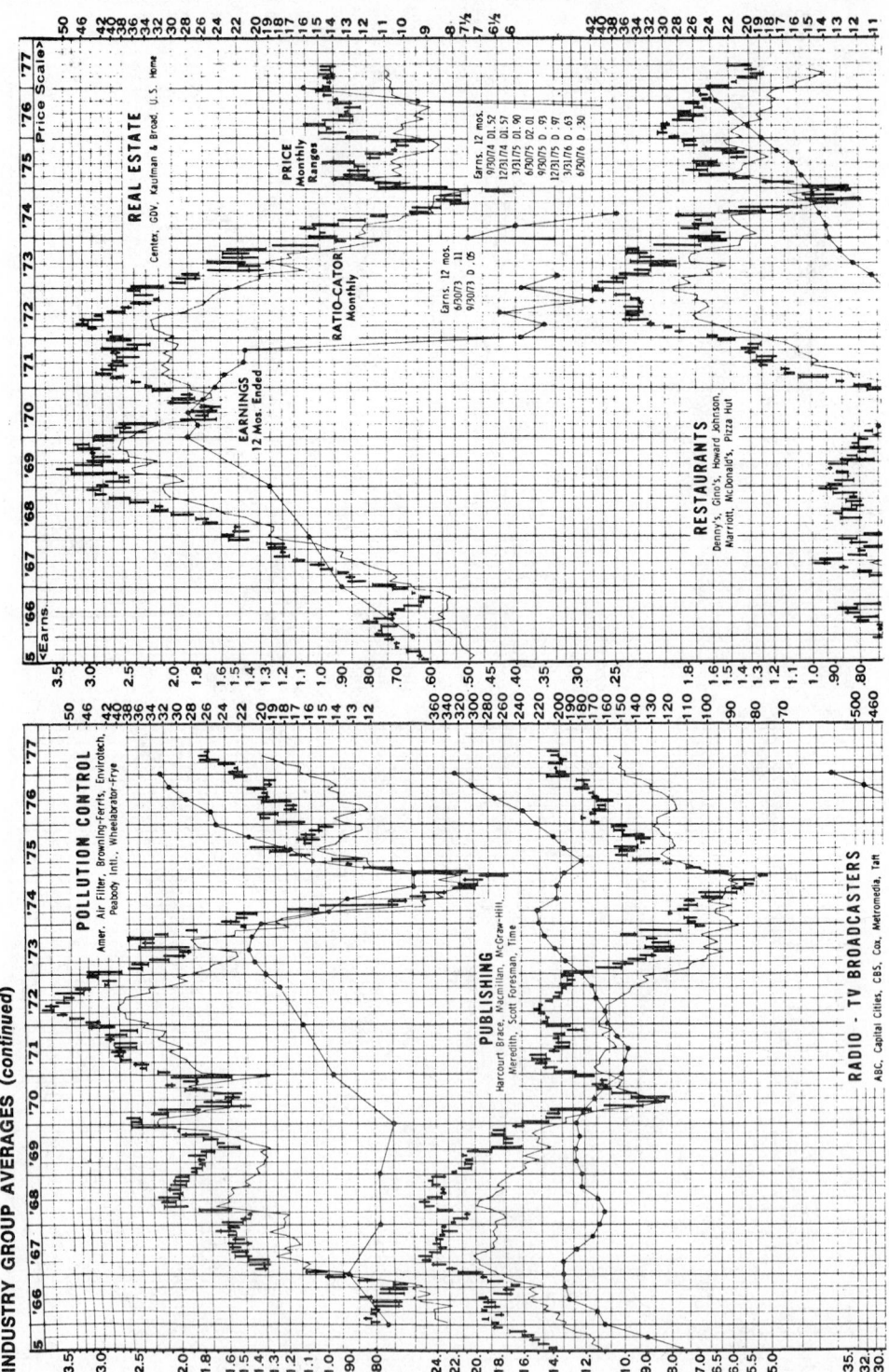

INDUSTRY GROUP AVERAGES (continued)

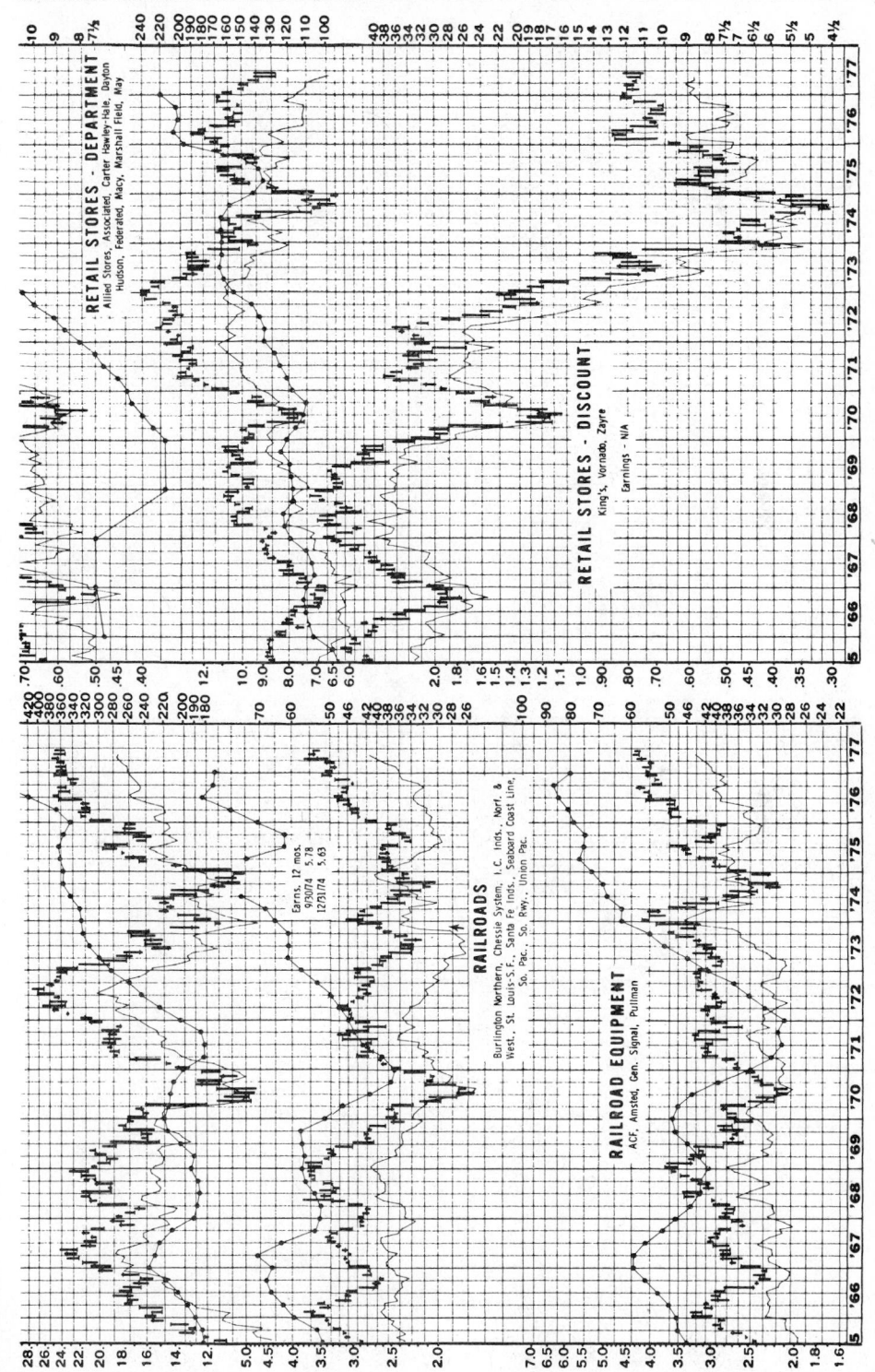

RETAIL STORES - DEPARTMENT
Allied Stores, Associated, Carter Hawley-Hale, Dayton Hudson, Federated, Macy, Marshall Field, May

RETAIL STORES - DISCOUNT
King's, Vornado, Zayre
Earnings - N/A

RAILROADS
Burlington Northern, Chessie System, I.C. Inds., Norf. & West., St. Louis-S.F., Santa Fe Inds., Seaboard Coast Line, So. Pac., So. Rwy., Union Pac.

Earns, 12 mos.
9/30/74   5.78
12/31/74 5.63

RAILROAD EQUIPMENT
ACF, Amsted, Gen. Signal, Pullman

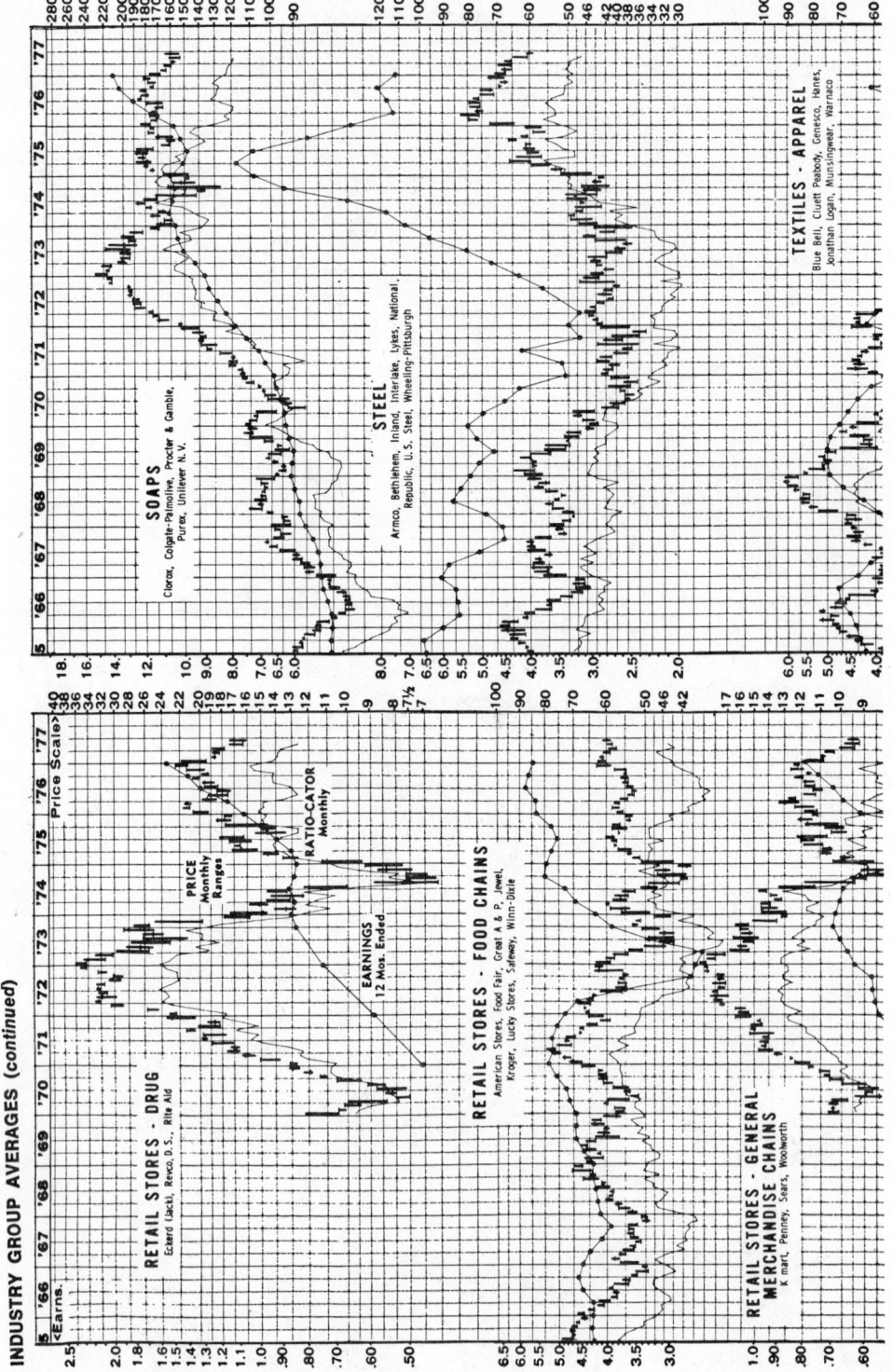

INDUSTRY GROUP AVERAGES (continued)

RETAIL STORES - DRUG
Eckerd (Jack), Revco, D.S., Rite Aid

PRICE
Monthly
Ranges

RATIO-CATOR
Monthly

Price Scale>

EARNINGS
12 Mos. Ended

Earns.

RETAIL STORES - FOOD CHAINS
American Stores, Food Fair, Great A & P, Jewel,
Kroger, Lucky Stores, Safeway, Winn-Dixie

RETAIL STORES - GENERAL
MERCHANDISE CHAINS
K mart, Penney, Sears, Woolworth

SOAPS
Clorox, Colgate-Palmolive, Procter & Gamble,
Purex, Unilever N.V.

STEEL
Armco, Bethlehem, Inland, Interlake, Lykes, National,
Republic, U.S. Steel, Wheeling-Pittsburgh

TEXTILES - APPAREL
Blue Bell, Cluett Peabody, Genesco, Hanes,
Jonathan Logan, Munsingwear, Warnaco

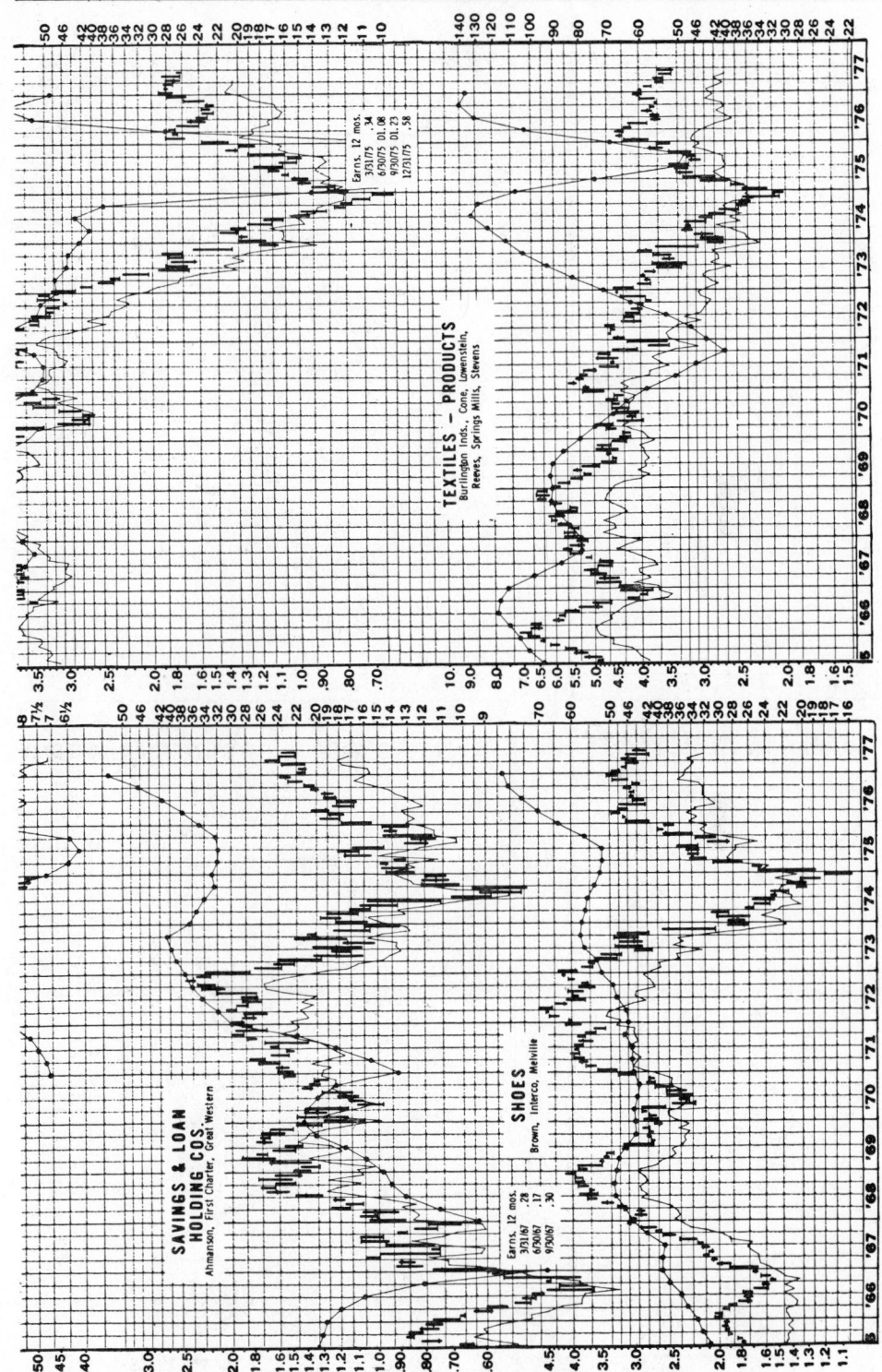

TEXTILES – PRODUCTS
Burlington Inds., Cone, Lowenstein,
Reeves, Springs Mills, Stevens

Earns. 12 mos.
3/31/75   .34
6/30/75 DL .08
9/30/75 DL .23
12/31/75   .58

SAVINGS & LOAN
HOLDING COS.
Ahmanson, First Charter, Great Western

SHOES
Brown, Interco, Melville

Earns. 12 mos.
3/31/67   .28
6/30/67   .17
9/30/67   .30

INDUSTRY GROUP AVERAGES (concluded)

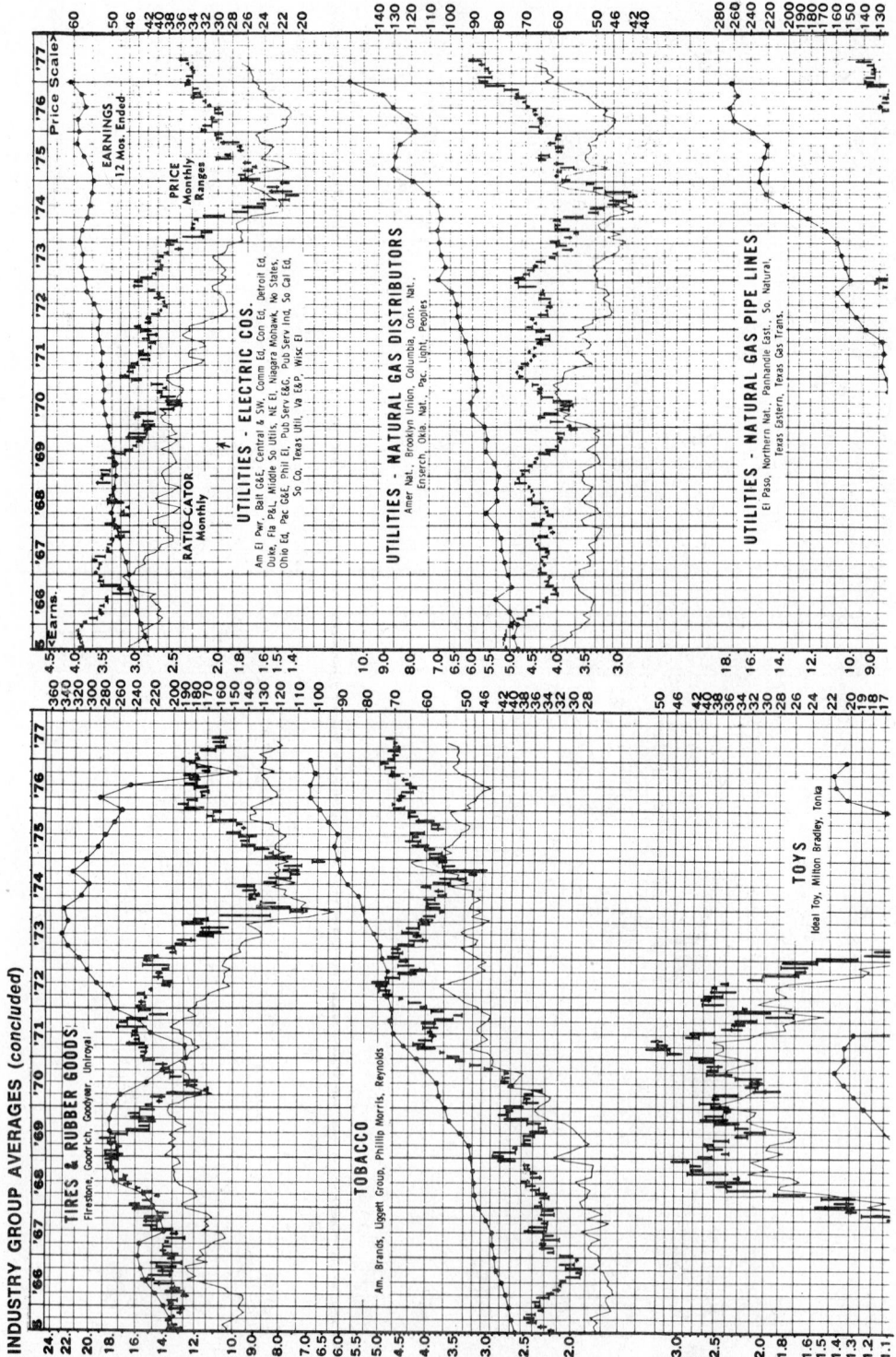

UTILITIES - ELECTRIC COS.

Am El Pwr, Balt G&E, Central & SW, Comm Ed, Con Ed, Detroit Ed,
Duke, Fla P&L, Middle So Utils, NE El, Niagara Mohawk, No States,
Ohio Ed, Pac G&E, Phil El, Pub Serv E&G, Pub Serv Ind, So Cal Ed,
So Co, Texas Util, Va E&P, Wisc El

UTILITIES - NATURAL GAS DISTRIBUTORS

Amer Nat, Brooklyn Union, Columbia, Cons. Nat.
Enserch, Okla. Nat., Pac. Light, Peoples

UTILITIES - NATURAL GAS PIPE LINES

El Paso, Northern Nat, Panhandle East, So. Natural,
Texas Eastern, Texas Gas Trans.

TIRES & RUBBER GOODS

Firestone, Goodrich, Goodyear, Uniroyal

TOBACCO

Am. Brands, Liggett Group, Phillip Morris, Reynolds

TOYS

Ideal Toy, Milton Bradley, Tonka

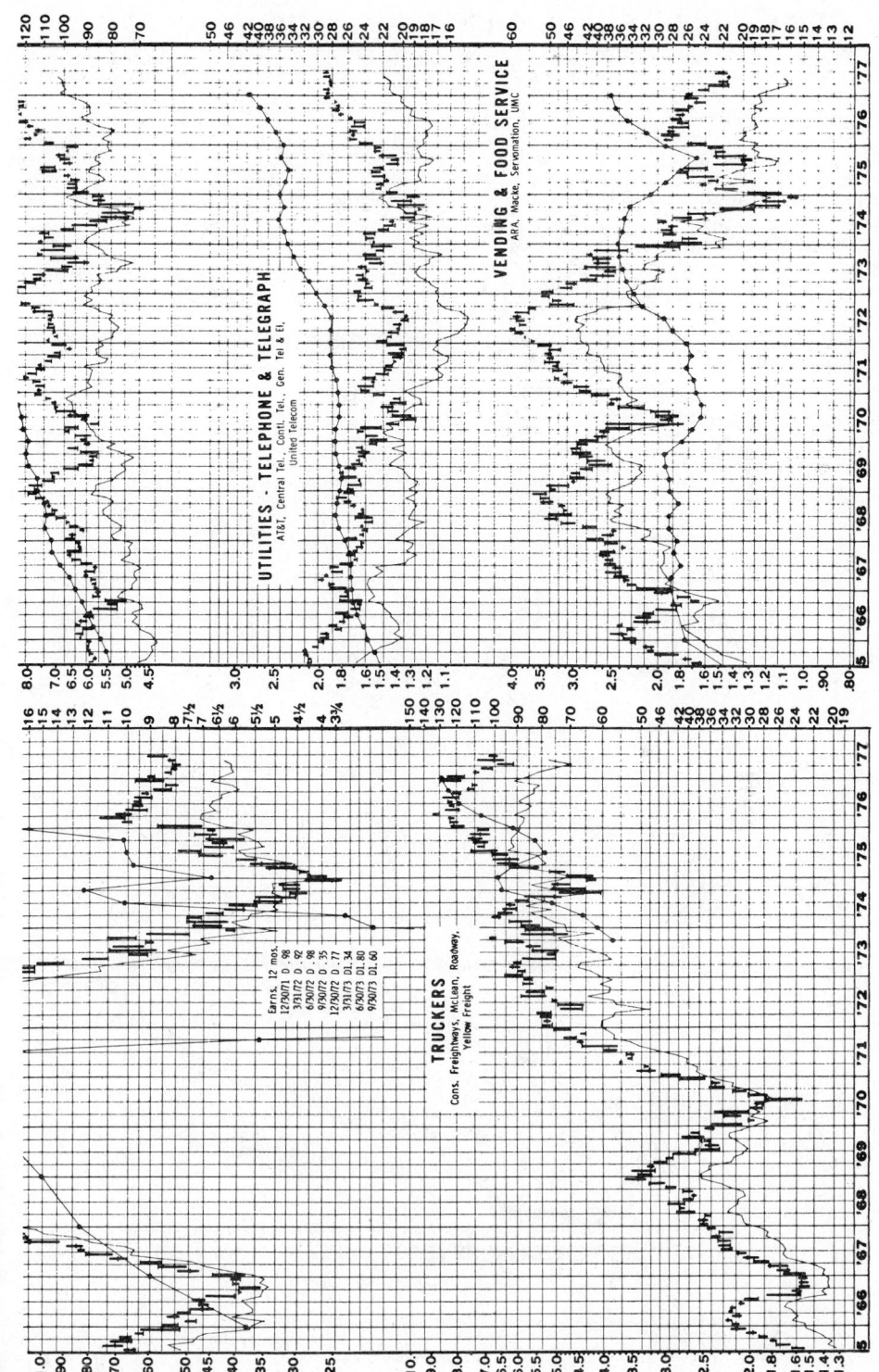

UTILITIES - TELEPHONE & TELEGRAPH
AT&T, Central Tel., Contl. Tel., Gen. Tel & El.,
United Telecom

VENDING & FOOD SERVICE
ARA, Macke, Servomation, UMC

TRUCKERS
Cons. Freightways, McLean, Roadway,
Yellow Freight

Earns. 12 mos.
12/50/71 0.98
3/31/72   0.92
6/30/72   0.98
9/30/72   0.35
12/50/72 0.77
3/31/73   D1.34
6/30/73   D1.80
9/50/73   D1.60

Investment Returns on Stocks, Bonds, and Bills

*Roger G. Ibbotson**

Our look at history consists of examining the returns of five capital market sectors. We measure total returns (capital gains plus income) on common stocks, long-term corporate bonds, long-term government bonds, U.S. Treasury bills, and rates of inflation on consumer goods. Comparing the returns from the various sectors gives us insights into the returns available from taking risk and the relationships between capital market returns and inflation.

* Graduate School of Business, University of Chicago, Chicago, Illinois 60637.

EXHIBIT 1: WEALTH INDEXES OF INVESTMENTS IN THE U.S. CAPITAL MARKETS, 1926–1976

Assumed initial Investment of $1 at year-end 1925 (Includes reinvestment Income)

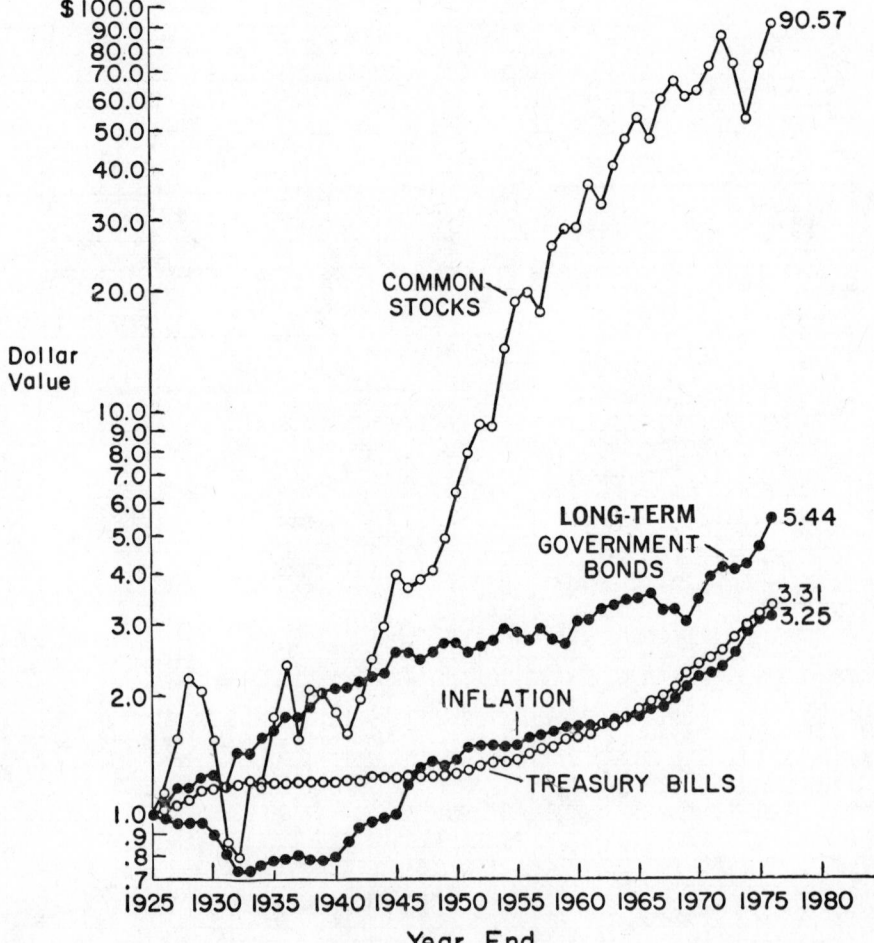

Source: *Stocks, Bonds, Bills, and Inflation: The Past (1926–1976), and the Future (1977–2000)*, by Roger G. Ibbotson and Rex Sinquefield, with a foreword by Jack L. Treynor, Financial Analysts Research Foundation, 1977, Charlottesville, VA 22906.

THE RISKS AND REWARDS

We display graphically the rewards and risks available from the U.S. capital markets over the past 51 years. Exhibit 1 shows the growth of an investment in common stocks, long-term government bonds, and Treasury bills as well as the increase in the inflation index over the 51-year period. Each of the series is initiated at $1 at year-end 1925. The vertical scale is logarithmic so that equal distances represent equal percentage changes anywhere along the axis. The graph vividly portrays that common stocks were the big winner over the entire period. If $1 were invested in stocks at year-end 1925 and all dividends reinvested, the dollar investment would have grown to $90.57 by year-end 1976. This phenomenal growth was not without substantial risk, especially during the earlier portion of the period. In contrast, long-term government bonds (with a constant 20-year maturity) exhibited much less risk, but grew to only $5.44.

A virtually riskless strategy (for those with short-term time horizons) has been to buy U.S. Treasury bills. However, Treasury bills have had a marked tendency to track inflation, with the result that their real (inflation adjusted) return is near zero for the entire 1926–1976 period. Note that the tracking is only prevalent over the latter portion of the period. During periods of deflation (such as the late 1920s and early 1930s) the Treasury bill returns were near zero, but not negative, since no one intentionally buys securities with negative yields. Beginning in the early 1940s, the yields (returns) on Treasury bills

were pegged by the government at low rates while high inflation was experienced. The government pegging ended with the U.S. Treasury–Federal Reserve Accord in March 1951.

We summarize the investment returns in Exhibit 2 by presenting the average annual returns over the 1926–1976 period. Common stocks returned a compounded (geometric mean) total return of 9.2 percent per year. The annual compound return from capital appreciation alone was 4.3 percent. After adjusting for inflation, annual compounded total returns were 6.7 percent per year.°

The average total return over any single year (arithmetic mean) for stocks was 11.6 percent, with positive returns recorded in two thirds of the years (34 out of 51 years). The risk or degree of return fluctuation is measured by the standard deviation as 22.4 percent. The frequency distribution (histogram) counts the number of years the returns fell in each 5 percent return increment. Note the wide variations in common stock returns relative to the other capital market sectors.

° Editor's note: Over the current decade the compounded growth rate for common stock with dividends reinvested has been considerably less than the long-term value of 9.2 percent. Thus from the beginning of 1967 to the end of 1976 the compounded growth rate has been 6.6 percent for common stock as compared to 5.4 percent for long-term corporate bonds and 5.6 percent for Treasury bills. All figures neglect taxes. The inflation rate during this period was 5.9 percent. After inflationary adjustments and income taxes, it is evident that all of these investments resulted in a net loss in terms of real income. Assuming a 40 percent tax rate and a 6 percent inflation rate, investments must earn 10 percent before taxes to break even.

EXHIBIT 2: BASIC SERIES, INVESTMENT TOTAL ANNUAL RETURNS, 1926–1976

Series	Geometric Mean	Arithmetic Mean	Standard Deviation	Distribution
Common Stocks	9.2%	11.6%	22.4%	
Long-Term Corporate Bonds	4.1%	4.2%	5.6%	
Long-Term Government Bonds	3.4%	3.5%	5.8%	
U.S. Treasury Bills	2.4%	2.4%	2.1%	
Inflation	2.3%	2.4%	4.8%	

-50%   0%   +50%

Source: Ibbotson and Sinquefield, *Stocks, Bonds, Bills, and Inflation.*

Annual stock returns ranged from 54.0 percent in 1933 to −43.3 percent in 1931.

A simple example illustrates the difference between geometric and arithmetic means. Suppose $1 were invested in a common stock portfolio that experiences successive annual returns of +50 percent and −50 percent. At the end of the first year the portfolio is worth $1.50. At the end of the second year, the portfolio is worth $0.75. The annual arithmetic mean is 0 percent, whereas the annual geometric mean (compounded return) is −13.4 percent. Naturally, it is the geometric mean that more directly measures the change in wealth over more than one period. On the other hand, the arithmetic mean is a better representation of typical performance over any single annual period.

The other capital market sectors also had returns commensurate with their risks. Long-term corporate bonds outperformed the default-free, long-term government bonds, which in turn outperformed the essentially riskless U.S. Treasury bills. Over the entire period the riskless U.S. Treasury bills had a return almost identical with the inflation rate. Thus, we again note that the real rate of interest (the inflation-adjusted riskless rate) has been on average very near 0 percent historically.

MEASUREMENT OF THE FIVE SERIES

The returns were computed by compounding monthly returns, with no adjustments made for transactions costs or taxes. We describe each of the five total return series which are listed annually in Exhibit 3.

COMMON STOCKS

The total return index is based upon Standard and Poor's (S&P) Composite Index with dividends reinvested monthly. To the extent that the 500 stocks currently included in the S&P Composite Index (prior to March 1957, there were 90 stocks) are representative of all stocks in the United States, the market value weighting scheme allows the returns of the index to correspond to the ag-gregate stock market returns in the U.S. economy.

LONG-TERM CORPORATE BONDS

We measure the total returns of a corporate bond index with approximately 20 years to maturity. We use Salomon Brothers' High Grade Long-Term Corporate Bond Index from its beginning in 1969 through 1976. For the period 1946–68 we backdate Salomon Brothers' index using Salomon Brothers' monthly yield data and similar methodology. For the period 1926–45 we compute returns using Standard and Poor's monthly high-grade corporate composite bond yield data, assuming a 4 percent coupon and a 20-year maturity.

LONG-TERM GOVERNMENT BONDS

To measure the total returns of long-term U.S. government bonds, we use the bond data obtained from the U.S. Government Bond File (constructed by Lawrence Fisher) at the Center for Research in Security Prices (CRSP) at the University of Chicago. We attempt to maintain a 20-year bond portfolio whose returns do not reflect the potential tax benefits, impaired negotiability, or the special redemption or call privileges frequently characterizing government bond prices and yields.

U.S. TREASURY BILLS

For the U.S. Treasury bill index, we again use the data in the CRSP U.S. Government Bond File. We measure one-month holding period returns for the shortest-term bills not less than one month in maturity. Since U.S. Treasury bills were not initiated until 1929, we use short-term coupon bonds whenever bill quotes are unavailable.

CONSUMER PRICE INDEX

We utilize the Consumer Price Index (CPI) to measure inflation. The CPI is constructed by the U.S. Department of Labor, Bureau of Labor Statistics, Washington, DC.

EXHIBIT 3: BASIC SERIES, INDEXES OF YEAR-END CUMULATIVE WEALTH, 1925–1976

| Year | Common Stocks | | Long-Term Government Bonds | | Long-Term Corporate Bonds | U.S. Treasury Bills | Consumer Price Index |
	Total Returns	Capital Appreciation Only	Total Returns	Capital Appreciation Only	Total Returns	Total Returns	Rates of Inflation
1925...	1.000	1.000	1.000	1.000	1.000	1.000	1.000
1926...	1.116	1.057	1.073	1.039	1.074	1.033	0.985
1927...	1.535	1.384	1.174	1.095	1.154	1.065	0.965
1928...	2.204	1.908	1.175	1.061	1.186	1.099	0.955
1929...	2.018	1.681	1.215	1.059	1.225	1.152	0.957
1930...	1.516	1.202	1.272	1.072	1.323	1.179	0.899
1931...	0.859	0.636	1.204	0.981	1.299	1.192	0.814
1932...	0.789	0.540	1.407	1.108	1.439	1.204	0.730
1933...	1.214	0.792	1.406	1.073	1.588	1.207	0.734
1934...	1.197	0.745	1.547	1.146	1.808	1.209	0.749
1935...	1.767	1.053	1.624	1.170	1.982	1.211	0.771
1936...	2.367	1.346	1.746	1.225	2.116	1.213	0.780
1937...	1.538	0.827	1.750	1.194	2.174	1.217	0.804
1938...	2.016	1.035	1.847	1.228	2.307	1.217	0.782
1939...	2.008	0.979	1.957	1.271	2.399	1.217	0.778
1940...	1.812	0.829	2.076	1.319	2.480	1.217	0.786
1941...	1.602	0.681	2.095	1.305	2.548	1.218	0.862
1942...	1.927	0.766	2.162	1.315	2.614	1.221	0.942
1943...	2.427	0.915	2.207	1.310	2.688	1.225	0.972
1944...	2.906	1.041	2.270	1.314	2.815	1.229	0.993
1945...	3.965	1.361	2.513	1.423	2.930	1.233	1.015
1946...	3.645	1.199	2.511	1.392	2.980	1.238	1.199
1947...	3.853	1.199	2.445	1.327	2.911	1.244	1.307
1948...	4.065	1.191	2.528	1.340	3.031	1.254	1.343
1949...	4.829	1.313	2.691	1.395	3.132	1.268	1.318
1950...	6.360	1.600	2.692	1.366	3.198	1.283	1.395
1951...	7.888	1.863	2.586	1.281	3.112	1.302	1.477
1952...	9.336	2.082	2.616	1.262	3.221	1.324	1.490
1953...	9.244	1.944	2.711	1.270	3.331	1.348	1.499
1954...	14.108	2.820	2.906	1.325	3.511	1.360	1.492
1955...	18.561	3.564	2.868	1.271	3.527	1.381	1.497
1956...	19.778	3.658	2.708	1.164	3.287	1.415	1.540
1957...	17.646	3.134	2.910	1.208	3.573	1.459	1.587
1958...	25.298	4.327	2.733	1.097	3.494	1.482	1.615
1959...	28.322	4.694	2.671	1.029	3.460	1.526	1.639
1960...	28.455	4.554	3.039	1.124	3.774	1.566	1.663
1961...	36.106	5.607	3.068	1.092	3.956	1.600	1.674
1962...	32.955	4.945	3.280	1.122	4.270	1.643	1.695
1963...	40.469	5.879	3.319	1.092	4.364	1.695	1.723
1964...	47.139	6.642	3.436	1.084	4.572	1.754	1.743
1965...	53.008	7.244	3.460	1.047	4.552	1.823	1.777
1966...	47.674	6.295	3.586	1.036	4.560	1.910	1.836
1967...	59.104	7.560	3.257	0.895	4.335	1.991	1.892
1968...	65.642	8.139	3.248	0.846	4.446	2.094	1.981
1969...	60.059	7.210	3.083	0.754	4.086	2.232	2.102
1970...	62.465	7.222	3.457	0.791	4.837	2.378	2.218
1971...	71.406	8.001	3.914	0.843	5.370	2.482	2.292
1972...	84.955	9.252	4.136	0.840	5.760	2.577	2.371
1973...	72.500	7.645	4.090	0.775	5.825	2.756	2.579
1974...	53.300	5.373	4.268	0.748	5.647	2.976	2.894
1975...	73.130	7.068	4.661	0.754	6.474	3.149	3.097
1976...	90.566	8.422	5.441	0.815	7.681	3.309	3.246

Source: Ibbotson and Sinquefield, *Stocks, Bonds, Bills, and Inflation.*

DIVIDEND INCREASE IN EACH OF LAST 10 YEARS (NYSE Issues)

	Closing Price April 4, 1977	Paid 1976 ($)	Indi-cated Rate ($)	Dividends Yield on Indi-cated Rate (%)	In-crease Last 10 Years (%)	Payout 5-Year Aver-age (%)	Per Share Earnings Last 12 Months ($)
Air Products & Chem..........	26	0.12N	0.20	0.8N	200	5	2.24
Alcon Laboratories...........	19	0.27	0.32	1.7	440	21	1.35
Allied Maintenance...........	13½	0.62	0.64	4.7	210	31	1.75
American Brands.............	43¾	2.80	2.92	6.7	55	53	4.54
Amer Bldg Mainten..........	10⅝	0.42K	0.52	4.9K	281	23	1.64
Amer Home Products........	29¼	1.00	1.10	3.8	163	54	1.75
Amer Hospital Sup...........	25½	0.38	0.56	2.2	123	23	1.72
AMP Inc....................	25	0.41	0.48	1.9	241	28	1.40
ARA Services................	39¾	1.13	1.32	3.3	156	26	3.99
Atlantic City Elec.............	21⅝	1.56	1.62	7.5	27	61	2.47
Avon Products...............	47	1.80	2.00	4.3	157	64	2.90
Baxter Travenol Labs........	31¾	0.21	0.24	0.8	200	13	1.85
Belding Heminway...........	7½	0.32N	0.36	4.8N	100	32	0.96
Central & South West........	16	1.20	1.26	7.9	50	65	1.75
Central Tel & Util............	25⅛	1.32	1.50	6.0	85	52	2.50
Cleveland Elec III............	33¼	2.56	2.64	7.9	47	72	3.57
Coca-Cola Co...............	76½	2.65	3.08	4.0	152	55	4.76
Colgate-Palmolive	24¾	0.82	0.88	3.6	148	41	1.95
Columbia Gas Sys...........	29¾	2.14	2.24	7.5	48	59	3.70
Cont'l Illinois................	52½	2.34	2.40	4.6	84	35	7.45
Dart Indus..................	32⅛	0.65N	1.00	3.1N	242	14	4.14
Diebold, Inc................	11⅝	0.44	0.50	4.3	131	23	1.28
Dillon Co's.................	31¼	0.92N	1.08	3.5N	300	41	2.46
Disney (Walt) Prod..........	34¾	0.11N	0.16	0.5N	175	5	2.36
Dr. Pepper.................	11⅞	0.40	0.44	3.7	400	48	0.81
Dun & Bradstreet Cos.......	28⅜	1.06	1.08	3.8	92	60	1.80
Echlin Mfg.................	22¾	0.46	0.60	2.6	155	26	2.01
Gen'l Amer Oil Texas........	54⅝	0.86N	1.00	1.8N	196	22	3.54
Gen'l Tire & Rubber..........	26⅝	1.07N	1.20	4.5N	62	28	4.99
Genuine Parts...............	32⅝	0.73	0.90	2.8	247	34	2.16
Georgia-Pacific	32⅜	0.71N	0.80	2.5N	195	30	2.17
Heinz (H.J.)................	29½	0.93	1.20	4.1	126	30	3.46
Heublein Inc................	26⅝	1.20	1.32	5.0	100	41	2.93
Holiday Inns................	11⅝	0.38	0.46	4.0	192	24	1.28
Int'l Business Machines.......	275¾	8.00	10.00	3.6	362	47	15.94
Int'l Flavors/Fragr............	19¾	0.33	0.44	2.2	312	33	1.03
Iowa Public Service..........	21½	1.69	1.80	8.4	36	72	2.22
Johnson & Johnson..........	66½	1.05K	1.10	1.7K	425	25	3.53
Kresge (S.S.)................	32⅜	0.30	0.32	1.0	233	16	2.15
Lawter Chemicals............	9¾	0.32	0.40	4.1	433	49	0.63
Longs Drug Stores............	26	0.46	0.48	1.8	475	27	1.62
Louisville Gas & El...........	25⅛	1.89	1.92	7.6	47	71	2.86
Lucky Stores................	15½	0.66N	0.68	4.4N	312	47	1.22
MAPCO, Inc.................	44¼	0.90	1.10	2.5	800	27	3.00
Melville Corp...............	23⅝	0.68	0.96	4.1	240	31	2.46
Minnesota Gas...............	21⅞	1.69	1.72	7.9	32	62	2.93
Minnesota Mining & Mfg......	49½	1.45	1.70	3.4	123	47	2.94
Missouri Public SV...........	16⅝	0.86N	1.00	6.0N	36	48	2.20
Nat'l Presto Indus............	49¾	1.40	2.00	4.0	218	23	8.09
Nevada Power...............	23¼	1.57	1.76	7.6	74	41	3.45
Nicor Inc...................	29	2.09	2.32	8.0	39	63	3.52
Oklahoma Gas & Elec........	18	1.44	1.48	8.2	44	71	1.88
Papercraft Corp..............	15	0.63N	0.80	5.3N	103	32	2.06
Pargas, Inc..................	18	0.95	1.00	5.6N	102	59	1.86
Pittston Co.................	33½	0.97U	1.25	3.7U	546	17	3.91

DIVIDEND INCREASE IN EACH OF LAST 10 YEARS (NYSE issues) (*continued*)

	Closing Price April 4, 1977	Paid 1976 ($)	Indi-cated Rate ($)	Yield on Indi-cated Rate (%)	In-crease Last 10 Years (%)	Payout 5-Year Aver-age (%)	Per Share Earnings Last 12 Months ($)
Portland Gen'l Elec..........	20	1.62	1.70	8.5	55	68	2.27
Rochester Gas & El..........	18	1.23N	1.28	7.1N	51	55	2.37
Rollins Inc.................	16¾	0.34	0.36	2.1	385	17	1.75
Royal Dutch Petrol...........	54⅝	3.58R	3.58	6.6	205	35	8.77
Sabine Corp................	25	0.35	0.50	2.0	191	18	2.08
Schering-Plough	36⅝	0.94	1.00	2.7	235	31	2.91
South'n Indiana G&E........	20⅜	1.21	1.32	6.5	77	48	2.72
Standard Brands............	28½	1.21	1.28	4.5	77	48	2.42
Standard Br Paint...........	34¼	0.38	0.48	1.4	245	18	2.02
Standex Int'l................	16⅛	0.71	0.80	5.0	317	23	2.61
Sun Co Inc.................	43½	1.61	2.00	4.6	172	18	7.33
Texas Indus................	15	0.98N	1.00	6.7N	44	58	1.04
Texas Utilities..............	19⅞	1.30	1.40	7.0	73	53	2.29
Tootsie Roll Indus...........	6⅞	0.38N	0.40	5.8N	31	50	0.68
Trans Union................	36	1.68	1.76	4.9	75	51	4.01
Unilever N.V................	51	2.55	2.84	5.6	157	34	8.60
United Telecommun..........	18¾	1.16	1.20	6.4	45	64	2.01
Winn-Dixie Stores...........	41	1.50	1.56	3.8	53	52	3.29

See footnotes on p. 201.
Source: *Growth Leaders on the Big Board*, New York Stock Exchange, 1977.

QUARTERLY DIVIDENDS FOR 40 YEARS OR MORE (NYSE issues)

	Closing Price April 4, 1977	Quarterly Payments Began	Paid 1976 ($)	Indi-cated Rate ($)	Yield on Indicated Rate (%)	Payout 5-Year Average (%)	Per Share Earnings Last 12 Months ($)
Aetna Life & Caslty......	29¼	1908	1.08	1.20	4.1	32	[123]3.91
Airco, Inc..............	29⅞	1917	1.07½	1.15	3.8	31	[124]4.68
Allied Chemical........	43½	1921	1.80	1.80	4.1	38	[124]4.52
American Brands........	43¾	1921	2.80	2.92	6.7	52	[124]4.54
American Can Co........	39⅜	1923	2.25	2.40	5.7	52	[125]5.10
Amer. District Teleg.....	25¼	1903	0.74	0.84	2.9	26	[12]2.39
Amer. Elec. Power.......	24	1910	2.01½	2.06	8.4	76	[12]2.66
Amer. Home Prods......	29¼	1926	1.00	1.10	3.8	55	[121]1.75
Amer. Natural Res.......	42⅛	1904	2.61½	2.80	6.6	51	[125]5.23
Amer. Sterilizer..........	9	1914	0.30	0.30	3.3	43	[120]0.59
Amer. Tel. & Tel........	62⅝	1882	3.70	4.20	6.7	61	[126]6.27
AMF, Inc...............	20¼	1927	1.24	1.24	6.1	52	[122]2.03
Anchor Hocking.........	28¼	1928	1.35	1.50	5.3	37	[124]4.06
Archer-Daniels/Midl	16⅞	1931	0.20	0.20	1.2	13	[122]2.26
Atlantic Richfield........	52¼	1927	1.42½	1.60	2.7	38	[125]5.04
Balt. Gas & Elec.........	25	1911	2.05	2.08	8.2	68	[23]3.08
BanCal Tri-State.........	20¾	1910	0.78½	0.60	3.8	y82	[120]0.76
Bank of New York.......	36⅝	1920	2.20	2.32	6.3	41	[125]5.34
Blue Bell..............	28⅜	1923	0.65	1.00	3.5	21	[124]4.99
Borden, Inc..............	32⅞	1924	1.35	1.40	4.1	45	[123]3.64
Boston Edison Co........	26⅛	1892	2.44	2.44	9.3	86	[122]2.73
Brown Group...........	22⅛	1923	1.25	1.40	6.3	54	[12]2.95
Burroughs Corp..........	60½	1906	0.66	0.80	1.3	13	[124]4.62
Carpenter Technol.......	36½	1908	1.70	2.00	5.5	35	[125]5.46
Cent. Hudson G. & E.....	20	1903	1.72	1.80	9.0	63	[122]2.68
Central Illinois Lt........	17⅞	1921	1.60	1.60	9.0	79	[2]2.00
Charter NY Corp.........	29	1867	2.00	2.12	7.3	47	[124]4.85

QUARTERLY DIVIDENDS FOR 40 YEARS OR MORE (NYSE issues) (continued)

				Dividends			
	Closing Price April 4, 1977	Quarterly Payments Began	Paid 1976 ($)	Indi- cated Rate ($)	Yield on Indicated Rate (%)	Payout 5-Year Average (%)	Per Share Earnings Last 12 Months ($)
Chase Manh'n Corp......	29⅞	1918	2.20	2.20	7.4	45	¹²3.28
Chemical N.Y. Corp......	40⅜	1849	2.88	2.88	7.1	50	¹²6.38
Chesebrough-Pond's	22⅛	1919	0.76	0.84	3.8	46	¹²1.69
Cinn. Bell Inc..........	25⅛	1879	1.60	1.60	6.4	55	¹²2.79
C.I.T. Financial..........	36⅝	1924	2.20	2.40	6.6	51	¹²4.54
Cleveland Elec. Ill........	33¼	1912	2.56	2.64	7.9	72	¹²3.57
Coca-Cola Co...........	76½	1921	2.65	3.08	4.0	56	¹²4.76
Combustion Eng'g.......	54	1912	1.95	2.00	3.6	40	¹²5.04
Commonw'l Edison......	29⅜	1890	2.37½	2.40	8.1	75	²3.28
Continental Group.......	36⅜	1923	1.85	2.00	5.1	48	¹²4.01
Conwood Corp..........	39	1903	2.25	2.40	5.8	53	¹²4.78
Corning Glass Wks.......	61¾	1922	1.50	1.52	2.5	43	¹²4.74
CPC Int'l...............	47⅜	1919	2.26	2.50	5.3	50	¹²5.15
Culbro Corp............	20	1909	1.29	1.32	6.5	53	¹²3.02
Dentsply Int'l...........	25½	1923	0.80	0.80	3.1	42	¹²2.31
Detroit Edison Co.......	15⅝	1909	1.45	1.45	9.3	85	²¹1.88
Dome Mines. Ltd........	49⅛	1920	g0.90	g0.90	1.8	25	¹²3.06
Dow Chemical..........	37	1912	0.90	1.00	2.4	25	¹²3.30
Duke Power............	20⅛	1926	1.52½	1.60	7.6	76	¹²2.40
DuPont (E.I.) Nem.......	123	1905	5.25	5.50	4.5	60	¹²9.30
Duquesne Light.........	19⅛	1913	1.72	1.72	9.0	75	¹²1.95
Eastman Kodak..........	67¾	1902	2.06	2.10	3.1	48	¹²4.03
Equifax Inc.............	27½	1917	2.20	2.20	8.0	77	¹²3.15
Equimark Corp..........	12⅜	1910	0.88	0.88	7.1	40	¹²1.70
Firestone Tire&Rub.......	20	1924	1.10	1.10	5.5	41	¹1.74
First Pennsylvania.......	16¾	1911	1.32	1.32	7.9	53	¹²1.60
Fisher Scientific........	12¾	1907	0.24	0.28	1.9	16	¹²2.16
Ft. Howard Paper.......	35	1922	0.62	0.72	2.1	23	¹²3.06
Freeport Minerals........	26½	1927	1.60	1.60	6.0	44	¹²3.03
General Electric.........	48⅝	1899	1.65	1.80	3.4	46	¹²4.12
General Foods..........	31½	1922	1.50	1.64	5.2	59	¹²3.45
General Mills...........	28¼	1927	0.72	0.88	3.1	34	²2.34
General Motors.........	66¾	1923	5.55	5.55	8.3	y63	¹²10.08
Grt. North. Nekoosa.....	29¼	1910	1.00	1.10	3.4	27	¹²3.80
Heller (W.E.) Intl........	18	1921	0.88	0.92	4.9	35	¹²2.39
Hercules Inc............	23⅜	1913	0.85	1.00	3.6	y40	¹²1.78
Hobart Corp............	20½	1906	0.89	0.92	4.3	42	¹²1.96
Household Finance......	19⅞	1926	1.12½	1.20	5.7	43	¹²2.87
Houston Indus..........	33¼	1922	1.61	1.76	4.8	46	²4.01
Huyck Corp............	14	1921	0.50	0.60	3.6	35	¹²1.23
Indust'l Nat'l Corp......	17	1921	1.20	1.20	7.1	y50	¹²2.22
Ingersoll-Rand Co........	73⅝	1919	2.68	2.80	3.8	44	¹²5.33
Interco, Inc.............	40⅛	1913	1.59	1.80	4.5	32	¹¹5.39
Int'l Business Mach......	275¾	1916	8.00	10.00	3.6	47	¹²15.94
Int'l Harvester...........	33¼	1910	1.70	1.85	5.6	40	¹5.83
Iowa Pwr & Light........	25	1916	2.00	2.10	8.4	65	¹²3.01
Jewel Companies........	23⅝	1928	1.25	1.30	5.3	43	¹3.14
Johnson Controls........	38¾	1901	0.95	1.40	3.6	37	¹²3.83
Kraft Inc...............	45⅜	1924	2.12	2.32	5.1	46	¹²4.86
Kroger Company........	25⅛	1910	1.38	1.44	5.7	49	¹²3.58
Liggett Group...........	31⅞	1912	2.50	2.50	7.8	67	¹²4.23
Lilly (Eli) & Co..........	42⅝	1904	1.25	1.42	3.3	40	¹²2.90
Ludlow Corp............	8	1886	0.40	0.40	5.0	y110	¹²0.87
Macy (R.H.) Co..........	32⅛	1927	1.17½	1.30	4.0	33	¹4.82
Mfrs. Hanover Corp.......	37⅞	1913	1.80	1.92	5.1	41	¹²4.82
Marsh & McLennan.....	56	1923	1.90	2.40	4.3	56	¹²3.41
May Dept. Stores.......	25⅛	1911	1.07	1.16	4.6	44	¹3.06
Melville Corp...........	23⅝	1917	0.68	0.96	4.1	32	¹²2.46

QUARTERLY DIVIDENDS FOR 40 YEARS OR MORE (NYSE issues) (continued)

	Closing Price April 4, 1977	Dividends					Per Share Earnings Last 12 Months ($)
		Quarterly Payments Began	Paid 1976 ($)	Indi- cated Rate ($)	Yield on Indicated Rate (%)	Payout 5-Year Average (%)	
Minnesota Mining & Mfg..	49½	1916	1.45	1.70	3.4	48	[1,2]2.94
Monsanto Co............	74⅝	1928	2.75	2.80	3.8	29	[1,2]10.05
Morgan (J. P.) & Co.....	50¼	1900	1.80	2.00	4.0	38	[1,2]5.04
Morton Norwich Pr......	19	1925	0.88	0.88	4.6	66	[1,2]d0.35
Mountain States Tel......	24¼	1911	1.64	1.88	7.8	62	[2]2.87
Nabisco Inc.............	48⅛	1899	2.37½	2.52	5.2	64	[1,2]4.82
Nat'l Fuel Gas.........	26	1903	2.11	2.16	8.3	56	[1,2]4.41
Nat'l-Standard	17⅛	1922	0.94½	1.04	6.1	42	[1,2]2.36
Nat'l Steel.............	41¾	1908	2.50	2.50	6.0	50	[2]4.53
New England T&T.......	33⅜	1886	2.36	2.60	7.8	86	[2]3.73
N L Industries.........	21	1906	1.05	1.20	5.7	46	[1,2]2.44
Norfolk & West'n Ry.....	32½	1910	1.713	1.76	5.4	57	[1,2]4.21
Northeast Utilities.......	10⅞	1927	1.016	1.016	9.3	70	[2]1.42
Olin Corp..............	39½	1926	1.36½	1.50	3.8	28	[1,2]6.07
Orange & Rock Util......	15½	1914	1.30	1.36	8.8	80	[1,2]1.89
Owens-Illinois Inc........	27⅛	1907	0.94	1.06	3.9	29	[1,2]3.42
Pacific Gas & Elec.......	23⅛	1919	1.88	2.00	8.7	60	[2]3.10
Pacific Lighting.........	19	1909	1.68	1.68	8.8	74	[1,2]2.48
Pacific Tel. & Tel.......	17⅞	1925	1.20	1.40	7.8	71	[2]2.09
Pennwalt Corp..........	34	1913	1.54	1.80	5.3	49	[1,2]3.56
Peter Paul.............	11⅞	1921	0.90	0.90	7.6	90	[1,2]1.40
Phila. Electric..........	19	1913	1.64	1.80	9.5	85	[1,2]1.91
Pillsbury Co............	36⅞	1927	1.04	1.16	3.1	36	[2]3.20
PPG Industries..........	53	1899	2.00	2.20	4.2	35	[1,2]7.28
Procter & Gamble........	76¼	1898	2.15	2.60	3.4	44	[1,2]5.38
Public Serv. E.&G........	22⅜	1920	1.78	1.80	8.0	73	[2]2.85
Pullman, Inc...........	33¼	1867	1.23	1.32	4.0	34	[1,2]2.77
Quaker Oats...........	21¾	1922	0.86	0.92	4.2	40	[1,2]2.99
Raybestos-Manh't'n	31⅛	1898	1.25	1.50	4.8	27	[1,2]5.38
Rexnord, Inc...........	36¾	1922	1.26	1.44	3.9	35	[1]5.02
Reynolds (R. J.) Ind......	63⅞	1901	3.13	3.28	5.1	42	[1,2]7.48
Richardson-Merrell	23¼	1925	0.67	0.70	3.0	30	[1,2]2.48
Safeway Stores.........	45⅛	1927	2.05	2.20	4.9	43	[1,2]4.07
San Diego Gas & El......	13⅞	1909	1.20	1.20	8.6	67	[1,2]2.14
Scott Paper............	16⅞	1926	0.72	0.76	4.5	36	[1,2]2.01
Sherwin-Williams	35⅛	1922	2.20	2.20	6.3	48	[1,2]1.53
South'n Cal. Ed..........	23⅜	1910	1.68	2.00	8.6	50	[1,2]3.70
Squibb Corp............	28	1903	0.91½	0.96	3.4	42	[1,2]2.40
Stand. Oil Calif..........	39½	1912	2.15	2.20	5.6	38	[1,2]5.18
Stand. Oil (Ind.).........	51⅝	1913	2.30	2.60	5.0	34	[1,2]6.09
Stanley Works..........	32¼	1895	1.13	1.17	3.6	34	[1,2]3.44
Stauffer Chemical........	46⅛	1915	1.35½	1.44	3.1	30	[1,2]5.20
Sterling Drug............	15	1913	0.70	0.70	4.7	49	[1,2]1.39
Sun Co................	43½	1912	1.61	2.00	4.6	19	[1,2]7.33
Tampa Electric..........	18	1911	1.10	1.12	6.2	54	[2]1.89
Texaco, Inc.............	26¾	1903	2.00	2.00	7.5	47	[1,2]3.20
Texas Utilities..........	19⅞	1919	1.30	1.40	7.0	54	[2]2.29
Texasgulf Inc...........	29¼	1921	1.20	1.20	4.1	34	[1,2]2.05
TI Corp...............	18⅞	1915	1.00	1.10	5.8	58	[1,2]3.03
Timkem Co.............	51⅝	1921	2.20	2.20	4.3	41	[1,2]5.45
Toledo Edison..........	25¼	1922	2.12	2.12	8.4	66	[1,2]2.82
Trans Union Corp.......	36	1919	1.68	1.76	4.9	51	[1,2]4.01
Travelers Corp..........	31⅛	1892	1.08	1.28	4.1	32	[1,2]3.51
Union Carbide..........	55¼	1918	2.50	2.80	5.1	37	[1,2]7.15
Union Electric..........	15⅛	1918	1.34	1.36	9.0	81	[1,2]1.86
Union Oil Calif..........	55	1916	2.07	2.20	4.0	29	[1,2]7.42
Union Pacific Corp.......	51⅛	1907	1.40	1.70	3.3	41	[1,2]4.02

QUARTERLY DIVIDENDS FOR 40 YEARS OR MORE (NYSE issues) (concluded)

	Closing Price April 4, 1977	Quarterly Payments Began	Paid 1976 ($)	Indicated Rate ($)	Yield on Indicated Rate (%)	Payout 5-Year Average (%)	Per Share Earnings Last 12 Months ($)
				Dividends			
United Illuminating......	26	1900	2.32	2.44	9.4	64	[1,2]2.97
U.S. Gypsum.............	24⅝	1919	1.60	1.60	6.5	71	[1,2]2.04
U.S. Tobacco Co.........	27⅞	1918	1.10	1.50	5.4	49	[1,2]2.25
Upjohn Company........	34½	1921	0.99	1.08	3.1	41	[1,2]2.62
Washington Gas Lt.......	22¾	1885	1.88	2.08	9.1	77	[1]3.06
Westvaco Corp..........	31⅞	1895	1.02½	1.10	3.5	32	[1]3.40
Woolworth (F. W.).......	25⅞	1912	1.20	1.40	5.4	40	[1]3.62
Wrigley (Wm.) Jr........	80⅝	1911	3.90	3.90	4.8	58	[1,2]7.82

See footnotes on p. 201.
Source: *Growth Leaders on the Big Board*, New York Stock Exchange, 1977.

INSTITUTIONAL FAVORITES 1976/1977 (NYSE issues)

	Closing Price April 4, 1977	Institutional Holdings Companies	Shares (000)	Indicated Dividend Rate ($)	Yield on Indicated Dividend (%)	Per Share Earnings Last 12 Months ($)	P-E Ratio
Int'l Business Machines.....	275¾	1.424	51,060	10.00	3.6	15.94	17
Exxon Corp................	50⅝	943	131,907	3.00	5.9	5.90	8
American Tel & Tel.........	62⅝	893	79,052	4.20	6.7	6.27	9
Eastman Kodak.............	67¾	852	49,961	2.10	3.1	4.03	16
General Motors............	66¾	855	73,492	5.55	8.3	10.08	6
General Electric...........	48⅝	818	61,177	1.80	3.7	4.12	11
Xerox Corp................	47⅝	670	34,233	1.20	2.5	4.51	10
Texaco, Inc...............	26¾	613	65,136	2.00	7.5	3.20	8
Sears, Roebuck & Co.......	60⅜	573	32,783	2.10	3.5	4.37	13
Atlantic Richfield..........	52¼	506	35,672	1.60	3.1	5.04	10
Citicorp	27¾	541	50,900	1.06	3.8	3.24	8
Merck & Co...............	55	515	30,389	1.50	2.7	3.38	16
Mobil Corp................	66¾	533	29,933	3.80	5.7	9.07	7
Dow Chemical.............	37	533	54,861	1.00	2.7	3.30	11
Minnesota Mining & Mfg.....	49½	501	36,327	1.70	3.4	2.94	16
Standard Oil (Ind.).........	51⅝	522	38,208	2.60	5.0	6.09	8
Ford Motor................	53⅜	429	41,620	3.20	6.0	10.45	5
Union Carbide.............	55¼	452	19,716	2.80	5.1	7.15	7
Phillips Petroleum..........	55⅛	454	20,664	2.00	3.6	5.39	10
General Tel & Elect........	29⅝	449	30,062	2.00	6.8	3.29	9
Kresge (S. S.).............	32⅜	442	54,236	0.32	1.0	2.15	15
Burroughs Corp............	60½	392	16,846	0.80	1.3	4.62	13
Gulf Oil...................	28¼	435	38,675	1.80	6.4	4.19	6
Amer Home Products.......	29¼	456	55,888	1.10	3.8	1.75	16
DuPont (EI) Nem...........	123	387	9,593	5.50	4.5	9.30	13
Caterpillar Tractor.........	54¾	396	37,659	1.50	2.7	4.45	12
Procter & Gamble..........	76¼	401	21,687	2.60	3.4	5.38	14
Continental Oil............	34¾	402	34,889	1.20	3.5	4.38	7
Standard Oil of Cal........	39½	421	33,976	2.20	5.6	5.18	7
Schlumberger, Ltd.........	59⅛	360	26,964	0.80	1.4	3.41	17
Warner-Lambert	26	406	22,694	1.00	3.8	2.01	12
Texas Utilities.............	19⅞	382	29,430	1.40	7.0	2.29	8
Philip Morris..............	53¼	369	25,737	1.30	2.4	4.47	11
Johnson & Johnson........	66½	344	16,177	1.10	1.7	3.53	18
Pfizer, Inc................	28⅛	386	21,714	0.96	3.4	2.28	12
Int'l Paper................	56	351	20,302	2.00	3.6	5.60	10
Halliburton Co.............	55⅝	345	23,372	1.24	2.2	5.22	10
Coca-Cola Co.............	76½	345	16,415	3.08	4.0	4.76	16
Goodyear Tire & Rub.......	19¾	345	25,480	1.10	5.6	1.69	11

INSTITUTIONAL FAVORITES 1976/1977 (NYSE issues) (continued)

	Closing Price April 4, 1977	Institutional Holdings		Indicated Dividend Rate ($)	Yield on Indicated Dividend (%)	Per Share Earnings Last 12 Months ($)	P-E Ratio
		Companies	Shares (000)				
Monsanto Co...............	74⅝	333	12,017	2.80	3.8	10.05	7
Avon Products.............	47	320	21,229	2.00	4.3	2.90	16
Tenneco, Inc..............	32¼	325	27,646	1.88	5.8	4.33	7
Alcan Aluminium Ltd........	26½	265	8,602	0.80	3.0	1.14	23
Lilly (ELI) & Co............	42⅝	298	24,109	1.42	3.3	2.90	14
Weyerhaeuser Co...........	38¾	321	3,331	0.80	2.1	2.32	16
McDonald's Corp...........	40½	285	18,646	0.10	0.2	2.72	14
Int'l Tel & Tel..............	31¾	331	25,940	1.76	5.5	3.95	8
Schering-Plough	36⅝	305	23,955	1.00	2.7	2.91	12
Penney (J. C.)..............	39¼	324	28,090	1.48	3.8	3.57	10
Commonw'l Edis............	29⅜	296	13,350	2.40	8.2	3.28	8
Bristol-Myers	62⅝	294	11,013	2.20	3.5	4.90	12
Reynolds (R. J.) Ind.........	63⅞	293	14,260	3.28	5.1	7.48	8
Florida Pwr & Light........	25	282	16,630	1.56	6.2	2.23	11
Federated Dept Stor........	39¼	281	18,310	1.46	3.7	3.50	11
Morgan (J.P.) & Co.........	50¼	272	14,133	2.00	4.0	5.04	9
U.S. Steel..................	45⅝	274	15,937	2.20	4.8	5.03	9
Southern Co...............	16½	288	12,061	1.46	8.8	1.77	9
Texas Instruments..........	82⅝	242	11,276	1.32	1.6	4.25	19
Deere & Co................	30½	263	24,241	1.10	3.6	3.94	7
Sperry Rand...............	35⅜	239	13,755	0.92	2.6	4.32	8
RCA Corp..................	28¼	269	13,399	1.20	4.2	2.30	12
Southern Cal Edison........	23⅜	257	15,231	2.00	8.6	3.70	6
Kerr-McGee	62⅝	239	8,225	1.25	2.0	5.19	12
Middle South Util...........	16	259	18,116	1.38	8.6	1.72	9
BankAmerica Corp..........	25⅛	257	35,801	0.80	3.2	2.40	10
CBS Inc...................	58½	227	9,161	2.00	3.4	5.75	10
Westinghouse Elec..........	18¾	242	17,323	0.97	5.2	2.54	7
Digital Equipment..........	41	211	20,566	—	—	2.22	18
Emerson Electric...........	33⅝	249	19,789	1.00	3.0	2.13	15
Central & South West.......	16	261	23,122	1.26	7.9	1.75	9
General Foods.............	31½	260	12,019	1.64	5.2	3.45	9
Georgia-Pacific	32⅜	250	26,005	0.80	2.5	2.17	14
Gillette Co.................	27¼	218	9,006	1.50	5.5	2.58	10
Colgate-Palmolive	24¾	263	19,798	0.88	3.6	1.95	12
Honeywell, Inc.............	46¾	204	6,307	1.60	3.4	4.53	10

Prices are high and low ranges for all of 1977 to cutoff date of table.

Yields and Indicated Rate are based on annual amount of dividends expected to be paid by the company based on most recent payment, assuming same rate will be continued over the next year.

Earnings, in general, are per share as reported by company. Net operating earnings are shown for banks: earnings before appropriation to general reserve for savings & loan associations; Foreign issues traded ADR are dollars per share, converted at prevailing exchange rate.

Per share earnings last 12 months indicates earnings through period indicated by superior number preceding figure: [1]for Jan., [2]for Feb., etc. Figure without superior number indicates fiscal year end.

Dividends—The following footnotes have been used in "Paid 1976" column:

K = Includes extra.

U = Includes extra and stock.

g = In Canadian funds, less 15% or 10% nonresidence tax re % Canadian ownership.

R = Less tax at origin.

N = Also stock.

% Payout 5-year average:

y = In certain years dividends exceeded available earnings.

Growth rate shows the compounded annual rate of per share earnings for the latest 5 years.

Source: *Growth Leaders on the Big Board*, New York Stock Exchange, 1977.

VICKERS FAVORITE 50

Rank by $ Value				Stocks	$ Value (millions)	No. Funds Holding	No. of Shares Held	Net Change in Holdings	Net Change by Insiders	Percent of Outstanding Stocks Held by Funds
June 30 1973	June 30 1977	March 31 1978	June 30 1978							
1	1	1	1	International Business Machines	1,531.10	319	5,934,490	−350,391	4.1	−700
4	2	2	2	American Telephone & Telegraph	611.34	177	10,339,831	−390,294	1.6	+352
2	3	3	3	Exxon Corporation	518.34	182	11,915,832	−534,420	2.7	−0−
6	5	5	4	Philip Morris	408.80	116	6,265,083	−227,950	10.5	+9,330
—	8	7	5	Schlumberger, Ltd.	345.53	114	4,220,248	+52,640	4.9	+18,500
7	4	4	6	General Motors Corporation	344.86	122	5,882,398	−554,750	2.0	−5,454
11	7	6	7	Ford Motor Company	329.33	88	7,178,819	+413,200	6.0	−31,717
12	6	8	8	General Electric Company	288.50	143	5,769,910	−173,067	2.5	−1,192
14	9	9	9	Atlantic Richfield Co.	259.43	103	5,294,449	+225,167	5.1	+19,344
—	15	20	10	Boeing Co.	256.58	67	4,946,100	−154,600	11.6	−6,038
3	19	11	11	Xerox Corp.	250.83	115	14,823,714	+400,021	6.0	−3,380
18	23	12	12	Du Pont (E.I.) De Nemours Co.	225.07	68	2,041,457	+95,124	4.3	−232
23	14	10	13	Phillips Petroleum Company	210.90	75	6,642,653	−300,140	4.3	−20
—	—	26	14	Smith Kline Corp.	208.87	51	2,555,015	−128,882	8.5	+53,892
13	24	18	15	Avon Products, Inc.	208.52	89	3,943,578	+189,490	6.8	+4,100
—	41	16	16	NCR Corp.	206.08	72	4,021,000	−167,900	15.4	+38,700
8	—	39	17	Polaroid Corp.	205.12	61	5,562,706	+612,700	16.9	+400
16	25	15	18	McDonald's Corp.	187.85	82	3,621,280	−298,550	9.0	−197,000
—	13	17	19	Halliburton Company	187.26	81	2,990,170	−113,290	5.1	−0−
9	31	22	20	Burroughs Corp.	183.09	89	2,542,945	−252,300	6.2	−1,700
44	29	27	21	Travelers Corp.	174.70	71	5,009,233	+121,200	11.6	+40,000
47	—	29	22	PepsiCo Inc.	171.64	88	5,970,084	−235,990	6.5	+11,999
37	10	21	23	Digital Equipment Corporation	169.44	77	3,693,593	−668,930	9.3	+7,425
—	36	23	24	Northwest Airlines, Inc.	166.39	53	6,220,072	−213,128	28.8	+10,600
19	—	43	25	Minnesota Mng. & Mfg. Co.	165.68	83	3,026,051	+335,342	2.6	−0−
27	21	13	26	General Tel. & Elec. Corp.	163.03	94	5,720,424	−450,055	4.2	−10,000
15	16	14	27	Mobil Corp.	161.99	98	2,677,491	−280,405	2.5	+2,500
50	32	34	28	Merck & Co.	158.53	94	2,888,998	+170,399	3.8	−300
43	45	42	29	Bristol Myers Co.	156.59	80	4,411,126	+361,900	6.8	−72,400
17	17	25	30	Standard Oil of Calif.	151.95	83	3,908,780	−33,314	2.3	+300

			No.	Company						
10	11	19	31	Texaco, Inc.	149.28	78	6,318,628	−230,594	2.3	− 37,780
—	20	32	32	Tenneco, Inc.	144.64	71	4,821,401	+144,880	5.1	− 3,626
41	—	47	33	Pfizer, Inc.	143.54	79	4,349,604	+244,500	6.2	− 7,706
45	22	30	34	Int'l Tel. & Tel. Co.	143.18	63	4,694,404	−418,624	4.4	+ 600
—	46	45	35	Amer. Broadcasting Co.	141.68	60	3,080,107	+105,750	17.2	+ 13,850
—	—	—	36	*General Dynamics Corp.	141.61	34	1,939,900	+332,000	18.2	− 3,513
—	—	49	37	Johnson & Johnson	138.17	70	1,713,749	+ 26,011	2.9	− 50,700
—	35	40	38	Standard Oil Co. (Indiana)	135.89	75	2,898,982	+157,784	2.0	+ 900
—	38	31	39	Union Oil of Calif.	135.82	46	2,889,750	−101,700	6.6	−0−
—	—	33	40	United Technologies Corp.	133.05	71	3,196,332	−683,341	8.4	+ 6,565
—	50	41	41	Martin Marietta Corp.	132.51	49	4,670,000	− 57,050	19.6	− 2,600
—	18	28	42	Reynolds (R.J.) Inds., Inc.	131.12	57	2,336,191	−302,900	4.8	− 957
—	—	—	43	*Motorola, Inc.	129.00	48	2,804,345	+308,698	9.2	+ 126
—	—	36	44	Abbott Laboratories	128.29	66	4,024,792	−674,300	6.8	+ 9,840
33	12	24	45	Union Carbide Corp.	127.28	94	3,416,870	−593,817	5.3	+ 500
21	48	37	46	Warner Lambert Co.	125.33	55	4,496,103	−217,400	5.7	− 1,030
—	—	—	47	*Federal Nat'l Mortgage Assn.	123.87	45	7,129,095	−375,740	14.3	−0−
24	—	50	48	Schering-Plough	121.62	63	3,830,644	− 81,800	7.1	− 400
—	—	—	49	*Caterpillar Tractor Co.	120.25	68	2,186,315	− 51,650	2.5	+ 3,475
26	43	48	50	Aetna Life & Casualty	118.89	63	3,048,445	−199,700	5.7	− 7,127

Displaced stocks: Allied Chemical Corp.-Continental Oil Co.-Gulf Oil Corp.-K mart Corp.

* Returned to list.

Source: Vickers Guide to Investment Company Portfolios. Copyright © 1978 by Vickers Associates, Inc. Reproduction hereof permitted only on written permission from Vickers Associates, Inc., The Copyright owner.

SUMMARY OF FAVORITE 50 BY INDUSTRY

DOLLAR VALUE OF STOCKS BY INDUSTRY TO TOTAL VALUE OF FAVORITE 50

Industry	6/30/78	3/31/78	6/30/77	6/30/73
Oil and natural gas	21.3%	24.6%	29.8%	17.8%
Office equipment	20.6	20.6	20.2	23.1
Chemicals and drugs	15.5	15.5	12.4	15.8
Utilities	6.9	7.9	7.6	5.4
Motors	6.0	6.6	6.3	6.0
Aerospace	5.9	4.1	2.8	—
Leisure	4.7	4.0	5.0	8.5
Miscellaneous	19.1	16.7	15.9	23.4
	100.0%	100.0%	100.0%	100.0%

Source: *Vickers Guide to Investment Company Portfolios.* Copyright © 1978 by Vickers Associates, Inc. Reproduction hereof permitted only on written permission from Vickers Associates, Inc., The Copyright owner.

FOREIGN SECURITIES LISTED ON THE NEW YORK STOCK EXCHANGE*

Alcan Aluminium Limited
Aluminum (Canada)

ASA Limited
Financial (Africa)

Bell Canada
Telecommunication services (Canada)

Benguet Consolidated, Inc.
Mining (Philippines)

British Petroleum Company Ltd.
Holding company-petroleum (Gt. Britain)

Campbell Red Lake Mines, Ltd.
Mining (Canada)

Canadian Pacific Limited
Railroad (Canada)

Carling O'Keefe Limited
Breweries (Canada)

Deltec International Limited
Foods, commodities (Gt. Britain)

Dome Mines, Limited
Mining (Canada)

EMI Limited
Electronics, records, entertainment (Gt. Britain)

Genstar Limited
Building (Canada)

Hudson Bay Mining & Smelting Co.
Mining (Canada) [2 issues]

Intercontinental Diversified Corp.
Homesites, casinos (Panama)

Inco Ltd.
Mining (Canada)

KLM Royal Dutch Airlines
Airline (Netherlands)

Kubota, Ltd.
Agricultural machinery; pipe (Japan)

Massey-Ferguson Ltd.
Agricul. mach., diesel eng. (Canada)

Matsushita Electric Industrial Co., Ltd.
Electronic products (Japan)

McIntyre Mines Ltd.
Mining (Canada)

Norlin Corporation
Holding company-various (Panama)

Northern Telecom Ltd.
Telecommunication equipment (Canada)

Northgate Exploration Limited
Mining (Canada)

Pacific Petroleums Ltd.
Petroleum & natural gas (Canada)

Pioneer Electronic Corporation
High fidelity stereo; audio (Japan)

Plessey Company Ltd.
Electronic equipment, systems (Great Britain)

Royal Dutch Petroleum Co.
Petroleum (Netherlands)

Schlumberger, N.V.
Petroleum (Netherlands)

Seagram Co. Ltd.
Distilleries (Canada)

"Shell" Transport and Trading Co., Ltd.
Petroleum (Gt. Britain)

Sony Corporation
Radios, recorders, televisions (Japan)

Unilever Limited
Foods, commodities (Gt. Britain)

Unilever, N.V.
Foods, commodities (Netherlands Antilles)

Walker (Hiram)-Gooderham & Worts, Ltd.
Distilleries (Canada)

Westcoast Transmission Co., Ltd.
Natural gas distributor (Canada)

Source: New York Stock Exchange *Fact Book.*
* Honda Motor Co. Ltd.—motorcycles, automobiles (Japan)—was recently listed on the NYSE.

MARGIN REQUIREMENTS

PERCENT OF MARKET VALUE AND EFFECTIVE DATES

Type of Security on Sale	Mar. 11, 1968	June 8, 1968	May 6, 1970	Dec. 6, 1971	Nov. 24, 1972	Jan. 3, 1974
Margin stocks..........................	70	80	65	55	65	50
Convertible bonds....................	50	60	50	50	50	50
Short sales...........................	70	80	65	55	65	50

Note. Regulations G, T, and U of the Federal Reserve Board of Governors, prescribed in accordance with the Securities Exchange Act of 1934, limit the amount of credit to purchase and carry margin stocks that may be extended on securities as collateral by prescribing a maximum loan value, which is a specified percentage of the market value of the collateral at the time the credit is extended. Margin requirements are the difference between the market value (100 percent) and the maximum loan value. The term "margin stocks" is defined in the corresponding regulation.

Regulation G and special margin requirements for bonds convertible into stocks were adopted by the Board of Governors effective March 11, 1968.

Source: *Federal Reserve Bulletin.*

LARGEST PERCENTAGE GAINS ON THE NEW YORK STOCK EXCHANGE

Issue	1977 Reported Share Volume*	Closing Market Price #		
		1977	1976	% Increase
Deltec International	1,244,000	$12½	$ 4¼	194.1%
Great Lakes Dredge & Dock ...	599,000	32⅛	11⅝	176.3
Intercont'l Diversified	421,900	15	6	150.0
Diamond M Company	2,850,500	42	17	147.1
Handleman Company	2,321,500	11⅜	4⅞	133.3
American Medicorp	8,925,000	21¼	9⅛	132.9
Amtel, Inc.	3,429,400	16¼	7	132.1
Johnson Controls	2,874,800	30⅝	13¼	131.1
Columbia Pictures	17,194,200	17⅞	7¾	130.6
C. I. Realty Investors	1,241,600	10⅝	4⅝	129.7
Ponderosa System	7,076,600	15⅞	7⅛	122.8
Oxford Industries	973,000	10½	4⅞	115.4
Rowan Companies	4,124,800	30⅝	14¼	114.9
Sonesta Int'l Hotels	1,353,200	7½	3½	114.3
Oak Industries	1,907,200	19¾	9½	107.9
Twentieth Century-Fox Film ...	16,069,400	21⅜	10⅜	160.0
Triangle Pacific	1,191,500	30	14⅝	105.1
MacDonald (E. F.) Company ...	2,060,300	10¼	5	105.0
SCA Services	5,010,900	5⅜	2⅝	104.8
Bangor Punta	2,307,300	23	11¼	104.4

* Old and new volume combined.
† Adjusted for stock dividends, splits, spinoffs, etc., where applicable.
Source: New York Stock Exchange *Fact Book.*

LARGEST PERCENTAGE LOSSES ON THE NEW YORK STOCK EXCHANGE

Issue	1977 Reported Share Volume*	Closing Market Price #		
		1977	1976	% Increase
Franklin Mint	10,029,100	$ 8⅜	$28⅞	71.0%
Johnson (E. F.) Company	1,923,400	5⅞	17⅛	65.7
Lykes Corporation	3,922,000	6¼	13¼	52.8
LTV Corporation	6,734,000	6⅜	13⅜	52.3
Tishman Realty & Constr.	1,118,400	7⅞	16⅛	51.2
Tesoro Petroleum	9,417,200	7⅞	16	50.8
Keystone Consolidated	366,000	10½	21⅛	50.3
Wheeling-Pittsburgh Steel	546,500	9¼	18½	50.0
Winnebago Industries	2,433,400	3¼	6½	50.0
Wyly Corporation	2,314,800	⅞	1¾	50.0
Holly Sugar	1,112,400	15¼	30¼	49.6
Zenith Radio	8,480,300	14½	27⅞	48.0
Phelps Dodge	7,720,500	21½	41	47.6
Inco Limited	10,761,700	17⅛	32⅝	47.5
Bethlehem Steel	16,227,100	21¼	40⅜	47.4
Amalgamated Sugar	379,900	18¾	35¼	46.8
Diversified Industries	858,400	1	1⅞	46.7
Fedders Corporation	4,297,100	4	7½	46.7
Farah Manufacturing	1,556,400	3⅛	5¾	45.7
Mobile Home Industries	1,092,400	2⅜	4⅜	45.7

* Old and new volume combined.
† Adjusted for stock dividends, splits, spinoffs, etc., where applicable.
Source: New York Stock Exchange *Fact Book*.

50 LEADING STOCKS IN MARKET VALUE (NYSE)
(December 31, 1977)

	Listed Shares	Market Value
	(mils.)	
Int'l Business Machines	148.4	$ 40,513
American Tel. & Tel.	647.5	39,172
Exxon Corp.	453.2	21,754
General Motors	287.7	18,053
General Electric	231.4	11,513
Sears, Roebuck	321.8	9,011
Eastman Kodak	161.6	8,280
Texaco Inc.	274.3	7,577
Standard Oil (Indiana)	150.0	7,446
Procter & Gamble	82.6	7,095
Mobil Corp.	105.9	6,726
Standard Oil of Calif.	170.5	6,608
Schlumberger, N. V.	88.6	6,447
du Pont de Nemours	48.5	5,839
Gulf Oil	211.9	5,642
Minnesota Mining & Mfg.	116.2	5,620
Atlantic Richfield	104.8	5,357
Dow Chemical	198.5	5,311
Shell Oil	146.3	4,901
Ford Motor	103.8	4,747
Caterpillar Tractor	86.3	4,733
Phillips Petroleum	153.7	4,708
American Home Products	167.8	4,678
Coca-Cola Company	122.6	4,567
Johnson & Johnson	58.6	4,497
Merck & Co.	75.8	4,208
General Tel. & Electronics	133.6	4,158
Getty Oil	22.1	3,840
Halliburton Co.	58.7	3,838
Morris (Philip) Inc.	59.9	3,708
Xerox Corp.	79.2	3,703
Weyerhaeuser Co.	128.6	3,553
Continental Oil	113.0	3,389
Int'l Tel. & Tel.	104.9	3,331
K mart Corp.	121.6	3,330
BankAmerica Corp.	146.3	3,329
Burroughs Corp.	40.4	2,948
Citicorp	127.8	2,923
Tenneco Inc.	94.9	2,919
Georgia-Pacific Corp.	102.7	2,914
Pacific Tel. & Tel.	168.6	2,866
Reynolds (R.J.) Industries	48.2	2,858
Avon Products	58.1	2,796
Union Carbide	64.7	2,660
U. S. Steel	84.2	2,651
Eli Lilly	69.5	2,634
American Express	71.5	2,582
American Electric Power	103.0	2,510
PepsiCo, Inc.	86.9	2,432
Southern Co.	136.1	2,415
Total	**6,942.8**	**$329,290**

Source: New York Stock Exchange *Fact Book*.

MUTUAL FUNDS: TEN-YEAR SELECTED PERFORMANCE

Each year column is subdivided into three figures: Net Asset Value per share · 12 mos. Divs from Income · 12 mos. Disb. fr. Cap. Gns(a).

QUARTER ENDED JUNE 30	1978 NAV	1977 NAV	1976 NAV	1975 NAV	1974 NAV	1973 NAV	1972 NAV	1971 NAV	1970 NAV	1969 NAV	1968 NAV
* Acorn Fund	17.93	16.17	12.65	10.04	8.07	8.95	14.86	12.90	7.31		
Afuture Fund	11.15	9.39	9.57	8.25	7.18	9.45	11.15	10.82	4.93	10.97	9.03
Affiliated Fund	7.39	8.22	8.33	7.22	5.79	6.21	6.92	7.42	5.78	8.37	9.58
American Birthright Trust	9.81	9.98	9.18	8.52	7.73	7.36	7.62	7.10	5.71	7.00	
* Amer. Gen. Cap. Growth	4.29	4.10	4.38	4.31	3.86	4.97	7.12	5.86	3.98		8.71
American Gen. Income Fd	6.26	6.72	6.39	6.00	5.79	6.69	7.55	7.59	6.30	8.09	
American Gen. Venture	16.87	12.38	10.87	9.26	6.29	6.69	15.15	12.25			
American Grth Fund (e)	4.19	5.61	5.16	4.67	4.82	5.92	6.22	5.69	4.68	7.08	8.32
American Investors Fund	4.40	5.92	5.13	5.06	3.83	4.53	6.01	5.69	4.35	9.16	9.94
American Mutual Fund	10.12	10.01	9.76	8.35	7.25	8.06	9.12	9.39	6.86	9.78	10.45
Anchor Growth Fund (b)	6.77	6.48	7.37	6.79	5.91	7.42	12.06	11.39	8.20	13.17	15.65
Anchor Income Fund (f)	6.87	7.53	7.17	6.55	6.14	7.22	8.13	8.13	6.56	9.14	10.29
Axe-Houghton Inco Fund	4.70	5.05	4.80	4.45	4.03	4.56	5.68	5.68	4.36	7.17	9.18
Axe-Houghton Fund B	7.73	8.17	7.55	6.74	6.33	6.96	8.00	8.03	6.14	9.26	11.52
Axe-Houghton Stock Fund	5.98	5.95	6.31	5.86	5.16	5.68	6.37	6.07	5.06	7.18	8.52
♠ D. L. Babson Income Trust	1.69	1.80	1.75	1.74	1.76	1.90	2.03	2.00	1.67	2.72	2.78
Boston Foundation Trust	9.21	9.63	9.25	8.86	7.94	10.45	11.08	11.45	10.58	12.36	14.11
Broad Street Investing	10.74	11.82	12.62	11.55	10.50	13.29	15.21	14.76	10.75	14.67	15.52
Bullock Fund	12.48	13.02	13.17	12.03	10.30	12.45	15.75	15.27	10.77	15.49	16.56
Canadian Fund	7.31	7.69	8.88	9.00	9.53	10.68	10.92	9.79	8.28	9.22	9.09
Capital Shares	6.94	6.30	5.59	4.95	4.09	5.30	6.68	6.55	5.04	7.15	7.86
Charter Fund	16.31	14.47	11.93	11.13	9.08	8.98	13.67	9.04	4.28	9.48	
Century Shares Trust	11.21	11.79	10.10	10.36	9.17	12.44	14.37	13.46	8.94	10.80	11.44
Chase Fund of Boston	6.28	6.38	6.84	6.87	5.70	7.81	12.01	10.49	6.49	12.30	14.57
Chemical Fund	7.26	7.13	8.36	8.71	8.46	10.42	10.80	9.42	7.16	9.08	9.92
Colonial Fund	8.99	9.42	9.92	9.48	8.93	9.64	11.11	11.09	8.73	12.21	14.43
Colonial Growth Shares	4.59	4.66	5.17	5.17	4.91	5.81	10.98	6.59	4.43	6.65	8.44
Commerce Income Shares	8.03	8.93	9.05	8.41	6.89	8.40	9.87	9.87	7.46	11.94	12.94
Composite Bond & Stock	8.51	9.09	8.72	8.03	7.26	8.22	8.87	9.36	7.16	9.70	12.26
Composite Fund	8.05	7.48	8.05	7.93	6.38	7.11	9.28	10.14	7.41	10.39	13.16
* Comstock Fund	7.04	6.11	5.43	4.55	3.22	3.12	4.48	4.41	3.48	5.36	
Concord Fund	13.84	13.14	11.27	8.84	7.97	8.94	11.45	11.98	9.06	17.51	22.19
Decatur Income Fund	11.85	12.68	11.63	9.80	8.36	9.60	13.21	12.08	9.53	12.67	14.38
Delaware Fund	11.41	11.55	11.17	9.47	7.83	9.21	13.21	13.40	9.93	14.10	16.73
DeVegh Mutual Fund	30.11	31.08	32.24	31.29	23.75	23.56	34.87	34.73	24.21	34.71	37.52
Directors Capital Fund	3.94	4.32	4.16	3.83	3.36	3.62	8.05	6.87	4.05	3.89	4.06
* Dividend Shares	2.72	3.06	3.30	3.06	2.88	2.88	3.89	3.77	2.97	3.11	25.47
Dodge & Cox Balanced Fund	20.85	22.33	21.96	19.61	17.65	20.62	23.17	22.36	18.13	23.60	15.30
Dreyfus Fund	12.18	12.15	11.98	10.91	8.76	10.44	12.87	12.63	9.30	13.23	11.91
Eaton & Howard Balanced	7.69	8.39	8.78	8.36	7.84	9.43	10.26	10.15	8.47	11.87	

- Eaton & Howard Income
- Eaton & Howard Stock
- Edie Special Growth Fund
- Energy Fund
- Enterprise Fund

- Evergreen Fund
- Fairfield Fund
- Fidelity Capital Fund
- Fidelity Fund
- Fidelity Trend Fund

- Financial Dynamics Fund
- Financial Industrial Inco Fund
- Financial Industrial Fund
- First Invest. Fund for Inc.
- First Investors Stock

- 44 Wall St Fund
- Founders Mutual Fund
- Frank C. Fds Dy Tech (c)
- Franklin Cust—Growth (c)
- Franklin Cust—Inc Shrs (c)

- Franklin Cust—Util Shrs(c)
- Fundamental Investors (d)
- General Securities
- Growth Industry Shrs
- Guardian Mutual Fund

- Guardian Pk. Ave. Fd.
- Hamilton H-DA
- Heritage Fund
- Herold Fund
- IDS Growth Fund

- IDS New Dimension Fund
- IDS Progressive Fund
- International Investors
- Investment Co. of America
- Invest. Trust of Boston

- Investors Mutual
- Investors Research Fund
- Investors Selective
- Investors Stock Fund
- Investors Variable Pay

- ISI Trust Fund
- Istel Fund
- Ivest Fund
- JP Growth Fund
- Johnston Mutual

- Keystone Series B-1
- Keystone Series B-2
- Keystone Series B-4
- Keystone Series K-1
- Keystone Series K-2

MUTUAL FUNDS: TEN-YEAR SELECTED PERFORMANCE (continued)

QUARTER ENDED JUNE 30. Each year group shows three columns: Net Asset Value per share | 12 mos. Divs from Income | 12 mos. Disb. fr. Cap. Gns(a).

Fund	1978 NAV	Divs	CapGns	1977 NAV	Divs	CapGns	1976 NAV	Divs	CapGns	1975 NAV	Divs	CapGns	1974 NAV	Divs	CapGns	1973 NAV	Divs	CapGns	1972 NAV	Divs	CapGns	1971 NAV	Divs	CapGns	1970 NAV	Divs	CapGns	1969 NAV	Divs	CapGns	1968 NAV
Keystone Series S-1	17.39	.65	.21	17.72	.63	.34	19.45	.44		19.25	.42	.30	17.33	.27	.37	22.56	.21	.75	22.42	.34		19.71	.42		14.54	.49	2.91	21.20	.43	1.21	23.50
Keystone Series S-3	8.42	.07		7.81	.17	.30	8.64			7.77	.18		5.83			7.09	.09	.76	9.61	.09		8.50	.13		5.72	.15	.69	8.50	.07	1.26	10.74
Keystone Series S-4	4.81	.07		3.96	.06		3.72	.04		3.33			2.81			3.69		.26	6.87			5.22	.02		3.28	.03		5.35	.03	.57	6.94
Lexington Growth Fund	12.00	.09		9.35	.05		7.78	.04		6.54	.07		4.86	.05		5.78	.04	2.87	11.05		1.09	10.40	.02		6.46	.05					16.48
Lexington Research Fund	14.51	.56		14.87	.54		15.09	.43		12.96	.40		11.24	.25		12.68	.34		17.30	.17	.55	16.65	.20		11.37	.11	.39	15.28	.13	1.26	7.59
Life Insurance Investors	8.75	.23	.155	7.53	.19	.061	6.06	.17	.03	6.28	.15	.025	5.37	.125	.175	7.56	.115		9.06	.10	.40	8.02	.12		5.53	.092		6.88	.072	2.13	8.06
Lindner Fund	23.18	.31	.562	17.26	.25		13.55	.25		10.20	.28		8.92	.19		9.76	.08		15.74	.22		11.36			7.63			8.82			13.62
* Loomis Sayles Cap Dev	12.54	.27		10.84	.18		10.77	.13		10.76	.15		10.07	.14	.37	12.41	.08	.42	13.86	.16		11.89	.21		7.99	.22	.30	12.15	.19	.98	
* Loomis Sayles Mutual	12.95	.61		13.16	.42	.08	13.68	.43		13.15	.43		12.37	.46		14.39	.42	.05	15.30	.42	.35	14.74	.44	.35	11.26	.51	.60	15.01	.51	.87	16.01
Lord Abbett Inco. Fd	3.20	.24	.16	3.60	.22	.19	3.31	.225		2.95	.18		2.62	.175		3.16	.17		3.49	.16	.10	3.33	.16		2.86	.155	.07	3.39	.155	.20	3.58
Magna Income Trust	9.15	.77		9.44	.70		8.65	.55		8.11	.60		7.61	.50		8.72	.47		9.14	.52		8.79	.53		7.65	.51		10.54	.40	.23	10.79
Massachusetts Fund	10.57	.54		10.75	.55		10.54	.49		9.88	.50		9.14	.49		11.25	.42	.35	12.10	.40		11.36	.40		8.81	.40	.18	11.07	.37	.96	12.95
Mass. Investors Grth. Stk.	8.78	.20	.264	8.47	.15	.256	9.77	.148	.224	10.33	.19	.37	9.51	.196		12.72	.196	.723	14.87	.176	.28	13.23	.21		9.07	.193	.295	12.20	.181	.201	12.97
* Mass. Investors Trust	9.60	.43	.155	10.40	.394	.217	11.37	.345	.168	10.32	.405	.19	9.23	.393	.15	10.89	.379	.618	12.59	.416	.347	14.32	.457	.974	11.68	.464		15.73	.442	1.135	17.15
* Mathers Fund	16.28	.41	.32	13.96	.33		11.80	.24		10.23	.13		7.95	.25		10.50	.33	1.07	17.12	.32	1.71	13.75	.19		8.83	.11	.60	12.01	.04	.67	13.31
MIF Fund	7.68	.39		8.47	.33		9.08	.33		7.66	.37		6.75	.13		7.50	.33		8.28	.33		8.85	.36		6.82	.39		9.49	.36	.72	10.14
MIF Growth Fund	4.26	.09		3.87	.08	.20	3.99	.08		3.58	.12		3.31	.11	.18	4.10	.08	.25	5.92	.08	.26	5.77	.10		4.05	.13	.08	5.99	.14	.26	6.56
MONY Fund	9.08	.225		9.24	.165		9.98	.148		9.67	.135		8.23	.065		10.09	.009	.351	13.47	.008	.21	11.91	.08								
* Mutual Shares	33.95	.60	1.95	30.41	.57	1.95	25.97	.50	1.05	20.52	.85		15.87	.30		14.50	.43	.55	16.78	.39	.252	16.24	.45	.21	11.35	.24	1.34	18.67	.135	3.185	16.48
* National Investors	6.40	.14	.24	6.36	.12	.24	6.84	.13	.14	6.65	.16		5.88	.12	.46	8.11	.10		10.00	.10	.32	8.44	.13	.21	5.79	.14	.28	7.88	.13	.58	8.32
* National Sec—Balanced	9.24	.48		9.56	.44		9.24	.38		7.93	.49		7.16	.49		8.53	.47		10.40	.48		10.85	.49		8.70	.47		10.79	.57	.50	12.15
* National Sec—Bond	4.38	.39		4.64	.39		4.32	.39		4.09	.38		4.08	.38		4.77	.40		5.16	.38		4.94	.33		4.53	.33		5.59	.29	.50	6.07
National Sec—Dividend	4.13	.27	.04	4.16	.255	.04	3.82	.25		3.28	.24		2.99	.205	.07	3.55	.20	.12	4.14	.21	.12	4.27	.22	.10	3.37	.23	.07	4.56	.22		5.41
National Sec—Growth	5.62	.155		5.63	.13		5.86	.13		5.64	.175		5.07	.195		4.38	.10	.45	9.94	.13	.35	9.44	.060	.25	6.92	.25		9.44	.24	1.25	11.84
National Sec—Income	7.57	.365		5.61	.43		5.13	.40		4.55	.325		4.16	.305		4.59	.30	.09	5.41	.29	.05	5.35	.28	.06	4.21	.27	.30	5.64	.27	.35	6.22
National Sec—Pfd.	7.20	.51		7.81	.41		6.87	.40		5.60	.43		5.28	.39		6.03	.40		7.28	.39	.07	7.28	.36		5.62	.38	.15	7.16	.37	.58	8.05
National Sec—Stock	7.79	.37	.04	8.28	.36	.12	7.99	.35		6.86	.34		5.72	.32		6.49	.32	.26	7.68	.32	.41	8.17	.34	.17	6.35	.35		6.91	.35	.55	9.51
Nation-Wide Securities	9.21	.53	.12	10.18	.51	.14	9.94	.50	.12	9.03	.50	.16	8.24	.47	.23	9.78	.49	.25	10.45	.49	.25	10.49	.49	.22	8.68	.48	.40	10.77	.35	.35	11.90
* Newton Growth Fund	12.85	.275		11.93	.185		11.48	.24		11.68	.35		10.75	.35		12.14		.988	21.44	.05		15.36	.28		11.53	.245	.41	14.96	.10	.47	16.53
* Nicholas Fund	20.29	.368		15.26	.33		13.37	.059		12.69	.101		9.90	.047		14.15			26.17			16.62			8.00						
* Northeast Investors Trust	13.96	1.28		14.94	1.28		14.15	1.245		13.51	1.19		13.21	1.15		15.37	1.15		15.80	1.14	.44	15.04	1.085		13.44	1.02	.938	16.43	.98	.436	17.60
* One William Street Fund	14.32	.325	.21	14.04	.27	.315	14.77	.30	.23	14.77	.395	.53	13.25	.345	.53	15.87	.305	1.035	17.51	.255		16.17	.295		11.32	.285	.445	16.23	.30	.735	17.44
Oppenheimer Fund	5.90	.23		6.20	.18		6.67	.11		6.25	.25		5.58	.145		6.91	.084	.542	9.24	.145	.095	8.61	.08		5.88	.085		7.85	.28	.44	6.66
Q-T-C Securities Fund Inc.	16.08	.37	.41	12.79	.39	.51	11.09	.30	.43	10.07	.25	.25	9.42	.19	.55	9.71	.18	.54	12.05	.12	.31	10.67	.32	.15	9.42	.25	.37	11.85	.31	.52	11.44
* Penn Square Mutual	7.49	.35	.42	8.19	.30	.37	8.36	.30	.59	7.19	.325		5.88	.255		6.41	.24	.138	7.34	.25	.235	8.20	.29	.134	6.57	.363	.172	8.63	.291	.925	9.25
* Pennsylvania Mutual	5.46	.055	.341	3.89	.124		3.24		.077	2.56		.938	1.64	.086		2.10		.692	4.53			4.88		.127	3.34			8.98			9.20
Philadelphia Fund	8.17	.179		7.43	.16	.31	7.43	.178		6.91	.147		4.97	.06		6.06	.07	.415	7.98	.079		7.90	.179		5.46	.263		7.50	.165	.73	7.83
Pilgrim Fund	10.79	.15		9.05	.06		7.51	.085		7.03	.10		6.02	.06		7.74	.045	.035	11.02	.05		10.05	.12		7.09	.04		9.68	.055	.98	11.60
* Pine Street Fund	10.04	.502	.295	10.91	.417	.32	10.72	.39	.315	10.30	.445	.155	8.76	.445	.178	9.67	.35	.275	10.04	.295	.311	11.46	.39	.54	8.53	.43	.17	13.58	.355	1.025	12.86
Pioneer Fund	14.33	.52	.475	14.35	.48	.45	13.91	.61	.22	11.81	.41	.22	9.79	.365	.58	11.28	.37	.60	12.23	.365	.54	11.97	.365	.27	9.18	.37	1.19	13.58			14.82
Pioneer II Fund	19.42	.42	.53	16.01	.42	.42	13.30	.19	.42	10.58	.17	.255	8.90	.17	.44	8.52	.16	1.68	12.26	.175	.525	10.04	.18		7.12	.07					
Pilgrowth Fund	11.05	.12		10.90	.295	.105	11.32	.345	.065	10.77	.385	.093	10.07	.27	.48	12.54	.19		15.06	.175	.39	13.52	.32	.90	10.07	.12		13.98	.25	.93	17.05
Plitrend Fund	10.48	.225	.10	8.45	.225	.055	7.22	.21	.10	6.57	.178		5.98	.25	.31	7.72	.16	.385	8.72	.16	.385	8.65	.16		6.07	.12		9.64	.11	1.37	11.58
* T. Rowe Price Growth Stk	10.84	.277	.246	10.20	.226	.21	11.27	.231		11.18	.229		10.10	.195	.105	12.77	.173	.54	16.43	.125	.315	13.94	.14	.20	9.20	.205	.285	12.28	.095	.385	12.91
* Rowe Price New Era Fund	10.74	.324		11.09			11.24	.279		11.50	.286		10.12	.184	.031	10.77	.105	.138	11.63	.16		10.37	.16		8.08	.16		9.81			
* Rowe Price New Horizons	9.70	.098		7.35	.071		7.18	.074		7.62	.091	.17	6.39	.055	.083	8.84	.042	.692	14.97	.057	.207	9.99	.053	.155	6.11	.07	.40	9.11	.06	.573	5.90
* Provident Fund for Income	3.76	.27	.30	4.04	.245		3.68	.25		3.39	.26	.05	3.20	.25	.18	3.81	.25	.207	5.06	.22	.18	4.87	.24		5.02	.12	.36	5.02	.22	.25	5.89
Puritan Fund	10.50	.665		11.32	.615	.21	10.62	.585	.10	9.73	.565		8.31	.56		9.03	.53	.32	10.54	.61		10.54	.50		8.31	.51		10.85	.46	.51	12.01

Putnam Fund
Putnam Growth Fund
Putnam Income Fund
Putnam Investors Fund
Research Capital Fund
* Revere Fund
Safeco Equity Fund
St. Paul Cap Fund
St. Paul Grth Fund
Scudder Int'l Invests
** Scudder Special Fund
** Scudder Shrn & Clark C Stk
Scudder Income Fund
Security Equity Fund
Security Invest Fund
* Selected Amer. Shares
Sentinel Apex Fund
Sentinel Bal Fund
Sentinel Com Stk Fund
Sequoia Fund
Shareholders Tr. of Boston
Sigma Capital Shares
Sigma Investment Shares
Sigma Trust Shares
Sigma Venture Shares
Sovereign Investors
* Stein Roe & Farnham Bal
Stein Roe & Farnham Stk
* Technology Fund
Templeton Growth Fund
* Twentieth Cent Growth Inv
Union Income Fund
United Accumulative
United Income Fund
United Science Fund
United Services Fund
Value Line Fund
Value Line Income Fund
Value Line Leveraged Grth
Value Line Special Sit
Vance Sanders Investors
Vance Sanders Common Stk
Vance Sanders Special Fd
Wall Street Growth Fund
Wash Mutual Investors
* Wellington Fund
* Windsor Fund
* WisconsinFund

Notes: (a) Capital gains distributions may include payments from other sources. (b) Paid 6% stock dividend in 1970. (c) Paid 5% stock dividend in 1971; 8% in 1972. (c) Paid 5% stock dividend in 1970. (d) Paid 5% stock dividend in 1971. (e) Paid 10% stock dividend in 1972. (f) Paid 3% stock dividend in 1972. All figures are adjusted for split-ups. Stock of record is used in determining in which period dividends and capital gains payments fall. To provide longer-term performance data, funds are not included in Quarterly Record until they have been offered publicly at least three years.

* Indicates no-load fund.

Source: *Barron's*, August 7, 1978.

WHAT IS IN A 10K AND OTHER SEC REPORTS

PART I OF 10K

1. **Business.** Identifies principal products and services of the company, principal markets and methods of distribution and, if "material," competitive factors, backlog and expectation of fulfillment, availability of raw materials, importance of patents, licenses, and franchises, estimated cost of research, number of employees, and effects of compliance with ecological laws; if there is more than one line of business, for each of the last five fiscal years a statement of total sales and net income for each line which, during either of the last two fiscal years, accounted for 10 percent or more of total sales or pretax income.

2. **Summary of operations.** Summary of operations for each of the last five fiscal years and any additional years required to keep the summary from being misleading (per share earnings and dividends are included). Includes explanatory material describing reasons for changes in revenues, earnings, etc.

3. **Properties.** Location and character of principal plants, mines, and other important properties and if held in fee or leased.

4. **Parents and subsidiaries.** List or diagram of all parents and subsidiaries and for each named, the percentage of voting securities owned, or other basis of control.

5. **Legal proceedings.** Brief description of material legal proceedings pending; when civil rights statutes are involved, proceedings must be disclosed.

6. **Increases and decreases in outstanding securities.** Information for each security, including reacquired securities, new issues, securities issued in exchange for property, services or other securities, and new securities resulting from modification of outstanding securities.

7. **Approximate number of equity security holders.** Holders of record for each class of equity securities as of the end of the fiscal year.

Source: *The National Investment Library*, New York.

8. **Executive officers of the registrant.** List of all executive officers, nature of family relationship between them, positions and offices held.

9. **Indemnification of directors and officers.** General effect under which any director or officer is insured or indemnified against any liability which he may incur in his capacity as such.

10. **Financial statements and exhibits filed.** Complete, audited annual financial information, and a list of exhibits filed.

PART II OF 10K

11. **Principal security holders and security holdings of management.** Identification of owners of 10 percent or more of any class of securities and of securities held by directors and officers according to amount and percent of each class.

12. **Directors of the registrant.** Name, office, term of office, and specific background data on each.

13. **Remuneration of directors and officers.** List of each director and three highest paid officers with aggregate annual remuneration exceeding $40,000—and total paid all officers and directors.

14. **Options granted to management to purchase securities.** Options granted to or exercised by directors and officers since the beginning of the fiscal year.

15. **Interest of management and others in certain transactions.** Material changes in significant transactions of such things as assets, pension, retirement, savings or other similar plans, or unusual loans.

SCHEDULES TO 10K

I. Marketable securities. Other security investments.

II. Amounts due from directors, officers, and principal holders of equity securities other than affiliates.

III. Investments in securities of affiliates.

IV. Indebtedness of affiliates (not current).

V. Property, plant, and equipment.

VI. Reserves for depreciation, depletion, and amortization of property, plant, and equipment.

VII. Intangible assets.

VIII. Reserves for depreciation and amortization of intangible assets.

IX. Bonds, mortgages, and similar debt.

X. Indebtedness to affiliates (not current).

XI. Guarantees of securities of other issuers.

XII. Reserves.

XIII. Capital shares.

XIV. Warrants or rights.

XV. Other securities.

XVI. Supplementary profit and loss information.

XVII. Income from dividends (equity in net profit and loss of affiliates).

OTHER REPORTS

12-K. The 12-K annual report is filed with the SEC by certain companies which are regulated by, and file reports with, the Federal Power Commission, Interstate Commerce Commission, and Federal Communications Commission. It is similar in content to the 10-K.

10-Q. This is the quarterly financial report filed by most companies, which, although unaudited, provides a continuing view of a company's financial position during the year. It must be filed within 45 days of the close of a fiscal quarter.

8-K. This is a report of unscheduled material events or corporate changes deemed of importance to shareholders or to the SEC—changes in control of the registrant; acquisition or disposition of assets; legal proceedings; changes in securities (i.e., collateral for registered securities); defaults upon senior securities; increase or decrease in the amount of securities outstanding; options to purchase securities; revaluation of assets; submission of matters to a vote of security holders; and any newly enacted requirements affecting the company's business.

Proxy statement. Provides official notification to stockholders of matters to be brought to a vote at shareholders meeting.

Registration statement. Discloses fully, all financial and relevant facts on a company, needed by investors to evaluate proposed sale of securities. Very detailed.

Commodities Market

COMMODITIES MARKETS AND TRADING INFORMATION

COMMODITY FUTURES TRADING INFORMATION*

Position limits: The Commodity Futures Trading Commission has established limits on the positions that may be held, and the daily trading position limits that may be made by a person in the aggregate of all accounts he owns, controls, or participates in directly or indirectly in any one contract month or all contract months combined. In addition to the CFTC limits, certain limits are imposed by some of the commodity exchanges.

Reportable positions: The Commodity Futures Trading Commission requires that reports be filed for each day on which a trade is made, for the day before, and one day after the positions are reached by a person in the aggregate of all accounts that person owns, controls, or participates in directly or indirectly.

Those commodities for which "Reportable Position" and "Position Limit" are indicated as pending just became regulated April 21, 1975. Reportable position size and position limits were not yet decided upon at the time of this publication.

Current Year	Key to Contract Months	Forward Year
F	January	A
G	February	B
H	March	C
J	April	D
K	May	E
M	June	I
N	July	L
Q	August	O
U	September	P
V	October	R
X	November	S
Z	December	T

DAILY PERMISSIBLE TRADING PRICE LIMITS AND PRICE RANGE

Price limitations are imposed by the various exchanges to prevent extreme price changes in any one day. When prices reach the trading limit, trading beyond that limit is stopped for that day. In nearly all markets the Board of Directors or Governors has the power to change the limits in emergencies.

In the current month the limitations are broadened in certain future contracts by permitting wider price ranges and in others by removing limitations entirely.

Explanation of variable trading limits in CBOT markets: If three or more contracts within a crop year (or all contracts in a crop year if there are less than three open contracts) close on the limit bid for three successive business days or on the limit sellers for three successive business days, then the limit would be raised to 150 percent of the current level for all contract months and remain there for three successive business days.

If three or more contract months (or all contracts in a crop year if there are less than three open contracts) in a given crop year close on the limit bid for the next three business days or on the limit sellers for three successive business days, then the limits will remain at 150 percent of the original level for another three-day period.

The limits would remain at 150 percent for successive periods of three business days until three or more contracts in a crop year (or all contracts in a crop year if there are less than three open contracts) do not close at the limit on one day during that period. If at any time during a three-day business period the three or more contract months (or all contracts in a crop year if there are less than three open contracts) do not close on the limit bid or limit sellers, then the limits would revert to their original level at the end of the three-day period.

Explanation of variable trading limits: I.M.M. (gold, copper, silver coins): Whenever on two successive days any contract month closes at the normal daily price limit

---

* Source: Clayton Brokerage Co. of St. Louis, Inc. The tables that follow are also provided by Clayton Brokerage Co., St. Louis, Mo.

The information contained herein is derived from the customs and practices of the commodity industry and is believed to be reliable. However, because of changing customs and practices in the commodity industry, those acting on this information are responsible for their own actions and must ascertain that the information is current and accurate. © Date of publication 9/77.

214

in the same direction (not necessarily the same contract month on both days) an expanded daily price-limit schedule shall go into effect as follows:

1. The third day's price limit in all contract months shall be 150 percent of the normal daily price limit.
2. If any contract month closes at its expanded daily price limit on the third day in the same direction, then the fourth day's expanded daily price limit and each successive day thereafter, shall be 200 percent of the normal daily price limit, so

long as any contract month closes at its expanded daily price limit.
3. Whenever the foregoing daily price limit schedule is in effect and no contract month closes at the price limit in the same direction which initiated or maintained the expanded schedule, then the normal daily price limit shall be reinstated on the following day.

I.M.M. (currencies): Same as above, though fourth day. On fifth day there is no limit, and on sixth day normal limit returns.

CHICAGO BOARD OF TRADE (CBOT)

141 West Jackson Boulevard
Chicago, Illinois 60604

Commodity	Exchange Trading Hours (CDT)	Ultronic Symbol	Delivery Months*	Usual Par Contract Grade(s)	Contract Size	Prices Quoted In	Minimum Fluctuation
Corn............	9:30–1:15	C₂C*	ZHKNU	#2 Yellow	5,000 bu	$¢/bu	$\frac{1}{4}$ ¢/bu
Oats............	9:30–1:15	C₂O*	ZHKNU	#1 White #1, 2 Heavy white	5,000 bu	$¢/bu	$\frac{1}{4}$ ¢/bu
Soybeans.......	9:30–1:15	C₃S*	XFHKNQU	#2 Yellow	5,000 bu	$¢/bu	$\frac{1}{4}$ ¢/bu
Soybean meal....	9:30–1:15	C₂SM*	VZFHKNQU	44% protein	100 tons (200,000 lbs)	$¢/ton	10¢/ton
Soybean oil.......	9:30–1:15	C₂BO*	VZFHKNQU	Regular—one grade	60,000 lbs (one tank car)	$¢/lb	$\frac{1}{100}$ ¢/lb
Wheat...........	9:30–1:15	C₁W*	NUZHK	#2 Soft red winter #2 Hard winter #1, 2 North spring	5,000 bu	$¢/bu	$\frac{1}{4}$ ¢/bu
Broilers, Iced.....	9:15–1:05	C₂IB*	FHKMNQUX	USDA Grade A 2½ to 3½ lbs whole eviscerated	30,000 lbs. (65 lb. boxes)	$¢/lb	$\frac{2.5}{100}$ ¢/lb
GNMA "Ginnie Maes".	8:50–1:30	C₂M*	HMUZ	HUD—1717 3/73 Mortgage backed certificates 8% yield	$100,000	% pts.	$\frac{1}{32}$%pt.
Commercial paper..........	8:30–1:35	C₃P*	HMUZ	A-1, P-1 90 day Commercial paper	$1,000,000	% pts.	0.01 % pt.
United States treasury bonds..........	8:40–1:30	C₁US*	HMUZ	15 year minimum	$100,000	% pts.	$\frac{1}{32}$% pt.
Gold............	8:25–1:30	C₂G*	FHKNUX	0.995 Fine	96.45 troy oz. (3–1 kilo bars)	$¢/oz	10¢/oz
Silver...........	9:00–1:25	C₂SI*	GJMQVZ	0.999 Fine	5,000 troy oz. (5 bars)	$¢/oz	$\frac{1}{10}$ ¢/oz
Plywood..........	9:00–1:00	C₂PW*	FHKNUX	½" CDX-standard exterior- 4–5 ply 4 x 8's Group 1	76,032 sq. ft. 36 (66 pc. units) (one boxcar load)	$\frac{$¢}{M\ sq.\ ft.}$	$\frac{10¢}{M\ sq.\ ft.}$

* Commodity Futures Trading Commission.
† Limit is removed from delivery month on the first notice day.
‡ Variable limit rule.

Dollar Value of		Usual Maximum Daily Permissible Price Limits above or below Previous Close‡		Usual Maximum Permissible Range between Session's High and Low‡		CFTC* Reportable Position Contracts	Position Limits Contracts	Seasonal	
Min Tick	1¢ Move	Cents	$	Cents	$			High	Low
12.50	50	10¢/bu	500	20¢/bu	1,000	100	600	NO	VXZ
12.50	50	6¢/bu	300	12¢/bu	600	40	600	ZFK	NO
12.50	50	30¢/bu	1,500	60¢/bu	3,000	100	600	KMN	UV
10.00	1	1,000¢/ton†	1,000	2,000¢/ton†	2,000	50	720	NU	VZ
6.00	600	1¢/lb†	600	2¢/lb†	1,200	50	540	KMN	UVX
12.50	50	20¢/bu	1,000	40¢/bu	2,000	100	600	XZF	MOU
7.50	300	2¢/lb†	600	4¢/lb†	1,200	25	300	NO	XZ
31.25	1,000	$\frac{3\%}{4}$ pt.†	750	1.5% pt.†	1,500	25	600		
25.00	10,000	25% pt.†	625	50% pt.†	1,250	25	No limit		
31.25	1,000	¾% pt.†	750	1.5% pt.†	1,500	25	No limit		
9.65	0.965	1,000¢/oz†	964.5	2,000¢/oz†	1,929	50	No limit	O	FG
5.00	50	20¢/oz†	1,000	40¢/oz†	2,000	100	No limit	O	FG
7.60	0.760	$\frac{700¢}{M\ sq.\ ft.}$†	532	$\frac{1,400¢}{M\ sq.\ ft.}$	1,064	25	600	Summer	Winter

First notice day............................. For all CBOT commodities is the last business day before the first business day of the delivery month.

First delivery day........................... For all CBOT commodities is the first business day of the delivery month.

Last trading day .... Commercial paper ⎫
Corn
GNMA
Oats
Plywood
Soybeans   ⎬ Eighth last business day of the delivery month
Soybean meal
Soybean oil
US T-bonds
Wheat   ⎭

Broilers   ⎫
Gold   ⎬ Fourth last business day of the delivery month
Silver   ⎭

Last notice day .... Commercial paper ⎫
GNMA   ⎬ Seventh last business day of the delivery month
Plywood
Soybean meal   ⎭

US T-Bonds   ⎫
Broilers
Corn
Gold
Oats   ⎬ Second last business day of the delivery month
Silver
Soybeans
Soybean oil
Wheat   ⎭

Last delivery day .... Commercial paper ⎫
GNMA
Plywood   ⎬ Sixth last business day of the delivery month
Soybean meal
US T-bonds   ⎭

Broilers   ⎫
Corn
Gold
Oats   ⎬ Last business day of the delivery month
Silver
Soybeans
Soybean oil
Wheat   ⎭

Currently Inactive CBOT Futures Contracts

Choice steers....................................	USDA Choice	40,000 lbs
Steer carcass beef..............................	USDA Choice	30,000 lbs
Cotton..	1" Staple	50,000 lbs
Cottonseed oil..................................	Summer Prime	60,000 lbs
Grain sorghum/milo..............................	#1, 2 Yellow	100,000 lbs
Loose lard......................................	Prime rendered	60,000 lbs
North Pacific—coast wheat.......................	#1 Hard	5,000 bu
Gulf hard red—winter wheat......................	#2	5,000 bu
Rye...	#2	5,000 bu
Stud lumber.....................................	10–15% utility	100,000 bd. ft.

Daily Permissible Trading Price Limits and Price Range

Price limitations are imposed by the various exchanges to prevent extreme price changes in any one day. When prices reach the trading limit, trading beyond that limit is stopped for that day. In nearly all markets the Board of Directors or Governors has the power to change the limits in emergencies.

In the current month the limitations are broadened in certain future contracts by permitting wider price ranges and in others by removing limitations entirely.

In CBOT markets, if three or more contracts within a crop year (or all contracts in a crop year if there are less than three open contracts) close on the limit bid for three successive business days or on the limit sellers for three successive business days, then the limit would be raised to 150 percent of the current level for all contract months and remain there for three successive business days.

If three or more contract months (or all contracts in a crop year if there are less than three open contracts) in a given crop year close on the limit bid for the next three business days or on the limit sellers for three successive business days, then the limits will remain at 150 percent of the original level for another three-day period.

The limits would remain at 150 percent for successive periods of three business days until three or more contracts in a crop year (or all contracts in a crop year if there are less than three open contracts) do not close at the limit on one day during that period. If at any time during a three-day business period the three or more contract months (or all contracts in a crop year if there are less than three open contracts) do not close on the limit bid or limit sellers, then the limits would revert to their original level at the end of the three-day period.

CHICAGO MERCANTILE EXCHANGE (CME)

444 WEST JACKSON BOULEVARD
CHICAGO, ILLINOIS 60606

Commodity	Exchange Trading Hours (CDT)	Ultronic Symbol	Delivery Months*	Uusual Par Contract Grade(s)	Contract Size	Prices Quoted In	Minimum Fluctuation
Cattle, live....	9:05–12:45	C_1LC*	GJMQVZ	USDA choice live steers	40,000 lbs. (1,050 lbs avg.)	$¢/lb	$\frac{2.5}{100}$ ¢/lb
Feeder cattle..	9:05–12:45	C_1FC*	HJKQUVX	USDA—minimum 80% choice and maximum 20% good	42,000 lbs. (650 lb avg)	$¢/lb	$\frac{2.5}{100}$ ¢/lb
Hogs, live.....	9:15–12:55	C_1LH*	GJMNQVZ	USDA 1, 2, 3, 4 barrows and gilts	30,000 lbs. (220 lb avg)	$¢/lb	$\frac{2.5}{100}$ ¢/lb
Pork bellies, frozen......	9:10–1:00	C_1PB*	GHKNQ	USDA seedless green—square cut—standard	36,000 lbs. (12 to 14 lb)	$¢/lb	$\frac{2.5}{100}$ ¢/lb
Eggs, shell....	9:20–1:00	C_1E*	All	USDA extras 90% Grade A large white	22,500 dozen (750 cases) (one carload)	$¢/doz	$\frac{5}{100}$ ¢/doz
Milo grain sorghum....	9:30–1:15	C_1MI*	NUZHK	#2 Yellow U.S.	400,000 lbs (7,273 bu)	$¢/cwt	$\frac{1}{4}$¢/cwt
Lumber.......	9:00–1:05	C_1LB*	FHKNUX	Kiln or air dried random 2 x 4's hem—fir—construction	100,000 bd. ft. (two boxcar loads)	$\frac{\$¢}{M \text{ bd. ft.}}$	$\frac{10¢}{M \text{ bd. ft.}}$
Potatoes (Idaho russets).....	9:00–12:50	C_1IP*	FHJKX	USDA No. 1 Size A ɔ" diameter	80,000 lbs. (one carload)	$¢/cwt	1¢/cwt
Turkeys, frozen......	9:10–12:45	C_1TT*	FHKQV	USDA Grade A young, dressed	36,000 lbs (16–24 lb avg)	$¢/16 lb	$\frac{2.5}{100}$¢/16 lb
Boneless beef........	9:05–12:45	C_1BB*	GJMQVZ	USDA Graded or Ungraded Steers or Heifer Trimmings	38,000 lbs.	$¢/lb	$\frac{2.5}{100}$ $/lb

* Commodity Futures Trading Commission.
† Limit is removed from delivery month on the first notice day.
‡ 65¢/lb and $1.30/lb during the last two trading days.
(1) 450 daily trading limit.
(2) 300 in any one delivery month, 1,125 daily trading limit or 450 in any one delivery month.
(3) 150 in G, H, N, and Q; 200 in K, 375 daily trading limit or 225 in G, H, N and Q, 300 in K.
(4) 150 net tons or short in all months combined, but no more than 550 in any one delivery month.
(5) 825 net of all delivery months when intermarket spreading.
(6) 300 in any one delivery month, 2,000 daily trading limit or 600 in any one delivery month.
(7) 150 in H, J, and K; 300 in F and X.
(8) 300 daily trading limit.

First notice day......

Boneless beef
Eggs
Cattle, feeder or live[B]
Milo
Pork Bellies
Turkeys
} First business day of the delivery month

Idaho potatoes — Sixth calendar day of the delivery month[A]

Hogs — M, T, W, T, business day on or after the sixth calendar day of the delivery month[B]

Lumber — First business day after the 16th calendar day of the delivery month

First delivery day....

Boneless beef
Eggs
Cattle, feeder or live[B]
Milo
Pork bellies
Turkeys
} First business day of the delivery month

Idaho potatoes — Sixth calendar day of the delivery month[A]

Cattle
Hogs
} M, T, W, T business day on or after the sixth calendar day of the delivery month[B]

Lumber — First business day after the 16th calendar day of the delivery month

Dollar Value of		Usual Maximum Daily Permissible Price Limits above or below Previous Close		Usual Maximum Permissible Range between Session's High and Low		CFTC* Reportable Position Contracts	Position Limits Contracts	Seasonal	
Min Tick	1¢ Move	Cents	$	Cents	$			High	Low
10.00	400	1.5¢/lb	600	3¢/lb	1,200	25	300(1)	Summer NO	Fall VX
10.50	420	1.5¢/lb	630	3¢/lb	1,260	25	300(1)	Summer NO	Fall VX
7.50	300	1.5¢/lb	450	3¢/lb	900	25	750(2)	MNO	VXZ
9.00	360	2.5¢/lb	720	4¢/lb	1,440	25	250(3)	MNO	VXZ
11.25	225	2¢/doz	450	4¢/doz	900	25	150(4)	VZ	JKM
10.0	40	15¢/cwt	600	30¢/cwt	1,200	25	550(5)	FGJ	UV
10.00	1	500¢†/M bd. ft.	500	1,000¢†/M bd. ft.	1,000	25	1,000(6)	Spring	Winter
8.00	8	50¢/cwt‡	400	100¢/cwt‡	800	25	350(7)	OU	FG
9.00	360	1.5¢/16 lb	540	3¢/16 lb	1,080	25	150(8)	XZ	NO
9.50	380	1.5¢ lb	470	3¢ lb	940	25	750	Summer	Fall

Last trading day..... Idaho potatoes — Fifth calendar day of the delivery month(C)
Lumber — 15th calendar day of the delivery month(C)
Cattle, Hogs — 20th calendar day of the delivery month(C)
Eggs, Milo — Eighth last business day of the delivery month
Boneless beef, Pork bellies, Turkeys — Sixth last business day of the delivery month

Last notice day....... Idaho potatoes — Fifth last business day of the delivery month
Lumber — Third last business day of the delivery month
Cattle, Hogs, Pork bellies — Second last business day of the delivery month
Boneless beef, Eggs, Idaho potatoes, Milo, Turkeys — Last business day of the delivery month

Last delivery day........................... For all CME commodities is the last business day of the delivery month

Currently Inactive CME Futures Contracts

Beef, frozen boneless...........	Domestic	36,000 lbs
Butter........................	Fresh or salted	40,000 lbs
Eggs, frozen,...................	Yolks, whites	36,000 lbs
Eggs, nest run.................	Large white A	22,500 dozen
Hams, frozen skinned..........	Uncured	36,000 lbs

(A) Or the first business day thereafter.
(B) Not a Friday, holiday, nor business day prior to a holiday.
(C) Or the first business day prior thereto.

INTERNATIONAL MONETARY MARKET OF THE CHICAGO MERCANTILE EXCHANGE

444 West Jackson Boulevard
Chicago, Illinois 60606

Commodity	Exchange Trading Hours (CDT)	Ultronic Symbol	Delivery Months*	Usual Par Contract Grade(s)	Contract Size	Prices Quoted In	Minimum Fluctuation
Gold..............	8:25–1:30	C₁GD*	HMUZ	0.995 Fine	100 troy oz.	$¢/oz	10¢/oz
Copper...........	8:45–1:00	C₁CR*	FHKNUX	Electrolytic ASTM standards	12,500 lbs	$¢/lb	$\frac{1}{10}$¢/lb
U.S. silver coins...	8:50–1:25	C₁UC*	HMUZ	Dimes, quarters, halfs, pre-1965	$5,000 (5 bags)	$¢/bag	$2/bag
U.S. Treasury bills.	8:35–1:35	C₁TB*	HMUZ	3-month 13-week U.S. Treasury bills	$1,000,000	%pts	0.01% pt

Foreign Currencies

Commodity	Exchange Trading Hours (CDT)	Ultronic Symbol	Delivery Months*	Usual Par Contract Grade(s)	Contract Size	Prices Quoted In	Minimum Fluctuation
British pound....	8:55–1:10	C₁BP*	HMUZ		25,000£	$/£	0.05¢/£
Canadian dollar..	8:55–1:10	C₁CD*	HMUZ		100,000CD	$/CD	0.01¢/CD
Deutsche Mark..	8:55–1:10	C₁DM*	HMUZ		125,000DM	$/DM	0.01¢/DM
Dutch guilder....	8:55–1:10	C₁DG*	HMUZ		125,000DG	$/DG	0.004¢/DG
French francs....	8:55–1:10	C₁FR*	HMUZ		250,000FF	$/FF	0.005¢/FF
Italian lira.......	8:55–1:10	C₁IC*	HMUZ		25,000,000IL	$/IL	0.00004$/IL
Japanese yen ...	8:55–1:10	C₁JY*	HMUZ		12,500,000JY	$/JY	0.0001¢/JY
Mexican peso...	8:55–1:10	C₁MP*	HMUZ		1,000,000MP	$/MP	0.001¢/MP
Swiss franc......	8:55–1:10	C₁SF*	HMUZ		125,000SF	$/SF	0.01¢/SF

* Commodity Futures Trading Commission.
† Limit is removed on the first notice day.
‡ See explanation below on daily permissible price limits and price range.
§ Limit is removed on the last trading day.
‖ $150 per bag on the last trading day.
Accumulation of positions: The positions of all accounts owned or controlled by a person or persons acting in concert or in which such person or persons have a proprietary or beneficial interest shall be cumulated. The Board may impose position limits for any such account or accounts as it deems appropriate.

Dollar Value of		Usual Maximum Daily Permissible Price Limits above or below Previous Close‡		Usual Maximum Permissible Range between Session's High and Low‡		Reportable Position Contracts	Position Limits Contracts #
Min Tick	1¢ Move	Cents	$	Cents	$		
10.00	1	1,000¢/oz†	1,000	2,000¢/oz†	2,000	25	
12.50	125	5¢/lb§	625	10¢/lb§	1,250	25	
10.00	0.05	10,000¢/bag‖	500	20,000¢/bag‖	1,000	25	
25.00	10,000	0.50% pts§	1,250	1.0% pts§	2,500	25	
12.50	250	5¢/£§	1,250	10¢/£§	2,500	25	
10.00	1,000	0.75¢/CD§	750	1.5¢/CD§	1,500	25	
12.50	1,250	0.6¢/DM§	750	1.2¢/DM§	1,500	25	
5.00	1,250	0.6¢/DG§	750	1.2¢/DG§	1,500	25	
12.50	2,500	0.5¢/FF§	1,250	1¢/FF§	2,500	25	
10.00	250,000	0.003¢/IL§	750	0.006¢/IL§	1,500	25	
12.50	125,000	0.006¢/JY§	750	0.012¢/JY§	1,500	25	
10.00	10,000	0.075¢/MP§	750	0.15¢/MP§	1,500	25	
12.50	1,250	0.6¢/SF§	750	1.2¢/SF§	1,500	25	

First notice day...... Copper ⎫
                       Gold   ⎬ First business day of the delivery month
                       Silver coins⎭

                       Foreign currencies⎫
                       T-Bills   ⎬ Last trading day of the delivery month

First delivery day..... Copper ⎫
                        Gold   ⎬ First business day of the delivery month
                        Silver coins⎭

                        Foreign currencies Third Wednesday of the delivery month or the first business day
                                            thereafter
                        T-Bills   First business day following the last trading day of the delivery
                                            month

Last trading day...... Copper ⎫
                       Gold   ⎬ Sixth last business day of the delivery month
                       Silver coins⎭

                       Foreign Currencies

                       British pound ⎫
                       Deutsche Mark │
                       Dutch guilder │
                       French franc ⎬ Two business days prior to the third Wednesday of the delivery
                       Italian lira │ month
                       Japanese yen │
                       Swiss franc   ⎭

                       Canadian dollar⎫ First business day prior to the third Wednesday of the delivery
                       Mexican peso   ⎭ month
                       T-Bills   Second business day following the Federal Reserve 3-month
                                         T-Bill auction of the third week of the delivery month or the
                                         third Wednesday of the delivery month or the first business
                                         day thereafter

KANSAS CITY BOARD OF TRADE (KCBT)

4800 Main Street
Kansas City, Missouri 64112

Commodity	Exchange Trading Hours (CDT)	Ultronic Symbol	Delivery Months*	Usual Par Contract Grade(s)	Contract Size	Prices Quoted In	Minimum Fluctuation
Wheat.....	9:30– 1:15	C₁KW*	NUZHK	#2 Dark hard red hard yellow winter	5,000 bu	$¢/bu	$\frac{1}{4}$ ¢/bu

* Commodity Futures Trading Commission.
† To the extent that the net position held or controlled by any one person in all futures in any one grain on any one market is shown to represent spreading in the same grain between markets, the limit on net position in all futures may be exceeded on such contract market, but in no case shall the excess result in a net position of more than 3 million bushels in all futures combined nor more than 2 million bushels in any one future.

First notice day.............. Last business day before first business day of the delivery month
First delivery day............ First business day of the delivery month
Last trading day.............. Eighth last business day of the delivery month

Last notice day....... Copper ⎫
                    Gold   ⎬ Last business day of the delivery month
                    Silver coins ⎭
                    Foreign currencies ⎫
                    T-Bills   ⎭ Last trading day of the delivery month

Last delivery day..... Copper ⎫
                    Gold   ⎬ Last business day of the delivery month
                    Silver coins ⎭
                    T-Bills   First business day following the last trading day of the delivery
                                           month
                    Foreign currencies Third Wednesday of the delivery month or the first business day
                                           thereafter

Daily Permissible Trading Price Limits and Price Range

Price limitations are imposed by the various exchanges to prevent extreme price changes in any one day. When prices reach the trading limit, trading beyond that limit is stopped for that day. In nearly all markets the Board of Directors or Governors has the power to change the limits in emergencies.

In the current month the limitations are broadened in certain future contracts by permitting wider price ranges and in others by removing limitations entirely.

I.M.M. (gold copper, silver coins, T-bills):   Whenever on two successive days any contract month closes at the normal daily price limit in the same direction (not necessarily the same contract month on both days) an expanded daily price-limit schedule shall go into effect as follows:

1. The third day's price limit in all contract months shall be 150 percent of the normal daily price limit.
2. If any contract month closes at its expanded daily price limit on the third day in the same direction, then the fourth day's expanded daily price limit and each successive day thereafter, shall be 200 percent of the normal daily price limit, so long as any contract month closes at its expanded daily price limit.
3. Whenever the foregoing daily price limit schedule is in effect and no contract month closes at the price limit in the same direction which initiated or maintained the expanded schedule, then the normal daily price limit shall be reinstated on the following day.

I.M.M. (currencies):   Same as above, though fourth day. On fifth day there is no limit, and on sixth day normal limit returns.

Dollar Value of		Usual Maximum Daily Permissible Price Limits above or below Previous Close		Usual Maximum Permissible Range between Session's High and Low		CFTC* Reportable Position	Position Limits	Seasonal	
Min Tick	1¢ Move	Cents	$	Cents	$	Contracts	Contracts	High	Low
12.50	50	25¢/bu	1,250	50¢/bu	2,500	100	600†	XZ	MN

Last notice day.............. Second last business day of the delivery month
Last delivery day............ Last business day of the delivery month

Currently Inactive KCBT Futures Contracts

Feeder cattle..	USDA Choice	42,000 lbs
Grain sorghum.......................................	#1, 2 Yellow or white	5,000 bu
Gulf wheat..	#2 Hard red	5,000 bu
Corn..	#2 Yellow	5,000 bu
Oats..	#3 White or red	5,000 bu
Soybeans..	#2 Yellow	5,000 bu

MID-AMERICA COMMODITY EXCHANGE

175 West Jackson Boulevard
Chicago, Illinois 60604

Commodity	Exchange Hours (CDT)	Delivery Months*	Usual Par Contract Grade(s)	Contract Size	Prices Quoted In	Minimum Fluctuation
Corn...............	9:30–1:30	ZHKNU	#2 Yellow	1,000 bu.	$¢/bu	⅛¢/bu
Oats...............	9:30–1:30	NUZHK	#1 White	5,000 bu.	$¢/bu	⅛¢bu
Soybeans..........	9:30–1:30	XFHKNQU	#2 Heavy white #2 Yellow	1,000 bu.	$¢/bu	⅛¢/bu
Wheat.............	9:30–1:30	NUZHK	#2 Soft or hard red winter #1, 2 North spring	1,000 bu.	$¢/bu	⅛¢/bu
Hogs, live..........	9:15–1:05	GHMNQVZ	#1, 2, 3, 4 USDA barrows and gilts	15,000 lbs. (220 lb. avg.)	$¢/16 lb.	$\frac{2.5 ¢/16 \text{ lb.}}{100}$
Gold...............	8:25–1:40	FHKNUX	0.995 Fine	32.15 Troy oz. (1 kilo bar)	$¢/oz.	10¢/oz.
Silver..............	8:40–1:50	FJHQVZ	0.999 Fine	1,000 troy oz.	$¢/oz.	$\frac{5 ¢/\text{oz.}}{100}$
U.S. silver coins.....	8:50–1:35	HMUZ	Dimes, quarters halfs, pre-1965	$5,000 (5 bags)	$/bag	1$/bag

* Commodity Futures Trading Commission.
† Limit is removed from delivery month on first notice day.
‡ Variable limit rule.
§ Limit is removed from delivery month on the last trading day.
‖ 400 in any one delivery month.

Dollar Value of		Usual Maximum Daily Permissible Price Limits above or below Previous Close‡		Usual Maximum Permissible Range between Session's High and Low		Reportable Position Contracts	Position Limits Contracts	Seasonal	
Min Tick	1¢ Move	Cents	$	Cents	$			High	Low
1.25	10	10¢/bu	100	20¢/bu	200	40	600	NQ	VXZ
1.25	50	6¢/bu	300	12¢/bu	600	40	400	ZFK	NQ
1.25	10	30¢/bu	300	60¢/bu	600	40	600	KMN	UV
1.25	10	20¢/bu	200	40¢/bu	400	40	600	XZF	MQU
3.75	150	1.5¢/lb	300	3¢/lb	600	25	800‖	MNQ	UXZ
3.22	0.32	1,000¢†/oz	321.5	2,000¢†/oz	643	100	None	Q	FG
0.50	10	20¢/oz†	200	40¢/oz†	400	100	None	Q	FG
5.00	0.05	15,000¢§/Bag	750	30,000¢§/Bag	1,500	50	None	—	—

First notice day................. Corn, Oats, Soybeans, Wheat, Gold, Silver — Last business day prior to the 1st business day of the delivery month

Silver coins — First business day of the delivery month
Live hogs — M,T,W,T business day on or after the sixth calender day of the delivery month (A)

First delivery day............... Corn, Oats, Soybeans, Wheat, Gold, Silver, Silver coins — First business day of the delivery month

Live hogs — M,T,W,T business day on or after the sixth calender day of the delivery month (A)

Last trading day................. Live hogs — 20th calender day of the delivery month (B)

Corn, Oats, Soybeans, Wheat — Eighth last business day of the delivery month

Silver coins — Sixth last business day of the delivery month

Gold, Silver — Fourth last business day of the delivery month

Last notice day.................. For all Mid-America commodities is the last business day of the delivery month

Last delivery day................ For all Mid-America commodities is the last business day of the delivery month

(A) Not a Friday, holiday, or business day prior thereto.
(B) Or the first business day prior thereto.
Currently inactive Mid-America futures contract: Rye #2 1000 bu.

MINNEAPOLIS GRAIN EXCHANGE (MGE)

400 South 4th Street
Minneapolis, Minnesota 55475

Commodity	Exchange Trading Hours (CDT)	Ultronic Symbol	Delivery Months*	Usual Par Contract Grade(s)	Contract Size	Prices Quoted In	Minimum Fluctuation
Wheat........	9:30–1:15	C₁MW*	NUZHK	#2 Northern spring U.S. 13.5% protein	5,000 bu	$¢/bu	$\frac{1}{8}$ ¢/bu
Durum wheat......	9:30–1:15	C₁MD*	NUZHK	#3 U.S. Hard amber durum	5,000 bu	$¢/bu	$\frac{1}{8}$ ¢/bu

* Commodity Futures Trading Commission.
† To the extent that the net position held or controlled by any one person in all futures in any one grain on any one market is shown to represent spreading in the same grain between markets, the limit on net position in all futures may be exceeded on such contract market, but in no case shall the excess result in a net position of more than 3 million bushels in all futures combined nor more than 2 million bushels in any one future.

First notice day.............. Last business day before first business day of the delivery month
First delivery day............ First business day of the delivery month
Last trading day............. Eighth last business day of the delivery month

NEW YORK COCOA EXCHANGE

127 John Street
New York, New York 10038

Commodity	Exchange Trading Hours (CDT)	Ultronic Symbol	Delivery Months*	Usual Par Contract Grade(s)	Contract Size	Prices Quoted In	Minimum Fluctuation
Cocoa.....	9:00–2:00	C₁CC*	HKNUZ	Standard beans African	30,000 lbs (200 sacks)	$¢/lb	$\frac{1}{100}$ ¢/lb
Rubber....	8:45–1:45	C₁NR*	FHKNUX	International #1 ribbed smoked sheets	33,000 lbs	$¢/lb	$\frac{5}{100}$ ¢/lb

* Commodity Futures Trading Commission.
† Limit is removed from delivery month on first notice day.

Dollar Value of		Usual Maximum Daily Permissible Price Limits above or below Previous Close		Usual Maximum Permissible Range between Session's High and Low		CFTC* Reportable Position	Position Limits	Seasonal	
Min Tick	1¢ Move	Cents	$	Cents	$	Contracts	Contracts	High	Low
6.25	50	20¢/bu	1,000	40¢/bu	2,000	40	600†	XZ	MN
6.25	50	20¢/bu	1,000	40¢/bu	2,000	40	600†	XZ	MN

Last notice day.............. Second last business day of the delivery month
Last delivery day............ Last business day of the delivery month

Currently Inactive MGE Futures Contracts

Barley..	#2 U.S.	5,000 bu
Corn..	#2 U.S. yellow	5,000 bu
Oats..	#2 U.S. white	5,000 bu
Rye...	#2 U.S.	5,000 bu
Soybeans...	#2 U.S. yellow	5,000 bu
Pork bellies, frozen.................................	Standard	36,000 lbs
Gold..	0.995 Fine	32,145 oz

Dollar Value of		Usual Maximum Daily Permissible Price Limits above or below Previous Close		Usual Maximum Permissible Range between Session's High and Low		CFTC* Reportable Position	Position Limits	Seasonal	
Min Tick	1¢ Move	Cents	$	Cents	$	Contracts	Contracts	High	Low
3.00	300	4¢/lb†	1,200	4¢/lb†	1,200	25	No limit	Z	KM
16.50	330	2¢/lb†	660	4¢/lb†	1,320	25	No limit		

First notice day..................	Cocoa	Seven business days before first business day of the delivery month
	Rubber	Two business days before the first business day of the delivery month
First delivery day...............	Cocoa } Rubber}	First business day of the delivery month
Last trading day.................	Cocoa } Rubber}	Eighth last business day of the delivery month
Last notice day..................	Cocoa	Eighth last business day of the delivery month
	Rubber	Third last business day of the delivery month
Last delivery day...............	Cocoa } Rubber}	Last business day of the delivery month

NEW YORK COFFEE AND SUGAR EXCHANGE

4 World Trade Center
New York, New York 10048

Commodity	Exchange Trading Hours (CDT)	Ultronic Symbol	Delivery Months*	Usual Par Contract Grade(s)	Contract Size	Prices Quoted In	Minimum Fluctuation
Coffee (C)..	8:45– 1:30	C_1C*	HKNUZ	Washed Arabic beans, Columbia, Mexico, S. America	37,500 lbs (250 sacks)	$¢/lb	$\frac{1}{100}$ ¢/lb
Sugar #11...	9:00– 1:45	C_1SE*	FHKNUV	World production raw bulk cane 96° average polarization	112,000 lbs (50 long tons)	$¢/lb	$\frac{1}{100}$ ¢/lb
Sugar #12...	9:00– 1:45	C_1SW*	FHKNUX	Foreign and domestic production raw bulk cane 96° average polarization	112,000 lbs (50 long tons)	$¢/lb	$\frac{1}{100}$ ¢/lb

* Commodity Futures Trading Commission.
† Limit is removed from delivery month on first business day prior to the delivery preceding month.
‡ Limit is removed from the calendar month prior to the delivery month.

First notice day......................... Sugar 11, 12 } Fifth last business day of the month prior to the
                                          Coffee (c)   } first business day of the delivery month
First delivery day...................... Coffee
                                          Sugar 11   } First business day of the delivery month
                                          Sugar 12   }
Last trading day........................ Sugar 12   Eighth calendar day of the month prior to the first
                                                       business day of the delivery month[1]
                                          Sugar 11   Last business day of the month prior to the first
                                                       business day of the delivery month
                                          Coffee (c)   Sixth last business day

COMMODITY EXCHANGE, INC. OF NEW YORK (COMEX)

4 World Trade Center
New York, New York 10048

Commodity	Exchange Hours (CDT)	Ultronic Symbol	Delivery Months*	Usual Par Contract Grade(s)	Contract Size	Prices Quoted In	Minimum Fluctuation
Copper..........	8:50– 1:00	C_1CP*	FHKNUZ	Electrolytic ASTM standards	25,000 lbs.	$¢/lb	$\frac{1}{10}$¢/lb
Gold............	8:25– 1:30	C_1GO*	GJMQVZ	0.995 fine	100 troy oz (3–1 kilo bars)	$¢/oz	10¢/oz
Silver..........	9:00– 1:15	C_1S*	FHKNUZ	0.999 fine	5,000 troy oz (5 bars)	$¢/oz	$\frac{1}{10}$¢/oz

* Commodity Futures Trading Commission.
† Limit is removed from the delivery month on the first business day prior to the first notice day.
‡ 4,000 in all months combined.

First notice day.......... For all Comex commodities is the last business day prior to the first business
                           day of the delivery month
First delivery day......... For all Comex commodities is the first business day of the delivery month
Last trading day.......... Copper }
                           Gold   } Fourth last business day of the delivery month
                           Silver }
Last notice day........... For all Comex commodities is the third last business day of the delivery month
Last delivery day......... For all Comex commodities is the last business day of the delivery month

Dollar Value of		Usual Maximum Daily Permissible Price Limits above or below Previous Close		Usual Maximum Permissible Range between Session's High and Low		CFTC* Reportable Position Contracts	Position Limits Contracts	Seasonal	
Min Tick	1¢ Move	Cents	$	Cents	$			High	Low
3.75	375	3¢/lb†	1,125	6¢/lb†	2,250	25	No limit	Winter	Spring
11.20	1,120	1¢/lb‡	1,120	2¢/lb‡	2,240	25	No limit	KZ	HU
11.20	1,120	1¢/lb‡	1,120	2¢/lb‡	2,240	25	No limit	KZ	HU

Last notice day...................... Sugar 11, 12 ⎫ First business day after the last trading day of the
                                      Coffee (c)   ⎬ delivery month
Last delivery day.................... Sugar 11, 12 ⎭ Last business day of the delivery month
                                      Coffee (c)
  (1) Or the first business day thereafter.

Currently Inactive Futures Contracts

Coffee (B)........................ Brazilian   32,500 lbs.
Coffee (U)........................ Robusta   32,500 lbs.
Molasses.......................... 48% sugar   40,000 gals.
Sugar #7.......................... Domestic   112,000 lbs.
Sugar #8.......................... World   112,000 lbs.
Sugar #10......................... Domestic   112,000 lbs.

Dollar Value of		Usual Maximum Daily Permissible Price Limits above or below Previous Close		Usual Maximum Permissible Range between Session's High and Low		CFTC* Reportable Position Contracts	Position Limits Contracts	Seasonal	
Min Tick	1¢ Move	Cents	$	Cents	$			High	Low
12.50	250	3¢/lb†	750	6¢/lb†	1,500	50	2,000‡	UV	FG
10.00	1	1,000¢/oz	1,000	2,000¢/oz	2,000	50	2,000‡	QX	FG
5.00	50	20¢/oz†	1,000	40¢/oz†	2,000	100	2,000‡	QX	FG

Currently Inactive Comex Futures Contracts

Hides....................... 40,000 lbs.
Lead........................ 60,000 lbs.
Mercury..................... 760 lbs.
Propane..................... 100,000 gals.
Rubber...................... 22,040 lbs.
Tin......................... 11,200 lbs.
Zinc........................ 60,000 lbs.

NEW YORK COTTON EXCHANGE (NYCE) AND THE CITRUS, PETROLEUM AND WOOL ASSOCIATES

4 WORLD TRADE CENTER
NEW YORK, NEW YORK 10100

Commodity	Exchange Trading Hours (CDT)	Ultronic Symbol	Delivery Months*	Usual Par Contract Grade(s)	Contract Size	Prices Quoted In	Minimum Fluctuation
Cotton #2	9:30–2:00	C₁CT*	VZHKN	U.S. middling 1¹₁₆″ white	50,000 lbs. (100 bales)	$¢/lb	1 ¢/lb / 100
Citrus Associates							
Frozen concentrated orange juice	9:15–1:45	C₁OJ*	FHKNUX	USDA Grade A Brix—51° 3% solids	15,000 lbs. 44 (55 gallon drums)	$¢/lb	5 ¢/lb / 100
Wool Associates							
Wool	9:00–1:30	C₁NW*	HKNVZ	64's 2¾″	6,000 lbs. (clean weight)	$¢/lb	1 ¢/lb / 10
Petroleum Associates							
Crude oil	8:50–1:20	C₁LO*	HMUZ	API 34° gravity 1.7% sulfur	5,000 barrels (42 U.S. gals/bbl.) 210,000 gals.	$¢/bbl.	1 ¢/bbl / 10
Liquified propane gas	8:45–1:35	C₁GP*	FKNUZ	NGPA-HD-5	100,000 gallons (pipe line bulk)	$¢/gal.	1 ¢/gal / 100

* Commodity Futures Trading Commission.
† Limit is removed from the delivery month on the first notice day.
‡ Limit is removed from the delivery month on the eighth day of delivery month.
§ Limit is removed from the delivery month on the last trading day.

First notice day	Crude oil	Ten business days prior to the first business day of the delivery month
	Cotton #2	
	Propane	Five business days before first day of delivery month(A)
	Wool	
	Orange juice	11th last business day after the last trading day of the delivery month
First delivery day ...	Crude oil	
	Cotton #2	First business day of the delivery month
	Propane	
	Wool	
	Orange juice	Fourth last business day of the delivery month
Last trading day	Crude oil	Last business day prior to first business day of the delivery month
	Cotton #2	17th last business day of the delivery month
	Wool	11th last business day of the delivery month
	Propane	15th calendar day of the delivery month(B)
	Orange juice	10th last business day of the delivery month

Dollar Value of		Usual Maximum Daily Permissible Price Limits above or below Previous Close		Usual Maximum Permissible Range between Session's High and Low		CFTC* Reportable Position Contracts	Position Limits Contracts	Seasonal	
Min Tick	1¢ Move	Cents	$	Cents	$			High	Low
5.00	500	2¢/lb†	1,000	4¢/lb†	2,000	50	300	NOZ	V
7.50	150	3¢/lb‡	450	3¢/lb‡	900	25	4,000	U	Z
6.00	50	10¢/lb‡	600	10¢/lb‡	600	25	4,000	Z	KM
5.00	50	25¢/bbl.	1,250	50¢/bbl	2,500	25	8,000		
10.00	1,000	1¢/gal§	1,000	2¢/gal§	2,000	25	4,000		

Last notice day..... Crude oil — Ten business days prior to the first business day of the delivery month

Cotton #2(A) — 12th last business day of the delivery month

Orange juice(A)
Propane(A)
Wool } Sixth last business day of the delivery month

Last delivery day... Crude oil — First business day of the delivery month

Cotton #2 — Seventh last business day of the delivery month

Orange juice
Propane
Wool } Last business day of the delivery month

(A) At least five business days prior to the delivery day.
(B) Or the first full business day prior thereto.

Currently Inactive NYCE Futures Contracts

Cotton #1......................... 15/16″ White   50,000 lbs

Tomato Paste Associates

Tomato Paste..................... Grade A 31–32% Solids   26,500 lbs

Wool Associates

Wool Crossbred....................   6,000 lbs
Wool Tops........................   5,000 lbs

Business and Economic Data

NEW YORK MERCANTILE EXCHANGE (NYME)

4 World Trade Center
New York, New York 10048

Commodity	Exchange Trading Hours (CDT)	Ultronic Symbol	Delivery Months*	Usual Par Contract Grade(s)	Contract Size	Prices Quoted In	Minimum Fluctuation
Potatoes (round white Maine)........	9:00– 12:30	C₁PO*	FHJKX	USDA No. 1 size A 2″ dia. min 4″ dia. max	50,000 lbs (1,000–50 lb sacks)	$¢/cwt	1¢/cwt
Platinum........	8:45– 12:30	C₁PT*	FJNV	99.8% pure sheet or bar	50 troy oz. (1 sheet or bar)	$¢/oz	10¢/oz
Gold...........	8:25– 1:30	C₁GL*	FHKNUZ	0.995 fine	32.151 troy oz. 1 kilo bar	$¢/oz	20¢/oz
Silver coins......	8:50– 1:20	C₁SR*	FJNV	Dimes, quarters, halves pre-1965 U.S.	$10,000 (10 bags)	$¢/bag	$1/bag
Palladium.......	9:20– 11:50	C₁PL*	HKMXUXZ	99.8% pure	100 troy oz. (4 sheets or ingots)	$¢/oz	5¢/oz
Imported frozen boneless beef.	9:15– 12:45	C₁IB*	All	Australia, Mexico Canada, Ireland, New Zealand full cow carcass less briskets and plates	36,000 lbs. 600 (60 lb boxes)	$¢/lb	$\frac{2}{100}$¢/lb
Foreign currency Belgium francs	9:20– 1:05	C₁NB*	HMUZ	3.5% max. Sulfur 3500 sec. max.	2,000,000 BF	$/BF	0.0005$/BF

* Commodity Futures Trading Commission.
† Limit is removed from delivery month on the last trading day
‡ $5.00 and $10.00 per ounce during the delivery month
§ $2.00 and $4.00 per lb. during the delivery month

First notice day........	Gold Potatoes (Maine)	First business day of the delivery month
	Boneless beef Palladium Platinum Silver coins	First business day after the last trading day of the delivery month
	Belgium francs	Last trading day of the delivery month
First delivery day.......	Gold Potatoes (Maine)	First business day of the delivery month
	Boneless beef Palladium Platinum Potatoes (Maine) Silver coins	First business day after the last trading day of the delivery month
	Belgium francs	Last trading day of the delivery month
Last trading day........	Potatoes (Maine)	Last business day prior to the first business day of the delivery month
	Palladium Platinum Silver coins	14th calendar day of the delivery month(A)
	Boneless beef	15th calendar day of the delivery month(A)
	Belgium francs	Second business day prior to the third Wednesday of the delivery month
	Gold	Third last business day of the delivery month
Last notice day........	Potatoes (Maine)	16th calendar day of the delivery month(A)
	Boneless beef Gold Silver coins	Third last business day of the delivery month
	Palladium Platinum	Last business day of the delivery month

Dollar Value of		Usual Maximum Daily Permissible Price Limits above or below Previous Close		Usual Maximum Permissible Range between Session's High and Low		Reportable Position Contracts	Position Limits Contracts	Seasonal	
Min Tick	1¢ Move	Cents	$	Cents	$			High	Low
5.00	5	50¢/ cwt†	250	100¢/ cwt†	500	25	350	K	U
5.00	0.50	1,000¢/ oz†	500	2,000¢/ oz†	1,000	25	None	Q	FG
6.43	0.32	1,000¢/ oz†	322	2,000¢/ oz†	644	50	None	Q	FG
10.00	0.10	15,000¢/ bag†	1,500	30,000¢/ bag†	3,000	50	None		
5.00	1	400¢/ oz†‡	400	800¢/ bag†‡	800	25	None	Q	FG
7.20	360	1.5¢/ lb†§	540	3¢/ lb†§	1,080	25	None		
10.00	20,000	0.0375 $/BF	750	0.075$ $/BF	1,500	25	None		

Last delivery day.......
  Belgium francs   Last trading day of the delivery month
  Potatoes (Maine) 20th calendar day of the delivery month(A)
  Boneless beef
  Gold
  Palladium
  Platinum   }Last business day of the delivery month
  Silver coins
  Belgium francs   Last trading day of the delivery month

(A) Or the first full business day prior thereto.

Currently Inactive NYME Futures Contracts

Aluminum	99.5% Pure	50,000 lbs
Apples	Red Delicious	840 cartons
Butter	Salted	30,000 lbs
Eggs, shell	Large	22,500 doz
Eggs, shell	Medium	6,000 doz
Heating oil	2.5% max sulfur	100 metric tons
Industrial fuel oil	3.5% max sulfur	100 metric tons
Nickel	Electrolytic 99.5%	2,000 lbs
Plywood	½" C.D.–4–5 Ply 4 x 8's	70,000 sq. ft.
Potatoes	Idaho russets	50,000 lbs
Potatoes	Long Island	45,000 lbs
Rice L	U.S. #5 long grain	100,000 lbs
Rice M	U.S. #5 medium grain	100,000 lbs

Foreign Currencies

British pound	25,000 BP
Canadian dollar	100,000 CD
Deutsche Mark	250,000 DM
Dutch guilder	125,000 DG
Italian lira	26,000,000 IL
Japanese yen	12,500,000 JY
Mexican peso	1,000,000 MP
Swiss franc	2,000,000 SW

MONTHLY AVERAGE SPOT PRICE CHARTS OF SELECTED COMMODITIES

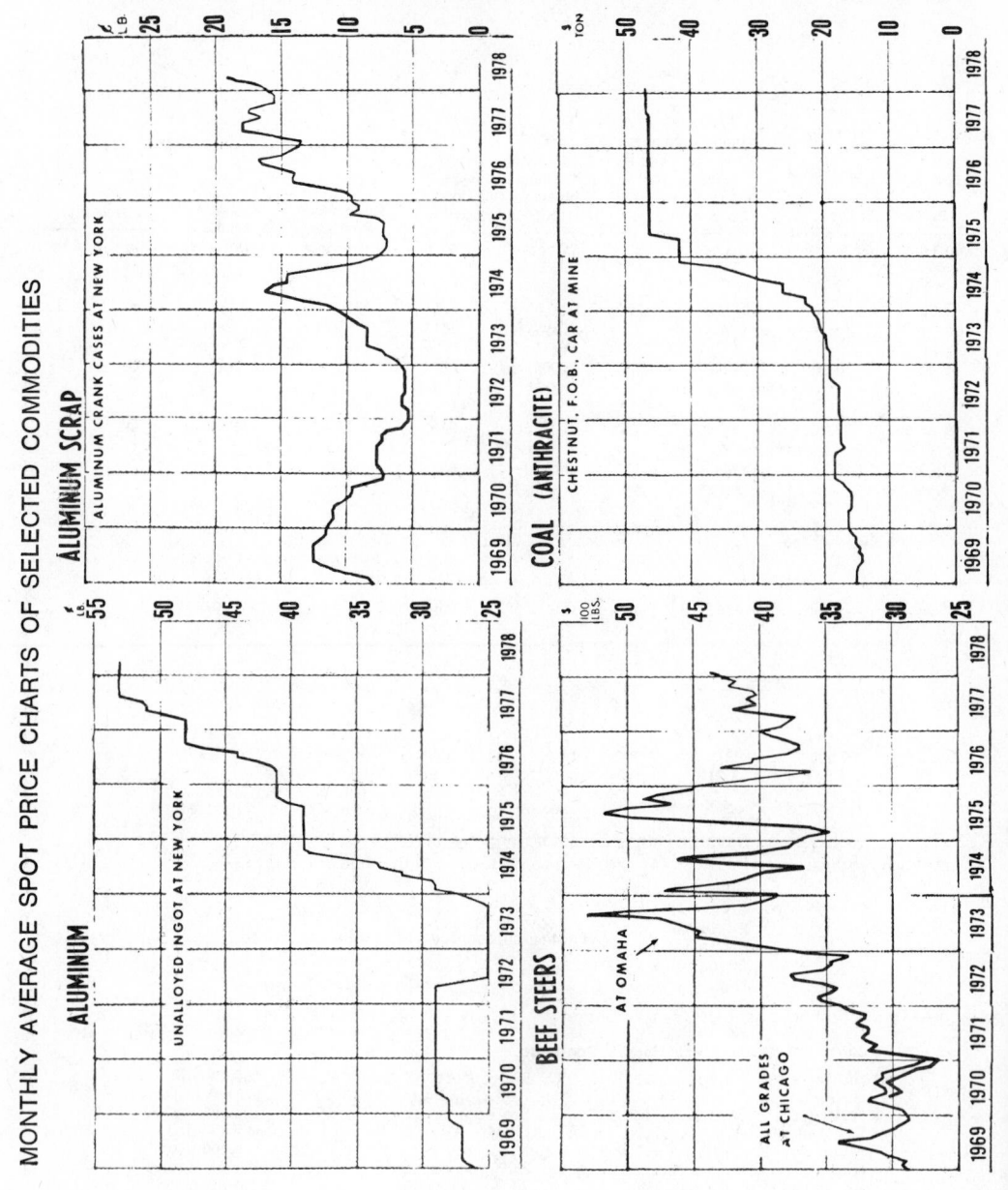

ALUMINUM SCRAP

ALUMINUM CRANK CASES AT NEW YORK

COAL (ANTHRACITE)

CHESTNUT, F.O.B., CAR AT MINE

ALUMINUM

UNALLOYED INGOT AT NEW YORK

BEEF STEERS

AT OMAHA

ALL GRADES
AT CHICAGO

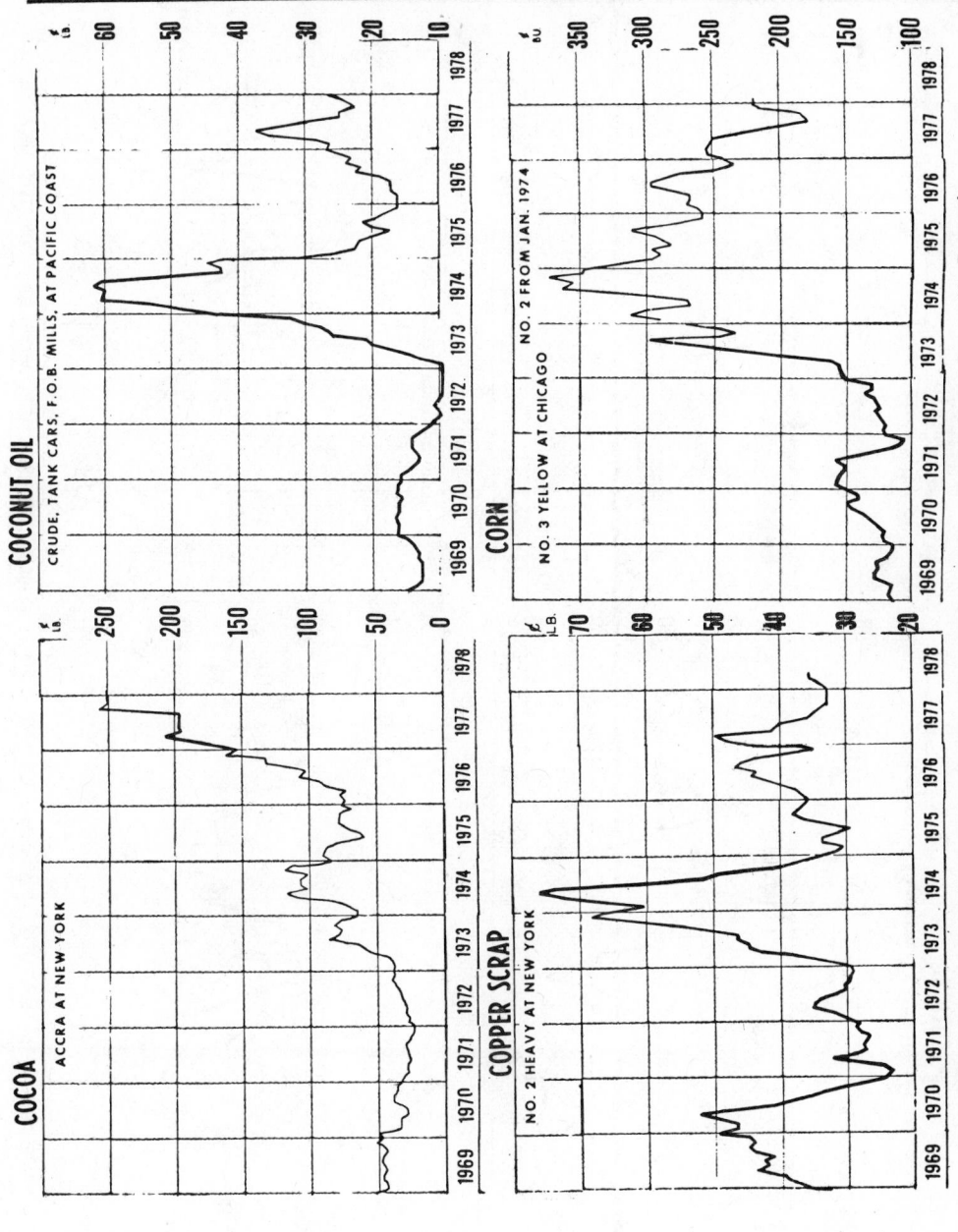

COCONUT OIL

CRUDE, TANK CARS, F.O.B. MILLS, AT PACIFIC COAST

CORN

NO. 3 YELLOW AT CHICAGO   NO. 2 FROM JAN. 1974

COCOA

ACCRA AT NEW YORK

COPPER SCRAP

NO. 2 HEAVY AT NEW YORK

Source: Reprinted from Commodity Year Book Statistical Abstract Service, a publication of Commodity Research Bureau, Inc., New York.

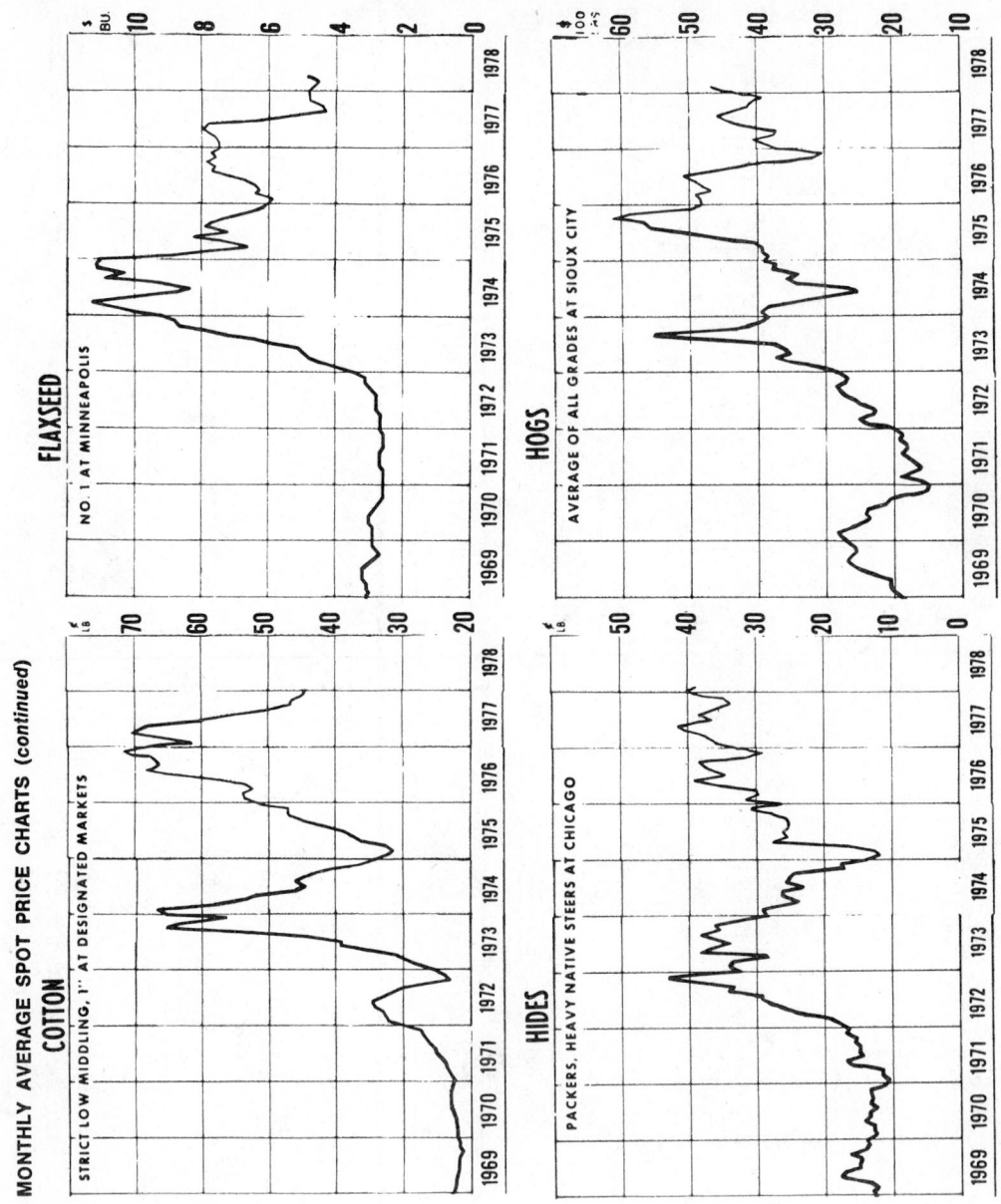

MONTHLY AVERAGE SPOT PRICE CHARTS *(continued)*

FLAXSEED
NO. 1 AT MINNEAPOLIS

COTTON
STRICT LOW MIDDLING, 1" AT DESIGNATED MARKETS

HOGS
AVERAGE OF ALL GRADES AT SIOUX CITY

HIDES
PACKERS, HEAVY NATIVE STEERS AT CHICAGO

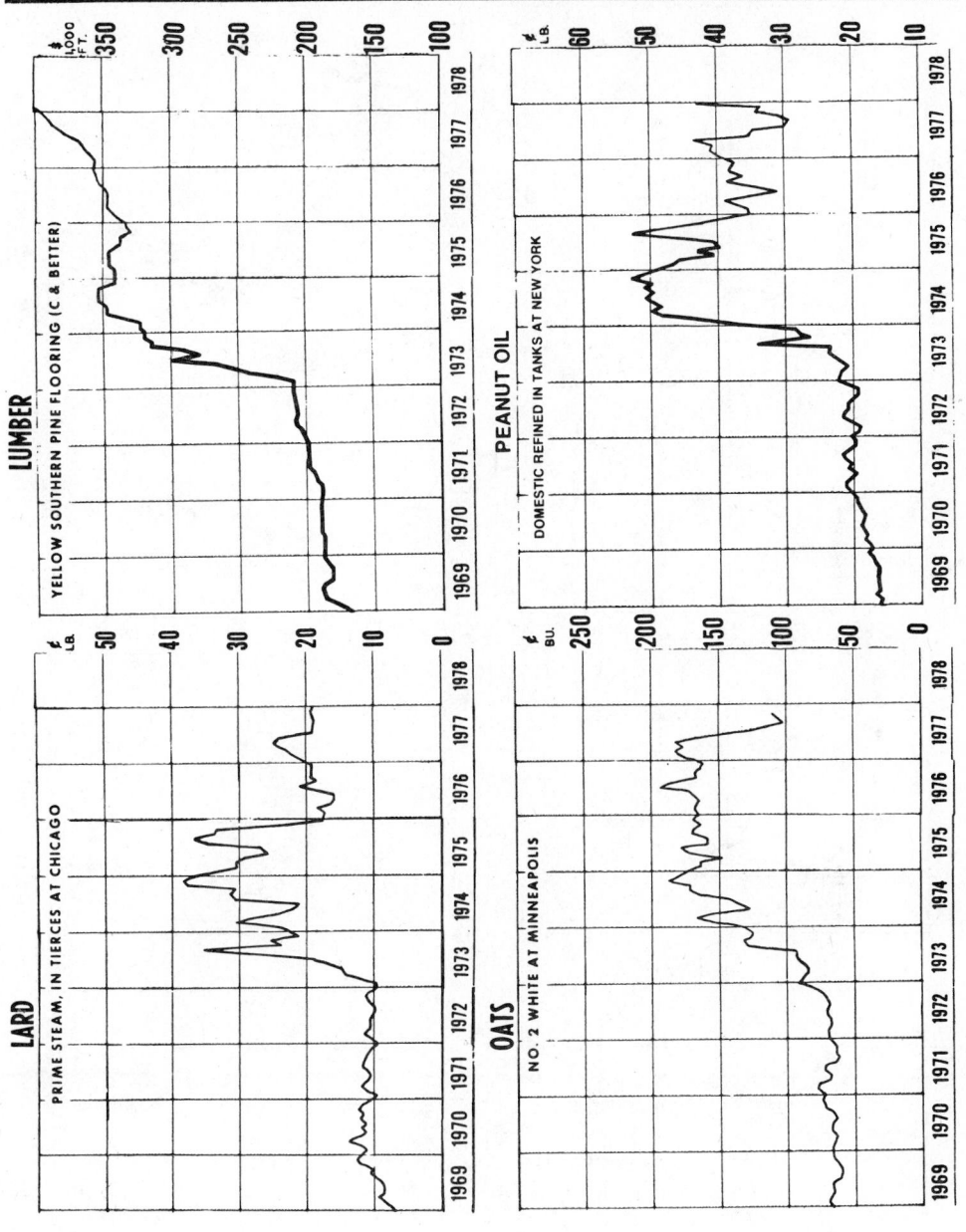

LUMBER
YELLOW SOUTHERN PINE FLOORING (C & BETTER)

LARD
PRIME STEAM, IN TIERCES AT CHICAGO

PEANUT OIL
DOMESTIC REFINED IN TANKS AT NEW YORK

OATS
NO. 2 WHITE AT MINNEAPOLIS

MONTHLY AVERAGE SPOT PRICE CHARTS (concluded)

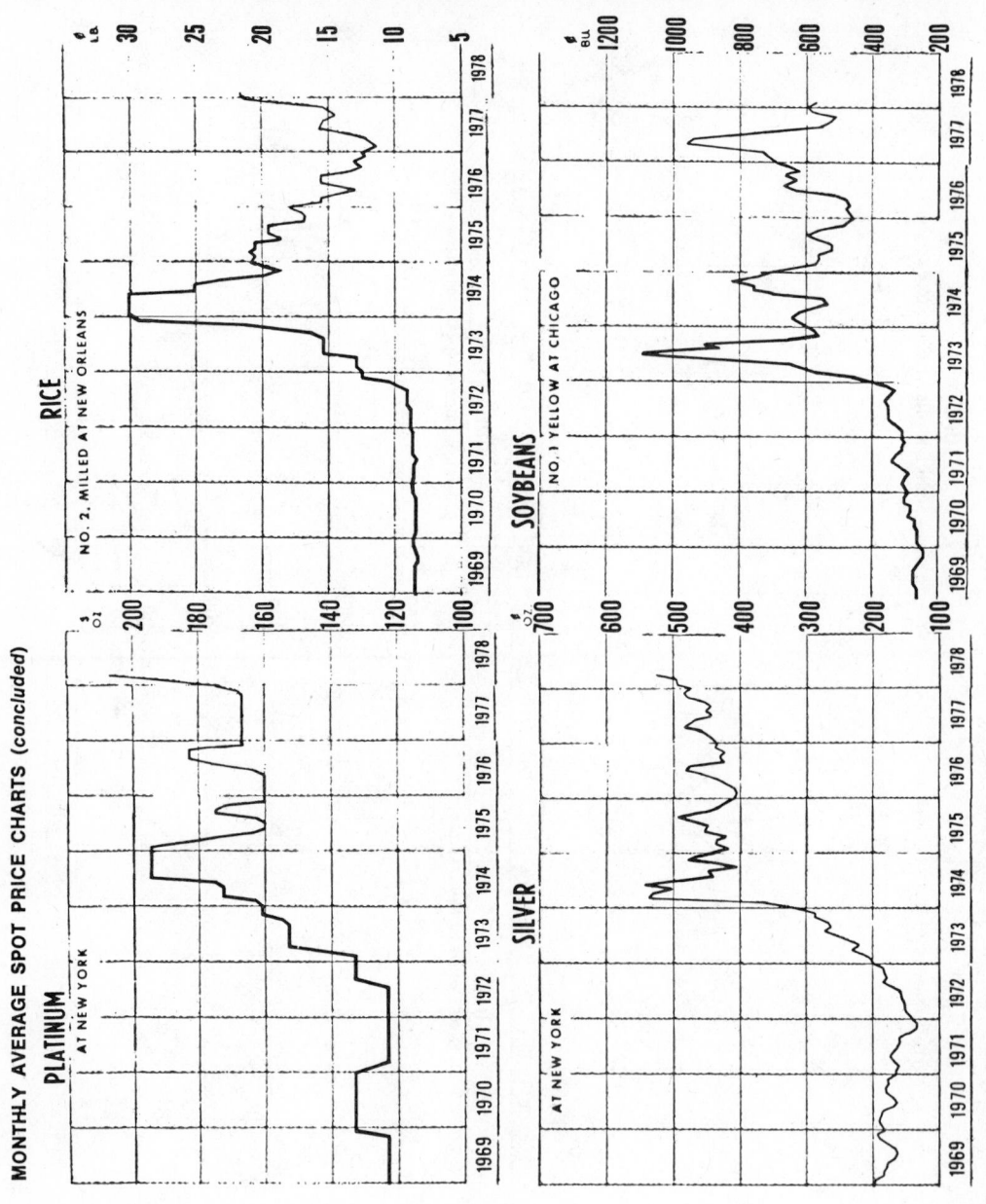

RICE — NO. 2, MILLED AT NEW ORLEANS

PLATINUM — AT NEW YORK

SOYBEANS — NO. 1 YELLOW AT CHICAGO

SILVER — AT NEW YORK

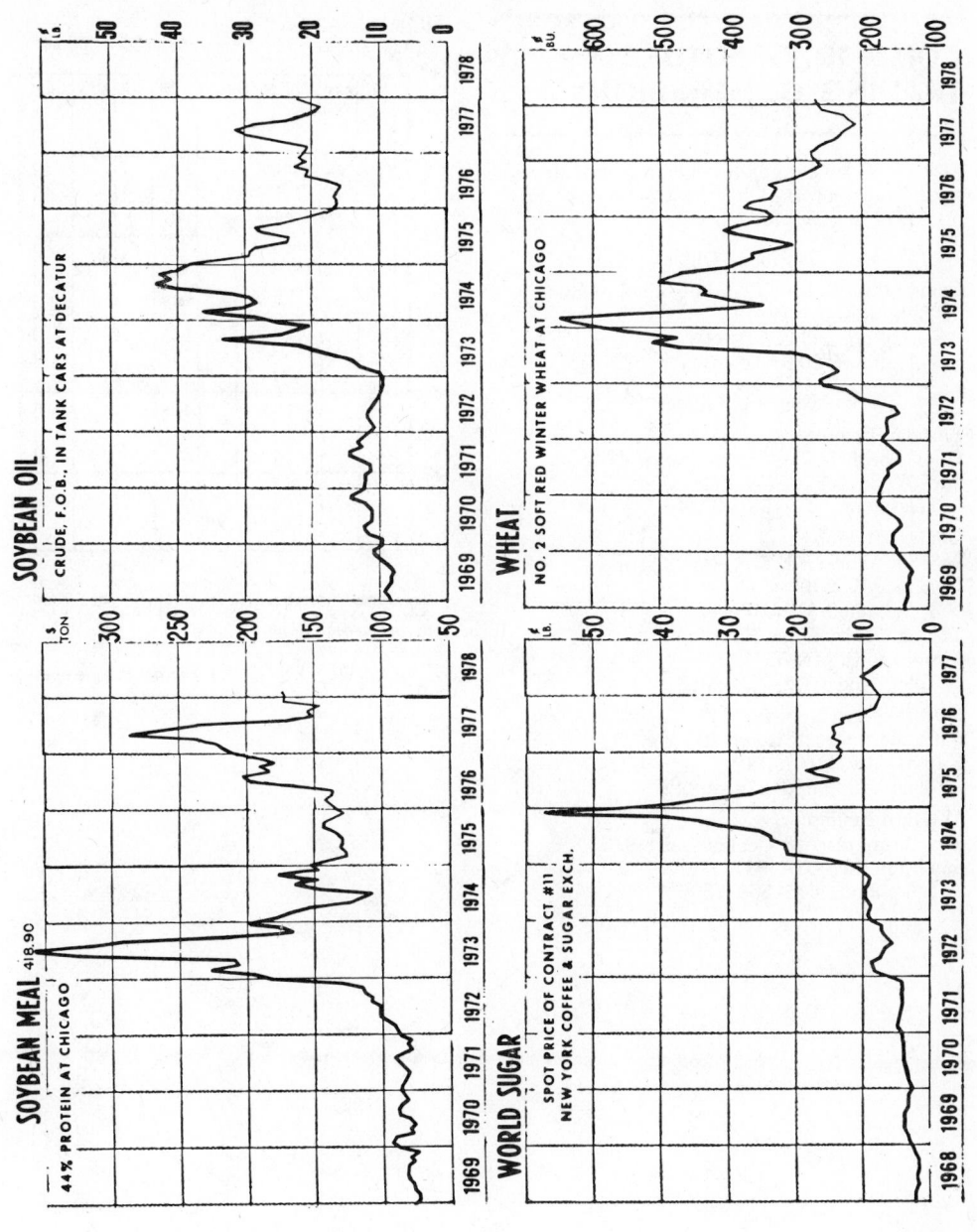

SOYBEAN OIL
CRUDE, F.O.B., IN TANK CARS AT DECATUR

WHEAT
NO. 2 SOFT RED WINTER WHEAT AT CHICAGO

SOYBEAN MEAL 418.90
44% PROTEIN AT CHICAGO

WORLD SUGAR
SPOT PRICE OF CONTRACT #11,
NEW YORK COFFEE & SUGAR EXCH.

COMMODITY FUTURES TRADING COMMISSION

Federal laws regulating commodity futures trading are enforced by the Commodity Futures Trading Commission.

National Office

Commodity Futures Trading Commission
2033 K Street, NW
Washington, DC 20581
   Telephone: 202–254–8631

Regional Offices

Eastern Region
One World Trade Center, Suite 4747
New York, NY 10048
   Telephone: 212–791–0784

Central Region
233 So. Wacker Drive, 46th Floor
Chicago, IL 60606
   Telephone: 312–353–5990
510 Grain Exchange Building
Minneapolis, MN 55415
   Telephone: 612–725–2025

Southwestern Region
4901 Main Street, Room 208
Kansas City, MO 64112
   Telephone: 816–374–2994

Western Region
Two Embarcadero Center, Suite 975
San Francisco, CA 94111
   Telephone: 415–556–7503

DOW JONES COMMODITY INDEXES

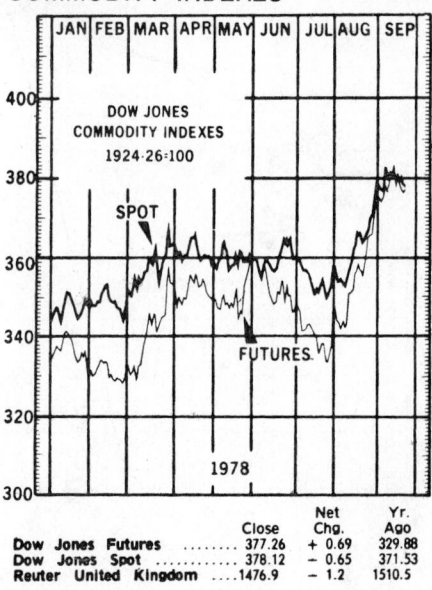

	Close	Net Chg.	Yr. Ago
Dow Jones Futures	377.26	+ 0.69	329.88
Dow Jones Spot	378.12	– 0.65	371.53
Reuter United Kingdom	1476.9	– 1.2	1510.5

Source: *The Wall Street Journal*, September 26, 1978.

FAIR PLAN
PLACEMENT FACILITIES

The FAIR plan (Fair Access to Insurance Requirements), operated by the insurance industry, re-insured by HUD, and regulated by the insurance department of your state, makes fire, extended coverage, and vandalism and mischief insurance available for eligible urban properties. Anyone who has property in an urban area and is having difficulty obtaining basic property insurance may apply by contacting a local insurance agent or the nearest FAIR plan facility listed. If the property does not qualify, you may be eligible for insurance at an increased rate until repairs are made, or you may qualify for financial assistance in bringing the property up to insurance standards.

California California FAIR Plan Association, 1930 Wilshire Boulevard, 6th Floor S/E Corner Wilshire & Westlake, Los Angeles, CA 90057; 213-484-1731

Connecticut Connecticut Insurance Placement Facility, 111 Founders Plaza, East Hartford, CT 06108; 203-528-9801

Delaware Insurance Placement Facility of Delaware, Public Ledger Building, Sixth and Chestnut Streets, Philadelphia, PA 19106; 215-627-6800

District of Columbia District of Columbia Property Insurance Facility, 1750 Pennsylvania Avenue NW, Washington, DC 20006; 202-393-4640

Georgia Georgia Underwriting Association, 1577 Northeast Freeway NE, P.O. Box 29851, Atlanta, GA 30329; 404-455-6310

Illinois Illinois FAIR Plan Association, 175 W. Jackson Boulevard, Room 2131, Chicago, IL 60604; 312-427-9614

Indiana Indiana Basic Property Insurance Underwriting Association, 701 Board of Trade Building, 143 N. Meridian Street, Indianapolis, IN 46204; 317-632-4533

Iowa Industry Placement Facility, Iowa FAIR Plan, 317 Insurance Exchange Building, 528 Fifth Avenue, Des Moines, IA 50309; 515-243-0109

Kansas Kansas All-Industry Placement Facility, 625 Polk Street, Topeka, KS 66603; 913-234-3405

Kentucky Kentucky Property Insurance Placement Facility, 312 Whitington Parkway, P.O. Box 7980, Louisville, KY 40207; 502-423-0220

Louisiana Louisiana Joint Reinsurance Association, P.O. Box 60730, New Orleans, LA 70160; 504-525-2391

Maryland Joint Insurance Association, Arlington Federal Building, 201 N. Charles Street, Baltimore, MD 21201; 301-539-6808

Massachusetts Massachusetts Property Insurance Underwriting Association, 3 Center Plaza, Boston, MA 02108; 617-723-3800

Michigan Michigan Basic Property Insurance Association, 300 Buhl Building, P.O. Box 86, Detroit, MI 48231; 313-965-3382

Minnesota Minnesota Property Insurance Placement Facility, 12 S. Sixth Street, Room 1229, Minneapolis, MN 55402; 612-338-7584

Missouri Missouri Property Insurance Placement Facility, 1400 Pierce Building, St. Louis, MO 63102; 314-621-7280

New Jersey New Jersey Insurance Underwriting Association, 744 Broad Street, Newark, NJ 07102; 201-622-3838

New Mexico New Mexico Property Insurance Program, Box 8351, Station C, Albuquerque, NM 87108; 505-265-7918

New York New York Property Insurance Underwriting Association, 110 William Street, New York, NY 10038; 212-233-7000

North Carolina North Carolina Insurance Underwriting Association, P.O. Box 1267, 226 S. Dawson Street, Raleigh, NC 27602; 919-834-4313

Ohio Ohio FAIR Plan Underwriting Association, 6230 Busch Boulevard, Columbus, OH 43265; 614-436-4530

Oregon Oregon FAIR Plan Underwriting Association, 8285 S.W. Nimbus Avenue, Beaverton, OR 97005; 503-643-5448

Pennsylvania Insurance Placement Facility of Pennsylvania, Public Ledger Building, Sixth and Chestnut Streets, Philadelphia, PA 19106; 215-627-6800

Puerto Rico Puerto Rico Fire & Allied Lines Underwriting Association, P.O. Box 1333, 420 Ochoa Building, San Juan, PR 00902; 723-1830

Rhode Island Rhode Island Joint Reinsurance Association, 198 Dyer Street, Providence, RI 02903; 401-331-9240

Virginia Virginia Property Insurance Association, Koger Executive Center, 1602 Rolling Hills Drive, Richmond, VA 23288; 703-288-7973

Washington Washington FAIR Plan, 809 Alaska Building, Seattle, WA 98104; 206-MA3-8121

Wisconsin Wisconsin Insurance Plan, 615 E. Michigan Street, Milwaukee, WI 53202; 414-276-3462

Money and Financial Institutions

INTEREST RATES AND BOND YIELDS

PERCENT PER ANNUM

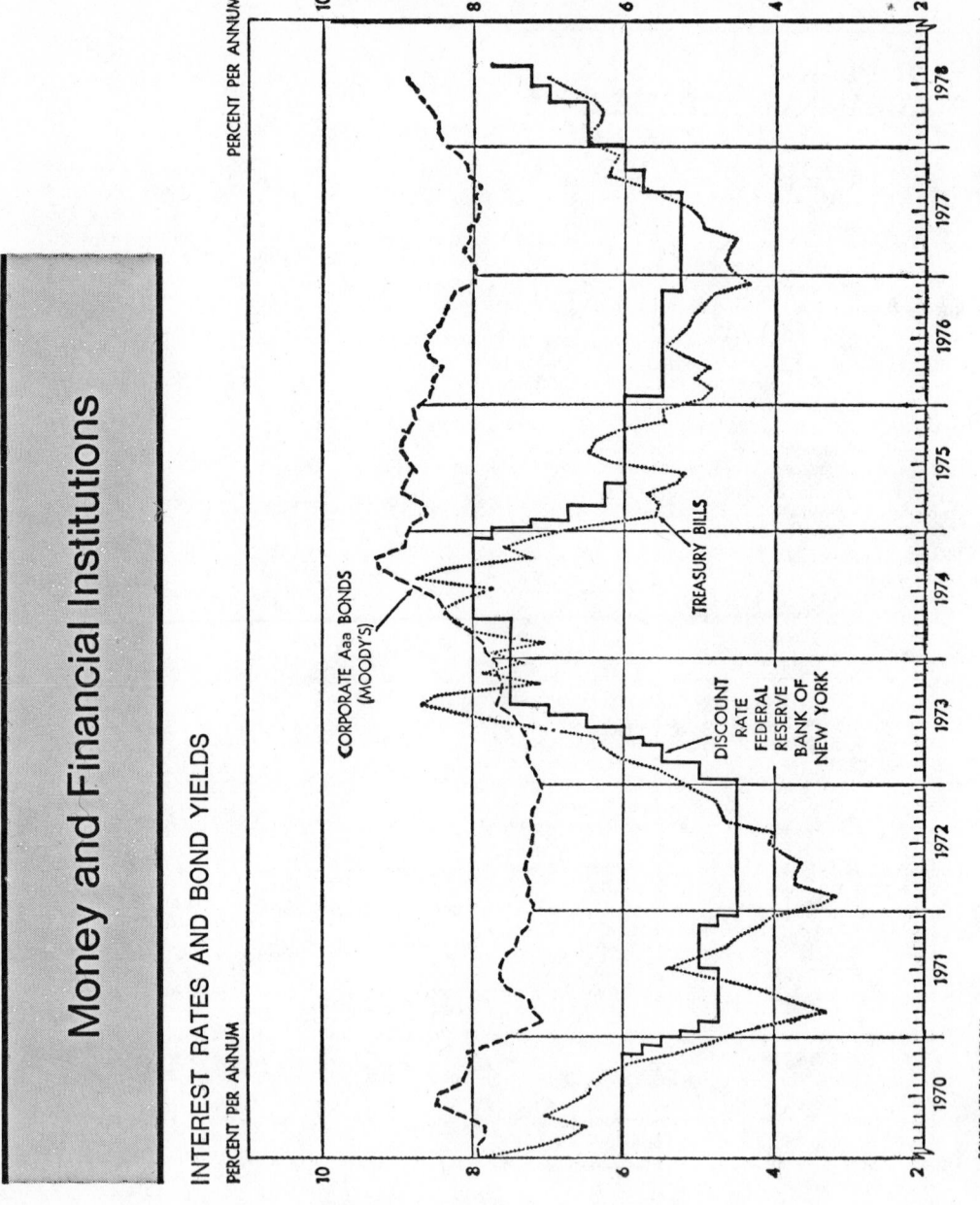

COUNCIL OF ECONOMIC ADVISERS

SOURCE: SEE TABLE BELOW

[Percent per annum]

Period	U.S. Treasury security yields			High-grade municipal bonds (Standard & Poor's)[3]	Corporate Aaa bonds (Moody's)	Prime commercial paper, 4–6 months	Discount rate (N.Y. F.R. Bank)[4]	Prime rate charged by banks[4]	New-home mortgage yields (FHLBB)[5]
	3-month bills[1]	Constant maturities[2] 3-year	Constant maturities[2] 10-year						
1972	4.071	5.72	6.21	5.27	7.21	4.69	4.50	5.25	7.60
1973	7.041	6.95	6.84	5.18	7.44	8.15	6.45	8.03	7.95
1974	7.886	7.82	7.56	6.09	8.57	9.87	7.83	10.81	8.92
1975	5.838	7.49	7.99	6.89	8.83	6.33	6.25	7.86	9.01
1976	4.989	6.77	7.61	6.49	8.43	5.35	5.50	6.84	8.99
1977	5.265	6.69	7.42	5.56	8.02	5.60	5.46	6.83	9.01
1977: July	5.146	6.51	7.33	5.50	7.94	5.41	5¼–5¼	6¾–6¾	9.00
Aug	5.500	6.79	7.40	5.46	7.98	5.84	5¼–5¾	6¾–7	9.02
Sept	5.770	6.84	7.34	5.37	7.92	6.17	5¾–5¾	7 –7¼	9.04
Oct	6.188	7.19	7.52	5.53	8.04	6.55	5¾–6	7¼–7¾	9.07
Nov	6.160	7.22	7.58	5.38	8.08	6.59	6–6	7¾–7¾	9.07
Dec	6.063	7.30	7.69	5.48	8.19	6.64	6–6	7¾–7¾	9.09
1978: Jan	6.448	7.61	7.96	5.60	8.41	6.79	6–6½	7¾–8	9.15
Feb	6.457	7.67	8.03	5.51	8.47	6.80	6½–6½	8–8	9.18
Mar	6.319	7.70	8.04	5.49	8.47	6.80	6½–6½	8–8	9.26
Apr	6.306	7.85	8.15	5.71	8.56	6.86	6½–6½	8–8	9.30
May	6.430	8.07	8.35	5.97	8.69	7.11	6½–7	8–8½	9.37
June	6.707	8.30	8.46	6.13	8.76	7.63	7–7	8½–9	9.46
July	7.074	8.54	8.64	6.18	8.88	7.91	7–7	9–9	9.57
Week ended:									
1978: July 28	6.935	8.55	8.63	6.12	8.88	7.92	7¼–7¼	9–9	----------
Aug 4	6.895	8.36	8.46	6.00	8.76	7.86	7¼–7¼	9–9	----------
11	6.808	8.21	8.39	5.90	8.66	7.84	7¼–7¼	9–9	----------
18	6.887	8.37	8.48	6.02	8.70	7.86	7¼–7¼	9–9	----------
25	7.267	8.35	8.37	5.96	8.69	7.95	7¼–7¾	9–9	----------

[1] Rate on new issues within period.
[2] Yields on the more actively traded issues adjusted to constant maturities by the Treasury Department.
[3] Weekly data are Wednesday figures.
[4] Average effective rate for year; opening and closing rate for month and week.
[5] Effective rate (in the primary market) on conventional mortgages, reflecting fees and charges as well as contract rate and assumed, on the average, repayment at end of 10 years. Rates beginning January 1973 not strictly comparable with prior rates.

Sources: Department of the Treasury, Board of Governors of the Federal Reserve System, Federal Home Loan Bank Board, Moody's Investors Service, and Standard & Poor's Corporation.

Source: *Economic Indicators*, Council of Economic Advisors.

INTEREST RATES: MONEY AND CAPITAL MARKETS
AVERAGES, PERCENT PER ANNUM

Instrument	1975	1976	1977	1978 Apr.	May	June	July	1978, week ending— July 1	July 8	July 15	July 22	July 29
Money market rates												
1 Federal funds [1]	5.82	5.05	5.54	6.89	7.36	7.60	7.81	7.78	7.72	7.72	7.94	7.88
Prime commercial paper [2]												
2 90- to 119-day	6.26	5.24	5.54	6.82	7.06	7.59	7.85	7.76	7.82	7.85	7.88	7.86
3 4- to 6-month	6.33	5.35	5.60	6.86	7.11	7.63	7.91	7.80	7.88	7.91	7.93	7.92
4 Finance company paper, directly placed, 3- to 6-month [3]	6.16	5.22	5.49	6.74	6.98	7.41	7.66	7.58	7.63	7.66	7.67	7.67
5 Prime bankers acceptances, 90-day [4]	6.30	5.19	5.59	6.92	7.32	7.75	8.02	7.94	8.01	8.06	8.05	7.97
Large negotiable certificates of deposit												
6 3-month, secondary market [5]	6.43	5.26	5.58	7.04	7.42	7.82	8.00	8.04	8.07	8.11	8.16	8.17
7 3-month, primary market [6]		5.15	5.52	6.85	7.24	7.68	8.00	8.00	8.00	8.00	8.00	8.00
8 Euro-dollar deposits, 3-month [7]	6.97	5.57	6.05	7.38	7.82	8.33	8.52	8.65	8.63	8.46	8.58	8.50
U.S. Government securities												
Bills: [8]												
Market yields:												
9 3-month	5.80	4.98	5.27	6.29	6.41	6.73	7.01	6.93	7.05	7.16	7.05	6.83
10 6-month	6.11	5.26	5.53	6.73	7.02	7.23	7.44	7.38	7.43	7.51	7.47	7.38
11 1-year	6.30	5.52	5.71	6.96	7.28	7.53	7.79	7.72	7.75	7.82	7.82	7.78
Rates on new issue: [9]												
12 3-month	5.838	4.989	5.265	6.306	6.430	6.707	7.074	6.967	7.058	7.188	7.113	6.935
13 6-month	6.122	5.266	5.510	6.700	7.019	7.200	7.471	7.396	7.447	7.515	7.497	7.425
14 Constant maturities: [10] 1-year	6.76	5.88	6.09	7.45	7.82	8.09	8.39	8.32	8.34	8.42	8.42	8.39
Capital market rates												
Government notes and bonds												
U.S. Treasury												
Constant maturities: [10]												
15 2-year	7.49		6.45	7.74	8.01	8.24	8.49	8.45	8.45	8.49	8.50	8.51
16 3-year	7.77	6.77	6.99	7.85	8.07	8.30	8.54	8.51	8.51	8.56	8.55	8.55
17 5-year	7.90	7.18	6.99	7.98	8.18	8.36	8.54	8.49	8.50	8.57	8.56	8.53
18 7-year	7.99	7.42	7.23	8.06	8.25	8.40	8.55	8.50	8.52	8.58	8.56	8.55
19 10-year	8.19	7.61	7.42	8.15	8.35	8.46	8.64	8.59	8.62	8.68	8.65	8.63
20 20-year		7.86	7.67	8.32	8.44	8.53	8.69	8.63	8.68	8.72	8.69	8.67
21 30-year				8.34	8.43	8.50	8.65	8.59	8.63	8.69	8.66	8.63

	Notes and bonds maturing in —[11]												
22	3 to 5 years	7.55	6.94	6.85	7.90	8.10	8.31	8.54	8.50	8.52	8.56	8.55	8.53
23	Over 10 years (long-term)	6.98	6.78	7.06	7.74	7.87	7.94	8.09	8.02	8.06	8.13	8.10	8.08
	State and local: Moody's series:[12]												
24	Aaa	6.42	5.66	5.20	5.41	5.57	5.73	5.80	5.85	5.85	5.85	5.75	5.74
25	Baa	7.62	7.49	6.12	5.88	6.14	6.44	6.45	6.50	6.50	6.52	6.40	6.38
26	Bond Buyer series [13]	7.05	6.64	5.68	5.80	6.03	6.22	6.28	6.29	6.31	6.32	6.26	6.24
	Corporate bonds												
27	Seasoned issues [14] All industries	9.57	9.01	8.43	8.88	9.02	9.13	9.22	9.16	9.18	9.21	9.24	9.23
	By rating groups:												
28	Aaa	8.83	8.43	8.02	8.56	8.69	8.76	8.88	8.82	8.85	8.90	8.89	8.88
29	Aa	9.17	8.75	8.24	8.73	8.84	8.95	9.07	9.00	9.01	9.06	9.08	9.10
30	A	9.65	9.09	8.49	8.93	9.05	9.18	9.33	9.22	9.26	9.31	9.37	9.36
31	Baa	10.61	9.75	8.97	9.32	9.49	9.60	9.60	9.58	9.60	9.59	9.59	9.61
	Aaa utility bonds:[15]												
32	New issue	9.40	8.48	8.19	8.90	8.95	9.09	9.14	9.16	9.18	9.17	9.12	9.08
33	Recently offered issues	9.41	8.49	8.19	8.85	8.98	9.07	9.18	9.18	9.20	9.22	9.19	9.10
	Dividend/price ratio												
34	Preferred stocks	8.38	7.97	7.60	8.06	8.11	8.31	8.42	8.38	8.39	8.48	8.38	8.42
35	Common stocks	4.31	3.77	4.56	5.42	5.20	5.19	5.25	5.32	5.38	5.28	5.18	5.14

[1] Weekly figures are 7-day averages of daily effective rates for the week ending Wednesday; the daily effective rate is an average of the rates on a given day weighted by the volume of transactions at these rates.
[2] Beginning Nov. 1977, unweighted average of offering rates quoted by five dealers. Previously, most representative rate quoted by those dealers.
[3] Averages of the most representative daily offering rates published by finance companies for varying maturities in this range.
[4] Average of the midpoint of the range of daily dealer closing rates offered for domestic issues; prior data are averages of the most representative daily offering rate quoted by dealers.
[5] Weekly figures (week ending Wednesday) are 7-day averages of the daily midpoints as determined from the range of offering rates; monthly figures are averages of total days in the month. Beginning Apr. 5, 1978, weekly figures are simple averages of offering rates.
[6] Posted rates, which are the annual interest rates most often quoted on new offerings of negotiable CD's in denominations of $100,000 or more by large New York City banks. Rates prior to 1976 not available. Weekly figures are for Wednesday dates.
[7] Averages of daily quotations for the week ending Wednesday.

[8] Except for new bill issues, yields are computed from daily closing bid prices. Yields for all bills are quoted on a bank-discount basis.
[9] Rates are recorded in the week in which bills are issued.
[10] Yields on the more actively traded issues adjusted to constant maturities by the U.S. Treasury, based on daily closing bid prices.
[11] Unweighted averages for all outstanding notes and bonds in maturity ranges shown, based on daily closing bid prices. "Long-term" includes all bonds neither due nor callable in less than 10 years, including a number of very low yielding "flower" bonds.
[12] General obligations only, based on figures for Thursday, from Moody's Investors Service.
[13] Twenty issues of mixed quality.
[14] Averages of daily figures from Moody's Investors Service.
[15] Compilation of the Board of Governors of the Federal Reserve System.

Issues included are long-term (20 years or more). New-issue yields are based on quotations on date of offering; those on recently offered issues (included only for first 4 weeks after termination of underwriter price restrictions), on Friday close-of-business quotations.

Source: *Federal Reserve Bulletin.*

MAXIMUM INTEREST RATES PAYABLE ON TIME AND SAVINGS DEPOSITS AT FEDERALLY INSURED INSTITUTIONS

PERCENT PER ANNUM

Type and maturity of deposit	Commercial banks				Savings and loan associations and mutual savings banks			
	In effect July 31, 1978		Previous maximum		In effect July 31, 1978		Previous maximum	
	Per cent	Effective date	Per cent	Effective date	Per cent	Effective date	Per cent	Effective date
1 Savings	5	7/1/73	4½	1/21/70	5¼	[7]	5	[8]
2 Negotiable orders of withdrawal (NOW) accounts[1]	5	1/1/74	[10]	....	5	1/1/74	[10]	....
3 Variable-rate time deposit of less than $100,000[2]	[9]	[9]	[9]	....	[9]	[9]	[9]	....
Other time (multiple- and single-maturity unless otherwise indicated)[3] 30-89 days:								
4 Multiple-maturity	5	7/1/73	4¼	1/21/70	[10]	....	[10]	....
5 Single-maturity	5	7/1/73	5	9/26/66	[10]	....	[10]	....
90 days to 1 year:								
6 Multiple-maturity	5½	7/1/73	5	7/20/66	4¾	[7]	5¼	1/21/70
7 Single-maturity	5½	7/1/73	5	9/26/66	4¾	[7]	5¼	1/21/70
8 1 to 2 years[4]	6	7/1/73	5½	1/21/70	6½	[7]	5¾	1/21/70
9 2 to 2½ years[4]	6½	7/1/73	5¾	1/21/70	6¾	[7]	6	1/21/70
10 2½ to 4 years[4]	6½	7/1/73	5¾	1/21/70	6¾	[7]	6	1/21/70
11 4 to 6 years[5]	7¼	11/1/73	[11]	....	7½	11/1/73	[11]	....
12 6 to 8 years[5]	7½	12/23/74	7¼	11/1/73	7¾	12/23/74	7½	11/1/73
13 8 years or more[5]	7¾	6/1/78	[10]	....	8	6/1/78	[10]	....
14 Governmental units (all maturities)	8	6/1/78	7¾	12/23/74	8	6/1/78	7¾	12/23/74
15 Individual retirement accounts and Keogh (H.R. 10) plans[6]	8	6/1/78	7¾	7/6/77	8	6/1/78	7¾	7/6/77

1 For authorized States only. Federally insured commercial banks, savings and loan associations, cooperative banks, and mutual savings banks were first permitted to offer NOW accounts on Jan. 1, 1974. Authorization to issue NOW accounts was extended to similar institutions throughout New England on Feb. 27, 1976.

2 Must have a maturity of exactly 26 weeks and a minimum denomination of $10,000, and must be nonnegotiable.

3 For exceptions with respect to certain foreign time deposits see the Federal Reserve BULLETIN for October 1962 (p. 1279), August 1965 (p. 1094), and February 1968 (p. 167).

4 A minimum of $1,000 is required for savings and loan associations, except in areas where mutual savings banks permit lower minimum denominations. This restriction was removed for deposits maturing in less than 1 year, effective Nov. 1, 1973.

5 $1,000 minimum except for deposits representing funds contributed to an Individual Retirement Account (IRA) or a Keogh (H.R. 10) Plan established pursuant to the Internal Revenue Code. The $1,000 minimum requirement was removed for such accounts in December 1975 and November 1976, respectively.

6 3-year minimum maturity.

7 July 1, 1973, for mutual savings banks; July 6, 1973, for savings and loan associations.

8 Oct. 1, 1966, for mutual savings banks; Jan. 21, 1970, for savings and loan associations.

9 Ceiling rate for commercial banks is the discount rate on most recently issued 6-month U.S. Treasury bills. Ceiling rate for savings and loan associations and mutual savings banks is ¼ per cent higher than the rate for commercial banks. The rates and effective dates for July were:

10 No separate account category.

11 Between July 1, 1973, and Oct. 31, 1973, there was no ceiling for certificates maturing in 4 years or more with minimum denominations of $1,000; however, the amount of such certificates that an institution could issue was limited to 5 per cent of its total time and savings deposits. Sales in excess of that amount, as well as certificates of less than $1,000, were limited to the 6½ per cent ceiling on time deposits maturing in 2½ years or more.

Effective Nov. 1, 1973, the present ceilings were imposed on certificates maturing in 4 years or more with minimum denominations of $1,000. There is no limitation on the amount of these certificates that banks can issue.

NOTE.—Maximum rates that can be paid by Federally insured commercial banks, mutual savings banks, and savings and loan associations are established by the Board of Governors of the Federal Reserve System, the Board of Directors of the Federal Deposit Insurance Corporation, and the Federal Home Loan Bank Board under the provisions of 12 CFR 217, 329, and 526, respectively. The maximum rates on time deposits in denominations of $100,000 or more were suspended in mid-1973. For information regarding previous interest rate ceilings on all types of accounts, see earlier issues of the Federal Reserve BULLETIN, the Federal Home Loan Bank Board Journal, and the Annual Report of the Federal Deposit Insurance Corporation.

Effective date	Rate	Effective date	Rate
1976—Nov. 1	6½	1977—Oct. 7	7½
Dec. 13	6¼	Oct. 24	7¾
1977—May 13	6½	1978—Jan. 10	8
31	6¾	May 5	8¼
1977—Aug. 22	7	May 26	8½
Sept. 16	7¼	June 16	8¾
		June 30	9

Source: *Federal Reserve Bulletin.*

PRIME RATE CHARGED BY BANKS ON SHORT-TERM BUSINESS LOANS

PERCENT PER ANNUM

Month	Average rate	Month	Average rate
1977—Jan.	6.25	1977—Nov.	7.75
Feb.	6.25	Dec.	7.75
Mar.	6.25	1978—Jan.	7.93
Apr.	6.41	Feb.	8.00
May	6.75	Mar.	8.00
June	6.75	Apr.	8.00
July	6.75	May	8.27
Aug.	6.83	June	8.63
Sept.	7.13	July	9.00
Oct.	7.52		

Source: *Federal Reserve Bulletin.*

INTEREST RATES CHARGED BY BANKS ON BUSINESS LOANS

PERCENT PER ANNUM

Center	All sizes 1976 Nov.	All sizes 1976 Aug.	1–9 1976 Nov.	1–9 1976 Aug.	10–99 1976 Nov.	10–99 1976 Aug.	100–499 1976 Nov.	100–499 1976 Aug.	500–999 1976 Nov.	500–999 1976 Aug.	1,000 and over 1976 Nov.	1,000 and over 1976 Aug.
Short-term rates												
1 All 35 centers	7.28	7.80	8.83	9.06	8.18	8.58	7.66	7.99	7.31	7.84	7.02	7.61
2 New York City	6.88	7.48	8.56	8.85	7.94	8.40	7.43	7.91	7.24	7.77	6.74	7.36
3 7 Other Northeast	7.62	8.18	9.22	9.41	8.34	8.84	7.88	8.25	7.49	8.16	7.34	7.98
4 8 North Central	7.28	7.70	8.45	8.65	8.12	8.50	7.69	7.85	7.36	7.71	7.03	7.55
5 7 Southeast	7.51	7.95	9.13	9.33	8.48	8.76	7.71	8.00	7.04	7.85	7.07	7.54
6 8 Southwest	7.33	7.75	8.51	8.83	7.82	8.24	7.39	7.80	7.21	7.61	7.12	7.55
7 4 West Coast	7.52	8.15	8.69	9.26	8.46	8.79	7.88	8.28	7.44	8.06	7.34	8.05
Revolving credit rates												
8 All 35 centers	7.19	7.87	8.37	8.70	8.14	8.33	7.60	8.02	7.41	7.80	7.12	7.88
9 New York City	7.18	8.14	7.23	7.25	7.86	8.26	7.21	7.70	6.97	7.56	7.19	8.19
10 7 Other Northeast	6.92	7.59	8.15	8.00	8.20	8.22	7.26	7.67	7.75	8.36	6.75	7.47
11 8 North Central	7.54	7.96	8.52	8.94	8.95	9.03	8.05	8.50	7.88	7.74	7.39	7.90
12 7 Southeast	7.05	7.48	8.31	8.75	8.09	8.40	7.56	8.16	6.77	....	6.83	7.13
13 8 Southwest	7.45	7.81	8.19	8.74	7.96	8.09	7.74	8.20	7.24	7.47	7.39	7.80
14 4 West Coast	7.11	7.73	8.77	9.10	7.85	8.08	7.58	7.95	7.45	7.91	7.01	7.68
Long-term rates												
15 All 35 centers	7.48	8.45	9.39	9.61	8.88	9.02	8.14	8.55	8.13	8.60	7.24	8.40
16 New York City	7.36	8.52	7.19	....	8.55	8.27	7.93	8.05	8.06	8.44	7.26	8.56
17 7 Other Northeast	6.64	8.62	9.22	9.40	8.84	9.43	7.95	8.93	8.99	7.50	5.73	8.70
18 8 North Central	7.66	8.05	9.20	8.83	9.03	9.07	8.35	8.26	6.77	8.36	7.32	7.92
19 7 Southeast	7.59	8.88	9.87	9.60	9.35	9.08	7.93	9.88	4.00	8.18	7.79	8.06
20 8 Southwest	7.73	8.42	10.54	10.85	9.05	9.04	8.28	8.23	8.44	8.69	7.20	8.30
21 4 West Coast	8.04	8.67	8.70	9.28	8.54	8.58	8.31	8.81	7.78	10.00	8.03	8.46

Size of loan (in thousands of dollars)

NOTE.—Weighted-average rates based on sample of loans made during first 7 days of the survey month.

Source: *Federal Reserve Bulletin.*

CREDIT RATINGS OF FIXED INCOME AND MONEY SECURITIES

KEY TO STANDARD & POOR'S MUNICIPAL BOND RATINGS

Standard & Poor's municipal bond ratings cover obligations of states and political subdivisions. Ratings are assigned to general obligation and revenue bonds. General obligation bonds are usually secured by all resources available to the municipality and the factors outlined in the rating definitions below are weighed in determining the rating. Because revenue bonds in general are payable from specifically pledged revenues, the essential element in the security for a revenue bond is the quantity and quality of the pledged revenues available to pay debt service. Although an appraisal of most of the same factors that bear on the quality of general obligation bond credit is usually appropriate in the rating analysis of a revenue bond, other factors are important, including particularly the competitive position of the municipal enterprise under review and the basic security covenants. Although a rating reflects our judgment as to the issuer's capacity for the timely payment of debt service, in certain instances it may also reflect a mechanism or procedure for an assured and prompt cure of a default, should one occur, i.e., an insurance program, federal or state guaranty, or the automatic withholding and use of state aid to pay the defaulted debt service.

AAA

Prime—These are obligations of the highest quality. They have the strongest capacity for timely payment of debt service.

General obligation bonds—In a period of economic stress, the issuers will suffer the smallest declines in income and will be least susceptible to autonomous decline. Debt burden is moderate. A strong revenue structure appears more than adequate to meet future expenditure requirements. Quality of management appears superior.

Revenue bonds—Debt service coverage has been, and is expected to remain, substantial. Stability of the pledged revenues is also exceptionally strong, due to the competitive position of the municipal enterprise or to the nature of the revenues. Basic se-

Source: *Fixed Income Investor*, Standard & Poor's Corporation.

curity provisions (including rate covenant, earnings test for issuance of additional bonds, debt service reserve requirements) are rigorous. There is evidence of superior management.

AA

High grade—The investment characteristics of general obligation and revenue bonds in this group are only slightly less marked than those of the prime quality issues. Bonds rated AA have the second strongest capacity for payment of debt service.

A

Good grade—Principal and interest payments on bonds in this category are regarded as safe. This rating describes the third strongest capacity for payment of debt service. It differs from the two ratings as shown below.

General obligation bonds—There is some weakness, in the local economic base, in debt burden, in the balance between revenues and expenditures, or in quality of management. Under certain adverse circumstances, any one such weakness might impair the ability of the issuer to meet debt obligations at some future date.

Revenue bonds—Debt service coverage is good, but not exceptional. Stability of the pledged revenues could show some variations because of increased competition or economic influences on revenues. Basic security provisions, while satisfactory, are less stringent. Management performance appears adequate.

BBB

Medium grade—This is the lowest investment grade security rating.

General obligation bonds—Under certain adverse conditions, several of the above factors could contribute to a lesser capacity for payment of debt service. The difference between A and BBB ratings is that the latter shows more than one fundamental weakness, or one very substantial fundamental weakness, whereas the former shows only one deficiency among the factors considered.

Revenue bonds—Debt service coverage is only fair. Stability of the pledged revenues could show substantial variations, with the revenue flow possibly being subject to erosion over time. Basic security provisions are no more than adequate. Management performance could be stronger.

BB

Lower medium grade—Bonds in this group have some investment characteristics, but they no longer predominate. For the most part this rating indicates a speculative, non-investment grade obligation.

B

Low grade—Investment characteristics are virtually nonexistent, and default could be imminent.

D

Defaults—Payment of interest and/or principal is in arrears.

NCR

No contract rating—No ratings are assigned to new offerings unless a contract is applied for.

Provisional ratings—The letter "p" following a rating indicates the rating is provisional, where payment of debt service requirements will be largely or entirely dependent upon the timely completion of the project.

For both municipal and corporate bond ratings, in order to provide more detailed indications of credit quality, traditional bond letter ratings may be modified by the addition of a plus or a minus sign, when appropriate, to show relative standing within the major rating categories, the only exceptions being in the AAA–Prime grade category and in the lesser categories below BB.

KEY TO STANDARD & POOR'S CORPORATE BOND RATINGS

Bank-quality bonds—Under present commercial bank regulations bonds rated in the top four categories (AAA, AA, A, BBB, or their equivalent) generally are regarded as eligible for bank investment.

AAA

Bonds rated AAA are highest grade obligations. They possess the ultimate degree of protection as to principal and interest. In the market they move with interest rates, and hence provide the maximum safety on all counts.

AA

Bonds rated AA also qualify as high-grade obligations, and in the majority of instances differ from AAA issues only in small degree. Here, too, prices move with the long-term money market.

Source: *Fixed Income Investor*, Standard & Poor's Corporation.

A

Bonds rated A are regarded as upper medium grade. They have considerable investment strength but are not entirely free from adverse effects of changes in economic and trade conditions. Interest and principal are regarded as safe. They predominantly reflect money rates in their market behavior, but also, to some extent, economic conditions.

BBB

The BBB, or medium grade, category is on the borderline between definitely sound obligations and those where the speculative element begins to predominate. These bonds have adequate asset coverage and normally are protected by satisfactory earnings. Their susceptibility to changing conditions, particularly to depressions, necessitates constant watching. In the market, the bonds are more responsive to business and trade conditions than to interest rates. This group is the lowest that qualifies for commercial bank investment.

BB

Bonds given a BB rating are regarded as lower medium grade. They have only minor investment characteristics. In the case of utilities, interest is earned consistently but by narrow margins. In the case of other types of obligors, charges are earned on average by fair margin, but in poor periods deficit operations are possible.

B

Bonds rated as low as B are speculative. Payment of interest cannot be assured under difficult economic conditions.

CCC–CC

Bonds rated CCC and CC are outright speculations, with the lower rating denoting the more speculative. Interest is paid, but continuation is questionable in periods of poor trade conditions. In the case of CC ratings, the bonds may be on an income basis and payment may be small.

C

The rating of C is reserved for income bonds on which no interest is being paid.

DDD–D

All bonds rated DDD, DD, and D are in default, with the rating indicating the relative salvage value.

NR—not rated.

Canadian corporate bonds are rated on the same basis as American corporate issues. The ratings measure the intrinsic value of the bonds, but they do not take into account exchange and other uncertainties.

KEY TO STANDARD & POOR'S PREFERRED STOCK RATINGS

Quality ratings on preferred stocks are expressed by symbols like those used in rating bonds. They are independent of Standard & Poor's bond ratings, however, in the sense that they are not necessarily graduated downward from the ratings accorded the issuing company's debt. They represent a considered judgment of the relative security of dividends but are not indicative of the protection of principal from market fluctuations. These ratings are as follows:

AAA	Prime	BB	Lower grade
AA	High grade	B	Speculative
A	Sound	C	Nonpaying
BBB	Medium grade		

To provide more detailed indications of credit quality, the traditional preferred stock letter ratings may be modified by the addition of a + or −, when appropriate, to show relative standing within the major rating categories, the only exceptions being in the AAA–Prime grade category and the lesser categories below BB.

KEY TO STANDARD & POOR'S COMMERCIAL PAPER RATINGS

These ratings are graded into four classifications ranging from A for the highest quality designations to B, C, and D for the lowest. Issuers rated A are further refined by the use of the numbers 1, 2, and 3, to denote relative strength within this highest classification, from A-1 down to A-3.

The requirements a company must meet to qualify for a given rating are as follows:

A RATING

1. Liquidity ratios are adequate to meet cash requirements.
   Liquidity ratios are basically as follows, broken down by the type of issuer:
   Industrial Company: acid-test ratio, current ratio, cash flow as a percent of current liabilities, short-term debt as a percent of current liabilities, short-term debt as a percent of current assets.

Utility: current liabilities as a percent of revenues, cash flow as a percent of current liabilities, short-term debt as a percent of capitalization.
   Finance Company: current ratio, current liabilities as a percent of net receivables, current liabilities as a percent of total liabilities.
2. The long-term senior debt rating is A or better; in some instances BBB credits may be allowed if other factors outweigh the BBB.
3. The issuer has access to at least two additional channels of borrowing.
4. Basic earnings and cash flow have an upward trend with allowances made for unusual circumstances.
5. Typically, the issuer's industry is well established and the issuer has a strong position within its industry.
6. The reliability and quality of management are unquestioned.

The relative strength or weakness of the above factors determines whether the issuer's commercial paper is rated A-1, A-2, or A-3.

B RATING

1. Liquidity ratios are good but not necessarily as high as in the A category.
2. The long-term senior debt rating is no less than BB.
3. Typically, the earnings growth record may be unimpressive and the potential of the company may not be fully developed. However, there is still demonstrated earning power.
4. The issuer has at least one alternative borrowing channel available.
5. The reliability and quality of management are at least average.

C RATING

1. There are wide swings in liquidity ratios from year to year.
2. The long-term senior debt rating is not of investment quality.
3. Maintenance of a satisfactory level of earnings is in some doubt due to management's ability, the burden of debt, competition, and other factors.
4. The flow of information and cooperation from management is barely acceptable and analysts may seriously question reliability and quality.

D RATING

Every indication is that the company will shortly be in default.

Source: *Fixed Income Investor,* Standard & Poor's Corporation.

KEY TO MOODY'S MUNICIPAL BOND RATINGS

Aaa

Bonds which are rated Aaa are judged to be of the best quality. They carry the smallest degree of investment risk and are generally referred to as "gilt edge." Interest payments are protected by a large or by an exceptionally stable margin and principal is secure. While the various protective elements are likely to change, such changes as can be visualized are most unlikely to impair the fundamentally strong position of such issues.

Aa

Bonds which are rated Aa are judged to be of high quality by all standards. Together with the Aaa group they comprise what are generally known as high grade bonds. They are rated lower than the best bonds because margins of protection may not be as large as in Aaa securities or fluctuation of protective elements may be of greater amplitude or there may be other elements present which make the long-term risks appear somewhat larger than in Aaa securities.

A

Bonds which are rated A possess many favorable investment attributes and are to be considered as upper medium grade obligations. Factors giving security to principal and interest are considered adequate, but elements may be present which suggest a susceptibility to impairment sometime in the future.

Baa

Bonds which are rated Baa are considered as medium grade obligations; i.e., they are neither highly protected nor poorly secured. Interest payments and principal security appear adequate for the present but certain protective elements may be lacking or may be characteristically unreliable over any great length of time. Such bonds lack outstanding investment characteristics and in fact have speculative characteristics as well.

Ba

Bonds which are rated Ba are judged to have speculative elements; their future cannot be considered as well-assured. Often the protection of interest and principal payments

Source: *Moody's Bond Record*, Moody's Investor Service, Inc.

may be very moderate, and thereby not well safeguarded during both good and bad times over the future. Uncertainty of position characterizes bonds in this class.

B

Bonds which are rated B generally lack characteristics of the desirable investment. Assurance of interest and principal payments or of maintenance of other terms of the contract over any long period of time may be small.

Caa

Bonds which are rated Caa are of poor standing. Such issues may be in default or there may be present elements of danger with respect to principal or interest.

Ca

Bonds which are rated Ca represent obligations which are speculative in a high degree. Such issues are often in default or have other marked shortcomings.

C

Bonds which are rated C are the lowest rated class of bonds, and issues so rated can be regarded as having extremely poor prospects of ever attaining any real investment standing.

CON. (. . .)

Bonds for which the security depends upon the completion of some act or the fulfillment of some condition are rated conditionally. These are bonds secured by (a) earnings of projects under construction, (b) earnings of projects unseasoned in operating experience, (c) rentals which begin when facilities are completed, or (d) payments to which some other limiting condition attaches. Parenthetical rating denotes probable credit stature upon completion of construction or elimination of basis of condition.

Those bonds in the A and Baa groups which Moody's believes possess the strongest investment attributes are designated by the symbols A1 and Baa1.

KEY TO MOODY'S SHORT-TERM LOAN RATINGS

MIG 1

Loans bearing this designation are of the best quality, enjoying strong protection from established cash flows of funds for their servicing or from established and broad-based access to the market for refinancing, or both.

MIG 2

Loans bearing this designation are of high quality, with margins of protection ample although not so large as in the preceding group.

MIG 3

Loans bearing this designation are of favorable quality, with all security elements accounted for but lacking the undeniable strength of the preceding grades. Market access for refinancing, in particular, is likely to be less well established.

MIG 4

Loans bearing this designation are of adequate quality, carrying specific risk but having protection commonly regarded as required of an investment security and not distinctly or predominantly speculative.

KEY TO MOODY'S CORPORATE BOND RATINGS

Aaa

Bonds which are rated Aaa are judged to be of the best quality. They carry the smallest degree of investment risk and are generally referred to as "gilt edge." Interest payments are protected by a large or by an exceptionally stable margin and principal is secure. While the various protective elements are likely to change, such changes as can be visualized are most unlikely to impair the fundamentally strong position of such issues.

Aa

Bonds which are rated Aa are judged to be of high quality by all standards. Together with the Aaa group they comprise what are generally known as high grade bonds. They are rated lower than the best bonds because margins of protection may not be as large as in Aaa securities or fluctuation of protective elements may be of greater amplitude or there may be other elements present which make the long-term risks appear somewhat larger than in Aaa securities.

A

Bonds which are rated A possess many favorable investment attributes and are to be

Source: *Moody's Bond Record*, Moody's Investor Service, Inc.

considered as upper medium grade obligations. Factors giving security to principal and interest are considered adequate, but elements may be present which suggest a susceptibility to impairment sometime in the future.

Baa

Bonds which are rated Baa are considered as medium grade obligations; i.e., they are neither highly protected nor poorly secured. Interest payments and principal security appear adequate for the present but certain protective elements may be lacking or may be characteristically unreliable over any great length of time. Such bonds lack outstanding investment characteristics and in fact have speculative characteristics as well.

Ba

Bonds which are rated Ba are judged to have speculative elements; their future cannot be considered as well-assured. Often the protection of interest and principal payments may be very moderate, and thereby not well safeguarded during both good and bad times over the future. Uncertainty of position characterizes bonds in this class.

B

Bonds which are rated B generally lack characteristics of the desirable investment. Assurance of interest and principal payments or of maintenance of other terms of the contract over any long period of time may be small.

Caa

Bonds which are rated Caa are of poor standing. Such issues may be in default or there may be present elements of danger with respect to principal or interest.

Ca

Bonds which are rated Ca represent obligations which are speculative in a high degree. Such issues are often in default or have other marked shortcomings.

C

Bonds which are rated C are the lowest rated class of bonds, and issues so rated can be regarded as having extremely poor prospects of ever attaining any real investment standing.

KEY TO MOODY'S PREFERRED STOCK RATINGS

Moody's Rating Policy Review Board extended its rating services to include quality designations on preferred stocks on October 1, 1973. The decision to rate preferred stocks, which Moody's had done prior to 1935, was prompted by evidence of investor interest. Moody's believes that its rating of preferred stocks is especially appropriate in view of the ever-increasing amount of these securities outstanding, and the fact that continuing inflation and its ramifications have resulted generally in the dilution of some of the protection afforded them as well as other fixed-income securities.

Because of the fundamental differences between preferred stocks and bonds, a variation of our familiar bond rating symbols is being used in the quality ranking of preferred stocks. The symbols, presented below, are designed to avoid comparison with bond quality in absolute terms. It should always be borne in mind that preferred stocks occupy a junior position to bonds within a particular capital structure.

Preferred stock rating symbols and their definitions are as follows:

aaa

An issue which is rated aaa is considered to be a top-quality preferred stock. This rating indicates good asset protection and the least risk of dividend impairment within the universe of preferred stocks.

aa

An issue which is rated aa is considered a high-grade preferred stock. This rating indicates that there is reasonable assurance that earnings and asset protection will remain relatively well maintained in the foreseeable future.

a

An issue which is rated a is considered to be an upper medium grade preferred stock. While risks are judged to be somewhat greater than in the aaa and aa classifications, earnings and asset protection are, nevertheless, expected to be maintained at adequate levels.

baa

An issue which is rated baa is considered to be medium grade, neither highly protected

Source: *Moody's Bond Record*, Moody's Investors Service, Inc.

nor poorly secured. Earnings and asset protection appear adequate at present but may be questionable over any great length of time.

ba

An issue which is rated ba is considered to have speculative elements and its future cannot be considered well assured. Earnings and asset protection may be very moderate and not well safeguarded during adverse periods. Uncertainty of position characterizes preferred stocks in this class.

b

An issue which is rated b generally lacks the characteristics of a desirable investment. Assurance of dividend payments and maintenance of other terms of the issue over any long period of time may be small.

caa

An issue which is rated caa is likely to be in arrears on dividend payments. This rating designation does not purport to indicate the future status of payments.

KEY TO MOODY'S COMMERCIAL PAPER RATINGS°

Moody's evaluates the salient features that affect a commercial paper issuer's financial and competitive position. Our appraisal includes, but is not limited to, the review of such factors as: quality of management, industry strengths and risks, vulnerability to business cycles, competitive position, liquidity measurements, debt structure, operating trends and access to capital markets. Differing degrees of weight are applied to these factors as deemed appropriate for individual situations.

Issuers rated in all three Prime categories are judged to be investment grade.

PRIME-1

Commercial paper issuers rated PRIME-1 are judged to be of the best quality. Their short-term debt obligations carry the smallest degree of investment risk. Margins of support

° The term "commercial paper" as used by Moody's means unsecured promissory obligations having a maximum maturity of 270 days, proceeds of which are normally employed to support current transactions or for bridge financing. Moody's makes no representation as to whether such commercial paper is by any other definition "commercial paper" or is exempt from registration under the Securities Act of 1933, as amended.

for current indebtedness are large or stable with cash flow and asset protection well assured. Current liquidity provides ample coverage of near-term liabilities and unused alternative financing arrangements are generally available. While protective elements may change over the intermediate or longer term, such changes are most unlikely to impair the fundamentally strong position of short-term obligations.

PRIME-2

Issuers in the commercial paper market rated PRIME-2 are of high quality. Protection for short-term note holders is assured with liquidity and value of current assets as well as cash generation in sound relationship to current indebtedness. They are rated lower

Source: *Moody's Bond Record,* Moody's Investors Service, Inc.

than the best commercial paper issuers because margins of protection may not be as large or because fluctuations of protective elements over the near or intermediate term may be of greater amplitude. Temporary increases in relative short and overall debt load may occur. Alternative means of financing remain assured.

PRIME-3

Commercial paper issuers rated PRIME-3 possess favorable investment attributes for short-term commitment. Liquidity considerations and cash generation provide satisfactory support for short-term debt repayment. While near-term investors are well-protected, elements may be present which suggest improvement or deterioration in support at sometime in the future. Alternative financing strategies have been outlined.

MONEY STOCK
BILLIONS OF DOLLARS* (RATIO SCALE)

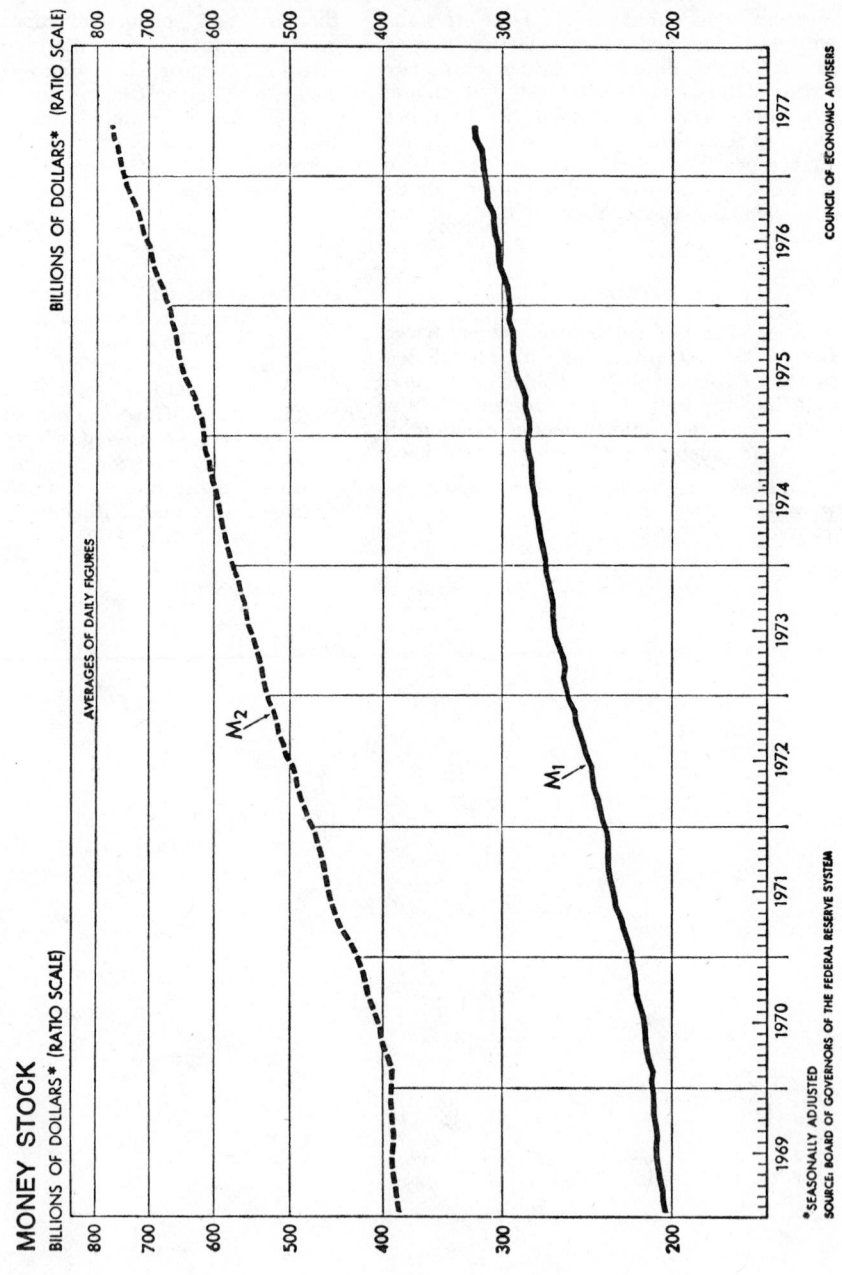

BILLIONS OF DOLLARS* (RATIO SCALE)

AVERAGES OF DAILY FIGURES

M₂

M₁

*SEASONALLY ADJUSTED
SOURCE: BOARD OF GOVERNORS OF THE FEDERAL RESERVE SYSTEM

COUNCIL OF ECONOMIC ADVISERS

[Averages of daily figures; billions of dollars, seasonally adjusted, except as noted]

Period	Overall measures *			Components and related items							Percent change †	
	M₁	M₂	M₃	Currency	Deposits at commercial banks				Deposits at nonbank thrift institutions	U.S. Government demand deposits (unadjusted)	M₁	M₂
					Demand	Time and savings						
						Total	Large CDs	Other				
1972: Dec	255.3	525.3	844.5	56.9	198.4	313.5	43.5	270.0	319.3	7.4	9.2	11.4
1973: Dec	270.5	571.4	919.6	61.5	209.0	363.9	63.0	300.9	348.1	6.3	6.0	8.8
1974: Dec	283.1	612.4	981.5	67.8	215.3	418.3	89.0	329.3	369.1	4.9	4.7	7.2
1975: Dec	294.8	664.3	1,092.6	73.7	221.0	451.7	82.1	369.6	428.3	4.1	4.1	8.5
1976: Dec	312.4	740.3	1,237.1	80.5	231.9	491.1	63.3	427.9	496.8	4.7	6.2	12.4
1976: May	303.5	695.7	1,149.7	77.3	226.2	460.7	68.6	392.1	454.0	3.8	5.4	10.4
June	303.2	698.2	1,156.5	77.5	225.6	465.3	70.2	395.1	458.2	4.8	5.8	10.5
July	305.0	705.2	1,168.8	78.1	226.9	469.0	68.9	400.1	463.6	3.5	6.7	10.7
Aug	306.5	710.4	1,180.8	78.6	227.9	468.9	65.0	403.9	470.5	3.7	6.6	9.7
Sept	306.9	716.3	1,193.9	79.2	227.7	472.5	63.1	409.4	477.6	5.0	6.0	10.1
Oct	310.4	725.9	1,210.7	79.8	230.6	477.8	62.3	415.5	484.8	4.0	5.8	10.5
Nov	310.4	732.3	1,223.4	80.2	230.2	484.2	62.2	422.0	491.0	4.2	4.6	10.8
Dec	312.4	740.3	1,237.1	80.5	231.9	491.1	63.3	427.9	496.8	4.7	6.2	12.4
1977: Jan	313.8	746.3	1,248.9	81.1	232.7	495.6	63.1	432.5	502.6	4.2	5.9	12.0
Feb	314.0	750.7	1,258.2	81.8	232.1	500.0	63.3	436.7	507.5	4.4	5.0	11.7
Mar	315.4	756.1	1,268.1	82.2	233.2	502.8	62.2	440.6	512.1	4.5	5.6	11.4
Apr	320.5	764.6	1,281.2	83.1	237.4	505.7	61.6	444.1	516.6	5.6	6.6	10.9
May ᵖ	320.7	767.6	1,288.8	83.6	237.1	509.2	62.3	446.9	521.2	3.8	6.7	9.9

* M₁ is currency plus demand deposits; M₂ is M₁ plus time deposits at commercial banks other than large certificates of deposit (CDs); and M₃ is M₂ plus deposits at nonbank thrift institutions.

† Annual changes are from December to December and monthly changes are from 6 months earlier at a seasonally adjusted annual rate.

Note.—Data revised beginning October 1976.

Source: Board of Governors of the Federal Reserve system.

Source: *Economic Indicators*, Council of Economic Advisors.

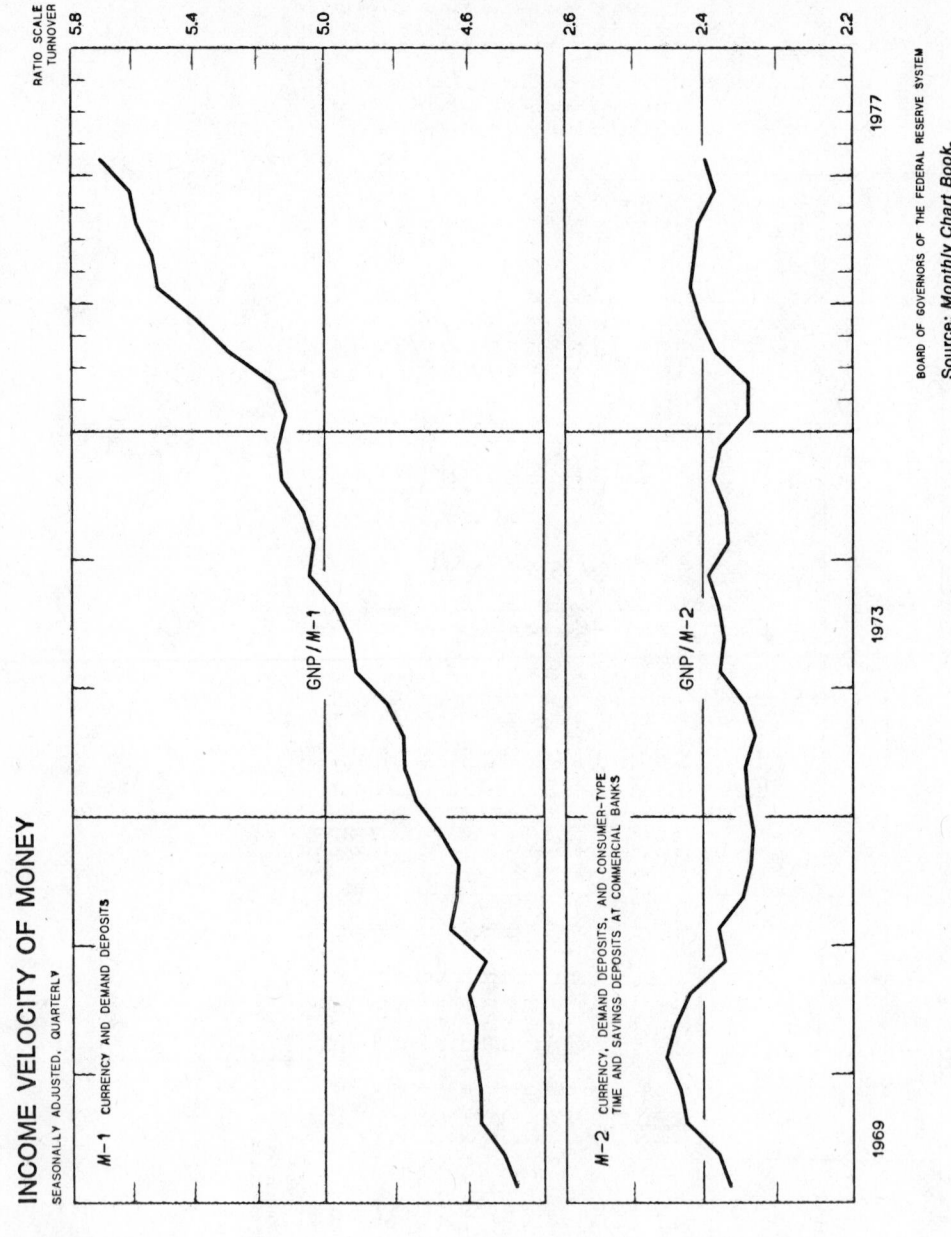

INCOME VELOCITY OF MONEY
SEASONALLY ADJUSTED, QUARTERLY

RATIO SCALE
TURNOVER

M-1 CURRENCY AND DEMAND DEPOSITS

GNP / M-1

M-2 CURRENCY, DEMAND DEPOSITS, AND CONSUMER-TYPE
TIME AND SAVINGS DEPOSITS AT COMMERCIAL BANKS

GNP / M-2

1969   1973   1977

BOARD OF GOVERNORS OF THE FEDERAL RESERVE SYSTEM

Source: *Monthly Chart Book.*

CURRENT ASSETS AND LIABILITIES OF NONFINANCIAL CORPORATIONS

Billions of dollars

End of period	Current assets							Current liabilities					Net working capital
	Total	Cash on hand and in banks¹	U.S. Government securities²	Receivables from U.S. Government³	Notes and accounts receivable	Inventories	Other current assets	Total	Advances and prepayments, U.S. Government³	Notes and accounts payable	Federal income tax liabilities	Other current liabilities⁵	
1970-----	492.3	50.2	7.7	4.2	201.9	193.3	35.0	304.9	6.6	204.7	10.0	83.6	187.4
1971-----	529.6	53.3	11.0	3.5	217.6	200.4	43.8	326.0	4.9	215.6	13.1	92.4	203.6
1972-----	573.5	57.5	9.3	3.4	240.0	215.2	48.1	352.2	4.0	230.4	15.1	102.6	221.3
1973-----	643.3	61.6	11.7	3.5	266.1	246.7	54.4	401.0	4.3	261.6	18.1	117.0	242.3
1974-----	712.2	62.7	11.7	3.5	289.7	288.0	56.6	450.6	5.2	287.5	23.2	134.8	261.5
1975-----	731.6	68.1	19.4	3.6	294.6	285.8	60.0	457.5	6.4	281.6	20.7	148.8	274.1
1976-----	816.8	77.0	26.4	4.3	323.9	315.4	69.8	499.9	7.0	295.9	26.8	170.2	316.9
1975: I---	698.4	60.6	12.1	3.2	281.9	285.2	55.4	438.0	5.3	271.2	21.8	139.8	260.4
II---	703.2	63.7	12.7	3.3	284.8	281.4	57.3	434.2	5.8	270.1	17.7	140.6	269.0
III--	716.5	65.6	14.3	3.3	294.7	279.6	59.0	444.7	6.2	273.4	19.4	145.6	271.8
IV---	731.6	68.1	19.4	3.6	294.6	285.8	60.0	457.5	6.4	281.6	20.7	148.8	274.1
1976: I---	753.5	68.4	21.7	3.6	307.3	288.8	63.6	465.9	6.4	280.5	23.9	155.0	287.6
II--	775.4	70.8	23.3	3.7	318.1	295.6	63.9	475.9	6.8	287.7	22.0	160.1	299.4
III-	791.8	71.1	23.9	4.3	324.2	302.1	66.3	484.1	7.0	284.7	24.9	167.5	307.7
IV--	816.8	77.0	26.4	4.3	323.9	315.4	69.8	499.9	7.0	295.9	26.8	170.2	316.9

¹ Includes time certificates of deposit.
² Includes Federal agency issues.
³ Receivables from and payables to the U.S. Government do not include amounts offset against each other on corporations' books or amounts arising from subcontracting which are not directly due from or to the U.S. Government. Wherever possible, adjustments have been made to include U.S. Government advances offset against inventories on corporations' books.
⁴ Includes marketable investments (other than Government securities and time certificates of deposit) as well as sundry current assets.
⁵ Includes commercial paper outstanding, the portion of long-term debt due in less than 1 year, and miscellaneous current liabilities not elsewhere classified.

Source: Securities and Exchange Commission.

Source: *Economic Indicators*, Council of Economic Advisors.

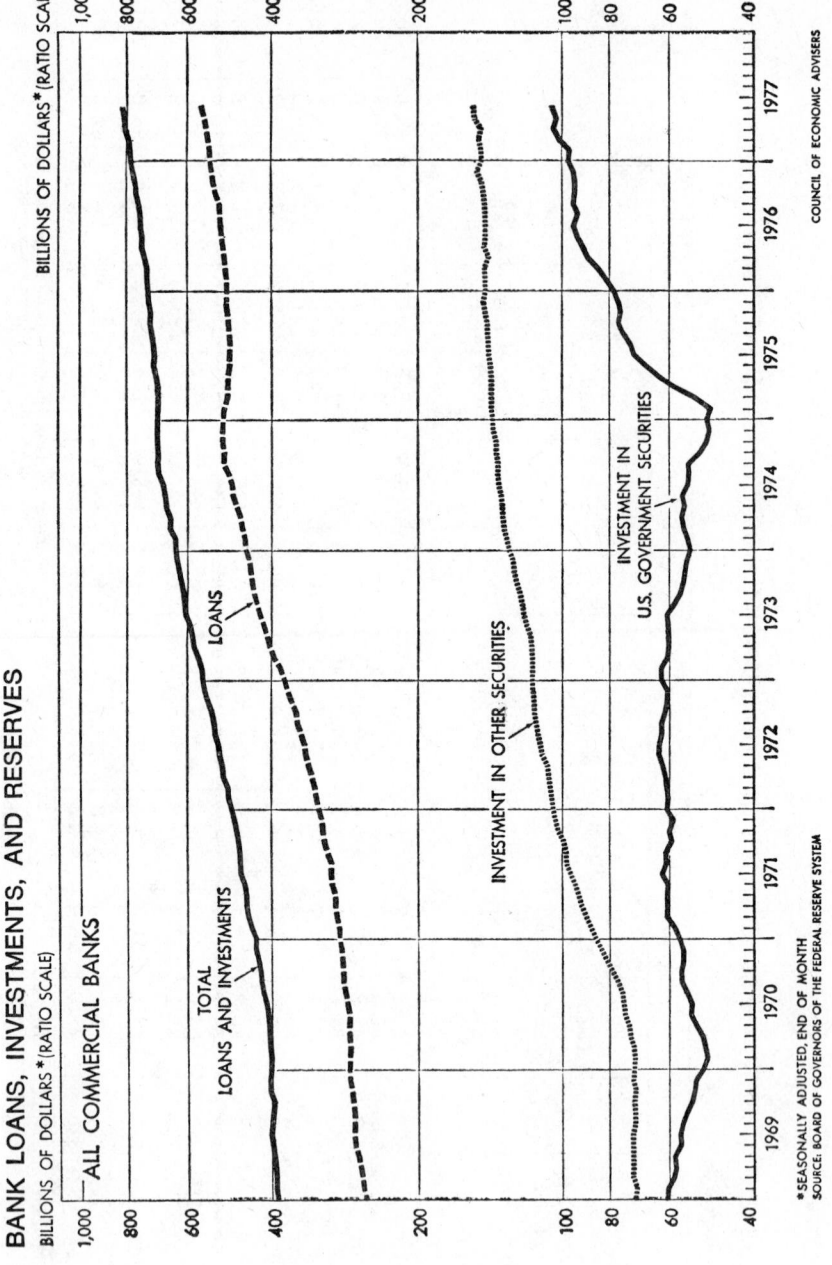

BANK LOANS, INVESTMENTS, AND RESERVES

BILLIONS OF DOLLARS* (RATIO SCALE)

ALL COMMERCIAL BANKS

TOTAL LOANS AND INVESTMENTS

LOANS

INVESTMENT IN OTHER SECURITIES

INVESTMENT IN U.S. GOVERNMENT SECURITIES

BILLIONS OF DOLLARS* (RATIO SCALE)

*SEASONALLY ADJUSTED, END OF MONTH
SOURCE: BOARD OF GOVERNORS OF THE FEDERAL RESERVE SYSTEM

COUNCIL OF ECONOMIC ADVISERS

[Billions of dollars, seasonally adjusted, except as noted]

Period	All commercial banks [1]					All member banks				
	Total loans and investments	Loans		Investments		Reserves [2][3]			Borrowings (millions of dollars, unadjusted) [2]	
		Total excluding interbank	Commercial and industrial	U.S. Government securities	Other securities	Total	Nonborrowed	Required	Total	Seasonal
1969	401.7	279.4	105.7	51.2	71.1	27.94	26.82	27.66	1,086	---
1970	435.5	292.0	110.0	57.8	85.7	29.12	28.79	28.87	321	---
1971	485.7	320.9	116.1	60.6	104.2	31.22	31.10	31.04	107	---
1972	558.0	378.9	130.2	62.6	116.5	31.41	30.36	31.12	1,049	---
1973	633.4	449.0	156.4	54.5	129.9	34.94	33.64	34.64	1,298	41
1974	[4]690.4	500.2	183.3	50.4	139.8	36.60	35.87	36.34	703	32
1975	721.1	496.9	176.0	79.4	144.8	34.73	34.60	34.46	127	13
1976	784.4	538.9	[5]179.5	97.3	148.2	34.95	34.90	34.68	62	12
1976: May	744.0	506.5	172.2	93.1	144.4	34.17	34.05	33.96	121	11
June	748.8	509.3	172.1	94.7	144.8	34.29	34.16	34.07	120	20
July	751.4	512.1	172.8	93.2	146.1	34.34	34.21	34.11	123	24
Aug	758.0	516.0	173.1	95.6	146.4	34.51	34.41	34.31	104	28
Sept	762.9	520.8	174.1	94.4	147.2	34.34	34.27	34.14	75	31
Oct	771.6	529.6	176.8	94.4	147.6	34.51	34.41	34.29	66	32
Nov	778.8	533.1	179.0	95.4	150.3	34.85	34.78	34.59	84	21
Dec	784.4	538.9	179.5	97.3	148.2	34.95	34.90	34.68	62	12
1977: Jan p	786.6	540.9	179.8	96.9	148.8	34.78	34.71	34.51	61	8
Feb p	796.4	545.4	181.2	101.5	149.5	34.40	34.33	34.20	79	12
Mar p	803.0	551.0	182.9	103.6	149.4	34.31	34.20	34.09	110	13
Apr p	812.4	557.7	184.9	102.8	151.9	34.68	34.61	34.49	73	14
May p	819.4	562.1	185.9	104.6	152.7	34.73	34.52	34.52	200	31

[1] Data are for end of period.
[2] Averages of daily figures. Annual data are for December.
[3] Member bank reserves series reflects actual reserve requirement percentages with no adjustment to eliminate the effect of changes in Regulations D and M.
[4] During 1974, total loans and investments were increased $0.6 billion due to a bank merger and were reduced $1.5 billion due to liquidation of a large bank.
[5] Loan reclassifications reduced these loans by $1.2 billion as of March 31, 1976.

Note.—Data revised beginning July 1976.

Source: Board of Governors of the Federal Reserve System.

Source: Economic Indicators, Council of Economic Advisors.

NEW SECURITY ISSUES: STATE AND LOCAL GOVERNMENT AND CORPORATE

Millions of dollars

Type of issue or issuer, or use	1974	1975	1976	1976				1977	
				Sept.	Oct.	Nov.	Dec.	Jan.	Feb.
				State and local government					
1 All issues, new and refunding [1]	24,315	30,607	35,313	2,819	3,544	3,345	2,352	3,429	3,150
By type of issue:									
2 General obligation	13,563	16,020	18,040	1,265	1,973	1,529	1,176	1,867	1,624
3 Revenue	10,212	14,511	17,140	1,549	1,551	1,807	1,166	1,552	1,518
4 Housing Assistance Administration [2]	461		133	5	20	9	10	10	
5 U.S. Govt. loans	79	76							8
By type of issuer:									
6 State	4,784	7,438	7,054	470	499	537	361	468	441
7 Special district and statutory authority	8,638	12,441	15,304	1,238	1,470	1,725	1,251	1,786	1,335
8 Municipalities, counties, townships, school districts	10,817	10,660	12,845	1,105	1,553	1,074	732	1,166	1,367
9 Issues for new capital, total	23,508	29,495	32,108	2,591	2,921	2,879	1,847	3,084	3,019
By use of proceeds:									
10 Education	4,730	4,689	4,900	356	428	351	334	489	502
11 Transportation	1,712	2,208	2,586	251	332	221	107	104	410
12 Utilities and conservation	5,634	7,209	9,594	747	632	1,333	723	1,050	935
13 Social welfare	3,820	4,392	6,566	767	676	574	233	483	580
14 Industrial aid	494	445	483	31	23	69	63	15	12
15 Other purposes	7,118	10,552	7,979	439	830	331	387	943	580

Corporate

16 All issues ³	38,313	53,619	53,356	4,817	4,431	3,047	6,480	3,989	2,708
17 Bonds	32,066	42,756	42,262	4,263	3,482	2,357	5,560	3,387	1,888
By type of offering:									
18 Public	25,903	32,583	26,453	2,100	2,729	1,256	2,568	2,786	1,108
19 Private placement	6,160	10,172	15,808	2,163	753	1,101	2,992	601	780
By industry group:									
20 Manufacturing	9,867	16,980	13,243	670	1,261	501	2,275	817	568
21 Commercial and miscellaneous	1,845	2,750	4,361	546	77	376	696	743	346
22 Transportation	1,550	3,439	4,357	1,212	240	193	564	165	47
23 Public utility	8,873	9,658	8,297	1,118	803	795	560	634	210
24 Communication	3,710	3,464	2,787	140	155	163	196	50	290
25 Real estate and financial	6,218	6,469	9,222	577	946	328	1,271	979	426
26 Stocks	6,247	10,863	11,094	554	949	690	920	602	820
By type:									
27 Preferred	2,253	3,458	2,789	136	276	282	308	103	128
28 Common	3,994	7,405	8,305	418	673	408	612	499	692
By industry group:									
29 Manufacturing	544	1,670	2,237	83	88	9	110	89	175
30 Commercial and miscellaneous	940	1,470	1,183	33	73	34	198	136	94
31 Transportation	22	1	24	7	......	......	......	......	......
32 Public utility	3,964	6,235	6,101	347	611	532	596	352	225
33 Communication	217	1,002	776	......	......	27	......	......	267
34 Real estate and financial	562	488	771	84	177	88	15	25	60

1 Par amounts of long-term issues based on date of sale.

2 Only bonds sold pursuant to the 1949 Housing Act, which are secured by contract requiring the Housing Assistance Administration to make annual contributions to the local authority.

3 Figures, which represent gross proceeds of issues maturing in more than 1 year, sold for cash in the United States, are principal amount or number of units multiplied by offering price. Excludes offerings of less than $100,000, secondary offerings, undefined or exempted issues as defined in the Securities Act of 1933, employee stock plans, investment companies other than closed-end, intracorporate transactions, and sales to foreigners.

SOURCES.—State and local government securities, Securities Industry Association; corporate securities, Securities and Exchange Commission.

Source: Federal Reserve Bulletin.

FUNDS RAISED IN U.S. CREDIT MARKETS

Billions of dollars; half-year data are at seasonally adjusted annual rates

Nonfinancial sectors

	Transaction category, or sector	1971	1972	1973	1974	1975	1976	1975 H1	1975 H2	1976 H1	1976 H2	
1	Total funds raised	151.0	176.9	197.6	188.8	210.4	271.6	184.2	236.5	256.6	286.3	1
2	*Excluding equities*	139.6	166.4	190.0	185.0	200.3	260.8	173.8	226.9	243.0	278.2	2
	By sector and instrument:											
3	U.S. Govt.	24.7	15.2	8.3	12.0	85.2	69.0	80.8	89.6	71.5	66.6	3
4	Public debt securities	26.0	14.3	7.9	12.0	85.8	69.1	82.0	89.7	71.5	66.9	4
5	Agency issues and mortgages	−1.3	1.0	.4	*	−.6	−.1	−1.2	−.1		−.3	5
6	All other nonfinancial sectors	126.3	161.7	189.4	176.8	125.2	202.6	103.4	146.9	185.0	219.7	6
7	Corporate equities	11.5	10.5	.7	3.8	10.1	10.8	10.5	9.6	13.6	8.1	7
8	Debt instruments	114.8	151.2	181.7	173.0	115.1	191.8	93.0	137.3	171.4	211.7	8
9	Private domestic nonfinancial sectors	121.1	157.7	183.1	161.6	112.2	181.1	94.9	129.4	169.1	192.5	9
10	Corporate equities	11.4	10.9	7.9	4.1	9.9	10.5	10.3	9.5	13.3	7.7	10
11	*Debt instruments*	109.7	146.8	175.3	157.5	102.3	170.5	84.6	119.9	155.8	184.8	11
12	*Debt capital instruments*	86.8	102.8	106.7	101.2	101.3	123.6	97.5	105.1	113.5	133.8	12
13	State and local obligations	17.5	15.4	16.3	19.6	17.3	17.2	16.2	18.4	18.1	16.4	13
14	Corporate bonds	18.8	12.2	9.2	19.7	27.2	22.8	33.4	21.0	20.7	25.0	14
	Mortgages:											
15	Home	28.6	42.6	46.4	34.6	40.8	64.4	33.5	48.1	58.1	70.7	15
16	Multifamily residential	9.7	12.7	10.4	7.0	−.1	−1.1	*	−.2	−1.6	.6	16
17	Commercial	9.8	16.4	18.9	15.1	10.9	11.7	8.7	13.1	9.8	13.5	17
18	Farm	2.4	5.6	5.5	5.1	5.0	6.4	5.6	4.8	5.1	7.6	18
19	*Other debt instruments*	22.8	44.0	68.6	56.3	1.0	46.9	−12.8	14.8	42.3	51.0	19
20	Consumer credit	11.6	18.6	21.7	9.8	8.5	20.5	−1.1	16.0	19.4	21.6	20
21	Bank loans n.e.c.	6.5	18.1	34.8	26.2	−14.5	5.7	−23.5	−5.5	2.2	12.7	21
22	Open market paper	−.4	.8	2.5	6.8	−2.2	3.5	−.2	−4.2	8.2	−1.3	22
23	Other	5.1	6.5	9.6	13.5	9.1	15.3	9.7	8.5	12.6	17.9	23
24	*By borrowing sector:*	121.1	157.7	183.1	161.6	112.2	181.1	94.9	129.4	169.1	192.5	24
25	State and local governments	17.8	15.2	14.8	18.6	14.9	16.8	13.9	15.9	16.4	17.2	25
26	Households	42.1	64.8	73.5	45.2	49.7	90.7	39.0	60.4	88.3	93.6	26
27	Farm	4.5	5.8	9.7	7.9	9.4	12.3	9.4	9.4	11.0	13.6	27
28	Nonfarm noncorporate	10.3	13.1	12.3	6.7	−1.2	4.7	−.8	3.2	4.2	4.8	28
29	Corporate	46.4	58.8	72.9	83.1	37.1	56.6	33.5	40.6	49.3	63.9	29
30	*Foreign*	5.2	4.0	6.2	15.3	13.0	21.5	8.5	17.4	15.9	27.2	30
31	Corporate equities	*	−.4	−.4	−.2	.2	.3	.1	.1	.3	.3	31
32	*Debt instruments*	5.2	4.4	6.4	15.5	12.8	21.2	8.4	17.3	15.6	26.9	32
33	Bonds	2.1	1.0	1.0	2.1	6.2	8.4	5.7	6.7	7.3	9.4	33
34	Bank loans n.e.c.	1.3	3.0	2.8	4.7	4.0	6.8	−.6	7.4	4.2	9.3	34
35	Open market paper		−1.0	.9	7.1	−.1	2.5	−1.2	1.0	.8	4.2	35
36	U.S. Govt. loans	1.8	1.5	1.7	1.6	2.8	3.6	3.3	2.2	3.2	4.0	36

Financial sectors

Line	Item										
37	Total funds raised	17.0	29.1	56.7	43.0	14.8	29.8	14.4	15.3	27.5	32.1
	By instrument:										
38	*U.S. Govt. related*	5.9	8.4	19.9	23.1	13.5	17.7	14.0	13.1	18.0	17.4
39	Sponsored credit agency securities	1.1	3.5	16.3	16.6	2.3	2.4	-1.4	3.3	3.9	7.9
40	Mortgage pool securities	4.8	4.9	3.6	5.8	10.3	15.7	11.5	9.2	14.2	17.2
41	Loans from U.S. Govt.	-.7		-.7	.7	.9	-.4	-1.1	.6	*	-.7
42	*Private financial sectors*	11.1	20.7	36.8	19.7	1.3	-.4	11.8	2.1	9.5	14.7
43	Corporate equities	3.5	2.8	1.5	1.0	1.2	1.2	1.2	2.1	9.1	3.3
44	*Debt instruments*	7.6	18.0	35.3	18.9	.1	1.8	10.3	1.0	7.2	11.4
45	Corporate bonds	3.8	5.1	3.5	2.1	2.9	10.3	2.5	3.3	7.2	4.4
46	Mortgages	2.1	1.7	-1.2	-1.3	-2.3	5.8	-4.7	3.4	-1.6	-2.8
47	Bank loans n.e.c.	3.5	6.8	14.0	7.5	-3.9	-1.9	7.6	-3.9	-3.6	-3.0
48	Open market paper and **Rp's**	-.9	4.4	11.8	3.9	-2.8	-3.3	7.3	-1.9	6.8	-8.8
49	Loans from FHLB's	-2.7	*	7.2	6.7	-4.0	7.8	2.6	-.6	-2.3	-1.7
	By sector:										
50	Sponsored credit agencies	1.1	3.5	16.3	17.3	3.2	2.0	2.5	4.0	3.9	.2
51	Mortgage pools	4.8	4.9	3.6	5.8	10.3	15.7	11.5	9.2	14.2	17.2
52	*Private financial sectors*	11.1	20.7	36.8	19.9	1.7	12.1	.4	2.1	9.9	14.7
53	Commercial banks	2.4	4.8	8.1	-1.1	1.7	7.6	5.7	-2.3	9.9	5.3
54	Bank affiliates	.4	.7	2.2	-3.5	.3	-.8	.9	.2	-1.5	2.4
55	Foreign banking agencies	-1.6	.8	5.1	2.9	-.3	.4	-7.8	3.6	-1.0	.7
56	Savings and loan associations	-.1	2.0	6.0	6.3	-2.1	-1.0	-.8	1.0	1.0	1.0
57	Other insurance companies	-.6	.6	9.4	4.5	-.9	6.1	-.8	-2.1	6.0	6.2
58	Finance companies	2.7	6.2	6.5	-1.5	.7	-2.1	-1.6	2.1	-1.8	-2.5
59	REIT's	2.9	6.3	-1.2	2.4	-1.8	-.3	-1.5	-2.1	-1.1	-1.8
60	Open-end investment companies	1.3	-.5			1.3		2.6	*	-1.7	.2
61	Money market funds										

All sectors

Line	Item										
62	Total funds raised, by instrument	168.1	206.0	254.3	231.8	225.2	301.4	198.6	251.8	284.1	318.4
63	Investment company shares	1.3	-.5	-1.2	-.5	.8	12.3	1.5	.1	-1.0	1.8
64	Other corporate equities	13.7	13.8	10.4	5.4	10.4	12.3	10.2	10.7	15.0	9.6
65	*Debt instruments*	153.7	192.8	245.2	227.0	214.0	288.7	187.0	241.0	270.2	307.0
66	U.S. Govt. securities	30.7	23.7	28.3	34.5	98.0	87.2	93.6	102.4	89.8	84.7
67	State and local obligations	17.5	15.4	16.6	19.6	17.3	17.2	16.2	18.4	18.1	16.4
68	Corporate and foreign bonds	23.5	18.4	13.6	23.9	36.3	37.0	41.6	31.0	35.2	38.8
69	Mortgages	52.5	76.6	79.9	60.5	59.0	85.4	49.1	69.0	75.7	95.2
70	Consumer credit	11.6	18.6	21.7	9.8	8.5	20.5	-1.1	16.0	19.4	21.6
71	Bank loans n.e.c.	12.1	27.8	51.6	38.4	-14.4	11.2	-27.6	-1.2	2.9	19.1
72	Open market paper and **Rp's**	4.9	4.1	15.2	17.8	.5	13.8	6.2	-5.1	15.8	11.8
73	Other loans	4.2	8.0	18.5	22.5	8.7	16.5	6.8	10.7	13.4	19.5

Source: Federal Reserve Bulletin.

MORTGAGE DEBT OUTSTANDING

Millions of dollars, end of period

	Type of holder, and type of property	1972	1973	1974	1975	1976 Q2	1976 Q3	1976 Q4	1977 Q1
1	All holders	603,417	682,321	742,504	801,640	ʳ840,813	ʳ864,345	ʳ888,958	ʳ910,625
2	1- to 4-family	372,793	416,883	449,937	491,568	ʳ521,705	ʳ541,224	ʳ558,415	ʳ574,534
3	Multifamily	82,572	92,877	99,851	100,471	ʳ100,790	ʳ100,344	ʳ102,380	ʳ102,591
4	Commercial	112,294	131,308	146,428	158,724	ʳ164,209	ʳ167,070	ʳ170,870	ʳ174,233
5	Farm	35,758	41,253	46,288	50,877	ʳ54,109	ʳ55,707	ʳ57,293	ʳ59,267
6	Major financial institutions	450,000	505,400	542,552	581,296	ʳ611,524	ʳ629,949	647,314	ʳ661,851
7	Commercial banks¹	99,314	119,068	132,105	136,186	143,699	147,636	150,869	154,007
8	1- to 4-family	57,004	67,998	74,758	77,018	82,900	86,013	87,897	89,725
9	Multifamily	5,778	6,932	7,619	5,915	6,107	6,201	6,336	6,468
10	Commercial	31,751	38,696	43,679	46,882	48,125	48,749	49,817	50,853
11	Farm	4,781	5,442	6,049	6,371	6,567	6,673	6,819	6,961
12	Mutual savings banks	67,556	73,230	74,920	77,249	78,838	80,249	81,734	82,273
13	1- to 4-family	46,229	48,811	49,213	50,025	51,326	52,250	53,217	53,568
14	Multifamily	10,910	12,343	12,923	13,792	13,674	13,915	14,173	14,266
15	Commercial	10,355	12,012	12,722	13,373	13,780	14,028	14,287	14,381
16	Farm	62	64	62	59	58	56	57	58
17	Savings and loan associations	206,182	231,733	249,293	278,693	ʳ299,296	ʳ311,847	323,130	ʳ333,697
18	1- to 4-family	167,049	187,750	201,553	224,710	ʳ241,623	ʳ251,629	ʳ260,895	ʳ270,094
19	Multifamily	20,783	22,524	23,683	25,417	ʳ26,817	ʳ27,505	ʳ28,436	ʳ29,032
20	Commercial	18,350	21,459	24,057	28,566	ʳ31,456	ʳ32,713	ʳ33,799	ʳ34,571
21	Life insurance companies	76,948	81,369	86,234	89,168	89,691	90,277	91,581	91,874
22	1- to 4-family	22,315	20,426	19,026	17,590	16,861	16,458	16,108	ʳ15,780
23	Multifamily	17,347	18,451	19,625	19,629	19,374	19,256	19,201	ʳ19,064
24	Commercial	31,608	36,496	41,256	45,196	46,456	47,322	48,854	ʳ49,405
25	Farm	5,678	5,996	6,327	6,753	7,000	7,181	7,418	ʳ7,625
26	Federal and related agencies	40,157	46,721	58,320	66,891	66,033	67,314	ʳ66,753	ʳ66,248
27	Government National Mortgage Assn.	5,113	4,029	4,846	7,438	5,557	5,068	4,241	ʳ4,013
28	1- to 4-family	2,513	1,455	2,248	4,728	3,165	2,486	1,970	ʳ1,670
29	Multifamily	2,600	2,574	2,598	2,710	2,392	2,582	2,271	ʳ2,343
30	Farmers Home Admin.	1,019	1,366	1,432	1,109	830	1,355	1,064	500
31	1- to 4-family	279	743	759	208	228	754	454	98
32	Multifamily	29	29	167	215	46	143	218	28
33	Commercial	320	218	156	190	151	133	72	64
34	Farm	391	376	350	496	405	325	320	310

35	Federal Housing and Veterans Admin...	3,338	3,476	4,015	4,970	5,111	5,092	5,150	5,406
36	1- to 4-family	2,199	2,013	2,009	1,990	1,781	1,716	1,676	1,732
37	Multifamily	1,139	1,463	2,006	2,980	3,330	3,376	3,474	3,674
38	Federal National Mortgage Assn...	19,791	24,175	29,578	31,824	32,028	32,962	32,904	32,830
39	1- to 4-family	17,697	20,370	23,778	25,813	26,112	27,030	26,934	26,836
40	Multifamily	2,094	3,805	5,800	6,011	5,916	5,932	5,970	5,994
41	Federal land banks	9,107	11,071	13,863	16,563	17,978	18,568	19,125	19,942
42	1- to 4-family	13	123	406	549	575	586	601	611
43	Farm	9,094	10,948	13,457	16,014	17,403	17,982	18,524	19,331
44	Federal Home Loan Mortgage Corp...	1,789	2,604	4,586	4,987	4,529	4,269	4,269	3,557
45	1- to 4-family	1,754	2,446	4,217	4,588	4,166	3,917	3,889	3,200
46	Multifamily	35	158	369	399	363	352	380	357
47	Mortgage pools or trusts²	14,404	18,040	23,799	34,138	41,225	44,960	49,801	54,811
48	Government National Mortgage Assn..	5,504	7,890	11,769	18,257	23,634	26,725	30,572	34,260
49	1- to 4-family	5,353	7,561	11,249	17,538	22,821	25,841	29,583	33,190
50	Multifamily	151	329	520	719	813	884	989	1,070
51	Federal Home Loan Mortgage Corp...	441	766	757	1,598	2,153	2,506	2,671	3,570
52	1- to 4-family	331	617	608	1,349	1,831	2,141	2,282	3,112
53	Multifamily	110	149	149	249	322	365	389	458
54	Farmers Home Admin...	8,459	9,384	11,273	14,283	15,438	15,729	16,558	16,981
55	1- to 4-family	5,017	5,458	6,782	9,194	9,670	9,587	10,219	10,423
56	Multifamily	131	138	116	295	541	535	532	530
57	Commercial	867	1,124	1,473	1,948	2,104	2,291	2,440	2,560
58	Farm	2,444	2,664	2,902	2,846	3,123	3,316	3,367	3,468
59	Individuals and others³	98,856	112,160	117,833	119,315	r122,031	r122,122	r125,090	127,715
60	1- to 4-family	45,040	51,112	53,331	56,268	r59,246	r60,816	r62,690	64,495
61	Multifamily	21,465	23,982	24,276	22,140	21,095	r19,298	r20,011	19,307
62	Commercial	19,043	21,303	23,085	22,569	r22,137	r21,834	r21,601	22,399
63	Farm	13,308	15,763	17,141	18,338	19,553	20,174	20,788	21,514

¹ Includes loans held by nondeposit trust companies but not bank trust departments.

² Outstanding principal balances of mortgages backing securities insured or guaranteed by the agency indicated.

³ Other holders include mortgage companies, real estate investment trusts, State and local credit agencies, State and local retirement funds, noninsured pension funds, credit unions, and U.S. agencies for which amounts are small or separate data are not readily available.

NOTE.—Based on data from various institutional and Govt. sources, with some quarters estimated in part by Federal Reserve in conjunction with the Federal Home Loan Bank Board and the Dept. of Commerce. Separation of nonfarm mortgage debt by type of property, if not reported directly, and interpolations and extrapolations where required, are estimated mainly by Federal Reserve. Multifamily debt refers to loans on structures of 5 or more units.

Source: *Federal Reserve Bulletin.*

CONSUMER INSTALLMENT CREDIT: TOTAL OUTSTANDING AND NET CHANGE

Millions of dollars

Holder, and type of credit	1974	1975	1976	1976 Sept.	Oct.	Nov.	Dec.	1977 Jan.	Feb.	Mar.
				Amounts outstanding (end of period)						
1 Total............................	155,384	162,237	178,775	172,918	173,930	175,333	178,775	177,975	178,252	179,695
By holder:										
2 Commercial banks..........	75,846	78,703	85,379	83,714	84,152	84,278	85,379	85,051	85,005	85,916
3 Finance companies.........	36,208	36,695	39,642	38,575	38,809	39,129	39,642	39,665	39,831	39,889
4 Credit unions..............	22,116	25,354	30,546	29,600	29,711	30,053	30,546	30,410	30,701	31,448
5 Retailers[1].................	17,933	18,002	19,178	17,012	17,205	17,726	19,178	18,693	18,322	18,068
6 Others[2]...................	3,281	3,483	4,030	4,017	4,053	4,147	4,030	4,156	4,393	4,374
By type of credit:										
7 *Automobile*...............	50,392	53,028	60,498	59,270	59,717	60,002	60,498	60,349	60,774	61,841
8 Commercial banks..........	30,994	31,534	35,313	34,701	35,009	35,095	35,313	35,284	35,492	36,232
9 Indirect................	18,687	18,353	19,642	19,495	19,611	19,575	19,642	19,566	19,640	20,005
10 Direct..................	12,306	13,181	15,671	15,206	15,398	15,520	15,671	15,719	15,852	16,227
11 Finance companies........	10,618	11,439	13,059	12,808	12,901	12,957	13,059	12,973	13,042	13,084
12 Credit unions............	8,414	9,653	11,633	11,270	11,311	11,442	11,633	11,579	11,690	11,976
13 Others.................	366	402	493	491	496	508	493	513	550	549
Mobile homes:										
14 Commercial banks........	8,972	8,704	8,233	8,340	8,294	8,254	8,233	8,146	8,094	8,076
15 Finance companies........	3,524	3,451	3,277	3,319	3,309	3,295	3,277	3,248	3,207	3,197
16 *Home improvement*.......	7,754	8,004	8,773	8,665	8,726	8,790	8,773	8,736	8,750	8,816
17 Commercial banks........	4,694	4,965	5,381	5,318	5,359	5,388	5,381	5,340	5,307	5,343
Revolving credit:										
18 Bank credit cards........	8,281	9,501	11,075	10,153	10,232	10,329	11,075	10,996	10,820	10,705
19 Bank check credit........	2,797	2,810	3,010	2,922	2,933	2,935	3,010	3,031	3,039	3,030
20 *All other*...............	73,664	76,738	83,910	80,249	80,719	81,728	83,910	83,469	83,568	84,031
21 Commercial banks, total..	20,108	21,188	22,368	22,280	22,325	22,277	22,368	22,254	22,253	22,531
22 Personal loans..........	13,771	14,629	15,606	15,450	15,534	15,517	15,606	15,590	15,590	15,769
23 Finance companies, total..	21,717	21,655	23,178	22,316	22,469	22,748	23,178	23,319	23,454	23,480
24 Personal loans..........	16,961	17,681	19,043	18,371	18,509	18,773	19,043	19,002	18,998	19,048
25 Credit unions............	13,037	14,937	17,993	17,438	17,505	17,706	17,993	17,915	17,993	18,524
26 Retailers...............	17,933	18,002	19,178	17,012	17,205	17,726	19,178	18,693	18,322	18,068
27 Others.................	869	956	1,193	1,203	1,215	1,271	1,193	1,288	1,453	1,428

Net change (during period)[3]

		8,952	6,843	16,539	1,481	1,564	1,243	1,823	1,918	2,022	2,717
28	Total	8,952	6,843	16,539	1,481	1,564	1,243	1,823	1,918	2,022	2,717
	By holder:										
29	Commercial banks	3,975	2,851	6,678	697	671	381	913	565	829	1,462
30	Finance companies	806	483	2,946	233	317	245	364	481	442	373
31	Credit unions	2,507	3,238	5,192	483	280	395	537	416	540	717
32	Retailers	1,538	69	1,176	24	263	98	64	249	118	238
33	Others	126	202	547	45	33	124	-55	207	93	-72
	By type of credit:										
34	*Automobile*	*327*	*2,631*	*7,470*	*605*	*528*	*477*	*1,013*	*758*	*884*	*1,201*
35	Commercial banks	-508	535	3,779	376	350	221	652	418	504	759
36	Indirect	-310	-340	1,289	125	117	70	330	160	239	385
37	Direct	-198	875	2,490	251	233	151	322	258	265	373
38	Finance companies	-100	821	1,620	28	77	98	146	99	161	194
39	Credit unions	958	1,239	1,980	172	105	144	207	174	213	267
40	Other	-23	36	91	28	-4	14	8	66	6	-19
	Mobile homes:										
41	Commercial banks	632	-268	-471	-53	-56	-43	32	-43	-26	16
42	Finance companies	168	-73	-174	-16	-16	-16	-16	-18	-43	3
43	*Home improvement*	*804*	*248*	*768*	*65*	*73*	*103*	*73*	*130*	*73*	*97*
44	Commercial banks	611	271	416	43	44	55	54	36	14	75
	Revolving credit:										
45	Bank credit cards	1,443	1,220	1,576	166	123	71	-33	28	170	293
46	Bank check credit	543	14	199	17	27	6	7	41	32	38
47	*All other*	*5,036*	*3,072*	*7,172*	*698*	*884*	*645*	*747*	*1,023*	*931*	*1,059*
48	Commercial banks, total	1,255	1,080	1,180	148	183	72	199	85	134	281
49	Personal loans	898	858	977	108	161	47	148	101	114	200
50	Finance companies, total	803	-64	1,523	223	258	163	236	401	320	175
51	Personal loans	479	717	1,362	198	237	161	113	178	129	168
52	Credit unions	1,473	1,900	3,056	297	166	239	313	227	312	428
53	Retailers	1,538	69	1,176	24	263	98	64	249	118	238
54	Others	-33	87	237	5	15	73	-66	60	48	-54

[1] Excludes 30-day charge credit held by retailers, oil and gas companies, and travel and entertainment companies.

[2] Mutual savings banks, savings and loan associations, and auto dealers.

[3] Net change equals extensions minus liquidations (repayments, charge-offs, and other credits); figures for all months are seasonally adjusted.

NOTE.—Total consumer noninstalment credit outstanding—credit scheduled to be repaid in a lump sum, including single-payment loans, charge accounts, and service credit—amounted to $39.0 billion at the end of 1976, $35.0 billion at the end of 1975, and $33.4 billion at the end of 1974. Comparable data for Dec. 31, 1977, will be published in the *Bulletin* for February 1978.

Source: *Federal Reserve Bulletin.*

THRIFT INSTITUTIONS AND LIFE INSURANCE COMPANIES, SELECTED ASSETS AND LIABILITIES

Millions of dollars, end of period

Account	1974	1975	1976	1976 Aug.	Sept.	Oct.	Nov.	Dec.	1977 Jan.	Feb.	Mar.	Apr.
Savings and loan associations												
1 Assets	295,545	338,233	391,999	376,188	379,747	385,013	389,173	391,999	398,299	403,591	409,357	414,276
2 Mortgages	249,301	278,590	323,130	307,766	311,847	315,742	319,273	323,130	326,056	329,086	333,703	338,922
3 Cash and investment securities[1]	23,251	30,853	35,660	35,815	35,209	36,442	36,605	35,660	38,252	39,505	39,656	38,975
4 Other	22,993	28,792	33,209	32,607	32,691	32,829	33,295	33,209	33,991	35,000	35,998	35,379
5 Liabilities and net worth	295,545	338,233	391,999	376,188	379,747	385,013	389,173	391,999	398,299	403,591	409,357	414,276
6 Savings capital	242,974	285,743	336,030	318,227	323,800	327,252	329,833	336,030	341,211	344,616	352,194	354,273
7 *Borrowed money*	24,780	20,634	19,087	18,856	19,083	18,810	18,715	19,087	18,455	18,256	18,283	18,841
8 FHLBB	21,508	17,524	15,708	15,495	15,832	15,636	15,571	15,708	15,029	14,661	14,325	14,788
9 Other	3,272	3,110	3,379	3,361	3,251	3,174	3,144	3,379	3,426	3,595	3,958	4,053
10 Loans in process	3,244	5,128	6,836	6,628	6,688	6,735	6,753	6,836	6,718	6,783	7,351	7,893
11 Other	6,105	6,949	8,015	11,197	8,779	10,531	11,918	8,015	9,667	11,418	8,833	10,292
12 Net worth[2]	18,442	19,779	22,031	21,280	21,398	21,685	21,954	22,031	22,248	22,518	22,696	22,977
13 MEMO: Mortgage loan commitments outstanding[3]	7,454	10,673	14,828	15,773	15,449	15,319	15,467	14,828	15,079	16,796	19,304	21,243
Mutual savings banks												
14 Assets	109,550	121,056	134,702	130,571	131,413	132,455	133,361	134,812	135,906	137,307	138,901	......
Loans: 15 Mortgage	74,891	77,221	81,554	79,781	80,145	80,543	80,884	81,630	81,826	81,982	82,273	......
16 Other	3,812	4,023	5,192	5,210	5,478	5,549	5,801	5,183	5,956	6,254	6,389	......
Securities: 17 U.S. Govt.	2,555	4,740	5,911	5,733	5,851	5,796	5,836	5,840	5,917	6,096	6,360	......
18 State and local government	930	1,545	2,420	2,339	2,359	2,429	2,466	2,417	2,295	2,366	2,431	......
19 Corporate and other[4]	22,550	27,992	33,676	32,319	32,432	32,793	33,074	33,793	34,475	35,088	35,928	......
20 Cash	2,167	2,330	2,374	1,552	1,581	1,695	1,668	2,355	1,800	1,835	1,823	......
21 Other assets	2,645	3,205	3,574	3,576	3,567	3,649	3,632	3,593	3,637	3,686	3,668	......
22 Liabilities	109,550	121,056	134,702	130,571	131,413	132,455	133,361	134,812	135,906	137,307	138,901	......

23 Deposits	98,701	109,873	122,802	118,225	119,590	120,360	120,971	122,877	123,864	124,728	126,687
24 Regular:[5]	98,221	109,291	121,874	117,203	118,510	119,346	120,125	121,961	122,874	123,721	125,624
25 Ordinary savings	64,286	69,653	74,483	72,872	73,484	73,610	73,857	74,535	74,621	75,038	76,260
26 Time and other	33,935	39,639	47,391	44,331	45,027	45,736	46,268	47,426	48,253	48,683	49,364
27 Other	480	582	928	1,022	1,080	1,014	846	916	989	1,007	1,063
28 Other liabilities	2,888	2,755	2,853	3,490	2,898	3,140	3,376	2,884	2,940	3,368	2,939
29 General reserve accounts	7,961	8,428	9,047	8,855	8,925	8,955	9,015	9,052	9,102	9,211	9,275
30 MEMO: Mortgage loan commitments outstanding[6]	2,040	1,803	2,439	2,459	2,671	2,548	2,553	2,439	2,584	2,840	3,161

Life insurance companies

31 Assets	263,349	289,304	320,555	309,295	312,044	313,960	316,505	320,555	322,489	324,164	326,453
Securities:											
32 Government[7]	10,900	13,758	17,270	16,902	16,862	17,329	17,565	17,270	17,549	17,817	18,059
33 United States[7]	3,372	4,736	5,156	5,922	5,150	5,448	5,606	5,156	5,291	5,382	5,283
34 State and local	3,667	4,508	5,551	5,324	5,364	5,446	5,467	5,551	5,614	5,666	5,626
35 Foreign[8]	3,861	4,514	6,563	6,286	6,348	6,435	6,492	6,563	6,644	6,769	7,150

Note. *Savings and loan associations:* Estimates by the FHLBB for all associations in the United States. Data are based on monthly reports of federally insured associations and annual reports of other associations. Even when revised, data for current and preceding year are subject to further revision.

Mutual savings banks: Estimates of National Association of Mutual Savings Banks for all savings banks in the United States. Data are reported on a gross-of-valuation-reserves basis.

Life insurance companies: Estimates of the Institute of Life Insurance for all life insurance companies in the United States. Annual figures are annual-statement asset values, with bonds carried on an amortized basis and stocks at year-end market value. Adjustments for interest due and accrued and for differences between market and book values are not made on each item separately but are included, in total, in "other assets."

Credit unions: Estimates by the National Credit Union Administration for a group of Federal and State-chartered credit unions that account for about 30 percent of credit union assets. Figures are preliminary and revised annually to incorporate recent benchmark data.

Source: *Federal Reserve Bulletin.*

THRIFT INSTITUTIONS AND LIFE INSURANCE COMPANIES, SELECTED ASSETS AND LIABILITIES (continued)

Account	1974	1975	1976	1976					1977			
				Aug.	Sept.	Oct.	Nov.	Dec.	Jan.	Feb.	Mar.	Apr.
Life insurance companies												
36 *Business*	119,637	135,317	157,625	150,303	152,125	153,298	154,502	157,625	159,464	160,683	161,319	
37 Bonds	97,717	107,256	123,149	117,806	118,706	120,358	121,659	123,149	125,892	127,542	128,584	
38 Stocks	21,920	28,061	34,476	32,497	33,419	32,940	32,843	34,476	33,572	33,141	32,735	
39 Mortgages	86,234	89,167	91,581	89,891	90,217	90,323	90,808	91,581	91,615	91,646	91,874	
40 Real estate	8,331	9,621	10,526	10,146	10,175	10,285	10,310	10,526	10,550	10,632	10,717	
41 Policy loans	22,862	24,467	25,849	25,383	25,505	25,607	25,710	25,849	25,921	26,051	26,221	
42 Other assets	15,385	16,971	17,704	16,670	17,160	17,118	17,610	17,704	17,390	17,335	18,263	
Credit unions												
43 **Total assets/liabilities and capital**	31,948	38,037	44,897	42,266	43,079	43,415	44,089	44,835	44,906	45,798	47,111	47,348
44 Federal	16,715	20,209	24,164	22,698	23,198	23,283	23,668	24,164	24,188	24,756	25,596	25,697
45 State	15,233	17,828	20,733	19,568	19,881	20,132	20,421	20,671	20,718	21,042	21,515	21,651
46 *Loans outstanding*	24,432	28,169	34,033	32,300	33,093	33,275	33,732	34,293	34,188	34,549	35,411	36,019
47 Federal	12,730	14,869	18,022	17,065	17,458	17,522	17,786	18,202	18,081	18,275	18,776	19,050
48 State	11,702	13,300	16,011	15,235	15,635	15,753	15,946	16,091	16,107	16,274	16,635	16,969
49 *Savings*	27,518	33,013	39,264	36,752	37,436	37,854	38,281	38,968	39,344	39,981	41,161	41,394
50 Federal (shares)	14,370	17,530	21,149	19,783	20,167	20,358	20,597	20,980	21,165	21,559	22,346	22,524
51 State (shares and deposits)	13,148	15,483	18,115	16,969	17,269	17,496	17,684	17,988	18,179	18,442	18,815	18,870

1 Stock of the Federal Home Loan Bank Board (FHLBB) is included in "other assets."
2 Includes net undistributed income, which is accrued by most, but not all, associations.
3 Excludes figures for loans in process, which are shown as a liability.
4 Includes securities of foreign governments and international organizations and nonguaranteed issues of U.S. government agencies.
5 Excludes checking, club, and school accounts.
6 Commitments outstanding (including loans in process) of banks in New York State as reported to the Savings Banks Assn. of the State of New York.
7 Direct and guaranteed obligations. Excuses federal agency issues not guaranteed, which are shown in this table under "business" securities.
8 Issues of foreign governments and their subdivisions and bonds of the International Bank for Reconstruction and Development.
Source: *Federal Reserve Bulletin.*

SOURCES AND USES OF FUNDS, NONFARM NONFINANCIAL CORPORATE BUSINESS

Billions of dollars; quarterly data are at seasonally adjusted annual rates

Period	Sources							Uses			Discrepancy (sources less uses)
	Total	Internal[1]	External					Total	Purchase of physical assets[4]	Increase in financial assets	
			Total	Credit market funds			Other				
				Total	Long-term[2]	Short-term[3]					
1970	105.1	58.9	46.2	41.5	32.6	8.9	4.8	96.1	80.6	15.4	9.0
1971	129.0	68.6	60.4	46.4	41.6	4.7	14.0	115.1	86.2	28.8	13.9
1972	154.0	80.8	73.2	58.8	41.4	17.3	14.4	137.5	101.0	36.5	16.4
1973	181.7	83.8	97.8	72.9	37.4	35.5	25.0	165.5	124.4	41.1	16.1
1974	183.0	77.6	105.4	83.1	39.6	43.5	22.2	169.9	134.6	35.3	13.1
1975	145.5	103.4	42.1	37.1	49.8	-12.8	5.0	130.9	95.7	35.2	14.5
1976	211.5	121.8	89.7	56.6	46.6	9.9	33.2	196.6	137.6	59.0	15.0
1975: I	83.5	83.5	.0	35.0	52.9	-18.0	-35.0	68.6	89.8	-21.2	14.9
II	130.7	101.5	29.2	32.1	54.4	-22.2	-2.9	115.3	80.9	34.4	15.4
III	171.0	113.6	57.4	31.1	37.9	-6.8	26.3	157.9	106.8	51.1	13.2
IV	196.7	114.9	81.8	50.0	54.0	-4.0	31.7	182.2	105.5	76.7	14.6
1976: I	199.3	120.6	78.7	46.8	48.2	-1.4	31.9	187.4	129.5	57.9	11.9
II	205.5	121.3	84.2	51.9	41.0	10.8	32.4	190.4	139.1	51.3	15.1
III	204.8	126.0	78.8	50.7	47.2	3.5	28.1	188.7	145.0	43.7	16.0
IV	236.6	119.5	117.1	77.2	50.2	26.9	40.0	219.5	136.9	82.6	17.1
1977: I p	232.6	118.6	114.0	80.6	37.9	42.8	33.4	216.1	142.9	73.2	16.5

[1] Undistributed profits (after inventory valuation and capital consumption adjustments), capital consumption allowances, and foreign branch profits.
[2] Stocks, bonds, and mortgages.
[3] Bank loans, commercial paper, finance company loans, bankers' acceptances, and Government loans.
[4] Plant and equipment, residential structures, inventory investment, and mineral rights.

Source: Board of Governors of the Federal Reserve System.

Source: Economic Indicators, Council of Economic Advisors.

Banks and Other Financial Institutions

25 LARGEST U.S. COMMERCIAL BANKING COMPANIES (ranked by assets)

Rank 1976	Company	Assets[1] ($000)	Deposits ($000)	Loans[2] ($000)	Employees[3] Number
1	BankAmerica Corp. (San Francisco)	73,912,940	60,749,814	39,162,515	66,877
2	Citicorp (New York)	64,281,504	49,136,069	40,323,078	46,600
3	Chase Manhattan Corp. (New York)	45,637,747	37,608,281	30,474,391	28,400
4	Manufacturers Hanover Corp. (New York)	31,482,813	26,192,219	17,442,699	18,359
5	J. P. Morgan & Co. (New York)	28,765,510	21,474,258	14,059,479	9,662
6	Chemical New York Corp.	26,613,774	20,873,796	14,451,207	15,500
7	Bankers Trust New York Corp.	22,248,581	17,694,400	11,581,079	12,520
8	Continental Illinois Corp. (Chicago)	21,974,815	15,817,127	12,914,138	9,942
9	First Chicago Corp.	19,834,052	14,063,432	11,807,317	8,188
10	Western Bancorp. (Los Angeles)	19,672,193	16,378,317	11,289,256	25,884†
11	Security Pacific Corp. (Los Angeles)	16,400,732	13,486,727	9,487,790	18,321†
12	Wells Fargo & Co. (San Francisco)	12,968,664	10,446,453	8,398,447	12,500
13	Crocker National Corp. (San Francisco)	10,771,223	9,067,345	6,665,374	11,570
14	Marine Midland Banks, Inc. (Buffalo)	10,718,881	9,095,019	6,348,444	10,062†
15	Charter New York Corp.	10,208,942	8,698,563	4,975,314	7,600
16	Mellon National Corp. (Pittsburgh)	9,352,661	6,689,174	5,382,424	6,156†
17	First National Boston Corp.	8,498,586	5,967,002	4,221,954	9,400
18	Northwest Bancorp. (Minneapolis)	8,358,181	6,627,076	4,693,526	9,598
19	First Bank System, Inc. (Minneapolis)	7,843,753	6,133,792	4,873,172	7,686†
20	National Detroit Corp.	7,552,509	5,839,629	3,923,826	5,470
21	First Pennsylvania Corp. (Philadelphia)	7,214,021	4,260,493	4,135,654	6,436
22	First International Bancshares, Inc. (Dallas)	7,166,576	5,626,238	3,464,913	3,983†
23	Republic of Texas Corp. (Dallas)	6,521,265	4,648,720	3,386,444	2,955
24	Seafirst Corp. (Seattle)	5,309,590	4,127,817	3,537,459	5,795
25	First City Bancorp. of Texas (Houston)	5,256,316	4,274,072	3,006,464	3,601

[1] As of December 31, 1976.

[2] Includes federal funds sold, U.S. securities purchased under agreements to resell, and mortgages; net of loan-loss reserves.

[3] Year-end total unless followed by a dagger (†), in which case average for the year.

[4] After securities transactions and extraordinary items.

[5] Sum of capital stock, surplus, and retained earnings at the end of the year.

[6] For all companies, the figures shown for 1976 and 1975 are the "primary" earnings per share that appear in the company's income statement. These figures are based on a weighted average of the number of common shares and common-stock equivalents outstanding during the year. "Common stock equivalents" generally include (a) convertible securities whose cash yield is less than two thirds of the prime rate as of the time the securities were issued and (b) options and warrants when the effect of their inclusion in the computation would reduce the "primary" earnings per share. Weighted averages are used for 1966 where these are available; where they are not, figures are based on a simple average of 1965 and 1966 year-end shares outstanding. Per-share earnings for 1975 and 1966 are adjusted for stock splits and stock dividends. They are not restated for mergers, acquisitions, or accounting changes made after 1966.

[7] Income before securities transactions.

Net Income[4] ($000)	Stockholders' Equity[5] ($000)	Net Income as Percent of Equity	Earnings per Share[6]				Growth Rate 1966-76[9] (Percent)	Total Return to Investors[10]	
			1976($)[7]	1976($)[8]	1975($)[8]	1966($)[7]		1976[11] (Percent)	1966-76 Average[11] (Percent)
336,771	2,421,593	13.9	2.40	2.41	2.19	0.83	11.20	46.07	13.67
401,352	2,660,719	15.1	3.24	3.21	2.83	0.98	12.70	14.20	11.86
116,412	1,667,092	7.0	3.28	3.63	5.42	3.14	0.44	19.34	1.58
143,062	1,086,867	13.2	4.82	4.82	4.80	2.00	9.19	41.56	10.04
202,683	1,455,548	13.9	5.04	5.04	4.76	1.76	11.09	8.51	13.39
92,614	885,874	10.5	6.38	6.40	6.64	4.14	4.42	51.26	5.45
56,528	724,710	7.8	4.76	4.66	5.82	4.86	(0.21)	39.49	1.06
128,013	914,067	14.0	7.45	7.28	6.49	2.92	9.82	69.38	10.34
105,640	955,563	11.1	2.35	2.67	2.72	1.12	7.69	31.50	8.89
87,783	865,309	10.1	3.78	3.68	3.20	2.16	5.76	74.64	4.64
76,328	713,774	10.7	3.58	3.58	3.16	2.09	5.53	69.83	3.77
63,511	545,862	11.6	3.16	3.16	2.83	1.51	7.66	80.52	7.65
46,272	443,053	10.4	3.63	3.71	3.63	2.48	3.88	37.95	5.01
13,151	428,982	3.1	0.74	1.04	1.19	2.67	(12.04)	(0.68)	(3.15)
42,826	397,744	10.8	4.85	4.87	5.14	3.17	4.34	40.11	4.48
64,087	670,215	9.6	6.62	6.54	6.25	3.72	5.93	20.00	6.52
43,452	524,314	8.3	3.55	3.59	3.60	2.54	3.40	37.53	5.22
65,382	519,774	12.6	5.26	5.23	4.85	2.14	9.41	35.64	13.25
63,434	516,368	12.3	4.25	4.26	4.16	1.70	9.60	11.63	12.71
51,124	470,699	10.9	4.38	4.30	4.29	1.96	8.37	46.38	9.04
23,116	296,424	7.8	1.64	1.76	1.39	1.44	1.31	19.64	6.17
56,039	382,861	14.6	3.80	3.78	3.50	1.04	13.83	20.33	15.25
46,207	335,240	13.8	3.99	4.06	4.01	1.22	12.58	20.99	10.00
36,366	274,033	13.3	4.05	4.04	4.65	1.48	10.59	40.48	11.66
31,921	257,753	12.4	3.43	3.44	3.05	1.32[12]	10.02	75.28	11.51

[8] After securities transactions and extraordinary items.

[9] Average annual growth rate, compounded. The 1976 figure on which the growth rate is based is income before securities transactions, but after a loan-loss provision. The 1966 figure does not reflect any loan losses.

[10] Total return includes both price appreciation and dividend yield, i.e., to an investor in the company's stock. The figures shown assume sales at the end of 1976 of stock owned at the end of 1966 or 1975. It has been assumed that any proceeds from cash dividends, the sale of rights and warrant offerings, and stock received in spin-offs were reinvested at the end of the year in which they were received. Returns are adjusted for stock splits, stock dividends, recapitalizations, and corporate reorganizations as they occur; however, no effort has been made to reflect the cost of brokerage commissions or of taxes. Results are listed as not available where shares are not publicly traded or traded on only a limited basis. Where corporations have more than one class of shares outstanding, only the more widely held and actively traded have been considered.

[11] Percentages are the returns received by the hypothetical investor described in footnote 10. The ten-year figures are annual averages, compounded. Where corporations were substantially reorganized—e.g., because of mergers—the predecessor companies used in calculating total return are the same as those cited in the footnotes dropped from the earnings-per-share figures.

[12] Figure is for First City National Bank of Houston.

Source: Reprinted from the 1977 Fortune Directory by special permission; © 1977 Time Inc.

25 LARGEST COMMERCIAL BANKING COMPANIES OUTSIDE THE UNITED STATES

Rank 1976	Bank	Country	Assets[1] ($000)	Increase (decrease) from Prior Year	
				In U.S. Dollars	In Local Currencies
1	Deutsche Bank[7]	Germany	44,593,275	27.63%	14.97%
2	Dai-Ichi Kangyo Bank[8,9]	Japan	43,012,074	18.14	11.78
3	Banque Nationale de Paris	France	41,424,423	5.76	17.53
4	Banco do Brasil[10]	Brazil	39,868,607	37.26	81.38
5	Crédit Lyonnais[10]	France	38,010,237	14.91	27.69
6	Fuji Bank[8]	Japan	37,233,164	17.35	11.03
7	Sumitomo Bank[8]	Japan	37,174,458	20.77	14.26
8	Société Générale[10]	France	36,880,569	10.09	22.33
9	Dresdner Bank[7]	Germany	36,006,195	27.30	14.68
10	Mitsubishi Bank[8]	Japan	34,984,443	15.99	9.74
11	Sanwa Bank[8]	Japan	34,407,282	17.44	11.11
12	Barclays Bank	Britain	32,863,410	(0.51)	18.36
13	Bank of Tokyo[8]	Japan	32,776,243	7.42	1.64
14	Westdeutsche Landesbank Girozentrale[7,10]	Germany	30,874,169	19.19	7.37
15	Industrial Bank of Japan[8,9]	Japan	30,045,333	25.51	18.75
16	Royal Bank of Canada[12]	Canada	29,656,169	19.69	14.36
17	National Westminster Bank	Britain	29,036,145	(2.12)	16.44
18	Mitsui Bank[8,9]	Japan	27,020,488	21.36	14.82
19	Canadian Imperial Bank of Commerce[12]	Canada	26,850,618	22.74	17.27
20	Tokai Bank[8]	Japan	26,848,948	17.24	10.92
21	Commerzbank[7]	Germany	26,809,506	24.37	12.05
22	Banca Nazionale del Lavoro[10]	Italy	24,188,717	(1.50)	25.22
23	Bayerische Vereinsbank[7]	Germany	24,045,840	29.30	16.48
24	Taiyo Kobe Bank[8,9]	Japan	23,939,555	15.40	9.18
25	Long-Term Credit Bank of Japan[8,9]	Japan	22,781,446	23.61	16.95

[1] Figures have been translated into U.S. dollars on the following basis: total assets, deposits, loans, and stockholders' equity have been converted using the market rate prevailing at each bank's fiscal year-end, which is December 31, 1976, unless otherwise noted. Net income has been converted using the average rate in the official exchange market during the bank's fiscal year. Figures for subsidiaries are included if they are more than 50 percent owned (unless there is a footnote to the contrary). Daiwa Bank, Mitsubishi Trust & Banking, Mitsui Trust & Banking, and Sumitomo Trust & Banking include holdings of major trusts in their assets.

[2] Figures for all German banks include their own bonds; so do the figures for Bank of Tokyo, Industrial Bank of Japan, and Long-Term Credit Bank of Japan. Banco do Brasil includes other borrowed funds. Figures for Swiss banks include medium-term notes.

[3] Includes loans to banks and money at call or available on short notice.

Deposits[2] ($000)	Loans[3] ($000)	Net Income[4] ($000)	Stock-holders' Equity[5] ($000)	Offices[6]	Employees
41,225,014	35,816,149	171,080	1,437,728	1,281	40,772
29,050,138	25,150,040	76,201	948,260	319	25,325
39,900,081	29,119,218	135,657	462,817	2,249	55,732
31,996,234	32,705,052	609,825	2,753,614	1,026	72,404
36,544,748	28,170,308	67,570	359,066	2,434	48,768
25,465,257	21,016,007	84,122	939,401	239	19,451
25,483,791	21,282,048	86,442	1,012,925	196	18,518
35,396,453	26,156,422	108,741	421,389	2,642	41,544
33,643,844	28,060,806	112,141	1,084,977	1,067	28,401
23,937,434	20,405,149	84,273	964,205	223	20,170
23,509,507	20,402,772	72,781	815,364	231	18,223
29,349,404	25,692,004	143,849	1,552,952	5,100	97,191[11]
20,256,916	18,278,498	76,239	572,247	195	13,066
29,020,837	23,720,998	58,871	796,556	13	7,100
24,273,407	18,113,440	61,841	685,709	20	4,994
27,042,748	18,335,238	93,529	751,806	1,567	34,010
26,167,500	24,234,919	152,146	1,586,526	4,000	68,921
17,775,963	14,469,420	45,776	586,369	161	12,871
24,550,200	16,822,570	112,267	657,792	1,784	32,784
17,887,815	16,144,198	52,166	597,026	217	15,637
25,420,172	22,894,307	88,956	754,610	861	19,207
21,075,961	13,641,653	26,864	797,550	294	16,750
22,683,226	21,018,422	46,746	511,992	391	10,300
16,779,204	14,453,173	41,408	531,723	325	17,339
18,973,199	15,276,270	60,778	573,503	17	3,161

[4] After taxes and excluding any minority interest.
[5] Sum of capital stock, surplus, and retained earnings at the end of the fiscal year.
[6] Includes head office, branches, and agencies.
[7] Excludes certain subsidiaries that are more than 50 percent owned.
[8] Figures are for fiscal year ending September 30, 1976.
[9] Parent company only.
[10] Government owned.
[11] Average for the year.
[12] Figures are for fiscal year ending October 31, 1976.
Source: Reprinted from the 1977 *Fortune Directory* by special permission; © 1977 Time Inc.

U.S. BANKS WITH FOREIGN BRANCHES†

ABU DHABI

Abu Dhabi
Bank of America NT&SA, San Francisco.
Citibank NA, New York.
First National Bank, Chicago.

ANGOLA

Luanda
First National City Bank, New York.

ANGUILLA

The Valley
Bank of America NT&SA, San Francisco.

ANTIGUA

St. Johns
First Pennsylvania Bank NA, Philadelphia.

ARGENTINA

Avellaneda
First National Bank of Boston.
Buenos Aires
Bank of America NT&SA, San Francisco.
Bank Leumi Trust Co., New York.
Bankers Trust Co., New York.
Chase Manhattan Bank NA, New York.
Chemical Bank, New York.
Citibank NA, New York.
Continental Illinois National Bank & Trust Co., Chicago.
First National Bank of Boston.
First Wisconsin National Bank, Milwaukee.
Irving Trust Co., New York.
Manufacturers Hanover Trust Co., New York.
Marine Midland Bank, New York.
Morgan Guaranty Trust Co., New York.
Republic National Bank, New York.
J. Henry Schroder Banking Corp., New York.
Wells Fargo Bank NA, San Francisco.
Cordoba
Citibank NA, New York.

Lomas de Zamora
Citibank NA, New York.
Mendoza
Citibank NA, New York.
Rosario
Citibank NA, New York.
First National Bank of Boston.

AUSTRALIA

Adelaide
National Bank of Detroit.
Brisbane
Citibank NA, New York.
Continental Illinois National Bank & Trust Co., Chicago.
Manufacturers National Bank, Detroit.
Melbourne
Bank of America NT&SA, San Francisco.
Bankers Trust Co., New York.
Chase Manhattan Bank NA, New York.
Citibank NA, New York.
Crocker National Bank, San Francisco.
First National Bank of Boston.
First National City Bank, New York.
Irving Trust Co., New York.
Mellon Bank, NA, Pittsburgh.
Morgan Guaranty Trust Co., New York.
National Bank of Detroit.
Security Pacific National Bank, Los Angeles.
United California Bank, Los Angeles.
Perth
Chase Manhattan Bank NA, New York.
Sydney
American Express International Banking Corp., New York.
American National Bank & Trust Co., Chicago.
Bank of America NT&SA, San Francisco.
Bankers Trust Co., New York.
Chase Manhattan Bank NA, New York.
Chemical Bank, New York.
Continental Illinois National Bank & Trust Co., Chicago.
Fidelity Bank, Philadelphia.
First National Bank, Chicago.
First National Bank of Boston.
First National City Bank, New York.
Manufacturers Hanover Trust Co., New York.
Marine Midland Bank, New York.
Mellon Bank NA, Pittsburgh.
Morgan Guaranty Trust Co., New York.
National Bank of Detroit.
Philadelphia National Bank.
Pittsburgh National Bank.
Provident National Bank, Philadelphia.
Seattle-First National Bank.
Security Pacific National Bank, Los Angeles.
°United California Bank, Los Angeles.
Wells Fargo Bank NA, San Francisco.

AUSTRIA

Vienna
American Express International Banking
Corp., New York.
Bank of America NT&SA, San Francisco.
Chase Manhattan Bank NA, New York.
Chemical Bank, New York.
Citibank NA, New York.
Continental Illinois National Bank & Trust
Co., Chicago.
First National Bank of Boston.
Philadelphia National Bank.

BAHAMAS

Eleuthera Island
Chase Manhattan Bank NA, New York.
Freeport
Chase Manhattan Bank NA, New York.
Citibank NA, New York.
Great Exuma
Chase Manhattan Bank NA, New York.
Nassau
Allied Bank, International, New York.
American Fletcher National Bank, Indian-
apolis.
American National Bank & Trust of New
Jersey, Morristown.
American Security and Trust Co., Wash-
ington.
Bank Leumi Trust Co., New York.
Bank of America NT&SA, San Francisco.
Bank of California NA, San Francisco.
Bank of New Orleans.
Bank of New York.
Bank of the Southwest NA, Houston.
Bank of Virginia Co., Richmond.
Bankers Trust Co., New York.
California First Bank, San Francisco.
Central National Bank, Cleveland.
Chase Manhattan Bank, NA, New York.
Chemical Bank, New York.
Citibank NA, New York.
Citizens & Southern National Bank, At-
lanta.
Cleveland Trust Co.
Commerce Union Bank, Nashville.
Connecticut Bank & Trust Co., Hartford.
Continental Illinois National Bank & Trust,
Chicago.
Detroit Bank & Trust Co.
Equibank NA, Pittsburgh.
Equitable Trust Co., Baltimore.
Exchange National Bank, Chicago.
Fidelity Bank, Philadelphia.
Fidelity Union Trust Co., Newark.
First & Merchants National Bank, Rich-
mond.
First City National Bank of Houston.
First National Bank of Arizona, Phoenix.
First National Bank of Boston.
First National Bank of Ft. Worth.

First National Bank of Memphis.
First National Bank in St. Louis.
First National Bank of St. Paul.
First National Bank & Trust Co., Tulsa.
First Union National Bank of North Caro-
lina, Charlotte.
Harris Trust & Savings Bank, Chicago.
Hartford National Bank & Trust Co.
Houston National Bank.
Indiana National Bank, Indianapolis.
International Bank, Washington, DC.
Liberty National Bank & Trust Co., Okla-
homa City.
Lloyds Bank California, Los Angeles.
Manufacturers Hanover Trust Co., New
York.
Manufacturers National Bank, Detroit.
Marine Midland Bank, New York.
Marine National Exchange Bank, Milwau-
kee.
Maryland National Bank, Baltimore.
Merchants National Bank & Trust Co., In-
dianapolis.
Morgan Guaranty Trust Co., New York.
National Bank of North America, New
York.
National Bank of Washington, Washington,
DC.
National City Bank, Cleveland.
New England Merchants National Bank,
Boston.
Northwestern National Bank, Minneapolis.
Omaha (Neb.) National Bank.
Philadelphia National Bank.
Pittsburgh National Bank.
Provident National Bank, Philadelphia.
Republic National Bank, Dallas.
Republic National Bank, New York.
Riggs National Bank, Washington, DC.
Seattle-First National Bank.
Security Pacific National Bank, Los Ange-
les.
Shawmut Bank of Boston NA.
Society National Bank, Cleveland.
Southeast First National Bank of Miami.
State Street Bank & Trust Co., Boston.
Sterling National Bank & Trust Co., New
York.
Sumitomo Bank of California, San Fran-
cisco.
Texas Commerce Bank NA, Houston.
Union Bank, Los Angeles.
Union Commerce Bank, Cleveland.
Union Trust Co., Stamford, Conn.
United Bank of Denver.
United California Bank, Los Angeles.
United States National Bank of Oregon,
Portland.
Valley National Bank, Phoenix.
Virginia National Bank, Norfolk.
Wells Fargo Bank NA, San Francisco.
Oakes Field
Citibank NA, New York.

BAHRAIN

Manama
American Express International Banking Corp., New York.
°Bank of America NT&SA, San Francisco.
Chase Manhattan Bank NA, New York.
°Chemical Bank, New York.
Citibank NA, New York.
Continental Illinois National Bank & Trust Co., Chicago.
°Texas Commerce Bank NA, Houston.

BANGLADESH

Chittagong
American Express International Banking Corp., New York.
Morgan Guaranty Trust Co., New York.
Dacca
American Express International Banking Corp., New York.
Citibank NA, New York.

BARBADOS

Bridgetown
Bank of America NT&SA, San Francisco.
Chase Manhattan Bank NA, New York.
Citibank NA, New York.
First National Bank, Chicago.
Holetown
Citibank NA, New York.

BELGIUM

Antwerp
American Express International Banking Corp., New York.
Bank of America NT&SA, San Francisco.
Bankers Trust Co., New York.
Chase Manhattan Bank NA, New York.
Citibank NA, New York.
Continental Illinois National Bank & Trust Co., Chicago.
First National Bank, Chicago.
Brussels
American Express International Banking Corp., New York.
Bank of America NT&SA, San Francisco.
Bankers Trust Co., New York.
Chase Manhattan Bank NA, New York.
Chemical Bank, New York.
Citibank NA, New York.
Continental Illinois National Bank & Trust Co., Chicago.
First National Bank of Boston.
First National Bank, Chicago.
First National Bank of Louisville.
Manufacturers Hanover Trust Co., New York.
Marine Midland Bank, New York.
Morgan Guaranty Trust Co., New York.

Security Pacific National Bank, Los Angeles.
United California Bank, Los Angeles.
Ghent
°Bankers Trust Co., New York.
Chase Manhattan Bank NA, New York.
International Bank, Washington, DC.
Hasselt
Citibank NA, New York.
Liege
°Bankers Trust Co., New York.
Chase Manhattan Bank NA, New York.
Citibank NA, New York.
Continental Illinois National Bank & Trust Co., Chicago.

BELIZE

Belize
Chase Manhattan Bank, NA, New York.

BENIN

Cotonou
Bank of America NT&SA, San Francisco.

BERMUDA

Hamilton
Chemical Bank, New York.
European-American Banking Corp., New York.
Morgan Guaranty Trust Co., New York.
Security Pacific National Bank, Los Angeles.
South Shore Bank, Quincy, Mass.

BOLIVIA

La Paz
Bank of America NT&SA, San Francisco.
Citibank NA, New York.
First National Bank of Boston.
Santa Cruz de la Sierra
Bank of America NT&SA, San Francisco.

BRAZIL

Bahia (Salvador)
Citibank NA, New York.
Belo Horizonte
Citibank NA, New York.
Brasilia
Citibank NA, New York.
Campinas
Citibank NA, New York.
First National Bank of Boston.
Curitiba
Citibank NA, New York.
Porto Alegre
Citibank NA, New York.
First National Bank of Boston.
Recife
Bank of America NT&SA, San Francisco.
Citibank NA, New York.

Rio de Janeiro
Bank of America NT&SA, San Francisco.
Bankers Trust Co., New York.
Chase Manhattan Bank NA, New York.
Chemical Bank, New York.
Citibank NA, New York.
Citizens & Southern National Bank, Atlanta.
European-American Banking Corp. & European-American Bank & Trust Co., New York.
First National Bank of Boston.
*First National Bank, Louisville.
Irving Trust Co., New York.
Manufacturers Hanover Trust Co., New York.
Marine Midland Bank, New York.
Mellon Bank NA, Pittsburgh.
Philadelphia National Bank.
Republic National Bank, New York.
J. Henry Schroder Banking Corp., New York.
Security Pacific National Bank, Los Angeles.
Union Bank, Los Angeles.
United California Bank, Los Angeles.
Santo Andre
Manufacturers Hanover Trust Co., New York.
Santos
Bank of America NT&SA, San Francisco.
Citibank NA, New York.
Sao Paulo
American National Bank & Trust Co., Chicago.
Bank Leumi Trust Co., New York.
Bank of America NT&SA, San Francisco.
Bankers Trust Co., New York.
Chase Manhattan Bank NA, New York.
Chemical Bank, New York.
Citibank NA, New York.
Continental Illinois National Bank & Trust Co., Chicago.
Crocker National Bank, San Francisco.
Fidelity Bank, Philadelphia.
First National Bank of Boston.
First National Bank, Chicago.
First National Bank, Dallas.
*First National Bank, Louisville.
First Pennsylvania Bank NA, Philadelphia.
*First Wisconsin National Bank, Milwaukee.
Harris Trust & Savings Bank, Chicago.
Manufacturers Hanover Trust Co., New York.
Marine Midland Bank, New York.
Midlantic National Bank, Newark.
Morgan Guaranty Trust Co., New York.
Philadelphia National Bank.
Pittsburgh National Bank.
Republic National Bank, Dallas.
Republic National Bank, New York.
J. Henry Schroder Banking Corp., New York.

Security Pacific National Bank, Los Angeles.
Wells Fargo Bank NA, San Francisco.

BRUNEI

Bandar Seri Begawan
Bank of America NT&SA, San Francisco.
Citibank NA, New York.
Kuala Belait
Citibank NA, New York.

BURUNDI

Bujumbura
Bank of America NT&SA, San Francisco.

CAMEROON

Yaounde
Bank of America NT&SA, San Francisco.
Bankers Trust Co., New York.
Citibank NA, New York.
Morgan Guaranty Trust Co., New York.

CANADA

Edmonton
Seattle-First National Bank.
Montreal
Bank of America NT&SA, San Francisco.
Citibank NA, New York.
First National Bank of Boston.
First Pennsylvania Bank NA, Philadelphia.
Manufacturers National Bank, Detroit.
Marine Midland Bank, New York.
South Shore Bank, Quincy, Mass.
St. Johns
Northern Trust Co., Chicago.
Toronto
American National Bank and Trust Co., Chicago.
Bank Leumi Trust Co., New York.
Bank of America NT&SA, San Francisco.
Bankers Trust Co., New York.
Chase Manhattan Bank NA, New York.
Chemical Bank, New York.
Detroit Bank & Trust Co.
Industrial National Bank, Providence.
Manufacturers National Bank, Detroit.
Manufacturers & Traders Trust Co., Buffalo.
Marine Midland Bank, New York.
Morgan Guaranty Trust Co.
National Bank of Detroit.
*Wells Fargo Bank NA, San Francisco.
Worcester County National Bank, Worcester.
Vancouver
Bank of America NT&SA, San Francisco.
Winnipeg
Northwestern National Bank, Minneapolis.

CAYMAN ISLANDS

George Town
American Express International Banking Corp., New York.
Arizona Bank, Phoenix.
Bank Leumi Trust Co., New York.
Bank of America NT&SA, San Francisco.
Bank of New York.
Bank of Tokyo Trust Co., New York.
Bank of Virginia Co., Richmond.
Barclays Bank of California, San Francisco.
Brown Brothers Harriman & Co., New York.
Capital National Bank, Houston.
Central National Bank, Chicago.
Central Penn National Bank, Philadelphia.
Chase Manhattan Bank NA, New York.
Citibank NA, New York.
Citizens and Southern National Bank, Atlanta.
City National Bank of Detroit.
Colonial Bank & Trust Co., Waterbury, Conn.
Commerce Union Bank, Nashville.
Continental Illinois National Bank & Trust Co., Chicago.
Crocker National Bank, San Francisco.
European-American Bank & Trust Co., New York.
First American National Bank, Nashville.
First National Bank, Atlanta.
First National Bank and Trust Co., Oklahoma City.
First National Bank in Dallas.
First National Bank of Birmingham.
First National Bank of Chicago.
First National Bank of Commerce, New Orleans.
First National Bank of Denver.
First National Bank of Louisville.
First National Bank of Maryland, Baltimore.
First National Bank of Oregon, Portland.
First National State Bank of New Jersey, Newark.
First New Haven National Bank.
First Pennsylvania Bank NA, Philadelphia.
First Virginia Bank, Falls Church.
Fort Worth National Bank.
Girard Bank, Philadelphia.
Hibernia Bank, New Orleans.
Huntington National Bank, Columbus.
Indiana National Bank, Indianapolis.
Industrial National Bank, Providence.
Industrial Valley Bank and Trust Co., Philadelphia.
International Bank, Washington, DC.
Irving Trust Co., New York.
La Salle National Bank, Chicago.
M&I Marshall & Ilsley Bank, Milwaukee.
Marine Midland Bank, New York.
°Mercantile National Bank at Dallas.

Mercantile Trust Co., St. Louis.
Midlantic National Bank, Newark.
National Central Bank, Lancaster.
New England Merchants National Bank, Boston.
New Jersey Bank NA, Paterson.
°Nordic American Banking Corp., New York.
North Carolina National Bank, Charlotte.
Northern Trust Co., Chicago.
Old Kent Bank & Trust Co., Grand Rapids.
J. Henry Schroder Banking Corp., New York.
Third National Bank, Nashville.
Trust Company Bank, Atlanta.
UBAF Arab American Bank, New York.
Union Commerce Bank, Cleveland.
Union Planters National Bank, Memphis.
United Jersey Bank, Hackensack.
United Virginia Bank, Richmond.
Wachovia National Bank & Trust Co. NA, Winston-Salem.
Winters National Bank & Trust Co., Dayton.
Worcester County National Bank, Worcester.

CENTRAL AFRICAN REPUBLIC

Bangui
Citibank NA, New York.

CHAD

N'Jamene
Citibank NA, New York.

CHANNEL ISLANDS

Guernsey
Allied Bank International, New York.
Chemical Bank, New York.
First National Bank of Boston.
First National Bank, Chicago.
Manufacturers Hanover Trust Co., New York.
Jersey
Bank of America NT&SA, San Francisco.
Chase Manhattan Bank NA, New York.
Citibank NA, New York.
St. Helier
Bank of America NT&SA, San Francisco.
Citibank NA, New York.

CHILE

Santiago
Bank of America NT&SA, San Francisco.
Citibank NA, New York.
European-American Banking Corp. & European-American Bank & Trust Co., New York.

°Manufacturers Hanover Trust Co., New York.

COLOMBIA

Barranquilla
Bank of America NT&SA, San Francisco.
Citibank NA, New York.
Marine Midland Bank, New York.
Philadelphia National Bank.

Bogota
American National Bank & Trust Co., Chicago.
Bankers Trust Co., New York.
Chase Manhattan Bank NA, New York.
Chemical Bank, New York.
Citibank NA, New York.
Citizens & Southern National Bank, Atlanta.
°Continental Illinois National Bank & Trust Co., Chicago.
European-American Banking Corp. & European-American Bank & Trust Co., New York.
First National Bank, Chicago.
First Wisconsin National Bank, Milwaukee.
Manufacturers Hanover Trust Co., New York.
Marine Midland Bank, New York.
New Jersey Bank NA, Paterson.
Pan American Bancshares, Inc., Miami.
Republic National Bank, New York.
J. Henry Schroder Banking Corp., New York.
Wells Fargo Bank NA, San Francisco.

Bucaramanga
Citibank NA, New York.

Cali
Bank of America NT&SA, San Francisco.
Citibank NA, New York.
Continental Illinois National Bank & Trust Co., Chicago.
First National Bank of Minneapolis.

Carrera Septima
Bank of America NT&SA, San Francisco.

Cartagena
Citibank NA, New York.
Marine Midland Bank, New York.

Chapinera
Bank of America NT&SA, San Francisco.

Cucuta
Citibank NA, New York.

Manizales
Fidelity Bank, Philadelphia.
Manufacturers National Bank, Detroit.
Wells Fargo Bank NA, San Francisco.

Medellin
Bank of America NT&SA, San Francisco.
Bankers Trust Co., New York.
Citibank NA, New York.
First National Bank of Boston.

Meta
Citibank NA, New York.

Pereira
Citibank NA, New York.

San Diego
Citibank NA, New York.

CONGO

Brazzaville
Bank of America NT&SA, San Francisco.
Morgan Guaranty Trust Co., New York.

COSTA RICA

San Jose
Bank of America NT&SA, San Francisco.
Chase Manhattan Bank NA, New York.
Citibank NA, New York.
First National Bank of Boston.
First Pennsylvania Bank NA, Philadelphia.
Marine Midland Bank, New York.

CYPRUS

Nicosia
'Bank of America NT&SA, San Francisco.
Citibank NA, New York.

DENMARK

Copenhagen
American Express International Banking Corp., New York.
Bank of America NT&SA, San Francisco.
Bankers Trust Co., New York.
Chase Manhattan Bank NA, New York.
Citibank NA, New York.
First National Bank of Boston.
°Philadelphia National Bank.

DOMINICAN REPUBLIC

Salcedo
Bank of America NT&SA, San Francisco.

Santiago de Los Caballeros
Bank of America NT&SA, San Francisco.
Chase Manhattan Bank NA, New York.
Citibank NA, New York.

Santo Domingo
Banco Popular de Puerto Rico, San Juan.
Bank of America NT&SA, San Francisco.
Chase Manhattan Bank NA, New York.
Citibank NA, New York.
°First National Bank of Boston.
Manufacturers Hanover Trust Co., New York.

DUBAI

Bander Taleb
Citibank NA, New York.

Deira
°Chemical Bank, New York.

Dubai
*American Express International Banking
Corp., New York.
Bank of America NT&SA, San Francisco.
Chase Manhattan Bank NA, New York.
Citibank NA, New York.
First National Bank, Chicago.
*First National Bank, Dallas.
Wells Fargo Bank NA, San Francisco.
Riqa
Citibank NA, New York.

ECUADOR
Ambato
Citibank NA, New York.
Cuenca
Citibank NA, New York.
Guayaquil
Bank of America NT&SA, San Francisco.
Citibank NA, New York.
Manufacturers Hanover Trust Co., New
York.
Wells Fargo Bank NA, San Francisco.
Quito
Bank of America NT&SA, San Francisco.
Citibank NA, New York.
Continental Illinois National Bank & Trust
Co., Chicago.
Wells Fargo Bank NA, San Francisco.

EGYPT
Cairo
American Express International Banking
Corp., New York.
*Bank of America NT&SA, San Francisco.
Chase Manhattan Bank NA, New York.
*Chemical Bank, New York.
Citibank NA, New York.
European-American Banking Corp. &
European-American Bank & Trust Co.,
New York.
First National Bank, Chicago.
Industrial National Bank, Providence.
Manufacturers Hanover Trust Co., New
York.

EL SALVADOR
San Salvador
*Bank of America NT&SA, San Francisco.
Citibank NA, New York.
Manufacturers Hanover Trust Co., New
York.

ENGLAND
Birmingham
American Express International Banking
Corp., New York.
Bank of America NT&SA, San Francisco.
Bankers Trust Co., New York.
Chemical Bank, New York.
Bradford
Bank of America NT&SA, San Francisco.

Brighton
First National Bank of Boston.
Bristol
First National Bank, Chicago.
Leicester
First National Bank, Chicago.
London
Allied Bank International, New York.
American Express International Banking
Corp., New York.
American National Bank & Trust Co.,
Chicago.
Bank Leumi Trust Co., New York.
Bank of America NT&SA, San Francisco.
Bank of California NA, San Francisco.
Bank of New York.
Bank of Tokyo Trust Co., New York.
Bankers Trust Co., New York.
Brown Brothers Harriman & Co., New
York.
Chase Manhattan Bank NA, New York.
Chemical Bank, New York.
Citibank NA, New York.
City National Bank, Detroit.
Cleveland Trust Co.
Colonial Bank and Trust Co., Waterbury.
Commerce Union Bank, Nashville.
Continental Illinois National Bank & Trust
Co., Chicago.
Crocker National Bank, San Francisco.
Detroit Bank & Trust Co.
*Equibank NA, Pittsburgh.
Fidelity Bank, Philadelphia.
First City National Bank, Houston.
First National Bank, Atlanta.
First National Bank of Boston.
First National Bank, Chicago.
First National Bank in Dallas.
First National Bank, Minneapolis.
*First National Bank in St. Louis.
First Pennsylvania Bank NA, Philadelphia.
First Union National Bank of North Caro-
lina, Charlotte.
First Wisconsin National Bank, Milwaukee.
Girard Bank, Philadelphia.
Harris Trust & Savings Bank, Chicago.
Indiana National Bank, Indianapolis.
*Industrial National Bank, Providence.
Irving Trust Co., New York.
LaSalle National Bank, Chicago.
Lloyds Bank California, Los Angeles.
Manufacturers Hanover Trust Co., New
York.
Manufacturers National Bank, Detroit.
Marine Midland Bank, New York.
Maryland National Bank, Baltimore.
Mellon Bank, NA, Pittsburgh.
Midlantic National Bank, Newark.
Morgan Guaranty Trust Co., New York.
National Bank of Detroit.
National City Bank, Cleveland.
North Carolina National Bank, Charlotte.
Northern Trust Co., Chicago.

Northwestern National Bank, Minneapolis.
Philadelphia National Bank.
Pittsburgh National Bank.
Rainier National Bank, Seattle.
Republic National Bank, Dallas.
Republic National Bank, New York.
Seattle-First National Bank.
Security Pacific National Bank, Los Angeles.
Shawmut Bank of Boston NA.
Southeast First National Bank of Miami.
State Street Bank & Trust Co., Boston.
Texas Commerce Bank NA, Houston.
Trust Company Bank, Atlanta.
Union Bank, Los Angeles.
Union Commerce Bank, Cleveland.
United California Bank, Los Angeles.
United States Trust Co. of New York.
Wells Fargo Bank NA, San Francisco.

Manchester
American Express International Banking Corp., New York.
Bank of America NT&SA, San Francisco.
Bankers Trust Co., New York.

Newcastle
First National Bank, Chicago.

Plymouth
Philadelphia National Bank.

Reading
Bank of America NT&SA, San Francisco.
*Security Pacific National Bank, Los Angeles.

Watford
First National Bank of Boston.

FIJI

Ba
Citibank NA, New York.

Lautoka
Citibank NA, New York.

Nadi
Citibank NA, New York.

Suva
Citibank NA, New York.

FINLAND

Helsinki
Chemical Bank, New York.
First National Bank of Boston.
Manufacturers Hanover Trust Co., New York.

FRANCE

Antibes
American Express International Banking Corp., New York.

Cannes
American Express International Banking Corp., New York.

Lille
Bank of America NT&SA, San Francisco.

Lyon
Bank of America NT&SA, San Francisco.
Chase Manhattan Bank NA, New York.

Marseilles
Bank of America NT&SA, San Francisco.

Nice
American Express International Banking Corp., New York.

Paris
American Express International Banking Corp., New York.
Bank Leumi Trust Co., New York.
Bank of America NT&SA, San Francisco.
Bank of the Southwest NA, Houston.
Bankers Trust Co., New York.
Central National Bank, Cleveland.
Chase Manhattan Bank NA, New York.
Chemical Bank, New York.
Citibank NA, New York.
Continental Illinois National Bank & Trust Co., Chicago.
Fidelity Bank, Philadelphia.
First National Bank in Dallas.
First National Bank of Boston.
First National Bank, Chicago.
French American Banking Corp., New York.
Girard Bank, Philadelphia.
Irving Trust Co., New York.
Manufacturers and Traders Trust Co., Buffalo.
Manufacturers Hanover Trust Co., New York.
Marine Midland Bank-New York.
Morgan Guaranty Trust Co., New York.
Northern Trust Co., Chicago.
Philadelphia National Bank.
Pittsburgh National Bank.
J. Henry Schroder Banking Corp., New York.
Security Pacific National Bank, Los Angeles.
United States Trust Co. of New York.
Wells Fargo Bank NA, San Francisco.

Strasbourg
Bank of America NT&SA, San Francisco.

GABON

Libreville
Bank of America NT&SA, San Francisco.
Citibank NA, New York.
Fidelity Bank, Philadelphia.
Morgan Guaranty Trust Co., New York.

GAMBIA

Bathurst
Bank of America NT&SA, San Francisco.

GERMANY, F.R.

Berlin
Citibank NA, New York.

Cologne
American Express International Banking Corp., New York.
*Bank of America NT&SA, San Francisco.
Duesseldorf
American Express International Banking Corp., New York.
Bank of America NT&SA, San Francisco.
Bankers Trust Co., New York.
Chase Manhattan Bank NA, New York.
Citibank NA, New York.
Continental Illinois National Bank & Trust Co., Chicago.
First National Bank, Chicago.
*Manufacturers Hanover Trust Co., New York.
Morgan Guaranty Trust Co., New York.
Frankfurt
American Express International Banking Corp., New York.
Bank Leumi Trust Co., New York.
Bank of America NT&SA, San Francisco.
Bankers Trust Co., New York.
Chase Manhattan Bank NA, New York.
Chemical Bank, New York.
Citibank NA, New York.
Continental Illinois National Bank & Trust Co., Chicago.
First National Bank of Boston.
First National Bank, Chicago.
First Pennsylvania Bank NA, Philadelphia.
First Wisconsin National Bank, Milwaukee.
Irving Trust Co., New York.
Manufacturers Hanover Trust Co., New York.
Marine Midland Bank, New York.
Mellon Bank, NA, Pittsburgh.
Morgan Guaranty Trust Co., New York.
National Bank of Detroit.
Nordic American Banking Corp., New York.
Republic National Bank, New York.
J. Henry Schroder Banking Corp., New York.
Security Pacific National Bank, Los Angeles.
Wells Fargo Bank NA, San Francisco.
Hamburg
American Express International Banking Corp., New York.
Bank of America NT&SA, San Francisco.
Bankers Trust Co., New York.
Chase Manhattan Bank NA, New York.
Citibank NA, New York.
Manufacturers Hanover Trust Co., New York.
Philadelphia National Bank.
Heidelberg
American Express International Banking Corp., New York.
Mainz-Mombach
American National Bank & Trust Co., Chicago.

First National Bank of Boston.
Munich
American Express International Banking Corp., New York.
Bank of America NT&SA, San Francisco.
Bankers Trust Co., New York.
Chase Manhattan Bank NA, New York.
Continental Illinois National Bank & Trust Co., Chicago.
First National Bank, Chicago.
*Manufacturers Hanover Trust Co., New York.
Morgan Guaranty Trust Co., New York.
*Security Pacific National Bank, Los Angeles.
State Street Bank & Trust Co., Boston.
Stuttgart
Bank of America NT&SA, San Francisco.
Chase Manhattan Bank NA, New York.
Citibank NA, New York.

GHANA

Accra
Citibank NA, New York.
Morgan Guaranty Trust Co., New York.

GREECE

Athens
American Express International Banking Corp., New York.
Bank of America NT&SA, San Francisco.
Chase Manhattan Bank NA, New York.
Continental Illinois National Bank & Trust Co., Chicago.
Citibank NA, New York.
First National Bank, Chicago.
Manufacturers Hanover Trust Co., New York.
Kypseli
Citibank NA, New York.
Piraeus
American Express International Banking Corp., New York.
Bank of America NT&SA, San Francisco.
Chase Manhattan Bank NA, New York.
Citibank NA, New York.
Continental Illinois National Bank & Trust Co., Chicago.
First National Bank, Chicago.
Salonica
American Express International Banking Corp., New York.
Bank of America NT&SA, San Francisco.
Chase Manhattan Bank NA, New York.
Thessaloniki
Citibank NA, New York.
Continental National City Bank, New York.

GUADELOUPE

Pointe-a-Pitre
Chase Manhattan Bank NA, New York.

GUAM

Agana
Bank of America NT&SA, San Francisco.
Bank of Hawaii, Honolulu.
California First Bank, San Francisco.
Chase Manhattan Bank NA, New York.
Citibank NA, New York.
First Hawaiian Bank, Honolulu.
Agat
Bank of Hawaii, Honolulu.
Dededo
First Hawaiian Bank, Honolulu.
Tamuning
Bank of America NT&SA, San Francisco.
Bank of Hawaii, Honolulu.
Citibank NA, New York.

GUATEMALA

Guatemala City
Bank of America NT&SA, San Francisco.
Citibank NA, New York.
First National Bank of Boston.
First National Bank, Chicago.

GUYANA

Georgetown
Chase Manhattan Bank NA, New York.

HAITI

Petionville
First National Bank of Boston.
Port-au-Prince
Banco Popular de Puerto Rico, San Juan.
Citibank NA, New York.
First National Bank of Boston.
First National Bank, Chicago.
Manufacturers Hanover Trust Co., New York.

HONDURAS

Comayaguela
Bank of America NT&SA, San Francisco.
San Pedro Sula
Bank of America NT&SA, San Francisco.
First National Bank of Boston.
Tegucigalpa
Bank of America NT&SA, San Francisco.
Chase Manhattan Bank NA, New York.
Citibank NA, New York.

HONG KONG

Hong Kong
Allied Bank International, New York.
American Express International Banking Corp., New York.
American National Bank & Trust Co., Chicago.
Bank of America NT&SA, San Francisco.

Bank Leumi Trust Co., New York.
Bankers Trust Co., New York.
Chase Manhattan Bank NA, New York.
Chemical Bank, New York.
Citibank NA, New York.
Continental Illinois National Bank & Trust Co., Chicago.
Crocker National Bank, San Francisco.
Fidelity Bank, Philadelphia.
First National Bank of Boston.
First National Bank, Chicago.
First National Bank of Oregon, Portland.
International Bank, Washington, DC.
Irving Trust Co., New York.
Manufacturers Hanover Trust Co., New York.
Marine Midland Bank, New York.
Morgan Guaranty Trust Co., New York.
National Bank of Detroit.
°National Bank of North America, New York.
North Carolina National Bank, Charlotte.
Northern Trust Co., Chicago.
Pacific National Bank of Seattle.
Rainier National Bank, Seattle.
°Republic National Bank, Dallas.
Security Pacific National Bank, Los Angeles.
Union Bank, Los Angeles.
United California Bank, Los Angeles.
Wells Fargo Bank NA, San Francisco.
Kowloon
American Express International Banking Corp., New York.

INDIA

Bombay
American Express International Banking Corp., New York.
Bank of America NT&SA, San Francisco.
Chase Manhattan Bank NA, New York.
Citibank NA, New York.
Fidelity Bank, Philadelphia.
First National Bank of Boston.
Calcutta
American Express International Banking Corp., New York.
Bank of America NT&SA, San Francisco.
Citibank NA, New York.
Madras
Bank of America NT&SA, San Francisco.
Citibank NA, New York.
New Delhi
American Express International Banking Corp., New York.
Bank of America NT&SA, San Francisco.
Citibank NA, New York.

INDONESIA

Jakarta
American Express International Banking Corp., New York.

Bank of America NT&SA, San Francisco.
Bankers Trust Co., New York.
Chase Manhattan Bank NA, New York.
Chemical Bank, New York.
Citibank NA, New York.
Continental Illinois National Bank & Trust Co., Chicago.
Crocker National Bank, San Francisco.
First National Bank, Chicago.
Manufacturers Hanover Trust Co., New York.
Marine Midland Bank, New York.
Morgan Guaranty Trust Co., New York.
United California Bank, Los Angeles.

Jakarta-Kota
American Express International Banking Corp., New York.
Chase Manhattan Bank NA, New York.

IRAN

Teheran
Bank of America NT&SA, San Francisco.
Bankers Trust Co., New York.
Chase Manhattan Bank NA, New York.
Chemical Bank, New York.
Citibank NA, New York.
Continental Illinois National Bank & Trust Co., Chicago.
European-American Banking Corp. & European-American Bank & Trust Co., New York.
First National Bank of Boston.
First National Bank, Chicago.
Irving Trust Co., New York.
Manufacturers Hanover Trust Co., New York.
Marine Midland Bank, New York.
Mellon Bank NA, Pittsburgh.
Philadelphia National Bank.
°United California Bank, Los Angeles.

IRELAND, NORTHERN

Belfast
Chase Manhattan Bank NA, New York.
Citibank NA, New York.

IRELAND, REPUBLIC

Cork
Citibank NA, New York.
Dublin
Bank of America NT&SA, San Francisco.
Chase Manhattan Bank NA, New York.
Citibank NA, New York.
First National Bank, Chicago.
First National Bank of Boston.
Marine Midland Bank, New York.
Philadelphia National Bank.
Shannon
Chase Manhattan Bank NA, New York.

ISRAEL

Jerusalem
Exchange National Bank, Chicago.
Tel-Aviv
Exchange National Bank, Chicago.
First Pennsylvania Bank NA, Philadelphia.

ITALY

Bari
Chase Manhattan Bank NA, New York.
Florence
American Express International Banking Corp., New York.
Milan
American Express International Banking Corp., New York.
Bank Leumi Trust Co., New York.
Bank of America NT&SA, San Francisco.
Bankers Trust Co., New York.
Chase Manhattan Bank NA, New York.
Chemical Bank, New York.
Citibank NA, New York.
Continental Illinois National Bank & Trust Co., Chicago.
First National Bank of Boston.
First National Bank, Chicago.
Marine Midland Bank, New York.
Morgan Guaranty Trust Co., New York.
Naples
American Express International Banking Corp., New York.
Rome
American Express International Banking Corp., New York.
Bankers Trust Co., New York.
Chase Manhattan Bank NA, New York.
Chemical Bank, New York.
Citibank NA, New York.
Continental Illinois National Bank & Trust Co., Chicago.
First National Bank, Chicago.
Manufacturers Hanover Trust Co., New York.
Marine Midland Bank, New York.
Morgan Guaranty Trust Co., New York.
Venice
American Express International Banking Corp., New York:

IVORY COAST

Abidjan
Bank of America NT&SA, San Francisco.
Bankers Trust Co., New York.
Chase Manhattan Bank NA, New York.
Citibank NA, New York.
Morgan Guaranty Trust Co., New York.

JAMAICA

Kingston
Bank of America NT&SA, San Francisco.
Chase Manhattan Bank NA, New York.

Citibank NA, New York.
Citizens & Southern National Bank, Atlanta.
Continental Illinois National Bank & Trust Co., Chicago.
First National Bank, Chicago.
International Bank, Washington, DC
Mandeville
Citibank NA, New York.
May Pen
Citibank NA, New York.
Montego Bay
Citibank NA, New York.
Ocho Rios
Citibank NA, New York.

JAPAN

Kobe
Bank of America NT&SA, San Francisco.
Nagoya
Citibank NA, New York.
Marine Midland Bank, New York.
Okinawa
American Express International Banking Corp., New York.
Bank of America NT&SA, San Francisco.
Osaka
Bank of America NT&SA, San Francisco.
Chase Manhattan Bank NA, New York.
Citibank NA, New York.
Tokyo
Allied Bank International, New York.
American Express International Banking Corp., New York.
Bank of America NT&SA, San Francisco.
Bank of California NA, San Francisco.
Bank of Hawaii, Honolulu.
Bankers Trust Co., New York.
Chase Manhattan Bank NA, New York.
Chemical Bank, New York.
Citibank NA, New York.
Continental Illinois National Bank & Trust Co., Chicago.
Crocker National Bank, San Francisco.
Fidelity Bank, Philadelphia.
First City National Bank Houston.
First Hawaiian Bank, Honolulu.
First National Bank of Boston.
First National Bank, Chicago.
First National Bank in Dallas.
*First Pennsylvania Bank NA, Philadelphia.
First Union National Bank of North Carolina, Charlotte.
*Harris Trust & Savings Bank, Chicago.
Irving Trust Co., New York.
Manufacturers Hanover Trust Co., New York.
Marine Midland Bank, New York.
Mellon Bank, NA, Pittsburgh.
Morgan Guaranty Trust Co., New York.
National Bank of Commerce, Seattle.
National Bank of Detroit.

Pacific National Bank of Washington, Seattle.
Republic National Bank, Dallas.
J. Henry Schroder Banking Corp. New York.
Seattle-First National Bank.
Security Pacific National Bank, Los Angeles.
Texas Commerce Bank NA, Houston.
Union Bank, Los Angeles.
United California Bank, Los Angeles.
Wells Fargo Bank NA, San Francisco.
Yokohama
Bank of America NT&SA, San Francisco.
Citibank NA, New York.

JORDAN

Amman
*American Express International Banking Corp., New York.
Citibank NA, New York.

KENYA

Nairobi
Bank of America NT&SA, San Francisco.
Citibank NA, New York.
Continental Illinois Bank & Trust Co., Chicago.
First National Bank, Chicago.
Manufacturers Hanover Trust Co., New York.

KOREA, REP.

Pusan
Chase Manhattan Bank NA, New York.
Citibank NA, New York.
Seoul
Bank of America NT&SA, San Francisco.
Bankers Trust Co., New York.
Chase Manhattan Bank NA, New York.
Citibank NA, New York.
Continental Illinois National Bank & Trust Co., Chicago.
First National Bank, Chicago.
Marine Midland Bank, New York.

KUWAIT

Kuwait City
*Bank of America NT&SA, San Francisco.
International Bank, Washington, DC
Philadelphia National Bank.
*State Street Bank & Trust Co., Boston.

LEBANON

Beirut
Bank of America NT&SA, San Francisco.
Chase Manhattan Bank NA, New York.
Chemical Bank, New York.

Citibank NA, New York.
Continental Illinois National Bank & Trust Co., Chicago.
European-American Banking Corp. & European-American Bank & Trust Co., New York.
Fidelity Bank, Philadelphia.
First National Bank of Boston.
First National Bank, Chicago.
International Bank, Washington, DC
Irving Trust Co., New York.
Manufacturers Hanover Trust Co., New York.
Marine Midland Bank, New York.
Morgan Guaranty Trust Co., New York.

LIBERIA

Harbel
Chase Manhattan Bank NA, New York.
Monrovia
Chase Manhattan Bank NA, New York.
Chemical Bank, New York.
Citibank NA, New York.
International Bank, Washington DC

LUXEMBOURG

Luxembourg
American Fletcher National Bank, Indianapolis.
Bank of America NT&SA, San Francisco.
Chase Manhattan Bank NA, New York.
Chemical Bank, New York.
Citibank NA, New York.
Continental Illinois National Bank & Trust Co., Chicago.
Fidelity Bank, Philadelphia.
First National Bank of Boston.
First Pennsylvania Bank NA, Philadelphia.
International Bank, Washington, DC
Manufacturers Hanover Trust Co., New York.
Marine Midland Bank, New York.
National Bank of Detroit.
Northwestern National Bank, Minneapolis.
Philadelphia National Bank.
Shawmut Bank of Boston NA.
Southeast First National Bank of Miami.
United States Trust Co. of New York.
Wells Fargo Bank NA, San Francisco.

MALAWI

Blantyre-Limbe
Bank of America NT&SA, San Francisco.

MALAYSIA

Kuala Lumpur
Bank of America NT&SA, San Francisco.
Chase Manhattan Bank NA, New York.
Citibank NA, New York.
Continental Illinois National Bank & Trust Co., Chicago.

Manufacturers Hanover Trust Co., New York.
Marine Midland Bank, New York.
Morgan Guaranty Trust Co., New York.
Seattle-First National Bank.
Security Pacific National Bank, Los Angeles.
Penang
Citibank NA, New York.

MALI

Bamako
Citibank NA, New York.

MARIANA ISLANDS

Saipan
Bank of America NT&SA, San Francisco.
Bank of Hawaii, Honolulu.
California First Bank, San Francisco.

MARSHALL ISLANDS

Majuro
Bank of America NT&SA, San Francisco.

MARTINIQUE

Fort-de-France
Bank of America NT&SA, San Francisco.
Chase Manhattan Bank, New York.

MAURITANIA

Nouakchott
Citibank NA, New York.

MAURITIUS

Port Louis
Citibank NA, New York.

MEXICO

Mexico City
American National Bank & Trust Co., Chicago.
Bank of America NT&SA, San Francisco.
°Bank of Virginia Co., Richmond.
Bankers Trust Co., New York.
Central National Bank of Cleveland.
Chase Manhattan Bank NA, New York.
Chemical Bank, New York.
Citibank NA, New York.
Continental Illinois National Bank & Trust Co., Chicago.
European-American Banking Corp. & European-American Bank & Trust Co., New York.
Exchange National Bank, Chicago.
Fidelity Bank, Philadelphia.
First National Bank of Boston.

First National Bank, Chicago.
First National Bank of Birmingham.
First National Bank of Commerce. New Orleans.
First National State Bank of New Jersey, Newark.
First Pennsylvania Bank NA, Philadelphia.
Girard Bank, Philadelphia.
Harris Trust & Savings Bank, Chicago.
Indiana National Bank, Indianapolis.
Manufacturers Hanover Trust Co., New York.
Marine Midland Bank, New York.
Mellon Bank, NA, Pittsburgh.
Morgan Guaranty Trust Co., New York.
New Jersey Bank NA, Paterson.
Provident National Bank, Philadelphia.
Republic National Bank, Dallas.
Republic National Bank, New York.
Security Pacific National Bank, Los Angeles.
Texas Commerce Bank NA, Houston.
Union Bank, Los Angeles.
United California Bank, Los Angeles.
Wells Fargo Bank NA, San Francisco.

MIDWAY ISLANDS

Midway
Bank of Hawaii, Honolulu.

MONACO

Monte Carlo
American Express International Banking Corp., New York.
Citibank NA, New York.

MOROCCO

Casablanca
Bank of America NT&SA, San Francisco.
Citibank NA, New York.
Continental Illinois National Bank & Trust Co., Chicago.
Rabat
Bank of America NT&SA, San Francisco.
Morgan Guaranty Trust Co., New York.
Tangier
Bank of America NT&SA, San Francisco.
Tetuan
Bank of America NT&SA, San Francisco.

NETHERLANDS

Amsterdam
American Express International Banking Corp., New York.
Bank of America NT&SA, San Francisco.
*Bankers Trust Co., New York.
Citibank NA, New York.
Chase Manhattan Bank NA, New York.

Continental Illinois National Bank & Trust Co., Chicago.
Crocker National Bank, San Francisco.
First National Bank, Chicago.
Morgan Guaranty Trust Co., New York.
*Security Pacific National Bank, Los Angeles.
The Hague
*Chemical Bank, New York.
Rotterdam
Bank of America NT&SA, San Francisco.
Citibank NA, New York.
Continental Illinois National Bank & Trust Co., Chicago.
First National Bank, Chicago.
Utrecht
American National Bank and Trust Co., Chicago.

NETHERLANDS ANTILLES

Aruba
Citibank NA, New York.
Curacao
Allied Bank International, New York.
Bank of America NT&SA, San Francisco.
Citibank NA, New York.
Manufacturers and Traders Trust Co., Buffalo.
Marine Midland Bank, New York.
St. Maarten
Chase Manhattan Bank NA, New York.

NEW CALEDONIA

Noumea
Bank of America NT&SA, San Francisco.
Bank of Hawaii, Honolulu.

NEW HEBRIDES

Vila
Bank of America NT&SA, San Francisco.
*First Hawaiian Bank, Honolulu.

NEW ZEALAND

Auckland
Bank of America NT&SA, San Francisco.
Chase Manhattan Bank NA, New York.
Security Pacific National Bank, Los Angeles.
Wells Fargo Bank NA, San Francisco.
Christchurch
Bank of America NT&SA, San Francisco.
Wellington
Bank of America NT&SA, San Francisco.
Morgan Guaranty Trust Co., New York.

NICARAGUA

Managua
Bank of America NT&SA, San Francisco.
Citibank NA, New York.

Philadelphia National Bank.
Wells Fargo Bank NA, San Francisco.

NIGER

Niamey
Citibank NA, New York.

NIGERIA

Kano
Bank of America NT&SA, San Francisco.
Lagos
Bank of America NT&SA, San Francisco.
Bankers Trust Co., New York.
Chase Manhattan Bank NA, New York.
Citibank NA, New York.
First National Bank, Chicago.
Port Harcourt
Bank of America NT&SA, San Francisco.
Morgan Guaranty Trust Co., New York.

NORWAY

Oslo
Citibank NA, New York.
Manufacturers Hanover Trust Co., New York.

OMAN

Matrah
Bank of America NT&SA, San Francisco.
Muscat
Citibank NA, New York.
Ruwi
°Citibank NA, New York.

PAKISTAN

Karachi
American Express International Banking Corp., New York.
Bank of America NT&SA, San Francisco.
Citibank NA, New York.
Continental Illinois National Bank & Trust Co., Chicago.
Morgan Guaranty Trust Co., New York.
Lahore
American Express International Banking Corp., New York.
Bank of America NT&SA, San Francisco.
Citibank NA, New York.

PANAMA

Balboa
Chase Manhattan Bank NA, New York.
Citibank NA, New York.
Canal Zone
Chase Manhattan Bank NA, New York.
Chitre
Chase Manhattan Bank NA, New York.

Colombia
Mercantile Trust Co., St. Louis.
Colon
Bank of America NT&SA, San Francisco.
Chase Manhattan Bank NA, New York.
Citibank NA, New York.
David
Bank of America NT&SA, San Francisco.
Chase Manhattan Bank NA, New York.
Citibank NA, New York.
La Concepcion
Chase Manhattan Bank NA, New York.
Las Tablas
Citibank NA, New York.
Panama City
Bank of America NT&SA, San Francisco.
Bankers Trust Co., New York.
Chase Manhattan Bank NA, New York.
Citibank NA, New York.
First National Bank of Boston.
First National Bank, Chicago.
Marine Midland Bank, New York.
Midlantic National Bank, Newark.
Philadelphia National Bank.
Security Pacific National Bank, Los Angeles.
Shawmut Bank of Boston, NA.
State Street Bank & Trust Co., Boston.
Wells Fargo Bank NA, San Francisco.
Penonome
Chase Manhattan Bank NA, New York.
Veraquas
Citibank NA, New York.

PARAGUAY

Asuncion
Bank of America NT&SA, San Francisco.
Citibank NA, New York.
Puerto Stroessner
Citibank NA, New York.

PERU

Lima
American National Bank & Trust Co., Chicago.
Bank of America NT&SA, San Francisco.
Citibank NA, New York.
Citizens & Southern National Bank, Atlanta.
Continental Illinois National Bank & Trust Co., Chicago.
First National Bank of Maryland, Baltimore.
Manufacturers Hanover Trust Co., New York.
Morgan Guaranty Trust Co., New York.
New Jersey Bank NA, West Paterson.
United California Bank, Los Angeles.

PHILIPPINES

Cebu
Citibank NA, New York.

Clark Air Force Base
  Citibank NA, New York.
Makati
  American Express International Banking
    Corp., New York.
  Bank of America NT&SA, San Francisco.
  Chemical Bank, New York.
  Citibank NA, New York.
  Marine Midland Bank-New York.
  Philadelphia National Bank.
Manila
  Bank of America NT&SA, San Francisco.
  Bank of California NA, San Francisco.
  Bankers Trust Co., New York.
  Chase Manhattan Bank NA, New York.
  Chemical Bank, New York.
  Citibank NA, New York.
  Continental Illinois National Bank & Trust
    Co., Chicago.
  Crocker National Bank, San Francisco.
  Fidelity Bank, Philadelphia.
  First National Bank of Boston.
  First National Bank, Chicago.
  Manufacturers Hanover Trust Co., New
    York.
  Marine Midland Bank, New York.
  Mellon Bank NA, Pittsburgh.
  Morgan Guaranty Trust Co., New York.
  National Bank of Detroit.
  °Pacific National Bank of Washington,
    Seattle.
  Philadelphia National Bank.
  °Rainier National Bank, Seattle.
  Security Pacific National Bank, Los An-
    geles.
  United California Bank, Los Angeles.
  Wells Fargo Bank NA, San Francisco.

POLAND

Warsaw
  First National Bank, Chicago.

PORTUGAL

Lisbon
  First National Bank of Boston.

PUERTO RICO

Arecibo
  Citibank NA, New York.
Bayamon
  Chase Manhattan Bank NA, New York.
  Citibank NA, New York.
Caguas
  Chase Manhattan Bank NA, New York.
  Citibank NA, New York.
Caparra
  Chase Manhattan Bank NA, New York.
Carolina
  Chase Manhattan Bank NA, New York.
  Citibank NA, New York.

Hato Rey
  Chase Manhattan Bank NA, New York.
Mayaguez
  Citibank NA, New York.
Ponce
  Chase Manhattan Bank NA, New York.
  Citibank NA, New York.
Rio Piedras
  Chase Manhattan Bank NA, New York.
San Juan
  Bank of America NT&SA, San Francisco.
  Chase Manhattan Bank NA, New York.
  Citibank NA, New York.
Santurce
  Chase Manhattan Bank NA, New York.
  First Pennsylvania Bank NA, Philadelphia.

QATAR

Doha
  Chase Manhattan Bank NA, New York.
  Citibank NA, New York.

RAS AL KHAIMAH

Ras Al Khaimah
  Citibank NA, New York.

ROUMANIA

Bucharest
  Manufacturers Hanover Trust Co., New
    York.

RWANDA

Kigali
  Bank of America NT&SA, San Francisco.
  Morgan Guaranty Trust Co., New York.

ST. KITTS

Basseterre
  Bank of America NT&SA, San Francisco.
Sandy Points
  °Bank of America NT&SA, San Francisco.

ST. LUCIA

Castries
  Chase Manhattan Bank NA, New York.

SAMOA (AMERICAN)

Pago Pago
  Bank of Hawaii, Honolulu.
  Citibank NA, New York.

SAUDI ARABIA

Jeddah
  Citibank NA, New York.
Riyadh
  Citibank NA, New York.

SCOTLAND

Edinburgh
American Express International Banking
Corp., New York.
Bank of America NT&SA, San Francisco.
*Chemical Bank, New York.
Continental Illinois National Bank & Trust
Co., Chicago.
First National Bank, Chicago.
*Manufacturers Hanover Trust Co., New
York.

SENEGAL

Dakar
Bank of America NT&SA, San Francisco.
Bankers Trust Co., New York.
Citibank NA, New York.
Fidelity Bank, Philadelphia.
Morgan Guaranty Trust Co., New York.

SHARJAH

Sharjah
Chase Manhattan Bank NA, New York.
Citibank NA, New York.
*First National Bank, Chicago.

SINGAPORE

Jurong
Citibank NA, New York.
Singapore
American Express International Banking
Corp., New York.
Bank of America NT&SA, San Francisco.
Bank of New York.
Bankers Trust Co., New York.
Chase Manhattan Bank NA, New York.
Chemical Bank, New York.
Citibank NA, New York.
Citizens & Southern National Bank, At-
lanta.
Continental Illinois National Bank & Trust
Co., Chicago.
*First National Bank of Boston.
First National Bank, Chicago.
First National Bank in Dallas.
First National Bank of Oregon, Portland.
First Pennsylvania Bank NA, Philadelphia.
Girard Bank, Philadelphia.
Harris Trust & Savings Bank, Chicago.
*Industrial National Bank, Providence.
Irving Trust Co., New York.
Marine Midland Bank, New York.
Morgan Guaranty Trust Co., New York.
Northern Trust Co., Chicago.
*Pacific National Bank of Washington
Seattle.
Pittsburgh National Bank.
Rainier National Bank, Seattle.
Republic National Bank, Dallas.
Seattle-First National Bank.

Security Pacific National Bank, Los An-
geles.
State Street Bank & Trust Co., Boston.
United California Bank, Los Angeles.
United States National Bank, Portland.
Wells Fargo Bank NA, San Francisco.

SOUTH AFRICA

Johannesburg
Bank Leumi Trust Co., New York.
Chase Manhattan Bank NA, New York.
Citibank NA, New York.
European-American Banking Corp. &
European-American Bank & Trust Co.,
New York.
First National Bank of Boston.

SPAIN

Barcelona
Bank of America NT&SA, San Francisco.
Continental Illinois National Bank & Trust
Co., Chicago.
*Security Pacific National Bank, Los An-
geles.
Bilbao
Bank of America NT&SA, San Francisco.
Madrid
Bank of America NT&SA, San Francisco.
Bankers Trust Co., New York.
Chase Manhattan Bank NA, New York.
Chemical Bank, New York.
Citibank NA, New York.
Continental Illinois National Bank & Trust
Co., Chicago.
First National Bank of Boston.
First National Bank, Chicago.
First National Bank of Miami.
Manufacturers Hanover Trust Co., New
York.
Marine Midland Bank, New York.
Morgan Guaranty Trust Co., New York.
Philadelphia National Bank.
United California Bank, Los Angeles.
Wells Fargo Bank NA, San Francisco.

SRI LANKA

Colombo
Citibank NA, New York.

SWEDEN

Stockholm
*Citibank NA, New York.
First National Bank of Boston.
First National Bank, Chicago.

SWITZERLAND

Basle
American Express International Banking
Corp., New York.

Geneva
American Express International Banking Corp., New York.
*American Fletcher National Bank, Indianapolis.
Bank Leumi Trust Co., New York.
Bank of America NT&SA, San Francisco.
Chase Manhattan Bank NA, New York.
Citibank NA, New York.
Continental Illinois National Bank & Trust Co., Chicago.
Fidelity Bank, Philadelphia.
First National Bank of Boston.
First National Bank, Chicago.
Marine Midland Bank, New York.
Morgan Guaranty Trust Co., New York.
Northern Trust Co., Chicago.
United States Trust Co. of New York.
Lausanne
American Express International Banking Corp., New York.
Citibank NA, New York.
Lugano
Bank of America NT&SA, San Francisco.
Citibank NA, New York.
Zug
Chemical Bank, New York.
Continental Illinois National Bank & Trust Co., Chicago.
Mellon Bank NA, Pittsburgh.
Zurich
American Express International Banking Corp., New York.
Bank Leumi Trust Co., New York.
Bank of America NT&SA, San Francisco.
Bankers Trust Co., New York.
Brown Brothers Harriman & Co., New York.
Chase Manhattan Bank NA, New York.
Chemical Bank, New York.
Citibank NA, New York.
Continental Illinois National Bank & Trust Co., Chicago.
First National Bank of Boston.
Girard Bank, Philadelphia.
Manufacturers Hanover Trust Co., New York.
Morgan Guaranty Trust Co., New York.
Seattle-First National Bank.

TAHITI

Papeete
Bank of Hawaii, Honolulu.
Tahiti
Citibank NA, New York.

TAIWAN

Taipei
American Express International Banking Corp., New York.

Bank of America NT&SA, San Francisco.
*Bank of California NA, San Francisco.
Bankers Trust Co., New York.
Chase Manhattan Bank NA, New York.
Chemical Bank, New York.
Citibank NA, New York.
Continental Illinois National Bank & Trust Co., Chicago.
Fidelity Bank, Philadelphia.
Irving Trust Co., New York.
Morgan Guaranty Trust Co., New York.
National Bank of Detroit.
*Pacific National Bank of Washington, Seattle.
*Security Pacific National Bank, Los Angeles.
United California Bank, Los Angeles.

THAILAND

Bangkok
Bank of America NT&SA, San Francisco.
Bankers Trust Co., New York.
Chase Manhattan Bank NA, New York.
Citibank NA, New York.
Continental Illinois National Bank & Trust Co., Chicago.
First National Bank, Chicago.
Manufacturers Hanover Trust Co., New York.
Philadelphia National Bank.
Security Pacific National Bank, Los Angeles.

TOGO

Lome
Bank of America NT&SA, San Francisco.
Citibank NA, New York.

TONGA

Nuku'Alofa
*Bank of Hawaii, Honolulu.

TRINIDAD & TOBAGO

Port of Spain
Chase Manhattan Bank NA, New York.
Citibank NA, New York.
International Bank, Washington, DC
San Fernando
Chase Manhattan Bank NA, New York.
Citibank NA, New York.

TRUK ISLANDS

Truk
Bank of America NT&SA, San Francisco.

TRUST TERRITORIES

Bank of Hawaii, Honolulu.

TUNISIA

Tunis
Bank of America NT&SA, San Francisco.
Bankers Trust Co., New York.
Morgan Guaranty Trust Co., New York

TURKEY

Istanbul
Bank of America NT&SA, San Francisco.
°Citibank NA, New York.
European-American Banking Corp. & European-American Bank & Trust Co., New York.
Fidelity Bank, Philadelphia.
Marine Midland Bank, New York.

UGANDA

Kampala
Citibank NA, New York.

UNION OF SOVIET SOCIALIST REPUBLICS

Moscow
Bank of America NT&SA, San Francisco.
Chase Manhattan Bank NA, New York.
Citibank NA, New York.

UPPER VOLTA

Ouagadougou
Bank of America NT&SA, San Francisco.
Citibank NA, New York.

URUGUAY

Montevideo
Bank of America, NT&SA, San Francisco.
Citibank NA, New York.

VENEZUELA

Caracas
American National Bank & Trust Co., Chicago.
Bank Leumi Trust Co., New York.
Bank of America NT&SA, San Francisco.
Bankers Trust Co., New York.
Chase Manhattan Bank NA, New York.
Chemical Bank, New York.

Citibank NA, New York.
Continental Illinois National Bank & Trust Co., Chicago.
°Crocker National Bank, San Francisco.
European-American Banking Corp. and European-American Bank & Trust Co., New York.
Fidelity Bank, Philadelphia.
First National Bank of Boston.
First National Bank, Chicago.
First National Bank of Louisville.
First Wisconsin National Bank, Milwaukee.
Irving Trust Co., New York.
Manufacturers Hanover Trust Co., New York.
Marine Midland Bank, New York.
Morgan Guaranty Trust Co., New York.
Northern Trust Co., Chicago.
°Republic National Bank, Dallas.
Republic National Bank, New York.
°Southeast First National Bank, Miami.
°Union Bank, Los Angeles.
°United California Bank, Los Angeles
Wells Fargo Bank NA, San Francisco.
Maracaibo
Citibank NA, New York.
Valencia
Citibank NA, New York.

VIRGIN ISLANDS (U.S.)

Charlotte Amalie
Bank of America NT&SA, San Francisco.
Chase Manhattan Bank NA, New York.
Citibank NA, New York.
First Pennsylvania Bank NA, Philadelphia.
Christiansted
Bank of America NT&SA, San Francisco.
Chase Manhattan Bank NA, New York.
Citibank NA, New York.
Cruz Bay
Chase Manhattan Bank NA, New York.
First Pennsylvania Bank NA, Philadelphia.
Frederiksted
Bank of America NT&SA, San Francisco.
Chase Manhattan Bank NA, New York.
First Pennsylvania Bank NA, Philadelphia.
Sunny Isle
Citibank NA, New York.

VIRGIN ISLANDS (BRITISH)

Tortola
Chase Manhattan Bank NA, New York.
First Pennsylvania Bank NA, Philadelphia.

WALES

Cardiff
First National Bank, Chicago.

YEMEN

Sana'a
Citibank NA, New York.

ZAIRE

Kinshasa
Citibank NA, New York.

Crocker National Bank, San Francisco.
Morgan Guaranty Trust Co., New York.
Philadelphia National Bank.

ZAMBIA

Lusaka
Citibank NA, New York.

FOREIGN BANKS WITH U.S. BRANCHES

The following is a compilation of foreign bank operations in the United States. It is listed alphabetically by state and type of activity and shows the home city of the parent bank. The list includes 233 foreign banks represented by 82 subsidiaries or affiliates (including 27 securities companies), 113 branches, 92 agencies, and 186 representative offices.

CALIFORNIA

SUBSIDIARIES OR AFFILIATES

ABD Securities Corp., New York: There is a Los Angeles branch of this firm owned by Algemene Bank Nederland NV, Amsterdam; Banque Bruxelles Lambert, Brussels; Bayerische Hypotheken- und Wechsel-Bank, Munich; and Dresdner Bank AG, Frankfurt.

Bank Julius Baer & Co., Ltd., Zurich: Owns 10 percent of Baer Holding AG of Zurich, which owns 100 percent of Baer Securities Corp., N.Y. and 100 percent of Baer American Banking Corp., a N.Y. investment company with a representative office in San Francisco.

Bank of Montreal, Montreal: Owns Bank of Montreal (California) with a head office and branch in San Francisco and branches in Los Angeles, Sacramento, and San Diego.

Bank of Tokyo, Ltd., Tokyo: Has a 74.7 percent interest in California First Bank which, in addition to its head office in San Francisco, has 101 offices, including 86 in southern California.

Banque Nationale de Paris, Paris: Owns French Bank of California, a state-chartered subsidiary with a head office in San Francisco and branches in Beverly Hills, Palo Alto, Newport Beach, and Los Angeles.

Barclays Bank International Ltd., subsidiary of **BARCLAYS BANK LTD.,** London: Owns Barclays Bank of California which, in addition to its head office in San Francisco, has 46 branches in 36 cities, towns, or unincorporated areas throughout the state.

The Becker and Warburg-Paribas Group Inc., New York: There is a Los Angeles branch office of Warburg Paribas Becker, Inc., and Los Angeles and San Francisco branch offices of A. G. Becker & Co. Inc., and Becker Securities Corp., all New York-

based subsidiaries of this holding company in which S. G. Warburg & Co. Ltd., London, and Compagnie Financiere de Paris et des Pays-Bas, Paris, hold interests.

Canadian Imperial Bank of Commerce, Toronto: Owns California Canadian Bank, San Francisco, which has 24 offices throughout the state.

Chartered Bank, London: Owns Chartered Bank of London, San Francisco, with seven branches in San Francisco, three in Vista, and one each in Los Altos, Los Angeles, Oakland, Poway, San Bruno, San Marcos, Walnut Creek, and San Diego.

Dai-Ichi Kangyo Bank Ltd., Tokyo: Owns 4½ percent of Japan California Bank, Los Angeles, in which about 37 major Japanese corporations, including Long-Term Credit Bank of Japan, Ltd., have minority interests. Japan California Bank has branches in San Jose and San Diego.

Daiwa Securities (America) Inc., New York: There is a Los Angeles branch office of this foreign-owned securities firm. (See "New York Subsidiaries or Affiliates" for ownership.)

European-American Banking Corp., New York: There are Los Angeles and San Francisco branch offices of this New York-headquartered firm which is owned by Amsterdam-Rotterdam Bank NV. Amsterdam; Creditanstalt Bankverein, Vienna; Deutsche Bank AG, Frankfurt/Main; Midland Bank Ltd., London; Societe Generale, Paris; and Societe Generale de Banque, Brussels.

Hongkong & Shanghai Banking Corp., Hong Kong: Owns the Hongkong Bank of California, a state-chartered subsidiary, with a head office in San Francisco, one branch in Los Angeles, and one branch each in Beverly Hills, Carson, Encino, North Hollywood, Sacramento, San Francisco, Silver Lake-Sunset, and Agana, Guam.

Korea Exchange Bank, Seoul: Has a wholly owned subsidiary, Korea Exchange Bank of California, in Los Angeles.

Lloyds Bank Ltd., London: Owns, through a holding company subsidiary, Lloyds First Western Corp., Wilmington, Lloyds Bank California, with a head office in Los Angeles and 97 branches in 69 cities throughout the state.

Long-Term Credit Bank of Japan Ltd., Tokyo: Owns 2½ percent of Japan California Bank, Los Angeles, in which 37 major Japanese corporations have minority interests. Japan California Bank has branches in San Jose and San Diego.

Mitsubishi Bank Ltd., Tokyo: Owns Mitsubishi Bank of California with a head office and branch in Los Angeles and branches in Gardena and San Francisco. Mitsubishi Bank of California acquired Hacienda Bank, of La

Reprinted with permission from *American Banker,* August 8, 1977. Compiled by Jeffrey Kutler.

Habra, with branches in La Habra, La Mirada, West Covina, Garden Grove, and Placentia on July 30, 1976.

Mitsui Bank Ltd., Tokyo: Has a wholly owned subsidiary, Mitsui Bank of California in Los Angeles.

New Japan Securities International Inc., New York: There is a Los Angeles branch office of this foreign-owned securities firm. (See "New York Subsidiaries or Affiliates" for ownership.)

Nikko Securities International Inc., New York: There are branch offices of this foreign-owned firm in Los Angeles and San Francisco. (See "New York Subsidiaries or Affiliates" for ownership.)

Nomura Securities International Inc., New York: There are branch offices of this foreign-owned firm in Los Angeles and San Francisco. (See "New York Subsidiaries or Affiliates" for ownership.)

Sanwa Bank Ltd., Osaka: Owns Sanwa Bank of California, a wholly owned commercial bank subsidiary with a head office in San Francisco, one branch in Los Angeles, and one branch each in Culver City, Oakland, Redondo Beach, Palm Beach, Sacramento, and San Jose.

Sogen-Swiss International Corp., New York: There are Los Angeles and San Francisco branches of this investment banking firm owned by Amsterdam-Rotterdam Bank; Societe Generale Alsacienne de Banque, Strasbourg; Societe Generale de Banque, Brussels; Societe Generale, Paris; and Swiss Credit Bank, Zurich.

Sumitomo Bank Ltd., Osaka: Owns the majority interest in Sumitomo Bank of California, San Francisco, which has 23 branches in 17 locations throughout the state.

Tokai Bank Ltd., Nagoya: Has a wholly owned subsidiary, Tokai Bank of California, Los Angeles, with two branches in Los Angeles, and one each in South Bay, Huntington Beach, Inglewood, Newport Beach, and Playa del Rey.

Toronto Dominion Bank, Toronto: Owns Toronto Dominion Bank of California with a head office in San Francisco and branches in Beverly Hills and Los Angeles.

Yamaichi International (America) Inc., New York: There is a Los Angeles branch office of this foreign-owned securities firm. (See "New York Subsidiaries or Affiliates" for ownership.)

AGENCIES

Algemene Bank Nederland, Amsterdam: In Los Angeles.

Banca Commerciale Italiana, Milan: In Los Angeles.

Banco de Comercio, S.A., Mexico City: In Los Angeles.

Banco di Roma, Rome: In San Francisco.

Banco do Brasil, Brasilia: In San Francisco and Los Angeles.

Banco do Estado do Sao Paolo, Brazil: In Los Angeles.

Banco Nacional de Mexico S.A., Mexico City: In Los Angeles.

Banco Popular de Puerto Rico, San Juan: In Los Angeles. This is the only agency on this list certified to accept insured domestic deposits.

Banco Real S.A., Sao Paulo: In Los Angeles.

Bangkok Bank Ltd., Thailand: In Los Angeles.

Bank Leumi Le-Israel B.M., Tel Aviv: In Beverly Hills.

Bank of British Columbia, Vancouver: In San Francisco.

Bank of Montreal, Montreal: In San Francisco.

Bank of Nova Scotia, Toronto: In San Francisco.

Bank of Tokyo Ltd., Tokyo: In Los Angeles and San Francisco.

Banque Nationale de Paris, Paris: In San Francisco.

Barclays Bank International Ltd., London: In San Francisco.

Bayerische Vereinsbank (Union Bank of Bavaria), Munich: In Los Angeles.

Canadian Imperial Bank of Commerce, Toronto: In San Francisco.

Chartered Bank, London: In San Francisco.

Credit Lyonnais, Paris: In Los Angeles.

Dai-ichi Kangyo Bank Ltd., Tokyo: In Los Angeles.

Daiwa Bank Ltd., Osaka: In Los Angeles.

Dresdner Bank AG, Frankfurt/Main: In Los Angeles.

Fuji Bank Ltd., Tokyo: In Los Angeles.

Hokkaido Takushoku Bank Ltd., Sapporo: In Los Angeles.

Hongkong & Shanghai Banking Corp., Hong Kong: In San Francisco.

Industrial Bank of Japan, Ltd., Tokyo: In Los Angeles.

Korea Exchange Bank, Seoul: In Los Angeles.

Kyowa Bank Ltd., Tokyo: In Los Angeles.

Metropolitan Bank & Trust Co., Manila: In Los Angeles.

Mitsubishi Bank Ltd., Tokyo: In Los Angeles.

Mitsui Bank Ltd., Tokyo: In Los Angeles.

National Westminster Bank Ltd., London: In San Francisco.

Philippine National Bank, Manila: In San Francisco.

Royal Bank of Canada, Montreal: In San Francisco.

Saitama Bank Ltd., Urawa: In Los Angeles.

Sanwa Bank Ltd., Osaka: In San Francisco.

Shanghai Commercial Bank Ltd., Hong Kong: In San Francisco.

Sumitomo Bank Ltd., Osaka: In San Francisco.

Swiss Bank Corp, Basle: In San Francisco.

Swiss Credit Bank, Zurich: In Los Angeles.

Taiyo Kobe Bank Ltd., Kobe: In Los Angeles.

Tokai Bank Ltd., Nagoya: In Los Angeles.

Toronto Dominion Bank, Toronto: In San Francisco.

REPRESENTATIVES

Banca Nazionale del Lavoro, Rome: In Los Angeles.

Banco Nacional de Mexico S.A., Mexico City: In Los Angeles.

Bank of New South Wales, Sydney: In San Francisco.

Bank of Nova Scotia, Toronto: In Los Angeles.

Bank of Seoul Ltd.: In Los Angeles.

Banque Nationale de Paris: In Beverly Hills.

Canadian Imperial Bank of Commerce, Toronto: In Los Angeles and San Francisco.

Long-Term Credit Bank of Japan, Ltd., Tokyo: In Los Angeles.

Mercantile Bank of Canada, Montreal: In Los Angeles.

Mitsubishi Trust & Banking Corp. Ltd., Tokyo: In Los Angeles.

Nippon Fudosan Bank Ltd., Tokyo: In Los Angeles.

Royal Bank of Canada, Montreal: In Los Angeles.

Royal Bank of Scotland Ltd., Edinburgh: In San Francisco.

Royal Trust Co., Montreal: In San Diego.

Swiss Bank Corp., Basle: In Los Angeles.

Swiss Credit Bank, Zurich: In Los Angeles.

Toronto Dominion Bank, Toronto: In Beverly Hills and San Francisco.

Union Bank of Switzerland, Zurich: In San Francisco.

DISTRICT OF COLUMBIA

SUBSIDIARIES OR AFFILIATES

Schroders Ltd., London: There is a Washington, DC, branch office of Schroder Naess and Thomas Division, investment counselors, of Schroders Inc., the New York based holding company subsidiary of Schroders, Ltd.

REPRESENTATIVES

Banco do Brasil, Brasilia: In Washington, DC.

Banco Real S.A., Sao Paulo: In Washington, DC.

Bank of Korea, Seoul: In Washington, DC.

Bank of Tokyo Ltd., Tokyo: In Washington, DC.

Export-Import Bank of Japan Ltd., Tokyo: In Washington, DC.

Istituto Mobiliare Italiano, Rome: In Washington, DC.

Japan Development Bank Ltd., Tokyo: In Washington, DC.

Societe Generale de Banque, Brussels: In Washington, DC.

FLORIDA

SUBSIDIARIES OR AFFILIATES

Royal Trust Co., Montreal: Has a Miami-based commercial bank holding company, Royal Trust Bank Corp., which holds the Royal Trust Bank of Tampa, the Royal Trust Bank of Miami NA, the Royal Trust Bank of St. Petersburg and the Royal Trust Bank of Palm Beach NA.

REPRESENTATIVES

Banco Central, S.A., Madrid: In Miami.

Bank Leumi Le-Israel B.M., Tel Aviv: In Miami.

Israel Discount Bank Ltd., Tel Aviv: In Miami.

GEORGIA

SUBSIDIARIES OR AFFILIATES

The Becker and Warburg-Paribas Group Inc., New York: There are Atlanta branch offices of A.G. Becker & Co. Inc., and Becker Securities Corp., New York-based subsidiaries of this holding company in which S. G. Warburg & Co. Ltd., London, and Compagnie Financiere de Paris et des Pays-Bas, Paris, hold interests.

Schroders Ltd., London: There is an Atlanta branch office of Schroder Naess and Thomas Division, investment counselors, of Schroders, Inc., the New York-based holding company subsidiary of Schroders Ltd.

AGENCIES

Barclays Bank International, London: In Atlanta.

GUAM

REPRESENTATIVES

Metropolitan Bank & Trust Co., Manila: In Agana.

HAWAII

SUBSIDIARIES OR AFFILIATES

Nomura Securities International Inc., New York: There is a Honolulu branch office of this foreign-owned firm. (See "New York Subsidiaries or Affiliates" for ownership.)

Sumitomo Bank Ltd., Osaka: Has a 13.44 percent interest in Central Pacific Bank, Honolulu.

AGENCIES

Philippine National Bank, Manila: In Honolulu.

REPRESENTATIVES

Bank of Tokyo Ltd.: In Honolulu.

ILLINOIS

SUBSIDIARIES OR AFFILIATES

ABD Securities Corp., New York: There is a Chicago branch office of this firm which is owned by Algemene Bank Nederland NV, Amsterdam; Banque Bruxelles Lambert, Brussels; Bayerische Hypotheken-und Wechsel-Bank, Munich; and Dresdner Bank, AG, Frankfurt/Main.

Banca Steinhauslin & Co., Florence: Through a holding company and a trust company, both based in Italy, owns Lombardfin S.p.A., Milan, a securities firm and a member of the Midwest Stock Exchange, Chicago.

Banco di Roma, Rome: Owns Banco di Roma (Chicago), in Chicago.

Bank of Tokyo Ltd., Tokyo: Has a 4.95 percent interest in the Chicago-Tokyo Bank, Chicago.

The Becker and Warburg-Paribas Group Inc., New York: There are Chicago branch offices of Warburg Paribas Becker Inc., A. G. Becker & Co., Inc., and Becker Securities Corp., New York-based subsidiaries of this holding company in which S. G. Warburg & Co. Ltd., London, and Compagnie Financiere de Paris et des Pays-Bas, Paris, hold interests.

Dai-ichi Kangyo Bank Ltd., Tokyo: Has a 97.85 percent interest in the First Pacific Bank of Chicago, Chicago.

Kleinwort Benson Inc., New York: There is a Chicago rep. office of this New York investment bank owned by Kleinwort Benson Ltd., London.

Yamaichi International (America) Inc., New York: There is a Chicago branch office of this foreign-owned firm. (See "New York Subsidiaries or Affiliates" for ownership.)

BRANCHES

(Foreign banking offices may open only in the Central Business District of Chicago and are not afforded branching privileges.)

Algemene Bank Nederland NV, Amsterdam.

Banca Commerciale Italiana, Milan.

Bank Leumi Le-Israel B.M., Tel Aviv.

Banque de L'Indochine et de Suez, Paris.

Banque Nationale de Paris, Paris.

Barclays Bank International Ltd., London.

Bayerische Vereinsbank (Union Bank of Bavaria), Munich.

Chartered Bank, London.

Commerzbank AG, Frankfurt/Main.

Credit Lyonnais, Paris.

Dresdner Bank AG, Frankfurt/Main.

Hongkong & Shanghai Banking Corp., Hong Kong.

International Commercial Bank of China, Taipei.

Korea Exchange Bank, Seoul.

Lloyds Bank International Ltd., London.

National Bank of Greece, Athens.

National Westminster Bank Ltd., London.

Sanwa Bank Ltd., Osaka.

State Bank of India, Bombay.

Sumitomo Bank Ltd., Osaka.

Swiss Bank Corp., Basle.

REPRESENTATIVES

(All in Chicago)
Allied Irish Banks, Ltd., Dublin.

Banca Nazionale del Lavoro, Rome.

Banco do Brasil, Brasilia.

Bank of Ireland, Dublin.

Bank of Montreal, Montreal.

Bank of Nova Scotia, Toronto.

Bank of Tokyo Ltd., Tokyo.

Canadian Imperial Bank of Commerce, Toronto.

Credito Italiano, Milan.

Dai-ichi Kangyo Bank Ltd., Tokyo.

Fuji Bank Ltd., Tokyo.

Hokkaido Takushoku Bank, Ltd., Sapporo.

Jugobanka, Belgrade.

Mitsubishi Bank Ltd., Tokyo.

Mitsui Bank, Ltd., Tokyo.

Royal Bank of Canada, Montreal.

Swiss Credit Bank, Zurich.

Taiyo Kobe Bank, Ltd., Kobe.

Toronto Dominion Bank, Toronto.

Union Bank of Switzerland, Zurich.

MARYLAND

SUBSIDIARIES OR AFFILIATES

Schroders Ltd., London: There is a Baltimore branch office of Schroder Naess and Thomas Division, investment counselors, of Schroders Inc., the New York-based holding company subsidiary of Schroders Ltd.

MASSACHUSETTS

SUBSIDIARIES OR AFFILIATES

ABD Securities Corp., New York: There is a Boston branch office of this firm owned by Algemene Bank Nederland NV, Amsterdam; Banque Bruxelles Lambert, Brussels; Bayerische Hypotheken-und Wechsel-Bank, Munich, and Dresdner Bank AG, Frankfurt/Main.

The Becker and Warburg-Paribas Group Inc., New York: There are Boston branch offices of A. G. Becker & Co. Inc., and Becker Securities Corp., New York-based subsidiaries of this holding company in which S. G. Warburg & Co. Ltd., London, and Compagnie Financiere de Paris et des Pays-Bas, Paris, hold interests.

Pictet & Cie., Geneva: Overseas Securities Co. Inc., with headquarters in Panama and administrative offices in Montreal and Geneva, is a member of the Boston Stock Exchange. The firm is owned by Pictet International Ltd., an affiliated company of the Swiss private bank.

Westdeutsche Landesbank Girozentrale, Duesseldorf: Owns RWS Securities, Inc., a brokerage firm and member of the Boston Stock Exchange.

BRANCHES

Barclays Bank International Ltd., London: In Boston.

NEW YORK

SUBSIDIARIES OR AFFILIATES

Algemene Bank Nederland NV., Amsterdam: Has an interest in ABD Securities Corp., New York, along with Banque Bruxelles Lambert, Brussels; Bayerische Hypotheken-und Wechsel-Bank, Munich; and Dresdner Bank AG, Frankfurt/Main. ABD has branches in Boston, Chicago, and Los Angeles.

Amsterdam-Rotterdam Bank NV, Amsterdam: Is one of six shareholding banks in European-American Bank and Trust Co., New York, which has 14 branches in Manhattan, two in the Bronx, three in Brooklyn, 10 in Queens, 46 in Nassau County, and 23 in Suffolk County, and European-American Banking Corp., which has a main office in New York and branches in Los Angeles and San Francisco. Also has an interest in SoGen Swiss International Corp., New York.

Banca Nazionale del Lavoro, Rome: Has a wholly owned subsidiary, The Italian Economic Corporation (T.I.E.C.) in New York City.

Banco Ambrosiano, Milan: Banco Ambrosiano Holding SA, Luxembourg, wholly owns Ultrafin International Corp., New York, an investment banking and brokerage firm.

Banco di Roma, Rome: Has a minority interest in the New York investment bank, Europartners Securities Corp. Commerzbank AG, Frankfurt/Main; Credit Lyonnais, Paris; Bank Leu Ltd., Zurich; and Nordic Bank Ltd., London, also hold participations.

Banco Union C.A., Caracas: Has minority interest in Union International Corp., a bank holding company in Wilmington, Delaware, which wholly owns Union Chelsea National Bank, which has its main office and two branches in New York City.

Bank Hapoalim B.M., Tel Aviv: Owns controlling interest in Ampal Investment Co., New York, which promotes investment and trade with Israel.

Bank Julius Baer & Co., Ltd., Zurich: Owns 100 percent of Baer Holding A.G., Zurich, which owns 100 percent of Baer Securities Corp., New York, and 100 percent of Baer American Banking Corp., an Article 12 investment company in New York with representative office in San Francisco.

Bank Leu Ltd., Zurich: Owns a minority interest in Europartners Securities Corp., New York. See Banco di Roma.

Bank Leumi Le-Israel B.M., Tel Aviv: Owns Bank Leumi Trust Co. of New York which operates five branches in Manhattan, one branch in Brooklyn, one branch and one limited service branch in Queens, one branch in the Bronx, and one branch in Hewlett, Long Island. There are offshore branches in Nassau, Bahamas and George Town, Cayman Islands. Also owns Leumi Securities Corp., New York, which specializes in Israeli securities and Israeli government bonds.

Bank of Montreal, Montreal: Owns Bank of Montreal Trust Co., New York.

Bank of Nova Scotia, Toronto: Owns 99.8 percent of The Bank of Nova Scotia Trust Co., New York.

Bank of Tokyo Ltd., Tokyo: Owns the majority interest in Bank of Tokyo Trust Co., New York, with five branches in Manhattan and one in London.

Bank Polska Kasa Opieki S.A., Warsaw: Owns Pekao Trading Corp., New York, licensed to receive and transmit funds.

Banque Arabe et Internationale D' In-

vestissement, Paris: Has a 10 percent interest (increased to 15.7 percent in 1977) in Reynolds Securities, International, Inc., parent of Reynolds Securities, Inc., New York. BAII, a merchant bank, is owned by a consortium of 31 financial institutions. BAII is 50 percent owned by Arab interests and 50 percent owned by banks in North and South America, Europe, and Japan.

Banque Bruxelles Lambert, Brussels. Has an interest in ABD Securities Corp., New York. (See Algemene Bank Nederland.) Compagnie Bruxelles Lambert, a holding company in Belgium, has an interest in the Drexel Burnham Lambert Group, Inc., which has a subsidiary, Drexel Burnham Lambert, Inc.

Banque de L'Indochine et de Suez, Paris: Has a 100 percent interest in Suez American Corp., New York, a firm specializing in underwriting and placement of securities and owns 20 percent of Blyth Eastman Dillon Co. Compagnie Financiere de Suez, a holding company, owns 100 percent of the bank and also owns 72 percent of Credit Industriel et Commercial, Paris, which has a representative office and branch in New York. Compagnie Financiere de Suez has a representative in New York City.

Banque de Paris et des Pays-Bas, Paris: This a major subsidiary of Compagnie Financiere de Paris et des Pays-Bas for which it holds a 25 percent interest in The Becker and Warburg-Paribas Group Inc., New York, a holding company for Warburg Paribas Becker Inc., New York, investment bankers, with offices also in Chicago and Los Angeles; A. G. Becker & Co. Inc., New York, dealers in fixed income securities, with offices also in Chicago, Los Angeles, San Francisco, Boston, Philadelphia, Houston and Atlanta; and Becker Securities Corp., New York, an equity securities firm with offices also in Chicago, Los Angeles, San Francisco, Boston, Milwaukee, and Atlanta. S. G. Warburg & Co. Ltd., London, also owns a 10 percent equity interest in The Becker and Warburg-Paribas Group.

Banque Nationale de Paris, Paris: Has a wholly owned subsidiary, the French American Banking Corp., New York, and is affiliated with its subsidiary, the French American Capital Corp., New York.

Banque Rothschild, Paris: Has an indirect interest in New Court Securities Corp., New York, along with N. M. Rothschild & Sons, London, and Pierson, Heldring & Pierson, Amsterdam.

Barclays Bank International Ltd., London: Has a wholly owned subsidiary, Barclays Bank of New York, New York, which has a head office and 30 branches in metropolitan New York and Westchester County.

Bayerische Hypotheken-und Wechsel-Bank, Munich: Has an interest in ABD Securities Corp., New York. (See Algemene Bank Nederland.)

Canadian Imperial Bank of Commerce, Toronto: Wholly owns Canadian Bank of Commerce Trust Co., New York.

Commerzbank AG, Frankfurt/Main: Has an interest in the New York investment bank, Europartners Securities Corp. (See Banco di Roma.)

Credit Lyonnais, Paris: Has an interest in the New York investment bank, Europartners Securities Corp. (See Banco di Roma.)

Creditanstalt Bankverein, Vienna: Is one of six shareholding banks in European-American Bank and Trust Co., New York, which has 14 branches in Manhattan, two in the Bronx, three in Brooklyn, 10 in Queens, 46 in Nassau County, and 23 in Suffolk County, and European-American Banking Corp., which has a main office in New York and branches in Los Angeles and San Francisco.

Daiwa Bank, Ltd., Osaka: Has a wholly-owned subsidiary Daiwa Bank Trust Co., New York.

Daiwa Securities Co. Ltd., Tokyo: The following banks are major shareholders of this company which has a wholly owned New York subsidiary, Daiwa Securities (America), Inc. with a branch office in Los Angeles: Sumitomo Bank Ltd., Osaka, 4.2 percent; Sumitomo Trust and Banking Co. Ltd. Osaka, 3.5 percent; Long-Term Credit Bank of Japan Ltd., Tokyo, 3.4 percent; Industrial Bank of Japan, Tokyo, 3.4 percent, and Yasuda Trust & Banking Co. Ltd., Tokyo, 2.1 percent.

Deutsche Bank AG, Frankfurt/Main: Is one of six shareholding banks in European-American Bank and Trust Co., New York, which has 14 branches in Manhattan, two in the Bronx, three in Brooklyn, 10 in Queens, 46 in Nassau County, and 23 in Suffolk County, and European-American Banking Corp., which has a main office in New York and branches in Los Angeles and San Francisco. Also owns 50 percent of UBS-DB Corp., New York, investment bankers.

Dresdner Bank AG, Frankfurt/Main: Has a 25 percent interest in ABD Securities Corp., New York. (See Algemene Bank Nederland.)

Robert Fleming & Co., Ltd., London: Owns Robert Fleming, Inc., New York, an investment banking firm.

Fuji Bank Ltd., Tokyo: Has a wholly owned subsidiary, the Fuji Bank and Trust Co., New York.

Hill Samuel & Co., Ltd., London: Owns Hill Samuel Inc., New York, which has a wholly owned subsidiary, Hill Samuel Securities Corp., New York.

Industrial Bank of Japan Ltd., Tokyo: Has a wholly owned subsidiary, Industrial Bank of Japan Trust Co. in New York City.

Industrial Discount Bank & Trust Co. Ltd., Kingstown, St. Vincent: Wholly owns Trafalgar Capital Corp., New York, which specializes in natural resource financing.

Israel Discount Bank Ltd., Tel Aviv: Owns the Israel Discount Trust Co., New York. Its holding company, IDB Bankholding Corp. Ltd., Tel Aviv, owns 84 percent of PEC Israel Economic Corporation, New York, which organizes, finances, and administers enterprises in Israel.

Kleinwort Benson Ltd., London: Has a wholly owned investment banking subsidiary, Kleinwort Benson, Inc., New York. Also holds Sharpes, Pixley Ltd., London, which has a wholly owned subsidiary, Sharpes, Pixley Inc., New York, bullion brokers.

Lloyds Bank International Ltd., London: Holds Balfour, Williamson Co., Ltd., London, which has a wholly owned subsidiary in Balfour, Williamson Inc., New York, export financiers. This bank is wholly owned by Lloyds Bank Ltd.

Midland Bank Ltd., London: Is one of six shareholding banks in European-American Bank and Trust Co., New York, which has 14 branches in Manhattan, two in the Bronx, three in Brooklyn, 10 in Queens, 46 in Nassau County, and 23 in Suffolk County, and European-American Banking Corp., which has a main office in New York and branches in Los Angeles and San Francisco.

National Bank of Greece, Athens: Has a major interest in the Atlantic Bank of New York, New York.

New Japan Securities Co. Ltd., Tokyo: The following banks are major shareholders in this company which has a wholly owned New York subsidiary, New Japan Securities International Inc., with a branch office in Los Angeles: Industrial Bank of Japan, Tokyo, 9.6 percent; Sumitomo Trust and Banking Co., Osaka, 9.0 percent, Daiwa Bank Ltd., Osaka, 6.9 percent, and Sanwa Bank Ltd., Osaka, 2.1 percent.

Nikko Securities Co. Ltd., Tokyo: The following banks are major shareholders in this company which has a wholly owned New York subsidiary, Nikko Securities International Inc., with branch offices in Los Angeles and San Francisco: Mitsubishi Bank Ltd., Tokyo, 2.5 percent; Industrial Bank of Japan, Tokyo, 2.3 percent; Fuji Bank Ltd., Tokyo, 2.3 percent; Tokai Bank Ltd., Nagoya, 2.3 percent; Mitsui Trust and Banking Co. Ltd., Tokyo, 2.3 percent; and Mitsubishi Trust and Banking Co. Ltd., Tokyo, 2.3 percent.

Nomura Securities Co., Ltd., Tokyo: The following banks are major shareholders in this company which has a 95 percent owned New York subsidiary, Nomura Securities International Inc., with branch offices in Los Angeles, San Francisco, and Honolulu (Bank of Tokyo holds the remaining 5 percent interest); Daiwa Bank Ltd., Osaka, 2.2 percent; Sanwa Bank Ltd., Osaka, 2.1 percent; Industrial Bank of Japan, Tokyo, 2.1 percent; Long-Term Credit Bank of Japan, Ltd., Tokyo, 2.1 percent; Mitsui Bank Ltd., Tokyo, 1.8 percent; and Mitsui Trust & Banking Co. Ltd., Tokyo, 1.5 percent.

Nordic Bank Ltd., London: This merchant bank, jointly owned by Den Norske Creditbank, Oslo; Kansallis-Osake-Pankki, Helsinki; and Svenska Handelsbanken, Stockholm, has an interest in Europartners Securities Corp., New York. (See Banco di Roma.)

Okasan Securities Co. Ltd., Tokyo: There is a New York representative office of this firm which has among its shareholders: Daiwa Bank Ltd., Osaka, 10 percent; Industrial Bank of Japan Ltd., Tokyo, 9.8 percent; and Mitsubishi Trust & Banking Corp., Tokyo, 10 percent.

Pierson, Heldring & Pierson, Amsterdam: Has an interest in New Court Securities Corp., New York. (See Banque Rothschild.)

N. M. Rothschild & Sons, London: Has an interest in New Court Securities Corp., New York. (See Banque Rothschild.)

Royal Bank of Canada, Montreal: Owns the Royal Bank and Trust Co., New York.

Schroders Ltd., London: Is the parent company for the London-based merchant bank, J. Henry Schroder Wagg & Co., having as its New York-based holding company, Schroders Inc. (including Schroder Naess & Thomas Division, investment counselors, with Atlanta, Washington, DC, and Baltimore offices), which has as its subsidiaries J. Henry Schroder Banking Corp., New York; Schroder Trust Co., New York; Schroder Capital Corp., New York; and Schroder Oil Financing & Investment Company, Inc., Houston.

Skandinaviska Enskilda Banken, Stockholm: Has a wholly owned subsidiary, Scandinavian Securities Corp., New York, engaged in a corporate finance and bond business.

N.V. Slavenburg's Bank, Rotterdam: Has a wholly owned subsidiary, the Slavenburg Corp., New York, engaged in commercial finance and factoring.

Societe Generale, Paris: Is one of six shareholding banks in European-American Bank and Trust Co., New York, which has 14 branches in Manhattan, two in the Bronx, three in Brooklyn, 10 in Queens, 46 in Nassau County, and 23 in Suffolk County, and European-American Banking Corp., which has a main office in New York and branches in Los Angeles and San Francisco. Also holds a majority interest in SoGen Swiss International

Corp., New York, an investment banking subsidiary with branches in Los Angeles and San Francisco.

Societe Generale Alsacienne de Banque, Strasbourg: Has an interest in SoGen Swiss International Corp., New York, an investment banking firm with branches in Los Angeles and San Francisco.

Societe Generale de Banque, Brussels: Is one of six shareholding banks in European-American Bank and Trust Co., New York, which has 14 branches in Manhattan, two in the Bronx, three in Brooklyn, 10 in Queens, 46 in Nassau County, 23 in Suffolk County, and European-American Banking Corp., which has a main office in New York and branches in Los Angeles and San Francisco. Also owns an interest in SoGen Swiss International Corp., New York investment banking subsidiary with branches in Los Angeles and San Francisco.

Svenska Handelsbanken, Stockholm: Wholly owns Nordic American Banking Corp., New York, the first subsidiary of a Scandinavian bank in the United States.

Swiss Bank Corp., Basle: Owns Basle Securities Corp., New York.

Swiss Credit Bank, Zurich: Owns Swiss American Securities Inc., New York, a securities firm, and has an interest in SoGen Swiss International Corp., New York, investment bankers with branches in Los Angeles and San Francisco.

Toronto Dominion Bank, Toronto: Owns Toronto Dominion Bank Trust Co., New York.

Trade Development Bank Holding S.A., Luxembourg: Has a 62 percent interest in Republic New York Corporation, parent of Republic National Bank of New York.

UBAF Arab American Bank, New York City: Is owned by a consortium of 16 Arab and European banks and four U.S. bank holding companies. It is 16 percent owned by Union de Banques Arabes et Francaises, Neuilly, France, and four other members of the UBAF Group. The following institutions own 7 percent or less: Alahli Bank of Kuwait; Arab African Bank; Arab Bank, Ltd.; Central Bank of Egypt; Central Bank of Oman; Commercial Bank of Syria; Libyan Arab Foreign Bank; National Bank of Abu Dhabi; Banque du Maroc; Riyad Bank, Ltd.; and Sudan Commercial Bank.

Union Bank of Switzerland, Zurich: Owns 50 percent of UBS-DB Corp., New York, investment bankers. Deutsche Bank AG owns the other 50 percent.

S. G. Warburg & Co., Ltd., London: Holds a 10 percent equity interest in The Becker and Warburg-Paribas Group Inc., New York, a holding company for Warburg Paribas Becker Inc., New York, investment

bankers, with offices also in Chicago and Los Angeles; A. G. Becker & Co. Inc., New York, dealers in fixed income securities, with offices also in Chicago, Los Angeles, San Francisco, Boston, Houston, Philadelphia, and Atlanta; and Becker Securities Corp., New York, an equity securities firm with offices also in Chicago, Los Angeles, San Francisco, Boston, Milwaukee, and Atlanta. Compagnie Financiere de Paris et des Pays-Bas also holds a 25 percent interest in The Becker and Warburg-Paribas Group.

Yamaichi Securities Co. Ltd., Tokyo: The following banks are major shareholders in this company which has a wholly owned New York subsidiary in Yamaichi International (America) Inc., with branch offices in Chicago and Los Angeles: Fuji Bank Ltd., Tokyo, 5 percent; Mitsubishi Bank Ltd., Tokyo, 5 percent; Industrial Bank of Japan, Tokyo, 5 percent; and Dai-Ichi Kangyo Bank Ltd., Tokyo, 3.3 percent; Yasuda Trust & Banking Co., Ltd., Tokyo, 2.2 percent; and Mitsubishi Trust & Banking Corp., Tokyo, 2.2 percent.

BRANCHES

(All in New York City)

Algemene Bank Nederland NV, Amsterdam: Two branches.

Banca Commerciale Italiana, Milan: One branch.

Banca Nazionale del Lavoro, Rome: One branch.

Banco Credito y Ahorro Ponceno, Ponce: One branch.

Banco de Bogota, Bogota: One branch.

Banco de la Nacion Argentina, Buenos Aires: One branch.

Banco de Ponce, Ponce: Ten branches: four in Manhattan, two in the Bronx, three in Brooklyn, and one in Queens.

Banco di Napoli, Naples: One branch.

Banco di Roma, Rome: One branch.

Banco do Brasil, Brasilia: One branch.

Banco Popular de Puerto Rico, San Juan: Eight branches: four in Manhattan, two in the Bronx, one in Brooklyn, and one in Queens.

Banco Real S.A., Sao Paulo: One branch.

Bank fuer Gemeinwirtschaft, Frankfurt: One branch.

Bank Hapoalim B.M., Tel Aviv: One branch.

Banque Francaise du Commerce Exterieur, Paris: One branch.

Banque Nationale de Paris, France: One branch.

Barclays Bank International Ltd., London: Two branches.

Bayerische Vereinsbank (Union Bank of Bavaria), Munich: One branch.

Berliner Handels-und Frankfurter Bank, Frankfurt: One branch.

Chartered Bank, London: One branch (another branch is maintained by Standard Chartered Bank, Ltd., London).

Commerzbank AG, Frankfurt/Main: One branch.

Credit Industriel et Commercial S.A., Paris: One branch.

Credit Lyonnais, Paris: One branch.

Credito Italiano, Milan: One branch.

Deutsche Genossenschafts Bank, Frankfurt: One branch.

Dresdner Bank AG, Frankfurt/Main: One branch.

Habib Bank Ltd., Karachi: One branch.

Hongkong & Shanghai Banking Corp., Hong Kong: Two branches.

Israel Discount Bank Ltd., Tel Aviv: Two branches.

Lloyds Bank International Ltd., London: One branch.

Long-Term Credit Bank of Japan, Ltd., Tokyo: One branch.

National Bank of Pakistan, Karachi: Two branches.

National Westminster Bank Ltd., London: One branch.

Philippine National Bank, Manila: One branch.

Standard Chartered Bank, Ltd., London: One branch.

State Bank of India, Bombay: One branch.

Swiss Bank Corp., Basle: Three branches.

Swiss Credit Bank, Zurich: One branch.

Tokyo Trust & Banking Co., Ltd., Tokyo: One branch.

Union Bank of Switzerland, Zurich: One branch.

Westdeutsche Landesbank Girozentrale, Duesseldorf: One branch.

Yasuda Trust & Banking Co., Ltd., Tokyo: One branch.

AGENCIES

(All in New York City)
Australia and New Zealand Banking Group, Ltd., Melbourne.

Banco de Bilbao, Bilbao.

Banco de Vizcaya, Bilbao.

Banco do Estado de Sao Paulo S.A., Sao Paulo.

Banco Hispano Americano, Madrid.

Banco Industrial de Venezuela, Caracas.

Banco Mercantil de Sao Paulo S.A., Sao Paulo.

Banco Nacional de Mexico S.A., Mexico City.

Banco Union C.A., Caracas.

Banco Urquijo S.A., Madrid.

Bangkok Bank Ltd., Bangkok.

Bank Leumi Le-Israel BM, Tel Aviv.

Bank Melli Iran, Teheran.

Bank of Montreal, Montreal.

Bank of New South Wales, Sydney.

Bank of Nova Scotia, Toronto.

Bank of Tokyo Ltd., Tokyo.

Bank Saderat Iran, Teheran.

Canadian Imperial Bank of Commerce, Toronto.

Commercial Bank of Korea, Seoul.

Thomas Cook Bankers Ltd., London.

Dai-ichi Kangyo Bank Ltd., Tokyo.

Daiwa Bank Ltd., Osaka.

Fuji Bank Ltd., Tokyo.

Grindlays Bank Ltd., London.

Hokkaido Takushoku Bank Ltd., Sapporo.

Industrial Bank of Japan Ltd., Tokyo.

International Commercial Bank of China, Taipei.

Korea Exchange Bank, Seoul.

Kyowa Bank Ltd., Tokyo.

Mitsubishi Bank Ltd., Tokyo.

Mitsubishi Trust and Banking Corp., Ltd., Tokyo.

Mitsui Bank Ltd., Tokyo.

Mitsui Trust and Banking Co., Ltd., Tokyo.

Overseas Union Bank Ltd., Singapore.

Royal Bank of Canada, Montreal.

Saitama Bank, Saitama.

Sumitomo Bank Ltd., Osaka.

Taiyo Kobe Bank Ltd., Kobe.

Tokai Bank Ltd., Nagoya.

Toronto Dominion Bank, Toronto.

REPRESENTATIVES

(All in New York City)
Allied Irish Banks, Ltd., Dublin.

Australia & New Zealand Banking Group Ltd., Melbourne.

Banca Catalana, Barcelona.

Banca Nazionale del Lavoro, Rome.

Banca Nazionale Dell'Agricoltura, Rome.

Banca Populare di Novara, Novara.

Banco Ambrosiano, Milan.

Banco Atlantico S.A., Barcelona.

Banco Central S.A., Madrid.

Banco Comercial Antioqueno, Medellin.

Banco Comercial Mexicano S.A., Mexico City.

Banco Credito y Ahorro Ponceno, Ponce.

Banco de Comercio, S.A., Mexico City.

Banco de Credito del Peru, Lima.

Banco de Santander, Santander.

Banco del Caribe C.A., Caracas.

Banco di Roma, Rome.

Banco di Sicilia, Palermo.

Banco Espanol de Credito, Madrid.

Banco Exterior de Espana, Madrid.

Foreign Banks with U.S. Branches 309

Banco Financiero e Industrial de Investimento S.A., Sao Paulo.
Banco Frances e Italiano de Colombia-Sudameris, Bogota.
Banco Frances e Italiano Para a America do Sul S.A. Sudameris, Sao Paulo.
Banco Frances e Italiano Para la America del Sud-Sudameris, Buenos Aires.
Banco Frances e Italiano Para la America del Sud-Sudameris, Montevideo.
Banco Industrial de Cataluna S.A., Barcelona.
Banco la Filantropica, Quito.
Banco Latino, C.A., Caracas.
Banco Mercantil de Panama-S.A. Sudameris, Panama City.
Banco Mercantil y Agricola, Caracas.
Banco Mexicano, Mexico City.
Banco Nacional de Descuento, Caracas.
Banco Paraguayo de Comercio-Sudameris S.A. Asuncion.
Banco Totta & Acores, Lisbon.
Bank Ekspor Impor Indonesia, Djakarta.
Bank Handlowy w Warszawie, Warsaw.
Bank Indonesia, Djakarta.
Bank Negara Indonesia 1946, Djakarta.
Bank of Ireland, Dublin.
Bank of Italy, Rome.
Bank of Japan, Tokyo.
Bank of Korea, Seoul.
Bank of N. T. Butterfield & Son Ltd., Hamilton, Bermuda.
Bank of Nova Scotia, Toronto.
Bank of the Western Hemisphere Ltd., St. Vincent (West Indies).
Banque Bruxelles Lambert, Brussels.
Banque de L'Union Europeenne, Paris.
Banque Francaise & Italienne Pour L'Amerique du Sud-Sudameris-S.A., Paris.
Banque Nationale de Paris, Paris.
Banque Vernes et Commercial de Paris, Paris.
Banque Worms et Cie, Paris.
Bayerische Hypotheken-und Wechsel-Bank, Munich.
Berliner Handels-und Frankfurter Bank, Frankfurt.
Bishops Internatonal Bank, Ltd., Nassau.
British Bank of the Middle East, London.
Cassa di Risparmio di Firenze, Florence.
Cassa di Risparmio di Genova e Imperia, Genoa.
Cassa di Risparmio di Torino, Turin.
Cassa di Risparmio di Verona, Vicenza e. Belluno, Verona.
Central Trust of China, Taipei.
Charterhouse Japhet Ltd., London.
Cho-Heung Bank, Ltd., Seoul.
Christiania Bank og Kreditkasse, Oslo.
Chuo Trust & Banking Co. Ltd., Tokyo.
Commercial Bank of Australia Ltd., Melbourne.

Commercial Banking Co. of Sydney Ltd., Sydney.
Commonwealth Trading Bank, Sydney.
Compania Financiera y Comercial Panameris, Panama City.
Credit Commercial de France, Paris.
Credit D'Escompte, Paris.
Credit General S.A. de Banque, Brussels.
Credit Industriel et Commercial S.A., Paris.
Credit Lyonnais, Paris.
Den Danske Bank, Copenhagen.
Deutsche Genossenschaftsbank, Frankfurt.
Hambros Bank Ltd., London.
Hamburgische Landesbank Girozentrale, Hamburg.
Hanil Bank Ltd., Seoul.
Hessische Landesbank-Girozentrale, Frankfurt.
Industrial Discount Bank & Trust Co., Ltd., Kingstown, St. Vincent.
Japan Development Bank Ltd., Tokyo.
Jugobanka, Belgrade.
Korea Development Bank, Seoul.
Kredietbank NV., Brussels.
Kredietbank S.A. Luxembourgeoise, Luxembourg.
Kredietbank (Suisse) S.A., Geneva.
Libra Bank Ltd., London.
Ljubljanska Banks, Ljubljana, Yugoslavia.
Lloyds Bank International Ltd., London.
Morgan Grenfell & Co. Ltd., London.
National Bank of Australasia Ltd., Melbourne.
National Bank of New Zealand Ltd., London.
National Westminster Bank Ltd., London.
Nedbank Ltd., Johannesburg.
Nederlandsche Middenstandsbank N.V., Amsterdam.
Nippon Fudosan Bank Ltd., Tokyo.
Norges Bank, Oslo.
Orion Bank Ltd., London.
Post-Och Kreditbanken, Stockholm.
Privatbanken A/S, Copenhagen.
Privredna Banka Sarajevo, Sarajevo, Yugoslavia.
Rea Brothers Ltd., London.
Royal Bank of Scotland Ltd., Edinburgh.
Sociedad Financiera Amerfin, Caracas.
Sudameris Chile Ltda., Santiago.
Toronto Dominion Bank, Toronto.
Union Bank of Switzerland, Zurich.
United Mizrahi Bank, Ltd., Tel Aviv.
Williams & Glyn's Bank Ltd., London.
World Banking Corp. Ltd., Nassau.

OHIO

REPRESENTATIVES

Bank of Nova Scotia, Toronto: In Cleveland.

OREGON

BRANCHES

Bank of Tokyo Ltd., Tokyo: One branch in Portland.

Canadian Imperial Bank of Commerce, Toronto: Two branches in Portland; one branch in Beaverton.

PENNSYLVANIA

SUBSIDIARIES OR AFFILIATES

The Becker and Warburg-Paribas Group Inc., New York: There is a Philadelphia branch office of A. G. Becker & Co., Inc., a New York-based subsidiary of this holding company in which S. G. Warburg & Co. Ltd., London, and Compagnie Financiere de Paris et des Pays-Bas, Paris, hold interests.

B. Metzler Seel. Sohn & Co., Frankfurt: Metzler Securities GmbH, a German company 85 percent owned by this private bank, is a member of the Philadelphia Stock Exchange and, as an associate member of the Boston Stock Exchange, has trading privileges over Boston's facilities.

REPRESENTATIVES

Charterhouse Japhet, Ltd., London: In Philadelphia.

PUERTO RICO

The Commonwealth's three largest indigenous banks have been granted branching privileges on the U.S. mainland: Banco Credito y Ahorro Ponceno and Banco de Ponce in New York State and Banco Popular de Puerto Rico in New York and California. They are not Federal Reserve members but are insured by the Federal Deposit Insurance Corp. (See index under each bank.)

SUBSIDIARIES OR AFFILIATES

Banco de Santander, Spain: Holds a majority interest in Banco de Santander-Puerto Rico, Hato Rey, which was formerly the First National Bank of Puerto Rico.

Bank of Nova Scotia, Toronto: Owns a minority of Banco Mercantil de Puerto Rico, Hato Rey, which has branches in Rio Piedras, Santurce, and Ponce.

BRANCHES

Bank of Nova Scotia, Toronto: In San Juan, Santurce, Fajardo, and Hato Rey.

Royal Bank of Canada, Montreal: In Hato Rey, San Juan, Santurce, Mayaguez, Guanica, and Puerto Nueva.

REPRESENTATIVES

Banco de Santander, Santander: In Hato Rey.

TEXAS

SUBSIDIARIES OR AFFILIATES

Schroder Oil Financing & Investment Company, Inc., Houston: Is a subsidiary of Schroders Inc., a New York-based holding company.

Tokyo Bancorp., International (Houston) Inc., Houston: Is a subsidiary of Bank of Tokyo, Ltd., organized as an agreement corporation.

REPRESENTATIVES

Algemene Bank Nederland, Amsterdam: In Houston.

Banca Nazionale del Lavoro, Rome.

Banco di Roma, Rome: In Houston.

Bank of Montreal, Montreal: In Houston.

Bank of Nova Scotia, Toronto: In Houston.

Bank of Scotland, Edinburgh: In Houston.

Bank of Tokyo Ltd., Tokyo: In Houston.

Canadian Imperial Bank of Commerce, Toronto: In Dallas.

Charterhouse Japhet Ltd., London: In Houston.

Credit Lyonnais, Paris.

Dai-ichi Kangyo Bank, Ltd., Tokyo.

Houston International Bank Luxembourg S.A., Luxembourg: In Houston.

Lloyds Bank International, Ltd., London.

Royal Bank of Canada, Montreal: In Dallas.

Royal Bank of Scotland, Edinburgh: In Houston.

Swiss Bank Corp., Basle: In Houston.

Taiyo Kobe Bank Ltd., Kobe: In Houston.

Toronto Dominion Bank, Toronto: In Houston.

U.S. VIRGIN ISLANDS

BRANCHES

Bank of Nova Scotia, Toronto: Three branches, St. Croix: two branches, St. Thomas.

Barclays Bank International Ltd., London: One branch, St. Thomas.

Royal Bank of Canada, Montreal: One branch, St. Croix.

WASHINGTON

BRANCHES

Bank of Tokyo Ltd., Tokyo: In Seattle.

Canadian Imperial Bank of Commerce, Toronto: In Seattle.

Chartered Bank, London: In Seattle.
Hongkong & Shanghai Banking Corp., Hong Kong: In Seattle.
Taiyo Kobe Bank Ltd., Kobe: In Seattle.

REPRESENTATIVES

Hokkaido Takushoku Bank Ltd., Sapporo: In Seattle.
Sumitomo Bank, Ltd., Osaka: In Seattle.

WISCONSIN

SUBSIDIARIES OR AFFILIATES

The Becker and Warburg-Paribas Group Inc., New York: There is a Milwaukee branch office of Becker Securities Corp., a New York-based subsidiary of this holding company in which S. G. Warburg & Co. Ltd., London, and Compagnie Financiere de Paris et des Pays-Bas, Paris, hold interests.

25 LARGEST DIVERSIFIED FINANCIAL COMPANIES
(ranked by assets)

Rank 1976	Company	Assets[1] ($000)	Revenues[2] ($000)	Net Income[3] ($000)	Stockholders' Equity[4] ($000)
1	Aetna Life & Casualty (Hartford)	18,191,490	7,179,407	212,966	1,744,676
2	Travelers Corp. (Hartford)	13,369,697	6,417,751	143,342	1,662,125
3	American Express (New York)	10,368,090	2,948,865	194,485	1,253,813
4	H. F. Ahmanson (Los Angeles)	7,908,871	683,912	68,269	560,356
5	INA (Philadelphia)	7,161,692	2,932,180	87,618	1,067,721
6	Merrill Lynch & Co. (New York)	6,617,787	1,124,929	106,608	632,072
7	Great Western Financial (Beverly Hills)	6,302,399	477,123	49,225	425,286
8	Loews (New York)	6,225,475	2,901,454	91,327	584,102
9	First Charter Financial (Beverly Hills)	6,208,187	479,249	71,504	551,510
10	Continental (New York)	5,673,742	2,422,248	107,594	1,490,066
11	Transamerica (San Francisco)	5,209,561	2,730,884	113,737	921,290
12	American General Insurance (Houston)	4,689,257	1,434,639	95,955	778,495
13	C.I.T. Financial (New York)	4,591,763	584,930	94,963	829,992
14	Imperial Corp. of America (San Diego)	4,273,124	335,872	40,724	307,784
15	City Investing (Beverly Hills)	4,215,439	2,535,093	53,145	805,792
16	Walter E. Heller International (Chicago)	3,931,402	395,080	27,808	243,219
17	Household Finance (Chicago)	3,513,863	577,237	133,954	1,002,661
18	First Boston (Philadelphia)	3,146,418	109,561	18,224	84,011
19	Beneficial (Wilmington)	2,727,893	536,558	100,407	791,246
20	St. Paul Companies	2,532,786	1,194,205	93,037	493,469
21	U.S. Fidelity & Guaranty (Baltimore)	2,341,814	1,352,448	84,530	564,178
22	American International Group (New York)	2,275,448	1,104,759	98,077	493,088
23	Gibraltar Financial Corp. of California (Beverly Hills)	2,242,094	170,417	16,778	136,440
24	Golden West Financial (Oakland, Calif.)	2,129,309	172,004	21,346	102,951
25	USLIFE (New York)	2,109,086	475,555	52,689	383,965

N.A. Not available.

[1] Total assets shown as of December 31, 1976, unless otherwise noted. Only assets of consolidated subsidiaries are included. Holding companies that own commercial banks or life insurance companies are listed here only when these subsidiaries represent less than 80 percent of assets.

[2] Total income during the year, including any consolidated nonfinancial revenues from manufacturing, retailing, etc., and revenues from discontinued operations when published. All companies on the list must have derived more than 50 percent of their revenues from two or more kinds of financial businesses and be publicly held.

[3] That is, after taxes, extraordinary items, and realized capital gains or losses. Figures in parentheses indicate net loss.

[4] Sum of capital stock, surplus, and retained earnings at the end of the fiscal year.

[5] Year-end total.

Net Income as Percent of Equity	Number of Employees[5]	Earnings per Share				Total Return to Investors	
		1976($)	1975($)	1966($)	Growth-Rate 1966–76[6] (percent)	1976[9] (percent)	1966–76 Average (percent)
12.2	30,700	3.97	2.01	0.79	17.52	55.37	7.26
8.6	28,598	3.26	2.19	2.32	3.46	50.56	2.68
15.5	33,593	2.70	2.29	0.46	19.36	12.86	16.44
12.2	3,400	3.00	1.92	N.A.	—	70.15	N.A.
8.2	23,800	3.79	2.75	1.72[7]	8.22	40.50	5.27
16.9	19,715	3.01	2.69	1.17	9.91	79.66	N.A.
11.6	1,831	3.30	1.53	0.69	16.94	76.23	11.44
15.6	23,200	7.05	5.14	0.39	33.57	73.45	29.96
13.0	1,900	2.42	1.70	0.43	18.86	44.26	12.78
7.2	21,135	4.03	3.25	2.00	7.26	31.54	10.61
12.3	25,800	1.74	1.13	1.03	5.38	79.17	5.64
12.3	8,660	4.05	2.19	2.21	6.24	54.87	1.78
11.4	23,500	4.54	4.32	2.75	5.14	47.04	8.59
13.2	1,250	2.98	2.06	0.64	16.63	62.11	12.43
6.6	37,500	1.80	1.47	0.36	17.46	102.31	6.58
11.4	4,958	2.39	2.64	1.06	8.47	(12.18)	12.00
13.4	10,000	2.87	2.42	1.66	5.63	41.41	4.73
21.7	1,036	5.55	4.86	1.50	13.98	56.92	13.90
12.7	8,900	4.52	3.34	2.28	7.08	62.04	4.68
18.9	8,325	4.44	2.60	0.95	16.67	19.00	8.23
15.0	8,449	3.44	1.98	1.40	9.41	72.12	11.48
19.9	14,000	3.88	3.11	0.11[8]	42.81	(4.46)	N.A.
12.3	943	1.95	1.18	0.47	15.29	109.63	9.32
20.7	1,060	4.18	2.22	0.29	30.58	62.00	N.A.
13.7	3,710	2.35	2.21	1.11	7.79	51.10	(0.52)

• Average annual growth rate, compounded. No figure is given if the company had a loss in either 1966 or 1976.
⁊ Figure is for Insurance Co. of North America.
• Figure is for American Home Assurance.
Source: Reprinted from the 1977 Fortune Directory by special permission; © 1977 Time Inc.

25 LARGEST LIFE INSURANCE COMPANIES (ranked by assets)

Rank 1976	Company	Assets[1] ($000)	Premium and Annuity Income[2] ($000)	Investment Net Income ($000)
1	Prudential (Newark)*	43,700,778	6,201,181	2,331,941
2	Metropolitan (New York)*	37,501,516	5,344,295	2,231,751
3	Equitable Life Assurance (New York)*	22,430,473	3,728,920	1,153,208
4	New York Life*	14,858,967	2,033,386	867,335
5	John Hancock Mutual (Boston)*	13,995,567	2,208,795	772,123
6	Aetna Life (Hartford)[7]	12,060,829	3,448,741	717,295
7	Connecticut General Life (Bloomfield)	8,781,042	1,970,268	511,835
8	Northwestern Mutual (Milwaukee)*	8,544,200	893,702	497,279
9	Travelers (Hartford)[8]	8,458,808	2,680,869	413,957
10	Massachusetts Mutual (Springfield)*	6,396,921	941,786	374,725
11	Mutual of New York*	5,418,453	879,531	305,643
12	Teachers Insurance & Annuity (New York)	5,184,311	703,738	374,607
13	New England Mutual (Boston)*	4,984,457	685,737	285,579
14	Bankers Life (Des Moines)*	4,132,090	1,049,826	257,444
15	Connecticut Mutual (Hartford)*	3,951,303	478,402	211,802
16	Mutual Benefit (Newark)*	3,783,199	721,764	218,708
17	Lincoln National Life (Fort Wayne)	3,483,474	758,090	207,838
18	Penn Mutual (Philadelphia)*	3,078,164	321,606	179,543
19	National Life & Accident (Nashville)	2,593,572	332,982	163,705
20	Occidental of California (Los Angeles)[9]	2,545,185	897,446	137,735
21	Western & Southern (Cincinnati)*	2,456,535	274,609	147,792
22	Continental Assurance (Chicago)[10]	2,429,209	774,447	123,524
23	Phoenix Mutual (Hartford)*	2,003,716	359,847	106,467
24	National Life (Montpelier)*	1,949,025	208,040	107,124
25	Franklin Life (Springfield, Ill.)	1,860,244	236,774	111,933

Data for all companies are on the "statutory" accounting basis required by state insurance regulatory authorities.

N.A. Not available.

* Indicates mutual company.

[1] As of December 31, 1976. Includes "separate accounts," i.e., funds, heavily invested in common stocks, that are segregated from other assets; they are designed primarily for pension plans.

[2] Includes premium income from life, accident, and health policies, from annuities, and from contributions to deposit administration funds and excludes income from "separate accounts."

Source: Reprinted from the 1977 Fortune Directory with special permission; © Time Inc.

Net Gain from Operations[3]			Life Insurance in Force[4]	Increase in Life Insurance in Force[5]		Number of Employees[6]
($000)	Mutual	Stock	($000)	($000)	Percent of Increase	
13,771	12		262,651,784	26,451,535	11.2	61,673
142,249	1		243,006,858	16,718,861	7.4	53,000
61,052	2		130,429,073	11,262,325	9.5	22,965
55,045	3		83,111,025	7,006,061	9.2	19,325
47,411	4		94,788,196	7,004,155	8.0	20,050
111,205		1	90,349,562	5,794,467	6.9	16,300
101,221		2	51,230,991	3,024,472	6.3	9,250
38,959	5		35,238,093	3,474,061	10.9	5,642
89,379		3	78,545,549	6,841,747	9.5	37,798
30,233	6		31,648,581	2,881,729	10.0	7,898
9,198	17		25,320,739	2,152,170	9.3	7,488
35,316		8	4,135,236	517,366	14.3	1,346
14,372	11		22,126,667	1,644,001	8.0	6,174
20,228	7		20,657,868	1,998,264	10.7	4,553
6,714	19		16,929,766	1,509,850	9.8	4,521
(889)	25		24,999,196	2,111,646	9.2	4,892
49,725		5	35,964,439	3,579,310	11.1	6,046
9,590	16		13,343,182	943,254	7.6	3,674
79,277		4	14,783,431	763,855	5.4	9,296
27,443		11	43,236,876	4,409,848	11.4	5,915
18,952	8		12,896,803	669,300	5.5	8,950
18,052		18	19,721,703	1,769,573	9.9	N.A.
4,948	24		19,476,322	2,509,666	14.8	2,443
16,949	10		8,343,738	446,973	5.7	2,118
43,338		6	11,224,332	841,981	8.1	4,404

[3] After dividends to policyholders and federal income taxes, excluding capital gains and losses. Figures in parentheses indicate net losses.

[4] Face value of all life policies as of December 31, 1976.

[5] Change between December 31, 1975, and December 31, 1976.

[6] Includes home office, field force, and full-time agents.

[7] Company is wholly owned by Aetna Life & Casualty (No. 1 on the Diversified-Financial list).

[8] Company is wholly owned by Travelers Corp. (No. 2 on the Diversified-Financial list).

[9] Company is wholly owned by Transamerica (No. 11 on the Diversified-Financial list).

[10] Company is 57 percent owned by Loews (No. 8 on the Diversified-Financial list).

Advertising and the Media

ADVERTISING AND MEDIA EXPENDITURES

Overall advertising expenditures experienced a rapid growth in the early 1950s. They rose at an annual rate of 10 percent, or twice as fast as during the ensuing 15 years. Starting with 1970, the rate again accelerated to 7.6 percent. The market share of the various media was greatly influenced by the introduction of television.

As a percent of total advertising expendi-

tures, television's share grew from 3 percent in 1950 to 18.6 percent in 1975 in spite of the higher cost of television advertising. Only in 1971, when the ban on cigarette advertising was imposed, did it suffer a loss in market share. Direct mail advertising experienced the least fluctuation throughout that period. The bulk of the advertising dollar is still concentrated in newspapers and the printed media.

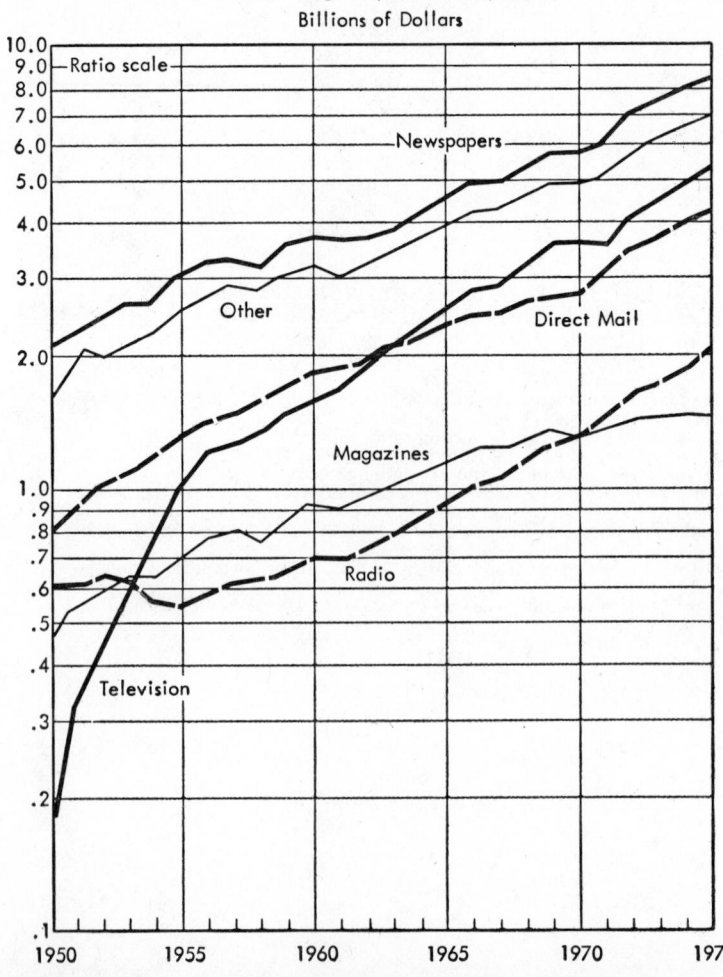

A. Advertising: Expenditures by Medium

Billions of Dollars

B. Breakdown of Advertising
By Selected Category – 1955 and 1975

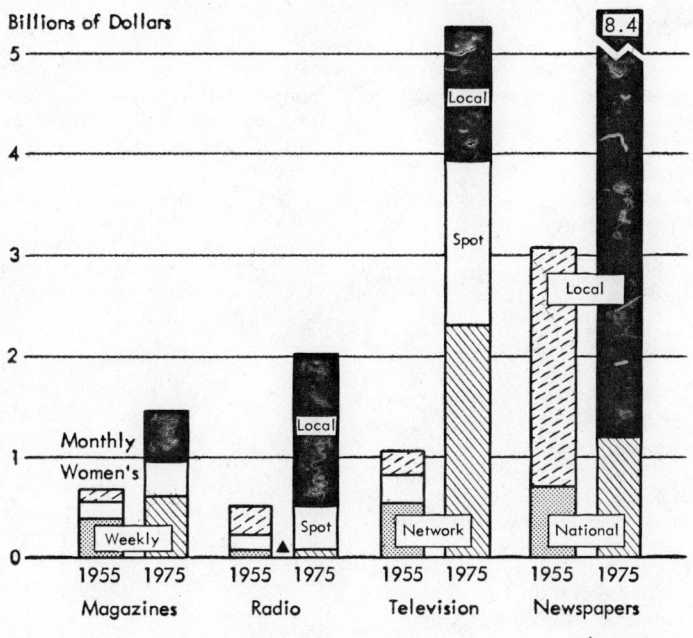

C. Advertising Expenditures
Outlays by Media

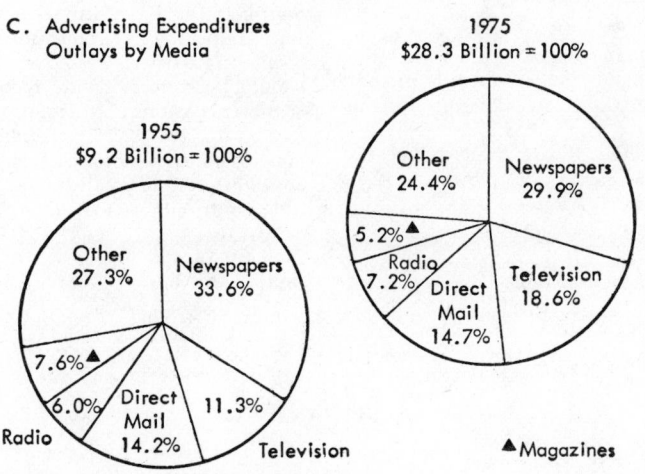

Source: The Conference Board.

WARNING SIGNALS FOR NEW PRODUCT INTRODUCTION

Any of the following answers should be warning signals for you.

From the consumer

1. "The price is too high."
2. "I don't know how to use it—I must be educated."
3. "Certainly it's a better product, but it's not quite worth the extra money."

From the trade

4. "The product will have a low rate of turnover."
5. "The product will disturb our business on established items—maybe destroy more business than it creates."
6. "We are afraid of the servicing problem this new item may create."
7. "The product is an unwanted addition to a field already crowded."
8. "There is no retail shelf space or floor space available for this product."
9. "The nature of the product is such that it must be sold in an odd size or shape, ill-suited to shipping or display facilities."
10. "This product cannot be sold without individual demonstration."

From company management

11. "It is difficult to procure (or procure *consistently*) the right raw materials for this product."
12. "It is difficult to project costs because the raw material market is subject to considerable price fluctuation."
13. "Plant production would be seriously hampered if changes were made to handle the manufacture of this new product."
14. "The product is good but impossible to package."
15. "The patent situation is confused and we would be vulnerable."
16. "The probable channel of distribution for this new product is not clearly defined."
17. "To make salesmen's time available for this product would jeopardize our established line."
18. "The new product does not hold promise of sufficient volume or frequency of purchase to maintain distribution."
19. "The trade-mark situation is unsatisfactory."
20. "Certain government regulations would make marketing of this product difficult."
21. "With this product we would be competing in a field dominated by strong, aggressive companies with superior marketing resources."

Profit Potential

It should be pointed out that some of these warnings can be readily identified as "facts," but others only as "conjectures." Before using them to arrive at a decision, conjectures should be converted into facts by market research, consumer research, and so forth. Even after this has been done, assuming the conclusion is favorable, a qualified financial specialist should analyze the product's probable contributions to company profit, and its ratio to capital investment required. The glamour of a new product and its profit potential are, unfortunately, often poles apart.

Source: *New Product Introduction for Small Business Owners,* Small Business Administration.

318

ADVERTISING EXPENDITURES, 1976 ($ millions, estimated)

Newspapers
- Total .... $ 9,910
- National 1,502
- Local 8,408

Magazines
- Total 1,789
- Weeklies 748
- Women's 457
- Monthlies 584

Farm Publications 86

Business papers 1,035

Outdoor
- Total 383
- National 252
- Local 131

Television
- Total 6,622
- Network 2,857
- Spot 2,125
- Local 1,640

Radio
- Total 2,277
- Network 104
- Spot 493
- Local 1,680

Direct mail 4,754

Miscellaneous
- Total 6,604
- National 3,453
- Local 3,151

Total
- National 18,450
- Local 15,010
- Grand total 33,460

Prepared for *Advertising Age* by Robert J. Coen, McCann-Erickson, Inc., July 1977. Reprinted with permission from the July 18, 1977 issue of *Advertising Age*, © Crain Communications, Inc., 1977.

ESTIMATE OF 1978 ADVERTISING VOLUME

	1978 (millions)	1977 (millions)	Percent change
Network television	$ 3,850	$ 3,460	+11 %
Spot television	2,560	2,204	+16
Magazines	2,510	2,162	+16
Newspapers	1,830	1,677	+ 9
Outdoor	320	290	+10
Other national media	12,705	11,297	+13
Total national advertisers	23,775	21,090	+12.7
All local advertisers	19,215	16,970	+13.2
Total, all advertising	$42,990	$38,060	+13.0%

Prepared by Robert J. Coen, VP, McCann-Erickson.
Reprinted with permission from the September 4, 1978 issue of *Advertising Age*, © Crain Communications, Inc., 1978.

EXAMPLES OF WEEKLY SPOT TV SCHEDULES IN THE TOP 100 TV MARKETS

30-Second Announcements	Cost	Gross Audience (000)				Cost per Thousand			
		Homes	Adults	Men	Women	Homes	Adults	Men	Women
10 Daytime M–F......	$ 70,840	33,850	37,510	10,090	27,420	$2.09	$1.89	$7.02	$2.58
5 Early evening.....	85,815	37,110	46,765	19,885	26,880	2.31	1.84	4.32	3.19
5 Nighttime.........	282,745	53,640	78,860	33,365	42,195	5.29	3.61	8.47	6.70
5 Late evening......	62,660	19,455	27,075	12,395	14,680	3.22	2.31	5.06	4.27
5 Weekend day.....	81,900	23,255	30,355	16,355	14,000	3.52	2.70	5.01	5.85

Source: TV Bureau of Advertising.

TOP 100 NATIONAL ADVERTISERS*

Rank	Company	Total	Magazines	Supplements	Network tv	Spot tv	Network radio	Outdoor
1.	Procter & Gamble Co.	$357,056.7	$16,273.6	$1,599.7	$193,423.3	$145,760.1	$324.2	$33.5
2.	General Foods Corp.	219,341.4	20,549.0	3,165.3	128,955.2	66,314.2		
3.	Bristol-Myers Co.	146,964.2	25,738.2	785.9	102,673.4	17,766.7	1,643.7	4,934.7
4.	General Motors Corp.	145,097.8	37,004.6	2,334.5	72,036.8	27,143.5	1,456.6	9.6
5.	American Home Products Corp.	139,106.7	6,429.6	263.3	97,467.6	33,489.6	89.9	2,018.8
6.	General Mills Inc.	110,443.9	10,972.9	1,084.7	58,324.7	39,962.1	2,069.3	
7.	Ford Motor Co.	103,647.5	21,298.0	18.7	50,059.9	28,182.8		
8.	Lever Bros. Co.	102,747.5	4,698.0	574.3	60,320.6	37,153.7		
9.	R. J. Reynolds Industries Inc.	102,318.9	41,909.6	19,367.1	5,843.0	6,366.5		28,832.7
10.	Sears, Roebuck & Co.	101,959.0	18,348.7	38.0	57,090.0	23,229.6	3,179.6	73.1
11.	Philip Morris Inc.	99,091.5	38,881.6	11,149.5	24,436.6	6,322.8	1,202.1	18,301.0
12.	Colgate-Palmolive Co.	89,664.5	8,171.8	949.8	41,680.3	37,642.8	5,102.5	17.7
13.	Warner-Lambert Co.	86,555.2	1,341.9	58.4	53,791.6	26,008.0	277.7	252.8
14.	McDonald's Corp.	81,831.4	228.2	178.9	32,329.9	47,529.5		1,287.2
15.	Ralston Purina Co.	79,095.0	6,353.6	1,237.3	54,668.5	16,210.3		625.3
16.	Heublein Inc.	78,116.4	17,196.0	222.3	25,859.8	26,482.7	222.2	8,355.6
17.	Chrysler Corp.	76,979.3	16,696.8		26,668.0	32,757.4	42.4	634.9
18.	Nabisco Inc.	75,169.8	4,134.5	945.3	55,528.3	14,463.1		56.2
19.	Gillette Co.	70,491.9	4,049.5	156.5	51,796.6	14,489.3		
20.	Sterling Drug Inc.	64,146.9	3,922.1	249.0	45,183.0	12,472.5	2,269.5	50.8
21.	PepsiCo Inc.	64,013.6	1,137.1	59.5	27,462.0	34,869.7		485.3
22.	American Telephone & Telegraph Co.	58,332.9	11,828.0	6.6	22,243.9	23,900.7	1,370.3	353.7
23.	Kraft Inc.	57,571.2	9,646.0	545.2	17,870.7	27,250.3	59.8	888.7
24.	B.A.T. Industries Ltd.	55,068.7	26,995.9	7,408.8	2,056.2	6,119.8	202.0	12,428.2
25.	Coca-Cola Co.	51,733.9	2,076.2	715.8	17,745.5	29,073.0	211.9	1,921.4
26.	Kellogg Co.	51,277.6	2,783.3	833.1	32,343.2	15,104.9		1.2
27.	Nestle Co.	50,853.8	2,291.8	1,207.0	32,091.2	15,241.5		22.3
28.	Pillsbury Co.	49,919.1	4,016.8	387.3	36,471.2	8,833.8	56.1	153.9
29.	American Brands Inc.	48,636.7	30,297.7	375.5	7,523.7	3,466.7	30.0	6,943.1
30.	Norton Simon Inc.	46,941.7	12,658.1	569.9	17,907.9	13,981.6	18.0	1,806.2
31.	Schering-Plough Corp.	44,933.2	6,046.2	101.5	22,292.7	12,832.9	2,323.4	1,336.5
32.	Johnson & Johnson	42,782.0	5,214.9	184.6	34,189.4	3,192.3		0.8
33.	Int'l Telephone & Telegraph Corp.	42,025.0	5,100.7	125.7	12,832.5	22,545.8	977.1	443.2
34.	Campbell Soup Co.	41,765.2	3,806.4	653.9	19,483.4	17,299.1	472.8	49.6
35.	Mobil Corp.	39,216.3	2,577.8	2,824.9	7,524.5	26,212.6		76.5
36.	Wm. Wrigley Jr. Co.	38,403.9	1,575.6		1,170.4	33,897.4	1,760.5	
37.	S. C. Johnson & Son Inc.	38,159.5	2,795.3	621.5	27,597.1	6,790.4	88.0	267.2
38.	Borden Inc.	37,581.2	4,294.0	319.3	15,765.8	16,045.7	805.7	350.7
39.	Liggett Group Inc.	37,484.6	15,001.0	1,231.4	9,496.9	5,848.5		5,906.8
40.	Esmark Inc.	37,163.2	2,023.3	536.3	25,691.8	8,849.1		62.7
41.	CBS Inc.	36,896.1	19,458.8	5,583.6	84.8	11,351.7	200.1	217.1
42.	Miles Labs Inc.	36,628.8	582.0	138.8	27,114.5	8,220.2	573.3	
43.	General Electric Co.	36,475.9	7,624.7	395.8	16,215.0	11,875.4	318.5	46.5
44.	Mars Inc.	36,474.2	1,693.2	277.1	7,317.6	27,090.8		95.5
45.	RCA Corp.	36,184.1	15,913.1	558.4	10,207.0	9,136.8	124.3	244.5
46.	Richardson-Merrell Inc.	36,141.1	2,514.8	101.7	24,583.4	8,292.8	648.4	
47.	Eastman Kodak Co.	35,631.4	11,824.6	180.5	20,445.6	2,538.3	406.3	236.1
48.	Volkswagenwerk A. G.	34,957.5	10,405.0	630.1	15,441.5	8,454.5		26.4
49.	Loews Corp.	34,626.0	20,413.0	4,812.1		236.4		9,164.5
50.	Clorox Co.	33,847.2	4,284.0	11.1	23,883.1	5,664.5		4.5

* Expenditures in thousands of dollars.

#	Company							
51	CPC International Inc.	33,837.5	3,873.6	813.5	12,866.3	16,072.8		211.3
52	Jos. Schlitz Brewing Co.	33,756.4	348.6	19.0	28,551.0	4,697.6		140.2
53	General Motors Corp. Local Dealers	33,506.6	42.4	87.1	—	30,955.6	—	2,421.5
54	U. S. Government	33,218.6	14,764.0	1,959.3	5,955.2	3,543.0	157.5	6,839.6
55	Chesebrough-Pond's Inc.	31,596.4	4,369.7	443.6	20,209.3	6,114.9	241.5	217.4
56	Morton-Norwich Products Inc.	31,050.8	2,658.2	165.2	22,590.2	5,388.7	238.3	10.2
57	Seagram Co. Ltd.	30,029.6	18,435.6	1,173.6	—	132.0	—	10,349.4
58	Carnation Co.	30,084.4	506.8	583.0	19,507.5	9,485.9	—	1.2
59	Revlon Inc.	29,817.3	7,534.1	146.9	10,791.9	10,919.1	425.3	
60	Quaker Oats Co.	29,548.8	4,165.5	1,043.9	13,184.5	11,153.0		1.9
61	American Motors Corp.	29,531.3	3,803.4		21,359.1	4,356.8		12.0
62	American Cyanamid Co.	29,359.9	5,872.9	209.0	17,179.8	6,078.0		20.2
63	Mattel Inc.	29,173.7	1,613.5		7,172.6	20,322.6		65.0
64	Anheuser-Busch Inc.	28,470.3	2,518.0	28.2	14,617.3	8,833.4		490.7
65	Toyota Motor Co. Ltd.	28,210.3	4,641.7	114.2	9,689.0	12,068.8	1,982.7	1,696.6
66	Block Drug Co. Inc.	28,157.2	3,446.1		17,940.0	6,771.1		
67	Hanes Corp.	27,151.5	4,352.8	592.4	16,314.1	5,355.4	536.8	10.4
68	Greyhound Corp.	26,290.1	3,734.7	66.3	14,684.8	5,403.2	2,390.7	233.3
69	Nissan Motor Co. Ltd.	25,649.6	4,443.7	111.7	14,682.3	5,655.4	523.2	28.1
70	H. J. Heinz Co.	25,340.7	573.2	512.9	13,042.6	11,183.9		
71	Polaroid Corp.	24,730.1	7,333.0	158.9	16,408.4	630.4	197.0	2.4
72	Noxell Corp.	23,924.6	3,713.4		14,816.8	5,394.4		
73	Standard Brands Inc.	23,826.4	3,071.1	78.6	8,828.5	9,210.8	1,770.2	867.2
74	North American Philips Corp.	23,284.8	1,528.4	664.3	10,969.7	10,113.8	563.1	8.6
75	J. C. Penney Co. Inc.	22,420.3	706.0		10,746.5	10,170.4	843.0	234.3
76	Time Inc.	22,355.0	14,125.7	362.5		7,023.8		
77	Exxon Corp.	21,643.7	3,765.3		13,401.6	4,209.4		267.4
78	Union Carbide Corp.	20,902.4	3,106.4	281.2	15,594.6	1,805.1	25.6	89.5
79	Avon Products Inc.	20,818.0	3,355.4	213.5	12,199.4	5,049.7		
80	SmithKline Corp.	20,394.5	1,140.3		13,851.8	2,105.1	3,296.0	1.3
81	Gulf & Western Industries Inc.	20,164.7	3,703.7	363.4	8,995.9	6,923.3	88.6	89.8
82	Federated Department Stores Inc.	19,364.4	887.6	2,732.8		15,678.4		65.6
83	Ford Motor Co. Local Dealers	19,159.0				18,064.7		1,094.3
84	A. H. Robins Co. Inc.	18,894.9	2,445.2	7.1		16,442.6		10.1
85	Pfizer Inc.	18,738.8	4,579.5		13,227.6	794.9	126.7	14.0
86	Beatrice Foods Co.	18,408.1	1,839.5	191.6	2,277.5	13,884.1	201.4	303.0
87	Royal Crown Cola Co.	18,053.5	121.0		5,063.9	12,565.6		6.8
88	Scott Paper Co.	17,909.9	501.7	554.7	7,217.6	9,629.1		1.1
89	Squibb Corp.	17,790.8	954.6	10.3	12,318.5	4,506.3		187.5
90	Goodyear Tire & Rubber Co.	17,765.3	1,332.2		10,893.2	4,242.3	1,110.1	84.9
91	American Express Co.	17,702.4	3,835.4	36.1	8,496.2	5,249.8		307.9
92	Consolidated Foods Corp.	17,528.9	1,469.5		3,349.6	12,342.7	59.2	
93	Panacolor Inc.	17,503.4	11,583.6	4,021.4		1,898.4		
94	Merck & Co. Inc.	16,972.2	806.2	84.6	15,324.8	754.0	94.3	2.6
95	British Leyland Motors Inc.	16,544.4	7,921.0	7.1	7,796.8	725.2		
96	North American Systems Inc.	16,495.9	309.4	139.3	14,819.4	1,227.8		11.0
97	Triangle Publications Inc.	15,958.5	435.3	25.1		15,487.1		
98	Ideal Toy Corp.	15,833.6	31.7		4,663.9	11,138.0		
99	Hiram Walker-Gooderham & Worts	15,782.5	11,071.1			141.3	1,755.9	4,570.1
100	S. S. Kresge Co.	15,648.3	1,689.4		1,224.4	10,974.1		4.5
	Top 100 total	$4,791,912.4	$740,139.5	$93,777.8	$2,286,013.7	$1,486,838.2	$45,153.3	$139,989.9

Source: Leading National Advertisers, Broadcast Advertisers Reports.
Reprinted with permission from the May 16, 1977 issue of Advertising Age, © Crain Communications, Inc., 1977.

TOP 25 ADVERTISING AGENCIES*

1977 World U.S. Income Rank	U.S. Income Rank	Agency	World Gross Income 1977	World Gross Income 1976	U.S. Gross Income 1977	U.S. Gross Income 1976	World Billing 1977	World Billing 1976	U.S. Billing 1977	U.S. Billing 1976	Data for U.S. only Capitalized Fees 1977	Capitalized Fees 1976	Total Employes 1977	Total Employes 1976
1	2	J. Walter Thompson Co.	$188.8	$155.8	$92.8	$76.9	$1,258.9	$1,038.9	$619.0	$512.5	$83.1	$69.2	2,190	2,090
2	1	Young & Rubicam	169.9	139.8	101.1	85.8	1,133.4	932.8	674.5	572.2	100.0	92.0	2,432	2,145
3	9	McCann-Erickson	162.6	133.6	51.1	44.3	1,083.5	889.9	339.6	294.7	64.0	50.0	1,078	1,071
4	5	Ogilvy & Mather International	127.7	106.0	62.9	51.8	872.2	713.7	450.5	364.9		—	1,452	1,250
5	3	Leo Burnett Co.	117.3	106.3	84.3	74.3	795.1	721.6	575.0	508.0	22.8	18.8	1,545	1,384
6	22	SSC&B Inc.	113.4	96.0	25.2	22.8	724.0	587.0	163.0	151.0	2.0	2.0	438	430
7	4	BBDO International	108.6	96.4	66.9	63.3	734.3	651.3	456.5	430.9	36.9	27.7	1,277	1,342
8	10	Ted Bates & Co.	101.0	93.5	45.4	44.4	751.2	700.2	373.3	349.6	29.7	24.9	1,018	996
9	6	Foote, Cone & Belding Communications	85.4	68.2	59.0	46.8	569.8	454.0	393.2	312.1	53.0	37.0	1,507	1,280
10	12	D'Arcy-MacManus & Masius	84.7	72.0	43.6	38.4	565.0	481.1	290.5	257.1	1.0	2.6	1,150	1,100
11	7	Grey Advertising	78.7	70.9	55.5	51.0	525.0	472.5	370.0	340.0	27.0	20.0	1,375	1,250
12	8	Doyle Dane Bernbach	73.4	65.2	52.3	46.2	491.0	430.3	350.0	308.3	27.3	16.0	—	1,150
13	11	Benton & Bowles	68.7	59.4	44.4	40.3	470.4	414.2	304.7	287.0	51.4	36.0	1,161	959
14	26	Compton Advertising	66.4	59.0	19.9	18.7	442.5	393.5	135.0	124.5	3.2	4.9	500	398
15	16	Campbell-Ewald Co.	59.5	43.0	33.5	25.1	396.9	287.1	224.0	167.7	41.0	25.0	807	656
16	21	Kenyon & Eckhardt	52.3	46.6	25.3	21.9	348.0	288.4	168.6	124.1	11.5	4.6	505	511
17	13	Dancer-Fitzgerald-Sample	43.0	40.0	40.0	38.0	330.0	303.5	305.0	253.5	105.0	100.0	909	694
18	28	Norman, Craig & Kummel	42.5	37.7	13.9	13.4	283.3	251.3	92.6	89.7	23.5	21.3	259	278
19	18	Needham, Harper & Steers	39.6	34.7	32.0	27.0	263.7	231.7	213.0	180.0	21.0	26.0	792	684
19	14	Wells, Rich, Greene	39.6	31.0	38.5	30.4	264.2	206.6	256.4	202.4	42.6	27.5	445	364
21	15	N W Ayer ABH International	36.8	31.4	36.8	31.4	256.1	220.5	245.7	209.3	50.7	43.3	998	929
22	19	Marsteller Inc.	36.0	28.8	27.1	21.9	240.2	192.2	180.6	136.3	40.0	30.0	766	631
23	17	William Esty Co.	33.0	26.4	33.0	26.4	220.0	176.0	220.0	176.0	—		590	460
24	23	Ketchum, MacLeod & Grove	29.9	26.6	23.0	21.3	202.4	186.1	153.6	142.3	27.8		644	681
25	20	Bozell & Jacobs International	27.3	22.6	27.0	22.4	182.0	150.1	180.5	148.8	43.0	28.3	830	700

* Figures shown in this table (in millions of dollars) represent the best information available to *Advertising Age* and are constructed either from answers to questionnaires (sometimes revised on the basis of other information) or on the best data available.
Reprinted with permission from the March 13, 1978 issue of *Advertising Age*, © Crain Communications, Inc., 1978.

TOP U.S. NEWSPAPERS: CIRCULATION

		Circulation	
		Weekday	Sunday
1.	New York News	1,911,565	2,752,739
2.	Los Angeles Times	1,018,563	1,300,260
3.	Chicago Sun-Times	574,587	694,227
4.	Chicago News	351,061	—
5.	New York Times	866,904	1,479,862
6.	Chicago Tribune	757,117	1,555,572
7.	Philadelphia Inquirer	411,938	861,600
8.	Philadelphia News	231,886	—
9.	Detroit News	643,792	826,304
10.	Detroit Free Press	620,153	716,325
11.	San Francisco Chronicle	470,003⎱	664,251
12.	San Francisco Examiner	155,108⎰	
13.	Kansas City Star	306,403	406,481
14.	Kansas City Times	332,045	—
15.	Philadelphia Bulletin	556,371	655,532
16.	New York Post	503,369	—
17.	Washington Post (D.C.)	555,030	766,241
18.	Milwaukee Journal	342,253	532,661
19.	Milwaukee Sentinel	164,617	—
20.	Boston Globe	459,568	630,061
21.	Miami Herald	435,424	534,853
22.	Miami News	77,663	—
23.	Minneapolis Tribune	227,336	610,408
24.	Minneapolis Star	246,233	—
25.	Pittsburgh Press	266,537	681,536
26.	Pittsburgh Post Gazette	190,370	—
27.	Newsday (L.I., N.Y.)	468,407	452,333
28.	Atlanta Journal	222,814⎱	535,587
29.	Atlanta Constitution	211,405⎰	
30.	Los Angeles Herald-Examiner...	338,372	336,462
31.	Cleveland Plain Dealer	381,082	457,963
32.	Louisville Courier Journal	210,528⎱	351,760
33.	Louisville Times	164,855⎰	
34.	Indianapolis Star	219,632*	355,216*
35.	Indianapolis News	155,492*	—
36.	Newark Star-Ledger	408,000*	588,722*

* Average for 3 months.

Source: Audit Bureau of Circulation's FAS-FAX Report, March 31, 1977 and May 27, 1977.

TOP U.S. MAGAZINES: CIRCULATION

	Circulation	
	1976*	1975†
TV Guide...	20,226,757	19,168,096
Reader's Digest..	17,887,299	18,142,923
National Geographic Magazine.........................	9,350,123	9,039,374
Women's Day..	8,582,538	8,167,108
Family Circle..	8,576,213	8,364,442
Better Homes and Gardens.............................	8,094,553	8,126,644
McCall's	6,524,126	6,801,287
Ladies' Home Journal..................................	6,088,117	7,067,039
Playboy	5,541,004	5,701,007
Good Housekeeping....................................	5,412,727	5,250,597
National Enquirer......................................	4,704,144	4,155,762
Penthouse	4,557,523	4,209,984
Redbook	4,527,049	4,562,760
Time	4,262,638	4,325,270
Newsweek	2,969,159	2,928,484
Senior Scholastic......................................	2,877,621	2,906,531
American Legion.......................................	2,670,967	2,660,002
American Home..	2,491,025	2,524,362
Cosmopolitan	2,465,145	2,095,201
Sports Illustrated......................................	2,274,246	2,267,547
U.S. News & World Report..............................	2,062,035	2,036,140
People	2,036,388	1,619,822
Field and Stream.......................................	1,998,936	1,992,994
Hustler	1,964,602	826,345
Glamour	1,946,078	1,740,026
Popular Science..	1,833,279	1,776,031
V.F.W. Magazine..	1,783,347	1,761,477
Outdoor Life...	1,776,309	1,797,642
Workbasket	1,772,618	1,778,379
Boys' Life..	1,684,821	1,877,572
Popular Mechanics.....................................	1,670,051	1,736,274
Today's Education......................................	1,647,976	1,647,976
Elks Magazine..	1,611,097	1,600,333
True Story...	1,607,272	1,702,146
Mechanics Illustrated..................................	1,577,852	1,547,892
Seventeen	1,519,136	1,520,135
Parents' Magazine......................................	1,508,153	1,509,215
Sport	1,388,088	1,395,086
Sunset	1,348,691	1,347,303
Southern Living..	1,338,779	1,225,747
Smithsonian	1,333,691	972,265
Ebony	1,290,060	1,285,525
Grit	1,231,162	1,202,346
Midnight	1,183,137	1,044,837
House & Garden..	1,134,926	1,070,136
Oui	1,115,882	1,279,625
Esquire	1,101,722	1,208,390
Psychology Today......................................	1,100,224	1,061,700
Nation's Business......................................	1,093,148	989,352
'Teen	1,019,587	821,114
Junior Scholastic......................................	1,012,087	1,076,105
Sports Afield/with Rod and Gun........................	1,000,767	1,123,686
Scouting	1,000,438	1,157,031
Photoplay	941,946	993,434
Family Health, incorporating Today's Health............	919,862	805,520

TOP U.S. MAGAZINES (continued)

	Circulation	
	1976*	1975†
Mademoiselle	903,220	888,597
Playgirl	900,927	1,042,451
Co-ed	889,406	899,439
Golf Digest	851,184	750,241
Hot Rod/with Rod and Custom	850,245	769,257
Apartment Life	772,752	589,762
Popular Photography	765,537	716,329
Family Handyman, incorporating Home Garden	n.a.‡	632,680
Business Week	762,352	761,737
Signature	751,487	751,546
Weight Watchers Magazine	741,960	614,520
TV Mirror	735,324	681,608
National Lampoon	731,690	839,560
Car & Driver	725,402	731,860
Lion Magazine, The	702,110	687,079
Motor Trend/combined with Car Life, Sports, Car Graphic, and Wheels Afield	701,142	709,886
Decorating & Craft Ideas	678,157	676,765
Scientific American	665,395	637,548
Simplicity Home Catalog	663,193	590,589
Forbes	646,490	629,084
Flower & Garden Magazine	· 636,094	499,877
Fortune	618,109	614,224
Gourmet	615,523	556,338
American Girl	609,818	618,828
Golf, incorporating Golfing	604,401	573,789
Jet	587,278	615,128
Argosy	583,256	625,530
Lutheran, The	556,022	546,344
House Beautiful	553,850	839,467
Harper's Bazaar	538,436	487,690
Modern Photography	534,447	515,666
Catholic Digest	526,452	532,168
Essence	500,477	450,402
Modern Romances	498,810	626,846
Saturday Review	497,875	481,487
New Yorker	492,048	490,876
Rolling Stone	488,897	451,124
Modern Screen	486,305	691,137
Vogue, incorporating Vanity Fair	461,418	704,147
Saturday Evening Post	460,454	483,240
Skiing Magazine	458,925	467,780
Rotarian	451,443	462,324
National Observer	434,516	463,924
Capper's Weekly	422,168	437,360
Viva	354,101	508,088

* Figures in this column are based on the total average paid circulation for the six months ending December 31, 1976.

† Figures in this column are based on the total average paid circulation for the six months ending December 31, 1975.

‡ Not available at press time.

Source: Audit Bureau of Circulation's FAS-FAX Report, December 31, 1976 and March 15, 1977.

RETAIL SALES IN 100 TOP MARKETS*

Population rank	SMSA	Group rank for total retail sales	% U.S. sales	% change 1976 vs. 1972	Food	Eating and drinking	Drug, proprietary stores	Gasoline service stations	General merchandise	Apparel, accessory stores	Furniture, home furnishings	Auto dealers	Bldg. matl., hardware, mobile homes
1	New York, N.Y.	1	3.69	20.3	$6,023,333	$2,949,704	$698,198	$1,045,338	$3,421,649	$2,119,606	$1,341,130	$2,441,144	$541,092
2	Los Angeles-Long Beach, Cal.	3	3.59	39.5	5,177,679	2,513,049	878,310	1,628,607	3,366,881	1,246,652	1,122,251	4,596,587	707,148
3	Chicago, Ill.	2	3.68	42.3	4,809,011	2,326,718	945,110	1,531,655	3,558,058	1,519,054	1,145,547	4,105,985	817,524
4	Philadelphia, Pa.	4	2.21	39.6	3,392,296	1,301,241	386,510	907,536	2,000,192	849,826	707,374	2,466,783	502,358
5	Detroit, Mich.	5	2.13	35.9	3,133,811	1,191,472	571,292	956,225	2,297,219	776,310	657,854	2,956,924	586,931
6	Boston-Lowell-Brockton-Lawrence, Mass.	6	1.86	35.3	2,754,744	1,206,663	320,400	756,073	1,675,154	686,916	609,375	1,908,215	471,034
7	San Francisco-Oakland, Cal.	7	1.67	43.9	2,567,886	1,211,573	439,382	731,458	1,593,332	629,618	520,624	1,896,611	324,829
8	Washington, D.C.	8	1.60	39.5	2,123,693	963,037	505,463	776,085	1,601,700	568,174	535,124	1,936,313	301,246
9	Nassau-Suffolk, N.Y.	10	1.38	33.6	2,230,812	735,745	202,107	601,992	1,538,537	491,744	447,551	1,331,645	296,081
10	Dallas-Fort Worth, Tex.	11	1.33	45.7	1,816,077	744,517	287,143	667,880	1,268,174	407,302	385,149	1,984,579	332,037
11	Houston, Tex.	9	1.46	83.4	2,118,721	752,213	252,080	663,671	1,605,949	440,058	431,304	2,151,231	397,904
12	St. Louis, Mo.	12	1.25	60.7	1,849,511	704,701	254,563	676,019	1,416,847	324,958	374,330	1,612,104	342,032
13	Pittsburgh, Pa.	13	1.07	45.2	1,611,594	556,551	228,494	515,623	1,280,049	340,006	318,681	1,297,711	253,764
14	Baltimore, Md.	18	0.94	33.5	1,435,679	593,433	225,374	455,431	973,391	291,638	278,616	1,059,477	158,115
15	Newark, N.J.	19	0.91	31.7	1,477,643	539,127	161,906	397,084	717,641	374,731	341,769	1,015,661	206,342
16	Minneapolis-St. Paul, Minn.	15	0.98	40.3	1,224,166	571,815	169,364	510,915	1,195,189	262,154	295,469	1,168,887	358,046
17	Cleveland, O.	14	0.98	46.0	1,516,228	593,598	205,210	479,980	1,174,724	285,122	282,858	1,190,982	184,964
18	Atlanta, Ga.	16	0.94	39.9	1,102,862	521,658	173,411	513,102	1,068,498	258,969	294,202	1,313,833	354,608
19	Anaheim-Santa Ana-Garden Grove, Cal.	17	0.94	59.5	1,300,595	663,366	199,021	450,469	961,964	249,189	294,046	1,233,784	310,949
20	San Diego, Cal.	22	0.77	56.3	1,040,054	491,816	175,622	352,781	801,356	201,305	256,918	1,045,459	291,164
21	Denver-Boulder, Colo.	23	0.75	42.3	980,921	442,714	172,246	312,819	757,955	206,720	253,919	1,046,709	330,121
22	Miami, Fla.	21	0.80	40.6	1,039,913	610,994	184,047	314,723	804,953	322,018	269,753	1,113,622	160,604
23	Seattle-Everett, Wash.	20	0.82	65.3	1,282,601	534,545	192,661	420,443	769,192	247,609	206,086	1,013,319	195,143
24	Tampa-St. Petersburg, Fla.	26	0.66	43.7	914,197	452,204	148,443	279,817	686,099	149,353	228,447	899,030	251,571
25	Milwaukee, Wis.	25	0.67	44.0	939,652	425,946	122,441	291,432	795,170	196,926	224,210	798,281	154,708
26	Cincinnati, O.	27	0.64	44.0	928,613	422,197	139,446	362,073	797,086	146,125	202,445	754,811	138,041
27	Buffalo, N.Y.	34	0.54	30.4	858,377	349,302	125,073	216,866	635,557	207,109	160,744	612,534	120,481
28	Kansas City, Mo.	30	0.61	29.2	818,546	331,683	124,332	342,239	645,326	190,402	157,520	848,407	167,394
29	Riverside-San Bernardino-Ontario, Cal.	31	0.60	52.8	936,860	376,338	120,250	361,652	159,919	171,694	171,694	763,438	235,641
30	Phoenix, Ariz.	29	0.62	48.5	891,936	356,838	154,333	261,389	612,995	139,758	214,845	844,714	256,658
31	San Jose, Cal.	28	0.63	53.2	959,446	343,252	138,974	296,582	662,223	231,062	222,924	797,824	169,312
32	Indianapolis, Ind.	24	0.72	76.8	921,922	422,621	166,123	415,019	770,337	160,985	198,840	985,010	213,810
33	Portland, Ore.	32	0.56	45.3	927,612	344,996	78,472	254,933	462,013	141,858	167,910	762,563	174,594
34	New Orleans, La.	36	0.50	42.2	884,389	317,584	117,564	216,426	491,281	220,464	146,091	561,607	103,402
35	Columbus, O.	35	0.54	41.7	730,573	344,738	98,197	263,641	675,931	141,005	168,362	705,060	150,356
36	Hartford, Conn.	37	0.49	33.9	716,063	268,873	112,579	252,093	453,591	168,938	149,508	543,626	124,108
37	San Antonio, Tex.	45	0.39	41.6	544,621	238,106	57,620	192,641	465,869	123,515	123,792	527,265	126,129
38	Rochester, N.Y.	40	0.45	34.5	717,938	246,836	96,606	194,049	432,505	124,235	136,740	604,483	118,195
39	Sacramento, Cal.	38	0.47	54.6	716,381	272,792	109,332	239,718	453,471	131,954	156,465	652,972	147,424
40	Louisville, Ky.	44	0.40	31.9	549,834	209,896	88,358	205,707	475,717	106,584	105,958	536,913	118,508
41	Fort Lauderdale-Hollywood, Fla.	33	0.55	67.9	784,545	432,866	122,412	213,574	560,196	179,882	220,967	655,915	146,780
42	Memphis, Tenn.	41	0.42	41.5	553,805	176,803	73,291	209,450	496,717	141,813	125,481	640,841	103,011
43	Providence-Warwick-Pawtucket, R.I.	47	0.39	37.9	570,104	226,773	82,134	170,107	382,317	139,048	117,661	409,730	120,882
44	Dayton, O.	52	0.35	26.8	532,722	218,753	54,010	184,608	441,409	84,136	114,831	457,506	79,158
45	Bridgeport-Stamford-Norwalk-Danbury, Conn.	39	0.45	47.4	704,236	227,116	82,176	208,784	379,252	172,521	145,337	462,504	151,024
46	Birmingham, Ala.	42	0.41	58.9	606,024	172,157	77,276	194,976	385,684	169,494	128,274	617,223	126,935
47	Albany-Schenectady-Troy, N.Y.	53	0.34	27.2	546,725	197,866	60,290	140,021	329,923	109,999	95,436	381,139	86,129
48	Salt Lake City-Ogden, Utah	48	0.38	51.4	512,296	209,728	148,995	172,193	324,744	94,964	142,579	562,943	154,195
49	Norfolk-Virginia Beach-Portsmouth, Va.	59	0.31	41.6	438,436	154,067	75,653	138,109	367,258	123,722	109,366	433,070	78,641
50	Toledo, O.	49	0.37	39.6	540,842	243,568	71,275	190,087	428,209	84,843	103,951	486,280	107,784

#	Market												
51	Greensboro-High Point-Winston-Salem, N.C.	51	0.36	40.8	489,505	163,639	72,974	181,099	276,865	516,036	119,762	131,923	145,890
52	Oklahoma City, Okla.	43	0.41	49.1	549,231	212,626	61,158	181,236	407,552	651,309	121,477	159,323	150,085
53	New Haven-West Haven, Conn.	50	0.36	33.7	574,581	194,428	67,106	172,889	343,758	363,583	119,785	148,894	97,910
54	Nashville-Davidson, Tenn.	46	0.39	51.8	549,934	187,328	78,199	218,197	386,873	587,719	108,217	130,852	132,277
55	Honolulu, Hawaii	56	0.32	40.6	446,958	325,553	99,388	123,008	398,932	292,372	84,988	112,154	34,005
56	Jacksonville, Fla.	55	0.32	35.0	417,169	179,922	90,544	188,493	255,901	522,552	86,262	87,000	106,295
57	Akron, O.	54	0.33	49.3	501,700	202,038	60,047	188,111	393,689	433,712	90,539	72,955	94,692
58	Worcester, Mass.	61	0.30	46.6	493,471	178,393	52,773	129,892	292,271	321,771	85,324	98,687	90,224
59	Gary-Hammond-East Chicago, Ind.	60	0.31	49.8	514,803	165,840	76,823	181,010	291,514	394,567	94,602	77,766	101,514
60	Syracuse, N.Y.	71	0.27	30.5	448,264	168,842	73,681	124,680	254,862	325,594	75,578	83,422	66,022
61	Northeast Pennsylvania	65	0.29	36.5	444,524	155,998	57,085	150,600	306,024	286,049	91,257	91,028	90,826
62	Allentown-Bethlehem-Easton, Pa.	70	0.27	32.6	417,308	144,100	43,358	131,551	310,109	301,185	83,575	68,687	76,641
63	Tulsa, Okla.	62	0.30	53.6	444,282	142,666	55,558	155,896	235,267	477,406	118,580	118,580	107,025
64	Jersey City, N.J.	105	0.17	11.7	278,188	117,757	35,772	73,223	128,954	136,427	61,271	117,543	26,268
65	Orlando, Fla.	57	0.32	53.6	400,772	187,734	64,263	180,459	303,235	506,358	95,716	63,525	112,995
66	New Brunswick-Sayreville-Perth Amboy, N.J.	69	0.27	34.7	471,216	146,890	49,885	134,928	373,362	209,036	66,960	103,584	75,789
67	Richmond, Va.	63	0.29	41.2	422,546	136,857	74,177	173,726	307,645	391,314	85,244	92,877	80,641
68	Springfield-Holyoke-Chicopee, Mass.	75	0.24	26.6	323,237	147,023	47,349	112,571	221,304	248,208	73,673	74,277	84,875
69	Charlotte-Gastonia, N.C.	58	0.31	43.2	409,948	129,265	65,194	138,209	313,408	496,533	92,219	100,663	98,096
70	Omaha, Neb.	78	0.23	23.1	300,910	156,583	59,233	128,489	282,828	277,636	98,151	70,488	57,452
71	Grand Rapids, Mich.	66	0.28	39.1	498,607	141,220	49,654	145,674	194,580	406,066	102,843	94,098	99,902
72	Youngstown-Warren, O.	64	0.29	67.5	408,595	159,774	54,388	143,341	396,470	377,176	94,378	80,309	72,728
73	Greenville-Spartanburg, S.C.	79	0.23	43.2	353,269	105,227	50,784	127,480	195,394	298,832	97,938	71,386	103,940
74	Wilmington, Del.	72	0.26	37.3	389,061	134,058	56,233	139,883	273,426	284,350	92,419	73,290	61,674
75	Flint, Mich.	68	0.28	50.2	423,639	137,902	67,353	143,269	288,584	405,351	83,592	83,813	108,038
76	Asbury Park-Long Branch, N.J.	73	0.08	49.3	118,933	35,830	14,947	43,690	86,180	114,857	22,123	19,522	39,082
77	New Bedford-Fall River, Mass.	93	0.20	37.6	316,375	113,768	37,604	86,668	167,137	208,584	68,479	68,486	63,800
78	Tucson, Ariz.	81	0.23	51.4	320,616	126,247	44,485	95,613	252,352	304,553	70,152	49,224	120,553
79	West Palm Beach-Boca Raton, Fla.	67	0.28	57.3	399,537	158,849	63,947	111,543	261,759	378,358	121,311	101,594	121,953
80	Paterson-Clifton-Passaic, N.J.	87	0.21	20.7	317,181	110,563	31,873	76,344	229,836	182,279	71,524	111,834	45,473
81	Raleigh-Durham, N.C.	77	0.23	46.5	335,086	104,345	51,792	114,259	227,227	323,843	76,352	78,234	95,631
82	Fresno, Cal.	74	0.24	60.8	343,560	135,594	75,027	128,647	215,828	293,195	86,443	69,279	88,405
83	Oxnard-Simi Valley-Ventura, Cal.	88	0.21	56.6	317,511	107,197	47,670	110,504	190,507	282,940	54,756	47,802	78,052
84	Lansing-East Lansing, Mich.	80	0.23	50.1	303,200	128,258	32,036	111,495	252,395	353,471	69,534	61,254	75,625
85	El Paso, Tex.	98	0.18	53.1	228,825	91,132	31,613	83,709	234,453	237,401	72,760	73,379	55,972
86	Knoxville, Tenn.	83	0.22	52.6	311,718	102,299	45,332	120,778	237,068	291,456	63,372	50,312	97,394
87	Harrisburg, Pa.	84	0.22	39.8	306,271	109,987	43,516	130,220	213,079	282,268	66,167	59,244	68,482
88	Tacoma, Wash.	104	0.17	41.4	235,284	112,916	35,096	94,798	168,113	228,026	54,900	40,105	45,693
89	Baton Rouge, La.	90	0.20	56.4	331,111	85,241	42,030	93,352	232,997	302,789	53,117	52,585	62,264
90	Mobile, Ala.	90	0.18	56.6	284,489	87,173	35,433	94,598	179,093	254,918	53,108	51,149	71,519
91	Johnson City-Kingsport-Bristol, Tenn.	102	0.17	56.8	250,569	65,643	32,960	90,628	171,349	247,093	53,702	46,198	117,790
92	Austin, Tex.	92	0.20	52.8	273,482	124,686	30,128	93,522	144,272	268,956	68,205	79,925	87,557
93	Canton, O.	76	0.24	84.6	333,516	137,070	37,617	118,812	257,308	337,615	74,164	83,714	73,033
94	Chattanooga, Tenn.	96	0.19	39.7	291,837	77,606	40,377	103,279	171,779	270,391	49,793	47,524	63,596
95	Albuquerque, N.M.	95	0.19	40.8	224,993	101,888	46,394	95,830	196,972	277,156	66,680	51,550	74,695
96	Wichita, Kan.	94	0.19	43.4	251,812	102,548	32,511	108,820	180,819	293,729	52,374	69,712	58,935
97	Fort Wayne, Ind.	82	0.22	69.6	296,431	141,119	48,641	113,191	242,674	311,142	83,341	68,874	68,187
98	Charleston, S.C.	109	0.16	51.5	248,138	62,193	26,354	80,397	172,436	212,403	46,782	46,767	73,510
99	Davenport-Rock Island-Moline, Ia., Ill.	97	0.19	48.1	255,116	128,326	43,692	128,729	179,096	245,042	53,190	42,781	59,789
100	Columbia, S.C.	103	0.17	47.7	220,473	76,748	25,407	92,533	184,713	261,388	50,603	48,709	78,677

* Compiled by Marketing Economics Institute, Inc.
Reprinted with permission from the December 12, 1977 issue of Advertising Age. © Crain Communications Inc., 1977.

RETAIL TRADE: TRENDS AND PROJECTIONS 1972–1978

SALES IN MILLIONS OF CURRENT DOLLARS

SIC Code		1972	1973	1974	1975	1976	1977[1]	Percent change 1976-77	1978[1]	Percent change 1977-78
52–59	Total Retail Trade	448,379	503,317	537,561	584,423	651,884	717,732	10	781,625	10
5311	Department Stores	46,302	52,292	55,855	60,719	68,011	75,452	11	82,667	10
5331	Variety Stores	7,756	8,212	8,715	9,120	8,259	8,878	8	9,499	7
5411	Grocery Stores	88,340	98,392	111,347	122,666	130,000	143,000	9	157,000	10
5611	Men's and Boys' Apparel Stores	5,198	5,609	5,665	6,085	6,300	6,704	6	7,106	6
5621-31	Women's Apparel, Accessory Stores	8,386	9,119	9,563	10,396	11,200	11,568	4	12,262	6
5712	Furniture Stores	9,321	10,439	10,982	10,087	12,113	13,448	11	14,658	9
5722	Household Appliances	4,634	5,124	5,222	5,083	5,620	6,126	9	6,677	9
5812-13	Eating and Drinking Places	33,891	37,925	41,821	47,514	52,290	57,519	10	63,271	10
5913	Drug Stores	14,523	15,474	16,745	18,014	19,704	21,674	10	23,625	9

* Estimated by Bureau of Domestic Commerce.
Source: *U.S. Industrial Outlook, 1978.*

RETAIL TRADE EMPLOYMENT, 1969–1977

IN THOUSANDS

	1969	1970	1971	1972	1973	1974	1975	1976	1977[1]	Percent change 1976–77
Total retail trade.	10,907	11,102	11,333	11,705	12,209	12,751	12,771	13,431	13,888	3
Department stores.	1,483	1,511	1,545	1,594	1,676	1,769	1,658	1,702	1,756	3
Variety stores.	318	312	319	330	339	334	309	309	309	0
Food stores.	1,517	1,561	1,585	1,651	1,709	1,752	1,774	1,877	1,915	2
Men's and boys' apparel stores.	126	131	131	132	133	135	137.4	140	143	2
Women's ready to wear stores.	270	269	276	287	296	289	292.1	298	301	1
Furniture stores.	288	288	289	297	308	328	313	318	323	2
Household appliances.	88	88	89	92	95	101	101	102	105	2
Eating and drinking places.	2,420	2,488	2,569	2,684	2,818	3,145	3,298	3,624	3,860	6
Drug stores.	446	453	456	470	481	467	470	478	483	1

* Estimated by Bureau of Domestic Commerce.
Source: U.S. Industrial Outlook, 1978.

WHOLESALE TRADE: TRENDS AND PROJECTIONS, 1967–78

SALES IN MILLIONS OF CURRENT DOLLARS

	1972	1973	1974	1975	1976	1977¹	Percent change 1976-77	1978¹	Percent change 1977-78¹
50-51	Merchant wholesalers, total....	289,199	364,858	448,127	439,000	482,549	536,590	11	590,000	10
	Durable good, total.........	138,446	167,713	202,341	185,922	210,864	238,610	13	265,000	11
501	Motor vehicles, equipment.....	27,001	30,891	32,928	33,610	38,874	46,288	19	51,275	11
502	Furniture, furnishings.........	6,303	6,891	7,012	6,691	7,698	8,470	10	9,470	12
503	Lumber, other construction materials.................	15,836	18,813	17,821	15,921	20,129	24,576	22	27,474	12
506	Electrical goods..........	19,066	22,475	26,347	24,246	28,861	31,018	7	33,430	8
507	Hardware, plumbing equipment................	13,471	15,696	17,997	17,196	19,340	22,667	17	26,475	17
508	Machinery, equipment supplies.	35,125	41,921	50,666	51,819	56,379	63,229	12	69,950	11
	Nondurable goods, total......	159,753	197,145	245,786	253,078	271,685	297,980	10	325,000	10
511	Paper, paper products.........	8,192	9,546	12,622	11,528	13,147	14,304	9	15,590	9
512	Drugs, chemicals............	11,750	13,081	15,343	15,117	16,824	18,476	10	20,360	10
513	Dry goods, apparel..........	13,008	14,035	15,107	15,466	17,295	18,625	8	20,300	9
514	Groceries and related products.	58,006	68,124	80,513	89,758	93,899	103,019	10	113,550	10
518	Beer, wines, spirits.........	15,506	15,762	18,296	20,161	21,615	22,946	6	24,825	8
	Total employment (000)²......	3,918	4,079	4,259	4,177	4,263	4,365	2	4,450	2

* Estimated by Bureau of Domestic Commerce.
† Includes employees in other distributive lines (approximately 25 percent of total) not defined as merchant wholesalers.
Because some trade lines are excluded, wholesalers by type of business do not add to durable and nondurable goods total.
Source: Bureau of the Census and Bureau of Labor Statistics. *U.S. Industrial Outlook, 1978.*

PROJECTED REGIONAL GROWTH PATTERNS

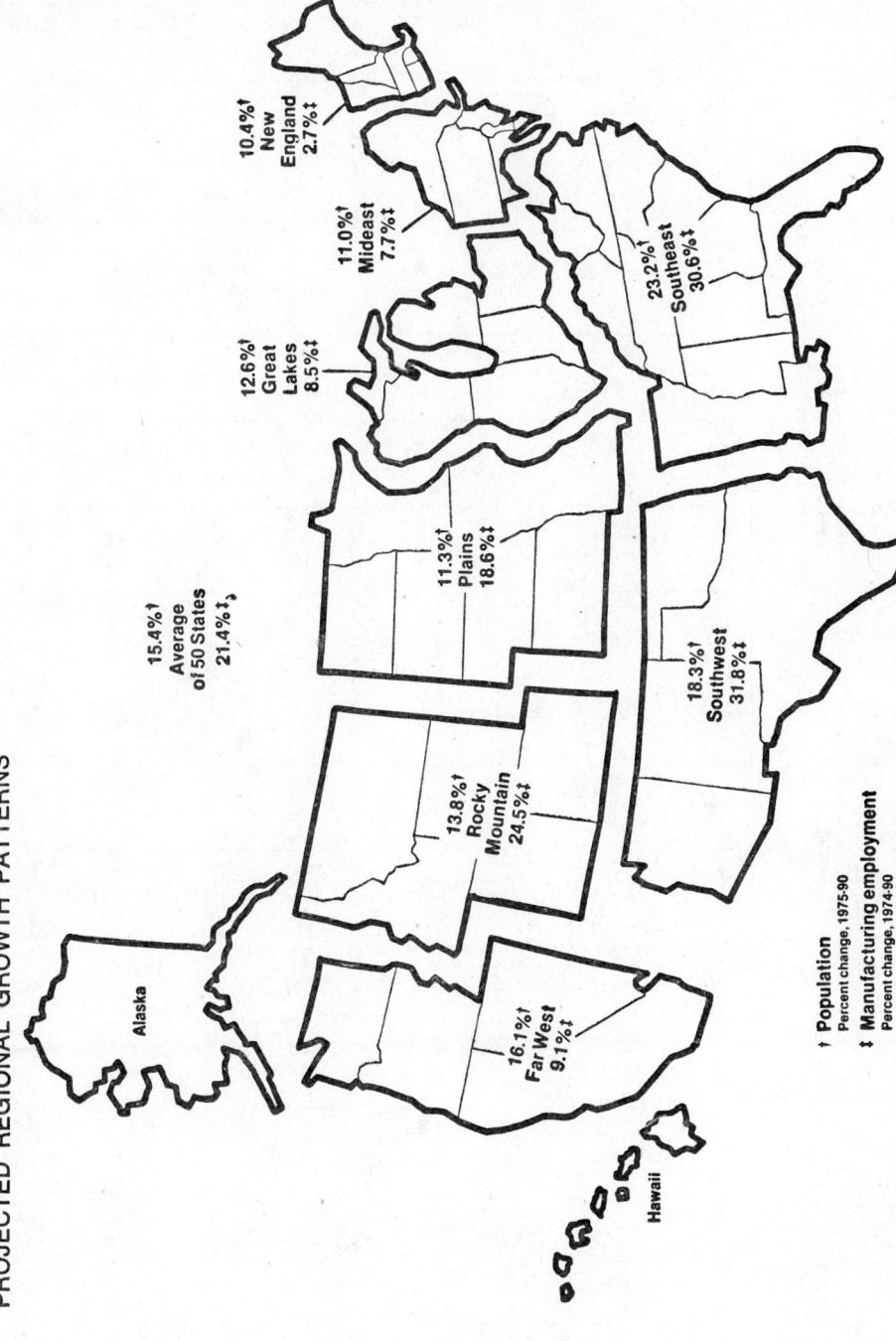

10.4%† New England 2.7%‡

11.0%† Mideast 7.7%‡

23.2%† Southeast 30.6%‡

12.6%† Great Lakes 8.5%‡

11.3%† Plains 18.6%‡

15.4%† Average of 50 States 21.4%‡

18.3%† Southwest 31.8%‡

13.8%† Rocky Mountain 24.5%‡

Alaska

16.1%† Far West 9.1%‡

Hawaii

† **Population**
Percent change, 1975-90

‡ **Manufacturing employment**
Percent change, 1974-90

Reprinted from the May 17, 1976 issue of *Business Week* by special permission © 1976 by McGraw-Hill, Inc., p. 112. Data: Bureau of Economic Analysis, *BW* est.

ESTIMATED AND PROJECTED POPULATION, BY AGE AND SEX, 1950–2000, AND ILLUSTRATIVE ZERO GROWTH PROJECTIONS, 1980–2050

In thousands, except percent. As of July 1. Includes Armed Forces abroad. The base date for the projections is 1974. These projections were prepared using the "cohort-component" method. Series I, II, and III assume a slight improvement in mortality, an annual net immigration of 400,000, and completed cohort fertility rates (i.e., average number of lifetime births per 1,000 women) that move toward the following levels: I–2,700; II–2,100; III–1,700. Series II–X differs from Series II only in that it assumes no net immigration. The Series II and II–X fertility assumption represents "replacement level" fertility (i.e., the level of fertility at which the population would exactly replace itself in the absence of net immigration). See also Historical Statistics, Colonial Times to 1970, series A 23–25 and A 29–37.

YEAR, SERIES, AND SEX	Total, all ages	Under 5 years	5–13 years	14–17 years	18–21 years	22–24 years	25–34 years	35–44 years	45–54 years	55–64 years	65 years and over	16 years and over	18 years and over	21 years and over	Median age (yr.)
TOTAL															
1950	152,271	16,410	22,423	8,444	8,947	7,129	24,036	21,637	17,453	13,396	12,397	109,141	104,994	98,341	30.2
1960	180,671	20,341	32,965	11,219	9,555	6,573	22,919	24,221	20,578	15,625	16,675	121,835	116,146	108,856	29.4
1970	204,879	17,156	36,636	15,910	14,705	9,978	25,293	23,142	23,310	18,664	20,085	142,949	135,177	124,024	27.9
1974	211,909	16,304	34,082	16,878	16,108	10,800	29,770	22,823	23,821	19,507	21,815	153,058	144,644	132,394	28.6
Percent of total:															
1950	100.0	10.8	14.7	5.5	5.9	4.7	15.8	14.2	11.5	8.8	8.1	71.7	69.0	64.6	(X)
1960	100.0	11.3	18.2	6.2	5.3	3.6	12.7	13.4	11.4	8.6	9.2	67.4	64.3	60.3	(X)
1970	100.0	8.4	17.9	7.8	7.2	4.9	12.3	11.3	11.4	9.1	9.8	69.8	66.0	60.5	(X)
1974	100.0	7.7	16.1	8.0	7.6	5.1	14.0	10.8	11.2	9.2	10.3	72.2	68.3	62.5	(X)
Projections:															
1980—I	225,705	20,001	30,441	15,753	17,097	12,344	36,157	25,702	22,640	21,047	24,523	167,659	159,511	146,638	29.5
II	222,769	17,259	30,245												29.9
III	220,356	14,981	30,112												30.3
1985—I	241,274	24,042	33,330	14,388	15,431	12,404	39,846	31,332	22,378	21,465	26,659	176,533	169,515	158,154	30.1
II	234,068	19,785	30,380												31.1
III	228,355	16,498	27,954												31.8
1990—I	257,663	25,447	41,282	13,538	14,519	10,644	41,062	36,545	25,213	20,479	28,933	183,745	177,396	166,433	30.8
II	245,075	34,096	34,643	12,941											32.3
III	235,581	16,339	29,383	12,463											33.4
2000—I	287,007	24,654	45,923	20,575	18,829	11,749	34,684	41,315	35,742	22,937	30,600	205,938	195,855	181,426	31.4
II	262,494	18,364	35,963	16,751	16,002	10,325	34,494					199,709	191,415	179,189	34.8
III	245,098	14,288	29,119	13,915	13,727	9,090	34,366					194,710	187,776	177,337	37.0
MALE															
1950	75,849	8,362	11,415	4,269	4,484	3,525	11,804	10,706	8,715	6,714	5,856	53,893	51,803	48,460	28.8
1960	89,320	10,339	16,762	5,682	4,810	3,284	11,327	11,872	10,142	7,559	7,542	59,413	56,536	52,859	28.5
1970	100,266	8,746	18,667	8,101	7,435	4,998	12,521	11,316	11,251	8,825	8,405	68,706	64,751	59,114	26.6
974	103,454	8,329	17,375	8,595	8,149	5,396	14,770	11,158	11,505	9,211	8,966	73,441	69,156	62,964	27.4
Projections:															
1980—I	109,979	10,237	15,544	8,031	8,647	6,166	17,967	12,557	10,996	9,920	9,914	80,322	76,167	69,659	28.4
II	108,474	8,832	15,444												28.8
III	107,238	7,664	15,375												29.1

Estimated and Projected Population (continued)

MALE—Con.															
1985—I	117,560	12,315	17,052	7,344	7,813	6,197	19,790	15,356	10,875	10,132	10,684	84,427	80,849	75,104	28.9
1985—II	113,866	10,132	15,541	7,344	7,813	6,197	19,790	15,356	10,875	10,132	10,684	84,427	80,849	75,104	29.8
1985—III	110,940	8,448	14,298	7,344	7,813	6,197	19,790	15,356	10,875	10,132	10,684	84,427	80,849	75,104	30.6
1990—I	125,605	13,042	21,144	6,923	7,364	5,316	20,389	17,937	12,253	9,719	11,518	87,740	84,496	78,938	29.5
1990—II	119,154	10,299	17,742	6,618	7,364	5,316	20,389	17,937	12,253	9,719	11,518	87,740	84,496	78,938	31.1
1990—III	114,290	8,373	15,048	6,373	7,364	5,316	20,389	17,937	12,253	9,719	11,518	87,740	84,496	78,938	32.2
2000—I	140,072	12,643	23,543	10,539	9,578	5,892	17,229	20,247	17,448	10,912	12,041	98,509	93,347	86,013	29.7
2000—II	127,521	9,416	18,433	8,579	8,138	5,174	17,133	20,247	17,448	10,912	12,041	95,339	91,094	84,880	33.3
2000—III	118,617	7,325	14,921	7,124	6,979	4,551	17,069	20,247	17,448	10,912	12,041	92,795	89,247	83,944	35.7
FEMALE															
1950	76,422	8,048	11,008	4,175	4,463	3,603	12,233	10,931	8,738	6,682	6,541	55,248	53,191	49,881	30.5
1960	91,352	10,002	16,203	5,537	4,745	3,289	11,591	12,349	10,436	8,067	9,133	62,422	59,610	55,997	30.3
1970	104,613	8,410	17,968	7,808	7,270	4,980	12,772	11,826	12,059	9,838	11,680	74,243	70,425	64,910	29.2
1974	108,455	7,976	16,708	8,283	7,958	5,404	15,000	11,665	12,315	10,296	12,849	79,617	75,488	69,430	29.8
Projections:															
1980—I	115,726	9,765	14,897	7,721	8,450	6,178	18,190	13,144	11,646	11,126	14,609	87,337	83,344	76,979	30.8
1980—II	114,295	8,428	14,802	7,721	8,450	6,178	18,190	13,144	11,646	11,126	14,609	87,337	83,344	76,979	31.1
1980—III	113,118	7,317	14,737	7,721	8,450	6,178	18,190	13,144	11,646	11,126	14,609	87,337	83,344	76,979	31.5
1985—I	123,714	11,727	16,278	7,044	7,618	6,206	20,055	15,975	11,504	11,332	15,975	92,105	88,666	83,050	31.4
1985—II	120,201	9,652	14,840	7,044	7,618	6,206	20,055	15,975	11,504	11,332	15,975	92,105	88,666	83,050	32.3
1985—III	117,415	8,050	13,656	7,044	7,618	6,206	20,055	15,975	11,504	11,332	15,975	92,105	88,666	83,050	33.0
1990—I	132,058	12,405	20,138	6,615	7,156	5,327	20,673	18,608	12,961	10,760	17,415	96,005	92,899	87,495	32.0
1990—II	125,921	9,797	16,901	6,324	7,156	5,327	20,673	18,608	12,961	10,760	17,415	96,005	92,899	87,495	33.5
1990—III	121,291	7,966	14,335	6,090	7,156	5,327	20,673	18,608	12,961	10,760	17,415	96,005	92,899	87,495	34.6
2000—I	146,935	12,011	22,380	10,036	9,251	5,857	17,455	21,067	18,294	12,025	18,558	107,430	102,508	95,413	33.1
2000—II	134,973	8,948	17,531	8,173	7,864	5,152	17,361	21,067	18,294	12,025	18,558	104,371	100,321	94,308	36.2
2000—III	126,481	6,963	14,198	6,791	6,749	4,539	17,297	21,067	18,294	12,025	18,558	101,915	98,529	93,394	38.2
SERIES II-X PROJECTIONS [1]															
1980	220,197	16,877	29,842	15,585	16,896	12,155	35,463	25,415	22,497	20,964	24,502	165,956	157,893	145,167	30.1
1985	229,057	19,113	29,460	14,084	15,089	12,104	38,617	30,630	22,070	21,294	26,593	173,264	166,399	155,290	31.3
1990	237,421	19,194	33,156	12,422	14,034	10,243	39,432	35,290	24,658	20,198	28,795	178,758	172,649	162,048	32.6
2000	249,061	17,048	33,632	15,734	14,993	9,601	32,149	39,170	34,226	22,285	30,223	190,436	182,648	171,183	35.4
2025	269,343	17,582	33,281	15,075	14,564	10,125	33,989	36,839	30,658	31,515	45,715	203,405	203,851	192,360	37.7
2050	269,999	17,812	32,978	14,774	14,547	10,353	34,574	35,509	32,156	31,492	45,805	211,748	204,435	193,440	37.8
Percent distribution in ultimate stationary population	100.0	6.7	12.0	5.3	5.3	4.0	13.1	12.9	12.4	11.3	17.0	78.6	76.0	72.0	37.8

X Not applicable. [1] Series II-X, which would reach zero growth around the middle of the twenty-first century, is one of many possible approaches to zero growth. Immediate cessation of net immigration, combined with replacement level fertility would not lead to immediate zero growth because the U.S. has a relatively young age structure (due to the post-World War II baby boom) which provides momentum for continued growth. Zero growth in 1975 (assuming no dramatic change in mortality) would require an annual total fertility rate of about 1,000 with net immigration at the current level, or about 1,200 with no net immigration. Total fertility rate in 1974 was between 1,800 and 1,900.

Source: U.S. Bureau of the Census, *Current Population Reports*, series P-25, Nos. 310, 311, 519, and 601.

Source: *Statistical Abstracts.*

Taxes

TAX FORMS TO USE

SS-4	Application for Employer Identification Number
SS-5	Application for Social Security Number
W-2	Wage and Tax Statement
W-2P	Statement for Recipients of Annuities, Pensions, or Retired Pay
W-3	Transmittal of Income and Tax Statements
W-4	Employee's Withholding Allowance Certificate
W-4E	Exemption From Withholding
W-4P	Annuitant's Request for Federal Income Tax Withholding
501	Federal Tax Deposit—Withheld Income and FICA Taxes
503	Federal Tax Deposit—Corporation Income Taxes
504	Federal Tax Deposit—Excise Taxes
508	Federal Tax Deposit—Federal Unemployment Taxes
720	Quarterly Federal Excise Tax Return
940	Employer's Annual Federal Unemployment Tax Return
941	Employer's Quarterly Federal Tax Return
941E	Quarterly Return of Withheld Federal Income Tax
966	Corporate Dissolution or Liquidation
1040	U.S. Individual Income Tax Return
1040ES	Declaration of Estimated Income Tax for Individuals
1040X	Amended U.S. Individual Income Tax Return
1041	U.S. Fiduciary Income Tax Return
1045	Application for Tentative Refund
1065	U.S. Partnership Return of Income
1087-DIV	Statement for Recipients of Dividends and Distributions
1087-INT	Statement for Recipients of Interest Income
1087-MISC	Statement for Recipients of Miscellaneous Income
1099-DIV	Statement For Recipients of Dividends and Distributions
1099-INT	Statement For Recipients of Interest Income
1099-MISC	Statement For Recipients of Miscellaneous Income
1099R	Statement For Recipients of Lump-sum Distributions from Profit-Sharing and Retirement Plans
1120	U.S. Corporation Income Tax Return
1120S	U.S. Small Business Corporation Income Tax Return
1120-W	(WORKSHEET) Corporation Estimated Income Tax
1120X	Amended U.S. Corporation Income Tax Return
1127	Application for Extension of Time for Payment of Tax
1128	Application for Change in Accounting Period
1138	Extension of Time for Payment of Taxes by Corporation Expecting a Net Operating Loss Carryback
1139	Corporation Application for Tentative Refund from Carryback of Net Operating Loss, Net Capital Loss, Unused Investment Credit, and Unused Work Incentive (WIN) Program Credit
1310	Statement of Claimant to Refund Due-Deceased Taxpayer
2106	Employee Business Expenses
2210	Underpayment of Estimated Tax by Individuals
2220	Underpayment of Estimated Income Tax by Corporations
2290	Federal Use Tax Return on Highway Motor Vehicles
2440	Disability Income (Sick-Pay) Exclusion
2553	Election by Small Business Corporation (as to taxable status under subchapter S of the Internal Revenue Code)

Source: Internal Revenue Service.

2688	Application for Extension of Time to File U.S. Individual Income Tax Return	4726	Maximum Tax on Earned Income
		4782	Employee Moving Expense Information
2848	Power of Attorney	4797	Supplemental Schedule of Gains and Losses
3115	Application for Change in Accounting Method		
		4798	Capital Loss Carryover
3435	Payer's Request for Identifying Number	4831	Rental Income
		4832	Class Life (ADR) System
3468	Computation of Investment Credit	4835	Farm Rental Income and Expenses
3903	Moving Expense Adjustment	4868	Application for Automatic Extension of Time to File U.S. Individual Income Tax Return
3921	Exercise of a Qualified or Restricted Stock Option		
		4876	Election to be Treated as a DISC
3922	Transfer of Stock Acquired by Certain Options	5006	Guideline Class Life System
		5329	Return for Individual Retirement Savings Arrangement
4070	Employee's Report of Tips to Employer		
		5452	Corporate Report of Nontaxable Dividends
4070A	Employee's Daily Record of Tips		
4136	Computation of Credit for Federal Tax on Gasoline, Special Fuels, and Lubricating Oil	5498	Statement of Account for Participants in Individual Retirement Accounts or Annuities
4137	Computation of Social Security Tax on Unreported Tip Income	5500	Annual Return/Report of Employee Benefits Plan (with 100 or more)
4219	Statement of Liability of Lender, Surety, or Other Person for Withholding Taxes	5500-C	Annual Return/Report of Employee Benefit Plan (less than 100 and no owner-employee)
4255	Tax from Recomputing a Prior Year Investment Credit	5500-K	Annual Return/Report of Employee Pension Benefit Plan for Sole Proprietorships and Partnerships (less than 100 and at least one owner-employee)
4562	Depreciation		
4571	Explanation for Late Filing of Return or Late Payment of Tax		
4625	Computation of Minimum Tax	5884	New Jobs Credit
4626	Computation of Minimum Tax—For Corporation and Fiduciaries	7004	Application for Automatic Extension of Time to File Corporation Income Tax Return
4683	U.S. Information Return on Foreign Bank, Securities, and Other Financial Accounts	7005	Application for Additional Extension of Time to File Corporation Income Tax Return
4684	Casualties and Thefts		

Congress Votes New Tax Bill: Summary

John Pierson

Congress has sent President Carter a tax-cut bill that satisfies most of his objections to earlier versions of the legislation.

The $18.7 billion reduction approved yesterday is even somewhat smaller in 1979 than the President demanded. It reduces the capital gains relief to the $2 billion range the White House specified. It salvages something of the minimum tax on capital gains and other preference items. It contains a more modest break for homeowners than the House-passed relief, which the administration called excessive. And it doesn't contain two provisions for which the President was said to be ready to veto the tax bill: tuition tax credits and tax cuts in the 1980s tied to federal spending restraint.

House-Senate conferees, who finished work on the bill at 4:02 yesterday morning, also deleted a provision for "indexing" capital gains against inflation, which Mr. Carter found troublesome.

On the other hand, the distribution of tax cuts among income classes isn't much broader than the Senate bill provided—apparently a sore point with the President. And the conferees approved a three-year delay in a key provision liberals won in 1976—the "carry-over" basis rule, which prevents billions of dollars of unrealized capital gains at death from escaping taxation forever.

White House Press Secretary Jody Powell said the other day that Mr. Carter wouldn't accept a "gutting" of the carry-over basis rule. But in the eyes of many observers, liberal and conservative, that's what the President will have to accept unless he decides to veto the bill.

INDIVIDUAL TAXES

The bill would cut individual taxes roughly $12.7 billion in 1979, business taxes $3.7 billion and capital gains taxes $2.2 billion. The capital gains cut would have been about $1 billion greater, except that Sen. Russell Long (D., La.), chairman of the Senate Finance Committee, persuaded everyone to assume revenue "feedback" to the Treasury as investors rushed to take advantage of lower tax rates on the sale of their stocks, real estate and other capital assets.

For individuals, the bill contains a higher exemption, a higher standard deduction, fewer

Source: *The Wall Street Journal*, October 16, 1978, pp. 3, 6, 24. © 1978 by Dow Jones Corporation. Reprinted by permission.

and wider tax brackets, rate cuts and an increase in the earned-income credit for the working poor, all effective Jan. 1.

For business, the bill would provide a cut in the top corporate rate to 46% from 48% next year, rate reductions for small corporations, a more generous investment credit and a new jobs credit targeted at the hard-core unemployed.

For investors, the tax bill reduces the maximum rate on capital gains to 28% from 49%. Most of the reduction happens Nov. 1. Capital gains rates would drop for lower-bracket taxpayers, too. Homeowners aged 55 or over would be allowed to avoid tax, once, on up to $100,000 of profit from a home sale, retroactive to last July 26.

By 1983, the reductions for all three groups would total close to $30 billion annually.

CARTER PROPOSALS

The bill contains pieces of four of the revenue-raising "reforms" President Carter proposed last January. It repeals the deduction for state and local gasoline taxes, tightens up a bit on tax shelters and taxes a portion of unemployment benefits received by middle-income persons.

It also repeals the business deduction for yachts, hunting lodges and other entertainment facilities, which was part of Mr. Carter's sweeping attack on "three-martini lunches" and other manifestations of "expense-account living."

Under great pressure from yacht builders and others, the conferees were ready to scuttle even this change, but in the end, the President insisted on at least a tattered remnant of his original banner.

The conferees acceded, but only after voting to retain the business deduction for country club dues.

When the conferees first sat down, they had before them a House-passed tax cut of about $16 billion, a Senate-passed cut of about $29 billion and a demand from Mr. Carter that they hold next year's reduction to no more than about $20 billion. What's more, the President wanted much smaller tax cuts in the 1980s than the Senate had passed.

The reductions approved by the Senate would have swelled to $55 billion a year by 1983 and to $130 billion if certain goals were met for holding down federal spending.

HOW BILL AFFECTS TYPICAL TAXPAYERS*

	Tax Liability					
	Single Person			Married Couple, Two Dependents		
Adjusted Gross Income	Under Present Law	Under Tax Bill	Reduction	Under Present Law	Under Tax Bill	Reduction
$ 5,000	$ 279	$ 250	$ 29	$ −300	$ −400	$ 100
8,000	810	787	23	120	84	36
10,000	1,199	1,177	22	446	374	72
15,000	2,126	2,047	79	1,330	1,233	97
20,000	3,232	3,115	117	2,180	2,013	167
25,000	4,510	4,364	146	3,150	2,901	249
30,000	5,950	5,718	232	4,232	3,917	315
35,000	7,500	7,220	281	5,464	5,065	399
40,000	9,233	8,886	347	6,848	6,312	536
50,000	12,985	12,559	426	9,950	9,323	627
60,000	16,835	16,392	443	13,496	12,634	862
70,000	20,685	20,242	443	17,330	16,395	935
80,000	24,535	24,092	443	21,180	20,178	1,002
90,000	28,385	27,942	443	25,030	24,028	1,002
100,000	32,235	31,792	443	28,880	27,878	1,002

* The table assumes that adjusted gross income is entirely from wages, salary, or self-employment. Capital gains aren't included. It also assumes deductions equal to 23 percent of income. The table was prepared by the staff of the Joint Committee on Taxation.

Along the way to shrinking the tax cut to suit Mr. Carter—and the congressional budget limit for the fiscal year that started Oct. 1—the conferees threw overboard the Senate's tax-cut–spending-cut provision, which the House had also instructed its conferees to accept. Instead, they approved a statement of "intention" to provide "significant" tax cuts in the years ahead, the economy permitting.

Earlier in the shrinking process, the conferees got . rid of the House-passed plan to index capital gains against inflation, the Senate's "out-year" cuts in the top corporate rate to 44%, more generous small-business depreciation contained in both bills, an extension of the general jobs tax credit, an increase in the credit for the elderly, $700 million of relief for the working poor, more than $5 billion of Senate-passed cuts mostly for the middle class, and the college tuition credit.

Meanwhile, they also cut about $1 billion from the capital gains relief approved by the Senate.

While this "squeezing out" process reduced the bill's impact on the budget, it didn't do much to broaden the way the overall cuts are distributed among different income classes. The spread is wider than that the House originally approved but about the same as that the Senate voted—still far from the kind of "progressivity" Mr. Carter had called for.

Republicans, who have proposed a 33% rate cut over three years, immediately called the $18.7 billion reduction too little. Senate GOP leader Howard Baker of Tennessee said that every family of four making more than $8000 next year will experience a net tax boost because of a scheduled Social Security tax increase and the tendency of inflation to push taxpayers into ever higher brackets.

At least one liberal organization, Ralph Nader's Tax Reform Research Group, called on Mr. Carter to veto the bill. "The tax bill reverses over 10 years of tax reform efforts," said director Robert Brandon.

"The long effort to eliminate the special treatment of capital gains—the biggest loophole in the tax system for the wealthy—would be dealt a knockout blow, unless the President rejects the bill," Mr. Brandon added.

One administration official, as bleary-eyed as the conferees, put it this way: "The conferees are like a bunch of college sophomores. They wait until the last minute, cram all night, and still flunk the exam."

But top administration officials were more cautious. Treasury Secretary Michael Blumenthal called the bill "much improved" from the House and Senate versions. Mr. Blumenthal said it was too soon to say what he would recommend to the President.

And presidential adviser Stuart Eizenstat said on CBS-TV's "Face the Nation" program that the final product is "much closer to the type of bill which we requested." Whether the conferees did enough to avoid a veto "remains to be seen," Mr. Eizenstat said.

The betting among Congressmen, too tired to think much about anything, was that Mr. Carter would sign.

Here is a summary of the bill approved by the conferees. Except as indicated, the provisions take effect Jan. 1, 1979. "Date of enactment" means the day President Carter signs the bill into law.

TAX CUTS

Individuals: The conferees agreed to raise the $750 personal exemption to $1,000 for each taxpayer and dependent. The higher exemption would replace the existing personal tax credit, which equals the greater of $35 per exemption or 2% of the first $9,000 of taxable income.

The zero bracket amount, formerly called the standard deduction, would rise to $2,300 from $2,200 for single taxpayers and $3,400 from $3,200 for married couples filing joint returns.

In addition, the conferees agreed to a new individual rate schedule. Currently, there are 25 brackets with rates from 14% to 70%. Single taxpayers pay from 14% on taxable income between $2,200 and $2,700 to 70% on taxable income exceeding $102,200. Couples filing joint returns pay from 14% on taxable income between $3,200 and $4,200 to 70% on taxable income over $203,200.

The conferees adopted a smaller number of wider brackets so that higher earnings wouldn't push taxpayers so quickly into higher brackets. Under the conference agreement, single taxpayers would have 16 brackets, ranging from 14% on taxable income between $2,300 and $3,400 to 70% on taxable income above $108,300. Couples would have 15 new brackets ranging from 14% on taxable income between $3,400 and $5,500 to 70% above $215,400. There would be rate cuts, too, in certain middle-income brackets.

Working poor: Currently, a taxpayer with a dependent qualifies for a credit equal to 10% of the first $4,000 of earned income, or a maximum credit of $400 a year. This "earned income credit" is phased out at income levels between $4,000 and $8,000. The credit is refundable, which means it can exceed a person's tax liability, in which case he gets a check from the Treasury at the year-end. The credit expires at the end of this year. The conferees voted to make the credit permanent and to increase it to 10% of the first $5,000 of income, or a maximum credit of $500, starting Jan. 1. The new credit would be phased out between $6,000 and $10,000 of income.

And starting July 1, the earned-income credit would be reflected in pay envelopes, instead of in a lump sum at year-end.

Corporations: The bill approved by the conferees would lower the top rate on corporate income to 46% from 48% next year.

The rate on the first $25,000 of corporate income would drop to 17% from 20%, and the rate on the second $25,000 would drop to 20% from 22%. In addition, there would be two new brackets for the third and fourth $25,000 of corporate income, which are currently taxed at the top 48% rate. The conferees agreed to make the rate 30% on the third $25,000 and 40% on the fourth $25,000.

Capital gains: The conferees accepted a package of changes that would reduce the top tax rate on individual capital gains—profits from sale of stock, real estate and other capital assets—to 28% from 49%. The bottom rate on gains would be cut to 5.6% from 7%, and there would be rate cuts in between, as well.

Under current law, income from certain capital transactions qualifies for preferential tax treatment. Half of an individual's net, long-term capital gains can be excluded from income before applying regular tax rates, which range from 14% to 70%. Thus, the regular tax on gains ranges from 7% to 35%, although taxpayers in brackets above 50% can choose to have the first $50,000 of gains taxed at no more than 25%. Meanwhile, the excluded half of gains is considered an item of tax "preference" subject to the existing add-on minimum tax and reducing the amount of earned income eligible for the 50% maximum tax ceiling. The interaction of the regular, minimum and maximum taxes can raise the rate on capital gains as high as 49.125%.

The conferees voted to raise the capital gains exclusion to 60%, starting next Nov. 1. They voted to repeal the alternative 25% rate on the first $50,000 of gains Jan. 1. They agreed to stop "poisoning" the maximum tax break with the excluded part of gains, also starting Jan. 1. They further agreed to subject the excluded 60% of gains as well as one other preference item—excess itemized deductions—to a new alternative minimum tax.

Individuals would pay this new alternative minimum tax only if it exceeded regular taxes plus the existing minimum tax, which would continue to apply to a modified list of eight other preferences. For capital gains and excess itemized deductions, the new alternative minimum tax would replace the existing add-on tax Jan. 1.

The new alternative tax would be applied to taxable income plus the excluded part of gains plus excess itemized deductions minus a $20,000 exemption. The rate would be 10% on the first $40,000, then 20% on the next $40,000 and 25% on amounts exceeding $80,000.

Corporate gains: Existing law doesn't allow corporations to exclude 50% of their capital gains. But it does provide an alternative 30% rate for gains of corporations subject to the top 48% rate on income. In addition, part of a corporation's gains are subject to a 15% minimum tax, which can raise the top rate on corporate capital gains to 31.125%.

The conferees agreed to reduce the alternative rate on corporate gains to 28% from 30%. As gains would remain subject to the corporate minimum tax, the maximum rate on capital gains of corporations would be reduced to 29.67%.

Home sales: Currently, someone who sells a house and buys a new one within 18 months doesn't pay any tax on his profit unless the new one costs less than he gets for his old one. Also, someone who has reached the age of 65 can avoid tax, once, on all his profit if he sells his house for less than $35,000. As the sale price rises above $35,000, there's a diminishing amount of capital gains relief for the elderly.

The conferees agreed to lower the age for the elderly tax break to 55 and permit a one-time exclusion of up to $100,000 of *profit* on a home sale, instead of a tax benefit based on $35,000 of *sales price*. To qualify, an individual would have to have owned and occupied the house for three of the previous five years. Profits on home sales wouldn't any longer be subject to the minimum tax. These changes would be retroactive to July 26, the day the House Ways and Means Committee approved a similar provision.

Current law limits homeowners to one tax-free "rollover" every 18 months. The conferees agreed to allow more than one rollover within 18 months if the homeowner moves for employment reasons.

Inherited property: The conferees voted to delay the "carry-over" basis provision of the Tax Reform Act of 1976, which raises capital gains taxes on people who sell inherited assets.

Prior to the 1976 act, the law permitted heirs to avoid income tax—but not estate tax —on appreciated property held until their benefactor's death. The heirs received a "step-up" in basis on the property they inherited. Thus, if they later sold, the only gain subject to tax was gain that occurred after death; gain before death was forgotten by the IRS. The 1976 act required an heir to use the same cost basis as the person who died, adjusted for death taxes paid. To ease the effects, Congress agreed to apply the new carry-over basis rules to gains occurring after 1976.

The conferees decided to delay the carry-over basis rules for three years, through 1979. Estates of people who died after Dec. 31,

1976, and before this bill's date of enactment would be subject to the old step-up rule, too, although they may have already filed returns under the carry-over rule. But the conferees promised to consider the problems of these estates early next year.

Investment credit: The conferees agreed to liberalize the investment credit and extend it to rehabilitation of certain buildings.

Current law permits a businessman to claim a credit generally equal to 10% of the cost of machinery and equipment. It doesn't apply to buildings. The credit can be used to offset the first $25,000 of tax liability and 50% of tax liability above $25,000. In 1981, the investment credit is due to drop to 7%, while the maximum amount of used property eligible for the credit is due to drop to $50,000 from $100,000.

The conferees decided to make the credit and the $100,000 used-property limit permanent. They also agreed to raise to 90% the amount of tax liability, in excess of $25,000, that can be offset, phasing in the higher ceiling at the rate of 10 percentage points a year. Thus, the offset would reach 90% by 1982. Utilities, airlines and railroads, which currently enjoy special increase limitations, could choose between the new law and existing law during the phase-in period. Finally, the conferees voted to make the investment credit available for money spent after Nov. 1, 1978, to rehabilitate industrial and commercial buildings that have been in use for at least 20 years.

Pollution: Under existing law, the 10% investment credit is cut to 5% for pollution-control facilities that the taxpayer elects to write off over five years. The conference committee agreed to allow the full 10% credit even where five-year amortization is elected. But the credit would be only 5% to the extent the facilities were financed with tax-exempt industrial development bonds.

Job credit: The conferees voted to replace the existing general jobs credit with a new credit targeted at certain hard-to-hire persons. An employer gets the existing credit, up to $2,100, for hiring anyone beyond certain base-period payroll. The existing credit expires Dec. 31.

Instead, there would be a credit up to $3,000 the first year of employment and up to $1,500 the second year. The credit would be available for each worker hired from eight target groups, including certain welfare recipients, Vietnam veterans, handicapped persons, young people and convicted felons. The credit would be in force during the three years 1979 through 1981 for employes hired after Sept. 26, 1978.

WIN credit: Present law gives employers a tax credit of up to 20% of wages paid in the first year of employment of certain welfare recipients and those who register for the work incentive, or WIN, program. The conferees agreed to make the WIN credit up to $3,000 in the first year and $1,500 in the second year for employers conducting a trade or business. For other employers, such as housewives hiring maids, the maximum credit would be $2,100 the first year.

Political gifts: Current law permits a taxpayer to take either a deduction or a credit for political contributions. The maximum deduction is $100, or $200 on a joint return. The credit equals half the contribution, up to a maximum of $25, or $50 on a joint return. The conferees agreed to double the maximum credit to $50, or $100 on a joint return. The alternative deduction would be retained.

Education: Under existing law, if an employer pays for an employe's schooling, the employe must pay tax on the money unless the schooling is needed for him to keep the same job. Aid that prepares him for a new job, even with the same company, is taxable. The conferees agreed to make employer-provided education help tax-free for five years starting Jan. 1. But this break wouldn't extend to living expenses or to courses involving sports, games or hobbies.

Industrial bonds: In general, interest on state and local government bonds is tax exempt. But interest on industrial development bonds is taxable, with certain exceptions. Issues of less than $1 million are tax exempt, and this limit can be increased to $5 million under certain conditions. The conferees agreed to raise the $5 million "small issue" limit to $10 million. Projects that have received urban development Action grants could use up to $10 million of industrial development bonds, after Sept. 30, 1979, even though the total capital expenditures reached $20 million.

Water bonds: Under current law, industrial development bonds to build water facilities are tax exempt if the water is available to the general public. The conferees agreed to expand the definition of "general public" to include industrial, agricultural and commercial users as well as electric utilities, effective the date of enactment.

New York electricity: The conferees agreed to a change in the rules so that the New York State Power Authority would be able to use tax-exempt industrial development bonds to supply electricity to New York City and adjacent Westchester County.

Refundings: Current law provides a tax exemption for industrial development bonds issued to build certain public projects. Issues to refund these issues also are tax exempt. But the IRS has proposed that certain issues refunded in advance of their redemption date lose their tax exemption. The conferees acted to retain the exempt status of advanced refundings of these public project bonds, effective the date of enactment.

Retirement: The conferees agreed to a number of changes that would liberalize the rules for individual retirement accounts, pension plans, tax-sheltered annuities and mutual fund stock held by retirement plans.

Current law requires pension plans to meet complex rules and reporting requirements if they want to receive favorable tax treatment. Current law also allows individuals who don't belong to a tax-qualified pension plan to deduct contributions to an individual retirement plan, or IRA. The rules for IRAs are simpler. The maximum annual deduction to an IRA is 15% of earned income or $1,500, whichever is less. Where a working spouse shares an IRA with a non-working spouse, the limit is 15% or $1,750.

The conferees agreed that instead of setting up a pension plan, an employer could make tax-deductible contributions to an employe's IRA. In that case, the IRA limits would be raised to the lesser of $7,500 or 15% of earned income. If employer contributions to an employe IRA were less than the normal IRA limits—15% or $1,500—the employee could make his own contributions to bring the annual amount up to that normal limit.

Current law limits annual benefits under a tax-qualified pension plan to the lesser of 100% of pay or $75,000, adjusted for inflation since 1974, which puts it at $90,150 this year. The conferees agreed to disregard the 100%-of-pay rule for employes under certain collectively bargained plans with at least 100 participants. In such cases, the $75,000 limit would be reduced to $37,500, adjusted for inflation.

Many tax-exempt charities and schools provide for employe retirement by purchasing annuity contracts or mutual fund stock. Mutual fund stock can't be distributed before an employe reaches age 65 unless he dies or becomes disabled. If he leaves his job, he can have his stock only if he has reached age 55. The conferees decided to permit distribution of mutual fund stock after an employe dies, becomes disabled, quits his job, reaches age 59½ or encounters hardship.

Currently, life insurance companies don't sell annuity contracts to state and local retirement plans, because the reserves maintained for such contracts receive less favorable tax treatment than reserves maintained for annuity contracts sold to other retirement plans. The conferees agreed to give contracts sold to state and local governments the same favorable treatment.

Current law permits a participant in a pension profit-sharing, stock-bonus or annuity plan to convert his share into an IRA or another employer-sponsored plan if he quits his job. But public school teachers and employes of other tax-exempt organizations who use tax-sheltered annuities aren't eligible for a tax-free switch. The conferees agreed to make them eligible, retroactive to Dec. 31, 1977.

Deferred pay: Under current law, taxpayers generally aren't required to count as income, and pay tax on, compensation until they actually receive it. Employes may agree in advance with their employers to receive compensation on a deferred basis rather than currently and thus avoid tax on it until later. But on Feb. 3, the Internal Revenue Service proposed new rules that generally would put a stop to these agreements.

The conferees approved changes aimed at preventing the IRS from carrying out its proposals. Thus, employes of state and local governments or tax-exempt rural electric cooperatives could defer a limited amount of compensation. Independent contractors working for these employers also could participate in these plans. Each participant would put aside up to $7,500 a year or one-third of his pay, whichever was less, and extra contributions would be permitted during the three years prior to retirement. Participants would have the right to make monthly, rather than annual elections to defer compensation. All plans would have until Jan. 1, 1982, to meet the requirements for eligibility.

The conferees didn't set any limits for deferred compensation plans of private employers. Participants in these plans would receive tax deferral under the rules in effect on Feb. 1, 1978. But tax-exempt organizations would remain potentially subject to the new rules proposed by the IRS Feb. 3.

The rules would be tightened for independent contractors, however. Existing law permits an employer to deduct, in the current year, deferred compensation set aside until a future year for an independent contractor. The conferees agreed to deny employers a deduction until the year the contractor receives the money.

In addition, the conferees agreed to clarify the tax treatment of "cafeteria" plans, which permit an employe to choose from a package of employer-provided fringe benefits, some of which may be taxable and some of which may be nontaxable. Under the conference agreement, employes wouldn't be taxed on employer contributions under a cafeteria plan to the extent the employe chooses nontaxable benefits. But executives and other highly paid employes would be taxed currently on amounts contributed to the plan, to the extent they could have chosen taxable benefits, unless rank-and-file workers are eligible to join the plan.

Finally, the conferees clarified the treatment of arrangements where the employe has the choice of getting cash or having the same amount contributed to a tax-deferred profit-sharing plan. These arrangements were questioned in proposed regulations issued by the IRS in 1972. Under the conference agreement, employes who chose profit sharing wouldn't be taxed on employer contributions, merely because they could have chosen cash, so long as the plan met certain eligibility standards. This provision would take effect Jan. 1, 1980, but there would be transition rules for plans in existence on Jan. 27, 1974.

Contractors: The IRS is currently locked in battle with employers and employes over whether real estate brokers, insurance salesmen, truckers and others are to be classified as employes or independent contractors. If they're contractors, their employers don't have to pay Social Security or unemployment insurance taxes on their behalf and don't have to withhold income or Social Security taxes from their pay. Otherwise they do.

The conferees agreed to forgive any pre-1979 taxes the IRS may have assessed against employers who had a "reasonable basis" for treating employes as independent contractors. The conference agreement also would extend this relief through 1979, and it would prohibit the IRS from issuing any new rules or regulations on the question before 1980 to give Congress time to come up with a permanent solution.

Tips: Under IRS rulings, restaurant operators are supposed to tell the IRS about all tips waiters report to the management, including tips entered on charge-account slips. The conferees agreed that restaurant operators won't have to report charge-account tips any more.

Child care: Current law gives working parents a tax credit for child-care costs. But payments to grandparents don't qualify for the credit. The conferees agreed to extend the credit to child-care payments to grandparents.

Capital losses: Under current law, taxpayers must use capital losses to offset capital gains. A limited amount, $3,000, of left-over capital losses can be used to offset ordinary income. But a special rule permits owners of small businesses to issue special stock and treat any loss on it as an ordinary loss up to $25,000 a year, or $50,000 on a joint return. The conferees agreed to raise these maximum amounts to $50,000, or $100,000 on a joint return. They agreed to increase the maximum amount of special stock that a business can issue to $1 million from $500,000. They also decided to repeal certain other requirements. These changes would be effective on the date of enactment.

Farms: The Tax Reform Act of 1976 required corporations engaged in farming to use accrual accounting instead of the cash method and to capitalize expenses incurred during the preproductive period, instead of deducting them immediately. Exceptions were provided for Subchapter S corporations, certain family-held corporations, those with gross receipts of less than $1 million and nurseries. In 1977, Congress provided temporary relief from the 1976 act for two large chicken farms: Hudson Foods of Arkansas and Halifax Foods of Maine. The conferees agreed to make that relief permanent. They also agreed to exempt sod farms and to exempt farmers, nurseries and florists—who use accrual accounting—from an IRS ruling requiring that growing crops be inventoried, retroactive to Dec. 31, 1977. These taxpayers could also change to the cash method without prior IRS approval as long as they acted before Jan. 1, 1981.

Pigpens: In general, buildings aren't eligible for the investment credit, and the IRS has specifically denied the credit for greenhouses, pigpens, milking parlors, chicken coops and the like. The conferees voted to overrule the IRS, making these structures eligible for the investment credit, retroactive to Aug. 15, 1971.

Co-ops: The conferees agreed to make the investment credit available to cooperatives without requiring, as current law does, that they first deduct patronage dividends. Such deductions reduce income and the value of the credit. The change would be effective Nov. 1, 1978.

Conrail: Under current law, investment credits aren't generally recaptured where assets are transferred in a tax-free reorganization. But Congress didn't think to apply this rule to the bankrupt railroads that transferred assets to Consolidated Rail Corp. on April 1, 1976. The conferees agreed to apply the no-recapture rule to those rail properties, retroactively.

In addition, the conferees voted to make it clear that the bankrupt railroads may use net operating losses carried over from earlier years to offset income they may realize on the certificates of value they are obtaining from Conrail.

Housing: Current law permits taxpayers who rehabilitate rental housing for low-income tenants to take a limited amount of depreciation deductions over five years under the straight-line method. This provision is due to expire Dec. 31. The conferees agreed to extend it for three more years. Expenditures made under a binding contract entered into

before the end of 1981 would qualify for a five-year write-off, even though the taxpayer didn't actually pay out the money until after 1981.

Mutual funds: Under current law, mutual funds are required to distribute at least 90% of their income to shareholders every year. Otherwise they pay a penalty. The conferees agreed to let a mutual fund pay a "deficiency dividend" in a later year if an IRS audit determined that the fund inadvertently paid out less than 90% of its income in the earlier year. This would take effect on the date of enactment.

Utilities: Under current law, water and sewage utilities can treat as nontaxable contributions to capital, rather than taxable income, the value of lines installed by developers and then given to the utilities. The conferees agreed to extend this same tax break to gas and electric utilities, retroactive to Jan. 31, 1976.

Net losses: In 1976, Congress moved to crack down on the practice of profitable corporations buying unprofitable ones to reduce their own taxes with losses carried over from the other company's earlier years. The conferees decided to delay the effective dates of the 1976 rules for two years. But taxpayers could elect to use the 1976 rules on certain

Liabilities: Under current law, when certain liabilities are transferred to a newly created corporation, a gain is recognized. The conferees agreed that, after the date of enactment, those liabilities wouldn't constitute a gain.

Railroads: Under current law, a taxpayer who leases railroad cars to a railroad may lose foreign tax credits if the lease produces a tax loss and the cars are used outside the U.S. This rule has led to an inefficient use of railroad cars between the U.S. and Canada and the U.S. and Mexico. The conferees agreed that the lessors wouldn't lose their foreign tax credits if the cars weren't used outside the U.S. for more than 90 days. This change would be effective on the date of enactment, or sooner at the option of the lessor.

Oil and gas drilling: In moving against tax "shelters" in 1976, Congress agreed to include, as an item of tax preference under the individual minimum tax, deductions for labor, fuel and other "intangible" costs of drilling for oil and gas. In 1977, under pressure from independent oil and gas producers, Congress voted temporarily to apply the new rule only to taxpayers whose main occupation wasn't in oil and gas operations. It did this by saying that, for 1977, individuals would have to include intangibles in their minimum tax base only to the extent that the deductions exceeded their oil and gas income.

The conferees agreed to make this provision permanent, starting last Jan. 1. Thus, the break would reduce both 1978 taxes under the existing 15% minimum tax and taxes in later years under the new alternative minimum tax.

The conferees went even further and agreed that oil and gas income won't be reduced, for the purposes of figuring the minimum tax, by intangible costs of drilling holes that turn out dry. Furthermore, producers could make an irrevocable election to capitalize intangible drilling costs for any oil and gas property, instead of deducting them immediately.

Deductions: One of the 10 preference items subject to the existing minimum tax is "excess" itemized deductions, defined as deductions—other than medical expenses and casualty losses—exceeding 60% of adjusted gross income. The conferees voted to remove state and local taxes from this preference item. But the benefit to taxpayers would be offset by the requirement that they deduct medical expenses, casualty losses and state and local taxes from adjusted gross income before applying the 60% test.

Stock options: Corporate executives and other recipients of certain qualified stock options would be allowed to treat the options as nonqualified, and thus avoid the minimum tax, under the conference agreement.

Maximum tax: Individual tax rates currently range from 14% to 70%, but "personal service" income is taxed at a maximum rate of 50%. Dividends, interest and other income from capital doesn't qualify for the maximum tax. But where an unincorporated business produces income from both capital and personal services, the taxpayer is allowed to treat up to 30% of the income as being from personal services. The conferees agreed to substitute a "reasonable" compensation test for the 30% rule.

Savings and loans: Current law provides U.S. citizens and corporations with tax breaks for interest received on deposits left with Puerto Rican branches of U.S. commercial banks. Under the conference agreement, interest from Puerto Rican branches of U.S. savings and loan associations would receive the same breaks, effective the date of the tax bill's enactment.

Foundations: Current law imposes a 4% tax on net investment income of U.S. private foundations. The conferees agreed to cut the rate to 2%, retroactive to Sept. 30, 1977.

In addition, the conferees agreed to exempt from the excise tax certain foundations that care for disabled persons, elderly persons, needy widows or children. This provision was designed to benefit the Sand Springs Home in Sand Springs, Okla.

Slot machines: Under present law, the federal government imposes a tax of $250 a year on each slot machine. If a state imposes a similar tax, the casino owner can use the state tax as a credit against up to 80% of the federal tax. The conferees agreed to increase the credit to 95% for two years starting June 30, 1978, and to repeal the federal tax altogether thereafter.

Charity: Under existing law, certain requirements must be met before a taxpayer can take a deduction for giving a split interest to charity. The conferees agreed that split-interest trusts created before Dec. 31, 1977, will have until the end of 1978 to be changed to meet the rules governing charitable deductions. This provision is designed to help Arkansas College.

"Widow's tax": Under present law, even if legal title to a farm or small business is jointly held by a husband and wife for many years and the wife contributes substantially to the enterprise, the entire value is deemed to be the husband's property. This may mean more estate tax. The conferees voted to permit a wife to "earn" an estate tax credit on jointly held property at the rate of 50% or $500,000 if she can demonstrate her participation in the enterprise. Husbands also would be allowed to earn the credit.

Estate tax: The conferees also agreed to a change intended to benefit the heirs of Ernest and Julio Gallo, owners of the Gallo Winery in California. Currently, heirs who inherit certain family companies can elect to pay estate taxes over 15 years. On part of the taxes due, the government charges only 4% interest. The conferees agreed to change the rules so that the Gallo family could qualify for this special treatment.

Liens: Current law permits owners of a family farm or business to have it valued at actual use rather than fair market value for purposes of determining how much estate tax is owed. Where this special treatment is elected, the Treasury has a lien on the property for up to 15 years. But banks are reluctant to lend money to owners of such property. The conferees agreed to permit the Treasury to subordinate its lien to that of a bank, for estates retroactive to Dec. 31, 1976.

Product liability: Current law permits a businessman to carry net operating losses back three years or forward seven years to offset income. Amounts accumulated to meet future casualty losses may be subject to a tax on excess accumulated earnings. The conferees agreed to let businessmen carry losses from product liability back 10 years, instead of three, as well as forward the usual seven years. In addition, they could set aside "reasonable" amounts of after-tax income as a reserve against future liability claims without triggering a penalty tax. These changes are effective starting Oct. 1, 1979.

Unsold magazines: Present law requires a publisher or distributor of magazines, paperback books or records, who uses accrual accounting, to count proceeds as income when shipments are made but to deduct unsold items only in the year they're returned. The conferees decided to let these taxpayers deduct unsold items on their previous year's taxes if the items are returned early in the following tax year. The change would be effective Oct. 1, 1979.

Discount coupons: Current law allows someone who issues premium coupons, and uses accrual accounting, to deduct the estimated cost of redeeming coupons outstanding at the close of the tax year. But the IRS has ruled that this break isn't available to taxpayers who issue "cents off" or other discount coupons. The conferees agreed to let issuers of the discount coupons take a current deduction for coupons outstanding at the end of the tax year and redeemed within the next six months.

Technical changes: The 1976 Tax Reform Act, especially the parts relating to estate taxes, was drafted in such haste that it contains "technical" mistakes. The conferees agreed to attach to the tax-cut bill the Senate version of a separate measure making technical corrections in the 1976 act.

Commodities: As part of the 1976 technical corrections, the conferees deleted a House-passed provision that would have required holders of futures contracts in silver and other nonagricultural commodities to keep their contracts one year, instead of six months, before becoming eligible for long-term capital-gains treatment.

Share the wealth: Currently there aren't any special provisions in the U.S. tax code for private corporations set up for the benefit of state residents. The conferees agreed to a five-year experiment to see whether general stock ownership corporations, or GSOCs, can contribute to broader distribution of wealth. States would charter these business corporations and hand out up to 10 shares to each state citizen. A GSOC would have to pay out 90% of its net income each year, and the shareholders rather than the corporation would be taxed on the income, after the manner of a partnership. The corporation would be required to withhold for the IRS 30% of every distribution to its shareholders. Net losses wouldn't flow through to the shareholders, but could be carried forward 10 years by the corporation.

Conservation: The conferees voted to provide tax exemption for payments received under certain federal and state programs aimed at clearing up water and abandoned mines, saving soil and forests, and the like.

Refunds: The conferees agreed to provide quick refunds to certain taxpayers who normally might have to wait for months or even years to get their money back. This would be effective upon enactment.

Medical students: Students entering medical school before 1979, under the Uniformed Services Health Professions Scholarship programs, aren't taxed on scholarship money received through 1982. The conferees agreed to extend this tax break for one more year. It would therefore, apply to students entering before 1980 and to amounts received through 1983.

Research: The IRS has ruled that amounts received as national research service awards under the Public Health Service Act of 1974 are taxable. The conferees voted to make these awards tax exempt for years 1974 through 1979.

Student loans: Currently, the federal government and some states lend money to would-be doctors, nurses and teachers to go to school and then forgive the loans if the recipients work in rural areas or urban slums. Any loans forgiven before 1979 aren't counted as income to the recipients. The conferees agreed to extend this tax break to loans made before 1983.

Co-op housing: The conferees accepted a change that would permit tenant-stockholders in cooperative housing corporations to continue deducting their share of real estate taxes and interest, even when vacancy rates are high, effective the date of enactment.

Alaska natives: The conferees agreed to give a tax break to corporations formed under the Alaska Native Claims Settlement Act, retroactive to Dec. 18, 1971.

Cows: The conferees voted tax relief for Michigan farmers whose cattle were poisoned with the chemical PBB. Current law permits a tax-free rollover of gain on the involuntary conversion of certain property, if the money is used to acquire similar property. The conferees agreed to permit this tax break for livestock, even where the proceeds—in this case insurance—are reinvested in other farm property, including real estate. The change would be retroactive to Jan. 1, 1975.

TAX INCREASES

Gasoline: The conferees agreed to repeal the deduction for state and local taxes on gasoline, diesel fuel and other motor fuels that aren't used for business purposes. The deduction that would be repealed is currently available only for taxpayers who itemize deductions.

Jobless pay: Unemployment compensation isn't taxed. The conferees voted to tax unemployment compensation received by single persons making more than $20,000 a year and couples making more than $25,000, if they file a joint return. The amount these taxpayers would have to include in their income and pay taxes on would equal half the amount by which their total income exceeded $20,000 in the case of a single person, or $25,000 for a couple.

Entertainment: The conferees agreed to repeal the existing business deduction for yachts, hunting lodges, fishing camps and other entertainment facilities. Country club dues would still be deductible, however.

At risk: As part of a crackdown on tax "shelters," Congress in 1976 passed certain "at risk" rules, which are meant to prevent a taxpayer from deducting losses that exceed his actual investment. The conferees agreed to extend these rules to all activities other than real estate. They also agreed to extend them to all corporations in which five or fewer individuals own more than 50% of the stock, except equipment-leasing companies. They also decided to require the IRS to "recapture" previously allowed losses, when the taxpayer subsequently reduces his risk to zero. The new recapture rule would apply only to losses deducted after Dec. 31, 1978.

Medical expenses: Currently, there isn't any tax on amounts received as reimbursement for medical bills under self-insured accident or health plans. The conferees agreed to end this tax exemption unless the plans are drawn up so that they don't discriminate in favor of executives and other top employes.

OTHER CHANGES

Employe stock: Under current law, employes aren't taxed on employer contributions to an employe stock-ownership plan, or ESOP, until the contributions are distributed. And corporations can get an additional one percentage point of investment credit, above the regular 10%, for contributing an equal amount to an ESOP, known as a TRASOP, that satisfies requirement of the Tax Reduction Act of 1975. Another one-half percentage point of investment credit is allowed for employe contributions to a TRASOP that are matched by employe contributions. The TRASOP law expires at the end of 1980.

The conferees agreed to extend the TRASOP provisions for three more years and to make a number of "technical" changes in both the TRASOP and ESOP rules.

Subchapter S: Under Subchapter S of the tax code, small corporations may elect to be taxed in the manner of partnerships. Tax isn't imposed on the corporation itself, but each shareholder pays tax on his share of any profits. The conferees agreed to increase the number of shareholders a Subchapter S corporation may have to 15 from 10, to count a husband and wife as one shareholder—regardless of how they hold their stock—and to let corporations elect Subchapter S status during the entire previous year and the first 75 days of the current year. Current law requires the election during the three months prior to the start of the current year.

Small tax: Tax cases involving deficiencies of less than $1,500 may be tried, informally, at the taxpayer's option, under the small tax-case procedures of the Tax Court. The conferees agreed to increase the eligible amount to $5,000.

Elderly help: The conferees agreed to authorize the IRS to help train volunteers from nonprofit organizations to assist persons over 60 in preparing their tax returns. The service could reimburse volunteers for transportation, meals and other expenses.

Partnerships: Under existing law, partnerships aren't taxed, but they must report to the IRS each partner's share of the partnership's income, deductions and credits. Each partner then is supposed to report these items on his own tax return. The conferees agreed to impose a penalty on partnerships that don't file timely or complete reports to the IRS. The penalty would be up to $250 multiplied by the number of partners. In addition, the conference agreement would extend from three to four years the amount of time the IRS has to assess additional tax on a partnership.

Judgments: At present, state and local governments haven't any way to find out whether their bonds are tax exempt in advance of issuing them. The conferees agreed to authorize the Tax Court and the U.S. Appeals Court for the District of Columbia to issue declaratory judgments on the tax status of proposed municipal bond issues.

Arbitrage: State and local governments often issue tax-exempt bonds and then, while waiting to spend the proceeds, invest the money in high-yielding Treasury or other bonds. These "arbitrage" bonds aren't tax exempt. Until 1976, some state and local governments diverted arbitrage profits to the bond underwriter or to charity. The IRS put a stop to the practice. The conferees agreed to permit profits on arbitrage arrangements that were under way before the IRS ruling to be given to public charities.

REITs: The conferees agreed to exempt real estate investment trusts from the penalty tax on gain from the sale of certain real estate assets.

Budget control: The conferees expressed the "intention" of the tax-writing committees of Congress to provide "significant" tax cuts for individuals if they're justified by economic conditions. The committees would consider the cuts if federal spending were kept within certain guidelines through 1983.

Studies: The conferees ordered the Treasury to conduct a number of studies. These include simplifying the filing of tax returns, using the tax code to help businessmen comply with health and safety rules, the effect of cuts in capital gains taxes and the tax treatment of foreigners who own or sell U.S. real estate.

TAX-FREE *VERSUS* TAXABLE INVESTMENTS

TAXABLE EQUIVALENT YIELDS

YOUR TOTAL TAX BRACKET* IS	AFTER TAX YIELDS														
	3.00	3.50	4.00	4.25	4.50	4.75	5.00	5.25	5.50	5.75	6.00	6.25	6.50	6.75	7.00
27%	4.11	4.80	5.48	5.82	6.17	6.51	6.85	7.19	7.54	7.88	8.22	8.56	8.91	9.25	9.59
31%	4.35	5.07	5.80	6.16	6.53	6.89	7.25	7.61	7.98	8.34	8.70	9.06	9.43	9.79	10.15
36%	4.69	5.47	6.24	6.63	7.02	7.41	7.80	8.19	8.58	8.97	9.36	9.75	10.14	10.53	10.92
40%	5.00	5.83	6.68	7.10	7.52	7.93	8.35	8.77	9.19	9.60	10.02	10.44	10.86	11.27	11.69
45%	5.45	6.36	7.28	7.74	8.19	8.65	9.10	9.56	10.01	10.47	10.92	11.38	11.83	12.29	12.74
48%	5.77	6.73	7.68	8.16	8.64	9.12	9.60	10.08	10.56	11.04	11.52	12.00	12.48	12.96	13.44
50%	6.00	7.00	8.00	8.50	9.00	9.50	10.00	10.50	11.00	11.50	12.00	12.50	13.00	13.50	14.00
52%	6.25	7.29	8.32	8.84	9.36	9.88	10.40	10.92	11.44	11.96	12.48	13.00	13.52	14.04	14.56
55%	6.67	7.78	8.88	9.44	9.99	10.55	11.10	11.66	12.21	12.77	13.32	13.88	14.43	14.99	15.54
57%	6.98	8.14	9.32	9.90	10.49	11.07	11.65	12.23	12.82	13.40	13.98	14.56	15.15	15.73	16.31
60%	7.50	8.75	10.00	10.63	11.25	11.88	12.50	13.13	13.75	14.38	15.00	15.63	16.25	16.88	17.50
61%	7.69	8.97	10.24	10.88	11.52	12.16	12.80	13.44	14.08	14.72	15.36	16.00	16.64	17.28	17.92
67%	9.09	10.61	12.12	12.88	13.64	14.39	15.15	15.91	16.66	17.42	18.18	18.94	19.70	20.45	21.21

This table gives the approximate yields which taxable securities must earn in various income brackets to produce after-tax yields equal to those on tax-free bonds yielding from 3.00% to 7.00%. This table is computed on the theory that the taxpayer's highest rate is applicable to the entire amount of any increase or decrease in his taxable income resulting from a switching from taxable to tax-free securities or vice versa.

* Federal and state income tax.

Employment Wages and Productivity

STATUS OF THE LABOR FORCE

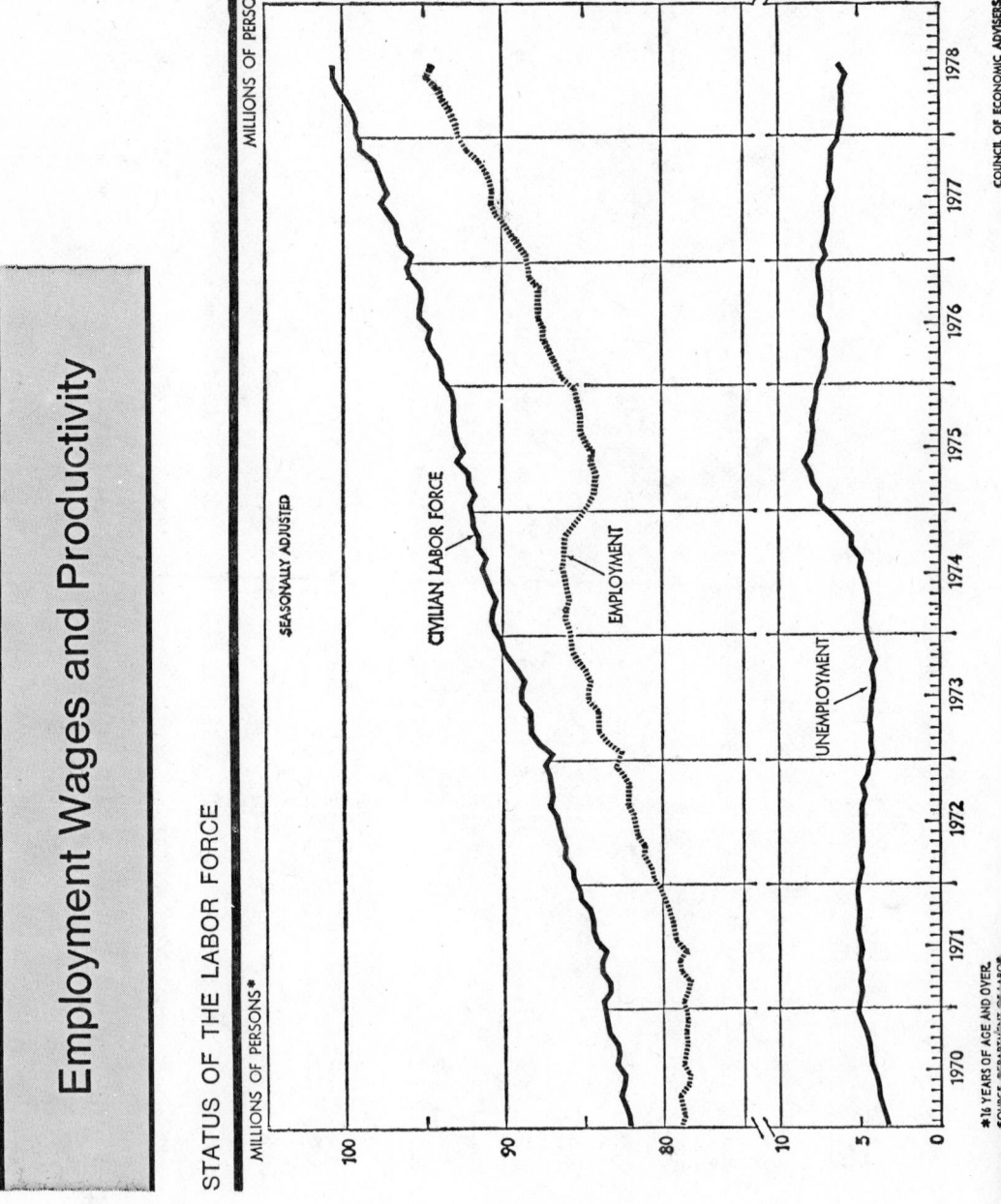

MILLIONS OF PERSONS*

SEASONALLY ADJUSTED

CIVILIAN LABOR FORCE

EMPLOYMENT

UNEMPLOYMENT

MILLIONS OF PERSONS*

*16 YEARS OF AGE AND OVER.

COUNCIL OF ECONOMIC ADVISERS

[Thousands of persons 16 years of age and over]

Period	Noninstitutional population	Civilian employment	Unemployment	Total labor force (including Armed Forces)	Civilian labor force	Civilian employment		Nonagricultural		Unemployment		Labor force participation rate (percent)[2]
						Total	Agricultural	Total	Part-time for economic reasons[1]	Total	15 weeks and over	
			Unadjusted					Seasonally adjusted				
1973	148,263	84,409	4,304	91,040	88,714	84,409	3,452	80,957	2,311	4,304	812	61.4
1974	150,827	85,935	5,076	93,240	91,011	85,935	3,492	82,443	2,709	5,076	937	61.8
1975	153,449	84,783	7,830	94,793	92,613	84,783	3,380	81,403	3,490	7,830	2,483	61.8
1976	156,048	87,485	7,288	96,917	94,773	87,485	3,297	84,188	3,272	7,288	2,339	62.1
1977	158,559	90,546	6,855	99,534	97,401	90,546	3,244	87,302	3,297	6,855	1,911	62.8
1977: July	158,682	92,372	6,941	99,442	97,307	90,588	3,206	87,382	3,464	6,719	1,824	62.7
Aug	158,899	92,315	6,757	99,751	97,614	90,793	3,224	87,569	3,253	6,821	1,800	62.8
Sept	159,114	91,247	6,437	99,887	97,756	91,088	3,199	87,889	3,306	6,668	1,834	62.8
Oct	159,334	92,230	6,221	100,205	98,071	91,383	3,243	88,140	3,263	6,688	1,848	62.9
Nov	159,522	92,473	6,346	101,009	98,877	92,214	3,357	88,857	3,285	6,663	1,829	63.3
Dec	159,736	92,623	5,880	101,048	98,919	92,609	3,323	89,286	3,220	6,310	1,797	63.3
1978: Jan*	159,937	91,053	6,897	101,228	99,107	92,881	3,354	89,527	2,986	6,226	1,688	63.3
Feb	160,128	91,185	6,739	101,217	99,093	93,003	3,242	89,761	3,193	6,090	1,568	63.3
Mar	160,313	91,964	6,479	101,536	99,414	93,266	3,310	89,956	3,164	6,148	1,463	63.3
Apr	160,504	93,180	5,685	101,902	99,784	93,801	3,275	90,526	3,327	5,983	1,384	63.5
May	160,713	93,851	5,457	102,374	100,261	94,112	3,235	90,877	3,243	6,149	1,358	63.7
June	160,928	95,852	6,326	102,671	100,573	94,819	3,473	91,346	3,458	5,754	1,231	63.8
July	161,148	96,202	6,438	102,734	100,618	94,425	3,387	91,038	3,330	6,193	1,292	63.8

[1] Persons at work. Economic reasons include slack work, material shortages, inability to find full-time work, etc.

[2] Total labor force as percent of noninstitutional population 16 years of age and over.

* Beginning 1978, data not strictly comparable with earlier data because of revisions in the household survey, which added about 250,000 to labor force and to employment.

Source: Economic Indicators, Council of Economic Advisors.

Source: Department of Labor, Bureau of Labor Statistics.

SELECTED UNEMPLOYMENT RATES

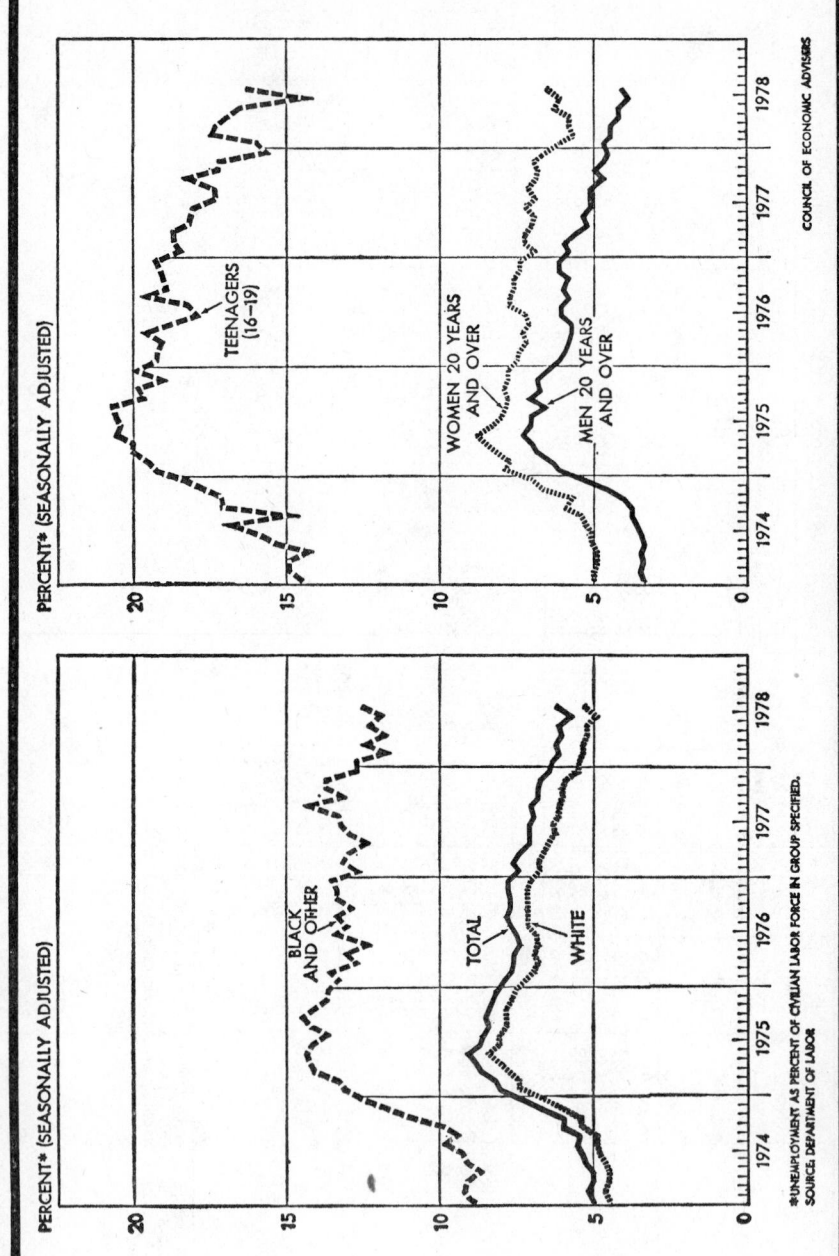

[Monthly data seasonally adjusted]

| Period | Unemployment rate (percent of civilian labor force in group) | | | | | | | | | | Labor force time lost (percent) [1] |
| | By sex and age | | | | By race | | By selected groups | | | | |
	Total (all civilian workers)	Men 20 years and over	Women 20 years and over	Both sexes 16–19 years	White	Black and other	Experienced wage and salary workers	Household heads	Full-time workers	Part-time workers	
1973	4.9	3.2	4.8	14.5	4.3	8.9	4.5	2.9	4.3	7.9	5.2
1974	5.6	3.8	5.5	16.0	5.0	9.9	5.3	3.3	5.1	8.6	6.1
1975	8.5	6.7	8.0	19.9	7.8	13.9	8.2	5.8	8.1	10.3	9.1
1976	7.7	5.9	7.4	19.0	7.0	13.1	7.3	5.1	7.3	10.1	8.3
1977	7.0	5.2	7.0	17.7	6.2	13.1	6.6	4.5	6.5	9.8	7.6
1977: July	6.9	5.1	6.9	17.3	6.1	13.3	6.4	4.4	6.5	9.3	7.5
Aug	7.0	5.1	7.1	17.3	6.1	14.3	6.5	4.5	6.6	9.0	7.6
Sept	6.8	4.7	6.9	18.3	6.0	13.1	6.3	4.4	6.4	9.7	7.4
Oct	6.8	5.0	6.8	17.3	6.0	13.7	6.5	4.4	6.4	9.6	7.4
Nov	6.7	4.7	6.9	17.2	5.9	13.7	6.3	4.2	6.2	9.6	7.3
Dec	6.4	4.6	6.6	15.6	5.5	12.7	6.0	4.0	5.9	8.9	7.0
1978: Jan	6.3	4.7	6.1	16.0	5.5	12.7	5.9	3.8	5.8	8.9	6.8
Feb	6.1	4.5	5.7	17.4	5.3	11.8	5.7	3.6	5.7	8.6	6.6
Mar	6.2	4.5	5.8	17.3	5.3	12.4	5.7	3.7	5.6	9.6	6.6
Apr	6.0	4.2	5.8	16.9	5.2	11.8	5.5	3.6	5.6	9.2	6.3
May	6.1	4.2	6.3	16.5	5.2	12.3	5.6	3.7	5.6	8.8	6.6
June	5.7	3.9	6.1	14.2	4.9	11.9	5.4	3.6	5.2	8.8	6.4
July	6.2	4.1	6.5	16.3	5.3	12.5	5.7	3.9	5.7	8.8	6.8

[1] Aggregate hours lost by the unemployed and persons on part-time for economic reasons as percent of potentially available labor force hours.

Source: Department of Labor, Bureau of Labor Statistics.

Source: *Economic Indicators*, Council of Economic Advisors.

EMPLOYMENT BY INDUSTRY DIVISION AND MAJOR MANUFACTURING GROUP, SEASONALLY ADJUSTED

Nonagricultural payroll data, in thousands

Industry division and group	1976 Apr.	May	June	July	Aug.	Sept.	Oct.	Nov.	Dec.	1977 Jan.	Feb.	Mar.	Apr.P
TOTAL	79,312	79,319	79,368	79,513	79,618	79,918	79,819	80,106	80,344	80,561	80,824	81,372	81,644
MINING	775	776	781	791	752	798	800	805	808	817	823	840	848
CONTRACT CONSTRUCTION	3,620	3,605	3,592	3,608	3,579	3,565	3,582	3,619	3,605	3,561	3,645	3,746	3,822
MANUFACTURING	19,008	19,000	18,984	18,945	18,979	19,100	18,941	19,065	19,095	ʳ19,211	19,233	19,399	19,481
Production workers	13,700	13,693	13,665	13,618	13,627	13,749	13,575	13,675	13,691	13,801	13,810	13,964	14,039
Durable goods	11,016	11,062	11,059	11,034	11,083	11,146	11,018	11,128	11,158	11,236	11,230	11,369	11,392
Production workers	7,871	7,916	7,905	7,878	7,911	7,975	7,833	7,929	7,955	8,026	8,011	8,131	8,153
Ordnance and accessories	160	160	158	156	157	156	155	156	156	156	156	156	157
Lumber and wood products	600	601	601	605	605	613	613	621	626	625	626	634	636
Furniture and fixtures	493	496	493	490	486	495	491	491	493	494	497	505	508
Stone, clay, and glass products	626	627	628	631	628	630	630	636	629	631	620	642	648
Primary metal industries	1,187	1,193	1,200	1,206	1,215	1,216	1,194	1,186	1,182	1,183	1,178	1,199	1,210
Fabricated metal products	1,387	1,392	1,390	1,387	1,394	1,404	1,387	1,396	1,404	1,413	1,416	1,432	1,436
Machinery, except electrical	2,056	2,068	2,069	2,084	2,090	2,115	2,078	2,106	2,107	2,125	2,134	2,135	2,144
Electrical equipment	1,830	1,837	1,837	1,815	1,843	1,848	1,849	1,860	1,863	1,874	1,888	1,909	1,917
Transportation equipment	1,742	1,747	1,743	1,728	1,737	1,737	1,695	1,749	1,766	1,790	1,766	1,808	1,792
Instruments and related products	509	512	513	512	510	512	511	514	517	521	524	525	520
Miscellaneous manufacturing	426	429	427	420	418	420	415	413	415	424	425	424	424
Nondurable goods	7,992	7,938	7,925	7,911	7,896	7,954	7,923	7,937	7,937	7,975	8,003	8,030	8,089
Production workers	5,829	5,777	5,760	5,740	5,716	5,774	5,742	5,746	5,736	5,775	5,799	5,833	5,886
Food and kindred products	1,707	1,712	1,718	1,719	1,715	1,711	1,706	1,711	1,710	1,721	1,727	1,729	1,732
Tobacco manufactures	76	76	75	80	78	76	76	75	75	74	73	72	73
Textile mill products	973	977	973	970	969	971	961	960	957	958	964	973	983
Apparel and other textile products	1,322	1,321	1,320	1,299	1,292	1,281	1,273	1,276	1,271	1,278	1,280	1,284	1,294
Paper and allied products	677	679	678	680	679	681	677	680	680	684	688	689	697
Printing and publishing	1,076	1,079	1,077	1,082	1,082	1,086	1,087	1,089	1,089	1,090	1,095	1,098	1,097
Chemicals and allied products	1,036	1,034	1,029	1,037	1,040	1,035	1,032	1,038	1,041	1,044	1,050	1,048	1,056
Petroleum and coal products	205	203	202	201	202	202	202	203	204	205	205	206	212
Rubber and plastics products, n.e.c.	641	578	577	572	572	643	645	642	647	656	656	665	678
Leather and leather products	279	279	276	271	267	268	264	263	263	265	265	266	267

TRANSPORTATION AND PUBLIC UTILITIES	4.510	4.503	4.482	4.508	4.501	4.528	4.506	4.519	4.553	4.549	4.553	4.567	4.575
WHOLESALE AND RETAIL TRADE	17,662	17,663	17,664	17,737	17,764	17,839	17,824	17,308	17,898	17,981	18,067	18,172	18,196
Wholesale trade	4,250	4,258	4,254	4,271	4,272	4,283	4,292	4,291	4,304	4,323	4,334	4,349	4,370
Retail trade	13,412	13,405	13,410	13,466	13,492	13,556	13,532	13,517	13,594	13,658	13,733	13,823	13,826
FINANCE, INSURANCE, AND REAL ESTATE	4,289	4,282	4,301	4,312	4,312	4,338	4,359	4,381	4,403	4,423	4,431	4,450	4,467
SERVICES[1]	14,536	14,567	14,610	14,664	14,751	14,798	14,819	14,873	14,936	15,010	15,068	15,153	15,200
Hotels and other lodging places	1,053	1,056	1,044	1,060	1,061	1,068	1,069	1,071	1,090	1,099	1,084	1,088	......
Personal services	826	824	822	823	c823	c817	c814	809	808	808	807	810	......
Medical and other health services	4,385	4,409	4,439	4,417	4,476	4,505	4,519	4,548	4,577	4,584	4,603	4,639	......
Educational services	1,262	1,255	1,248	1,248	1,252	1,266	1,283	1,277	1,271	1,269	1,282	1,283	......
GOVERNMENT	14,912	14,923	14,954	14,948	14,980	14,952	14,988	15,036	15,046	15,009	15,004	15,045	15,055
Federal	2,733	2,730	2,728	2,723	2,732	2,728	2,730	2,734	2,720	2,721	2,721	2,725	2,724
State and local	12,179	12,193	12,226	12,225	12,248	12,224	12,258	12,302	12,326	12,288	12,283	12,320	12,331

c = corrected.

Source: *Monthly Labor Review*, U.S. Department of Labor, Bureau of Labor Statistics.

LABOR TURNOVER RATES IN MANUFACTURING, 1974 TO DATE

Per 100 employees

Year	Annual average	Jan.	Feb.	Mar.	Apr.	May	June	July	Aug.	Sept.	Oct.	Nov.	Dec.
Total accessions													
1974	4.2	4.2	3.6	4.0	4.4	5.1	5.4	4.8	5.4	4.9	3.8	2.4	1.8
1975	3.7	3.0	2.7	3.2	3.7	3.9	4.5	4.5	5.1	4.6	3.7	2.8	2.2
1976	3.9	3.8	3.5	4.2	3.9	4.4	4.8	4.2	5.1	4.4	3.5	3.0	2.2
1977	....	3.7	3.7	p4.2									
New hires													
1974	3.2	3.2	2.7	3.0	3.3	3.9	4.3	3.7	4.2	3.9	2.9	1.7	1.0
1975	2.0	1.3	1.2	1.3	1.6	2.0	2.5	2.6	3.1	3.0	2.4	1.7	1.3
1976	2.6	2.1	2.1	2.6	2.5	3.0	3.6	2.8	3.5	3.2	2.5	1.9	1.3
1977	....	2.2	2.1	p2.7									
Total separations													
1974	4.8	4.9	4.0	4.4	4.2	4.4	4.2	4.9	6.1	5.4	5.0	5.0	5.2
1975	4.2	6.2	4.5	4.2	4.0	3.9	3.6	4.4	4.6	4.3	4.0	3.5	3.4
1976	3.8	3.7	3.1	3.5	3.5	3.4	3.5	4.3	4.9	4.6	4.1	3.4	3.5
1977	....	3.9	3.4	p3.5									
Quits													
1974	2.3	2.2	1.9	2.3	2.4	2.6	2.5	2.5	4.0	3.2	2.2	1.4	0.9
1975	1.4	1.1	.9	1.0	1.1	1.3	1.3	1.5	2.4	2.0	1.6	1.2	.9
1976	1.7	1.3	1.2	1.5	1.6	1.7	1.8	1.8	2.8	2.4	1.7	1.2	1.0
1977	....	1.4	1.3	p1.6									
Layoffs													
1974	1.5	1.7	1.2	1.1	0.9	0.8	0.8	1.4	1.1	1.2	1.8	1.4	3.6
1975	2.1	4.1	2.9	2.5	2.1	1.8	1.5	2.0	1.3	1.4	1.6	1.7	1.9
1976	1.3	1.6	1.1	1.1	1.1	.9	.9	1.6	1.1	1.3	1.5	1.5	1.8
1977	....	1.7	1.4	p1.0									

Source: *Monthly Labor Review*, U.S. Department of Labor, Bureau of Labor Statistics.

LABOR TURNOVER RATES IN MANUFACTURING, BY MAJOR INDUSTRY GROUP

Per 100 employees

Major industry group	Accession rates — Total Mar. 1976	Total Feb. 1977	Total Mar. 1977p	New hires Mar. 1976	New hires Feb. 1977	New hires Mar. 1977p	Separation rates — Total Mar. 1976	Total Feb. 1977	Total Mar. 1977p	Quits Mar. 1976	Quits Feb. 1977	Quits Mar. 1977p	Layoffs Mar. 1976	Layoffs Feb. 1977	Layoffs Mar. 1977p
Manufacturing	4.2	3.7	4.2	2.6	2.1	2.7	3.5	3.4	3.5	1.5	1.3	1.3	1.1	1.4	1.0
Seasonally adjusted	4.4	4.6	4.5	3.0	2.9	3.1	3.8	4.1	3.8	1.8	1.9	1.9	1.1	1.4	1.0
Durable goods	4.0	3.7	4.1	2.3	1.9	2.5	3.2	3.3	3.1	1.2	1.1	1.1	1.1	1.4	.8
Ordnance and accessories	1.6	1.8		.9	.9		1.7	2.0		.5	.5		.6	1.0	
Lumber and wood products	6.6	5.1	6.6	4.8	3.3	5.0	5.3	4.7	5.1	2.7	2.1	2.1	1.6	1.8	1.2
Furniture and fixtures	5.6	4.7	5.1	4.5	3.4	3.8	5.1	4.5	5.1	3.1	2.3	2.3	.9	1.4	1.0
Stone, clay, and glass products	5.0	5.0	6.4	2.4	1.9	2.9	3.3	4.9	3.2	1.3	1.0	1.0	1.2	3.1	1.0
Primary metal industries	4.0	3.9	4.3	1.3	1.0	1.4	2.6	3.3	2.2	.6	.5	.5	1.1	2.0	.8
Fabricated metal products	4.4	4.2		2.8	2.2		3.7	3.8		1.4	1.2		1.4	1.7	
Machinery, except electrical	2.9	2.7	2.7	1.6	1.7	2.0	2.6	2.4	2.4	.9	.8	.9	1.0	1.0	.6
Electrical equipment	3.6	2.9		2.0	1.6		2.7	2.7		1.1	.9		.7	.9	
Transportation equipment	4.3	3.9		2.3	1.9		3.3	3.4		1.1	1.0		1.2	1.5	
Instruments and related products	2.6	2.5	2.9	2.0	1.8	2.3	2.1	2.3	2.9	.9	.8	1.0	.4	.5	.7
Miscellaneous manufacturing	5.3	5.0	4.9	3.7	2.9	3.1	4.1	4.0	4.2	2.0	1.8	1.8	1.3	1.4	1.4
Nondurable goods	4.3	3.7	4.2	3.0	2.3	2.9	3.9	3.5	4.0	2.0	1.5	1.5	1.1	1.3	1.2
Food and kindred products	5.0	4.1	5.1	3.1	2.3	3.1	5.0	4.2	5.3	2.1	1.7	1.7	2.2	1.9	2.4
Tobacco manufactures	1.6	1.0		1.1	.5		4.0	6.0		.6	.3		2.7	5.0	
Textile mill products	5.5	4.0	4.8	4.2	2.8	3.8	4.8	3.8	4.3	3.1	2.1	2.1	.6	.8	.6
Apparel and other products	6.0	5.7	5.9	4.2	3.3	3.7	5.2	5.1	5.6	2.9	2.3	2.3	1.4	2.0	.9
Paper and allied products	3.1	2.5	2.6	2.1	1.4	1.8	2.5	2.4	2.4	1.0	.8	.8	.9	1.0	.6
Printing and publishing	2.8	2.7	3.0	2.0	2.1	2.3	2.6	2.6	2.5	1.4	1.3	1.3	.7	.8	.6
Chemicals and allied products	2.1	1.9	1.9	1.5	1.2	1.4	1.6	1.5	1.5	.7	.5	.5	.4	.5	.3
Petroleum and coal products	2.0	1.8	2.3	1.4	1.3	1.7	1.6	1.7	1.6	.6	.6	.6	.3	.4	.3
Rubber and plastics products, n.e.c	5.2	4.1	5.1	3.7	2.9	3.7	4.0	3.7	4.5	2.1	1.7	1.7	.9	1.1	1.1
Leather and leather products	7.0	5.6	6.4	5.3	3.4	4.5	6.0	5.3	5.7	3.5	2.6	2.6	1.2	1.8	1.4

Source: *Monthly Labor Review*, U.S. Department of Labor, Bureau of Labor Statistics.

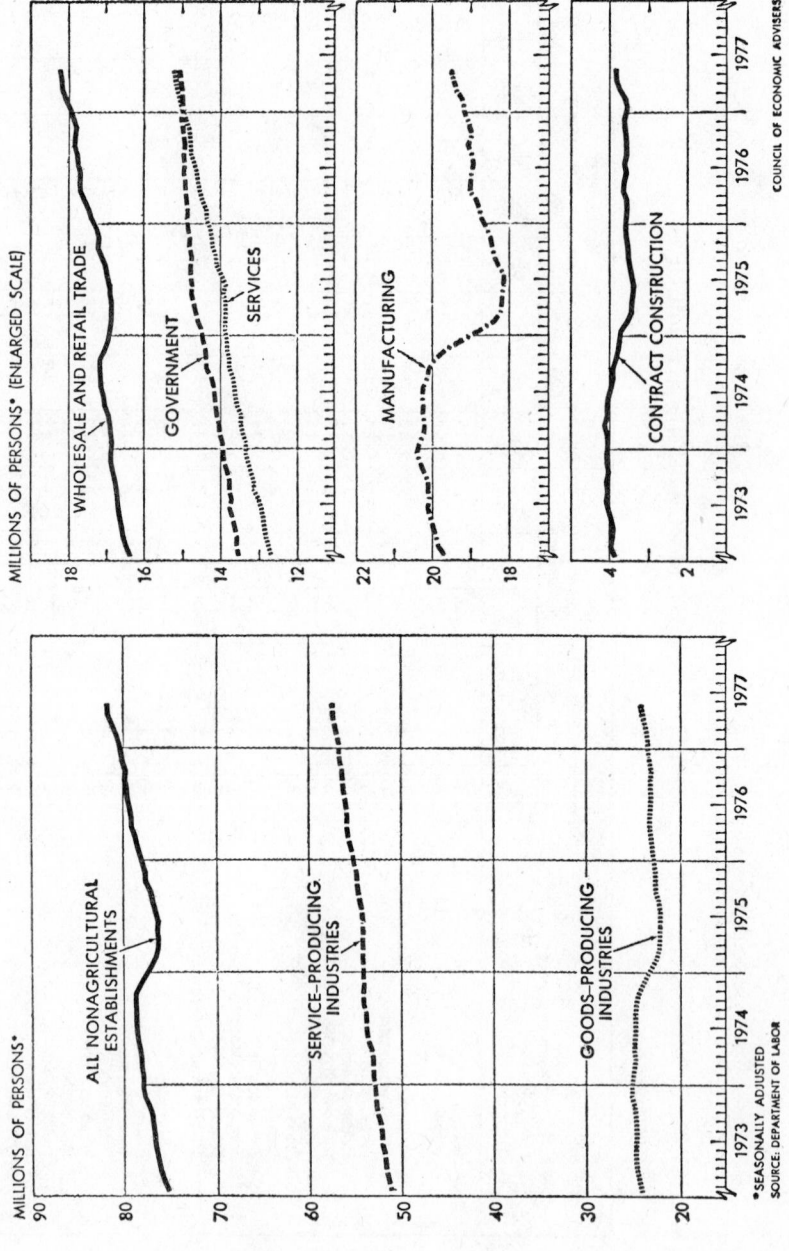

NONAGRICULTURAL EMPLOYMENT

MILLIONS OF PERSONS*

*SEASONALLY ADJUSTED
SOURCE: DEPARTMENT OF LABOR

MILLIONS OF PERSONS* (ENLARGED SCALE)

COUNCIL OF ECONOMIC ADVISERS

[Thousands of wage and salary workers;[1] seasonally adjusted]

Period	Total nonagricultural employment	Goods-producing industries					Service-producing industries						
		Total[2]	Contract construction	Manufacturing			Total	Transportation and public utilities	Wholesale and retail trade	Finance, insurance, and real estate	Services	Government	
				Total	Durable goods	Non-durable goods						Federal	State and local
1972	73,714	23,546	3,831	19,090	11,006	8,084	50,167	4,517	15,975	3,943	12,392	2,684	10,655
1973	76,896	24,727	4,015	20,068	11,839	8,229	52,169	4,644	16,674	4,091	13,021	2,663	11,073
1974	78,413	24,697	3,957	20,046	11,895	8,151	53,715	4,696	17,017	4,208	13,617	2,724	11,459
1975	77,051	22,603	3,512	18,347	10,679	7,668	54,448	4,498	17,000	4,223	14,006	2,748	11,973
1976	79,443	23,332	3,594	18,956	11,026	7,930	56,111	4,509	17,694	4,316	14,644	2,733	12,215
1976: May	79,319	23,381	3,605	19,000	11,062	7,938	55,938	4,503	17,663	4,282	14,567	2,730	12,193
June	79,368	23,357	3,592	18,984	11,059	7,925	56,011	4,482	17,664	4,301	14,610	2,728	12,226
July	79,513	23,344	3,608	18,945	11,034	7,911	56,169	4,508	17,737	4,312	14,664	2,723	12,225
Aug	79,618	23,310	3,579	18,979	11,083	7,896	56,308	4,501	17,764	4,338	14,751	2,732	12,248
Sept	79,918	23,323	3,565	19,100	11,146	7,954	56,455	4,528	17,839	4,359	14,798	2,728	12,224
Oct	79,819	23,323	3,582	18,941	11,018	7,923	56,496	4,506	17,824	4,381	14,819	2,730	12,258
Nov	80,106	23,489	3,619	19,065	11,128	7,937	56,617	4,519	17,808	4,403	14,873	2,734	12,302
Dec	80,344	23,508	3,605	19,095	11,158	7,937	56,836	4,553	17,898	4,423	14,936	2,720	12,326
1977: Jan	80,561	23,589	3,561	19,211	11,236	7,975	56,972	4,549	17,981	4,431	15,010	2,721	12,288
Feb	80,824	23,701	3,645	19,233	11,230	8,003	57,123	4,553	18,067	4,453	15,068	2,721	12,283
Mar	81,395	24,005	3,759	19,404	11,370	8,034	57,390	4,568	18,189	4,459	15,149	2,725	12,306
Apr p	81,605	24,163	3,835	19,481	11,392	8,089	57,442	4,568	18,194	4,477	15,171	2,719	12,331
May p	81,792	24,244	3,848	19,547	11,445	8,102	57,548	4,578	18,214	4,477	15,202	2,717	12,360

[1] Includes all full- and part-time wage and salary workers in nonagricultural establishments who worked during or received pay for any part of the pay period which includes the 12th of the month. Excludes proprietors, self-employed persons, domestic servants, and personnel of the Armed Forces. Total derived from this table not comparable with estimates of nonagricultural employment of the civilian labor force, which include proprietors, self-employed persons, and domestic servants; which count persons as employed when they are not at work because of industrial disputes; and which are based on a sample of the working-age population, whereas the estimates in this table are based on reports from employing establishments.

[2] Includes mining, not shown separately.

Source: Department of Labor, Bureau of Labor Statistics.

Source: Economic Indicators, Council of Economic Advisors.

PRICE, WAGE, AND PRODUCTIVITY: SUMMARY OF CHANGES 1968–1977

Percent change, seasonally adjusted annual rate

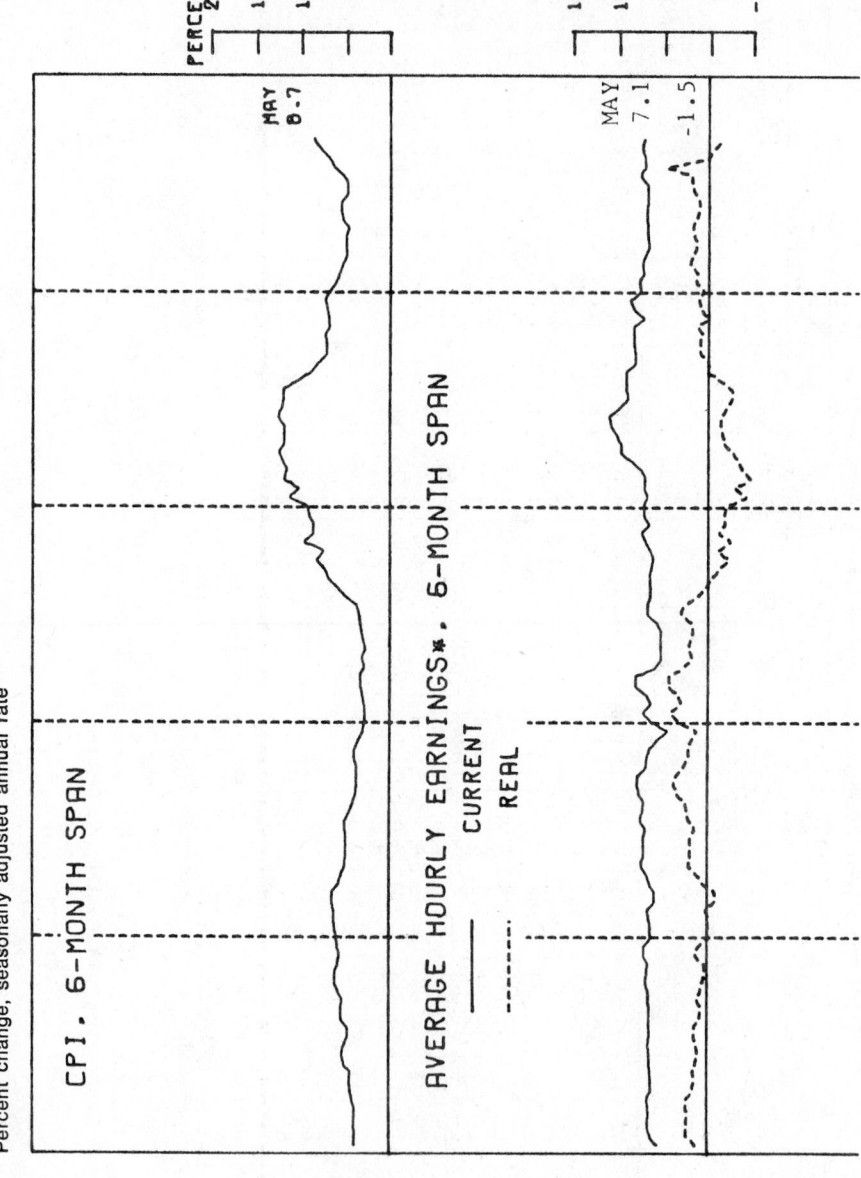

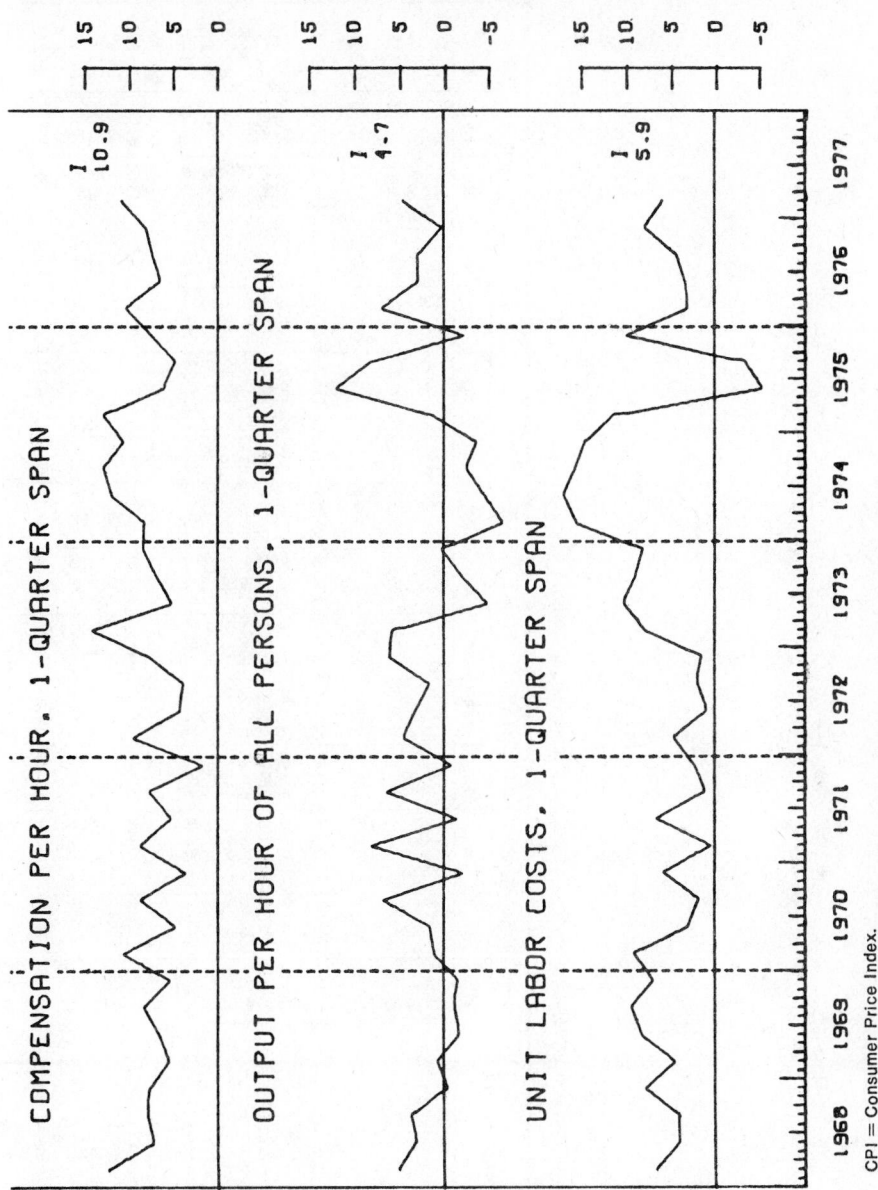

CPI = Consumer Price Index.
Source: *Chartbook on Prices, Wages, and Productivity*, Bureau of Labor Statistics.

WEEKLY EARNINGS, BY INDUSTRY DIVISION AND MAJOR MANUFACTURING GROUP

Gross averages, production or nonsupervisory workers on private nonagricultural payrolls

Industry division and group	Annual average		1976									1977			
	1975	1976	Apr.	May	June	July	Aug.	Sept.	Oct.	Nov.	Dec.	Jan.	Feb.	Mar.P	Apr.P
TOTAL PRIVATE	$163.89	$176.29	$171.12	$174.36	$176.54	$177.88	$178.97	$179.55	$180.28	$180.50	$182.73	$179.48	$182.73	$183.45	$184.53
MINING	249.57	274.78	267.76	269.88	270.50	272.85	259.15	289.08	287.33	288.63	293.23	286.62	292.71	294.50	294.19
CONTRACT CONSTRUCTION	265.35	284.93	278.25	283.09	288.04	291.07	292.21	287.41	299.87	289.25	289.98	269.84	288.41	287.31	288.51
MANUFACTURING	189.51	207.60	198.74	205.82	208.06	208.00	208.40	212.93	211.20	215.20	220.05	212.94	216.66	220.70	220.80
Durable goods	205.09	225.33	214.24	224.54	227.28	224.78	225.99	229.80	228.17	232.31	238.71	229.50	233.92	238.68	239.32
Ordnance and accessories	216.00	232.80	220.81	229.55	232.37	232.88	232.53	235.17	239.13	243.98	251.68	244.82	246.04	250.51	252.35
Lumber and wood products	167.35	189.34	180.80	186.24	193.26	194.32	196.10	195.77	197.72	193.91	197.15	191.57	197.38	194.22	194.53
Furniture and fixtures	142.13	154.03	148.19	151.70	154.44	151.65	156.39	156.33	157.53	157.92	162.31	151.06	156.00	159.68	158.00
Stone, clay, and glass products	198.53	217.95	212.16	218.29	221.01	219.60	222.44	224.80	226.97	225.09	225.36	214.50	225.48	228.93	232.25
Primary metal industries	246.80	276.08	274.19	275.26	279.60	280.03	280.95	283.56	276.69	279.68	283.50	281.20	285.22	293.45	297.05
Fabricated metal products	201.60	221.00	207.64	221.40	224.67	220.05	223.86	226.59	222.89	226.73	231.54	219.85	225.03	230.11	230.70
Machinery, except electrical	219.22	236.74	224.80	233.29	235.66	234.60	237.39	240.26	240.20	246.45	253.38	243.41	248.63	250.66	248.66
Electrical equipment	180.91	196.40	185.64	193.76	195.05	193.55	198.00	200.80	202.21	205.84	210.64	201.76	208.35	208.64	208.68
Transportation equipment	242.61	272.06	251.77	275.40	279.06	273.00	266.67	276.81	272.41	280.98	295.64	282.17	281.67	298.92	298.07
Instruments and related products	180.12	196.75	188.42	195.77	195.62	196.66	196.98	198.19	199.49	203.59	210.73	201.45	207.06	205.02	205.53
Miscellaneous manufacturing	145.16	155.19	150.10	154.41	154.41	154.37	154.00	154.37	157.93	160.34	164.27	159.42	167.03	168.20	165.21

Nondurable goods	168.78	183.92	176.72	180.85	182.03	183.85	184.24	189.12	188.16	190.70	194.53	189.59	192.76	194.04	194.72
Food and kindred products	184.17	199.89	192.27	196.00	197.78	200.38	202.69	205.32	203.62	205.64	208.98	204.62	207.23	207.11	208.03
Tobacco manufactures	171.38	185.60	195.07	195.45	199.79	169.00	172.33	175.77	181.50	185.55	193.03	184.21	206.75	206.39	209.25
Textile mill products	133.28	147.17	136.93	144.59	146.11	148.03	148.50	148.93	149.71	152.40	154.73	150.52	154.37	155.54	155.96
Apparel and other textile products	111.97	121.40	117.28	121.00	122.06	120.68	121.75	122.85	123.20	123.90	124.26	119.60	125.32	126.74	124.95
Paper and allied products	207.58	230.23	218.82	225.68	229.61	231.38	233.20	237.71	235.61	239.41	243.95	237.84	239.55	242.53	245.23
Printing and publishing	198.32	213.38	206.64	212.25	211.88	213.19	215.27	218.86	216.95	220.00	224.44	219.04	222.38	224.47	221.49
Chemicals and allied products	219.63	245.02	240.61	240.86	242.94	244.50	243.72	253.68	251.26	254.56	258.49	255.85	256.47	258.96	261.25
Petroleum and coal products	267.07	301.31	300.46	300.04	300.04	303.74	299.46	309.02	306.00	307.10	309.10	307.84	318.93	324.44	332.78
Rubber and plastics products, n.e.c.	172.70	188.03	177.30	176.58	177.39	175.56	176.44	198.37	199.75	204.52	209.92	206.35	207.74	207.65	207.77
Leather and leather products	120.80	128.31	126.17	131.33	129.65	127.53	127.31	126.32	125.96	127.75	129.90	123.88	131.40	131.40	131.04
TRANSPORTATION AND PUBLIC UTILITIES	234.43	257.75	251.46	252.41	256.80	259.69	265.02	265.06	265.20	267.33	269.33	264.65	270.95	268.13	271.20
WHOLESALE AND RETAIL TRADE	126.75	133.39	130.99	132.33	133.51	136.62	136.51	135.74	135.20	135.46	137.97	136.78	138.60	139.02	139.68
Wholesale trade	188.75	200.98	196.86	199.82	199.95	203.18	203.19	204.61	204.34	205.50	208.26	208.29	209.52	209.37	211.53
Retail trade	108.22	113.96	112.35	112.29	114.02	116.82	117.15	115.88	115.43	115.34	118.63	116.00	117.69	118.06	118.76
FINANCE, INSURANCE, AND REAL ESTATE	150.75	159.58	158.84	160.01	158.84	160.01	162.36	160.67	161.85	161.04	162.58	166.34	165.88	165.07	165.43
SERVICES	137.23	146.06	143.19	144.96	145.82	146.88	146.88	148.07	148.74	149.97	150.97	153.18	153.97	153.38	154.51

Source: *Monthly Labor Review*, U.S. Department of Labor, Bureau of Labor Statistics.

HOURS AND EARNINGS, BY INDUSTRY DIVISION, 1947–1976

Gross averages, production or nonsupervisory workers on nonagricultural payrolls

Year	Total private			Mining			Contract construction			Manufacturing		
	Average weekly earnings	Average weekly hours	Average hourly earnings	Average weekly earnings	Average weekly hours	Average hourly earnings	Average weekly earnings	Average weekly hours	Average hourly earnings	Average weekly earnings	Average weekly hours	Average hourly earnings
1947	$45.58	40.3	$1.131	$59.94	40.8	$1.469	$58.87	38.2	$1.541	$49.17	40.4	$1.217
1948	49.00	40.0	1.225	65.56	39.4	1.664	65.27	38.1	1.713	53.12	40.0	1.328
1949	50.24	39.4	1.275	62.33	36.3	1.717	67.56	37.7	1.792	53.88	39.1	1.378
1950	53.13	39.8	1.335	67.16	37.9	1.772	69.68	37.4	1.863	58.32	40.5	1.440
1951	57.86	39.9	1.45	74.11	38.4	1.93	76.96	38.1	2.02	63.34	40.6	1.56
1952	60.65	39.9	1.52	77.59	38.6	2.01	82.86	38.9	2.13	67.16	40.7	1.65
1953	63.76	39.6	1.61	83.03	38.8	2.14	86.41	37.9	2.28	70.47	40.5	1.74
1954	64.52	39.1	1.65	82.60	38.6	2.14	88.91	37.2	2.39	70.49	39.6	1.78
1955	67.72	39.6	1.71	89.54	40.7	2.20	90.90	37.1	2.45	75.70	40.7	1.86
1956	70.74	39.3	1.80	95.06	40.8	2.33	96.38	37.5	2.57	78.78	40.4	1.95
1957	73.33	38.8	1.89	98.65	40.1	2.46	100.27	37.0	2.71	81.59	39.8	2.05
1958	75.08	38.5	1.95	96.08	38.9	2.47	103.78	36.8	2.82	82.71	39.2	2.11
1959	78.78	39.0	2.02	103.68	40.5	2.56	108.41	37.0	2.93	88.26	40.3	2.19
1960	80.67	38.6	2.09	105.44	40.4	2.61	113.04	36.7	3.08	89.72	39.7	2.26
1961	82.60	38.6	2.14	106.92	40.5	2.64	118.08	36.9	3.20	92.34	39.8	2.32
1962	85.91	38.7	2.22	110.43	40.9	2.70	122.47	37.0	3.31	96.56	40.4	2.39
1963	88.46	38.8	2.28	114.40	41.6	2.75	127.19	37.3	3.41	99.63	40.5	2.46
1964	91.33	38.7	2.36	117.74	41.9	2.81	132.06	37.2	3.55	102.97	40.7	2.53
1965	95.06	38.8	2.45	123.52	42.3	2.92	138.38	37.4	3.70	107.53	41.2	2.61
1966	98.82	38.6	2.56	130.24	42.7	3.05	146.26	37.6	3.89	112.34	41.3	2.72
1967	101.84	38.0	2.68	135.89	42.6	3.19	154.95	37.3	4.11	114.90	40.6	2.83
1968	107.73	37.8	2.85	142.71	42.6	3.35	164.49	37.3	4.41	122.51	40.7	3.01
1969	114.61	37.7	3.04	155.23	43.0	3.61	181.54	37.9	4.79	129.51	40.6	3.19
1970	119.46	37.1	3.22	164.40	42.7	3.85	195.45	37.3	5.24	133.73	39.8	3.36
1971	127.28	37.0	3.44	172.14	42.4	4.06	211.67	37.2	5.69	142.44	39.9	3.57
1972	136.16	37.1	3.67	187.43	42.5	4.41	222.51	36.9	6.03	154.69	40.6	3.81
1973	145.43	37.1	3.92	201.03	42.5	4.73	235.69	37.0	6.37	166.06	40.7	4.08
1974	154.45	36.6	4.22	220.90	42.4	5.21	249.08	36.9	6.75	176.40	40.0	4.41
1975	163.89	36.1	4.54	249.57	42.3	5.90	265.35	36.6	7.25	189.51	39.4	4.81
1976	176.29	36.2	4.87	274.78	42.8	6.42	284.93	37.1	7.68	207.60	40.0	5.19

Year	Transportation and public utilities			Wholesale and retail trade			Finance, insurance, and real estate			Services		
1947				$38.07	40.5	$0.940	$43.21	37.9	$1.140			
1948				40.80	40.4	1.010	45.48	37.9	1.200			
1949				42.93	40.5	1.060	47.63	37.8	1.260			
1950				44.55	40.5	1.100	50.52	37.7	1.340			
1951				47.79	40.5	1.18	54.67	37.7	1.45			
1952				49.20	40.0	1.23	57.08	37.8	1.51			
1953				51.35	39.5	1.30	59.57	37.7	1.58			
1954				53.33	39.5	1.35	62.04	37.6	1.65			
1955				55.16	39.4	1.40	63.92	37.6	1.70			
1956				57.48	39.1	1.47	65.68	36.9	1.78			
1957				59.60	38.7	1.54	67.53	36.7	1.84			
1958				61.76	38.6	1.60	70.12	37.1	1.89			
1959¹				64.41	38.8	1.66	72.74	37.3	1.95			
1960				66.01	38.6	1.71	75.14	37.2	2.02			
1961				67.41	38.3	1.76	77.12	36.9	2.09			
1962				69.91	38.2	1.83	80.94	37.3	2.17			
1963				72.01	38.1	1.89	84.38	37.5	2.25			
1964	$118.37	41.1	$2.88	74.28	37.9	1.96	85.79	37.3	2.30	$69.84	36.0	$1.94
1965	125.14	41.3	3.03	76.53	37.7	2.03	88.91	37.2	2.39	73.60	35.9	2.05
1966	128.13	41.2	3.11	79.02	37.1	2.13	92.13	37.3	2.47	77.04	35.5	2.17
1967	131.22	40.5	3.24	81.76	36.5	2.24	95.46	37.0	2.58	80.38	35.1	2.29
1968	138.85	40.6	3.42	86.40	36.0	2.40	101.75	37.0	2.75	83.97	34.7	2.42
1969	148.15	40.7	3.64	90.78	35.6	2.55	108.70	37.1	2.93	90.57	34.7	2.61
1970	155.93	40.5	3.85	95.66	35.3	2.71	113.34	36.8	3.08	96.66	34.4	2.81
1971	169.24	40.2	4.21	100.39	35.1	2.86	120.66	36.9	3.27	103.28	34.2	3.02
1972	187.92	40.5	4.64	105.65	35.1	3.01	126.88	37.1	3.42	110.14	34.1	3.23
1973	204.62	40.6	5.04	111.04	34.7	3.20	132.10	36.9	3.58	117.64	34.0	3.46
1974	218.29	40.2	5.43	118.33	34.1	3.47	140.19	36.7	3.82	127.46	33.9	3.76
1975	234.43	39.6	5.92	126.75	33.8	3.75	150.75	36.5	4.13	137.23	33.8	4.06
1976	257.75	39.9	6.46	133.39	33.6	3.97	159.58	36.6	4.36	146.06	33.5	4.36

¹ Data include Alaska and Hawaii beginning in 1959.

Source: *Monthly Labor Review*, U.S. Department of Labor, Bureau of Labor Statistics.

HOURLY EARNINGS, BY INDUSTRY DIVISION AND MAJOR MANUFACTURING GROUP

Gross averages, production or nonsupervisory workers on private nonagricultural payrolls

Industry division and group	Annual average		1976									1977			
	1975	1976	Apr.	May	June	July	Aug.	Sept.	Oct.	Nov.	Dec.	Jan.	Feb.	Mar.P	Apr.P
TOTAL PRIVATE	$4.54	$4.87	$4.78	$4.83	$4.85	$4.86	$4.89	$4.96	$4.98	$5.00	$5.02	$5.07	$5.09	$5.11	$5.14
MINING	5.90	6.42	6.33	6.35	6.32	6.39	6.29	6.60	6.56	6.62	6.71	6.76	6.76	6.77	6.81
CONTRACT CONSTRUCTION	7.25	7.68	7.50	7.61	7.60	7.68	7.71	7.81	7.85	7.86	7.88	7.96	7.88	7.85	7.84
MANUFACTURING	4.81	5.19	5.07	5.12	5.15	5.20	5.21	5.31	5.28	5.34	5.42	5.46	5.43	5.49	5.52
Durable goods	5.14	5.55	5.41	5.49	5.53	5.55	5.58	5.66	5.62	5.68	5.78	5.81	5.79	5.85	5.88
Ordnance and accessories	5.23	5.72	5.59	5.64	5.64	5.75	5.77	5.85	5.89	5.98	6.05	6.06	6.06	6.14	6.14
Lumber and wood products	4.28	4.71	4.52	4.61	4.76	4.81	4.83	4.87	4.87	4.86	4.88	4.95	4.91	4.88	4.90
Furniture and fixtures	3.75	3.98	3.91	3.93	3.96	3.97	4.01	4.05	4.06	4.07	4.13	4.15	4.16	4.18	4.18
Stone, clay and glass products	4.89	5.29	5.20	5.26	5.30	5.33	5.36	5.43	5.43	5.45	5.47	5.50	5.54	5.57	5.61
Primary metal industries	6.17	6.80	6.77	6.73	6.77	6.83	6.92	6.95	6.90	6.94	7.00	7.03	7.06	7.14	7.21
Fabricated metal products	5.04	5.43	5.27	5.40	5.44	5.42	5.46	5.54	5.49	5.53	5.62	5.58	5.57	5.64	5.67
Machinery, except electrical	5.36	5.76	5.62	5.69	5.72	5.75	5.79	5.86	5.83	5.91	5.99	6.01	6.02	6.04	6.05
Electrical equipment	4.58	4.91	4.76	4.82	4.84	4.90	4.95	5.02	5.03	5.07	5.15	5.16	5.17	5.19	5.23
Transportation equipment	6.02	6.54	6.31	6.48	6.52	6.50	6.52	6.67	6.58	6.69	6.94	6.95	6.87	7.05	7.03
Instruments and related products	4.56	4.87	4.77	4.81	4.83	4.88	4.90	4.93	4.95	4.99	5.09	5.10	5.10	5.10	5.10
Miscellaneous manufacturing	3.79	4.01	3.95	3.99	3.99	4.02	4.00	4.02	4.06	4.08	4.18	4.24	4.25	4.28	4.28

Nondurable goods	4.35	4.68	4.59	4.59	4.62	4.69	4.70	4.80	4.80	4.84	4.90	4.95	4.93	4.95	4.98
Food and kindred products	4.57	4.96	4.88	4.90	4.92	4.96	4.98	5.02	5.04	5.09	5.16	5.22	5.22	5.23	5.28
Tobacco manufactures	4.51	4.91	5.12	5.13	5.23	5.00	4.62	4.65	4.69	4.87	5.04	5.16	5.37	5.46	5.58
Textile mill products	3.40	3.67	3.52	3.57	3.59	3.71	3.75	3.78	3.79	3.81	3.83	3.83	3.84	3.85	3.87
Apparel and other textile products	3.19	3.41	3.37	3.38	3.40	3.39	3.42	3.49	3.49	3.50	3.52	3.57	3.55	3.57	3.57
Paper and allied products	4.99	5.43	5.26	5.31	5.39	5.47	5.50	5.58	5.57	5.62	5.66	5.69	5.69	5.72	5.77
Printing and publishing	5.36	5.69	5.60	5.66	5.65	5.67	5.71	5.79	5.77	5.82	5.86	5.92	5.93	5.97	5.97
Chemicals and allied products	5.37	5.89	5.77	5.79	5.84	5.92	5.93	6.04	6.04	6.09	6.14	6.18	6.18	6.21	6.25
Petroleum and coal products	6.42	7.14	7.12	7.11	7.11	7.13	7.13	7.22	7.20	7.26	7.29	7.40	7.63	7.67	7.83
Rubber and plastics products, n.e.c.	4.35	4.62	4.50	4.36	4.38	4.40	4.40	4.85	4.86	4.94	5.01	5.07	5.03	5.04	5.08
Leather and leather products	3.23	3.44	3.41	3.42	3.43	3.41	3.45	3.48	3.47	3.50	3.53	3.57	3.60	3.61	3.60
TRANSPORTATION AND PUBLIC UTILITIES	5.92	6.46	6.35	6.39	6.42	6.46	6.56	6.61	6.63	6.65	6.65	6.70	6.74	6.72	6.78
WHOLESALE AND RETAIL TRADE	3.75	3.97	3.91	3.95	3.95	3.96	3.98	4.04	4.06	4.08	4.07	4.17	4.20	4.20	4.22
Wholesale trade	4.89	5.18	5.10	5.15	5.14	5.17	5.21	5.26	5.28	5.31	5.34	5.41	5.40	5.41	5.48
Retail trade	3.34	3.55	3.50	3.52	3.53	3.54	3.55	3.61	3.63	3.65	3.65	3.73	3.76	3.76	3.77
FINANCE, INSURANCE, AND REAL ESTATE	4.13	4.36	4.34	4.36	4.34	4.36	4.40	4.39	4.41	4.40	4.43	4.52	4.52	4.51	4.52
SERVICES	4.06	4.36	4.30	4.34	4.34	4.32	4.32	4.42	4.44	4.49	4.52	4.60	4.61	4.62	4.64

Source: *Monthly Labor Review,* U.S. Department of Labor, Bureau of Labor Statistics.

HOURLY EARNINGS INDEX FOR PRODUCTION OR NONSUPERVISORY WORKERS ON PRIVATE NONAGRICULTURAL PAYROLLS, BY INDUSTRY DIVISION

Seasonally adjusted data: 1967 = 100

Industry	1976									1977				Percent change	
	Apr.	May	June	July	Aug.	Sept.	Oct.	Nov.	Dec.	Jan.	Feb.	Mar.P	Apr.P	Mar. 1977 to Apr. 1977	Apr. 1976 to Apr. 1977
TOTAL PRIVATE (in current dollars)	182.4	183.6	184.3	185.6	186.8	187.5	188.4	189.7	190.6	192.7	193.2	194.1	195.2	0.6	7.0
Mining	195.7	197.0	196.9	199.1	202.3	203.8	205.5	205.0	206.8	207.8	210.2	210.0	211.9	.9	8.3
Contract construction	183.3	185.2	185.8	188.0	187.1	186.4	187.9	189.2	189.5	192.4	190.8	191.1	191.9	.4	4.7
Manufacturing	181.9	182.5	183.6	185.4	186.7	188.1	188.4	189.8	191.0	192.3	193.3	194.5	195.4	.5	7.4
Transportation and public utilities	195.7	198.1	199.0	199.9	200.9	201.6	202.4	203.7	203.1	205.1	206.2	207.0	208.9	.9	6.8
Wholesale and retail trade	176.0	177.2	177.5	178.8	179.8	180.8	182.1	183.4	184.6	186.4	187.6	188.3	189.4	.6	7.6
Finance, insurance, and real estate	169.1	170.5	169.2	170.8	173.1	172.0	173.5	173.1	172.9	176.5	175.7	175.9	176.7	.4	4.5
Services	185.9	187.4	188.3	188.3	189.8	190.0	191.3	193.0	194.6	197.7	197.7	199.0	200.0	.5	7.6
TOTAL PRIVATE (in constant dollars)	108.3	108.3	108.3	108.5	108.7	108.7	108.9	109.3	109.4	109.7	109.0	108.8	108.6	-.2	.2

NOTE: Hourly Earnings Index data have been revised slightly as a result of corrections in the computerized data file and the introduction of more precision in the processing system.

Source: *Monthly Labor Review*, U.S. Department of Labor, Bureau of Labor Statistics.

TOTAL AND PER CAPITA PERSONAL INCOME AND QUARTERLY TOTAL PERSONAL INCOME, BY STATES AND REGIONS

State and region	Total personal income				Per capita personal income			
	Millions of dollars			Per-cent change	Dollars			Per-cent change
	1974 r	1975 p	1976 p	1975-76	1974 r	1975 r	1976 p	1975-76
United States	1,159,478	1,257,535	1,382,457	9.9	5,486	5,903	6,441	9.1
New England	68,820	74,106	80,536	8.7	5,668	6,080	6,590	8.4
Connecticut	19,999	21,558	22,981	6.6	6,481	6,965	7,373	5.9
Maine	4,760	5,070	5,762	13.6	4,536	4,785	5,385	12.5
Massachusetts	32,782	35,290	38,251	8.4	5,658	6,066	6,585	8.6
New Hampshire	4,082	4,396	4,912	11.7	5,051	5,375	5,973	11.1
Rhode Island	5,044	5,457	6,021	10.3	5,377	5,888	6,498	10.4
Vermont	2,152	2,337	2,610	11.7	4,602	4,962	5,480	10.4
Mideast	254,577	274,290	297,897	8.6	5,968	6,430	6,975	8.5
Delaware	3,628	3,906	4,244	8.6	6,284	6,745	7,290	8.1
District of Columbia	5,077	5,552	6,069	9.3	7,044	7,752	8,648	11.6
Maryland	24,426	26,469	29,161	10.2	5,973	6,459	7,036	8.9
New Jersey	45,711	49,135	53,327	8.5	6,243	6,716	7,269	8.2
New York	110,782	118,953	128,397	7.9	6,120	6,564	7,100	8.2
Pennsylvania	64,953	70,276	76,699	9.1	5,485	5,941	6,466	8.8
Great Lakes	234,448	251,116	278,076	10.7	5,732	6,128	6,793	10.9
Illinois	70,000	75,703	83,459	10.2	6,272	6,792	7,432	9.4
Indiana	28,143	30,042	33,175	10.4	5,297	5,656	6,257	10.6
Michigan	53,302	56,490	63,678	12.7	5,846	6,169	6,994	13.4
Ohio	58,896	62,747	68,759	9.6	5,481	5,832	6,432	10.3
Wisconsin	24,107	26,134	29,006	11.0	5,281	5,674	6,293	10.9
Plains	89,284	96,582	103,022	6.7	5,361	5,788	6,130	5.9
Iowa	15,884	17,437	18,478	6.0	5,561	6,076	6,439	6.0
Kansas	12,758	13,706	15,003	9.5	5,630	6,046	6,495	7.4
Minnesota	21,351	22,835	24,394	6.8	5,469	5,817	6,153	5.8
Missouri	24,082	26,146	28,693	9.7	5,047	5,490	6,005	9.4
Nebraska	8,270	9,413	9,690	2.9	5,379	6,106	6,240	2.2
North Dakota	3,629	3,680	3,474	-5.6	5,698	5,781	5,400	-6.6
South Dakota	3,311	3,364	3,290	-2.2	4,860	4,924	4,796	-2.6
Southeast	223,043	241,378	267,060	10.6	4,740	5,054	5,544	9.7
Alabama	15,317	16,799	18,711	11.4	4,285	4,648	5,105	9.8
Arkansas	9,055	9,770	10,700	9.5	4,379	4,617	5,073	9.9
Florida	43,742	47,069	51,434	9.3	5,406	5,640	6,108	8.3
Georgia	23,393	24,981	27,691	10.8	4,797	5,072	5,571	9.8
Kentucky	15,310	16,590	18,588	12.0	4,564	4,886	5,423	11.0
Louisiana	16,766	18,555	20,680	11.5	4,456	4,895	5,386	10.0
Mississippi	8,984	9,568	10,771	12.6	3,850	4,079	4,575	12.2
North Carolina	24,996	26,833	29,582	10.2	4,650	4,922	5,409	9.9
South Carolina	12,181	13,006	14,599	12.2	4,390	4,615	5,126	11.1
Tennessee	18,918	20,559	22,894	11.4	4,560	4,909	5,432	10.7
Virginia	26,389	28,732	31,581	9.9	5,375	5,786	6,276	8.5
West Virginia	7,993	8,916	9,822	10.2	4,479	4,946	5,394	9.1
Southwest	90,226	100,503	112,902	12.3	5,019	5,486	6,040	10.1
Arizona	11,121	11,822	13,208	11.7	5,152	5,316	5,817	9.4
New Mexico	4,810	5,467	6,089	11.4	4,299	4,768	5,213	9.3
Oklahoma	12,933	14,263	15,650	9.7	4,823	5,259	5,657	7.6
Texas	61,362	68,951	77,956	13.1	5,106	5,635	6,243	10.8
Rocky Mountain	29,193	31,738	35,124	10.7	5,223	5,585	6,072	8.7
Colorado	13,955	15,200	16,797	10.5	5,549	5,998	6,503	8.4
Idaho	4,104	4,248	4,756	12.0	5,150	5,177	5,726	10.6
Montana	3,743	4,062	4,215	3.8	5,079	5,433	5,600	3.1
Utah	5,350	5,954	6,731	13.0	4,539	4,938	5,482	11.0
Wyoming	2,042	2,274	2,625	15.4	5,644	6,079	6,723	10.6
Far West	162,415	178,794	197,850	10.7	5,976	6,487	7,048	8.6
California	126,956	139,388	154,173	10.6	6,090	6,596	7,164	8.6
Nevada	3,536	3,950	4,475	13.3	6,159	6,673	7,337	10.0
Oregon	12,156	13,163	14,743	12.0	5,390	5,752	6,331	10.1
Washington	19,768	22,292	24,458	9.7	5,648	6,284	6,772	7.8
Alaska	2,402	3,355	3,888	15.9	7,037	9,535	10,178	6.7
Hawaii	5,069	5,674	6,101	7.5	6,010	6,658	6,969	4.7

r Revised.   p Preliminary.

Source: *Survey of Current Business,* Department of Commerce, Bureau of Economic Analysis.

PRODUCTIVITY AND RELATED DATA. PRIVATE BUSINESS ECONOMY

1967=100; quarterly data seasonally adjusted

Period	Output[1]		Hours of all persons[2]		Output per hour of all persons		Compensation per hour[3]		Unit labor costs		Implicit price deflator[4]	
	Total private business	Private non-farm business	Total private business	Private non-farm business	Total private business	Private non-farm business	Total private business	Private non-farm business	Total private business	Private non-farm business	Total private business	Private non-farm business
1966	98.0	98.1	100.3	100.0	97.8	98.1	94.7	94.5	96.8	96.4	97.2	96.8
1967	100.0	100.0	100.0	100.0	100.0	100.0	100.0	100.0	100.0	100.0	100.0	100.0
1968	105.1	105.4	101.7	102.1	103.3	103.2	107.6	107.3	104.1	103.9	103.9	104.0
1969	108.3	108.6	104.5	105.3	103.7	103.1	115.1	114.3	111.0	110.9	108.8	108.7
1970	107.4	107.4	102.8	104.0	104.5	103.3	123.3	121.9	118.1	118.1	113.9	114.0
1971	110.3	110.3	102.3	103.7	107.8	106.3	131.5	129.9	121.9	122.2	118.9	119.2
1972	117.6	117.9	106.0	107.6	111.0	109.5	138.9	137.4	125.2	125.5	123.2	122.9
1973	124.5	125.0	110.1	112.2	113.1	111.4	150.3	148.1	132.9	133.0	130.3	128.0
1974	120.8	121.1	110.6	112.7	109.2	107.5	164.3	162.0	150.4	150.8	143.8	142.0
1975	118.1	118.0	106.1	108.0	111.3	109.2	179.9	177.4	161.6	162.4	157.5	156.4
1976	126.1	126.2	108.9	111.4	115.7	113.2	193.7	190.5	167.4	168.2	164.6	163.9
1975: I	114.2	114.4	105.7	107.8	108.1	106.0	176.1	173.1	162.9	163.3	154.5	154.0
II	116.7	116.6	104.9	106.9	111.2	109.0	178.7	176.1	160.7	161.5	155.9	155.0
III	120.1	119.9	105.9	107.7	113.4	111.4	180.8	178.9	159.5	160.6	158.4	157.0
IV	121.2	121.3	107.5	109.7	112.8	110.6	184.2	181.4	163.3	164.1	160.9	159.3
1976: I	124.2	124.3	108.2	111.0	114.7	112.0	188.8	185.4	164.6	165.4	161.7	161.0
II	125.8	126.0	108.9	111.2	115.5	113.0	191.8	188.9	166.0	166.8	163.8	162.5
III	126.8	126.9	108.9	111.3	116.3	114.0	195.3	192.1	167.8	168.5	165.4	164.8
IV	127.5	127.5	109.5	112.2	116.4	113.6	199.2	195.4	171.1	171.9	167.4	167.2
1977: I	130.0	130.1	110.4	113.3	117.8	114.8	204.4	200.2	173.6	174.4	169.4	168.6

Percent change; quarterly data at seasonally adjusted annual rates

	[1]											
1966	5.5	6.0	2.3	3.3	3.2	2.5	7.0	6.1	3.7	3.4	3.2	2.9
1967	2.0	1.9	.3	.0	2.3	1.9	5.6	5.8	3.3	3.8	2.9	2.9
1968	5.1	5.4	1.7	2.1	3.3	3.2	7.6	7.3	4.1	3.9	3.9	3.4
1969	3.0	5.0	2.7	3.2	.3	-.2	7.0	6.5	6.6	6.6	4.7	4.5
1970	-.9	-1.1	-1.6	-1.2	.7	-.2	7.2	6.7	6.4	6.5	4.7	4.9
1971	2.8	2.7	.4	1.3	3.2	2.9	6.6	6.6	3.2	3.5	4.4	4.5
1972	6.6	6.9	3.6	3.7	2.9	3.0	5.7	5.8	2.7	2.7	3.6	3.1
1973	5.9	6.0	3.4	4.3	9.1	1.7	8.2	7.8	6.2	6.0	5.8	4.1
1974	-3.0	-3.1	.4	.4	-3.4	-3.5	9.3	9.4	13.2	13.4	10.3	11.0
1975	-2.3	-2.6	-4.1	-4.1	1.9	1.6	9.5	9.5	7.5	7.7	9.5	10.1
1976	6.8	6.9	2.7	3.1	4.0	3.7	7.7	7.4	3.6	3.6	4.5	4.8
1975: I	-11.2	-11.3	-12.5	-12.3	1.4	1.1	12.9	11.6	11.3	10.4	11.3	13.5
II	8.9	7.9	2.7	3.5	12.0	1.8	6.1	7.1	-5.2	-4.2	3.5	2.6
III	12.3	12.1	3.9	2.9	8.1	8.9	4.8	6.4	-3.1	-2.3	6.6	5.3
IV	3.6	4.5	5.9	7.6	2.1	-2.8	7.6	5.8	10.0	8.9	6.6	6.2
1976: I	10.2	10.5	2.9	4.8	7.0	5.4	10.4	9.0	3.1	3.4	2.1	4.3
II	5.5	5.4	2.6	1.0	2.9	4.6	6.5	7.7	3.5	3.2	5.2	3.6
III	2.9	3.0	2.1	4.0	2.9	1.2	7.5	7.1	4.5	4.3	3.9	5.8
IV	2.3	1.9	2.1	3.2	.3	-1.2	8.2	7.0	8.0	8.3	5.5	5.5
1977: I	8.0	8.3	3.2	4.1	4.7	4.1	10.9	10.3	5.9	6.0	4.8	3.5

[1] Output refers to gross domestic product originating in the sector in 1972 dollars.

[2] Hours of all persons in private industry engaged in production, including hours of proprietors and unpaid family workers. Estimates based primarily on establishment data.

[3] Wages and salaries of employees plus employers' contributions for social insurance and private benefit plans. Also includes an estimate of wages, salaries, and supplemental payments for the self-employed.

Source: *Economic Indicators*, Council of Economic Advisors.

[4] Current dollar gross domestic product divided by constant dollar gross domestic product.

NOTE.—Percent changes are from preceding period and are based on original data; they therefore may differ slightly from percent changes based on indexes shown here.

Source: Department of Labor, Bureau of Labor Statistics.

LABOR–MANAGEMENT DATA

Definitions are applicable to the exhibits on pages 371–74.

Data on wage changes apply to private nonfarm industry agreements covering 1,000 workers or more. Data on wage and benefit changes *combined* apply only to those agreements covering 5,000 workers or more. **First-year wage settlements** refer to pay changes going into effect within the first 12 months after the effective date of the agreement. **Changes over the life of the agreement** refer to total agreed upon settlements (exclusive of potential cost-of-living escalator adjustments) expressed at an average annual rate. **Wage-rate changes** are expressed as a percent of straight-time hourly earnings, while **wage and benefit changes** are expressed as a percent of total compensation.

Effective wage-rate adjustments going into effect in major bargaining units measure changes actually placed into effect during the reference period, whether the result of a newly negotiated increase, a deferred increase negotiated in an earlier year, or a cost-of-living escalator adjustment. Average adjustments are affected by workers receiving no adjustment, as well as by those receiving increases or decreases.

Work stoppages include all known strikes or lockouts involving six workers or more and lasting a full shift or longer. Data cover all workers idle one shift or more in establishments directly involved in a stoppage. They do not measure the indirect or secondary effect on other establishments whose employees are idle owing to material or service shortages.

WAGE AND BENEFIT SETTLEMENTS IN MAJOR COLLECTIVE BARGAINING UNITS, 1971–1977
In Percent

Sector and measure	Annual average						Quarterly average					
							1975	1976				1977p
	1971	1972	1973	1974	1975	1976	IV	I	II	III	IV	I
Wage and benefit settlements, all industries:												
First-year settlements	13.1	8.5	7.1	10.7	11.4	8.5	14.0	10.5	8.9	10.0	6.8	8.5
Annual rate over life of contract	8.8	7.4	6.1	7.8	8.1	6.6	8.7	8.0	7.2	7.4	5.2	6.7
Wage rate settlements, all industries:												
First-year settlements	11.6	7.3	5.8	9.8	10.2	8.4	11.0	9.7	8.2	9.6	7.1	7.6
Annual rate over life of contract	8.1	6.4	5.1	7.3	7.8	6.4	8.0	7.9	6.7	7.2	4.9	6.5
Manufacturing:												
First-year settlements	10.9	6.6	5.9	8.7	9.8	8.9	9.2	9.5	10.9	11.0	6.7	7.8
Annual rate over life of contract	7.3	5.6	4.9	6.1	8.0	6.0	7.1	7.2	7.6	7.4	4.3	6.4
Nonmanufacturing (excluding construction):												
First-year settlements	12.2	8.2	6.0	10.2	11.9	8.6	12.1	11.4	8.0	8.5	9.2	8.1
Annual rate over life of contract	8.6	7.3	5.4	7.2	8.0	7.2	8.3	9.3	6.7	7.2	7.7	7.4
Construction:												
First-year settlements	12.6	6.9	5.0	11.0	8.0	6.1	9.1	6.9	5.6	7.0	6.4	2.5
Annual rate over life of contract	10.8	6.0	5.1	9.6	7.5	6.2	9.4	6.8	5.9	6.6	7.3	2.8

Source: *Monthly Labor Review*, U.S. Department of Labor, Bureau of Labor Statistics.

WORK STOPPAGES, 1946–1977

Month and year	Number of stoppages		Workers involved		Days idle	
	Beginning in month or year	In effect during month	Beginning in month or year (thousands)	In effect during month (thousands)	Number (thousands)	Percent of estimated working time
1946	4,985	....	4,600	....	116,000	1.04
1947	3,693	....	2,170	....	34,600	.30
1948	3,419	....	1,960	....	34,100	.28
1949	3,606	....	3,030	....	50,500	.44
1950	4,843	....	2,410	....	38,800	.33
1951	4,737	....	2,220	....	22,900	.18
1952	5,117	....	3,540	....	59,100	.48
1953	5,091	....	2,400	....	28,300	.22
1954	3,468	....	1,530	....	22,600	.18
1955	4,320	....	2,650	....	28,200	.22
1956	3,825	....	1,900	....	33,100	.24
1957	3,673	....	1,390	....	16,500	.12
1958	3,694	....	2,060	....	23,900	.18
1959	3,708	....	1,880	....	69,000	.50
1960	3,333	....	1,320	....	19,100	.14
1961	3,367	....	1,450	....	16,300	.11
1962	3,614	....	1,230	....	18,600	.13
1963	3,362	....	941	....	16,100	.11
1964	3,655	....	1,640	....	22,900	.15
1965	3,963	....	1,550	....	23,300	.15

1966	4,405	.....	1,960	.....	25,400	.15
1967	4,595	.....	2,870	.....	42,100	.25
1968	5,045	.....	2,649	.....	49,018	.28
1969	5,700	.....	2,481	.....	42,869	.24
1970	5,716	.....	3,305	.....	66,414	.37
1971	5,138	.....	3,280	.....	47,589	.26
1972	5,010	.....	1,714	.....	27,066	.15
1973	5,353	.....	2,251	.....	27,948	.14
1974	6,074	.....	2,778	.....	47,991	.24
1975	5,031	.....	1,746	.....	31,237	.16
1976	5,600	.....	2,500	.....	38,000	.19
1976: March	438	630	152	189	1,688	.09
April	583	787	464	521	3,148	.18
May	577	836	164	344	3,706	.23
June	571	931	240	421	4,488	.25
July	523	977	312	607	5,219	.31
August	508	847	123	407	3,824	.22
September	525	778	373	486	4,566	.27
October	537	790	161	421	4,138	.27
November	400	679	262	430	3,228	.19
December	251	466	89	158	1,770	.10
1977: January	351	518	109	176	1,160	.07
February	314	549	158	260	1,356	.09
March^p	391	600	221	340	2,094	.11

Source: Monthly Labor Review, U.S. Department of Labor, Bureau of Labor Statistics.

EFFECTIVE WAGE ADJUSTMENTS GOING INTO EFFECT IN MAJOR COLLECTIVE BARGAINING UNITS, 1972 TO DATE

In percent

Sector and measure	Average annual changes						Average quarterly changes							
							1976		1977				1978f	
	1972	1973	1974	1975	1976	1977	III	IV	I	II	III	IV	I	II
Total effective wage rate adjustment, all industries	6.6	7.0	9.4	8.7	8.1	8.0	2.5	1.5	1.2	2.9	2.7	1.1	1.3	2.3
Change resulting from—														
Current settlement	1.7	3.0	4.8	2.8	3.2	3.0	.8	.9	.3	1.0	1.3	.5	.4	.4
Prior settlement	4.2	2.7	2.6	3.7	3.2	3.2	1.0	.4	.5	1.4	1.0	.3	.6	1.4
Escalator provision	.7	1.3	1.9	2.2	1.6	1.7	.7	.3	.3	.6	.5	.3	.3	.5
Manufacturing	5.6	7.3	10.3	8.5	8.5	8.4	2.5	2.4	1.2	2.9	2.7	1.4	1.3	2.0
Nonmanufacturing	7.4	6.7	8.6	8.9	7.7	7.6	2.6	.8	1.1	2.9	2.7	.8	1.2	2.6

NOTE: Because of rounding and compounding, the sums of individual items may not equal totals.

Source: *Monthly Labor Review*, U.S. Department of Labor, Bureau of Labor Statistics.

LABOR CONTRACT
EXPIRATION DATES

Contract Identifying Name	Workers
January 1979	
AM INSULATED WIRE CORP & N E CABLE CORP MA & RI	1,200
ATLANTIC RICHFIELD CO & ARCO PIPE LINE CO INTER	2,200
ATLANTIC RICHFIELD CO CA	1,100
CHICAGO NEWSPAPER PUBLISHERS ASSN CHICAGO IL	1,100
ERWIN MILLS ERWIN NC	1,800
FIRST NATIONAL STORES INC MA	1,700
FIRST NATIONAL STORES INC MA	1,950
GENL TELEPHONE CO OF WISCONSIN	1,500
GOVERNMENT SERVICES INC DC MD & VA	1,000
GULF OIL CO–US PORT ARTHUR REFINERY TX	2,500
HONEYWELL INC MINNEAPOLIS & ST PAUL MN	5,700
I-A INDEP MEAT MARKETS MO & IL	1,400
I-A MASS SHOE MFRS MA	1,000
ITT GWALTNEY SMITHFIELD VA	1,000
MOBIL OIL CORP BEAUMONT REFINERY YARD UNIT TX	1,700
NATL UNION ELECTRIC CORP EUREKA DIV IL	1,500
NORTHERN ILLINOIS GAS COMPANY IL	1,850
SHELL OIL CO CALIF	1,150
SHELL OIL CO SHELL CHEM CO D HOUSTON TX	2,000
STANDARD OIL CO AMOCO OIL CO TEXAS	1,350
STANDARD OIL CO AMOCO OIL CO WHITING REF IN	1,250
SUN SHIPBLDG & DRY DOCK CO P & M CHESTER PA	2,700
SUNBEAM CORP SUNBEAM APPLIANCE CO IL	1,600
TEXACO INC PLT & TERML PORT ARTHUR TX	3,800
UNION CARBIDE CORP CHEM & PLASTICS OPERATIONS WV	1,200
February 1979	
AGC OF MASS AND 1 OTH MA	4,200
ANHEUSER-BUSH INC ST LOUIS MO	1,350
CENTRAL TELE CO OF FL	1,100
CONSTR INDUSTRIES OF MA	4,200
DENNISON MFG CO NATL BLANK BOOK CO HOLYOKE MA	1,000
DESOTO INC FORT SMITH FURNITURE DIV AR	1,350
EXXON CORP BAYWAY REF & CHEM PLT LINDEN NJ	1,000
FOUNDATION-MARINE CONTRS ASSN NEW ENG MA NH ME	4,200
GATES LEARJET CORP WICHITA KS	1,700
I-A BAKERIES LOS ANGELES CA	4,000
JEWELRY MFRS ASSN INC & 1 OTH NY NJ & CONN	2,600
LADISH CO CUDAHY WI	1,900
NORRIS INDUSTRIES INC VERNON FACILITY CA	1,600
NORTHROP WORLDWIDE AIRCRAFT SERVICES INC AL	1,200
PROCTER & GAMBLE CO IVORYDALE & ST BERNARD PLTS OH	2,200
RETAIL APPAREL MERCHANTS ASSN NY	1,800
RETAILAPPAREL MERCHANTS ASSN NYC NY	2,500
SLIPPER & PLAYWEAR ASSN NYC NY	2,500
STANDARD OIL CO OF IND AMOCO OIL CO ILL	1,200
STOP & SHOP COS INC MA RI CT ME NH & VT	8,000
March 1979	
AGC OF AM N Y STATE CHPTR	7,200

* I-A designates industry area with more than one company in the same area; D means division· and AGC stands for Associated General Contractors.
Source: U.S. Department of Labor.

LABOR CONTRACT EXPIRATION DATES (*continued*)

Contract Identifying Name	Workers
AGC OF AM NY STATE CHPTR INC...	1,000
AGC OF AM NY STATE CHPTR INC...	6,500
AGC OF AM NY STATE CHPTR...	4,600
AGC OF AM SO FLORIDA CHPTR BROWARD..	2,000
AGC OF AM SOUTH FLORIDA CHPTR...	2,200
CALIF METAL TRADES ASSN FOUNDRY...	1,300
CALIF METAL TRADES ASSN FRESNO & MADERA CA................................	1,800
CALIF TRUCKING ASSN...	2,800
CENTRAL PENN MOTOR CARRIERS CONFERENCE INC................................	9,900
CIN GAS & ELEC CO & 1 OTH OH & KY...	1,650
EDITION BOOKBINDERS OF NY INC...	1,000
EXXON CORP EXXON CO USA BATON ROUGE REF & CHEM LA.........................	2,450
FIRST NATL STORES INC...	2,450
FMC CORP CRANE & EXCAVATOR DIV CEDAR RAPIDS IA............................	1,150
GENL FOODS CORP MAXWELL HOUSE DIV HOBOKEN NJ..............................	1,000
I-A CAROLINA FREIGHT COUNCIL CITY CARTAGE SUPP NC&SC......................	6,700
I-A CAROLINA FREIGHT COUNCIL O-T-R SUPP AGMT NC & SC......................	6,350
I-A CENTRAL STATES AREA LOCAL CARTAGE SUPP AGMT INT.......................	67,000
I-A CENTRAL STATES AREA O-T-R MOTOR FREIGHT SUPP INT......................	41,000
I-A CENTRAL STATES IRON-STEEL SPEC COMMD AGMT.............................	25,000
I-A EASTERN CONF AREA IRN & STEEL RIDER AGMT..............................	350,000
I-A JOINT AREA CARTAGE AGMT IL & IN.......................................	2,200
I-A LOCAL CARTAGE AGMT FOR HIRE & PRI CARRIERS IL.........................	8,000
I-A MASTER RAI-TRUCK FREIGHT AGMT...	3,500
I-A MD-DC CITY PICKUP & DELIVERY SUPP AGMT DC & MD........................	4,000
I-A MD-DC O-T-R SUPP AGMT DC & MD...	1,000
I-A NATL MASTER FREIGHT LOCAL CARTAGE PHILA PA & VIC......................	5,000
I-A NEW ENGLAND FREIGHT SUPP AGMT...	1,600
I-A NJ-NY AREA GENL TRUCKING SUPP AGMT....................................	38,000
I-A NO NEW ENGLAND GENL FREIGHT AGMT SUPP.................................	1,600
I-A NY STATE TEAMSTERS FREIGHT DIV LOCAL CARTAGE..........................	8,000
I-A NY STATE TEAMSTERS FREIGHT DIV O-T-R SUPP.............................	12,000
I-A SO CONF LOCAL FREIGHT FORWARDING GARAGE...............................	75,000
I-A SO CONF LOCAL FREIGHT FORWARDING OFF EES..............................	7,000
I-A SO CONF LOCAL FREIGHT FORWARDING PICKUP...............................	40,000
I-A SO CONF O-T-R MOTOR FREIGHT SUPP AGMT.................................	25,000
I-A WESTERN STATES AREA LOCAL CARTAGE SUPPLEMENT..........................	46,000
I-A WESTERN STATES AREA O-T-R MOTOR FREIGHT SUPP INT......................	19,000
I-A WESTERN STATES AREA OFFICE SUPP.......................................	6,500
I-A WESTERN STATES AUTOMOTIVE SHOP-TRUCK AGMT.............................	2,400
ILLINOIS TRUCKING ASSNS INC & 1 OTH OFF...................................	2,100
ILLINOIS TRUCKING ASSNS INC HWY DRIVERS...................................	6,200
INGERSOLL-RAND CO PAINTED POST NY...	1,700
LABORERS NEGOTIATG COMM OF AGR OF IN INC..................................	1,400
LEVER BROTHERS CO HAMMOND IN..	1,050
LEVER BROTHERS CO MASTER NJ MD CA MO......................................	2,650
MARINE TOWING & TRANSP EMPLRS ASSN OIL TANKRS NY..........................	1,000
MARINE TOWING & TRANSP EMPLRS ASSN OPERS TUG..............................	2,000
MATTEL INC CA...	2,000
MERCHANTS FAST MOTOR LINES INC TX...	1,050
ROCKWELL INTL CORP ADMIRAL CORP APPLIANCE D IL............................	3,500
VIRGINIA ELECTRIC & POWER CO VA...	3,800
WASH METAL TRADES INC INTRA WASH..	1,200
WESTERN PENN MOTOR CARRIERS LOCAL CARTAGE SUP.............................	4,200
WESTERN PENN MOTOR CARRIERS O-T-R AGMT....................................	2,800

April 1979

AFFILIATED HOSPITALS OF SAN FRANCISCO CA..................................	2,600
AGC ARKANSAS CHPT AR..	1,050
AGC EAST TENN INC KNOXVILLE BRANCH TN & NC................................	3,200
AGC EAST TENN KNOXVILLE BRANCH..	1,500
AGC OF AM BATON ROUGE CHPTR LA..	2,500

LABOR CONTRACT EXPIRATION DATES (continued)

AGC OF AM WISCONSIN CHPT...	2,300
ASSOC PRODUCERS & PACKERS INC WA...............................	3,050
AVCO CORP AVCO LYCOMING ENG GROUP STRATFORD CT................	1,350
BTEA & 1 OTH CUYAHOGA & GEAUGA COUNTIES OH....................	3,000
BTEA & 2 OTHS OH..	4,000
CARTAGE EXCHANGE OF CHICAGO INC & OTHS IL......................	3,100
CENTURY BRASS PRODS INC WATERBURY & NEW MILFORD..............	1,700
CHICAGO BEER WHOLESALERS ASSN IL................................	1,350
CHICAGO MIDWEST MEAT ASSN IL.....................................	4,300
CIRCLE F INDUSTRIES INC TRENTON & BORDENTOWN NJ................	1,000
CLEVE PLUMBING CONTRS ASSN OH...................................	1,200
EAST BAY RESTAURANT ASSN INC CONTRA COSTA CA...................	1,500
EMHART INDUS INC BERLIN PLANT HARDWARE DIV CT...................	1,250
FIRESTONE TIRE & RUBBER CO MASTER AGMT..........................	18,000
FOOD MART–WALDBAUM INC CT & MA..................................	1,500
FRUEHAUF CORP MD SHIPBLDG & DRYDOCK CO BALT....................	1,300
GENL TELEPHONE CO OF IND INC IN..................................	2,000
GOODRICH BF CO OH IN OK PA.......................................	10,500
GOODYEAR TIRE & RUBBER CO...	24,000
GTE AUTOMATIC ELEC CO IL..	1,100
GTE AUTOMATIC ELEC CO NORTHLAKE IL..............................	2,400
I-A INDUSTRIAL MAINTENANCE CONTRS AGMT SEATTLE WA..............	1,200
I-A MEAT INDUSTRY INDEPENDENT SHOPS IN CHI IL....................	1,100
I-A RACE TRACK CLUBS 15 PARI-MUTUEL CLKS CA......................	1,700
ICE CREAM COUNCIL 13 COS IL & IN.................................	1,000
LYNCHBURG FNDRY CO LYNCHBURG VA................................	1,200
LYNCHBURG FNDRY CO RADFORD PLT VA..............................	1,100
MASON CONTRS ASSN CLEVELAND OH.................................	1,800
MECH CONTRS ASSN OF CLEVE INC OH...............................	1,750
NECA GREATER CLEVELAND CHAPT OH................................	1,600
NO AM ROYALTIES INC WHELAND FOUNDRY DIV TN.....................	1,150
NORTHWEST BREWERS ASSN WA.......................................	1,000
OHIO CONTRS ASSN HVY & HWY CLEVELAND..........................	2,000
OHIO CONTRS ASSN–AGC OF AM INC OH & WV........................	1,400
PARKE DAVIS & CO DETROIT ALLEN PARK & ROCHESTER MI.............	1,200
REALTY ADVISORY BD ON LAB RELS INC APT BLDGS...................	10,000
RELIANCE ELEC CO DODGE MFG DIV MISHAWAKA IN....................	1,100
REXNORD INC WEST MILWAUKEE OPERS WI............................	2,200
ROCKWELL INTL CORP COLLINS RADIO GROUP DALLAS TX..............	1,550
SCHIFFLI LACE & EMBROIDERY MFRS ASSN INC NJ.....................	2,200
TEXTRON INC FAFNIR BEARING DIV NEW BRITAIN CT....................	3,000
UNIROYAL INC P & M NATIONWIDE....................................	15,000
UNITED PARCEL SERVICE INC CENTRAL AREA MO......................	1,000
UNITED PARCEL SERVICE INC CENTRAL STATES........................	1,100
UNITED PARCEL SERVICE INC CHICAGO IL............................	3,700
UNITED PARCEL SERVICE INC NO CALIF...............................	1,800
UNITED PARCEL SERVICE NO & SO OHIO..............................	1,600
UPHOLSTERED FURNITURE MFRS ASSN OF SO CA.......................	2,200
WAGNER ELECTRIC CORP & 1 OTH ST LOUIS MO.......................	1,900
WHITIN MACHINE WORKS INC WHITINSVILLE MA........................	1,150
WISCONSIN ROAD BLDRS ASSN LABOR RELATIONS DIV WI...............	1,300

May 1979

AFFILIATED DRESS MFRS INC & 2 OTHS INTER.........................	27,000
AGC & OTHERS AZ...	15,000
AGC OF AM HVY CONSTR SECTION LABOR RELS DIV AL................	1,400
AGC OF MASS INC & 1 OTH MA & NH................................	10,000
ALABAMA DRY DOCK & SHIPBUILDING CO MOBILE AL...................	2,700
ALLIED CONST EMPLRS ASSN INC WI..................................	2,850
AM STANDARD INC 6 PLTS CHINAWARE DEPTS.........................	1,400
ARKANSAS POWER & LIGHT CO AR....................................	2,100
ASSN OF KNITTED FABRIC MFRS INC NYC.............................	1,200

LABOR CONTRACT EXPIRATION DATES (*continued*)

Contract Identifying Name	Workers
ASSN OF RAIN APPAREL CONTRS INC NY NY.....................................	3,500
ASSOC STEEL ERECTORS CHICAGO IL...	2,350
BTEA WESTCH & PUTNAM BLDG CONSTR NY....................................	1,600
CALIF BREWERS ASSN & OTHS..	1,000
CARRIER AIR CONDITIONING CO MCMINNVILLE TN............................	1,800
CONST EMPLRS LABOR RELS ASSN OF NYS INC SYRACUSE NY..................	1,300
CONSTR INDUS OF MASS INC..	1,500
DEL MONTE CORP PLTS...	1,800
DIAMOND FRUIT GROWERS INC OR...	1,200
E R SQUIBB & SONS INC LAWRENCEVILLE NJ.................................	2,100
GENL TIRE & RUBBER CO OH & TX...	2,800
GREATER BLOUSE SKT & UNGMT ASSN INC NY NY..............................	1,250
GREATER BLOUSE SKIRT & UNDERGARMENT ASSN INC...........................	15,000
GREATER BLOUSE SKT & UNGMT ASSN INC NY NY..............................	12,000
HOMESTAKE MINING CO MINING OPERATIONS LEAD SD.........................	1,200
HOSPITAL SERVICE & MEDICAL-SURGICAL PLANS OF NJ........................	1,500
HOTEL ASSN OF NY CITY INC NY..	24,000
I-A DENVER RETAIL GROCERS CO..	9,000
I-A FOOD INDUSTRY MI..	7,500
I-A NATL MASTER AUTOMOBILE TRANSPORTERS AGMT..........................	3,000
I-A REST & BARS EVERETT WA..	1,500
I-A REST & BARS WHATCOM SKAGIT & ISLAND CNTYS WA.......................	2,000
INDUS EMPLRS & DISTRIBUTORS ASSN CALIF.................................	1,500
INDUS EMPLRS AND DISTRIBUTORS ASSN CA.................................	3,000
INGERSOLL-RAND TORRINGTON CO CT...	1,800
INGERSOLL-RAND TORRINGTON CO CT...	3,000
IRONWORKERS EMPLOYERS ASSN OF WESTERN PENN............................	2,200
KEYSTONE BLDG CONTRS ASSN INC HARRISBURG PA...........................	1,500
LOS ANGELES COAT & SUIT MFRS ASSN CA...................................	1,500
MASON CONTRS ASSN OF ALLEGHENY CNTY PA.................................	1,000
MASON CONTRS ASSN OF MILWAUKEE & 1 OTH WI..............................	1,050
MASTER BLDRS ASSN OF WESTERN PA INC....................................	1,000
MASTER BUILDERS ASSN OF WESTERN PA.....................................	7,000
MASTER BUILDERS ASSN OF WESTERN PA.....................................	12,000
MECHANICAL CONTRS ASSN ROCHESTER.......................................	1,000
MID-AM REGIONAL BARG ASSN IL...	24,850
MID-AM REGIONAL BARG BLDRS ASSN OF CHICAGO IL..........................	1,900
NATL ASSN OF BLOUSE MFRS..	7,500
NATL SKIRT & SPORTSWEAR ASSN...	35,000
NATL TEA CO STANDARD GROCERY DIV IL & IN...............................	3,000
NATL WOMENS NECKWEAR & SCARF ASSN NY...................................	1,000
NEEDLE TRADES EMPLRS ASSN MA...	1,000
NEW ENGLAND APPAREL ASSN RI & MASS.....................................	3,000
NY COAT & SUIT ASSN NY NJ CT & PA.......................................	25,000
PA ELECTRIC CO PA...	1,900
PA POWER & LIGHT CO EASTERN PA...	4,500
POPULAR PRICE DRESS CONTRS ASSN INC....................................	50,000
POTOMAC ELECTRIC POWER CO DC...	3,100
ROCKWELL INTL CORP COLLINS RADIO GRP C RPDS IA.........................	4,800
ROPER CORP ROPER EASTERN GRP MD..	1,100
SAN FRANCISCO EMPLOYERS COUNCIL CA.....................................	2,000
SPERRY RAND CORP UNIVAC DIV ST PAUL MN.................................	2,400
SQUIBB E R & SONS INC P & M NJ..	2,100
STANLEY WORKS CT..	2,500
WHIRLPOOL CORP ST JOSEPH MI DIV PLTS...................................	1,600

June 1979

Contract Identifying Name	Workers
AGC NEV CHAP & 2 OTHS SO NEV...	1,600
AGC UTAH CHPT UT..	1,400
AGRIPAC INC OR..	2,600
ALLIED CHEM CORP INDUS CHEM D SYRACUSE WKS............................	1,400
ALMACS INC RI MA CT...	2,000

LABOR CONTRACT EXPIRATION DATES (*continued*)

AM MOTORS CORP AM GENERAL CORP SUB IN	1,800
ASSN OF CONTRNG PLUMBERS OF THE CITY OF NY	3,800
ASSN OF STEEL ERECTORS & HVY EQUIP OPERS GA	1,150
ASSOC GARMENT INDUS OF ST LOUIS DRESS BRANCH IL & MO	4,500
BELT ASSN INC NEW YORK NY	1,800
CALIF PROCESSORS INC CA	55,000
CHIC PNEUMATIC TOOL CO UTICA NY	1,200
COPELAND CORPORATION INTRASTATE OH	3,100
DIAMOND-SUNSWEET INC STOCKTON CA	1,200
DUNLOP TIRE & RUBBER CORP BUFFALO NY	1,000
FMC CORP INDUSTRIAL CHEM DIV S CHARLESTON WV	1,300
FROZEN FOOD EMPLOYERS ASSN WATSONVILLE CA	3,500
GENERAL TIRE & RUBBER CO IND PRODS DIV WABASH IN	1,100
GENL DYNAMICS CORP ELECTRIC BOAT DIV CT	5,000
GENL ELEC CO BATTERY BUS DEPT GAINESVILLE FL	1,200
GENL ELEC CO MED SYS BUSN DIV MILWAUKEE WI	1,650
GENL ELEC CO NATL AGMT	17,200
GENL ELEC CO NATL AGMT INTER	70,200
GENL ELECTRIC CO CHICAGO & CICERO IL	2,000
GENL TELE CO OF KENTUCKY	1,200
GENL TIME CORP WESTCLOX DIV PERU	1,100
GF BUSINESS EQUIPMENT INC YOUNGSTOWN OH	1,300
GREAT A&P TEA CO INC NEW ENGLAND	1,800
HILLS SUPERMARKETS INC LONG ISLAND & QUEENS NY	1,300
I-A CHICAGO AREA GROCERY STORES (5) CHIC IL	7,100
I-A GROCERY AGMT QUAD-CITIES IA & IL	1,900
I-A MASTER CEMENT & ALL DRY BULK COMMODITIES	3,500
I-A WEST COAST P & P CONVERT INDUS MULTIPLE	6,000
I-A WHOLESALE GROCERS CHAIN STORE & 1 OTH MN	1,000
ILLINOIS ASSN OF HEALTH CARE FACILITIES IL	3,000
JACKSONVILLE SHIPYARDS INC FL	1,900
JORDAN MARSH CO BOSTON MA	1,200
KANSAS CITY GARMENT MFRS ASSN COAT & SUIT GROUP MC	1,500
KANSAS CITY GARMENT MFRS ASSN KANSAS CITY MO	1,000
KELLY-SPRINGFIELD TIRE CO CUMBERLAND MD	2,000
KEYSTONE BLDG CONTRS ASSN & 1 OTH PA	1,500
MAGNAVOX CO MAGNAVOX GOVT & IND ELECTRONICS CO IN	1,450
MANSFIELD TIRE & RUBBER CO MANSFIELD OH	1,000
MANUFACTURING WOODWRKS ASSN GR NY & 1 OTH	2,200
NATL ASSN OF DOLL MFRS INC NEW YORK NY	6,500
NATL HAND EMBROIDERY & NOVELTY MFRS ASSN INC NY	5,000
NEW ENG SPORTSWEAR MFRS ASSN BOSTON MA	3,600
OHIO VALLEY CONSTR EMPLRS CNCL INC OH WV & PA	3,050
PHILCO-FORD CORP ELECTRONICS D LANSDALE PA	1,000
PLUMBING CONTRS ASSN OF METRO ST LOUIS MO	1,300
SEATTLE AREA HOSP CNCL SEATTLE WASH	2,200
SMACCNA LOS ANGELES CHPTR & 1 OTH ASSN CA	2,450
STOCKHAM VALVES & FITTING INC BIRMINGHAM AL	1,650
STOP & SHOP COS INC DBA BRADLESS CT & W MA	1,850
STUFFED TOY MFRS INC NY	1,300
UN PAINTING CONTRS ASSN KS NE & WY	1,100
VARSITY TRANSIT INC NY DIV	2,800
WATSONVILLE EMPLRS FROZEN FOOD ASSN CA	3,500
WOODWARD & LOTHROP METROP DC AREA	10,000

July 1979

ALLEN-BRADLEY CO MILWAUKEE WI	5,000
ARMSTRONG RUBBER CO MASTER AGMT	3,750
ARTIC ENTERPRISES INC THIEF RIVER FALLS MN	1,000
ASSN OF MOTION PICTURE & TV PRODUCERS INC CA	1,650
ASSN OF MOTION PICTURE & TV PRODUCERS OFF CA	1,000
BABCOCK & WILCOX CO POWER GENERATION GROUP OH	2,600
BATH IRON WORKS CORP BATH & BRUNSWICK ME	2,500

LABOR CONTRACT EXPIRATION DATES (*continued*)

Contract Identifying Name*	Workers
CESSNA AIRCRAFT CO WICHITA KS	6,100
ESCO CORP PORTLND OR	1,050
FAIRCHILD INDUSTRIES INC FARMINGDALE NY	2,050
FERNANDES SUPER MARKETS MA & RI	2,150
GENL ELECTRIC CO EVENDALE OH	1,050
GENL ELECTRIC CO EVENDALE OH	3,000
GREATER ST LOUIS AUTOMOTIVE ASSN MO & IL	2,500
HAMILTON INDUS TWO RIVERS WI	1,000
HOLLOW METAL DOOR & BUCK ASSN INC NY	1,600
HOUSTON SHEET METAL CONTRS ASSN INC TX	1,000
I-A DRIED FRUIT INDUSTRY DEL MONTE-MAYFAIR CA	1,200
I-A GARAGE ATTENDENTS AGMT IL	1,300
I-A MAJOR SHOE CHAIN STORES NY	1,100
I-A MISSOURI RIVER BASIN AGMT	3,100
KORVETTES INC KORVETTES DEPT STORE DIV NY	4,500
KROGER CO CIN-DAYTON MARKETING AREA OH	2,250
MONTEREY PENINSULA HOTEL & REST ASSOC INC CA	2,050
NATIONAL FOOTBALL LEAGUE MANAGEMENT COUNCIL	1,100
NCR CORP TERMINAL SYSTEMS DIV ITHACA NY	1,000
OLIN CORP NEW HAVEN & BRANFORD CT	1,200
OREGON DRAYMEN & WAREHOUSEMENS ASSN OR	1,700
STOP & SHOP COS INC DBA BRADLEES NEW ENG	3,000
UNION CARBIDE CORP NUCLEAR DIV PADUCAH PL KY	1,200
VORNADO CORP NON-FOOD STORES INTERSTATE	6,500
WESTERN UNION TELEGRAPH CO NATL	7,700
WESTERN UNION TELEGRAPH CO NY NJ	1,000
WESTINGHOUSE ELEC CORP	13,200
WESTINGHOUSE ELEC CORP AEROSPACE DIV MD	1,600
WESTINGHOUSE ELEC CORP BEAVER PLT PA	1,900
WESTINGHOUSE ELEC CORP INTERSTATE	1,000
WESTINGHOUSE ELEC CORP NATL AGMT	6,600
WESTINGHOUSE ELECTRIC CORP MASTER AGMT	33,000
WHIRLPOOL CORP ST PAUL DIV MN	1,500

August 1979

ARMOUR & CO MASTER AGMT	6,200
BETHLEHEM STEEL CORP SHIPBUILDING DEPT BEAUMONT TX	1,150
BUCYRUS-ERIE CO IN PA & WI	2,400
CLUETT PEABODY & CO INC ARROW CO DIV	5,000
DUBUQUE PACKING CO DUBUQUE IA	2,550
GATES RUBBER CO DENVER CO	3,200
GOODYEAR AEROSPACE CORP AKRON OH	1,300
ILLINOIS FOOD RETAILERS ASSNS IND FOOD STORES	4,350
JOHN MORRELL & CO INTER	6,200
NATL NECKWEAR CONFERENCE NY	1,500
OSCAR MAYER & CO DAVENPORT PLT IA DIST	1,800
OSCAR MAYER & CO MADISON PLT WI	3,150
PITTSB FORGINGS CO GREENVILLE STEEL CAR CO PA	1,000
PUBLIX SHIRT CORP PA TN & GA	1,000
RATH PACKING CO TX NC & GA	1,850
SWIFT & CO & ESTECH INC MASTER AGMT	3,500
TRANE COMPANY LA CROSSE WI	1,800
WILSON FOODS CORP MASTER AGMT	6,500
3M COMPANY MN MINING & MFG CO D ST PAUL MN	2,000

September 1979

ACME-CLEVELAND CORP NATL ACME CO DIV OH	1,250
AGC AL BLDG CONSTRUCTION AGMT	4,000
BRONX REALTY ADVISORY BOARD INC NEW YORK	4,000
CATERPILLAR TRACTOR CO TOWMOTOR CORP CENTRAL AGMT	30,550
CHI & SUBURGAN REFUSE DISPOSAL ASSN IL	1,400
CHRYSLER CORP PARTS DEPOTS	2,200
CHRYSLER CORP PLANT GUARDS NATION-WIDE	1,000

CHRYSLER CORP PRODUCTION-MAINTENANCE.................................... 100,000
CHRYSLER CORPORATION ENGINEERING...................................... 4,500
CHRYSLER CORPORATION OFFICE & CLERICAL................................ 3,500

DEERE & CO IOWA & ILLINOIS.. 25,400
FOOD EMPLRS CNCL INC FOOD INDUS OFF AGMT CA........................... 1,400
FOOD EMPLRS CNCL INC FOOD INDUS WAREH AGMT CA......................... 3,500
FOOD EMPLRS CNCL INC WHSALE DELVRY DRVRS AGMT CA...................... 1,100
FORD MOTOR CO BODY ENGINEERING DEARBORN MI............................ 1,000
FORD MOTOR CO MASTER INTERSTATE....................................... 150,200
GENL DYNAMICS CORP ELEC BOAT DIV CT................................... 1,500
GENL ELEC CO TUBE DEPT OWENSBORO KY................................... 1,250
GENL MOTORS CORP INLAND DIV DAYTON OH................................. 5,400
GENL MOTORS CORP MASTER AGMT INTERSTATE............................... 400,000

GENL MOTORS CORP OH NY & NJ... 28,500
GTE SYLVANIA OTTAWA OH.. 1,350
HYGRADE FOODS PRODUCTS CORP IO MI & WA FL............................. 1,500
I-A DRESS AGMT SAN FRANCISCO CA....................................... 2,750
I-A HOTELS RESTAURANT & TAVERNS FRESNO CA............................. 1,850

I-A TABEL AND ART GLASSWARE MANUFACTURERS............................. 1,600
INTL HARVESTER CO CLER & TECH... 2,500
INTL HARVESTER CO DEPOT & DISTRIBUTION CONTRACT....................... 1,350
INTL HARVESTER CO MAIN LABR AGMT PROD-MAINT........................... 36,500
KAISER STEEL CORP P & M EES EAGLE MT MINE CA.......................... 1,200

KELLY-SPRINGFIELD TIRE CO TYLER TX.................................... 1,250
SPERRY RAND CORP NY & CA.. 1,250

October 1979
AMERICAN ENKA CORP LOWLAND TENN....................................... 2,400
CESSNA AIRCRAFT CO HUTCHINSON KS...................................... 1,600
CHRYSLER CORP DAYTON.. 2,000
COLONIAL STORES INC RALEIGH DIV NC.................................... 1,150
GENL MOTORS CORP PLT PROTECTION EES INTER............................. 2,500

GENL TIRE & RUBBER CO P & M MAYFIELD KY............................... 1,400
I-A CHINAWARE MANUFACTURERS GROUP NY PA & OH.......................... 1,450
I-A OIL PETRO CHEM & LIQUID PROD DRVRS AGMT IN........................ 2,000
I-A RETAIL MEAT MARKETS FROZEN FOOD LOCKER CA......................... 1,500
I-A RETL BUTCHERS—FISH & POULTRY AGMT SF CA........................... 3,500

I-A SOUTHEASTERN STATES BOILERMAKER EMPLRS............................ 2,600
MAC TRUCKS INC MASTER SHOP AGMT PA NJ MD & CA......................... 8,650
MASSEY-FERGUSON INC MASTER IL MI OH & IA.............................. 1,600
METRO CONTAINER COUNCIL INC... 1,700
MONFORT OF COLORADO INC MONFORT PACKAGING CO.......................... 1,000

PITTSBURGH BUILDINGS ASSN PA.. 1,800
RUBBERMAID INC WOOSTER OH... 1,150
TRW INC TAPCO-VALVES-MAIN PLANT-REPLACEMENT OH........................ 3,900
TRW INC VAN DYKE PLANT STERLING HEIGHTS MI............................ 1,150
WISC PUBLIC SERVICE CORP.. 1,100

November 1979
ALLIS-CHALMERS CORP LA PORTE IN....................................... 1,000
ALLIS-CHALMERS CORP WEST ALLIS WI..................................... 3,700
ARMSTRONG CORK CO LANCASTER PA FLOOR PLANT............................ 1,800
CARRIER CORP SYRACUSE NY.. 2,600
CHICAGO BAKERY EMPLOYERS LABOR COUNCIL IL............................. 1,050

COLGATE-PALMOLIVE CO JERSEY CITY PLT NJ............................... 1,250
FOOD EMPLOYERS COUNCIL INC LOS ANGELES CA............................. 6,000
GREATER BOSTON HOTEL & MOTOR INN ASSN MA.............................. 3,200
HOTEL & MOTEL ASSN OF GREATER ST LOUIS MO............................. 1,750
I-A CENTRAL STATES AREA TANK TRUCK AGMT INTER......................... 3,000

I-A COTTON GARMENT & OUTERWEAR AGMT PHILA PA.......................... 2,000
I-A EASTERN AREA TANK HAUL PA MD NJ & WV.............................. 3,000
I-A FILM EXCHANGE EMPLOYEES AGMT INTERSTATE........................... 1,400
I-A INDEP HOTELS CONTRACT ST LOUIS MO................................. 1,000
I-A LINEN SUPPLIERS NJ.. 1,050

LABOR CONTRACT EXPIRATION DATES (*concluded*)

Contract Identifying Name	Workers
I-A MILWAUKEE AREA RETAIL MEAT INDUSTRY WI	1,400
I-A RETAIL DISTRIBUTION AGMT S DIEGO CA	1,300
METRO TAXICAB BOARD OF TRADE NEW YORK CITY NY	17,000
PROCTER & GAMBLE MFG CO WOODBRIDGE NJ	1,000
ST LOUIS REST OWNERS ASSN MO	1,450
U S POTTERS ASSN PA OH & WV	3,000

December 1979

DANA CORP MASTER AGMT PA OH MI IN IL & WI	8,000
GTE SYLVANIA INC SMITHFELD NC	1,100
HUGHES AIRCRAFT CO CA	8,000
I-A GROCERY & DELICATESSEN SAN FRANCISCO CA	3,000
I-A RETAIL FOOD STORE AGMT SAN JOSE CA	6,100
INTL TELE & TELE GENL CONTROLS DIV CA	1,300
LOEWS THEATRES INC LORILLARD DIV LOUISVILLE KY	1,500
METRO PACKAGE STORE ASSN INC NY	1,000
MFRS INDUS RELS ASSN MO OH MA IL & MI	4,500
MICH CONSOLIDATED GAS CO DETROIT & ANN ARBOR MI	1,600
NECA INC WESTERN PENN CHPTR	1,350
RCA CORP NATL AGMT IN CA PA NJ OH & FL	15,000
STANDARD PLASTIC PRODS INC SO PLAINFIELD NJ	1,100

UNION ADDRESSES
AND MEMBERSHIP

Actors and Artistes of America; Associated (AFL-CIO)
1500 Broadway
New York, NY 10036
  Membership: 77,024

Actors' Equity Association
1500 Broadway
New York, NY 10023
  Membership: 76,000

Air Line Employees Association
5600 S. Central Avenue
Chicago, IL 60638
  Membership: 9,200

Air Line Pilots Association (AFL-CIO)
Pilot Division
1625 Massachusetts Avenue NW
Washington, DC 20036
  Membership: 27,639

Aluminum Workers International Union (AFL-CIO)
Paul Brown Building
818 Olive Street
St. Louis, MO 63101
  Membership: 29,500

American Federation of Television and Radio Artists
1350 Avenue of the Americas
New York, NY 10019
  Membership: 23,714

Asbestos Workers; International Association of Heat and Frost Insulators and (AFL-CIO)
505 Machinists Building
1300 Connecticut Avenue NW
Washington, DC 20036
  Membership: 18,833

Association of Flight Attendants
1625 Massachusetts Avenue NW
Washington, DC 20036
  Membership: 12,900

Automobile, Aerospace and Agricultural Implement Workers of America; International Union, United (Ind.)
8000 East Jefferson Avenue
Detroit, MI 48214
  Membership: 1,393,501

Source: *Directory of National Unions and Employee Associations,* 1978, Supplement to Bulletin 1937, Bureau of Labor Statistics, U.S. Department of Labor.

Bakery and Confectionery Workers' International Union of America (AFL-CIO)
1828 L Street NW
Washington, DC 20036
  Membership: 145,836

Barbers, Beauticians, and Allied Industries, International Association (AFL-CIO)
7050 West Washington Street
Indianapolis, IN 46214
  Membership: 50,000

Boilermakers, Iron Ship Builders, Blacksmiths, Forgers and Helpers; International Brotherhood of (AFL-CIO)
New Brotherhood Building
8th Street at State Avenue
Kansas City, KS 66101
  Membership: 132,000

Brick and Clay Workers of America; The United (AFL-CIO)
150 E. Mound Street
Columbus OH 43215
  Membership: 16,160

Bricklayers, and Allied Craftsmen; International Union of (AFL-CIO)
815 15th Street NW
Washington, DC 20005
  Membership: 149,000

Broadcast Employees and Technicians; National Association of (AFL-CIO)
1601 Connecticut Avenue NW
Washington, DC 20009
  Membership: 8,900

Carpenters and Joiners of America; United Brotherhood of (AFL-CIO)
101 Constitution Avenue NW
Washington, DC 20001
  Membership: 820,000

Cement, Lime and Gypsum Workers International Union; United (AFL-CIO)
7830 W. Lawrence Avenue
Chicago, IL 60656
  Membership: 36,644

Chemical Workers Union; International (AFL-CIO)
1655 W. Market Street
Akron, OH 44313
  Membership: 84,949

Classified School Employees; American Association of (Ind.)
1730 Rhode Island Avenue NW
Washington, DC 20036
  Membership: 96,723

Clothing Workers of America; Amalgamated (AFL-CIO)
15 Union Square
New York, NY 10003
  Membership: 365,000

Communications Workers of America (AFL-CIO)
1925 K Street NW
Washington, DC 20006
Membership: 443,278

Distillery, Rectifying, Wine and Allied Workers' International Union of America (AFL-CIO)
66 Grand Avenue
Englewood, NJ 07631
Membership: 33,000

Distributive Workers of America (Ind.)
13 Astor Place
New York, NY 10003
Membership: 50,000

Education Association; National (Ind.)
1201 16th Street NW
Washington, DC 20036
Membership: 1,165,617

Electrical, Radio and Machine Workers; International Union of (AFL-CIO)
1126 16th Street NW
Washington, DC 20036
Membership: 290,000

Electrical, Radio, and Machine Workers of America; United (Ind.)
11 E. 51st Street
New York, NY 10022
Membership: 165,000

Electrical Workers; International Brotherhood of (AFL-CIO)
1125 15th Street NW
Washington, DC 20005
Membership: 956,579

Elevator Constructors; International Union of (AFL-CIO)
12 S. 12th Street
Philadelphia, PA 19107
Membership: 17,683

Farm Workers of America; United (AFL-CIO)
P.O. Box 62
Keene, CA 93531
Membership: 20,000

Fire Fighters; International Association of (AFL-CIO)
1750 New York Avenue NW
Washington, DC 20006
Membership: 160,258

Firemen and Oilers; International Brotherhood of (AFL-CIO)
VFM Building
200 Maryland Avenue NE
Washington, DC 20002
Membership: 44,000

Furniture Workers of America; United (AFL-CIO)
700 Broadway
New York, NY 10003
Membership: 30,503

Garment Workers of America; United (AFL-CIO)
200 Park Avenue South
New York, NY 10003
Membership: 25,000

Glass and Ceramic Workers of North America; United (AFL-CIO)
556 E. Town Street
Columbus, OH 43215
Membership: 42,943

Glass Bottle Blowers Association of the United States and Canada (AFL-CIO)
608 E. Baltimore Pike
Media, PA 19063
Membership: 78,883

Glass Workers' Union of North America; American Flint (AFL-CIO)
1440 S. Byrne Road
Toledo, OH 43614
Membership: 36,000

Government Employees; American Federation of (AFL-CIO)
1325 Massachusetts Avenue NW
Washington, DC 20005
Membership: 292,809

Government Employees; National Association of (Ind.)
285 Dorchester Avenue
Boston, MA 02127
Membership: 100,000

Grain Millers; American Federation of (AFL-CIO)
4949 Olson Memorial Highway
Minneapolis, MN 55422
Membership: 36,000

Graphic Arts International Union (AFL-CIO)
1900 L Street NW
Washington, DC 20036
Membership: 106,441

Hatters, Cap and Millinery Workers International Union; United (AFL-CIO)
245 5th Avenue
New York, NY 10016
Membership: 15,000

Hotel and Restaurant Employees and Bartenders International Union (AFL-CIO)
120 E. 4th Street
Cincinnati, OH 45202
Membership: 458,029

Industrial Workers of America; International
Union Allied (AFL-CIO)
3520 W. Oklahoma Avenue
Milwaukee, WI 53215
Membership: 86,000

Iron Workers; International Association of
Bridge and Structural (AFL-CIO)
1750 New York Avenue NW
Washington, DC 20006
Membership: 175,611

Jewelry Workers' Union; International (AFL-CIO)
8 W. 40th Street
New York, NY 10018
Membership: 12,500

Laborers' International Union of North America (AFL-CIO)
905 16th Street NW
Washington, DC 20006
Membership: 600,000

Ladies' Garment Workers' Union; International (AFL-CIO)
1710 Broadway
New York, NY 10019
Membership: 427,568

Lathers; International Union of Wood, Wire
and Metal (AFL-CIO)
815 16th Street NW
Washington, DC 20006
Membership: 13,767

Laundry and Dry Cleaning International
Union (AFL-CIO)
Carlton House
550 Grant Street
Pittsburgh, PA 15219
Membership: 22,556

Laundry, Dry Cleaning and Dye House
Workers' International Union
360 N. Michigan Avenue
Chicago, IL 60601
Membership: 37,354

Leather Goods, Plastic and Novelty Workers'
Union; International (AFL-CIO)
265 W. 14th Street
New York, NY 10011
Membership: 39,200

Letter Carriers of the United States of America; National Association of (AFL-CIO)
100 Indiana Avenue NW
Washington, DC 20001
Membership: 220,000

Locomotive Engineers; Brotherhood of (Ind.)
1112 Brotherhood of Locomotive Engineers
Building
Cleveland, OH 44114
Membership: 37,600

Longshoremen's and Warehousemen's Union;
International (Ind.)
1188 Franklin Street
San Francisco, CA 94109
Membership: 58,000

Longshoremen's Association; International
(AFL-CIO)
17 Battery Place
New York, NY 10004
Membership: 60,000

Machinists and Aerospace Workers; International Association of (AFL-CIO)
1300 Connecticut Avenue NW
Washington, DC 20036
Membership: 757,564

Maintenance of Way Employees; Brotherhood of (AFL-CIO)
12050 Woodward Avenue
Detroit, MI 48203
Membership: 142,289

Marble, Slate and Stone Polishers, Rubbers
and Sawyers, Tile and Marble Setters'
Helpers and Terrazzo Workers' Helpers;
International Association of (AFL-CIO)
801 N. Pitt Street
Alexandria, VA 22314
Membership: 9,000

Marine and Shipbuilding Workers of America; Industrial Union of (AFL-CIO)
1126 16th Street NW
Washington, DC 20036
Membership: 21,000

Maritime Union of America; National (AFL-CIO)
346 W. 17th Street
New York, NY 10011
Membership: 45,000

Meat Cutters and Butcher Workmen of North
America; Amalgamated (AFL-CIO)
2800 N. Sheridan Road
Chicago, IL 60657
Membership: 528,631

Metal Polishers, Buffers, Platers and Allied
Workers International Union (AFL-CIO)
5578 Montgomery Road
Cincinnati, OH 45212
Membership: 10,000

Mine Workers of America; United (Ind.)
900 15th Street NW
Washington, DC 20005
Membership: 213,113

Molders' and Allied Workers' Union; International (AFL-CIO)
1225 E. McMillan Street
Cincinnati, OH 45206
Membership: 67,000

Musicians; American Federation of (AFL-CIO)
1500 Broadway
New York, NY 10036
 Membership: 315,000

Newspaper Guild; The (AFL-CIO)
1125 15th Street NW
Washington, DC 20005
 Membership: 32,535

Nurses' Association; American (Ind.)
2420 Pershing Road
Kansas City, MO 64108
 Membership: 156,665

Office and Professional Employees International Union (AFL-CIO)
265 W. 14th Street
New York, NY 10011
 Membership: 82,500

Oil, Chemical and Atomic Workers International Union (AFL-CIO)
P.O. Box 2812
1636 Champa Street
Denver, CO 80201
 Membership: 172,000

Operating Engineers; International Union of (AFL-CIO)
1125 17th Street NW
Washington, DC 20036
 Membership: 401,537

Painters and Allied Trades of the United States and Canada; International Brotherhood of (AFL-CIO)
United Unions Building
1750 New York Avenue NW
Washington, DC 20006
 Membership: 207,844

Paperworkers International Union; United (AFL-CIO)
163–03 Horace Harding Expressway
Flushing, NY 11365
 Membership: 389,427

Pattern Makers' League of North America (AFL-CIO)
1000 Connecticut Avenue NW
Washington, DC 20036
 Membership: 11,311

Plant Guard Workers of America; International Union, United (Ind.)
25510 Kelly Road
Roseville, MI 48066
 Membership: 20,000

Plasterers' and Cement Masons' International Association of the United States and Canada; Operative (AFL-CIO)
1125 17th Street NW
Washington, DC 20036
 Membership: 68,000

Plumbing and Pipe Fitting Industry of the United States and Canada; United Association of Journeymen and Apprentices of the (AFL-CIO)
901 Massachusetts Avenue NW
Washington, DC 20001
 Membership: 228,000

Police; Fraternal Order of (Ind.)
G–3136 W. Pasadena Avenue
Flint, MI 48504
 Membership: 125,000

Postal Supervisors; National Association of (Ind.)
P.O. Box 23456, L'Enfant Plaza Station
Washington, DC 20024
 Membership: 32,965

Postal Workers Union; American (AFL-CIO)
817 14th Street NW
Washington, DC 20005
 Membership: 238,763

Pottery and Allied Workers; International Brotherhood of (AFL-CIO)
(affiliated with Seafarer's International Union, effective June 21, 1976)

Printing and Graphic Communications Union; International (AFL-CIO)
1730 Rhode Island Avenue NW
Washington, DC 20036
 Membership: 123,000

Professional Air Traffic Controllers Organization
2100 M Street NW
Washington, DC 20037
 Membership: 21,000

Railroad Signalmen; Brotherhood of (AFL-CIO)
601 W. Golf Road
Mt. Prospect, IL 60056
 Membership: 12,000

Railway, Airline and Steamship Clerks, Freight Handlers, Express and Station Employees; Brotherhood of (AFL-CIO)
O'Hare International Transportation Center
6300 River Road
Rosemont, IL 60018
 Membership: 238,355

Railway Carmen of the United States and Canada; Brotherhood (AFL-CIO)
Carmen's Building
4929 Main Street
Kansas City, MO 64112
 Membership: 103,992

Retail Clerks International Association (AFL-CIO)
Suffridge Building
1775 K Street NW
Washington, DC 20006
 Membership: 633,221

Retail, Wholesale and Department Store Union (AFL-CIO)
101 W. 31st Street
New York, NY 10001
Membership: 197,840

Retail Workers Union; United (Ind.)
9865 W. Roosevelt Road
Westchester, IL 60153
Membership: 21,000

Roofers, Damp and Waterproof Workers Association; United Slate, Tile and Composition (AFL-CIO)
1125 17th Street NW
Washington, DC 20036
Membership: 26,448

Rubber, Cork, Linoleum and Plastic Workers of America; United (AFL-CIO)
URWA Building
South High Street
Akron, OH 44308
Membership: 182,949

Screen Actors Guild
7750 Sunset Boulevard
Hollywood, CA 90046
Membership: 26,610

Seafarers' International Union of North America (AFL-CIO)
675 4th Avenue
Brooklyn, NY 11232
Membership: 80,000

Service Employees' International Union (AFL-CIO)
900 17th Street NW
Washington, DC 20006
Membership: 484,000

Sheet Metal Workers' International Association (AFL-CIO)
United Unions Building
1750 New York Avenue NW
Washington, DC 20006
Membership: 153,000

Shoe Workers of America; United (AFL-CIO)
120 Boylston Street
Boston, MA 02116
Membership: 40,000

Shoe Workers' Union; Boot and (AFL-CIO)
(merged with the Retail Clerks International Association, effective September 1, 1977)

State, County and Municipal Employees; American Federation of (AFL-CIO)
1625 L Street NW
Washington, DC 20036
Membership: 529,035

Steelworkers of America; United (AFL-CIO)
Five Gateway Center
Pittsburgh, PA 15222
Membership: 1,400,000

Stove, Furnace and Allied Appliance Workers' International Union of North America (AFL-CIO)
2929 S. Jefferson Avenue
St. Louis, MO 63118
Membership: 9,139

Teachers; American Federation of (AFL-CIO)
11 Dupont Circle NW
Washington, DC 20036
Membership: 248,521

Teamsters, Chauffeurs, Warehousemen and Helpers of America; International Brotherhood of (Ind.)
25 Louisiana Avenue NW
Washington, DC 20001
Membership: 1,854,659

Technical Engineers; International Federation of Professional and (AFL-CIO)
1126 16th Street NW
Washington, DC 20036
Membership: 17,700

Telecommunications International Union (Ind.)
P.O. Box 5462
Hamden, CT 16518
Membership: 50,000

Telegraph Workers; United (AFL-CIO)
701 Gude Drive
Rockville, MD 20850
Membership: 18,000

Textile Workers of America; United (AFL-CIO)
420 Common Street
Lawrence, MA 01842
Membership: 52,000

Textile Workers Union of America (AFL-CIO)
(merged into Clothing and Textile Workers Union, effective June 3, 1976)

Theatrical Stage Employees and Moving Picture Machine Operators of the United States and Canada; International Alliance of (AFL-CIO)
1515 Broadway
Suite 601
New York, NY 10036
Membership: 62,000

Tobacco Workers International Union (AFL-CIO)
1522 K Street NW
Washington, DC 20005
Membership: 33,565

Transit Union; Amalgamated (AFL-CIO)
5025 Wisconsin Avenue NW
Washington, DC 20016
    Membership: 130,000

Transport Workers Union of America (AFL-CIO)
1980 Broadway
New York, NY 10023
    Membership: 150,000

Transportation Union; United (AFL-CIO)
14600 Detroit Avenue
Cleveland, OH 44107
    Membership: 248,088

Typographical Union; International (AFL-CIO)
P.O. Box 157
Colorado Springs, CO 80901
    Membership: 115,273

Upholsterers' International Union of North America (AFL-CIO)
25 N. Fourth Street
Philadelphia, PA 19106
    Membership: 59,000

Utility Workers Union of America (AFL-CIO)
815 16th Street NW
Washington, DC 20006
    Membership: 60,000

Western Pulp and Paper Workers; Association of (Ind.)
1430 Southwest Clay
Portland, OR 97201
    Membership: 20,202

Woodworkers of America; International (AFL-CIO)
1622 N. Lombard Street
Portland, OR 97217
    Membership: 105,790

UNIT LABOR COSTS—TRADE RIVALS' CHECKLIST*

The pattern of world production is changing—and in ways that don't escape the public's notice. But few seem to realize that the changes are building up to new battles for world markets. Lately, almost like scouts sent ahead of the main forces, government officials and economic experts here and abroad have shown an unusual interest in methods of comparing the competitive strength of the major trading powers.

* Reproduced from Citibank's Monthly Economic Letter, September 1978.

One striking change in the international arena has been the swift industrialization of several developing countries, notably some on Asia's outer rim. From these countries comes a rising flood of manufactured goods at rock-bottom prices. This export drive has bored into the markets of the world's most powerful industrial nations—and helped to trigger shakeouts in some of their industries, both in home markets and export sectors.

By now, it's well known that Japan's electronics industry virtually has given up assembling the low-priced transistor radios that once were a staple Japanese export. Thousands upon thousands of these sets are now pouring out of factories in Hong Kong, South Korea and Taiwan.

Leading German manufacturers of machinery are beginning to face a similar situation. Some of their less sophisticated products are now being outpriced by standard machines, of acceptable quality, produced in rapidly industrializing countries—and also in Eastern European nations.

Meanwhile, in several of the most advanced countries, cyclical and structural problems are bedeviling long-established industries such as steel and shipbuilding. These problems were not caused by the competitive exports of developing countries. But as such exports proliferate, the problems don't get easier to solve.

Thus, on many fronts, the positions held by the top industrial nations are under heavy pressure. But these nations are combat veterans of many a long trade war. They aren't about to surrender.

In fact, it looks as if some of them are starting a counteroffensive. Quite visibly in Japan and Germany, less clearly in other leading countries, industries that have come under attack are beginning to upgrade their output —that is, they are shifting away from the production of standard, relatively unsophisticated items and toward increasingly high-technology products and luxury goods.

But if the industrial countries swing away from direct competition with low-cost exports from less-developed lands, they run the risk of colliding more frequently with each other. For some industries in the United States, the implications could be especially serious. From now on, producers in other industrial nations may move more aggressively into such product lines as computers, anti-pollution equipment, sophisticated electronics and high-technology machinery. For years, these lines have been dominated mainly by U.S. manufacturers.

In short, among the top countries, the competition for markets—and for investments— seems bound to be rough for a long time to come. And the question now appears to be: Which of them is going to gain, and which

EXHIBIT 1
COMPENSATION: WHERE IT ROSE FASTER*

	Hourly Compensation (in U.S. Dollars)			Percent Rise 1970–77 in Real Terms (and in Local Currency)
	1970	1976	1977	
Belgium	$2.31	$7.65	$ 9.02	61%
Britain	1.65	3.40	3.62	21
Canada	3.71	7.63	7.80	27
Denmark	2.55	6.23	7.69	28
France	2.09	5.63	6.16	43
Germany	2.30	6.62	7.84	48
Italy	2.12	5.21	6.00	70
Japan	1.11	3.58	4.35	44
Netherlands	2.46	8.08	9.40	48
Sweden	3.33	9.38	10.30	48
Switzerland	2.28	6.97	7.43	21
United States	4.91	8.00	8.71	12

* Data are estimates of compensation—or in some cases, of labor costs—per hour worked, and they relate essentially to all employees in manufacturing. In right-hand column, increases in real terms were obtained by adjusting for inflation, as measured by a consumer price index or its equivalent.
Sources: U.S. Bureau of Labor Statistics, Citibank estimates.

will lose, from the adjustments that are getting under way?

Against this background, it's easy to see why interest has revived in methods of comparing the competitive strength of industrial countries. And one classic method is to compare their unit labor costs—that is, labor costs per unit of output. Within the past few months, comparative studies of these costs have been published by the Bank of England and by the Organization for Economic Cooperation and Development.

As its contribution to the discussion, Citibank presents its fifth annual survey of unit labor costs in manufacturing for leading industrial countries—based essentially on the latest data from the U.S. Bureau of Labor Statistics. The results are summed up in Exhibits 3 and 6. Both tables reveal trends that favor the United States over its main rivals.

Hasty conclusions are to be avoided, however. Unit labor costs are not the ultimate guide to a country's competitive standing. And obviously, a quick glance at the trends won't tell a company's executives which country is the right one to site a new plant or where to cut back on capital investment.

But in manufacturing, a company's prices as well as its profit margins are determined to a large extent by its labor costs—because, in most industries, labor is a primary direct

EXHIBIT 2
FRINGES: HOW MUCH THEY ADD TO COSTS*
Percent of average hourly earnings

	Pay for Leave Time	Bonuses	Employer Outlays		Add-on to Earnings
			Social Security	Company Programs	
Belgium	21.0%	5.8%	36.5%	0.7%	64.3%
Britain	9.3	†	7.1	2.9	18.5
Canada	9.3	0.2	4.6	5.6	20.4
France	13.7	4.8	36.5	5.6	62.3
Germany	16.6	5.1	24.6	1.6	48.0
Italy	18.6	15.7	51.0	1.1	86.7
Japan	†	†	5.9	4.1	13.2
Netherlands	20.0	6.9	22.8	9.4	60.2
Sweden	12.8	†	27.1	5.2	49.5
United States	8.8	0.6	9.1	11.5	30.0

* Data are from surveys covering production workers in manufacturing, except Japan and the Netherlands, where all employees are covered. Total add-on includes minor costs and taxes not itemized in table.
† Bonuses in Britain included under hourly earnings; in Sweden, under leave-time pay. Bonuses and leave-time pay in Japan included under hourly earnings.
Source: U.S. Bureau of Labor Statistics.

EXHIBIT 3
THE 1970–1977 SCOREBOARD: RESULTS OF SEVEN YEARS' PLAY IN THE UNIT-LABOR-COST GAME*

| | Exchange-Rate Movement Against U.S. Dollar | Percent Rise Hourly Compensation In | | Percent Rise Output Per Man-Hour | Percent Rise Unit Labor Costs In | |
		Local Currency	U.S.$		Local Currency	U.S.$
Belgium	+39%	181%	290%	65%	71%	137%
Britain	−27	202	120	17	159	88
Canada	− 2	110	106	25	68	65
Denmark	+25	142	202	43	69	111
France	+12	162	194	42	85	108
Germany	+57	117	241	46	48	133
Italy	−29	298	183	38	189	105
Japan	+34	193	291	41	107	178
Netherlands	+47	159	282	53	69	149
Sweden	+16	166	209	26	112	146
Switzerland	+80	80	224	31	37	147
United States	—	75	75	21	44	44

* Data are for manufacturing industry and cover basically all employed and self-employed persons in the United States and Canada, wage earners in Switzerland, and all employees in the other countries.
Sources: U.S. Bureau of Labor Statistics, Citibank estimates.

cost factor in production. Since surveys indicate where these key costs are rising more slowly, they are likely to influence corporate decisions. This would explain why they attract attention now, when competition among countries is rough.

International trends in unit labor costs depend on changes in three factors: compensation, productivity and exchange rates. A country's unit labor costs are calculated by dividing its average hourly compensation by its average rate of productivity—or output per hour worked. Since average rates of money wages rise regularly in all industrial countries, unit labor costs get an upward push from rising compensation. Gains in productivity tend to limit—and at times, reverse—this upward pressure.

But one country's labor costs may be compared with another's only if the costs are expressed in a common currency. This makes exchange rates a critical factor.

For example, the percent rise in Swiss unit labor costs in Swiss francs during 1970–77 was smaller than the percent rise in U.S. unit labor costs in dollars. But a comparison between the two percentages is meaningless. And in fact, when the conversion is made into a common currency—the dollar is the currency used for this purpose in Exhibit 3—the result shows unit labor costs shooting up much faster in Switzerland than in the United States.

In this exhibit, the first column shows how strongly the Swiss franc and several other leading currencies rose against the dollar. The last two columns on the right indicate how exchange-rate movements against the dollar have affected intercountry trends in unit labor costs during 1970–77.

For the same seven-year period, productivity gains in the United States tended to lag those in other countries, except Britain. But hourly compensation rose more slowly in the United States than in all other leading nations shown in the table.

A more detailed picture of increases in compensation is given in Exhibit 1. The hourly rates in this table are estimates of compensation—or in a few cases, of labor costs, where required to reflect the impact of payroll taxes.

Hourly compensation is an especially useful indicator. It includes not only gross pay but also employer contributions to social security and all sorts of employee benefit programs, plus other costs properly attributed to labor.

EXHIBIT 4
SOME TAXMEN TAKE MORE
Percent of GNP In 1975

	Direct Taxes	Social Security Contributions	Total
Belgium	25.5%	12.1%	37.6%
Britain	29.6	6.5	36.1
Canada	30.0	3.4	33.4
Denmark	37.7	0.7	38.4
France	21.1	13.4	34.5
Germany	23.2	13.2	36.4
Italy	20.2	14.8	35.0
Japan	16.1	5.3	21.4
Netherlands	28.8	19.6	48.4
Norway	30.0	13.6	43.6
Sweden	35.2	9.0	44.2
Switzerland	20.1	8.7	28.8
United States ...	24.3	7.2	31.5

Source: West German Finance Ministry, *Finanzbericht 1977.*

FIVE VIEWS OF THE LABOR-COST SCENE

The international landscape of unit labor costs undergoes some interesting changes as the beholder moves from one currency into another. In the table below, the 1970–77 increase in each country's unit labor costs was first expressed in the country's currency, then was converted into sterling, deutschemarks, etc. For every country the percent rise—as measured in five key currencies—is listed under each currency's symbol.

	£	FF	DM	Y	$
Belgium ...	225%	110%	51%	78%	137%
Britain	159	68	20	41	88
Canada	126	46	5	24	65
Denmark ...	190	88	34	58	111
France	186	85	32	56	108
Germany ...	219	106	48	74	133
Italy	181	83	31	54	105
Japan	279	145	76	107	178
Netherlands .	241	121	59	87	149
Sweden	237	118	56	84	146
Switzerland .	237	118	56	84	147
United States	98	28	–7	8	44

Employers' outlays for fringe benefits are heavier in some countries than in others, as shown by Exhibit 2. The data in this table were drawn from surveys conducted in Sweden in 1976, in the United States in 1974 and in the other listed countries between 1971–73.

In certain countries, the cost of fringe benefits is relatively low, but taxation is heavy. Exhibit 4 gives an idea of how direct taxes—and contributions to social security—tend to vary from one country to another.

INSTANT REPLAY

An overview of the international arena is provided by the charts in Exhibit 5. They show how unit-labor-cost trends have affected the competitive standing of six major trading countries. In each chart a top line traces the movements in an index of a leading country's unit labor costs, measured in dollars.

A bottom line plots changes in a second index, showing how the country's unit costs moved relative to those in 13 other leading nations. To obtain this second index, the home country's index was divided by a trade-weighted average of the indexes of the 13 other countries. When the bottom line rises, it signals a deterioration in the home country's relative position. A dip in the line indicates an improvement.

The gap between the top and bottom lines in each chart reveals how trade patterns modulate the impact of labor-cost differences. For instance, the top lines of European countries

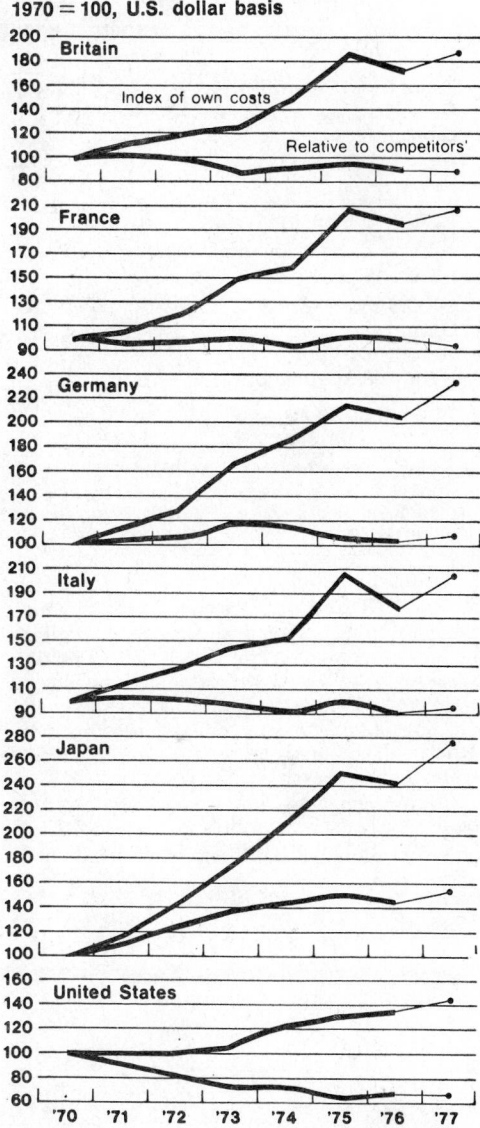

EXHIBIT 5
COMPARING LABOR-COST TRENDS: YOUR RIVALS HAVE COSTS, TOO*

1970 = 100, U.S. dollar basis

* Top lines plot changes in dollar-based index of each country's unit labor costs in manufacturing. Bottom lines reflect changes in this index relative to trade-weighted index. Weighting, adapted by OECD from IMF model, allows for competition among 14 countries on bilateral basis and in third markets.

rise sharply as their costs rise in dollar terms. But their bottom-line trends are almost flat, since they trade heavily with each other. In the U.S. chart, the bottom line's downward slope confirms that, since 1970, the U.S. position has improved considerably in terms of the trade-weighted index of 13 other countries.

EXHIBIT 6
TRENDS IN MANUFACTURING: A BUSINESS CYCLE'S IMPACT ON UNIT LABOR COSTS*

	Britain	Canada	France	Germany	Italy	Japan	United States
1977 vs. 1976							
Labor input (hours).......	2.1%	− 0.9%	− 1.7%	− 1.0%	2.0%	− 1.5%	3.7%
Output...................	0.4	3.1	2.0	3.2	2.5	4.5	6.4
Output per hour..........	− 1.6	4.0	3.8	4.2	0.5	6.1	2.6
Hourly compensation.....	10.0	10.1	12.6	9.2	22.6	9.6	9.0
Unit labor costs in							
National currency........	11.8	5.9	8.5	4.9	22.0	3.3	6.3
U.S. dollars..............	8.1	− 1.8	5.4	13.7	14.7	14.4	6.3
1976 vs. 1975							
Labor input (hours).......	− 2.4	1.7	− 1.3	− 0.8	4.6	0.7	4.4
Output...................	1.0	5.1	8.0	7.4	12.4	13.8	9.3
Output per hour..........	3.5	3.3	9.4	8.2	7.5	13.0	4.7
Hourly compensation.....	18.1	12.7	15.3	6.0	18.4	8.8	8.8
Unit labor costs in							
National currency........	14.2	9.1	5.4	− 2.0	10.2	− 3.7	3.9
U.S. dollars..............	− 7.3	12.6	− 5.5	− 4.4	−13.4	− 3.6	3.9

* Data are for same categories of workers as in Exhibit 3. Changes in labor input reflect changes in employment and hours worked. For Italy, changes in 1977 based on data for three quarters. British and French compensation include tax adjustments borne by employers.
    Source: U.S. Bureau of Labor Statistics.

For 1976 and 1977, a closer look at comparative trends among seven major trading nations is provided in Exhibit 6. Broadly speaking, the data suggest that the long-term improvement in the competitiveness of U.S. unit labor costs suffered a setback in 1976. But by and large, this improvement seems to have resumed last year.

Many significant contrasts can be observed between intercountry trends in 1976 and those in 1977. Frequently, these contrasts reflect differences in the ways the seven countries responded to the cyclical upswing.

In view of the dollar's precipitous decline in currency markets since January, the chances are that the data for 1978 will show a further overall improvement in the U.S. competitive position—when gauged by dollar-based trends in unit labor costs. But perhaps the burning question now is how durable this latest improvement will be.

Price Data

Definitions are applicable to the exhibits on pages 395–419 and 422.

Price data are gathered by the Bureau of Labor Statistics from retail and primary markets in the United States. Price indexes are given in relation to a base period (1967 = 100, unless otherwise noted).

DEFINITIONS

The **Consumer Price Index** is a monthly statistical measure of the average change in prices in a fixed market basket of goods and services. Effective with the January 1978 index, the Bureau of Labor Statistics began publishing CPI's for two groups of the population. One index, a new CPI for All Urban Consumers, covers 80 percent of the total noninstitutional population; and the other index, a revised CPI for Urban Wage Earners and Clerical Workers, covers about half the new index population. The All Urban Consumers index includes, in addition to wage earners and clerical workers, professional, managerial, and technical workers, the self-employed, short-term workers, the unemployed, retirees, and others not in the labor force.

The CPI is based on prices of food, clothing, shelter, fuel, drugs, transportation fares, doctor's and dentist's fees, and other goods and services that people buy for day-to-day living. The quantity and quality of these items are kept essentially unchanged between major revisions so that only price changes will be measured. Prices are collected from over 18,000 tenants, 24,000 retail establishments, and 18,000 housing units for property taxes in 85 urban areas across the country. All taxes directly associated with the purchase and use of items are included in the index. Because the CPI's are based on the expenditures of two population groups in 1972–73, they may not accurately reflect the experience of individual families and single persons with different buying habits.

Though the CPI is often called the "Cost-of-Living Index," it measures only price change, which is just one of several important factors affecting living costs. Area indexes do not measure differences in the level of prices among cities. They only measure the average change in prices for each area since the base period.

Producer Price Indexes measure average changes in prices received in primary markets of the United States by producers of commodities in all stages of processing. The sample used for calculating these indexes contains about 2,800 commodities and about 10,000 quotations per month selected to represent the movement of prices of all commodities produced in the manufacturing, agriculture, forestry, fishing, mining, gas and electricity, and public utilities sectors. The universe includes all commodities produced or imported for sale in commercial transactions in primary markets in the United States.

Producer Price Indexes can be organized by stage of processing or by commodity. The stage of processing structure organizes products by degree of fabrication (that is, finished goods, intermediate or semifinished goods, and crude materials). The commodity structure organizes products by similarity of end-use or material composition.

To the extent possible, prices used in calculating Producer Price Indexes apply to the first significant commercial transaction in the United States, from the production or central marketing point. Price data are generally collected monthly, primarily by mail questionnaire. Most prices are obtained directly from producing companies on a voluntary and confidential basis. Prices generally are reported for the Tuesday of the week containing the 13th day of the month.

In calculating Producer Price Indexes, price changes for the various commodities are averaged together with implicit quantity weights representing their importance in the total net selling value of all commodities as of 1972. The detailed data are aggregated to obtain indexes for stage of processing groupings, commodity groupings, durability of product groupings, and a number of special composite groupings.

Price indexes for the output of selected SIC industries measure average price changes in commodities produced by particular industries, as defined in the *Standard Industrial Classification Manual 1972* (Washington, U.S. Office of Management and Budget, 1972). These indexes are derived from several price series, combined to match the economic activity of the specified industry and weighted by the value of shipments in the industry. They use data from comprehensive industrial

393

censuses conducted by the U.S. Bureau of the Census and the U.S. Department of Agriculture.

NOTES ON THE DATA

Beginning with the May issue of the *Review*, regional CPI's cross classified by population size, were introduced. These indexes will enable users in local areas for which an index is not published to get a better approximation of the CPI for their area by using the appropriate population size class measure for their region. The cross-classified indexes will be published bimonthly.

For further details about the new and the revised indexes and a comparison of various aspects of these indexes with the old unrevised CPI, see *Facts About the Revised Consumer Price Index,* a pamphlet in the Consumer Price Index Revision 1978 series. See also *The Consumer Price Index: Concepts and Content Over the Years,* Report 517, revised edition (Bureau of Labor Statistics, May 1978).

For interarea comparisons of living costs at three hypothetical standards of living, see the family budget data published in the *Handbook of Labor Statistics, 1977,* Bulletin 1966 (Bureau of Labor Statistics, 1977), tables 122–133. Additional data and analysis on price changes are provided in the *CPI Detailed Report* and *Producer Prices and Price Indexes,* both monthly publications of the Bureau.

As of January 1976, the Wholesale Price Index (as it was then called) incorporated a revised weighting structure reflecting 1972 values of shipments. From January 1967 through December 1975, 1963 values of shipments were used as weights.

For a discussion of the general method of computing consumer, producer, and industry price indexes, see *BLS Handbook of Methods for Surveys and Studies,* Bulletin 1910 (Bureau of Labor Statistics, 1976), chapters 13–15. See also John F. Early, "Improving the measurement of producer price change," *Monthly Labor Review,* April 1978, pp. 7–15. For industry prices, see also Bennett R. Moss, "Industry and Sector Price Indexes," *Monthly Labor Review,* August 1965, pp. 974–82.

PRODUCER PRICE INDEXES, FOR SPECIAL COMMODITY GROUPINGS

1967 = 100 unless otherwise specified

Commodity group	Annual average 1977	1977							1978					
		June	July	Aug.	Sept.	Oct.	Nov.	Dec.	Jan.	Feb.	Mar.	Apr.	May	June
All commodities—less farm products	193.7	194.0	194.6	195.1	195.8	196.8	197.4	198.4	200.1	r201.7	203.0	203.0	206.6	207.9
All foods	186.8	188.0	189.1	187.2	187.0	187.2	188.3	190.5	193.4	198.6	199.6	199.2	206.6	208.9
Processed foods	186.8	189.7	190.2	188.3	187.7	188.2	188.7	192.3	194.1	198.7	199.6	199.6	207.1	209.3
Selected textile mill products (Dec. 1975 = 100)	106.7	107.1	106.5	106.9	107.4	107.7	107.4	107.7	107.9	107.9	107.6	107.6	108.3	108.4
Hosiery	107.1	109.2	104.0	104.2	104.5	104.9	104.9	104.9	105.3	105.1	106.1	106.1	106.3	105.7
Underwear and nightwear	152.2	151.5	151.5	155.0	155.0	155.2	155.2	155.2	155.8	156.9	157.1	157.1	157.5	158.8
Chemicals and allied products, including synthetic rubber and manmade fibers and yarns	185.0	185.7	185.9	186.2	186.2	186.4	186.6	186.8	186.9	187.7	188.4	188.4	190.2	190.7
Pharmaceutical preparations	133.4	133.6	133.9	133.9	134.1	134.6	135.2	135.6	136.8	r137.9	138.3	138.3	138.7	140.0
Lumber and wood products, excluding millwork and other wood products	258.8	247.7	258.3	268.1	282.1	272.9	265.1	273.2	281.7	287.8	288.3	288.3	291.8	297.2
Special metals and metal products[1]	193.7	192.1	193.8	195.0	195.9	198.3	198.5	199.4	200.7	r203.1	204.2	204.2	207.4	208.1
Fabricated metal products	198.9	197.2	199.8	200.9	203.0	203.3	204.0	204.9	206.0	208.8	210.8	210.8	213.9	214.5
Copper and copper products	152.9	158.2	155.5	153.4	147.3	144.4	144.3	145.9	150.3	151.1	151.3	151.3	153.0	154.6
Machinery and motive products	176.6	175.2	175.9	176.9	177.9	181.8	182.6	183.1	184.5	r185.2	185.9	185.9	188.3	189.4
Machinery and equipment, except electrical	197.7	196.9	198.1	199.2	200.2	202.0	203.6	204.7	206.4	207.6	208.7	208.7	211.4	213.0
Agricultural machinery, including tractors	199.7	197.5	198.0	200.3	202.4	203.5	208.0	209.4	209.9	210.7	210.3	210.3	211.3	212.2
Metalworking machinery	205.7	206.0	206.7	208.2	210.0	211.0	212.9	214.5	217.9	r219.1	220.6	220.6	224.4	226.9
Numerically controlled machine tools (Dec. 1971 = 100)	167.6	168.0	168.1	168.1	169.7	169.8	170.9	173.2	173.2	r173.3	173.8	173.8	175.2	177.8
Total tractors	210.9	208.6	211.0	212.3	211.1	213.7	217.2	219.8	220.4	221.3	220.2	220.2	224.8	225.4
Agricultural machinery and equipment less parts	196.9	194.7	195.6	197.9	199.6	200.7	204.5	205.8	206.3	r207.1	206.9	206.9	208.2	209.3
Farm and garden tractors less parts	201.5	198.5	199.8	202.6	205.8	206.6	208.6	209.1	210.0	211.4	211.4	211.4	212.0	212.0
Agricultural machinery excluding tractors less parts	198.5	196.8	197.6	198.8	199.8	201.2	207.8	209.9	210.0	210.4	209.5	209.5	210.9	212.5
Industrial valves	217.5	217.3	217.4	218.9	219.5	220.7	222.6	223.2	224.6	225.6	225.6	225.6	227.8	230.6
Industrial fittings	213.4	218.6	218.6	217.8	214.0	213.8	213.8	213.8	219.2	225.5	227.0	227.0	229.2	231.4
Abrasive grinding wheels	194.2	191.5	191.5	191.5	191.5	202.6	203.8	203.8	204.0	r204.4	205.1	205.1	205.1	205.1
Construction materials	204.9	202.5	206.1	208.4	212.0	210.8	210.2	211.8	215.8	r219.9	221.9	221.9	226.2	228.4

[1] Metals and metal products, agricultural machinery and equipment, and motor vehicles and equipment.

Source: *Monthly Labor Review*, U.S. Department of Labor, Bureau of Labor Statistics.

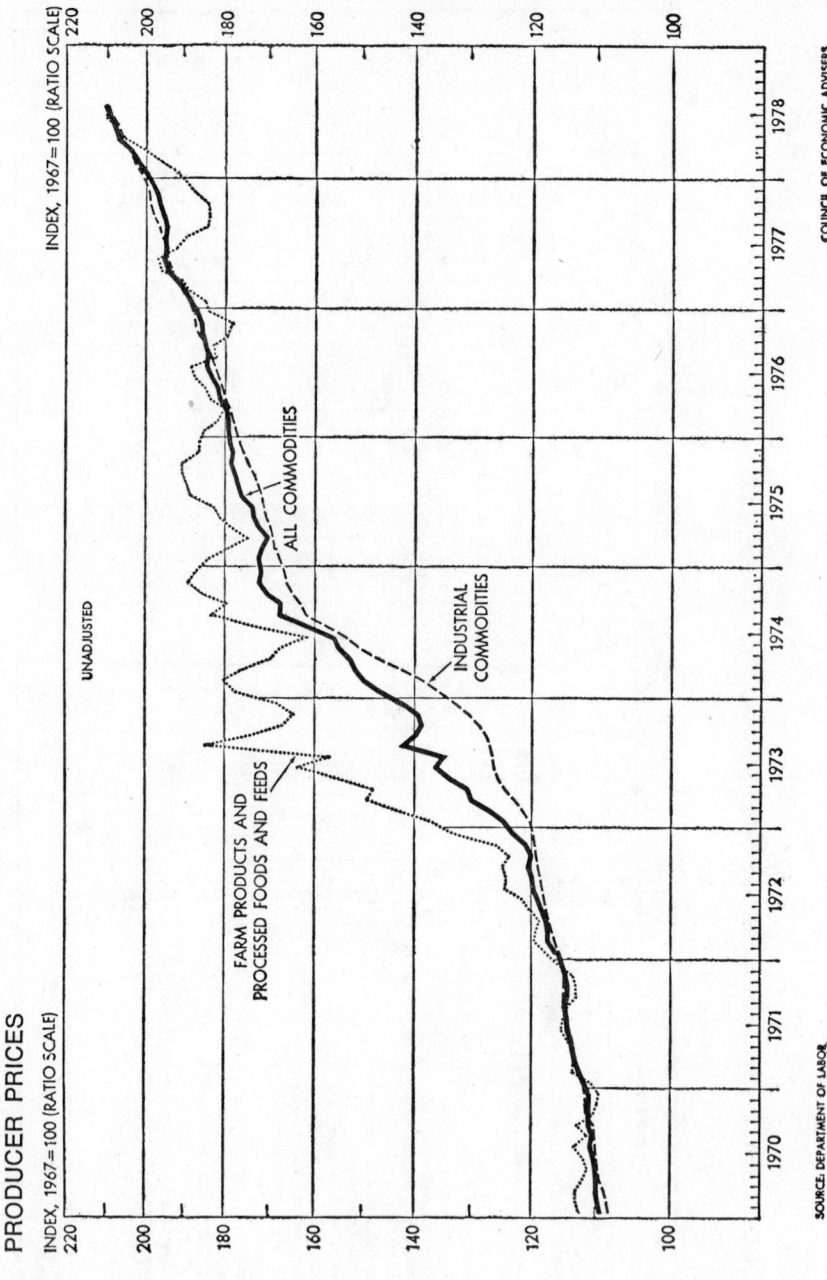

PRODUCER PRICES

INDEX, 1967=100 (RATIO SCALE)

INDEX, 1967=100 (RATIO SCALE)

UNADJUSTED

ALL COMMODITIES

INDUSTRIAL COMMODITIES

FARM PRODUCTS AND PROCESSED FOODS AND FEEDS

SOURCE: DEPARTMENT OF LABOR

COUNCIL OF ECONOMIC ADVISERS

[1967=100]

Period	All commodities	Farm products and processed foods and feeds	Industrial commodities	Finished goods		Excluding consumer foods			Intermediate materials, supplies, and components		Crude materials for further processing		
				Total	Consumer foods	Total	Consumer goods	Capital equipment[1]	Total	Excluding foods and feeds[2]	Total	Foodstuffs and feedstuffs	Other
Unadjusted													
1970	110.4	111.7	110.0	110.3	113.5	109.1	107.7	112.0	109.9	109.9	112.3	112.3	112.7
1971	114.0	113.9	114.1	113.7	115.3	113.1	111.4	116.6	114.1	114.3	115.1	115.1	117.0
1972	119.1	122.4	117.9	117.2	121.7	115.4	113.4	119.5	118.7	118.9	127.6	127.6	128.0
1973	134.7	159.1	125.9	127.9	146.4	120.2	118.5	123.5	131.6	128.1	174.0	174.0	162.5
1974	160.1	177.4	153.8	147.5	166.9	139.4	138.6	141.0	162.9	159.5	196.1	196.1	208.9
1975	174.9	184.2	171.5	163.4	181.0	156.2	153.1	162.5	180.0	178.6	196.9	196.9	206.9
1976	183.0	183.1	182.4	170.3	180.2	165.5	161.8	173.2	189.3	189.5	205.1	205.1	233.6
1977	194.2	188.8	195.1	180.6	189.1	176.2	172.1	184.5	201.7	202.4	214.3	214.3	258.4
Seasonally adjusted													
1977: July	194.8	188.7	195.9	181.1	189.9	176.5	172.6	184.5	202.2	203.2	209.8	185.8	255.4
Aug	194.6	184.3	196.9	181.5	189.3	177.2	173.2	185.4	202.6	204.2	206.3	180.2	255.6
Sept	195.3	184.0	197.8	182.1	189.2	178.2	174.1	186.4	203.5	205.3	205.7	179.8	254.4
Oct	196.3	184.0	199.1	183.2	189.5	179.5	174.8	188.9	204.3	206.1	207.4	182.2	254.9
Nov	197.1	187.0	199.3	184.5	191.9	180.3	175.4	189.9	205.2	206.4	214.4	189.9	260.9
Dec	198.2	189.4	200.0	185.3	192.6	181.2	176.1	191.3	206.0	207.4	217.2	191.1	266.3
1978: Jan	200.1	192.2	201.6	186.6	194.8	182.2	177.1	192.2	207.9	209.2	221.6	196.4	269.4
Feb	202.1	196.8	202.9	188.6	200.7	183.0	177.6	193.5	209.7	210.9	228.7	205.6	272.1
Mar	203.7	200.0	204.1	189.6	202.1	183.9	178.3	194.6	211.3	211.9	231.7	209.2	276.2
Apr	206.4	205.5	206.0	191.9	205.8	185.7	180.7	195.6	212.3	213.0	238.3	217.0	278.7
May	207.9	207.7	207.3	193.3	206.8	187.2	182.1	197.3	213.6	214.1	238.9	217.1	279.7
June	209.4	210.4	208.5	194.7	209.1	188.3	182.9	198.9	214.3	215.1	243.1	221.3	284.4
July	210.6	210.5	209.9	195.7	208.4	189.8	184.8	199.9	215.4	216.0	241.7	215.7	291.0

[1] Formerly called producer finished goods.

[2] Excludes intermediate materials for food manufacturing and manufactured animal feeds.

NOTE.—Data revised for March 1978.

Source: Department of Labor, Bureau of Labor Statistics.

Source: Economic Indicators, Council of Economic Advisors.

PRODUCER PRICE INDEXES, BY COMMODITY GROUPINGS

1967 = 100 unless otherwise specified

Code	Commodity group	Annual average 1977	June (1977)	July	Aug.	Sept.	Oct.	Nov.	Dec.	Jan (1978)	Feb.	Mar.	Apr.	May	June
	All commodities	194.2	194.5	194.8	194.6	195.3	196.3	197.1	198.2	200.1	202.1	203.8	206.4	207.9	209.4
	All commodities (1957–59 = 100)	206.0	206.3	206.6	206.5	207.2	208.2	209.0	210.2	212.3	214.4	216.2	219.0	220.6	222.2
	Farm products and processed foods and feeds	188.8	191.5	188.7	184.3	184.4	184.3	187.0	189.4	192.2	196.8	200.3	205.5	207.7	210.4
	Industrial commodities	195.1	194.7	195.9	196.9	197.8	199.1	199.3	200.0	201.6	202.9	204.1	206.0	207.3	208.5
	FARM PRODUCTS AND PROCESSED FOODS AND FEEDS														
01	Farm products	192.5	192.8	190.2	181.8	182.0	182.0	185.6	188.3	192.2	198.9	205.3	213.6	215.7	219.5
01-1	Fresh and dried fruits and vegetables	192.2	176.3	182.1	176.5	182.9	188.0	193.5	169.5	196.6	204.2	201.6	227.3	220.3	230.2
01-2	Grains	165.2	157.7	151.1	140.5	144.2	144.7	164.6	167.3	169.1	170.8	178.9	198.7	189.2	188.1
01-3	Livestock	173.0	172.3	180.5	175.2	172.9	177.5	171.6	182.7	188.2	202.1	208.3	218.1	230.3	236.2
01-4	Live poultry	175.4	182.7	193.7	176.1	181.7	170.5	162.7	157.8	170.2	188.8	187.9	196.0	194.5	221.6
01-5	Plant and animal fibers	202.3	197.3	195.3	180.3	165.8	166.9	164.1	161.0	171.0	174.4	186.9	181.0	191.8	192.9
01-6	Fluid milk	202.6	199.3	202.7	205.0	206.7	209.6	209.8	210.1	208.4	209.7	219.7	212.1	212.1	212.1
01-7	Eggs	162.0	141.4	156.6	162.0	163.3	137.6	149.4	166.3	145.2	170.3	167.4	152.3	141.2	127.5
01-8	Hay, hayseeds, and oilseeds	234.3	270.2	207.7	196.0	178.2	178.8	193.5	196.9	198.4	191.5	209.5	216.6	219.6	220.4
01-9	Other farm products	325.4	341.7	335.0	292.0	317.1	296.3	303.3	302.5	284.6	277.2	274.1	269.4	269.6	271.8
02	Processed foods and feeds	186.1	190.1	187.2	184.9	184.4	184.3	186.9	189.3	191.5	194.9	196.8	200.2	202.5	204.6
02-1	Cereal and bakery products	173.2	171.1	171.9	172.1	174.6	175.5	179.9	182.1	183.3	185.0	185.7	188.6	188.2	189.0
02-2	Meats, poultry, and fish	182.0	189.5	189.5	182.7	182.8	184.7	183.4	190.8	193.6	205.4	204.6	211.7	220.4	226.2
02-3	Dairy products	173.4	174.3	175.1	175.3	175.6	175.9	176.9	178.2	178.0	178.7	180.3	184.5	184.5	185.4
02-4	Processed fruits and vegetables	187.3	187.7	188.3	190.4	191.1	190.4	193.1	194.4	194.3	194.5	195.6	196.4	197.3	198.7
02-5	Sugar and confectionery	177.5	176.3	171.3	178.8	174.3	170.1	178.5	179.0	185.8	193.8	192.9	196.9	197.1	198.0
02-6	Beverages and beverage materials	200.9	207.9	204.7	205.5	204.8	205.0	201.7	201.3	202.1	201.3	200.0	200.1	199.5	200.0
02-71	Animal fats and oils	267.0	279.9	258.7	252.0	243.6	276.5	270.0	263.2	250.2	262.8	284.7	310.1	279.7	290.4
02-72	Crude vegetable oils	197.5	229.6	181.0	180.7	155.2	164.3	175.0	196.6	185.9	184.6	223.9	219.5	232.1	219.7
02-73	Refined vegetable oils	198.9	219.2	182.0	173.3	162.6	179.7	189.9	212.1	221.7	224.9	230.3	221.8	228.8	224.6
02-74	Vegetable oil end products	198.6	216.3	208.7	199.9	201.1	195.1	190.4	197.4	194.5	193.9	206.6	216.8	219.8	217.9
02-8	Miscellaneous processed foods	190.0	192.9	194.4	194.3	194.2	193.9	192.0	191.9	193.5	194.1	195.8	193.3	200.7	199.9
02-9	Manufactured animal feeds	205.0	225.4	188.3	175.7	174.7	168.5	193.8	187.3	194.3	186.9	200.8	197.8	194.0	198.0
	INDUSTRIAL COMMODITIES														
03	Textile products and apparel	154.0	154.6	154.5	154.6	155.1	155.2	155.3	155.8	156.5	157.0	157.3	157.5	158.4	158.9
03-1	Synthetic fibers[1]	107.4	109.2	108.9	109.3	109.4	109.2	109.3	109.3	110.0	109.9	110.5	109.8	110.2	109.1
03-2	Processed yarns and threads[1]	100.9	103.4	103.4	102.8	102.1	101.2	100.4	100.5	100.6	101.1	101.1	101.3	101.0	101.3
03-3	Grey fabrics[1]	104.7	104.4	104.9	103.3	103.0	103.7	105.2	107.2	108.9	109.9	112.2	113.9	117.1	117.8
03-4	Finished fabrics[1]	103.9	104.8	104.6	104.6	104.4	104.3	103.5	103.6	103.6	103.7	102.9	103.1	103.2	102.9
03-81	Apparel	147.3	147.3	147.3	147.8	148.4	148.6	149.1	149.4	150.1	150.0	150.0	150.3	150.8	151.7
03-82	Textile housefurnishings	171.5	169.4	169.4	170.8	174.4	175.2	175.3	175.3	175.4	175.8	176.7	176.4	177.0	178.7

Code															
04	Hides, skins, leather, and related products	179.5	179.4	180.0	180.2	179.6	179.2	180.0	181.5	185.8	187.2	188.1	192.2	193.8	195.5
04-1	Hides and skins	286.8	288.8	291.5	288.3	274.4	266.6	273.2	291.9	300.4	298.2	296.0	320.5	321.7	346.5
04-2	Leather	201.1	202.3	198.7	200.3	200.5	196.4	197.0	200.4	210.8	211.9	215.3	217.4	217.3	217.4
04-3	Footwear	168.8	168.2	169.8	169.9	170.0	171.2	171.6	171.6	173.4	175.7	176.2	180.5	181.4	181.6
04-4	Other leather and related products	163.4	163.7	163.8	164.2	164.5	164.4	164.7	164.7	170.3	170.5	171.7	171.9	176.0	176.6
05	Fuels and related products and power	302.2	304.3	307.0	309.5	309.9	310.7	310.5	312.0	312.8	312.9	315.3	317.3	319.6	322.8
05-1	Coal	389.4	390.5	393.0	394.2	395.1	398.5	400.6	402.0	403.8	404.9	407.2	426.6	432.4	434.6
05-2	Coke	379.4	386.1	386.1	386.1	386.1	386.1	386.1	386.1	388.4	400.9	400.9	400.9	418.8	418.8
05-3	Gas fuels	387.9	386.6	391.8	400.9	405.2	406.2	414.0	422.3	420.4	417.7	423.6	428.7	428.9	428.1
05-4	Electric power	232.9	234.3	239.0	244.6	242.8	242.1	237.6	237.0	239.5	242.6	250.0	250.8	252.8	256.5
05-61	Crude petroleum	274.2	271.8	270.8	273.3	276.1	278.6	282.9	288.1	288.8	289.7	293.4	294.3	295.5	298.8
05-7	Petroleum products, refined	308.1	312.2	313.8	313.1	313.2	314.2	313.6	313.9	314.3	312.9	311.1	311.6	314.4	318.0
06	Chemicals and allied products	192.7	193.9	193.6	193.6	193.2	193.7	193.9	194.1	194.1	195.2	196.2	197.0	198.6	199.1
06-1	Industrial chemicals	223.9	224.2	224.6	224.5	224.1	224.9	225.1	225.3	224.3	224.2	224.1	224.4	223.6	224.6
06-21	Prepared paint	182.4	181.7	183.9	183.9	185.1	185.1	186.7	185.9	186.1	189.3	189.5	191.6	192.6	192.6
06-22	Paint materials	205.9	209.3	206.6	206.8	204.7	203.8	204.3	206.1	205.0	204.5	207.7	209.3	210.8	211.9
06-3	Drugs and pharmaceuticals	140.5	140.8	141.2	141.2	141.4	141.8	142.3	142.9	144.1	145.0	145.3	146.2	146.6	147.8
06-4	Fats and oils, inedible	279.0	318.8	281.9	268.9	246.9	260.9	265.4	266.1	263.2	281.5	294.6	301.3	315.2	313.2
06-5	Agricultural chemicals and chemical products	187.7	189.0	188.5	188.6	189.9	190.2	188.2	187.1	187.5	189.1	190.8	192.1	203.3	202.4
06-6	Plastic resins and materials	197.4	197.6	200.2	200.2	200.1	199.8	199.4	198.7	198.8	198.3	199.4	199.1	200.6	200.9
06-7	Other chemicals and allied products	175.6	176.0	175.9	176.4	176.5	176.6	177.4	178.0	178.6	180.4	181.4	181.8	182.0	182.6
07	Rubber and plastic products	167.5	167.5	168.9	169.3	169.5	170.2	170.2	170.0	170.2	170.2	171.3	172.7	173.7	174.4
07-1	Rubber and rubber products	173.5	173.0	174.9	175.5	176.2	177.2	177.3	177.4	178.0	178.0	179.0	181.8	184.3	185.3
07-11	Crude rubber	171.5	171.8	172.4	172.8	176.6	176.6	177.5	177.2	177.6	181.5	181.8	181.3	181.9	185.1
07-12	Tires and tubes	169.7	168.0	171.4	172.0	172.0	172.0	171.7	172.1	172.3	170.9	172.2	175.0	178.7	179.3
07-13	Miscellaneous rubber products	176.6	177.2	177.8	178.4	178.9	180.9	181.7	181.7	182.6	182.9	184.0	187.7	189.5	190.2
07-21	Plastic construction products[3]	133.2	134.1	136.5	136.7	136.0	136.1	135.7	134.7	134.6	134.6	134.8	134.7	134.7	135.6
07-22	Unsupported plastic film and sheeting[3]	160.3	160.3	160.9	161.0	161.2	161.6	161.6	161.5	161.2	161.2	162.7	162.8	162.1	162.3
07-23	Laminated plastic sheets, high pressure[3]	141.2	142.4	143.1	142.9	142.0	142.1	142.6	142.2	142.1	142.8	143.2	144.6	145.0	145.1
08	Lumber and wood products	236.2	228.8	235.6	242.7	252.9	247.8	243.3	249.2	256.4	263.7	266.0	269.5	273.4	278.5
08-1	Lumber	276.5	264.8	275.9	286.4	301.7	294.2	284.8	291.0	300.4	308.5	312.5	316.7	316.5	320.8
08-2	Millwork	193.6	192.4	192.2	194.8	197.8	200.6	202.5	204.2	209.2	219.4	225.0	233.7	240.5	244.9
08-3	Plywood	212.0	202.7	211.9	219.8	230.4	221.8	213.5	225.8	231.9	233.3	226.3	220.3	228.4	236.0
08-4	Other wood products	184.3	185.4	185.6	186.5	189.7	189.8	189.8	191.0	194.6	199.0	202.1	204.8	208.8	214.0

See footnotes at end of table.

PRODUCER PRICE INDEXES, BY COMMODITY GROUPINGS (continued)

Code	Commodity group	Annual average 1977	1977 June	July	Aug.	Sept.	Oct.	Nov.	Dec.	1978 Jan	Feb.	Mar.	Apr.	May	June
	INDUSTRIAL COMMODITIES—Continued														
09	Pulp, paper, and allied products	186.4	187.3	187.8	187.8	188.1	188.7	188.2	187.6	188.0	[r]188.6	189.8	191.6	193.0	193.3
09-1	Pulp, paper, and products, excluding building paper and board	187.4	188.4	188.8	188.6	188.7	189.2	188.7	188.0	188.3	[r]188.6	189.6	191.4	192.7	193.1
09-11	Woodpulp	281.8	285.8	285.8	282.1	277.5	276.0	275.5	266.6	262.9	[r]262.2	262.8	263.0	262.5	262.5
09-12	Wastepaper	187.2	186.3	186.3	183.6	187.3	191.1	201.3	208.0	209.9	210.8	202.9	183.0	182.5	182.6
09-13	Paper	194.3	194.3	195.4	196.2	196.0	197.4	197.2	196.9	197.5	[r]198.1	199.0	202.8	204.3	205.4
09-14	Paperboard	176.5	179.5	180.6	179.3	178.8	177.8	173.6	170.8	170.7	[r]172.1	174.1	176.5	178.0	178.6
09-15	Converted paper and paperboard products	176.5	177.5	177.4	177.5	178.1	178.6	178.3	178.3	178.9	179.0	180.2	181.9	183.3	183.4
09-2	Building paper and board	157.0	153.8	157.8	162.5	166.8	168.9	168.3	170.7	175.0	180.1	186.6	188.6	190.7	192.0
10	Metals and metal products	209.0	207.7	210.6	211.7	212.6	211.8	212.0	213.3	215.2	219.1	221.1	223.8	224.4	225.2
10-1	Iron and steel	230.3	227.0	232.1	233.2	236.0	234.4	233.5	235.7	237.9	[r]244.8	247.2	251.7	251.7	252.1
10-13	Steel mill products	229.9	225.4	233.4	234.4	237.5	237.5	237.3	237.3	237.5	246.4	248.5	252.8	253.3	253.6
10-2	Nonferrous metals	195.4	197.3	198.0	198.5	195.1	193.6	194.2	195.1	198.0	199.7	201.1	202.9	203.2	205.2
10-3	Metal containers	218.2	216.9	217.5	218.3	225.1	226.5	227.1	227.1	227.2	233.7	236.8	236.8	239.1	239.2
10-4	Hardware	185.3	184.6	187.0	186.8	187.6	186.8	188.0	189.5	193.4	194.0	194.0	196.4	197.3	197.6
10-5	Plumbing fixtures and brass fittings	186.6	186.1	189.3	189.9	190.8	190.9	191.2	192.0	192.4	[r]194.8	196.0	197.7	198.2	198.9
10-6	Heating equipment	165.5	164.5	165.4	166.0	166.8	168.0	168.3	169.3	171.3	[r]170.7	171.1	172.5	173.7	173.6
10-7	Fabricated structural metal products	206.8	204.9	207.9	210.1	211.9	211.8	212.2	213.3	214.5	218.9	221.5	224.7	225.1	226.0
10-8	Miscellaneous metal products	196.4	194.5	196.9	198.1	199.8	200.5	201.5	202.2	202.7	[r]203.9	206.1	207.4	209.0	209.7
11	Machinery and equipment	181.7	180.7	181.8	182.8	183.8	185.4	186.8	187.5	189.3	[r]190.3	191.4	192.4	193.7	195.1
11-1	Agricultural machinery and equipment	197.7	195.9	196.6	198.6	200.4	201.4	205.3	206.3	206.7	207.7	207.6	208.6	209.2	209.6
11-2	Construction machinery and equipment	213.7	212.0	213.9	215.3	214.7	217.2	220.8	223.0	223.5	[r]224.8	224.9	227.9	229.8	230.7
11-3	Metalworking machinery and equipment	198.5	197.9	199.3	200.8	202.3	203.5	204.9	206.0	208.3	[r]209.5	210.5	212.0	213.5	215.3
11-4	General purpose machinery and equipment	201.7	201.7	202.8	203.7	204.6	205.5	206.8	207.4	208.9	[r]210.2	211.1	211.9	214.1	215.8
11-6	Special industry machinery and equipment	202.8	201.9	202.8	203.8	204.1	209.5	209.9	211.8	213.5	[r]214.4	216.7	217.9	219.3	222.2
11-7	Electrical machinery and equipment	154.1	152.0	154.1	154.6	155.7	157.3	157.9	158.0	160.0	[r]160.7	161.7	162.4	163.3	164.5
11-9	Miscellaneous machinery	180.7	179.7	180.7	181.9	183.3	184.0	185.1	185.9	188.1	[r]189.3	191.2	191.5	192.5	193.6

Code	Commodity														
12	Furniture and household durables	151.4	151.5	151.4	152.6	152.7	153.0	153.8	154.2	156.5	†156.7	157.4	158.3	158.4	159.2
12-1	Household furniture	162.2	162.2	162.9	163.2	163.3	164.1	165.1	166.4	168.2	†168.8	168.9	169.9	170.6	172.3
12-2	Commercial furniture	185.9	186.7	184.4	191.0	190.8	190.8	192.2	192.2	194.9	†195.1	198.8	200.5	200.5	200.5
12-3	Floor coverings	136.4	135.8	136.1	136.5	136.6	137.1	138.1	138.3	139.8	†139.8	140.1	141.7	141.9	142.3
12-4	Household appliances	144.9	144.8	145.7	146.6	147.5	147.8	148.0	148.0	149.5	†149.8	150.9	152.1	152.1	152.3
12-5	Home electronic equipment	87.7	88.4	86.8	86.8	86.4	86.2	86.6	86.5	89.0	†88.7	88.5	88.5	87.4	87.4
12-6	Other household durable goods	190.1	189.9	190.7	191.4	191.4	191.7	192.5	193.5	198.1	†198.0	198.1	198.1	199.9	202.1
13	Nonmetallic mineral products	200.4	200.6	201.7	202.5	204.3	205.4	205.7	206.6	212.9	†215.1	215.8	218.0	219.1	221.7
13-11	Flat glass	160.8	161.6	160.0	161.1	161.1	162.5	164.0	168.2	168.2	†170.3	170.3	172.8	172.8	172.8
13-2	Concrete ingredients	198.8	199.9	200.6	200.9	201.0	201.3	201.5	201.5	209.7	†210.7	211.1	215.2	215.9	216.3
13-3	Concrete products	191.8	191.0	192.8	193.5	194.0	195.0	195.4	195.7	202.9	†205.2	205.9	207.8	209.4	211.4
13-4	Structural clay products excluding refractories	179.8	180.2	183.8	184.5	185.7	187.8	185.1	185.5	189.6	†190.4	193.5	193.7	194.2	195.5
13-5	Refractories	199.6	196.5	197.3	198.5	207.1	208.5	210.3	209.3	209.6	†210.1	210.7	211.0	211.3	211.3
13-6	Asphalt roofing	253.0	246.2	253.5	253.5	267.1	275.2	275.2	275.2	277.4	†277.4	277.6	283.6	287.5	289.4
13-7	Gypsum products	183.5	187.1	186.6	189.8	193.7	201.6	203.2	204.9	209.7	†215.9	217.0	221.2	228.2	230.2
13-8	Glass containers	214.3	218.1	218.1	218.1	218.1	218.5	218.5	218.5	236.6	†236.3	236.5	236.5	236.5	249.0
13-9	Other nonmetallic minerals	250.5	250.4	251.5	253.7	257.6	256.1	256.0	257.3	260.7	†267.3	268.6	269.1	269.9	274.2
14	Transportation equipment[1]	161.3	159.5	159.6	160.7	161.5	167.8	168.1	168.3	169.1	†169.5	169.6	170.5	172.1	172.5
14-1	Motor vehicles and equipment	163.7	161.9	161.9	163.2	163.9	170.7	170.7	170.9	171.3	†171.8	171.9	172.8	174.7	175.2
14-4	Railroad equipment	233.5	232.0	234.2	235.2	235.2	238.7	238.7	239.7	243.7	†244.6	244.6	250.2	250.9	251.0
15	Miscellaneous products	164.4	163.5	163.9	164.2	166.0	168.4	168.9	169.7	171.6	†171.3	172.5	181.2	182.4	183.6
15-1	Toys, sporting goods, small arms, ammunition	155.2	154.9	155.2	155.7	155.5	156.7	156.8	157.0	159.6	†161.4	162.0	162.3	162.3	162.9
15-2	Tobacco products	180.0	175.3	175.7	175.8	186.8	189.6	189.6	190.1	190.6	†191.3	190.9	191.4	191.4	195.1
15-3	Notions	172.4	172.4	172.6	172.9	172.9	172.9	172.8	172.8	180.7	180.7	181.5	181.5	181.5	181.5
15-4	Photographic equipment and supplies	139.9	140.4	141.2	141.0	140.6	140.7	140.7	141.5	142.1	142.6	142.7	144.4	144.7	146.0
15-9	Other miscellaneous products	167.4	167.1	167.0	167.5	167.7	173.1	174.1	175.0	177.5	174.1	177.5	206.5	210.7	211.1

[1] December 1975 = 100.
[2] December 1969 = 100.
[3] December 1970 = 100.
[4] December 1968 = 100.

Source: *Monthly Labor Review*, U.S. Department of Labor, Bureau of Labor Statistics.

PRICE INDEXES FOR THE OUTPUT OF SELECTED SIC INDUSTRIES

1967 = 100 unless otherwise specified

Month columns: the first seven months (June–Dec.) are for 1977; the last six months (Jan.–June) are for 1978.

1972 SIC code	Industry	Annual average 1977	June	July	Aug.	Sept.	Oct.	Nov.	Dec.	Jan.	Feb.	Mar.	Apr.	May	June
	MINING														
1011	Iron ores (12/75 = 100)	116.6	117.1	117.1	117.1	117.1	117.1	117.1	117.1	117.1	117.1	117.1	119.7	120.2	122.8
1092	Mercury ores (12/75 = 100)	117.5	103.7	89.6	104.2	117.7	121.7	114.6	106.2	109.6	137.5	122.9	122.9	127.1	122.9
1211	Bituminous coal and lignite	388.7	389.7	392.3	393.5	394.4	397.9	400.1	401.6	403.4	404.5	406.9	426.8	432.8	434.9
1311	Crude petroleum and natural gas	317.0	314.6	315.8	321.8	325.0	326.4	331.4	338.1	337.5	338.7	346.4	350.2	351.7	351.4
1442	Construction sand and gravel	178.7	179.0	179.8	179.9	180.7	181.2	181.1	181.2	187.1	189.3	189.8	189.8	193.3	194.3
1455	Kaolin and ball clay (6/76 = 100)	104.1	104.1	104.1	104.1	105.2	105.9	105.9	105.9	107.1	107.4	107.4	107.4	109.4	109.4
	MANUFACTURING														
2011	Meat packing plants	177.9	180.3	184.4	178.3	176.3	183.7	180.4	188.5	190.9	202.7	202.6	213.1	223.5	229.6
2013	Sausages and other prepared meats	172.8	178.7	183.6	183.4	183.4	182.6	189.3	194.6	196.9	210.5	207.7	208.6	215.4	215.0
2016	Poultry dressing plants	172.1	177.1	187.1	173.1	177.4	168.8	161.6	158.5	167.7	182.3	183.0	188.3	187.9	209.3
2021	Creamery butter	183.9	186.9	187.2	187.6	187.4	190.8	188.6	191.0	188.7	187.8	193.3	197.4	198.2	198.9
2022	Cheese natural and processed (12/72 = 100)	152.0	151.9	153.9	154.0	155.1	155.3	155.4	158.1	157.6	159.6	162.1	164.2	164.4	165.0
2024	Ice cream and frozen desserts (12/72 = 100)	143.8	145.3	145.3	145.3	145.3	145.3	147.7	148.4	148.5	148.5	149.1	153.2	154.4	154.9
2033	Canned fruits and vegetables	179.4	180.8	180.4	180.3	181.2	181.9	183.9	184.8	185.3	186.1	187.0	188.5	189.7	192.1
2034	Dehydrated food products (12/73 = 100)	125.0	127.3	126.3	128.7	127.3	124.6	117.7	117.9	118.3	116.1	116.8	117.4	118.3	116.8
2041	Flour mills (12/71 = 100)	130.6	127.4	123.3	119.1	122.6	117.7	135.8	133.6	135.9	137.6	140.2	148.6	144.5	145.4
2044	Rice milling	170.9	170.7	169.5	163.0	168.4	173.1	225.9	245.5	245.5	245.5	245.5	237.8	221.7	221.7
2048	Prepared foods, n.e.c. (12/75 = 100)	109.6	119.0	106.0	96.5	95.3	92.8	102.7	102.7	104.7	102.1	108.8	108.9	106.1	110.0
2061	Raw cane sugar	147.3	137.4	130.4	158.1	148.6	134.4	134.4	134.4	173.0	193.0	182.6	193.4	187.6	190.4
2063	Beet sugar	158.0	158.5	147.7	154.8	154.6	148.6	160.4	173.6	176.9	203.5	187.1	187.3	187.3	188.3
2067	Chewing gum	203.4	203.8	203.4	203.4	203.4	203.7	203.7	203.7	203.9	203.5	204.1	204.1	223.0	223.0
2074	Cottonseed oil mills	185.8	223.9	174.9	160.3	139.2	146.2	168.4	163.9	171.9	168.2	179.3	170.6	175.8	173.9
2075	Soybean oil mills	232.4	271.8	192.0	193.8	183.6	174.6	210.3	202.2	213.2	197.6	231.6	229.9	235.5	225.2
2077	Animal and marine fats and oils	268.8	297.0	248.6	243.0	239.2	243.2	259.6	245.1	250.3	257.2	283.5	280.2	280.0	285.3
2083	Malt	208.5	217.7	210.1	199.4	188.7	188.7	188.7	188.7	188.7	180.7	180.7	180.7	180.7	180.7
2085	Distilled liquor, except brandy (12/75 = 100)	100.9	100.6	100.6	100.6	101.7	101.8	101.7	101.7	102.7	106.1	106.1	106.1	106.8	106.8
2091	Canned and cured seafoods (12/73 = 100)	129.7	135.2	135.4	134.9	135.3	134.5	136.2	136.8	136.6	136.5	134.8	135.0	135.3	136.3
2092	Fresh or frozen packaged fish	292.3	291.0	295.3	275.1	285.2	276.7	280.9	291.4	286.4	280.8	284.1	290.2	291.8	293.8
2095	Roasted coffee (12/72 = 100)	314.7	353.4	335.9	335.0	328.9	327.7	306.7	302.7	302.8	285.9	276.4	275.8	267.2	267.2
2098	Macaroni and spaghetti	167.0	168.1	168.1	168.1	168.1	168.1	168.1	168.1	171.2	174.2	174.2	174.2	174.1	174.2
2111	Cigarettes	195.4	180.1	180.2	180.2	192.8	196.0	196.0	196.1	196.2	196.5	196.5	196.6	196.6	200.7
2121	Cigars	130.6	130.3	131.6	133.2	133.4	133.4	133.8	135.7	140.5	141.1	136.7	138.7	138.8	139.4
2131	Chewing and smoking tobacco	199.4	197.9	201.8	201.9	202.0	202.0	202.0	207.3	208.2	219.3	219.2	219.2	223.9	223.9
2211	Weaving mills, cotton (12/72 = 100)	173.5	173.7	174.2	174.2	174.6	174.1	174.1	175.8	175.8	176.9	178.0	177.5	177.6	179.4
2251	Women's hosiery, except socks (12/75 = 100)	97.2	101.0	91.0	91.0	91.1	91.1	91.1	91.1	91.1	91.1	91.2	91.2	91.2	90.4
2254	Knit underwear mills	156.2	155.8	155.7	160.1	160.3	160.3	160.4	160.4	161.6	163.0	163.2	163.2	163.4	164.1
2257	Circular knit fabric mills (6/76 = 100)	98.7	100.0	98.9	99.1	99.0	99.2	97.8	97.6	96.7	98.1	97.8	98.1	98.3	98.3

Code	Product														
2261	Finishing plants, cotton (6/76 = 100)	108.6	110.0	110.0	110.0	109.3	108.2	109.6	109.9	109.3	109.2	109.5	109.4	109.6	109.4
2262	Finishing plants, synthetics, silk (6/76 = 100)	99.5	100.2	100.0	100.0	99.5	99.1	99.6	99.9	99.3	99.0	98.8	99.7	100.1	100.6
2271	Woven carpets and rugs (12/75 = 100)	108.6	108.1	108.1	108.1	108.0	111.4	108.0	111.4	111.5	111.5	111.6	115.6	115.7	115.7
2272	Tufted carpets and rugs	121.2	120.6	120.6	121.1	121.4	122.9	122.0	123.0	123.5	123.5	123.8	126.0	125.5	126.0
2281	Yarn mills, except wool (12/71 = 100)	165.9	168.5	168.5	165.9	163.9	162.0	162.4	162.0	162.4	163.4	164.7	166.1	167.1	167.5
2282	Throwing and winding mills (6/76 = 100)	97.9	102.1	102.1	102.6	101.4	99.4	101.4	99.8	99.5	100.0	99.5	98.0	96.3	96.8
2284	Thread mills (6/76 = 100)	110.8	112.5	112.4	112.2	112.3	112.2	112.2	112.2	112.2	112.3	110.0	112.7	112.7	112.8
2321	Men's and boys' shirts and nightwear	177.5	177.6	177.7	177.8	179.1	179.6	179.1	179.7	179.9	179.8	179.8	179.8	180.0	179.0
2322	Men's and boys' underwear	172.0	171.2	171.1	176.5	176.6	176.7	176.6	176.8	178.0	180.2	180.2	180.2	180.2	181.1
2323	Men's and boys' neckwear (12/75 = 100)	100.3	100.0	103.5	100.0	100.0	100.0	100.0	100.0	100.0	100.0	100.0	100.0	100.4	103.4
2327	Men's and boys' separate trousers	147.7	147.7	147.9	147.9	148.0	148.1	148.0	148.3	148.8	148.3	148.3	152.6	152.4	152.6
2341	Women's and children's underwear (12/72 = 100)	128.2	128.0	128.0	128.8	128.8	129.2	128.9	129.2	129.4	129.5	129.8	129.8	130.2	130.9
2342	Brassieres and allied garments (12/75 = 100)	107.3	107.4	108.4	108.4	108.4	109.4	108.4	109.4	109.4	111.1	111.1	111.6	111.6	111.7
2381	Fabric dress and work gloves	199.7	200.8	200.8	201.2	202.1	203.2	202.7	204.9	207.8	208.3	208.3	211.1	211.7	212.5
2421	Sawmills and planing mills (12/71 = 100)	195.0	186.2	194.9	202.8	213.8	199.7	206.0	203.2	216.6	218.5	221.1	223.8	224.4	228.5
2436	Softwood veneer and plywood (12/75 = 100)	134.7	126.1	133.7	141.0	149.5	135.5	142.3	146.9	150.1	151.4	145.2	138.5	145.6	150.6
2439	Structural wood members, n.e.c. (12/75 = 100)	120.0	118.0	116.3	119.3	123.1	128.2	128.2	128.2	128.3	132.4	133.4	133.0	133.1	135.4
2448	Wood pallets and skids (12/75 = 100)	119.6	120.0	120.5	122.2	124.7	124.5	124.6	125.6	128.8	134.8	138.2	141.8	146.4	152.8
2451	Mobile homes (12/74 = 100)	116.8	116.7	117.3	118.0	118.1	119.8	119.0	121.2	122.4	123.0	123.6	124.7	124.8	125.2
2492	Particleboard (12/75 = 100)	120.0	113.6	120.4	128.3	137.7	135.1	137.5	138.3	149.0	155.6	165.8	168.5	169.0	172.0
2511	Wood household furniture (12/71 = 100)	141.6	141.7	142.0	142.2	142.3	144.7	143.3	146.1	147.2	147.3	147.3	148.3	150.1	151.9
2512	Upholstered household furniture (12/71 = 100)	136.6	137.1	137.1	137.1	137.1	138.5	137.7	138.6	139.6	140.2	140.2	141.5	141.4	143.0
2515	Mattresses and bedsprings	145.5	144.7	146.7	146.7	146.7	148.0	148.0	149.7	154.4	154.4	154.2	154.3	154.4	155.1
2521	Wood office furniture	178.6	179.5	180.1	181.0	185.0	184.4	181.0	184.4	186.0	186.8	190.5	193.2	193.2	193.2
2611	Pulp mills (12/73 = 100)	185.4	187.1	187.1	186.5	187.0	183.2	183.7	181.2	178.2	177.6	180.0	178.3	177.9	179.9
2621	Paper mills, except building (12/74 = 100)	110.7	110.9	111.4	111.7	111.4	111.6	111.8	111.3	111.3	111.7	112.2	113.2	113.9	114.5
2631	Paperboard mills (12/74 = 100)	104.5	106.1	106.6	105.9	105.5	103.1	105.0	101.6	101.5	102.3	103.4	104.7	105.5	105.9
2647	Sanitary paper products	234.6	238.2	238.3	238.3	238.4	238.5	238.4	238.5	240.0	241.2	243.5	246.6	249.8	249.8
2654	Sanitary food containers	163.2	164.5	164.5	164.8	164.8	164.5	164.8	164.5	164.9	164.9	168.9	170.3	169.8	169.8
2655	Fiber cans, drums, and similar products (12/75 = 100)	114.5	114.6	114.4	115.4	116.4	118.5	118.5	118.5	119.8	120.2	120.2	120.6	121.8	121.8
2812	Alkalies and chlorine (12/73 = 100)	198.9	198.9	199.5	199.5	199.7	199.4	200.5	198.8	198.3	195.8	197.0	196.1	198.3	199.5
2821	Plastics materials and resins (6/76 = 100)	102.3	102.4	103.6	103.6	103.7	103.5	103.6	103.1	103.2	103.0	103.5	103.5	104.2	104.4
2822	Synthetic rubber	169.1	170.6	171.1	171.7	172.4	174.1	173.8	174.2	174.5	177.8	177.7	177.8	178.1	179.3
2824	Organic fiber, noncellulosic	106.7	109.1	108.9	109.5	109.4	108.7	109.1	108.7	109.0	108.9	109.4	108.2	108.2	106.7
2873	Nitrogenous fertilizers (12/75 = 100)	97.7	98.8	99.0	98.9	99.0	96.0	98.1	95.2	94.6	96.5	98.4	98.4	97.7	97.1
2874	Phosphatic fertilizers	159.9	160.2	160.3	164.0	164.2	162.2	164.8	158.0	160.2	162.1	165.6	166.2	165.9	165.4
2875	Fertilizers, mixing only	176.7	176.7	176.9	176.8	177.1	178.8	179.3	180.6	180.6	179.9	180.3	181.8	181.8	182.0
2892	Explosives	200.3	199.8	199.7	200.2	200.1	199.8	200.2	213.3	213.1	214.4	215.0	214.6	214.1	214.1
2911	Petroleum refining (6/76 = 100)	113.8	115.1	116.0	116.0	116.1	116.5	116.4	116.8	117.1	116.8	116.3	116.5	117.2	118.2
2951	Paving mixtures and blocks (12/75 = 100)	107.4	106.8	107.7	109.0	109.9	110.0	110.2	110.5	112.3	114.8	114.4	114.8	116.1	116.6

PRICE INDEXES FOR THE OUTPUT OF SELECTED SIC INDUSTRIES (continued)

1972 SIC code	Industry	Annual average 1977	1977							1978					
			June	July	Aug.	Sept.	Oct.	Nov.	Dec.	Jan.	Feb.	Mar.	Apr.	May	June
2952	Asphalt felts and coatings (12/75 = 100)	111.1	108.2	111.2	111.3	117.3	120.9	121.0	121.0	121.8	121.8	122.0	124.7	126.4	127.1
3011	Tires and inner tubes (12/73 = 100)	146.0	144.6	147.4	147.8	147.8	147.8	147.6	147.9	148.2	147.1	148.2	150.5	153.5	154.1
3021	Rubber and plastic footwear (12/71 = 100)	148.7	146.2	146.4	149.1	150.4	153.6	154.7	154.7	154.9	154.9	154.9	156.4	156.4	157.2
3031	Reclaimed rubber (12/73 = 100)	147.8	149.4	148.4	148.8	149.5	152.1	151.7	151.6	151.6	152.9	150.7	152.3	151.4	152.5
3142	House slippers (12/75 = 100)	109.3	106.3	111.5	111.5	111.5	111.7	111.7	111.7	118.5	119.5	120.7	121.6	121.6	121.6
3143	Men's footwear, except athletic (12/75 = 100)	115.1	114.8	116.1	116.2	116.2	117.5	117.9	118.0	119.5	122.3	122.4	125.2	125.4	125.7
3144	Women's footwear, except athletic	151.9	151.8	152.7	152.7	152.7	153.6	153.9	153.9	154.0	154.8	154.9	161.6	164.0	164.0
3171	Women's handbags and purses (12/75 = 100)	102.9	103.5	103.5	103.5	103.5	103.5	103.5	103.5	105.7	105.7	105.7	105.7	114.3	114.3
3211	Flat glass (12/71 = 100)	132.1	132.5	130.8	132.0	132.0	135.1	137.9	137.9	137.9	140.1	140.1	142.9	142.9	142.9
3221	Glass containers	214.2	218.0	218.0	218.0	218.0	218.5	218.5	218.5	236.8	236.2	236.5	236.5	236.5	248.9
3241	Cement, hydraulic	227.7	229.8	230.8	231.0	231.0	230.9	230.7	230.7	243.0	243.0	241.0	248.5	248.5	248.5
3251	Brick and structural clay tile	201.8	199.4	205.5	206.8	209.6	211.4	212.9	213.0	209.9	221.3	226.3	226.6	227.2	227.4
3253	Ceramic wall and floor tile (12/75 = 100)	108.0	111.6	111.6	111.6	111.6	113.5	104.8	104.8	104.9	104.9	106.0	106.0	106.0	108.3
3255	Clay refractories	203.5	200.6	201.2	202.6	209.6	212.1	213.7	213.7	214.2	214.9	216.1	216.3	217.0	216.9
3259	Structural clay products, n.e.c.	165.3	166.8	168.9	168.9	168.8	168.3	168.4	170.6	169.5	172.4	172.4	172.7	174.8	176.0
3261	Vitreous plumbing fixtures	174.2	172.2	175.9	177.9	180.4	180.6	180.7	181.4	182.0	183.6	186.9	188.5	188.7	190.4
3262	Vitreous china food utensils	233.2	234.7	234.7	234.7	234.7	234.7	247.0	247.0	256.2	256.2	256.2	256.2	267.4	267.4
3263	Fine earthenware food utensils	207.7	213.3	213.3	213.3	213.3	213.5	217.3	217.3	218.7	218.7	218.8	218.8	220.4	220.6
3269	Pottery products, n.e.c. (12/75 = 100)	108.7	110.6	110.6	110.7	110.7	110.7	114.5	114.6	116.8	116.8	116.8	116.8	119.6	119.6
3271	Concrete block and brick	183.9	184.5	187.8	185.7	185.7	186.1	188.6	188.6	191.8	193.4	195.5	196.2	198.7	200.4
3273	Ready-mixed concrete	195.7	194.7	196.4	197.8	198.6	198.9	198.8	199.2	206.7	209.6	210.1	211.7	212.7	215.0
3274	Lime (12/75 = 100)	117.7	118.6	117.6	117.5	117.2	118.9	118.9	119.9	123.1	125.4	127.9	128.6	128.6	129.0
3275	Gypsum products	183.9	187.4	187.0	190.1	194.0	201.9	203.5	205.2	210.0	214.0	217.4	221.5	228.6	230.6
3291	Abrasive products (12/71 = 100)	162.1	160.9	161.9	162.3	162.5	166.2	166.6	166.9	167.7	169.1	170.2	170.7	170.6	170.9
3297	Nonclay refractories (12/74 = 100)	123.4	121.4	122.1	122.8	128.9	129.1	129.1	129.2	129.3	129.6	129.7	130.0	130.0	130.0
3312	Blast furnaces and steel mills	236.9	232.5	240.5	241.2	244.5	244.4	244.2	244.6	244.7	253.4	255.4	260.2	261.2	261.6
3313	Electrometallurgical products (12/75 = 100)	95.6	95.6	95.6	95.5	94.7	94.8	93.9	93.8	92.6	92.6	92.6	92.6	93.5	94.1
3316	Cold finishing of steel shapes	220.6	215.8	225.9	226.9	227.1	227.1	227.0	227.0	226.6	235.5	235.6	239.1	239.5	239.5
3317	Steel pipes and tubes	232.2	228.8	228.9	234.7	241.7	241.7	241.6	241.9	241.7	247.7	250.8	253.6	254.4	254.5
3321	Gray iron foundries (12/68 = 100)	218.3	217.5	217.5	217.8	223.2	223.0	223.0	223.4	226.9	227.9	226.4	228.4	229.9	230.8
3333	Primary zinc	240.2	237.6	238.0	236.3	237.8	222.0	217.7	216.9	216.9	216.8	207.8	207.8	208.0	217.5
3334	Primary aluminum	205.1	205.4	209.2	211.0	214.3	213.7	213.7	213.7	213.7	213.7	213.9	215.5	216.1	216.1
3351	Copper rolling and drawing	164.8	170.1	170.4	167.0	161.4	157.6	158.8	159.5	163.3	164.7	165.1	166.7	167.9	170.3
3353	Aluminum sheet plate and foil (12/75 = 100)	122.4	120.9	125.3	125.8	126.2	126.2	128.1	128.1	129.6	130.4	132.6	135.8	135.9	136.4
3354	Aluminum extruded products (12/75 = 100)	121.2	119.7	125.0	125.6	125.7	125.6	126.3	126.3	130.2	130.7	132.6	133.4	133.0	133.4
3355	Aluminum rolling, drawing, n.e.c. (12/75 = 100)	112.7	111.0	115.3	115.3	115.6	115.3	115.2	115.2	115.4	115.5	118.0	118.3	118.3	119.3
3411	Metal cans	218.7	217.8	219.2	220.2	223.9	226.2	226.9	227.0	223.1	230.2	233.2	233.2	234.2	234.5
3425	Hand saws and saw blades (12/72 = 100)	137.7	138.6	138.8	138.8	139.2	140.0	140.1	140.2	141.4	143.1	145.1	145.8	146.7	147.7
3431	Metal sanitary ware	196.1	195.6	196.9	197.6	199.2	199.5	200.5	201.0	201.0	203.4	206.1	207.5	208.6	208.9
3465	Automotive stampings (12/75 = 100)	110.0	108.7	110.2	111.6	113.0	113.3	113.5	113.5	113.6	114.0	115.1	116.0	117.8	117.8

Code	Industry														
3482	Small arms ammunition (12/75 = 100)	110.8	109.0	110.0	110.5	111.3	112.1	112.8	112.8	119.2	119.2	119.2	119.2	116.7	118.4
3493	Steel springs, except wire	189.3	186.6	188.9	190.5	192.8	196.2	196.4	196.6	197.0	200.0	200.4	202.6	203.0	203.2
3494	Valves and pipe fittings (12/71 = 100)	172.6	173.2	173.9	174.4	174.1	174.8	176.0	176.4	178.2	180.1	180.6	181.6	182.7	184.6
3498	Fabricated pipe and fittings	245.2	246.0	246.1	246.1	247.5	249.0	249.1	249.1	249.9	252.6	258.1	263.6	263.6	263.7
3519	Internal combustion engines, n.e.c.	196.9	194.7	197.4	199.2	202.6	202.6	204.1	204.2	211.1	212.4	213.6	214.3	214.8	216.6
3531	Construction machinery (12/76 = 100)	104.6	103.8	104.7	105.3	105.3	106.5	108.2	109.1	109.4	110.1	110.1	111.6	112.5	112.9
3532	Mining machinery (12/72 = 100)	192.2	190.6	192.3	193.7	195.4	196.6	197.7	198.0	198.8	199.7	205.1	205.6	207.5	208.4
3533	Oilfield machinery and equipment	240.4	239.9	240.6	242.8	243.3	244.1	246.2	252.2	253.3	255.6	256.8	258.3	260.8	262.3
3534	Elevators and moving stairways	191.0	191.5	192.0	192.3	193.1	193.7	194.3	194.7	197.6	198.1	198.1	198.8	199.5	205.1
3542	Machine tools, metal forming types (12/71 = 100)	189.8	191.3	192.3	193.7	195.4	196.3	196.8	197.3	201.5	203.0	206.6	207.9	209.3	211.0
3546	Power driven hand tools (12/76 = 100)	104.2	104.0	104.6	105.0	105.1	105.4	106.1	106.2	108.7	109.0	109.2	109.7	110.1	110.4
3552	Textile machinery (12/69 = 100)	169.3	168.9	170.9	171.4	171.2	171.5	171.9	172.9	174.2	174.5	174.6	175.7	175.7	176.5
3553	Woodworking machinery (12/72 = 100)	155.9	154.6	155.7	157.2	158.4	159.0	159.0	161.3	162.0	161.8	164.1	164.8	166.8	167.4
3576	Scales and balances, excluding laboratory	167.7	166.6	167.9	169.8	170.8	171.4	171.4	173.5	175.2	176.4	176.9	177.6	177.7	177.5
3592	Carburetors, pistons, rings, valves (6/76 = 100)	110.1	110.4	110.5	111.5	112.7	113.4	115.8	115.9	121.9	122.2	125.1	126.3	126.4	128.4
3612	Transformers	150.4	149.9	151.6	152.4	152.1	153.0	154.6	154.6	155.9	155.7	155.3	155.6	155.8	158.1
3623	Welding apparatus, electric (12/72 = 100)	169.0	168.0	170.0	171.5	171.7	172.7	173.4	173.4	173.3	173.7	174.0	174.2	176.9	177.5
3631	Household cooking equipment (12/75 = 100)	109.8	109.0	109.8	110.8	111.8	111.8	111.8	111.9	112.8	112.8	112.6	113.2	113.1	113.5
3632	Household refrigerators, freezers (6/76 = 100)	104.3	103.6	104.2	104.3	106.1	106.6	106.7	106.7	106.9	106.9	108.3	108.3	109.7	109.7
3633	Household laundry equipment (12/73 = 100)	134.3	135.0	135.4	136.5	136.2	136.2	136.6	136.6	136.8	137.9	137.9	139.5	139.5	139.6
3635	Household vacuum cleaners	128.7	128.5	128.6	130.5	130.3	130.4	130.4	130.4	137.3	133.0	135.1	135.3	135.4	135.4
3636	Sewing machines (12/75 = 100)	102.5	101.7	102.6	103.6	103.6	104.0	104.0	104.0	106.7	106.7	106.7	110.4	111.3	111.3
3641	Electric lamps	193.6	193.9	197.6	199.2	199.3	199.2	199.2	199.2	201.8	207.2	212.6	212.6	212.7	212.9
3644	Noncurrent-carrying wiring devices (12/72 = 100)	166.9	166.0	168.4	168.6	168.6	169.1	168.7	169.0	170.3	173.4	179.2	182.5	183.7	186.7
3646	Commercial lighting fixtures (12/75 = 100)	106.0	105.9	107.1	107.1	107.3	107.3	107.4	107.2	107.7	110.1	110.6	110.7	110.9	111.0
3648	Lighting equipment, n.e.c. (12/75 = 100)	107.8	107.2	108.3	109.3	109.5	109.5	110.7	110.8	110.8	111.5	111.9	112.0	112.2	112.3
3671	Electron tubes receiving type	181.2	178.8	178.3	178.3	185.3	185.4	185.7	188.8	190.5	190.6	190.7	190.5	197.2	203.7
3674	Semiconductors and related devices	91.0	91.0	90.2	90.1	90.2	90.1	90.0	87.8	87.9	87.5	87.5	85.4	85.3	85.0
3675	Electronic capacitors (12/75 = 100)	106.7	106.0	106.1	106.6	106.7	108.4	109.6	110.3	110.5	110.5	110.5	111.6	111.0	111.0
3676	Electronic resistors (12/75 = 100)	110.6	110.0	110.0	110.0	111.7	112.8	112.9	113.3	113.6	113.7	113.7	114.3	114.8	114.3
3678	Electronic connectors (12/75 = 100)	108.9	109.3	109.4	109.5	109.9	110.6	111.2	111.9	113.0	114.0	117.0	116.9	117.0	119.2
3692	Primary batteries, dry and wet	162.1	162.0	162.1	161.5	161.5	161.5	161.5	161.6	161.5	161.6	161.7	161.8	161.9	161.9
3711	Motor vehicles and car bodies (12/75 = 100)	108.4	107.1	107.1	107.2	107.2	113.5	113.4	113.5	113.5	113.5	113.6	113.5	115.4	115.7
3942	Dolls (12/75 = 100)	99.3	99.6	99.6	99.6	99.6	99.7	99.7	99.6	99.5	100.5	102.0	103.2	103.2	104.0
3944	Games, toys, and children's vehicles	161.0	161.5	161.8	161.9	162.0	162.5	162.6	162.7	163.9	170.2	170.6	171.5	172.5	173.0
3955	Carbon paper and inked ribbons (12/75 = 100)	102.5	103.2	103.2	102.5	102.6	102.6	103.2	103.2	103.2	103.3	103.4	105.1	105.3	105.3
3995	Burial caskets (6/76 = 100)	105.4	104.4	105.6	105.6	105.6	106.3	109.1	109.2	110.2	111.2	111.4	111.4	111.7	112.3
3996	Hard surface floor coverings (12/75 = 100)	110.1	109.8	111.8	111.8	111.1	111.1	111.2	111.8	115.6	115.6	115.6	115.6	115.6	116.0

Source: *Monthly Labor Review*, U.S. Department of Labor, Bureau of Labor Statistics.

CONSUMER PRICES
INDEX, 1967=100 (RATIO SCALE)

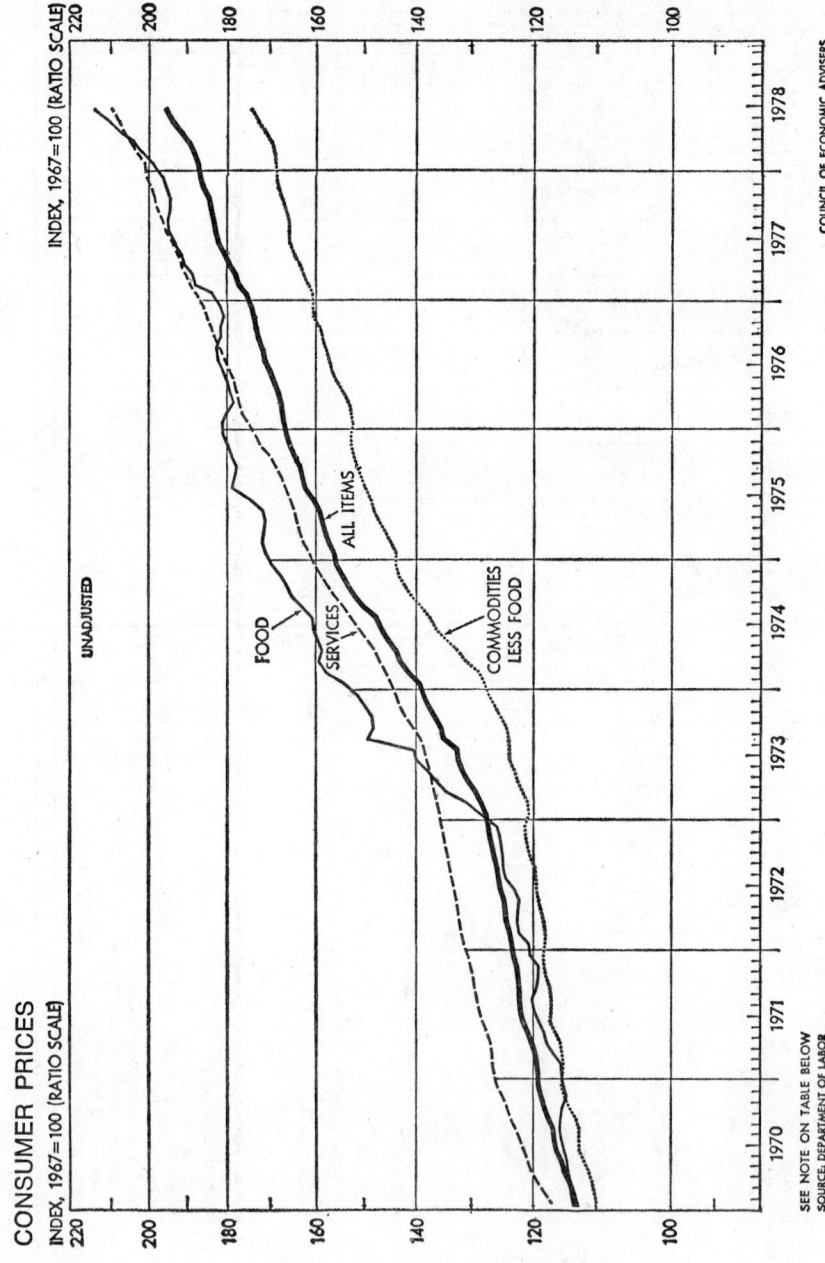

INDEX, 1967=100 (RATIO SCALE)

UNADJUSTED

FOOD

SERVICES

ALL ITEMS

COMMODITIES LESS FOOD

1970 1971 1972 1973 1974 1975 1976 1977 1978

SEE NOTE ON TABLE BELOW
SOURCE: DEPARTMENT OF LABOR

COUNCIL OF ECONOMIC ADVISERS

[1967=100]

Period	All items	Food	Commodities less food	Services	All commodities	Food — All	Food at home	Food away from home	Commodities less food — All	Durable	Non-durable	Services
	Unadjusted					*Seasonally adjusted*						
1970	116.3	114.9	112.5	121.6	113.5	114.9	113.7	119.9	112.5	111.8	113.1	121.6
1971	121.3	118.4	116.8	128.4	117.4	118.4	116.4	126.1	116.8	116.5	117.0	128.4
1972	125.3	123.5	119.4	133.3	120.9	123.5	121.6	131.1	119.4	118.9	119.8	133.3
1973	133.1	141.4	123.5	139.1	129.9	141.4	141.4	141.4	123.5	121.9	124.8	139.1
1974	147.7	161.7	136.6	152.1	145.5	161.7	162.4	159.4	136.6	130.6	140.9	152.1
1975	161.2	175.4	149.1	166.6	158.4	175.4	175.8	174.3	149.1	145.5	151.7	166.6
1976	170.5	180.8	156.6	180.4	165.2	180.8	179.5	186.1	156.6	154.3	158.3	180.4
1977	181.5	192.2	165.1	194.3	174.7	192.2	190.2	200.3	165.1	163.2	166.5	194.3
1977: June	181.8	193.6	165.4	193.7	175.1	193.8	191.9	200.9	165.1	163.3	166.4	194.3
July	182.6	194.6	165.6	195.3	175.2	193.5	191.3	201.8	165.4	163.4	166.9	195.7
Aug	183.3	195.2	166.0	196.3	175.7	194.3	192.0	203.0	165.7	163.6	167.2	196.8
Sept	184.0	194.5	166.7	197.7	176.2	194.7	192.3	203.8	166.2	163.9	167.8	197.9
Oct	184.5	194.4	167.4	198.5	176.7	195.0	192.5	204.5	166.8	164.4	168.6	198.7
Nov	185.4	195.6	168.1	199.5	177.5	196.0	193.5	205.1	167.6	165.1	169.4	199.5
Dec	186.1	196.3	168.4	200.5	178.3	196.7	194.2	206.1	168.4	166.0	169.9	200.3
1978: Jan	187.2	199.2	168.6	202.0	179.9	199.2	197.0	208.4	169.5	167.6	170.6	201.5
Feb	188.4	202.0	168.8	203.5	180.8	201.6	199.5	210.5	169.9	168.7	170.1	203.0
Mar	189.8	204.2	170.0	204.9	182.3	204.3	202.5	212.5	170.9	169.5	171.2	204.7
Apr	191.5	207.5	171.3	206.5	184.0	208.1	207.3	214.0	171.8	170.4	172.1	206.6
May	193.3	210.3	173.0	208.0	185.6	211.2	211.1	215.8	172.8	171.8	172.8	208.7
June	195.3	213.8	174.4	209.9	187.2	214.0	214.0	218.2	173.9	173.2	173.5	210.5

NOTE.—Beginning January 1978 data relate to all urban consumers. Earlier data relate to urban wage earners and clerical workers.

Source: Department of Labor, Bureau of Labor Statistics.
Source: Economic Indicators, Council of Economic Advisors.

CONSUMER PRICE INDEX FOR URBAN WAGE EARNERS AND CLERICAL WORKERS, ANNUAL AVERAGES AND CHANGES, 1967–1977

1967 = 100

Year	All Items		Food and beverages		Housing		Apparel and upkeep		Transportation		Medical care		Entertainment		Other goods and services	
	Index	Percent change	Index	Percent change	Index	Percent change	Index	Percent change	Index	Percent change	Index	Percent change	Index	Percent change	Index	Percent change
1967	100.0	-----	100.0	-----	100.0	-----	100.0	-----	100.0	-----	100.0	-----	100.0	-----	100.0	-----
1968	104.2	4.2	103.6	3.6	104.0	4.0	105.4	5.4	103.2	3.2	106.1	6.1	105.7	5.7	105.2	5.2
1969	109.8	5.4	108.8	5.0	110.4	6.2	111.5	5.8	107.2	3.9	113.4	6.9	111.0	5.0	110.4	4.9
1970	116.3	5.9	114.7	5.4	118.2	7.1	116.1	4.1	112.7	5.1	120.6	6.3	116.7	5.1	116.8	5.8
1971	121.3	4.3	118.3	3.1	123.4	4.4	119.8	3.2	118.6	5.2	128.4	6.5	122.9	5.3	122.4	4.8
1972	125.3	3.3	123.2	4.1	128.1	3.8	122.3	2.1	119.9	1.1	132.5	3.2	126.5	2.9	127.5	4.2
1973	133.1	6.2	139.5	13.2	133.7	4.4	126.8	3.7	123.8	3.3	137.7	3.9	130.0	2.8	132.5	3.9
1974	147.7	11.0	158.7	13.8	148.8	11.3	136.2	7.4	137.7	11.2	150.5	9.3	139.8	7.5	142.0	7.2
1975	161.2	9.1	172.1	8.4	164.5	10.6	142.3	4.5	150.6	9.4	168.6	12.0	152.2	8.9	153.9	8.4
1976	170.5	5.8	177.4	3.1	174.6	6.1	147.6	3.7	165.5	9.9	184.7	9.5	159.8	5.0	162.7	5.7
1977	181.5	6.5	188.0	6.0	186.5	6.8	154.2	4.5	177.2	7.1	202.4	9.6	167.7	4.9	172.2	5.8

Source: *Monthly Labor Review*, U.S. Department of Labor, Bureau of Labor Statistics.

CONSUMER PRICE INDEX FOR ALL URBAN CONSUMERS AND REVISED CPI FOR URBAN WAGE EARNERS AND CLERICAL WORKERS, U.S. CITY AVERAGE—GENERAL SUMMARY AND GROUPS, SUBGROUPS, AND SELECTED ITEMS

1967 = 100 unless otherwise specified

| General summary | All Urban Consumers | | | | | | | Urban Wage Earners and Clerical Workers (revised) | | | | | | |
| | 1977 | | 1978 | | | | | 1977 | | 1978 | | | | |
	May	Dec.	Jan.	Feb.	Mar.	Apr.	May	May	Dec.	Jan.	Feb.	Mar.	Apr.	May
All items	180.6	186.1	187.2	188.4	189.8	191.5	193.3	180.6	186.1	187.1	188.4	189.7	191.4	193.3
Food and beverages	187.5	191.9	194.6	197.3	199.5	202.6	205.2	187.5	191.9	194.5	197.1	199.2	202.2	205.1
Housing	184.6	192.4	193.8	195.0	196.7	198.3	199.9	184.6	192.4	193.8	195.0	196.7	198.1	199.8
Apparel and upkeep	153.4	158.2	155.7	154.5	156.5	158.4	159.8	153.4	158.2	155.4	154.5	156.0	158.1	159.7
Transportation	178.1	178.8	179.0	179.4	179.9	181.1	183.2	178.1	178.8	179.1	179.5	180.0	181.3	183.4
Medical care	200.5	209.3	211.2	213.2	214.5	215.7	216.9	200.5	209.3	211.2	213.2	214.3	215.6	217.0
Entertainment	166.6	171.0	171.9	172.9	174.1	175.6	176.2	166.6	171.0	171.7	173.7	174.1	175.3	175.6
Other goods and services	170.4	177.8	178.5	179.0	179.3	179.8	180.4	170.4	177.8	178.4	179.1	179.6	180.1	180.6
Commodities	174.3	178.3	179.2	180.2	181.6	183.5	185.5	174.3	178.3	179.1	180.1	181.5	183.4	185.4
Commodities less food and beverages	165.7	169.5	169.6	169.8	170.9	172.3	174.0	165.7	169.5	169.5	169.8	170.8	172.1	173.8
Nondurables less food and beverages	167.5	172.5	171.7	171.5	172.7	173.7	174.7	167.5	172.5	171.7	171.6	172.6	173.6	174.7
Durables	163.4	165.9	166.6	167.2	168.3	169.9	172.0	163.4	165.9	166.7	167.1	168.2	169.7	171.8
Services	192.2	200.5	202.0	203.5	204.9	206.5	208.0	192.2	200.5	202.0	203.6	205.0	206.4	207.9
Rent, residential	152.2	157.9	158.8	159.7	160.5	161.5	162.7	152.2	157.9	158.8	159.7	160.5	161.4	162.6
Household services less rent	209.5	220.0	221.8	223.7	226.0	228.3	230.6	209.5	220.0	221.7	223.8	226.0	228.2	230.6
Transportation services	187.4	192.9	193.7	194.7	194.9	195.3	195.5	187.4	192.9	194.0	195.1	195.2	195.5	195.7
Medical care services	214.6	224.2	226.5	228.7	229.9	231.3	232.5	214.6	224.2	226.5	228.6	229.7	231.0	232.5
Other services	170.9	177.5	178.8	179.9	180.7	181.7	182.5	170.9	177.5	178.6	180.3	181.1	182.4	183.0
Special indexes:														
All items less food	177.3	183.1	183.8	184.7	185.9	187.4	189.0	177.3	183.1	183.8	184.7	185.8	187.2	188.8
All items less mortgage interest costs	178.5	183.6	184.7	185.8	187.1	188.8	190.5	178.5	183.6	184.6	185.8	187.0	188.7	190.4
Commodities less food	164.7	168.4	168.6	168.8	170.0	171.3	173.0	164.7	168.4	168.5	168.8	169.9	171.2	172.8
Nondurables less food	165.7	170.3	169.7	169.6	170.7	171.8	172.8	165.7	170.3	169.6	169.7	170.7	171.8	172.8
Nondurables less food and apparel	174.5	179.3	179.7	180.3	181.0	181.7	182.6	174.5	179.3	179.6	180.3	181.1	181.7	182.5
Nondurables	178.3	182.9	183.9	185.1	186.8	188.8	190.7	178.3	182.9	183.8	185.1	186.6	188.7	190.7
Services less rent	199.4	208.2	209.8	211.4	213.0	214.6	216.2	199.4	208.2	209.8	211.6	213.0	214.6	216.1
Services less medical care	188.6	196.7	198.0	199.5	200.9	202.5	204.0	188.6	196.7	198.0	199.6	201.0	202.4	203.9
Domestically produced farm foods	178.0	181.8	184.2	188.1	190.7	193.3	198.2	178.0	181.8	184.2	188.1	190.7	193.3	198.2
Selected beef cuts	163.6	169.0	171.6	176.9	180.5	188.0	198.8	163.6	169.0	171.6	176.9	180.5	188.0	198.8
Energy	206.6	211.3	211.8	213.0	214.3	215.7	217.7	206.6	211.3	211.7	212.8	214.1	215.4	217.5
All items less energy	178.8	184.4	185.6	186.7	188.2	190.0	191.7	178.8	184.4	185.5	186.8	188.1	189.9	191.7
All items less food and energy	174.7	180.6	181.4	182.2	183.4	184.9	186.4	174.7	180.6	181.3	182.2	183.3	184.7	186.3
Commodities less food and energy	160.6	164.5	164.6	164.9	166.2	167.6	169.3	160.6	164.5	164.6	164.9	166.1	167.5	169.2
Energy commodities	203.9	206.5	206.8	206.7	206.6	207.2	208.5	203.9	206.5	206.7	206.5	206.5	207.0	208.4
Services less energy	190.8	199.1	200.6	202.0	203.3	204.7	206.1	190.8	199.1	200.6	202.1	203.2	204.6	206.0
Purchasing power of the consumer dollar, 1967 = $1	$0.554	$0.537	$0.534	$0.531	$0.527	$0.522	$0.517	$0.554	$0.537	$0.534	$0.531	$0.527	$0.522	$0.517

CONSUMER PRICE INDEX—U.S. CITY AVERAGE (continued)

General summary	All Urban Consumers							Urban Wage Earners and Clerical Workers (revised)						
	1977		1978					1977		1978				
	May	Dec.	Jan.	Feb.	Mar.	Apr.	May	May	Dec.	Jan.	Feb.	Mar.	Apr.	May
FOOD AND BEVERAGES	187.5	191.9	194.6	197.3	199.5	202.6	205.2	187.5	191.9	194.5	197.1	199.2	202.2	205.1
Food	191.7	196.3	199.2	202.0	204.2	207.5	210.3	191.7	196.3	199.0	201.8	203.9	207.1	210.2
Food at home	189.8	193.7	197.0	200.1	202.5	206.5	209.7	189.8	193.7	196.8	199.8	202.2	206.0	209.5
Cereals and bakery products	182.5	189.0	191.3	193.1	194.4	195.2	197.5	182.5	189.0	191.1	193.3	194.7	195.7	198.4
Cereal and cereal products	-----	100.0	102.0	103.0	105.2	105.9	106.9	-----	100.0	101.0	104.1	105.4	106.1	107.1
Flour and prepared flour mixes	-----	100.0	101.7	103.3	103.8	105.0	106.6	-----	100.0	101.7	103.8	104.6	105.4	106.8
Cereal	-----	100.0	101.3	103.5	104.0	104.1	104.6	-----	100.0	101.3	103.4	104.1	104.6	105.1
Rice, pasta, and cornmeal	-----	100.0	103.0	105.5	108.1	109.4	110.5	-----	100.0	100.9	105.2	108.0	108.7	110.1
Bakery products	-----	100.0	101.0	101.6	102.2	102.4	103.7	-----	100.0	100.1	101.7	102.7	102.7	104.3
White bread	162.8	164.5	166.2	166.8	167.5	168.0	171.6	162.8	164.5	165.4	166.4	166.7	167.7	171.4
Other breads	-----	100.0	100.8	100.5	102.1	102.3	103.9	-----	100.0	101.4	101.6	103.1	103.1	105.3
Fresh biscuits, rolls, and muffins	-----	100.0	101.4	101.8	102.6	103.3	104.2	-----	100.0	102.2	101.8	103.0	103.5	105.2
Fresh cakes and cupcakes	-----	100.0	100.7	101.7	101.3	101.8	103.0	-----	100.0	100.9	102.0	102.0	102.7	103.8
Cookies	-----	100.0	100.8	100.8	101.8	102.4	103.0	-----	100.0	100.8	101.8	102.3	103.2	104.3
Crackers and bread and cracker products	-----	100.0	100.2	101.4	101.6	102.0	103.8	-----	100.0	100.3	101.1	101.2	101.5	104.4
Fresh sweetrolls, coffeecake, and donuts	-----	100.0	100.9	103.1	102.7	102.9	103.4	-----	100.0	100.6	103.6	103.3	104.1	105.1
Frozen and refrigerated bakery products and fresh pies, tarts, and turnovers	-----	100.0	101.6	101.9	102.9	102.8	103.0	-----	100.0	101.1	100.9	102.8	102.7	102.6
Meats, poultry, fish, and eggs	174.0	179.4	184.2	189.0	193.1	199.0	202.8	174.0	179.4	184.1	188.5	192.8	198.5	202.2
Meats, poultry, and fish	175.9	182.1	186.7	191.7	196.0	202.8	207.4	175.9	182.1	186.6	191.3	195.7	202.2	206.8
Meats	171.3	178.3	183.1	188.7	193.6	200.8	206.2	171.3	178.3	183.2	188.4	193.3	200.2	205.8
Beef and veal	162.8	168.0	171.1	177.0	182.0	191.9	201.0	162.8	168.0	171.9	177.6	182.9	192.5	202.0
Ground beef other than canned	158.3	159.0	161.3	171.6	178.5	190.1	199.8	158.3	159.0	161.6	171.2	180.0	190.7	210.0
Chuck roast	163.8	167.1	170.7	180.8	184.7	192.6	202.1	163.8	167.1	174.8	182.9	189.4	196.1	208.0
Round roast	156.3	161.4	168.1	170.1	173.0	179.7	185.5	156.3	161.4	168.4	172.5	173.4	181.6	186.9
Round steak	162.9	167.3	170.2	175.0	177.5	188.1	195.8	162.9	167.3	170.3	175.2	176.8	186.4	193.0
Sirloin steak	162.0	169.4	173.0	174.2	177.6	192.2	204.1	162.0	169.4	173.1	174.6	188.8	193.1	205.4
Other beef and veal	-----	100.0	100.0	103.3	106.4	111.7	116.8	-----	100.0	101.8	103.6	106.2	114.4	116.7
Pork	182.0	191.7	199.6	205.2	208.4	211.5	211.3	182.0	191.7	198.7	204.0	207.7	210.6	210.4
Bacon	188.2	190.1	203.4	211.9	228.8	237.5	233.3	188.2	190.1	202.7	211.2	233.3	238.8	234.4
Pork chops	171.7	177.5	185.8	219.6	192.6	192.0	196.6	171.7	177.5	184.9	193.1	191.9	191.9	195.5
Ham other than canned	-----	100.0	99.8	99.6	99.4	97.7	95.1	-----	100.0	100.1	100.1	100.2	97.5	96.2
Sausage	212.3	224.0	231.2	239.6	249.3	253.4	257.7	212.3	224.0	228.7	234.9	245.9	250.0	253.1
Canned ham	192.2	208.5	215.3	218.6	218.8	221.4	221.6	192.2	208.5	215.0	217.1	217.1	218.2	214.4
Other pork	-----	100.0	106.0	109.6	110.3	111.7	112.5	-----	100.0	105.4	108.3	109.7	111.6	111.9

Item														
Other meats	206.2	201.6	195.4	189.4	185.9	183.2	175.1	208.8	204.5	198.5	191.2	186.5	182.3	175.1
Frankfurters	200.9	194.2	185.5	174.9	168.8	164.4	161.2	204.4	197.7	188.8	176.8	170.5	164.4	161.2
Bologna, liverwurst, and salami	112.4	109.4	107.0	102.8	101.1	100.0	----	113.3	110.4	108.5	103.5	101.3	100.0	----
Other lunchmeats	107.7	105.5	103.4	102.2	101.1	100.0	----	108.9	107.5	104.9	102.7	101.7	100.0	----
Lamb and organ meats	114.3	113.8	108.8	106.1	104.2	100.0	----	115.4	113.7	109.9	107.5	103.0	100.0	----
Poultry	169.2	167.5	162.2	159.4	155.7	153.6	157.6	171.0	169.3	163.9	161.5	157.5	153.6	157.6
Fresh whole chicken	172.0	171.3	162.4	158.6	152.9	152.2	160.2	175.8	174.7	165.7	163.0	156.2	152.2	160.2
Fresh and frozen chicken parts	109.0	107.4	105.9	103.9	101.5	100.0	----	109.2	108.1	105.4	103.6	101.9	100.0	----
Other poultry	107.0	105.7	103.5	102.8	102.5	100.0	----	107.8	106.2	105.0	104.2	103.0	100.0	----
Fish and seafood	270.3	271.8	267.7	267.2	267.1	262.6	248.8	272.8	271.6	267.4	266.5	266.3	262.6	248.8
Canned fish and seafood	102.5	102.3	101.4	101.1	100.9	100.0	----	103.6	102.7	101.5	101.7	101.1	100.0	----
Fresh and frozen fish and seafood	103.2	104.3	102.3	102.2	102.2	100.0	----	104.0	103.9	102.0	101.4	101.6	100.0	----
Eggs	145.9	155.2	160.1	157.8	156.2	148.6	152.8	147.4	155.3	160.7	159.1	156.1	148.6	152.8
Dairy products	183.5	181.6	179.4	178.9	177.9	176.9	173.1	183.5	181.6	179.3	178.8	177.7	176.9	173.1
Fresh milk and cream	103.6	102.4	101.2	100.9	100.4	100.0	----	103.7	102.7	101.4	101.0	100.6	100.0	----
Fresh whole milk	169.6	167.6	165.8	165.2	164.5	163.7	161.5	170.1	168.3	166.3	166.5	164.8	163.7	161.5
Other fresh milk and cream	103.5	102.3	101.1	100.7	100.2	100.0	----	103.7	102.3	100.7	100.0	100.4	100.0	----
Processed dairy products	104.0	103.0	101.6	101.5	100.8	100.0	----	103.7	102.6	101.3	101.1	100.3	100.0	----
Butter	174.2	173.0	170.3	169.6	169.6	167.8	162.7	174.4	173.3	170.3	169.3	169.6	167.8	162.7
Cheese	103.2	102.8	101.7	101.3	100.7	100.0	----	103.2	102.5	101.3	101.2	100.5	100.0	----
Ice cream and related products	105.8	103.6	101.9	102.3	100.9	100.0	----	104.7	102.1	100.9	100.7	99.4	100.0	----
Other dairy products	103.4	102.4	101.4	101.2	100.4	100.0	----	103.1	102.9	102.1	101.6	100.2	100.0	----
Fruits and vegetables	219.4	209.9	203.1	200.8	196.1	192.5	195.1	219.3	210.9	203.8	200.9	197.2	192.5	195.1
Fresh fruits and vegetables	233.6	215.9	203.8	200.0	192.6	188.0	200.8	233.3	217.3	204.6	200.3	195.0	188.0	200.8
Fresh fruits	222.3	206.6	201.4	191.6	185.4	186.5	185.8	222.4	207.1	200.5	191.0	189.1	186.5	185.8
Apples	237.9	213.5	203.6	190.3	183.4	176.5	193.0	216.6	217.8	204.7	190.0	185.1	176.5	193.0
Bananas	207.2	206.3	203.2	202.6	161.0	160.2	176.2	208.5	209.1	203.4	177.3	162.8	160.2	176.2
Oranges	211.6	201.6	207.0	98.9	196.0	198.9	164.3	211.2	199.9	203.2	199.6	201.3	198.9	164.3
Other fresh fruits	114.9	105.6	101.5	207.6	97.4	100.0	----	114.8	105.6	101.5	99.0	99.9	100.0	----
Fresh vegetables	243.9	224.4	206.1	187.2	199.1	189.5	213.1	243.5	227.0	208.5	209.1	200.5	189.5	213.1
Potatoes	200.1	191.8	188.1	245.5	184.3	180.1	226.6	201.4	191.8	187.9	187.7	184.5	180.1	226.6
Lettuce	341.4	252.0	195.3	210.1	210.1	205.6	149.7	330.0	268.4	209.0	253.2	215.8	205.6	149.7
Tomatoes	235.3	213.0	190.3	212.0	212.0	206.5	219.8	234.6	205.7	185.8	157.3	208.9	206.5	219.8
Other fresh vegetables	125.8	127.8	123.1	119.2	108.6	100.0	----	127.5	128.5	123.7	119.6	109.5	100.0	----
Processed fruits and vegetables	205.3	205.1	204.0	203.5	201.7	199.2	186.7	205.9	205.7	204.6	203.2	201.5	199.2	186.7
Processed fruits	104.2	103.8	103.1	102.8	101.4	100.0	----	104.1	103.9	103.1	102.5	101.3	100.0	----
Frozen fruit and fruit juices	107.4	106.1	105.2	104.5	102.9	100.0	----	106.9	106.3	105.5	104.4	103.1	100.0	----
Fruit juices and other than frozen	103.6	104.0	102.6	102.6	100.2	100.0	----	103.4	103.5	102.3	101.8	100.0	100.0	----
Canned and dried fruits	102.1	101.6	101.9	101.6	101.3	100.0	----	102.5	102.3	102.1	101.6	101.2	100.0	----
Processed vegetables	102.2	102.3	101.9	101.6	101.2	100.0	----	102.6	102.7	102.4	101.9	101.0	100.0	----
Frozen vegetables	102.8	102.6	101.9	101.2	100.7	100.0	----	102.8	102.4	101.8	100.8	101.0	100.0	----

CONSUMER PRICE INDEX—U.S. CITY AVERAGE (continued)

General summary	All Urban Consumers							Urban Wage Earners and Clerical Workers (revised)						
	1977		1978					1977		1978				
	May	Dec.	Jan.	Feb.	Mar.	Apr.	May	May	Dec.	Jan.	Feb.	Mar.	Apr.	May
FOOD AND BEVERAGES—Continued														
Food—Continued														
Food at home—Continued														
Fruits and vegetables—Continued														
Cut corn and canned beans except lima	.....	100.0	101.2	101.5	103.0	103.1	103.1	.....	100.0	101.9	101.4	102.4	102.9	102.6
Other canned and dried vegetables	.....	100.0	101.2	102.2	102.4	102.6	102.3	.....	100.0	101.0	101.8	101.5	101.8	101.7
Other foods at home	236.3	241.7	244.0	246.0	247.9	249.6	250.4	236.3	241.7	244.0	245.8	247.3	249.1	250.2
Sugar and sweets	230.1	239.7	244.9	248.1	251.7	254.9	256.4	256.4	239.7	244.9	248.6	252.1	254.4	256.4
Candy and chewing gum	.....	100.0	101.4	102.8	104.1	105.6	106.8	.....	100.0	101.5	102.8	103.7	105.4	106.7
Sugar and artificial sweeteners	.....	100.0	104.7	106.8	109.2	111.0	110.4	.....	100.0	104.6	107.3	110.3	111.0	110.9
Other sweets	.....	100.0	101.0	101.3	102.1	102.8	103.4	.....	100.0	100.7	101.4	102.2	102.0	103.0
Fats and oils	188.5	196.1	198.1	198.9	200.4	204.5	207.9	188.5	196.1	198.0	198.6	200.0	205.1	208.8
Margarine	201.8	211.5	213.9	214.8	214.9	221.6	226.7	201.8	211.5	213.9	214.3	214.7	223.4	226.2
Nondairy substitutes and peanut butter	.....	100.0	100.8	100.9	101.3	102.3	102.5	.....	100.0	100.9	100.8	100.8	101.6	102.9
Other fats, oils, and salad dressings	.....	100.0	101.1	101.6	102.9	104.8	106.7	.....	100.0	100.9	101.5	102.4	105.0	107.5
Nonalcoholic beverages	334.6	334.3	337.1	339.5	341.7	342.9	341.6	334.6	334.3	336.9	338.5	340.0	340.8	340.4
Cola drinks, excluding diet cola	201.6	206.0	209.1	210.5	213.6	216.8	216.8	201.6	206.0	209.2	209.9	211.7	214.5	215.6
Carbonated drinks, including diet cola	.....	100.0	101.3	102.9	104.1	106.0	106.2	.....	100.0	100.6	102.0	103.1	104.7	104.9
Roasted coffee	486.2	457.5	453.1	450.2	446.5	433.2	424.6	486.2	457.5	452.7	449.5	446.1	431.6	423.4
Freeze dried and instant coffee	334.3	383.2	383.3	382.5	378.3	372.3	367.0	334.3	383.2	382.9	381.8	379.0	371.1	366.5
Other noncarbonated drinks	.....	100.0	101.2	103.1	104.2	105.0	105.3	.....	100.0	101.5	102.8	103.6	104.7	105.0
Other prepared foods	173.8	180.8	181.9	183.5	184.7	185.6	187.0	173.8	180.8	182.1	183.8	184.8	186.1	187.3
Canned and packaged soup	.....	100.0	100.3	101.3	101.2	101.2	101.7	.....	100.0	100.4	101.3	100.8	101.5	101.6
Frozen prepared foods	.....	100.0	100.9	101.6	102.9	102.5	104.4	.....	100.0	100.6	101.6	102.7	102.7	104.0
Snacks	.....	100.0	100.4	101.3	101.5	102.1	102.2	.....	100.0	100.1	101.3	101.4	102.4	102.2
Seasonings, olives, pickles, and relish	.....	100.0	101.5	102.6	103.3	103.7	104.0	.....	100.0	101.6	103.2	103.9	104.1	104.7
Other condiments	.....	100.0	100.3	101.5	102.6	103.6	104.3	.....	100.0	101.4	102.4	103.2	104.3	105.0
Miscellaneous prepared foods	.....	100.0	100.5	101.6	102.1	103.1	103.8	.....	100.0	100.5	101.6	102.2	103.0	103.9
Other canned and packaged prepared foods	.....	100.0	100.4	100.9	101.5	102.4	103.4	.....	100.0	100.5	100.7	101.4	102.5	103.9
Food away from home	199.3	206.2	208.2	210.5	212.3	214.0	215.8	199.3	206.2	208.1	210.2	211.9	213.5	215.6
Lunch	.....	100.0	101.2	102.4	103.3	104.0	104.7	.....	100.0	100.9	101.8	102.5	103.3	104.3
Dinner	.....	100.0	101.0	102.1	102.9	103.7	104.5	.....	100.0	101.2	102.2	103.0	103.7	104.6
Other meals and snacks	.....	100.0	100.6	101.6	102.6	103.8	105.0	.....	100.0	100.7	101.9	102.9	103.8	105.0

Item														
Alcoholic beverages	159.2	158.2	156.8	155.3	154.1	153.2	150.3	159.2	157.9	156.5	155.4	154.2	153.2	150.3
Alcoholic beverages at home	104.0	103.4	102.5	101.6	100.6	100.0	....	103.8	103.1	102.3	101.5	100.7	100.0	....
Beer and ale	153.6	152.8	151.2	149.3	148.6	147.2	145.9	152.9	152.1	150.8	148.6	147.8	147.2	145.9
Whiskey	122.1	121.0	120.6	120.6	119.6	118.8	117.2	122.5	121.2	120.7	120.8	120.2	118.8	117.2
Wine	179.2	177.8	175.3	173.9	169.3	167.4	159.9	177.6	176.6	174.2	173.9	169.4	167.4	159.9
Other alcoholic beverages	101.7	101.5	101.3	101.2	100.8	100.0	....	102.2	101.2	101.2	100.8	100.4	100.0	....
Alcoholic beverages away from home	103.5	102.7	101.4	100.4	100.3	100.0	....	104.4	103.1	101.5	100.9	100.3	100.0	....
HOUSING	199.8	198.1	196.7	195.0	193.8	192.4	184.6	199.9	198.3	196.7	195.0	193.8	192.4	184.6
Shelter	206.5	204.5	202.9	201.3	200.0	198.2	188.9	206.6	204.7	202.9	201.3	200.0	198.2	188.9
Rent, residential	162.6	161.4	160.5	159.7	158.8	157.9	152.2	162.7	161.5	160.5	159.7	158.8	157.9	152.2
Other rental costs	204.3	202.9	202.2	200.1	197.0	192.2	185.3	204.4	202.7	202.0	200.1	197.2	192.2	185.3
Lodging while out of town	208.3	206.8	206.1	203.1	199.1	192.2	185.3	208.9	206.8	206.2	203.4	194.4	192.2	185.3
Tenants' insurance	100.9	101.0	101.2	101.0	100.2	100.0	....	100.8	100.8	101.0	100.8	100.2	100.0	....
Homeownership	222.5	220.2	218.3	216.5	215.1	213.0	202.3	222.5	220.4	218.3	216.4	215.0	213.0	202.3
Home purchase	193.4	191.7	190.6	189.1	188.1	186.2	177.7	193.4	191.7	190.5	189.0	188.1	186.2	177.7
Financing, taxes, and insurance	251.0	248.0	245.1	242.6	240.7	238.1	222.9	250.8	247.7	244.8	242.4	240.5	238.1	222.9
Property insurance	103.2	102.6	101.6	101.4	100.5	100.0	....	103.2	102.5	101.6	101.3	100.6	100.0	....
Property taxes	193.3	192.7	192.3	191.6	190.3	189.6	181.1	193.0	192.4	191.9	191.2	190.2	189.6	181.1
Contracted mortgage interest cost	106.6	105.0	103.5	102.2	101.3	100.0	....	106.6	105.0	103.4	102.2	101.3	100.0	....
Mortgage interest rates	143.5	142.7	141.5	140.8	140.4	140.0	136.4	143.6	142.7	141.5	140.8	140.4	140.0	136.4
Maintenance and repairs	228.7	226.6	224.4	223.3	221.9	220.9	212.8	229.6	228.4	225.5	223.5	222.4	220.9	212.8
Maintenance and repair services	246.7	244.0	241.6	239.9	237.9	236.9	227.1	247.8	246.0	242.6	239.8	238.3	236.9	227.1
Maintenance and repair commodities	187.8	187.1	185.2	185.3	184.9	184.0	179.7	187.4	187.4	185.9	185.9	185.6	184.0	179.7
Paint and wallpaper, supplies, tools, and equipment	101.7	101.0	100.6	101.3	100.7	100.0	....	101.7	101.7	100.8	101.2	101.0	100.0	....
Lumber, awnings, glass, and masonry	104.3	104.5	102.5	99.9	100.6	100.0	....	103.5	103.5	102.3	101.7	100.9	100.0	....
Plumbing, electrical, heating, and cooling supplies	100.3	99.7	98.4	99.9	100.6	100.0	....	99.8	99.4	99.3	99.8	100.4	100.0	....
Miscellaneous supplies and equipment	101.2	100.7	99.9	99.5	100.2	100.0	....	101.6	101.8	101.3	101.0	100.9	100.0	....
Fuel and other utilities	215.7	214.1	212.7	210.6	208.4	207.6	200.2	215.5	213.9	212.6	210.6	208.5	207.6	200.2
Fuels	247.1	244.4	242.2	239.1	235.9	234.7	226.4	246.8	244.2	242.1	239.2	235.9	234.7	226.4
Fuel oil, coal, and bottled gas	295.6	296.5	297.1	296.9	295.1	291.9	282.6	295.6	296.6	297.2	296.9	295.2	291.9	282.6
Fuel oil	293.5	293.9	294.0	293.6	292.0	288.7	279.4	293.5	294.0	294.1	293.7	292.1	288.7	279.4
Other fuels	99.3	100.5	101.6	101.8	101.0	100.0	....	99.3	100.5	101.6	101.7	101.7	100.0	....
Gas (piped) and electricity	232.8	229.4	226.7	223.1	219.6	218.9	210.9	232.5	229.2	226.6	223.3	219.7	218.9	210.9
Electricity	204.3	201.0	198.8	195.1	191.7	190.7	185.4	203.6	200.6	198.1	195.1	191.6	190.7	185.4
Utility (piped) gas	261.8	258.5	255.2	252.3	249.2	249.2	238.2	262.2	258.6	255.4	252.6	249.3	249.2	238.2

CONSUMER PRICE INDEX—U.S. CITY AVERAGE (continued)

General summary	All Urban Consumers							Urban Wage Earners and Clerical Workers (revised)						
	1977		1978					1977		1978				
	May	Dec.	Jan.	Feb.	Mar.	Apr.	May	May	Dec.	Jan.	Feb.	Mar.	Apr.	May
HOUSING—Continued														
Fuel and other utilities—Continued														
Other utilities and public services	150.4	156.0	156.3	156.8	157.3	157.7	157.7	150.4	156.0	156.3	156.8	157.4	157.8	157.8
Telephone services	131.0	132.2	132.1	132.4	132.4	132.7	132.7	131.0	132.2	132.1	132.4	132.4	132.8	132.7
Local charges	....	100.0	100.1	100.9	100.8	101.2	101.1	....	100.0	100.1	100.9	100.8	101.2	101.1
Interstate toll calls	....	100.0	99.4	99.5	99.2	99.0	99.0	....	100.0	99.4	99.2	99.3	99.1	99.1
Intrastate toll calls	....	100.0	100.2	99.9	99.7	100.3	100.2	....	100.0	100.1	100.1	99.6	100.2	100.1
Water and sewerage maintenance	203.8	221.5	224.4	225.8	229.1	229.5	229.9	203.8	221.5	224.2	225.8	229.4	229.7	230.2
Household furnishings and operations	166.5	171.0	171.3	172.1	173.6	175.0	176.0	166.5	171.0	171.4	172.0	173.6	174.6	175.4
Housefurnishings	147.1	150.2	149.7	150.1	151.5	152.8	153.6	147.1	150.2	150.0	150.2	151.8	152.6	153.1
Textile housefurnishings	154.6	160.4	155.8	159.3	162.3	160.4	160.7	154.6	160.4	157.8	159.3	162.9	161.4	160.6
Household linens	....	100.0	96.5	98.0	100.7	99.5	98.9	....	100.0	96.8	98.3	100.6	99.5	99.4
Curtains, drapes, slipcovers, and sewing materials	....	100.0	100.3	100.7	101.6	100.5	101.5	....	100.0	100.1	100.5	102.7	101.9	101.0
Furniture and bedding	158.0	160.8	159.4	160.0	161.8	164.6	165.7	158.0	160.8	160.1	160.4	162.6	163.8	164.8
Bedroom furniture	....	100.0	100.1	100.9	101.1	102.2	103.6	....	100.0	99.8	99.1	100.7	101.4	102.0
Sofas	....	100.0	100.4	99.9	99.8	102.4	102.7	....	100.0	100.6	99.6	101.9	102.5	103.4
Living room chairs and tables	....	100.0	99.2	98.7	99.3	100.8	101.3	....	100.0	99.8	99.5	100.8	100.8	101.0
Other furniture	....	100.0	97.1	98.3	101.6	103.7	104.1	....	100.0	98.3	100.0	101.1	102.8	103.5
Appliances including TV and sound equipment	125.6	127.3	127.8	127.7	128.4	129.1	130.0	125.6	127.3	127.8	127.5	128.1	128.8	129.7
Television and sound equipment	....	100.0	100.4	100.4	100.9	101.4	101.3	....	100.0	100.6	100.5	100.7	101.2	101.1
Television	101.6	101.2	101.1	101.0	101.4	101.5	101.3	101.6	101.2	101.3	100.7	100.8	101.3	101.1
Sound equipment	....	100.0	100.9	101.0	101.5	102.4	102.4	....	100.0	101.1	101.4	101.7	102.0	102.1
Household appliances	139.6	142.7	143.1	143.0	144.0	144.8	146.9	139.6	142.7	142.8	142.4	143.4	144.4	146.4
Refrigerators and home freezer	138.9	143.1	141.5	142.0	143.4	143.0	145.4	138.9	143.1	142.3	143.1	144.6	144.9	146.8
Laundry equipment	....	100.0	100.9	101.3	101.7	102.1	102.6	....	100.0	100.6	101.0	101.4	101.9	102.8
Other household appliances	....	100.0	100.8	100.2	100.9	101.9	103.8	....	100.0	100.1	99.1	99.7	100.8	102.6
Stoves, dishwashers, vacuums, and sewing machines	....	100.0	101.4	100.6	101.4	102.9	104.9	....	100.0	100.5	99.6	100.5	101.8	103.2
Office machines, small electric appliances, and air conditioners	....	100.0	100.1	99.6	100.2	100.9	102.5	....	100.0	99.7	98.5	98.9	99.5	101.9
Other household equipment	....	100.0	100.0	100.3	101.1	102.6	102.7	....	100.0	100.2	100.5	101.8	102.6	102.2
Floor and window coverings, infants' laundry cleaning and outdoor equipment	....	100.0	99.9	100.9	100.8	101.3	100.9	....	100.0	100.7	100.9	100.5	101.0	97.5
Clocks, lamps, and decor items	....	100.0	100.1	99.9	101.2	101.1	101.7	....	100.0	99.7	100.1	101.6	100.7	101.2
Tableware, serving pieces, and nonelectric kitchenware	....	100.0	100.4	100.4	101.5	104.8	104.9	....	100.0	100.3	101.0	103.1	105.3	105.2
Lawn equipment, power tools, and other hardware	....	100.0	99.4	99.9	100.6	101.5	101.8	....	100.0	100.1	99.9	101.1	101.0	101.8

Item													
Housekeeping supplies	191.1	198.2	199.2	200.2	202.3	203.5	204.6	191.1	198.2	199.1	200.1	201.9	203.2	204.3
Soaps and detergents	184.7	189.9	189.9	191.1	194.3	195.6	196.7	184.7	189.9	190.1	191.2	193.8	194.2	195.2
Other laundry and cleaning products	-----	100.0	100.9	101.8	102.1	102.6	102.2	-----	100.0	100.5	101.3	101.8	102.2	101.9
Cleansing and toilet tissue, paper towels and napkins	-----	100.0	100.4	100.8	101.7	103.2	104.9	-----	100.0	100.3	100.9	101.3	103.2	104.8
Stationery, stationery supplies, and gift wrap	-----	100.0	100.3	100.7	101.0	101.8	101.9	-----	100.0	100.0	101.4	101.6	102.6	103.2
Miscellaneous household products	-----	100.0	100.7	101.0	102.4	102.7	103.1	-----	100.0	101.5	102.2	102.5	103.1	103.2
Lawn and garden supplies	-----	100.0	100.6	101.1	102.8	102.4	103.5	-----	100.0	99.7	100.2	101.4	101.4	102.5
Housekeeping services	206.3	212.9	215.0	216.9	218.3	220.0	221.7	206.3	212.9	215.3	216.9	218.2	219.8	221.5
Postage	225.6	225.6	225.6	225.6	225.6	225.6	225.6	225.6	225.6	225.6	225.6	225.6	225.6	225.6
Moving, storage, freight, household laundry, and drycleaning services	-----	100.0	101.2	102.2	102.4	103.0	103.6	-----	100.0	102.0	102.7	103.0	103.5	104.3
Appliance and furniture repair	-----	100.0	101.0	101.4	101.7	102.0	102.3	-----	100.0	100.6	100.9	101.3	101.7	101.9
APPAREL AND UPKEEP	153.4	158.2	155.7	154.5	156.5	158.4	159.8	153.4	158.2	155.4	154.5	156.0	158.1	159.7
Apparel commodities	150.9	155.3	152.3	150.7	152.8	154.8	156.1	150.9	155.3	152.0	150.8	152.3	154.4	156.1
Apparel commodities less footwear	149.7	154.5	151.1	149.2	151.4	153.5	154.8	149.7	154.5	150.8	149.3	150.9	153.2	155.0
Men's and boys'	154.3	157.8	154.7	153.9	155.8	156.7	157.7	154.3	157.8	155.0	154.1	155.4	156.6	157.6
Men's	-----	100.0	98.0	97.6	99.0	99.6	100.3	-----	100.0	98.2	98.0	99.1	99.9	100.5
Suits, sport coats, and jackets	-----	100.0	97.1	96.9	98.7	100.1	100.7	-----	100.0	97.6	97.6	99.7	100.7	100.8
Coats and jackets	-----	100.0	95.4	94.4	94.7	96.4	99.7	-----	100.0	95.4	94.9	94.9	96.3	99.0
Furnishings and special clothing	-----	100.0	99.5	100.4	100.5	100.8	101.6	-----	100.0	99.5	99.8	99.9	100.3	101.2
Shirts	-----	100.0	99.1	98.1	100.3	100.2	101.0	-----	100.0	99.6	98.9	100.7	102.0	102.2
Dungarees, jeans, and trousers	-----	100.0	97.9	97.0	99.1	99.2	99.4	-----	100.0	98.1	97.7	98.6	99.2	99.5
Boys'	-----	100.0	98.2	97.0	97.5	97.8	98.4	-----	100.0	98.1	96.4	96.6	96.9	97.6
Coats, jackets, sweaters, and shirts	-----	100.0	97.2	93.4	94.6	95.4	95.7	-----	100.0	96.8	92.6	92.6	94.3	94.8
Furnishings	-----	100.0	99.4	98.8	98.7	99.5	101.2	-----	100.0	99.6	98.4	98.8	99.4	100.7
Suits, trousers, sport coats, and jackets	144.7	100.0	98.4	99.1	99.4	99.1	99.5	144.7	100.0	98.7	98.5	98.8	98.0	98.7
Women's and girls'	-----	150.4	146.0	142.7	145.4	149.0	150.7	-----	150.4	144.8	142.7	144.7	148.2	150.8
Women's	154.0	100.0	97.2	94.9	96.8	99.5	100.7	154.0	100.0	96.5	95.4	96.7	99.2	101.3
Coats and jackets	-----	161.1	153.0	144.4	145.2	163.7	173.5	-----	161.1	147.2	143.9	144.5	162.2	175.7
Dresses	-----	159.4	153.8	150.5	156.2	160.3	160.1	-----	159.4	152.2	152.4	156.6	159.2	159.0
Separates and sportswear	-----	100.0	97.5	96.3	97.7	98.9	99.0	-----	100.0	97.3	96.9	97.2	98.2	99.0
Underwear, nightwear, and hosiery	-----	100.0	99.9	100.0	100.8	100.6	100.8	-----	100.0	100.0	100.3	100.9	101.1	101.2
Suits	-----	100.0	94.3	87.3	90.6	93.9	97.2	-----	100.0	93.7	87.0	90.9	94.4	100.9

CONSUMER PRICE INDEX—U.S. CITY AVERAGE (continued)

General summary	All Urban Consumers 1977 May	1977 Dec.	1978 Jan.	Feb.	Mar.	Apr.	May	Urban Wage Earners and Clerical Workers (revised) 1977 May	1977 Dec.	1978 Jan.	Feb.	Mar.	Apr.	May
APPAREL AND UPKEEP—Continued														
Apparel commodities—Continued														
Apparel commodities less footwear—Continued														
Girls'		100.0	96.7	95.0	96.5	97.3	97.8		100.0	95.7	92.7	94.5	95.6	95.7
Coats, jackets, dresses, and suits		100.0	95.1	91.1	97.2	97.2	96.8		100.0	93.2	88.3	95.8	95.3	94.6
Separates and sportswear		100.0	97.0	97.7	95.2	96.4	97.8		100.0	96.0	93.8	91.1	93.4	94.7
Underwear, nightwear, hosiery, and accessories		100.0	98.8	97.7	97.8	99.0	99.4		100.0	99.1	98.0	98.2	99.9	99.3
Infants' and toddlers'	207.6	216.5	211.3	208.7	213.8	215.5	215.9	207.6	216.5	213.2	209.9	211.6	215.2	215.9
Other apparel commodities	150.9	154.6	154.5	154.6	155.3	155.7	156.4	150.9	154.6	155.2	155.1	155.5	156.6	158.0
Sewing materials and notions		100.0	98.9	97.0	96.4	97.7	97.6		100.0	99.9	98.5	97.6	98.1	98.9
Jewelry and luggage		100.0	100.4	101.2	102.1	101.9	102.6		100.0	100.6	101.1	101.9	102.7	103.7
Footwear	157.0	159.6	158.8	159.3	160.7	161.7	163.4	157.0	159.6	158.5	159.1	159.8	161.1	162.0
Men's		100.0	99.4	99.6	100.2	101.2	102.3		100.0	99.4	100.2	100.3	101.8	102.7
Boys' and girls'		100.0	100.0	100.3	100.5	100.7	101.8		100.0	99.7	100.3	100.3	100.6	101.6
Women's		100.0	99.3	99.7	101.2	101.9	102.8		100.0	98.9	98.7	99.9	100.5	100.5
Apparel services	168.0	175.5	177.1	179.2	180.4	181.7	184.1	168.0	175.5	177.5	179.2	180.4	181.8	182.9
Laundry and drycleaning other than coin operated		100.0	101.7	102.9	103.8	104.7	105.7		100.0	101.7	103.0	103.8	104.9	105.7
Other apparel services		100.0	99.9	100.6	101.1	101.4	103.7		100.0	100.3	100.7	101.2	101.5	101.9
TRANSPORTATION	178.1	178.8	179.0	179.4	179.9	181.1	183.2	178.1	178.8	179.1	179.5	180.0	181.3	183.4
Private	177.7	178.0	178.2	178.6	179.1	180.3	182.6	177.7	178.0	178.3	178.7	179.2	180.5	182.8
New cars	141.4	150.5	150.9	151.2	151.1	151.2	152.5	141.4	150.5	151.0	151.1	151.1	151.2	152.2
Used cars	191.4	170.7	169.8	170.0	172.3	177.3	184.6	191.4	170.7	169.8	170.0	172.3	177.3	184.6
Gasoline	189.2	190.1	190.0	189.5	189.4	190.2	191.8	189.2	190.1	190.0	189.5	189.4	190.1	191.7
Automobile maintenance and repair	202.3	210.4	212.0	214.1	215.3	216.3	217.7	202.3	210.4	212.5	215.3	216.3	217.0	218.3
Body work		100.0	100.7	102.3	102.6	102.7	103.7		100.0	101.0	102.0	102.7	102.9	104.2
Automobile drive train, brake, and miscellaneous mechanical repair		100.0	101.3	103.9	103.3	103.9	104.4		100.0	101.5	103.5	104.1	104.8	105.2
Maintenance and servicing		100.0	100.6	101.1	102.0	102.3	103.1		100.0	100.7	101.8	102.2	102.3	102.8
Power plant repair		100.0	100.6	101.6	102.1	102.6	103.2		100.0	100.2	102.2	102.7	103.1	103.6
Other private transportation	176.3	181.2	181.7	182.5	182.5	182.6	182.8	176.3	181.2	181.9	182.7	182.7	183.0	182.9
Other private transportation commodities	150.2	154.7	154.9	155.8	156.5	156.8	158.2	150.2	154.7	155.2	156.2	157.5	158.3	158.7
Motor oil, coolant, and other products		100.0	100.1	100.7	101.6	102.1	102.0		100.0	99.2	99.5	101.3	101.0	101.2
Automobile parts and equipment		100.0	100.0	100.8	101.1	101.2	102.3		100.0	100.5	101.2	101.9	102.6	102.8
Tires	135.0	138.1	137.9	138.9	139.5	139.6	141.5	135.0	138.1	138.6	139.6	140.6	141.9	142.1
Other parts and equipment		100.0	100.6	101.0	101.3	101.6	102.0		100.0	101.0	101.4	102.1	102.1	102.6

Item														
Other private transportation services	184.9	190.0	190.6	191.4	191.1	191.3	191.1	184.9	190.0	190.8	191.5	191.2	191.4	191.1
Automobile insurance	209.5	214.7	215.3	216.2	215.6	215.6	214.2	209.5	214.7	215.4	216.2	215.7	215.8	214.4
Automobile finance charges	…	100.0	100.3	100.9	100.8	101.0	102.1	…	100.0	100.3	100.7	100.6	100.8	101.5
Automobile rental, registration, and other fees	…	100.0	100.3	100.7	100.8	101.1	101.3	…	100.0	100.7	100.7	101.1	101.2	101.5
State registration	142.2	142.2	142.3	142.5	142.8	142.8	142.8	142.2	142.2	142.3	142.5	142.7	142.8	142.8
Drivers' license	…	100.0	100.0	100.0	100.9	100.9	103.4	…	100.0	100.0	100.0	101.2	101.2	103.2
Vehicle inspection	…	100.0	107.8	110.1	110.1	110.0	110.3	…	100.0	109.5	111.5	111.5	111.5	111.7
Other vehicle related fees	…	100.0	100.1	100.6	100.8	101.2	101.4	…	100.0	101.3	101.8	101.8	101.6	102.2
Public	181.5	185.7	186.6	186.8	187.2	187.3	187.4	181.5	185.7	186.6	186.8	187.3	187.3	187.4
Airline fare	180.7	190.3	191.5	191.5	191.7	192.0	191.8	180.7	190.3	191.3	191.4	191.5	191.7	191.6
Intercity bus fare	211.2	232.6	233.7	235.4	238.2	238.7	239.3	211.2	232.6	233.6	235.1	238.2	238.5	239.1
Intracity mass transit	179.1	179.5	179.6	179.4	179.9	179.8	179.8	179.1	179.5	179.5	179.4	180.0	179.9	180.0
Taxi fare	188.2	194.4	198.8	201.1	201.3	201.2	202.0	188.2	194.4	201.2	204.0	204.1	203.9	204.3
Intercity train fare	173.6	190.8	190.5	190.5	190.7	190.8	193.6	173.6	190.8	190.6	190.5	190.7	190.8	193.8
MEDICAL CARE	200.5	209.3	211.2	213.2	214.5	215.7	216.9	200.5	209.3	211.2	213.2	214.3	215.6	217.0
Medical care commodities	133.3	137.9	138.8	140.1	141.0	141.8	142.7	133.3	137.9	138.6	140.0	141.0	142.2	143.2
Prescription drugs	121.2	125.8	127.0	128.5	129.4	130.1	130.7	121.2	125.8	126.8	128.5	129.6	130.7	131.4
Anti-infective drugs	…	100.0	100.7	101.9	102.3	103.3	103.6	…	100.0	100.3	101.9	102.2	103.7	104.2
Tranquilizers and sedatives	…	100.0	101.6	102.5	103.3	103.8	103.9	…	100.0	101.0	102.3	103.2	104.2	104.6
Circulatories and diuretics	…	100.0	100.5	101.2	101.6	101.6	102.2	…	100.0	100.4	101.1	101.7	101.9	102.7
Hormones, diabetic drugs, biologicals, and prescription medical supplies	…	100.0	101.6	103.8	105.2	106.4	106.9	…	100.0	101.5	103.8	105.5	106.7	107.3
Pain and symptom control drugs	…	100.0	101.1	102.2	103.0	103.3	103.9	…	100.0	100.9	102.5	103.4	103.6	103.8
Supplements, cough and cold preparations, and respiratory agents	…	100.0	100.3	101.0	101.7	102.0	102.6	…	100.0	100.6	101.4	102.0	102.7	103.6
Nonprescription drugs and medical supplies	…	100.0	100.4	101.1	101.7	102.2	103.0	…	100.0	100.3	101.0	101.7	102.6	103.4
Eyeglasses	…	100.0	100.5	100.6	100.5	101.2	101.5	…	100.0	100.2	100.6	101.2	101.7	101.9
Internal and respiratory over-the-counter drugs	147.9	152.4	153.3	154.7	156.1	156.8	158.0	147.9	152.4	153.0	154.2	155.5	156.8	158.2
Nonprescription medical equipment and supplies	…	100.0	99.8	100.7	101.0	102.2	103.0	…	100.0	100.1	101.2	101.5	102.9	104.1
Medical care services	214.6	224.2	226.5	228.7	229.9	231.3	232.5	214.6	224.2	226.5	228.6	229.7	231.0	232.5
Professional services	192.4	200.5	201.9	203.5	204.5	205.7	206.6	192.4	200.5	202.1	203.8	204.8	205.8	207.2
Physicians' services	204.3	213.5	215.4	217.1	218.4	219.6	220.6	204.3	213.5	215.7	217.3	218.4	219.6	221.3
Dental services	183.2	190.9	191.8	193.4	194.0	195.2	196.0	183.2	190.9	192.1	194.1	195.0	196.1	197.4
Other professional services	…	100.0	100.6	101.3	102.0	102.7	102.8	…	100.0	100.2	101.0	101.4	101.7	102.1
Other medical care services	241.6	253.0	256.3	259.3	260.7	262.3	263.9	241.6	253.0	256.1	258.8	260.1	261.5	263.2
Hospital and other medical services	…	100.0	101.5	102.8	103.4	103.9	104.7	…	100.0	101.4	102.6	103.0	103.6	104.3
Hospital room	295.9	311.9	316.5	320.9	323.2	323.3	327.1	295.9	311.9	316.3	320.3	321.2	322.6	325.6
Other hospital and medical care services	…	100.0	101.6	102.8	103.4	104.1	104.5	…	100.0	101.4	102.6	103.1	103.8	104.2

CONSUMER PRICE INDEX—U.S. CITY AVERAGE (concluded)

General summary	All Urban Consumers							Urban Wage Earners and Clerical Workers (revised)						
	1977		1978					1977		1978				
	May	Dec.	Jan.	Feb.	Mar.	Apr.	May	May	Dec.	Jan.	Feb.	Mar.	Apr.	May
ENTERTAINMENT	166.6	171.0	171.9	172.9	174.1	175.6	176.2	166.6	171.0	171.7	173.7	174.1	175.3	175.6
Entertainment commodities	167.7	172.9	173.3	174.3	175.5	177.3	178.0	167.7	172.9	173.5	175.1	175.3	176.1	176.3
Reading materials	----	100.0	100.9	100.2	101.3	102.2	102.1	----	100.0	100.8	100.0	101.1	102.0	101.9
Newspapers	189.4	196.6	197.1	197.4	197.8	198.9	199.7	189.4	196.6	196.9	197.1	197.4	198.4	199.3
Magazines, periodicals, and books	----	100.0	101.7	100.1	102.1	103.4	102.6	----	100.0	101.6	99.7	102.1	103.5	102.7
Sporting goods and equipment	----	100.0	100.1	100.4	101.1	103.0	103.8	----	100.0	100.7	101.3	99.6	99.8	100.1
Sport vehicles	----	100.0	100.0	100.4	101.1	103.7	104.6	----	100.0	100.9	101.5	98.9	99.0	99.4
Indoor and warm weather sport equipment	----	100.0	100.4	100.6	100.8	101.4	102.4	----	100.0	100.2	100.2	100.0	99.8	100.0
Bicycles	147.0	146.2	146.6	147.4	148.6	149.3	150.8	147.0	146.2	147.2	149.1	149.0	149.5	150.3
Other sporting goods and equipment	----	100.0	100.0	100.1	100.4	101.8	102.0	----	100.0	100.3	100.6	100.1	100.8	101.0
Toys, hobbies, and other entertainment	----	100.0	100.0	101.4	101.9	102.5	102.9	----	100.0	100.0	101.8	102.5	103.0	103.2
Toys, hobbies, and music equipment	----	100.0	99.2	101.6	102.4	103.5	104.2	----	100.0	99.1	101.9	103.0	104.0	104.1
Photographic supplies and equipment	----	100.0	101.2	102.4	102.5	102.3	103.1	----	100.0	100.9	102.2	102.4	102.0	102.9
Pet supplies and expense	----	100.0	100.5	100.2	100.7	100.9	100.3	----	100.0	101.0	101.4	101.8	101.7	101.6
Entertainment services	165.0	168.7	170.2	171.3	172.4	173.4	174.0	165.0	168.7	169.6	172.2	172.9	174.9	175.1
Fees for participant sports	----	100.0	100.6	101.4	101.8	102.7	103.1	----	100.0	100.2	101.7	102.2	104.1	104.3
Admissions	----	100.0	102.1	102.5	103.7	103.6	104.1	----	100.0	101.7	102.0	103.2	103.9	104.2
Other entertainment services	----	100.0	100.2	100.6	100.9	102.0	102.1	----	100.0	99.8	103.3	101.8	102.1	102.0
OTHER GOODS AND SERVICES	170.4	177.8	178.5	179.0	179.3	179.8	180.4	170.4	177.8	178.4	179.1	179.6	180.1	180.6
Tobacco products	166.2	173.0	173.3	173.6	173.6	173.9	174.0	166.2	173.0	173.2	173.4	173.7	173.9	174.1

Cigarettes	169.1	175.7	175.8	176.0	176.0	176.2	176.2	169.1	175.7	175.8	175.9	176.1	176.3	176.4
Other tobacco products and smoking accessories	----	100.0	100.7	101.6	101.7	102.8	103.1	----	100.0	100.5	101.3	101.9	102.7	103.0
Personal care	169.5	176.3	177.2	177.7	178.2	179.1	180.3	169.5	176.3	177.1	178.2	178.9	179.7	180.7
Toilet goods and personal care appliances	166.1	172.3	173.0	173.1	173.2	173.5	174.9	166.1	172.3	173.0	173.9	174.5	174.7	175.5
Products for the hair, hairpieces, and wigs	----	100.0	101.1	100.7	100.5	100.4	100.3	----	100.0	100.5	100.7	100.8	100.4	100.0
Dental and shaving products	----	100.0	99.9	100.3	100.2	101.6	103.5	----	100.0	101.9	103.0	103.6	103.9	104.9
Cosmetics, bath and nail preparations, manicure and eye makeup implements	----	100.0	100.3	100.1	100.4	99.8	100.6	----	100.0	99.6	99.7	99.9	100.2	100.9
Other toilet goods and small personal care appliances	----	100.0	100.3	101.0	101.3	101.7	102.6	----	100.0	100.3	101.4	102.2	102.3	103.2
Personal care services	173.0	180.5	181.4	182.4	183.1	184.6	185.6	173.0	180.5	181.4	182.5	183.4	184.8	186.1
Beauty parlor services for women	173.6	182.5	183.3	184.7	185.1	186.7	187.9	173.6	182.5	183.5	185.1	185.7	187.0	188.4
Haircuts and other barber shop services for men	----	100.0	100.7	100.9	101.6	102.3	102.7	----	100.0	100.4	100.6	101.4	102.2	102.8
Personal and educational expenses	181.3	191.3	192.5	193.1	193.5	193.6	193.9	181.3	191.3	192.5	193.2	193.6	193.7	194.1
School books and supplies	165.8	177.8	179.9	180.2	180.5	180.6	180.7	165.8	177.8	180.3	180.6	181.0	181.2	181.2
Personal and educational services	185.5	195.0	196.0	196.7	197.1	197.2	197.6	185.5	195.0	195.9	196.7	197.1	197.3	197.7
Tuition and other school fees	----	100.0	100.6	100.8	100.8	100.9	100.9	----	100.0	100.7	100.7	100.8	100.9	100.9
College tuition	----	100.0	100.7	100.8	100.6	100.6	100.6	----	100.0	100.8	100.8	100.8	100.9	100.9
Elementary and high school tuition	----	100.0	100.2	100.6	100.6	100.6	100.6	----	100.0	100.7	100.4	100.4	100.4	100.4
Personal expenses	----	100.0	100.1	101.4	102.1	102.4	103.3	----	100.0	100.1	101.5	102.1	102.5	103.4
Special indexes:														
Gasoline, motor oil, coolant and other products	187.5	188.7	188.6	188.2	188.1	188.9	190.5	187.5	188.7	188.6	188.2	188.1	188.7	190.3
Insurance and finance	208.7	220.1	221.9	223.5	225.0	227.0	229.0	208.7	220.1	220.0	223.5	225.0	226.9	228.7
Utilities and public transportation	185.5	191.9	192.5	194.3	196.1	197.4	198.9	185.5	191.9	192.5	194.3	196.2	197.6	199.2
Housekeeping and home maintenance services	222.7	231.3	233.1	234.8	237.0	239.7	241.5	222.7	231.3	232.9	234.8	236.4	238.4	240.7

C = Corrected.

Source: *Monthly Labor Review*, U.S. Department of Labor, Bureau of Labor Statistics.

PRICES RECEIVED AND PAID BY FARMERS

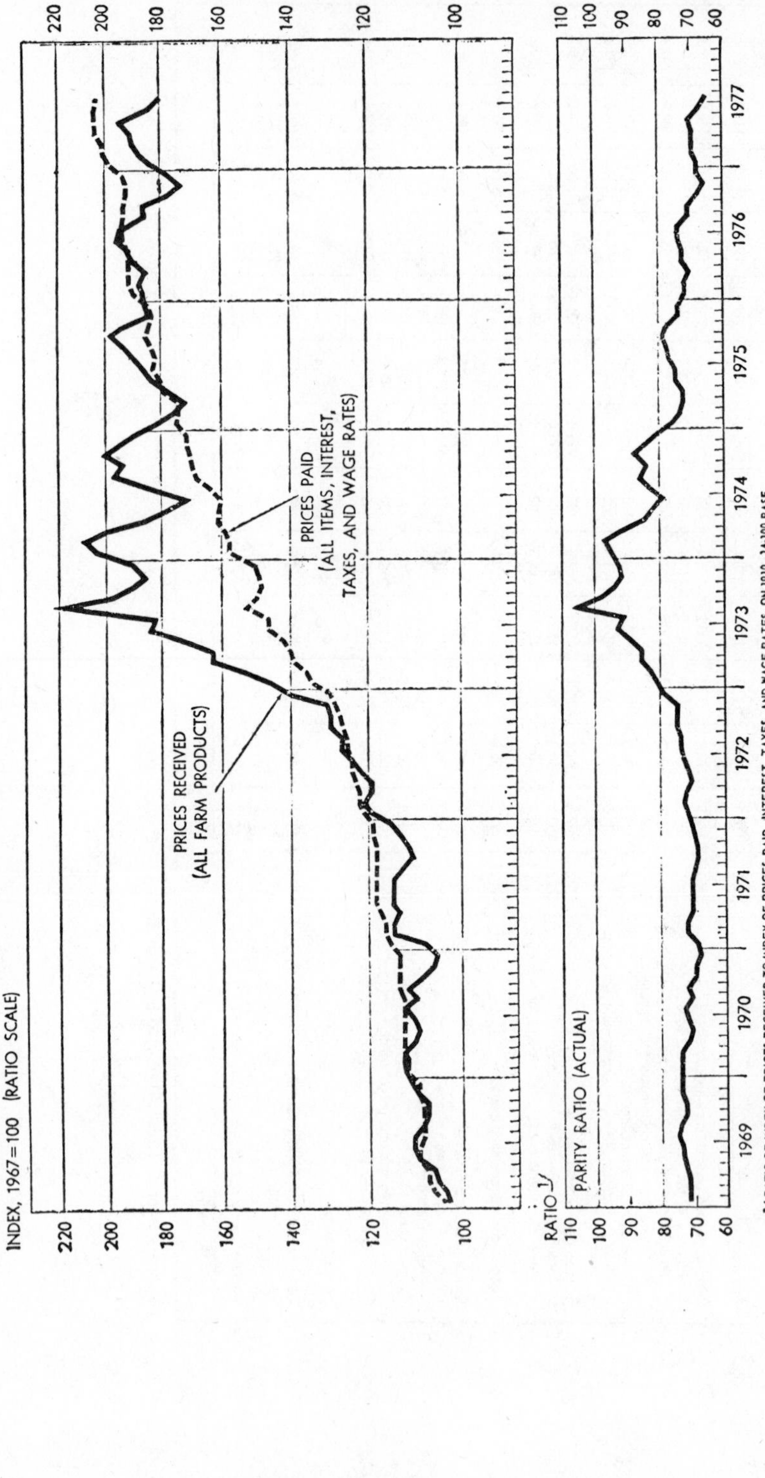

INDEX, 1967=100 (RATIO SCALE)

PRICES PAID
(ALL ITEMS, INTEREST,
TAXES, AND WAGE RATES)

PRICES RECEIVED
(ALL FARM PRODUCTS)

RATIO 1/

PARITY RATIO (ACTUAL)

1/ RATIO OF INDEX OF PRICES RECEIVED TO INDEX OF PRICES PAID, INTEREST, TAXES, AND WAGE RATES, ON 1910-14=100 BASE.

SOURCE: DEPARTMENT OF AGRICULTURE

COUNCIL OF ECONOMIC ADVISERS

Period	Prices received by farmers			Prices paid by farmers			Parity ratio [1]	
	All farm products	Crops	Livestock and products	All items, interest, taxes, and wage rates	Family living items	Production items	Actual	Adjusted [2]
	Index, 1967 = 100							
1969	107	97	117	108	109	104	73	79
1970	110	100	118	112	114	108	72	77
1971	113	108	118	118	118	113	71	75
1972	125	114	136	125	123	121	74	79
1973	179	175	183	144	133	146	91	94
1974	192	224	165	164	151	166	86	87
1975	185	201	172	180	166	182	76	76
1976	186	197	177	192	176	193	71	72
1976: July 15	194	214	179	194	177	196	74	74
Aug 15	186	201	175	193	177	194	71	72
Sept 15	186	204	172	193	178	194	71	72
Oct 15	178	195	165	192	179	192	68	69
Nov 15	173	186	162	192	180	191	66	67
Dec 15	178	190	169	193	181	193	68	68
1977: Jan 15	183	198	170	198	182	196	68	69
Feb 15	187	203	174	200	(3)	199	69	70
Mar 15	190	211	171	201	(3)	201	69	70
Apr 15	191	214	172	204	(3)	204	69	70
May 15	194	214	176	204	(3)	205	70	70
June 15	184	198	173	204	(3)	203	67	67
July 15	180	181	179	203	(3)	201	65	66

[1] Percentage ratio of index of prices received by farmers to index of prices paid, interest, taxes, and wage rates on 1910-14=100 base.
[2] The adjusted parity ratio reflects Government payments made directly to farmers.
[3] Index discontinued. Consumer price index (Department of Labor) substituted in calculating total prices paid beginning January 1977.
Source: Department of Agriculture.

Source: *Economic Indicators*, Council of Economic Advisors.

CONSUMER PRICE INDEX—U.S. CITY AVERAGE, AND SELECTED AREAS

1967 = 100 unless otherwise specified

Area¹	All Urban Consumers 1977 May	Dec.	1978 Jan.	Feb.	Mar.	Apr.	May	Urban Wage Earners and Clerical Workers (revised) 1977 May	Dec.	1978 Jan.	Feb.	Mar.	Apr.	May
U.S. city average²	180.6	186.1	187.2	188.4	189.8	191.5	193.3	180.6	186.1	187.1	188.4	189.7	191.4	193.3
Anchorage, Alaska (10/67=100)	----	----	179.2	----	180.7	----	184.2	----	----	179.2	----	180.8	----	184.0
Atlanta, Ga.	----	184.5	----	186.1	----	188.5	----	----	184.5	----	186.5	----	188.9	----
Baltimore, Md.	----	190.7	----	----	195.7	----	198.0	----	190.7	----	----	195.7	----	198.4
Boston, Mass.	----	----	187.5	----	188.2	----	190.7	----	----	187.5	----	187.8	----	190.2
Buffalo, N.Y.	181.3	----	----	187.5	----	189.0	----	181.3	----	----	187.5	----	189.2	----
Chicago, Ill.-Northwestern Ind.	174.4	180.0	182.5	184.2	186.3	187.3	189.0	174.4	180.0	182.4	183.8	185.6	186.6	188.2
Cincinnati, Ohio-Ky.-Ind.	----	186.7	----	----	192.3	----	197.5	----	186.7	----	----	192.3	----	197.6
Cleveland, Ohio	179.9	----	----	186.6	----	190.3	----	179.9	----	----	186.6	----	190.7	----
Dallas-Ft. Worth, Tex.	179.4	----	----	186.7	----	189.3	----	179.4	----	----	186.7	----	189.7	----
Denver-Boulder, Colo.	----	----	192.3	----	195.1	----	198.5	----	----	192.3	----	195.7	----	199.5
Detroit, Mich.	179.3	184.4	185.0	185.6	188.4	190.2	192.3	179.3	184.4	185.0	185.8	187.9	189.8	192.1
Honolulu, Hawaii	----	174.9	----	178.0	----	181.4	----	----	174.9	----	177.5	----	181.3	----
Houston, Tex.	----	----	----	183.8	----	188.9	----	----	----	----	184.4	----	188.6	----
Kansas City, Mo.-Kansas	----	182.7	----	----	----	----	----	----	182.7	----	----	----	----	----
Los Angeles-Long Beach, Anaheim, Calif.	178.5	184.4	185.5	186.5	187.4	189.6	191.5	178.5	184.4	185.6	186.8	187.1	188.9	191.2
Miami, Fla. (11/77=100)	----	----	100.7	----	102.2	----	102.8	----	----	100.6	----	102.3	----	103.3
Milwaukee, Wis.	178.0	----	183.5	----	186.3	----	188.7	178.0	----	184.0	----	186.5	----	189.5
Minneapolis-St. Paul, Minn.-Wis.	184.6	188.8	189.8	190.8	192.2	193.5	194.6	184.6	188.8	189.8	190.8	191.9	192.8	193.7
New York, N.Y.-Northeastern N.J.	179.0	----	184.9	----	187.0	----	190.0	179.0	----	184.6	----	187.2	----	190.8
Northeast, Pa. (Scranton)	----	----	----	----	----	----	----	----	----	----	----	----	----	----
Philadelphia, Pa.-N.J.	183.1	186.9	187.6	188.2	189.6	190.8	191.7	183.1	186.9	187.4	188.7	189.7	191.5	192.6
Pittsburgh, Pa.	----	----	187.9	----	191.7	----	195.3	----	----	184.9	----	191.9	----	196.1
Portland, Oreg.-Wash.	----	----	----	----	184.0	----	189.5	----	----	----	----	184.0	----	187.9
St. Louis, Mo.-Ill.	180.6	180.6	188.9	----	191.4	----	195.5	180.6	180.6	188.9	----	191.2	----	195.4
San Diego, Calif.	----	----	----	----	191.4	----	195.5	----	----	----	----	191.2	----	195.4
San Francisco-Oakland, Calif.	----	187.3	----	189.2	----	192.8	----	----	187.3	----	189.5	----	192.4	----
Seattle-Everett, Wash.	176.2	----	184.1	----	187.2	----	193.5	176.2	----	183.8	----	186.8	----	192.5
Washington, D.C.-Md.-Va.	182.2	----	190.2	----	191.5	----	194.7	182.2	----	189.5	----	191.4	----	196.7

¹The areas listed include not only the central city but the entire portion of the Standard Metropolitan Statistical Area, as defined for the 1970 Census of Population, except that the Standard Consolidated Area is used for New York and Chicago.

²Average of 85 cities.

Source: *Monthly Labor Review*, U.S. Department of Labor, Bureau of Labor Statistics.

Economic Indicators

COMPOSITE INDEXES AND THEIR COMPONENTS

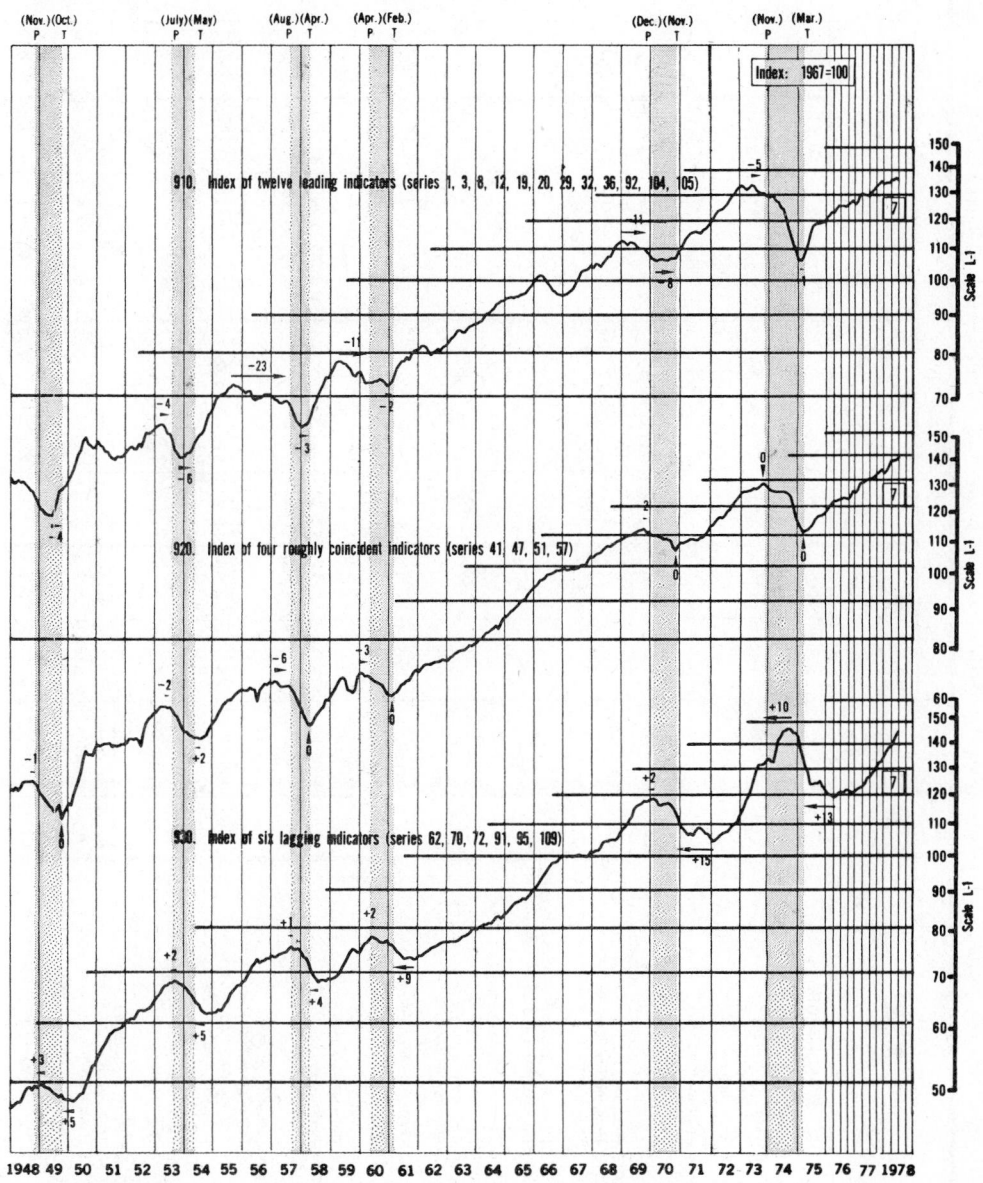

Source: *Business Conditions Digest.*

SUMMARY OF RECENT DATA AND CURRENT CHANGES FOR PRINCIPAL INDICATORS

Series title	Timing classification[3]	Unit of measure	Basic data[1] 1976	1977	4th Q 1977	1st Q 1978	2d Q 1978	May 1978	June 1978	July 1978	Percent change May to June 1978	June to July 1978	4th Q to 1st Q 1978	1st Q to 2d Q 1978	Series number
I. CYCLICAL INDICATORS															
A. Composite Indexes															
910. Twelve leading indicators	L,L,L	1967=100	124.7	130.9	134.8	134.8	136.5	136.4	137.1	136.1	0.5	-0.7	0.0	1.3	910
920. Four coincident indicators	C,C,C	do.	122.3	130.1	133.3	134.0	138.3	138.2	138.6	139.6	0.3	0.7	0.5	3.2	920
930. Six lagging indicators	Lg,Lg,Lg	do.	120.7	126.9	132.3	137.3	141.6	141.6	143.8	146.0	1.6	1.5	3.8	3.1	930
Leading Indicator Subgroups:															
913. Marginal employment adjustments	L,L,L	do.	96.2	96.9	97.6	97.3	97.8	97.8	97.2	97.0	-0.6	-0.2	-0.3	0.5	913
914. Capital investment commitments	L,L,L	do.	106.7	111.7	114.1	113.7	113.8	113.4	114.8	113.5	1.2	-1.1	-0.4	0.1	914
915. Inventory investment and purchasing	L,L,L	do.	102.0	107.9	103.5	105.2	106.1	106.3	106.0	105.0	-0.3	-0.9	1.6	0.9	915
916. Profitability	L,L,L	do.	108.1	107.8	106.9	103.4	107.0	107.4	106.9	107.8	-0.5	-0.1	-3.3	3.5	916
917. Money and financial flows	L,L,L	do.	107.9	112.2	115.3	112.4	110.7	110.7	110.3	110.2	-0.4	-0.1	-2.5	-1.5	917
B. Cyclical Indicators by Economic Process															
B1. Employment and Unemployment															
Marginal Employment Adjustments:															
*1. Average workweek, prod. workers, mfg.	L,L,L	Hours	40.0	40.3	40.5	40.0	40.4	40.3	40.4	40.4	0.2	0.0	-1.2	1.0	1
21. Avg. weekly overtime, prod. workers, mfg.[2]	L,C,L	do.	3.1	3.4	3.5	3.7	3.5	3.5	3.5	3.5	0.0	0.0	-0.2	-0.2	21
2. Accession rate, per 100 employees, mfg.[3]	L,L,L	Percent	3.9	4.0	4.1	4.0	4.0	4.1	3.8	3.9	-0.3	0.1	-0.1	-0.0	2
*5. Avg. weekly initial claims (inverted[4])	L,C,L	Thousands	384	371	351	340	335	328	346	375	-5.5	-8.4	3.1	1.5	5
*3. Layoff rate, per 100 employ., mfg. (inv.[4])[3]	L,L,L	Percent	1.3	1.1	1.0	0.9	1.0	0.9	1.0	1.0	0.0	0.0	0.1	-0.1	3
4. Quit rate, per 100 employees, mfg.[3]	L,Lg,U	do.	1.7	1.8	1.9	2.0	2.2	2.1	2.1	2.0	0.0	-0.1	0.1	0.2	4
Job Vacancies:															
60. Ratio, help-wanted advertising to persons unemployed[2]	L,Lg,U	Ratio	0.390	0.517	0.608	0.674	0.728	0.697	0.761	0.716	0.064	-0.045	0.066	0.054	60
46. Help-wanted advertising	L,Lg,U	1967=100	95	118	134	139	146	144	147	149	2.1	1.4	3.7	5.0	46
Comprehensive Employment:															
48. Employee hours in nonagri. establishments	U,C,C	Ar. bil. hrs.	151.48	156.53	158.58	159.27	162.95	162.53	163.39	164.24	0.5	0.5	0.4	2.3	48
42. Persons engaged in nonagri. activities	U,C,C	Thousands	84,188	87,302	88,761	89,748	90,916	90,877	91,346	91,038	0.5	-0.3	1.1	1.3	42
*41. Employees on nonagri. payrolls	C,C,C	do.	79,443	82,142	83,192	84,107	85,485	85,466	85,767	86,031	0.4	0.3	1.1	1.6	41
40. Employees in mfg., mining, construction	L,C,U	do.	23,332	24,229	24,497	24,757	25,444	25,429	25,552	25,637	0.5	0.3	1.1	2.8	40
90. Ratio, civilian employment to total population of working age[2]	U,Lg,U	Percent	56.06	57.11	57.71	58.11	58.64	58.56	58.92	58.60	0.36	-0.32	0.40	0.53	90
Comprehensive Unemployment:															
37. Total unemployed (inverted[4])	L,Lg,U	Thousands	7,288	6,855	6,554	6,155	5,962	6,149	5,754	6,193	6.4	-7.6	6.1	3.1	37
43. Unemployment rate, total (inverted[4])[2]	L,Lg,U	Percent	7.7	7.0	6.6	6.2	5.9	6.1	5.7	6.2	0.4	-0.5	0.4	0.3	43
45. Avg. weekly insured unemploy. rate (inv.[4])[3]	L,Lg,U	do.	4.5	3.9	3.8	3.5	3.1	3.0	3.1	3.4	-0.1	-0.3	0.3	0.4	45
*91. Avg. duration of unemployment (inverted[4])	Lg,Lg,Lg	Weeks	15.8	14.3	13.8	12.6	12.1	12.1	12.0	11.8	0.8	1.7	8.7	4.0	91
44. Unemploy. rate, 15 weeks and over (inv.[4])[3]	Lg,Lg,Lg	Percent	2.5	2.0	1.8	1.6	1.3	1.4	1.2	1.3	0.2	-0.1	0.2	0.3	44

B2. Production and Income

Comprehensive Output and Income:

No.	Series	Unit	Code	(1)	(2)	(3)	(4)	(5)	(6)	(7)	(8)	(9)	(10)	(11)	(12)
50.	GNP in 1972 dollars	A.r., bil. dol.	C,C,C	1.9	0.0	...	...	1139.3	1127.7	1126.7	1380.5	1354.2	1354.5	1332.7	1271.0
52.	Personal income in 1972 dollars	do.	C,C,C	1.1	0.2	1.0	0.1	987.6	980.9	978.4	1127.2	1114.7	1112.4	1086.8	1037.7
51.	Pers. income less transfer pay, 1972 dollars	do.	C,C,C	1.5	0.3	0.7	0.3	...	...	...	979.4	964.7	961.6	938.4	892.0
53.	Wages and salaries in mining, mfg., and construction, 1972 dollars	do.	C,C,C	3.2	0.5	0.7	0.2	247.4	245.8	245.3	245.7	238.0	236.7	232.3	221.1

Industrial Production:

No.	Series	Unit	Code	(1)	(2)	(3)	(4)	(5)	(6)	(7)	(8)	(9)	(10)	(11)	(12)
*47.	Industrial production, total	1967=100.	C,C,C	3.1	0.2	0.5	0.5	145.3	144.6	143.9	143.9	139.6	139.3	137.1	129.8
73.	Industrial production, durable mfrs.	do.	C,C,C	4.1	-0.4	0.8	0.7	139.6	138.5	137.6	137.7	132.3	132.8	129.5	121.7
74.	Industrial production, nondurable mfrs.	do.	C,L,U	2.1	-0.3	0.0	0.3	154.3	154.3	153.8	153.6	150.6	150.2	148.1	140.9
49.	Value of goods output, 1972 dollars	A.r., bil. dol.	C,C,C	2.5	-1.3	...	...	...	...	...	627.2	611.8	620.1	608.4	576.5

Capacity Utilization:

No.	Series	Unit	Code	(1)	(2)	(3)	(4)	(5)	(6)	(7)	(8)	(9)	(10)	(11)	(12)
82.	Capacity utilization rate, mfg., FRB[3]	Percent.	L,C,U	1.7	-0.8	...	...	...	...	...	83.8	82.1	82.9	82.4	80.2
83.	Capacity utilization rate, mfg., BEA[3]	do.		NA				...	...	...	NA	84	82	83	81
84.	Capacity utilization rate, materials, FRB[3]	do.	L,C,U	2.8	-0.5	...	...	...	...	...	84.5	81.7	82.2	81.9	80.4

B3. Consumption, Trade, Orders, and Deliveries

Orders and Deliveries:

No.	Series	Unit	Code	(1)	(2)	(3)	(4)	(5)	(6)	(7)	(8)	(9)	(10)	(11)	(12)
6.	New orders, durable goods	Bil. dol.	L,L,L	5.0	3.4	-6.4	-1.7	64.44	68.84	70.04	69.64	66.35	64.18	59.78	50.97
7.	New orders, durable goods, 1972 dollars	do.	L,L,L	2.7	0.9	-7.1	-2.2	38.06	40.98	41.92	41.69	40.60	40.22	38.48	35.14
*8.	New orders, cons. goods and mtls., 1972 dol.	do.	L,L,L	2.8	2.6	-3.1	-1.9	35.88	37.04	37.76	37.80	36.76	35.83	35.27	32.56
25.	Chg. in unfilled orders, durable goods[5]	do.	L,L,L	-0.27	0.55	-2.96	-2.07	-0.41	2.55	4.62	3.57	3.84	3.29	1.53	0.30
96.	Mfrs.' unfilled orders, durable goods[5]	Bil. dol., EOP	L,Lg,U	5.5	6.2	-0.2	1.2	206.66	207.07	204.52	207.07	196.36	184.83	184.83	166.44
32.	Vendor performance[2] (11)	Percent.	L,L,L	.3	8	-10		56	66	64	65	62	54	55	54

Consumption and Trade:

No.	Series	Unit	Code	(1)	(2)	(3)	(4)	(5)	(6)	(7)	(8)	(9)	(10)	(11)	(12)
56.	Manufacturing and trade sales	Bil. dol.	C,C,C	6.3	2.0	NA	0.4	NA	253.20	252.09	252.09	237.15	232.42	223.60	200.25
*57.	Manufacturing and trade sales, 1972 dollars	do.	C,C,C	3.6	-0.3	NA	-0.3	NA	153.85	154.30	154.30	148.92	149.39	146.15	138.36
75.	Industrial production, consumer goods	1967=100.	C,L,U	2.4	-1.0	0.3	-0.1	147.3	146.9	147.1	147.2	143.8	145.3	143.4	136.2
54.	Sales of retail stores	Mil. dol.	C,L,U	4.5	-0.1	0.2	-0.1	64,421	64,271	64,229	64,193	61,402	61,473	59,029	53,542
59.	Sales of retail stores, 1972 dollars	do.	U,L,U	12.2	-2.2	-0.3	-0.5	42,606	42,733	42,963	42,968	42,044	43,008	41,735	39,806
55.	Personal consumption expend., autos	A.r., bil. dol.	L,C,C	-1.0	-0.2	...	...	82.4	80.0	82.9	70.8	63.1	63.2	61.8	52.8
58.	Index of consumer sentiment (11)	I Q 1966=100	L,L,L		-1.0	3.0	-3.5	...	...	...	81.5	82.3	83.1	86.8	85.4

B4. Fixed Capital Investment

Formation of Business Enterprises:

No.	Series	Unit	Code	(1)	(2)	(3)	(4)	(5)	(6)	(7)	(8)	(9)	(10)	(11)	(12)
*12.	Net business formation	1967=100.	L,L,L	-0.7	0.4	NA	2.2	NA	135.1	132.2	133.1	134.0	133.4	127.4	117.6
13.	New business incorporations	Number.	L,L,L	4.1	-3.0	NA	7.7	NA	41,257	38,320	39,358	37,801	38,987	36,509	31,244

SUMMARY OF RECENT DATA AND CURRENT CHANGES FOR PRINCIPAL INDICATORS (continued)

Series title	Timing classification[3]	Unit of measure	Average 1976	Average 1977	4th Q 1977	1st Q 1978	2d Q 1978	May 1978	June 1978	July 1978	May to June 1978	June to July 1978	4th Q to 1st Q 1978	1st Q to 2d Q 1978	Series number
I. CYCLICAL INDICATORS—Con.															
B4. Fixed Capital Investment—Con.															
Business Investment Commitments:															
10. Contracts and orders, plant and equipment	L,L,L	Bil. dol.	15.24	18.17	19.12	21.35	20.32	21.60	20.21	20.68	-6.4	2.3	11.7	-4.8	10
*20. Contr. and orders, plant and equip., 1972 dol.	L,L,L	do.	10.79	12.13	12.42	13.59	12.83	13.62	12.69	12.79	-6.8	0.8	9.4	-5.6	20
24. New orders, cap. goods indus., nondefense	L,L,L	do.	12.48	15.20	16.39	17.30	17.90	18.12	18.16	16.70	0.2	-8.0	5.6	3.5	24
27. New orders, capital goods industries, nondefense, 1972 dollars	L,L,L	do.	8.89	10.20	10.70	11.07	11.34	11.48	11.44	10.38	-0.3	-9.3	3.5	2.4	27
9. Construction contracts, commercial and industrial buildings, floor space	L,C,U	Mil. sq. ft.	51.43	62.96	68.57	74.28	82.80	88.41	83.27	74.82	-5.8	-10.1	8.3	11.5	9
11. New capital appropriations, mfg.	U,Lg,U	Bil. dol.	12.45	16.14	17.20	17.82	NA	...	...	...	...	...	3.6	NA	11
97. Backlog of capital appropriations, mfg.[5]	C,Lg,Lg	Bil. dol., EOP	47.53	57.52	57.52	61.99	NA	...	...	...	...	...	7.8	NA	97
Business Investment Expenditures:															
61. Business expend., new plant and equipment	C,Lg,Lg	Ar., bil. dol.	120.49	135.80	138.11	144.25	148.88	...	...	...	...	...	4.4	3.2	61
69. Machinery and equipment sales and business construction expenditures	C,Lg,Lg	do.	171.23	196.20	207.37	211.88	226.42	222.36	231.31	NA	4.0	NA	2.2	6.9	69
76. Industrial production, business equip.	C,Lg,U	1967=100.	136.3	149.2	153.4	154.7	160.3	160.2	161.3	162.8	0.7	0.9	0.8	3.6	76
86. Nonresid. fixed investment, total, 1972 dol.	C,Lg,C	Ar., bil. dol.	118.9	129.8	132.5	133.8	140.4	...	...	...	...	...	1.0	4.9	86
Residential Construction Commitments and Investment:															
28. New private housing units started, total	L,L,L	Ar., thous.	1,538	1,987	2,146	1,721	2,114	2,054	2,124	2,085	3.4	-1.8	-19.8	22.8	28
*29. New building permits, private housing	L,L,L	1967=100.	111.8	145.3	154.6	135.2	148.1	137.6	156.9	140.6	14.0	-10.4	-12.5	9.5	29
89. Fixed investment, residential, 1972 dol.	L,L,L	Ar., bil. dol.	47.8	57.7	60.3	59.5	60.1	...	...	...	...	...	-1.3	1.0	89
B5. Inventories and Inventory Investment															
Inventory Investment:															
30. Chg. in business inventories, 1972 dol.[2]	L,L,L	do.	6.7	8.9	7.5	12.3	12.0	...	...	...	...	...	4.8	-0.3	30
*36. Change in inventories on hand and on order, 1972 dollars (smoothed[6])[2]	L,L,L	do.	6.22	9.78	11.71	14.97	24.69	26.82	23.67	NA	-3.15	NA	3.26	9.72	36
31. Chg. in book value, mfg. and trade inven.[2]	L,L,L	do.	25.6	25.6	17.7	44.2	39.9	44.2	18.9	NA	-25.3	NA	26.5	-4.3	31
38. Chg. in mtl. stocks on hand and on order[2]	L,L,L	Bil. dol.	0.52	0.88	0.90	1.76	2.18	2.54	2.17	0.46	-0.37	-1.71	0.86	0.42	38
Inventories on Hand and on Order:															
71. Mfg. and trade inventories, total[5]	Lg,Lg,Lg	Bil. dol., EOP	309.24	334.78	334.78	345.84	355.80	354.23	355.80	NA	0.4	NA	3.3	2.9	71
*70. Mfg. and trade invent., total, 1972 dol.[5]	Lg,Lg,Lg	do.	225.20	233.75	233.75	237.28	240.12	239.97	240.12	NA	0.1	NA	1.5	1.2	70
65. Mfrs.' inventories of finished goods[5]	Lg,Lg,Lg	do.	54.11	58.91	58.91	59.88	61.62	61.06	61.62	62.12	0.9	0.8	1.6	2.9	65
77. Ratio, inventories to sales, mfg. and trade, constant dollars[2]	Lg,Lg,Lg	Ratio.	1.60	1.57	1.56	1.58	1.55	1.56	1.56	NA	0.0	NA	0.02	-0.03	77
78. Materials and supplies, stocks on hand and on order[5]	L,Lg,Lg	Bil. dol., EOP	132.40	142.90	142.90	148.17	154.70	152.53	154.70	155.16	1.4	0.3	3.7	4.4	78

B6. Prices, Costs, and Profits

Series	Class.	Unit														No.
Sensitive Commodity Prices															
*92. Chg. in sensitive prices (smoothed⁶)¹²	L,L,L	Percent.	1.17	0.75	0.70	1.47	0.97	0.92	1.08	1.24	0.16	0.16	0.72	-0.50	92
23. Industrial materials prices ⑬	U,L,L	1967=100.	200.7	206.5	210.4	219.8	220.1	217.8	222.1	224.7	2.0	1.2	6.4	0.1	23
Stock Prices															
*19. Stock prices, 500 common stocks ⑪	L,L,L	1941-43=10	102.01	93.95	98.20	89.35	95.93	97.41	97.66	97.19	0.3	-0.5	-4.9	7.4	19
Profits and Profit Margins															
16. Corporate profits after taxes	L,L,L	A.r., bil. dol.	91.7	104.4	102.1	102.1	117.3						-2.2	14.9	16
18. Corp. profits after taxes, 1972 dollars	L,L,L	do.	67.3	70.8	70.9	68.0	76.4						-4.0	12.4	18
79. Corp. profits after taxes, with IVA and CCA	L,C,L	do.	62.7	74.3	72.3	62.6	75.3						-15.7	20.3	79
80. ...do......in 1972 dol.	L,C,L	do.	46.4	50.8	50.5	42.2	49.5						-16.9	17.3	80
15. Profits (after taxes) per dol. of sales, mfg.²	L,C,L	Cents.	5.4	5.4	5.3	5.0	NA					0.0	-0.4	NA	15
17. Ratio, price to unit labor cost, mfg.	L,L,L	1967=100.	122.7	121.7	122.2	119.2	122.1	122.1	122.8	122.8	0.6	0.0	-2.1	2.4	17
Cash Flows															
34. Net cash flow, corporate	L,L,L	A.r., bil. dol.	150.9	167.5	164.4	166.5	182.5						-0.6	9.6	34
35. Net cash flow, corporate, 1972 dollars	L,L,L	do.	107.6	109.5	110.4	107.2	115.6						-2.1	7.8	35
Unit Labor Costs and Labor Share															
63. Unit labor cost, private business sector	Lg,Lg,Lg	1967=100.	169.2	183.8	180.1	191.4	194.7						4.1	1.7	63
68. Labor cost (cur. dol.) per unit of gross domestic product (1972), nonfin corp.	Lg,Lg,Lg		0.891	0.973	0.952	1.008	1.019					0.5	3.6	1.1	68
*62. Labor cost per unit of output, mfg.	Lg,Lg,Lg	Dollars. 1967=100.	145.9	159.3	155.6	165.7	165.7	165.7	165.9	166.8	0.1		4.0	0.0	62
64. Compensation of employees as percent of national income²	Lg,Lg,Lg	Percent.	76.2	76.1	76.1	77.4	76.5						1.3	-0.9	64

B7. Money and Credit

Series	Class.	Unit													No.
Money															
85. Change in money supply (M1)²	L,L,L	Percent.	0.50	0.56	0.63	0.36	0.91	0.66	0.49	0.46	-0.17	-0.03	-0.20	0.55	85
102. Change in money supply plus time deposits at commercial banks (M2)²	L,C,U	do.	0.90	0.61	0.74	0.55	0.75	0.65	0.65	0.71	0.0	0.06	-0.06	0.20	102
*104. Chg. in total liquid assets (M7) (smoothed⁶)²	L,L,L	do.	0.85	1.10	0.93	0.94	0.80	0.79	0.82	0.82	0.03	0.0	-0.16	-0.14	104
*105. Money supply (M1), 1972 dollars	L,L,L	Bil. dol.	223.6	227.1	225.0	225.9	225.5	225.6	224.7	224.6	-0.4	0.0	-0.5	-0.2	105
106. Money supply (M2), 1972 dollars	L,L,L	do.	517.1	544.2	537.1	543.0	540.6	540.5	539.2	540.3	-0.2	0.2	-0.2	-0.4	106
Velocity of Money															
107. Ratio, GNP to money supply (M1)²	C,C,C	Ratio.	5.586	5.835	5.786	5.854	5.979					0.003	0.019	0.125	107
108. Ratio, pers. income to money supply (M2)²	C,Lg,C	do.	1.962	1.981	1.964	1.991	2.014	2.014	2.017	2.031	0.014		0.010	0.023	108
Credit Flows															
33. Change in mortgage debt²	L,L,L	A.r., bil. dol.	53.34	90.31	81.14	83.58	96.54	98.44	104.48	NA	6.04	NA	-6.73	12.96	33
112. Change in business loans²	L,L,L	do.	-4.40	9.37	8.68	19.39	27.04	32.98	25.96	3.44	-7.02	-22.52	10.02	7.65	112
113. Change in consumer installment debt²	L,L,L	do.	19.98	32.86	30.77	36.61	45.47	46.28	45.50	NA	-0.78	NA	3.75	8.86	113
110. Total private borrowing	L,L,L	do.	199.25	307.02	283.74	275.72	NA						-10.2	NA	110

SUMMARY OF RECENT DATA AND CURRENT CHANGES FOR PRINCIPAL INDICATORS (continued)

Series title	Timing classifi- cation[3]	Unit of measure	Average 1976	Average 1977	4th Q 1977	1st Q 1978	2d Q 1978	May 1978	June 1978	July 1978	May to June 1978	June to July 1978	4th Q to 1st Q 1978	1st Q to 2d Q 1978	Series number
I. CYCLICAL INDICATORS—Con.															
B7. Money and Credit—Con.															
Credit Difficulties:															
14. Liabilities of business failures (inv.[4]) ⑪	L,L,L	Mil. dol.	250.94	257.94	161.43	232.58	NA	NA	NA	NA	NA	NA	-44.1	NA	14
39. Delinquency rate, instal. loans (inv.[4])[2,3]	L,L,L	Percent, EOP	2.40	2.36	2.36	2.51	2.44	2.28	2.44	NA	-0.16	NA	-0.15	0.07	39
Bank Reserves:															
93. Free reserves (inverted[4])[1,2] ⑪	L,U,U	Mil. dol.	134	-253	-690	-162	-808	-975	-974	-1,084	-1	110	-528	646	93
94. Borrowing from the Federal Reserve[2] ⑪	L,Lg,U	do.	84	462	906	410	959	1,227	1,111	1,286	-116	175	-496	549	94
Interest Rates:															
119. Federal funds rate[2] ⑪	L,Lg,Lg	Percent	5.05	5.54	6.51	6.76	7.28	7.36	7.60	7.81	0.24	0.21	0.25	0.52	119
114. Treasury bill rate[2] ⑪	C,Lg,Lg	do.	5.00	5.26	6.14	6.41	6.48	6.43	6.71	7.07	0.28	0.36	0.27	0.07	114
115. Treasury bond yields[2] ⑪	C,Lg,Lg	do.	6.78	7.06	7.16	7.58	7.85	7.86	7.94	8.10	0.08	0.16	0.42	0.27	115
116. Corporate bond yields[2] ⑪	Lg,Lg,Lg	da.	8.59	8.20	8.29	8.70	9.01	9.00	9.15	9.27	0.15	0.12	0.41	0.31	116
117. Municipal bond yields[2] ⑪	Lg,Lg,Lg	do.	6.64	5.68	5.57	5.65	6.02	6.03	6.22	6.28	0.19	0.06	0.08	0.37	117
118. Mortgage yields, residential[2] ⑪	U,Lg,Lg	do.	8.82	8.59	8.87	8.88	NA	9.67	9.45	9.92	NA	NA	NA	NA	118
67. Bank rates on short-term bus. loans[2] ⑪	Lg,Lg,Lg	do.	7.52	7.97	8.59	8.88	9.13	9.01	9.13	NA	0.44	NA	0.29	0.25	67
*109. Average prime rate charged by banks[2] ⑪	Lg,Lg,Lg	do.	6.84	6.82	7.67	7.98	8.30	8.27	8.63	9.00	0.36	0.37	0.31	0.32	109
Outstanding Debt															
66. Consumer installment debt[5]	Lg,Lg,Lg	Bil. dol., EOP	179.93	210.70	210.70	219.85	231.22	227.42	231.22	NA	1.7	NA	4.3	5.2	66
*72. Commercial and industrial loans outstanding, weekly reporting large comm. banks	Lg,Lg,Lg	Bil. dol.	116.36	121.66	124.97	128.50	134.73	134.93	137.07	137.36	1.6	0.2	2.8	4.8	72
*95. Ratio, consumer instal. debt to pers. income[2]	Lg,Lg,Lg	Percent	12.35	12.83	13.05	13.27	13.52	13.52	13.64	NA	0.12	NA	0.22	0.25	95
II. OTHER IMPORTANT ECONOMIC MEASURES															
B. Prices, Wages, and Productivity															
B1. Price Movements															
310. Implicit price deflator, GNP		1972=100	133.8	141.6	144.6	147.1	150.9						1.7	2.6	310
320. Consumer prices (CPI), all items ⑪		1967=100	170.5	181.5	185.5	188.4	193.3	193.3	195.3	196.7	1.0	0.7	1.7	2.6	320
320c. Change in CPI, all items, S/A[2]		Percent	0.4	0.5	0.4	0.7	0.9	0.9	0.9	0.5	0.0	-0.4	0.3	0.2	320c
322. CPI, food		1967=100	180.8	192.2	195.9	201.5	210.9	211.1	213.9	213.8	1.3	-0.0	2.9	4.7	322
330. Wholesale prices (WPI), all commodities ⑪		do.	183.0	194.2	197.2	202.0	207.9	207.9	209.4	210.6	0.7	0.6	2.4	2.9	330
331. WPI, crude materials		do.	205.1	214.3	213.0	227.3	240.1	238.2	243.1	241.7	1.8	-0.6	6.7	5.6	331
332. WPI, intermediate materials		do.	189.3	201.7	205.1	209.6	213.4	213.6	214.3	215.4	0.3	0.5	2.7	1.8	332
333. WPI, producer finished goods		do.	173.2	184.5	190.0	193.5	197.3	197.3	198.9	199.9	0.8	0.5	1.8	2.0	333
334. WPI, consumer finished goods		do.	169.0	178.9	181.9	186.0	191.6	191.5	192.9	193.9	0.7	0.5	2.9	3.0	334

B2. Wages and Productivity

No.	Series	Unit													
340	Average hourly earnings, production workers, private nonfarm economy	do.	185.0	198.5	204.2	209.0	211.9	212.8	213.9	215.6	0.5	0.8	2.4	1.9	340
341	Real average hourly earnings, production workers, private nonfarm economy	do.	108.5	109.4	110.2	110.7	110.0	109.9	109.5	109.8	-0.4	0.3	0.5	-0.6	341
345	Average hourly compensation, nonfarm bus.	do.	192.4	208.5	214.5	220.6	225.0	...	...	...	...	...	2.8	2.0	345
346	Real avg. hourly compo, nonfarm business	do.	112.9	114.9	115.8	116.6	116.2	...	...	...	...	...	-1.2	-0.6	346
370	Output per hour, private business sector	do.	116.1	118.1	119.1	117.7	117.9	...	...	...	...	...	0.5	0.2	370

C. Labor Force, Employment, and Unemployment

No.	Series	Unit													
441	Total civilian labor force	Millions	94.77	97.39	98.62	99.20	100.20	100.26	100.57	100.62	0.3	0.0	0.6	1.0	441
442	Total civilian employment	do.	87.48	90.55	92.07	93.05	94.24	94.11	94.82	94.43	0.8	-0.4	-1.1	1.3	442
37	Number of persons unemployed	Thousands	7,288	6,855	6,554	6,155	5,962	6,149	5,754	6,193	-6.4	7.6	-6.1	-3.1	37
444	Unemployed males, 20 years and over	do.	3,041	2,727	2,522	2,424	2,182	2,232	2,089	2,178	-6.4	4.3	-3.9	-10.0	444
445	Unemployed females, 20 years and over	do.	2,546	2,487	2,461	2,153	2,268	2,333	2,302	2,432	-1.3	5.6	-12.5	5.3	445
446	Unemployed persons, 16-19 years of age	do.	1,701	1,642	1,570	1,578	1,512	1,584	1,363	1,583	-14.0	16.1	0.5	-4.2	446

Labor Force Participation Rates:

No.	Series	Unit													
451	Males, 20 years and over [1]	Percent	79.8	79.7	79.9	79.9	79.9	79.9	79.9	79.6	0.0	-0.3	0.0	0.0	451
452	Females, 20 years and over [2]	do.	47.0	48.1	48.6	49.0	49.5	49.5	49.6	49.7	0.1	0.1	0.4	0.5	452
453	Both sexes, 16-19 years of age [3]	do.	54.6	56.2	57.0	56.7	58.0	58.3	58.4	58.9	0.1	0.5	-0.3	1.3	453

D. Government Activities
D1. Receipts and Expenditures

No.	Series	Unit													
501	Federal Government receipts	A.r., bil. dol	331.4	374.4	385.5	396.2	423.5	...	...	...	...	...	2.8	6.9	501
502	Federal Government expenditures	do.	385.2	422.6	444.1	448.8	448.6	...	...	...	...	...	1.1	0.0	502
500	Federal Government surplus or deficit [1]	do.	-53.8	-48.1	-58.6	-52.6	-25.2	...	...	...	...	...	6.0	27.4	500
511	State and local government receipts	do.	266.3	296.0	307.9	315.7	327.3	...	...	...	...	...	2.5	3.7	511
512	State and local government expenditures	do.	246.3	266.6	278.9	284.2	297.5	...	...	...	...	...	1.9	4.7	512
510	State and local govt. surplus or deficit [2]	do.	20.7	29.6	29.0	31.5	29.8	...	...	...	...	...	2.5	-1.7	510

D2. Defense Indicators

No.	Series	Unit													
517	Defense Department obligations	Mil. dol	8,977	9,879	10,186	10,547	10,304	10,987	9,819	NA	-10.6	NA	3.5	-2.3	517
525	Military prime contract awards	do.	4,096	4,580	5,219	4,834	NA	6,614	NA	NA	NA	NA	-7.4	NA	525
548	New orders, defense products	do.	2,476	2,868	4,092	3,337	3,849	4,078	3,437	2,332	-15.7	-32.2	-18.5	15.3	548
564	National defense purchases	A.r. bil. dol	86.8	94.3	97.1	97.9	98.6	...	...	...	...	...	0.8	0.7	564

E. U.S. International Transactions
E1. Merchandise Trade

No.	Series	Unit													
602	Exports, total except military aid	Mil. dol	9,572	10,101	9,945	10,283	11,838	11,754	12,126	11,792	3.2	-2.8	3.4	15.1	602
604	Exports of agricultural products	do.	1,925	1,985	1,840	NA	NA	NA	NA	NA	NA	NA	NA	NA	604
606	Exports of nonelectrical machinery	do.	1,838	1,852	1,801	NA	NA	NA	NA	NA	NA	NA	NA	NA	606
612	General imports, total	do.	10,044	12,315	12,823	13,507	14,070	13,992	13,723	14,779	-1.9	7.7	5.3	4.2	612
614	Imports of petroleum and products	do.	2,658	3,462	3,370	NA	NA	NA	NA	NA	NA	NA	NA	NA	614
616	Imports of automobiles and parts	do.	1,096	1,323	1,457	NA	NA	NA	NA	NA	NA	NA	NA	NA	616

SUMMARY OF RECENT DATA AND CURRENT CHANGES FOR PRINCIPAL INDICATORS (concluded)

Series title	Unit of measure	Average 1975	Average 1976	Average 1977	1st Q 1977	2d Q 1977	3d Q 1977	4th Q 1977	1st Q 1978	2d Q 1978	Percent change 3d Q to 4th Q 1977	Percent change 4th Q 1977 to 1st Q 1978	Percent change 1st Q 1978 to 2d Q 1978	Series number
II. OTHER IMPORTANT ECONOMIC MEASURES—Con.														
E2. Goods and Services Movements Except Transfers Under Military Grants														
618. Merchandise exports	Mil. dol.	26,772	28,674	30,138	29,478	30,630	31,012	29,434	30,664	35,014	-5.1	4.2	14.2	618
620. Merchandise imports	do.	24,510	31,012	37,914	36,496	37,258	38,265	39,639	41,865	42,978	3.6	5.6	2.7	620
622. Merchandise trade balance[2]	do.	-2,262	-2,338	-7,776	-7,018	-6,628	-7,253	-10,205	11,201	-7,964	-2,952	-996	3,237	622
651. Income on U.S. investments abroad	do.	6,340	7,311	8,025	7,796	8,088	8,220	7,997	9,432	NA	-2.7	17.9	NA	651
652. Income on foreign investment in the U.S.	do.	3,141	3,328	3,648	3,197	3,601	3,610	4,185	4,665	NA	15.9	11.5	NA	652
668. Exports of goods and services	do.	38,914	42,819	45,804	44,751	46,285	47,135	45,046	48,137	NA	-4.4	6.9	NA	668
669. Imports of goods and services	do.	33,149	40,478	48,432	46,374	47,712	48,726	50,916	53,837	NA	4.5	5.7	NA	669
667. Balance on goods and services[2]	do.	5,765	2,340	-2,628	-1,623	-1,427	-1,591	-5,870	-5,700	NA	-4,279	170	NA	667
A. National Income and Product														
A1. GNP and Personal Income														
50. GNP in 1972 dollars	A.r. bil. dol.	1202.3	1271.0	1332.7	1306.7	1325.5	1343.9	1354.5	1354.2	1380.5	0.8	0.0	1.9	50
200. GNP in current dollars	do.	1528.8	1700.1	1887.2	1806.8	1867.0	1916.8	1958.1	1992.0	2083.2	2.2	1.7	4.6	200
213. Final sales, 1972 dollars	do.	1212.1	1264.4	1323.8	1300.9	1315.5	1331.7	1347.1	1341.8	1368.5	1.2	-0.4	2.0	213
224. Disposable personal income, current dollars	do.	1086.7	1184.4	1303.0	1248.0	1285.3	1319.1	1359.6	1391.6	1433.3	3.1	2.4	3.0	224
225. Disposable personal income, 1972 dollars	do.	859.7	890.1	926.3	904.8	918.6	931.9	949.6	952.1	959.9	1.9	0.3	0.8	225
217. Per capita GNP in 1972 dollars	A.r. dollars	5,630	5,906	6,145	6,044	6,119	6,191	6,226	6,215	6,324	0.6	-0.2	1.8	217
227. Per capita disposable pers. income, 1972 dol.	do.	4,025	4,136	4,271	4,185	4,241	4,293	4,365	4,370	4,397	1.7	-0.1	0.6	227
A2. Personal Consumption Expenditures														
231. Total, 1972 dollars	A.r. bil. dol.	774.6	819.4	857.7	846.6	849.5	858.0	876.6	873.5	887.3	2.2	-0.4	1.6	231
233. Durable goods, 1972 dollars	do.	112.7	125.5	137.8	134.9	136.2	136.9	143.0	137.8	145.6	4.5	-3.6	5.9	233
238. Nondurable goods, 1972 dollars	do.	306.6	320.2	330.4	327.1	327.2	329.2	333.1	333.3	336.6	2.7	-1.4	1.0	238
239. Services, 1972 dollars	do.	355.3	373.2	389.5	384.6	386.0	391.8	395.6	402.4	404.8	1.0	1.7	0.6	239
230. Total, current dollars	do.	979.1	1090.2	1206.5	1167.7	1188.6	1214.5	1255.2	1276.7	1324.9	3.4	1.7	3.8	230
232. Durable goods, current dollars	do.	132.6	156.6	178.4	173.2	175.6	177.4	187.2	183.5	198.0	5.5	-2.0	7.9	232
236. Nondurable goods, current dollars	do.	408.9	442.6	479.0	465.9	473.6	479.7	496.9	501.4	519.8	3.6	0.9	3.7	236
237. Services, current dollars	do.	437.5	491.0	549.2	528.6	539.4	557.5	571.1	591.8	607.1	2.4	3.6	2.6	237
A3. Gross Private Domestic Investment														
241. Total, 1972 dollars	do.	142.6	173.4	196.3	186.1	197.1	201.7	200.3	205.7	212.5	-0.7	2.7	3.3	241
243. Total fixed investment, 1972 dollars	do.	152.4	166.8	187.4	180.3	187.1	189.5	192.8	193.4	200.5	1.7	0.3	3.7	243
30. Change in business inventories, 1972 dol.[2]	do.	-9.8	6.7	8.9	5.8	10.0	12.2	7.5	12.3	12.0	-4.7	4.8	-0.3	30
240. Total, current dollars	do.	190.9	243.0	297.8	272.5	295.6	309.7	313.5	322.7	344.0	1.2	2.9	6.6	240
242. Total fixed investment, current dollars	do.	201.6	232.8	282.3	262.2	278.6	287.4	300.5	306.0	325.1	4.4	1.8	6.2	242
245. Chg. in bus. inventories, current dol.[2]	do.	-10.7	10.2	15.6	10.3	17.0	21.9	13.1	16.7	18.9	-8.8	3.6	2.2	245

A4. Government Purchases of Goods and Services

Series No.	Title	Unit												
261.	Total, 1972 dollars	do....	262.6	262.8	269.2	262.8	267.9	271.7	274.5	272.1	271.9	1.0	-0.9	-0.1
263.	Federal Government, 1972 dollars	do....	96.5	96.6	101.6	98.7	101.3	102.9	103.6	101.2	97.1	0.7	-2.3	-4.1
267.	State and local governments, 1972 dollars	do....	166.1	165.2	167.6	164.1	166.6	168.8	170.9	170.2	174.7	1.2	-0.1	0.1
260.	Total, current dollars	do....	338.4	359.5	394.0	375.0	388.8	399.5	412.5	416.7	424.5	3.3	-1.0	1.9
262.	Federal Government, current dollars	do....	123.1	129.9	145.1	138.3	142.9	146.8	152.2	151.5	147.2	3.7	-0.5	-2.8
266.	State and local governments, current dollars	do....	215.4	229.6	248.9	236.7	245.9	252.7	260.3	265.2	277.3	3.0	1.9	4.6

A5. Foreign Trade

Series No.	Title	Unit												
256.	Exports of goods and services, 1972 dollars	do....	90.0	95.9	98.2	97.1	98.9	100.8	96.0	99.1	106.1	-4.8	3.2	7.1
257.	Imports of goods and services, 1972 dollars	do....	67.5	80.5	88.7	85.9	87.9	88.2	92.9	96.2	97.3	5.3	3.6	1.1
255.	Net exports of goods and serv., 1972 dol.[2]	do....	22.6	15.4	9.5	11.2	11.0	12.5	3.1	2.9	8.9	-9.4	-0.2	6.0
252.	Exports of goods and services, current dol.	do....	147.3	163.2	175.5	170.9	178.1	180.8	172.1	181.7	200.9	-4.8	5.6	10.6
253.	Imports of goods and services, current dol.	do....	126.9	155.7	186.6	179.4	184.0	187.8	195.2	205.8	211.1	3.9	5.4	2.6
250.	Net exports of goods and serv., current dol.[2]	do....	20.4	7.4	-11.1	-8.5	-5.9	-7.0	-23.2	-24.1	-10.2	-16.2	-0.9	13.9

A6. National Income and its Components

Series No.	Title	Unit												
220.	National income	do....	1215.0	1359.2	1515.3	1447.5	1499.3	1537.6	1576.9	1603.1	1683.6	2.6	1.7	5.0
280.	Compensation of employees	do....	931.1	1036.8	1153.4	1107.9	1140.5	1165.8	1199.7	1241.0	1287.5	2.9	3.4	3.7
282.	Proprietors' income with IVA and CCA	do....	87.0	88.6	99.8	95.6	98.9	97.2	107.3	105.0	110.1	10.4	-2.1	4.9
286.	Corporate profits with IVA and CCA	do....	95.9	127.0	144.2	129.9	143.7	154.8	148.2	110.1	159.5	-4.3	-10.5	20.3
284.	Rental income of persons with CCA	do....	22.4	22.5	22.5	22.5	22.4	22.4	22.7	22.8	22.2	1.3	-0.4	-2.6
288.	Net interest	do....	78.6	84.3	95.4	91.7	93.7	97.3	99.0	101.7	104.5	1.7	2.7	2.8

A7. Saving

Series No.	Title	Unit												
290.	Gross saving (private and govt.)	do....	195.4	237.5	272.2	251.8	276.8	285.5	274.7	284.2	319.7	-3.8	3.5	12.5
295.	Business saving	do....	176.2	202.6	223.9	207.4	221.1	236.5	230.6	222.9	240.4	-2.5	-3.3	7.9
292.	Personal saving	do....	83.6	68.0	66.9	52.2	67.5	74.3	73.7	82.4	74.6	-0.8	11.8	-9.5
298.	Government surplus or deficit[3]	do....	-64.4	-33.2	-18.6	-7.8	-11.8	-25.2	-29.6	21.1	4.6	-4.4	8.5	25.7
293.	Personal saving rate[3]	Percent....	7.7	5.7	5.1	4.2	5.3	5.6	5.4	5.9	5.2	-0.2	0.5	-0.7

NOTE. Series are seasonally adjusted except for those indicated by ⑪ which appear to contain no seasonal movement. Series indicated by an asterisk (*) are included in the major composite indexes. Dollar values are in current dollars unless otherwise specified. For complete series titles (including composition of the composite indexes) and sources, see "Titles and Sources of Series" at the back of BCD. NA = not available. a = anticipated. EOP = end of period. A.r. = annual rate. S/A = seasonally adjusted (used for special emphasis). IVA = inventory valuation adjustment. CCA = capital consumption adjustment. NIA = national income accounts.

[1] For a few series, data shown here have been rounded to fewer digits than those shown elsewhere in BCD. Annual figures published by the source agencies are used if available.
[2] Differences rather than percent changes are shown for this series.
[3] The three-part timing code indicates the timing classification of the series at peaks, at troughs, and at all turns: L = leading; C = roughly coincident; Lg = lagging; U = unclassified.
[4] Inverted series. Since this series tends to move counter to movements in general business activity, signs of the changes are reversed.
[5] End-of-period series. The annual figures (and quarterly figures for monthly series) are the last figures for the period.
[6] This series is a weighted 4-term moving average (with weights 1, 2, 2, 1) placed at the terminal month of the span.

Source: *Business Conditions Digest.*

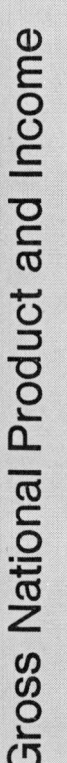

Gross National Product and Income

GROSS NATIONAL PRODUCT

BILLIONS OF DOLLARS (RATIO SCALE)
BILLIONS OF DOLLARS (RATIO SCALE)
•SEASONALLY ADJUSTED ANNUAL RATES
2,200
2,000
1,800
1,600
1,400
1,200
1,000
GNP
IN CURRENT DOLLARS
GNP
IN 1972 DOLLARS
1970
1971
1972
1973
1974
1975
1976
1977
1978

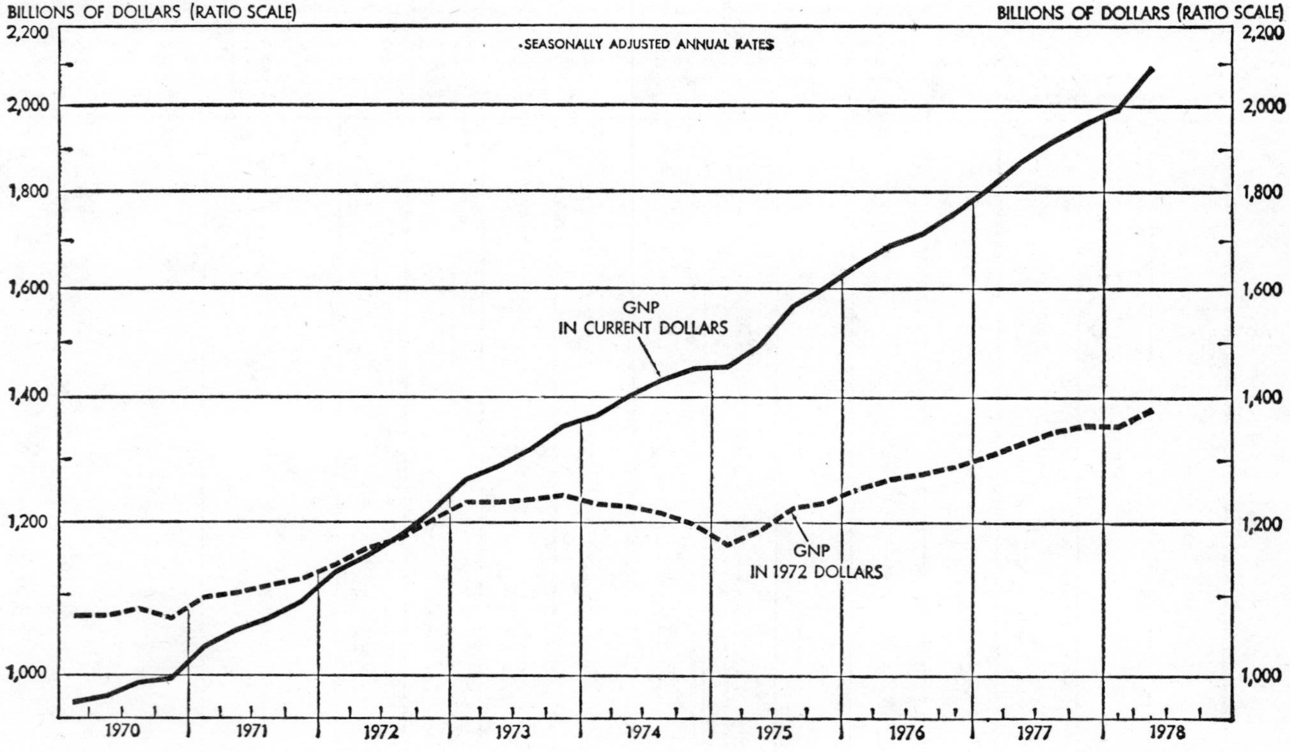

SOURCE: DEPARTMENT OF COMMERCE

COUNCIL OF ECONOMIC ADVISERS

[Billions of current dollars; quarterly data at seasonally adjusted annual rates]

Period	Gross national product	Personal consumption expenditures	Gross private domestic investment	Exports and imports of goods and services			Government purchases of goods and services					Final sales
				Net exports	Exports	Imports	Total	Federal			State and local	
								Total	National defense [1]	Non-defense		
1967-------	796.3	490.4	120.8	4.9	45.6	40.6	180.2	90.9	71.5	19.5	89.3	786.2
1968-------	868.5	535.9	131.5	2.3	49.9	47.7	198.7	98.0	76.9	21.2	100.7	860.8
1969-------	935.5	579.7	146.2	1.8	54.7	52.9	207.9	97.5	76.3	21.2	110.4	926.2
1970-------	982.4	618.8	140.8	3.9	62.5	58.5	218.9	95.6	73.5	22.1	123.2	978.6
1971-------	1,063.4	668.2	160.0	1.6	65.6	64.0	233.7	96.2	70.2	26.0	137.5	1,057.1
1972-------	1,171.1	733.0	188.3	-3.3	72.7	75.9	253.1	102.1	73.5	28.6	151.0	1,161.7
1973-------	1,306.6	809.9	220.0	7.1	101.6	94.4	269.5	102.2	73.5	28.7	167.3	1,288.6
1974-------	1,412.9	889.6	214.6	6.0	137.9	131.9	302.7	111.1	77.0	34.1	191.5	1,404.0
1975-------	1,528.8	979.1	190.9	20.4	147.3	126.9	338.4	123.1	83.7	39.4	215.4	1,539.6
1976-------	1,700.1	1,090.2	243.0	7.4	163.2	155.7	359.5	129.9	86.8	43.1	229.6	1,689.9
1977-------	1,887.2	1,206.5	297.8	-11.1	175.5	186.6	394.0	145.1	94.3	50.8	248.9	1,871.6
1977: I---	1,806.8	1,167.7	272.5	-8.5	170.9	179.4	375.0	138.3	91.9	46.4	236.7	1,796.5
II--	1,867.0	1,188.6	295.6	-5.9	178.1	184.0	388.8	142.9	93.7	49.3	245.9	1,850.0
III-	1,916.8	1,214.5	309.7	-7.0	180.8	187.8	399.5	146.8	94.4	52.4	252.7	1,894.9
IV--	1,958.1	1,255.1	313.5	-23.2	172.1	195.2	412.5	152.2	97.1	55.1	260.3	1,945.0
1978: I---	1,992.0	1,276.7	322.7	-24.1	181.7	205.8	416.7	151.5	97.9	53.6	265.2	1,975.3
II--	2,083.2	1,324.9	344.0	-10.2	200.9	211.1	424.5	147.2	98.6	48.6	277.3	2,064.3

[1] This category corresponds closely with budget outlays for national defense.

Source: Department of Commerce, Bureau of Economic Analysis.

Source: *Economic Indicators*, Council of Economic Advisors.

GROSS NATIONAL PRODUCT IN 1972 DOLLARS

Billions of 1972 dollars; quarterly data at seasonally adjusted annual rates

Period	Gross national product	Personal consumption expenditures	Gross private domestic investment			Net exports	Exports of goods and services		Government purchases of goods and services			Final sales
			Nonresidential fixed	Residential fixed	Change in business inventories		Exports	Imports	Total	Federal	State and local	
1967	1,007.7	603.2	103.5	37.2	12.0	3.5	54.2	50.7	248.3	125.3	123.1	995.7
1968	1,051.8	633.4	108.0	42.8	8.7	-.4	58.5	58.9	259.2	128.3	130.9	1,043.1
1969	1,078.8	655.4	114.3	43.2	10.6	-1.3	62.2	63.5	256.7	121.8	134.9	1,068.2
1970	1,075.3	668.9	110.0	40.4	4.3	1.4	67.1	65.7	250.2	110.7	139.5	1,071.0
1971	1,107.5	691.9	108.8	52.2	6.6	-.6	67.9	68.5	249.4	103.9	145.5	1,100.9
1972	1,171.1	733.0	116.8	62.0	9.4	-3.3	72.7	75.9	253.1	102.1	151.0	1,161.7
1973	1,235.0	767.7	131.0	59.7	16.5	7.6	87.4	79.9	252.5	96.6	155.9	1,218.5
1974	1,217.8	760.7	130.6	45.0	8.0	15.9	93.0	77.1	257.7	95.8	161.8	1,209.9
1975	1,202.3	774.6	113.6	38.8	-9.8	22.6	90.0	67.5	262.6	96.5	166.1	1,212.1
1976	1,271.0	819.4	118.9	47.8	6.7	15.4	95.9	80.5	262.8	96.6	166.2	1,264.4
1977	1,332.7	857.7	129.8	57.7	8.9	9.5	98.2	88.7	269.2	101.6	167.6	1,323.8
1977: I	1,306.7	846.6	126.8	53.5	5.8	11.2	97.1	85.9	262.8	98.7	164.1	1,300.9
II	1,325.5	849.5	129.1	58.0	10.0	11.0	98.9	87.9	267.2	101.3	166.8	1,315.5
III	1,343.9	858.0	130.8	58.8	12.2	12.5	100.8	88.2	271.7	102.9	168.8	1,331.7
IV	1,354.5	876.6	132.5	60.3	7.5	3.1	96.0	92.9	274.5	103.6	170.9	1,347.1
1978: I	1,354.2	873.5	133.8	59.5	12.3	2.9	99.1	96.2	272.1	101.2	170.8	1,341.8
II	1,380.5	887.3	140.4	60.1	12.0	8.9	106.1	97.3	271.9	97.1	174.7	1,368.5

Source: *Economic Indicators*, Council of Economic Advisors.

IMPLICIT PRICE DEFLATORS FOR GROSS NATIONAL PRODUCT

1972 = 100

Period	Gross national product	Personal consumption expenditures				Gross private domestic investment		Exports and imports of goods and services		Government purchases of goods and services	
		Total	Durable goods	Non-durable goods	Services	Nonresidential fixed	Residential fixed	Exports	Imports	Federal	State and local
1966	76.76	79.3	85.7	80.1	76.5	76.8	74.6	82.8	79.7	70.1	68.4
1967	79.02	81.3	87.4	81.9	78.8	79.3	77.0	84.0	80.1	72.6	72.5
1968	82.57	84.6	90.7	85.3	82.0	82.6	80.7	85.3	80.9	76.4	76.9
1969	86.72	88.5	93.1	89.4	86.1	86.6	87.7	87.9	83.3	80.0	81.1
1970	91.36	92.5	95.5	93.6	90.5	91.3	90.6	93.1	89.1	86.4	88.3
1971	96.02	96.6	99.0	96.6	95.8	96.4	94.9	96.6	93.5	92.6	94.5
1972	100.00	100.0	100.0	100.0	100.0	100.0	100.0	100.0	100.0	100.0	100.0
1973	105.80	105.5	101.6	107.9	104.7	103.8	110.8	116.2	118.2	105.8	107.3
1974	116.41	116.9	108.3	124.0	113.5	116.1	122.3	148.6	169.6	117.1	119.0
1975	127.25	126.3	117.7	133.7	122.7	132.1	133.2	163.4	187.4	130.0	129.8
1976	133.75	132.7	124.4	138.0	131.0	138.2	143.9	169.3	194.7	138.0	138.7
1975: III	128.07	127.3	118.2	135.1	123.6	132.7	132.8	163.4	186.6	130.4	131.0
IV	130.27	129.1	120.2	136.2	125.9	134.5	135.9	163.7	187.3	134.2	132.9
1976: I	131.29	130.3	121.8	136.4	128.0	136.2	139.0	164.6	189.2	135.4	135.4
II	132.96	131.7	123.8	136.9	129.8	137.5	142.9	168.1	190.4	136.7	137.7
III	134.40	133.4	124.9	138.5	132.0	138.7	145.3	171.1	198.1	138.3	139.7
IV	136.30	135.2	127.0	139.9	134.0	140.5	147.7	173.0	200.8	141.6	141.9
1977: I	138.19	137.4	128.9	142.2	136.2	142.2	155.3	174.5	207.4	143.3	144.8

Source: Department of Commerce, Bureau of Economic Analysis.

Source: *Economic Indicators*, Council of Economic Advisors.

CHANGES IN GNP AND GNP PRICE MEASURES

Percent change from previous period; quarterly data at seasonally adjusted annual rates

Period	Gross national product					Gross domestic product				
	Current dollars	Constant (1972) dollars	Implicit price deflator	Chain price index	Fixed-weighted price index (1972 weights)	Current dollars	Constant (1972) dollars	Implicit price deflator	Chain price index	Fixed-weighted price index (1972 weights)
1966	9.4	5.9	3.3	3.1	2.9	9.6	6.1	3.3	3.1	3.0
1967	5.8	2.7	2.9	3.4	3.0	5.7	2.7	3.0	3.1	3.0
1968	9.1	4.4	4.5	4.4	4.3	9.1	4.4	4.5	4.4	4.4
1969	7.7	2.6	5.0	5.0	5.2	7.8	2.6	5.1	5.0	5.2
1970	5.0	-.3	5.4	5.3	5.2	5.0	-.3	5.3	5.3	5.0
1971	8.2	3.0	5.1	5.0	4.9	8.1	2.8	5.1	5.0	4.9
1972	10.1	5.7	4.1	4.1	4.0	10.1	5.8	4.7	4.1	4.0
1973	11.6	5.5	5.8	6.0	4.0	11.5	5.4	5.7	5.9	5.9
1974	8.1	-1.4	9.7	9.9	10.2	7.9	-1.3	9.3	9.6	9.9
1975	8.2	-1.3	9.6	9.5	9.4	8.5	-1.1	9.7	9.5	9.4
1976	11.6	6.0	5.3	5.6	5.6	11.4	5.9	5.2	5.6	5.6
1976: I	13.2	8.8	4.1	4.9	4.6	12.4	8.3	3.8	4.8	4.6
II	10.2	5.1	4.9	5.3	5.2	10.5	5.2	5.4	5.4	5.2
III	8.6	3.9	4.6	4.6	4.8	8.2	3.7	4.4	4.5	4.6
IV	6.7	1.2	5.4	5.9	6.0	6.9	1.3	4.5	6.0	6.1
1977: I	13.2	7.5	5.3	6.9	7.1	12.6	7.2	5.0	6.7	7.0
II	13.7	6.1	7.1	7.0	7.0	13.6	6.1	7.1	7.0	7.0

Note.—Annual changes from previous year and quarterly changes from previous quarter.

Source: Department of Commerce, Bureau of Economic Analysis.

Source: *Economic Indicators*, Council of Economic Advisors.

PERSONAL CONSUMPTION EXPENDITURES

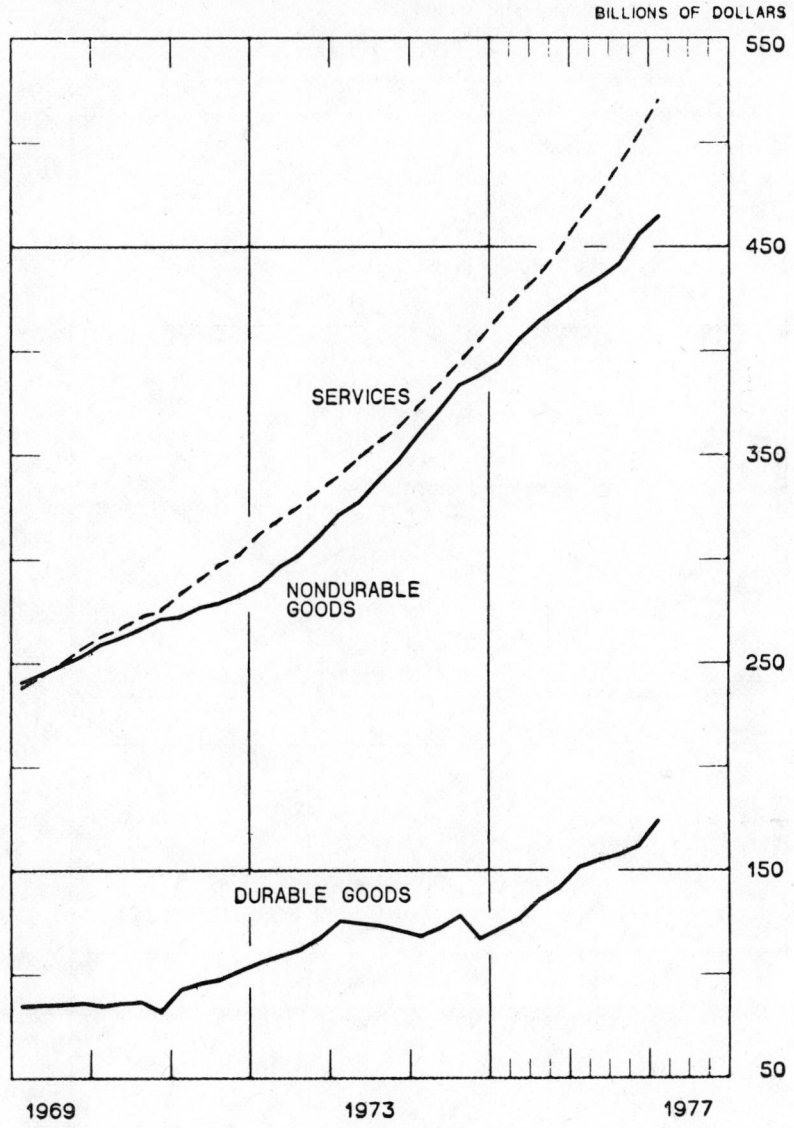

BILLIONS OF DOLLARS

SERVICES

NONDURABLE GOODS

DURABLE GOODS

550

450

350

250

150

50

1969   1973   1977

BOARD OF GOVERNORS OF THE FEDERAL RESERVE SYSTEM

Source: *Monthly Chart Book.*

SELECTED COMPONENTS OF GNP
Seasonally adjusted annual rates, quarterly

INVESTMENT

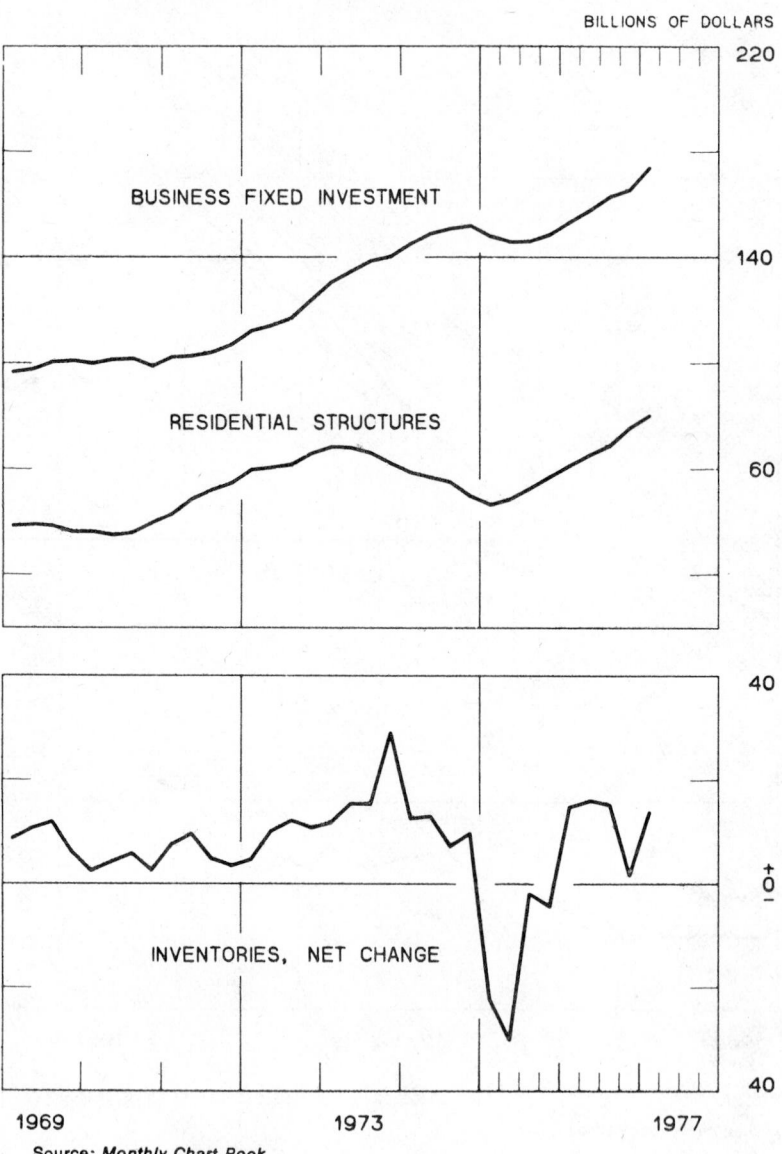

BILLIONS OF DOLLARS

Source: *Monthly Chart Book.*

GOVERNMENT PURCHASES

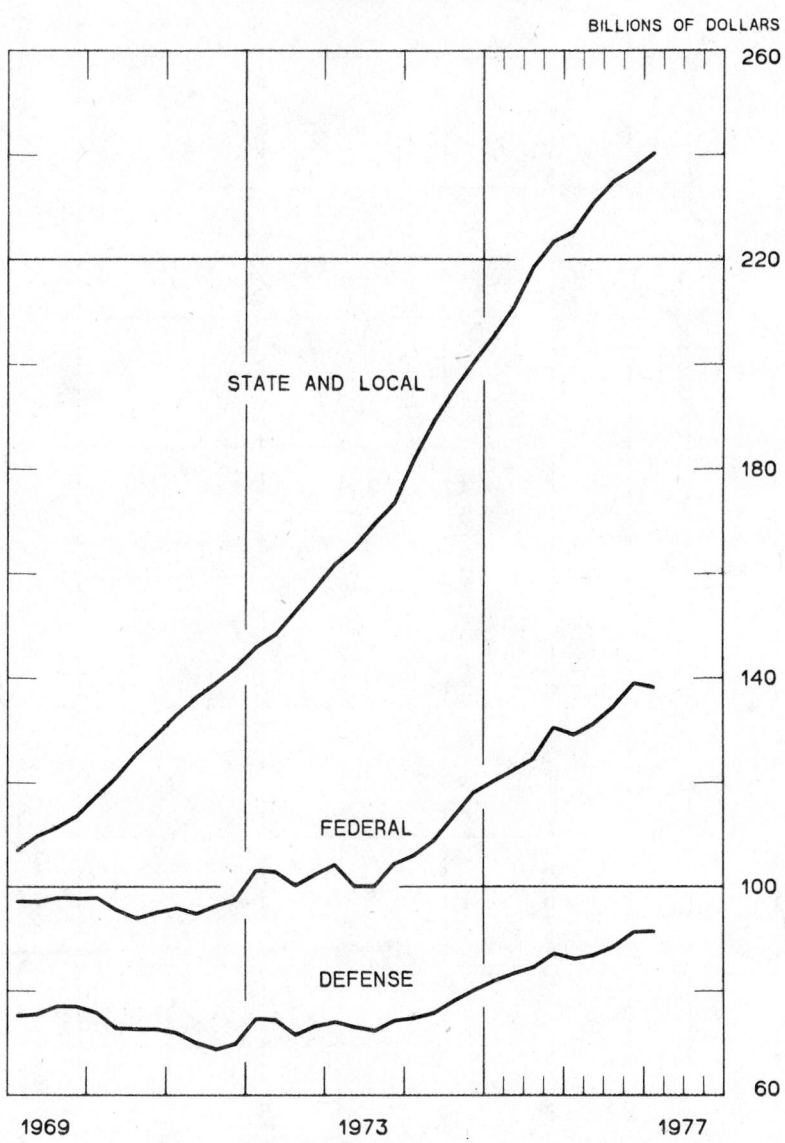

BILLIONS OF DOLLARS

STATE AND LOCAL

FEDERAL

DEFENSE

1969   1973   1977

BOARD OF GOVERNORS OF THE FEDERAL RESERVE SYSTEM

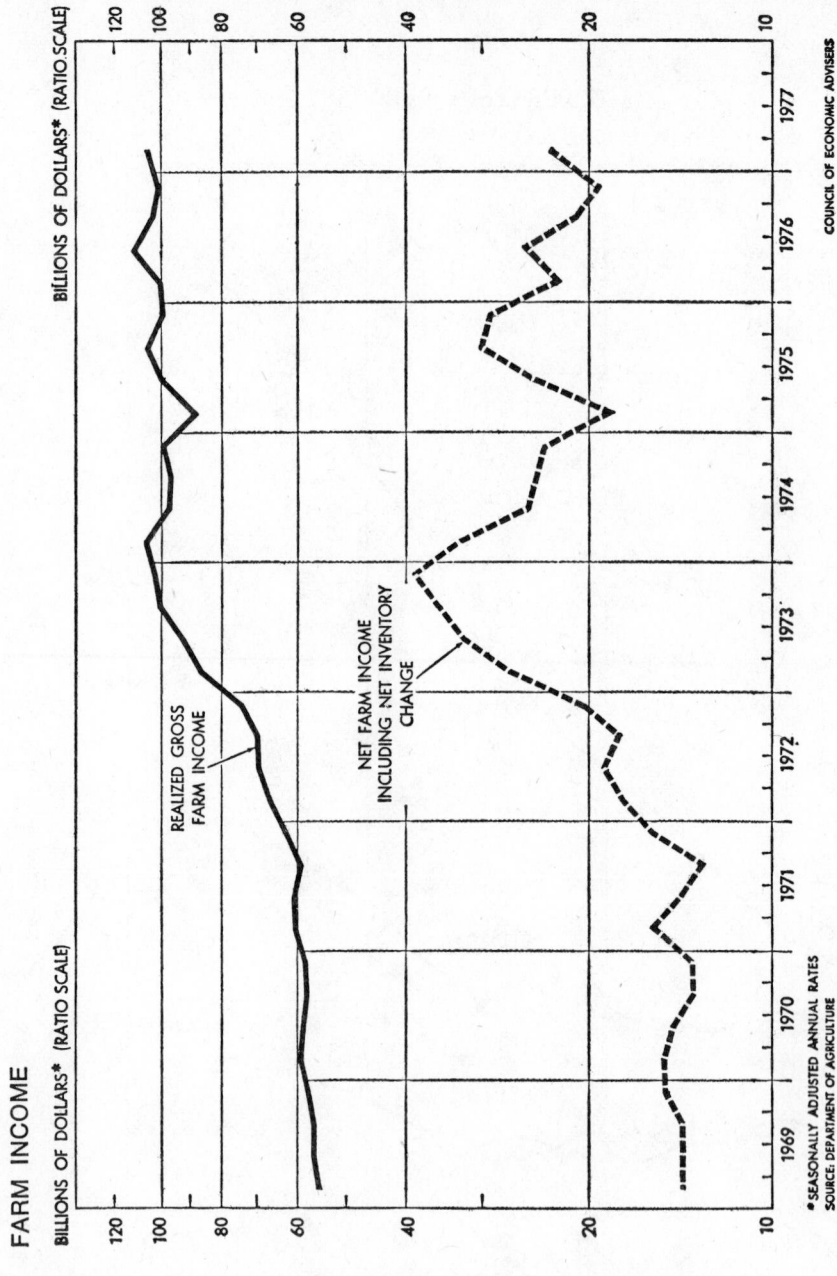

FARM INCOME

BILLIONS OF DOLLARS* (RATIO SCALE)

BILLIONS OF DOLLARS* (RATIO SCALE)

REALIZED GROSS
FARM INCOME

NET FARM INCOME
INCLUDING NET INVENTORY
CHANGE

*SEASONALLY ADJUSTED ANNUAL RATES
SOURCE: DEPARTMENT OF AGRICULTURE

COUNCIL OF ECONOMIC ADVISERS

[Quarterly data at seasonally adjusted annual rates]

Period	Personal income received by total farm population			Income received from farming								Net income per farm including net inventory change[3]	
	From all sources	From farm sources	From nonfarm sources	Realized gross					Net to farm operators		Current dollars	1967 dollars[4]
				Total[1]	Cash receipts from marketings			Production expenses	Excluding net inventory change	Including net inventory change[2]		
					Total	Livestock and products	Crops					
	Billions of dollars										Dollars	
1969	26.9	12.9	13.9	56.3	48.2	28.6	19.6	42.1	14.2	14.3	4,766	4,372
1970	27.4	13.0	14.4	58.6	50.5	29.6	21.0	44.4	14.1	14.2	4,790	4,202
1971	28.7	13.4	15.3	60.6	52.9	30.6	22.3	47.4	13.2	14.6	5,030	4,263
1972	34.4	16.8	17.6	70.1	61.1	35.7	25.5	52.3	17.8	18.7	6,504	5,288
1973	48.6	29.0	19.5	95.5	87.1	45.9	41.1	65.6	29.9	33.3	11,727	8,817
1974	45.1	23.5	21.5	100.2	92.6	41.4	51.3	72.4	27.8	26.5	9,371	6,206
1975	45.5	22.8	22.7	98.2	89.6	42.9	46.7	75.5	22.7	25.6	9,100	5,482
1976	44.0	20.0	24.0	104.2	94.8	47.0	47.8	80.9	23.3	22.0	7,920	4,500
1975: III	----	----	----	105.2	96.5	45.0	51.5	76.8	28.4	30.0	10,680	6,320
IV	----	----	----	99.6	90.8	46.4	44.4	75.7	23.9	29.1	10,360	6,060
1976: I	----	----	----	101.5	92.4	46.6	45.8	79.0	22.5	22.5	8,100	4,710
II	----	----	----	111.1	101.8	49.6	52.2	82.5	28.6	25.6	9,210	5,300
III	----	----	----	113.3	93.8	47.2	46.6	81.5	21.8	20.8	7,490	4,230
IV	----	----	----	100.9	91.3	44.5	46.8	80.6	20.3	19.3	6,950	3,860
1977: I	----	----	----	105.6	95.9	45.3	50.6	83.1	22.5	23.0	8,360	4,570

[1] Cash receipts from marketings, Government payments, and nonmoney income furnished by farms.
[2] Inventory of crops and livestock valued at the average price for the year.
[3] Based on Census of Agriculture definition of a farm. The number of farms is held constant within a year.
[4] Income in current dollars divided by the index of prices paid by farmers for family living items on a 1967 base. As of January 1977 movement is based on the overall change in the consumer price index.

Source: Department of Agriculture.

Source: *Economic Indicators*, Council of Economic Advisors.

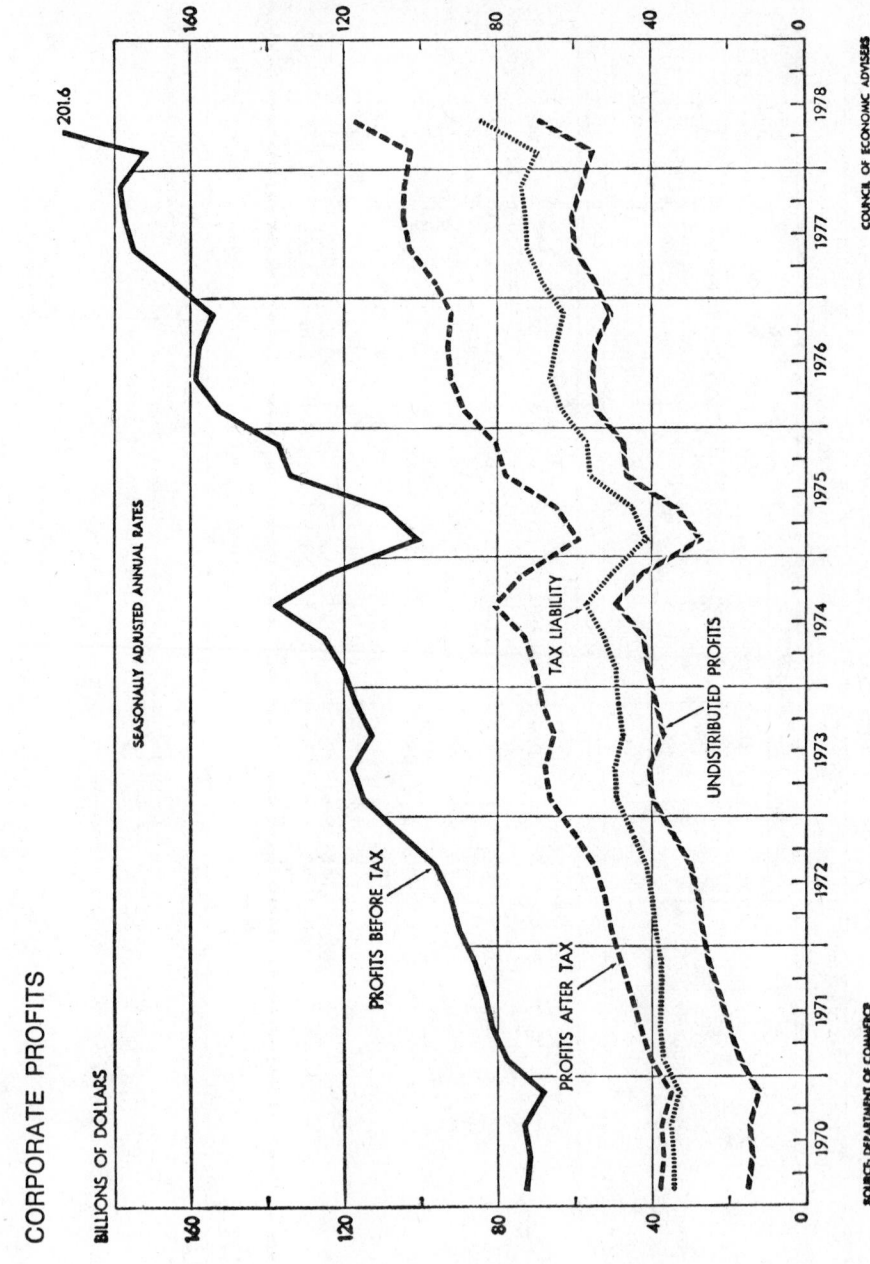

CORPORATE PROFITS

BILLIONS OF DOLLARS

SEASONALLY ADJUSTED ANNUAL RATES

PROFITS BEFORE TAX

PROFITS AFTER TAX

TAX LIABILITY

UNDISTRIBUTED PROFITS

201.6

SOURCE: DEPARTMENT OF COMMERCE

COUNCIL OF ECONOMIC ADVISERS

[Billions of dollars; quarterly data at seasonally adjusted annual rates]

Period	Profits (before tax) with inventory valuation adjustment						Profits before tax	Tax liability	Profits after tax				Inventory valuation adjustment
	Total[2]	Domestic industries							Total	Dividends	Undistributed profits	
		Total	Financial	Nonfinancial								
				Total[3]	Manufacturing	Wholesale and retail trade						
1967	75.6	72.6	9.0	63.6	37.9	8.9	77.3	32.5	44.9	20.1	24.7	−1.7
1968	82.1	78.9	10.4	68.5	41.2	10.1	85.6	39.4	46.2	21.9	24.2	−3.4
1969	77.9	74.2	11.3	62.9	36.8	10.1	83.4	39.7	43.8	22.6	21.2	−5.5
1970	66.4	62.6	12.6	50.1	27.1	9.4	71.5	34.5	37.0	22.9	14.1	−5.1
1971	76.9	72.4	14.1	58.2	32.4	11.7	82.0	37.7	44.3	23.0	21.3	−5.0
1972	89.6	84.7	15.4	69.3	40.6	13.3	96.2	41.5	54.6	24.6	30.0	−6.6
1973	97.2	90.4	16.2	74.1	44.1	14.7	115.8	48.7	67.1	27.8	39.3	−18.6
1974	86.5	76.9	14.4	62.5	36.6	12.9	126.9	52.4	74.5	31.0	43.6	−40.4
1975	107.9	101.8	13.0	88.9	48.3	20.7	120.4	49.8	70.6	31.9	38.7	−12.4
1976	141.4	133.2	17.5	115.6	65.6	24.0	155.9	64.3	91.7	37.9	53.8	−14.5
1977	159.1	149.5	20.9	128.6	74.7	24.0	173.9	71.8	102.1	43.7	58.4	−14.8
1977: I	144.5	134.8	19.7	115.1	66.4	20.6	164.8	68.3	96.5	41.5	55.0	−20.3
II	158.5	148.1	19.9	128.1	77.4	22.8	175.1	72.3	102.8	42.7	60.1	−16.6
III	169.9	159.5	21.9	137.6	74.7	30.6	177.5	72.8	104.8	44.1	60.6	−7.7
IV	163.5	155.6	21.9	133.7	80.2	22.1	178.3	73.9	104.4	46.3	58.1	−14.8
1978: I	148.7	139.2	22.7	116.6	69.8	16.7	172.1	70.0	102.1	47.0	55.1	−23.5
II[p]	176.7	167.3	24.3	143.0	---	---	201.6	84.2	117.3	48.1	69.2	−24.9

[2] Includes rest of the world, not shown separately.
[3] Includes industries not shown separately.

Source: Department of Commerce, Bureau of Economic Analysis.

Source: Economic Indicators, Council of Economic Advisors.

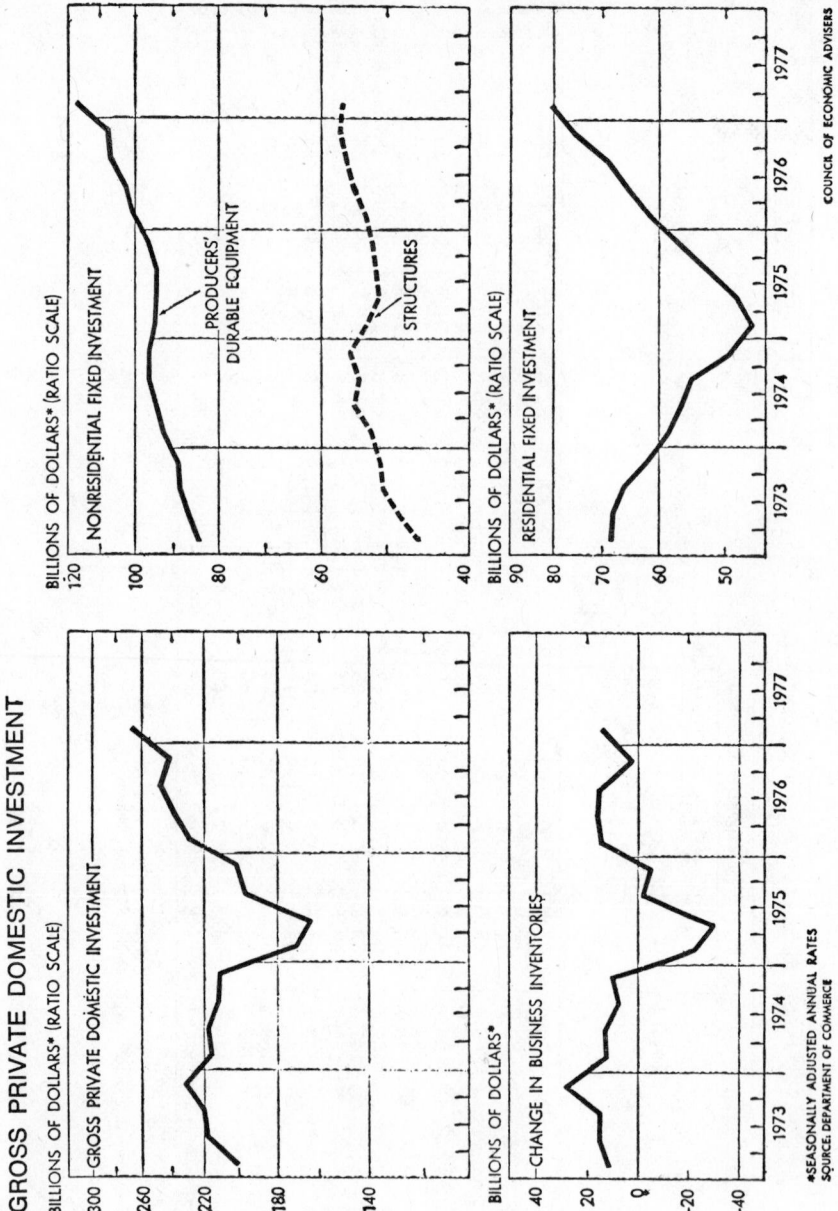

GROSS PRIVATE DOMESTIC INVESTMENT

*SEASONALLY ADJUSTED ANNUAL RATES
SOURCE: DEPARTMENT OF COMMERCE

COUNCIL OF ECONOMIC ADVISERS

[Billions of dollars; quarterly data at seasonally adjusted annual rates]

Period	Gross private domestic investment	Nonresidential fixed investment Total	Structures Total	Structures Non-farm	Producers' durable equipment Total	Producers' durable equipment Non-farm	Residential fixed investment Total	Non-farm structures	Farm structures	Producers durable equipment	Change in business inventories Total	Non-farm
1966	124.5	81.4	29.2	28.1	52.2	47.9	28.7	27.4	0.7	0.7	14.3	14.5
1967	120.8	82.1	29.5	28.2	52.6	48.0	28.6	27.2	.7	.7	10.1	9.4
1968	131.5	89.3	31.6	30.4	57.7	53.4	34.5	33.1	.6	.8	7.7	7.6
1969	146.2	98.9	35.7	34.3	63.3	58.9	37.9	36.3	.7	.9	9.4	9.2
1970	140.8	100.5	37.7	36.1	62.8	58.1	36.6	35.1	.6	.9	3.8	3.7
1971	160.0	104.1	39.3	37.8	64.7	59.9	49.6	47.9	.7	1.0	6.4	5.1
1972	188.3	116.8	42.5	41.1	74.3	69.1	62.0	60.3	.7	1.1	9.4	8.8
1973	220.0	136.0	49.0	46.9	87.0	80.1	66.1	64.3	.6	1.2	17.9	14.7
1974	215.0	149.2	54.1	51.8	95.1	87.2	55.1	52.7	1.0	1.3	10.7	12.2
1975	183.7	147.1	52.0	49.8	95.1	86.9	51.2	49.0	.8	1.3	−14.6	−17.6
1976	239.6	160.0	55.3	53.0	104.7	95.9	67.7	65.1	1.1	1.6	11.9	11.9
1975: III	196.7	146.1	51.8	49.6	94.3	86.7	52.6	50.2	1.0	1.4	−2.0	−4.2
IV	201.4	148.7	52.1	49.9	96.6	88.0	57.0	54.2	1.4	1.4	−4.3	−9.5
1976: I	229.6	153.4	53.2	51.0	100.2	91.3	61.3	58.6	1.2	1.5	14.8	12.7
II	239.2	157.9	54.2	52.5	103.0	94.1	65.3	62.9	.9	1.5	16.0	17.3
III	247.0	163.0	56.0	53.7	107.0	98.0	68.9	66.3	1.0	1.6	15.1	15.6
IV	242.8	165.6	57.0	54.8	108.6	100.2	75.5	72.7	1.2	1.6	1.7	2.2
1977: I	267.9	173.9	56.6	54.4	117.4	107.8	80.2	77.4	1.1	1.7	13.8	13.0

Source: Department of Commerce, Bureau of Economic Analysis.

Source: *Economic Indicators*, Council of Economic Advisors.

EXPENDITURES FOR NEW PLANT AND EQUIPMENT

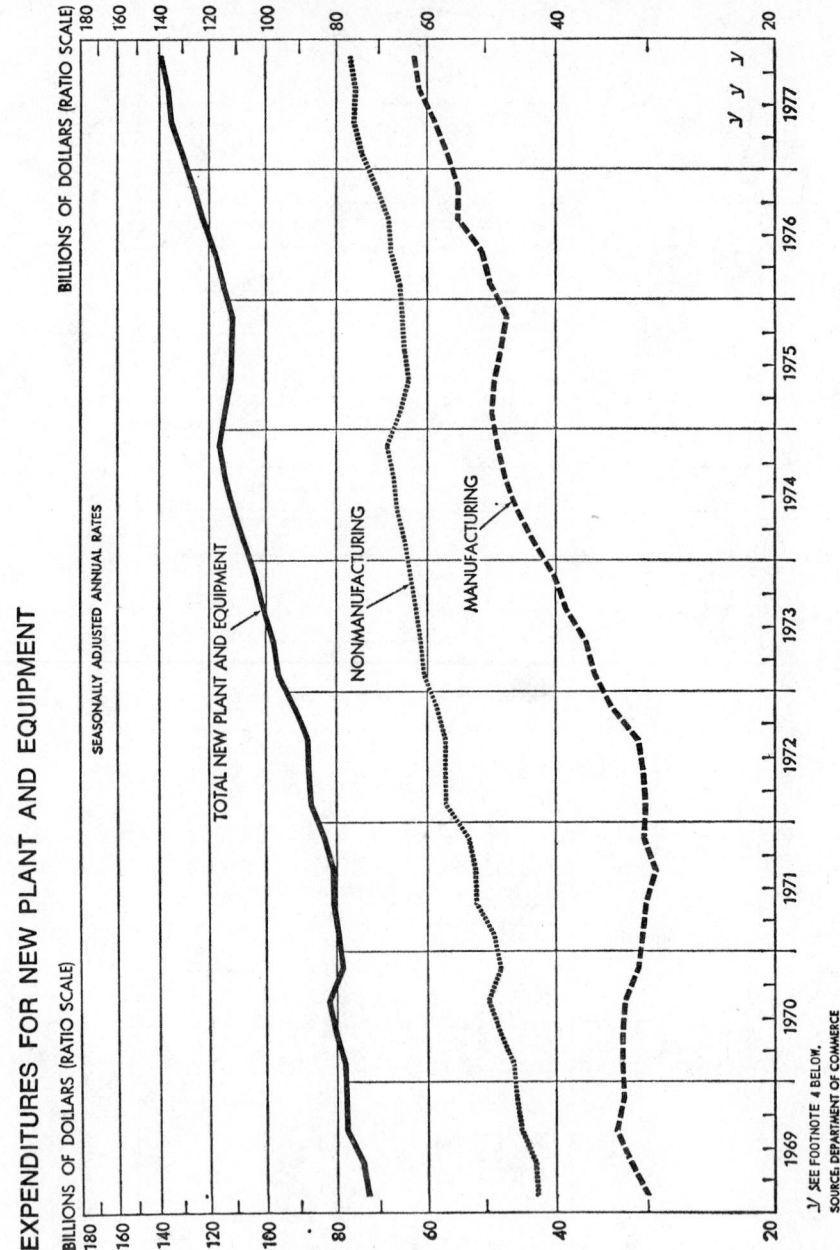

[Billions of dollars; quarterly data at seasonally adjusted annual rates]

Period	Total [1]	Expenditures for plant and equipment — Manufacturing			Nonmanufacturing						Starts of plant and equipment projects [3]	
		Total	Durable goods	Non-durable goods	Total	Mining	Transportation	Public utilities	Communication	Commercial and other [2]	Manufacturing	Public utilities
1970	79.71	31.95	15.80	16.15	47.76	1.89	6.04	13.14	10.10	16.59	29.18	17.20
1971	81.21	29.99	14.15	15.84	51.22	2.16	4.93	15.30	10.77	18.05	28.00	22.22
1972	88.44	31.35	15.64	15.72	57.09	2.42	5.72	17.00	11.89	20.07	35.21	28.60
1973	99.74	38.01	19.25	18.76	61.73	2.74	6.03	18.71	12.85	21.40	47.57	38.13
1974	112.40	46.01	22.62	23.39	66.39	3.18	6.66	20.55	13.96	22.05	52.49	45.74
1975	112.78	47.95	21.84	26.11	64.82	3.79	7.57	20.14	12.74	20.60	48.24	34.50
1976 [4]	120.49	52.48	23.68	28.81	68.01	4.00	7.45	22.28	13.30	20.99	51.05	29.66
1977 [4]	*135.34*	*59.91*	*27.44*	*32.47*	*75.42*	*4.41*	*6.83*	*26.11*	*15.34*	*22.75*		
1976: I	114.72	49.21	21.63	27.58	65.51	3.83	6.55	21.91	12.54	20.68	11.64	3.43
II	118.12	50.64	22.54	28.09	67.48	3.83	8.24	21.85	12.62	20.94	12.77	8.56
III	122.55	54.78	24.59	30.20	67.76	4.21	7.25	21.67	13.64	20.99	13.22	7.54
IV	125.22	54.44	25.50	28.93	70.78	4.13	7.53	23.46	14.30	21.36	12.88	10.22
1977: I	130.16	56.43	26.30	30.13	73.74	4.24	7.29	25.35	14.19	22.67	15.26	9.76
II [4]	*134.46*	*58.62*	*26.42*	*32.20*	*75.84*	*4.42*	*6.60*	*25.65*	*{39.16}*			
III [4]	*136.91*	*61.77*	*28.30*	*33.46*	*75.14*	*4.54*	*6.74*	*25.72*	*{38.14}*			
IV [4]	*139.08*	*62.33*	*28.59*	*33.74*	*76.75*							

[1] Excludes agricultural business; real estate operators; medical, legal, educational, and cultural service; and nonprofit organizations. These figures do not agree precisely with the nonresidential fixed investment data in gross national product estimates, mainly because those data include investment by farmers, professionals, nonprofit institutions, and real estate firms, and certain outlays charged to current account.

[2] Includes trade, service, construction, finance, and insurance.

[3] Starts are estimated by adding changes in carryover to expenditures during given period.

[4] Expenditures estimates based on expected capital expenditures as reported by business in late April and May 1977.

NOTE.—Annual totals is the sum of unadjusted quarterly totals. Estimates (as noted in footnote 4) include adjustments when necessary for systematic biases in expectations data.

Source: Department of Commerce, Bureau of Economic Analysis.

Source: *Economic Indicators*, Council of Economic Advisors.

SOURCES OF PERSONAL INCOME

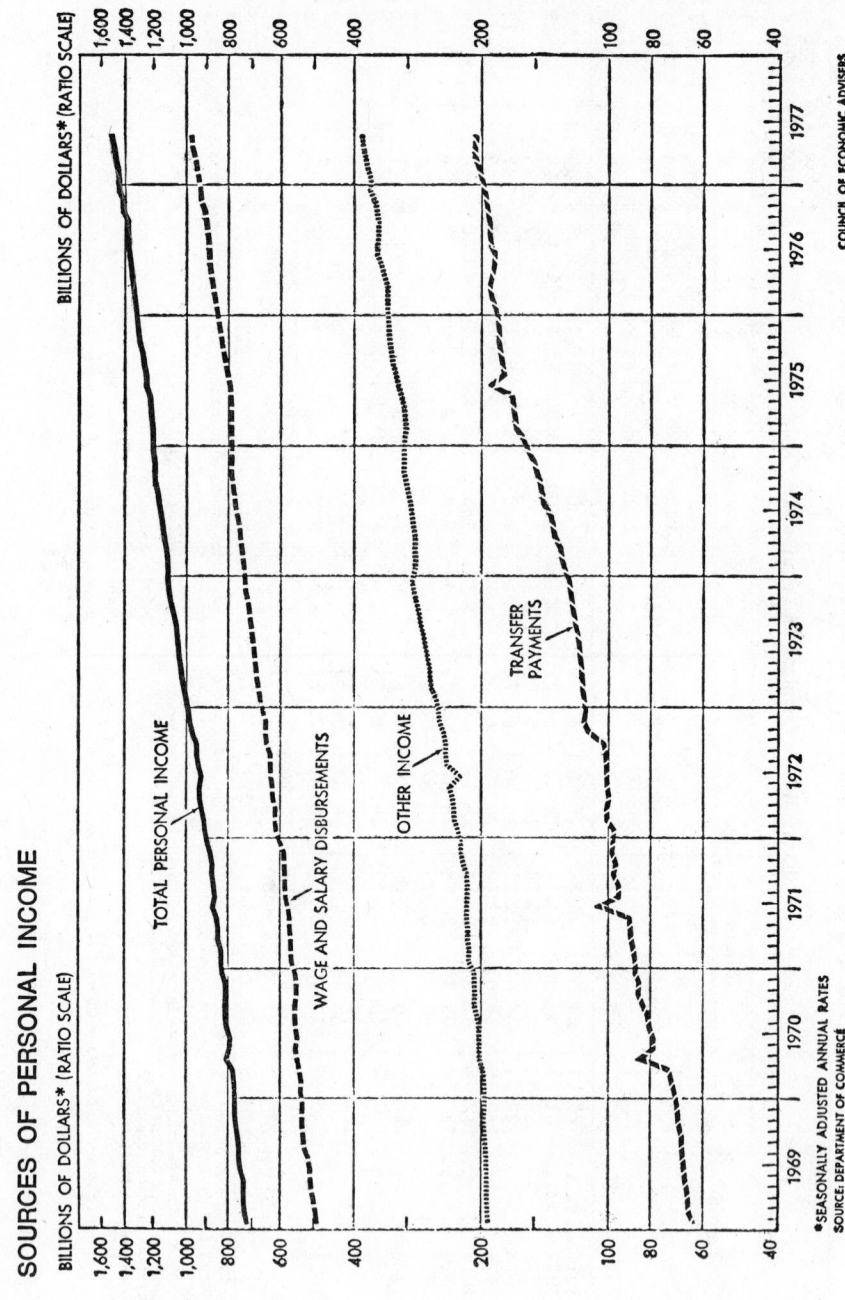

BILLIONS OF DOLLARS* (RATIO SCALE)

BILLIONS OF DOLLARS* (RATIO SCALE)

TOTAL PERSONAL INCOME

WAGE AND SALARY DISBURSEMENTS

OTHER INCOME

TRANSFER PAYMENTS

*SEASONALLY ADJUSTED ANNUAL RATES
SOURCE: DEPARTMENT OF COMMERCE

COUNCIL OF ECONOMIC ADVISERS

[Billions of dollars; monthly data at seasonally adjusted annual rates]

Period	Total personal income	Wage and salary disbursements [1]	Other labor income [1][2]	Proprietors' income [3]		Rental income of persons [4]	Dividends [4]	Personal interest income	Transfer payments [5]	Less: Personal contributions for social insurance	Nonfarm personal income [6]
				Farm	Nonfarm						
1969	745.8	514.6	28.2	13.9	52.3	18.1	22.6	55.9	66.5	26.3	725.8
1970	801.3	546.5	32.0	13.9	51.2	18.6	22.9	64.3	79.9	28.0	780.7
1971	859.1	579.4	36.2	14.3	53.4	20.1	23.0	69.3	94.1	30.8	838.0
1972	942.5	633.8	42.0	18.0	58.1	21.5	24.6	74.6	104.1	34.2	917.3
1973	1,052.4	701.3	48.7	32.0	60.4	21.6	27.8	84.1	118.9	42.2	1,011.9
1974	1,153.3	765.0	55.5	25.8	61.1	21.0	30.8	101.4	140.3	47.6	1,117.3
1975	1,249.7	806.7	62.5	24.9	65.3	22.4	32.1	110.7	175.2	50.0	1,213.4
1976	1,375.3	890.4	70.1	22.8	73.8	23.5	35.1	122.0	191.3	54.9	1,340.0
1976: May	1,362.9	883.3	69.0	27.5	72.5	23.4	33.9	120.7	187.1	54.4	1,323.3
June	1,370.4	883.1	69.7	31.6	73.4	22.7	35.2	121.5	186.8	54.3	1,326.6
July	1,380.8	892.7	70.4	26.0	73.8	23.4	35.2	123.0	191.3	54.4	1,342.5
Aug	1,385.5	897.4	71.1	21.0	74.4	23.2	35.4	125.2	192.9	55.2	1,351.8
Sept	1,391.7	903.5	71.7	18.1	74.9	23.6	35.6	126.9	192.9	55.5	1,360.8
Oct	1,404.2	911.3	72.4	18.6	75.4	24.0	36.1	127.8	194.4	55.9	1,372.7
Nov	1,421.4	921.5	73.2	19.6	76.8	24.3	36.5	128.7	197.3	56.7	1,388.6
Dec	1,439.5	930.1	74.1	22.7	78.2	24.5	40.5	128.7	198.0	57.3	1,403.4
1977: Jan	1,441.3	933.4	74.9	23.1	77.6	25.0	37.0	129.8	199.4	59.0	1,404.5
Feb	1,464.2	946.9	75.8	24.1	79.7	25.2	37.6	131.7	202.8	59.6	1,426.2
Mar	1,486.5	961.0	76.8	24.7	81.4	25.2	38.1	133.3	206.3	60.4	1,447.8
Apr	1,497.7	970.2	77.8	24.1	82.0	24.6	38.1	134.5	207.1	60.9	1,459.4
May p	1,507.2	979.2	78.8	23.5	83.0	25.8	38.7	135.6	204.2	61.4	1,469.4

[1] The total of wage and salary disbursements and other labor income differs from compensation of employees in that it excludes employer contributions for social insurance and the excess of wage accruals over wage disbursements.

[2] Consists of employer contributions to private pension, health, and welfare funds; workmen's compensation; directors' fees; and a few other minor items.

[3] With inventory valuation and capital consumption adjustments.

[4] With capital consumption adjustment.

[5] Consists mainly of social insurance benefits, direct relief, and veterans payments.

[6] Personal income exclusive of farm proprietors' income, farm wages, farm other labor income, and agricultural net interest.

Source: Department of Commerce, Bureau of Economic Analysis.

Source: Economic Indicators, Council of Economic Advisors.

DISPOSITION OF PERSONAL INCOME

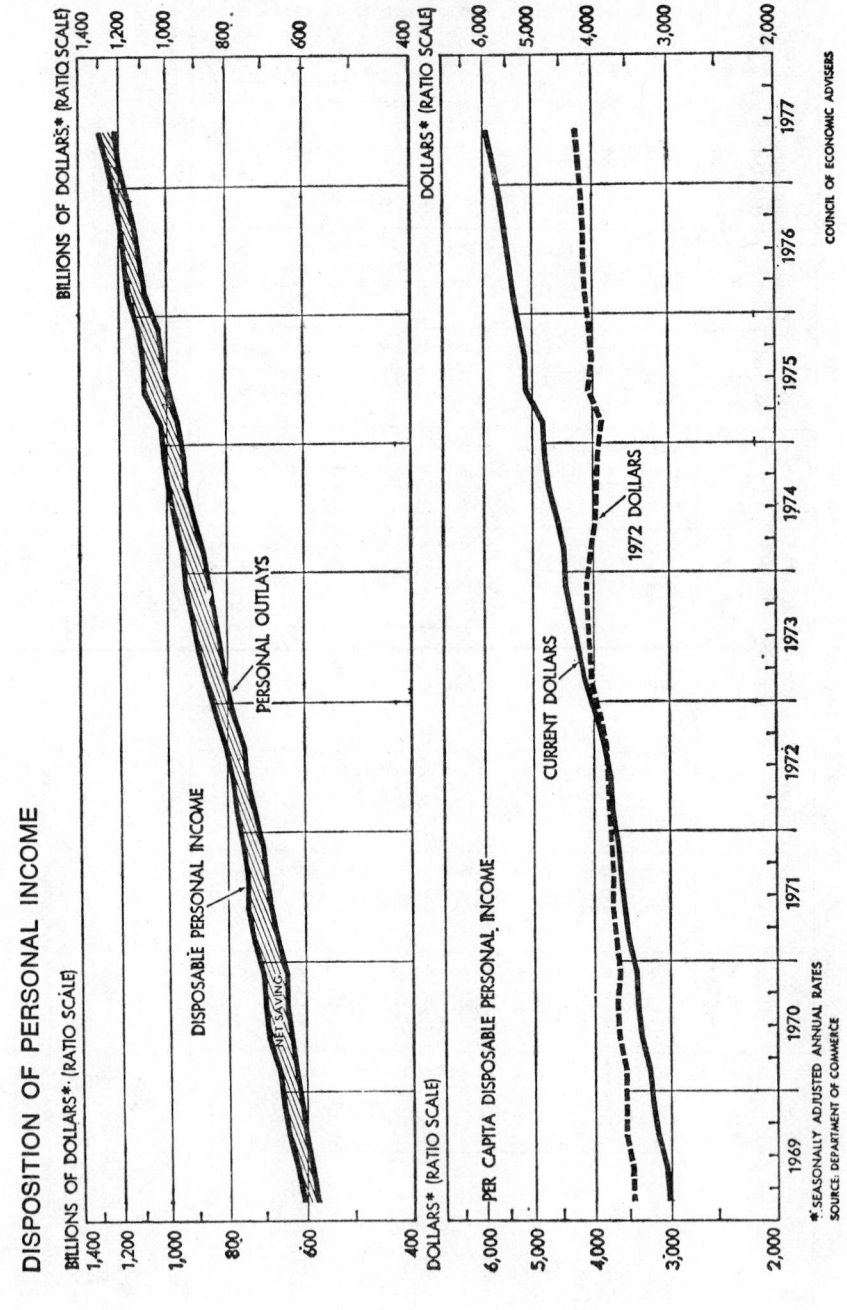

BILLIONS OF DOLLARS* (RATIO SCALE)

BILLIONS OF DOLLARS* (RATIO SCALE)

PERSONAL OUTLAYS

DISPOSABLE PERSONAL INCOME

NET SAVING

DOLLARS* (RATIO SCALE)

DOLLARS* (RATIO SCALE)

PER CAPITA DISPOSABLE PERSONAL INCOME

CURRENT DOLLARS

1972 DOLLARS

1969   1970   1971   1972   1973   1974   1975   1976   1977

*SEASONALLY ADJUSTED ANNUAL RATES
SOURCE: DEPARTMENT OF COMMERCE

COUNCIL OF ECONOMIC ADVISERS

Period	Personal income	Less: Personal tax and nontax payments	Equals: Disposable personal income	Less: Personal outlays[1]	Equals: Personal saving	Per capita disposable personal income		Per capita personal consumption expenditures		Percent change in real per capita disposable personal income	Saving as percent of disposable personal income	Population (thousands)[2]
						Current dollars	1972 dollars	Current dollars	1972 dollars			
	Billions of dollars					Dollars						
1968	685.2	97.1	588.1	550.1	38.1	2,930	3,464	2,670	3,156	2.8	6.5	200,706
1969	745.8	115.8	630.4	595.3	35.1	3,111	3,515	2,860	3,234	1.5	5.6	202,677
1970	801.3	115.3	685.9	635.4	50.6	3,348	3,619	3,020	3,265	3.0	7.4	204,878
1971	859.1	116.3	742.8	685.5	57.3	3,588	3,714	3,227	3,342	2.6	7.7	207,053
1972	942.5	141.2	801.3	751.9	49.4	3,837	3,837	3,510	3,510	3.3	6.2	208,846
1973	1,052.4	150.8	901.7	831.3	70.3	4,285	4,062	3,849	3,648	5.9	7.8	210,410
1974	1,154.9	170.3	984.6	913.0	71.7	4,646	3,973	4,197	3,589	-2.2	7.3	211,945
1975	1,253.4	169.0	1,084.4	1,004.2	80.2	5,077	4,014	4,591	3,629	1.0	7.4	213,566
1976	1,382.7	196.9	1,185.8	1,119.9	65.9	5,511	4,137	5,084	3,817	3.1	5.6	215,191
					Seasonally adjusted annual rates							
1976: I	1,338.1	184.8	1,153.3	1,080.9	72.4	5,374	4,107	4,921	3,761	4.5	6.3	214,608
II	1,366.7	192.6	1,174.1	1,103.8	70.3	5,462	4,130	5,017	3,794	2.3	6.0	214,948
III	1,393.9	200.6	1,193.3	1,128.5	64.8	5,540	4,135	5,117	3,820	.5	5.4	215,380
IV	1,432.2	209.5	1,222.6	1,166.3	56.3	5,665	4,177	5,277	3,891	4.1	4.6	215,827
1977: I	1,476.8	224.4	1,252.4	1,201.0	51.4	5,793	4,202	5,423	3,933	2.4	4.1	216,206
II	1,517.2	224.8	1,292.5	1,223.9	68.5	5,967	4,268	5,512	3,943	6.4	5.3	216,602

[1] Includes personal consumption expenditures, interest paid by consumers to business, and personal transfer payments to foreigners (net).
[2] Includes Armed Forces abroad. Annual data are for July 1 through 1973 and are averages of quarterly data beginning 1974. Quarterly data are for middle of period.

Source: Department of Commerce (Bureau of Economic Analysis and Bureau of the Census).

Source: *Economic Indicators*, Council of Economic Advisors.

PERSONAL CONSUMPTION EXPENDITURES

Billions of dollars except as noted; quarterly data at seasonally adjusted annual rates

Period	Total personal consumption expenditures	Durable goods			Nondurable goods				Services	Retail sales of new passenger cars (millions of units)	
		Total durable goods[1]	Motor vehicles and parts	Furniture and household equipment	Total nondurable goods[1]	Food	Clothing and shoes	Gasoline and oil		Domestics	Imports
1966	464.8	67.7	30.1	27.7	204.7	106.6	36.6	16.0	192.4	8.4	0.7
1967	490.4	69.0	29.7	29.5	212.6	109.6	38.2	17.0	208.1	7.6	.8
1968	535.9	80.5	35.8	32.6	230.4	118.3	41.8	18.4	225.6	8.6	1.0
1969	579.7	85.9	37.7	35.0	247.0	126.1	45.1	20.4	247.2	8.5	1.3
1970	618.8	84.9	34.9	36.7	264.7	136.3	46.6	22.0	269.1	7.1	1.6
1971	668.2	97.1	43.8	39.4	277.7	140.6	50.5	23.4	293.4	8.7	1.6
1972	733.0	111.2	50.6	44.8	299.3	150.4	55.1	24.9	322.4	9.3	1.8
1973	809.9	123.7	55.2	50.7	333.8	168.1	61.3	27.8	352.3	9.7	1.9
1974	887.5	121.6	47.9	54.7	376.2	189.9	65.1	36.3	389.6	7.5	1.4
1975	973.2	131.2	53.2	57.6	409.1	209.5	70.0	38.9	432.4	7.1	1.6
1976	1,079.7	156.5	70.7	63.0	440.4	224.4	75.4	41.5	482.8	8.6	1.5
1975: III	987.3	136.0	56.3	58.2	414.6	211.8	71.3	39.2	436.7	7.6	1.6
IV	1,012.0	141.8	59.2	60.6	421.6	215.2	73.0	39.9	448.6	7.7	1.4
1976: I	1,043.6	151.4	68.0	61.2	429.1	219.2	73.5	40.1	463.2	8.9	1.3
II	1,064.7	155.0	70.4	62.3	434.8	223.1	73.2	40.3	474.9	8.7	1.4
III	1,088.5	157.6	71.7	62.9	441.8	225.2	75.9	41.6	489.1	8.6	1.5
IV	1,122.0	162.0	72.7	65.6	456.0	230.2	79.0	44.1	504.0	8.3	1.7
1977: I	1,159.1	174.0	83.6	66.6	464.7	236.4	78.9	44.2	520.4	9.5	1.8

Source: Department of Commerce, Bureau of Economic Analysis.

1 Total includes other items not shown separately.

Source: Economic Indicators, Council of Economic Advisors.

NATIONAL INCOME

Billions of dollars; quarterly data at seasonally adjusted annual rates

Period	National income	Compensation of employees [1]	Proprietors' income with inventory valuation and capital consumption adjustments		Rental income of persons with capital consumption adjustment	Corporate profits with inventory valuation and capital consumption adjustments					Net interest
						Total	Profits with inventory valuation adjustment and without capital consumption adjustment			Capital consumption adjustment	
			Farm	Non-farm			Total	Profits before tax	Inventory valuation adjustment		
1967	655.8	471.9	12.1	48.9	19.4	79.3	75.6	77.3	−1.7	3.7	24.3
1968	714.4	519.8	12.0	51.4	18.6	85.8	82.1	85.6	−3.4	3.7	26.8
1969	767.9	571.4	13.9	52.3	18.1	81.4	77.9	83.4	−5.5	3.5	30.8
1970	798.4	609.2	13.9	51.2	18.6	67.9	66.4	71.5	−5.1	1.5	37.5
1971	858.1	650.3	14.3	53.4	20.1	77.2	76.9	82.0	−5.0	.3	42.8
1972	951.9	715.1	18.0	58.1	21.5	92.1	89.6	96.2	−6.6	2.5	47.0
1973	1,064.6	799.2	32.0	60.4	21.6	99.1	97.2	115.8	−18.6	1.9	52.3
1974	1,136.0	875.8	25.4	60.9	21.4	83.6	86.5	126.9	−40.4	−2.9	69.0
1975	1,215.0	931.1	23.5	63.5	21.4	95.9	107.9	120.4	−12.4	−12.0	78.6
1976	1,359.2	1,036.8	18.4	70.2	22.5	127.0	141.4	155.9	−14.5	−14.4	84.3
1977	1,515.3	1,153.4	20.2	79.5	22.5	144.2	159.1	173.9	−14.8	−14.9	95.4
1977: I	1,447.5	1,107.9	19.4	76.1	22.5	129.9	144.5	164.8	−20.3	−14.6	91.7
II	1,499.3	1,140.5	20.0	78.9	22.4	143.7	158.5	175.1	−16.6	−14.8	93.7
III	1,537.6	1,165.8	16.5	80.8	22.4	154.8	169.9	177.5	−7.7	−15.0	97.3
IV	1,576.9	1,199.7	25.1	82.3	22.7	148.2	163.5	178.3	−14.8	−15.3	99.0
1978: I	1,603.1	1,241.0	21.9	83.1	22.8	132.6	148.7	172.1	−23.5	−16.1	101.7
II ᵖ	1,683.6	1,287.5	24.0	86.0	22.2	159.5	176.7	201.6	−24.9	−17.2	104.5

[1] Includes employer contributions for social insurance.

Source: Department of Commerce, Bureau of Economic Analysis.

Source: *Economic Indicators*, Council of Economic Advisors.

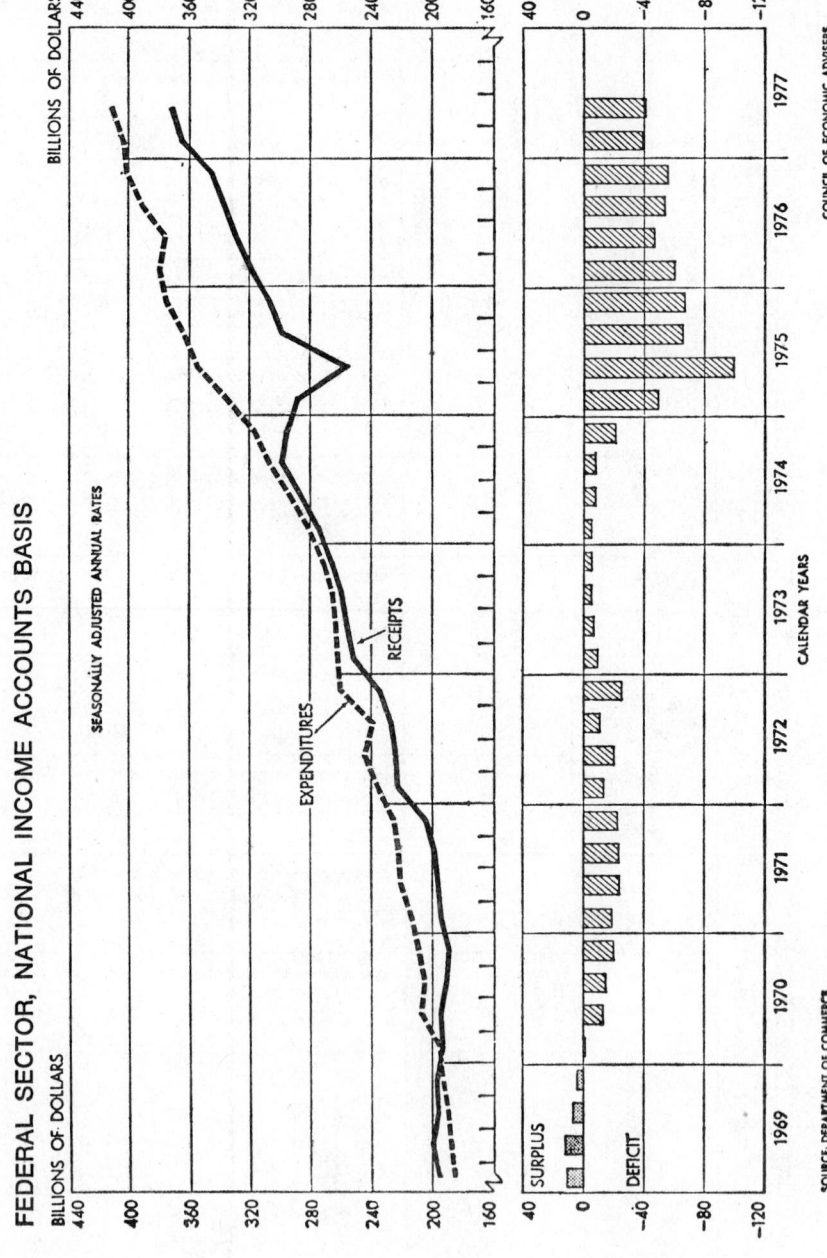

FEDERAL SECTOR, NATIONAL INCOME ACCOUNTS BASIS

BILLIONS OF DOLLARS

SEASONALLY ADJUSTED ANNUAL RATES

BILLIONS OF DOLLARS

EXPENDITURES

RECEIPTS

SURPLUS

DEFICIT

CALENDAR YEARS

SOURCE: DEPARTMENT OF COMMERCE

COUNCIL OF ECONOMIC ADVISERS

[Billions of dollars; quarterly data at seasonally adjusted annual rates]

Period	Federal Government receipts					Federal Government expenditures							Surplus or deficit (—), national income and product accounts
	Total	Personal tax and nontax receipts	Corporate profits tax accruals	Indirect business tax and nontax accruals	Contributions for social insurance	Total	Purchases of goods and services	Transfer payments	Grants-in-aid to State and local governments	Net interest paid	Subsidies less current surplus of Government enterprises	Less: Wage accruals less disbursements	
Fiscal year:													
1974	271.8	122.6	43.7	21.4	84.2	278.8	104.6	104.7	41.6	19.8	8.0	−0.2	−7.0
1975	283.6	127.3	42.1	22.1	92.1	328.7	117.9	134.2	48.4	21.9	5.7	−.4	−45.0
1976	314.1	137.2	52.2	24.2	100.5	372.3	126.5	156.8	57.5	25.4	6.1	−.0	−58.2
Calendar year:													
1972	227.5	108.2	36.6	20.0	62.8	244.7	102.1	83.2	37.5	14.6	7.8	.5	−17.3
1973	258.3	114.6	43.0	21.2	79.4	265.0	102.2	95.8	40.6	18.2	8.2	.0	−6.7
1974	288.6	131.1	45.9	21.7	89.9	299.3	111.1	117.6	43.9	20.9	5.3	.5	−10.7
1975	286.9	125.6	43.1	24.0	94.2	357.1	123.3	149.1	54.6	23.3	6.7	—	−70.2
1976	332.3	147.3	55.9	23.4	105.7	386.3	130.1	162.0	61.0	27.2	5.9	.0	−54.0
1976: I	318.4	138.0	54.4	22.7	103.2	378.7	127.6	160.2	58.5	26.2	6.2	.0	−60.3
II	329.1	143.9	57.0	23.2	105.0	375.3	128.5	157.8	56.8	26.7	5.5	.0	−46.2
III	337.1	150.3	56.9	23.7	106.2	390.6	130.2	163.9	63.1	27.3	6.1	.0	−53.5
IV	344.5	157.1	55.1	23.8	108.4	400.4	134.2	166.3	65.5	28.5	6.0	.0	−55.9
1977: I	364.9	170.0	55.4	24.2	115.4	403.7	136.3	170.7	62.0	28.6	6.1	.0	−38.8
IIp	370.9	168.6	59.6	24.6	118.1	411.5	143.6	169.3	63.6	29.1	5.9	.0	−40.6

Source: *Economic Indicators*, Council of Economic Advisors.

FEDERAL BUDGET: PROCEDURE AND TIMETABLE
Congressional Budget Timetable

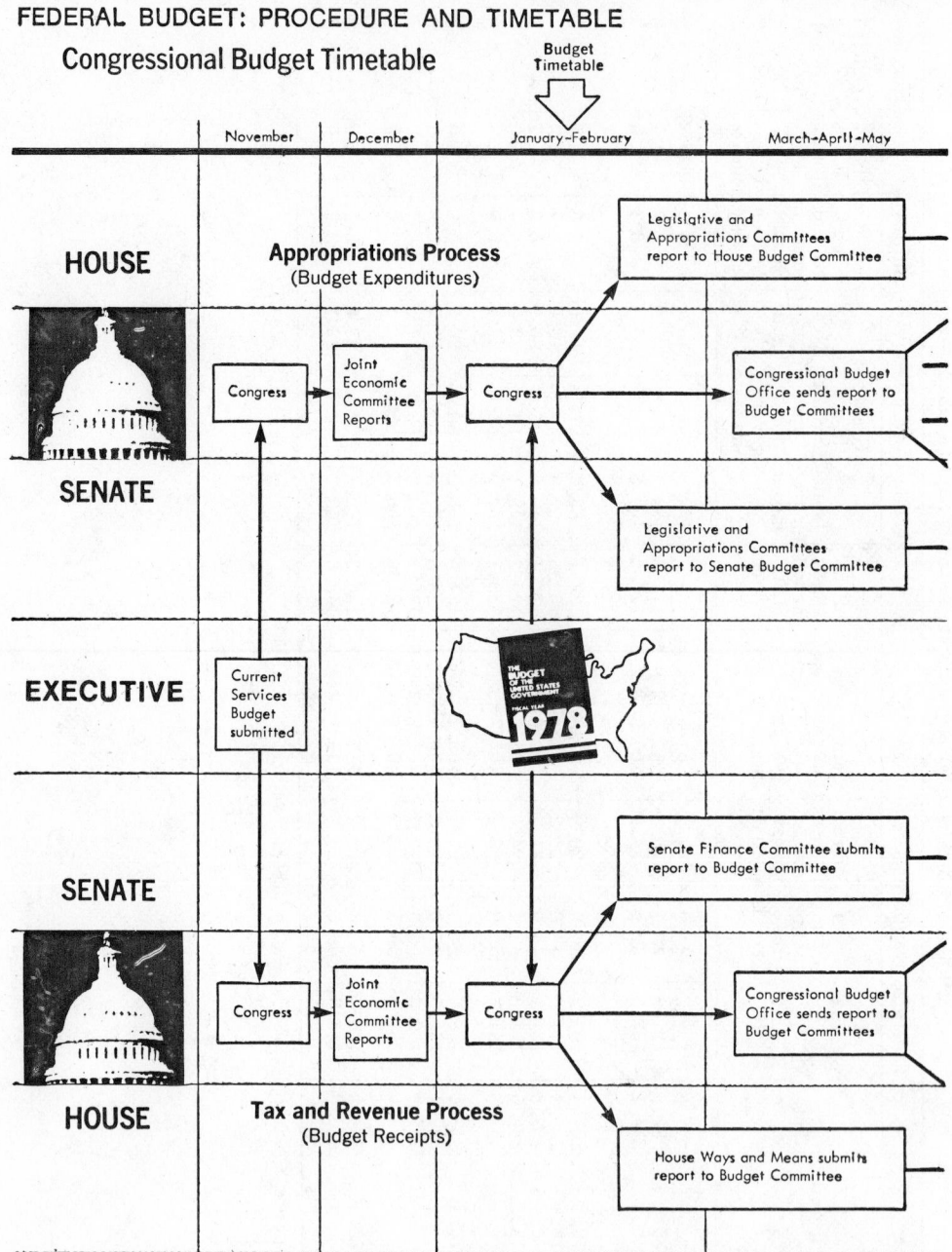

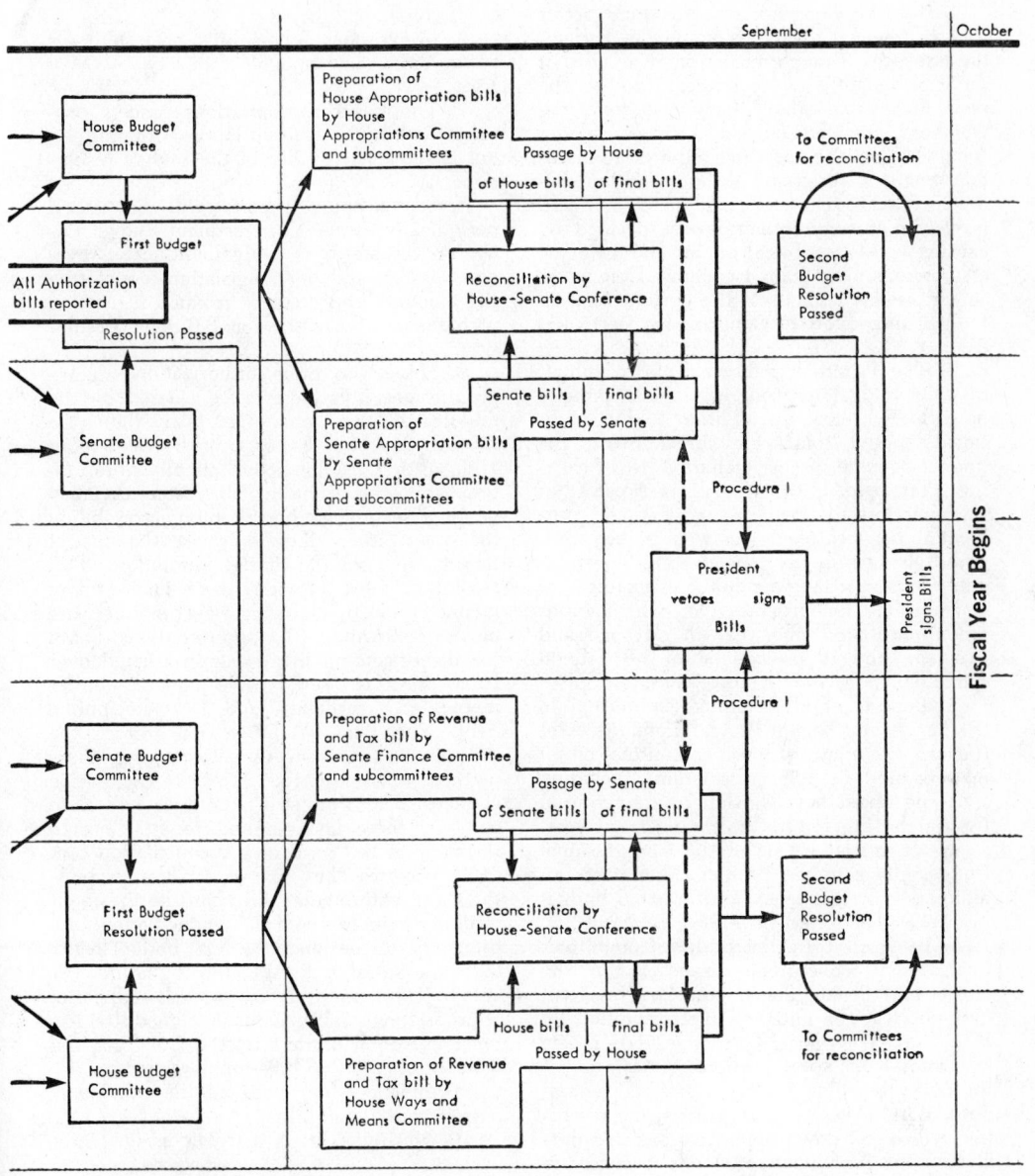

September | October

House Budget Committee

First Budget

All Authorization bills reported

Resolution Passed

Senate Budget Committee

Preparation of House Appropriation bills by House Appropriations Committee and subcommittees

Passage by House
of House bills | of final bills

Reconciliation by House-Senate Conference

Senate bills | final bills
Passed by Senate

Preparation of Senate Appropriation bills by Senate Appropriations Committee and subcommittees

To Committees for reconciliation

Second Budget Resolution Passed

Procedure I

President

vetoes   signs

Bills

President signs Bills

Fiscal Year Begins

Procedure I

Senate Budget Committee

First Budget Resolution Passed

House Budget Committee

Preparation of Revenue and Tax bill by Senate Finance Committee and subcommittees

Passage by Senate
of Senate bills | of final bills

Reconciliation by House-Senate Conference

House bills | final bills
Passed by House

Preparation of Revenue and Tax bill by House Ways and Means Committee

Second Budget Resolution Passed

To Committees for reconciliation

Source: The Conference Board, "The Federal Budget: Its Impact on the Economy," Michael E. Levy, assisted by Delos R. Smith.

CONGRESSIONAL BUDGET ACT OF 1974: THE NEW BUDGET PROCESS IN TEN STEPS

1. To give Congress an earlier and better start in reviewing and reshaping the budget, the Executive Branch must submit a "current services budget" by November 10th for the new fiscal year that starts the following October 1st. The current services budget should project the spending required to maintain ongoing programs throughout the following fiscal year at existing commitment levels, or at commitment levels specified by existing legislation based on current economic assumptions. The Joint Economic Committee should review and assess the current services budget and report to Congress by December 31st.

2. The President will continue to submit his new budget to Congress in late January or early February. In addition to the traditional budget totals and breakdowns, the budget document must include a list of existing "tax expenditures"—i.e., estimates of revenues lost to the Treasury through preferential tax treatment—as well as any proposed changes in tax expenditures. The budget must also contain estimates of expenditures for programs for which funds are appropriated one year in advance and five-year budget projections of all federal spending under existing programs.

3. Reports of all standing committees to the House and Senate Budget Committees of the spending plans of those committees on all matters under their jurisdiction, including spending under new legislation, are required by March 15th for the upcoming fiscal year.

4. An annual report of the Congressional Budget Office to the Budget Committees on alternative budget levels and national budget priorities is required on or before April 1st.

5. By April 15th, the Budget Committees must report concurrent resolutions to the House and Senate floors, and Congress will have to clear the initial budget resolution by May 15th. This initial budget resolution sets target totals for appropriations, outlays, taxes, the budget surplus or deficit, and the federal debt. Within these overall targets, the resolution will break down appropriations and outlays by the functional categories used in the President's budget document, as well as by classifications used by the appropriations subcommittees for the 13 appropriations bills. The resolution will include any recommended changes in tax revenues and in the level of the federal debt ceiling.

6. Committees report bills or resolutions authorizing new budget authority by May 15th.

7. The basic appropriations process proceeds within the Appropriations Committees, but is subject to targets of the budget resolution.

8. Scorekeeping reports will be issued periodically by the Congressional Budget Office on the status of budget authority, revenue, outlays and debt legislation, comparing the amounts and changes in such legislation with the First Congressional Budget Resolution.

9. Subject to prior authorization, all appropriations bills have to be cleared by the middle of September—no later than the seventh day after Labor Day. By September 15th, after finishing action on all appropriations and other spending bills, Congress must adopt a second, and final, budget resolution that may either affirm or revise the budget targets set by the initial resolution. This resolution must provide for a final budget reconciliation by changing either one or more of the following: (1) appropriations (both for the upcoming fiscal year or carried over from previous fiscal years) and/or entitlements; (2) revenues; and (3) the public debt. The final resolution will direct the committees that have jurisdiction over these matters to report the necessary legislative changes. The Budget Committees will then combine these changes and report them to the floor in the form of a reconciliation bill.

If Congress has withheld all appropriations and entitlement bills from the President until passage of the final reconciliation bill, then this bill becomes the final budget legislation, subject to Presidential signature (or veto). If, on the other hand, each individual appropriations bill has been signed by the President upon passage by the Congress, the final reconciliation bill—upon signature by the President—supersedes all the previously passed individual bills.

10. The new fiscal year begins on October 1st.

Production, Construction, and Business Activity

LABOR FORCE PARTICIPATION RATES OF MEN AND WOMEN
16 YEARS AND OVER, 1950–1976

Annual average

Year	Percent of civilian noninstitutional population in the labor force	
	Men	Women
1950	86.4	33.9
1951	86.5	34.6
1952	86.3	34.7
1953	86.0	34.4
1954	85.5	34.6
1955	85.3	35.7
1956	85.5	36.9
1957	84.8	36.9
1958	84.2	37.1
1959	83.7	37.1
1960	83.3	37.7
1961	82.9	38.1
1962	82.0	37.9
1963	81.4	38.3
1964	81.0	38.7
1965	80.7	39.3
1966	80.4	40.3
1967	80.4	41.1
1968	80.1	41.6
1969	79.8	42.7
1970	79.7	43.3
1971	79.1	43.3
1972	79.0	43.9
1973	78.8	44.7
1974	78.7	45.6
1975	77.9	46.3
1976	77.5	47.3

Source: *Monthly Labor Review*, U.S. Department of Labor, Bureau of Labor Statistics.

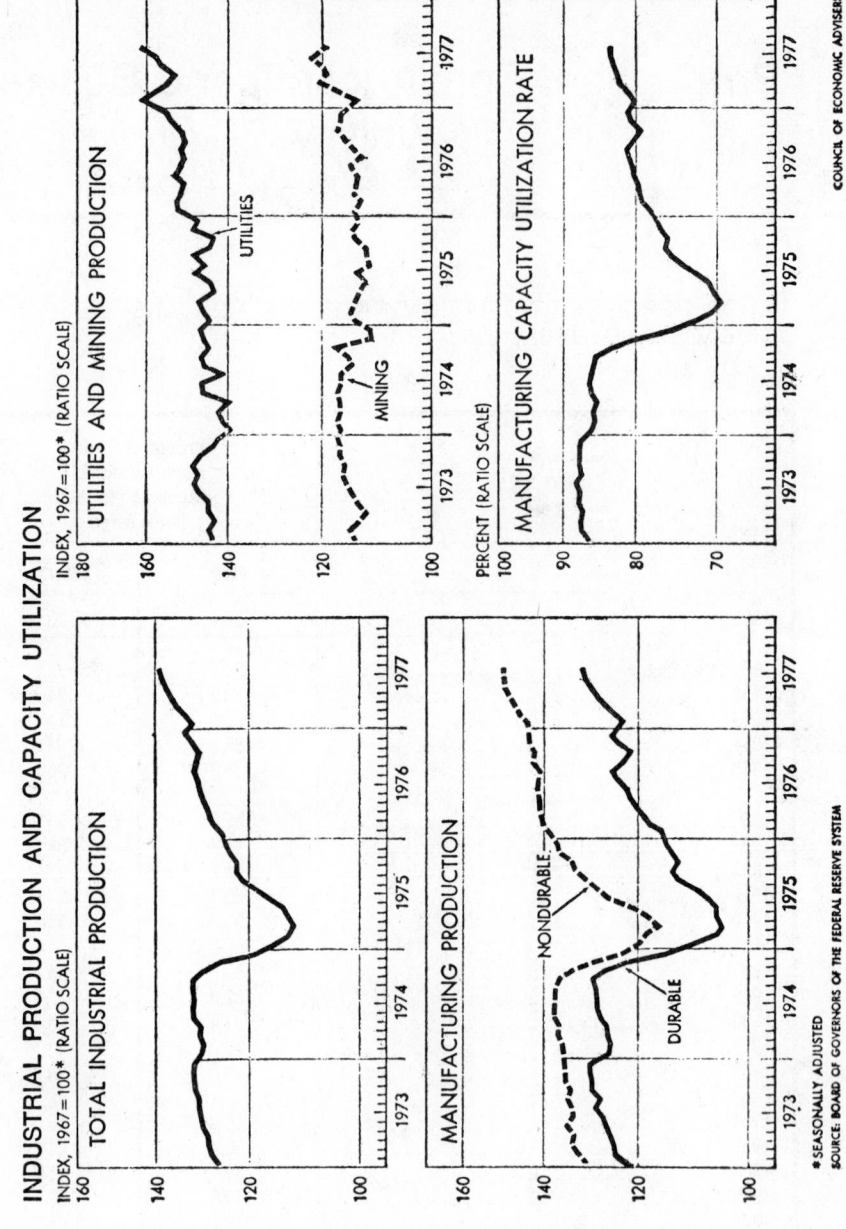

INDUSTRIAL PRODUCTION AND CAPACITY UTILIZATION

INDEX, 1967=100* (RATIO SCALE)

INDEX, 1967=100* (RATIO SCALE)

UTILITIES AND MINING PRODUCTION

TOTAL INDUSTRIAL PRODUCTION

MANUFACTURING PRODUCTION

MANUFACTURING CAPACITY UTILIZATION RATE

PERCENT (RATIO SCALE)

UTILITIES

MINING

NONDURABLE

DURABLE

* SEASONALLY ADJUSTED

SOURCE: BOARD OF GOVERNORS OF THE FEDERAL RESERVE SYSTEM

COUNCIL OF ECONOMIC ADVISERS

[Seasonally adjusted]

Period	Total industrial production — Index, 1967=100	Total industrial production — Percent change from year earlier	Industry production indexes, 1967=100 — Manufacturing — Total	Manufacturing — Durable	Manufacturing — Non-durable	Mining	Utilities	Manufacturing capacity utilization rate, percent[1] — Federal Reserve series — Total manufacturing	Federal Reserve series — Materials	Commerce series[2]	Wharton series[3]
1967 proportion	100.00	---	87.95	61.98	35.97	6.36	5.69				
1971	109.6	1.7	108.2	102.4	116.6	109.8	130.5	78.0	83.1	80	86.4
1972	119.7	9.2	118.9	113.7	126.5	114.1	139.4	83.1	88.0	83	91.8
1973	129.8	8.4	129.8	127.1	133.8	114.7	145.5	87.5	92.4	86	97.1
1974	129.3	-.4	129.4	125.7	134.6	115.3	143.7	84.2	87.7	83	93.0
1975	117.8	-8.9	116.3	109.3	126.4	112.8	146.0	73.6	73.6	77	80.4
1976	129.8	10.2	129.4	121.4	141.0	114.1	151.7	80.1	80.3	81	87.4
1976: July	130.7	10.4	131.0	124.2	141.1	112.5	150.8	80.9	81.2	---	---
Aug	131.3	8.5	131.6	125.1	140.9	114.4	151.3	81.1	81.6	---	---
Sept	130.8	7.1	130.7	122.4	142.6	115.7	150.1	80.4	81.0	80	88.1
Oct	130.4	6.7	129.9	121.5	142.2	116.7	151.2	79.7	80.3	---	---
Nov	131.8	6.7	131.9	123.8	143.5	116.2	154.0	80.8	80.3	---	---
Dec	133.1	7.0	132.8	125.2	143.7	116.2	155.5	81.2	80.1	81	87.7
1977: Jan	132.1	5.1	131.5	123.0	143.7	113.2	161.5	80.2	79.1	---	---
Feb	133.2	4.6	132.9	124.0	145.7	116.5	158.8	80.8	80.0	---	---
Mar	135.2	5.5	135.2	126.8	147.0	120.2	154.2	82.1	81.6	83	88.3
Apr	136.2	6.1	136.0	127.9	147.8	119.2	153.1	82.3	82.0	---	---
May	137.4	6.0	137.4	129.3	149.1	120.0	156.4	82.9	82.7	---	---
June ²	138.3	6.3	138.3	130.6	149.3	122.3	157.7	83.3	83.1	---	90.7
July ²	139.0	6.4	138.8	131.3	149.6	119.3	161.3	83.4	83.0	---	---

1 Output as percent of capacity.
2 Annual data are averages of four monthly indexes.
3 Quarterly data entered in last month of quarter. Annual data are averages of quarterly data.

Sources: Board of Governors of the Federal Reserve System, Department of Commerce (Bureau of Economic Analysis), and Wharton School of Finance.

Source: Economic Indicators, Council of Economic Advisors.

INDUSTRIAL PRODUCTION—MAJOR MARKET GROUPS AND SELECTED MANUFACTURERS

1967 = 100, seasonally adjusted

Period	Total	Products								Materials	Supplementary group: Energy total
		Final products					Intermediate products			
		Consumer goods			Equipment					
		Total	Durable goods	Non-durable goods	Total	Business	Total	Construction supplies		
1967 proportion	*47.82*	*27.68*	*7.89*	*19.79*	*20.14*	*12.63*	*12.89*	*6.42*	*39.29*	*12.23*
1969	109.6	109.8	115.0	107.7	109.3	112.5	112.9	112.3	112.5	111.1
1970	105.3	109.0	106.1	110.1	100.1	107.0	112.9	111.0	109.2	117.0
1971	106.3	114.7	118.8	113.1	94.7	104.1	116.7	116.8	111.3	119.5
1972	115.7	124.4	133.8	120.6	103.8	118.0	126.5	128.4	122.3	125.2
1973	124.4	131.5	146.2	125.6	114.5	134.2	137.2	139.8	133.0	128.3
1974	125.1	128.9	135.3	126.3	120.0	142.4	135.3	134.5	132.4	125.5
1975	118.2	124.0	121.4	125.1	110.2	128.2	123.1	116.3	115.5	125.5
1976	127.3	136.8	141.5	134.9	114.3	136.1	136.8	132.0	130.5	129.0
1976: May	127.3	137.4	143.2	135.1	113.5	134.6	135.0	130.9	130.6	129.3
June	127.6	137.8	144.2	135.1	113.8	135.0	135.9	131.8	131.1	129.7
July	127.6	136.8	141.8	134.8	114.9	136.9	137.6	133.1	132.2	128.4
Aug	128.3	137.5	143.7	134.9	115.7	137.7	137.8	134.1	133.0	129.0
Sept	127.4	136.2	138.4	135.3	115.2	137.5	138.7	134.3	132.5	128.6
Oct	127.4	136.9	139.4	135.8	114.4	135.9	138.3	134.0	131.6	128.6
Nov	129.8	139.1	143.7	137.1	116.9	140.2	138.8	135.7	131.9	130.7
Dec	132.1	142.0	151.2	138.4	118.6	143.2	139.8	135.5	131.9	132.2
1977: Jan	130.8	140.2	145.1	138.3	117.8	142.0	141.8	136.1	130.7	133.0
Feb	131.8	141.0	146.1	138.9	119.0	143.1	141.8	135.7	132.4	132.4
Mar	133.3	143.0	152.3	139.1	119.8	144.4	141.9	136.4	135.4	132.4
Apr ᵖ	134.0	143.0	152.4	139.5	121.6	146.7	143.0	137.8	136.8	132.1
May ᵖ	135.2	143.6	152.8	140.0	123.6	149.3	144.8	139.6	138.5	132.4

[1967=100, seasonally adjusted]

Period	Durable manufactures								Nondurable manufactures			
	Primary metals		Fabricated metal products	Nonelectrical machinery	Electrical machinery	Transportation equipment		Lumber and products	Apparel products	Printing and publishing	Chemicals and products	Foods
	Total	Iron and steel				Total	Motor vehicles and parts					
1967 proportion	*6.57*	*4.21*	*5.93*	*9.15*	*8.05*	*9.27*	*4.50*	*1.64*	*3.81*	*4.72*	*7.74*	*8.75*
1969	113.8	112.6	107.9	109.3	111.9	108.4	116.5	107.9	106.7	107.4	118.4	106.1
1970	106.6	104.7	102.4	104.4	108.1	89.5	92.3	105.6	101.4	107.0	120.4	108.9
1971	100.2	96.1	103.5	100.2	107.7	97.9	118.6	113.8	104.7	107.1	125.9	112.8
1972	112.1	107.1	112.1	116.0	122.2	108.2	135.8	120.8	109.4	112.7	143.6	116.8
1973	126.7	122.3	124.7	133.7	143.1	118.3	148.8	126.0	117.3	118.2	154.5	120.9
1974	123.1	119.8	124.2	140.1	143.8	108.7	128.2	116.2	114.3	118.2	159.4	124.0
1975	96.4	95.8	109.9	125.1	116.5	97.4	111.1	107.6	107.6	113.3	147.3	123.4
1976	108.0	104.4	123.3	134.7	131.7	110.6	140.7	125.1	126.1	120.7	169.4	132.0
1976: May	113.2	110.7	121.4	134.0	131.8	112.9	144.3	123.0	130.3	120.5	166.6	131.2
June	111.5	110.0	124.0	133.5	132.0	112.6	146.5	120.3	126.8	119.7	170.0	130.5
July	116.9	115.3	124.6	135.6	131.0	113.3	148.5	124.6	125.6	122.0	167.6	131.8
Aug	118.6	116.2	125.8	136.8	135.3	115.0	150.6	128.1	123.7	120.6	170.4	133.4
Sept	114.1	110.3	126.6	136.8	133.7	104.4	130.2	128.7	122.5	120.6	170.5	135.7
Oct	109.9	105.1	123.5	134.1	135.0	104.7	129.3	130.7	126.4	119.2	170.6	134.7
Nov	107.3	103.1	126.7	137.5	135.8	112.7	145.8	129.0	125.9	119.3	174.2	134.7
Dec	102.7	95.6	128.2	141.2	135.6	118.2	156.4	127.5	128.0	123.1	173.5	134.3
1977: Jan	100.0	89.8	125.7	139.5	134.0	113.5	145.5	132.7	123.6	124.3	172.0	135.5
Feb	100.4	91.3	126.0	139.4	137.6	113.4	145.4	132.2	125.2	122.4	175.1	137.1
Mar	107.2	97.9	127.8	140.4	138.1	120.5	161.2	132.1	123.5	124.0	177.5	138.5
Apr ᵖ	112.3	104.4	129.1	142.7	139.7	119.7	158.2	132.5	------	123.6	177.6	139.3
May ᵖ	117.3	111.5	130.7	145.4	141.7	120.8	158.5	------	------	125.0	------	------

Source: Board of Governors of the Federal Reserve System.

Source: *Economic Indicators*, Council of Economic Advisors.

NEW PRIVATE HOUSING AND VACANCY RATES

Period	Total new construction expenditures	Private					Federal, State, and local	Construction contracts[2]	
		Total	Residential		Commercial and industrial	Other		Total value index (1967=100)	Commercial and industrial floor space (millions of square feet)
			Total[1]	New housing units					
			Billions of dollars						
1970	94.9	66.8	31.9	24.3	16.3	18.6	28.1	123.1	743
1971	110.0	80.1	43.3	35.1	17.0	19.8	29.9	145.4	727
1972	124.1	93.9	54.3	44.9	18.1	21.5	30.2	165.3	854
1973	137.9	105.4	59.7	50.1	21.7	24.0	32.5	179.5	1,010
1974	138.5	100.2	50.4	40.6	23.8	26.0	38.3	169.7	840
1975	132.0	93.0	46.5	34.4	20.8	25.7	39.0	167.9	555
1976	144.8	108.4	59.9	46.7	19.5	29.0	36.4	194.1	602
	Seasonally adjusted annual rates							Seasonally adjusted	Seasonally adjusted annual rates
1976: Apr	144.5	106.6	58.9	44.2	19.8	27.9	37.9	208	634
May	143.4	107.2	58.8	43.9	19.3	29.1	36.2	205	632
June	145.4	106.5	58.7	45.4	18.7	29.1	38.9	187	646
July	140.9	104.1	57.0	46.9	18.7	28.5	36.8	217	627
Aug	141.9	104.5	55.2	46.5	19.9	29.4	37.3	189	609
Sept	146.6	109.0	59.1	48.8	19.7	30.2	37.6	203	582
Oct	148.5	114.5	65.4	51.1	19.0	30.1	34.0	237	618
Nov	152.8	118.8	69.2	52.7	19.0	30.6	34.1	186	631
Dec	152.2	118.9	70.0	54.3	19.3	29.7	33.3	183	658
1977: Jan	137.1	107.2	63.4	50.0	18.3	25.5	29.9	203	643
Feb	148.9	116.4	69.1	56.5	18.8	28.5	32.5	207	615
Mar [p]	159.3	125.7	75.0	62.0	21.1	29.6	33.6	207	809
Apr [p]	163.4	128.3	77.1	63.5	21.0	30.2	35.1	250	671

[1] Includes nonhousekeeping residential construction and additions and alterations, not shown separately.

[2] F. W. Dodge series. Relates to 50 States beginning 1969 for value index and beginning 1971 for floor space.

Note.—New construction expenditures data prior to 1973 not comparable with later data.

Sources: Department of Commerce (Bureau of the Census) and McGraw-Hill Information Systems Company, F. W. Dodge Division.

Source: *Economic Indicators*, Council of Economic Advisors.

NEW CONSTRUCTION

Period	Total new construction expenditures	Private Total	Private Residential Total¹	Private Residential New housing units	Private Commercial and industrial	Private Other	Federal, State, and local	Construction contracts² Total value index (1967=100)	Construction contracts² Commercial and industrial floor space (millions of square feet)
	Billions of dollars								
1971	110.0	80.1	43.3	35.1	17.0	19.8	29.9	145.4	727
1972	124.1	93.9	54.3	44.9	18.1	21.5	30.2	165.3	854
1973	137.9	105.4	59.7	50.1	21.7	24.0	32.5	179.5	1,010
1974	138.5	100.2	50.4	40.6	23.8	25.9	38.3	169.7	840
1975	134.5	93.7	46.5	34.4	20.8	26.4	40.9	167.9	555
1976	148.8	110.5	60.5	47.3	19.9	30.0	38.3	199.4	592
1977	172.6	134.7	81.0	65.7	22.5	31.3	37.8	252.2	738
	Seasonally adjusted annual rates							*Seasonally adjusted*	*Seasonally adjusted annual rates*
1977: June	175.8	136.6	82.6	66.6	22.8	31.2	39.2	307	733
July	176.4	137.3	82.9	67.1	23.4	31.0	39.1	209	702
Aug	176.4	137.6	82.9	67.1	23.8	30.9	38.8	267	853
Sept	177.8	138.3	83.0	67.6	24.1	31.2	39.4	279	813
Oct	176.7	139.2	84.2	69.3	24.1	30.9	37.4	244	757
Nov	178.1	140.6	85.2	70.7	24.3	31.1	37.4	258	847
Dec	179.0	142.3	87.4	72.8	22.8	32.1	36.8	299	864
1978: Jan	171.7	135.3	79.7	65.0	22.4	33.2	36.4	283	996
Feb	177.9	142.2	85.6	70.9	22.8	33.8	35.7	266	814
Mar	184.8	147.1	87.6	72.5	25.4	34.1	37.7	254	863
Apr	192.9	151.3	90.0	74.4	26.4	34.9	41.5	279	921
May ᵖ	198.3	153.2	91.3	75.3	27.3	34.7	45.1	332	1,061
June ᵖ	200.5	156.6	92.4	76.6	29.9	34.2	43.9	249	999
July ᵖ								286	898

¹ Includes nonhousekeeping residential construction and additions and alterations, not shown separately.
² F. W. Dodge series. Relates to 50 States beginning 1969 for value index and beginning 1971 for floor space.

NOTE.—New construction expenditures data prior to 1973 not comparable with later data.

Sources: Department of Commerce (Bureau of the Census) and McGraw-Hill Information Systems Company, F. W. Dodge Division.

Source: *Economic Indicators*, Council of Economic Advisors.

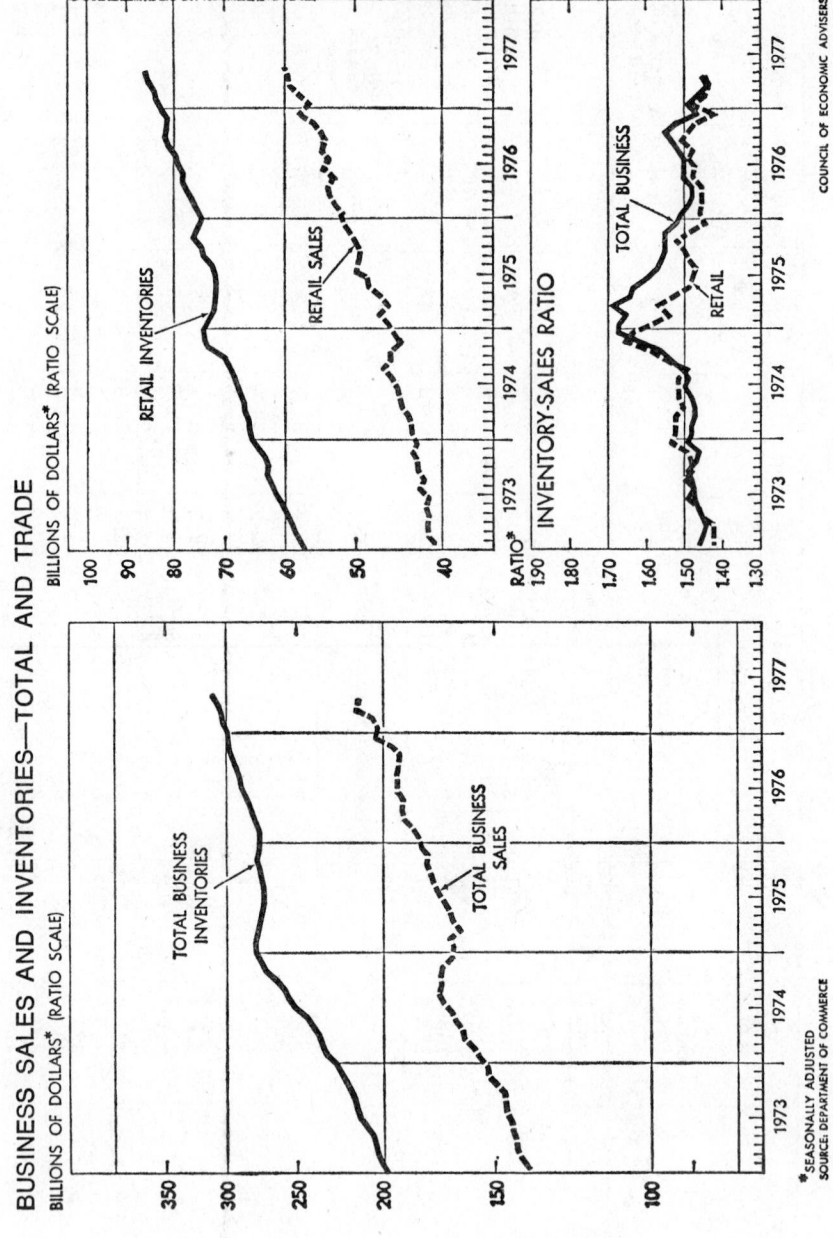

BUSINESS SALES AND INVENTORIES—TOTAL AND TRADE
BILLIONS OF DOLLARS* (RATIO SCALE)

*SEASONALLY ADJUSTED
SOURCE: DEPARTMENT OF COMMERCE

COUNCIL OF ECONOMIC ADVISERS

Period	Total business[1] Sales[2]	Total business[1] Inventories[3]	Wholesale Sales[2]	Wholesale Inventories[3]	Retail Sales[2] Total	Retail Sales[2] Durable goods stores	Retail Sales[2] Non-durable goods stores	Retail Inventories[3] Total	Retail Inventories[3] Durable goods stores	Retail Inventories[3] Non-durable goods stores	Inventory-sales ratio[4] Total business[1]	Inventory-sales ratio[4] Retail
			Millions of dollars, seasonally adjusted									
1971	112,323	184,756	22,327	29,695	34,071	10,985	23,086	52,571	23,864	28,707	1.61	1.47
1972	125,269	198,045	24,862	32,817	37,365	12,472	24,893	57,156	26,056	31,100	1.52	1.46
1973	145,297	227,926	30,400	38,302	41,943	14,190	27,754	65,229	29,593	35,636	1.46	1.46
1974	166,771	278,386	37,344	46,564	44,815	13,943	30,872	73,851	34,301	39,550	1.51	1.53
1975	172,511	275,484	36,583	45,115	48,702	15,060	33,642	74,676	34,474	40,202	1.60	1.51
1976	192,720	299,123	40,212	50,131	54,324	17,847	36,476	82,405	38,224	44,181	1.50	1.46
1976: Apr	191,404	283,062	39,530	46,826	53,696	18,046	35,650	78,102	35,462	42,640	1.48	1.45
May	190,445	285,693	39,386	47,799	52,868	17,419	35,419	78,406	35,547	42,859	1.50	1.48
June	193,360	289,138	40,780	48,645	53,983	17,803	36,180	79,375	35,863	43,512	1.50	1.47
July	193,302	290,866	40,616	48,805	53,754	17,699	36,055	79,917	36,523	43,394	1.50	1.49
Aug	194,302	293,308	40,581	49,006	54,643	18,208	36,435	81,118	37,515	43,603	1.51	1.48
Sept	193,868	296,537	41,381	49,723	54,100	17,481	36,619	81,848	37,822	44,026	1.53	1.51
Oct	192,591	298,179	40,676	49,847	54,634	17,559	37,075	81,658	37,518	44,140	1.55	1.49
Nov	196,477	298,941	40,796	50,167	55,573	18,157	37,416	81,660	37,933	43,727	1.52	1.47
Dec	204,365	299,123	41,767	50,131	57,898	19,730	38,168	82,405	38,224	44,181	1.46	1.42
1977: Jan	202,066	301,970	41,931	50,872	56,660	19,024	37,636	83,616	38,931	44,685	1.49	1.48
Feb	207,567	303,985	43,233	51,658	58,175	19,764	38,411	83,878	38,912	44,966	1.46	1.44
Mar	214,844	307,325	43,879	52,549	59,522	20,687	38,835	85,397	39,613	45,784	1.43	1.43
Apr[p]	213,542	310,066	44,417	53,286	59,572	20,333	39,239	86,033	39,581	46,452	1.45	1.44
May[p]	---	---	---	---	59,998	20,440	39,558	---	---	---	---	---

[1] The term "business" also includes manufacturing.
[2] Monthly average for year and total for month.
[3] Book value, end of period, seasonally adjusted.
[4] For annual periods, ratio of weighted average inventories to average monthly sales; for monthly data, ratio of inventories at end of month to sales for month.

Source: Department of Commerce (Bureau of Economic Analysis and Bureau of the Census).

Source: Economic Indicators, Council of Economic Advisors.

MANUFACTURERS' SHIPMENTS, INVENTORIES, AND NEW ORDERS

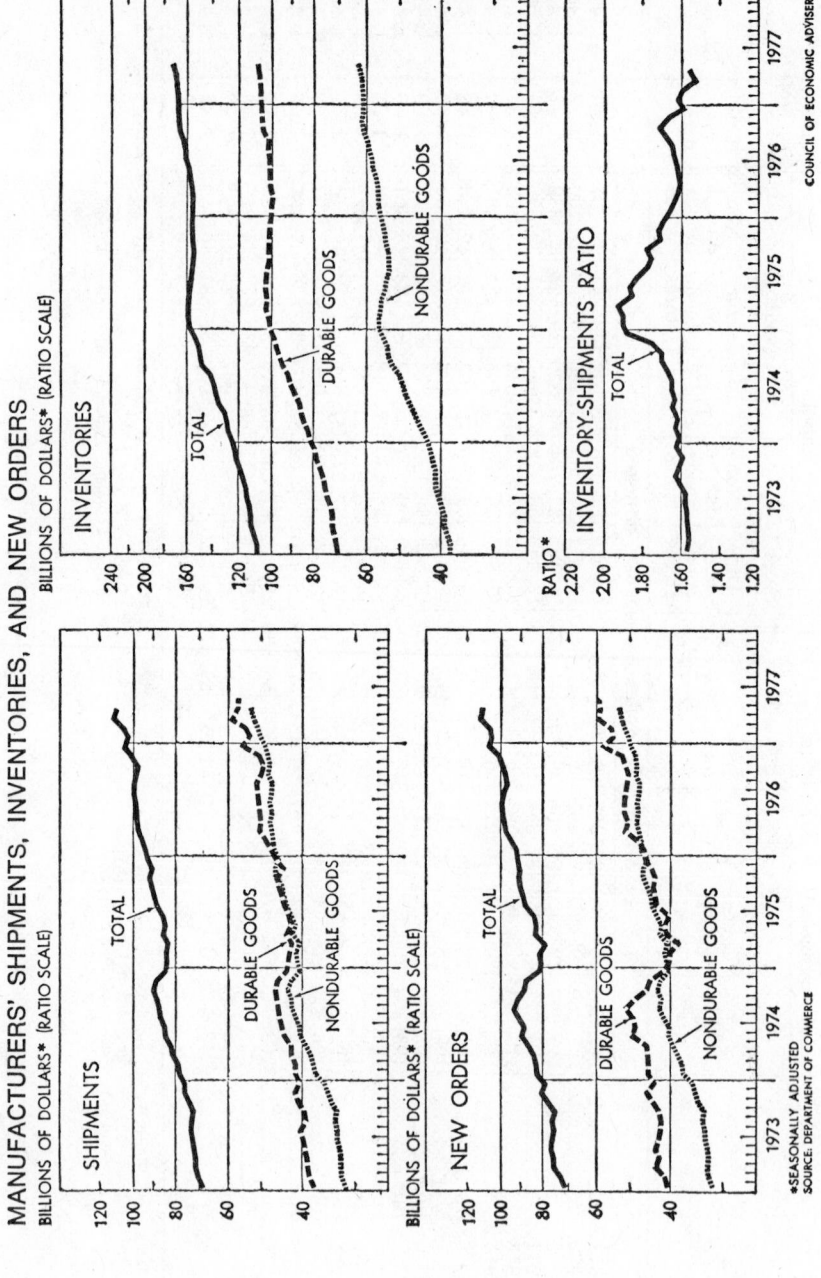

BILLIONS OF DOLLARS* (RATIO SCALE)

INVENTORIES

BILLIONS OF DOLLARS* (RATIO SCALE)

240
200
160
120
100
80
60
40

TOTAL
DURABLE GOODS
NONDURABLE GOODS

INVENTORY-SHIPMENTS RATIO

RATIO*
2.20
2.00
1.80
1.60
1.40
1.20

TOTAL

BILLIONS OF DOLLARS* (RATIO SCALE)

SHIPMENTS

120
100
80
60
40

TOTAL
DURABLE GOODS
NONDURABLE GOODS

BILLIONS OF DOLLARS* (RATIO SCALE)

NEW ORDERS

120
100
80
60
40

TOTAL
DURABLE GOODS
NONDURABLE GOODS

1973 1974 1975 1976 1977

*SEASONALLY ADJUSTED
SOURCE: DEPARTMENT OF COMMERCE

COUNCIL OF ECONOMIC ADVISERS

Period	Manufacturers' shipments [1]			Manufacturers' inventories [2]			Manufacturers' new orders [1]				Manufacturers' unfilled orders [3]	Manufacturers' inventory-shipments ratio [4]
	Total	Durable goods	Non-durable goods	Total	Durable goods	Non-durable goods	Total	Durable goods		Non-durable goods		
								Total	Capital goods industries, non-defense			
	Millions of dollars, seasonally adjusted											
1971	55,925	29,973	25,953	102,490	66,149	36,341	55,937	29,951	7,575	25,986	107,656	1.83
1972	63,042	34,042	28,999	108,072	70,098	37,974	64,246	35,142	8,947	29,104	122,362	1.67
1973	72,954	39,704	33,250	124,395	81,218	43,177	76,988	42,888	11,169	33,329	161,766	1.58
1974	84,612	44,043	40,569	157,971	101,780	56,191	86,988	46,570	12,656	40,418	190,271	1.66
1975	87,226	43,912	43,313	155,693	100,310	55,382	85,659	42,164	10,899	43,495	171,438	1.80
1976	98,184	50,392	47,792	166,587	105,729	60,858	98,513	50,697	12,837	47,816	175,453	1.64
1976: Apr--	98,178	50,146	48,033	158,134	101,033	57,101	98,415	50,245	12,476	48,170	170,687	1.61
May--	98,191	50,558	47,634	159,488	101,502	57,986	99,025	51,354	12,666	47,670	171,520	1.62
June--	98,597	50,606	47,990	161,118	102,429	58,689	99,135	51,249	12,607	47,886	172,059	1.63
July--	98,932	51,090	47,842	162,144	102,856	59,288	98,811	51,180	13,778	47,631	171,938	1.64
Aug--	99,078	51,648	47,430	163,184	103,282	59,902	97,554	50,380	12,690	47,174	170,414	1.65
Sept--	98,387	50,060	48,328	164,966	104,117	60,850	98,476	50,068	13,468	48,409	170,503	1.68
Oct--	97,281	49,267	48,014	166,674	105,589	61,085	99,244	50,993	14,302	48,252	172,468	1.71
Nov--	100,108	51,427	48,681	167,114	106,128	60,986	100,973	52,424	12,878	48,549	173,333	1.67
Dec--	104,700	55,520	49,180	166,587	105,729	60,858	106,825	57,265	14,112	49,560	175,453	1.59
1977: Jan--	103,475	53,247	50,228	167,482	106,562	60,920	105,194	54,943	14,778	50,251	177,179	1.62
Feb--	106,159	54,729	51,430	168,449	107,222	61,227	106,601	55,159	14,335	51,442	177,623	1.59
Mar--	111,443	59,051	52,392	169,379	107,685	61,694	111,927	59,299	14,667	52,628	178,105	1.52
Apr--	109,553	56,677	52,876	170,747	108,190	62,557	111,625	58,730	14,932	52,895	180,168	1.56
May⁹	---------	56,839	--------	--------	--------	--------	--------	59,050	14,832	--------	--------	--------

[1] Monthly average for year and total for month. Shipments are the same as sales.
[2] Book value, end of period.
[3] End of period.
[4] For annual periods, ratio of weighted average inventories to average monthly shipments; for monthly data, ratio of inventories at end of month to shipments for month.

Source: Department of Commerce, Bureau of the Census.

Source: Economic Indicators, Council of Economic Advisors.

Federal, State, and Local Finance

FEDERAL BUDGET RECEIPTS AND OUTLAYS AND DEBT

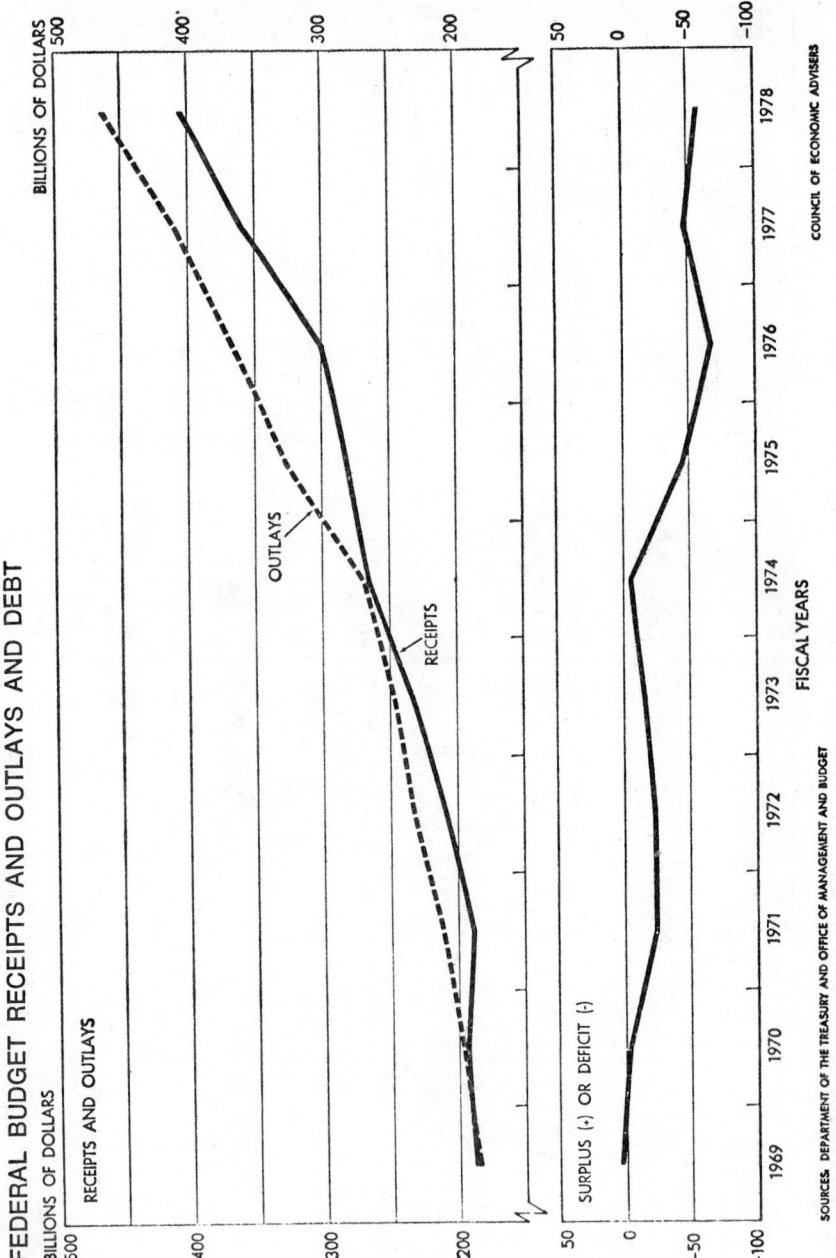

BILLIONS OF DOLLARS

RECEIPTS AND OUTLAYS
BILLIONS OF DOLLARS

500

400

300

200

OUTLAYS

RECEIPTS

SURPLUS (+) OR DEFICIT (-)

50

0

-50

-100

1969 1970 1971 1972 1973 1974 1975 1976 1977 1978

FISCAL YEARS

SOURCES: DEPARTMENT OF THE TREASURY AND OFFICE OF MANAGEMENT AND BUDGET

COUNCIL OF ECONOMIC ADVISERS

[Billions of dollars]

Period	Receipts	Outlays	Surplus or deficit (−)	Federal debt (end of period)	
				Total [1]	Held by the public
Fiscal year or period:					
1969	187.8	184.5	3.2	367.1	279.5
1970	193.7	196.6	−2.8	382.6	284.9
1971	188.4	211.4	−23.0	409.5	304.3
1972	208.6	232.0	−23.4	437.3	323.8
1973	232.2	247.1	−14.8	468.4	343.0
1974	264.9	269.6	−4.7	486.2	346.1
1975	281.0	326.1	−45.1	544.1	396.9
1976	300.0	366.5	−66.5	631.9	480.3
Transition quarter	81.8	94.7	−13.0	646.4	498.3
1977 (estimates):					
Current estimates, April 1977 [2]	359.5	408.2	−48.7	727.0	571.3
Third Concurrent Resolution [3]	356.6	409.2	−52.6		
1978 (estimates):					
Current estimates, April 1977 [2]	404.7	462.6	−57.9	802.4	637.1
First Concurrent Resolution [4]	396.3	461.0	−64.7		
October 1975–May 1976	190.1	244.7	−54.6	621.5	475.9
October 1976–May 1977 [5]	223.4	266.4	−43.1	683.0	531.7

[1] Excludes non-interest-bearing public debt securities held by IMF.
[2] Estimates from Current Budget Estimates, April 1977, Office of Management and Budget.
[3] Third Concurrent Resolution on the Budget—Fiscal year 1977, revised May 17, 1977.
[4] First Concurrent Resolution on the Budget—Fiscal year 1978, May 17, 1977.
[5] First 8 months of fiscal year 1977.

Sources: Department of the Treasury and Office of Management and Budget, except as noted.

Source: *Economic Indicators*, Council of Economic Advisors.

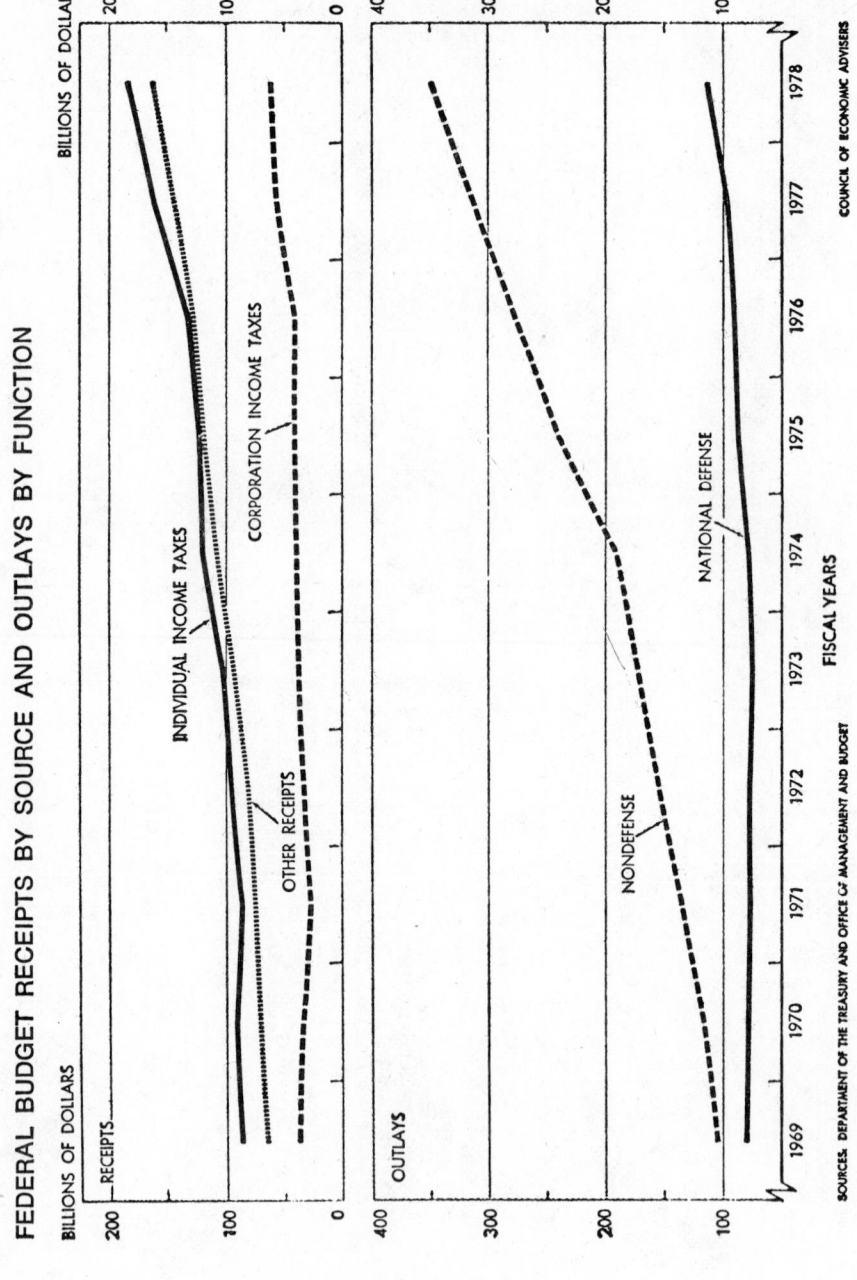

FEDERAL BUDGET RECEIPTS BY SOURCE AND OUTLAYS BY FUNCTION

[Billions of dollars]

Period	Receipts				Outlays						
	Total	Individual income taxes	Corporation income taxes	Other	Total	National defense		International affairs	Health and income security	Interest	Other
						Total	Department of Defense, military				
Fiscal year or period:											
1969	187.8	87.2	36.7	63.9	184.5	80.2	77.9	3.8	49.0	15.8	35.7
1970	193.7	90.4	32.8	70.5	196.6	79.3	77.2	3.6	56.1	18.3	39.3
1971	188.4	86.2	26.8	75.4	211.4	76.8	74.5	3.1	70.1	19.6	41.8
1972	208.6	94.7	32.2	81.7	232.0	77.4	75.2	3.9	81.4	20.6	48.8
1973	232.2	103.2	36.2	92.8	247.1	75.1	73.3	3.5	91.8	22.8	53.9
1974	264.9	119.0	38.6	107.4	269.6	78.6	77.6	4.8	106.5	28.1	51.7
1975	281.0	122.4	40.6	118.0	326.1	86.6	85.0	5.9	136.3	31.0	66.4
1976	300.0	131.6	41.4	127.0	366.5	90.0	88.0	5.1	160.9	34.6	76.0
Transition quarter	81.8	38.8	8.5	34.5	94.7	22.5	21.9	2.0	41.5	7.2	21.5
1977 ¹	359.5	160.1	55.0	144.4	408.2	97.1	96.2	6.6	177.7	37.8	89.0
1978 ¹	404.7	183.0	61.3	160.4	462.6	112.8	109.1	7.2	193.3	40.9	108.4
October 1975–May 1976 ²	190.1	81.9	23.4	84.8	244.7	59.7	59.0	3.0	109.4	22.9	49.9
October 1976–May 1977 ²	223.4	97.1	29.8	96.4	266.4	62.9	63.1	3.4	117.8	24.1	58.1

¹ Estimates from *Current Budget Estimates, April 1977.*
² First 8 months of fiscal year 1977.

Source: Department of the Treasury and Office of Management and Budget.

Source: *Economic Indicators,* Council of Economic Advisors.

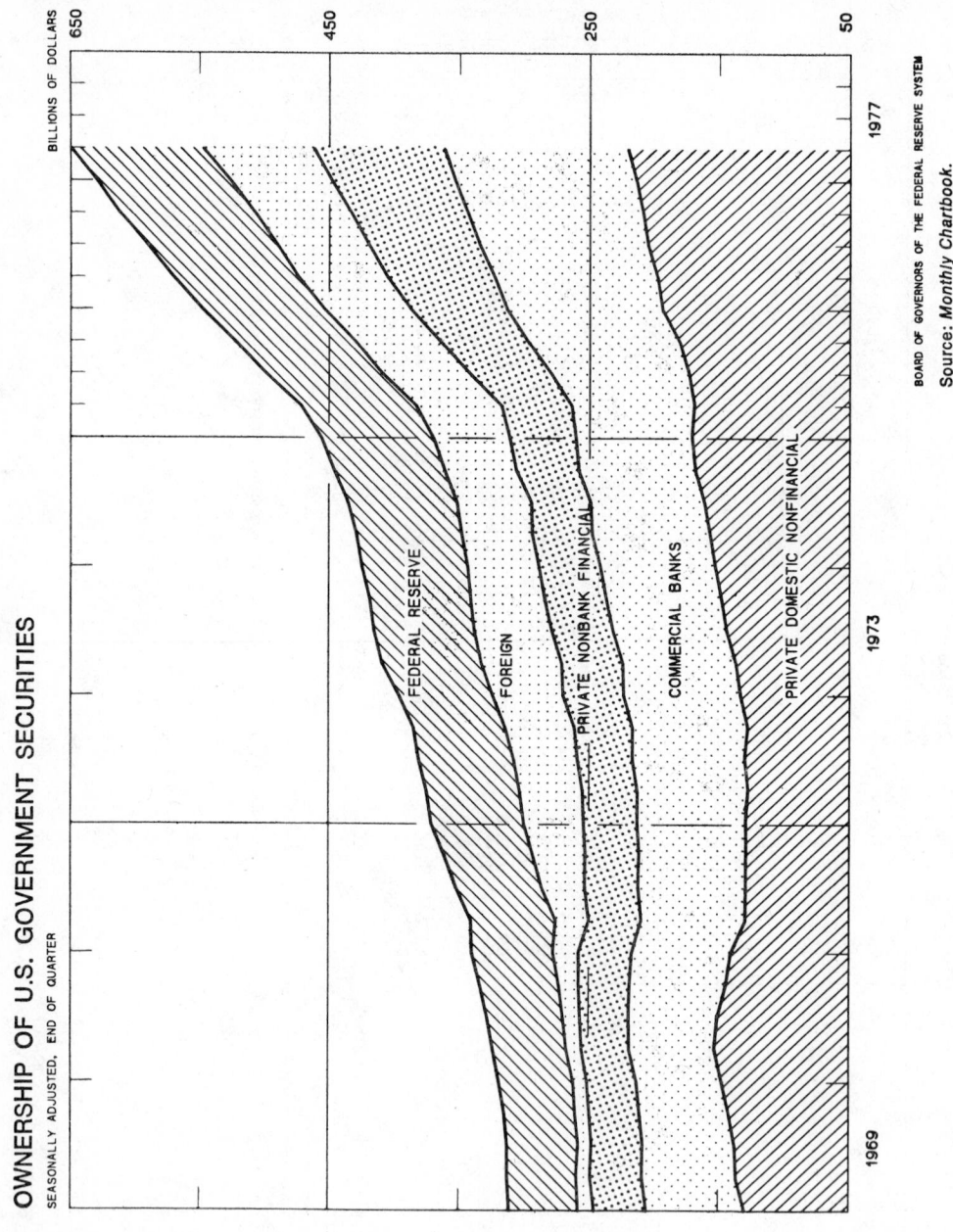

OWNERSHIP OF U.S. GOVERNMENT SECURITIES
SEASONALLY ADJUSTED, END OF QUARTER

BILLIONS OF DOLLARS

650

450

250

50

1969   1973   1977

FEDERAL RESERVE

FOREIGN

PRIVATE NONBANK FINANCIAL

COMMERCIAL BANKS

PRIVATE DOMESTIC NONFINANCIAL

BOARD OF GOVERNORS OF THE FEDERAL RESERVE SYSTEM

Source: *Monthly Chartbook.*

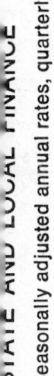

STATE AND LOCAL FINANCE

Seasonally adjusted annual rates, quarterly

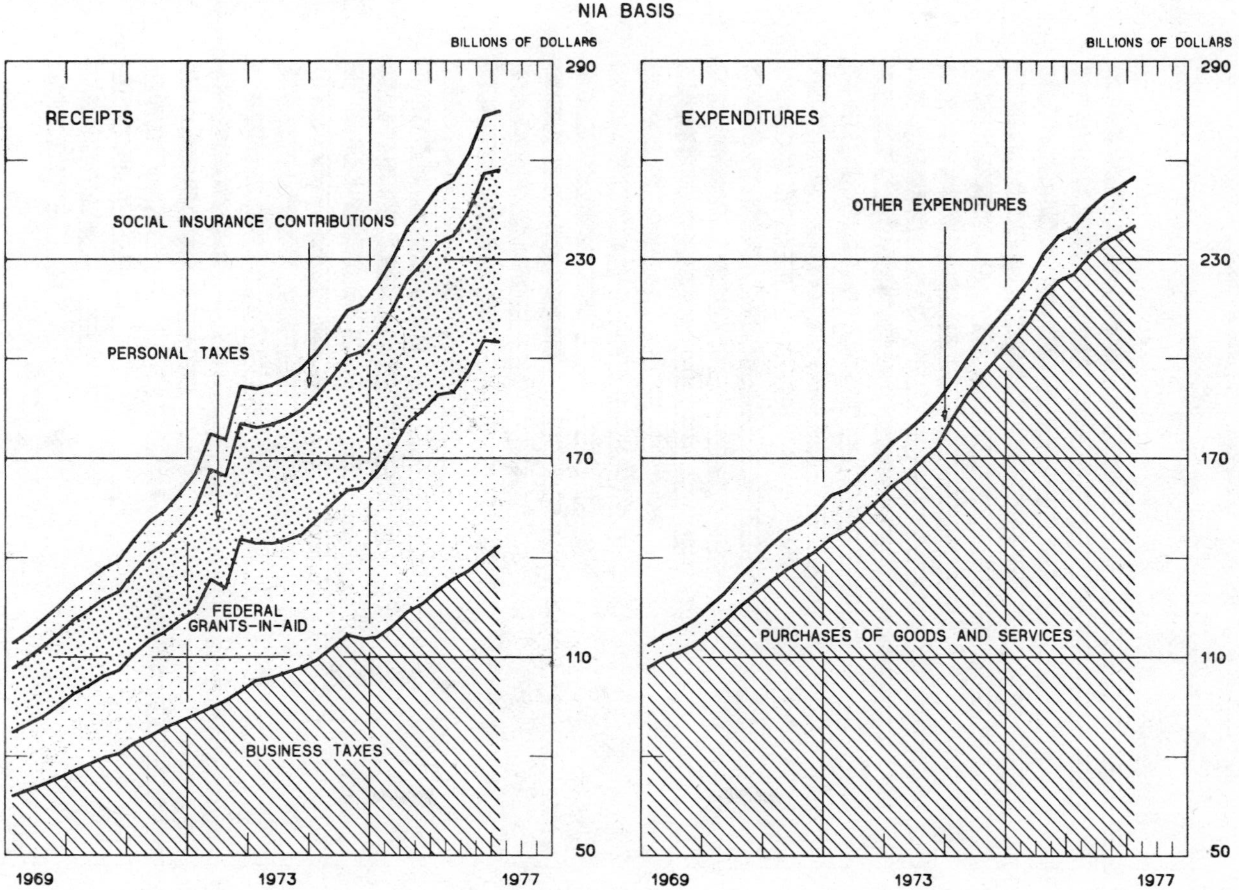

NIA BASIS

BILLIONS OF DOLLARS

RECEIPTS

SOCIAL INSURANCE CONTRIBUTIONS

PERSONAL TAXES

FEDERAL GRANTS-IN-AID

BUSINESS TAXES

EXPENDITURES

OTHER EXPENDITURES

PURCHASES OF GOODS AND SERVICES

BILLIONS OF DOLLARS

BOARD OF GOVERNORS OF THE FEDERAL RESERVE SYSTEM

Source: *Monthly Chartbook.*

STATE AND LOCAL GOVERNMENT SECURITY ISSUES

Gross proceeds

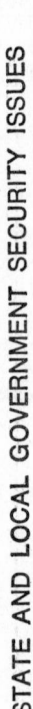

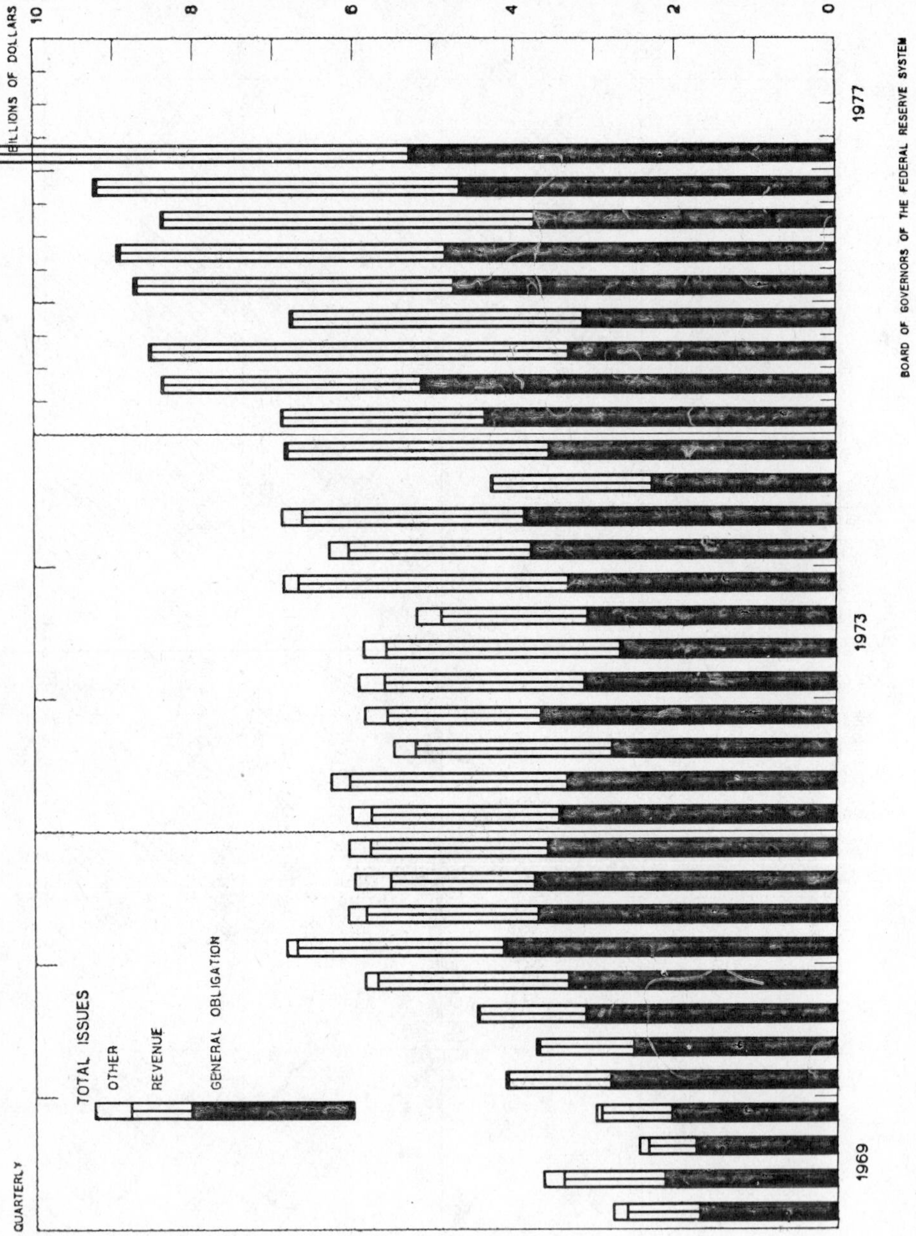
QUARTERLY
BILLIONS OF DOLLARS
10
8
6
4
2
0
TOTAL ISSUES
OTHER
REVENUE
GENERAL OBLIGATION
1969
1973
1977
BOARD OF GOVERNORS OF THE FEDERAL RESERVE SYSTEM

Source: *Monthly Chartbook.*

International Business and Trade

FINANCING EXPORTS

Many sources of financial assistance are available to exporters. First, of course, is your own working capital or bank line of credit. Use of your own facilities may, however, restrict your total cash availability even if you were to establish a separate export line of credit with your bank.

Commercial Banks More than 250 U.S. banks have qualified international banking departments with specialists familiar with particular foreign countries and experts in different types of commodities and transactions. These banks, located in all major U.S. cities, maintain correspondent relationships with smaller banks throughout the United States. This banking network enables any exporter to find assistance (for himself or his overseas customer) for his export financing needs. The larger banks also maintain correspondent relationships with banks in most foreign countries or operate their own overseas branches, providing a direct channel to overseas customers.

Factoring Houses Exporters should also be aware of factoring houses that deal in accounts receivable of American exporters. Although possibly charging higher fees, they will purchase your receivables, often without recourse, assuring you of prompt payment for your export sale.

Export Management Companies Export management companies not only will act as your export representative, but some of these professional export houses also will carry the financing for the export sale, again assuring you of immediate payment and removing from your company any foreign credit risk. For names of export management companies in your area, you may write to The National Federation of Export Management Companies, P.O. Box 7612, Washington, D.C. 20044.

Eximbank The U.S. Government also participates in the financing of America's exports. The Export-Import Bank of the United States (Eximbank) offers direct loans for large projects and equipment sales that usually require longer term financing. It cooperates with commercial banks in the United States and abroad in providing a number of financial arrangements to help U.S. exporters offer credit to their overseas buyers. It provides export credit guarantees to commercial banks that finance export sales; and, through the Foreign Credit Insurance Association (FCIA), provides insurance to American exporters which enables them to extend credit terms to their overseas buyers. In all cases, the Bank must find a "reasonable assurance of repayment" as a precondition of participating in the transaction.

Eximbank regulation and conditions of assistance are, of course, subject to change. For more information, consult your commercial bank, or write directly to the Export-Import Bank of the United States, 811 Vermont Avenue, NW., Washington, D.C. 20571. Telex 89-461.

Foreign Credit Insurance Association The FCIA administers the U.S. export credit insurance program on behalf of its member insurance companies and the Government-owned Eximbank. The private insurers cover the normal commercial credit risks, mainly the insolvency of or the prolonged payment default by the overseas buyer. Eximbank assumes all liability for the political risks including, in addition to exchange transfer delay, such hazards as war, revolution, or similar hostilities; unforeseen withdrawal or nonrenewal of a license to export or import; requisition, expropriation, confiscation, or intervention in the business of the buyer by a governmental authority; transport or insurance charges caused by interruption or diversion of shipment; and certain other government acts which may prevent or unduly delay payment and which are beyond the control of the seller or the buyer.

One of FCIA's major forms of coverage is the master policy, designed to provide under one policy substantially automatic coverage for all of an exporter's sales to overseas buyers both short- and medium-term, on credit terms ranging up to 5 years. The policy may provide political risks coverage only, or comprehensive risks coverage.

For information on other types of policies offered by FCIA, exporters should consult with FCIA at One World Trade Center, 9th Floor, New York, N.Y. 10048.

Source: Excerpted from *A Basic Guide to Exporting*, U.S. Department of Commerce.

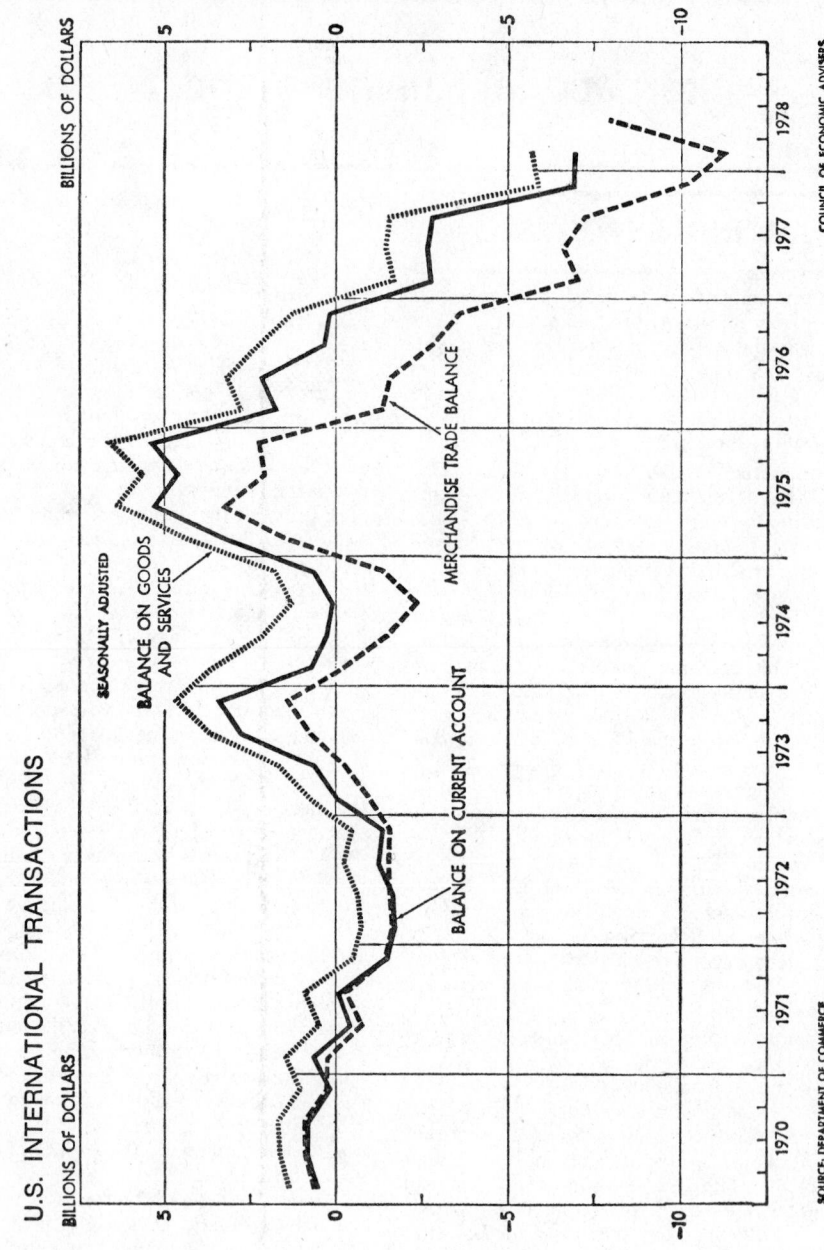

U.S. INTERNATIONAL TRANSACTIONS

BILLIONS OF DOLLARS

BILLIONS OF DOLLARS

SEASONALLY ADJUSTED

BALANCE ON GOODS AND SERVICES

MERCHANDISE TRADE BALANCE

BALANCE ON CURRENT ACCOUNT

SOURCE: DEPARTMENT OF COMMERCE

COUNCIL OF ECONOMIC ADVISERS

[Millions of dollars; quarterly data seasonally adjusted]

Period	Merchandise [1][2]			Investment income [3]			Net military transactions	Net travel and transportation receipts	Other services, net [3]	Balance on goods and services [1]	Remittances, pensions, and other unilateral transfers [1]	Balance on current account
	Exports	Imports	Net balance	Receipts	Payments	Net						
1971	43,319	-45,579	-2,260	12,688	-5,436	7,252	-2,893	-2,315	2,509	2,294	-3,701	-1,407
1972	49,381	-55,797	-6,416	14,694	-6,544	8,150	-3,621	-3,028	2,789	-2,125	-3,854	-5,979
1973	71,410	-70,499	911	21,697	-9,655	12,042	-2,287	-3,086	3,185	10,766	-3,881	6,885
1974	98,306	-103,649	-5,343	27,541	-12,084	15,457	-2,080	-3,105	3,975	8,905	-7,186	1,719
1975	107,088	-98,041	9,047	25,359	-12,564	12,795	-876	-2,522	4,617	23,060	-4,615	18,445
1976	114,694	-124,047	-9,353	29,244	-13,311	15,933	312	-2,245	4,714	9,361	-5,022	4,339
1977	120,554	-151,658	-31,104	32,100	-14,593	17,507	1,334	-3,044	4,749	-10,514	-4,708	-15,221
1977: I	29,478	-36,496	-7,018	7,796	-3,197	4,599	568	-907	1,136	-1,623	-1,126	-2,749
II	30,630	-37,258	-6,628	8,088	-3,601	4,487	295	-759	1,171	-1,427	-1,243	-2,670
III	31,012	-38,265	-7,253	8,220	-3,610	4,610	467	-677	1,260	-1,591	-1,277	-2,868
IV	29,434	-39,639	-10,205	7,997	-4,185	3,812	5	-701	1,183	-5,870	-1,064	-6,934
1978: I p	30,664	-41,865	-11,201	9,432	-4,665	4,767	307	-824	1,252	-5,700	-1,254	-6,954
II p	35,014	-42,978	-7,964									

[1] Excludes military grants.
[2] Adjusted from Census data for differences in timing and coverage.
[3] Fees and royalties from U.S. direct investments abroad or from foreign direct investments in the United States are excluded from investment income and included in other services, net.

Source: *Economic Indicators*, Council of Economic Advisors.

NOTE.—Merchandise trade data revised for 1977. Other data to be revised later.

Source: Department of Commerce, Bureau of Economic Analysis.

FOREIGN TRADE OF THE UNITED STATES

Unless otherwise stated in footnotes below, data through 1974 and descriptive notes are as shown in the 1975 edition of BUSINESS STATISTICS	1976	1977	1977				
	Annual		June	July	Aug.	Sept.	Oct.
VALUE OF EXPORTS							
Exports (mdse.), incl. reexports, total♂.....mil. $..	114,992.4	r121,212.3	r10,282.4	r9,742.8	r8,987.1	r10,371.1	r9,557.4
Excl. Dept. of Defense shipments........do....	114,802.3	r121,150.4	r10,279.3	r9,739.6	r8,984.1	r10,367.5	r9,554.3
Seasonally adjusted.................do....	....	....	r10,090.6	r10,372.3	r9,683.2	r11,038.6	r9,357.4
By geographic regions:							
Africa..................................do....	5,205.6	5,545.6	458.9	486.7	413.4	541.6	378.6
Asia....................................do....	29,728.5	31,428.9	2,679.5	2,577.5	2,413.1	2,526.6	2,246.8
Australia and Oceania...................do....	2,689.9	2,876.5	215.0	244.8	249.6	278.2	237.5
Europe.................................do....	35,900.6	36,296.0	3,087.9	2,745.3	2,434.2	3,009.4	2,586.7
Northern North America.................do....	24,111.0	25,752.1	2,322.8	1,817.9	1,768.3	2,145.2	2,381.3
Southern North America.................do....	8,368.0	8,660.5	708.2	794.8	737.3	809.2	767.2
South America...........................do....	8,595.4	9,274.8	765.3	817.6	818.9	1,021.1	672.1
By leading countries:							
Africa:							
Egypt................................do....	810.0	982.4	73.9	101.6	65.5	78.4	43.2
Republic of South Africa............do....	1,347.6	1,054.4	76.3	87.8	82.8	84.0	77.3
Asia; Australia and Oceania:							
Australia, including New Guinea......do....	2,199.2	2,375.6	181.6	202.3	210.3	233.2	196.2
India................................do....	1,135.8	778.6	94.3	62.7	46.3	48.7	62.3
Pakistan.............................do....	394.3	292.7	21.4	38.1	16.5	14.8	21.2
Malaysia.............................do....	535.6	560.7	37.4	45.1	45.2	49.0	79.7
Indonesia............................do....	1,034.6	763.2	77.4	65.9	53.3	51.8	67.6
Philippines..........................do....	818.2	875.9	83.3	69.2	88.2	88.8	54.8
Japan................................do....	10,144.7	10,522.1	814.0	871.6	787.4	801.9	752.2
Europe:							
France...............................do....	3,446.3	3,503.2	287.5	247.2	245.6	321.4	247.9
German Democratic Republic (formerly E. Germany)........................mil. $..	64.9	36.1	.9	4.5	1.3	.3	3.1
Federal Republic of Germany (formerly W. Germany) ....mil. $..	5,730.8	5,982.0	523.8	448.9	428.5	501.9	440.8
Italy................................do....	3,071.1	2,787.5	227.7	182.5	169.9	208.1	175.9
Union of Soviet Socialist Republics....do....	2,309.6	1,627.5	107.5	91.4	48.4	88.8	39.2
United Kingdom.......................do....	4,801.2	5,380.1	568.9	465.7	382.4	440.0	387.6
North and South America:							
Canada...............................do....	24,106.4	25,748.8	2,322.5	1,817.6	1,768.1	2,144.8	2,381.0
Latin American Republics, total♀......do....	15,487.4	16,346.5	1,340.6	1,486.9	1,419.4	1,676.1	1,305.5
Argentina............................do....	543.7	731.1	78.9	65.2	65.6	59.5	65.9
Brazil...............................do....	2,808.8	2,482.3	174.8	225.1	218.8	317.8	132.3
Chile................................do....	507.7	520.2	34.3	40.0	50.7	45.1	52.6
Colombia.............................do....	702.7	782.0	63.4	60.8	64.6	85.2	72.9
Mexico...............................do....	4,990.0	4,806.1	371.8	477.6	408.6	418.2	454.8
Venezuela............................do....	2,627.8	3,170.5	272.1	288.3	259.6	354.4	228.6
Exports of U.S. merchandise, total♂.........do....	113,318.5	117,962.7	10,040.1	9,347.6	8,708.6	10,148.0	9,119.1
Excluding military grant-aid............do....	113,128.4	117,900.9	10,037.1	9,344.4	8,705.7	10,144.4	9,116.5
Agricultural products, total.............do....	22,997.6	23,671.0	1,882.1	1,748.9	1,541.6	1,733.8	1,705.1
Nonagricultural products, total.........do....	90,320.9	94,291.8	8,158.0	7,598.8	7,167.0	8,414.2	7,414.0
By commodity groups and principal commodities:							
Food and live animals♀ ....mil. $..	15,710.1	r14,115.7	1,148.0	1,165.1	r1,137.1	r1,247.6	987.5
Meats and preparations (incl. poultry).do....	798.0	796.9	62.6	67.0	67.5	75.3	65.1
Grains and cereal preparations........do....	10,910.9	8,754.8	718.3	725.1	684.0	777.7	556.1

r Revised.   1 Annual total reflects revisions not distributed to the monthly data.
2 Beginning Jan. 1978, data are based on a new classification system and include nonmonetary gold; the overall total and the commodity groups (but not the items within the groups) have been revised back to Jan. 1977 to reflect these changes.
  ♂ Data may not equal the sum of the geographic regions, or commodity groups and principal commodities, because of revisions to the totals not reflected in the component items.
  ♀ Includes data not shown separately.

		1978						
Nov.	Dec.	Jan.	Feb.	Mar.	Apr.	May	June	July
·9,692.6	·11,399.9	20,366.9	9,518.5	12,079.4	12,069.7	12,494.6	12,457.3	10,944.7
·9,690.2	·11,396.1	20,364.4	9,514.6	12,074.2	12,064.2	12,478.9	12,477.3	10,934.0
·9,477.9	·10,999.0	210,014.3	9,922.4	10,912.1	11,634.9	11,753.7	12,125.7	11,792.5
430.0	518.9							
2,423.4	3,277.1							
228.3	289.7							
2,755.3	3,488.3							
2,222.7	1,990.1							
755.2	849.2							
779.7	891.6							
68.2	86.2							
72.7	81.1							
163.4	244.2							
74.0	92.4							
17.7	9.3							
40.9	53.6							
74.3	62.3							
67.2	85.5							
875.8	1,067.4							
281.1	318.3							
8.3	1.6							
459.0	590.1							
234.4	252.0							
134.7	173.4							
370.1	504.2							
2,222.5	1,990.0							
1,398.1	1,590.7							
73.2	73.3							
202.5	211.6							
40.9	49.7							
59.8	79.8							
437.6	488.0							
283.1	316.7							
9,478.3	11,131.5							
9,475.8	11,127.7							
2,081.5	2,323.9							
7,396.8	8,807.6							
1,142.9	1,348.2	21,132.7	1,271.5	1,465.7	1,472.8	1,684.2	1,737.1	1,540.6
67.3	77.5							
677.9	856.9							

FOREIGN TRADE OF THE UNITED STATES (continued)

Unless otherwise stated in footnotes below, data through 1974 and descriptive notes are as shown in the 1975 edition of BUSINESS STATISTICS	1976	1977	1977				
	Annual		June	July	Aug.	Sept.	Oct.
Beverages and tobacco_____do____	1,523.5	1,846.8	142.5	156.6	155.6	201.8	67.3
Crude materials, inedible, exc. fuels ♀ ....do____	10,890.7	r13,086.3	r1,071.8	r 937.1	r 720.5	822.7	r1,042.7
Cotton, raw, excl. linters and waste____do____	1,048.7	1,529.5	167.5	98.4	61.6	67.0	45.9
Soybeans, exc. canned or prepared_____do____	3,315.4	4,393.2	294.8	223.3	133.4	113.6	448.1
Metal ores, concentrates, and scrap____do____	1,284.9	1,197.0	140.6	125.0	89.5	104.5	82.2
Mineral fuels, lubricants, etc. ♀ _____mil. $__	4,225.8	r4,183.6	398.1	r 398.4	333.7	401.8	r 367.0
Coal and related products_____do____	2,988.2	2,730.4	295.5	258.8	206.7	259.7	259.0
Petroleum and products_____do____	997.6	1,275.6	98.3	108.8	109.2	134.1	92.3
Oils and fats, animal and vegetable_____do____	978.1	1,308.7	120.1	r 126.2	102.8	105.7	98.1
Chemicals_____do____	9,958.7	r10,812.3	917.6	r 945.7	r 878.7	r1,064.9	737.2
Manufactured goods ♀¶_____do____	11,206.1	r10,857.0	r 949.0	r 854.2	r 831.6	r1,014.3	r 742.5
Textiles_____do____	1,970.9	1,958.9	169.6	156.9	140.0	194.8	120.7
Iron and steel_____do____	1,906.8	1,660.5	139.5	132.0	133.7	152.7	113.1
Nonferrous base metals_____do____	1,088.4	1,058.4	93.4	87.0	80.2	97.2	61.4
Machinery and transport equipment, total mil. $__	49,501.2	r50,247.6	r4,261.0	r3,798.7	r3,622.4	r4,303.4	r4,157.9
Machinery, total ♀ _____do____	31,290.8	32,516.6	2,753.7	2,627.7	2,432.5	2,860.0	2,442.6
Agricultural_____do____	2,107.7	1,871.1	163.4	156.9	125.5	147.3	125.7
Metalworking_____do____	949.2	730.3	59.8	55.0	48.2	68.9	42.3
Construction, excav. and mining__do____	4,945.3	4,405.5	374.2	362.2	305.4	404.6	298.0
Electrical_____do____	9,278.5	10,285.3	851.6	844.2	778.4	901.7	819.5
Transport equipment, total_____do____	18,210.4	18,520.0	1,572.2	1,204.8	1,244.7	1,507.5	1,794.0
Motor vehicles and parts_____do____	10,954.2	11,796.5	1,037.8	786.7	711.8	1,048.9	1,119.5
Miscellaneous manufactured articles_____do____	6,574.9	r8,233.9	724.5	r 683.6	651.3	744.4	r 670.7
Commodities not classified_____do____	2,749.4	r4,313.6	335.1	515.7	375.5	250.9	493.7
VALUE OF IMPORTS							
General imports, total_____do____	120,677.6	r147,685.0	14,046.4	r12,430.5	12,044.5	r12,452.4	r12,497.5
Seasonally adjusted_____do____			13,334.3	r12,482.9	12,101.4	r12,941.6	r12,586.9
By geographic regions:							
Africa_____do____	12,644.0	17,023.9	1,583.7	1,306.1	1,382.5	1,466.8	1,264.3
Asia_____do____	39,366.8	49,421.7	4,625.6	4,228.9	4,593.1	4,382.4	4,117.3
Australia and Oceania_____do____	1,671.2	1,719.6	142.6	148.0	179.5	149.9	145.3
Europe_____do____	23,645.6	28,330.9	2,603.8	2,376.6	2,631.8	2,389.1	2,229.2
Northern North America_____do____	26,246.8	29,375.4	2,791.4	2,238.5	2,146.1	2,487.5	2,495.9
Southern North America_____do____	9,348.9	11,590.7	1,005.5	901.3	992.4	808.8	842.3
South America_____do____	7,760.6	9,343.1	816.4	664.8	734.7	790.3	718.6
By leading countries:							
Africa:							
Egypt_____do____	92.5	170.0	18.6	16.2	12.9	27.9	36.9
Republic of South Africa_____do____	924.8	1,268.8	93.1	101.6	100.2	117.1	111.7
Asia; Australia and Oceania:							
Australia, including New Guinea_____do____	1,285.7	1,264.2	104.8	95.1	127.1	117.2	124.7
India_____do____	708.3	781.1	75.0	63.1	64.3	67.2	63.8
Pakistan_____do____	69.8	57.0	5.1	7.4	4.2	3.7	3.1
Malaysia_____do____	939.6	1,321.6	117.0	109.9	143.6	113.1	102.5
Indonesia_____do____	3,004.3	3,491.3	319.8	340.4	272.4	296.7	207.5
Philippines_____do____	882.9	1,103.2	110.8	89.5	99.0	120.2	71.4
Japan_____do____	15,504.2	18,622.7	1,619.8	1,520.7	1,763.3	1,624.2	1,620.4
Europe:							
France_____do____	2,508.8	3,030.7	268.5	270.6	298.4	250.3	281.3
German Democratic Republic (formerly E. Germany)_____mil. $__	13.6	16.7	1.4	.8	1.3	2.2	.9
Federal Republic of Germany (formerly W. Germany)_____mil. $__	5,592.0	7,215.3	661.7	625.5	648.7	627.0	605.6
Italy_____do____	2,529.8	3,037.5	276.9	243.1	311.3	252.9	221.0
Union of Soviet Socialist Republics____do____	220.2	234.4	21.0	24.8	26.0	10.9	16.0
United Kingdom_____do____	4,254.3	5,067.9	507.0	416.2	498.1	459.1	380.3

Revised. ♀ Includes data not shown separately.
¶ Manufactured goods-- classified chiefly by material.

		1978						
Nov.	Dec.	Jan.	Feb.	Mar.	Apr.	May	June	July
142.4	282.6	²138.0	168.0	213 6	144.3	143.6	141.5	161.6
ʳ1,131.5	1,179.6	²1,049.8	1,063.4	1,337.5	1,388.6	1,466.5	1,353.9	992.5
103.1	156.6							
520.0	355.3							
69.9	111.5							
362.1	315.3	188.9	141.0	165.2	284.5	363.6	424.0	321.7
243.4	181.0							
103.9	118.0							
112.5	116.0	96.0	97.2	141.5	145.4	119.3	132.1	130.7
736.0	1,037.4	830.2	883.2	1,031.1	971.3	1,018.7	1,083.4	1,077.2
815.4	ʳ977.1	829.9	848.4	1,067.7	988.7	1,100.4	1,092.5	939.5
135.7	185.5							
138.7	136.7							
69.4	103.3							
ʳ4,074.7	ʳ4,768.7	3,852.0	3,941.9	5,144.4	5,098.2	5,132.2	5,075.2	4,486.8
2,644.2	3,064.7							
135.7	159.3							
41.9	73.8							
320.8	404.7							
878.5	971.2							
1,501.5	1,787.3							
1,015.4	995.8							
692.9	741.8	665.6	689.6	878.5	854.6	908.8	857.2	777.9
312.3	434.8	433.6	237.5	390.4	511.1	312.8	395.0	351.6
ʳ12,270.1	ʳ13,372.0	12,717.7	13,286.4	14,547.3	14,486.0	14,199.2	14,514.5	14,703.9
ʳ12,406.6	13,474.2	12,380.9	14,440.2	13,699.3	14,496.1	13,992.1	13,722.7	14,779.3
1,494.8	1,476.6							
3,826.3	4,503.6							
101.9	215.0							
2,029.4	2,783.4							
2,765.3	2,573.5							
893.5	990.0							
686.7	764.4							
15.8	2.1							
129.0	155.7							
86.4	155.3							
79.2	66.1							
3.1	5.3							
109.6	130.8							
250.3	283.3							
91.3	119.1							
1,559.1	1,807.1							
223.4	300.2							
.7	2.6							
569.1	771.3							
215.1	279.0							
18.8	12.5							
333.9	472.0							

FOREIGN TRADE OF THE UNITED STATES (concluded)

Unless otherwise stated in footnotes below, data through 1974 and descriptive notes are as shown in the 1975 edition of BUSINESS STATISTICS	1976	1977	1977				
	Annual		June	July	Aug.	Sept.	Oct.
North and South America:							
Canada..od....	26,237.1	29,355.7	2,789.0	2,231.7	2,142.8	2,485.7	2,494.8
Latin American Republics, total ♀....do....	13,228.3	16,335.3	1,424.7	1,197.2	1,304.1	1,268.9	1,210.8
Argentina..do....	307.9	383.3	28.5	33.5	37.3	26.3	35.0
Brazil...do....	1,736.6	2,245.9	193.5	168.0	182.2	141.2	155.2
Chile..do....	221.6	260.8	17.6	24.2	18.5	18.5	19.1
Colombia...do....	654.8	821.6	62.4	41.2	35.7	51.1	77.4
Mexico ....do....	3,598.1	4,684.8	417.4	344.5	369.5	322.5	377.6
Venezuela ....do....	3,574.4	4,071.9	348.4	296.6	343.9	411.3	311.1
By commodity groups and principal commodities:							
Agricultural products, total.............mil. $..	11,179.3	13,538.3	1,251.7	1,010.5	1,019.9	1,013.3	835.6
Nonagricultural products, total..........do....	109,510.4	133,278.4	12,318.0	10,849.3	11,641.6	11,462.4	10,978.1
Food and live animals ♀..................do....	10,267.6	12,557.8	1,156.8	980.3	884.8	873.7	812.9
Cocoa or cacao beans.......................do....	357.9	485.5	43.6	38.7	37.9	25.3	36.1
Coffee..do....	2,632.3	3,860.9	360.5	244.7	215.1	177.5	152.7
Meats and preparations......................do....	1,447.0	1,273.2	102.7	106.4	112.9	111.4	82.8
Sugar...do....	1,154.0	1,079.1	78.8	86.2	89.6	108.4	89.4
Beverages and tobacco.....................do....	1,623.7	1,669.4	145.5	111.2	162.3	182.9	137.8
Crude materials, inedible, exc. fuels ♀...do....	7,014.1	8,486.2	839.1	714.7	771.3	744.6	737.4
Metal ores.......................................do....	2,250.9	2,234.4	246.1	306.5	238.9	197.8	181.8
Paper base stocks.............................do....	1,275.5	1,252.4	127.2	94.8	113.6	91.4	90.3
Textile fibers...................................do....	249.3	225.1	24.4	20.2	23.5	15.7	12.6
Rubber...do....	520.0	650.3	58.2	60.3	40.5	62.3	59.6
Minerals fuels, lubricants, etc..........do....	33,999.6	44,537.2	4,305.8	3,911.3	3,651.4	3,720.5	3,634.9
Petroleum and products.....................do....	31,797.9	41,526.1	3,779.3	3,331.2	3,556.4	3,538.6	3,172.3
Oils and fats, animal and vegetable......do....	463.9	530.7	70.6	41.8	52.6	41.7	29.6
Chemicals..do....	4,772.4	4,970.4	449.2	399.4	421.8	436.4	349.1
Manufactured goods ♀ ◄...................do....	17,621.9	21,367.0	2,010.5	1,784.1	1,863.5	1,888.7	1,869.3
Iron and steel..................................do....	4,347.6	5,804.4	568.9	488.2	528.2	593.5	511.9
Newsprint..do....	1,742.4	1,871.8	174.0	139.4	160.3	149.1	156.9
Nonferrous metals.............................do....	3,506.3	3,938.4	365.1	334.7	371.7	307.9	300.2
Textiles...do....	1,634.9	1,772.4	156.3	141.2	169.2	156.6	139.3
Machinery and transport equipment....mil. $..	29,824.7	36,406.8	3,419.1	2,995.2	2,761.3	2,995.9	3,301.5
Machinery, total ♀..........................do....	15,184.5	17,663.8	1,623.5	1,490.3	1,534.7	1,531.2	1,505.9
Metalworking....................................do....	362.1	433.5	37.1	32.6	39.8	39.7	32.9
Electrical...do....	7,424.3	8,432.0	781.7	733.8	741.4	766.6	761.3
Transport equipment.......................do....	14,640.2	17,829.9	1,671.1	1,391.4	1,317.9	1,343.7	1,563.5
Automobiles and parts.......................do....	13,104.0	15,842.0	1,474.2	1,234.5	1,118.3	1,193.8	1,387.9
Miscellaneous manufactured articles.....do....	12,564.1	13,809.4	1,257.0	1,261.8	1,231.2	1,257.4	1,341.1
Commodities not classified................do....	2,537.7	3,335.7	392.7	230.7	244.2	308.4	280.5
Indexes							
Exports (U.S. mdse., excl. military grant-aid):							
Unit value...................................1967=100..	202.1	►211.8	212.6	211.3	211.0	212.2	210.6
Quantity..do....	182.7	►181.7	184.9	173.2	161.5	187.2	169.5
Value...do....	369.1	►384.7	393.0	365.9	340.9	397.2	357.0
General imports:							
Unit value..do....	248.8	►269.2	268.7	270.4	273.3	273.4	272.6
Quantity..do....	182.1	►204.2	227.3	197.0	207.6	204.7	194.7
Value...do....	452.9	►549.8	610.9	532.7	567.4	559.5	530.8
Shipping Weight and Value							
Waterborne trade:							
Exports (incl. reexports):							
Shipping weight...............thous. sh. tons..	283,070	►274,429	24,062	24,085	21,624	24,610	22,218
Value..mil. $..	64,712	►65,387	5,617	5,490	4,880	5,947	4,151
General imports:							
Shipping weight...............thous. sh. tons..	517,450	►612,798	56,066	49,434	54,324	53,204	49,016
Value..mil. $..	81,171	►103,038	9,495	8,488	9,281	8,773	7,906

Source: *Survey of Current Business.*

		1978						
Nov.	Dec.	Jan.	Feb.	Mar.	Apr.	May	June	July
2,763.7	2,572.4	--------	--------	--------	--------	--------	--------	--------
1,262.6	1,445.8	--------	--------	--------	--------	--------	--------	--------
39.8	43.2	--------	--------	--------	--------	--------	--------	--------
125.8	223.6	--------	--------	--------	--------	--------	--------	--------
14.1	33.6	--------	--------	--------	--------	--------	--------	--------
68.4	86.1	--------	--------	--------	--------	--------	--------	--------
428.0	451.0	--------	--------	--------	--------	--------	--------	--------
283.2	252.7	--------	--------	--------	--------	--------	--------	--------
803.1	1,309.8	--------	--------	--------	--------	--------	--------	--------
10,995.4	11,997.4	--------	--------	--------	--------	--------	--------	--------
901.6	1,294.6	1,126.9	1,111.4	1,257.5	1,161.5	1,143.4	1,045.9	1,126.1
21.0	23.0	--------	--------	--------	--------	--------	--------	--------
221.0	316.0	--------	--------	--------	--------	--------	--------	--------
63.0	157.5	--------	--------	--------	--------	--------	--------	--------
76.3	185.4	--------	--------	--------	--------	--------	--------	--------
105.0	159.8	138.1	162.4	174.7	201.5	189.2	212.7	177.4
715.2	781.2	650.4	675.2	768.5	712.4	841.4	769.8	788.0
218.1	205.0	--------	--------	--------	--------	--------	--------	--------
115.8	95.2	--------	--------	--------	--------	--------	--------	--------
7.7	18.0	--------	--------	--------	--------	--------	--------	--------
31.5	69.5	--------	--------	--------	--------	--------	--------	--------
3,702.9	3,153.0	3,422.2	3,502.3	3,431.2	3,513.5	3,234.1	3,471.5	3,380.1
3,322.1	3,223.0	--------	--------	--------	--------	--------	--------	--------
39.0	41.1	29.3	46.6	46.0	42.7	51.5	46.7	49.4
311.6	549.0	418.9	472.7	604.2	611.6	583.9	547.2	546.9
1,763.0	2,117.6	1,982.9	2,195.4	2,334.1	2,383.0	2,359.3	2,301.0	2,418.3
557.7	612.1	--------	--------	--------	--------	--------	--------	--------
175.6	176.6	--------	--------	--------	--------	--------	--------	--------
311.3	377.4	--------	--------	--------	--------	--------	--------	--------
118.8	181.3	--------	--------	--------	--------	--------	--------	--------
3,190.1	3,643.1	3,392.7	3,573.2	4,050.7	4,085.5	4,020.4	4,132.9	4,108.2
1,399.2	1,668.8	--------	--------	--------	--------	--------	--------	--------
31.2	46.7	--------	--------	--------	--------	--------	--------	--------
685.7	763.9	--------	--------	--------	--------	--------	--------	--------
1,645.5	1,766.3	--------	--------	--------	--------	--------	--------	--------
1,480.9	1,535.4	--------	--------	--------	--------	--------	--------	--------
1,118.9	1,305.4	1,227.9	1,293.7	1,511.1	1,439.7	1,460.0	1,651.5	1,782.5
414.6	327.2	328.4	253.5	369.2	334.8	316.0	335.2	327.0
213.0	215.4	219.9	219.6	219.4	223.0	224.0	--------	--------
174.2	202.3	164.1	162.8	211.1	208.2	213.9	--------	--------
371.0	435.7	360.8	357.5	463.3	464.2	479.0	--------	--------
275.5	271.1	275.6	282.5	288.1	288.1	287.2	--------	--------
192.5	220.6	207.2	211.6	227.0	226.3	222.5	--------	--------
530.3	598.0	571.0	597.8	653.8	651.9	639.1	--------	--------
22,978	24,594	18,144	18,930	--------	--------	--------	--------	--------
4,625	6,371	4,947	5,108	--------	--------	--------	--------	--------
48,176	56,856	44,657	45,953	--------	--------	--------	--------	--------
7,312	10,620	8,680	9,132	--------	--------	--------	--------	--------

International Business and Financial Comparisons

ANNUAL PERCENT CHANGE IN MANUFACTURING UNIT LABOR COSTS, 12 COUNTRIES, 1960–1976

Country	Unit labor costs				1976²		Unit labor costs in U.S. dollars				1976	
	1960–73¹	1974	1975	1976	1st half	2d half	1960–73¹	1974	1975	1976	1st half	2d half
United States........	2.1	14.4	11.0	0.9	-2.7	3.0	2.1	14.4	11.0	0.9	-2.7	3.0
Canada...............	1.9	12.3	14.7	8.9	8.9	8.8	2.0	14.8	10.2	12.3	11.4	13.2
Japan................	3.8	29.2	18.6	-3.7	-3.3	-4.0	5.2	20.1	16.5	-3.6	-5.9	-1.2
France...............	3.2	14.0	19.2	1.3	.6	1.4	2.9	5.3	33.8	-9.1	-8.7	-10.0
Germany..............	3.5	8.9	7.5	-2.6	-5.1	-.4	5.9	11.7	13.1	-5.0	-13.2	4.0
Italy................	5.1	18.7	34.9	10.2	.....	.....	5.4	6.1	34.5	-13.4	.....	.....
United Kingdom.......	4.2	22.8	33.3	11.8	15.0	8.5	2.6	17.2	26.6	-9.2	-7.2	-11.1
Six foreign countries.....	3.3	17.4	18.7	1.7	.....	.....	4.3	13.0	19.4	-5.5	.....	.....
Belgium..............	3.4	14.2	16.8	.....	1.0	³2.7	4.5	14.0	23.8	.....	-10.1	³.2
Denmark..............	3.9	15.2	12.9	.5	-1.3	2.4	3.9	14.1	19.7	-4.2	-11.2	2.8
Netherlands..........	4.8	11.3	18.2	.....	1.0	³-5.0	6.1	15.3	25.7	.....	-9.6	³-6.6
Sweden...............	3.1	13.7	21.9	20.3	27.2	14.0	3.8	11.7	30.4	14.4	14.4	15.0
Switzerland..........	3.2	11.0	11.6	-6.0	-11.0	-1.0	4.5	18.0	28.3	-2.5	-12.0	6.9
Eleven foreign countries........	3.4	16.8	18.6	.....	.....	.....	4.4	13.3	20.4	.....	.....	.....
Nine European countries........	3.7	13.7	18.8	.....	.....	.....	4.6	11.2	22.2	.....	.....	.....

¹ Percent changes computed from the least squares trend of the logarithms of the index numbers.
² Percent change over same period of 1975.
³ Third quarter.
NOTE: Dashes indicate data not available.

COMMERCIAL PAPER RATES, UNITED STATES AND CANADA

MONTHLY AVERAGES

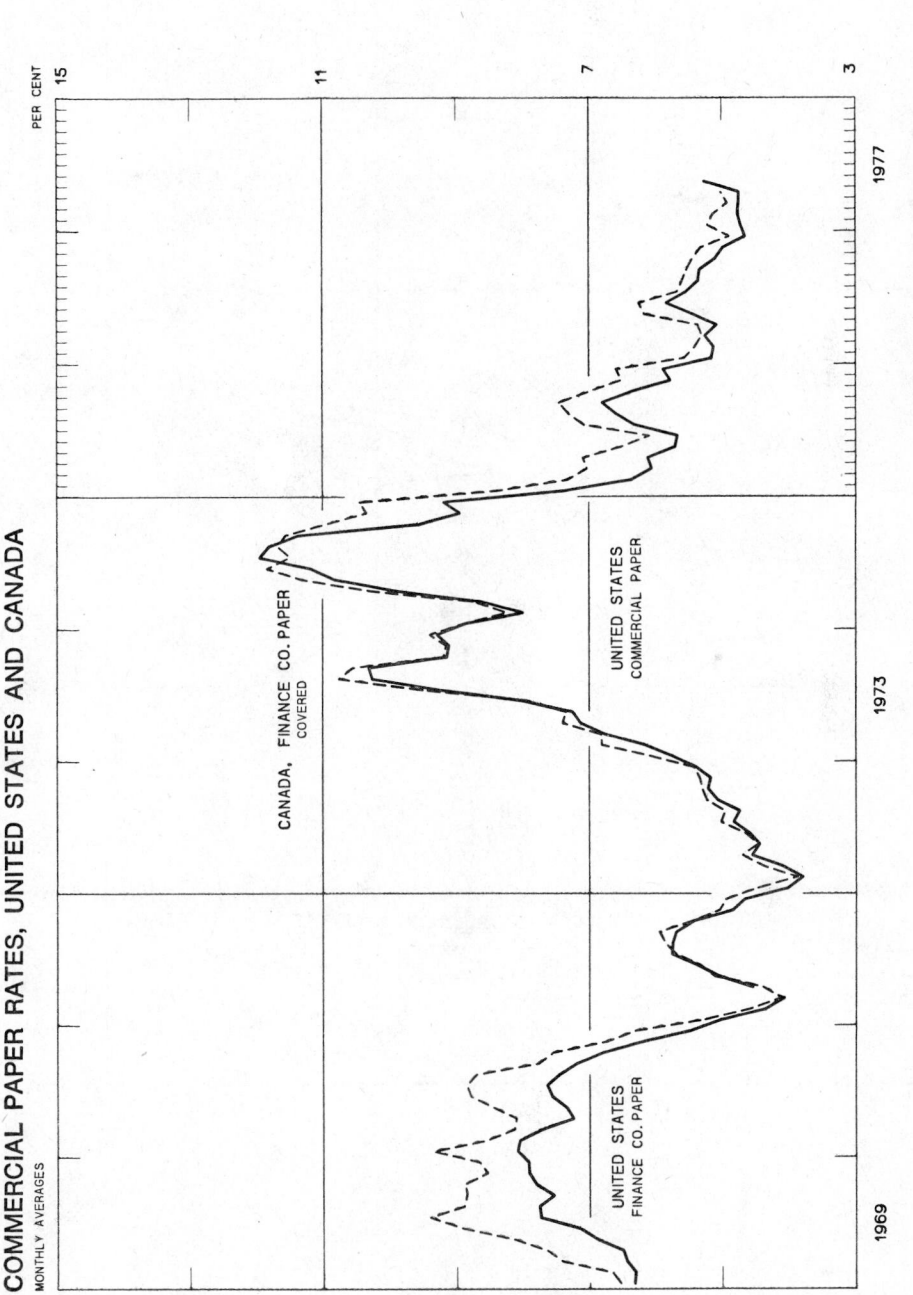

PER CENT

CANADA, FINANCE CO. PAPER
COVERED

UNITED STATES
COMMERCIAL PAPER

UNITED STATES
FINANCE CO. PAPER

BOARD OF GOVERNORS OF THE FEDERAL RESERVE SYSTEM

Source: Monthly Chartbook.

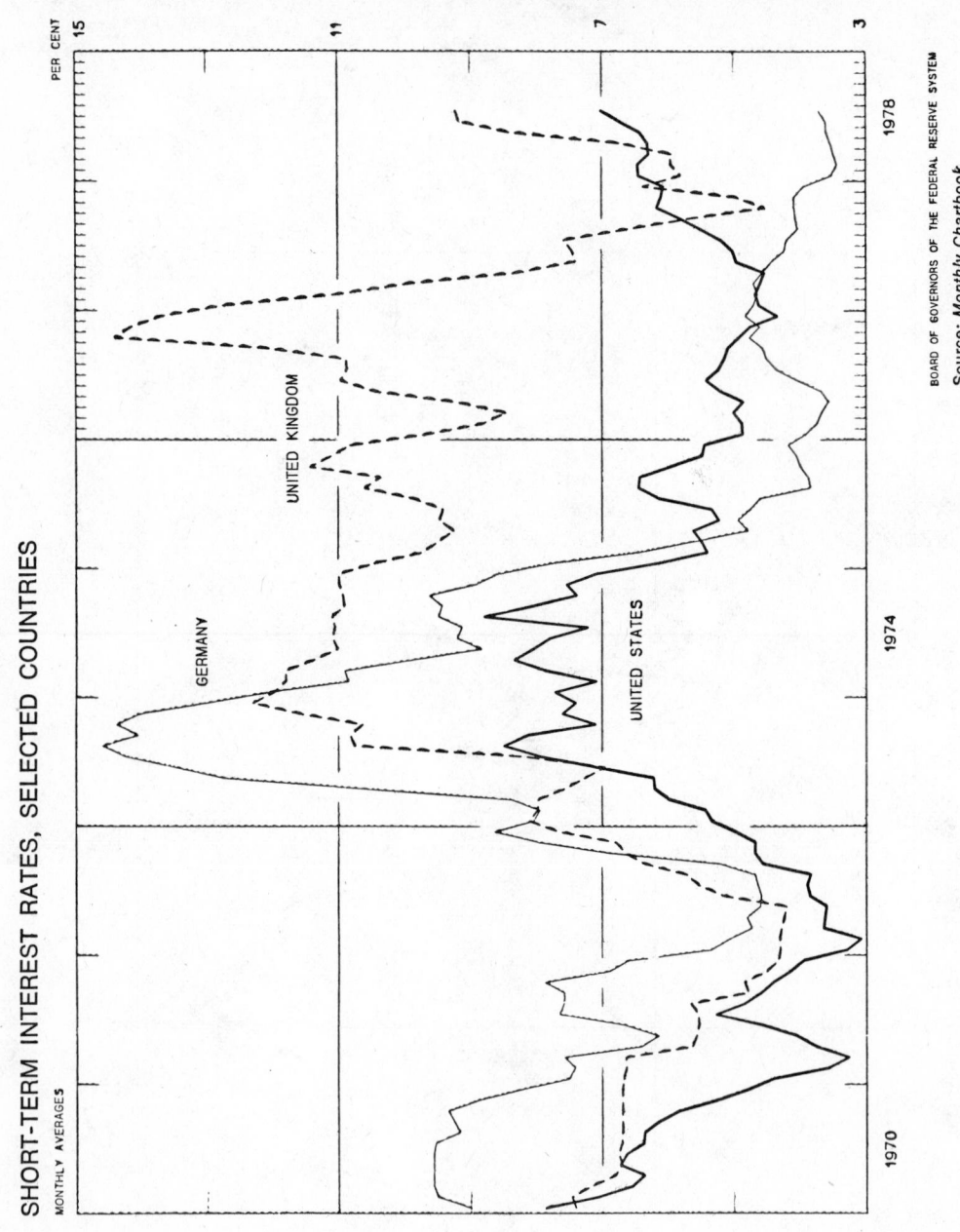

SHORT-TERM INTEREST RATES, SELECTED COUNTRIES

MONTHLY AVERAGES

PER CENT

15

11

7

3

UNITED KINGDOM

GERMANY

UNITED STATES

1978

1974

1970

BOARD OF GOVERNORS OF THE FEDERAL RESERVE SYSTEM

Source: Monthly Chartbook.

TREASURY BILL RATES

Bond-equivalent yields, at or near end of month

	1975 Dec	1976 Dec	1977 Dec	1978 Jan	Feb	Mar	Apr	May	Jun	Jul	Aug
United States	5.27	4.41	6.33	6.59	6.56	6.46	6.49	6.78	7.14	6.98	7.74
Canada	8.64	8.14	7.17	7.18	7.30	7.73	8.19	8.20	8.26	8.66	8.97
Japan	5.68	5.68	4.15	4.15	4.15	3.39	3.39	3.39	3.39	3.39	3.39
Australia	7.19	8.73	8.35	8.35	8.35	8.35	8.35	8.35	8.35	8.35	8.35
United Kingdom	10.78	13.98	6.42	5.86	6.07	6.03	7.10	8.64	9.50	9.31	8.68
Belgium	6.05	10.00	9.25	7.75	6.75	5.75	5.75	5.60	5.75	6.35	7.00
Ireland	10.23	14.28	6.74	6.14	6.18	6.22	6.26	8.46	9.06	9.55	9.55
Italy	n.a.	17.74	11.80	11.80	11.80	12.26	11.60	11.80	11.34	11.10	10.89
Netherlands	5.00	5.63	6.00	4.50	4.88	4.87	4.10	4.10	4.38	4.87	n.a.
Sweden	4.81	9.75	9.21	8.66	8.13	8.13	7.61	6.61	6.62	6.09	6.09
Brazil	25.10	38.58	38.08	36.09	36.11	36.09	36.01	35.90	35.82	37.05	38.40
Korea	n.a.	n.a.	16.88	16.88	16.88	16.88	16.88	16.88	17.01	17.01	17.01
Philippines	9.62	9.78	10.04	10.29	9.54	11.00	11.11	11.01	10.76	10.78	n.a.
Singapore	3.36	2.99	3.17	3.19	3.16	3.16	3.19	3.18	3.21	3.25	3.31
South Africa	7.05	7.94	8.17	8.22	8.22	8.26	8.24	8.26	8.27	8.26	7.91

Source: Reprinted, with permission, from *World Financial Markets*, a publication of the Morgan Guaranty Trust Company of New York.

REPRESENTATIVE MONEY MARKET RATES

Bond-equivalent yields on major short-term (mostly 3–4 month) money market instruments, other than Treasury bills, at or near end of month

	1975 Dec	1976 Dec	1977 Dec	1978 Jan	Feb	Mar	Apr	May	Jun	Jul	Aug
United States	5.91	4.75	6.84	6.96	6.96	6.96	6.96	7.49	7.88	7.89	8.28
Canada	9.86	8.42	7.38	7.33	7.49	8.11	8.48	8.53	8.53	8.63	9.42
Japan	8.00	7.00	5.25	4.87	4.87	4.25	4.12	4.25	4.37	4.50	4.62
Australia	8.50	9.75	9.75	9.75	9.50	10.90	10.75	10.60	10.20	9.80	9.80
United Kingdom	10.69	14.38	6.50	6.37	7.06	6.69	8.31	9.50	10.00	9.87	9.19
Belgium	6.20	10.50	9.50	8.00	7.00	6.50	5.75	3.75	6.00	6.25	7.10
France	6.50	10.00	9.19	10.00	10.75	8.25	8.50	8.06	8.06	7.37	7.31
Germany	4.20	4.80	3.60	3.50	3.40	3.55	3.55	3.65	3.75	3.75	3.70
Ireland	11.06	14.69	6.75	6.62	7.19	7.37	8.37	9.62	11.37	10.69	10.50
Italy	7.88	16.63	11.75	11.25	11.37	11.75	11.87	11.75	11.75	11.75	11.75
Netherlands	5.63	5.88	6.25	5.10	5.38	5.45	4.69	4.93	4.75	6.87	6.37
Spain	11.43	11.36	12.06	13.80	8.20	5.30	8.40	12.50	17.10	24.50	37.20
Switzerland	3.31	1.84	2.02	0.87	0.50	0.75	1.00	1.37	1.62	1.87	0.87
Brazil	28.96	45.44	46.93	40.29	40.29	40.29	40.72	40.72	41.01	41.74	41.74
Hong Kong	4.88	5.50	5.73	5.99	5.51	5.61	5.68	5.73	5.97	5.82	5.97
Korea	16.99	16.99	16.88	16.88	16.88	16.88	16.88	16.88	17.01	17.01	17.01
Philippines	16.06	15.47	11.96	11.32	10.66	10.62	10.36	10.91	10.73	10.66	n.a.
Singapore	4.56	3.75	4.81	4.19	4.87	4.75	4.19	4.81	5.00	5.37	6.18
South Africa	8.68	9.73	9.00	9.42	9.73	9.63	9.00	8.68	8.58	8.58	8.28

Source: Reprinted, with permission, from *World Financial Markets*, a publication of the Morgan Guaranty Trust Company of New York.

LONG-TERM GOVERNMENT BOND YIELDS, SELECTED COUNTRIES

MONTHLY

PER CENT

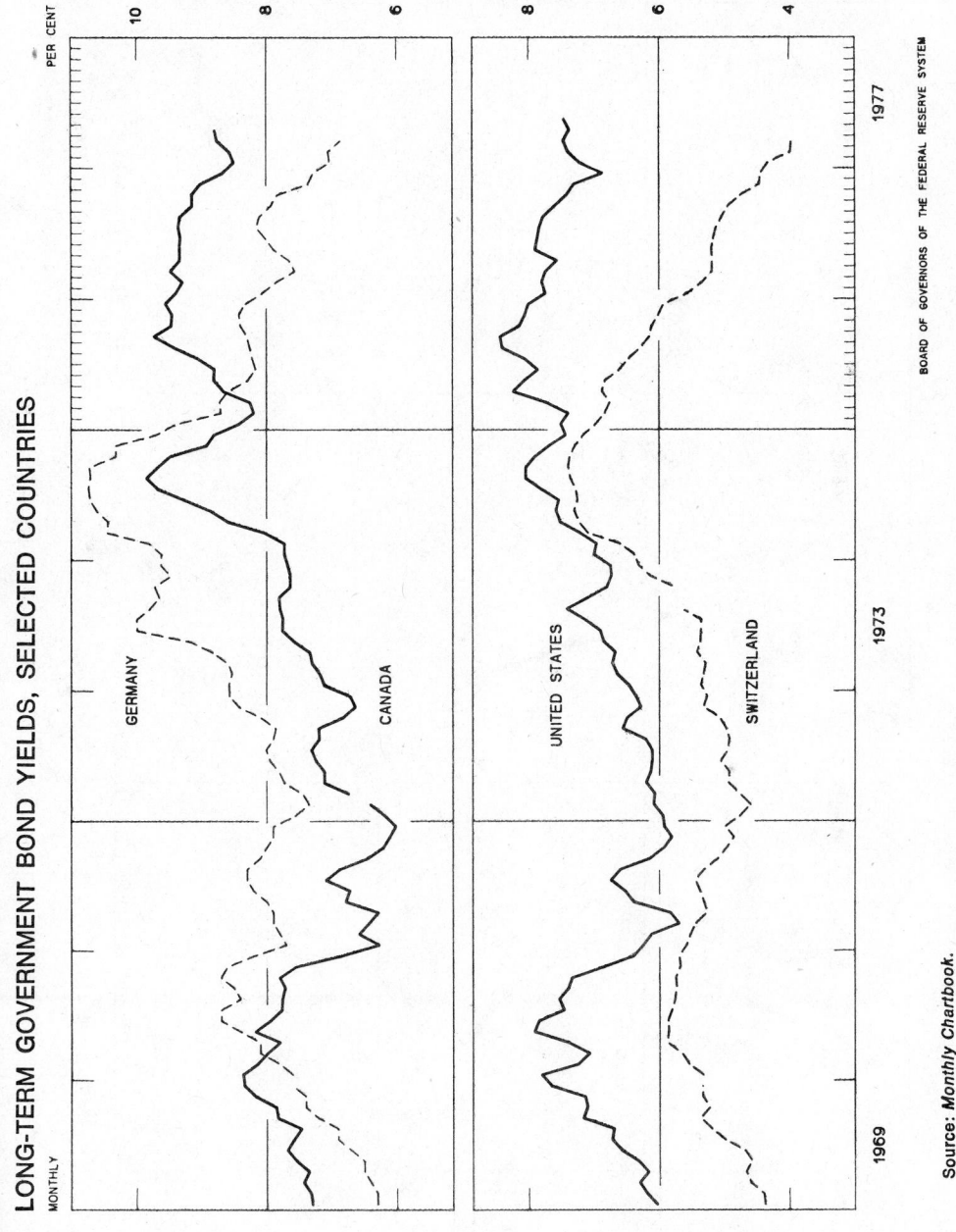

GERMANY

CANADA

UNITED STATES

SWITZERLAND

1969   1973   1977

BOARD OF GOVERNORS OF THE FEDERAL RESERVE SYSTEM

Source: *Monthly Chartbook.*

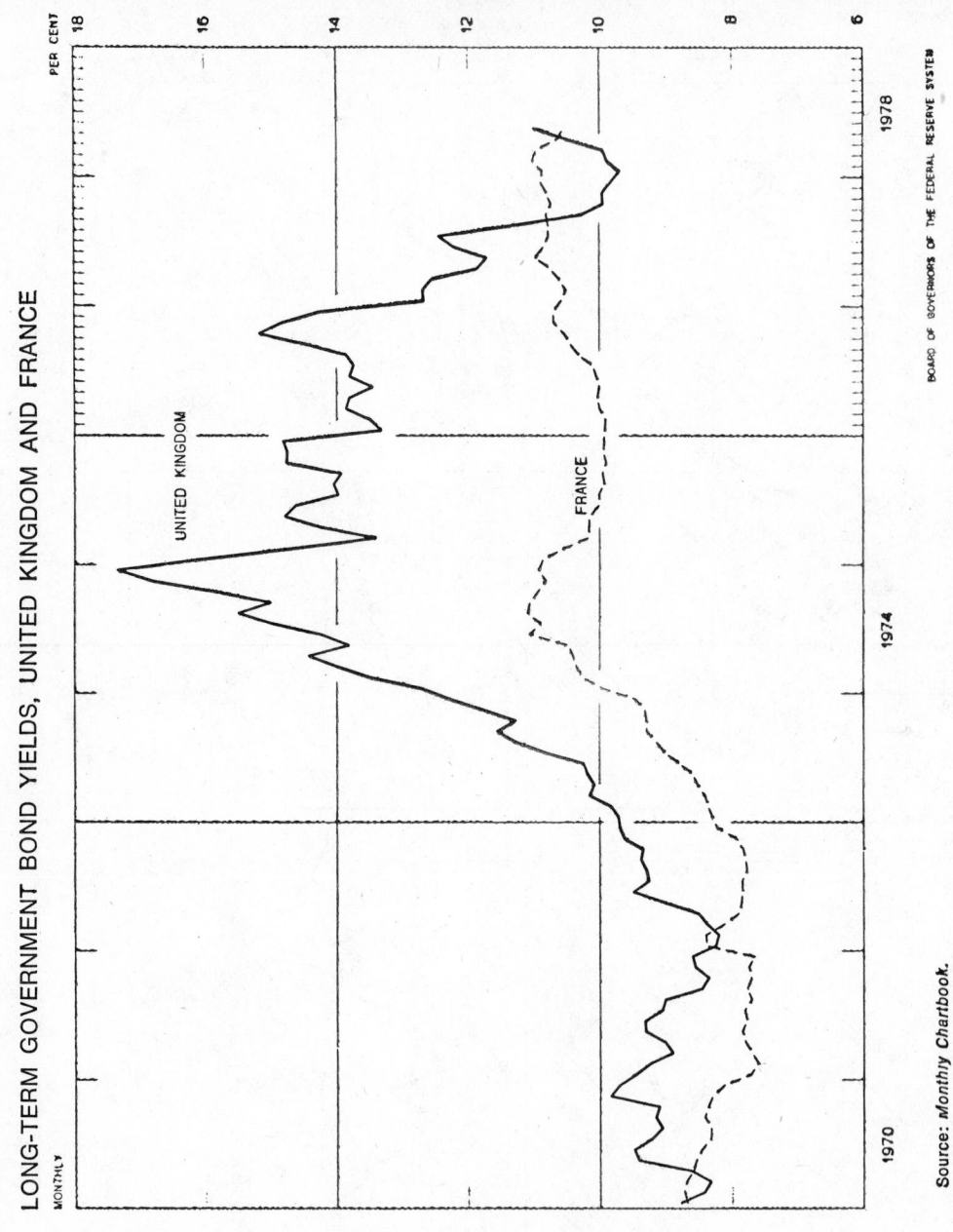

LONG-TERM GOVERNMENT BOND YIELDS, UNITED KINGDOM AND FRANCE

MONTHLY

PER CENT

UNITED KINGDOM

FRANCE

1970   1974   1978

BOARD OF GOVERNORS OF THE FEDERAL RESERVE SYSTEM

Source: Monthly Chartbook.

FOREIGN GOVERNMENT BOND YIELDS

Long-term issues, at or near end of month

	1975 Dec	1976 Dec	1977 Dec	1978 Jan	Feb	Mar	Apr	May	Jun	Jul	Aug
United States	8.05	7.20	7.97	8.20	8.22	8.28	8.39	8.47	8.60	8.56	8.90
Canada	9.49	8.47	8.77	9.08	9.14	9.17	9.22	9.23	9.23	9.17	9.16
Japan	9.01	8.55	6.12	5.75	5.73	5.60	5.51	5.56	5.76	5.64	5.65
Australia	10.00	10.50	9.50	9.20	9.20	9.20	9.10	9.10	9.10	9.00	9.00
United Kingdom	13.71	14.31	10.53	11.00	11.36	11.54	12.21	12.42	12.39	12.22	12.23
Belgium	8.72	9.30	8.76	8.71	8.54	8.30	8.25	8.22	8.22	8.25	8.45
France	10.18	11.04	11.07	11.25	11.36	11.07	10.75	10.76	10.60	10.49	10.40
Germany	8.73	7.28	5.52	5.44	5.33	5.30	5.41	5.53	5.73	6.37	6.24
Italy	11.37	13.92	10.82	11.10	11.07	11.07	10.96	10.89	10.80	10.80	10.70
Netherlands	8.61	8.40	8.11	7.73	7.54	7.46	7.27	7.40	7.35	7.70	n.a.
Austria	9.41	8.55	9.00	8.91	8.82	8.65	8.50	8.25	7.95	7.82	n.a.
Denmark	12.58	14.57	16.55	16.30	16.60	15.22	14.98	14.95	14.98	15.14	15.50
Finland	9.75	10.92	10.25	10.55	10.54	10.74	10.72	9.78	9.84	9.89	9.93
Ireland	14.64	15.49	11.30	11.68	12.29	12.28	12.89	13.26	13.31	12.62	n.a.
Norway	7.29	7.25	8.37	8.40	8.34	8.46	8.59	8.63	8.54	8.57	8.39
Sweden	9.15	9.61	9.84	9.86	9.87	10.08	10.17	n.a.	n.a.	n.a.	n.a.
Switzerland	5.81	4.43	3.75	3.66	3.53	3.50	3.40	3.47	3.40	3.37	3.31
Brazil	33.30	38.39	37.30	37.22	41.24	33.71	37.93	39.07	42.05	41.33	40.24
Philippines	13.67	13.41	13.40	13.40	13.40	13.40	13.40	13.40	13.40	13.40	13.40
Venezuela	7.02	7.04	7.24	7.24	7.24	7.24	7.24	n.a.	n.a.	n.a.	n.a.

Source: Reprinted, with permission, from *World Financial Markets*, a publication of the Morgan Guaranty Trust Company of New York.

FOREIGN CORPORATE BOND YIELDS

Long-term issues, at or near end of month

	1975 Dec	1976 Dec	1977 Dec	1978 Jan	Feb	Mar	Apr	May	Jun	Jul	Aug
United States	8.55	7.35	8.30	8.45	8.60	8.60	8.80	8.90	8.95	8.60	8.60
Canada	11.06	9.58	9.71	9.96	9.94	9.95	9.96	9.95	9.95	9.87	9.89
Japan	9.39	8.77	6.36	6.22	6.25	6.38	6.33	6.29	6.21	6.15	6.02
Australia	12.50	12.00	11.00	10.75	10.50	10.50	10.50	10.40	10.40	10.40	10.00
United Kingdom	15.72	15.96	11.88	11.85	12.23	12.20	12.69	12.95	12.98	12.97	12.84
Belgium	10.24	11.88	9.85	9.69	9.50	9.26	9.08	9.23	9.16	9.34	9.59
France	10.85	11.39	12.09	12.14	12.28	12.08	11.69	11.58	11.39	11.15	10.93
Germany	8.63	7.47	5.92	5.76	5.75	5.68	5.71	5.76	5.73	6.34	6.30
Italy	11.94	16.90	10.71	11.14	10.97	10.75	11.10	10.87	10.54	10.28	10.20
Netherlands	8.52	8.22	7.90	7.57	7.38	7.29	7.07	7.13	7.15	7.43	n.a.
Norway	7.73	7.65	8.59	8.66	8.73	8.81	8.79	8.87	8.58	8.45	8.53
Spain	10.99	10.86	11.58	12.22	12.58	12.55	12.36	11.93	12.18	12.50	12.57
Sweden	9.14	9.82	9.83	9.78	9.81	10.02	10.06	10.12	10.15	10.18	9.86
Switzerland	7.08	5.50	4.96	4.73	4.66	4.76	4.74	4.79	4.81	4.77	4.76
Korea	n.a.	21.70	19.60	20.70	20.70	20.80	21.40	21.40	24.00	24.00	26.00
Mexico	13.97	15.56	17.56	16.77	16.24	15.33	16.67	16.30	16.08	16.24	18.84
Venezuela	10.18	10.37	10.39	10.39	10.38	10.47	10.66	10.78	10.76	10.95	11.48

Source: Reprinted, with permission, from *World Financial Markets*, a publication of the Morgan Guaranty Trust Company of New York.

ECONOMIC AND BUSINESS INDICATORS OF DEVELOPED COUNTRIES*

Unless otherwise specified in the tables, the following definitions apply. **Industrial production:** Covers mining, manufacturing and electricity, gas and water (major divisions 2 and 3; groups 4101 and 4102 of the International Standard Industrial Classification), but not building or civil engineering. Indexes are adjusted for number of working days in the month. **Employment:** Includes members of the armed forces. **International liquidity:** Reserve position in IMF includes oil facility lending.

CONVENTIONAL SIGNS

In graphs:
* = Seasonally adjusted series.
S = Affected by strike.
B = Break in continuity of series.
In tables:
(e) = Secretariat estimates.

---

* All exhibits in this section are reproduced with permission from *Main Economic Indicators*, Organisation for Economic Co-operation and Development, Paris, July 1977.
Note: Captions on data in this section taken from the O.E.C.D. *Main Economic Indicators* appear in both French and English.

.. = For data: not available.
For rates of change: either rate over 100 percent or not calculated because data affected by strike or other special event.
— = Nil or negligible.
• = Decimal point.
In tables and graphs:
$ = U.S. dollar.
Cent = U.S. cent.
£ = Pound sterling.

ABBREVIATIONS

O.E.C.D. MAIN COUNTRY GROUPINGS
E.E.C.: European Economic Community: Belgium, Denmark, France, Germany, Ireland, Italy, Luxembourg, the Netherlands, and the United Kingdom.
O.E.C.D.-Europe: All European member countries of O.E.C.D., i.e., countries in E.E.C. plus Austria, Finland, Greece, Iceland, Norway, Portugal, Spain, Sweden, Switzerland, and Turkey.
North America: Canada and the United States.
O.E.C.D.-Total: All member countries of O.E.C.D., i.e., countries in O.E.C.D.-Europe and in North America plus Japan, Australia, and New Zealand.

OTHER
Orig. = Series prior to seasonal adjustment.
Adj. = Series adjusted for seasonal variations.
Billion = Thousand million.
Tons = Metric tons.

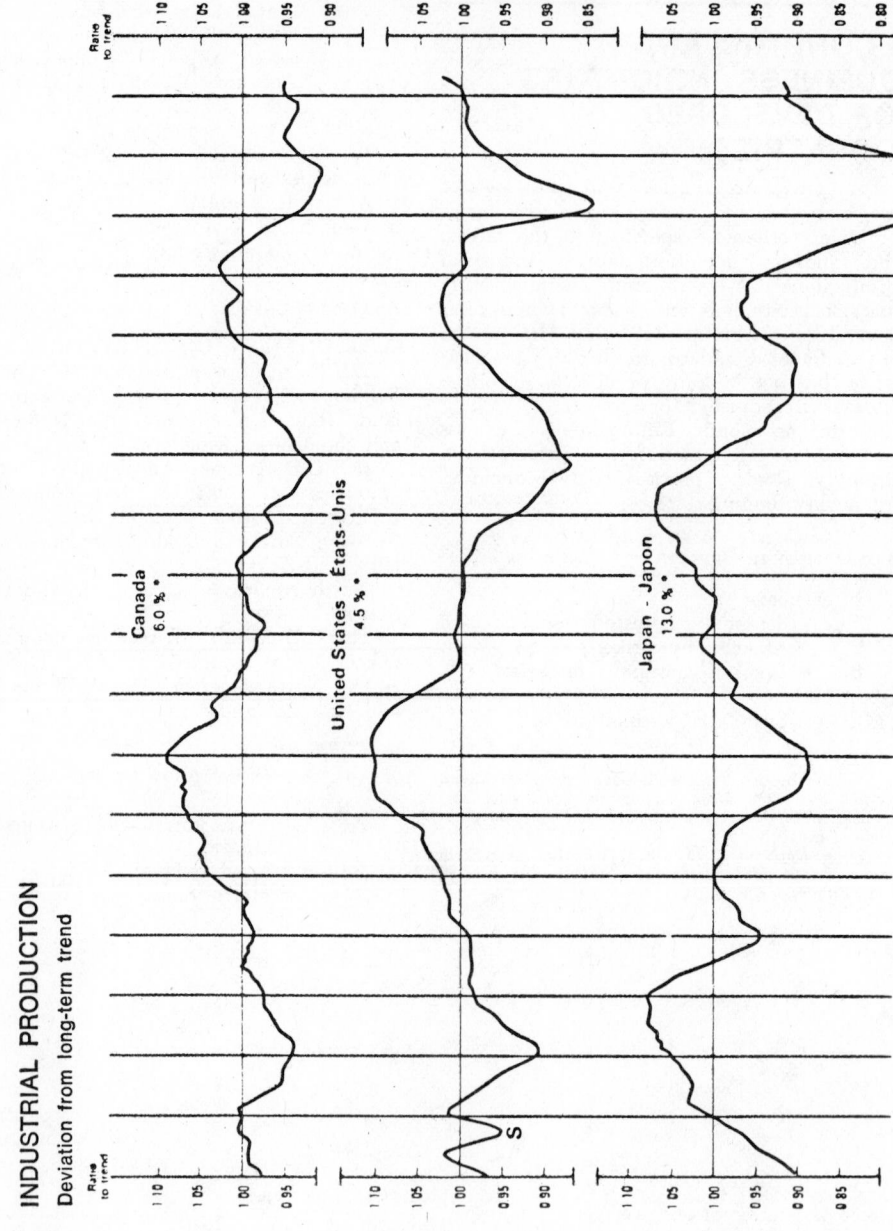

INDUSTRIAL PRODUCTION
Deviation from long-term trend

Canada
60 %*

United States - États-Unis
45 %*

Japan - Japon
130 %*

Ratio to trend

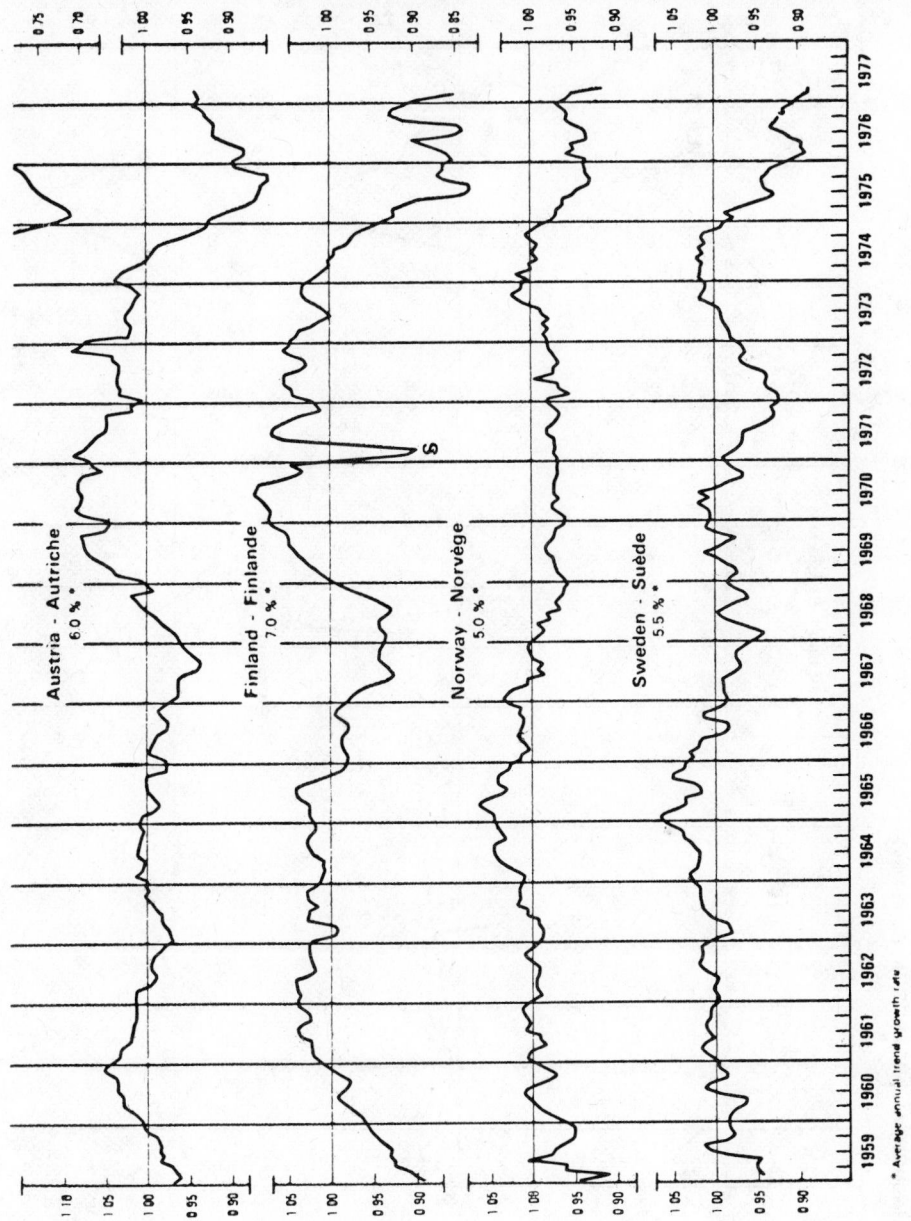

Austria - Autriche
60 %*

Finland - Finlande
70 %*

Norway - Norvège
50 %*

Sweden - Suède
55 %*

* Average annual trend growth rate

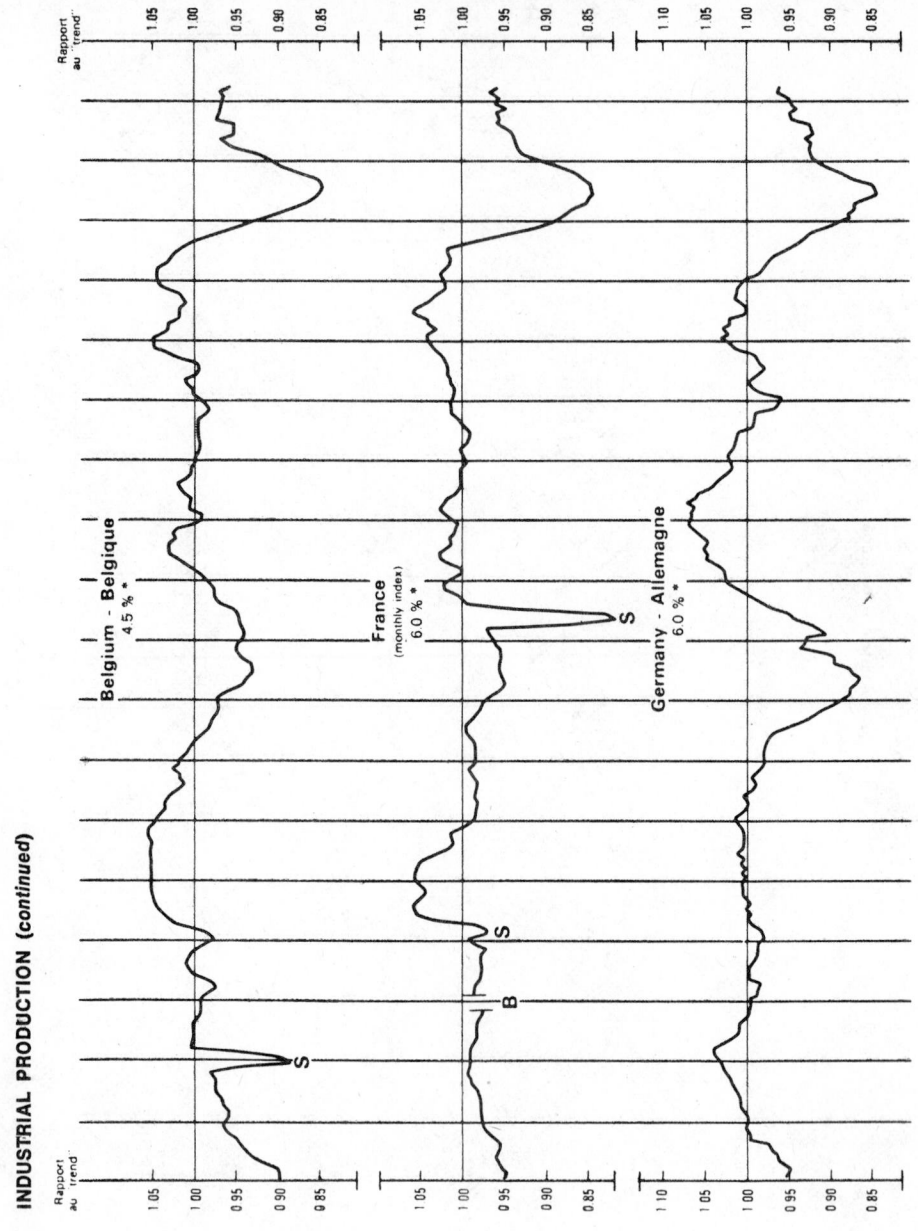

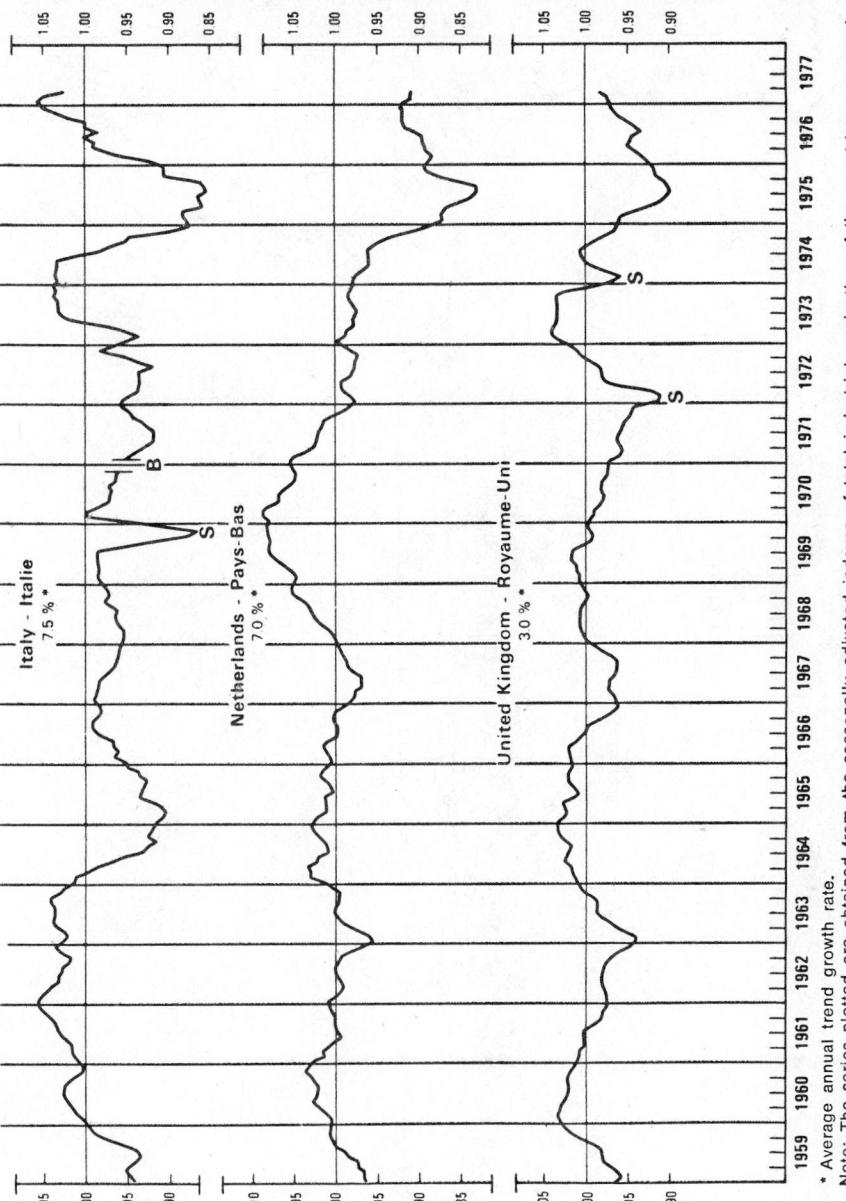

Italy - Italie
7.5 %*

Netherlands - Pays-Bas
7.0 %*

United Kingdom - Royaume-Uni
3.0 %*

* Average annual trend growth rate.
Note: The series plotted are obtained from the seasonally adjusted indexes of total industrial production of the countries concerned.
The long-term trend of each series is first calculated and a three-month moving average of the original series is then divided by this trend.

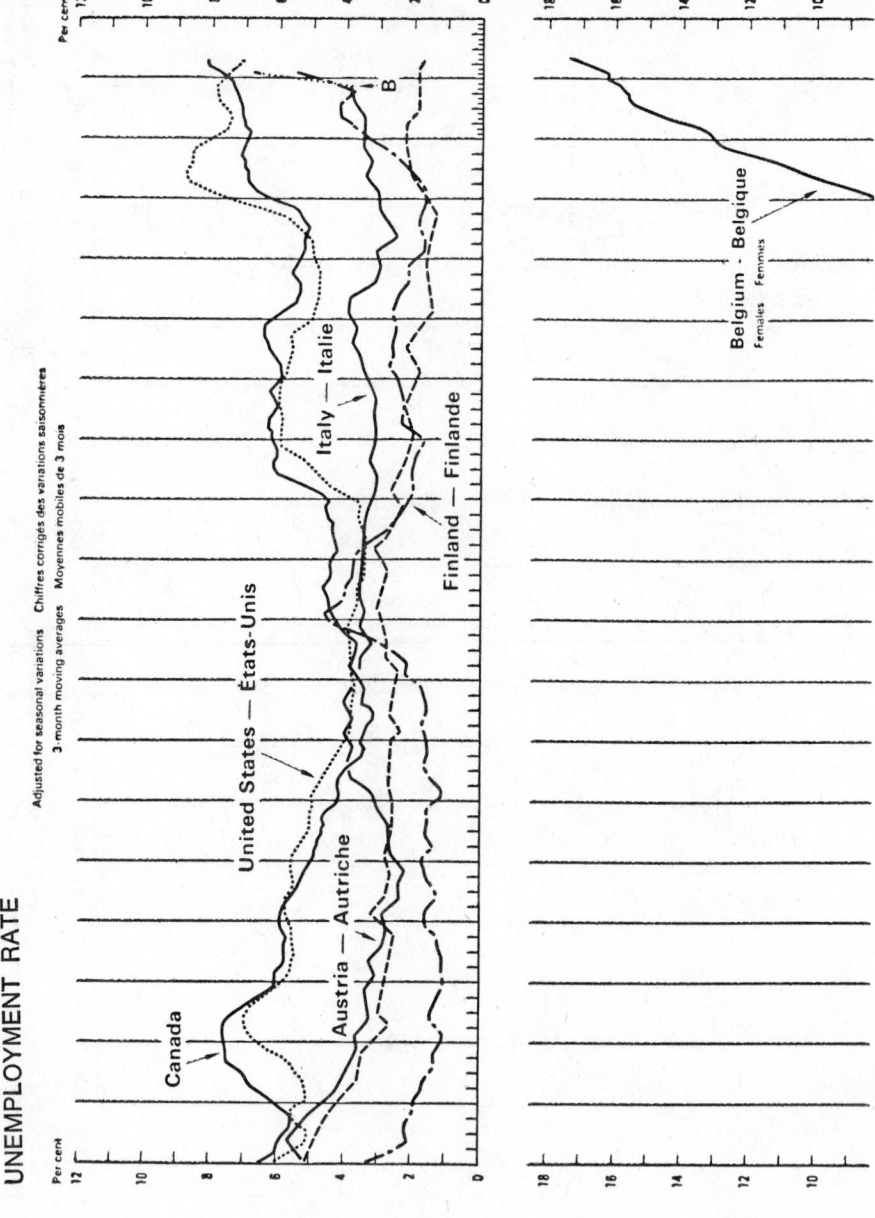

UNEMPLOYMENT RATE

Adjusted for seasonal variations   Chiffres corrigés des variations saisonnières
3-month moving averages   Moyennes mobiles de 3 mois

Per cent

Canada

United States — États-Unis

Austria — Autriche

Italy — Italie

Finland — Finlande

B

Belgium · Belgique
Females Femmes

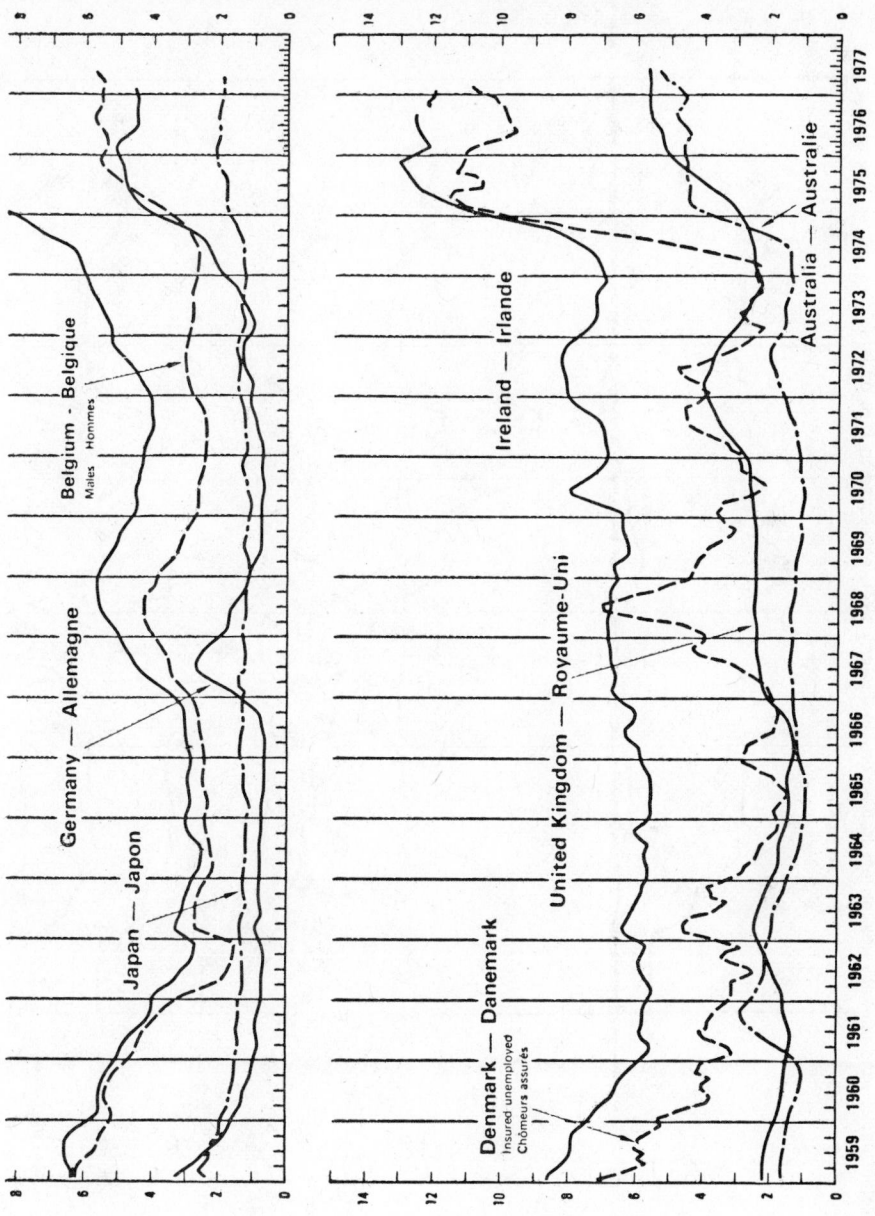

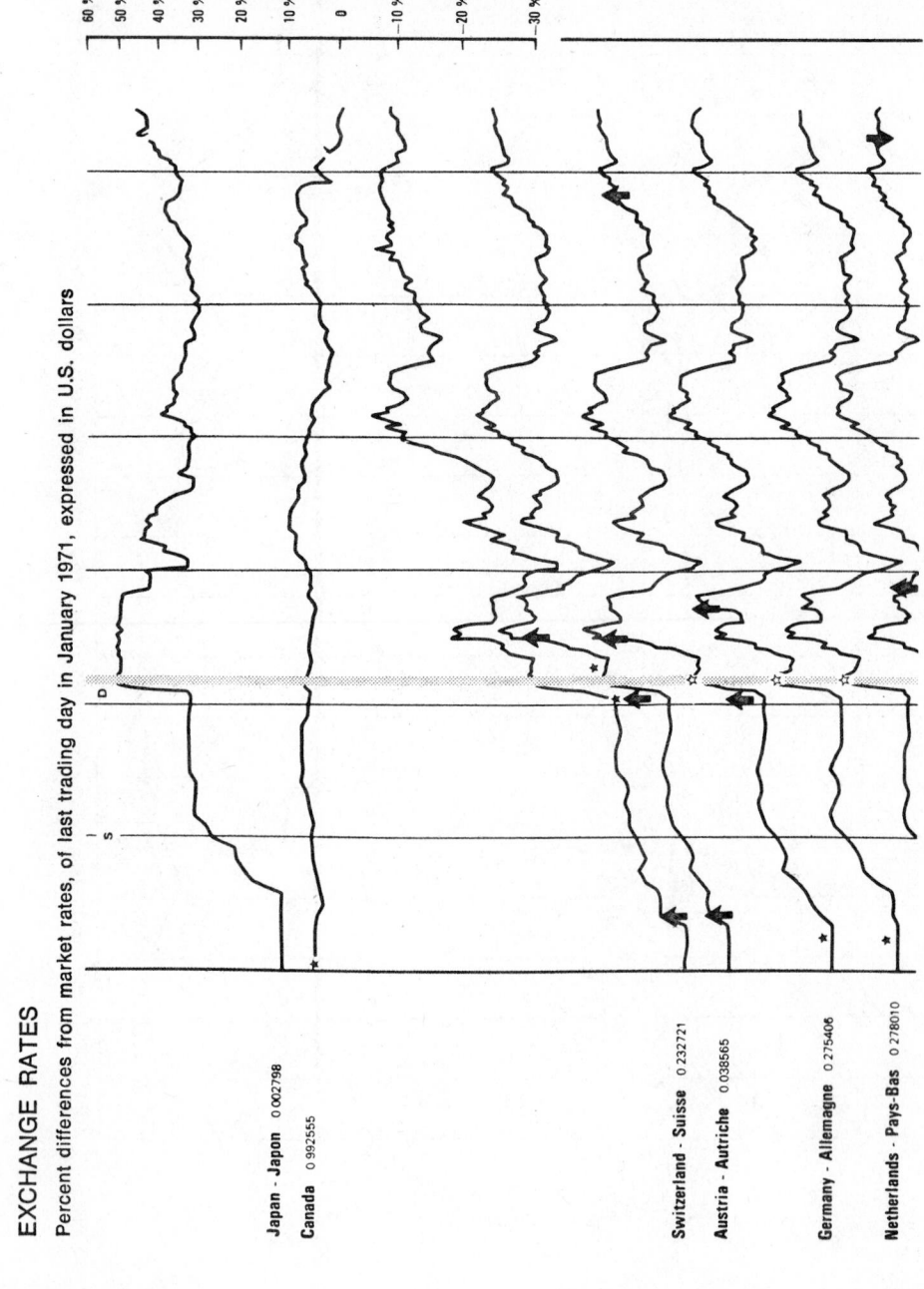

EXCHANGE RATES

Percent differences from market rates, of last trading day in January 1971, expressed in U.S. dollars

Échelle semi-logarithmique Semi-logarithmic scale

60 %
50 %
40 %
30 %
20 %
10 %
0
-10 %
-20 %
-30 %

Japan - Japon 0.002798
Canada 0.992555

Switzerland - Suisse 0.232721
Austria - Autriche 0.038565

Germany - Allemagne 0.275406
Netherlands - Pays-Bas 0.278010

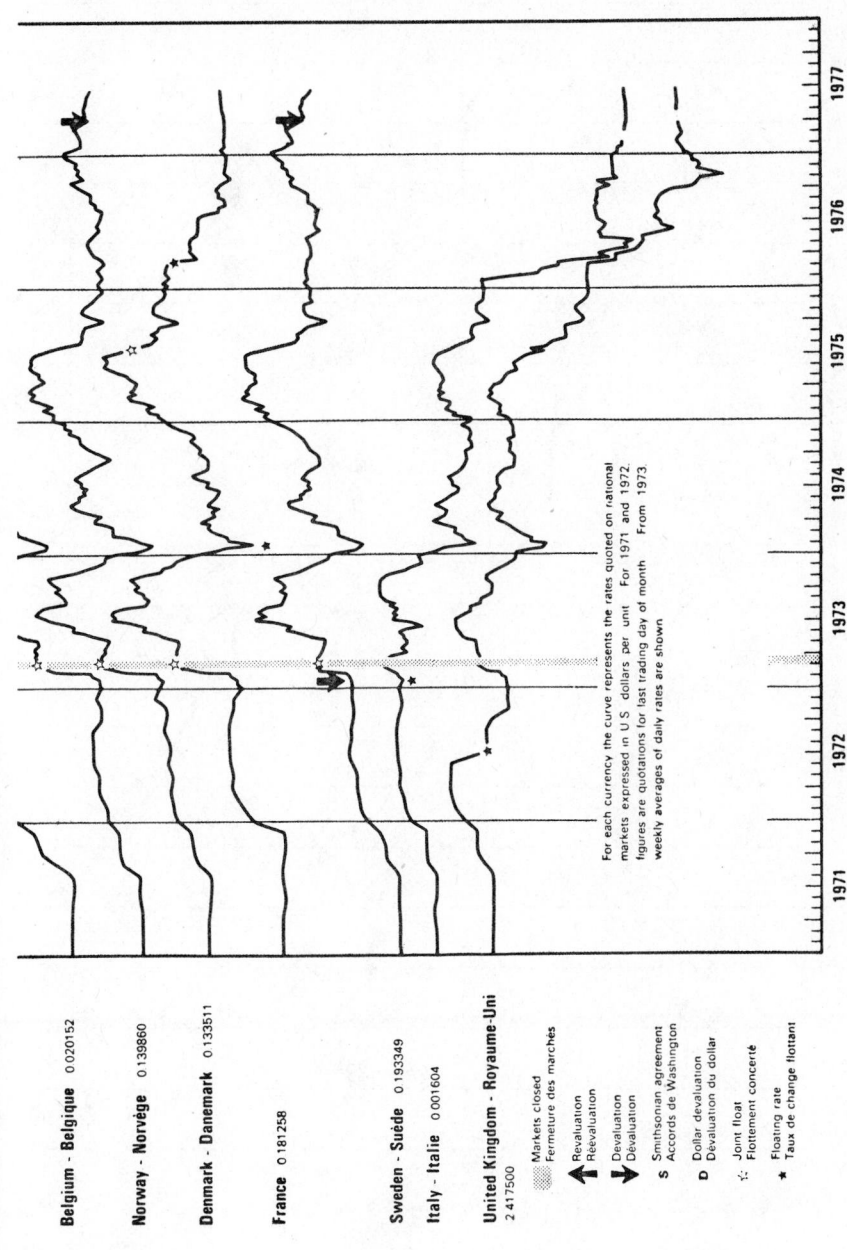

Belgium - Belgique 0.020152

Norway - Norvège 0.139860

Denmark - Danemark 0.133511

France 0.181258

Sweden - Suède 0.193349

Italy - Italie 0.001604

United Kingdom - Royaume-Uni
2.417500

Markets closed
Fermeture des marchés

Revaluation
Réévaluation

Devaluation
Dévaluation

s Smithsonian agreement
Accords de Washington

D Dollar devaluation
Dévaluation du dollar

Joint float
Flottement concerté

★ Floating rate
Taux de change flottant

For each currency the curve represents the rates quoted on national
markets expressed in U.S. dollars per unit   For 1971 and 1972,
figures are quotations for last trading day of month   From 1973
weekly averages of daily rates are shown

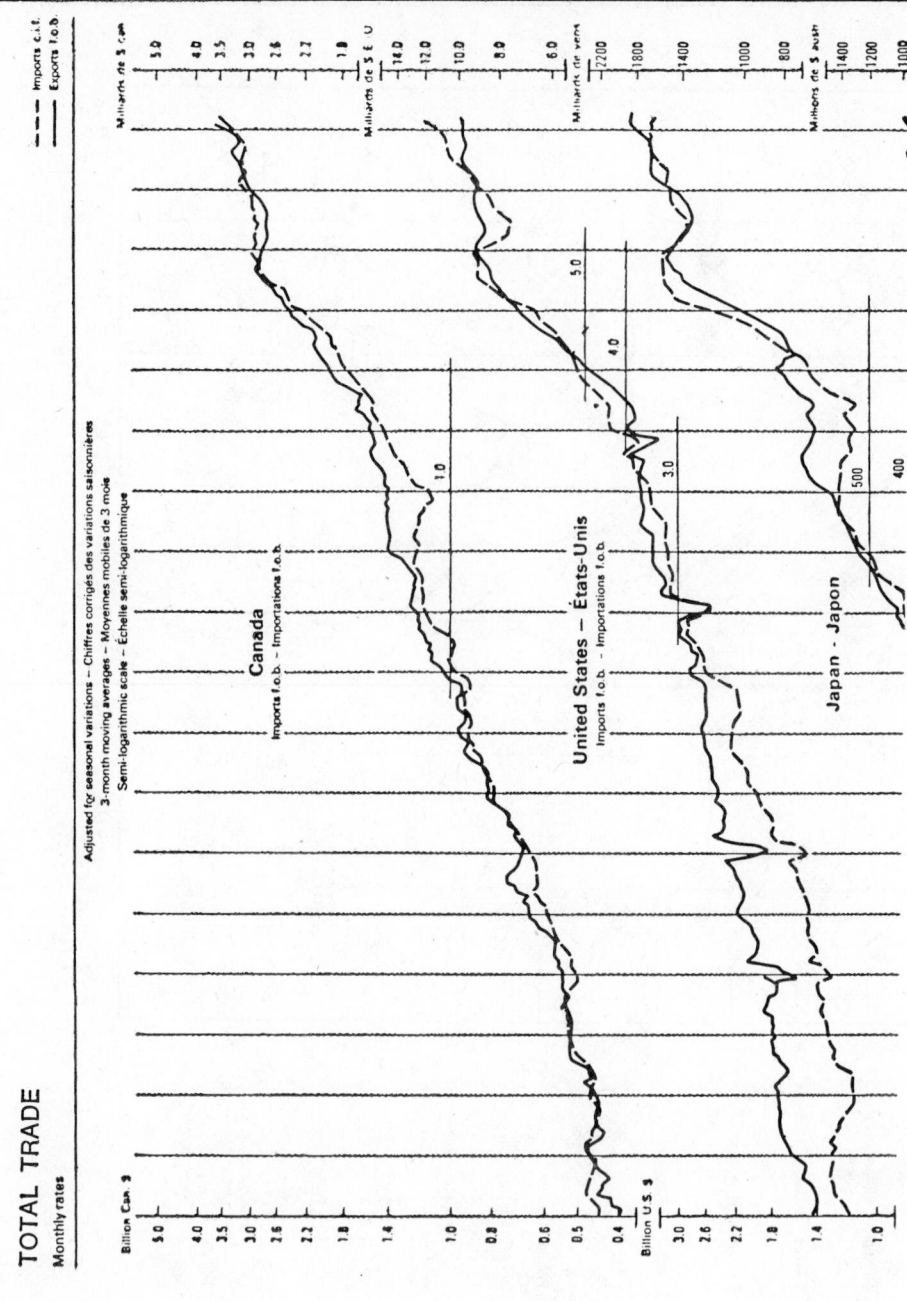

TOTAL TRADE
Monthly rates

Imports c.i.f.
Exports f.o.b.

Adjusted for seasonal variations – Chiffres corrigés des variations saisonnières
3-month moving averages – Moyennes mobiles de 3 mois
Semi-logarithmic scale – Échelle semi-logarithmique

Canada
Imports f.o.b. – Importations f.o.b.

United States – États-Unis
Imports f.o.b. – Importations f.o.b.

Japan – Japon

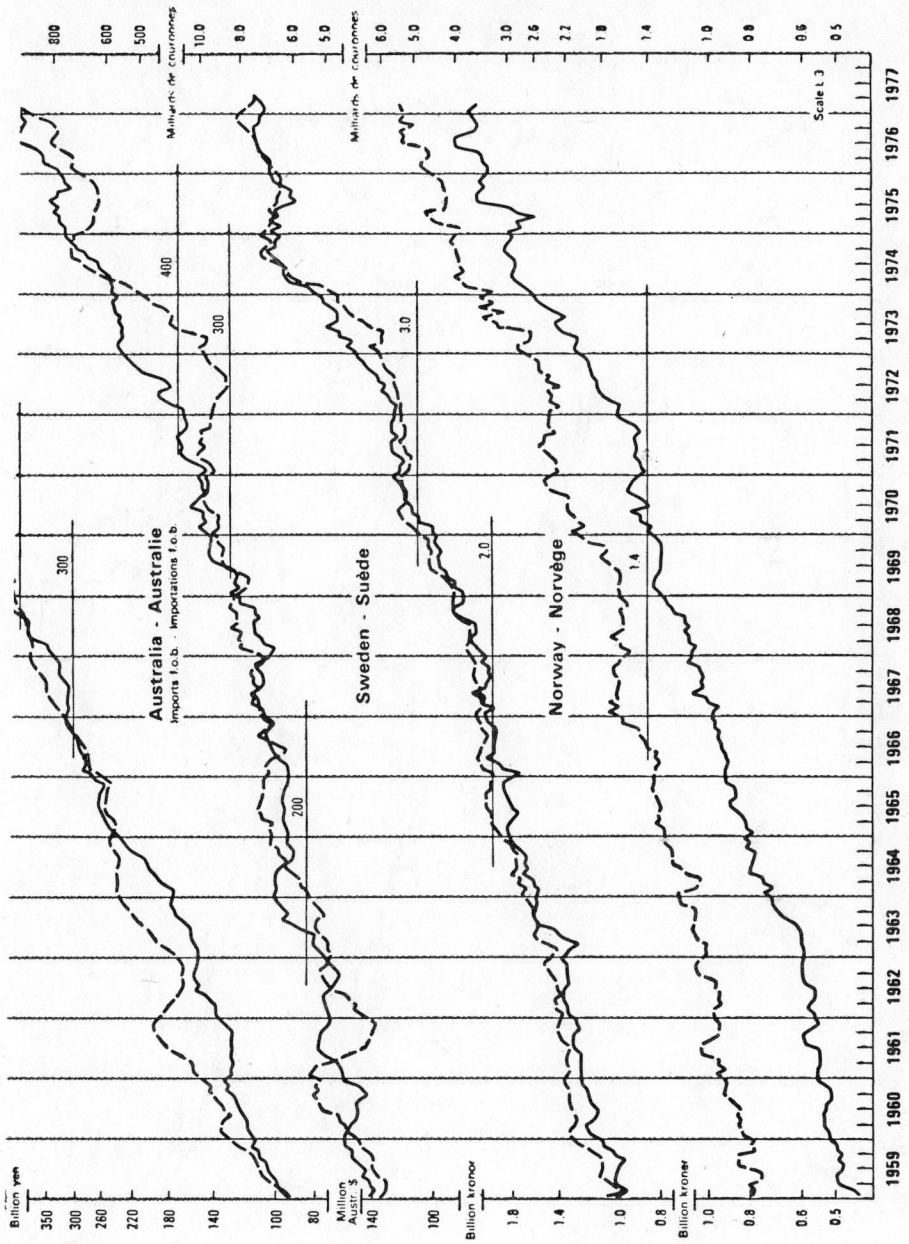

Australia - Australie
Imports f.o.b. · Importations f.o.b.

Sweden - Suède

Norway - Norvège

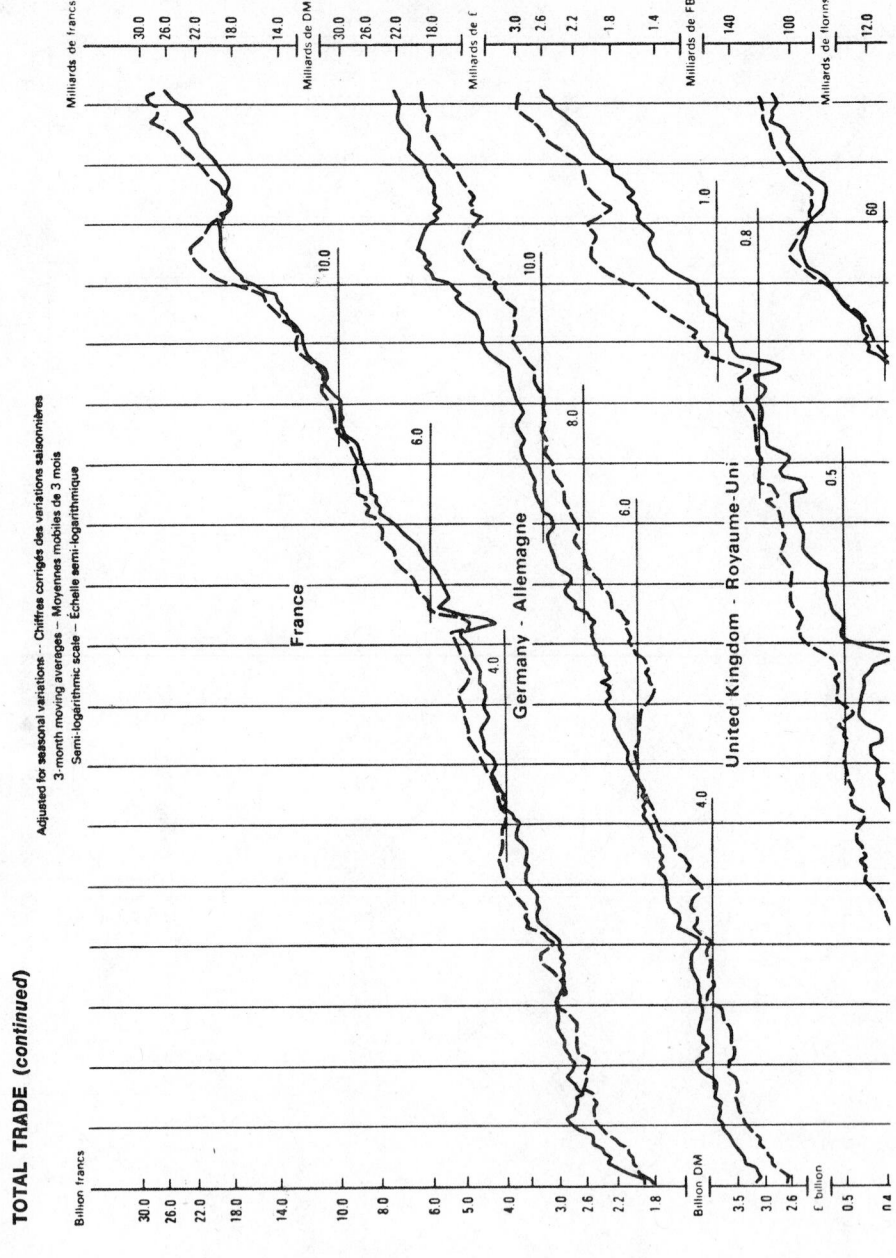

TOTAL TRADE (continued)

Adjusted for seasonal variations -- Chiffres corrigés des variations saisonnières
3-month moving averages -- Moyennes mobiles de 3 mois
Semi-logarithmic scale -- Échelle semi-logarithmique

Billion francs — Milliards de francs

France

Germany - Allemagne

United Kingdom - Royaume-Uni

Billion DM — Milliards de DM

£ billion — Milliards de £

Milliards de FB

Milliards de florins

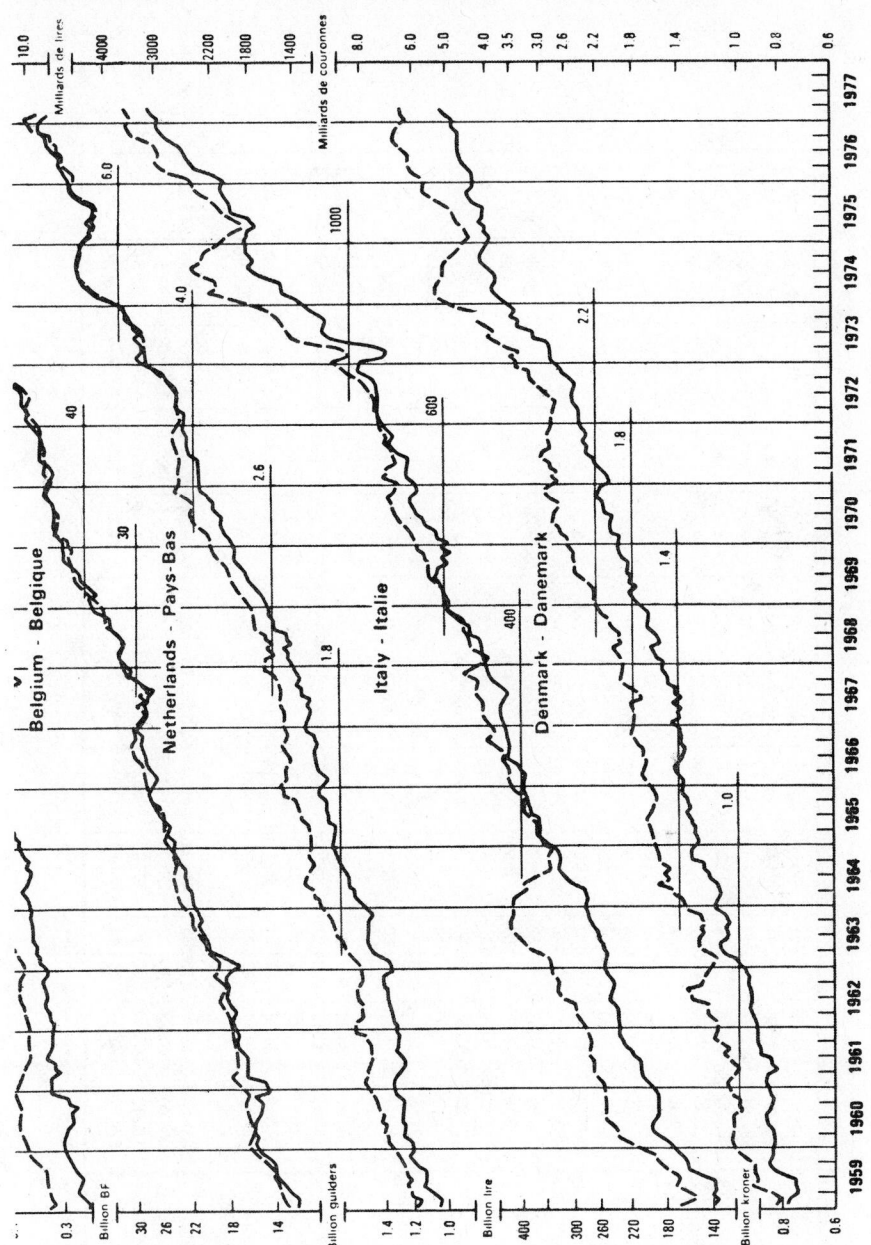

GROSS DOMESTIC PRODUCT

	at 1970 prices and 1970 exchange rates — aux prix et aux taux de change de 1970 (Billion dollars - Milliards de dollars)							Volume (2) 1976/1975 annual % — % annuel	at current prices and exchange rates — aux prix et taux de change courants (Billion dollars - Milliards de dollars)			
	1970	1971	1972	1973	1974	1975	1976(3)		1973	1974	1975	1976(3)
Canada	82.80	88.26	93.21	99.89	103.04	103.59	108.5	4.75	123.49	149.20	159.68	189.4
United States - Etats-Unis	981.20	1009.56	1067.61	1125.54	1107.82	1090.07	1158.2	6.25	1302.14	1405.48	1513.83	1688.8
Japan - Japon	197.87	212.32	231.19	253.87	251.10	257.03	272.5	6	407.82	454.48	490.63	553.0
Australia - Australie	34.80	36.73	37.86	40.23	41.10	41.32	42.6	3	65.65	79.30	84.24	92.9
New Zealand - Neuvelle-Zélande	6.25	6.41	6.69	7.18	7.38	7.52	7.2	-4	11.91	13.31	13.24	12.4
Austria - Autriche	14.35	15.11	16.07	17.00	17.70	17.35	18.0	4	27.24	32.82	37.57	40.4
Belgium - Belgique	25.80	26.83	28.30	30.09	31.30	30.67	31.6	3	45.51	53.40	62.25	67.2
Denmark - Danemark	15.57	16.14	16.84	17.34	17.38	17.25	18.0	4.5	27.30	30.22	35.45	38.2
Finland - Finlande	10.35	10.60	11.34	12.08	12.59	12.61	12.6	0.3	17.44	22.39	26.59	28.4
France	141.54	149.04	157.62	166.03	170.81	169.06	177.5	5	250.01	265.61	335.71	346.5
Germany - Allemagne	188.39	193.86	200.36	210.53	212.00	205.28	216.6	5.5	347.31	385.69	424.92	453.3
Greece - Grèce	9.96	10.67	11.62	12.47	12.02	12.76	13.4	5.25	16.34	18.97	20.86	22.2
Iceland - Islande	0.49	0.55	0.59	0.62	0.65	0.64	0.6	-0.9	1.06	1.39	1.25	1.4
Ireland - Irlande	3.89	4.05	4.26	4.44	4.45	4.44	4.6	3.25	6.54	6.70	7.76	7.8
Italy - Italie	92.38	93.81	96.77	103.36	106.92	102.92	107.6	4.5	140.90	152.60	172.10	163.6
Luxembourg	1.07	1.10	1.15	1.23	1.27	1.17	1.2	3.1	1.86	2.18	2.20	2.4
Netherlands - Pays-Bas	31.68	33.07	34.36	36.39	37.28	36.86	38.3	4.0	60.13	69.59	81.20	88.3
Norway - Norvège	11.17	11.67	12.26	12.74	13.42	13.87	14.7	5.9	19.32	23.27	28.30	30.8
Portugal	6.19	6.55	7.12	7.90	8.07	7.78			11.37	13.29	14.62	
Spain - Espagne	36.95	38.72	42.02	45.56	47.86	48.22	49.2	2	70.95	85.64	101.04	102.8
Sweden - Suède	32.95	33.19	34.04	35.24	36.65	36.94	37.5	1.5	50.42	56.19	69.36	73.8
Switzerland - Suisse	21.03	21.89	22.59	23.28	23.62	21.87	21.7	-0.8	41.07	47.36	54.16	56.6
Turkey - Turquie	12.85	14.08	15.03	15.71	17.04	18.57	20.0	7.8	20.74	28.97	35.45	38.9
United Kingdom - Royaume-Uni	121.49	124.57	127.77	135.39	135.74	133.97	136.0	1.5	175.81	190.80	227.79	215.0
O.E.C.D.-Total - O.C.D.E.-Total	2081.04	2158.77	2276.66	2414.11	2417.20	2391.76	2508.1(4)	5.2(4)	3242.31	3588.86	4000.19	4314.1(4)
North America - Amérique du Nord	1064.00	1097.82	1160.82	1225.43	1210.86	1193.66	1266.7	6.1	1425.63	1554.68	1673.51	1878.2
O.E.C.D.-Europe - O.C.D.E.-Europe	778.12	805.50	840.10	887.40	906.76	892.23	919.0(4)	3.9(4)	1331.31	1487.09	1738.57	1777.6(4)
E.E.C. - C.E.E.	621.82	642.47	667.43	704.80	717.14	701.62	731.4	4.2	1055.38	1156.78	1349.37	1382.3

1. Sources: National Accounts of O.E.C.D. Countries. 1975 Vol I. countries submissions and Secretariat estimates.
2. Various base years. GDP/GNP Growth rate
3. Provisional figures.
4. Excluding Portugal

World Population and GNP by Country

WORLD POPULATION DATA

Region or Country [1]	Population Estimate Mid-1977 (millions) [2]	Birth Rate [3]	Death Rate [3]	Rate of Natural Increase (annual, percent) [1]	Number of Years to Double Population [5]	Population Projection to 2000 (millions) [6]	Infant Mortality Rate [7]	Population under 15 Years (percent) [8]	Population over 64 Years (percent) [8]	Life Expectancy at Birth (years)	Urban Population (percent) [9]	Per Capita Gross National Product (US$) [10]
WORLD	4,083	30	12	1.8	38	6,182	103	36	6	59	38	1,530
AFRICA	423	45	19	2.6	27	811	154	44	3	46	24	400
NORTHERN AFRICA	100	42	14	2.8	25	185	130	44	3	53	39	570
Algeria	17.8	48	15	3.2	22	36.5	142	48	3	53	52	780
Egypt	38.9	36	12	2.3	30	63.9	116	41	3	52	45	310
Libya	2.7	48	9	3.9	18	5.2	130	49	4	55	30	5,080
Morocco	18.3	48	16	3.2	22	35.5	130	46	2	53	38	470
Sudan	16.3	48	18	3.0	23	32.7	141	45	3	51	13	290
Tunisia	6.0	34	11	2.3	30	10.8	125	45	4	55	47	760
WESTERN AFRICA	125	49	23	2.6	27	243	175	45	3	42	19	300
Benin (Dahomey)	3.3	50	23	2.7	26	6.0	185	46	4	41	14	140
Cape Verde	0.3	29	9	2.0	35	0.4	79	48	5	50	8	470
Gambia	0.6	42	21	2.1	33	0.9	165	41	2	44	14	190
Ghana	10.4	47	20	2.7	26	21.1	156	47	4	48	31	460
Guinea	4.7	47	23	2.4	29	8.5	175	43	3	41	20	130
Guinea-Bissau	0.5	40	25	1.5	46	0.8	208	37	4	38	23	390
Ivory Coast	7.0	46	21	2.5	28	13.2	164	43	3	44	20	500
Liberia	1.7	50	21	2.9	24	3.0	159	42	3	45	28	410
Mali	5.9	50	26	2.4	29	11.0	188	49	2	38	13	90
Mauritania	1.4	45	25	2.0	35	2.4	187	42	6	38	23	310
Niger	4.9	52	26	2.7	26	9.6	200	43	3	38	9	130
Nigeria	66.6	49	23	2.7	26	134.9	180	45	2	41	18	310
Senegal	5.3	46	21	2.5	28	9.3	159	43	3	44	32	370
Sierra Leone	3.2	45	21	2.4	29	5.8	136	43	3	44	15	200
Togo	2.3	51	23	2.7	26	4.6	127	46	3	41	15	270
Upper Volta	6.4	48	26	2.3	30	11.0	182	43	3	38	4	90
EASTERN AFRICA	120	46	19	2.7	26	239	151	44	3	45	12	220
Burundi	3.9	41	20	2.1	33	7.2	150	44	2	40	2	100
Comoros	0.3	45	20	2.5	28	0.5	160	43	3	46	10	260
Ethiopia	29.4	43	18	2.5	28	53.8	181	44	3	42	12	100
Kenya	14.4	49	16	3.3	21	31.5	119	46	3	50	10	220
Madagascar	7.9	50	21	2.9	24	16.4	102	35	3	44	14	200
Malawi	5.3	48	24	2.4	29	9.9	142	35	3	43	10	150
Mauritius	0.9	25	8	1.7	41	1.2	46	41	4	63	44	580
Mozambique	9.5	43	20	2.3	30	17.4	165	43	3	44	6	310
Reunion	0.5	28	7	2.1	33	0.7	47	43	4	63	51	1,550
Rhodesia	6.8	48	14	3.4	20	15.2	122	48	2	52	20	540
Rwanda	4.5	51	22	2.9	24	8.7	133	44	3	41	3	90
Seychelles	0.1	33	9	2.4	29	0.1	39	43	6	65	26	520
Somalia	3.4	47	22	2.6	27	6.5	177	45	2	41	28	100
Tanzania, United Rep. of	16.0	47	22	2.5	28	33.1	162	47	2	44	7	170
Uganda	12.4	43	16	2.7	26	24.7	160	44	3	50	7	250
Zambia	5.2	50	19	3.1	22	11.3	160	46	3	46	36	540

WORLD POPULATION DATA (continued)

Region or Country[1]	Population Estimate Mid-1977 (millions)[2]	Birth Rate[3]	Death Rate[3]	Rate of Natural Increase (annual, percent)[4]	Number of Years to Double Population[5]	Population Projection to 2000 (millions)[6]	Infant Mortality Rate[7]	Population under 15 Years (percent)[8]	Population over 64 Years (percent)[8]	Life Expectancy at Birth (years)	Urban Population (percent)[9]	Per Capita Gross National Product (US$)[10]
MIDDLE AFRICA	48	44	22	2.3	30	88	165	43	3	42	24	270
Angola	6.3	47	24	2.3	30	11.7	203	42	3	38	18	680
Cameroon, United Rep. of	6.7	40	22	1.8	38	11.6	137	40	3	41	20	270
Central African Republic	1.9	43	22	2.1	33	3.3	190	42	3	41	36	230
Chad	4.2	44	24	2.0	35	6.9	160	40	3	38	14	120
Congo, People's Rep. of	1.4	45	21	2.4	29	2.7	180	42	3	44	40	500
Equatorial Guinea	0.3	37	20	1.7	41	0.5	165	37	3	44	45	320
Gabon	0.5	32	22	1.0	69	0.7	178	32	4	41	32	2,240
Sao Tome and Principe	0.1	45	11	3.4	20	0.1	64	—	—	53	16	570
Zaire	26.3	45	20	2.5	28	50.5	160	44	3	44	26	150
SOUTHERN AFRICA	30	40	16	2.5	28	57	119	41	4	51	44	1,220
Botswana	0.7	46	23	2.3	30	1.4	97	48	6	56	12	330
Lesotho	1.1	39	20	1.9	36	1.8	114	40	4	46	3	180
Namibia	0.9	44	23	2.1	33	1.7	177	41	4	41	32	800
South Africa	26.1	40	15	2.5	28	51.2	117	41	4	52	48	1,320
Swaziland	0.5	49	22	2.7	26	1.0	149	48	3	44	8	470
ASIA	2,325	32	12	2.0	35	3,584	116	38	4	56	26	530
SOUTHWEST ASIA	89	42	14	2.8	25	166	114	44	4	55	44	1,370
Bahrain	0.3	43	8	3.5	20	0.6	78	44	3	63	78	2,440
Cyprus	0.6	17	9	0.8	87	0.8	29	29	9	71	42	1,180
Gaza	0.4	49	16	3.3	21	0.9	—	53	5	52	87	—
Iraq	11.8	44	11	3.2	22	24.3	99	48	3	53	64	1,280
Israel	3.6	28	7	2.1	33	5.5	22	33	7	72	82	3,580
Jordan	2.9	48	15	3.3	21	5.9	97	48	3	53	42	460
Kuwait	1.1	44	5	3.9	18	2.9	44	44	2	69	56	11,510
Lebanon	2.8	40	10	3.0	23	5.6	59	41	5	64	60	1,070
Oman	0.8	50	19	3.1	22	1.6	138	—	—	—	5	2,070
Qatar	0.1	50	19	3.1	22	0.2	138	—	—	—	69	8,320
Saudi Arabia	7.6	50	20	2.9	24	14.8	152	45	3	45	21	3,010
Syria	7.8	45	15	3.0	23	16.0	93	49	4	57	46	660
Turkey	41.9	39	12	2.7	26	72.4	119	42	4	57	43	860
United Arab Emirates	0.2	50	18	3.2	22	0.5	138	—	—	—	52	10,480
Yemen	5.6	50	21	2.9	24	11.0	152	45	3	45	9	210
Yemen, Democratic	1.8	50	21	2.9	24	3.5	152	48	4	45	33	240
MIDDLE SOUTH ASIA	864	37	14	2.3	30	1,473	125	41	3	49	20	200
Afghanistan	20.0	43	21	2.2	32	36.1	182	44	3	40	15	130
Bangladesh	83.3	47	20	2.7	26	154.9	132	43	3	47	9	110
Bhutan	1.2	44	20	2.3	30	2.1	—	42	3	44	3	70
India	622.7	34	13	2.1	33	1,023.7	122	40	3	50	21	150
Iran	34.8	44	16	2.8	25	66.1	139	47	3	51	44	1,440
Maldives	0.1	50	23	2.7	26	0.2	—	44	2	.	11	100
Nepal	13.2	43	20	2.3	30	23.2	169	40	3	44	4	110
Pakistan	74.5	44	15	2.9	24	145.5	121	46	3	51	26	140
Sri Lanka	14.1	28	8	2.0	35	20.7	45	39	4	68	22	150

WORLD POPULATION DATA (continued)

Region or Country[1]	Population Estimate Mid-1977 (millions)[2]	Birth Rate[3]	Death Rate[3]	Rate of Natural Increase (annual, percent)[4]	Number of Years to Double Population[5]	Population Projection to 2000 (millions)[6]	Infant Mortality Rate[7]	Population under 15 Years (percent)[8]	Population over 64 Years (percent)[8]	Life Expectancy at Birth (years)[8]	Urban Population (percent)[9]	Per Capita Gross National Product (US$)[10]
SOUTHEAST ASIA	332	38	14	2.4	29	574	116	43	3	52	21	260
Burma	31.8	40	16	2.4	29	53.3	126	40	4	50	22	110
Democratic Kampuchea (Cambodia)	8.0	47	19	2.8	25	14.7	127	45	3	45	12	70
East Timor	0.7	44	23	2.1	33	1.2	184	42	3	40	11	150
Indonesia	136.9	38	14	2.4	29	226.9	137	44	2	48	18	180
Lao People's Republic (Laos)	3.5	45	23	2.2	32	5.8	123	42	3	40	15	70
Malaysia	12.6	35	7	2.8	25	21.6	75	45	3	63	27	720
Philippines	44.3	35	8	2.7	26	83.7	74	43	3	58	32	370
Singapore	2.3	18	5	1.3	53	3.1	14	34	4	68	100	2,510
Thailand	44.4	35	11	2.4	29	84.6	89	45	3	58	13	350
Vietnam, Socialist Rep. of	47.3	42	20	2.1	33	78.9	—	41	4	50	22	160
EAST ASIA	1,040	26	10	1.6	43	1,371	22	33	6	63	31	820
China, People's Rep. of[11]	850	27	10	1.7	41	1,126	—	33	6	62	24	350
Hong Kong	4.5	20	5	1.4	50	5.9	17	31	5	71	92	1,720
Japan	114.2	17	6	1.1	63	133.4	10	24	8	74	72	4,460
Korea, Dem. People's Rep. of	16.7	36	9	2.6	27	27.5	—	42	4	61	43	430
Korea, Rep. of	35.9	24	7	1.7	41	52.9	47	40	3	65	48	550
Macao	0.3	25	7	1.8	38	0.4	78	38	5	—	97	310
Mongolia	1.5	40	10	3.0	23	2.7	—	44	3	61	46	700
Taiwan (Rep. of China)[12]	16.6	23	5	1.8	38	22.0	26	43	3	69	63	890
NORTH AMERICA	240	15	9	0.6	116	294	16	26	10	72	74	7,020
Canada	23.5	16	7	0.8	87	31.6	15	27	8	73	76	6,650
United States	216.7	15	9	0.6	116	262.5	16	26	10	72	74	7,060
LATIN AMERICA	336	36	9	2.7	26	608	78	42	4	62	59	1,030
MIDDLE AMERICA	85	42	8	3.4	20	174	70	46	3	62	56	1,060
Costa Rica	2.1	29	5	2.4	29	3.6	38	44	4	68	41	910
El Salvador	4.3	40	8	3.2	22	8.6	58	46	3	58	39	450
Guatemala	6.4	43	12	3.1	22	12.2	80	45	3	53	34	650
Honduras	3.3	49	15	3.5	20	6.9	117	47	2	54	31	350
Mexico	64.4	42	7	3.5	20	134.6	66	46	3	63	62	1,190
Nicaragua	2.3	48	14	3.4	20	4.8	123	48	3	53	49	720
Panama	1.8	31	5	2.6	27	3.2	40	43	4	66	50	1,060
CARIBBEAN	28	30	9	2.1	33	44	75	41	5	64	45	970
Bahamas	0.2	20	5	1.4	50	0.3	35	44	3	66	58	2,600
Barbados	0.2	19	8	1.1	63	0.3	38	34	9	69	44	1,260
Cuba	9.6	22	6	1.6	43	14.9	29	37	6	70	60	800
Dominican Republic	5.0	46	11	3.5	20	10.7	98	48	3	58	44	720
Grenada	0.1	26	8	1.9	36	0.1	32	—	—	63	15	370
Guadeloupe	0.3	28	7	2.1	33	0.5	44	40	5	60	48	1,240
Haiti	5.3	36	16	2.0	35	7.9	150	42	4	50	20	180
Jamaica	2.1	30	7	2.3	30	2.8	26	46	6	68	37	1,290
Martinique	0.4	22	7	1.6	43	0.5	32	41	5	65	50	1,540
Netherlands Antilles	0.2	20	5	1.5	46	0.4	28	38	5	62	48	1,590
Puerto Rico	3.2	23	6	1.7	41	4.1	24	37	7	72	58	2,300
Trinidad and Tobago	1.0	24	6	1.8	38	1.3	34	40	4	66	12	1,900

WORLD POPULATION DATA (continued)

Region or Country [1]	Population Estimate Mid-1977 (millions) [2]	Birth Rate [3]	Death Rate [3]	Rate of Natural Increase (annual, percent) [4]	Number of Years to Double Population [5]	Population Projection to 2000 (millions) [6]	Infant Mortality Rate [7]	Population under 15 Years (percent) [8]	Population over 64 Years (percent) [8]	Life Expectancy at Birth (years)	Urban Population (percent) [9]	Per Capita Gross National Product (US$) [10]
TROPICAL SOUTH AMERICA	183	37	9	2.8	25	337	84	43	3	61	59	960
Bolivia	4.8	44	18	2.6	27	8.7	108	42	4	47	34	320
Brazil	112.0	37	9	2.8	25	205.0	82	42	3	61	59	1,010
Colombia	25.2	33	9	2.5	28	47.1	97	43	3	61	64	550
Ecuador	7.5	42	10	3.2	22	14.7	78	45	4	60	41	550
Guyana	0.8	32	7	2.4	29	1.3	40	44	3	68	40	560
Paraguay	2.8	40	9	3.1	22	5.3	65	45	4	62	37	570
Peru	16.6	41	12	2.9	24	31.2	110	45	3	56	55	810
Surinam	0.4	37	7	3.0	23	0.9	30	50	4	66	50	1,180
Venezuela	12.7	37	6	3.1	22	23.2	49	45	3	65	74	2,220
TEMPERATE SOUTH AMERICA	40	23	9	1.4	50	52	63	31	7	67	79	1,340
Argentina	26.1	23	9	1.3	53	32.9	59	29	8	68	80	1,590
Chile	11.0	24	8	1.6	43	15.8	77	36	5	63	76	760
Uruguay	2.8	21	10	1.1	63	3.4	45	28	9	70	81	1,330
EUROPE	478	15	10	0.4	173	539	22	24	12	71	65	4,090
NORTHERN EUROPE	82	13	11	0.2	347	90	14	24	13	72	74	4,590
Denmark	5.1	14	10	0.4	173	5.4	12	23	13	74	80	6,920
Finland	4.8	14	9	0.5	139	4.8	10	23	10	71	58	5,100
Iceland	0.2	21	7	1.4	50	0.3	11	30	9	74	86	5,620
Ireland	3.2	22	11	1.1	63	4.0	17	31	11	71	52	2,420
Norway	4.0	14	10	0.4	173	4.5	11	24	14	74	45	6,540
Sweden	8.2	13	11	0.2	347	9.2	8	21	15	75	81	7,880
United Kingdom	56.0	12	12	0.1	693	61.9	16	24	14	72	78	3,840
WESTERN EUROPE	152	12	11	0.1	693	169	15	23	13	71	77	6,150
Austria	7.5	12	13	0.0	—	8.1	21	24	15	71	52	4,720
Belgium	9.9	12	12	0.0	—	10.7	16	23	14	71	87	6,070
France	53.4	14	11	0.4	173	61.7	12	24	14	72	70	5,760
Germany, Federal Rep. of	61.2	10	12	-0.2	—	65.5	20	22	14	71	88	6,610
Luxembourg	0.4	11	12	-0.1	—	0.4	15	20	13	70	69	6,050
Netherlands	13.9	13	8	0.5	139	16.1	11	26	11	74	77	5,590
Switzerland	6.2	12	9	0.4	173	6.9	12	23	12	73	55	8,050
EASTERN EUROPE	108	18	11	0.7	99	122	26	23	11	70	57	2,800
Bulgaria	8.8	17	10	0.6	116	9.9	23	22	11	71	59	2,040
Czechoslovakia	15.0	20	12	0.8	87	16.9	21	23	12	71	67	3,710
German Democratic Republic	16.7	11	14	-0.4	—	17.7	16	22	16	71	75	4,230
Hungary	10.7	18	12	0.6	116	11.1	33	20	12	70	50	2,480
Poland	34.7	19	9	1.0	69	40.2	25	24	9	70	54	2,910
Romania	21.7	20	9	1.1	63	25.9	35	25	9	69	43	1,300
SOUTHERN EUROPE	136	17	9	0.8	87	158	26	26	10	71	52	2,470
Albania	2.5	33	8	2.5	28	4.1	87	40	5	67	34	600
Greece	9.1	16	9	0.7	99	9.8	24	24	12	72	65	2,360
Italy	56.5	15	10	0.5	139	61.9	21	24	12	72	53	2,940
Malta	0.3	19	10	0.9	77	0.3	19	26	9	70	94	1,220
Portugal	9.2	20	11	0.9	77	10.4	38	27	10	69	26	1,610
Spain	36.5	18	8	1.0	69	45.4	14	28	10	72	61	2,700
Yugoslavia	21.8	18	9	1.0	69	25.7	40	26	8	68	39	1,480

WORLD POPULATION DATA (concluded)

Region or Country [1]	Population Estimate Mid-1977 (millions) [2]	Birth Rate [3]	Death Rate [3]	Rate of Natural Increase (annual, percent) [4]	Number of Years to Double Population [5]	Population Projection to 2000 (millions) [6]	Infant Mortality Rate [7]	Population under 15 Years (percent) [8]	Population over 64 Years (percent) [8]	Life Expectancy at Birth (years)	Urban Population (percent) [9]	Per Capita Gross National Product (US$) [10]
USSR	259	18	9	0.9	77	314	28	26	9	69	60	2,620
OCEANIA	22	22	9	1.3	53	32	55	32	7	67	71	4,490
Australia	13.9	17	8	0.9	77	19.6	16	28	8	71	86	5,640
Fiji	0.6	29	7	2.2	32	0.8	21	40	3	70	38	920
New Zealand	3.2	18	8	1.0	69	4.4	16	30	9	72	81	4,680
Papua New Guinea	2.9	41	17	2.4	29	5.1	159	45	2	48	11	450
Samoa, Western	0.2	35	7	2.8	25	0.3	40	51	3	63	21	320
Solomon Islands	0.2	36	9	2.7	26	0.4	52	44	3	—	9	310

General Notes

World Population Data Sheets of various years should not be used as a time series. Because every attempt is made to use the most recent and most accurate information, data sources vary and radical changes in numbers and rates from year to year may reflect improved source material, revised data, or a later base year for computation, rather than yearly changes

Sources of data: Aside from the population estimates and projections (see footnotes 2 and 6), number of years to double population (see footnote 5), and per capita Gross National Product (see footnote 10), almost all of the data in this table were reported in the following United Nations (UN) publications: Demographic Yearbook, 1973, 1974, and 1975 editions; Population and Vital Statistics Report, Data Available as of 1 January 1977, Statistical Papers, Series A, Vol. XXIX, No. 1; Trends and Prospects in Urban and Rural Population, 1950-2000, as Assessed in 1973-1974, ESA/P/WP.54, 25 April 1975; Selected World Demographic Indicators by Countries, 1950-2000, ESA/P/WP.55, 28 May 1975; and Single-Year Population Estimates and Projections for Major Areas, Regions and Countries of the World, 1950-2000, ESA/P/WP.56, 6 October 1975. The source for any figure shown on the Data Sheet may be obtained by writing or telephoning the Population Reference Bureau

Figures for the regions and the world: Population totals take into account small areas not listed on the Data Sheet. Totals may also not equal the sums of their parts because of independent rounding. All other data are weighted averages for countries for which data are available

Dashes indicate data are unavailable.

Footnotes

[1] The Data Sheet lists all UN members and all geopolitical entities with a population larger than 200,000.

[2] Based on a population total from a very recent census or on the most recent official country or UN estimate; for almost all countries the estimate was for mid-1975. Each estimate was updated by the Population Reference Bureau to mid-1977 by applying the same rate of growth as indicated by population change during part or all of the period since 1970

[3] Annual number of births or deaths per 1,000 population. For the more developed countries, with complete or nearly complete registration of births and deaths, nearly all the rates shown pertain to 1974 or 1975. For nearly all the developing countries, with incomplete registration, the rates refer to the 1970-75 period and are cited in Statistical Papers, Series A, as having been prepared by the United Nations. These rates were used in the medium variant estimates and projections as assessed by the United Nations in 1973 (UN, Selected World Demographic Indicators . . .). These figures should be considered as rough approximations only

[4] Birth rate minus the death rate. Since the rates were based on unrounded birth and death rates, some rates do not exactly equal the difference between the birth and death rates shown because of rounding.

[5] Based on the rate of natural increase shown and assuming no change in the rate.

[6] Except for the United States, estimated by the Population Reference Bureau by applying the percentage increase in the population 1977-2000 implied by the UN medium variant projections to the population total as estimated for mid-1977. For the United States, the figure shown is the Series II projection given in the U.S. Bureau of the Census, Projections of the Population of the United States: 1975 to 2050, P-25, No. 601, October 1975.

[7] Annual number of deaths to infants under one year of age per 1,000 live births. For countries with complete or nearly complete registration of births and deaths, nearly all rates pertain to 1974 or 1975. For many developing countries with incomplete registration, rates are the latest available estimates generally obtained from the UN sources noted above: from World Health Organization, World Health Statistics Report, Vol. 29, No. 4, 1976; or from International Statistical Programs Center, U.S. Bureau of the Census, World Population: 1973, May 1974, and World Population: 1975, June 1976

[8] The "dependency ratio" for each country or region can be derived by adding the percentages under 15 years and over 64 years and dividing by the complement. For the world as a whole, for example, 36% + 6% : 58% gives a figure of 72 persons in the "dependent ages" for each 100 persons in the "working ages" of 15 to 65.

[9] The percentage of the total population living in areas defined as urban by each country.

[10] The figures given for the individual countries were released by the World Bank on December 27, 1976. They refer to 1975 except for 18 of the smaller countries for which the data refer to 1974. The figures are published in the eleventh edition of the World Bank Atlas Population, Per Capita Product, and Growth Rates, 1977

[11] In the absence of official information, the UN medium variant estimates as assessed in 1973 are given here for the birth and death rates. Some observers, however, consider the birth rate of 27 per 1,000 population too high at the present time because of China's rigorous family planning program. The population estimate for mid-1977 is also the medium variant estimate after subtracting the estimated mid-1977 total for Taiwan. However, population estimates for those provinces that have recently been announced through Chinese radio and newspapers strongly suggest that a more valid estimate would be 30 to 50 million higher than that given here. It is expected that the 1978 Data Sheet will show a revised estimate based on further information from China or new estimates by the UN.

[12] The UN does not show figures for Taiwan. These figures were separately estimated on the basis of official Taiwan data. The population was assumed to increase to 2000 at the same rate as that of the People's Republic of China

Source: 1977 World Population Data Sheet, courtesy of the Population Reference Bureau, Inc.

PER CAPITA GROSS NATIONAL PRODUCT AT MARKET PRICES—AMOUNT (1974) AND AVERAGE ANNUAL GROWTH RATES (1960–74 AND 1965–74)

COUNTRIES WITH POPULATIONS OF 1,000,000 OR MORE. GNP PER CAPITA ROUNDED TO NEAREST US$10.

Country	GNP per capita Amount (US$)	Growth rates (%) 1960–74	1965–74	Country	GNP per capita Amount (US$)	Growth rates (%) 1960–74	1965–74
Switzerland	7,870	2.9	2.9	Portugal	1,630	7.4	7.6
Sweden	7,240	3.2	2.8	Hong Kong	1,610	6.6	5.4
United States	6,670	2.9	2.4				
Denmark	6,430	3.8	3.4	Argentina	1,520	2.8	2.9
Germany, Federal				Yugoslavia	1,310	4.9	5.4
Republic of	6,260	3.7	3.9	Iran	1,250	6.7	7.7
				South Africa	1,210	2.9	2.5
Canada	6,190	3.7	3.5	Jamaica	1,190	3.6	4.5
Norway	5,860	3.7	3.4				
Belgium	5,670	4.5	4.9	Uruguay	1,190	0.5	0.8
France	5,440	4.4	4.8	Iraq	1,110	4.0	4.8
Australia	5,330	3.2	3.4	Romania	1,100	N.A.	8.0
				Mexico[3]	1,090	3.3	2.8
Netherlands, The	5,250	4.0	4.1	Lebanon[4]	1,070	3.1	3.7
Finland	4,700	4.6	5.2				
Libyan Arab Republic	4,440	12.5	6.5	Panama	1,000	4.1	3.7
Austria	4,410	4.4	5.0	Brazil	920	4.0	6.3
New Zealand	4,310	2.1	1.8	Costa Rica	840	2.9	3.7
				Chile	830	1.7	1.3
Japan	4,070	8.8	8.5	China, Republic of	810	6.5	6.9
German Democratic							
Republic[1,2]	3,950	3.1	3.0	Turkey	750	3.9	4.3
United Kingdom	3,590	2.3	2.2	Peru	740	2.0	1.8
Israel	3,460	5.3	5.8	Algeria	730	1.3	4.5
Czechoslovakia[1,2]	3,330	2.4	2.5	Angola	710	3.7	3.2
				Cuba[1,2]	710	−0.9	−0.6
Saudi Arabia	2,830	8.4	9.2				
Italy	2,820	4.2	4.0	Malaysia	680	3.9	3.8
Poland[1,2]	2,510	4.0	4.5	Nicaragua	670	3.0	1.5
Spain	2,490	5.8	5.4	Dominican Republic	650	3.1	5.5
USSR[1,2]	2,380	3.8	3.4	Tunisia[5]	650	3.9	5.4
				Mongolia[1,2]	610	0.8	1.8
Ireland	2,320	3.6	3.6				
Singapore	2,240	7.6	10.0	Guatemala	580	3.3	3.8
Puerto Rico	2,230	5.3	4.7	Syrian Arab Republic	560	4.0	4.2
Hungary[1,2]	2,180	3.2	2.9	Albania[1,2]	530	4.4	5.0
Greece	2,090	6.8	6.5	Zambia	520	2.3	1.0
				Rhodesia	520	1.9	3.5
Venezuela	1,960	2.4	2.2				
Bulgaria[1,2]	1,780	4.5	3.5	Paraguay	510	2.0	2.5
Trinidad and Tobago	1,700	2.1	2.2	Colombia	500	2.6	3.4

PER CAPITA GROSS NATIONAL PRODUCT AT MARKET PRICES (continued)

Country	GNP per capita			Country	GNP per capita		
	Amount (US$)	Growth rates (%)			Amount (US$)	Growth rates (%)	
		1960–74	1965–74			1960–74	1965–74
Ecuador.............	480	2.4	2.1	Sierra Leone[7]..........	190	1.6	1.4
Korea, Republic of....	480	7.3	8.7	Madagascar..........	180	0.1	0.3
Papua New Guinea....	470	4.2	4.1	Yemen Arab			
Congo, People's				Republic[1]...........	180	N.A.	N.A.
Republic of the.....	470	2.8	4.0	Indonesia.............	170	2.4	4.1
Ivory Coast..........	460	3.5	2.7	Haiti................	170	−0.1	0.7
Jordan..............	430	0.9	−2.5	Tanzania[8].............	160	2.6	2.3
Morocco.............	430	1.8	2.8	Zaire................	150	2.6	2.9
Ghana...............	430	−0.2	0.3	Viet Nam, Socialist			
El Salvador..........	410	1.8	1.0	Republic of[1,2]........	150	0.3	−0.8
Liberia..............	390	2.2	4.1	India................	140	1.1	1.3
Korea, Democratic				Lesotho[1]..............	140	4.2	3.7
People's				Sri Lanka.............	130	2.1	2.0
Republic of[1,3].......	390	4.4	3.5	Pakistan..............	130	3.4	2.5
Mozambique[1]........	340	2.8	3.5	Malawi...............	130	3.9	4.7
Honduras............	340	1.6	2.2	Benin, People's			
Senegal..............	330	−1.1	−0.9	Republic of[1]..........	120	0.7	0.8
Philippines...........	330	2.4	2.7	Guinea...............	120	0.0	0.1
Thailand.............	310	4.6	4.3	Niger.................	120	−1.8	−3.8
China, People's				Afghanistan...........	110	0.5	1.1
Republic of[1,2].......	300	5.2	4.6	Nepal................	100	0.4	0.0
Mauritania...........	290	3.8	1.3	Ethiopia..............	100	2.2	1.5
Nigeria..............	280	2.9	6.0	Chad.................	100	−1.2	−1.5
Egypt, Arab				Bangladesh...........	100	−0.5	−1.9
Republic of.........	280	1.5	1.0	Burma...............	100	0.7	0.8
Bolivia..............	280	2.5	2.2	Burundi[1].............	90	1.3	1.3
Cameroon............	250	4.4	2.8	Somalia[1].............	90	−0.3	1.1
Togo................	250	4.4	2.8	Upper Volta...........	90	−0.1	−0.5
Uganda.............	240	1.8	0.7	Rwanda[1].............	80	−0.2	1.4
Sudan[1]..............	230	1.7	4.3	Mali.................	80	0.9	0.4
Yemen, People's				Cambodia[1,4]...........	70	−2.7	−6.2
Democratic				Bhutan[1]..............	70	−0.3	−0.2
Republic of[1,6].......	220	N.A.	−4.3	Lao People's Democratic			
Central African				Republic[1,4]..........	70	1.8	2.0
Empire.............	210	0.4	0.8				
Kenya...............	200	3.2	3.5				

[1] Estimates of GNP per capita and its growth rate are tentative.
[2] For estimation of GNP per capita, see Technical Note, *World Bank Atlas, 1976*, p. 22 (1818 H Street NW Washington, DC 20433).
[3] Estimate of GNP per capita does not reflect the significant devaluation of the peso in August 1976.
[4] GNP per capita estimated on the 1972–74 base period.
[5] GNP per capita growth rate relates to 1961–74.
[6] GNP per capita growth rate relates to 1969–74.
[7] GNP per capita growth rate relates to 1964–74.
[8] Mainland Tanzania.
Source: *World Bank Atlas*, World Bank.

Economic Indicators by Country*

Unless otherwise specified in the tables, the following definitions apply.

Geographical coverage: Belgium-Luxembourg: Foreign finance, foreign trade, and balance-of-payments statistics refer to the Belgo-Luxembourg Economic Union. **United Kingdom:** Great Britain and Northern Ireland.

* All exhibits in this section are reproduced with permission from: *Main Economic Indicators,* Organisation for Economic Co-operation and Development, Paris, July 1977.

Subject definitions: Construction: Excludes civil engineering. **Internal trade:** Wholesale sales exclude indirect taxes; retail sales include them. **Time lost through labor disputes:** Excludes time lost due to shortages or strikes in related industries. **Internal trade:** Wholesale sales exclude indirect taxes; retail sales include them. **Official reserves:** Gross holdings of gold, special drawing rights, and foreign exchange plus reserve position in I.M.F. **Foreign trade:** Special trade.

AUSTRALIA

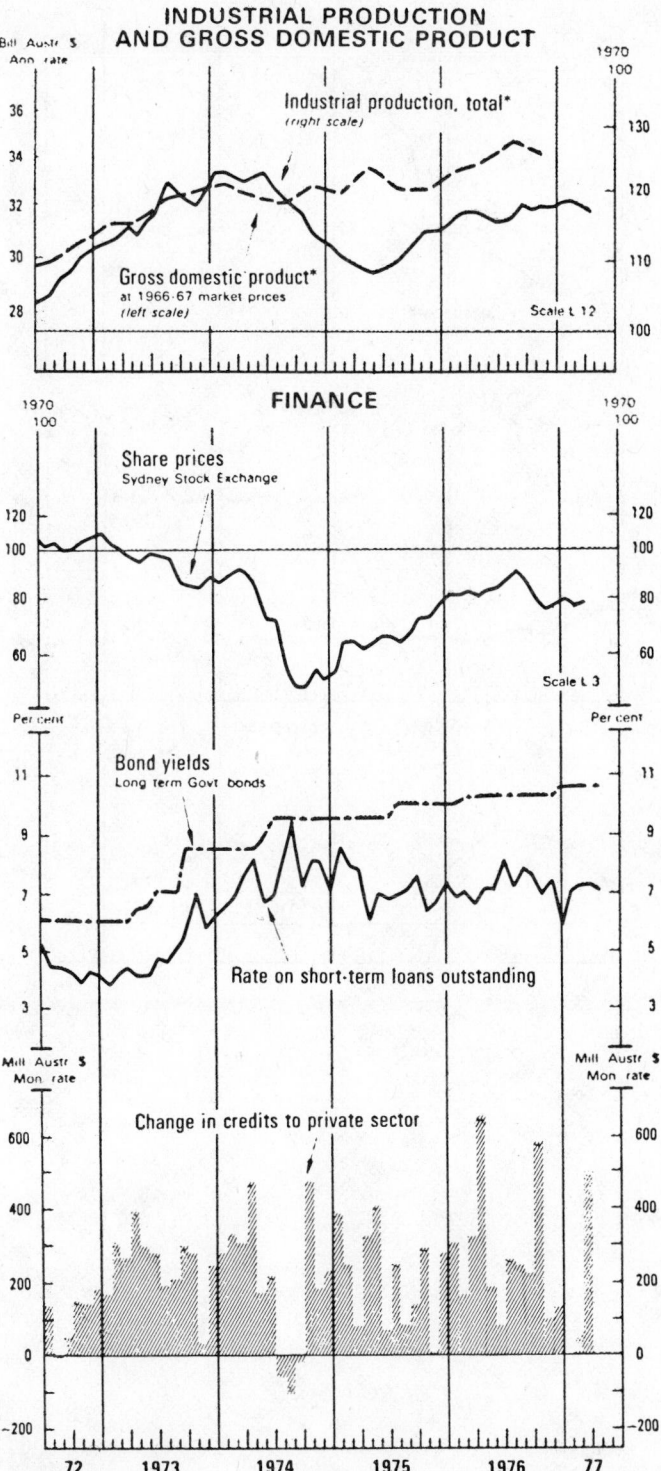

INDUSTRIAL PRODUCTION AND GROSS DOMESTIC PRODUCT

Bill Austr $
Ann rate

1970
100

Industrial production, total*
(right scale)

Gross domestic product*
at 1966-67 market prices
(left scale)

Scale L 12

FINANCE

1970
100

1970
100

Share prices
Sydney Stock Exchange

Scale L 3

Per cent

Per cent

Bond yields
Long term Govt bonds

Rate on short-term loans outstanding

Mill Austr $
Mon rate

Mill Austr $
Mon rate

Change in credits to private sector

72 1973 1974 1975 1976 77

AUSTRALIA (*continued*)

PRICES AND WAGES

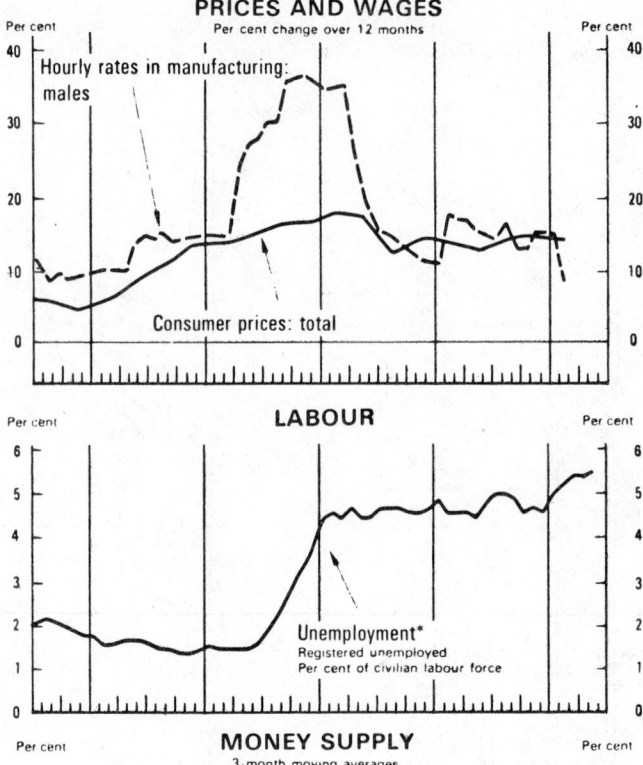

LABOUR

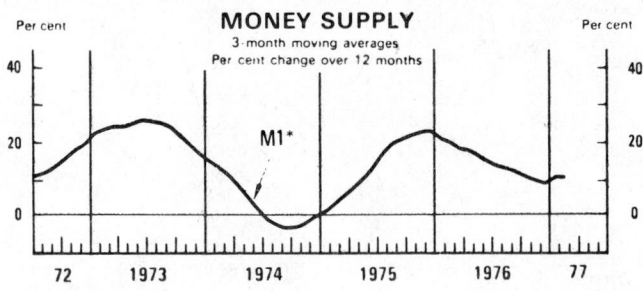

MONEY SUPPLY

AUSTRALIA (*concluded*)

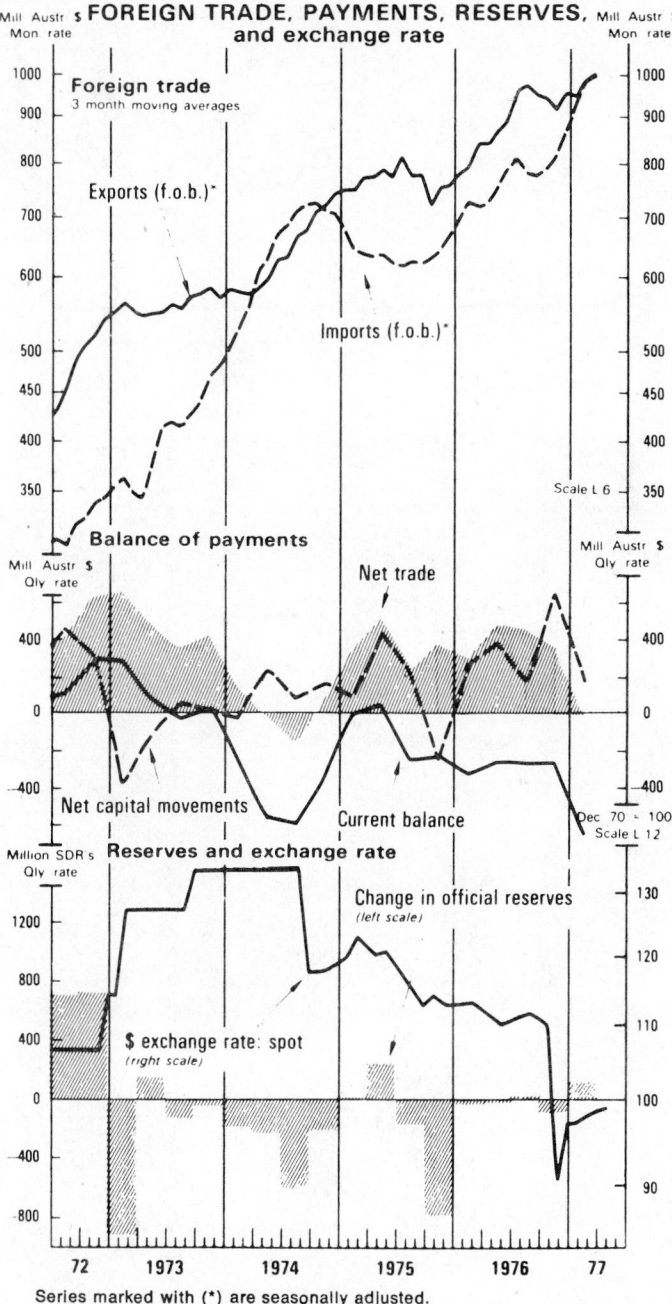

Mill Austr s
Mon rate

FOREIGN TRADE, PAYMENTS, RESERVES,
and exchange rate

Mill Austr $
Mon rate

Foreign trade
3 month moving averages

Exports (f.o.b.)*

Imports (f.o.b.)*

Scale L 6

Balance of payments

Mill Austr $
Qly rate

Net trade

Mill Austr $
Qly rate

Net capital movements

Current balance

Dec 70 = 100
Scale L 12

Million SDR s
Qly rate

Reserves and exchange rate

Change in official reserves
(left scale)

$ exchange rate: spot
(right scale)

Series marked with (*) are seasonally adjusted.

AUSTRIA

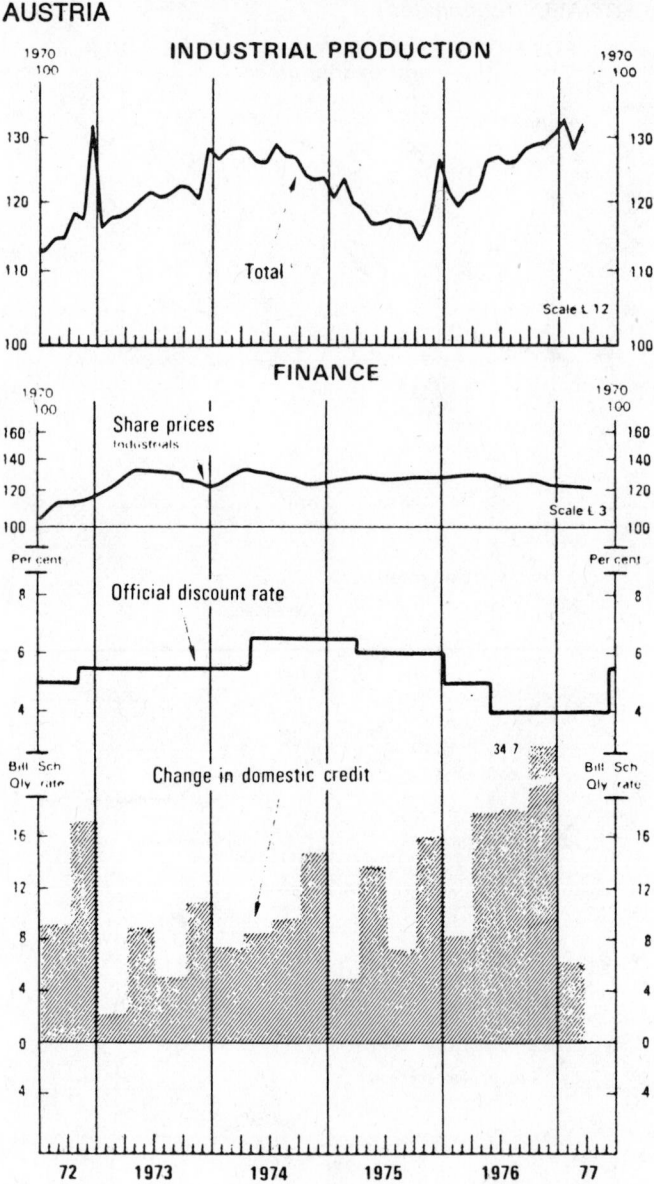

INDUSTRIAL PRODUCTION

1970 100

130

120

110

Total

Scale L 12

100

1970 100

130

120

110

100

FINANCE

1970 100

Share prices
Industrials

160
140
120
100

Scale L 3

1970 100

160
140
120
100

Per cent

8

Official discount rate

6

4

Per cent

8

6

4

Bill Sch
Qly rate

Change in domestic credit

34 7

Bill Sch
Qly rate

16

12

8

4

0

4

16

12

8

4

0

4

72   1973   1974   1975   1976   77

AUSTRIA *(continued)*

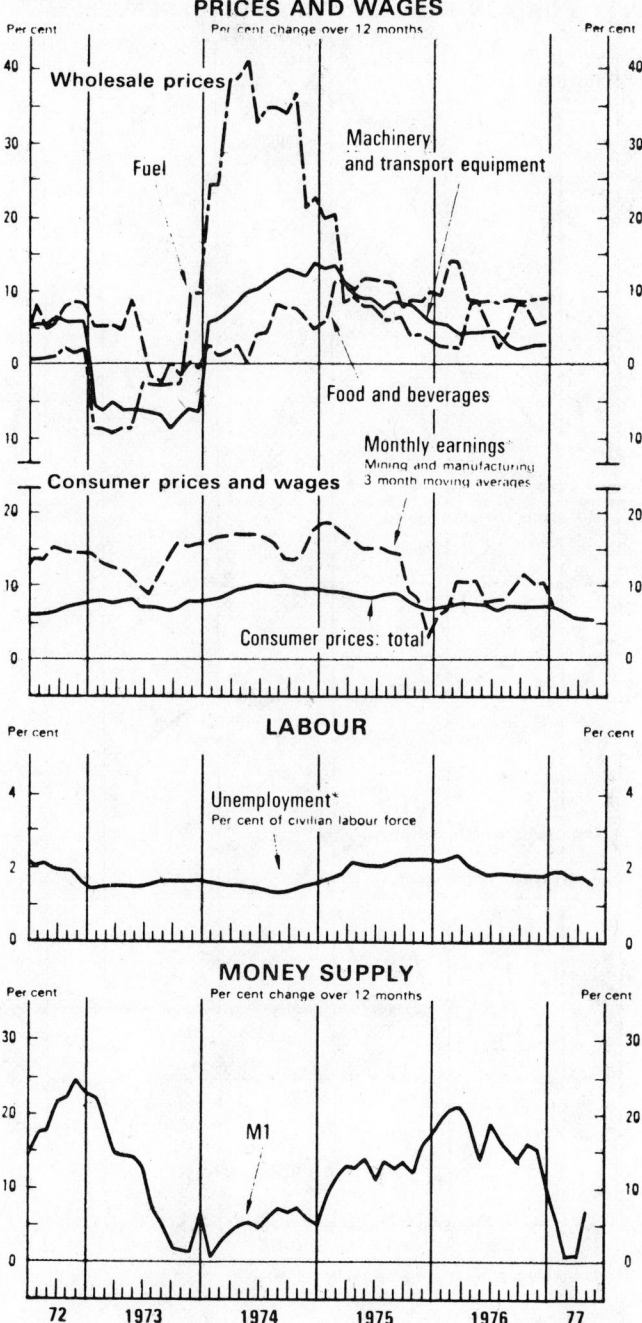

PRICES AND WAGES

Per cent change over 12 months

Wholesale prices

Fuel

Machinery and transport equipment

Food and beverages

Monthly earnings
Mining and manufacturing
3 month moving averages

Consumer prices and wages

Consumer prices: total

LABOUR

Unemployment*
Per cent of civilian labour force

MONEY SUPPLY

Per cent change over 12 months

M1

72   1973   1974   1975   1976   77

AUSTRIA (*concluded*)

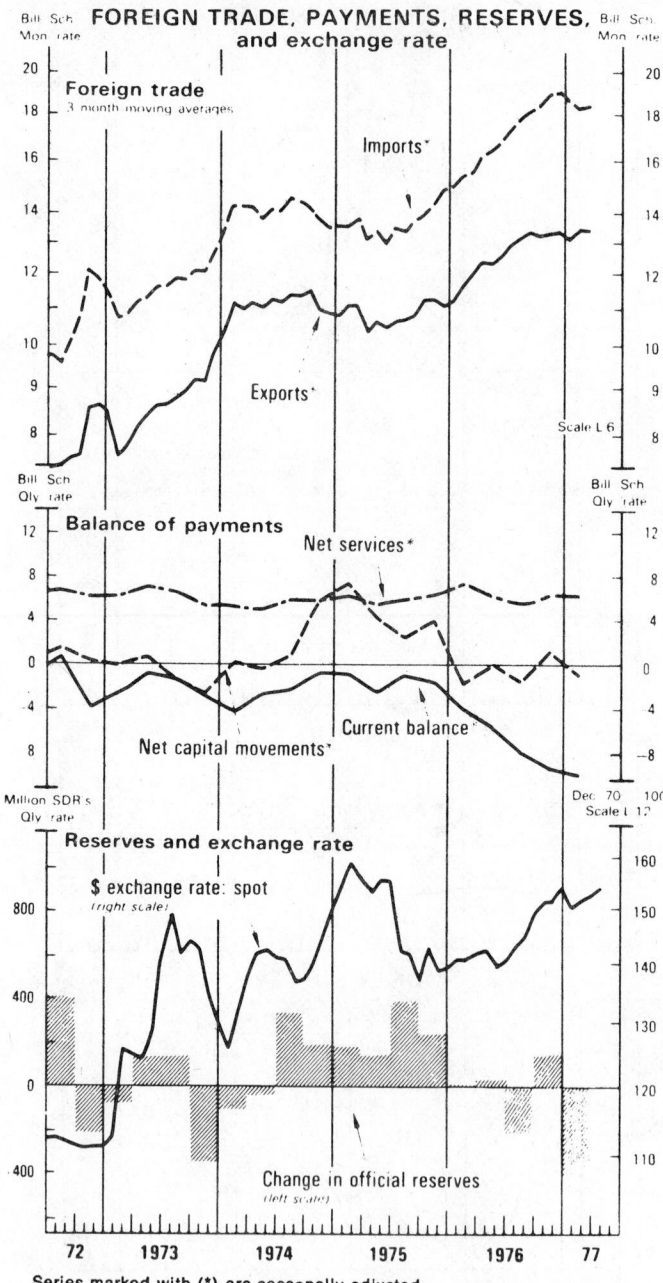

**FOREIGN TRADE, PAYMENTS, RESERVES,
and exchange rate**

Series marked with (*) are seasonally adjusted.

BELGIUM

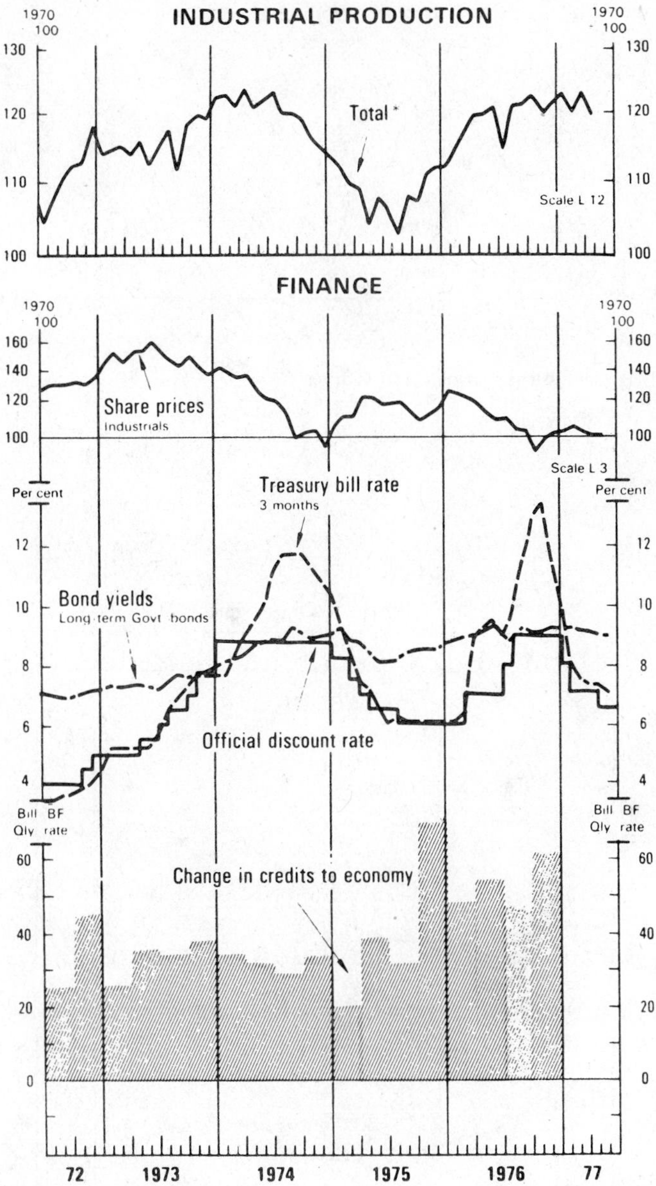

INDUSTRIAL PRODUCTION

1970
100

1970
100

130

130

120

120

Total

110

110

Scale L 12

100

100

FINANCE

1970
100

1970
100

160

160

140

140

Share prices
Industrials

120

120

100

100

Scale L 3

Per cent

Per cent

Treasury bill rate
3 months

12

12

Bond yields
Long-term Govt. bonds

10

10

8

8

Official discount rate

6

6

4

4

Bill BF
Qly rate

Bill BF
Qly rate

Change in credits to economy

60

60

40

40

20

20

0

0

72 1973 1974 1975 1976 77

BELGIUM (*continued*)

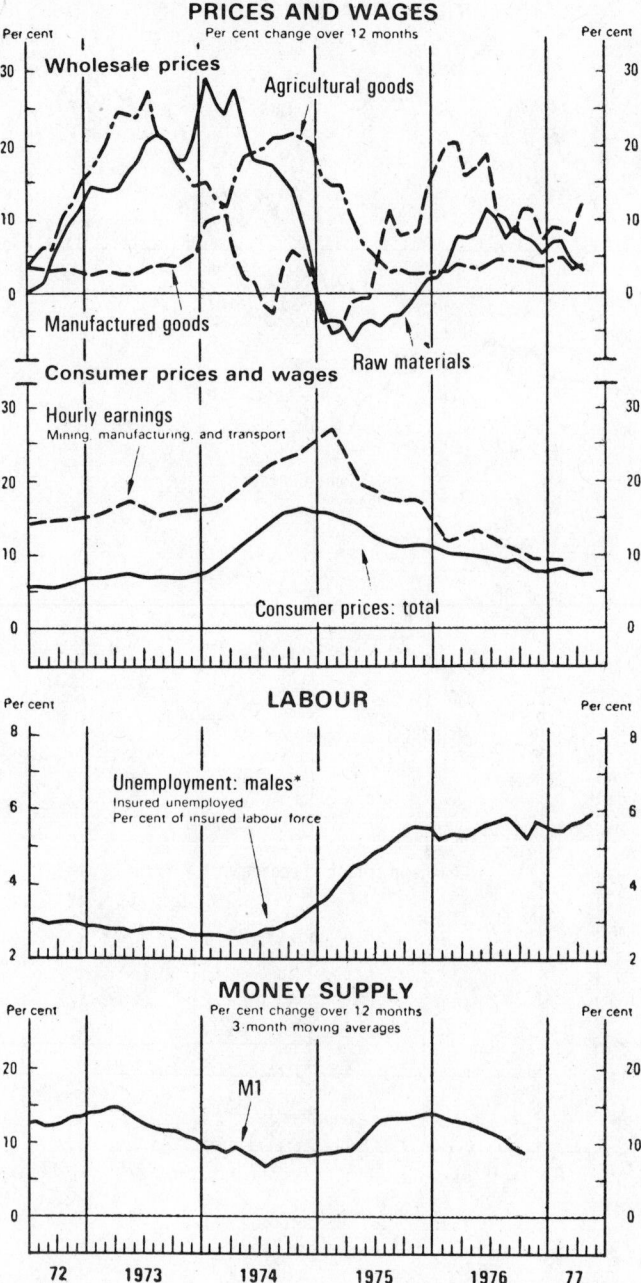

PRICES AND WAGES

Per cent change over 12 months

Wholesale prices

Agricultural goods

Manufactured goods

Raw materials

Consumer prices and wages

Hourly earnings
Mining, manufacturing, and transport

Consumer prices: total

LABOUR

Unemployment: males*
Insured unemployed
Per cent of insured labour force

MONEY SUPPLY

Per cent change over 12 months
3-month moving averages

M1

72 1973 1974 1975 1976 77

BELGIUM (*concluded*)

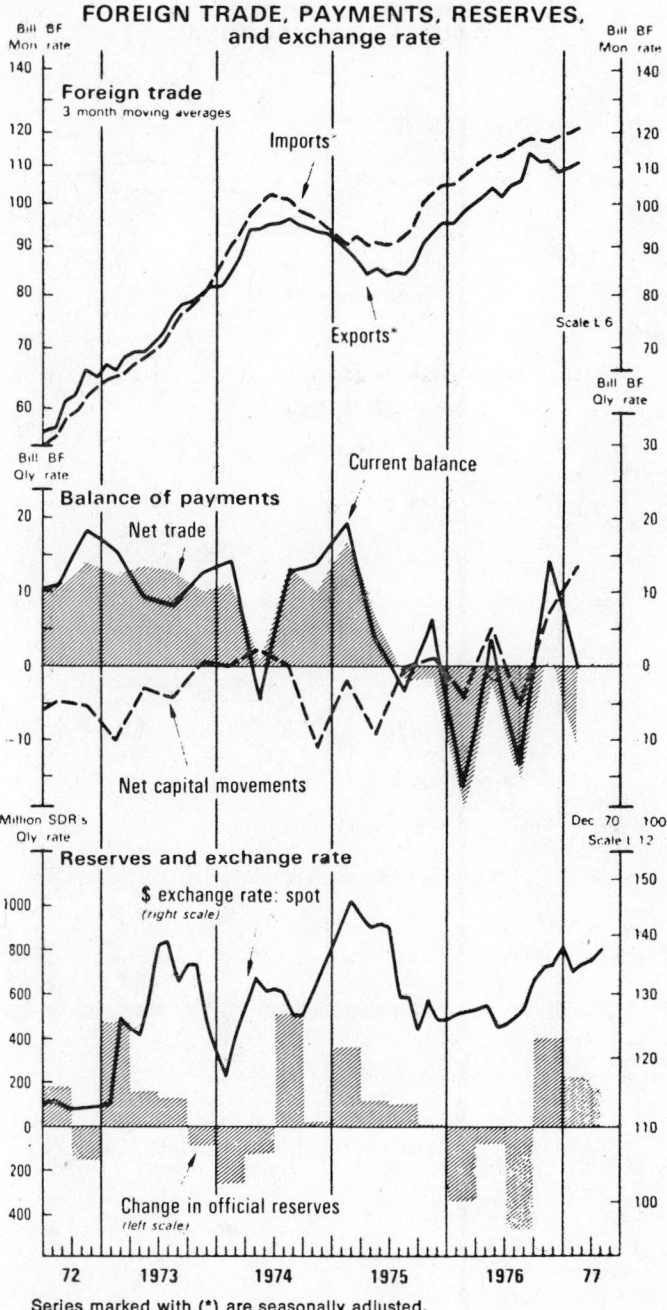

FOREIGN TRADE, PAYMENTS, RESERVES, and exchange rate

Series marked with (*) are seasonally adjusted.

CANADA

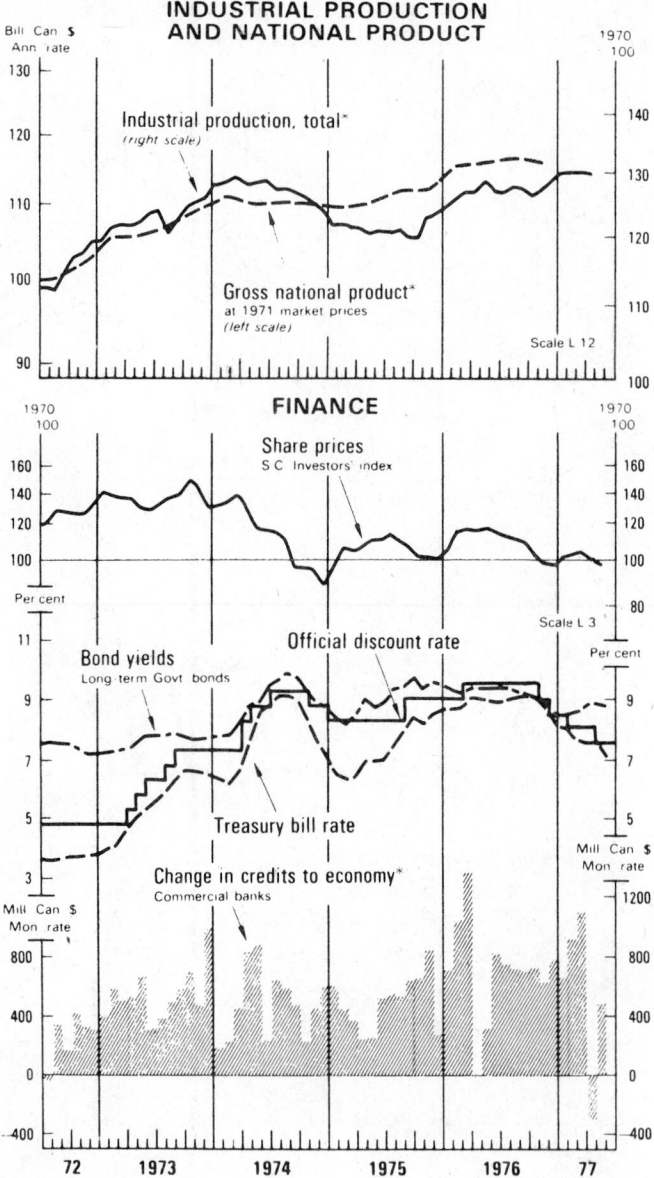

INDUSTRIAL PRODUCTION AND NATIONAL PRODUCT

Bill Can $
Ann rate

Industrial production, total*
(right scale)

Gross national product*
at 1971 market prices
(left scale)

Scale L 12

1970
100

FINANCE

1970
100

Share prices
S C Investors' index

Scale L 3

Per cent

Bond yields
Long term Govt bonds

Official discount rate

Treasury bill rate

Change in credits to economy*
Commercial banks

Mill Can $
Mon rate

Mill Can $
Mon rate

72   1973   1974   1975   1976   77

CANADA (continued)

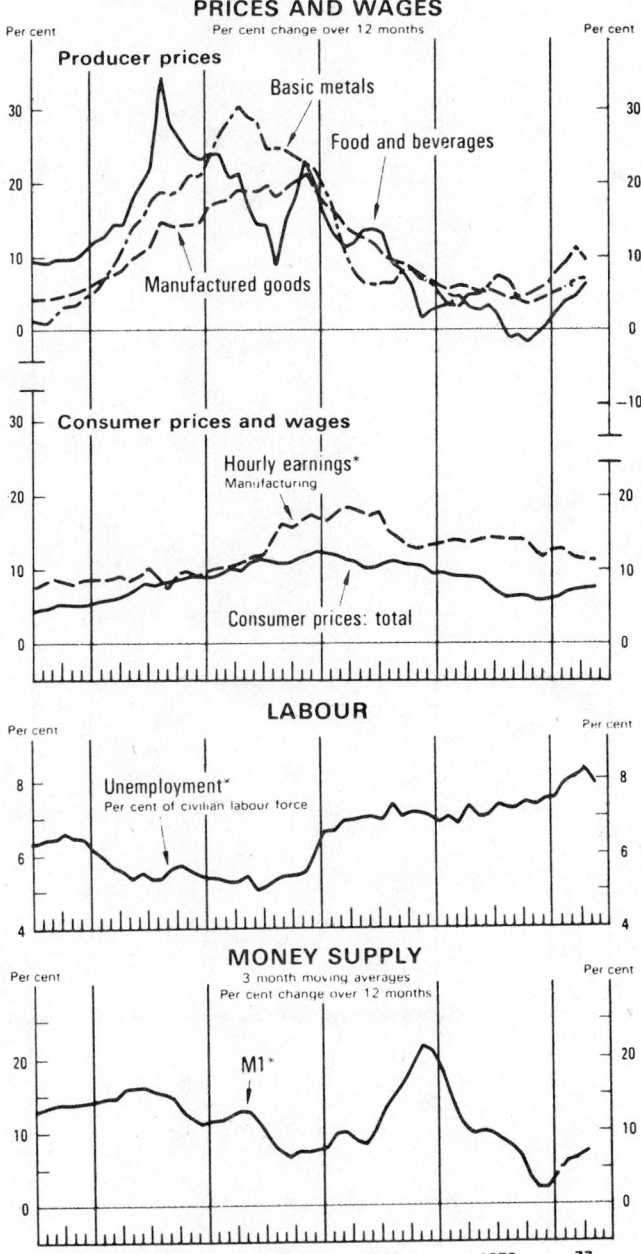

PRICES AND WAGES

Per cent change over 12 months

Per cent — Producer prices — Per cent

Basic metals

Food and beverages

Manufactured goods

Consumer prices and wages

Hourly earnings*
Manufacturing

Consumer prices: total

LABOUR

Per cent — Per cent

Unemployment*
Per cent of civilian labour force

MONEY SUPPLY

3 month moving averages
Per cent change over 12 months

Per cent — Per cent

M1*

72   1973   1974   1975   1976   77

CANADA (*concluded*)

FOREIGN TRADE, PAYMENTS, RESERVES, and exchange rate

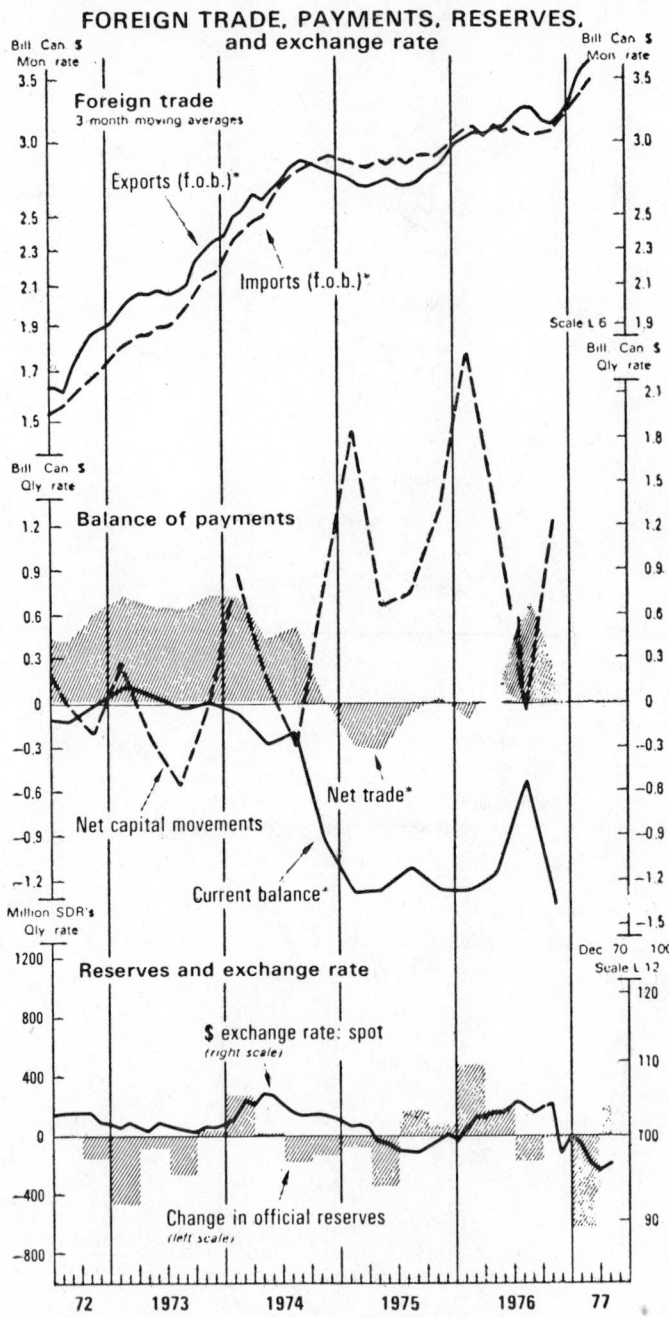

Series marked with (*) are seasonally adjusted.

DENMARK

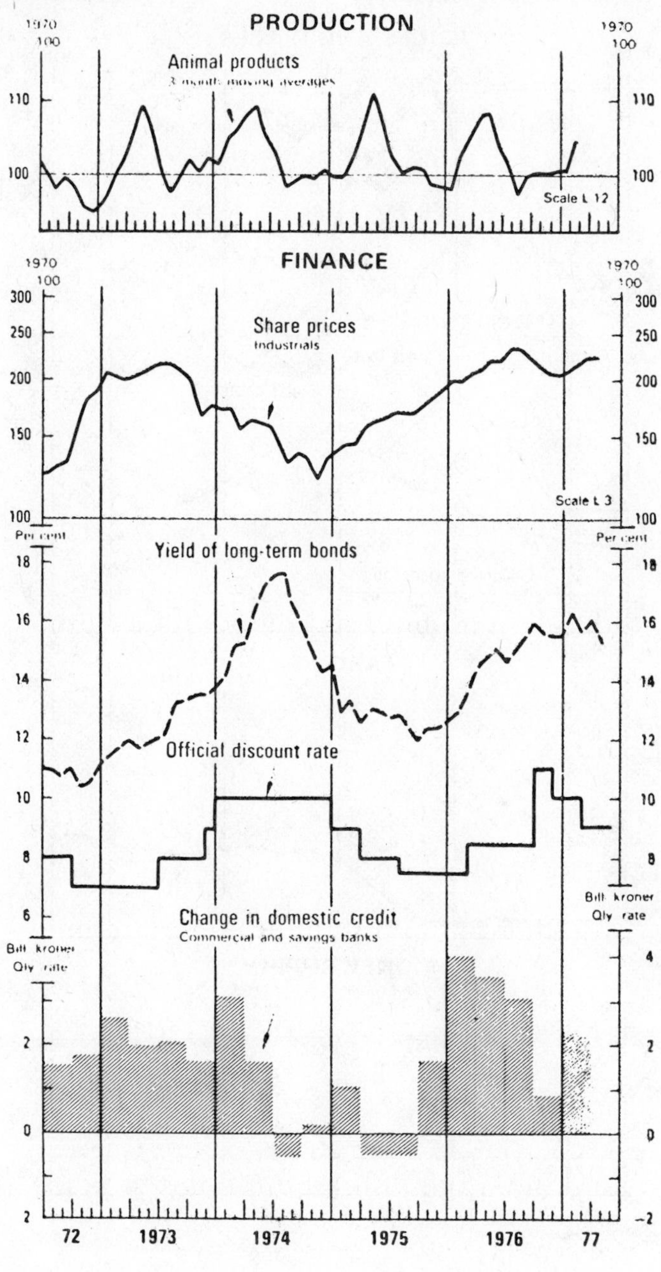

PRODUCTION

1970
100

1970
100

Animal products
3 month moving averages

110

110

100

100

Scale L 12

FINANCE

1970
100

1970
100

300

300

250

250

Share prices
Industrials

200

200

150

150

Scale L 3

100

100

Per cent

Per cent

18

18

Yield of long-term bonds

16

16

14

14

12

12

Official discount rate

10

10

8

8

Bill. kroner
Qly. rate

6

Change in domestic credit
Commercial and savings banks

Bill. kroner
Qly. rate

4

2

2

0

0

2

-2

72   1973   1974   1975   1976   77

DENMARK (*continued*)

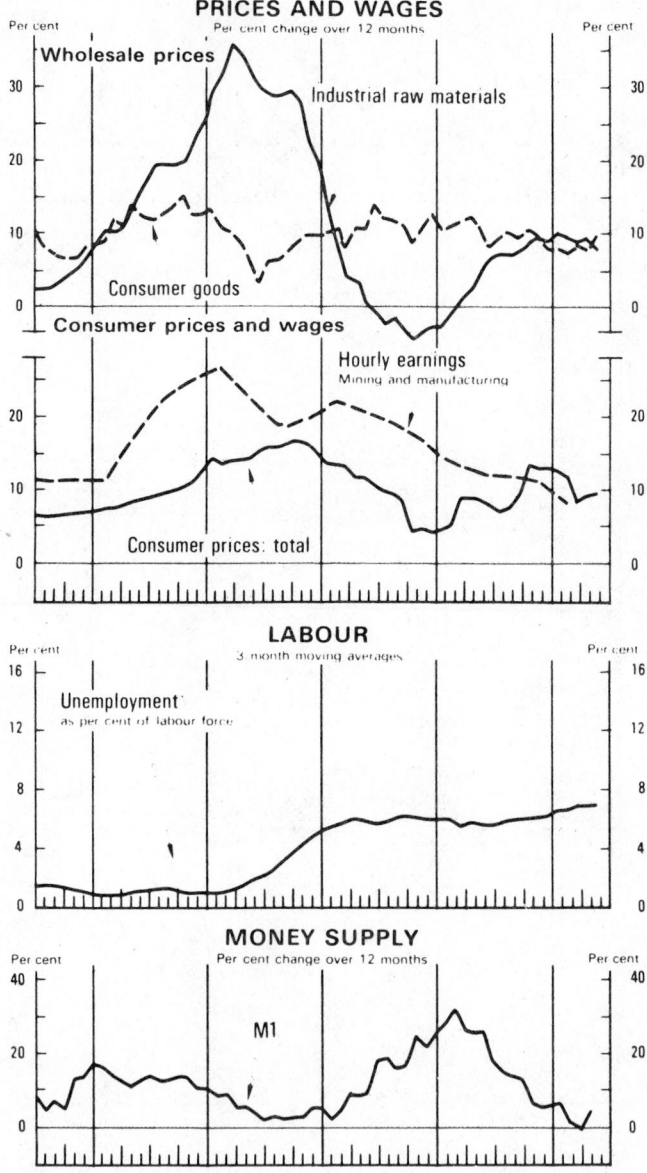

PRICES AND WAGES
Per cent change over 12 months

Wholesale prices

Industrial raw materials

Consumer goods

Consumer prices and wages

Hourly earnings
Mining and manufacturing

Consumer prices: total

LABOUR
3-month moving averages

Unemployment
as per cent of labour force

MONEY SUPPLY
Per cent change over 12 months

M1

72 1973 1974 1975 1976 77

DENMARK (*concluded*)

FOREIGN TRADE, PAYMENTS, RESERVES,
and exchange rate

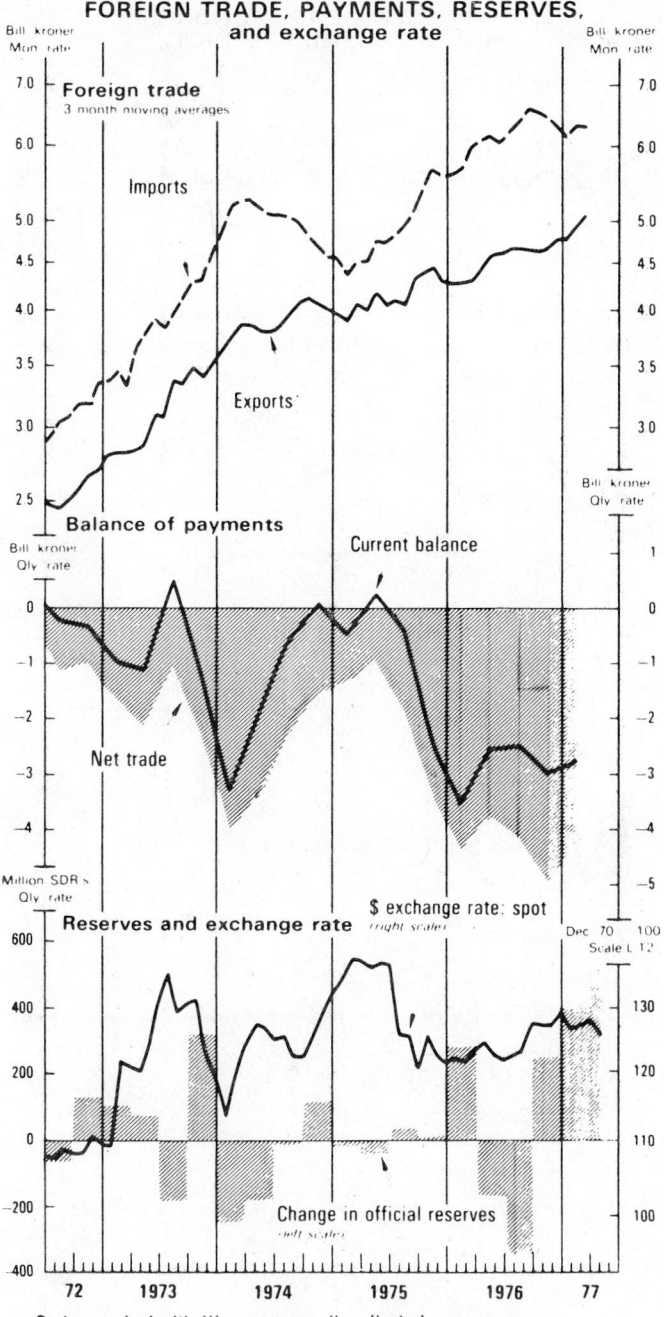

Series marked with (*) are seasonally adjusted.

FINLAND

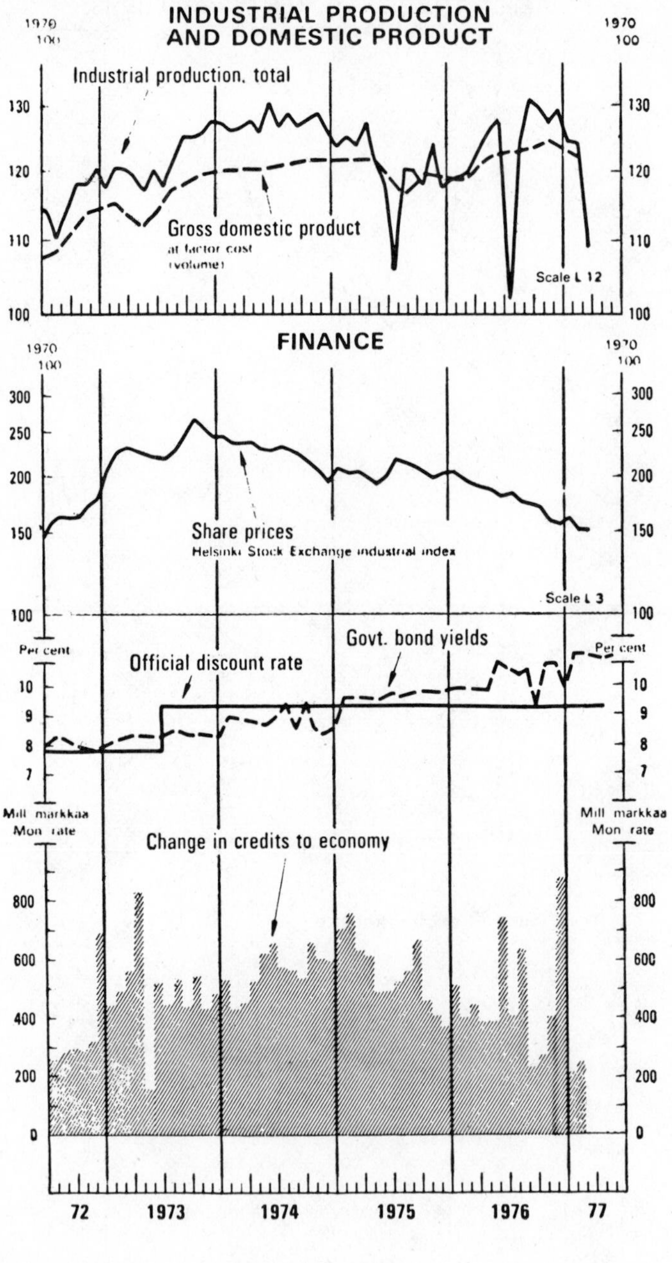

INDUSTRIAL PRODUCTION AND DOMESTIC PRODUCT

1970
100

1970
100

Industrial production, total

Gross domestic product
at factor cost
(volume)

Scale L 12

130
120
110
100

130
120
110
100

FINANCE

1970
100

1970
100

300
250
200
150
100

300
250
200
150
100

Share prices
Helsinki Stock Exchange industrial index

Scale L 3

Per cent

Per cent

Govt. bond yields

Official discount rate

10
9
8
7

10
9
8
7

Mill markkaa
Mon rate

Mill markkaa
Mon rate

Change in credits to economy

800
600
400
200
0

800
600
400
200
0

72   1973   1974   1975   1976   77

FINLAND (*continued*)

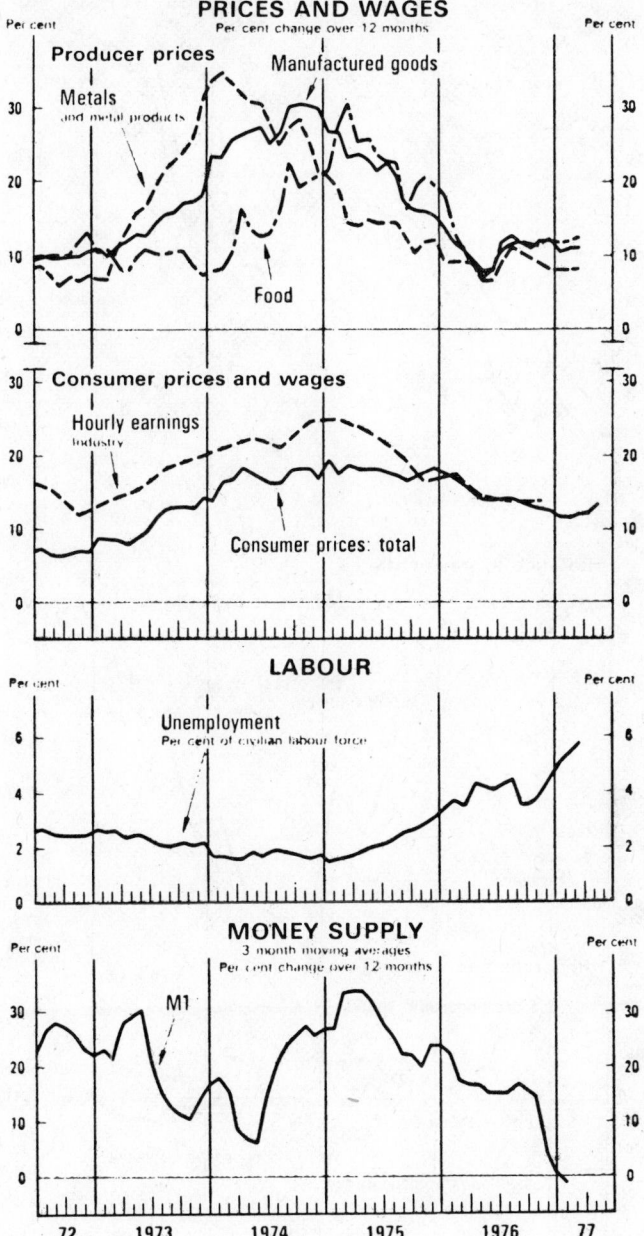

PRICES AND WAGES
Per cent change over 12 months

Per cent

Producer prices

Metals
and metal products

Manufactured goods

30

20

10

0

Food

Per cent

30

20

10

0

---

30 Consumer prices and wages

Hourly earnings
Industry

20

10

0

Consumer prices: total

30

20

10

0

LABOUR

Per cent

Unemployment
Per cent of civilian labour force

6

4

2

0

Per cent

6

4

2

0

MONEY SUPPLY
3 month moving averages
Per cent change over 12 months

Per cent

M1

30

20

10

0

Per cent

30

20

10

0

72   1973   1974   1975   1976   77

FINLAND (concluded)

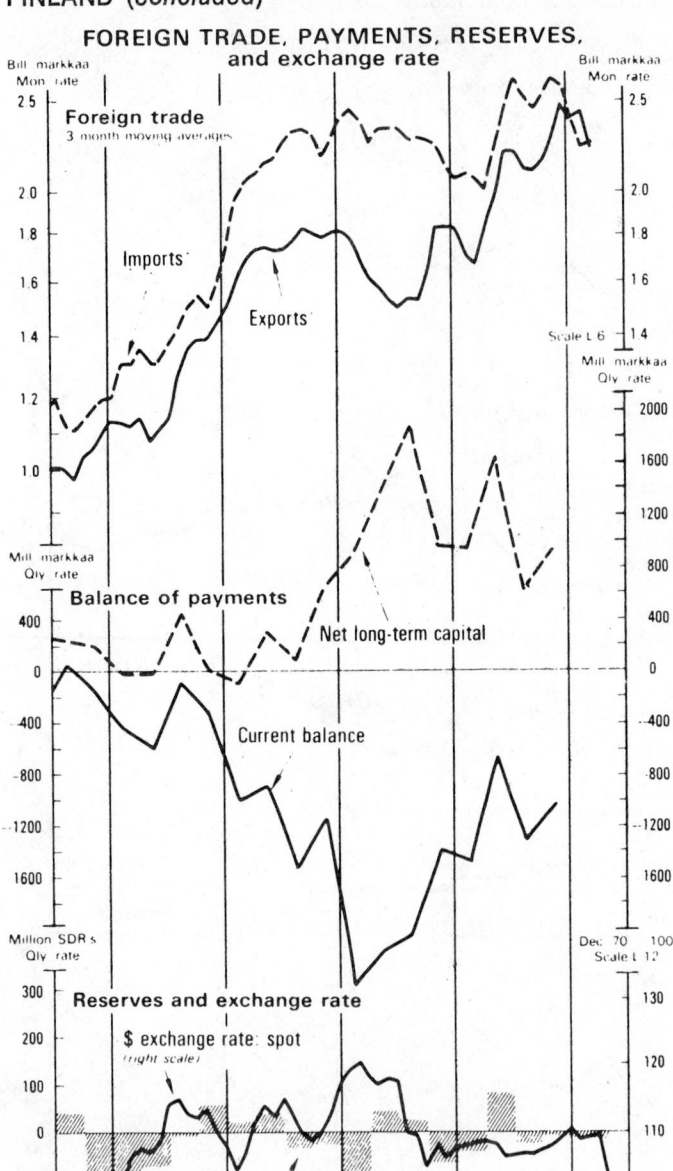

FOREIGN TRADE, PAYMENTS, RESERVES, and exchange rate

Series marked with (*) are seasonally adjusted.

FRANCE

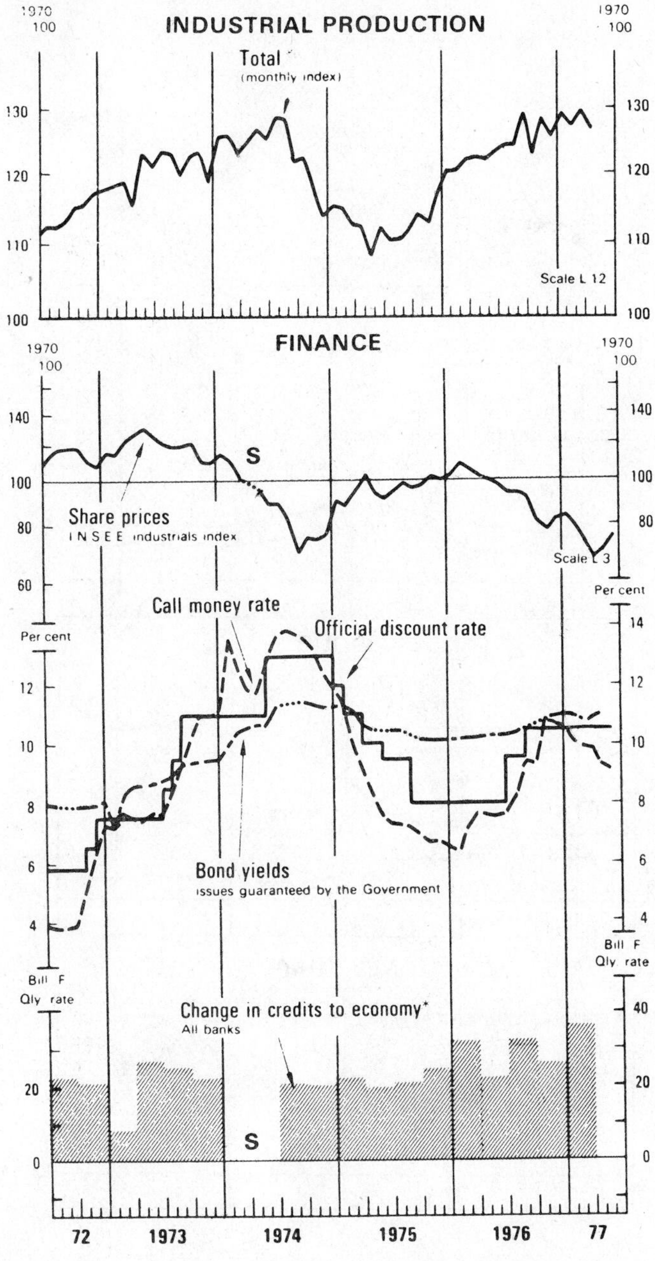

INDUSTRIAL PRODUCTION

1970
100

1970
100

Total
(monthly index)

130

130

120

120

110

110

Scale L 12

100

100

FINANCE

1970
100

1970
100

140

140

100

100

S

80

80

Share prices
I N S E E industrials index

Scale L 3

60

Per cent

Per cent

Call money rate

Official discount rate

14

12

12

10

10

8

8

Bond yields
issues guaranteed by the Government

6

6

4

4

Bill F
Qly rate

Bill F
Qly rate

Change in credits to economy*
All banks

40

20

20

S

0

0

72 **1973** **1974** **1975** **1976** 77

FRANCE (*continued*)

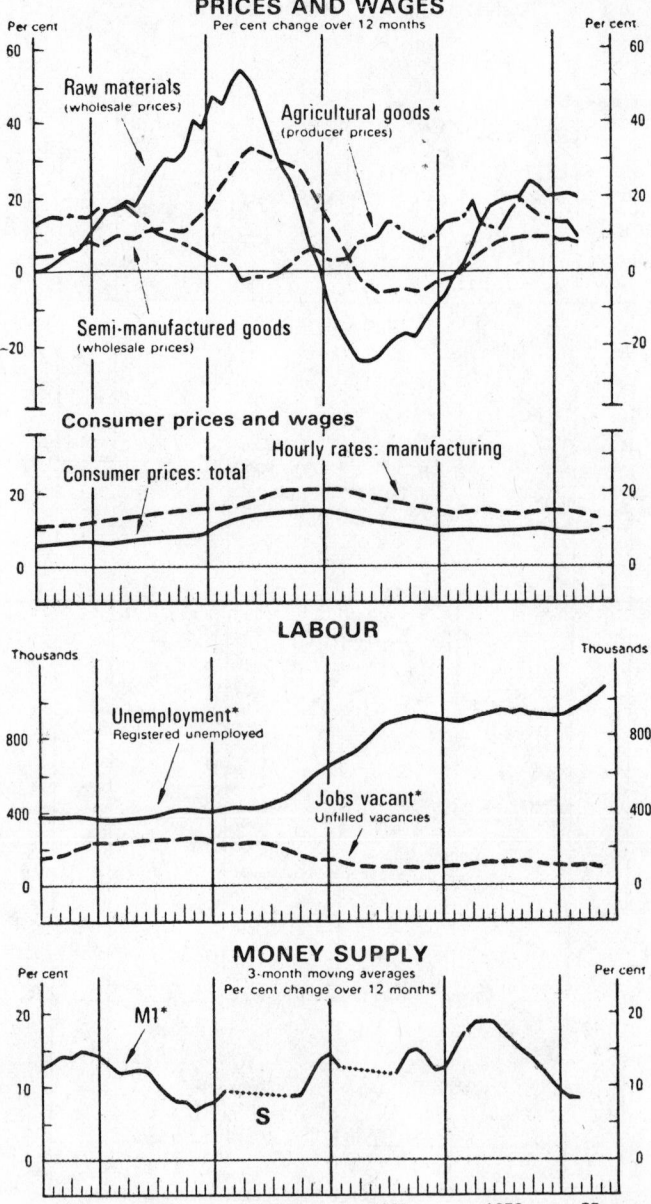

PRICES AND WAGES

Per cent change over 12 months

Raw materials
(wholesale prices)

Agricultural goods*
(producer prices)

Semi-manufactured goods
(wholesale prices)

Consumer prices and wages

Hourly rates: manufacturing

Consumer prices: total

LABOUR

Thousands

Unemployment*
Registered unemployed

Jobs vacant*
Unfilled vacancies

MONEY SUPPLY

3-month moving averages
Per cent change over 12 months

M1*

S

72   1973   1974   1975   1976   77

FRANCE (concluded)

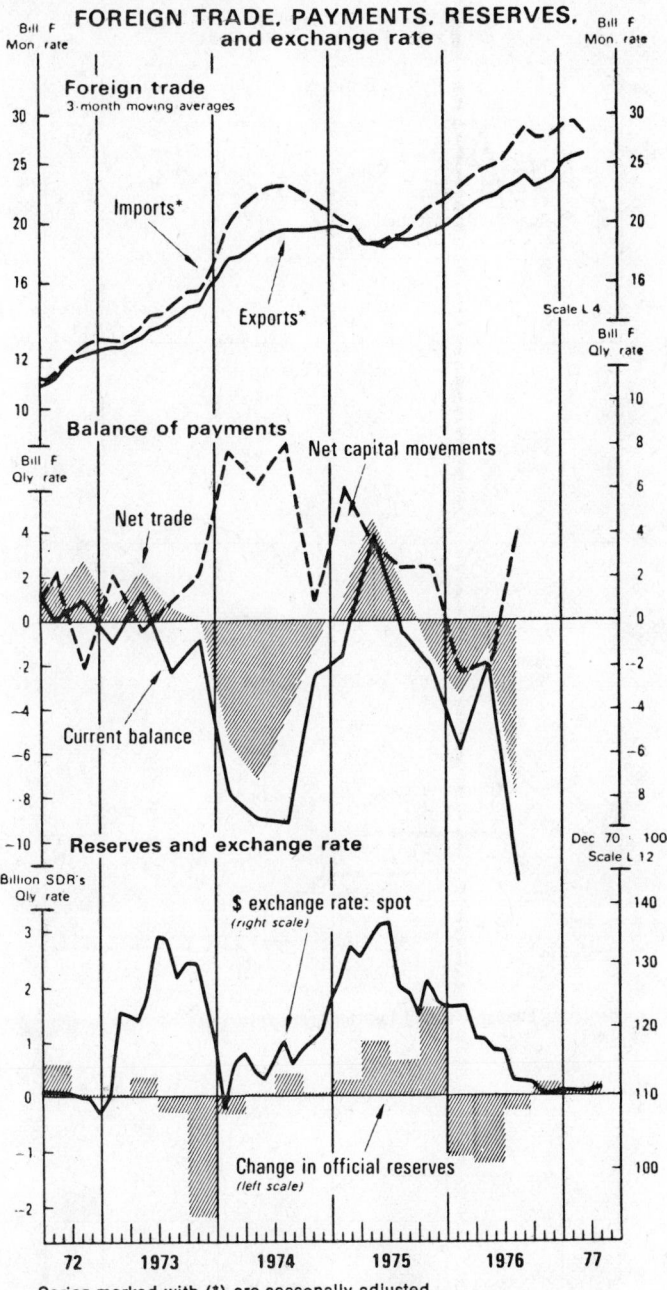

FOREIGN TRADE, PAYMENTS, RESERVES, and exchange rate

Bill F
Mon rate

Foreign trade
3-month moving averages

Imports*

Exports*

Scale L 4

Bill F
Qly rate

Balance of payments

Net capital movements

Net trade

Current balance

Reserves and exchange rate

Billion SDR's
Qly rate

$ exchange rate: spot
(right scale)

Change in official reserves
(left scale)

Dec 70 = 100
Scale L 12

72   1973   1974   1975   1976   77

Series marked with (*) are seasonally adjusted.

GERMANY

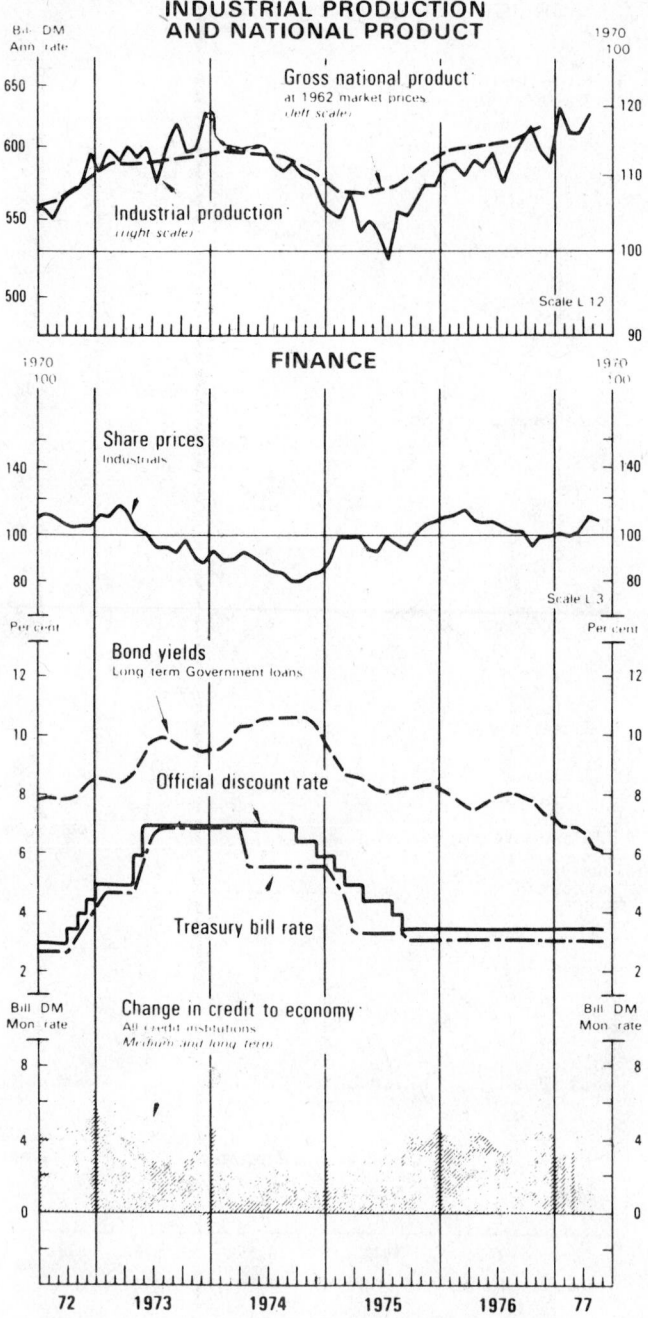

INDUSTRIAL PRODUCTION AND NATIONAL PRODUCT

Bil. DM Ann. rate

1970 100

650

120

Gross national product
at 1962 market prices
(left scale)

600

110

Industrial production
(right scale)

550

100

500

Scale L 12

90

FINANCE

1970 100

1970 100

Share prices
Industrials

140

140

100

100

80

80

Scale L 3

Per cent

Per cent

Bond yields
Long term Government loans

12

12

10

10

Official discount rate

8

8

6

6

Treasury bill rate

4

4

2

2

Bil. DM Mon. rate

Change in credit to economy
All credit institutions
Medium and long term

Bil. DM Mon. rate

8

8

4

4

0

0

72   1973   1974   1975   1976   77

GERMANY (*continued*)

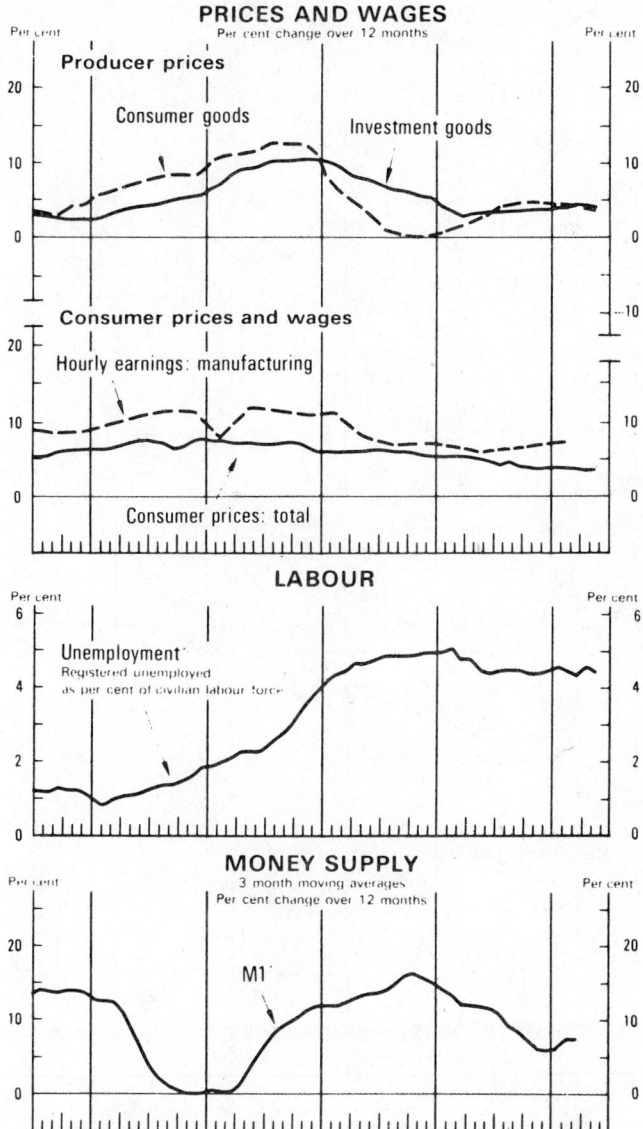

PRICES AND WAGES
Per cent change over 12 months

Producer prices

Consumer goods

Investment goods

Consumer prices and wages

Hourly earnings: manufacturing

Consumer prices: total

LABOUR

Unemployment
Registered unemployed
as per cent of civilian labour force

MONEY SUPPLY
3 month moving averages
Per cent change over 12 months

M1

72   1973   1974   1975   1976   77

GERMANY (concluded)

FOREIGN TRADE, PAYMENTS, RESERVES, and exchange rate

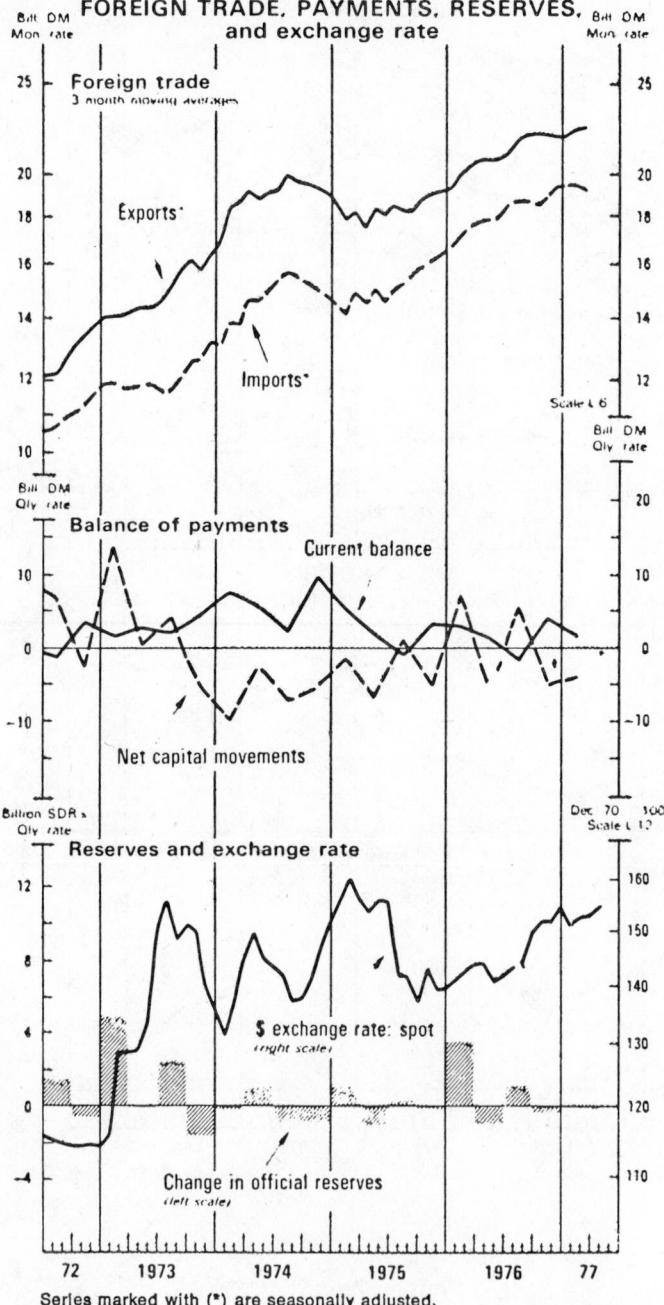

Series marked with (*) are seasonally adjusted.

GREECE

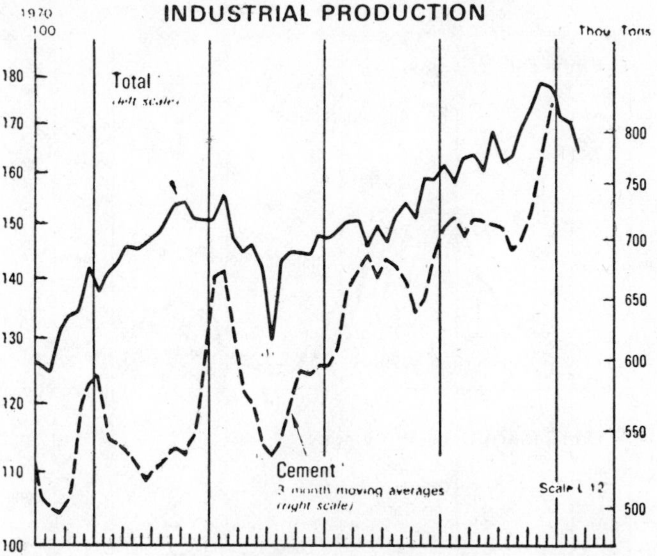

1970
100

INDUSTRIAL PRODUCTION

Thou. Tons

Total
(left scale)

180
170
160
150
140
130
120
110
100

800
750
700
650
600
550
500

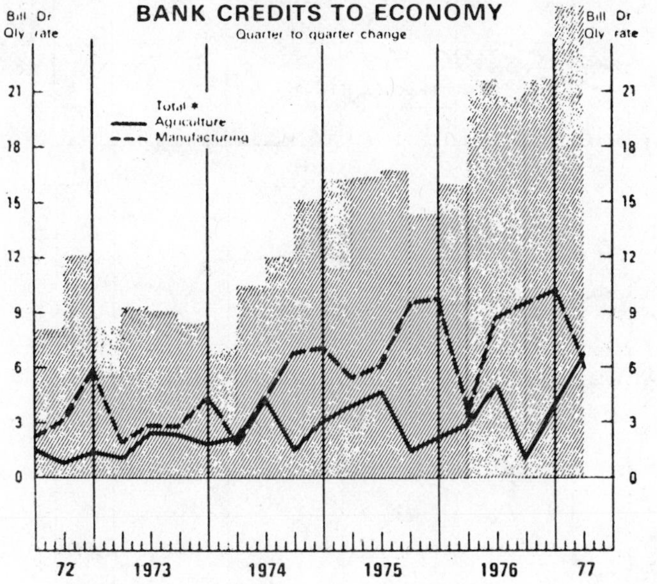

Cement
3 month moving averages
(right scale)

Scale (12

BANK CREDITS TO ECONOMY

Bill Dr
Qly rate

Bill Dr
Qly rate

Quarter to quarter change

Total *
Agriculture
Manufacturing

21
18
15
12
9
6
3
0

21
18
15
12
9
6
3
0

72   1973   1974   1975   1976   77

1. See note on country table

GREECE (continued)

PRICES AND WAGES

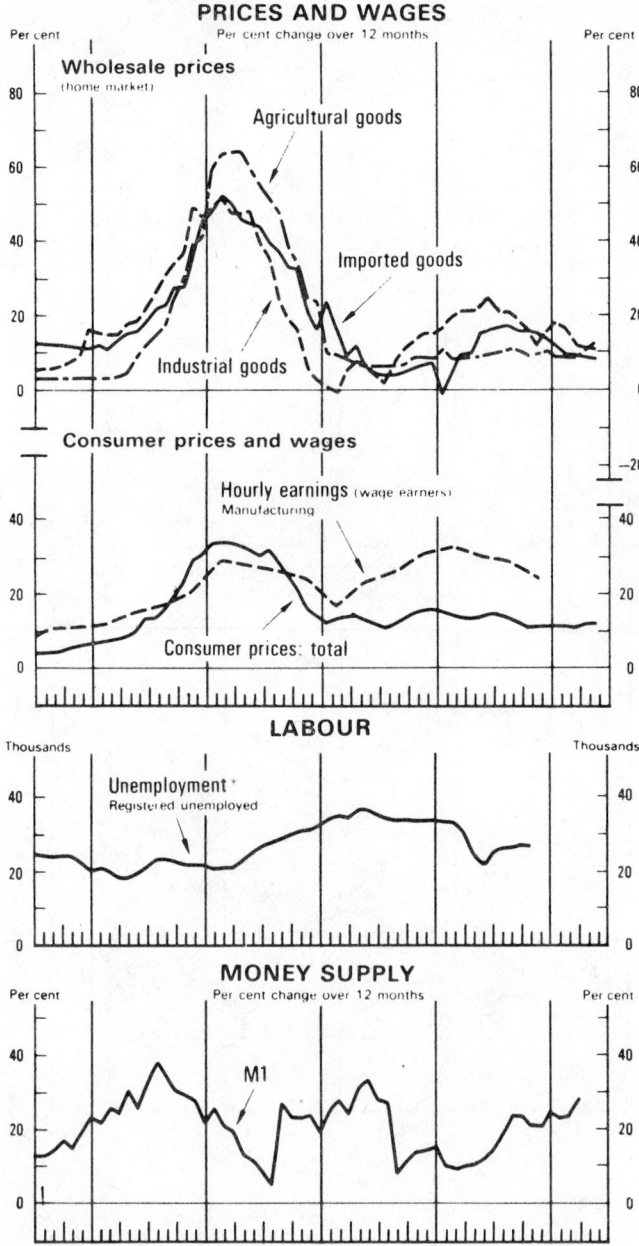

Per cent change over 12 months

Wholesale prices (home market)

Agricultural goods

Imported goods

Industrial goods

Consumer prices and wages

Hourly earnings (wage earners)
Manufacturing

Consumer prices: total

LABOUR

Thousands

Unemployment
Registered unemployed

MONEY SUPPLY

Per cent — Per cent change over 12 months

M1

72 1973 1974 1975 1976 77

GREECE (*concluded*)

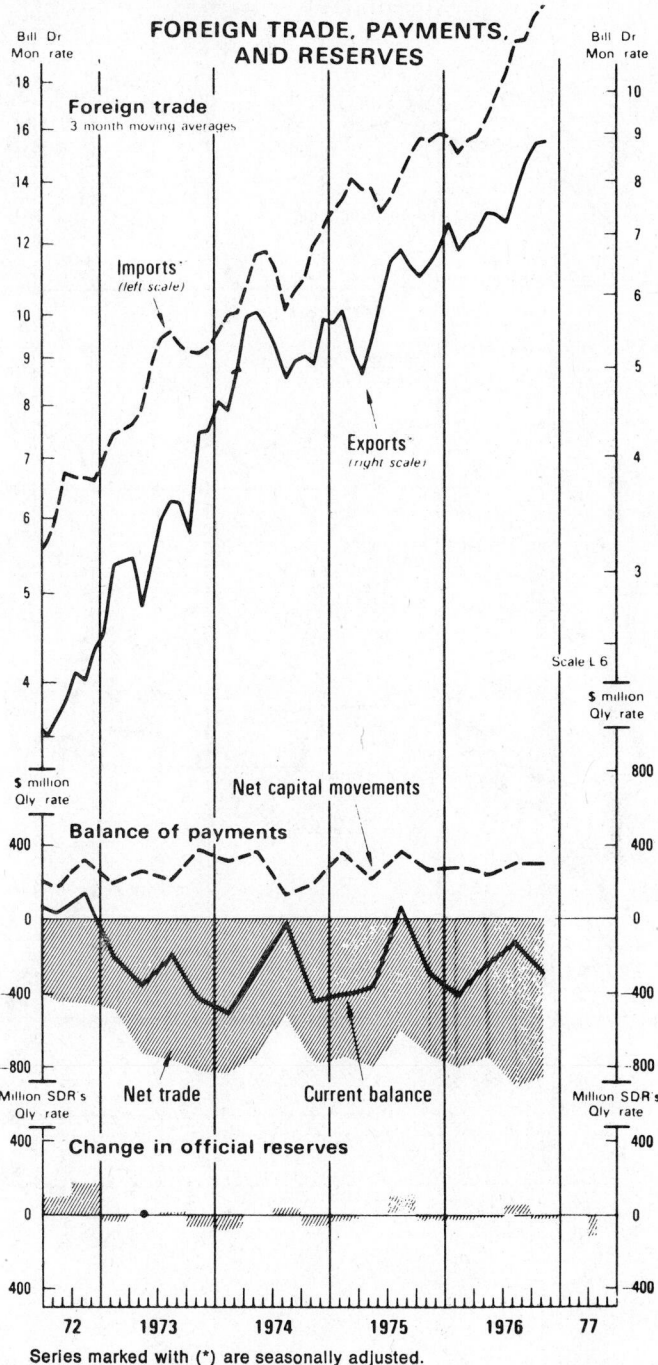

FOREIGN TRADE, PAYMENTS, AND RESERVES

Bill Dr Mon rate

Foreign trade
3 month moving averages

Imports*
(left scale)

Exports*
(right scale)

Scale L 6

$ million Qly rate

Net capital movements

Balance of payments

Net trade

Current balance

Million SDR s Qly rate

Change in official reserves

Series marked with (*) are seasonally adjusted.

IRELAND

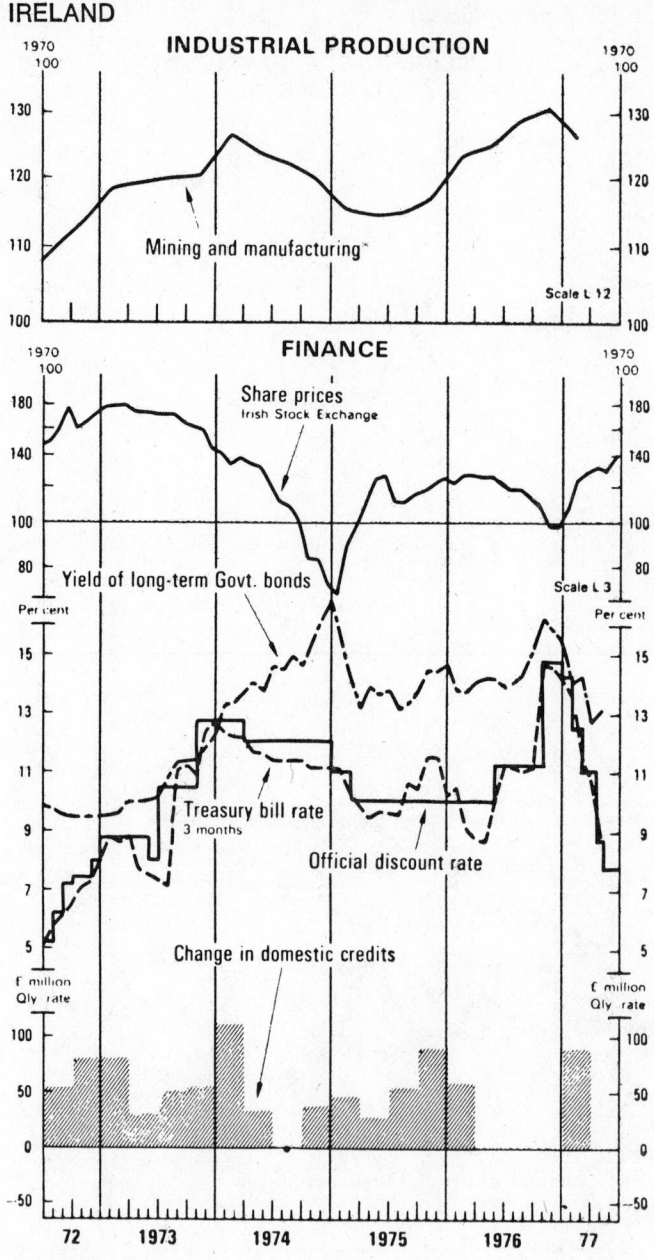

INDUSTRIAL PRODUCTION

Mining and manufacturing

Scale L 12

FINANCE

Share prices
Irish Stock Exchange

Yield of long-term Govt. bonds

Scale L 3

Treasury bill rate
3 months

Official discount rate

Change in domestic credits

IRELAND (continued)

PRICES AND WAGES

Per cent change over 4 quarters

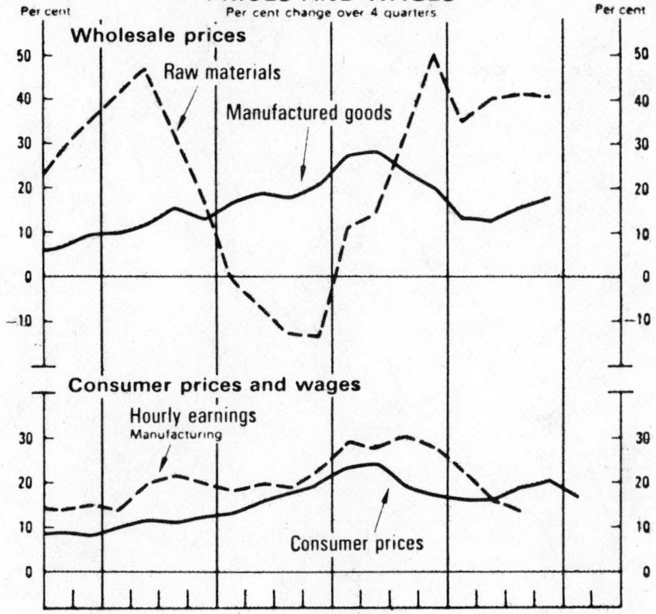

Wholesale prices

Per cent

Raw materials

Manufactured goods

50
40
30
20
10
0
−10

Consumer prices and wages

Hourly earnings
Manufacturing

Consumer prices

30
20
10
0

LABOUR

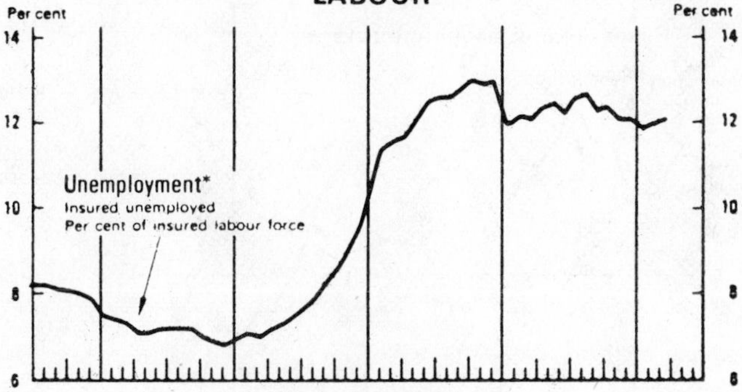

Per cent

14

12

10

8

6

Unemployment*
Insured unemployed
Per cent of insured labour force

MONEY SUPPLY

3-month moving averages
Per cent change over 12 months

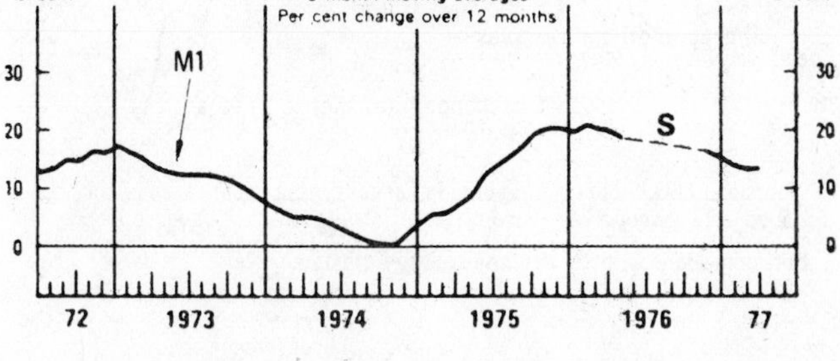

Per cent

30

20

10

0

M1

S

72   1973   1974   1975   1976   77

IRELAND (*concluded*)

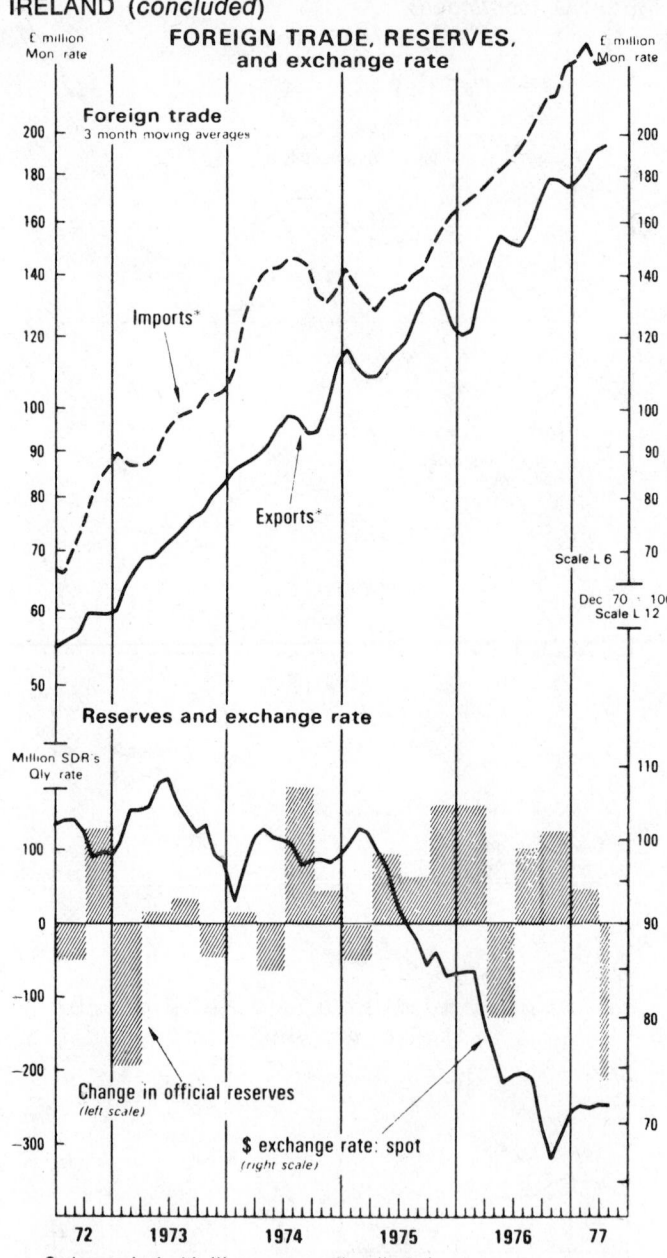

FOREIGN TRADE, RESERVES, and exchange rate

£ million
Mon rate

Foreign trade
3 month moving averages

Imports*

Exports*

Scale L 6

Dec 70 · 100
Scale L 12

Reserves and exchange rate

Million SDR's
Qly rate

Change in official reserves
(left scale)

$ exchange rate: spot
(right scale)

Series marked with (*) are seasonally adjusted.

ITALY

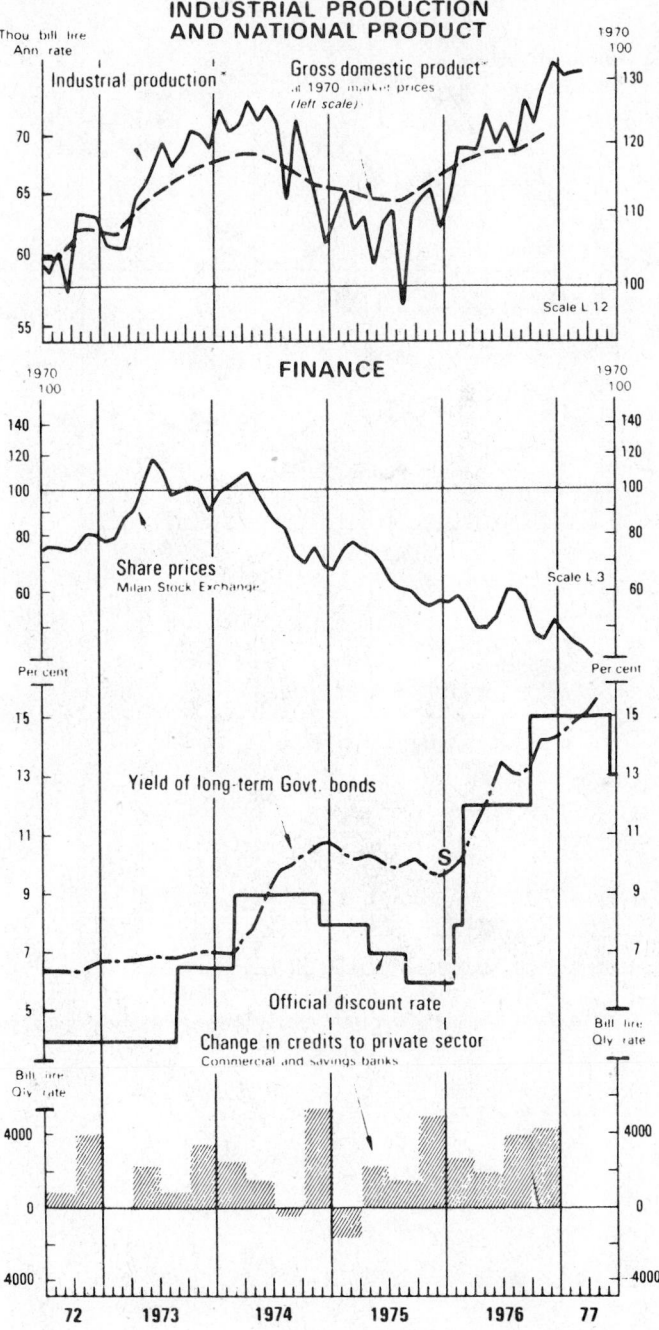

INDUSTRIAL PRODUCTION AND NATIONAL PRODUCT

Thou bill lire
Ann rate

Industrial production

Gross domestic product
at 1970 market prices
(left scale)

1970
100

Scale L 12

FINANCE

1970
100

1970
100

Share prices
Milan Stock Exchange

Scale L 3

Per cent

Per cent

Yield of long-term Govt. bonds

S

Official discount rate

Change in credits to private sector
Commercial and savings banks

Bill lire
Qty rate

Bill lire
Qty rate

72   1973   1974   1975   1976   77

ITALY (*continued*)

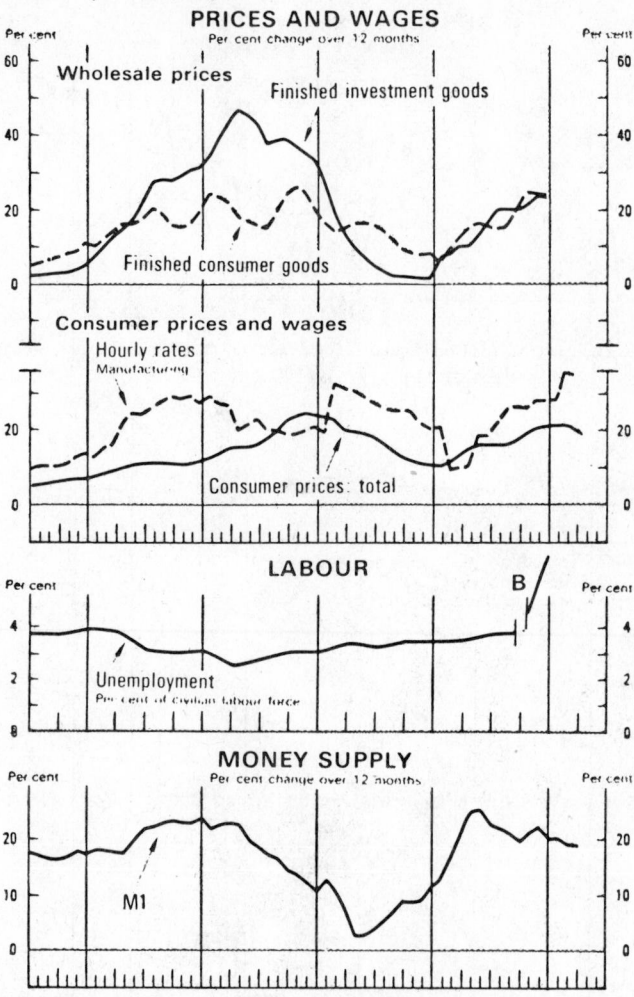

ITALY (concluded)

FOREIGN TRADE, PAYMENTS, RESERVES, and exchange rate

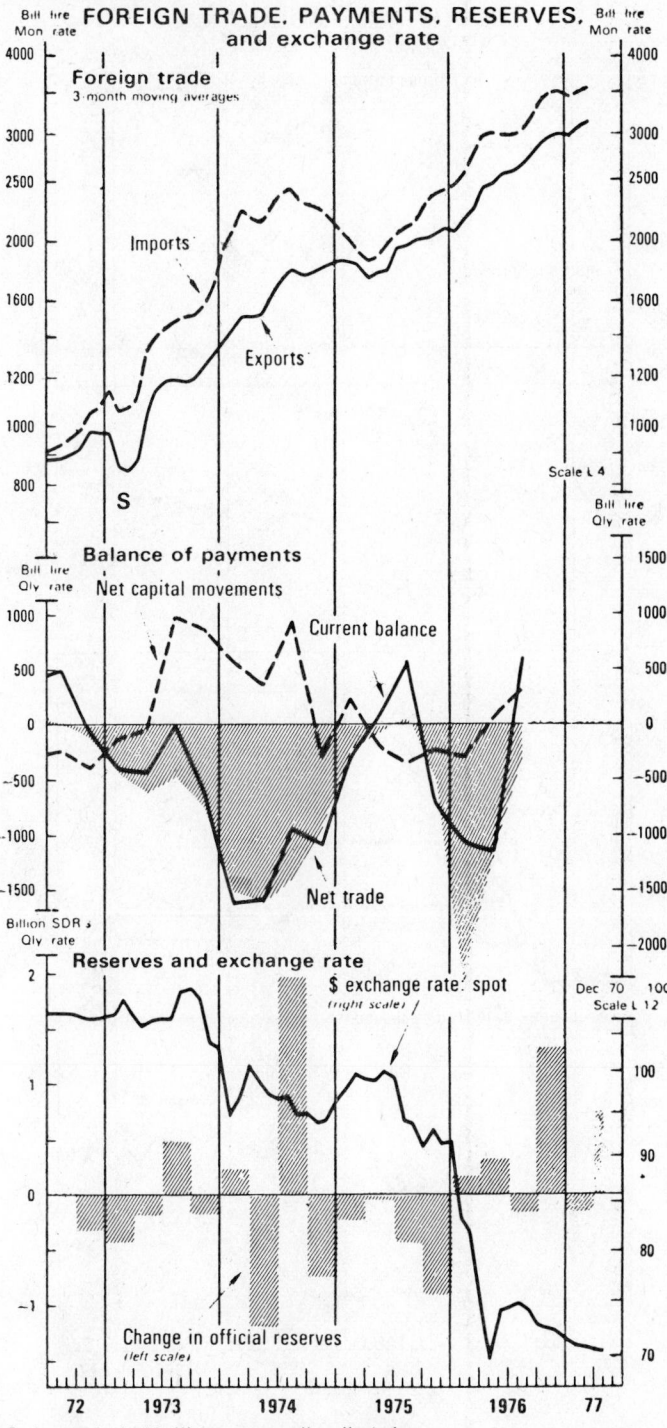

Foreign trade
3-month moving averages

Imports

Exports

Scale L 4

Balance of payments

Net capital movements

Current balance

Net trade

Reserves and exchange rate

$ exchange rate: spot
(right scale)

Dec 70 100
Scale L 12

Change in official reserves
(left scale)

Series marked with (*) are seasonally adjusted.

JAPAN

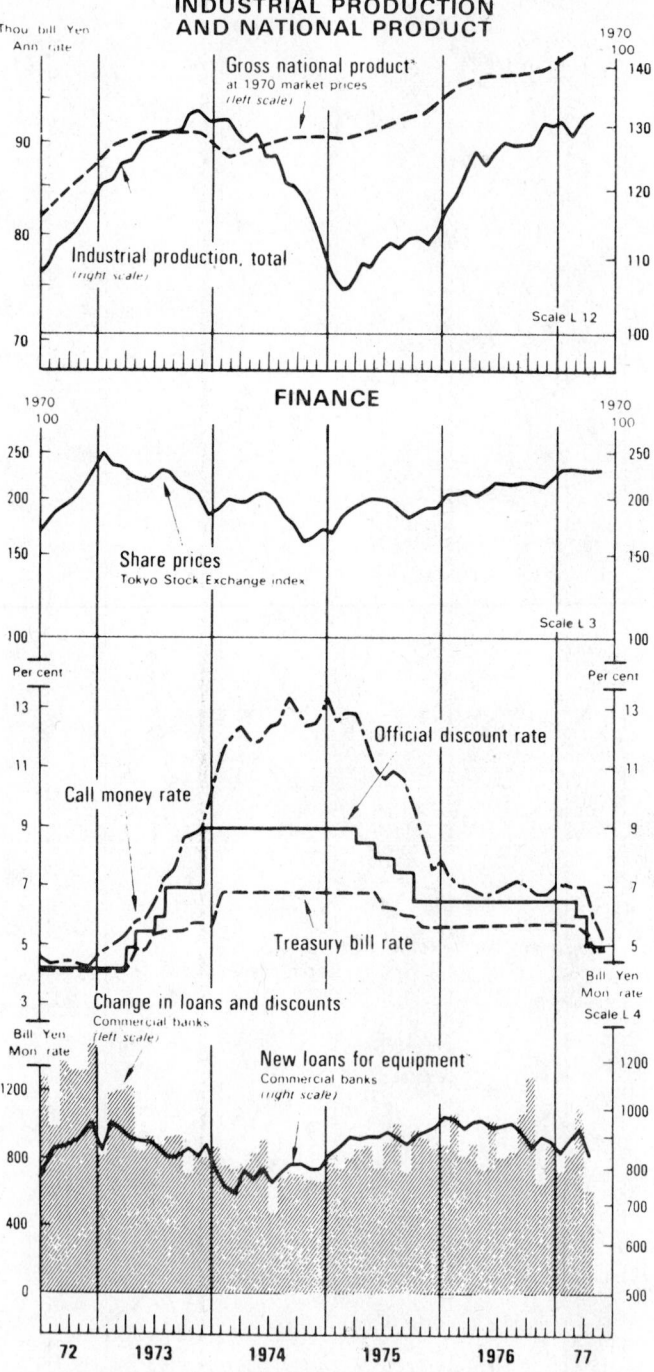

INDUSTRIAL PRODUCTION AND NATIONAL PRODUCT

Thou. bill. Yen
Ann. rate

1970 = 100

Gross national product*
at 1970 market prices
(left scale)

Industrial production, total
(right scale)

Scale L 12

FINANCE

1970 = 100

Share prices
Tokyo Stock Exchange index

Scale L 3

Per cent

Official discount rate

Call money rate

Treasury bill rate

Change in loans and discounts
Commercial banks
(left scale)

New loans for equipment
Commercial banks
(right scale)

Bill Yen
Mon. rate

Scale L 4

72   1973   1974   1975   1976   77

JAPAN *(continued)*

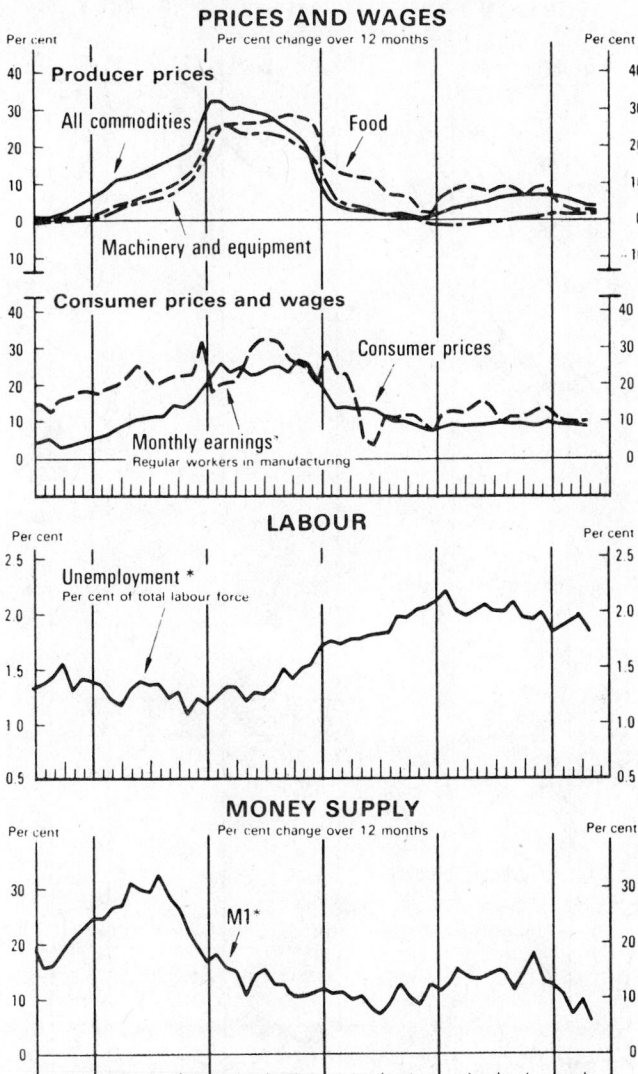

PRICES AND WAGES

Per cent   Per cent change over 12 months   Per cent

Producer prices

All commodities   Food

Machinery and equipment

Consumer prices and wages

Consumer prices

Monthly earnings`
Regular workers in manufacturing

LABOUR

Per cent   Per cent

Unemployment *
Per cent of total labour force

MONEY SUPPLY

Per cent   Per cent change over 12 months   Per cent

M1*

72   1973   1974   1975   1976   77

JAPAN (*concluded*)

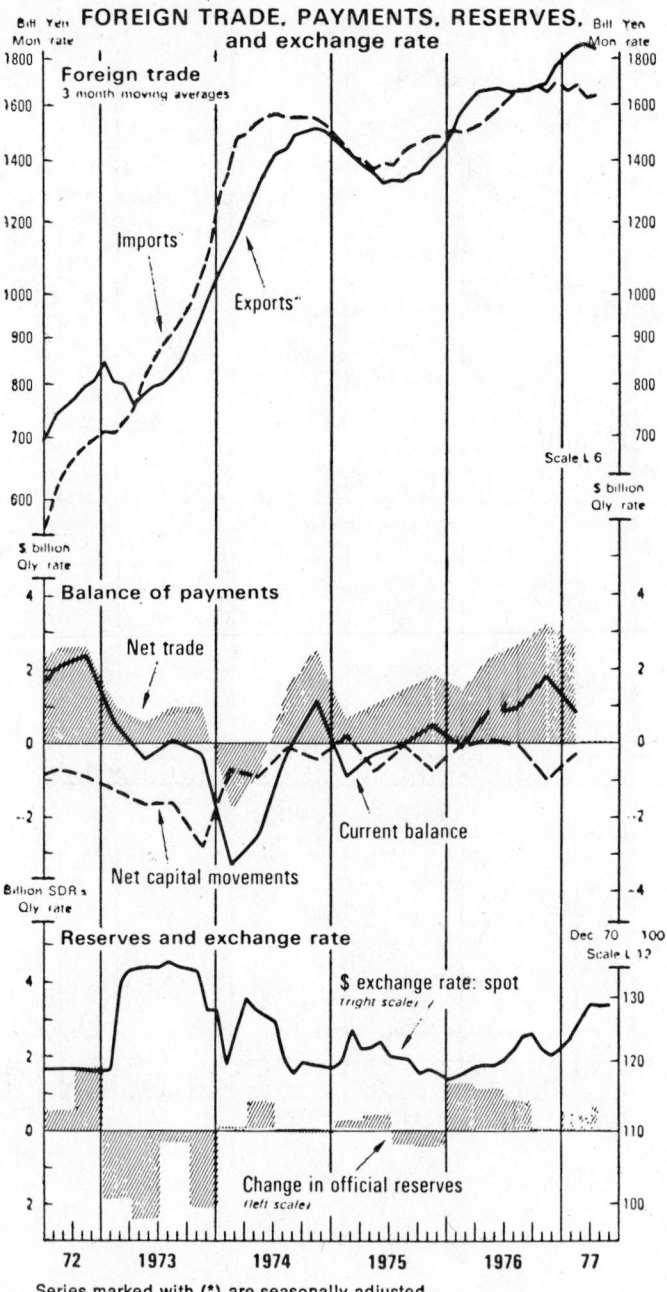

FOREIGN TRADE, PAYMENTS, RESERVES, and exchange rate

Series marked with (*) are seasonally adjusted.

NETHERLANDS

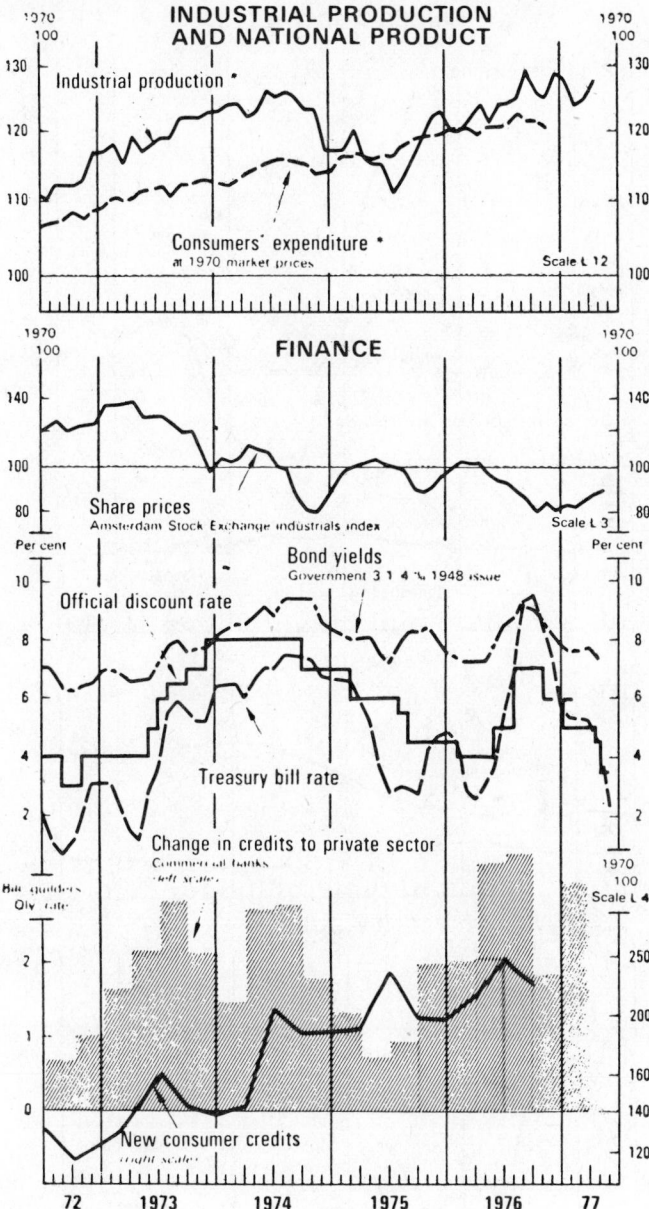

INDUSTRIAL PRODUCTION AND NATIONAL PRODUCT

Industrial production

Consumers' expenditure
at 1970 market prices

Scale L 12

FINANCE

Share prices
Amsterdam Stock Exchange industrials index

Scale L 3

Bond yields
Government 3 1 4 % 1948 issue

Official discount rate

Treasury bill rate

Change in credits to private sector
Commercial banks
left scale

New consumer credits
credit scale

Scale L 4

72 1973 1974 1975 1976 77

NETHERLANDS (*continued*)

PRICES AND WAGES

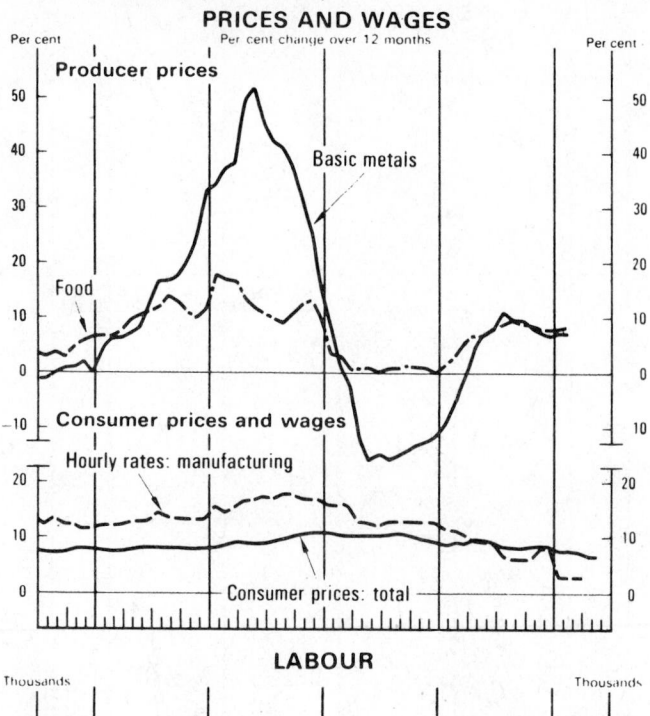

LABOUR

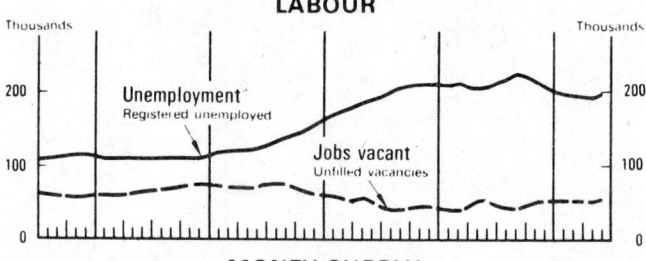

MONEY SUPPLY

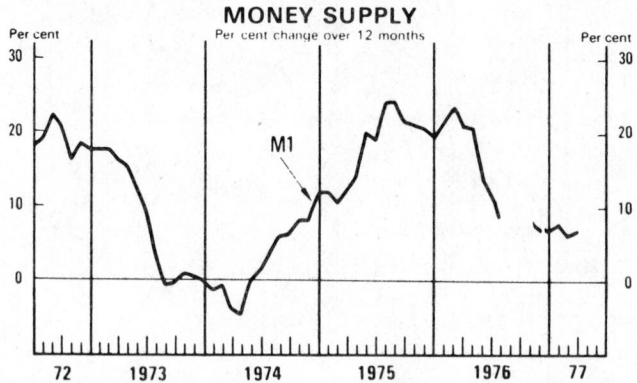

NETHERLANDS (*concluded*)

FOREIGN TRADE, PAYMENTS, RESERVES, and exchange rate

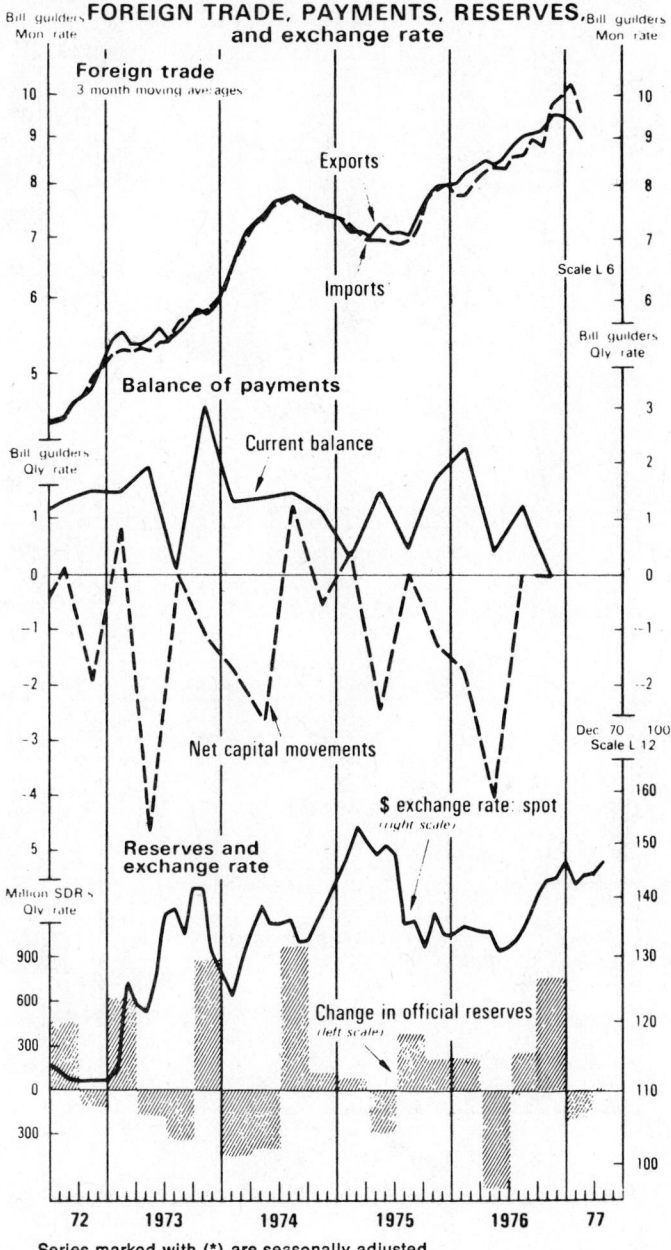

Series marked with (*) are seasonally adjusted.

NEW ZEALAND

COMMODITY OUTPUT

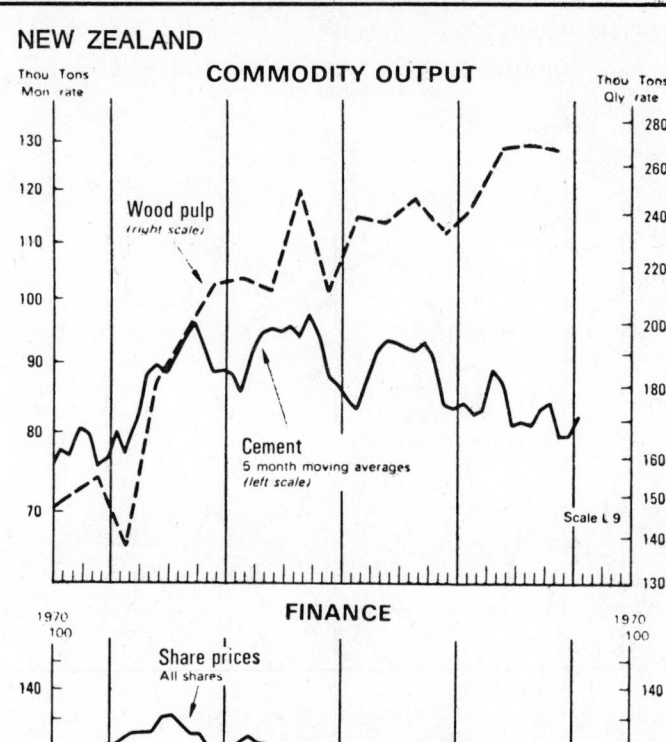

Thou Tons
Mon rate

Thou Tons
Qly rate

Wood pulp
(right scale)

Cement
5 month moving averages
(left scale)

Scale L 9

FINANCE

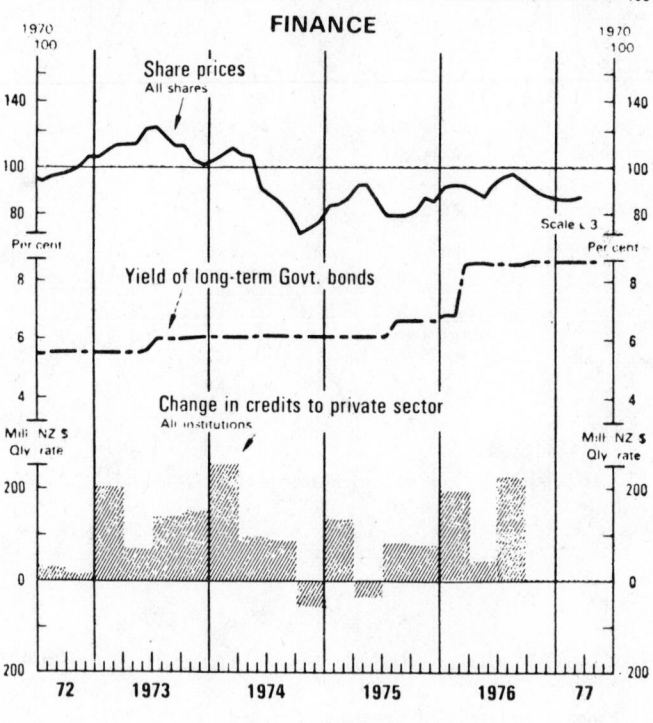

1970
100

1970
100

Share prices
All shares

Scale L 3

Per cent

Per cent

Yield of long-term Govt. bonds

Change in credits to private sector
All institutions

Mill NZ $
Qly rate

Mill NZ $
Qly rate

72   1973   1974   1975   1976   77

NEW ZEALAND (*continued*)

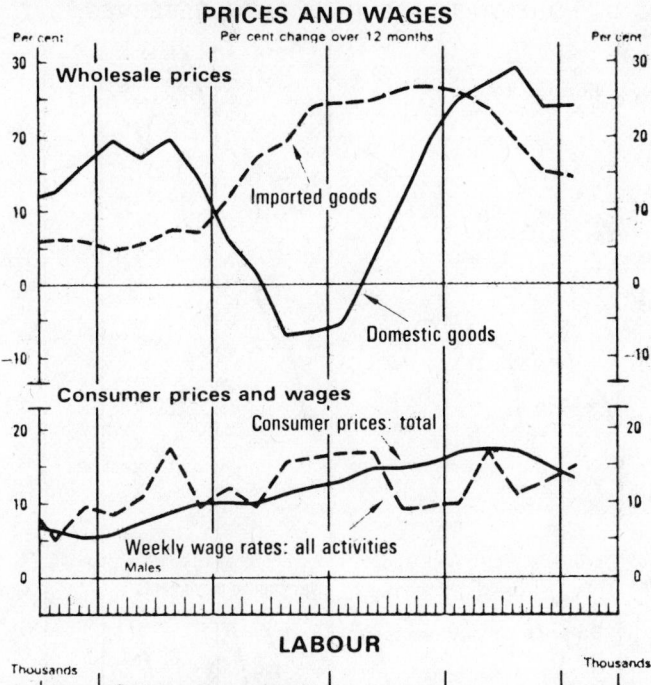

PRICES AND WAGES

Per cent change over 12 months

Wholesale prices

Imported goods

Domestic goods

Consumer prices and wages

Consumer prices: total

Weekly wage rates: all activities
Males

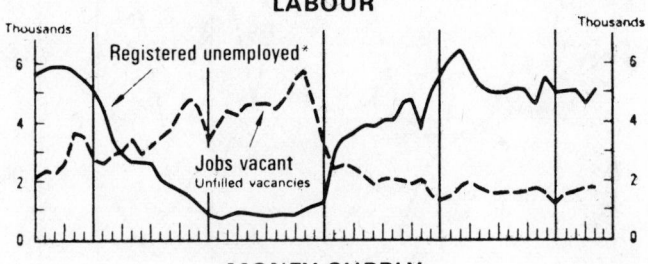

LABOUR

Thousands

Registered unemployed

Jobs vacant
Unfilled vacancies

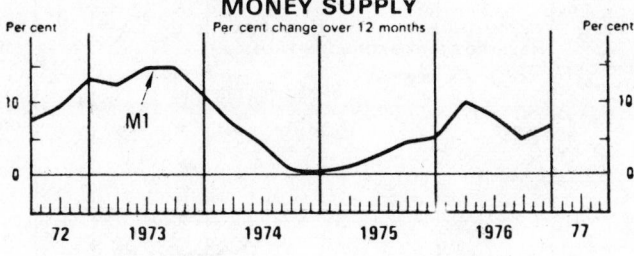

MONEY SUPPLY

Per cent change over 12 months

M1

72   1973   1974   1975   1976   77

NEW ZEALAND (*concluded*)

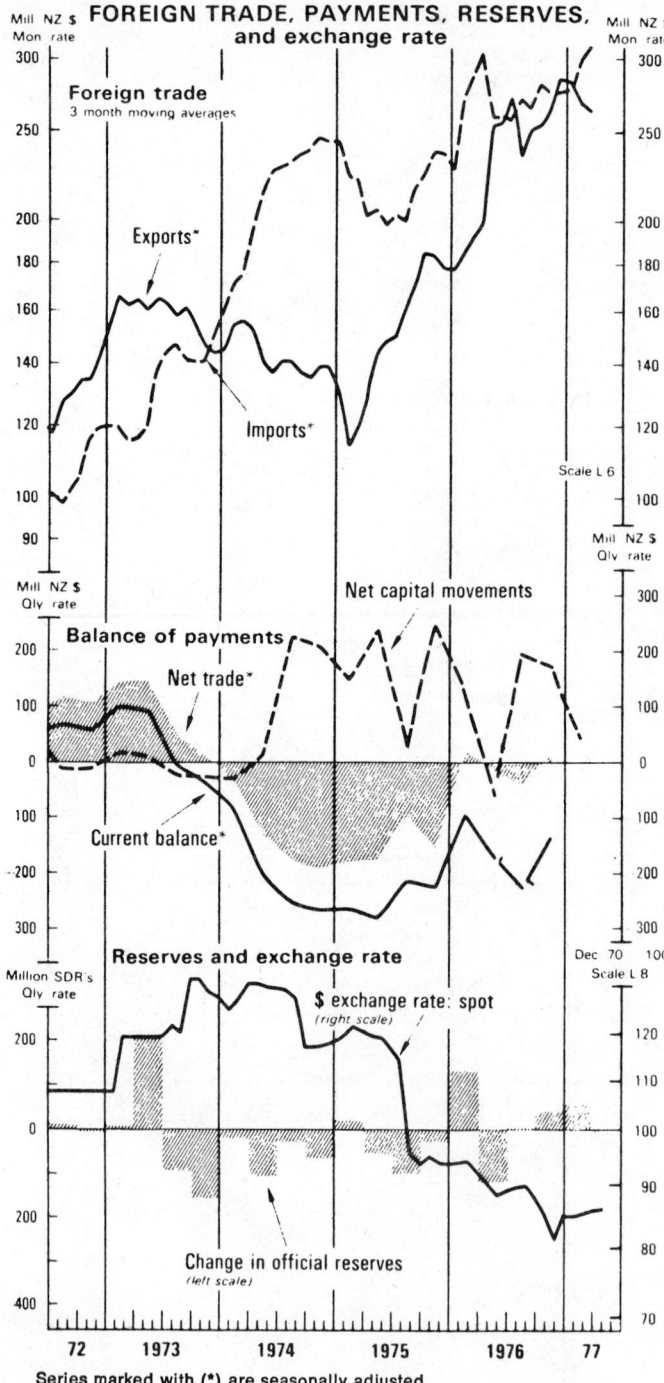

FOREIGN TRADE, PAYMENTS, RESERVES, and exchange rate

Mill NZ $
Mon rate

Foreign trade
3 month moving averages

Exports*

Imports*

Scale L 6

Mill NZ $
Qly rate

Balance of payments

Net capital movements

Net trade*

Current balance*

Dec 70   100
Scale L 8

Reserves and exchange rate

Million SDR's
Qly rate

$ exchange rate: spot
(right scale)

Change in official reserves
(left scale)

72   1973   1974   1975   1976   77

Series marked with (*) are seasonally adjusted.

NORWAY

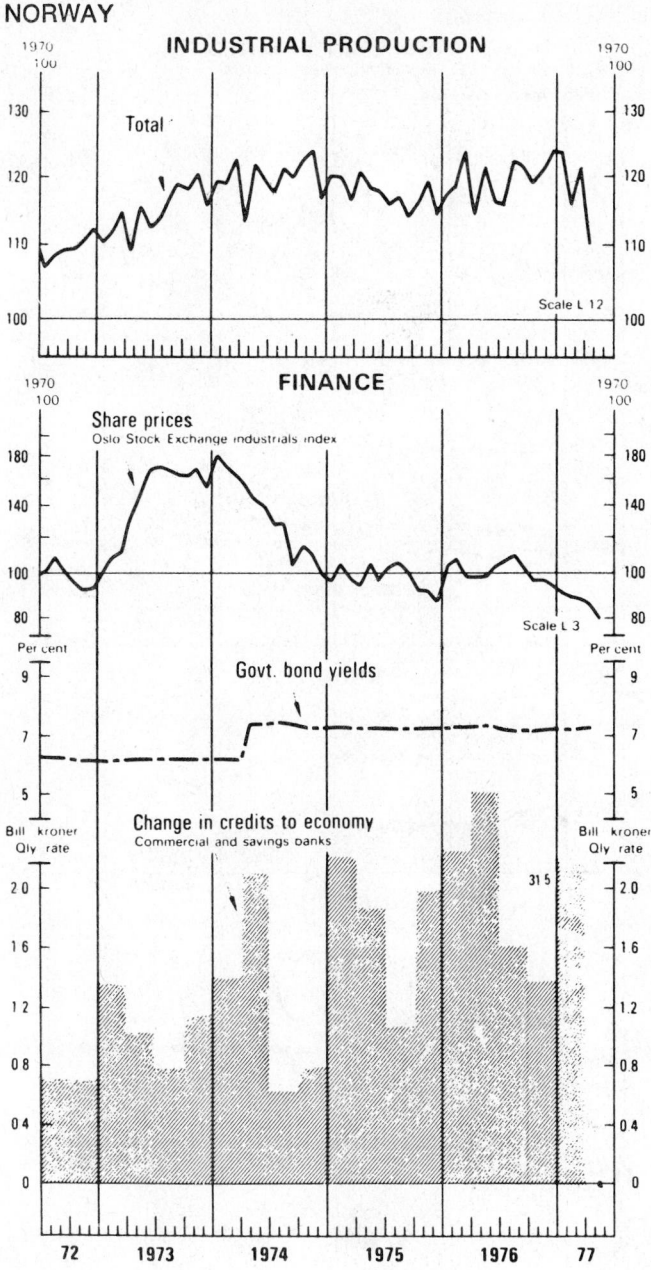

INDUSTRIAL PRODUCTION

1970 100

Total

Scale L 12

FINANCE

1970 100

Share prices
Oslo Stock Exchange industrials index

Scale L 3

Per cent

Govt. bond yields

Per cent

Bill kroner
Qly rate

Change in credits to economy
Commercial and savings banks

31 5

Bill kroner
Qly rate

72   1973   1974   1975   1976   77

NORWAY (continued)

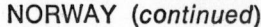

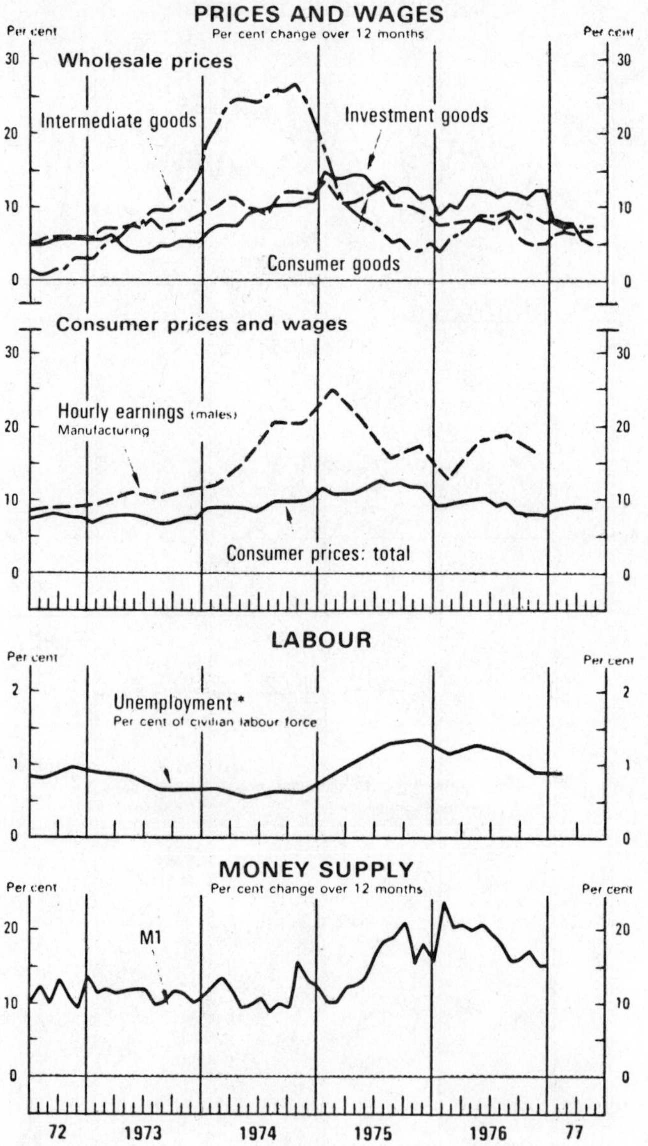

PRICES AND WAGES

Per cent change over 12 months

Wholesale prices

Intermediate goods

Investment goods

Consumer goods

Consumer prices and wages

Hourly earnings (males)
Manufacturing

Consumer prices: total

LABOUR

Unemployment *
Per cent of civilian labour force

MONEY SUPPLY

Per cent change over 12 months

M1

72 1973 1974 1975 1976 77

NORWAY (concluded)

Bill kroner
Mon rate

FOREIGN TRADE, PAYMENTS, RESERVES, and exchange rate

Bill kroner
Mon rate

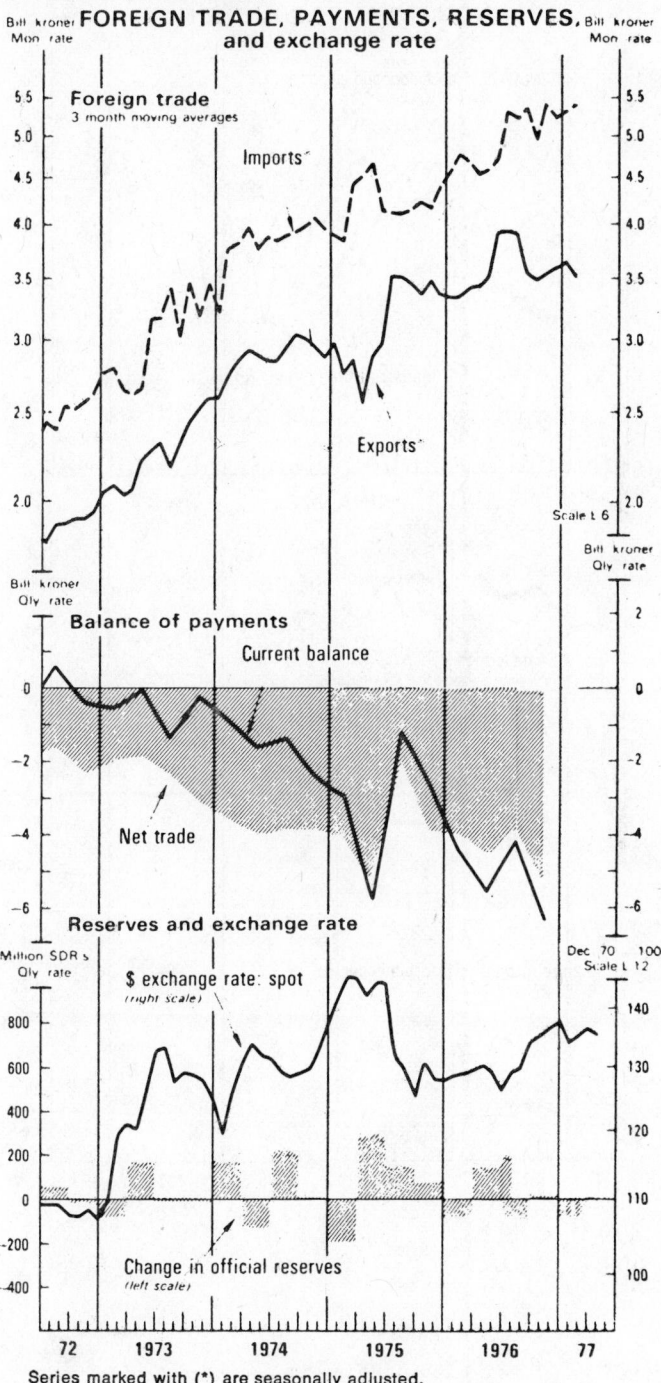

Series marked with (*) are seasonally adjusted.

SPAIN

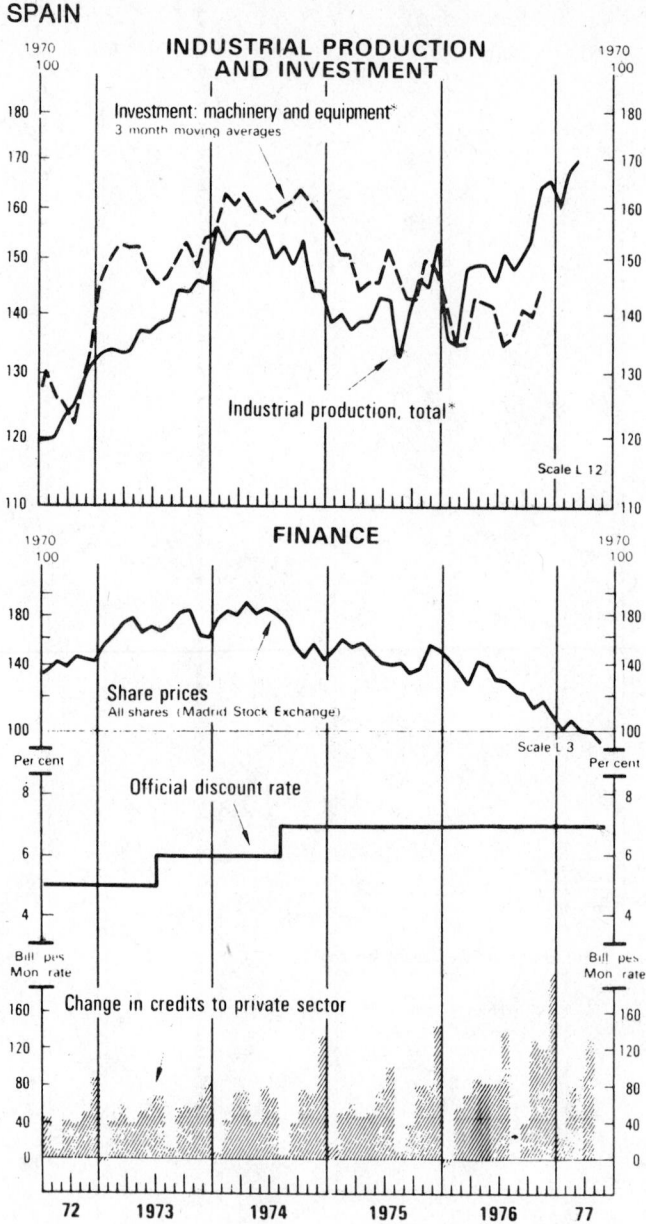

INDUSTRIAL PRODUCTION AND INVESTMENT

Investment: machinery and equipment*
3 month moving averages

Industrial production, total*

Scale L 12

FINANCE

Share prices
All shares (Madrid Stock Exchange)

Scale L 3

Per cent

Official discount rate

Bill pes
Mon rate

Change in credits to private sector

Bill pes
Mon rate

SPAIN (continued)

PRICES AND WAGES

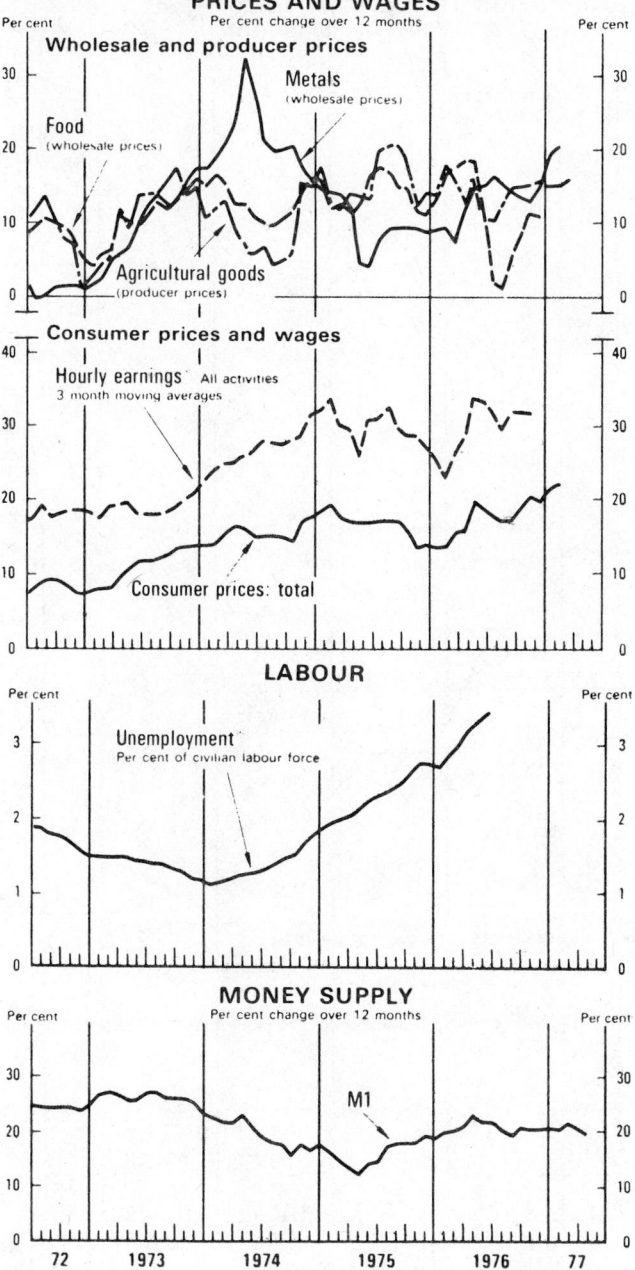

Per cent change over 12 months

Wholesale and producer prices

Food (wholesale prices)

Metals (wholesale prices)

Agricultural goods (producer prices)

Consumer prices and wages

Hourly earnings: All activities 3 month moving averages

Consumer prices: total

LABOUR

Unemployment Per cent of civilian labour force

MONEY SUPPLY

Per cent change over 12 months

M1

72   1973   1974   1975   1976   77

SPAIN (concluded)

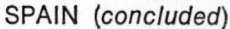

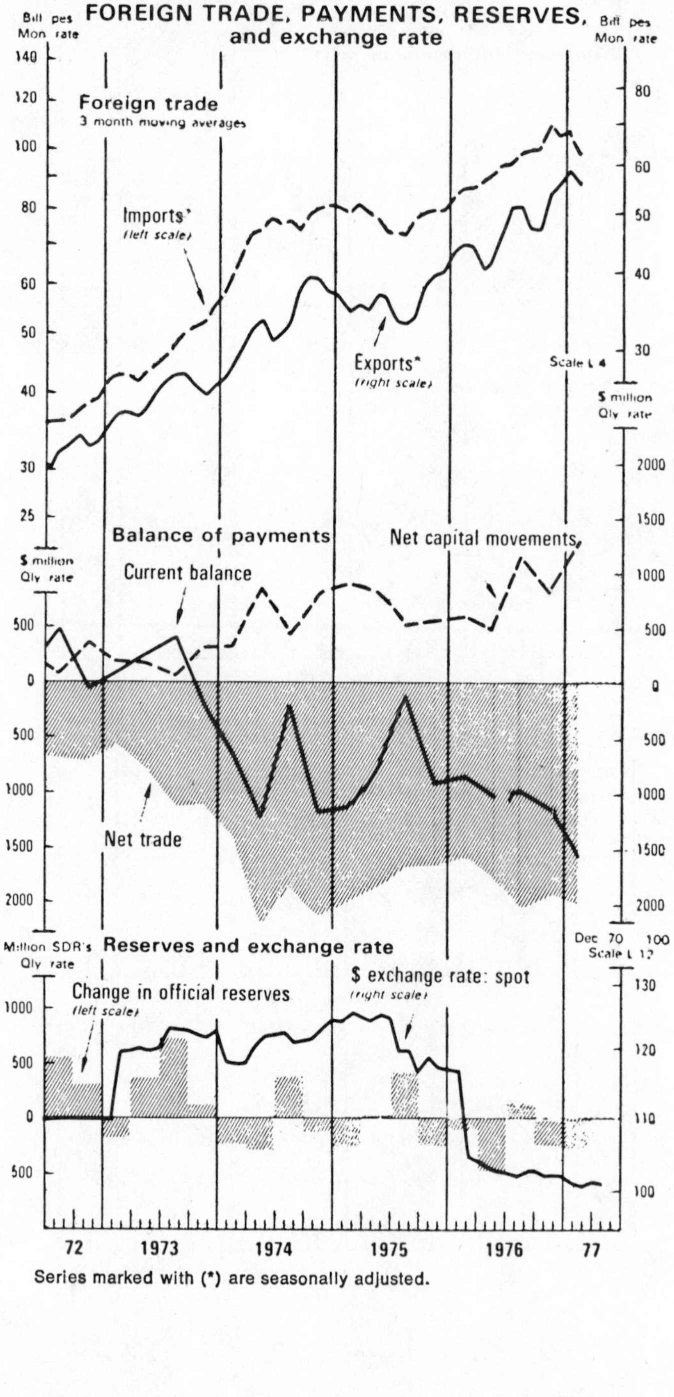

FOREIGN TRADE, PAYMENTS, RESERVES,
and exchange rate

Bill pes
Mon rate

Bill pes
Mon rate

Foreign trade
3 month moving averages

Imports*
(left scale)

Exports*
(right scale)

Scale L 4

$ million
Qly rate

$ million
Qly rate

Balance of payments

Net capital movements

Current balance

Net trade

Million SDR's
Qly rate

Reserves and exchange rate

Dec 70   100
Scale L 12

Change in official reserves
(left scale)

$ exchange rate: spot
(right scale)

72   1973   1974   1975   1976   77

Series marked with (*) are seasonally adjusted.

SWEDEN

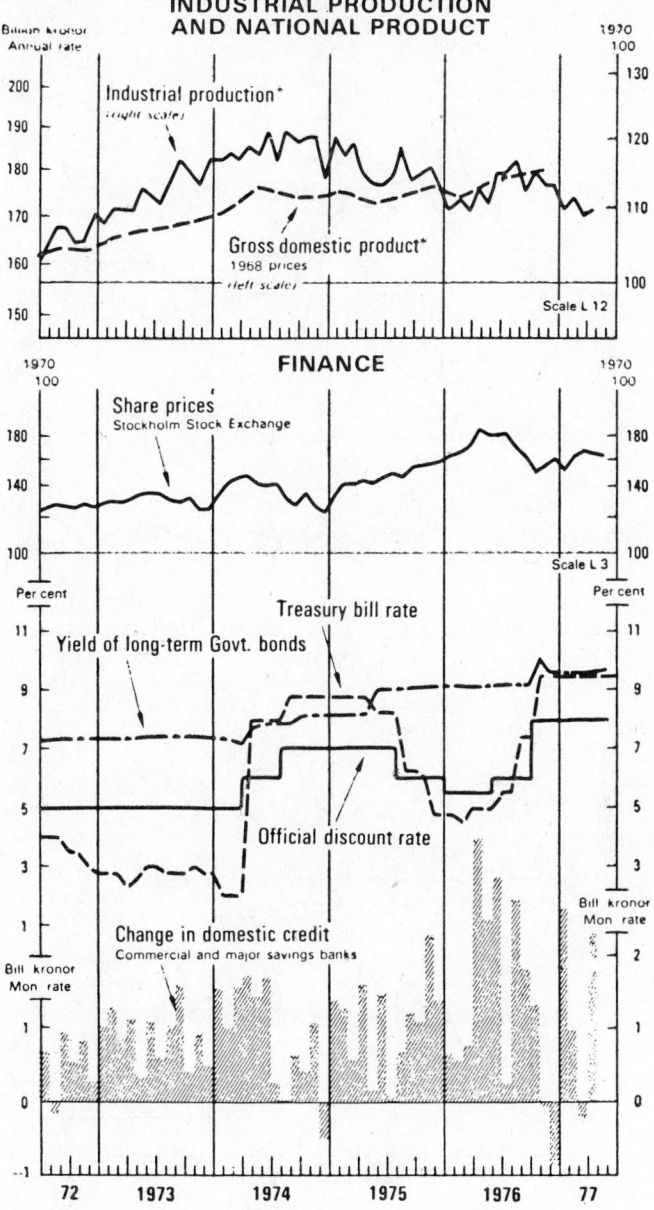

INDUSTRIAL PRODUCTION AND NATIONAL PRODUCT

Billion kronor
Annual rate

1970
100

Industrial production*
(right scale)

Gross domestic product*
1968 prices
(left scale)

Scale L 12

FINANCE

1970
100

1970
100

Share prices
Stockholm Stock Exchange

Scale L 3

Per cent

Per cent

Yield of long-term Govt. bonds

Treasury bill rate

Official discount rate

Change in domestic credit
Commercial and major savings banks

Bill kronor
Mon. rate

Bill kronor
Mon. rate

72   1973   1974   1975   1976   77

SWEDEN (*continued*)

PRICES AND WAGES

Per cent
Per cent change over 12 months
Per cent
Producer prices
Basic metals
Manufactured goods
Metal products
Textiles
50
40
30
20
10
0
−10
Consumer prices and wages
Consumer prices: total
Hourly earnings
20
10
0

LABOUR

Per cent
Per cent
Unemployment
Per cent of civilian labour force
4
2
0

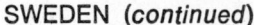

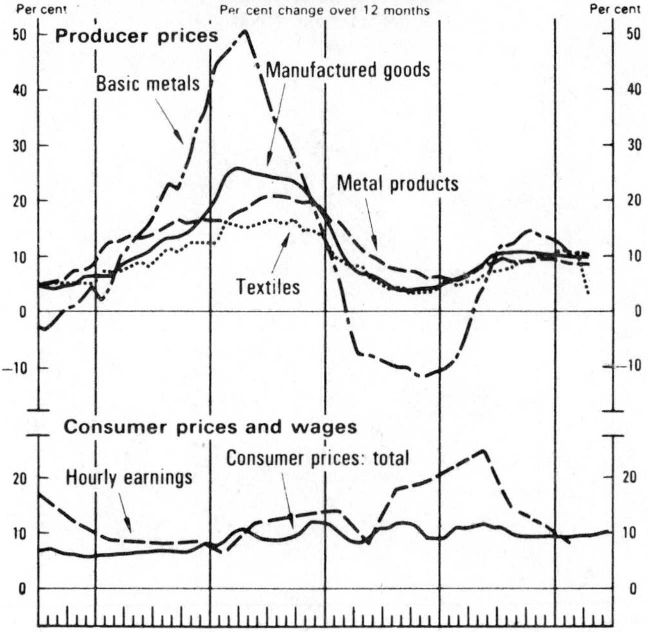

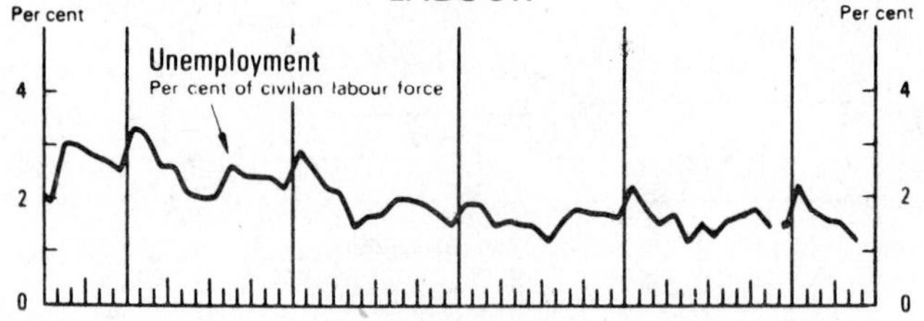

MONEY SUPPLY

Per cent change over 12 months
Per cent
Per cent
M1
20
10
0
72
1973
1974
1975
1976
77

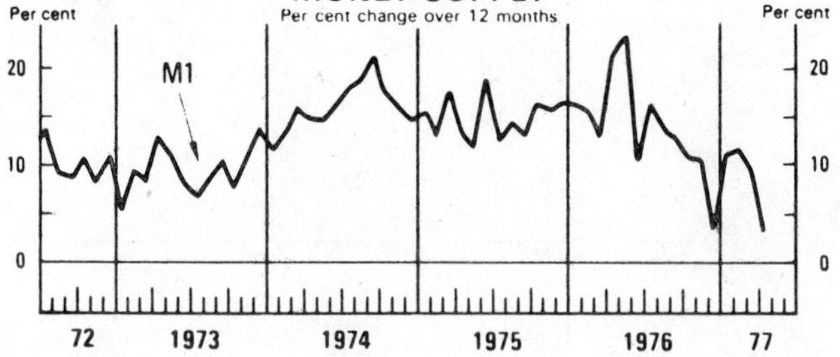

SWEDEN (*concluded*)

FOREIGN TRADE, PAYMENTS, RESERVES, and exchange rate

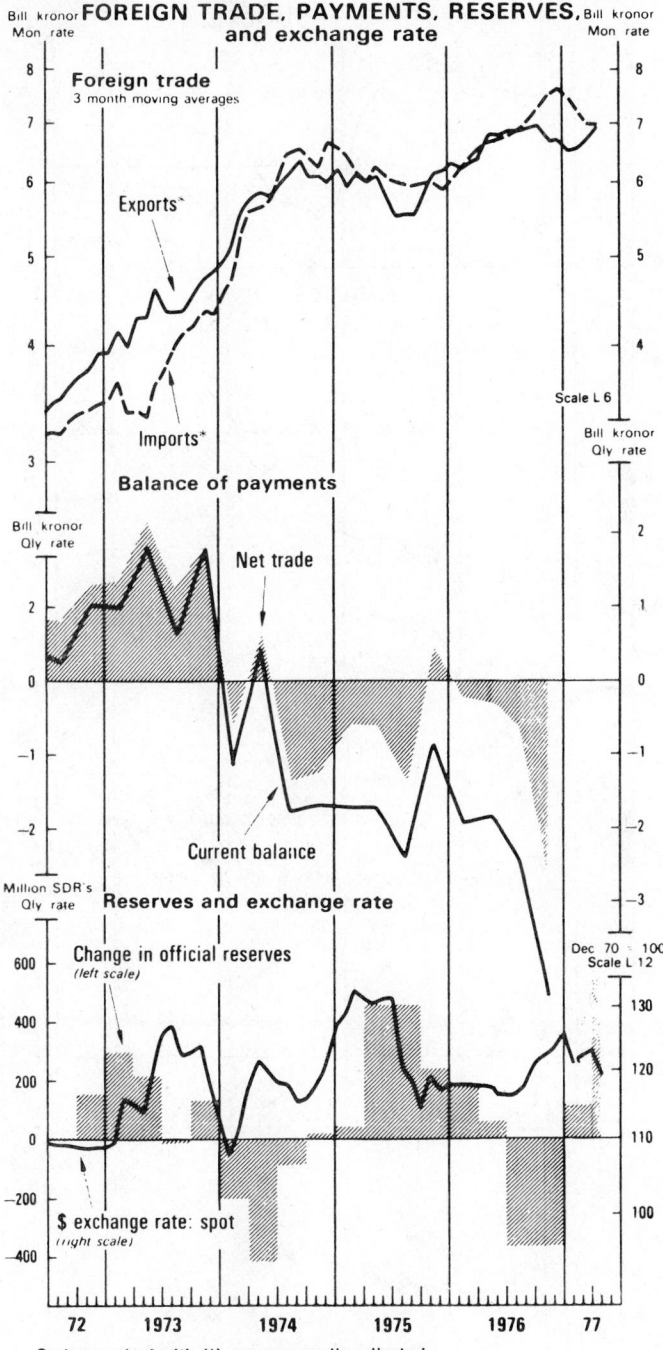

Series marked with (*) are seasonally adjusted.

SWITZERLAND

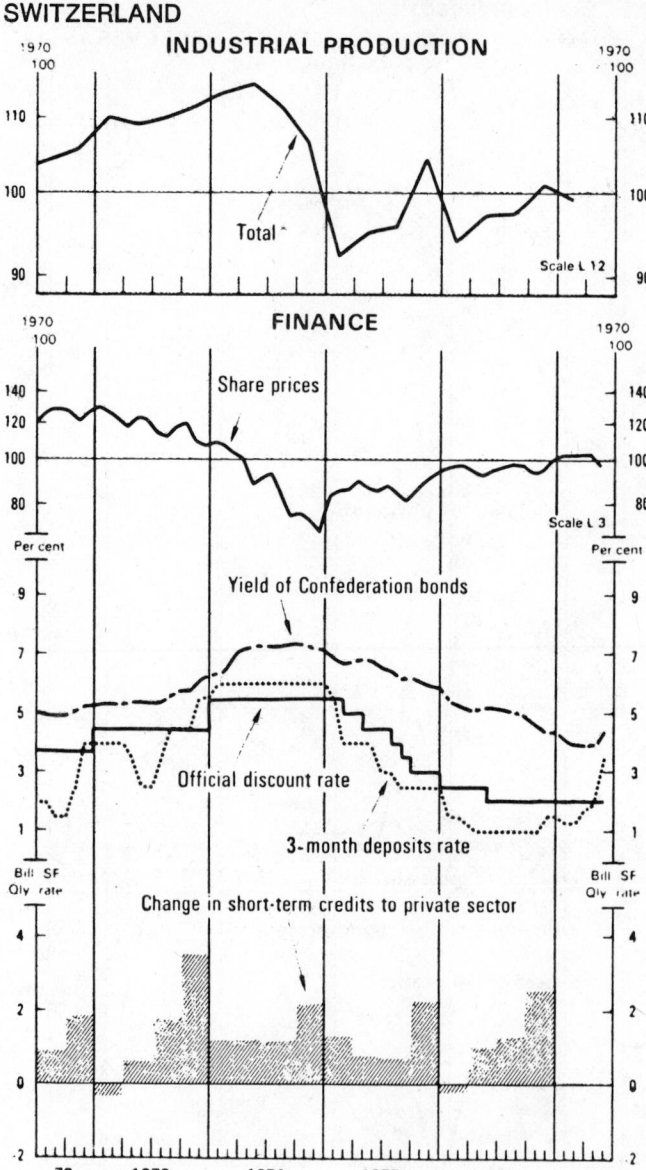

INDUSTRIAL PRODUCTION

Total

FINANCE

Share prices

Yield of Confederation bonds

Official discount rate

3-month deposits rate

Change in short-term credits to private sector

SWITZERLAND (*continued*)

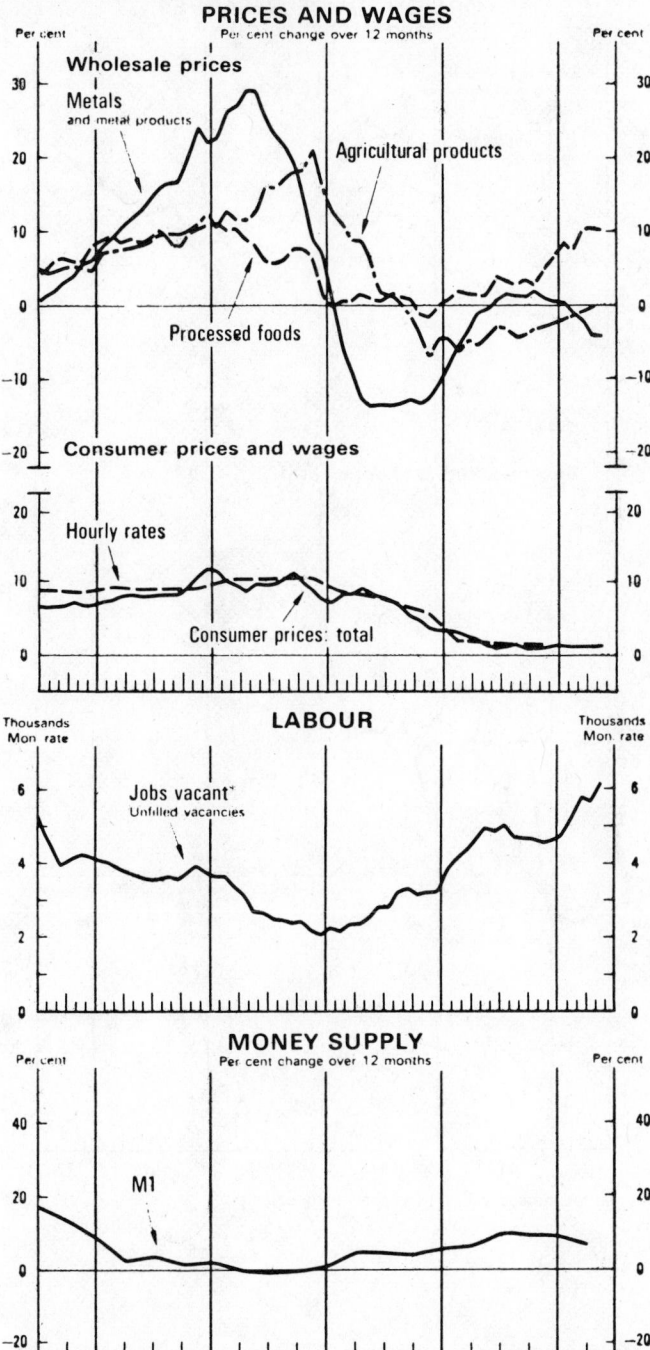

PRICES AND WAGES
Per cent change over 12 months

Wholesale prices

Metals and metal products

Agricultural products

Processed foods

Consumer prices and wages

Hourly rates

Consumer prices: total

LABOUR
Thousands Mon. rate

Jobs vacant
Unfilled vacancies

MONEY SUPPLY
Per cent change over 12 months

M1

72   1973   1974   1975   1976   77

SWITZERLAND (*concluded*)

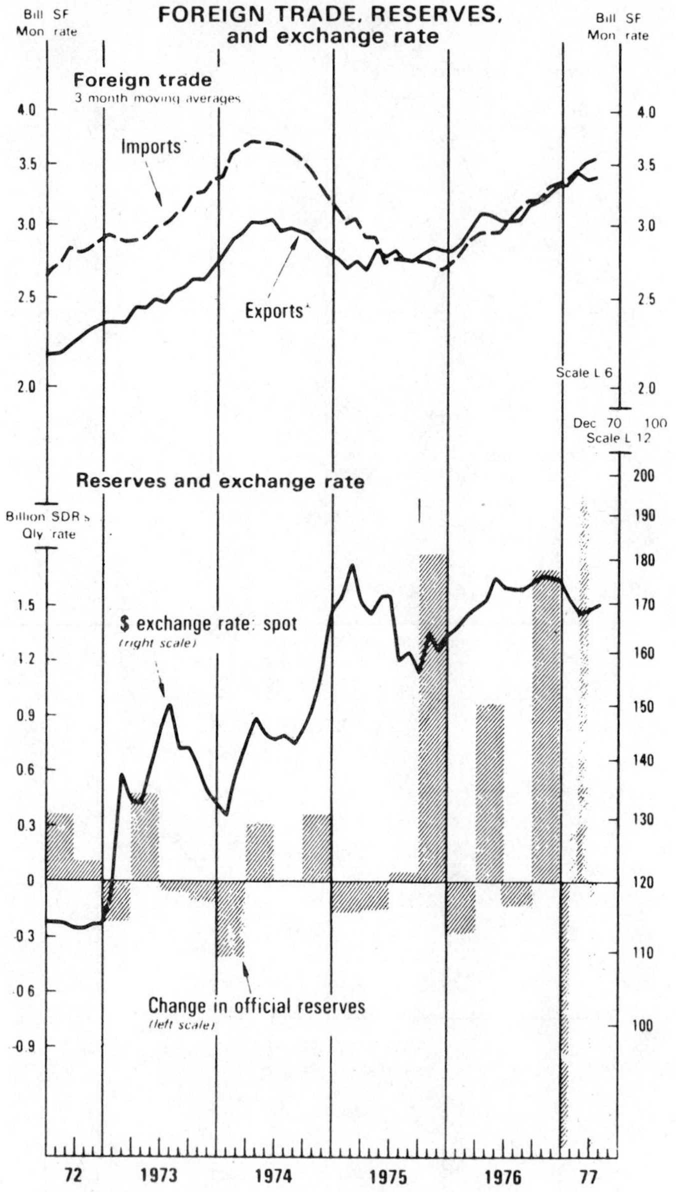

FOREIGN TRADE, RESERVES, and exchange rate

Bill SF
Mon rate

Bill SF
Mon rate

Foreign trade
3 month moving averages

Imports

Exports

4.0

3.5

3.0

2.5

2.0

Scale L 6

Dec 70   100
Scale L 12

Reserves and exchange rate

Billion SDR s
Qly rate

$ exchange rate: spot
(right scale)

Change in official reserves
(left scale)

1.5

1.2

0.9

0.6

0.3

0

-0.3

-0.6

-0.9

200

190

180

170

160

150

140

130

120

110

100

72   1973   1974   1975   1976   77

Series marked with (*) are seasonally adjusted.

UNITED KINGDOM

INDUSTRIAL PRODUCTION
AND NATIONAL PRODUCT

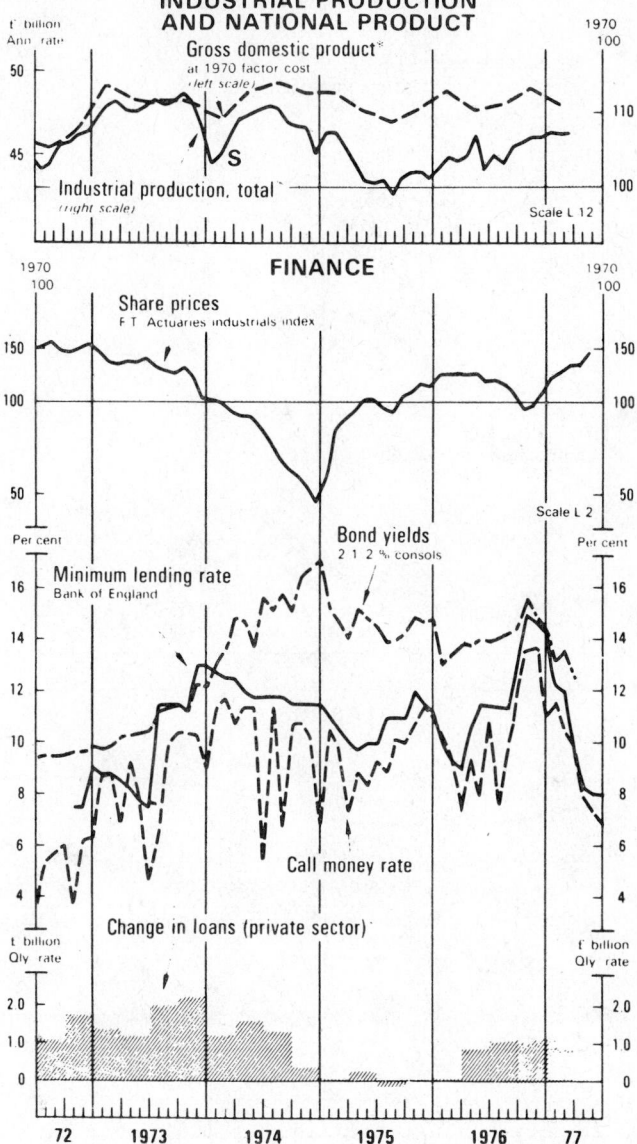

£ billion
Ann. rate

Gross domestic product*
at 1970 factor cost
(left scale)

50

45

S

Industrial production, total
(right scale)

1970
100

110

100

Scale L 12

FINANCE

1970
100

Share prices
F T Actuaries industrials index

150

100

50

1970
100

150

100

50

Scale L 2

Per cent

Minimum lending rate
Bank of England

16

14

12

10

8

6

4

Bond yields
2 1 2 % consols

Call money rate

Per cent

16

14

12

10

8

6

4

£ billion
Qly. rate

Change in loans (private sector)

2.0

1.0

0

£ billion
Qly. rate

2.0

1.0

0

72   1973   1974   1975   1976   77

UNITED KINGDOM (*continued*)

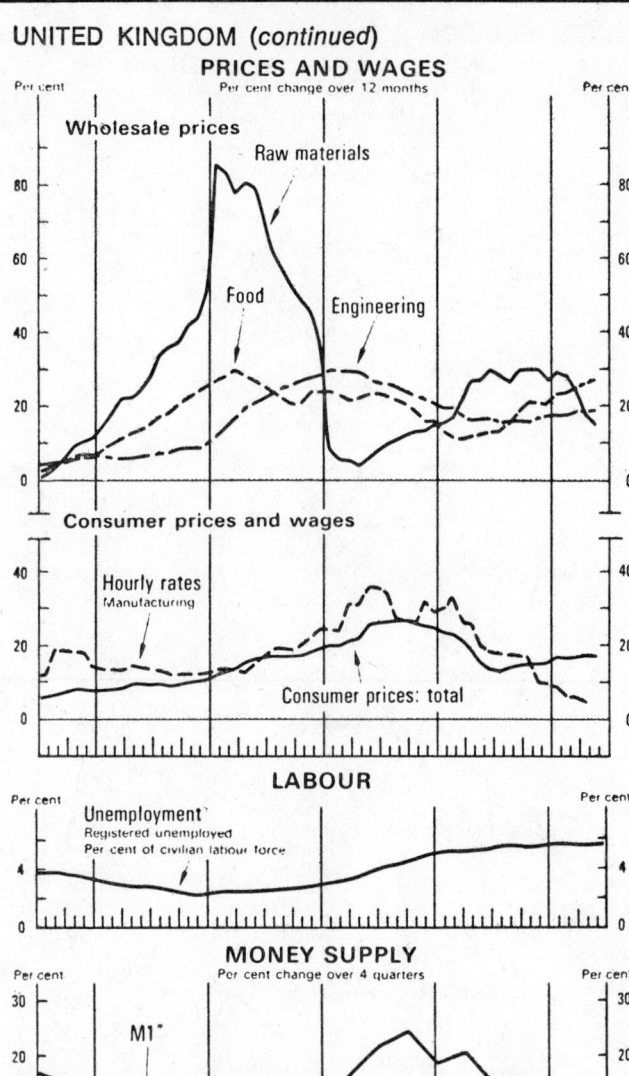

PRICES AND WAGES

Per cent · Per cent change over 12 months · Per cent

Wholesale prices

Raw materials

Food

Engineering

Consumer prices and wages

Hourly rates
Manufacturing

Consumer prices: total

LABOUR

Per cent · Per cent

Unemployment
Registered unemployed
Per cent of civilian labour force

MONEY SUPPLY

Per cent · Per cent change over 4 quarters · Per cent

M1*

72   1973   1974   1975   1976   77

UNITED KINGDOM (*concluded*)

FOREIGN TRADE, PAYMENTS, RESERVES, and exchange rate

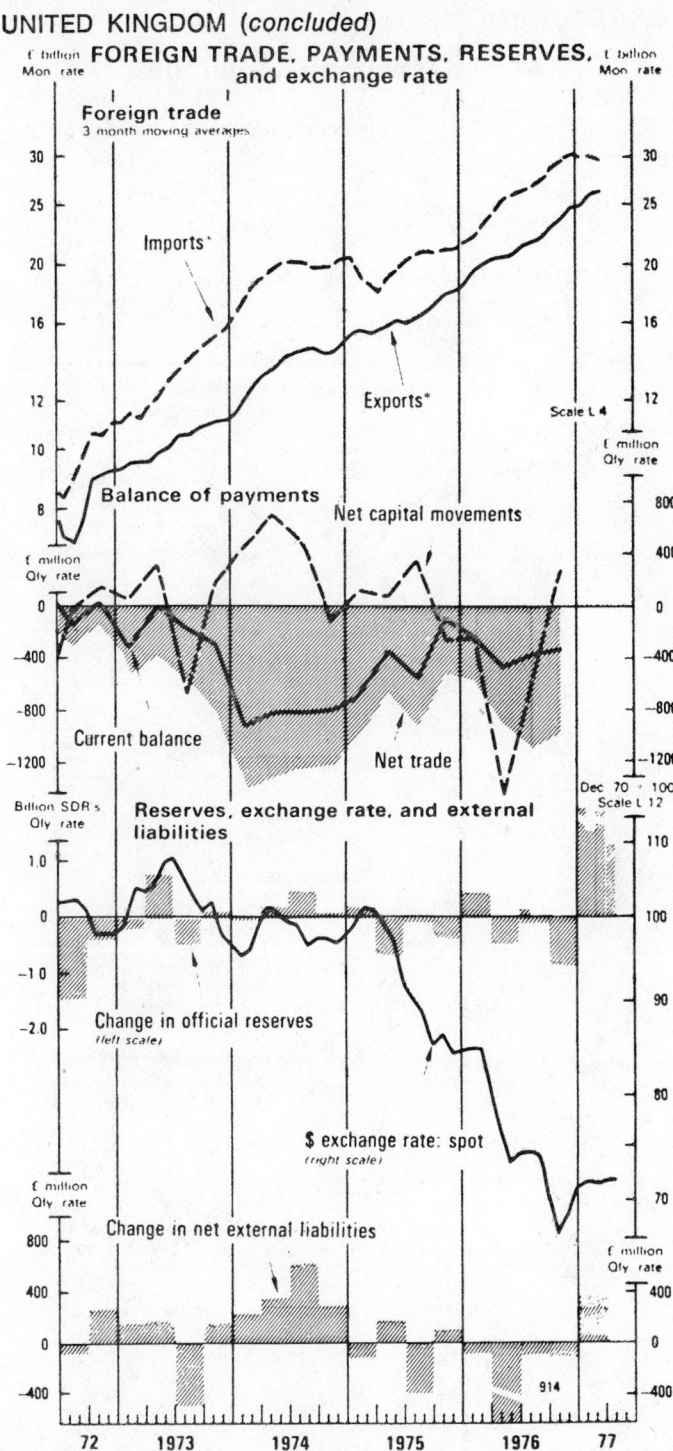

Series marked with (*) are seasonally adjusted.

UNITED STATES

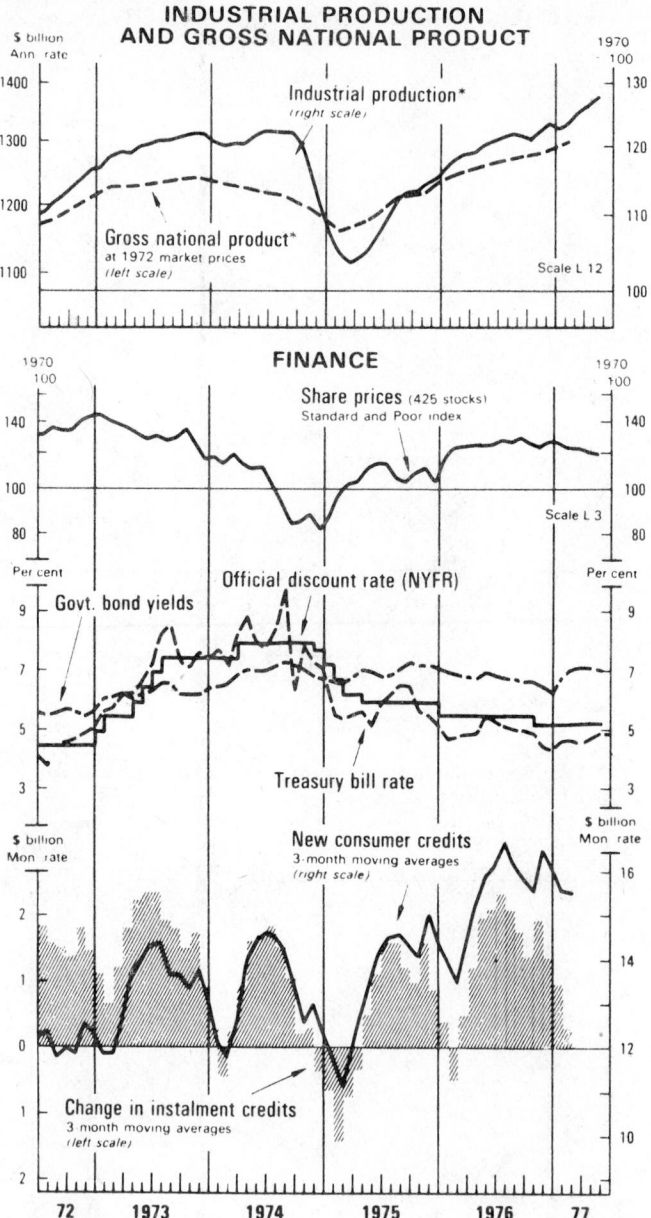

INDUSTRIAL PRODUCTION
AND GROSS NATIONAL PRODUCT

$ billion
Ann rate

1970
= 100

1400   130

Industrial production*
(right scale)

1300   120

1200   110

Gross national product*
at 1972 market prices
(left scale)

1100   Scale L 12   100

FINANCE

1970
100

1970
100

Share prices (425 stocks)
Standard and Poor index

140   140

100   Scale L 3   100

80   80

Per cent   Per cent

Official discount rate (NYFR)

9   9

Govt. bond yields

7   7

5   5

Treasury bill rate

3   3

$ billion
Mon rate

$ billion
Mon rate

New consumer credits
3-month moving averages
(right scale)

16

2

14

1

0   12

Change in instalment credits
3-month moving averages
(left scale)

1   10

2

72   1973   1974   1975   1976   77

UNITED STATES (*continued*)
PRICES AND WAGES

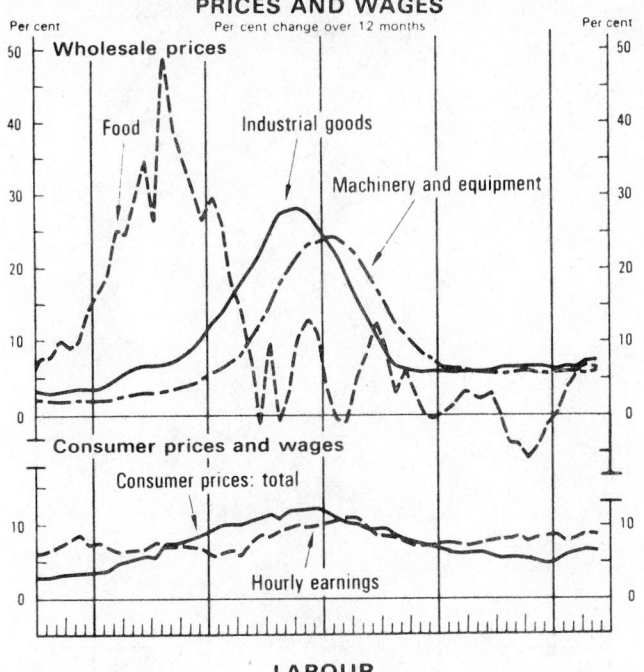

LABOUR

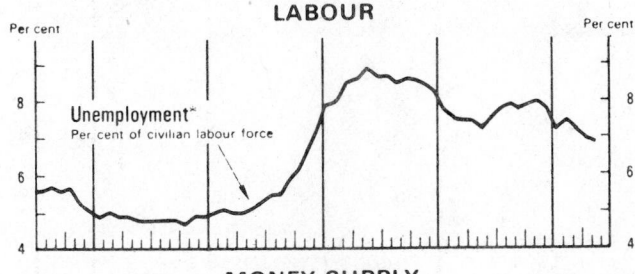

MONEY SUPPLY

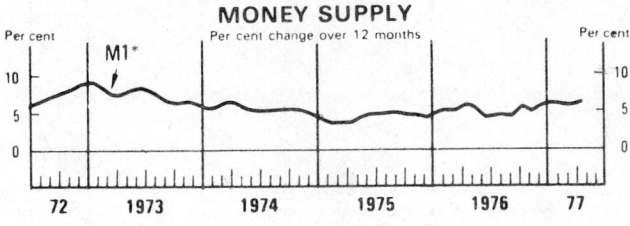

UNITED STATES (*concluded*)
FOREIGN TRADE, PAYMENTS, ASSETS, AND LIABILITIES

S billion
Mon rate

S billion
Mon rate

Foreign trade
3 month moving averages

Exports (f.o.b.)*

Imports (f.o.b.)*

Scale L 6

S billion
Qly rate

S billion
Qly rate

Current balance*

Balance of payments

Net trade*

Billion SDR's
Qly rate

Billion SDR's
Qly rate

Assets and liabilities

Change in official reserves

S billion
Qly rate

S billion
Qly rate

Change in short-term liabilities to foreigners

72 1973 1974 1975 1976 77

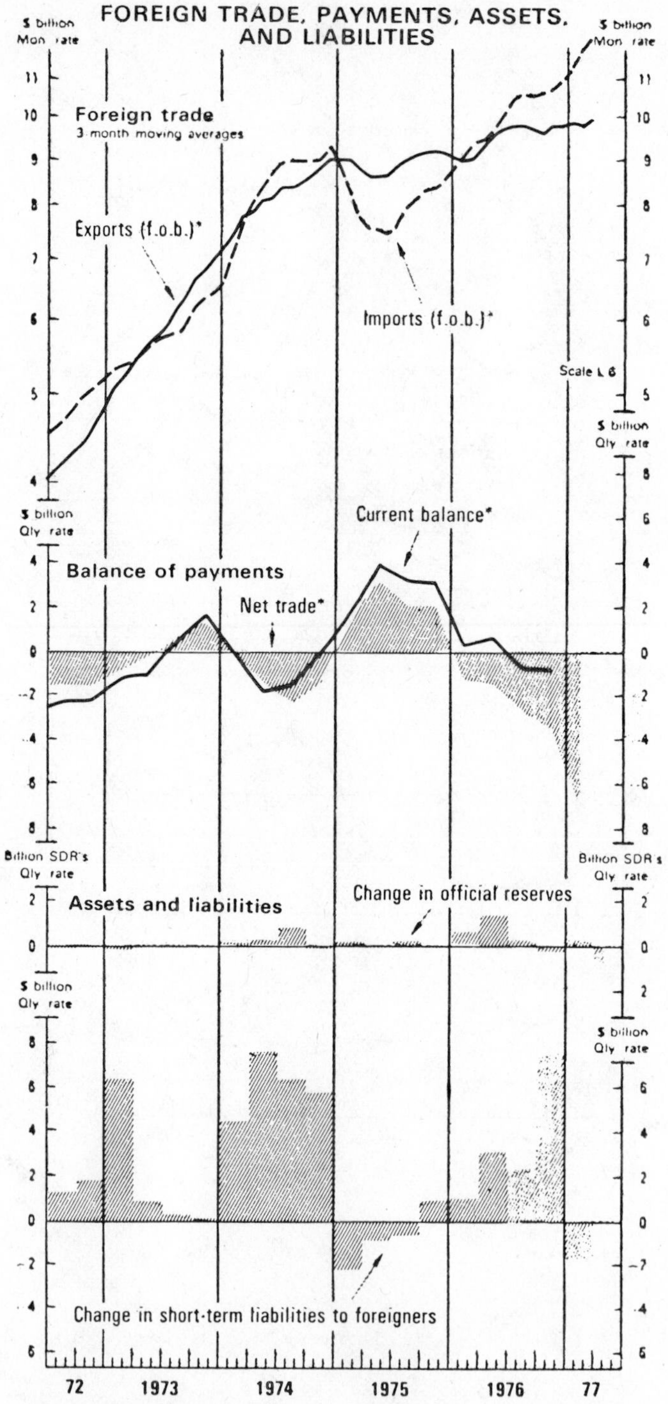

Series marked with (*) are seasonally adjusted.

Business Information Directory

GENERAL INFORMATION SOURCES

Government publications referred to below may be obtained from the Government Printing Office (GPO), Washington, DC, 20402, unless otherwise indicated.

GENERAL SOURCES

The *United States Government Manual* is an annual publication. It describes the organization, purposes, and programs of most government agencies and lists top personnel. Available from the GPO.

Washington Information Directory is an annual publication listing, by topic, organizations and publications which provide information on a wide range of subjects. It also lists congressional committee assignments, regional federal offices, embassies, and state and local officials. Published by the Congressional Quarterly, Inc., 1414 22nd Street NW, Washington, DC 20037.

Statistical Abstracts of the United States, published annually, is the standard summary on the social, political, and economic statistics of the United States. It includes data from both government and private sources. Appendix II gives a comprehensive list of sources. (GPO)

Professional and trade organizations and publications are a major source of contacts and information. Key directories to these sources are listed below.

Encyclopedia of Associations, published by Gale Research Co., Book Tower, Detroit, MI 48226.

The World Guide to Trade Associations gives a comprehensive national and international listing of associations. Published by R. R. Bowker Co., 1880 Avenue of the Americas, New York, NY 10036.

Ulrich's International Periodical Directory covers both domestic and foreign periodicals. Published by R. R. Bowker Co., 1880 Avenue of the Americas, New York, NY 10036.

Standard Periodical Directory covers U.S. and Canadian periodicals. Published by Oxbridge Communications, Inc., 183 Madison Avenue, New York, NY 10016.

Ayer's Directory of Newspapers and Periodicals provides titles of trade newspapers and periodicals. Published by Ayer Press, W.

Washington Square, Philadelphia, PA 19106.

Standard Rate and Data Service provides information on periodical circulation and advertising rates. Published by Standard Rates and Data Service, Inc., 5201 Old Orchard Road, Skokie, IL 60076.

Listings of trade directories are given in the following guides:

Guide to American Directories, published by B. Klein Publications, Inc., P.O. Box 8503, Coral Springs, FL 33065.

Trade Directories of the World provides an international listing of directories. Published by Croner Publications, 211–03 Jamaica Avenue, Queens Village, NY 11428.

Encyclopedia of Business Information, a comprehensive single-volume source, is updated periodically. Available from Gale Research Co., Book Tower, Detroit, MI 48226.

BUSINESS AND ECONOMICS INFORMATION

Business and economic information is provided by the following key references.

Survey of Current Business is a major publication which is supplemented on a weekly basis with *Current Statistics.* The publication contains articles as well as comprehensive statistics on all aspects of the economy, including data on the GNP, employment, wages, prices, finance, foreign trade, and production by industrial sector (GPO).

Business Conditions Digest is a monthly with an extensive collection of charts and tables on the national income and products, leading coincident and lagging cyclical indicators, foreign trade, prices, wages, analytical ratios, and international production and stock prices. (GPO)

Economic Indicators is a monthly summary-type publication prepared by the Council of Economic Advisors. It contains charts and tables on natural output, income, spending, employment, unemployment, wages, industrial production, construction, prices, money, credit, federal finance, and international statistics. (GPO)

Federal Reserve Bulletin is a monthly issued by the Federal Reserve System, containing articles and very extensive tabulated data on all aspects of the monetary situation, credit, mortgage markets, interest rates, and stock and bond yields. A monthly *Chart Book* is available which contains charts of financial and monetary data. Both are available from the Division of Administrative Services, Board of Governors, Federal Reserve System, Washington, DC 20551.

Monthly Labor Review. This monthly publication provides articles and statistics on employment, productivity, wages, earnings, prices, wage settlements, and work stoppages. (GPO)

U.S. Industrial Outlook is an annual providing evaluations and projections of all major industrial and commercial segments of the domestic economy. (GPO)

Quarterly Financial Report of Manufacturing Corporations is issued by the Securities and Exchange Commission and the Federal Trade Commission. It covers corporate financial statistics including sales, profits, assets, and financial ratios, classified by industry group and size. (GPO)

Current Industrial Reports are a series of over 100 monthly, quarterly, semiannual, and annual reports on major products manufactured in the United States. For subscription, contact the Bureau of the Census, U.S. Department of Commerce, Washington, DC 20233. (GPO)

Annual Survey of Manufacturers. General statistics of manufacturing activity for industry groups, individual industries, states, and geographical regions are provided. (GPO)

County Business Patterns is an annual publication on employment and payrolls, which includes a separate paperbound report for each state. (GPO)

Foreign Trade is a Bureau of the Census publication giving monthly reports on U.S. foreign trade. (GPO)

Population: Current Report is a series of monthly and annual reports covering population changes and socioeconomic characteristics of the population. (GPO)

Retail Sales: Current Business Report is a weekly report which provides retail statistics. (GPO)

Wholesale Trade, Sales and Inventories: Current Business Report provides a monthly report on wholesale trade. (GPO)

Directory of Marketing Research Houses and Services is an annual available from the American Marketing Association, 420 Lexington Avenue, New York, NY 10022.

CORPORATE INFORMATION

The major sources of information on publicly held corporations (as well as government and municipal issues) are: *Moody's Investor Services, Inc.*, owned by Dun & Bradstreet, 99 Church Street, New York, NY 10007, and *Standard & Poor's Corp.*, owned by McGraw-Hill, 345 Hudson Street, New York, NY 10014.

Standard & Poor's *Corporate Records* and Moody's *Manuals* are large multivolume works published annually and kept up to date with daily (for Standard & Poor's) or semiweekly (for Moody's) reports. The services provide extensive coverage of industrials, public utilities, transportation, banks, and financial companies. Also included are municipal and government issues.

In addition, the above corporations provide computerized data services and magnetic tapes. Compustat tapes, containing major corporate financial data, are available from Investor's Management Services, Inc., Denver, CO, a subsidiary of Standard & Poor's. Time-sharing access to Compustat and other financial data bases is available through Interactive Data Corporation, Waltham, MA.

The 10-K and other corporate reports are filed with the Securities and Exchange Commission and are available at local SEC offices, investor relations departments of publicly traded companies, as well as various private services, such as Disclosure Inc., Reliance Group, 280 Park Avenue, New York, NY, which provides a complete microfiche service.

Major trade directories include the *Thomas Register of American Manufacturers* (published by Thomas Register of American Manufacturers, 1 Pennsylvania Plaza, New York, NY) and Dun & Bradstreet's *Reference Book of Manufacturers.*

Thomas Register includes in one volume an alphabetical listing of manufacturers, giving address, phone number, product, subsidiaries, plant location, and an indication of assets.

Dun & Bradstreet's *Reference Book* covers similar information, including sales and credit. Dun & Bradstreet also publishes directories on transportation and apparel trades, the *Million Dollar Directory* (a listing of firms with a net worth of $1 million or more), and a *Middle Market Directory* (a listing of firms with a net worth of $500,000 to $1 million).

FEDERAL GOVERNMENT DEVELOPMENTS

Commerce Business Daily. This daily provides information on contract awards and subcontract opportunities, Defense Department awards, and surplus sales. (GPO)

Federal Register. This daily provides information on federal agency regulations and other legal documents (GPO).

CQ Weekly Report. This major service follows every important piece of legislation through both houses of Congress and reports on the political and lobbying pressures being applied. Available from the Congressional Quarterly Service, 1414 22nd Street, Washington, DC 20037.

Daily Report for Executives. A daily series of reports giving Washington developments that affect all aspects of business operations. Available from the Bureau of National Affairs, Inc., 1231 25th Street NW, Washington, DC 20037.

Two major services, the *Bureau of National Affairs, Inc.* (address above) and the *Commerce Clearing House, Inc.* (4025 West Patterson Avenue, Chicago, IL 60646), publish a large number of valuable weekly loose-leaf reports covering developments in all aspects of law, government regulations, and taxation.

INDEX PUBLICATIONS

Indexes of a wide variety of articles appearing in periodicals, trade presses, and financial services dealing with corporations, industry, and finance are given in the following:

Business Periodicals Index published by H. W. Wilson Co., 550 University Avenue, Bronx, NY.

Funk and Scott Index of Corporations and Industries, published by Predicast, Inc., 11001 Cedar Street, Cleveland, OH.

Major newspaper indexes are:

New York Times Index published by the New York Times Company, 229 W. 43rd Street, New York, NY 10036 (semimonthly, cumulates annually).

Wall Street Journal Index published by Dow Jones & Co. Inc., 22 Cortland Street, New York, NY 10007 (monthly).

USEFUL CONTACTS FOR BUSINESS INFORMATION

Association Addresses of any organization may be obtained by writing the Director of Information Central, American Society of Association Executives, 1101 East 16th Street NW, Washington, DC 20036, or calling 202–659–3333.

Congressional action information can be obtained from several sources. The Bill Status Office will provide information on whether legislation has been introduced, who sponsored it, and its current status. For House action, call 202–225–1772; for Senate action, call 202–224–2971.

Cloakrooms of both houses will provide details on what is happening on the floor of the chamber. House cloakrooms: Democrat 202–225–7400; Republican 202–225–7430. Senate cloakrooms: Democrat 202–224–8541; Republican 202–224–8601.

Corporate reports filed with the SEC can be ordered at 35¢ per page from the National Investment Library, 80 Wall Street, New York, NY 10005; or call 212–254–1700.

Service also provided by Disclosure Inc., 4827 Rugby Avenue, Bethesda, MD 20014, or call 301–951–0100.

The Commerce Department's Ombudsman operates throughout the entire government complex to assist both business and consumers. Services include dissemination of information and reports such as *Outlook '78*. Write Office of the Ombudsman, U.S. Department of Commerce, Washington, DC 20230, or call 202–377–3176.

European Community country information is available free from the European Community Information Service, 2100 M Street NW, Washington, DC 20037; or call 202–862–9500.

Economic data and indicators provided on a weekly, monthly, or quarterly basis may be obtained as released. Telephone numbers of the offices publishing and producing the information are given in the table below.

Department and Information	Telephone Number
Agriculture Department	
To order publications	202–447–4021
Agricultural prices	202–447–3570
Bureau of Economic Analysis	
Business Conditions Digest	202–523–0535
Defense Indicators	202–523–0535
Gross national product (preliminary)	202–523–0669
Personal income	202–523–0669
Merchandise trade balance, balance of payments basis	202–523–0668
Bureau of Labor Statistics	
To order publications	202–523–1221
Consumer price index	202–523–7827
Employment situation	202–523–1944
Wholesale price index	202–523–1795
Census Bureau	
To order publications	202–763–5853
Construction expenditures	202–763–5717
Manufacturers shipments, inventories, and orders	202–763–5850
Housing starts	202–763–5731
Advance report on durable goods, manufacturers shipments, and orders	202–763–5850
Advance monthly retail sales	202–763–5359
Export and import merchandise trade	202–763–5140
Monthly wholesale trade	202–763–5294
Federal Reserve	
To order publications	202–452–3245
Money stock measures	202–452–3591
Consumer credit	202–452–2458
Industrial production and related data	202–452–3153
Capacity utilization in manufacturing	202–452–3197
Joint Economic Committee	202–224–3081
To obtain latest economic information (employment, housing starts, price indices, retail sales, industrial production)	

Economic news and highlights of the day are provided by phone from the Department of Commerce; call 202–393–1847.

The Energy Information Center will provide free information on energy and related matters. Write National Energy Information Center, Room 1407, Federal Building NW, Washington, DC 20461, or call 202–566–9820.

Foreign trade information as well as gen-eral business data are provided by the World Trade Information Center, One World Trade Center, New York, NY 10048, which maintains extensive data banks. The charge for a preliminary search is about $10. Call 212–466–3063.

The Bureaus of International Commerce and East-West Trade of the Department of Commerce provide country and regional trade information as shown in the following table.

BIC Country Marketing Manager

Region	Telephone Number
Africa	
West and Central Africa	202–377–4388
East and South Africa	202–377–4927
Europe	
France and the Benelux countries	202–377–4504
Germany and Austria	202–377–3187
Italy, Greece, and Turkey	202–377–3944
Nordic countries	202–377–3848
Spain, Portugal, Switzerland, and Yugoslavia	202–377–2795
United Kingdom and Canada	202–377–3415
Far East	
Australia and New Zealand	202–377–3646
East and South Asia	202–377–5401
Japan	202–377–2896
Southeast Asia	202–377–2522
Latin America	
Brazil, Argentina, Paraguay, and Uruguay	202–377–5427
Mexico, Central America, and Panama	202–377–2313
Remainder of South America and Caribbean countries	202–377–2995
North Africa	202–377–5737
Near East	
Bahrain, Iraq, Jordan, Kuwait, Lebanon, Oman, Peoples Democratic Republic of Yemen, Qatar, Saudi Arabia, Syria, United Arab Emirates, and Yemen Arab Republic	202–377–5767
Iran, Israel, and Egypt	202–377–3752
Eastern Europe	202–377–2645
USSR	202–377–4655
Peoples Republic of China	202–377–3583

Source: U.S. Department of Commerce.

Industry information statistics and details on specific industries can be obtained from the Director of Business Research and Analysis, Department of Commerce, Washington, DC 20230; or call 202–377–2786.

Technical and scientific information is provided by the National Technical Information Service of the Department of Commerce, 5285 Port Royal Road, Springfield, VA 22161, which handles requests about government-sponsored research of all kinds. For $100 it will research a subject. If a search has been done, a copy will be provided for $25. Call 703–557–4650. For rush orders, call 703–557–4700.

The reference section of the Library of Congress, Science and Technology Division, 10 First Street SE, Washington DC 20540 provides answers to specific questions; call 202–426–5580. The National Referral Center provides names, addresses, and descriptions of information resources; call 202–426–5670.

Population information on all aspects of national and world population is provided by the Population Reference Bureau, Inc., 1754 N Street NW, Washington, DC 20036, or call 202–638–5500.

Smithsonian Institution, Science Information Exchange provides, at a fee to cover costs, information both on individuals currently working in specific fields and on sources of research support; it also covers general research trends. Write 1730 M Street NW, Washington, DC 20036, or call 202–381–4211.

The Washington Information Research Service provides reports and guidance to information on a fee basis. Write Washington Researchers, 910 17th Street NW, Washington, DC 20006, or call 202–452–0025.

Federal Information Centers (FICS) located in key cities throughout the country are a joint venture of the U.S. General Services Administration and the U.S. Civil Services. Each center is a focal point for obtaining information about the federal government and often about state and local governments. A member of the center's staff can either provide information or direct inquiries to an expert who can. Some centers have specialists who speak foreign languages. The coordinator of the FICS is located at 18th and F Streets, NW, Washington, DC 20405; call 202–566–1937. The Federal Information Centers and their telephone numbers are listed below.

Alabama
Birmingham: 322–8591. Toll-free tieline to Atlanta, GA.
Mobile: 438–1421. Toll-free tieline to New Orleans, LA.

Arizona
Phoenix: (602) 261–3313. Federal Building, 230 N. First Avenue 85025.
Tucson: 622–1511. Toll-free tieline to Phoenix, AZ.

Arkansas
Little Rock: 378–6177. Toll-free tieline to Memphis, TN.

California
Los Angeles: (213) 688–3800. Federal Building, 300 N. Los Angeles Street 90012.
Sacramento: (916) 440–3340. Federal Building, U.S. Courthouse, 650 Capitol Mall 95814.
San Diego: (714) 293–6030. 880 Front Street 92188.
San Francisco: (415) 556–6600. Federal Building, U.S. Courthouse, 450 Golden Gate Avenue 94102.
San Jose: 275–7422. Toll-free tieline to San Francisco, CA.

Colorado
Colorado Springs: 471–9491. Toll-free tieline to Denver, CO.
Denver: (303) 837–3602. Federal Building, 1961 Stout Street 80204.
Pueblo: 544–9523. Toll-free tieline to Denver, CO.

Connecticut
Hartford: 527–2617. Toll-free tieline to New York, NY.
New Haven: 624–4720. Toll-free tieline to New York, NY.

District of Columbia
Washington: (202) 755–8660. Seventh and D Streets SW, Room 5716, 20407.

Florida
Fort Lauderdale: 522–8531. Toll-free tieline to Miami, FL.
Jacksonville: 354–4756. Toll-free tieline to St. Petersburg, FL.
Miami: (305) 350–4155. Federal Building, 51 Southwest First Avenue 33130.
St. Petersburg: (813) 893–3495. William C. Cramer Federal Building, 144 First Avenue S. 33701.
Tampa: 229–7911. Toll-free tieline to St. Petersburg, FL.
West Palm Beach: 833–7566. Toll-free tieline to Miami, FL.

Georgia
Atlanta: (404) 526–6891. Federal Building, 275 Peachtree Street NE 30303.

Hawaii
Honolulu: (808) 546–8620. Federal Building, 300 Ala Moàna Boulevard, P.O. Box 50091, 96850.

Illinois
Chicago: (312) 353–4242. Everett Mc-Kinley Dirksen Building, 219 S. Dearborn Street 60604.

Indiana
Indianapolis: (317) 269–7373. Federal Building, 575 North Pennsylvania 46204.

Iowa
Des Moines: 282–9091. Toll-free tieline to Omaha, NB.

Kansas
Topeka: 232–7229. Toll-free tieline to Kansas City, MO.
Wichita: 263–6931. Toll-free tieline to Kansas City, MO.

Kentucky
Louisville: (502) 582–6261. Federal Building, 600 Federal Place 40202.

Louisiana
New Orleans: (504) 589–6696. Federal Building, Room 1210, 701 Loyola Avenue 70113.

Maryland
Baltimore: (301) 962–4980. Federal Building, 31 Hopkins Plaza 21201.

Massachusetts
Boston: (617) 223–7121. J. F. K. Federal Building, Cambridge Street, Lobby, 1st Floor 02203.

Michigan
Detroit: (313) 226–7016. McNamara Federal Building, 477 Michigan Avenue 48226.

Minnesota
Minneapolis: (612) 725–2073. Federal Building and U.S. Courthouse, 110 S. Fourth Street 55401.

Missouri
Kansas City: (816) 374–2466. Federal Building, 601 East Twelfth Street 64106.
St. Joseph: 233–8206. Toll-free tieline to Kansas City, MO.
St. Louis: (314) 425–4106. Federal Building, 1520 Market Street 63103.

Nebraska
Omaha: (402) 221–3353. Federal Building, U.S. Post Office, and Courthouse, 215 N. 17th Street 68102.

New Jersey
Newark: (201) 645–3600. Federal Building, 970 Broad Street 07102.
Trenton: 396–4400. Toll-free tieline to Newark, NJ.

New Mexico
Albuquerque: (505) 766–3091. Federal Building and U.S. Courthouse, 500 Gold Avenue SW 87101.
Santa Fe: 983–7743. Toll-free tieline to Albuquerque, NM.

New York
Albany: 463–4421. Toll-free tieline to New York, NY.
Buffalo: (716) 842–5770. Federal Building, 111 West Huron Street 14202.
New York: (212) 264–4464. Lobby, Federal Building, 26 Federal Plaza 10007.
Rochester: 546–5075. Toll-free tieline to Buffalo, NY.
Syracuse: 476–8545. Toll-free tieline to Buffalo, NY.

North Carolina
Charlotte: 376–3600. Toll-free tieline to Atlanta GA.

Ohio
Akron: 375–5638. Toll-free tieline to Cleveland, OH.
Cincinnati: (513) 684–2801. Federal Building, 550 Main Street 45202.
Cleveland: (216) 522–4040. Federal Building, 1240 E. Ninth Street 44199.
Columbus: 221–1014. Toll-free tieline to Cincinnati, OH.
Dayton: 223–7377. Toll-free tieline to Cincinnati, OH.
Toledo: 241–3223. Toll-free tieline to Cleveland, OH.

Oklahoma
Oklahoma City: (405) 231–4868. U.S. Post Office and Courthouse, 201 N.W. 3rd Street 73102.
Tulsa: 584–4193. Toll-free tieline to Oklahoma City, OK.

Oregon
Portland: (503) 221–2222. Federal Building, 1220 S.W. Third Avenue 97204.

Pennsylvania
Philadelphia: (215) 597–7042. Federal Building, 600 Arch Street 19106.
Pittsburgh: (412) 644–3456. Federal Building, 1000 Liberty Avenue 15222.
Scranton: 346–7081. Toll-free tieline to Philadelphia, PA.

Rhode Island
Providence: 331–5565. Toll-free tieline to Boston, MA.

Tennessee
Chattanooga: 265–8231. Toll-free tieline to Memphis, TN.
Memphis: (901) 534–3285. Clifford Davis Federal Building, 167 N. Main Street 38103.
Nashville: 242–5056. Toll-free tieline to Memphis, TN.

Texas
Austin: 472–5494. Toll-free tieline to Houston, TX.
Dallas: 749–2131. Toll-free tieline to Fort Worth, TX.

Fort Worth: (817) 334–3624. Fritz Garland Lanham Federal Building, 819 Taylor Street 76102.

Houston: (713) 226–5711. Federal Building, U.S. Courthouse, 515 Rusk Avenue 77002.

San Antonio: 224–4471. Toll-free tieline to Houston, TX.

Utah

Ogden: 399–1347. Toll-free tieline to Salt Lake City, UT.

Salt Lake City: (801) 524–5353. Federal Building, Lobby, 125 S. State Street 84138.

Washington

Seattle: (206) 442–0570. Federal Building, 915 Second Avenue 98174.

Tacoma: 383–5230. Toll-free tieline to Seattle, WA.

Wisconsin

Milwaukee: 271–2273. Toll-free tieline to Chicago, IL.

RECENTLY OPENED CENTERS

California

Santa Ana: 836–2386. Toll-free tieline to Los Angeles, CA.

Florida

Orlando: 422–1800. Toll-free line to St. Petersburg, FL.

Indiana

Gary/Hammond: 883–4110. Toll-free tieline to Indianapolis, IN.

Michigan

Grand Rapids: 451–2628. Toll-free tieline to Detroit, MI

New Jersey

Paterson/Passaic: 523–0717. Toll-free tieline to Newark, NJ.

Pennsylvania

Allentown/Bethlehem: 821–7785. Toll-free tieline to Philadelphia, PA.

Virginia

Newport News: 244–0480. Toll-free tieline to Norfolk, VA.

Norfolk: (804) 441–6723. Stanwick Building, 3661 E. Virginia Beach Boulevard 23502.

Richmond: 643–4928. Toll-free tieline to Norfolk, VA.

Roanoke: 982–8591. Toll-free tieline to Norfolk, VA.

INFORMATION SOURCES IN THE U.S. DEPARTMENT OF COMMERCE

Subject	Source	Telephone Number
Aeronautical charting	NOAA	301–443–8708
Agriculture census	CEN	301–763–7273
Air-quality research	NOAA	303–499–1000
Appliance labeling	NBS	301–921–3181
Applied technology	NBS	301–921–3181
Arab boycott	ITA	202–377–2253
Atmospheric remote sensing	NOAA	303–499–1000
Atmospheric research	NOAA	303–499–1000
Atomic, nuclear, isotopic research	NBS	301–921–3181
Automation technology	NBS	301–921–3181
Balance of payments	BEA	202–523–0777
Broadcast news	SEC	202–377–5610
Building technology	NBS	301–921–3181
Business censuses	CEN	301–763–7273
Business development loans	EDA	202–377–5113
Business Conditions Digest	BEA	202–523–0777
Capital equipment	ITA	202–377–3259
Censuses	CEN	301–763–7273
Climate monitoring	NOAA	303–499–1000
Coal gasification	NBS	301–921–3181
Coastal zone management	NOAA	202–634–4239
Commerce Technical Advisory Board (CTAB)	S&T	202–377–5065
Commodity statistics	ITA	202–377–3259
Computer science and technology	NBS	301–921–3181
Construction and forest products	ITA	202–377–3259
Consumer goods	ITA	202–377–3259
Consumer products safety	NBS	301–921–3181
Corporate profits	BEA	202–523–0777
Data (fire)	NFPCA	202–634–7663
Disaster research	NBS	301–921–3181
Domestic Business Development, Bureau of	ITA	202–377–3259
East-west trade	ITA	202–377–4654
Economic affairs	OCE	202–377–2235
Economic censuses	CEN	301–763–7273
Economic development programs	EDA	202–377–5113
Education statistics	CEN	301–763–7273
Education and training (fire)	NFPCA	202–634–7663
Energy (conservation)	NBS	301–921–3181
Energy (inventions)	NBS	301–921–3181
Environment (pollution)	NBS	301–921–3181
Environment affairs	S&T	202–377–4335
Environment data services	NOAA	302–634–7305
Environmental research	NOAA	303–499–1000
Environmental satellites	NOAA	301–443–8243
Employment and unemployment surveys	CEN	301–763–7273
Exports awards	ITA	202–377–2253
Export Development, Bureau of	ITA	202–377–2253
Export information	ITA	202–377–2253
Export licenses	ITA	202–377–4654
Expositions (international)	USTS	202–377–4987
Failure analysis	NBS	301–921–3181
Federal economic indicators	OCE	202–377–2235
Field operations	ITA	202–377–2253
Fire prevention	NFPCA	202–634–7663
Fire protection (see also Research and Education)	NBS	301–921–3181
Flash floods	NOAA	301–427–7622
Foreign investment statistics	BEA	202–523–0777
Foreign trade analysis	ITA	202–377–2253
Foreign trade statistics	CEN	301–763–7273

INFORMATION SOURCES IN THE U.S. DEPARTMENT OF COMMERCE (*continued*)

Subject	Source	Telephone Number
Freedom of information	SEC	202–377–5659
Frequency allocations (federal use)	NTIA	202–395–5800
Geodetic surveys	NOAA	301–443–8708
Government finances (state and local)	CEN	301–763–7273
Grants to local government	EDA	202–377–5113
Great Lakes research	NOAA	303–499–1000
Gross national product	BEA	202–523–0777
Health	NBS	301–921–3181
Housing and construction statistics	CEN	301–763–7273
Hurricane research	NOAA	303–499–1000
Hurricane warning	NOAA	301–427–7622
Hydrology, Office of	NOAA	301–427–7622
Import programs	ITA	202–377–3259
Income, family	CEN	301–763–7273
Income, personal (national and regional)	BEA	202–523–0777
Industry surveys	CEN	301–763–7273
Information policy	NTIA	202–395–5800
Input-output analysis	BEA	202–523–0777
Interdepartment Radio Advisory Committee (IRAC)	NTIA	202–395–5800
International finance, investment, and marketing	ITA	202–377–2253
International investment statistics	BEA	202–523–0777
Investment services	ITA	202–377–2253
Laser information	NBS	301–921–3181
Law enforcement standards	NBS	301–921–3181
Leading economic indicators	BEA	202–523–0777
Manufacturing industry (by commodity)	ITA	202–377–3259
Marine ecosystem studies	NOAA	303–499–1000
Marine mammals	NOAA	202–634–7281
Marine technology	NOAA	301–443–8243
Maritime technology	MARAD	202–377–2746
Materials research	NBS	301–921–3181
Meteorological center	NOAA	301–427–7622
Metric	NBS	301–921–3181
Minority business programs	OMBE	202–377–3024
National marine fisheries	NOAA	202–634–7281
Nautical charts	NOAA	301–443–8708
News releases and speeches	SEC	202–377–4901
Occupation and industry statistics	CEN	301–763–7273
Ombudsman for business	ITA	202–277–3259
Overseas business opportunities	ITA	202–377–2253
Patent and trademarks	PAT	703–557–3428
Patents, government-owned, foreign filing	PAT	703–557–4735
Plant and equipment expenditures	BEA	202–523–0777
Pollution abatement and control expenditures	BEA	202–523–0777
Population information	CEN	301–763–7273
Product standards	S&T	202–377–3221
Public works projects	EDA	202–377–5113
Publications, sales and distribution	SEC	202–377–5494
Radiation measurements	NBS	301–921–3181
Regional Planning Commissions	SEC	202–377–4901
Research (economic)	OCE	202–377–2235
Research and data (fire)	NFPCA	202–634–7663
Research (maritime)	MARAD	202–377–2746
Resource and Trade Assistance, Bureau of	ITA	202–377–3259
Retail, wholesale, and service trade statistics	CEN	301–763–7273
Satellites	NOAA	301–443–8243
Science and technology	S&T	202–377–5065
Sea grants	NOAA	202–634–4034
Secretarial statements	SEC	202–377–4901
Service industries (statistics)	ITA	202–377–3259
Ship operations shipbuilding	MARAD	202–377–2746
Solar forcasts	NOAA	303–499–1000
Space environment research	NOAA	303–499–1000
Spectrum management	NTIA	202–395–5800
Standard reference materials	NBS	301–921–3181
Statistical reporter	OFSPS	202–673–7965
Stratospheric research	NOAA	303–499–1000

INFORMATION SOURCES IN THE U.S. DEPARTMENT OF COMMERCE (*concluded*)

Subject	Source	Telephone Number
Survey of current business	BEA	202–523–0777
Technical document sales (all government agencies)	NTIS	202–557–4600
Technical help to exporters	NTIS	703–557–4733
Technology transfer to developing countries	NTIS	202–724–3366
Telecommunications applicators	NTIA	202–395–5800
Telecommunications policy (international and domestic)	NTIA	202–395–5800
Telecommunications research	NTIA	202–395–5800
Telecommunications technology	NTIA	202–395–5800
Textiles	ITA	202–377–3259
Time and frequency (standards)	NBS	303–323–3198
Tornado and severe storms research	NOAA	303–499–1000
Tornado warning	NOAA	301–427–7622
Tourism, international and domestic	USTS	202–377–4987
Trade adjustment assistance	EDA	202–377–5133
Trade fairs, trade centers and missions	ITA	202–377–2253
Trademarks	PAT	703–557–3428
Trade negotiations	ITA	202–377–2253
Trade zone board	ITA	202–377–3259
Transportation equipment	ITA	202–377–3259
Travel to and in USA	USTS	202–377–4987
Weather modification (cloud seeding)	NOAA	301–443–8243
Weather service	NOAA	301–427–7622
Weights and measures	NBS	301–921–3181

Abbreviations

BEA	Bureau of Economic Analysis
CEN	Bureau of the Census
EDA	Economic Development Administration
ITA	Industry and Trade Administration
MARAD	Maritime Administration
NBS	National Bureau of Standards
NFPCA	National Fire Prevention and Control Administration
NOAA	National Oceanic and Atmospheric Administration
NTIA	National Telecommunications and Information Administration
NTIS	National Technical Information Service
OCE	Office of Chief Economist
OFSPS	Office of Federal Stat. Policy and Standards
OMBE	Office of Minority Business Enterprise
PAT	Patent and Trademark Office
SEC	Office of the Secretary
S&T	Office of the Assistant Secretary for Science and Technology
USTS	United States Travel Service

ADDRESSES OF U.S. DEPARTMENT OF COMMERCE INFORMATION SOURCES

Office of Assistant Secretary for Science and Technology
Main Commerce Building
14th and Constitution Avenues
Washington, DC 20230
Telephone: 202–377–3914

Office of the Chief Economist
Main Commerce Building
14th and Constitution Avenues
Washington, DC 20230
Telephone: 202–377–2235

Bureau of the Census
Federal Office Building No. 3
Suitland, MD 20230
Telephone: 301–763–7273

Bureau of Economic Analysis
Tower Building
1401 K Street NW
Mailing Address:
U.S. Department of Commerce
14th and Constitution Avenues
Washington, DC 20230
Telephone: 202–523–0777

Industry and Trade Administration
  Main Commerce Building
  14th and Constitution Avenues
  Washington, DC 20230
  Telephone: 202–377–3808
Economic Development Administration
  Main Commerce Building
  14th and Constitution Avenues
  Washington, DC 20230
  Telephone: 202–377–5113
Maritime Administration
  Main Commerce Building
  14th and Constitution Avenues
  Washington, DC 20230
  Telephone: 202–377–2746
National Bureau of Standards
  Administration Building
  National Bureau of Standards
  Washington, DC 20234
  Telephone: 301–921–3181
National Fire Prevention and Control Administration
  2400 M Street NW
  Mailing Address:
  U.S. Department of Commerce
  14th and Constitution Avenues
  Washington, DC 20230
  Telephone: 202–634–7663

National Oceanic and Atmospheric Administration
  6010 Executive Boulevard
  Washington Science Center
  Rockville, MD 20852
  Telephone: 301–443–8243
National Technical Information Service
  Pennsylvania Building
  425 13th Street NW
  Washington, DC 20004
  Telephone: 202–724–3366
Office of Minority Business Enterprise
  Main Commerce Building
  14th and Constitution Avenues
  Washington, DC 20230
  Telephone: 202–377–3024
Office of Telecommunications
  1800 G Street NW
  Washington, DC 20005
  Telephone: 202–395–5800
Patent and Trademark Office
  Crystal Plaza
  2021 Jefferson Davis Highway
  Arlington, VA 20231
  Telephone: 703–557–3428
United States Travel Service
  Main Commerce Building
  14th and Constitution Avenue
  Washington, DC 20230
  Telephone: 202–377–4987

SALES FORECASTING—
TEN METHODS

1. *Canvass current and prospective buyers* for their purchasing plans. Works best for high-ticket industrial products. Too expensive when there are many customers.

2. *Experts* (such as company executives, dealers) submit supporting data with their forecasts.

3. *Industry forecasts* prepared by a trade association. Figure average market share for past years. Apply that to the current forecast for each product.

4. *Statistical correlation analysis.* Requires a computer. The forecaster uses it to analyze past trends in population, income, prices and company marketing expenditures. It provides a forecast when current figures are entered.

5. *Market indexing.* Works like statistical correlation analysis, but figures are scaled down to provide a forecast for a region.

6. *Market testing.* Expensive. Use it only when the cost of failure in the marketplace would exceed the cost of the test. *Advantage:* A well designed test can evaluate several market strategies simultaneously.

7. *Past sales.* Multiply the previous year's sales by the average annual increase in prior years. Only works in a stable market.

8. *Product-in-use.* Use it if the product is used with some other product. Knowing how many automobiles are in use, for example, is an accurate guide to the purchase of replacement tires.

9. *Sales force estimates* each customer's buying potential. Keep records of forecasts and actual purchases to identify the optimists and pessimists and adjust in the future.

10. *Trend and cycle analysis.* It takes a computer to process large amounts of data on long-term trends, sales cycles, seasonal changes and unpredictable events.

Source: *Sales Manager's Bulletin,* Bureau of Business Practices, 24 Rope Ferry Road, Waterford, CT 06385, © 1977.

STATE INFORMATION GUIDE

Regional Directories

Central Atlantic States Manufacturing Directory, T. K. Sanderson Organization, 200 E. 25 Street, Baltimore, MD 21218

Commercial Classified Directory and Buyers Guide 1977, Commercial Classified Publishers, Inc., 225 Broadway, New York, NY 10007

Daltons' Greater Philadelphia Industrial Directory, Dalton Corp., 2925 N. Broad Street, Philadelphia, PA 19132

Directory of Central Atlantic States Manfacturers, Manufacturers' News, Inc., 3 E. Huron Street, Chicago, IL 60611; George D. Hall Company, 20 Kilby Street, Boston, MA 02109

Directory of New England Manufacturers, The, George D. Hall Company, 20 Kilby Street, Boston, MA 02109

Eastern Manufacturers' and Industrial Directory, Bell Directory Publishers, Inc., 2112 Broadway, New York, NY 10023

Midwest Manufacturers' and Industrial Directory, Industrial Directory Publishers, 1002 Park Avenue Building, Detroit, MI 48226

New England Apparel Directory, Register Publication, Inc., 99 Chauncey Street, Boston, MA 02111

New England Industrial Service Directory, George D. Hall Company, 20 Kilby Street, Boston, MA 02109

New England Manufacturers Directory, Manufacturers' News, Inc., 3 E. Huron Street, Chicago, IL 60611

State Sales Guides, Dun & Bradstreet, Inc., 99 Church Street, New York, NY 10007

Survey of Industries in Texarcana (Arkansas-Texas), Texarkana Chamber of Commerce, Box 1468, Texarkana, AK 75501

Alabama

STATE CAPITOL, MONTGOMERY, AL 36130
(205) 832–6011

° Refers throughout this section to the Small Business Administration regional office.
† Refers throughout this section to the Small Business Administration field office.

INFORMATION OFFICES

Department of Commerce/Economic Development
Alabama Development Office
State Capitol
Montgomery, AL 36130
Taxation
Department of Revenue
Administrative Building
Montgomery, AL 36130
State Chamber of Commerce
Alabama Chamber of Commerce
468 S. Perry Street
P. O. Box 76
Montgomery, AL 36101
Small Business Administration
908 S. 20th Street†
Birmingham, AL 35205

PUBLICATIONS

Economic Abstract of Alabama, University of Alabama, Center for Business and Economic Research, University, AL 35486

Income and Population in Alabama (irregular publication), Bureau of Business Research, University of Alabama, University, AL 35486

Alabama Business (income statistics, annual), Center for Business and Economic Research, P.O. Box AK, University, AL 35486

Alabama Labor Market (employment statistics, monthly), Department of Industrial Relations, Montgomery, AL 36104

INDUSTRIAL AND BUSINESS DIRECTORIES

Alabama Directory of Mining and Manufacturing, Alabama Development Office, State Capitol, Montgomery, AL 36130

Alabama Industrial Directory, Manufacturers' News, Inc., 3 E. Huron Street, Chicago, IL 60611; State Industrial Directories Corp., 2 Penn Plaza, New York, NY 10001

Alabama International Trade Directory, Alabama State Chamber of Commerce, P.O. Box 76, Montgomery, AL 36101

Birmingham Industrial Directory, Birmingham Chamber of Commerce, 1914 6th Avenue, Birmingham, AL 35203

Alaska

STATE CAPITOL, JUNEAU, AK 99811
(907) 465–2111

INFORMATION OFFICES

Department of Commerce/Economic Development
Department of Commerce & Economic Development
Pouch D
Juneau, AK 99811
Taxation
Department of Revenue
Pouch S
Juneau, AK 99811
State Chamber of Commerce
Alaska State Chamber of Commerce
310 2nd Street
Juneau, AK 99801
Small Business Administration
Anchorage, Alaska†
1016 W. 6th Avenue
Anchorage, AK 99501

Fairbanks, Alaska
501½ 2d Avenue
Fairbanks, AK 99701

PUBLICATIONS

Alaska Statistical Review, Department of Economic Development, Division of Economic Enterprise, Juneau, AK 99801
Current Population Estimates by Census Divisions (population statistics, annual), Department of Labor, Employment Security Division, Research and Analysis Section, Box 3–7000, Juneau, AK 99801
Alaska Review of Business and Economic Conditions Series (income statistics, five times a year), Institute of Social, Economic and Government Research, University of Alaska, Fairbanks, AK 99701
Alaska Workforce Estimates by Industry and Area (employment statistics, annual), Employment Security Division, Department of Labor, Juneau, AK 99801
Alaska's Manpower Outlook—1970s Regional Population and Employment Estimates 1961–1980 (employment statistics, annual), Employment Security Division, Department of Labor, Juneau, AK 99801

INDUSTRIAL AND BUSINESS DIRECTORIES

Alaska Directory of Commercial Establishments, Manufacturers' News, Inc., 3 E. Huron Street, Chicago, IL 60611; State Industrial Directories Corp., 2 Penn Plaza, New York, NY 10001
Alaska Petroleum and Industrial Directory, 409 W. Northern Lights Boulevard, Anchorage, AK 99811

Arizona

STATE CAPITOL, PHOENIX, AZ 85007
(602) 271–4900

INFORMATION OFFICES

Department of Commerce/Economic Development
Office of Economic Planning and Development
1700 W. Washington Avenue
Phoenix, AZ 85007
Taxation
Department of Revenue
State Capitol
Phoenix, AZ 85007
State Chamber of Commerce
Arizona State Chamber of Commerce
3216 N. Third Street
Phoenix, AZ 85012
Small Business Administration
112 N. Central Avenue†
Phoenix, AZ 85004

PUBLICATIONS

Arizona Statistical Review, Valley National Bank, Economic Research Department, P.O. Box 71, Phoenix, AZ 85001
Arizona Basic Economic and Manpower Data (annual), Arizona Department of Economic Security, P.O. Box 6123, Phoenix, AZ 85005
Arizona Review (income statistics, monthly), Division of Economic and Business Research, University of Arizona, Tucson, AZ 85721
Arizona Newsletter (income statistics, monthly), Arizona Department of Economic Security, Research Institute Statistics Bureau, P.O. Box 6123, Phoenix, AZ 85005
Phoenix Area Manpower Newsletter (income statistics, monthly), Arizona Department of Economic Security, Research Institute Statistics Bureau, P.O. Box 6123, Phoenix, AZ 85005
Tucson Area Manpower Newsletter (income statistics, monthly), Arizona Department of Economic Security, Research Institute Statistics Bureau, P.O. Box 6123, Phoenix, AZ 85005
Arizona Indicator (income statistics, monthly), Arizona Department of Economic Security, Research Institute Statistics Bureau, P.O. Box 6123, Phoenix, AZ 85005
Manpower Newsletter (employment statistics, monthly), Unemployment Compensations

Division, Employment Security Commission, Phoenix, AZ 85005

INDUSTRIAL AND BUSINESS DIRECTORIES

Arizona Directory of Industries, Manufacturers' News, 3 E. Huron Street, Chicago, IL 60611

Arizona Directory of Manufacturers, Manufacturers' News, Inc., 3 E. Huron Street, Chicago, IL 60611; State Industrial Directories Corp., 2 Penn Plaza, New York, NY 10001

Arizona Exports and Imports, Office of Economic Planning and Development, 1700 W. Washington Avenue, Phoenix, AZ 85007

Arizona USA International Trade Directory, Arizona State Department of Economic Planning and Development, 1700 W. Washington Avenue, Phoenix, AZ 85007

Directory of Arizona Manufacturers, Phoenix Chamber of Commerce, Phoenix, AZ 85001

Arkansas

STATE CAPITOL, LITTLE ROCK, AR 72201
(501) 371-3000

INFORMATION OFFICES

Department of Commerce/Economic Development
  Department of Commerce
  1501 N. University Avenue
  Little Rock, AR 72207

  Department of Industrial Development
  205 State Capitol
  Little Rock, AR 72201
Taxation
  Division of Revenue Services
  Department of Finance and Administration
  7th and Wolfe Streets
  Little Rock, AR 72201
State Chamber of Commerce
  Arkansas State Chamber of Commerce
  911 Wallace Building
  Little Rock, AR 72201
Small Business Administration
  611 Gaines Street†
  Little Rock, AR 72201

PUBLICATIONS

Arkansas Almanac, Arkansas Almanac, Inc., Little Rock, AR 72114

Arkansas Business Economic Review (population statistics, quarterly), Bureau of

Business and Economic Research, University of Arkansas, Fayetteville, AR 72701

Annual Estimates of Total Personal and Per Capita Income (annual), Industrial Research and Extension Center, University of Arkansas, P.O. Box 3017, Little Rock, AR 72203

Arkansas Current Employment Development (monthly), Employment Security Division, Department of Labor, Little Rock, AR 72203

Employment and Payroll (quarterly), Employment Security Division, Department of Labor, Little Rock, AR 72203

INDUSTRIAL AND BUSINESS DIRECTORIES

Arkansas Directory of Industries, Manufacturers' News, 3 E. Huron Street, Chicago, IL 60611

Directory of Arkansas Manufacturers, Arkansas Industrial Development Commission, P.O. Box 1784, Little Rock, AR 72203; State Industrial Directories Corp., 2 Penn Plaza, New York, NY 10001

California

STATE CAPITOL, SACRAMENTO, CA 95814
(916) 445-4711

INFORMATION OFFICES

Department of Commerce/Economic Development
  Commission for Economic Development
  1400 10th Street
  Sacramento, CA 95814
Taxation
  Franchise Tax Board
  920 23d Street
  Sacramento, CA 95814

  Board of Equalization
  1020 N Street
  Sacramento, CA 95814
State Chamber of Commerce
  California Chamber of Commerce
  455 Capitol Mall
  P.O. Box 1736
  Sacramento, CA 95808
Small Business Administration
  450 Golden Gate Avenue*
  San Francisco, CA 94102

  211 Main Street†
  San Francisco, CA 94105

1229 N Street
Fresno, CA 93721

350 S. Figueroa Street†
Los Angeles, CA 90071

880 Front Street†
San Diego, CA 92188

2800 Cottage Way
Sacramento, CA 95825

PUBLICATIONS

California Statistical Abstract, Department of Finance, Budget Division, Sacramento, CA 95801

California's Population (annual), Population Research Unit, Department of Finance, Sacramento, CA 95814

The UCLA Forecast for the Nation and California (income statistics, annual), UCLA Business Forecasting Project, Graduate School of Management, UCLA, Los Angeles, CA 90024

California Economic Indicators (income statistics, quarterly), California Department of Finance, 1025 P Street, Sacramento, CA 95814

California Employment and Payroll (quarterly), Department of Human Resources Development, 800 Capitol Mall, Sacramento, CA 95810

California Labor Market Bulletin Statistical Supplement (employment statistics, monthly), Department of Human Resources Development, 800 Capitol Mall, Sacramento, CA 95810

Taxable Sales in California (sales statistics, quarterly), State Board of Equalization, P.O. Box 1799, Sacramento, CA 95814

INDUSTRIAL AND BUSINESS DIRECTORIES

California Handbook, Center for California Public Affairs, 226 W. Foothill Boulevard, Claremont, CA 91711

California International Business Directory, Center for International Business, 333 S. Flower Street, Los Angeles, CA 90071

California Manufacturers Register, Time-Mirror Press, 1115 S. Boyle Avenue, Los Angeles, CA 90023; Manufacturers' News, Inc., 3 E. Huron Street, Chicago, IL 50611; State Industrial Directories Corp., 2 Penn Plaza, New York, NY 10001

Los Angeles Area Chamber of Commerce Southern California Business Directory and Buyers Guide, Los Angeles Chamber of Commerce, 404 S. Bixel Street, Los Angeles, CA 95113

San Francisco Manufacturers Directory, San Francisco Chamber of Commerce, 333 Pine Street, San Francisco, CA 94577

Colorado

STATE CAPITOL, DENVER, CO 80203
(303) 892-9911

INFORMATION OFFICES

Department of Commerce/Economic Development
    Division of Commerce and Development
    Department of Local Affairs
    Centennial Building
    1313 Sherman Street
    Denver, CO 80203
Taxation
    Administrative Division
    Department of Revenue
    1375 Sherman Street
    Denver, CO 80203
State Chamber of Commerce
    Colorado Association of Commerce and Industry
    1390 Logan Street
    Denver, CO 80203
Small Business Administration
    1405 Curtis Street*
    Denver, CO 80202

    721 19th Street†
    Denver, CO 80202

PUBLICATIONS

Colorado Year Book, State Planning Division, Denver, CO 80200

Colorado Year Book (population statistics, annual), Denver Chamber of Commerce, 1301 Walton Street, Denver, CO 80202

Annual Report—Colorado Department of Revenue (income statistics, annual), Colorado Department of Revenue, 1375 Sherman Street, Denver, CO 80203

Colorado's Current Monthly Estimate of Nonfarm Employment (monthly), Colorado Division of Employment, 1210 Sherman Street, Denver, CO 80203

Colorado Manpower Review (employment statistics, monthly), Colorado Division of Employment, 1210 Sherman Street, Denver, CO 80202

Sales Tax Statistical Summary (annual), Department of Revenue, Denver, CO 80203

INDUSTRIAL AND BUSINESS DIRECTORIES

Colorado Industrial Capability Register, Public Affairs Department, Colorado Interstate Gas Co., P.O. Box 1087, Colorado Springs, CO 80901

Directory of Colorado Manufacturers, Business Research Division, University of Colorado, Boulder, CO 80309; State Industrial Directories Corp. 2 Penn Plaza, New York, NY 10001

Connecticut

STATE CAPITOL, HARTFORD, CT 06115
(203) 566–2211

INFORMATION OFFICES

Department of Commerce/Economic Development
  Department of Commerce
  210 Washington Street
  Hartford, CT 06106
Taxation
  Tax Department
  92 Farmington Avenue
  Hartford, CT 06115
State Chamber of Commerce
  Connecticut Business and Industry Association
  60 Washington Street
  Hartford, CT 06106
Small Business Administration
  1 Financial Plaza†
  Hartford, CT 06103

PUBLICATIONS

Connecticut Market Data, Connecticut Development Commission, Hartford, CT 06100
Weekly Health Bulletin (population statistics, annual), Public Health, Education Section, State Department of Health, State Office Building, Hartford, CT 06115
Connecticut Area Trends in Employment and Unemployment (income statistics, annual), Research and Information, Connecticut Labor Department, Hartford, CT 06115
Labor Situation (employment statistics, monthly), Employment Security Division, Department of Labor, Wethersfield, CT 06109
Sales and Use Tax Information (sales statistics, quarterly), State Tax Department, 92 Farmington Avenue, Hartford, CT 06115

INDUSTRIAL AND BUSINESS DIRECTORIES

Classified Business Directory—State of Connecticut, Connecticut Directory Co., Inc., 322 Main Street, Stamford, CT 06901
Connecticut Classified Business Directory,
Connecticut Directory Co., Inc., 322 Main Street, Stamford, CT 06901
Connecticut State Industrial Directory, Manufacturers' News, 3 E. Huron Street, Chicago, IL 06011; State Industrial Directories Corp., 2 Penn Plaza, New York, NY 10001
Directory of Connecticut Manufacturing Establishments, Connecticut Department of Labor, 200 Folly Brook Boulevard, Wethersfield, CT 06109

Delaware

LEGISLATIVE HALL, DOVER, DE 19901
(302) 678–4000

INFORMATION OFFICES

Department of Commerce/Economic Development
  Division of Economic Development
  Department of Community Affairs and Economic Development
  630 State College Road
  Dover, DE 19901
Taxation
  Department of Finance
  Division of Revenue
  601 Delaware Avenue
  Wilmington, DE 19899
State Chamber of Commerce
  Delaware State Chamber of Commerce, Inc.
  1102 West Street
  Wilmington, DE 19801
Small Business Administration
  844 King Street
  Wilmington, DE 19801

PUBLICATIONS

Statistical Abstract for the State of Delaware, Delaware State Planning Office, Dover, DE 19901
Estimates of the Population of Delaware Counties (population statistics, annual), Superintendent of Documents, U.S. Government Printing Office, Washington, DC 20402
Delaware Economic Indicators (income statistics, quarterly), Delaware State Planning Office, Thomas Collins Building, 530 S. DuPont Highway, Dover, DE 19901
Employment, Hours and Earnings (employment statistics, monthly), Employment Security Commission, Department of Labor, Wilmington, DE 19899

INDUSTRIAL AND BUSINESS DIRECTORIES

Delaware Directory of Commerce and Industry, Delaware State Chamber of Commerce, 1102 West Street, Wilmington, DE 19801

Delaware State Industrial Directory, State Industrial Directories Corp., 2 Penn Plaza, New York, NY 10001

Florida

STATE CAPITOL, TALLAHASSEE, FL 32304
(904) 488–1234

INFORMATION OFFICES

Department of Commerce/Economic Development
Department of Commerce
Collins Building
Tallahassee, FL 32304

Division of Economic Development
Department of Commerce
Collins Building
Tallahassee, FL 32304

Taxation
Department of Revenue
Carlton Building
Tallahassee, FL 32304

State Chamber of Commerce
Florida State Chamber of Commerce
311 S. Calhoun Street
Tallahassee, FL 32301

Small Business Administration
2222 Ponce de Leon Boulevard†
Coral Gables, FL 33134

1902 N. Trask Street
Tampa, FL 33607

400 W. Bay Street†
Jacksonville, FL 32202

701 Clematis Street
West Palm Beach, FL 33402

PUBLICATIONS

Florida Statistical Abstract, University of Florida, Bureau of Economic and Business Research, Gainesville, FL 32601

Business and Economic Dimension (population statistics, three times per year), Bureau of Economic and Business Research, University of Florida, Gainesville, FL 32601

Population Studies (three times per year), Bureau of Economic and Business Research, University of Florida, Gainesville, FL 32601

Florida State Abstract (population statistics, annual), Bureau of Economic and Business Research, University of Florida, Gainesville, FL 32601

Florida Statistical Abstract (income statistics, annual), University of Florida Press, 15 NW 15th Street, Gainesville, FL 32601

Business and Economic Dimensions (income statistics, annual), Bureau of Economic and Business Research, Gainesville, FL 32611

Economic Report of the Governor (income statistics, quarterly), Department of Administration, Division of Budget, The Capitol, Tallahassee, FL 32304

Florida Employment and Payrolls (annual), Department of Commerce Office of Research and Statistics, Caldwell Building, Tallahassee, FL 32304

Florida Employment Statistics (monthly), Department of Commerce Office of Research and Statistics, Caldwell Building, Tallahassee, FL 32304

Report of the Comptroller, State of Florida (sales statistics, annual), Comptroller, State of Florida, Tallahassee, FL 32304

INDUSTRIAL AND BUSINESS DIRECTORIES

Directory of Florida Industries, Manufacturers' News, Inc., 3 E. Huron Street, Chicago, IL 60611; Florida State Chamber of Commerce, P.O. Box 5497, Tallahassee, FL 32301; State Industrial Directories Corp., 2 Penn Plaza, New York, NY 10001

Florida Industries Guide, McHenry Publishing Co., Inc., Box 935, Orlando, FL 32802

Georgia

STATE CAPITOL, ATLANTA, GA 30334
(404) 656–2000

INFORMATION OFFICES

Department of Commerce/Economic Development
Department of Industry and Trade
1400 N. Omni Boulevard
Atlanta, GA 30303

Taxation
Department of Revenue
270 Washington Street, SW
Atlanta, GA 30334

State Chamber of Commerce
Georgia Chamber of Commerce
1200 Commerce Building
Atlanta, GA 30303

Small Business Administration
1401 Peachtree Street, NE °
Atlanta, GA 30309

1720 Peachtree Street NE
Atlanta, GA 30309

PUBLICATIONS

Georgia Statistical Abstract, University of
Georgia, Division of Research, College of
Business Administration, Athens, GA 30602
Georgia Vital Statistics (population statistics,
annual), Management and Analysis Unit,
Department of Human Resources, 47 Trin-
ity Avenue, SW, Atlanta, GA 30334
Georgia Statistical Abstract (income statis-
tics, annual), U.S. Bureau of Economic
Analysis, Regional Economic Division, Di-
vision of Research, College of Business Ad-
ministration, University of Georgia, Athens,
GA 30602
Employment and Earnings (employment sta-
tistics, annual), Employment Security
Agency, Department of Labor, Atlanta, GA
30303
*Employment and Wages Insured by the
Georgia Employment Security Law* (quarterly), Employment Security Agency, Department of Labor, Atlanta, GA 30303

INDUSTRIAL AND BUSINESS DIRECTORIES

*Directory of Associations in Georgia, 1974–
1975,* Basic Data Research, Industrial Development Division, Engineering Experiment Station, Atlanta, GA 30332
Georgia Manufacturing Directory, Georgia
Bureau of Industry and Trade, P.O. Box
38097, Atlanta, GA 30332; Manufacturers'
News, 3 E. Huron Street, Chicago, IL
60611; State Industrial Directories Corp.,
2 Penn Plaza, New York, NY 10001
Georgia World Trade Directory, Georgia
Chamber of Commerce, 1200 Commerce
Building, Atlanta, GA 30303

Hawaii

STATE CAPITOL BUILDING, HONOLULU, HI
96813
(808) 548–2211

INFORMATION OFFICES

**Department of Commerce/Economic Devel-
opment**
Department of Planning and Economic Development
250 S. King Street
Honolulu, HI 96813

Taxation
Department of Taxation
425 Queen Street
Honolulu, HI 96813
State Chamber of Commerce
Chamber of Commerce of Hawaii
735 Bishop Street
Dillingham Building
Honolulu, HI 96813
Small Business Administration
1149 Bethel Street†
Honolulu, HI 96813

PUBLICATIONS

*State of Hawaii Data Book, A Statistical Ab-
stract* (income statistics, annual), State of
Hawaii Department of Planning and Economic Development, P.O. Box 2359, Honolulu, HI 96804
Labor—Area Summary (employment statistics, monthly), Department of Labor, Industrial Relations, Honolulu, HI 96813
Employment and Payrolls in Hawaii (annual), Department of Labor, Industrial
Relations, Honolulu, HI 96813

INDUSTRIAL AND BUSINESS DIRECTORIES

Directory of Manufacturers, State of Hawaii,
Chamber of Commerce of Hawaii, Dilling-
ham Building, 735 Bishop Street, Honolulu,
HI 96813
Hawaii Business Directory, Hawaii Business
Directory, Inc., Box 2057, Honolulu, HI
96805
Hawaii Directory of Manufacturers, Manu-
facturers' News, Inc., 3 E. Huron Street,
Chicago, IL 60611; State Industrial Direc-
tories Corp., 2 Penn Plaza, New York, NY
10001

Idaho

STATE CAPITOL, BOISE, ID 83720
(208) 384–2411

INFORMATION OFFICES

**Department of Commerce/Economic Devel-
opment**
Division of Tourism and Industrial Devel-
opment
108 State House
Boise, ID 83720
Taxation
Department of Revenue and Taxation
5257 Fairview Avenue
Boise, ID 83722

State Chamber of Commerce
Idaho Association of Commerce and Industry
805 Idaho Street
Boise, ID 83720
Small Business Administration
216 N. 8th Street†
Boise, ID 83701

PUBLICATIONS

Idaho Statistical Abstract, University of Idaho, Bureau of Business and Economic Research, Moscow, ID 83843
Estimates of the Population of Idaho Counties (population statistics, annual), Superintendent of Documents, U.S. Government Printing Office, Washington, DC 20402
Annual Wages in Idaho (employment statistics, annual), Department of Employment, State of Idaho, P.O. Box 7189, Boise, ID 83707
Distribution by Industry of Covered Workers in Idaho (employment statistics, annual), Department of Employment, State of Idaho, P.O. Box 7189, Boise, ID 83707
Distribution by Industry of Wages Paid for Covered Employment in Idaho (annual), Department of Employment, State of Idaho, P.O. Box 7189, Boise, ID 83707
Idaho Manpower Review (employment statistics, monthly), Department of Employment, State of Idaho, P.O. Box 7189, Boise, ID 83707
Monthly Employment by Industry and County (quarterly), Department of Employment, State of Idaho, P.O. Box 7189, Boise, ID 83707
Centerpoint; Focus on Business and Economics (quarterly), Center for Business and Research, University of Idaho, Moscow, ID 83843

INDUSTRIAL AND BUSINESS DIRECTORIES

Idaho Manufacturers Directory, Manufacturers' News, Inc., 3 E. Huron Street, Chicago, IL 60611; State Industrial Directories Corp., 2 Penn Plaza, New York, NY 10001
Manufacturing Directory of Idaho, Center for Business and Research, University of Idaho, Moscow, ID 83843

Illinois

STATE HOUSE, SPRINGFIELD, IL 62706
(217) 782–2000

INFORMATION OFFICES

Department of Commerce/Economic Development
Commerce Commission
527 E. Capitol Avenue
Springfield, IL 62706

Department of Business and Economic Development
222 S. College Street
Springfield, IL 62706
Taxation
Department of Revenue
1500 S. 9th Street
Springfield, IL 62706
State Chamber of Commerce
Illinois State Chamber of Commerce
20 N. Wacker Drive
Chicago, IL 60606
Small Business Administration
219 S. Dearborn Street†
Chicago, IL 60604
1 North Old State Capitol Plaza
Springfield, IL 62701

PUBLICATIONS

Statistical Abstract, Office of Planning and Analysis, Bureau of the Budget, 216 E. Monroe Street, Springfield, IL 62706
Vital Statistics of Illinois (population statistics, annual), Illinois Department of Health, 353 W. Jefferson Street, Springfield, IL 62761
Uniform Demographic and Economic Data (income statistics, annual), Office of Planning and Analysis, Bureau of the Budget, 216 E. Monroe Street, Springfield, IL 62706
Gross State Product (income statistics, quarterly), Department of Business and Economic Development, 222 S. College Street, Springfield, IL 62706
Employment and Annual Payrolls of Firms Covered by Illinois Unemployment Act, by Industry and County (annual), Illinois Bureau of Employment Security, Department of Labor, Chicago, IL 62606
Illinois Employment Report (monthly), Illinois Bureau of Employment Security, Department of Labor, Chicago, IL 62606
Report of Department of Revenue (sales statistics, annual), Department of Revenue, Springfield, IL 62706
Retailer's Occupation Tax, Use Tax and Service Use Tax: Report No. 1 (sales-statistics, quarterly), Department of Revenue, Springfield, IL 62706
Illinois State and Regional Economic Data Book, Department of Business and Economic Development, 222 S. College Street, Springfield, IL 62706

INDUSTRIAL AND BUSINESS DIRECTORIES

Chicago Buyers' Guide, Chicago Association of Commerce and Industry, 130 S. Michigan Avenue, Chicago, IL 60603

Chicago Cook County and Illinois Industrial Directory, National Publishing Corp., 3150 Des Plaines Avenue, Des Plaines, IL 60018

Chicago Geographic Edition, Manufacturers' News, Inc., 3 E. Huron Street, Chicago, IL 60611; State Industrial Directories Corp., 2 Penn Plaza, New York, NY 10001

Illinois Industrial Directory, Illinois Industrial Directories National Publishing Corp., 3150 Des Plaines Avenue, Des Plaines, IL 60018

Illinois Manufacturers Directory, Manufacturers' News, Inc., 3 E. Huron Street, Chicago, IL 60611; State Industrial Directories Corp., 2 Penn Plaza, New York, NY 10001

Illinois Services Directory, Manufacturers' News, Inc., 3 E. Huron Street, Chicago, IL 60611

International Buyers' Directory to Illinois Products, Department of Business and Economic Development, 222 S. College Street, Springfield, IL 62706

Indiana

STATE HOUSE, INDIANAPOLIS, IN 46204
(317) 633–4000

INFORMATION OFFICES

Department of Commerce/Economic Development
Department of Commerce
State House
Indianapolis, IN 46204
Taxation
Department of Revenue
State Office Building
Indianapolis, IN 46204
State Chamber of Commerce
Indiana State Chamber of Commerce, Inc.
201–212 Board of Trade Building
Indianapolis, IN 46204
Small Business Administration
575 N. Pennsylvania Street†
Indianapolis, IN 46204

PUBLICATIONS

Statistical Abstract of Indiana Counties, Indiana State Chamber of Commerce, Indianapolis, IN 46200

Estimates of Population of the Indiana Counties (population statistics, annual), Superintendent of Documents, Government Printing Office, Washington, DC 20402

Indiana Business Review (income statistics, annual), Division of Research, School of Business, Indiana University, Bloomington, IN 47401

Data Supplement to the Indiana Business Review (quarterly), Division of Research, School of Business, Indiana University, Bloomington, IN 47401

Covered Employment and Payrolls (employment statistics, quarterly), Employment Security Division, Research and Statistics Section, Indianapolis, IN 46204

Indiana Labor Market Information (employment statistics, quarterly), Employment Security Division, Research and Statistics Section, Indianapolis, IN 46204

Indiana Fact Book, Indiana State Planning Service Agency, Harrison Office Building, Indianapolis, IN 46204

INDUSTRIAL AND BUSINESS DIRECTORIES

Indiana Industrial Directory, Manufacturers' News, Inc., 3 E. Huron Street, Chicago, IL 60611; Indiana State Chamber of Commerce, 201–212 Board of Trade Building, Indianapolis, IN 46204; State Industrial Directories Corp., 2 Penn Plaza, New York, NY 10001

Iowa

STATE CAPITOL, DES MOINES, IA 50319
(515) 281–5011

INFORMATION OFFICES

Department of Commerce/Economic Development
Commerce Commission
Valley Bank Building
Fourth and Walnut Streets
Des Moines, IA 50319

Development Commission
250 Jewett Building
914 Grand Avenue
Des Moines, IA 50319
Taxation
Department of Revenue
Lucas Building
East 21st and Walnut Streets
Des Moines, IA 50319
Small Business Administration
210 Walnut Street†
Des Moines, IA 50309

PUBLICATIONS

Statistical Profile of Iowa, Iowa Development Commission, Research Division, Des Moines, IA 50319

Iowa Detailed Report of Vital Statistics (population statistics, annual), Records and Statistics Division, Iowa State Department of Health, Lucas State Office Building, Des Moines, IA 50319

The Construction of Personal Income Estimates for Counties: A Study in Economic Statistics (income statistics), Bureau of Business and Economic Research, College of Business Administration, The University of Iowa, Iowa City, IA 52242

Iowa Employment and Earnings (employment statistics, monthly), Iowa Employment Security Commission, Des Moines, IA 50310

Report of Iowa Employment Security Commission (annual), Iowa Employment Security Commission, Des Moines, IA 50319

Retail Sales and Use Tax Annual Report (sales statistics, quarterly), Research and Statistics Division, Iowa Department of Revenue, Lucas State Office Building, Des Moines, IA 50319

INDUSTRIAL AND BUSINESS DIRECTORIES

Directory of Iowa Manufacturers, Iowa Development Commission, 250 Jewett Building, 914 Grand Avenue, Des Moines, IA 50319

Iowa Manufacturers Directory, Manufacturers' News, Inc., 3 E. Huron Street, Chicago, IL 60611; State Industrial Directories Corp., 2 Penn Plaza, New York, NY 10001

Kansas

State House, Topeka, KS 66612
(913) 296–0111

INFORMATION OFFICES

Department of Commerce/Economic Development
  Department of Economic Development
  503 Kansas Avenue
  Topeka, KS 66603
Taxation
  Department of Revenue
  State Office Building
  Topeka, KS 66612

State Chamber of Commerce
  Kansas Association of Commerce and Industry
  500 First National Tower
  1 Townsite Plaza
  Topeka, KS 66603
Small Business Administration
  110 E. Waterman Street†
  Wichita, KS 67202

PUBLICATIONS

Kansas Statistical Abstract, University of Kansas, Institute for Social and Environment Studies, Lawrence, KS 66045

Intensive Facts About Kansas (population statistics, annual), Kansas Association of Commerce and Industry, 708 Jackson Street, Topeka, KS 66603

Annual Economic Report of the Governor (income statistics, annual), Office of Economic Analysis, Kansas State University, Manhattan, KS 66502

Annual Manpower Planning Report (employment statistics, annual), Employment Security Division, Department of Labor, Topeka, KS 66603

Area Manpower Reviews (employment statistics, biennial), Employment Security Division, Department of Labor, Topeka, KS 66603

INDUSTRIAL AND BUSINESS DIRECTORIES

Directory of Kansas Manufacturers and Products, Kansas Department of Economic Development, State Office Building, Topeka, KS 66603; State Industrial Directories Corp., 2 Penn Plaza, New York, NY 10001

Directory of Manufacturers, Wichita Kansas, Wichita Area Chamber of Commerce, 300 Miller Building, Wichita, KS 67202

Kentucky

State Capitol, Frankfort, KY 40601
(502) 564–3130

INFORMATION OFFICES

Department of Commerce/Economic Development
  Department of Commerce
  Capitol Plaza Tower
  Frankfort, KY 40601
Taxation
  Department of Revenue
  Capitol Annex
  Frankfort, KY 40601

State Chamber of Commerce
  Kentucky Chamber of Commerce
  Versailles Road
  Frankfort, KY 40601
Small Business Administration
  600 Federal Place†
  Louisville, KY 40202

PUBLICATIONS

Deskbook of Kentucky Economic Statistics,
  Department of Economic Development,
  Frankfort, KY 40601
Kentucky Vital Statistics (population statis-
  tics, annual), Kentucky Vital Statistics,
  Kentucky Department of Health, Office of
  Biostatistics, 275 E. Main Street, Frank-
  fort, KY 40601
Kentucky Employment Statistics (monthly),
  Human Resource Agency, Bureau of Em-
  ployment Security, Department of Eco-
  nomic Securities, Frankfort, KY 40601
*Number of Workers in Manufacturing In-
  dustries and Total Wages Covered by Kentucky Unemployment Insurance Law Classified by Industry and County* (quarterly),
  Human Resource Agency, Bureau of Employment Security, Department of Economic Securities, Frankfort, KY 40601
Department of Revenue Annual Report (sales
  statistics, annual), Department of Revenue,
  Frankfort, KY 40601

INDUSTRIAL AND BUSINESS DIRECTORIES

Exporters Directory, Kentucky Department
  of Commerce, Capitol Plaza Tower, Frankfort, KY 40601
Kentucky Directory of Manufacturers, Department of Commerce, Capitol Plaza Tower,
  Frankfort, KY 40601; and from Manufacturers' News, 3 E. Huron Street, Chicago,
  IL 60611; State Industrial Directories
  Corp., 2 Penn Plaza, New York, NY 10001

Louisiana

STATE CAPITOL, BATON ROUGE, LA 70804
(504) 389-6601

INFORMATION OFFICES

**Department of Commerce/Economic Devel-
opment**
  Department of Commerce and Industry
  State Land and Natural Resources Build-
    ing
  Baton Rouge, LA 70804
Taxation
  Department of Revenue
  Capitol Annex
  Baton Rouge, LA 70804

State Chamber of Commerce
  Louisiana Association of Business and In-
    dustry
  P.O. Box 3988
  Baton Rouge, LA 70821
Small Business Administration
  1001 Howard Avenue†
  New Orleans, LA 70113

U.S. Post Office and Courthouse
  Fannin Street
  Shrevesport, LA 71163

PUBLICATIONS

Statistical Abstract of Louisiana, Louisiana
  State University, Division of Business and
  Economic Research, New Orleans, LA
  70122
*Statistical Report of the Bureau of Vital
  Statistics* (population statistics, annual),
  Division of Tabulation and Analysis, Bu-
  reau of Vital Statistics, P.O. Box 60603,
  New Orleans, LA 70164
The Louisiana Economy (income statistics,
  annual), Research Division, College of Ad-
  ministration and Business, Louisiana Tech
  University, Ruston, LA 71270
*Employment and Total Wages Paid by Em-
  ployees Subject to the Louisiana Employ-
  ment Security Law* (employment statistics, quarterly), Department of Employment Security, Baton Rouge, LA 70804
Louisiana Labor Market (monthly), Department of Employment Security, Baton
  Rouge, LA 70804

INDUSTRIAL AND BUSINESS DIRECTORIES

Louisiana Directory of Manufacturers, Department of Commerce and Industry, State
  Land and Natural Resources Building,
  Baton Rouge, LA 70804; and from Manufacturers' News, Inc., 3 E. Huron Street,
  Chicago, IL 60611; State Industrial Directories Corp., 2 Penn Plaza, New York, NY
  1001
Louisiana International Trade Directory, International House, New Orleans, LA 70150

Maine

STATE HOUSE, AUGUSTA, ME 04333
(207) 289-1110

INFORMATION OFFICES

**Department of Commerce/Economic Devel-
opment**
  Development Office
  Executive Office
  State House
  Augusta, ME 04333

Taxation
  Bureau of Taxation
  Department of Finance and Administration
  State Office Building
  Augusta, ME 04333
State Chamber of Commerce
  Maine State Chamber of Commerce
  477 Congress Street
  Portland, ME 04111
Small Business Administration
  40 Western Avenue†
  Augusta, ME 04430

PUBLICATIONS

Maine Economic Data Book, Department of Commerce and Industry, Augusta, ME 04330

Maine Vital Statistics (population statistics, annual), Department of Health and Welfare, Augusta, ME 04330

Employment, Wages Contribution Under Employment Security Program (employment statistics, annual), Employment Security Commission in the State Department of Manpower Affairs, Union Street, Augusta, ME 04330

Maine Manpower (employment statistics, monthly), Employment Security Commission in the State Department of Manpower Affairs, Union Street, Augusta, ME 04330

Sales and Use Tax Assessments (sales statistics, monthly), Bureau of Taxation, Sales Tax Division, State Office Building, Augusta, ME 04330

Facts About Industrial Maine, Maine State Development Office, Augusta, ME 04330

INDUSTRIAL AND BUSINESS DIRECTORIES

Census of Maine Manufacturers, Maine Bureau of Labor and Industry, Augusta, ME 04333

Maine Marketing Guide, State Development Office, State Office Building, Augusta, ME 04333

Maine Register, Tower Publishing Company, 163 Middle Street, Portland, ME 04111

Maine State Industrial Directory, State Industrial Directories Corp., 2 Penn Plaza, New York, NY 10001; Manufacturers' News, Inc., 3 E. Huron Street, Chicago, IL 60611

Portland Directory, Tower Publishing Company, 163 Middle Street, Portland, ME 04111

Maryland

STATE HOUSE, ANNAPOLIS, MD 21401
(301) 267–0100

INFORMATION OFFICES

Department of Commerce/Economic Development
  Department of Economic and Community Development
  1748 Forest Drive
  Annapolis, MD 21401
Taxation
  Comptroller of the Treasury
  State Treasury Building
  80 Calvert Street
  Annapolis, MD 21404
State Chamber of Commerce
  Maryland State Chamber of Commerce
  60 West Street
  Annapolis, MD 21401
Small Business Administration
  7800 York Road†
  Towson, MD 21204

PUBLICATIONS

Maryland Statistical Abstract, Department of Economic and Community Development, Annapolis, MD 21200

Maryland Vital Statistics (population statistics, annual), Maryland Center for Health Statistics, Department of Health and Hygiene, 610 N. Howard Street, Baltimore, MD 21201

Employment and Payrolls Covered by the Unemployment Insurance Law of Maryland (employment statistics, quarterly), Department of Employment and Social Services, Baltimore, MD 21201

Maryland Labor Market Trends (employment statistics, monthly), Department of Employment and Social Services, Baltimore, MD 21201

Statistical Report of Retail Sales Tax Division (sales statistics, annual), Comptroller of the Treasury, State Office Building, Baltimore, MD 21201

An Economic and Social Atlas of Maryland, Department Economic and Community Development, 2525 Riva Road, Annapolis, MD 21401

INDUSTRIAL AND BUSINESS DIRECTORIES

Directory of Maryland Exporters-Importers, Maryland Department of Economics and Community Development, 2525 Riva Road, Annapolis, MD 21401

Directory of Maryland Manufacturers, Maryland Department of Economic and Community Development, 2525 Riva Road, Annapolis, MD 21401

Maryland State Industrial Directory, State Industrial Directories Corp., 2 Penn Plaza, New York, NY 10001

Massachusetts

STATE HOUSE, BOSTON, MA 02133
(617) 727-2121

INFORMATION OFFICES

Department of Commerce/Economic Development
Department of Commerce and Development
Leverett Saltonstall Building
100 Cambridge Street
Boston, MA 02202

Office of Economic Affairs
212 State House
Boston, MA 02133
Taxation
Department of Corporations and Taxation
Leverett Saltonstall Building
100 Cambridge Street
Boston, MA 02202
Small Business Administration
150 Causeway Street†
Boston, MA 02203

302 High Street
Holyoke, MA 01040

PUBLICATIONS

Fact Book, Department of Commerce and Development, Boston, MA 02202
Annual Report of Vital Statistics of the Commonwealth of Massachusetts (population statistics, annual), Office of Health Statistics, Lemuel Shattuck Hospital, 170 Morton Street, Jamaica Plain, MA 02130
City and Town Monographs (income statistics, annual), Massachusetts Department of Commerce and Development, 100 Cambridge Street, Boston, MA 02202
Employment News Letter (employment statistics, monthly), Division of Statistics, Department of Labor and Industries, Boston, MA 02202

INDUSTRIAL AND BUSINESS DIRECTORIES

Directory of Directors in the City of Boston and Vicinity, Bankers Service Co., 14 Beacon Street, Boston, MA 02108
Directory of Manufacturers in Greater Boston, Industrial and Research Department, Greater Boston Chamber of Commerce, 125 High Street, Boston, MA 02110

Directory of Massachusetts Manufacturers, George D. Hall Company, 20 Kilby Street, Boston, MA 02109
Massachusetts Directory of Manufacturers, Manufacturers' News, Inc., 3 E. Huron Street, Chicago, IL 60611
Massachusetts State Industrial Directory, State Industrial Directories Corp., 2 Penn Plaza, New York, NY 10001

Michigan

STATE CAPITOL, LANSING, MI 48913
(517) 373-1837

INFORMATION OFFICES

Department of Commerce/Economic Development
Department of Commerce
525 W. Ottawa Street
Lansing, MI 48909
Taxation
Bureau of Collection
Department of Treasury
Treasury Building
Lansing, MI 48922
State Chamber of Commerce
Michigan State Chamber of Commerce
501 S. Capitol Avenue
Lansing, MI 48933
Small Business Administration
477 Michigan Avenue†
Detroit, MI 48226

540 W. Kaye Avenue
Marquette, MI 49885

PUBLICATIONS

Michigan Statistical Abstract, Bureau of Business and Economic Research, Michigan State University, Graduate School of Business Administration, Division of Research, East Lansing, MI 48823
County Population Data (population statistics, annual), Department of Management and Budget, Lewis Cass Building, Lansing, MI 48913
Michigan Statistical Abstract (income statistics, biennial), Bureau of Business and Economic Research, Michigan State University, East Lansing, MI 48823
Annual Report of Michigan Employment Security (employment statistics, monthly), Employment Security Commission, Detroit, MI 48202
Michigan Manpower Review (employment statistics, monthly), Employment Security Commission, Detroit, MI 48202

Annual Report of Michigan Department of Treasury Annual Report (sales statistics, annual), Michigan Department of Treasury, Lansing, MI 48933

Research and Statistical Bulletin (sales statistics, monthly), Michigan Department of Treasury, Lansing, MI 48933

INDUSTRIAL AND BUSINESS DIRECTORIES

Directory of Michigan Manufacturers, Manufacturers' News, Inc., 3 E. Huron Street, Chicago, IL 60611; Manufacturers Publishing Co., 8543 Puritan Avenue, Detroit, MI 48238

Harris Michigan Manufacturers Industrial Directory, Harris Publishing Company, 33140 Aurora Road, Cleveland, OH 44139

Minnesota

STATE CAPITOL, ST. PAUL, MN 55155
(612) 296–6013

INFORMATION OFFICES

Department of Commerce/Economic Development
Department of Commerce
Metro Square Building
St. Paul, MN 55101

Department of Economic Development
480 Cedar Street
St. Paul, MN 55101
Taxation
Department of Revenue
Centennial Office Building
St. Paul, MN 55145
State Chamber of Commerce
Minnesota Association of Commerce and Industry
Hanover Building
480 Cedar Street
St. Paul, MN 55101
Small Business Administration
12 S. 6th Street†
Minneapolis, MN 55402

PUBLICATIONS

Minnesota State Statistical Abstract, Minnesota State Planning Agency, Office of Local and Urban Affairs, St. Paul, MN 55103

Minnesota Vital Statistics (population statistics, annual), Section of Health Statistics, Department of Health, 717 Delaware Street, SE, Minneapolis, MN 55440

Employment Trends, A Manpower Analysis (employment statistics, monthly), Minne-

sota Department of Employment Services, 390 N. Robert Street, St. Paul, MN 55101

Minnesota Pocket Data Book, Minnesota State Planning Agency, Office of Local and Urban Affairs, St. Paul, MN 55103

Minnesota Statistical Profile, Minnesota Department of Economic Development, 480 Cedar Street, St. Paul, MN 551011

INDUSTRIAL AND BUSINESS DIRECTORIES

Minnesota Directory of Manufacturers, Manufacturers' News, Inc., 3 E. Huron Street, Chicago, IL 60611; Documents Section, State of Minnesota, 140 Centennial Building, St. Paul, MN 55155; State Industrial Directories Corp., 2 Penn Plaza, New York, NY 10001

Mississippi

NEW CAPITOL, JACKSON, MS 39205
(601) 354–7011

INFORMATION OFFICES

Department of Commerce/Economic Development
Department of Agriculture and Commerce
1604 Sillers Building
Jackson, MS 39205

Economic Development Division
Research and Development Center
3825 Ridgewood Road
Jackson, MS 39205
Taxation
Tax Commission
102 Woolfolk Building
Jackson, MS 39201
State Chamber of Commerce
P.O. Box 1849
Standard Life Building
Jackson, MS 39205
Small Business Administration
111 Fred Haise Boulevard
Biloxi, MS 39530

200 E. Pascagoula Street†
Jackson, MS 39201

PUBLICATIONS

Mississippi Statistical Abstract, State College, College of Business and Industry, Division of Research, Mississippi State, MS 39762

Annual Bulletin of Vital Statistics (population statistics, annual), State Board of Health, Statistical Services Unit, P.O. Box 1700, Jackson, MS 39205

Mississippi Business Review (income statistics, annual), Division of Business Research, College of Business and Industry, Mississippi State University, P.O. Box 5288, State College, MS 39762

Mississippi Covered Employment and Wages (employment statistics monthly), Mississippi Employment Security Commission, P.O. Box 1699, Jackson, MS 39205

Monthly Employment and Quarterly Wages of Workers Covered by the Mississippi Employment Law (annual), Mississippi Employment Security Commission, P.O. Box 1699, Jackson, MS 39205

Quarterly Bulletin on Employment and Wages of Workers Covered by the Mississippi Employment Security Law (quarterly), Mississippi Employment Security Commission, Jackson, MS 39205

Annual Service Bulletin (sales statistics, annual), State Tax Commission, P.O. Box 960, Jackson, MS 39205

INDUSTRIAL AND BUSINESS DIRECTORIES

Mississippi International Trade Directory, Mississippi Marketing Council, Box 849, Sillers State Office Building, Jackson, MS 39205

Mississippi Manufacturers Directory, Manufacturers' News, Inc., 3 E. Huron Street, Chicago, IL 60611; Public Information Office, Mississippi Research and Development Center, Jackson, MS 39205; State Industrial Directories Corp., 2 Penn Plaza, New York, NY 10001

Missouri

STATE CAPITOL, JEFFERSON CITY, MO 65101 (314) 751-2151

INFORMATION OFFICES

Department of Commerce/Economic Development
Division of Commerce and Industrial Development
Department of Consumer Affairs, Regulations and Licenses
803 Jefferson Building
Jefferson City, MO 65101
Taxation
Department of Revenue
State Office Building
Jefferson City, MO 65101
State Chamber of Commerce
Missouri Chamber of Commerce
P.O. Box 149
Jefferson City, MO 65101

Small Business Administration
911 Walnut Street*
Kansas City, MO 64106
1150 Grand Avenue†
Kansas City, MO 64106
Mercantile Tower†
1 Mercantile Center
St. Louis, MO 63101

PUBLICATIONS

Data for Missouri Counties, University of Missouri, Extension Division, Columbia, MO 65201

Missouri Vital Statistics (population statistics; annual), Missouri Center for Health Statistics, Broadway State Office Building, Jefferson City, MO 65101

Personal Income (income statistics, annual), Public Affairs Information Service, 311 Middle Hall, University of Missouri at Columbia, Columbia, MO 65201

Missouri State and Area Labor Trends (employment statistics, monthly), Missouri Division of Employment Security, Jefferson City, MO 65101

Report of Sales and Use Tax Collection (sales statistics, annual) Department of Revenue, Division of Collectors, Jefferson City, MO 65101

INDUSTRIAL AND BUSINESS DIRECTORIES

Kansas City, Missouri Metropolitan Area Contacts Influential Reference Boom, Contacts Influential, Inc., 809 P Street, Lincoln, NB 68508

Missouri Directory of Manufacturers, Manufacturers' News, Inc., 3 E. Huron Street, Chicago, IL 60611

Missouri Directory of Manufacturers and Mining, Informative Data Company, 4401 Hampton Avenue, St. Louis, MO 63109; State Industrial Directories, 2 Penn Plaza, New York, NY 10001

Montana

STATE CAPITOL, HELENA, MT 59601 (406) 449-2511

INFORMATION OFFICES

Department of Commerce/Economic Development
Office of Commerce
State Capitol Building
Helena, MT 59601
Department of Community Affairs
Human Resources Division
1424 9th Avenue
Helena, MT 59601

State Chamber of Commerce
Montana Chamber of Commerce
P.O. Box 1730
Helena, MT 59601
Small Business Administration
618 Helena Avenue†
Helena, MT 59601

PUBLICATIONS

Montana Data Book, Montana State Division
of Planning and Economic Development,
Helena, MT 59601
Unpublished estimates on population, Department of Labor and Industry, Employment Security Division, Helena, MT 59601
Montana Personal Income Series (income
statistics, annual), Information Systems
Bureau, Montana Department of Inter-
governmental Relations, Capital Station,
Helena, MT 59601
Montana Labor Market Supplements (employment statistics, annual), Department
of Labor and Industry, Employment Security Division, Research and Analysis Sec-
tion, Helena, MT 59601
Montana Labor Market (employment statistics, monthly), Department of Labor and
Industry, Employment Security Division,
Research and Analysis Section, Helena, MT
59601
Montana County Profiles (county reports,
regional summaries, periodically updated),
Montana State Division of Research and
Information Systems, Helena, MT 59601

INDUSTRIAL AND BUSINESS DIRECTORIES

Montana Directory of Manufacturers, Re-
search and Information Systems Division,
Department of Community Affairs, State
Capitol, Helena, MT 59601; State Indus-
trial Directories Corp., 2 Penn Plaza, New
York, NY 10001

Nebraska

STATE CAPITOL, LINCOLN, NB 68509
(402) 471–2311

INFORMATION OFFICES

**Department of Commerce/Economic Devel-
opment**
Department of Economic Development
301 Centennial Mall South
Lincoln, NB 68509
Taxation
Department of Revenue
301 Centennial Mall South
Lincoln, NB 68509

State Chamber of Commerce
Nebraska Association of Commerce and In-
dustry
P.O. Box 81556
Lincoln, NB 68501
Small Business Administration
19th and Farnam Streets†
Empire State Building
Omaha, NB 68102

PUBLICATIONS

Nebraska Statistical Handbook, Nebraska De-
partment of Economic Development, Division of Research, Box 94666, Lincoln, NB
68509
Population and Economic Base Study (income statistics, selected years), Nebraska
Department of Economic Development,
Division of Research, P.O. Box 94666, Lincoln, NB 68508
A New Business Activity Index for Nebraska
(income statistics, annual), Bureau of
Business Research, University of Nebraska,
Lincoln, NB 68508
Nebraska Work Force Trends (employment
statistics, monthly), Department of Labor,
Division of Employment, Lincoln, NB
68501

INDUSTRIAL AND BUSINESS DIRECTORIES

*Directory of Nebraska Manufacturers and
Their Products*, Manufacturers' News, Inc.,
3 E. Huron Street, Chicago, IL 60611
Directory of Nebraska Manufacturers, State
Department of Economic Development,
Lincoln, NB 68509; State Industrial Direc-
tories Corp., 2 Penn Plaza, New York, NY
10001
Manufacturers and Wholesales Directory,
Lincoln Chamber of Commerce, 200 Lin-
coln Building, Lincoln, NB 68508

Nevada

LEGISLATIVE BUILDING, CARSON CITY, NV
89710
(702) 885–5000

INFORMATION OFFICES

**Department of Commerce/Economic Devel-
opment**
Department of Commerce
321 Nye Building
Carson City, NV 89710

Department of Economic Development
State Capitol
Carson City, NV 89710
Taxation
Tax Commission
1100 E. William Street
Carson City, NV 89710
State Chamber of Commerce
Nevada Chamber of Commerce Association
P.O. Box 3499
Reno, NV 89505
Small Business Administration
301 E. Stewart†
Las Vegas, NV 89101

PUBLICATIONS

Nevada Community Profiles, Department of Economic Development, Carson City, NV 89701

Nevada Manpower Report (employment statistics, monthly), Employment Security Department, Carson City, NV 89701

Nevada Employment and Payroll (annual), Employment Security Department, Carson City, NV 89701

County Data Files (irregular update), Department of Economic Development, Carson City, NV 89701

INDUSTRIAL AND BUSINESS DIRECTORIES

Nevada Industrial Directory, Department of Economic Development, State Capitol, Carson City, NV 89701; Manufacturers' News, Inc., 3 E. Huron Street, Chicago, IL 60611

Nevada Directory of Business, Manufacturers' News, Inc., 3 E. Huron Street, Chicago, IL 60611

New Hampshire

STATE HOUSE, CONCORD, NH 03301
(603) 271-1110

INFORMATION OFFICES

Department of Commerce/Economic Development
Division of Economic Development
Department of Resources and Economic Development
State House Annex
Concord, NH 03301
Taxation
Department of Revenue
19 Pillsbury Street
Concord, NH 03301
State Chamber of Commerce
Business and Industry Association of New Hampshire

540 Chestnut Street
Manchester, NH 03101
Small Business Administration
55 Pleasant Street†
Concord, NH 03301

PUBLICATIONS

Resident Population Figures (population statistics, annual), Office of Comprehensive Planning, State Planning, State House Annex, Concord, NH 03301

Employment and Unemployment in New Hampshire (monthly), Department of Employment Security, Concord, NH 03301

Employment and Wage by County (quarterly), Department of Employment Security, Concord, NH 03301

Economic Conditions in New Hampshire Local Areas (employment statistics, quarterly), Department of Employment Security, Concord, NH 03301

New Hampshire Economic Indicators, Department of Resources and Economic Development, State House Annex, Concord, NH 03301

INDUSTRIAL AND BUSINESS DIRECTORIES

Made in New Hampshire, New Hampshire Office of Industrial Development, Department of Resources, State House Annex, Concord, NH 03301

New Hampshire Register, Tower Publishing Company, 163 Middle Street, Portland, ME 04111

New Hampshire State Industrial Directory, Manufacturers' News, Inc., 3 E. Huron Street, Chicago, IL 60611; State Industrial Directories Corp., 2 Penn Plaza, New York, NY 10001

New Jersey

STATE HOUSE, TRENTON, NJ 08625
(609) 292-2121

INFORMATION OFFICES

Department of Commerce/Economic Development
Division of Economic Development
Department of Labor and Industry
John Fitch Plaza
Trenton, NJ 08625
Taxation
Division of Taxation
Department of Treasury
State House
Trenton, NJ 08625

State Chamber of Commerce
New Jersey State Chamber of Commerce
5 Commerce Street
Newark, NJ 07102
Small Business Administration
970 Broad Street†
Newark, NJ 07102

1800 E. Davis Street
Camden, NJ 08104

PUBLICATIONS

Economic Facts Book, Office of Business Economics, Trenton, NJ 08625
New Jersey Population Estimates (population statistics, annual), Economic Development, Office of Business Economics, P.O. Box 845, Trenton, NJ 08625
County Data Sheets (income statistics, annual), Office of Business Economics, Division of Economic Development, New Jersey, Department of Labor and Industry, P.O. Box 845, Trenton, NJ 08625
Covered Employment Trends in New Jersey (employment statistics, quarterly), New Jersey Department of Labor and Industry, Division of Planning and Research, P.O. Box 359, Trenton, NJ 08625
New Jersey Covered Employment Trends by Geographic Areas of the State (employment statistics, annual), Department of Labor and Industry, Bureau of Research Statistics, Trenton, NJ 08625
New Jersey Employment and the Economy (monthly), Department of Labor and Industry, Bureau of Research Statistics, Trenton, NJ 08625

INDUSTRIAL AND BUSINESS DIRECTORIES

New Jersey State Industrial Directory, Manufacturers' News, Inc., 3 E. Huron Street, Chicago, IL 60611; State Industrial Directories Corp., 2 Penn Plaza, New York, NY 10001

New Mexico

STATE CAPITOL, SANTA FE, NM 87503
(505) 827–4011

INFORMATION OFFICES

Department of Commerce/Economic Development
Department of Development
Bataan Memorial Building
Sante Fe, NM 87503
Taxation
Bureau of Revenue
Manuel Lujan Sr. Building
Santa Fe, NM 87501

State Chamber of Commerce
Association of Commerce and Industry of New Mexico
117 Quincy NE
Albuquerque, NM 87108
Small Business Administration
5000 Marble Avenue NE†
Albuquerque, NM 87110

PUBLICATIONS

New Mexico Statistical Abstract, University of New Mexico, Bureau of Business Research, Albuquerque, NM 87131
New Mexico Blue Book (population statistics, biennial), Office of the Secretary of State, 400 Legislative Executive Building, Santa Fe, NM 87501
Income and Employment in New Mexico, Selected Years (New Mexico Studies in Business and Economics, No. 22—income statistics, biennial), Bureau of Business and Economic Research, University of New Mexico, Albuquerque, NM 87131
New Mexico Socio and Economic Statistics (income statistics, published irregularly), New Mexico State Planning Office, Executive Legislative Building, Santa Fe, NM 87501
New Mexico Manpower Review (employment statistics, monthly), Research and Statistics Section, Employment Security Commission of New Mexico, P.O. Box 1928, Albuquerque, NM 87103
The State of New Mexico Bureau of Revenue Receipts and Disbursements Monthly Statement (sales statistics, monthly), Bureau of Revenue, Santa Fe, NM 87501

INDUSTRIAL AND BUSINESS DIRECTORIES

Directory of New Mexico Manufacturing and Mining, Manufacturers' News, Inc., 3 E. Huron Street, Chicago, IL 60611; New Mexico Department of Development, Bataan Memorial Building, Sante Fe, NM 87503; State Industrial Directories Corp., 2 Penn Plaza, New York, NY 10001

New York

STATE CAPITOL, ALBANY, NY 12224
(518) 474–2121

INFORMATION OFFICES

Department of Commerce/Economic Development
Department of Commerce
99 Washington Avenue
Albany, NY 12245

Division of Industrial and Corporate Development

99 Washington Avenue
Albany, NY 12245

Taxation
State Tax Commission
Department of Taxation and Finance
State Campus Building #9
Albany, NY 12227

State Chamber of Commerce
Empire State Chamber of Commerce, Inc.
150 State Street
Albany, NY 12207

Small Business Administration
26 Federal Plaza†
New York, NY 10007

111 W. Heron Street
Buffalo, NY 14202

100 S. Clinton Street†
Syracuse, NY 13202

180 State Street
Elmira, NY 14901

Twin Towers Building
Albany, NY 12207

425 Broad Hollow Road
Melville, NY 11746

100 State Street
Rochester, NY 14614

PUBLICATIONS

New York State Statistical Yearbook, Division of Budget, Office of Statistical Coordination, Albany, NY 12207

Vital Statistics of New York State (population statistics, annual), Office of Biostatistics, State Department of Health, Albany, NY 12208

Personal Income in Areas and Counties of New York State (income statistics, annual), New York State Department of Commerce, 99 Washington Avenue, Albany, NY 12245

New York Employment Review (employment statistics, monthly), Division of Research and Statistics, 370 7th Avenue, New York, NY 10001

INDUSTRIAL AND BUSINESS DIRECTORIES

New York and Surrounding Territory Classified Business Directory, New York Directory Co., Inc., 1440 Broadway, New York, NY 10018

New York Classified Business Directory, New York Directory Co., Inc., 1440 Broadway New York, NY 10018

New York State Industrial Directory, State Industrial Directories Corp., 2 Penn Plaza, New York, NY 10001; Manufacturers'

News, Inc., 3 E. Huron Street, Chicago, IL 60611

North Carolina

STATE LEGISLATIVE BUILDING, RALEIGH, NC 27602
(919) 829–1110

INFORMATION OFFICES

Department of Commerce/Economic Development
Department of Commerce
417 N. Boylan Avenue
Raleigh, NC 27603

Department of Natural and Economic Resources
Division of Economic Development
P.O. Box 27687
Raleigh, NC 27611

Taxation
Department of Revenue
2 S. Salisbury Street
Raleigh, NC 22760

State Chamber of Commerce
North Carolina Citizen's Association
P.O. Box 2508
Raleigh, NC 27602

Small Business Administration
230 S. Tryon Street†
Charlotte, NC 28202

215 S. Evans Street
Greenville, NC 27834

PUBLICATIONS

North Carolina State Statistical Abstract, Department of Administration, Office of the State Budget and Association for Coordinating Interagency Statistics, Raleigh, NC 27601

Vital Statistics (population statistics, annual), North Carolina State Board of Health, Division of Administration Service, Public Health Statistical Section, Raleigh, NC 27611

Statistics of Taxation (income statistics, biennial), Tax Research Division, North Carolina Department of Revenue, Raleigh, NC 27640

North Carolina Insured Employment and Wage Payments (employment statistics, quarterly), Bureau of Employment Security Research, Employment Security Commission, P.O. Box 25903, Raleigh, NC 27611

North Carolina Insured Employment and Wage Payments (annual), Bureau of Employment Security Research, Employment

Security Commission, P.O. Box 25903, Raleigh, NC 27611

Labor Force Estimates by County Area and State (annual), Bureau of Employment Security Research, Employment Security Commission, P.O. Box 25903, Raleigh, NC 27611

Statistics of Taxation (sales statistics, biennial), Division of Tax Research, North Carolina Department of Revenue, Revenue Building, Raleigh, NC 27640

INDUSTRIAL AND BUSINESS DIRECTORIES

Directory of North Carolina Manufacturing Firms, North Carolina Department of Natural and Economic Resources, Raleigh, NC 27611; State Industrial Directories Corp., 2 Penn Plaza, New York, NY 10001; Manufacturers' News, Inc., 3 E. Huron Street, Chicago, IL 60611

North Carolina World Trade Directory, Department of Natural and Economic Resources, Raleigh, NY 27611

North Dakota

STATE CAPITOL, BISMARK, ND 58505
(701) 224-2000

INFORMATION OFFICES

Department of Commerce/Economic Development
Department of Business and Industrial Development
523 E. Bismark Avenue
Bismarck, ND 58505
Taxation
Tax Department
State Capitol
Bismarck, ND 58505
State Chamber of Commerce
Greater North Dakota Association—State Chamber of Commerce
P.O. Box 2467
Fargo, ND 58102
Small Business Administration
653 2d Avenue N.†
Fargo, ND 58102

PUBLICATIONS

North Dakota Growth Indicators, Business and Industrial Development Department, Bismarck, ND 58505
Population estimates are available annually from Business and Industrial Development

Department, 523 E. Bismark Avenue, Bismarck, ND 58505

Area Report of Employment and Total Wages by County and Industry (employment statistics, quarterly), Employment Security Bureau, Bismarck, ND 58505

Labor Market Trends (employment statistics, monthly), Employment Security Bureau, Bismarck, ND 58505

INDUSTRIAL AND BUSINESS DIRECTORIES

North Dakota Business Directory, Box 736, W. Fargo, ND 58078

North Dakota Manufacturers Directory, North Dakota Business and Industrial Development, 523 E. Bismark Avenue, Bismark, ND 58505; Manufacturers' News, Inc., 3 E. Huron Street, Chicago, IL 60611; State Industrial Directories Corp., 2 Penn Plaza, New York, NY 10001.

Ohio

STATE HOUSE, COLUMBUS, OH 43215
(614) 466-2000

INFORMATION OFFICES

Department of Commerce/Economic Development
Department of Commerce
180 E. Broad Street
Columbus, OH 43215

Department of Economic and Community Development
30 E. Broad Street
Columbus, OH 43215
Taxation
Department of Taxation
30 E. Broad Street
Columbus, OH 43215
State Chamber of Commerce
Ohio Chamber of Commerce
Huntington Bank Building
17 South High Street
Columbus, OH 43215
Small Business Administration
550 Main Street
Cincinnati, OH 45202

1240 E. 9th Street†
Cleveland, OH 44199

85 Marconi Boulevard†
Columbus, OH 43215

PUBLICATIONS

Statistical Abstract of Ohio, Department of Development, Economic Research Division, Columbus, OH 43215

Population Estimates for Ohio (population statistics, annual), Department of Economics and Community Development, Human Resources Development Division, Bureau of Research and Analysis, 8 E. Long Street, Columbus, OH 43215

Bulletin of Business Research (income statistics, monthly), Center for Business and Economic Research, The Ohio State University, 1775 College Road, Columbus, OH 43210

Ohio Labor Market Information (employment statistics, monthly), Ohio Bureau of Employment Services, 1455 Front Street, Columbus, OH 43216

Ohio Labor Market Information (employment statistics, quarterly), Ohio Bureau of Employment Services, 1455 Front Street, Columbus, OH 43216

Annual Report of Ohio Department of Taxation (sales statistics, annual), Department of Taxation, Columbus, OH 43215

INDUSTRIAL AND BUSINESS DIRECTORIES

Akron, Ohio Membership Directory and Buyers Guide, Akron Area Chamber of Commerce, Windsor Publications, 20229 Erwin Street, Woodland Hills, CA 91364

Directory of Manufacturers in the Toledo Area, Toledo Area Chamber of Commerce, 218 Huron Street, Toledo, OH 43604

Directory of Ohio Manufacturers, Harris Publishing Co., 33140 Aurora Road, Cleveland, OH 44139; Manufacturers' News, Inc., 3 E. Huron Street, Chicago, IL 60611

Manufacturers Directory, Columbus Area Chamber of Commerce, 50 W. Broad Street, Columbus, OH 43215

Ohio and International Trade, International Trade and Development Department, 65 S. Front Street, Columbus, OH 43215

Oklahoma

State Capitol, Oklahoma City, OK 73105 (405) 521-2011

INFORMATION OFFICES

Department of Commerce/Economic Development
Department of Industrial Development
500 Will Rogers Building
Oklahoma City, OK 73105

Department of Economic and Community Affairs
5500 N. Western Avenue
Oklahoma City, OK 73118

Taxation
Tax Commission
2102 N. Lincoln Boulevard
Oklahoma City, OK 73105
State Chamber of Commerce
Oklahoma State Chamber of Commerce
4020 North Lincoln Building
Oklahoma City, OK 73105
Small Business Administration
200 N.W. 5th Street†
Oklahoma City, OK 73102

PUBLICATIONS

Statistical Abstract of Oklahoma, University of Oklahoma, Bureau for Business and Economic Research, Norman, OK 73069

Oklahoma Population Estimates (population statistics, annual), Research and Planning Division, Oklahoma Employment Security Commission, Will Rogers Memorial Office Building, Oklahoma City, OK 73105

Oklahoma Business Bulletin (income statistics, monthly), Bureau for Business and Economic Research, Norman, OK 73069

Oklahoma Labor Market (employment statistics, monthly), Employment Security Commission, Oklahoma City, OK 73105

Oklahoma Labor Newsletter (employment statistics, monthly), Employment Security Commission, Oklahoma City, OK 73105

Oklahoma Sales Tax Statistical Report (sales statistics, annual), Oklahoma Tax Commission, Oklahoma City, OK 73102

INDUSTRIAL AND BUSINESS DIRECTORIES

Oklahoma Directory of Manufacturers and Products, Manufacturers' News, Inc., 3 E. Huron Street, Chicago, IL 60611; Industrial Development Department, 500 Will Rogers Building, Oklahoma City, OK 73105; State Industrial Directories Corp., 2 Penn Plaza, New York, NY 10001

Tulsa Area Manufacturers Directory, Metro Tulsa Chamber of Commerce, 616 S. Boston Avenue, Tulsa, OK 74119

Oregon

State Capitol, Salem, OR 97310 (503) 378-3131

INFORMATION OFFICES

Department of Commerce/Economic Development
Department of Commerce
Labor and Industries Building
Salem, OR 97310

Department of Economic Development
317 S. W. Alder Street
Portland, OR 97204
Taxation
Department of Revenue
204 State Office Building
Salem, OR 97310
State Department of Commerce
Associated Oregon Industries, Inc.
1149 Court Street, NE
Salem, OR 97301
Small Business Administration
1220 SW Third Avenue
Portland, OR 97204

PUBLICATIONS

Oregon Economic Statistics, University of Oregon, Bureau of Business and Research, 140 Commonwealth Hall, Eugene, OR 97403

Oregon Blue Book (population statistics, annual), State Capitol Building, Room 112, Salem, OR 97310

Oregon Covered Employment and Payrolls by Industry and County (employment statistics, quarterly), Department of Employment, Salem, OR 97310

Oregon's Labor Market (monthly), Department of Employment, Salem, OR 97310

INDUSTRIAL AND BUSINESS DIRECTORIES

International Trade Directory of Oregon and Southern Washington, Chamber of Commerce, 824 SW 5th Avenue, Portland, OR 97204

Oregon Manufacturers Directory, Department of Economic Development, 317 SW Alder Street, Portland, OR 97204; State Industrial Directories Corp., 2 Penn Plaza, New York, NY 10001; Manufacturers' News, Inc., 3 E. Huron Street, Chicago, IL 60611

Pennsylvania

MAIN CAPITOL BUILDING, HARRISBURG, PA 17120
(717) 787-2121

INFORMATION OFFICES

Department of Commerce/Economic Development
Department of Commerce
419 S. Office Building
Harrisburg, PA 17120

Bureau of Economic Development
Department of Commerce
412 S. Office Building
Harrisburg, PA 17120
Taxation
Department of Revenue
207 Finance Building
Harrisburg, PA 17120
State Chamber of Commerce
Pennsylvania Chamber of Commerce
222 N. Third Street
Harrisburg, PA 17101
Small Business Administration
231 St. Asaphs Road†
1 Bala Cynwyd Plaza
Bala Cynwyd, PA 19004

1500 N. 2d Street
Harrisburg, PA 17102

1000 Liberty Avenue†
Pittsburgh, PA 15222

Penn Place
20 N. Pennsylvania Avenue
Wilkes-Barre, PA 18702

PUBLICATIONS

Pennsylvania Statistical Abstract, Department of Commerce, Bureau of Statistics, Harrisburg, PA 17120

Population Estimates (annual), Office of State Planning and Development, Harrisburg, PA 17120

Pennsylvania Projection Series: Personal Income (income statistics, biennial), Office of State Planning and Development, Box 1323, Harrisburg, PA 17120

Employment and Wages of Workers Covered by the Pennsylvania Unemployment Compensation Law by County and Industry (employment statistics, annual), Bureau of Employment Security, Department of Labor and Industry, Harrisburg, PA 17121

Pennsylvania Employment and Earnings (monthly), Bureau of Employment Security, Department of Labor and Industry, Harrisburg, PA 17121

Statistical Data Sheet (employment statistics, quarterly), Bureau of Employment Security, Department of Labor and Industry, Harrisburg, PA 17121

INDUSTRIAL AND BUSINESS DIRECTORIES

Directory of Pennsylvania Manufacturing Exporters, Department of Commerce, 222 N. 3d Street, Harrisburg, PA 17120

Industrial Directory of the Commonwealth of Pennsylvania, Bureau of Management Services, State Book Store, Box 1365, Harrisburg, PA 17125

Pennsylvania State Industrial Directory, State Industrial Directories, Corp., 2 Penn Plaza, New York, NY 10001; Manufacturers' News, Inc., 3 E. Huron Street, Chicago, IL 60611

Rhode Island

STATE HOUSE, PROVIDENCE, RI 02903
(401) 277-2000

INFORMATION OFFICES

Department of Commerce/Economic Development
  Department of Economic Development
  1 Weybosset Hill
  Providence, RI 02903
Taxation
  Division of Taxation
  Department of Administration
  CIC Complex
  Providence, RI 02908
State Chamber of Commerce
  Rhode Island Chamber of Commerce
  206 Smith Street
  Providence, RI 02908
Small Business Administration
  57 Eddy Street†
  Providence, RI 02903

PUBLICATIONS

Rhode Island Basic Economic Statistics, Rhode Island Development Council, Providence, RI 02903
Employment Bulletin (employment statistics, monthly), Division of Statistics and Census, Department of Labor, Providence, RI 02903
Sales Tax Collection by City or Town and County (sales statistics, monthly), Rhode Island Office of Admission Processing and Methods, State House, Providence, RI 02901
Sales Tax Collection by Kind of Business (monthly), Rhode Island Office of Admission Processing and Methods, State House, Providence, RI 02901

INDUSTRIAL AND BUSINESS DIRECTORIES

Rhode Island Directory of Manufacturers and List of Nonmanufacturing Establishments, Rhode Island Development Council, Roger Williams Building, 1 Weybosset Hill, Providence, RI 02903
Rhode Island State Industrial Directory, State Industrial Directories Corp., 2 Penn Plaza, New York, NY 10001

South Carolina

STATE HOUSE, COLUMBIA, SC 29201
(803) 758-0221

INFORMATION OFFICES

Department of Commerce/Economic Development
  South Carolina State Development Board
  1301 Gervais Street
  Columbia, SC 29201
Taxation
  Tax Commission
  John C. Calhoun Office Building
  Columbia, SC 29201
State Chamber of Commerce
  South Carolina Chamber of Commerce
  1002 Calhoun Street
  Columbia, SC 29201
Small Business Administration
  1801 Assembly Street†
  Columbia, SC 29201

PUBLICATIONS

South Carolina Statistical Abstract, Budget and Control Board, Division of Research and. Statistical Services, Columbia, SC 29201
Annual Report of the State Board of Health (population statistics, annual), Division of Vital Statistics, State Board of Health, State Office Building, Columbia, SC 29201
Average Monthly Coverage Employment and Total Payroll (employment statistics, annual), Employment Security Commission, Columbia, SC 29202
The South Carolina Labor Market (employment statistics, monthly), Employment Security Commission, Columbia, SC 29202
Report to the Governor and General Assembly (sales statistics, annual), South Carolina Tax Commission, Columbia, SC 29201
Economic Report for South Carolina, Budget and Control Board, Division of Research and Statistical Services, Columbia, SC 29201
Inventory of Statistical Series of North Carolina, Budget and Control Board, Division of Research and Statistical Services, Columbia, SC 29201

INDUSTRIAL AND BUSINESS DIRECTORIES

Industrial Directory of South Carolina, South Carolina State Development Board, 1301 Gervais Street, Columbia, SC 29201; State Industrial Directories Corp., 2 Penn Plaza, New York, NY 10001

South Carolina International Trade Directory, South Carolina State Development Board, 1301 Gervais Street, Columbia, SC 29201

South Dakota

STATE CAPITOL, PIERRE, SD 57501
(605) 224-3011

INFORMATION OFFICES

Department of Commerce/Economic Development
Department of Commerce and Consumer Affairs
State Capitol
Pierre, SD 57501

Department of Economic and Tourism Development
State Office Building #2
Pierre, SD 57501

Division of Industrial Development
S. Cliff Street
Sioux Falls, SD 57103
Taxation
Department of Revenue
Capitol Lake Plaza
Pierre, SD 57501
State Chamber of Commerce
Greater South Dakota Association
P. O. Box 190
Pierre, SD 57501
Small Business Administration
8th and Main Avenue†
Sioux Falls, SD 57102

515 9th Street
Rapid City, SD 57701

PUBLICATIONS

South Dakota Economic and Business Abstract, University of South Dakota, Business Research Bureau, Vermillion, SD 57069
Annual estimates of population statistics are available from the Department of Manpower Affairs, Employment Security Division, 607 N. Fourth Street, Pierre, SD 57501
Annual Report of Employment Security Department of South Dakota (employment statistics, annual), South Dakota Department of Manpower Affairs, Employment Security Division, 607 N. 4th Street, Aberdeen, SD 57401
Labor Bulletin: An Analysis of Current Labor Statistics in South Dakota (monthly), South Dakota Department of Manpower

Affairs, Employment Security Division, 607 N. 4th Street, Aberdeen, SD 57401
South Dakota Facts, University of South Dakota, Business Research Bureau, Vermillion, SD 57069

INDUSTRIAL AND BUSINESS DIRECTORIES

Directory of South Dakota Industries, Manufacturers' News, Inc., 3 E. Huron Street, Chicago, IL 60611; State Industrial Directories Corp., 2 Penn Plaza, New York, NY 10001
South Dakota Manufacturers and Processors Directory, South Dakota Industrial Development Division, 620 S. Cliff Street, Sioux Falls, SD 57104

Tennessee

STATE CAPITOL, NASHVILLE, TN 37219
(615) 741-3011

INFORMATION OFFICES

Department of Commerce/Economic Development
Department of Economic and Community Development
1007 Andrew Jackson Building
Nashville, TN 37219
Taxation
Department of Revenue
927 Andrew Jackson Building
Nashville, TN 37219
State Chamber of Commerce
State Chamber Division of the Tennessee Taxpayers Association
1070 Capitol Hill Building
Nashville, TN 37219
Small Business Administration
502 S. Gay Street
Knoxville, TN 37902

404 James Robertson Parkway†
Nashville, TN 37219

167 N. Main Street
Memphis, TN 38103

PUBLICATIONS

Tennessee Statistical Abstract, University of Tennessee, Center for Business and Economic Research, Knoxville, TN 37916
Tennessee Survey of Business (population statistics, annual), Center for Business and

Economic Research, University of Tennessee, Knoxville, TN 37916

Population statistics are available from Statistical Service, State Department of Public Health, Cordell Hull Office Building, Nashville, TN 37219

Mid-South Quarterly Business Review (income statistics, quarterly), Bureau of Business and Economic Research, College of Business Administration, Memphis State University, Memphis, TN 38111

Basic Employment Security Data—State of Tennessee with County Data (employment statistics, annual), Department of Employment Security, Nashville, TN 37219

The Labor Market Report (employment statistics, monthly), Department of Employment Security, Nashville, TN 37219

Comparative Statement of Collected Revenue (sales statistics, monthly), Department of Revenue, Nashville, TN 37242

Sales and Use Tax (sales statistics, monthly), Department of Revenue, Nashville, TN 37242

Tennessee Pocket Data Book, University of Tennessee, Center for Business and Economic Research, Knoxville, TN 37916

INDUSTRIAL AND BUSINESS DIRECTORIES

Directory of Tennessee Industries, Manufacturers' News, Inc., 3 E. Huron Street, Chicago, IL 60611; State Industrial Directories Corp, 2 Penn Plaza, New York, NY 10001

Tennessee Directory of Manufacturers, Industrial Development Division, Andrew Jackson Building, Nashville, TN 37219

Texas

STATE CAPITOL, AUSTIN, TX 78701
(512) 475-2323

INFORMATION OFFICES

Department of Commerce/Economic Development
Industrial Commission
714 Sam Houston State Office Building
Austin, TX 78701
Taxation
Comptroller of Public Accounts
104 LBJ State Office Building
Austin, TX 78711
State Chamber of Commerce
East Texas Chamber of Commerce
P.O. Box 1592
Longview, TX 75601

Lower Rio Grand Valley Chamber of Commerce
P.O. Box 975
Weslaco, TX 78596

South Texas Chamber of Commerce
1011 Northwest Loop 410
San Antonio, TX 78213

Texas State Chamber of Commerce
1004 International
Life Building
Austin, TX 78712

West Texas Chamber of Commerce
P.O. Box 1561
760 Cedar Street
Abilene, TX 79604

Small Business Administration
1720 Regal Row*
Dallas, TX 75235

1100 Commerce Street†
Dallas, TX 75202

4100 Rio Bravo
El Paso, TX 79901

1 Allen Center†
Houston, TX 77002

222 E. Van Buren Street†
Lower Rio Grand Valley
Harlingen, TX 78550

3105 Leopard Street†
Corpus Christi, TX 78408

1205 Texas Avenue†
Lubbock, TX 79408

100 S. Washington Street†
Marshall, TX 75670

727 E. Durango†
San Antonio, TX 78205

PUBLICATIONS

Texas Almanac, Dallas Morning News, Dallas, TX 75201

Population Estimates for Texas (annual), Population Research Center, University of Texas, Austin, TX 78712

Annual population estimates are available from the Division of Vital Statistics, State Department of Health, Austin, TX 78756

Employment, Establishments and Wages Covered by the Texas Unemployment Compensation Act (quarterly), Texas Employment Commission, Austin, TX 78701

A *Brief Guide to Business Regulations and Services in Texas,* Texas Industrial Commission, 714 Sam Houston Building, Austin, TX 78701

Texas Facts: The Book on Profitable Plant Locations, Texas Industrial Commission, 714 Sam Houston Office Building, Austin, TX 78711

Texas Labor Market Employment Trends and Outlook (monthly), Texas Employment Commission, Austin, TX 78701

INDUSTRIAL AND BUSINESS DIRECTORIES

Dallas Business Guide, Dallas Chamber of Commerce, Fidelity Tower, Dallas, TX 75201

Directory of Texas Manufacturers, Bureau of Business Research, University of Texas, Austin, TX 78712; State Industrial Directories Corp., 2 Penn Plaza, New York, NY 10001

Fort Worth Directory of Manufacturers, Fort Worth Area Chamber of Commerce, 700 Throckmorton Street, Fort Worth, TX 76102

Texas Exporter-Importer Directory, Gulf International Trades, Box 52717, Houston, TX 77052

Texas Manufacturers Directory, Manufacturers' News, Inc., 3 E. Huron Street, Chicago, IL 60611

Utah

STATE CAPITOL, SALT LAKE CITY, UT 84114
(801) 533-4000

INFORMATION OFFICES

Department of Commerce/Economic Development
Trade Commission
Department of Business Regulation
330 E. 4th South Street
Salt Lake City, UT 84111

Department of Development Services
104 State Capitol
Salt Lake City, UT 84114
Taxation
Tax Commission
200 State Office Building
Salt Lake City, UT 84134
Small Business Administration
125 S. State Street
Salt Lake City, UT 84111

PUBLICATIONS

Statistical Abstract, University of Utah, Bureau of Economic and Business Research, Salt Lake City, UT 84112

Utah Economic and Business Review (population statistics, annual), Utah Population Work Committee, Utah Committee on Industrial and Unemployment Planning, 174 Social Hall Avenue, Salt Lake City, UT 84111

Personal Income in Utah and Utah's Counties (income statistics, three to four years), Bureau of Economic and Business Research, University of Utah, Salt Lake City, UT 84112

Utah Department of Employment Security Annual Report (employment statistics, annual), Department of Employment Security, Salt Lake City, UT 84147

Employment News Letter (monthly), Department of Employment Security, Salt Lake City, UT 84147

Statistical Review of Government in Utah, Utah Foundation, 32 First South Street, Salt Lake City, 84111

INDUSTRIAL AND BUSINESS DIRECTORIES

Directory of Utah Manufacturers, Manufacturers' News, Inc., 3 E. Huron Street, Chicago, IL 60611; Department of Employment Security, 1234 S. Main Street, Salt Lake City, UT 84147

Vermont

STATE HOUSE, MONTPELIER, VT 05602
(802) 828-1110

INFORMATION OFFICES

Department of Commerce/Economic Development
Agency of Development and Community Affairs
Department of Economic Development
109 State Street
Montpelier, VT 05602
Taxation
Department of Taxes
Agency of Administration
109 State Street
Montpelier, VT 05602
State Chamber of Commerce
Vermont State Chamber of Commerce
P.O. Box 37
Montpelier, VT 05602
Small Business Administration
87 State Street†
Montpelier, VT 05602

PUBLICATIONS

Vermont Facts and Figures, Department of Budget and Management, Montpelier, VT 05602

The Vermont Labor Market (employment statistics, monthly), Department of Employment Security, Montpelier, VT 05602

INDUSTRIAL AND BUSINESS DIRECTORIES

Vermont Directory of Manufacturers, Vermont Agency of Development and Community Affairs, Montpelier, VT 05602

Vermont State Industrial Directory, Manufacturers' News, Inc., 3 E. Huron Street, Chicago, IL 60611; State Industrial Directories Corp., 2 Penn Plaza, New York, NY 10001

Vermont Yearbook, The National Survey, Chester, VT 05143

Virginia

STATE CAPITOL, RICHMOND, VA 23219
(804) 786-0000

INFORMATION OFFICES

Department of Commerce/Economic Development
Division of Industrial Development
1010 State Office Building
Richmond, VA 23219
Taxation
Department of Taxation
State Office Building
Richmond, VA 23219
State Chamber of Commerce
Virginia State Chamber of Commerce
611 E. Franklin Street
Richmond, VA 23219
Small Business Administration
400 N. 8th Street†
Richmond, VA 23240

PUBLICATIONS

Estimates of Population, Virginia Counties and Cities (annual), Tayloe Murphy Institute, Graduate School of Business Administration, University of Virginia, Charlottesville, VA 22903

Personal Income Estimates for Virginia (annual), Tayloe Murphy Institute, Graduate School of Business Administration, University of Virginia, Box 3430, Charlottesville, VA 22903

Personal Income Estimates for Virginia SMSAs and Non-SMSAs Counties (annual), Tayloe Murphy Institute, Graduate School of Business Administration, University of Virginia, Box 3430, Charlottesville, VA 22903

Personal Income Estimates for Virginia Counties and Cities (annual), Tayloe Murphy Institute, Graduate School of Business Administration, University of Virginia, Box 3430, Charlottesville, VA 22903

Covered Employment and Wages (employment statistics, quarterly), Manpower Research Division, Virginia Employment Commission, Richmond, VA 23214

Trends in Employment, Hours and Earnings in Virginia (monthly), Manpower Research

Division, Virginia Employment Commission, Richmond, VA 23214

INDUSTRIAL AND BUSINESS DIRECTORIES

Industrial Directory of Virginia, Chamber of Commerce, 611 E. Franklin Street, Richmond, VA 23219

Virginia Industrial Directory, Manufacturers' News, Inc., 3 E. Huron Street, Chicago, IL 60611; State Industrial Directories Corp., 2 Penn Plaza, New York, NY 10001

Washington

LEGISLATIVE BUILDING, OLYMPIA, WA 98501
(206) 753-5000

INFORMATION OFFICES

Department of Commerce/Economic Development
Department of Commerce and Economic Development
101 General Administration Building
Olympia, WA 98504
Taxation
Department of Revenue
General Administration Building
Olympia, WA 98504
State Chamber of Commerce
Association of Washington Business
1414 S. Cherry Street
Olympia, WA 98501
Small Business Administration
710 2d Avenue°
Seattle, WA 98104

915 2d Avenue†
Seattle, WA 98174

651 U.S. Courthouse†
Spokane, WA 99210

PUBLICATIONS

The Research Council's Handbook, Washington State Research Council, Olympia, WA 98504

Vital Statistics Summary (population statistics, annual), Bureau of Vital Statistics, Health Service Division, 214 General Administration Building, Olympia, WA 98504

Estimates of Personal Income for SMSAs and Non-SMSAs Counties—State of Washington (income statistics, annual), Office of Program and Fiscal Management, Population Studies Division, House Office Building, Olympia, WA 98504

Employment and Payrolls in Washington State by County and Industry (employment statistics, quarterly), Employment Security Department, Olympia, WA 98504

The Washington Labor Market (monthly), Employment Security Department, Olympia, WA 98504

Annual Report of the Tax Commission (sales statistics, annual), Washington State Department of Revenue, General Administration Building, Olympia, WA 98504

State of Washington Pocket Data Book, Washington State Office of Program Planning and Fiscal Management, Olympia, WA 98504

INDUSTRIAL AND BUSINESS DIRECTORIES

Directory of Washington Manufacturers, State Department of Commerce and Economic Development, General Administration Building, Olympia, 98504

Washington State International Trade Directory, Washington State Department of Commerce and Economic Development, Olympia, WA 98504

Washington State Manufacturers Directory, Manufacturers' News, Inc., 3 E. Huron Street, Chicago, IL 60611

West Virginia

STATE CAPITOL, CHARLESTON, WV 25303
(304) 348-3456

INFORMATION OFFICES

Department of Commerce/Economic Development
    Department of Commerce
    State Office Building #6
    Charleston, WV 25305
Taxation
    Tax Department
    West Wing
    State Capitol
    Charleston, WV 25305
State Chamber of Commerce
    P.O. Box 2789
    1101 Kanawha Valley Building
    Charleston, WV 25330
Small Business Administration
    Charleston National Plaza
    Charleston, WV 25301

    109 N. 3d Street†
    Clarksburg, WV 26301

PUBLICATIONS

The Statistical Handbook, West Virginia Research League, Inc., Charleston, WV 25414
Annual population estimates are available from the Division of Resource Manage-

ment, Agricultural Economics Committee, West Virginia University, Morgantown, WV 26505

West Virginia Work Force Annual Average (employment statistics, annual), Research and Statistics Division, 112 California Avenue, Charleston, WV 25305

Employment Wages Covered by West Virginia Unemployment Compensation Law (annual), Research and Statistics Division, 112 California Avenue, Charleston, WV 25305

West Virginia Statistical Handbook, West Virginia University, Bureau of Business Research, Morgantown, WV 26505

INDUSTRIAL AND BUSINESS DIRECTORIES

West Virginia Manufacturing Directory, Department of Commerce, State Office Building #6, Charleston, WV 25305; State Industrial Directories Corp., 2 Penn Plaza, New York, NY 10001

Wisconsin

STATE CAPITOL, MADISON, WI 53702
(608) 266-2211

INFORMATION OFFICES

Department of Commerce/Economic Development
    Department of Business Development
    123 W. Washington Avenue
    Madison, WI 53702
Taxation
    Department of Revenue
    201 E. Washington Avenue
    Madison, WI 53703
State Chamber of Commerce
    Wisconsin Association of Manufacturers and Commerce
    111 E. Wisconsin Avenue
    Milwaukee, WI 53202
Small Business Administration
    122 W. Washington Avenue†
    Madison, WI 53703

    500 S. Barstow Street
    Eau Claire, WI 54701

    735 W. Wisconsin Avenue
    Milwaukee, WI 53233

PUBLICATIONS

Wisconsin Statistical Abstract, Department of Administration, Information Systems Unit, W. Wilson Street, Madison, WI 53702

Wisconsin Blue Book (population statistics, biennial), Legislative Reference Bureau, 201 N. State Capitol Street, Madison, WI 53702

Wisconsin Statistical Abstract (income statistics, biennial), Information Systems Unit, Wisconsin Department of Administration, 1 W. Wilson Street, Madison, WI 53702

Wisconsin Work Force (employment statistics, monthly), Bureau of Research and Statistics Administration, Madison, WI 53701

INDUSTRIAL AND BUSINESS DIRECTORIES

Classified Directory of Wisconsin Manufacturers, Wisconsin Association of Manufacturers and Commerce, 111 E. Wisconsin Avenue, Milwaukee, WI 53202; State Industrial Directories Corp., 2 Penn Plaza, New York, NY 10001

Wisconsin Manufacturers Directory, Manufacturers' News, Inc., 3 E. Huron Street, Chicago, IL 60611

Wyoming

STATE CAPITOL, CHEYENNE, WY 82002
(307) 777–7011

INFORMATION OFFICES

Department of Commerce/Economic Development
Department of Economic Planning and Development
Barrett Building
Cheyenne, WY 82002

Taxation
Department of Revenue and Taxation
2200 Carey Avenue
Cheyenne, WY 82002

Small Business Administration
100 E. B Street†
Casper, WY 82601

PUBLICATIONS

Wyoming Data Book, University of Wyoming, Division of Business and Economic Research, Laramie, WY 82070

Report of Employment and Wages E.S.—202 (income statistics, quarterly), Employment Security Commission, State Capitol Building, P.O. Box 2760, Casper, WY 82602

Employment and Total Payrolls by Industry Selected from Employer Quarterly Reports (employment statistics, quarterly), Employment Security Commission, P.O. Box 2760, Casper, WY 82601

Wyoming Labor Force Trends (monthly), Employment Security Commission, P.O. Box 2760, Casper, WY 82601

Biennial Report of the State Board of Equalization of the State of Wyoming (sales statistics, annual), Wyoming Board of Equalization, Department of Revenue, Supreme Court Building, Cheyenne, WY 82002

INDUSTRIAL AND BUSINESS DIRECTORIES

Wyoming Directory of Manufacturing and Mining, Manufacturers' News, Inc., 3 E. Huron Street, Chicago, IL 60611; Department of Economic Planning and Development, 720 W. 18th Street, Cheyenne, WY 82001; State Industrial Directories Corp. 2 Penn Plaza, New York, NY 10001

Puerto Rico

CAPITOL, SAN JUAN, PR 00904
(809) 723–6040

INFORMATION OFFICES

Department of Commerce/Economic Development
Department of Commerce
Box S 4275
San Juan, PR 00905

Economic Development Administration
Box 2350
San Juan, PR 00936

Taxation
Income Tax Bureau
Department of Treasury
San Juan, PR 00905

Chamber of Commerce
Camara De Comercie de Puerto Rico
P.O. Box 3789
San Juan, PR 00904

Small Business Administration
Federal Office Building
Hato Rey, PR 00918

PUBLICATIONS

Statistical Yearbook, Bureau of Statistics, Planning Board, Santurce, PR 00909

INDUSTRIAL AND BUSINESS DIRECTORIES

Puerto Rico Official Industrial and Trade Directory, Manufacturers' News, Inc., 3 E. Huron Street, Chicago, IL 60611; Witcom Group, Inc., 210 Ponce de Leon Avenue, San Juan, PR 00901

INTERNATIONAL INFORMATION SOURCES

Businessmen seeking information about foreign commercial opportunities or sources of business contacts have available a number of government and private services that are described in this and subsequent sections. The extensive nature of these services is not always fully appreciated by members of the business community. For example, one of the more underutilized services is that provided by the Domestic and International Business Administration (DIBA) of the Department of Commerce, described below. This agency is particularly helpful in establishing initial contacts and in evaluating foreign markets. Other key information sources given in subsequent sections of the *Business Almanac* are:

1. Foreign regional offices at the U.S. Department of State.
2. Foreign embassies, State Department desk officers, and foreign consulates in the United States.
3. Foreign chambers of commerce in the United States.
4. U.S. commercial banks with foreign offices in the countries of interest.
5. U.S. offices of foreign commercial banks.

Businessmen traveling abroad will find the following services of help in initiating contacts:

1. U.S. trade centers and commercial offices, U.S. Department of Commerce.
2. Commercial offices at U.S. embassies or consulates.

Foreign credit information sources are provided at the end of this section.

DEPARTMENT OF COMMERCE

Address: Constitution and 14th Street NW, Washington, DC 20230. Information phone: 202–377–2253.

The central information source within the Department of Commerce is the **Domestic and International Bureau Administration** (DIBA), established in 1972 to promote the growth of U.S. industry and commerce, both foreign and domestic. The DIBA consists of the following bureaus.

International Economic Policy and Research (IEPR) assists the department in research, analysis, and formulation of international economic programs.

The Bureau of International Commerce (BIC) helps U.S. business to sell its goods in international markets by providing commercial, economic, and marketing information. BIC conducts export development activities including the management of trade fairs and permanent trade centers (locations listed below). In addition, BIC organizes trade missions for groups of businessmen interested in specific markets. Businesses interested in attracting foreign capital or in seeking foreign investment opportunities can also get help from BIC.

World Traders Data Reports: BIC provides very helpful reports on foreign firms in its *World Traders Data Reports* (WTDRS). Each report contains detailed commercial information on individual firms, including financial and credit references. The complete name and address of the foreign firm must be submitted when ordering WTDRS. To order, write Bureau of International Commerce, Room 1033 EID/WTDR, Washington, DC 20230.

Foreign Traders Index: Information on more than 140,000 foreign importing organizations in 130 countries is stored in BIC's *Foreign Traders Index* (FTI), a computerized file. New information on listed firms and information on newly identified firms are constantly added to the index. The information in the file is collected and supplied to Commerce by the U.S. Foreign Service—Department of State.

Most of the lists or services described here are products of the *Foreign Traders Index.* Some, however, are prepared from special source material.

Export Mailing List Service: U.S. firms wishing to make export contacts may obtain lists of foreign organizations selected by electronic data processing techniques from the *Foreign Traders Index.* Selection of firms in one or more countries or geographic areas may be made according to the products or product groups handled by the foreign organizations.

The information is available either on pressure-sensitive mailing labels or in standard printout format.

Data Tape Service: U.S. firms with computer facilities may purchase magnetic tapes containing information on all firms in selected countries or in all countries covered in the *Foreign Traders Index.* This service makes it possible for users to retrieve various segments of data from the *Foreign Traders Index* through their own computer facilities.

The Agent/Distributor Service: BIC's

Agent/Distributor Service (A/DS) helps U.S. firms find agents or distributors for their products in almost every country of the world. U.S. commercial officers overseas will identify up to three foreign firms that have expressed interest in a specific U.S. proposal. The charge for this service is $25.

Application forms (DIB-424P) may be obtained from any Commerce Department district office. Trade specialists at district offices will help a U.S. firm prepare an application. They will offer guidance and determine whether there are factors to discourage a business relationship.

Trade List Service: The names and addresses of foreign distributors, agents, purchasers, and other firms, classified by products they handle and services they offer, are made available to U.S. firms through printed *Trade Lists* (TL). Some of the lists are produced from information in the *Foreign Traders Index.* Others are prepared from data compiled in connection with BIC's export promotion programs and from other sources.

Trade Opportunities Program: Up-to-the-minute direct sales leads and representation opportunities from overseas are now available to interested U.S. companies through a computerized mail service, the *Trade Opportunities Program* (TOP). A U.S. businessman, as a subscriber to TOP, specifies the products and the countries for which he wants trade opportunities, and that information is fed into the TOP computer.

Foreign Market Reports: Reports on commodities, industries, and economic conditions prepared by U.S. foreign service officers, and in-depth foreign market surveys prepared by private research organizations on a contract basis for BIC or by BIC's market research officers and U.S. foreign service officers are available for a nominal fee. Monthly indices list the reports and surveys in three sections—a numerical listing of documents, a country section, and the Standard Industrial Classification (SIC), and/or a general subject matter section.

Business Counseling Services: Counseling services are provided by the U.S. Departments of Commerce and State in Washington, DC, and by the Commerce district offices located in major commercial and industrial centers throughout the United States and Puerto Rico.

The Business Counseling Section of BIC's Office of Export Development in Washington offers guidance, in-depth counseling, and scheduling of appointments with appropriate Commerce officials as well as with officials in other agencies. This is a one-stop service designed to give the businessman a maximum amount of information in a minimum of time.

An important part of this program is an Export Information Reference Room where businessmen can review a wide range of major foreign projects under consideration by international financial institutions—World Bank Group, Inter-American Development Bank, Asian Development Bank, and the United Nations Development Programme.

For further information on all of the above services, contact the nearest Department of Commerce District Office.

The Bureau of Resources and Trade Assistance (BRTA) administers programs to aid domestic firms adversely affected by increased imports resulting from trade concessions granted by the U.S. government. The bureau also handles matters involving the fiber, textile, and apparel sectors of the economy.

The Bureau of Domestic Business Development (BDBD) collects and maintains factual data on U.S. industries, both domestic and international, in such categories as production, pricing, inventories, labor, marketing, finance, taxation, size, and location.

The Office of the Ombudsman in BDBD is a focal point for handling inquiries for business information as well as suggestions and complaints. Call 202–377–3176.

The Bureau of East-West Trade (BEWT) coordinates programs and provides information with regard to commercial relations with the socialist nations. The BEWT also manages export administration and issues export licenses, where required, for shipment to the Soviet bloc and China.

Information on specific countries may be obtained by calling the country marketing manager of BIC listed by region on page 581. Assistance or information about marketing in these countries may be obtained by dialing these key people directly.

DISTRICT OFFICES OF THE U.S. DEPARTMENT OF COMMERCE

Albuquerque, NM, 87102, 505 Marquette Avenue NW, Suite 1015. 505-766-2386.

Anchorage, AK, 99501, 632 Sixth Avenue, 412 Hill Building. 907-265-5307.

Atlanta, GA, 30309, 1365 Peachtree Street NE, Suite 600. 404-881-7000.

Baltimore, MD, 21202, 415 U.S. Customhouse, Gay and Lombard Streets. 301-962-3560.

Birmingham, AL, 35205, 908 S. 20th Street, Suite 200-201, 205-254-1331.

Boston, MA, 02116, 10th Floor, 441 Stuart Street. 617-223-2312.

Buffalo, NY, 14202, 1312 Federal Building, 111 W. Huron Street. 716-842-3208.

Source: **U.S. Department of Commerce.**

Charleston, WV, 25301, 3000 New Federal Office Building, 500 Quarrier Street. 304-343-6181, Ext. 375.

Cheyenne, WY, 82001, 6022 O'Mahoney Federal Center, 2120 Capitol Avenue. 307-778-2220, Ext. 2151.

Chicago, IL, 60603, 1406 Mid-Continental Plaza Building, 55 E. Monroe Street. 312-353-4450.

Cincinnati, OH, 45202, 10504 Federal Office Building, 550 Main Street. 513-684-2944.

Cleveland, OH, 44114, Room 600, 666 Euclid Avenue. 216-522-4750.

Columbia, SC, 29204, Forest Center, 2611 Forest Drive. 803-765-5345.

Dallas, TX, 75242, Room 7A5, 1100 Commerce Street. 214-749-1515.

Denver, CO, 80202, Room 165, New Custom House, 19th and Stout Streets. 303-837-3246.

Des Moines, IA, 50309, 609 Federal Building, 210 Walnut Street. 515-284-4222.

Detroit, MI, 48226, 445 Federal Building, 231 W. Lafayette. 313-226-3650.

Greensboro, NC, 27402, 203 Federal Building, W. Market Street, P.O. Box 1950. 919-378-5345.

Hartford, CT, 06103, Room 610-B, Federal Office Building, 450 Main Street. 203-244-3530.

Honolulu, HI, 96850, 4106 Federal Building, 300 Ala Moana Boulevard, P.O. Box 50026. 808-546-8694.

Houston, TX, 77002, 2625 Federal Building, 515 Rusk Street. 713-226-4231.

Indianapolis, IN, 46204, 357 U.S. Courthouse & Federal Office Building, 46 E. Ohio Street. 317-269-6214.

Los Angeles, CA, 90049, Room 800, 11777 San Vicente Boulevard. 213-824-7591.

Memphis, TN, 38103, Room 710, 147 Jefferson Avenue. 901-521-3213.

Miami, FL, 33130, Room 821, City National Bank Building, 25 W. Flagler Street. 305-350-5267.

Milwaukee, WI, 53203, 605 Federal Building, U.S. Courthouse, 517 E. Wisconsin Avenue. 414-224-3473.

Minneapolis, MN, 55401, 218 Federal Building, 110 S. Fourth Street. 612-725-2113.

New Orleans, LA, 70130, 432 International Trade Mart, No 2 Canal Street. 504-589-6546.

New York, NY, 10007, 37th Floor, Federal Office Building, 26 Federal Plaza, Foley Square. 212-264-0634.

Newark, NJ, 07102, Gateway Building (4th floor) Market Street & Penn Plaza. 201-645-6214.

Omaha, NE, 68102, 1815 Capitol Avenue, Capitol Plaza, Suite 703A. 402-221-3665.

Philadelphia, PA, 19106, 9448 Federal Building, 600 Arch Street. 215-597-2850.

Phoenix, AZ, 85073, 2950 Valley Center Bank Building, 201 N. Central Avenue. 602-261-3285.

Pittsburgh, PA, 15222, 2002 Federal Building, 1000 Liberty Avenue. 412-644-2850.

Portland, OR 97204, Room 618, 1220 SW Third Avenue. 503-221-3001.

Reno, NV, 89509, 2028 Federal Building, 300 Booth Street. 702-784-5203.

Richmond, VA, 23240, 8010 Federal Building, 400 N. 8th Street. 804-782-2246.

St. Louis, MO, 63105, 120 S. Central Avenue. 314-425-3302.

Salt Lake City, UT, 84138, 1203 Federal Building, 125 S. State Street. 801-524-5116.

San Francisco, CA, 94102, Federal Building, Box 36013, 450 Golden Gate Avenue. 415-556-5860.

San Juan, PR, 00918, Room 659, Federal Building, Chardon Avenue. 809-753-4555.

Savannah, GA, 31402, 235 U.S. Courthouse and Post Office Building, 125-29 Bull Street. 912-232-4321, Ext. 204.

Seattle, WA, 98109, 706 Lake Union Building, 1700 Westlake Avenue North. 206-442-5615.

PUBLICATIONS

The following publications on international commerce are available from the Government Printing Office, Washington, DC 20402.

PUBLICATIONS, DEPARTMENT OF COMMERCE

Foreign Trade Report FT 410: U.S. Exports Commodity by Country is one of the best sources for locating export markets. These monthly publications provide a statistical record of the shipments of all merchandise from the United States to foreign countries.

Market Share Reports. These annual reports provide a five-year record of U.S. participation in foreign markets for manufactured products. Both country and product series are available.

International Economic Indicators and Competitive Trends is a quarterly report providing basic international data.

Overseas Business Reports (OBR). These reports provide a great deal of basic background data for businessmen who are evaluating export markets. Each OBR discusses separate topics for a single country. About 80 reports per year are issued.

Global Market Surveys are in-depth reports covering 20 to 30 of the best foreign markets for a single industry or a group of related industries.

Foreign Economic Trends is an in-depth series of country-by-country reports prepared annually or semiannually by the U.S. Foreign Service of the Department of State that covers individually almost every country in the world. It gives the latest data on GNP, foreign trade, and wages and prices.

Special Reports. The BIC and other DIBA agencies of the Department of Commerce publish special reports detailing economic data, marketing, and trade opportunities.

Index to Business International Publications is an index to materials appearing in *Overseas Business Reports, Global Market Surveys, Foreign Economic Trends,* and *Special Reports.*

Country Market Surveys are in-depth reports covering the most promising U.S. export opportunities.

Producer Goods Research is in-depth reports covering the best foreign sales opportunities for the U.S. producer goods industry.

Consumer Goods Research is in-depth reports covering the best foreign sales opportunities for U.S. consumer goods industry.

International Marketing News Memo. This includes information bulletins received directly from the U.S. Foreign Service—reports prepared by U.S. businessmen or Department of Commerce officers. Reports cover a wide variety of industries, products, and countries.

Commerce America (formerly *Commerce Today*). This biweekly is the Commerce Department's principal periodical for domestic and international business news.

Commerce Business Daily is a daily record containing synopses of U.S. government procurement limitations, subcontracting leads, contract awards, sales of surplus property, and foreign business opportunities.

Business Service Check List. Published weekly, this publication lists books, pamphlets, and reports by the Department of Commerce.

International Marketing Events includes brief market summaries of trade promotion events, organized by the Office of International Marketing (BIC), which contain a detailed calendar of upcoming foreign fairs and exhibits. The publication includes:

1. U.S. trade center exhibits—scheduled exhibits of U.S. manufacturers at U.S. trade centers (permanent product exhibit facilities operated by the U.S. Department of Commerce).
2. Commercial and industrial fairs—events held in conjunction with established international trade fairs or important national trade fairs.
3. Trade missions—organized business trips led by staff officers selected by the Commerce Department.
4. Catalog events—U.S. government-organized display of U.S. company catalogs in foreign markets.
5. In-store promotions—marketing events for U.S.-manufactured consumer goods held in foreign retail establishments.

DEPARTMENT OF STATE

Address: 2201 C Street NW, Washington, DC 20520. Locator phone: 202–632–9884.

Current information relating to political, commercial, and economic developments in foreign countries and trade agreements is provided by a large staff of national specialists in the Department of State.

A convenient way of obtaining information or contacting personnel is to call the Bureau of Economic and Business Affairs, 202–632–0396, for guidance to the appropriate source.

Business persons travelling abroad desiring to initiate contacts at foreign locales should contact the U.S. commercial attaché overseas.

U.S. TRADE CENTERS AND COMMERCIAL OFFICES, DEPARTMENT OF STATE

Athens
Regional Trade Development Office for the Near East
91 Vasilissi Sophia Boulevard (at the Embassy)
Athens, Greece

Beirut
U.S. Trade Center
(Temporary location due to political unrest in Lebanon)
Commercial Section
American Embassy
91 Vasilissis Sophias Street
Athens, Greece

Cologne
International Marketing Center
ABC House
1–9 Bahnhofstrasse
D5000 Cologne 1, Germany

London
U.S. Trade Center
4/5 Langham Place
London W1N8AE, United Kingdom

Mexico City
U.S. Trade Center
Liverpool No. 31
Apartado Postal
M-2805
Mexico City 6, D.F., Mexico

Milan
U.S. Trade Center
Via Gattamelata, 5
20149 Milan, Italy

Source: **U.S. Department of Commerce.**

Moscow
U.S. Commercial Office
15 Chaykovskovo
Moscow, USSR
Nagoya
American Commercial Information Office
Nagoya Aichi Sangyo Boekikan Building,
4th Floor 106
Marunouchi 3-chome, Naka-ku
Nagoya, Japan
Osaka
U.S. American Merchandise Display
Sankei Kaikan Building
27, Umeda-Cho, Kita-Ku
Osaka, Japan
Paris
U.S. Trade Center
123 Avenue Charles de Gaulle
92200 Neuilly
Paris, France
Sao Paulo
U.S. Trade Center
Avenida Paulista, 2439
Edificio Eloy Chavez
CEP 01311 Sao Paulo, Brazil
Seoul
U.S. Trade Center
82 Sejon-Ro
Seoul, Korea
Singapore
U.S. Trade Center
Malayan Credit House
96 Somerset Road
Singapore 9, Singapore
Sydney
International Marketing Center
T&G Building
Hyde Park Square
Park Street
Sydney, N.S.W. 2000
Australia
Taipei
U.S. Trade Center
261 Nanking East Road
Section 3
Taipei, Taiwan
Tehran
U.S. Trade Center
61 Elizabeth Boulevard
Tehran, Iran
Tokyo
U.S. Trade Center
Tameike-Tokyu Building
1–14 Akasaka 1 Chome
Minato-ku, Tokyo 107
Japan
Vienna
U.S. Department of Commerce Trade Fair
Support Office
Vienna I, Friedrich Schmidt Platz 2
Austria

Warsaw
U.S. Trade Development and Technical In-
formation Office
Ulica Wiejska, 20
Warsaw, Poland

PUBLICATIONS

*Background Notes of the Countries of the
World* gives profiles of foreign countries.
Key Officers of Foreign Service Posts lists
the addresses and phone numbers of all
American embassies and consulates and their
key personnel.
Department of State Bulletin is a weekly
publication devoted to the latest developments in international politics and trade
agreements.

UNITED STATES INTERNATIONAL TRADE COMMISSION

Address: 701 E Street NW, Washington,
DC 20436. Information phone: 202–523–
0161.
Formerly the U.S. Tariff Commission, the
name was changed to the U.S. International
Trade Commission in 1974.

The commission is given broad powers
of investigation relating to the customs
laws of the United States and foreign
countries, the volume of importation in
comparison with domestic production and
consumption, the conditions, causes, and
effects relating to competition of foreign
industries with those of the United States
and all other factors affecting competition
between articles of the United States and
imported articles.

Source: *Government Organization Manual.*

Businesspersons who believe they have
been injured by unfair trade methods from
abroad may file a complaint with this commission.
Summaries of trade and tariff information
may be obtained directly from the commission.
The following agencies are important in
arranging trade financing and credit insurance:

EXPORT-IMPORT BANK

Address: 811 Vermont Avenue NW,
Washington, DC 20471. Phone: 202–382–
8400.

FOREIGN CREDIT INSURANCE ASSOCIATION (FCIA)

Address: One World Trade Center, New
York, NY 10048. Phone: 212–432–6200.

The Export-Import Bank, established in 1934, is an independent agency of the U.S. government with the basic mission of encouraging U.S. exports. The policies of the bank recognize that credit terms are as important to foreign buyers as price and quality, and that U.S. exporters should be provided with financing that is competitive with that offered by foreign competitors. The bank cooperates with and supplements private capital sources. Loans to exporters are generally for specific purposes and most offer reasonable assurance of repayment.

A number of programs are offered by the Eximbank, including direct credit to foreign buyers, credit guarantees of commercial banks, loans to exporters, export credit insurance, and discount loans.

Credit insurance protection for exporters is provided by FCIA, an association of commercial insurance companies formed by the Eximbank and the insurance industry in 1961. Policies issued by FCIA insure repayment if the foreign buyer should default. The exporter may use FCIA insurance as collateral for obtaining a commercial loan.

The Eximbank will make a preliminary commitment concerning the amount it will guarantee or lend, a feature of particular value to U.S. importers submitting proposals in response to a foreign bid. The bank is also helpful in providing credit information on foreign buyers.

PUBLICATION

Eximbank: How it Works (free on writing to the Export-Import Bank).

OVERSEAS PRIVATE INVESTMENT CORPORATION (OPIC)

Address: 1129 20th Street NW, Washington, DC. Information phone: 202–632–1854.

OPIC, established in 1971, is an independent agency of the U.S. government with the mission of reducing or eliminating private investment risks in the developing countries. OPIC insures U.S. investors against political risks of expropriation, inconvertability of local currency holdings, and damage from war, revolution, or insurrection. The agency offers lenders protection by guaranteeing payment of principal, interest, and loans.

The corporation offers investment information and counseling to businesses and participates in the cost of locating and developing projects.

INTERNATIONAL ORGANIZATIONS

UNITED NATIONS (UN)

Address: New York, NY 10017. Information phone: 212-754-1234.

The UN and its affiliated organizations publish a large number of reports and statistical tables covering all member nations. Publications may be obtained by writing: Sales Section, United Nations Publications, New York, NY 10017. A periodic check list of UN publications is available on request.

PUBLICATIONS

Journal of Development Planning.
Guidelines for Contracting for Industrial Projects in Developing Countries.
World Economic Survey.
Annual Bulletin of Exports of Chemical Products.
Annual Bulletin of Coal Statistics for Europe.
Statistics of World Trade in Steel.
Annual Bulletin of Gas Statistics for Europe.
Annual Bulletin of Electric Energy Statistics for Europe.
Economic Bulletin for Europe.
Economic Bulletin for Asia and the Pacific.
Quarterly Bulletin of Statistics for Asia and the Pacific.
Statistical Yearbook for Asia and the Pacific.
Demographic Yearbook.
Yearbook of International Trade Statistics Vol. I: Trade by Country; Vol. II: Trade by Commodity.
Monthly Bulletin of Statistics provides monthly statistics on 70 subjects from more than 200 countries and territories together with special tables illustrating important economic developments. Quarterly data for significant world and regional aggregates are also prepared regularly for the bulletin.
Statistical Yearbook is a comprehensive compilation of international statistics relating to: population and manpower; agricultural, mineral, and manufacturing production; construction; energy; trade; transport; communications; consumption; balance of payments; wages and prices; national accounts; finance; development assistance; health; housing; education; science and technology; and culture.
Population and Vital Statistics Reports (quarterly).
Yearbook of National Accounts Statistics.
Yearbook of International Trade Statistics.
Yearbook of Construction Statistics.

Commodity Trade Statistics (quarterly).
World Trade Annual.
The Growth of World Industry: Vol. I General Industrial Statistics; Vol. II Commodities Production Data.

INTERNATIONAL MONETARY FUND (IMF)

Address: 19th and H Streets NW, Washington, DC 20431. Phone: 202-477-7000.

The IMF was organized in 1945 with the purpose of promoting international monetary cooperation and consultation. The fund also seeks to facilitate the expansion of international trade and currency exchange stability. The fund issues Special Drawing Rights (SDR), a form of reserve currency used by central banks for settling balance of payment obligations.

PUBLICATIONS

The IMF issues a broad range of publications (some in conjunction with the World Bank Group) of interest to the business community.
Foreign Trade Statistics. Series A. This monthly bulletin provides a breakdown of overall trade by main commodity categories and available indices of foreign trade unit values and volumes. *Series B. Trade by Commodities. Analytical Abstracts* (quarterly). *Series C. Trade by Commodities. Market Summaries* (yearly).
Provisional Oil Statistics (quarterly).
The Annual Report of the Executive Directors reviews the funds' activities, policies, organization, and administration and surveys the world economy, with special emphasis on international liquidity, payments problems, exchange rates, and world trade.
Annual Report on Exchange Restrictions reviews developments in exchange controls and restrictions and other measures that may have direct implications for the balance of payments of member countries.
International Financial Statistics (monthly) reports for most countries of the world current data needed for analyzing problems of international payments and inflation and deflation, i.e., data on exchange rates, international liquidity, money and banking, international trade, prices, production, government finance, interest rates, and other items. Information is presented in country tables for each country and in tables with area and world aggregates. Charts on each country page show recent changes in important series.

Balance of Payments Yearbook presents statistics in a standard form, expressed in a common unit of account, for countries that report information to the fund on their balance of payments transactions. In the tables that are designated as "standard presentations," these transactions are classified in terms of objective criteria; in the tables designated as "analytic presentations," they are regrouped to facilitate further analysis and certain cumulative balances are drawn.

Direction of Trade is published jointly by the International Monetary Fund and the International Bank for Reconstruction and Development. The monthly issues provide the latest available information on each country's direction of trade, with comparative data for the corresponding period of the preceding year.

The *IMF Survey* is a topical report of the fund's activities (including all press releases, texts of communiques and major statements, SDR valuations, and exchange rates) presented in the broader context of developments in national economics and international finance.

ORGANIZATION FOR ECONOMIC COOPERATION AND DEVELOPMENT (OECD)

Address: 2 Rue Andre Pascal, Paris, France.

The OECD, established in 1961, is an outgrowth of the Organization for European Economic Cooperation, set up under the Marshall Plan in 1948. It consists of 24 developed countries: Canada, United States, Japan, Australia, New Zealand, Austria, Belgium, Denmark, England, Finland, France, West Germany, Greece, Iceland, Italy, Luxembourg, Netherlands, Norway, Portugal, Spain, Sweden, Turkey, Switzerland, and Yugoslavia. Together, the OECD countries account for 20 percent of world population, 60 percent of world industrial production, and 73 percent of world trade.

PUBLICATIONS

OECD Observer is intended for people who are interested in and concerned with economic and social planning in the broadest sense and who want to have relevant information in the most succinct form possible. It presents in readable fashion the entire range of OECD's work—in economic affairs, trade, manpower, social affairs, science and education, the environment, financial affairs, and development assistance. (Published bimonthly.)

The *OECD Economic Outlook* is a twice yearly, detailed survey of economic trends and prospects for the immediate future.

OECD Financial Statistics supplies complete, up-to-date, authoritative information on financial markets in 16 European countries, the United States, Canada, and Japan. (Published yearly with bimonthly supplements.)

OECD Economic Surveys is an annual analysis of the economic policy of each OECD country as seen by the others.

Main Economic Indicators, a monthly publication, is an essential source of statistics for the student of the international business cycle.

GENERAL AGREEMENT ON TRADE AND TARIFFS (GATT)

Address: International Trade Center, Geneva, Switzerland.

GATT is a multilateral trade treaty (entered into force in 1948) among 83 countries providing for the reduction of tariffs and other trade barriers, standardization of trade procedures, and the resolution of trade disputes. GATT publishes *Compilations of Basic Information on Export Markets; Guide to Sources of Foreign Trade Information; Analytical Bibliography: A Compendium of Sources: International Trade Statistics;* and *World Directory of Industry and Trade Associations.*

COMMERCIAL ORGANIZATIONS

DUN & BRADSTREET

Address: 99 Church Street, New York, NY Phone: 212–285–7000.

Dun & Bradstreet provides a number of valuable services and publications in the area of international business, i.e., international credit reports on companies, international marketing guides and services, and directories of foreign firms. Dun & Bradstreet publishes the comprehensive annual, *Exporters Encyclopedia*, with monthly supplements. It details the rules and regulations in over 220 world markets and is arranged alphabetically by country and market area. *Principal International Businesses* is a useful marketing publication providing addresses, lines of business, sales figures, and other information on nearly 50,000 foreign firms.

INTERNATIONAL REPORTS

Address: 200 Park Avenue South, New York, NY 10003.

International Reports publishes reports on sources of worldwide export credit insurance, foreign investment guarantees, and export financing under the title of *Insurance in International Finance*.

It also publishes the monthly *International Commercial Finance Service*, containing extensive information and data on financing and interest rates, surveys of credit ratings, and foreign payment records of individual countries.

BUSINESS INTERNATIONAL

Address: One Dag Hammarskjold Plaza, New York, NY 10017. Phone: 212–750–6300.

Business International publishes a series of weekly reports: *Business International* (a global view of business); *Business Europe; Business Latin America; Business Asia; Eastern Europe Report; Business China* (People's Republic); *Business International Money Report; Investing, Licensing, Trading Report;* and *Financing Foreign Operations.* It publishes a multivolume series, *Doing Business with Eastern Europe.*

COMMERCE CLEARING HOUSE

Address: 4025 West Peterson Avenue, Chicago, IL 60646. Phone: 312–267–9010.

Commerce Clearing House publishes a number of widely used looseleaf series updated on a weekly or monthly basis. In the international field these include: *Euromarket News; Doing Business in Europe; Balance of Payment Reports; Common Market Reports;* and *Income Taxes World Wide.* It also publishes a number of detailed tax and legal guides for specific countries, i.e., Canada, Mexico, Australia, England, and Germany.

OTHER PUBLICATIONS

Europa Year Book is an annual two-volume work covering a wide range of commercial, economic, and political statistics and information about every country in the world. Volume I deals with international organizations and the countries of Europe, while Volume II covers Africa, the Americas, Asia, and Australia. It is published by Europe Publications, Ltd., 18 Bedford Square, London, England.

Jane's Major Companies of Europe is an annual providing extensive information about all major European companies. It is available from Jane's Yearbooks, 8 Shepherdess, London N1 7LW, England.

SOURCES OF INTERNATIONAL CREDIT INFORMATION

Export Information Division, Domestic and International Business Administration, U.S. Department of Commerce, Washington, DC.

Dun & Bradstreet (address given above).

FCIB-NACM Corp., 475 Park Avenue South, New York, NY 10015.

Major commercial banks (see section on international officers of U.S. commercial banks for listing).

COST-OF-LIVING INDEXES FOR AMERICANS LIVING ABROAD

INDEXES OF LIVING COSTS ABROAD, EXCLUDING HOUSING AND EDUCATION, MAY 1977
Washington, D.C. = 100

Country and city	Survey date	Monetary unit	Rate of exchange per US$1	Local index
Argentina: Buenos Aires	May 1976	Peso	245	69
Australia: Canberra	Nov. 1976	Dollar	0.9174	112
Belgium: Brussels	Aug. 1976	Franc	38.0	147
Brazil: Sao Paulo	July 1976	Cruzeiro	10.9	111
Canada: Ottawa	Sept. 1976	Dollar	0.97	111
France: Paris	May 1976	Franc	4.90	139
Germany: Frankfurt	Feb. 1976	Mark	2.50	148
Hong Kong: Hong Kong	Dec. 1975	Dollar	5.04	116
India: New Delhi	Aug. 1976	Rupee	8.90	94
Italy: Rome	Apr. 1975	Lira	630	123
Japan: Tokyo	Feb. 1976	Yen	300	154
Mexico: Mexico, D.F.	Feb. 1977	Peso	22.0	78
Netherlands: The Hague	Feb. 1976	Guilder	2.70	126
Philippines: Manila	Dec. 1976	Peso	7.40	88
South Africa: Johannesburg	Feb. 1975	Rand	0.6711	105
Spain: Madrid	July 1976	Peseta	68.0	106
Sweden: Stockholm	June 1976	Krona	4.38	164
Switzerland: Geneva	Mar. 1976	Franc	2.50	162
United Kingdom: London	May 1976	Pound	0.5714	95
Venezuela: Caracas	Aug. 1976	Bolivar	4.28	136

SOURCE: U.S. Department of State, Allowances Staff.

Source: *Monthly Labor Review,* Department of Labor, Bureau of Labor Statistics, September 1977.

FAST MATCH CHART

A QUICK, EASY WAY TO MATCH YOUR INTERNATIONAL BUSINESS REQUIREMENTS TO THE APPROPRIATE GOVERNMENT PROGRAMS OR SERVICES DESIGNED TO SATISFY THOSE NEEDS

IF YOU ARE SEEKING INFORMATION REGARDING ➡

USE ⬇

	Potential Markets	Market Research*	Direct Sales Leads	Agents/Distributors	Licenses	Credit Analysis	Financial Assistance	Risk Insurance	Tax Incentives
Foreign Trade Statistics (FT-410)	•								
Global Market Surveys	•	•							
Foreign Market Reports	•	•							
Market Share Reports	•	•							
Foreign Economic Trends	•	•							
Commerce America	•	•	•	•	•				
Commercial Exhibitions	**	**	•	•	•				
Overseas Business Reports (OBR)		•							
Overseas Private Investment Corp.		•					•	•	
Commerce Business Daily			•						
New Product Information Service			•	•	•				
Trade Opportunity Program (TOP)			•	•	•				
Industry Trade Lists			•	•	•				
Special Trade Lists			•	•	•				
Export Mailing List Service (EMLS)			•	•	•				
Agent/Distributor Service (ADS)				•					
World Trader Data Report (WTDR)						•			
Export—Import Bank							•	•	
Foreign Credit Insurance Assoc. (FCIA)								•	
Domestic Int'l. Sales Corp. (DISC)							•		•
Western Hemisphere Trading Corp.									•

* Foreign Trade Outlook; Market Profiles; Industry Trends; Distribution and Sales Channels; Transportation Facilities; Local Business Practices and Customs; Investment Criteria; Import Procedures and Trade Regulations; and Industrial Property Rights.

** Research material developed regarding a planned exhibition and released to support promotional activities.

Cost of services may be obtained from Commerce District Offices.

Source: Domestic and International Business Administration, U.S. Department of Commerce.

Selected Business and Trade Organizations

Academy of Motion Picture Arts and Sciences
8949 Wilshire Boulevard
Beverly Hills, CA 90211

Administrative Management Society
Willow Grove, PA 19090

Advertising Research Foundation
3 E. 54th Street
New York, NY 10022

Aerospace Industries Association of America
1725 DeSales Street NW
Washington, DC 20036

Air Freight Forwarders Association of
America
1730 Rhode Island Avenue NW
Washington, DC 20036

Air Transport Association of America
1709 New York Avenue NW
Washington, DC 20006

Allied Trades of the Baking Industry
5240 W. Irving Park Road
Chicago, IL 60641

Aluminum Association
750 Third Avenue
New York, NY 10017

American Accounting Association
653 S. Orange Avenue
Sarasota, FL 33577

American Advertising Federation
1225 Connecticut Avenue NW
Washington, DC 20036

American Apparel Manufacturers Association
1611 N. Kent Street
Arlington, VA 22209

American Arbitration Association
140 W. 51st Street
New York, NY 10020

American Association of Advertising Agencies
200 Park Avenue
New York, NY 10017

American Association of Attorney–Certified
Public Accountants
1 Old Country Road
Carle Place, NY 11514

American Association of Equipment Lessors
5635 W. Douglas Avenue
Milwaukee, WI 53218

American Association of Meat Processors
224 E. High Street
Elizabethtown, PA 17022

American Automobile Association
8111 Gatehouse Road
Falls Church, VA 22042

American Bankers Association
1120 Connecticut Avenue NW
Washington, DC 20036

American Booksellers Association
800 Second Avenue
New York, NY 10017

American Building Contractors Association
2476 Overland Avenue
Los Angeles, CA 90064

American Bureau of Metal Statistics
420 Lexington Avenue
New York, NY 10017

American Bureau of Shipping
45 Broad Street
New York, NY 10004

American Business Communication
Association
University of Illinois
Urbana, IL 61801

American Business Women's Association
9100 Ward Parkway
Kansas City, MO 64114

American Chemical Society
1155 16th Street NW
Washington, DC 20036

American Dairy Association
6300 N. River Road
Rosemont, IL 60018

American Dental Trade Association
1140 Connecticut Avenue NW
Washington, DC 20036

American Federation of Small Business
407 S. Dearborn Street
Chicago, IL 60605

American Finance Association
Graduate School of Business Administration
New York University
100 Trinity Place
New York, NY 10006

American Gas Association
1515 Wilson Boulevard
Arlington, VA 22209

American Importers Association
420 Lexington Avenue
New York, NY 10017

American Industrial Real Estate Association
5670 Wilshire Boulevard
Los Angeles, CA 90036

American Institute of Banking
1120 Connecticut Avenue NW
Washington, DC 20036

American Institute of Certified Public
  Accountants
1211 Avenue of the Americas
New York, NY 10036

American Institute of Chemical Engineers
345 E. 47th Street
New York, NY 10017

American Institute of Food Distribution
28–06 Broadway
Fair Lawn, NJ 07410

American Institute of Management
125 E. 38th Street
New York, NY 10016

American Institute of Marine Underwriters
99 John Street
New York, NY 10038

American Institute of Real Estate Appraisers
530 Michigan Avenue
Chicago, IL 60611

American Insurance Association
85 John Street
New York, NY 10038

American Iron and Steel Institute
1000 16th Street, NW
Washington, DC 20036

American Management Association
135 W. 50th Street
New York, NY 10020

American Marketing Association
222 S. Riverside Plaza
Chicago, IL 60606

American Meat Institute
1600 Wilson Boulevard
Arlington, VA 22209

American Mining Congress
1100 Ring Building
1200 18th Street NW
Washington, DC 20036

American National Cattlemen's Association
1001 Lincoln Street
Denver, CO 80203

American Paper Institute
260 Madison Avenue
New York, NY 10016

American Petroleum Institute
2101 L Street NW
Washington, DC 20037

American Production and Inventory Control
  Society, Inc.
2600 Virginia Avenue NW
Washington, DC 20037

American Railway Engineering Association
59 E. Van Buren Street
Chicago, IL 60605

American Retail Federation
1616 H Street NW
Washington, DC 20006

American Savings and Loan League
733 15th Street NW
Washington, DC 20011

American Society for Metals
Metals Park, OH 44073

American Society for Personnel
  Administration
19 Church Street
Berea, OH 44017

American Society for Training and
  Development
6414 Ordana Road
Madison, WI 53705

American Society of Association Executives
1101 16th Street NW
Washington, DC 20045

American Society of Bank Directors
National Press Building
Washington, DC 20045

American Society of Chartered Life
  Underwriters
270 Bryn Mawr Avenue
Bryn Mawr, PA 19010

American Society of Civil Engineers
345 E. 47th Street
New York, NY 10017

American Society of International Executives
901 Poplar Street
Philadelphia, PA 19107

American Society of Mechanical Engineers
345 E. 47th Street
New York, NY 10017

American Society of Newspaper Editors
1350 Sullivan Trail
Easton, PA 18042

American Stock Association
86 Trinity Place
New York, NY 10006

American Textile Machinery Association
1730 M Street NW
Washington, DC 20036

American Textile Manufacturers Institute
400 S. Tryon Street
Charlotte, NC 28285

American Tin Trade Association
733 Third Avenue
New York, NY 10017

American Translators Association
P.O. Box 129
Croton-On-Hudson, NY 10520

American Trucking Association, Inc.
1616 P Street NW
Washington, DC 20036

Appraisers Association of America
541 Lexington Avenue
New York, NY 10022

Associated Builders and Contractors
1156 15th Street NW
Washington, DC 20005

Associated Equipment Distributors
615 W. 22nd Street
Oak Brook, IL 60521

Associated General Contractors of America
1957 E Street NW
Washington, DC 20006

Associated Press, Inc.
50 Rockefeller Plaza
New York, NY 10020

Association for Corporate Growth
999 Bedford Street
Stamford, CT 06905

Association for Systems Management
24587 Bagley Road
Cleveland, OH 44138

Association of American Publishers, Inc.
1 Park Avenue
New York, NY 10016

Association of American Railroads
American Railroads Building
1920 L Street NW
Washington, DC 20036

Association of Consulting Management
    Engineers, Inc.
347 Madison Avenue
New York, NY 10017

Association of Data Processing Service
    Organizations

210 Summit Avenue
Montvale, NJ 07645

Association of Executive Recruiting
    Consultants, Inc.
30 Rockefeller Plaza
New York, NY 10020

Audit Bureau of Circulations
123 N. Wacker Drive
Chicago, IL 60606

Automotive Information Council
28333 Telegraph Road
Southfield, MI 48076

Automotive Market Research Council
Torrington Co.
31313 Northwest Highway
Farmington, MI 48021

Automotive Service Industry Association
230 N. Michigan Avenue
Chicago, IL 60601

Automotive Trade Association Managers
2000 K Street NW
Chevy Chase, MD 20015

Bank Administration Institute
303 S. Northwest Highway
Park Ridge, IL 60068

Bank Marketing Association
309 W. Washington Street
Chicago, IL 60606

Bankers Association for Foreign Trade
1101 16th Street NW
Washington, DC 20036

Business Professional Advertising Association
205 E. 42nd Street
New York, NY 10017

Business Roundtable, The
405 Lexington Avenue
New York, NY 10017

Can Manufacturers Institute
1625 Massachusetts Avenue NW
Washington, DC 20036

Car and Truck Renting and Leasing
    Association
1725 K Street NW
Washington, DC 20006

Casualty Actuarial Society
200 E. 42nd Street
New York, NY 10017

Chamber of Commerce of U.S.A.
1615 H Street NW
Washington, DC 20006

Clothing Manufacturers Association of the
    U.S.A.

135 W. 50th Street
New York, NY 10020

Computer and Business Equipment
    Manufacturer's Association
1828 L Street NW
Washington, DC 20036

Conference of American Small Business
    Organizations, Inc.
407 S. Dearborn Street
Chicago, IL 60605

Construction Specifications Institute
1150 17th Street NW
Washington, DC 20036

Copper Development Association
405 Lexington Avenue
New York, NY 10017

Copper Trade Association
235 E. 42nd Street
New York, NY 10017

Cotton Foundation, The
1918 North Parkway
Memphis, TN 38112

Council of Better Business Bureaus, Inc.
1150 17th Street NW
Washington, DC 20036

Council of the Americas
680 Park Avenue
New York, NY 10021

Dairy and Food Industries Supply
    Associations, Inc.
5530 Wisconsin Avenue NW
Chevy Chase, MD 20015

Data Processing Management Association
505 Busse Highway
Park Ridge, IL 60068

Direct Mail/Marketing Association
6 E. 43rd Street
New York, NY 10017

Distilled Spirits Council of the United States
1300 Pennsylvania Building
425 13th Street NW
Washington, DC 20004

Drug, Chemical and Allied Trades
    Association
42–40 Bell Boulevard
Bayside, NY 11361

Electronic Industries Association
2001 Eye Street NW
Washington, DC 20006

Engineering Foundation
345 E. 47 Street
New York, NY 10017

Farm and Industrial Equipment Institute
410 N. Michigan Avenue
Chicago, IL 60611

Farm Equipment Manufacturers Association
230 S. Bemiston Avenue
St. Louis, MO 63105

FCIB-NACM
    (formerly Foreign Credit Interchange
    Bureau)
475 Park Avenue, So.
New York, NY 10016

Fertilizer Institute, The
1015 18th Street NW
Washington, DC 20036

Financial Analysts Federation
219 E. 42nd Street
New York, NY 10017

Financial Executives Institute
633 Third Avenue
New York, NY 10017

Food Distribution Research Society
780 Prospect Street
Winnetka, IL 60093

Food Service Executive Association
2827 Rupp Drive
Fort Wayne, IN 46805

Foreign Credit Insurance Association
1 World Trade Center
New York, NY 10048

General Agreement on Tariffs and Trade
Villa Le Bocage
Palais Des Nations
CH-1211
Geneva 10, Switzerland

Health Insurance Association of America
1701 K Street NW
Washington, DC 20006

Independent Bankers Association of America
P.O. Box 267
Sauk Centre, MN 56378

Independent Grocers Alliance Distributing
    Company
5725 E. River Road
Chicago, IL 60631

Industrial Management Society
570 Northwest Highway
Des Plaines, IL 60016

Information Industry Association
4720 Montgomery Lane
Bethesda, MD 20014

Institute of Chartered Financial Analysts
P.O. Box 3668
University of Virginia
Charlottesville, VA 22903

Institute of Electrical and Electronic
    Engineers
345 E. 47th Street
New York, NY 10017

Institute of Financial Education, The
111 E. Wacker Drive
Chicago, IL 60601

Institute of Gas Technology
3424 State Street
Chicago, IL 60616

Institute of Internal Auditors
5500 Diplomat Circle
Orlando, FL 32810

Institute of Life Insurance
277 Park Avenue
New York, NY 10017

Institute of Management Consultants
347 Madison Avenue
New York, NY 10017

Institute of Management Sciences, The
146 Westminster Street
Providence, RI 02903

Institute of Real Estate Management
430 N. Michigan Avenue
Chicago, IL 60611

Insurance Accounting and Statistical
  Association
Mutual Plaza
Durham, NC 27701

Insurance Services Office
2 World Trade Center
New York, NY 10048

International Advertising Association Inc.
475 5th Avenue
New York, NY 10017

International Airfreight Agents Association
P.O. Box 359
Springfield, NJ 07081

International Air Transport Association
1000 Sherbrooke Street, W.
Montreal, PQ, Canada H3A2R4

International Association of Drilling
  Contractors
7400 Harwin
Houston, TX 77036

International Association of Exchange
  Dealers
16 Boulevard Montmarte
Paris, France

International Bankers Association
422 Washington Building
15th and New York Avenue NW
Washington, DC 20005

International Chamber of Commerce
30 Cours Albert Ier
Paris, France

International Chamber of Commerce, Inc.,
  U.S. Council of the

1212 Avenue of the Americas
New York, NY 10036

International Coffee Organization
22 Berners Street
London WIP 4DD, England

International Confederation of Associations
  of Experts and Consultants
13 Boulevard D'Anvers
B-1000, Brussels, Belgium

International Consumer Credit Association
375 N. Jackson Avenue
St. Louis, MO 63130

International Copper Research Association
825 Third Avenue
New York, NY 10022

International Council of Shopping Centers
445 Park Avenue
New York, NY 10022

International Executive Service Corps
622 Third Avenue
New York, NY 10017

International Executives Associations, Inc.
1 World Trade Center
New York, NY 10048

International Federation of Forwarding
  Agents Association
P.O. Box 177
Ch-8026 Zurich, Switzerland

International Foundation of Employee
  Benefit Plans
18700 Blue Mound Road
Brookfield, WI 53005

International Franchise Association
7315 Wisconsin Avenue
Washington, DC 20014

International Industrial Television Association
Summit Avenue
Summit, NJ 07901

International Iron and Steel Institute
Avenue Hamoir 14
B-1180, Brussels, Belgium

International Lead Zinc Research
  Organization, Inc.
292 Madison Avenue
New York, NY 10017

International Magnesium Association
C/O Bell Publicom
1406 Third National Building
Dayton, OH 45402

International Management Council
Y.M.C.A.
291 Broadway
New York, NY 10007

International Personnel Management
Association
1313 E. 60th Street
Chicago, IL 60637

Investment Company Institute
Suffridge Building
1775 K Street NW
Washington, DC 20006

Iron and Steel Society
345 E. 47th Street
New York, NY 10017

Machinery and Allied Products Institute
1200 18th Street NW
Washington, DC 20036

Manufactured Housing Institute
P.O. Box 201
Chantilly, VA 22021

Manufacturing Chemists Association
1825 Connecticut Avenue NW
Washington, DC 20009

Mass Retailing Institute
570 7th Avenue
New York, NY 10018

Master Brewers Association of America
4513 Vernon Boulevard
Madison, WI 53705

Master Furriers Guild of America
101 W. 30th Street
New York, NY 10001

Milk Industry Foundation
910 17th Street NW
Washington, DC 20006

Minicomputer Industry National Interchange
2460 Limoine Avenue
Ft. Lee, NJ 07024

Mortgage Bankers Association of America
1125 15th Street NW
Washington, DC 20005

Motor and Equipment Manufacturers
Association
222 Cedar Lane
Teaneck, NJ 97666

Motor Vehicle Manufacturers Association
of the United States
320 New Center Building
Detroit, MI 48202

National Academy of Television Arts and
Sciences
291 S. LaCienega Boulevard
Beverly Hills, CA 90211

National Aeronautic Association
806 15th Street NW
Washington, DC 20005

National Agri-Marketing Association
800 W. 47th Street
Kansas City, MO 64112

National Air Transportation Associations
1156 15th Street NW
Washington, DC 20005

National Alcoholic Beverage Control
Association
5454 Wisconsin Avenue NW
Bethesda, MD 20015

National Apartment Association
1825 K Street NW
Washington, DC 20006

National Association of Accountants
919 Third Avenue
New York, NY 10022

National Association of Alcoholic Beverage
Importers
1025 Vermont Avenue NW
Washington, DC 20005

National Association of Bank Women
111 E. Wacker Drive
Chicago, IL 60601

National Association of Broadcasters
1771 N Street NW
Washington, DC 20036

National Association of Business Economists
28349 Chagrin Boulevard
Cleveland, OH 44122

National Association of Credit Management
475 Park Avenue So.
New York, NY 10016

National Association of Electric Companies
1140 Connecticut Avenue NW
Washington, DC 20036

National Association of Export Management
Companies
65 Liberty Street
New York, NY 10005

National Association of Food Chains
1725 I Street NW
Washington, DC 20006

National Association of Food Equipment
Manufacturers
c/o Smith, Bucklin & Associates, Inc.
111 E. Wacker Drive
Chicago, IL 60601

National Association of Furniture
Manufacturers
8401 Connecticut Avenue
Chevy Chase, MD 20015

National Association of Home Builders of the
U.S.

15th and M Streets
Washington, DC 20005

National Association of Independent Food
    Retailers
434 W. 8 Mile Road
Detroit, MI 48220

National Association of Insurance Agents
85 John Street
New York, NY 10038

National Association of Investment Clubs
1515 E. 11 Mile Road
Royal Oak, MI 48067

National Association of Life Underwriters
1922 F Street NW
Washington, DC 20006

National Association of Manufacturers
1776 F Street NW
Washington, DC 20006

National Association of Mutual Insurance
    Agents
640 Investment Building
1511 K Street NW
Washington, DC 20005

National Association of Mutual Savings Banks
200 Park Avenue
New York, NY 10017

National Association of Pharmaceutical
    Manufacturers
747 Third Avenue
New York, NY 10017

National Association of Photographic
    Manufacturers
600 Mamaroneck Avenue
Harrison, NY 10528

National Association of Purchasing
    Management
11 Park Place
New York, NY 10007

National Association of Real Estate Brokers
1025 Vermont Avenue NW
Washington, DC 20005

National Association of Realtors
430 N. Michigan Avenue
Chicago, IL 60611

National Association of Retail Druggists
1 E. Wacker Drive
Chicago, IL 60601

National Association of Retail Grocers of the
    United States
2000 Spring Road
Oak Brook, IL 60521

National Association of Securities Dealers,
    Inc.

1735 K Street NW
Washington, DC 20006

National Association of Small Business
    Investment Companies
512 Washington Building
Washington, DC 20005

National Association of Women's and
    Childrens' Apparel Salesmen
1819 Peachtree Street NE
Atlanta, GA 30309

National Automobile Dealers Association
8400 Westpark Drive
McLean, VA 22101

National Business Aircraft Association
401 Pennsylvania Building
Pennsylvania Avenue at 13th Street NW
Washington, DC 20004

National Business Forms Association
433 E. Monroe Avenue
Alexandria, VA 22301

National Business League
4324 Georgia Avenue NW
Washington, DC 20011

National Cable Television Association
918 16th Street NW
Washington, DC 20006

National Canners Association
1133 20th Street NW
Washington, DC 20036

National Coal Association
1130 17th Street NW
Washington, DC 20036

National Coffee Association of U.S.A.
120 Wall Street
New York, NY 10005

National Consumer Finance Association
1000 16th Street NW
Washington, DC 20036

National Contract Management Association
2001 Jefferson Davis Highway
Arlington, VA 22202

National Council for Small Business
    Management Development
University of Wisconsin—Extension
929 N. Sixth Street
Milwaukee, WI 53203

National Council of Salesmen's Organizations
127 John Street
New York, NW 10038

National Customs Brokers and Forwarders
    Association of America, Inc.
1 World Trade Center
New York, NY 10048

National Electrical Manufacturers
    Association

155 E. 44th Street
New York, NY 10017

National Environmental Systems Contractors
  Association
1501 Wilson Boulevard
Arlington, VA 22209

National Export Traffic League, Inc.
507 5th Avenue
New York, NY 10017

National Federation of Independent Business
150 W. 20th Avenue
San Mateo, CA 94403

National Food Brokers Association
1916 M Street NW
Washington, DC 20036

National Foreign Trade Council, Inc.
10 Rockefeller Plaza
New York, NY 10020

National Foundation For Consumer Credit
1819 H Street NW
Washington, DC 20006

National Glass Dealers Association
1000 Connecticut Avenue
Washington, DC 20036

National Home Furnishing Association
405 Merchandise Mart Plaza
Chicago, IL 60654

National Independent Automobile Dealers
  Association
Koger Executive Center
3700 National Drive
Raleigh, NC 27612

National Industrial Recreation Association
20 N. Wacker Drive
Chicago, IL 60606

National Knitted Outerwear Association
51 Madison Avenue
New York, NY 10010

National Licensed Beverage Association
1025 Vermont Avenue NW
Washington, DC 20005

National Liquor Stores Association
1025 Vermont Avenue NW
Washington, DC 20005

National Management Association
2210 Arbor Boulevard
Dayton, OH 45439

National Office Products Association
1500 Wilson Boulevard
Arlington, VA 22209

National Press Club
National Press Building

529 14th Street NW
Washington, DC 20045

National Restaurant Association
1 IBM Plaza
Chicago, IL 60611

National Retail Hardware Association
964 N. Pennsylvania Street
Indianapolis, IN 46204

National Retail Merchants Association
100 W. 31st Street
New York, NY 10001

National Secretaries Association
2440 Pershing Road
Kansas City, MO 64108

National Small Business Association
1225 19th Street NW
Washington, DC 20036

National Sporting Goods Association
717 N. Michigan Avenue
Chicago, IL 60611

National Surplus Dealers Association
2561 N. Clark Street
Chicago, IL 60614

National Tool, Die and Precision Machining
  Association
9300 Livingston Road
Washington, DC 20022

National Trade Show Exhibitors Association
4902 Tollview Drive
Rolling Meadows, IL 60008

National Waterways Conference, Inc.
1130 17th Street NW
Washington, DC 20036

Organization of the Petroleum Exporting
  Countries
Dr. Karl Lueger–Ring 10
A-1010, Vienna 1, Austria

Over-The-Counter Information Bureau
2 Broadway
New York, NY 10005

Overseas Automotive Club
475 Park Avenue, So.
New York, NY 10016

Overseas Press Club of America, Inc.
55 E. 43rd Street
New York, NY 10017

Overseas Sales and Marketing Association of
  America
7440 N. Long Avenue
Skokie, IL 60076

Packaging Institute
342 Madison Avenue
New York, NY 10017

Pan-American Coffee Bureau
1350 Avenue of the Americas
New York, NY 10019

Pharmaceutical Manufacturers Association
1155 15th Street NW
Washington, DC 20005

Planning Executives Institute
5500 College Corner Pike
Oxford, OH 45056

Prestressed Concrete Institute
20 N. Wacker Drive
Chicago, IL 60606

Printing Industries of America
1730 N. Lynn Street
Arlington, VA 22209

Public Relations Society of America
845 Third Avenue
New York, NY 10022

Retail Advertising Conference
P.O. Box 1666
Gainesville, GA 30501

Robert Morris Associates
(National Association of Bank Loan and
Credit Officers)
Philadelphia National Bank Building
Philadelphia, PA 19107

Rubber Manufacturers Association
1901 Pennsylvania Avenue NW
Washington, DC 20006

Sales and Marketing Executives International
380 Lexington Avenue
New York, NY 10017

Sales Association of the Chemical Industry,
Inc.
79 Madison Avenue
New York, NY 10017

Savings and Loan Foundation, Inc.
1111 E Street NW
Washington, DC 20004

Securities Industry Association
20 Broad Street
New York, NY 10005

Service Corps of Retired Executives
1441 L Street NW
Washington, DC 20416

Silver Institute
1001 Connecticut Avenue NW
Washington, DC 20036

Society for Advancement of Management
135 W. 50th Street
New York, NY 10020

Society of Actuaries
208 S. LaSalle Street
Chicago, IL 60604

Society of Real Estate Appraisers
7 So. Dearborn Street
Chicago, IL 60603

Specialty Equipment Manufacturers
Association
11001 E. Valley Mall
El Monte, CA 91734

Sugar Association, Inc.
1511 K Street NW
Washington, DC 20005

Super Market Institute
303 E. Ohio Street
Chicago, IL 60611

Synthetic Organic Chemical Manufacturers
Association
1075 Central Park Avenue
Scarsdale, NY 10583

Tanners' Council of America
411 Fifth Avenue
New York, NY 10016

Technical Association of the Pulp and Paper
Industry
1 Dunwoody Park
Atlanta, GA 30341

Television Information Office
745 Fifth Avenue
New York, NY 10022

Tennessee Valley Public Power Association
Pioneer Building
Chattanooga, TN 37402

Textile Information Users Council
P.O. Box 7793
Greensboro, NC 27407

Tool and Die Institute
777 Busse Highway
Park Ridge, IL 60068

Toy Manufacturers of America
200 Fifth Avenue
New York, NY 10010

Transportation Association of America
1101 17th Street
Washington, DC 20036

Truck Body and Equipment Association
5530 Wisconsin Avenue
Chevy Chase, MD 20015

Underwriters Laboratories
207 E. Ohio Street
Chicago, IL 60611

United Fresh Fruit and Vegetable Association
1019 19th Street NW
Washington, DC 20036

United Press International
220 E. 42nd Street
New York, NY 10017

United States League of Savings Associations
111 E. Wacker Drive
Chicago, IL 60601

U.S. Diplomatic Offices Abroad

An American business person traveling abroad may enlist the services of officers at a U.S. embassy, consulate general's office, or consulate, depending on the area in which he is traveling. At most large embassies, the commercial attaché can assist business persons by providing introductions to local business people and information on local legal requirements and the potential of a particular product. In smaller embassies, consulate general's offices, or consulates, specific persons within the economic section perform similar services if there is no designated commercial officer.

Although much of the information provided by these officers abroad can be obtained from the U.S. Department of Commerce prior to foreign travel, U.S. diplomatic officers stationed abroad provide useful on-the-spot assistance.

Abbreviations are given at the end of this section.

Afghanistan
Kabul (E), Wazir Akbar Khan Mina. Telephone: 24230-9.

Algeria
Algiers (E), 4 Chemin Cheikh Bachir Brahimi (ex Beaurepaire). Telephone: 601425/601255/601186/601716/ 601828/603670.
Oran (C), 14 Place Bamako. Telephone: 355502/352665.

Angola
Luanda (CG), Avenida Paulo Dias de Novais, No. 42, 13th and 14th Floors. Telephone: 72494 and 73155. Post temporarily closed.

Argentina
Buenos Aires (E), Saramiento 663 (1613). Telephone: 477-8811.

Australia
Canberra (E), Moonah Place, Canberra, A.C.T. 2600; APO San Francisco 96404. Telephone: (062) 73-3711.
Melbourne (CG), 24 Albert Road, South Melbourne, Victoria 3205; APO San Francisco 96405. Telephone: 699-2244.
Sydney (CG), 37 Pitt Street, P.O. Box R-223, Royal Exchange, Sydney, N.S.W. 2000; APO San Francisco 96209. Telephone: (02) 241-1031.

Source: Listing from "Key Officers of Foreign Service Posts," Department of State, March 1978.

Brisbane (C), 141 Queen Street, Brisbane, 4000. Telephone: (07)-221-1338.
Perth (C), 264 St. George's Terrace. Telephone: 22-4466.

Austria
Vienna (E), IX Boltzmangasse 16 A-1091. Telephone: (222) 346611, 347511.
Salzburg (C), 1 Franz Josefs, Kai, Room 302. Telephone: 46461.
Vienna (IAEA), VIII, Schmidgasse 14. Telephone: (222) 346611, 347511.
Vienna (UNIDO), Boltzmanngasse 16. Telephone: (222) 346611, 347511.

Bahamas
Nassau (E), Mosmar Building, Queen Street. Telehpone (809) 322-1700 and 322-1181.

Bahrain
Manama (E), Shaikh Isa Road, P.O. Box 431, FPO New York 09526. Telephone: 714151. Com. Off. Telephone: 713323.

Bangladesh
Dacca (E), Adamjee Court Building, (5th floor), Montijheel Commercial Area, G.P.O. Box 323, Ramna. Telephone: 244220 through 244229.

Barbados
Bridgetown (E), P.O. Box 302, FPO New York 09553. Telephone 63574-7. Telex 259 USEMB BG1 WB.

Belgium
Brussels (E), 27 Boulevard du Regent, APO New York 09667. Telephone: 513-3830.
U.S. Mission to the North Atlantic Treaty Organization (USNATO), Autoroute de Zaventem, B-1110 Brussels or APO New York 09667. Telephone: 02-241-00-40.
U.S. Mission to the European Communities (USEC), 40 Boulevard du Regent, 1000 Brussels. Telephone: 513-38-30.
Antwerp (CG), 64-68 Frankrijklei, APO New York 09667. Telephone: (031) 321800.

Belize
Belize City (CG), Gabourel Lane and Hutson Streets. Telephone: 3261.

Benin
Cotonou (E), Rue Caporal Anani Bernard, Boite Postale 2012. Telephone: 31-26-92/3.

Bermuda
Hamilton (CG), Vallis Building, Front Street, FPO New York 09560. Telephone: 5-1342.

Bolivia
La Paz (E), Banco Popular Del Peru Building, Corner of Calles Mercado y Colon, APO New York 09867. Telephone: 50251.

Botswana
Gaborone (E), P.O. Box 90. Telephone: 2944/7.

Brazil
Brasilia (E), Lote No. 3, Avenida das Nocoes, APO New York 09676. Telephone (0612) 230120.

Rio De Janeiro (CG), Avenida Presidente Wilson, 147, APO New York 09676. Telephone: (021) 252-8055, 252-8056, 252-8057.

Sao Paulo (CG), Edifício Conjunto Nacional Rua Padre João Manuel 20; SP, APO New York 09676. Telephone: 289-3155, 289-3355, 289-3560, 289-3722.

Belem (C), Avenida Oswaldo Cruz 165. Telephone: 230800.

Porto Alegre (C), Rua Uruguai 155 (11th Floor), APO New York 09676. Telephone: (0512) 24-0655, 24-0509, 24-0054.

Recife (C), Rua Goncalves Maia 163. Telephone: 21-14-12/3, 22-66-12, 22-65-77.

Salvador (C), Edificio Fundacao Politecnica Bloco. A, 4th floor, Avenida Sete de Setembro 73/79. Telephone: (071) 3-4908, 3-4911.

Bulgaria
Sofia (E), 1 Stamboliski Boulevard. Telephone: 88-48-01 to 05.

Burma
Rangoon (E), 581 Merchant Street. Telephone: 18055.

Mandalay (C), 71st Street and South Moat Road. Telephone: 555.

Burundi
Bujumbura (E), Chaussee Prince Louise Rwagasore, Boite Postale 1720. Telephone: 34-54.

Cameroon
Yaounde (E), Rue Nachtigal, Boite Postale 817. Telephone: 221633/220512.

Douala (C), 21 Avenue du Gen. De Gaulle, Boite Postale 4006. Telephone: 423434/425331.

Canada
Ottawa (E), 100 Wellington Street. Telephone: (613) 238-5335 K1P 5T1.

Calgary, Alberta (CG), Room 1050-615 Macleod Trail SE, Calgary, Alberta, Canada T2G 4T8. Telephone: (403) 266-8962.

Halifax, Nova Scotia (CG), Suite 910, Cogswell Tower, Scotia Square, Halifax, NS, Canada B3J 3K1. Telephone: (902) 429-2480-1.

Montreal, Quebec (CG), Suite 1122, South Tower, Place Desjardins, P.O. Box 65, Montreal H5B 1G1, Canada. Telephone: (514) 281-1886.

Montreal (ICAO), 1000 Sherbrooke W. Room 753. Telephone: 285-8304.

Quebec, Quebec (CG), 1 Avenue Ste-Genevieve, GIR 4A7. Telephone: (418) 692-2095.

Toronto, Ontario (CG), 360 University Avenue. Telephone: (416) 595-1700, Eco/Com. Off. Telephone: (416) 595-1224.

Vancouver, British Columbia (CG), 1199 West Hastings Street, V6E 2Y4. Telephone: (604) 685-4311.

Winnipeg, Manitoba (CG), 6 Donald Street. Telephone: 475-3344/8, 284-3039.

Central African Empire
Bangui (E), Place de la Republique Centrafricaine. Telephone: 2050, 2051.

Ceylon
See Sri Lanka

Chad
N'djamena (E), Rue du Lt. Col. Colonna D'Ornano, B.P. 413. Telephone: 30-91/2/3/4.

Chile
Santiago (E), Codina Building, 1343 Agustinas. Telephone: 82801-4.

China
Taipei (E), 2 Chung Hsiao W Road, Second Section, APO San Francisco 96263. Telephone: 331 3551-9.

Peking (LO), Kuang Hua Lu, Department of State, Washington, DC 20520. Telephone: 522-033.

Colombia
Bogota (E), Calle 37, 8-40, APO New York 09895. Telephone: 329-100.

Cali (C), Edificio Pielroja, Carrera 3, No. 11-55, APO New York 09895. Telephone: 88-11-36/7.

Medellin (C), Edificio Santa Helena, Calle 52 No. 49–27. Mailing Address: Apartado Aereo 980. Telephone: 313-188.

Barranquilla (C) Edificio Seguros Tequendama Calle 34 No. 44–63 (10th Floor), Apartado Aereo 2306, APO New York 09895. Telephone: 56599.

Congo, Democratic Republic of the
See Zaire

Congo, People's Republic of the
Brazzaville (E), Avenue du 28 Aout 1940. Telephone: 31-06. The embassy will remain closed until further notice. The Federal Republic of Germany serves as protective power for the United States in the Republic of the Congo.

Costa Rica
San Jose (E), Avenida 3 and Calle 1, APO New York 09883. Telephone: 22-55-66.

Cyprus
Nicosia (E), Therissos Street and Dositheos Street, FPO New York 09530. Telephone 65151/5.

Czechoslovakia
Prague (E), Trziste 15-12548 Praha, Amembassy, Prague, c/o Amcongen, APO New York 09757. Telephone: 53 66 41/8.

Dahomey
See Benin

Denmark
Copenhagen (E), Dag Hammarskjolds Alle 24, APO New York 09170. Telephone: 12 31 44.

Dominican Republic
Santo Domingo (E), Corner of Calle Cesar Nicolas Pensen & Calle Leopoldo Navarra, APO New York 09899. Telephone: 682-2171.

Ecuador
Quito (E), 120 Avenida Patria. Telephone: 230-020.
Guayaquil (CG), Casilla X. Telephone: 511570.

Egypt (Arab Republic of)
Cairo (E), 5 Sharia Latin America, Box 10, FPO New York 09527. Telephone: 28211/9.
Alexandria (CG), 110 Avenue Horreya. Telephone: 25306, 25607, 28458.
Port Said (C), Apt. 4, 8 Sharia Aby El Feda Metarch El Baher. Telephone: 8000, 8586, 8622.

El Salvador
San Salvador (E), 1230, 25 Avenida Norte APO New York 09889. Telephone: 25-7100.

Equatorial Guinea
Malabo (E), Armengol Coll and Asturias Streets. The embassy will remain closed until further notice. The Spanish State serves as protective power for the United States in Republic of Equatorial Guinea.

Ethiopia
Addis Ababa (E), Entoto Street, P.O. Box 1014, APO New York 09319. Telephone: 110666.
Asmara (CG), 32 Franklin D. Roosevelt Street, P.O. Box 22, FPO New York 09545. Telephone: 110855.

Fiji
Suva (E), Ratu Sukuna House, (7th Floor), MacArthur Street, P.O. Box 218. Telephone: 25-304/6.

Finland
Helsinki (E), Itainen Puistotie 14A, APO New York 09664. Telephone: 171931.

France
Paris (E), 2 Avenue Gabriel 75382, Paris Cedex 08, APO New York 09777. Telephone: 296-1202, 261-8075.
Paris (UNESCO), 2 Avenue Gabriel. Telephone: 265-74-00.
Paris (USOECD), 19 rue de Franqueville. Telephone: 524-8200.
Bordeaux (CG), No. 4 rue Espirit-des Lois. Telephone: 56/52.65.95.
Lyon (CG), 7 Quai General Sarrail 69454, Lyon CEDEX 3. Telephone: 24-68-49.
Marseille (CG), No. 9 Rue Armeny 13006. Telephone: 33-78-33,37.
Nice (C), No. 3 Rue Dr. Barety. Telephone: 88-89-55.
Strasbourg (CG), 15 Avenue d'Alsace 67082, Strasbourg CEDEX or APO New York 09777. Telephone: (88) 35.31.04, 05, 06.

French West Indies
Martinique (C), 14 Rue Blenac, Boite Postale 561, Fort de France 97206. Telephone: 71.93.01, 71.93.03.

Gabon
Libreville (E), Blvd. de la Mer, Boite Postale 4000. Telephone: 72-20-03/4, 72-13-37, 72-03-48.

Gambia, The
Banjul (E), 16 Buckle Street, P.O. Box 596. Telephone: 526-7.

German Democratic Republic
Berlin (E), 108 Berlin, Neustaedtische Kirchstrasse 4-5. Telephone: 2202741.

Germany, Federal Republic of
Bonn (E), Deichmannsaue, 5300 Bonn 2, APO New York 09080. Telephone: (02221) 89 55.
Berlin (M), Clayallee 170, D-1000 Berlin 33 (Dahlem), APO New York 09742. Telephone: (030) 832 40 87, COM UNIT: Telephone: (030) 819-7561.
Bremen (CG), President-Kennedy-Platz 1, 2800 Bremen 1; Box 1, APO New York 09069. Telephone: (0421) 32 00 01.
Dusseldorf (CG), Cecilienallee 5, 4000 Duesseldorf 30 Box 515, APO New York 09080. Telephone: (0211) 49 00 81.
Frankfurt am Main (CG), Siemayerstrasse 21, 6000 Frankfurt, APO New York 09757. Telephone: (0611) 74 0071. After hours: Telephone: (0611) 74 50 04.
Hamburg (CG), Alsterufer 27/28, 2000 Hamburg 36, Box 2 APO New York 09069. Telephone: (040) 44 10 61.
Munich (CG), Koeniginstrase 5, 8000 Muenchen 22, APO New York 09108. Telephone: (089) 2 30 11.
Stuttgart (CG), Urbanstrasse 7, 7000 Stuttgart, APO New York 09154. Telephone: (0711) 21 02 21.

Ghana
Accra (E), Liberia & Kinbu Roads, P.O. Box 194. Telephone: 66811, Com Off: Telephone: 66125.

Greece
Athens (E), 91 Vasilissis Sophias Boulevard or APO New York 09253. Tele-

phone 712951 or 718401 (Area Code from U.S.: 01130-1).

Thessaloniki (CG), 59 Vasileos Constantinou Street, APO New York 09693. Telephone: 273-941

Guatemala

Guatemala (E), 7-01 Avenida de la Reforma, Zone 10, APO New York 09891. Telephone: 31-15-41.

Guinea

Conakry (E), 2d Boulevard and 9th Avenue, Boite Postale 603. Telephone: 415-20 through 24.

Guinea-Bissau

Bissau (E) Avenida Domingos Ramos, C.P. 297. Telephone: 28-16/7.

Guyana

Georgetown (E), 31 Main Street. Telephone: 62687, Ext. 26.

Haiti

Port-au-Prince (E), Harry Truman Boulevard. Telephone: 20200.

Honduras

Tegucigalpa (E), Avenido La Paz, APO New York 09887. Telephone: 22-3121/22/23/24/27.

Hong Kong

Hong Kong (CG), 26 Garden Road, FPO San Francisco 96659. Telephone: 239011.

Hungary

Budapest (E), Szabadsag Ter 12; American Embassy, APO New York 09757. Telephone: 329-375.

Iceland

Reykjavik (E), Laufasvegur 21, FPO New York 09571. Telephone: 24083.

India

New Delhi (E), Shanti Path, Chanakyapuri 21. Telephone: 690351.

Bombay (CG), Lincoln House, 78 Bhulabhai Desai Road. Telephone: 363611-363618.

Calcutta (CG), 5/1 Ho Chi Minh Sarani, Calcutta 700071. Telephone: 44-3611-44-3616.

Madras (CG), Mount Road-6. Telephone: 83041.

Indonesia

Jakarta (E), Medan Merdeka Selatan 5, APO San Francisco 96356. Telephone: 40001-9.

Medan (C), Djalan Imam Bondjol 13. Telephone: 22290.

Surabaya (C), Djalan Roya Drive, Sutomo 33. Telephone: Selatan 836, 837, Darmo 7545.

Iran

Tehran (E), 260 Takhte Jamshid Avenue, P.O. Box 50; or Box 2000, APO New York 09205. Telephone: 820091/9, 824-001, 820-091, 829-051.

Isfahan (C), Trade Center Building, Room 201-203, Corner Pahlavi & Chahar Bgh

Boulevards. Telephone: 32079-9.

Shiraz (C), Charkhabi Building, Bagh Eram Avenue (near Eram Garden) P.O. Box 500. Telephone: 32023-4.

Tabriz (C), Shahnaz Avenue, APO New York 09205. Telephone: 2101, 5487.

Iraq

Baghdad (USINT), Belgian Embassy, 52/5/35 Masbah-Opp. For. Ministry Club, P.O. Box 2447 Alwiyah, Baghdad, Iraq. Telephone: 96138/9. The embassy is closed. The Government of Belgium serves as protective power for the United States in Iraq. The Belgian Embassy in Baghdad includes an American interests Section staffed by American personnel.

Basra, The consulate at Basra will remain closed until further notice.

Ireland

Dublin (E), 42 Elgin Road, Ballsbridge. Telephone: Dublin 688777.

Israel

Tel Aviv (E), 71 Hayarkon Street. Telephone: 54338.

Italy

Rome (E), Via V. Veneto 119/A, 00187-Rome; APO New York 09794. Telephone: (06) 4674. USIS: Via Boncompagni 2, 00187-Rome.

Genoa (CG), Banca d'America e d'Italia Building, Piazza Portello 6; Box G, APO New York 09794. Telephone: (010) 282-741 through 282-745.

Milan (CG) Plazza Delia Republica 32, APO New York 09689. Telephone: (02) 652-841 through 652-845.

U.S. Information Service: Via Bigli 11/A. Telephone: 795051.

Naples (CG), Piazza della Republica 80122 Naples; Box 18, FPO New York 09521. Telephone: (081) 660966.

Palermo (CG), Via Vaccarini 1, 90143; APO New York 09794 (c/o AmEmbassy Rome-P). Telephone: 291532-35.

Florence (C), Lungamo Amerigo Vespucci 38, APO New York 09019. Telephone: (055) 298-276.

Trieste (C), Via Valdirivo 19 (Fourth Floor), APO New York 09293. Telephone: (040) 68728/29.

Turin (C), Via Alfieri 17, 10121 Torino Box T, APO New York 09794. Telephone: (011) 543-600, 543-610, 513-367.

Ivory Coast

Abidjan (E), 5, Rue Jesse Owens, Boite Postale 1712. Telephone: 32-46-30.

Jamaica

Kingston (E), Jamaica Mutual Life Center, 2 Oxford Road. Telephone: 929-4850.

Japan

Tokyo (E), 13-go, No. 14, Akasaka 1-

chome Minato-ku, APO San Francisco 96503. Telephone: 583-7141.

Naha, Okinawa (CG), No. 2129, Gusu-kuma, Urasoe City, APO San Francisco 96248. Telephone: 0988-77-8142, 0988-77-8627.

Osaka-Kobe (CG), APO San Francisco 96503.

Osaka Office: 9th Floor, Sankei Building, 27, Umedo-cho, Kita-Ku, Osaka (530). Telephone: (06) 341-2754/7.

Kobe Office: 10, Kano-cho 6-chome, Ikuta-ku, Kobe (650). Telephone: (078) 331-6865/8.

Fukuoka (C), 5-26 Ohori 2 chome, Chuo-ku, Fukuoka-shi 810, or Box 10, FPO Seattle 98766. Telephone: (092) 751-9331.

Sapporo (C), North 1 West 13, APO San Francisco 96503. Telephone: 221-5121/3.

Jerusalem
Jerusalem (CG), 2 offices-18 Agron Road. Telephone: 226312; Nablus Road. Telephone: 282231/272681 (both offices via Israel).

Jordan
Amman (E), Jebel Amman, P.O. Box 354. Telephone: 44371-6.

Kenya
Nairobi (E), Cotts House, Wabera Street, P.O. Box 30137. Telephone: 334141.

Korea
Seoul (E), Sejong-Ro, APO San Francisco 96301. Telephone: 72-2601 thru 72-2619.

Kuwait
Kuwait (E), P.O. Box 77 SAFAT. Telephone: 424156/8.

Laos
Vientiane (E), Rue Bartholonie, Boite Postale 114. Telephone: 3126, 3570. Box V, APO San Francisco 96346.

Lebanon
Beirut (E), Corniche at Rue Ain Mreisseh. Telephone: 361-800.

Lesotho
Maseru (E), P.O. Box MS 333. Telephone: 2666/3954.

Liberia
Monrovia (E), United Nations Drive, APO New York 09155. Telephone: 22991, 22992-3-4.

Libya
Tripoli (E), Shari Mohammad Thabit, P.O. Box 289. Telephone: 34021/6.

Luxembourg
Luxembourg (E), 22 Boulevard. Emmanuel Servais, APO New York 09132. Telephone: 40123-4-5-6-7.

Madagascar
Tananarive (E), 14 and 16 rue Rainitovo, Antsohavola, Boite Postale 620. Telephone: 212-57.

Malawi
Lilongwe (E), P.O. Box 30016. Telephone: 30396/30166.

Malaysia
Kuala Lumpur (E), A.I.A. Building. Jalan Ampang, P.O. Box No. 35. Telephone: 26321.

Mali
Bamako (E), Rue Testard and Rue Mohamed V. Telephone: 246-63/4, 248-34, 248-45.

Malta
Valletta (E), 2d floor, Development House, St. Anne Street, Floriana, Malta, FPO New York 09534. Telephone: 623653, 620424, 623216.

Mauritania
Nouakchott (E), Boite Postale 222. Telephone: 52660/52663.

Mauritius
Port Louis (E), Anglo-Mauritius House (6th floor) Intendance Street. Telephone: 2-3218/9.

Mexico
Mexico, D.F. (E), Paseo de la Reforma 305, Mexico 5, D.F. Telephone: 553-3333.

Guadalajara (CG), Jal: Progreso 175. Telephone: 25-29-98, 25-27-00.

Hermosillo (CG), Son.; Isssteson Building 3d Floor, Miguel Hidalgo Y Costilla No. 15. Telephone: 3-89-22/23/24/25.

Monterrey (CG), N.L., Avenido Constitucion 411 Poniente. Telephone: 4306 50/59.

Tijuana (CG), B.C., Topachula 96. Telephone: 386-1001.

Ciudad Juarez (CG), Chi., 2286 Avenue 16 de Septiembre. Telephone: 34048.

Matamoros (C), Tamps.; Avenue Primera No. 232. Telephone 2-52-50/1/2.

Mezatlan (C), Sin.; 6 Circunvalacion No. 6 (at Venustiana Carranza). Telephone: 1-26-85, 1-26-87.

Merida (C), Yuc.; Paseo Montejo 453. Apartado Postal 1301. Telephone: 2-70-11, 2-70-78.

Nuevo Laredo (C), Tamps.; Avenida Allende 3330, Col. Jardin. Telephone: 2-00-05.

Morocco
Rabat (E), Avenue de Marrakech, Box 99, FPO New York 09544. Telephone: 30361, 30362.

Casablanca (CG), 8 Boulevard Moulay Youssef or Box 80, FPO 09544. Telephone: 2-605-21/23, 260562, 278457.

Tangier (CG), Chemin des Amoureux. Telephone: (09) 359-04.

Mozambique
Maputo (E), 35 Rua Da Mesquita, 2d floor. Telephone: 26051, 2, 3.

Nepal

Kathmandu (E), Pani Pokhari. Telephone: 11199, 12718, 11603, 11604.

Netherlands

The Hague (E), 102 Longe Voorhout, APO New York 09159. Telephone: 62-49-11.

Amsterdam (CG), Museumplein 19, APO New York 09159. Telephone: 790321.

Rotterdam (CG), Vlasmarkt 1, APO New York 09159. Telephone: 11.75.60.

Netherlands Antilles

Curacao (CG), St. Anna Boulevard 19, P.O. Box 158 vice John B. Gorsirawea 1. Telephone: 13066.

New Zealand

Wellington (E), 29 Fitzherbert Terrace, Thorndon, P.O. Box 1190. Telephone: 722-068.

Auckland (CG), 5th Floor, Old Northern Building. Society Building, Queen and Wellesley Streets, or P.O. Box 7140 Wellesley St., P.O. Telephone: 375-102, 30-992.

Nicaragua

Managua (E), Km. 4-1/2 Carretera Sur., APO New York 09885. Telephone: 23061-8, 23881-7.

Niger

Niamey (E) (No street address) Boite Postale 201. Telephone: 72-26-61/62/63/64; 71-26-70.

Nigeria

Lagos (E), 1 King's College Road, P.O. Box 554. Telephone: 57320.

Enugu (C). The consulate at Enugu is closed. Direct inquiries to American Embassy, Lagos.

Ibadan (C), Barclay's Bank Building. P.M.B. 5221. Telephone: 24101 through 24103.

Kaduna (C), 5 Ahmadu Bello Way. Telephone: 23373-7.

Norway

Oslo (E), Drammensveien 18, Oslo 1, or APO New York 09085. Telephone: 56-68-80.

Oman

Muscat (E), P.O. Box 966. Telephone: 722021.

Pakistan

Islamabad (E), Diplomatic Enclave Ramna 4. Telephone: 26161-26179.

Karachi (CG), 8 Abdullah Haroon Road. Telephone: 515081.

Lahore (CG), 50 Zafar All Road, Gullberg 5. Telephone: 81081-5.

Peshawar (C), 11 Hospital Road. Telephone: 73061/73405.

Panama

Panama (E), Avenida Balboa Y Calle 38, Apartado 6959, R.P. 5. Telephone: Panama 25-3600.

Papua New Guinea

Port Moresby (E), Armit Street P.O. Box 3492. Telephone: 211455, 211594, 211654.

Paraguay

Asuncion (E), 1776 Mariscal Lopez Avenue; APO New York 09881. Telephone: 21041/9.

Peru

Lima (E), Corner Avenidas Inca Garcilaso de la Vega & Espana, P.O. Box 1995. Telephone: 286000.

Philippines

Manila (E), 1201 Roxas Boulevard, APO San Francisco 96528. Telephone: 598-011.

Asian Development Bank (Manila).

Cebu (C), 3d Floor, Philippine American Life Insurance Building, Jones Avenue, APO San Francisco 96528. Telephone: 7-95-10/24.

Poland

Warsaw (E), Aleje Ujazdowskie 29/31; AmEmbassy Warsaw, c/o AmConGen, APO New York 09757. Telephone: 283041-9.

Krakow (C), Ulica Stolarka 9, 31043 Krakow, or AmConsul Krakow, c/o Amcongen, APO New York 09757. Telephone: 57793, 59764.

Poznan (C) Ulica Chopina 4, or c/o Amcongen, APO New York 09757. Telephone: 595-86, 591-62.

Portugal

Lisbon (E), Avenida Duque de Loule No. 39, APO New York 09678. Telephone: 555141.

Oporto (C), Apartado No. 88, Rua Julio Dinis 826-30. Telephone: 6-3094, 6-3095, 6-3096.

Ponta Delgada, Sao Miguel, Azores (C), Avenida D. Henrique, APO New York. Telephone: 22216, 22217.

Qatar

Doha (E), Farig Bin Omran (opp. TV station), P.O. Box 2399. Telephone: 87701, 87702, 87703.

Romania

Bucharest (E), Strada Tudor Arghezi 7-9, or AmConGen (Buch), APO New York 09757. Telephone: 12-40-40.

Rwanda

Kigali (E), Boulevard de la Revelution, B.P. Telephone: 5601.

Saudi Arabia

Jidda (E), Palestine Road, Ruwais, APO New York 09697. Telephone: 53410, 54110, 52188, 52396, 62589. Commercial Office: Palestine Road (opposite Embassy), P.O. Box 149. Telephone: 51553.

Dhahran (CG), Between Aramco Headquarters and Dhahran Int'l Airport, P.O. Box 81, or APO New York 09616. Telephone: 43200, 43452, 43613.

Senegal
Dakar (E), Boite Postale 49, BIAO Building, Place de l' Independance. Telephone: 26344.

Seychelles
Victoria (E), Box 148, APO New York 09030. Telephone: 23921/2.

Sierra Leone
Freetown (E), Corner Walpole and Siaka Stevens Street. Telephone: 26481.

Singapore
Singapore (E), 30 Hill Street, FPO San Francisco 96699. Telephone: 30251.

Somalia
Mogadiscio (E), Corso Primo Luglio. Telephone: 2811.

South Africa
Pretoria (E), Thibault House, 225 Pretorius Street. Telephone: 48-4266.
Cape Town (CG), Broadway Industries Center, Heerengracht, Foreshore. Telephone: 021-471280.
Durban (CG), Durban Bay House, 29th Floor, 333 Smith Street, Durban 4001. Telephone: 324727/8/9.
Johannesburg (CG), 11th Floor, Kine Center, Commissioner and Kruis Street, P.O. Box 2155. Telephone: (011) 21-1684/7.

Spain
Madrid (E), Serrano 75, APO New York 09285. Telephone: 276 3400, 276 3600.
Barcelona (CG), Via Layetana 33, APO New York 09284. Telephone: 319-9550.
Seville (CG), Paseo de las Delicias No. 7, APO New York 09282. Telephone: 954-23-18-85.
Bilbao (C), Avenida de Ejercito, 11-3rd Floor, Deusto-Bilbao, 14; APO New York 09285. Telephone: 435-8300, 8308, 8309.

Sri Lanka
Colombo (E), 44 Galle Road, Colombo 3, P.O. Box 106. Telephone: 26211 through 26218.

Sudan
Khartoum (E), Gamhouria Avenue, P.O. Box 699. Telephone: 74611 and 74700.

Surinam
Paramaribo (E), Dr. Sophie Redmondstraat 13, P.O. Box 1821. Telephone: 73024, 75620.

Swaziland
Mbabane (E), Embassy House, P.O. Box 199, Allister Miller Street. Telephone: 2272-3-4.

Sweden
Stockholm (E), Strandvagen 101. Telephone: (08) 63.05.20.
Goteborg (C), Sodra Hamngaton 53. Telephone: (031) 80-38-60.

Switzerland
Bern (E), Jubilaeumstrasse 93, 3005 Bern. Telephone: (031) 430011.
Zurich (CG), Zolikerstrasse 141. Telephone: 55-25-66.
Geneva (BO), 80 Rue du Lausanne. Telephone: 32 70 20. (This office offers no commercial services.)
Geneva (U.S. Delegation to Multilateral Trade Negotiations) 1-3 Ave. de la Paix. Telephone: 32-09-70.
Geneva (U.S. Mission to the European Office of the UN and Other International Organizations), 80 Rue du Lausanne. Telephone: 32.70.20.

Syria
Damascus (E), Abu Rumaneh, Al Monsur Street, No. 2, P.O. Box 29. Telephone: 332315, 332814.
Aleppo (CG). The Consulate General in Aleppo will remain closed until further notice.

Tanzania
Dar es Salaam (E), National Bank of Commerce Building, City Drive, P.O. Box 9123. Telephone: 22775.
Zanzibar (C), 83A Tuzungumzeni Square, P.O. Box 4. Telephone: 2118, 2119.

Thailand
Bangkok (E), 95 Wireless Road, APO San Francisco 96346. Telephone 252-5040, 252-5171. Com. Off: "R" Floor, Shell Building, 140 Wireless Road. Telephone: 251-9260/2.
Chiang Mai (C), Vidhayanond Road, APO San Francisco 96272. Telephone: 235566-7.
Songkhla (C), 9 Sadao Road. Telephone: 311-589.
Udorn (C), 35/6 Supakitjanya Road, WBO 96237. Telephone: 221548.

Togo
Lome (E), Rue Pelletier Caventou & rue Vouban, Boite Postale 852. Telephone: 29-91.

Trinidad and Tobago
Port-of-Spain (E), 15, Queen's Park West, P.O. Box 752. Telephone: 62-26371.

Tunisia
Tunis (E), 144 Avenue de la Liberte. Telephone: 282.566.

Turkey
Ankara (E), 110 Ataturk Boulevard, APO New York 09254. Telephone: 26 54 70.
Instanbul (CG), 104-108 Mesrutiyet Caddesi, Tepebasi. Telephone: 43-62-00/09.
Izmir (CG), 386 Ataturk Caddesi, APO New York 09224. Telephone: 132135/7.
Adana (C), Ataturk Caddesi. Telephone: 14702/3, 14818.

Uganda
Kampala (E), P.O. Box 7007 Embassy House, 9-11 Parliament Avenue. Tele-

phone: 54451. The embassy will remain closed until further notice. The Federal Republic of Germany serves as protective power for the United States in Uganda.

Union of Soviet Socialist Republics
Moscow (E), Ulitsa Chaykovskogo 19/21/23, or APO New York 09862. Telephone: 252-00-11 to 252-00-19. Commercial Office: Ulitsa Chaykovskogo 15. Telephone: 255-48-48/255-46-60.
Leningrad (CG) UL, Petra Lavrova St. 15; Box L, APO New York 09664. Telephone: 272-4548.

United Arab Emirates
Abu Dhabi (E), Shaikh Khalid Building, Corniche Road, P.O. Box 4009. Telephone: 61534/35.
Dubai (BO), Al Futtaim Building, Creek Road, Deira, P.O. Box 5343. Telephone: 29003.

United Kingdom
London, England (E), 24/31 Grosvenor Square, W. 1A 1AE; or Box 40 FPO New York 09510. Telephone: (01) 499-9000.
Belfast, Northern Ireland (CG), Queen's House, 14 Queen Street, BT1 6EQ. Telephone: Belfast (0232) 28239.
Edinburgh, Scotland (CG), 3 Regent Terrace, EH 7 5BW. Telephone: 031-556 8315.

United States
New York (USUN), 799 United Nations Plaza, New York, NY 10017. Telephone: (212) 826-4524.
Washington, DC (USOAS), Department of State. Telephone: (202) 632-9376.

Upper Volta
Ouagadougou (E), Boite Postale 35. Telephone: 35442/4/6.

Uruguay
Montevideo (E), Calle Lauro Muller 1776, APO New York 09879. Telephone: 40-90-51, 40-91-26.

Venezuela
Caracas (E), Avenida Francisco de Miranda and Avenida Principal de la Floresta, APO New York 09893. Telephone: 284-7111.
Maracaibo (C), Edificio Matema, 1 Piso, Avenida 15 Calle 78, or APO New York 09893. Telephone: (061) 51-65-06/7.

Yemen (Aden)
Aden. The embassy will remain closed until further notice. The Government of Great Britain serves as protective power for the United States in the Yemen People's Republic.

Yemen Arab Republic
Sana (E), Box 33 FPO New York 09545.

Taiz (BO). The Embassy Branch Office in Taiz will remain closed until further notice.

Yugoslavia
Belgrade (E), Kneza Milosa 50. Telephone: 645655.
Zagreb (CG), Brace Kavorica 2. Telephone: 444-800.

Zaire
Kinshasa (E), 310 Avenue des Aviateurs, APO New York 09662. Telephone: 25881-2-3-4-5-6
Bukavu (C), Mobutu Avenue, Boite Postale 3037, APO New York 09662. Telephone: 2594.
Lubumbashi (C), 1029 Boulevard de L'Ueac, Boite Postale 1196, APO New York 09662. Telephone: 2324, 2325.

Zambia
Lusaka (E), P.O. Box 1617. Telephone: 50222.

Abbreviations

BO	Branch office (of embassy)
C	Consulate
COM. OFF.	Commercial Office
CG	Consulate General
E	Embassy
IAEA	International Atomic Energy Agency
ICAO	International Civil Aviation Organization
LO	Liaison Office
M	Mission
UNESCO	United Nations Educational, Scientific and Cultural Organization
UNIDO	United Nations Industrial Development Organization
USEC	United States Mission to European Communities
USINT	United States Interests Sections
USNATO	United States Mission to the North Atlantic Treaty Organization
USOAS	Permanent Mission of the United States of America to the Organization of American States
USOECD	United States Mission to the Organization for Economic Cooperation and Development
USUN	United States Mission to the United Nations

Foreign Diplomatic Offices in the United States

The chancery is the name designating the building that houses the major components of the embassy in which the ambassador works.

A foreign consulate or embassy in the United States is where commercial, economic, and cultural information about a country can be obtained. It is also the place where an American can generally obtain a visa if one is needed for a particular country.

The State Department desk officer working at the U.S. State Department provides input for policy decisions relating to a specific country. Persons interested in doing business with a foreign country should contact the State Department desk officer (listed below) for that particular country. It is this officer who can direct him to additional sources of information at, for example, the Department of Commerce or the Agency for International Aid.

All chancery addresses in this section are, of course, in Washington, DC; all telephone numbers given in this section are in the 202 area code, unless otherwise indicated. Street addresses for foreign consulates throughout the United States are listed in local telephone directories.

Afghanistan
Chancery: 2341 Wyoming Avenue, NW 20008; 234-3770.
State Department Desk Officer: 632-9552.
Albania
State Department Desk Officer: 632-1457.
Algeria
Chancery: 2118 Kalorama Road, NW 20008; 234-7246.
State Department Desk Officer: 632-0304.
Andorra
State Department Desk Officer: 632-2633.
Angola, Republic of
State Department Desk Officer: 632-0725.
Argentina
Chancery: 1600 New Hampshire Avenue, NW 20009; 387-0705.
State Department Desk Officer: 632-9166.
Consulates:
California: Los Angeles, San Francisco.

Source: "Foreign Consular Offices in the United States," "Diplomatic List," and U.S. Department of State information.

Florida: Miami.
Illinois: Chicago.
Louisiana: New Orleans.
Maryland: Baltimore.
New York: New York.
Puerto Rico: San Juan.
Texas: Houston.
Australia
Chancery: 1601 Massachusetts Avenue, NW 20036; 797-3000.
State Department Desk Officer: 632-9690.
Consulates:
California: San Francisco.
District of Columbia: Washington.
Hawaii: Honolulu.
Illinois: Chicago.
New York: New York.
Austria
Chancery: 2343 Massachusetts Avenue, NW 20008; 483-4474.
State Department Desk Officer: 632-2005.
Consulates:
California: Los Angeles, San Francisco.
District of Columbia: Washington.
Florida: Miami.
Georgia: Atlanta.
Hawaii: Honolulu.
Illinois: Chicago.
Louisiana: New Orleans.
Massachusetts: Boston.
Michigan: Detroit.
New York: New York.
Ohio: Cleveland.
Oregon: Portland.
Puerto Rico: San Juan.
Washington: Seattle.
Bahamas, The Commonwealth of the
Chancery: Suite 865, 600 New Hampshire Avenue, NW 20037; 338-3940.
State Department Desk Officer: 632-8451.
Consulates:
District of Columbia: Washington.
Florida: Miami.
Bahrain, State of
Chancery: 2600 Virginia Avenue, NW 20037; 965-4930.
State Department Desk Officer: 632-1334.
Consulate: New York: New York.
Bangladesh
Chancery: 3421 Massachusetts Avenue, NW 20007; 337-6644.
State Department Desk Officer: 632-0466.

Consulate: New York: New York.

Barbados
Chancery: 2144 Wyoming Avenue, N.W. 20008; 387-7373.
State Department Desk Officer: 632-8451.
Consulates:
California: Los Angeles.
District of Columbia: Washington.
Florida: West Palm Beach.
Georgia: Atlanta.
Illinois: Chicago.
Massachusetts: Boston.
Michigan: Detroit.
New York: New York.

Belgium
Chancery: 3330 Garfield Street, NW 20008; 333-6900.
State Department Desk Officer: 632-0498.
Consulates:
Alabama: Mobile.
Alaska: Anchorage.
Arizona: Phoenix.
California: Los Angeles, San Diego, San Francisco.
Canal Zone: Colón, Panama.
Colorado: Denver.
District of Columbia: Washington.
Florida: Miami, Tampa.
Georgia: Atlanta.
Hawaii: Honolulu.
Illinois: Chicago, Moline.
Indiana: Mishawaka.
Iowa: Des Moines.
Kentucky: Louisville.
Louisiana: New Orleans.
Maryland: Baltimore.
Massachusetts: Boston.
Michigan: Detroit.
Minnesota: Minneapolis.
Missouri: Kansas City, St. Louis.
New York: New York.
Ohio: Cleveland.
Oklahoma: Oklahoma City.
Oregon: Portland.
Pennsylvania: Philadelphia, Pittsburgh.
Puerto Rico: San Juan.
Texas: Dallas, Houston.
Utah: Morgan.
Virgin Islands: St. Thomas.
Virginia: Norfolk.
Washington: Seattle.
Wisconsin: Milwaukee.

Benin, Peoples Republic of (Dahomey)
Chancery: 2737 Cathedral Avenue, NW 20008; 232-6656.
State Department Desk Officer: 632-0842.
Consulate: New York: New York.

Bhutan
State Department Desk Officer: 632-0653.

Bolivia
Chancery: 3014 Massachusetts Avenue, N.W. 20008; 483-4410.
State Department Desk Officer: 632-3076.

Consulates:
Alabama: Mobile.
Arkansas: Little Rock.
California: Los Angeles, San Diego, San Francisco, San Leandro.
Connecticut: Hartford.
District of Columbia: Washington.
Florida: Miami, Orlando, Palm Beach, Tampa.
Georgia: Atlanta.
Hawaii: Honolulu.
Illinois: Chicago.
Iowa: West Des Moines.
Louisiana: New Orleans.
Maryland: Baltimore, Rockville.
Massachusetts: Boston.
Missouri: Kansas City, St. Louis.
New York: New York.
Ohio: Akron.
Oklahoma: Oklahoma City.
Pennsylvania: Philadelphia.
Puerto Rico: San Juan.
Texas: Dallas, Houston, San Antonio.
Utah: Logan.
Virginia: Richmond.
Washington: Seattle.

Botswana
Chancery: Suite 404, 4301 Connecticut Avenue, NW 20008; 244-4990.
State Department Desk Officer: 632-0916.
Consulate: California: Los Angeles.

Brazil
Chancery: 3006 Massachusetts Avenue, NW 20008; 797-0100.
State Department Desk Officer: 632-1245.
Consulates:
California: Los Angeles, San Francisco.
District of Columbia: Washington.
Florida: Miami.
Georgia: Atlanta, Savannah.
Illinois: Chicago.
Louisiana: New Orleans.
Massachusetts: New Bedford.
New York: New York.
Pacific Islands: Hong Kong.
Puerto Rico: San Juan.
Texas: Houston.
Virginia: Norfolk.

Brunei
State Department Desk Officer: 632-3276.

Bulgaria
Chancery: 2100 16th Street, NW 20009; 387-7969.
State Department Desk Officer: 632-1457.

Burma
Chancery: 2300 S Street, NW 20008; 332-9044.
State Department Desk Officer: 632-3276.
Consulate: New York: New York.

Burundi
Chancery: 2717 Connecticut Avenue, NW 20008; 387-4477.
State Department Desk Officer: 632-3138.

Consulate: Illinois: Chicago.
Cambodia (see Khmer Republic)
Cameroon
 Chancery: 2349 Massachusetts Avenue, NW 20008; 265-8790.
 State Department Desk Officer: 632-0996.
Canada
 Chancery: 1746 Massachusetts Avenue, NW 20036; 785-1400.
 State Department Desk Officer: 632-2170.
 Consulates:
  California: Los Angeles, San Francisco.
  District of Columbia: Washington.
  Georgia: Atlanta.
  Illinois: Chicago.
  Louisiana: New Orleans.
  Massachusetts: Boston.
  Michigan: Detroit.
  Minnesota: Minneapolis.
  New York: Buffalo, New York.
  Ohio: Cleveland.
  Pennsylvania: Philadelphia.
  Puerto Rico: San Juan.
  Texas: Dallas.
  Washington: Seattle.
Cape Verde, Republic of
 Chancery: 1120 Connecticut Avenue, NW 20036; 659-3148.
 State Department Desk Officer: 632-8436.
Central African Empire
 Chancery: 1618 22d Street NW 20008; 265-5637.
 State Department Desk Officer: 632-3138.
 Consulate: Missouri: St. Louis.
Ceylon (see Sri Lanka)
Chad, Republic of
 Chancery: 2600 Virginia Avenue, NW 20037; 331-7697.
 State Department Desk Officer: 632-3066.
Chile
 Chancery: 1732 Massachusetts Avenue, NW 20036; 785-1746.
 State Department Desk Officer: 632-2575.
 Consulates:
  Arizona: Phoenix.
  California: Los Angeles, San Diego, San Francisco, Santa Clara.
  Colorado: Denver.
  District of Columbia: Washington.
  Florida: Miami, Miami Beach.
  Hawaii: Honolulu.
  Illinois: Chicago.
  Louisiana: New Orleans.
  Massachusetts: Boston.
  Michigan: Detroit.
  New York: New York.
  Puerto Rico: San Juan.
  Texas: Dallas, Galveston, Houston.
  Utah: Salt Lake City.
  Washington: Seattle.
China, People's Republic of
 Embassy: 2300 Connecticut Avenue, NW 20008; 797-9000 (as of March 1, 1979).

State Department Desk Officer: 632-1004.
China, Republic of (Taiwan)
 Chancery: 2311 Massachusetts Avenue, NW 20008; 667-9000.
 State Department Desk Officer: 632-7710.
 Consulates:
  American Samoa: Pago Pago.
  California: Calexico, Los Angeles, San Francisco.
  District of Columbia: Washington.
  Georgia: Atlanta.
  Guam: Agaña.
  Hawaii: Honolulu.
  Illinois: Chicago.
  Massachusetts: Boston.
  Michigan: Detroit.
  Missouri: Kansas City.
  New York: New York.
  Oregon: Portland.
  Texas: Houston.
  Washington: Seattle.
Colombia
 Chancery: 2118 Leroy Place, NW 20008; 387-5828.
 State Department Desk Officer: 632-3023.
 Consulates:
  California: Los Angeles, San Francisco.
  Connecticut: Stamford.
  District of Columbia: Washington.
  Florida: Coral Gables, Miami, Tampa.
  Georgia: Atlanta, Savannah.
  Illinois: Chicago.
  Louisiana: New Orleans.
  Maryland: Baltimore.
  Massachusetts: Boston.
  Michigan: Detroit.
  Minnesota: Minneapolis, Rochester.
  Missouri: Kansas City.
  New York: New York, North Babylon.
  Ohio: Cleveland.
  Pennsylvania: Philadelphia.
  Puerto Rico: Mayagüez, San Juan.
  Texas: Houston.
  West Virginia: Wheeling.
Comores, The
 Chancery: The Comores interests in the United States are represented by Tanzania, 2010 Massachusetts Avenue, NW 20036; 872-1005.
 State Department Desk Officer: 632-3040.
Congo (Brazzaville)
 Chancery: Congo (Brazzaville) interests in the United States are represented by Germany (West), 4645 Reservoir Road, NW 20007; 331-3000.
 State Department Desk Officer: 632-2216.
Congo (Kinshasa) (see Zaire)
Costa Rica
 Chancery: 2112 S Street, NW 20008; 234-2945.
 State Department Desk Officer: 632-5221.
 Consulates:
  Alabama: Mobile.

California: Atherton, Concord, Los Angeles, Riverside, San Diego, San Fernando, San Francisco, San Jose, Stanford.
Canal Zone: Cristóbal.
Colorado: Denver.
Connecticut: Hartford.
District of Columbia: Washington.
Florida: Coral Gables, Miami, Tampa.
Georgia: Atlanta.
Hawaii: Honolulu.
Illinois: Chicago.
Kentucky: Lexington.
Louisiana: New Orleans.
Maryland: Baltimore, Cecilton.
Massachusetts: Boston, Springfield.
Michigan: Detroit, Saginaw.
Minnesota: St. Paul.
Missouri: Kansas City, St. Louis.
Nevada: Las Vegas.
New Mexico: Santa Fe.
New York: Buffalo, New York.
Ohio: Columbus.
Oregon: Portland.
Pennsylvania: Philadelphia, Pittsburgh, State College.
Puerto Rico: Ponce, San Juan.
Tennessee: Nashville.
Texas: Dallas, Fort Worth, Houston, San Antonio.
Utah: Salt Lake City.
Virginia: Richmond.
Washington: Seattle.
Wisconsin: Milwaukee.
Wyoming: Cheyenne.

Cuba
Chancery: Cuba's interests in the United States are represented by Czechoslovakia, 3900 Linnean Avenue, NW 20008; 363-6315.
State Department Desk Officer: 632-1476.

Cyprus
Chancery: 2211 R Street, NW 20008; 462-5772.
State Department Desk Officer: 632-1429.
Consulates:
California: Piedmont.
District of Columbia: Washington.
Massachusetts: Boston.
Missouri: St. Louis.
New York: New York.

Czechoslovakia
Chancery: 3900 Linnean Avenue, NW 20008; 363-6315.
State Department Desk Officer: 632-1457.

Dahomey (see Benin)

Denmark
Chancery: 3200 Whitehaven Street, NW 20008; 234-4300.
State Department Desk Officer: 632-1194.
Consulates:
Alabama: Mobile.
Alaska: Anchorage.

Arizona: Scottsdale.
California: Los Angeles, San Diego, San Francisco.
Colorado: Denver.
District of Columbia: Washington.
Florida: Jacksonville, Miami, Tampa.
Georgia: Atlanta.
Hawaii: Honolulu.
Illinois: Chicago.
Iowa: Des Moines.
Louisiana: New Orleans.
Maryland: Baltimore.
Massachusetts: Boston.
Michigan: Detroit.
Minnesota: Minneapolis.
Missouri: Kansas City, St. Louis.
Nebraska: Omaha.
New York: New York.
Ohio: Cleveland.
Oregon: Portland.
Pennsylvania: Philadelphia.
Puerto Rico: San Juan.
Rhode Island: Providence.
South Carolina: Charleston.
Texas: Dallas, Houston.
Utah: Salt Lake City.
Virgin Islands: Charlotte Amalie, St. Thomas; Christiansted, St. Croix.
Virginia: Norfolk.
Washington: Seattle.
Wisconsin: Milwaukee.

Dominican Republic
Chancery: 1715 22d Street, NW 20008; 332-6280.
State Department Desk Officer: 632-2130.
Consulates:
Alabama: Mobile.
California: Culver City, Hollywood, Los Angeles, Pasadena, San Diego, San Francisco, Santa Monica.
Connecticut: Bridgeport.
District of Columbia: Washington.
Florida: Coral Gables, Fort Pierce, Gainesville, Hollywood, Jacksonville, Miami, Miami Beach, Panama City, Sarasota, South Miami, Tallahassee, West Palm Beach.
Georgia: Atlanta, Savannah.
Hawaii: Honolulu.
Illinois: Chicago, Wheaton.
Indiana: East Chicago, Fort Wayne.
Louisiana: Baton Rouge, Lake Charles, New Orleans.
Maryland: Annapolis, Baltimore.
Massachusetts: Boston.
Michigan: Detroit.
Minnesota: Rochester.
Missouri: St. Louis.
Montana: Great Falls.
New Mexico: Albuquerque.
New York: New York, New Rochelle.
North Carolina: Charlotte.
Ohio: Cincinnati, Cleveland, Columbus.

Oregon: Portland.
Pennsylvania: Philadelphia, Wyndmoor.
Puerto Rico: Arecibo, Bayamon, Guanica, Enseneda, Guayama, Humacao, Juana Diaz, Mavaguez, Ponce, San Juan.
Rhode Island: Providence.
Tennessee: Memphis, Nashville.
Texas: Corpus Christi, Dallas, **Fort** Worth, Galveston, Houston.
Virgin Islands: Charlotte Amalie, St. Thomas.
Virginia: Richmond.
Washington: Seattle.
Wisconsin: Milwaukee.

Ecuador
Chancery: 2535 15th Street, NW 20009; 234-7200.
State Department Desk Officer: 632-5864.
Consulates:
California: Los Angeles, San Diego, San Francisco.
District of Columbia: Washington.
Florida: Miami, Tampa.
Illinois: Chicago.
Louisiana: New Orleans.
Maryland: Baltimore.
Massachusetts: Boston.
Michigan: Detroit.
New York: Buffalo.
Ohio: Cincinnati.
Pennsylvania: Philadelphia.
Puerto Rico: San Juan.
South Carolina: Lake City.
Texas: Houston.
Virginia: Norfolk.
Washington: Seattle.

Egypt, Arab Republic of
Chancery: 2310 Decatur Place, NW 20008; 232-5400.
State Department Desk Officer: 632-1169.
Consulates:
District of Columbia: Washington.
California: San Francisco.
New York: New York.

El Salvador
Chancery: 2308 California Street, NW 20008; 265-3480.
State Department Desk Officer: 632-8148.
Consulates:
Alabama: Mobile.
Arizona: Phoenix.
California: Burlingame, Hollywood, Los Angeles, Oakland, San Diego, San Francisco.
Colorado: Denver.
District of Columbia: Washington.
Florida: Fort Lauderdale, Hollywood, Miami, St. Petersburg, Tampa.
Georgia: Atlanta.
Hawaii: Honolulu.
Illinois: Chicago.
Kentucky: Louisville.

Louisiana: New Orleans.
Maryland: Baltimore.
Michigan: Detroit.
Minnesota: Minneapolis.
Missouri: St. Louis.
Nevada: Reno.
New York: New York.
Oregon: Portland.
Pennsylvania: Philadelphia.
Puerto Rico: Bayamon, San Juan.
Texas: Dallas, Houston, Laredo, Pasadena, San Antonio.
Virgin Islands: Charlotte Amalie.
Virginia: Richmond.
Washington: Seattle.
Wisconsin: Madison.

Equatorial Guinea
Chancery: Equatorial Guinea's interests in the United States are represented by Cameroon, 2349 Massachusetts Avenue, NW 20008; 265-8790.
State Department Desk Officer: 632-0996.

Estonia
Consulate General's Office: 9 Rockefeller Plaza, New York, NY 10020; (212) 247-1450.
State Department Desk Officer: 632-1739.
Consulates:
California: Los Angeles.
New York: New York.

Ethiopia
Chancery: 2134 Kalorama Road 20008; 234-2281.
State Department Desk Officer: 632-3355.
Consulate: California: San Francisco.

Fiji
Chancery: Suite 520, 1629 K Street, NW 20006; 296-3928.
State Department Desk Officer: 632-9690.
Consulate: New York: New York.

Finland
Chancery: 1900 24th Street, NW 20008; 462-0556.
State Department Desk Officer: 632-1194.
Consulates:
Alabama: Mobile.
Alaska: Anchorage.
Arizona: Phoenix.
California: Los Angeles, San Diego, San Francisco.
Colorado: Denver.
Florida: Jacksonville, Lake Worth, Tampa.
Hawaii: Honolulu.
Illinois: Chicago.
Louisiana: New Orleans.
Maryland: Baltimore.
Massachusetts: Boston, Fitchburg.
Michigan: Detroit, Hancock, Ishpeming.
Minnesota: Duluth, Minneapolis.
Missouri: Kansas City.
New York: New York.

North Carolina: Wilmington.
Ohio: Ashtabula, Cleveland.
Oregon: Astoria, Portland.
Puerto Rico: San Juan.
Texas: Dallas, Houston.
Utah: Salt Lake City.
Virgin Islands: St. Thomas.
Virginia: Alexandria, Newport News.
Washington: Seattle.

France
Chancery: 2535 Belmont Road, NW 20008; 234-0990.
State Department Desk Officer: 632-0751.
Consulates:
Alabama: Birmingham, Mobile, Montgomery.
Alaska: Anchorage, Juneau.
American Samoa: Pago Pago.
Arizona: Phoenix.
Arkansas: Little Rock.
California: Los Angeles, Sacramento, San Diego, San Francisco.
Colorado: Denver.
Connecticut: Hartford.
Delaware: Dover.
District of Columbia: Washington.
Florida: Jacksonville, Miami, Tampa.
Georgia: Atlanta, Savannah.
Hawaii: Honolulu.
Illinois: Chicago.
Indiana: Indianapolis.
Iowa: Des Moines.
Kentucky: Louisville.
Louisiana: Lafayette, New Orleans, Shreveport.
Maine: Portland.
Maryland: Baltimore.
Massachusetts: Boston.
Michigan: Detroit.
Minnesota: Minneapolis.
Missouri: Kansas City, St. Louis.
Montana: Missoula.
Nebraska: Omaha.
Nevada: Las Vegas, Reno.
New Mexico: Albuquerque.
New York: Albany, Buffalo, New York, Rochester.
North Dakota: Bismarck.
Ohio: Cincinnati, Cleveland, Columbus.
Oklahoma: Oklahoma City, Tulsa.
Oregon: Portland.
Pennsylvania: Bethlehem, Philadelphia.
Puerto Rico: Mayagüez, Ponce, San Juan.
South Carolina: Charleston.
Tennessee: Nashville.
Texas: Amarillo, Austin, Dallas, Houston, Laredo, San Antonio.
Utah: Salt Lake City.
Virgin Islands: Charlotte Amalie.
Virginia: Norfolk.
Washington: Seattle.
West Virginia: Wheeling.

Wisconsin: Milwaukee.
Wyoming: Rock Springs.

Gabon, Republic of
Chancery: 2034 20th Street, NW 20009; 797-1000.
State Department Desk Officer: 632-0996.
Consulate: New York: New York.

Gambia, The Republic of
State Department Desk Officer: 632-2865.
Consulate: New York: Stanfordville.

German Democratic Republic (East)
Chancery: 1717 Massachusetts Avenue, NW 20036; 232-3134.
State Department Desk Officer: 632-2721.

Germany, Federal Republic of (West)
Chancery: 4645 Reservoir Road, NW 20007; 331-3000.
State Department Desk Officer: 632-2155.
Consulates:
Alaska: Anchorage.
Arizona: Phoenix.
California: Los Angeles, San Diego, San Francisco.
Canal Zone: Colon, Panama.
Caribbean Islands: Kingston, Jamaica.
Colorado: Denver.
District of Columbia: Washington.
Florida: Jacksonville, Miami.
Georgia: Atlanta, Savannah.
Hawaii: Honolulu.
Illinois: Chicago.
Kansas: Kansas City.
Louisiana: New Orleans.
Massachusetts: Boston.
Michigan: Detroit.
Minnesota: Minneapolis.
New Mexico: Santa Fe.
New York: Buffalo, New York.
Ohio: Cincinnati, Cleveland.
Oklahoma: Oklahoma City.
Oregon: Portland.
Pacific Islands: Manila, Philippines.
Pennsylvania: Philadelphia, Pittsburgh.
Puerto Rico: San Juan.
Tennessee: Memphis.
Texas: Dallas, Houston.
Utah: Salt Lake City.
Virginia: Norfolk.
Washington: Seattle, Spokane.

Ghana
Chancery: 2460 16th Street, NW 20009; 462-0761.
State Department Desk Officer: 632-8436.
Consulate: New York: New York.

Great Britain
Chancery: 3100 Massachusetts Avenue, NW 20008; 462-1340.
State Department Desk Officer: 632-2622.
Consulates:
California: Los Angeles, San Francisco.
District of Columbia: Washington.
Georgia: Atlanta.
Illinois: Chicago.

Louisiana: New Orleans.
Maryland: Baltimore.
Massachusetts: Boston.
Michigan: Detroit.
Missouri: Kansas City, St. Louis.
New York: New York.
Ohio: Cleveland.
Oregon: Portland.
Pacific Islands: Nuku' alofa, Tonga.
Pennsylvania: Philadelphia.
Puerto Rico: San Juan.
Texas: Dallas, Houston.
Virgin Islands: St. Thomas.
Virginia: Norfolk.
Washington: Seattle.

Greece
Chancery: 2221 Massachusetts Avenue, NW 20008; 667-3168.
State Department Desk Officer: 632-1563.
Consulates:
California: San Francisco.
Canal Zone: Colon, Panama.
District of Columbia: Washington.
Illinois: Chicago.
Louisiana: New Orleans.
Massachusetts: Boston.
New York: New York.

Grenada
Chancery: 927 15th Street, NW 20005; ·347-3198.
State Department Desk Officer: 632-8451.

Guatemala
Chancery: 2220 R Street, NW 20008; 332-2865.
State Department Desk Officer: 632-0467.

Consulates:
Alabama: Mobile.
California: Los Angeles, San Diego, San Francisco, San Mateo.
Colorado: Denver.
Florida: Jacksonville, Miami, Orlando, Pensacola.
Georgia: Atlanta.
Hawaii: Honolulu.
Illinois: Chicago.
Louisiana: New Orleans.
Maryland: Baltimore.
Massachusetts: Boston.
Michigan: Detroit.
Minnesota: Minneapolis.
Missouri: St. Louis.
New York: New York.
Pennsylvania: Philadelphia, Pittsburgh.
Puerto Rico: San Juan.
Rhode Island: Providence.
Tennessee: Memphis.
Texas: Abilene, Brownsville, Corpus Christi, Dallas, Fort Worth, Galveston, Houston, Laredo, San Antonio, San Juan.
Washington: Seattle.

Guinea
Chancery: 2112 Leroy Place, NW 20008; 483-9420.
State Department Desk Officer: 632-0842.

Guinea-Bissau
Chancery: % Permanent Mission of Guinea-Bissau to the United Nations, Suite 604, 211 E. 43d Street, New York, NY 10017; (212) 661-3977.
State Department Desk Officer: 632-8436.

Guyana
Chancery: 2490 Tracy Place, NW 20008; 265-6900.
State Department Desk Officer: 632-3449.
Consulates:
California: Los Angeles.
Indiana: East Chicago.
New York: New York.
Texas: Waco.

Haiti
Chancery: 4400 17th Street, NW 20011; 723-7000.
State Department Desk Officer: 632-2130.
Consulates:
Alabama: Mobile.
California: San Francisco.
Colorado: Denver.
Florida: Miami.
Illinois: Chicago.
Indiana: Evansville.
Louisiana: New Orleans.
Massachusetts: Boston.
Michigan: Detroit.
New York: New York.
Ohio: Cleveland.
Pennsylvania: Easton, Philadelphia.
Puerto Rico: San Juan.
Texas: Houston.
Virgin Islands: Charlotte Amalie.
Virginia: Hampton.

Honduras
Chancery: Suite 408, 4301 Connecticut Avenue NW 20008; 966-7700.
State Department Desk Officer: 632-0552.
Consulates:
Alabama: Birmingham, Mobile.
Arizona: Tucson.
California: Burlingame, La Habra, Los Angeles, Oakland, San Francisco, San Diego.
Canal Zone: Balboá, Cristóbal.
Colorado: Denver.
District of Columbia: Washington.
Florida: Coral Gables, Gainesville, Miami, Tampa.
Georgia: Atlanta.
Hawaii: Honolulu.
Illinois: Chicago.
Louisiana: Metairie, New Orleans.
Maryland: Baltimore.
Massachusetts: Boston.
Michigan: Detroit.
Missouri: St. Louis.

Nevada: Las Vegas.
New York: New York.
Ohio: Cincinnati, Cleveland.
Oregon: Portland.
Pennsylvania: Philadelphia, Pittsburgh.
Puerto Rico: Cayey, Ponce, San Juan.
Rhode Island: Providence.
Texas: Brownsville, Houston, San Antonio.
Washington: Seattle.

Hungary
Chancery: 3910 Shoemaker Street, NW 20008; 362-6730.
State Department Desk Officer: 632-1739.
Consulates:
District of Columbia: Washington.
New York: New York.

Iceland
Chancery: 2022 Connecticut Avenue, NW 20008; 265-6653.
State Department Desk Officer: 632-1774.
Consulates:
California: Los Angeles, San Francisco.
Colorado: Boulder.
Florida: Boca Raton.
Georgia: Atlanta.
Illinois: Chicago.
Massachusetts: Boston.
Michigan: Detroit.
Minnesota: Minneapolis.
New York: New York.
Oregon: Portland.
Pennsylvania: Philadelphia.
Texas: Dallas, Houston.
Virginia: Norfolk.
Washington: Seattle.

India
Chancery: 2107 Massachusetts Avenue, NW 20008; 265-5050.
State Department Desk Officer: 632-1289.
Consulates:
California: San Francisco.
District of Columbia: Washington.
New York: New York.
Ohio: Cleveland.

Indonesia
Chancery: 2020 Massachusetts Avenue, NW 20036; 293-1745.
State Department Desk Officer: 632-3276.
Consulates:
California: San Francisco
Hawaii: Honolulu.
New York: New York.

Iran
Chancery: 3005 Massachusetts Avenue, NW 20008; 797-6500.
State Department Desk Officer: 632-0488.
Consulates:
California: San Francisco.
District of Columbia: Washington.
Illinois: Chicago.
New York: New York.
Texas: Houston.

Iraq
Chancery: Iraq's interests in the United States are represented by India, 2107 Massachusetts Avenue, NW 20008; 265-5050. An Iraqi Interests Section is located at 1801 P Street, NW 20036; 483-7500.
State Department Desk Officer: 632-0695.

Ireland
Chancery: 2234 Massachusetts Avenue, NW 20008; 483-7639.
State Department Desk Officer: 632-1194.
Consulates:
California: San Francisco.
Illinois: Chicago.
Massachusetts: Boston.
Missouri: Kansas City.
New York: New York.

Israel
Chancery: 1621 22d Street, NW 20008; 483-4100.
State Department Desk Officer: 632-2647.
Consulates:
California: Los Angeles, San Francisco.
District of Columbia: Washington.
Georgia: Atlanta.
Illinois: Chicago.
Massachusetts: Boston.
New York: New York.
Pennsylvania: Philadelphia.
Texas: Houston.

Italy
Chancery: 1601 Fuller Street, NW 20009; 234-1935.
State Department Desk Officer: 632-8210.
Consulates:
Alabama: Mobile.
Alaska: Anchorage.
Arizona: Phoenix.
California: Bakersfield, Berkeley, Los Angeles, Monterey, Sacramento, San Diego, San Francisco, San Jose, Santa Barbara, Stockton.
Colorado: Denver.
Connecticut: Hartford.
Florida: Jacksonville, Miami, Tampa.
Georgia: Atlanta.
Hawaii: Honolulu.
Illinois: Chicago.
Indiana: Indianapolis.
Louisiana: New Orleans.
Maine: Portland.
Maryland: Baltimore.
Massachusetts: Boston, Springfield, Worcester.
Michigan: Detroit.
Missouri: Kansas City, St. Louis.
Nevada: Reno.
New Jersey: Newark, Trenton.
New Mexico: Albuquerque.
New York: Albany, Buffalo, New York, Rochester.
Ohio: Cincinnati, Cleveland.

Oregon: Portland.
Pennsylvania: Philadelphia, Pittsburgh.
Puerto Rico: San Juan.
Texas: Dallas, Galveston, Houston.
Utah: Salt Lake City.
Virginia: Norfolk.
Washington: Seattle.

Ivory Coast
Chancery: 2424 Massachusetts Avenue, NW 20008; 483-2400.
State Department Desk Officer: 632-0842.
Consulates:
California: Los Angeles, San Francisco.
Michigan: Detroit.
Missouri: St. Louis.
Oregon: Portland.

Jamaica
Chancery: 1666 Connecticut Avenue, NW 20009; 387-1010.
State Department Desk Officer: 632-2620.
Consulates:
California: Los Angeles, Sacramento.
District of Columbia: Washington.
Florida: Miami.
Illinois: Chicago.
New York: New York.

Japan
Chancery: 2520 Massachusetts Avenue, NW 20008; 234-2266.
State Department Desk Officer: 632-3152.
Consulates:
Alabama: Mobile.
Alaska: Anchorage.
American Samoa: Pago Pago.
California: Los Angeles, San Diego, San Francisco.
Colorado: Denver.
Florida: Miami.
Georgia: Atlanta.
Guam: Agaña.
Hawaii: Honolulu.
Illinois: Chicago.
Louisiana: New Orleans.
Massachusetts: Boston.
Michigan: Detroit.
Minnesota: Minneapolis.
Missouri: Kansas City, St. Louis.
New York: New York.
Ohio: Cleveland.
Oregon: Portland.
Pennsylvania: Philadelphia.
Puerto Rico: San Juan.
Texas: Houston.
Washington: Seattle.

Jordan
Chancery: 2319 Wyoming Avenue, NW 20008; 265-1606.
State Department Desk Officer: 632-0791.
Consulates:
Arizona: Scottsdale.
District of Columbia: Washington.

Florida: Palm Beach.
Texas: Houston.

Kenya
Chancery: 2249 R Street, NW 20009; 387-6101.
State Department Desk Officer: 632-0857.
Consulates:
California: Los Angeles.
New York: New York.

Khmer Republic (Cambodia)
State Department Desk Officer: 632-3132.

Korea, North and South
State Department Desk Officer: 632-2110.

Korea, Republic of
Chancery: 2320 Massachusetts Avenue, NW 20008; 483-7383.
State Department Desk Officer: 632-2110.
Consulates:
Alabama: Mobile.
Alaska: Anchorage.
Arizona: Phoenix.
California: La Jolla, Los Angeles, San Francisco.
Colorado: Denver.
District of Columbia: Washington.
Florida: Miami, Tampa.
Georgia: Atlanta.
Guam: Agaña.
Hawaii: Honolulu.
Illinois: Chicago.
Louisiana: New Orleans.
Massachusetts: Boston.
Michigan: Detroit.
Minnesota: Minneapolis.
Missouri: St. Louis.
New York: New York.
Ohio: Cleveland.
Oklahoma: Oklahoma City.
Oregon: Portland.
Pennsylvania: Philadelphia.
Puerto Rico: San Juan.
Texas: Dallas, Houston, San Antonio.

Kuwait
Chancery: 2940 Tilden Street, NW 20008; 966-0702.
State Department Desk Officer: 632-1794.
Consulate: New York: New York.

Laos
Chancery: 2222 S Street, NW 20008; 332-6416.
State Department Desk Officer: 632-3132.

Latvia
Chancery: 4325 17th Street, NW 20011; 726-8213.
State Department Desk Officer: 632-1739.
Consulates:
California: Los Angeles.
District of Columbia: Washington.

Lebanon
Chancery: 2560 28th Street, NW 20008; 332-0300.
State Department Desk Officer: 632-1018.
Consulates:

California: Los Angeles.
Illinois: Chicago.
Michigan: Detroit.
New Jersey: Orange.
New York: New York.
North Carolina: Goldsboro.
Oregon: Portland.
Puerto Rico: San Juan.
Texas: Dallas, Houston.

Lesotho
Chancery: Suite 300, Caravel Building, 1601 Connecticut Avenue, NW 20009; 462-4190.
State Department Desk Officer: 632-0916.
Consulates:
California: San Francisco.
Colorado: Denver.
Missouri: St. Louis.
Pennsylvania: Philadelphia.
Texas: Houston.

Liberia
Chancery: 5201 16th Street, NW 20011; 723-0437.
State Department Desk Officer: 632-8354.
Consulates:
California: Los Angeles.
District of Columbia: Washington.
Illinois: Chicago.
Louisiana: New Orleans.
Michigan: Detroit.
New York: New York.
Pennsylvania: Philadelphia.
Texas: Houston, Port Arthur.

Libya
Chancery: 1118 22d Street, NW 20037; 452-1290.
State Department Desk Officer: 632-9373.

Liechtenstein
Chancery: Liechtenstein's interests in the United States are represented by Switzerland, 2900 Cathedral Avenue, NW 20008; 462-1811.
State Department Desk Officer: 632-2005.

Lithuania
Chancery: 2622 16th Street, NW 20009; 234-5860.
State Department Desk Officer: 632-1739.
Consulates:
California: Los Angeles.
Illinois: Chicago.
New York: New York.

Luxembourg
Chancery: 2200 Massachusetts Avenue, NW 20008; 265-4171.
State Department Desk Officer: 632-0498.
Consulates:
California: Los Angeles.
Connecticut: New Haven.
Illinois: Chicago.
Missouri: Kansas City.
New York: New York.
Pennsylvania: Pittsburgh.
Texas: Fort Worth.

Madagascar, Democratic Republic of
Chancery: 2374 Massachusetts Avenue, NW 20008; 265-5525.
State Department Desk Officer: 632-3040.
Consulates:
California: San Francisco.
Illinois: Chicago.
New York: New York.

Malawi
Chancery: 1400 20th Street, NW 20036; 296-5530.
State Department Desk Officer: 632-8851.
Consulates:
California: Los Angeles, San Francisco.
District of Columbia: Washington.
Texas: Houston.

Malaysia
Chancery: 2401 Massachusetts Avenue, NW 20008; 234-7600.
State Department Desk Officer: 632-3276.
Consulates:
California: Los Angeles, San Francisco.
District of Columbia: Washington.
Hawaii: Honolulu.
Oregon: Portland.

Maldive, Republic of
State Department Desk Officer: 632-2351.

Mali
Chancery: 2130 R Street, NW 20008; 332-2249.
State Department Desk Officer: 632-2865.

Malta
Chancery: 2017 Connecticut Avenue, NW 20008; 462-3611.
State Department Desk Officer: 632-1726.
Consulates:
California: Los Angeles, San Francisco.
Michigan: Detroit.
Minnesota: St. Paul.
New York: New York.

Mauritania
Chancery: 2129 Leroy Place, NW 20008; 232-5700.
State Department Desk Officer: 632-2865.

Mauritius
Chancery: Suite 134, 4301 Connecticut Avenue, NW 20008; 244-1491.
State Department Desk Officer: 632-8851.

Mexico
Chancery: 2829 16th Street, NW 20009; 234-6000.
State Department Desk Officer: 632-9364.
Consulates:
Alabama: Mobile.
Arizona: Douglas, Nogales, Phoenix, Tucson.
California: Calexico, Fresno, Los Angeles, Sacramento, San Bernardino, San Diego, San Francisco, San Jose.
Colorado: Denver.
District of Columbia: Washington.
Florida: Miami, Tampa.

Georgia: Atlanta, Columbus.
Illinois: Chicago.
Louisiana: New Orleans.
Massachusetts: Boston.
Michigan: Detroit.
Minnesota: Rochester.
Missouri: Kansas City, St. Louis.
Nevada: Reno.
New Jersey: Newark.
New Mexico: Albuquerque.
New York: Buffalo, New York.
Ohio: Cincinnati, Cleveland.
Oklahoma: Oklahoma City.
Oregon: Portland.
Pennsylvania: Philadelphia, Pittsburgh.
Puerto Rico: San Juan.
Tennessee: Memphis, Nashville.
Texas: Austin, Brownsville, Corpus Christi, Dallas, Del Rio, Eagle Pass, El Paso, Fort Worth, Galveston, Houston, Laredo, Lubbock, McAllen, Presidio, San Angelo, San Antonio.
Virginia: Norfolk, Richmond.
Washington: Seattle, Spokane.
Wisconsin: Green Bay, Madison, Milwaukee.

Monaco
Diplomatic relations with Monaco are maintained by the United States Consulate in Nice, France.
State Department Desk Officer: 632-1726.
Consulates:
California: Los Angeles, San Francisco.
District of Columbia: Washington.
Florida: Palm Beach.
Hawaii: Honolulu.
Illinois: Chicago.
Louisiana: New Orleans.
Massachusetts: Boston.
New York: New York.
Pennsylvania: Philadelphia.
Puerto Rico: San Juan.
Texas: Dallas.
Utah: Salt Lake City.

Mongolia
State Department Desk Officer: 632-1436.

Morocco
Chancery: 1601 21st Street, NW 20009; 462-7979.
State Department Desk Officer: 632-0279.
Consulates:
New York: New York.
Texas: Dallas.

Mozambique, Peoples' Republic of
State Department Desk Officer: 632-8434.

Nauru
State Department Desk Officer: 632-9690.
Consulates:
California: San Francisco.
Guam: Agáña.
Hawaii: Honolulu.

Nepal
Chancery: 2131 Leroy Place, NW 20008; 667-4550.
State Department Desk Officer: 632-0653.
Consulates:
California: San Francisco.
Illinois: Chicago.

Netherlands
Chancery: 4200 Linnean Avenue, NW 20008; 244-5300.
State Department Desk Officer: 632-0498.
Consulates:
California: Los Angeles, San Diego, San Francisco.
Canal Zone: Colon, Panama; Panama, Panama.
District of Columbia: Washington.
Florida: Jacksonville, Miami.
Hawaii: Honolulu.
Illinois: Chicago.
Louisiana: New Orleans.
Maryland: Baltimore.
Massachusetts: Boston.
Michigan: Detroit, Grand Rapids.
Minnesota: St. Paul.
Missouri: Kansas City, St. Louis.
New York: Buffalo, New York.
Ohio: Cleveland.
Oregon: Portland.
Pennsylvania: Philadelphia, Pittsburgh.
Puerto Rico: Ponce, San Juan.
Texas: Houston.
Utah: Salt Lake City.
Virgin Islands: Charlotte Amalie.
Virginia: Norfolk.
Washington: Seattle.

New Zealand
Chancery: 19 Observatory Circle, NW 20008; 265-1721.
State Department Desk Officer: 632-9690.
Consulates:
California: Los Angeles, San Francisco.
District of Columbia: Washington.
New York: New York.

Nicaragua
Chancery: 1627 New Hampshire Avenue, NW 20009; 387-4371.
State Department Desk Officer: 632-3381.
Consulates:
Alabama: Mobile.
Arizona: Phoenix.
California: Garden Grove, Los Angeles, Pasadena, San Francisco, San Mateo.
Colorado: Denver.
District of Columbia: Washington.
Florida: Miami, Palm Beach, Tallahassee, Tampa.
Georgia: Atlanta.
Hawaii: Honolulu.
Illinois: Chicago.
Louisiana: Baton Rouge, Metairie, New Orleans.
Maryland: Baltimore.

Massachusetts: Boston, Framingham, Springfield.
Minnesota: Rochester.
Missouri: St. Louis.
New Jersey: Fort Lee, Linden, Ridgewood.
New York: New York.
Ohio: Cleveland.
Oregon: Portland.
Pennsylvania: Philadelphia, Pittsburgh.
Puerto Rico: Bayamón, Mayaguez, San Juan.
Rhode Island: Providence.
Texas: Austin, Brownsville, Corpus Christi, Dallas, El Paso, Fort Worth, Galveston, Houston, San Antonio.
Washington: Seattle.
Wisconsin: Madison, Milwaukee.

Niger
Chancery: 2204 R Street, NW 20008; 483-4224.
State Department Desk Officer: 632-3066.
Consulate: New York: New York.

Nigeria
Chancery: 2201 M Street, NW 20037; 223-9300.
State Department Desk Officer: 632-3406 and 632-3468.
Consulates:
California: San Francisco.
New York: New York.

Northern Rhodesia (see Zambia)

Norway
Chancery: 4200 Wisconsin Avenue, NW 20016; 966-9550.
State Department Desk Officer: 632-1774.
Consulates:
Alabama: Mobile.
Alaska: Anchorage, Juneau.
Arizona: Phoenix.
California: Los Angeles, San Diego, San Francisco.
Canal Zone: Balboa.
Colorado: Denver.
District of Columbia: Washington.
Florida: Jacksonville, Miami, Pensacola, Tampa.
Georgia: Savannah.
Hawaii: Honolulu.
Illinois: Chicago.
Iowa: Des Moines.
Louisiana: Baton Rouge, New Orleans.
Maine: Portland.
Maryland: Baltimore.
Massachusetts: Boston.
Michigan: Detroit.
Minnesota: Duluth, Minneapolis.
Mississippi: Gulfport.
Montana: Billings.
Nebraska: Omaha.
New Mexico: Albuquerque.
New York: New York.
North Carolina: Wilmington.

North Dakota: Fargo.
Ohio: Cleveland.
Oklahoma: Tulsa.
Oregon: Portland.
Pennsylvania: Philadelphia.
Puerto Rico: Ponce, San Juan.
South Carolina: Charleston.
South Dakota: Sioux Falls.
Tennessee: Nashville.
Texas: Corpus Christi, Dallas, Galveston, Houston, Point Comfort, Port Arthur.
Utah: Salt Lake City.
Virgin Islands: Charlotte Amalie.
Virginia: Newport News, Norfolk.
Washington: Seattle.
Wisconsin: Madison, Milwaukee.

Oman
Chancery: 2342 Massachusetts Avenue, NW 20008; 387-1980.
State Department Desk Officer: 632-1334.
Consulate: New York: New York.

Pakistan
Chancery: 2315 Massachusetts Avenue, NW 20008; 332-8330.
State Department Desk Officer: 632-2441.
Consulates:
Massachusetts: Boston.
New York: New York.
Texas: Houston.

Panama
Chancery: 2862 McGill Terrace, NW 20008; 483-1407.
State Department Desk Officer: 632-4980.
Consulates:
Alabama: Mobile.
Arizona: Phoenix.
California: Beverly Hills, Long Beach, Los Angeles, Oakland, San Diego, San Francisco.
Colorado: Denver.
District of Columbia: Washington.
Florida: Coral Gables, Fort Lauderdale, Miami, Miami Beach, Panama City.
Illinois: Chicago.
Louisiana: New Orleans.
Maine: Portland.
Maryland: Baltimore.
Massachusetts: Boston.
Michigan: Detroit.
New York: New York, Rochester.
Ohio: Cleveland.
Oregon: Portland.
Pennsylvania: Philadelphia, Pittsburgh.
Puerto Rico: San Juan.
Rhode Island: Coventry.
Texas: Brownsville, Dallas, El Paso, Houston, San Antonio.
Virginia: Alexandria, Norfolk.

Papua New Guinea
Chancery: 3122 Davenport Street, NW 20008; 966-3020.
State Department Desk Officer: 632-9690.

Paraguay
Chancery: 2400 Massachusetts Avenue, NW 20008; 483-6960.
State Department Desk Officer: 632-1551.
Consulates:
Alaska: Anchorage.
California: San Francisco.
Colorado: Denver.
Florida: Fort Lauderdale, Miami.
Illinois: Chicago.
Louisiana: New Orleans.
Massachusetts: Boston.
Michigan: Detroit.
New York: New York.
Puerto Rico: San Juan.
Texas: Dallas.
Washington: Seattle.

Peru
Chancery: 1700 Massachusetts Avenue, NW 20036; 833-9860.
State Department Desk Officer: 632-3360.
Consulates:
Alabama: Mobile.
Arizona: Tucson.
California: Los Angeles, San Francisco, Santa Barbara.
Colorado: Denver.
Delaware: Wilmington.
Florida: Cocoa Beach, Miami.
Georgia: Atlanta.
Hawaii: Honolulu.
Illinois: Chicago.
Louisiana: New Orleans.
Massachusetts: Boston.
Minnesota: Minneapolis.
New York: New York.
Oklahoma: Tulsa.
Oregon: Portland.
Pennsylvania: Philadelphia.
Puerto Rico: Cahuas, Ponce, San Juan.
Texas: Dallas, Fort Worth, Houston.
Utah: Salt Lake City.
Washington: Seattle.

Philippines
Chancery: 1617 Massachusetts Avenue, NW 20036; 483-1414.
State Department Desk Officer: 632-1221.
Consulates:
California: Los Angeles, San Francisco.
District of Columbia: Washington.
Guam: Agáña.
Hawaii: Honolulu.
Illinois: Chicago.
Louisiana: New Orleans.
New York: New York.
Washington: Seattle.

Poland
Chancery: 2640 16th Street, NW 20009; 234-3800.
State Department Desk Officer: 632-3191.
Consulates:
District of Columbia: Washington.
Illinois: Chicago.

New York: New York.

Portugal
Chancery: 2125 Kalorama Road, NW 20008; 265-1643.
State Department Desk Officer: 632-0718.
Consulates:
California: Los Angeles, San Francisco.
Connecticut: Waterbury.
District of Columbia: Washington.
Hawaii: Honolulu.
Illinois: Chicago.
Louisiana: New Orleans.
Massachusetts: Boston, New Bedford.
New Jersey: Newark.
New York: New York.
Pennsylvania: Philadelphia.
Rhode Island: Providence.
Texas: Houston.

Qatar
Chancery: Suite 1180, 600 New Hampshire Avenue, NW 20037; 338-0111.
State Department Desk Officer: 632-1794.

Rumania
Chancery: 1607 23d Street, NW 20008; 232-4747.
State Department Desk Officer: 632-3298.
Embassy at Washington, DC, has charge of the interests of Romanian nationals in the United States.

Rwanda
Chancery: 1714 New Hampshire Avenue, NW 20009; 232-2882.
State Department Desk Officer: 632-3138.

Samoa (see Western Samoa)

San Marino
State Department Desk Officer: 632-2253.
Consulates:
District of Columbia: Washington.
Michigan: Detroit.
New York: New York.

Sao Tome e Principe
State Department Desk Officer: 632-0996.

Saudi Arabia
Chancery: 1520 18th Street, NW 20036; 483-2100.
State Department Desk Officer: 632-3121.
Consulates:
District of Columbia: Washington.
New York: New York.

Senegal
Chancery: 2112 Wyoming Avenue, NW 20008; 234-0540.
State Department Desk Officer: 632-2865.
Consulates:
Arizona: Phoenix.
California: Los Angeles, San Francisco.
Colorado: Denver.
Connecticut: Bridgeport.
Florida: Miami.
Georgia: Atlanta.
Illinois: Chicago.
Louisiana: New Orleans.

Maryland: Baltimore.
Massachusetts: Boston, Marlboro.
Missouri: St. Louis.
Nebraska: Lincoln.
Nevada: Reno.
Oregon: Salem.
Texas: Prairie View.
Utah: Salt Lake City.
Vermont: Burlington.
Virginia: Richmond.
Wisconsin: Madison.

Sierra Leone
Chancery: 1701 19th Street, NW 20009; 265-7700.
State Department Desk Officer: 632-8354.
Consulates:
Missouri: Kansas City.
New York: New York.

Singapore
Chancery: 1824 R Street, NW 20009; 667-7555.
State Department Desk Officer: 632-3276.

Somalia
Chancery: Suite 710, 600 New Hampshire Avenue, NW 20037; 234-3261.
State Department Desk Officer: 632-0849.
Consulate: New York: New York.

South Africa, Republic of
Chancery: 3051 Massachusetts Avenue, NW 20008; 232-4400.
State Department Desk Officer: 632-3275.
Consulates:
Alabama: Mobile.
California: Los Angeles, San Francisco.
Louisiana: New Orleans.
Massachusetts: Boston.
New York: New York.
Oregon: Portland.
Texas: Houston.

Southern Rhodesia
State Department Desk Officer: 632-8252.

Spain
Chancery: 2700 15th Street, NW 20009; 265-0190.
State Department Desk Officer: 632-2633.
Consulates:
Alabama: Mobile.
California: Los Angeles, San Francisco.
Connecticut: Stamford.
District of Columbia: Washington.
Florida: Miami.
Illinois: Chicago.
Louisiana: New Orleans.
Massachusetts: Boston, Northboro.
Michigan: Detroit.
Missouri: Kansas City, St. Louis.
New York: New York.
Puerto Rico: Mayagüez, Ponce, San Juan.
Texas: Houston, Port Arthur.

Spanish Guinea (see Equatorial Guinea)

Sri Lanka (Ceylon)

Chancery: 2148 Wyoming Avenue, NW 20008; 483-4025.
State Department Desk Officer: 632-2351.
Consulates:
California: Los Angeles.
Illinois: Chicago.
Louisiana: New Orleans.

Sudan
Chancery: Site 400, 600 New Hampshire Avenue, NW 20037; 338-8565.
State Department Desk Officer: 632-0668.
Consulate: New York: New York.

Surinam, Republic of
Chancery: 2600 Virginia Avenue, NW 20037; 338-6980.
State Department Desk Officer: 632-3449.

Swaziland
Chancery: 4301 Connecticut Avenue, NW 20008; 362-6683.
State Department Desk Officer: 632-0916.

Sweden
Chancery: Suite 1200, 600 New Hampshire Avenue, NW 20037; 965-4100.
State Department Desk Officer: 632-0529.
Consulates:
Alabama: Mobile.
Alaska: Anchorage.
Arizona: Phoenix.
California: Los Angeles, San Diego, San Francisco.
Colorado: Denver.
Florida: Jacksonville, Miami, Tampa.
Georgia: Atlanta, Savannah.
Hawaii: Honolulu.
Illinois: Chicago.
Louisiana: New Orleans.
Maine: Portland.
Maryland: Baltimore.
Massachusetts: Boston.
Michigan: Detroit.
Minnesota: Duluth, Minneapolis.
Missouri: Kansas City, St. Louis.
Nebraska: Omaha.
New York: Buffalo, Jamestown, New York.
Ohio: Cincinnati, Cleveland.
Oregon: Portland.
Pennsylvania: Philadelphia.
Puerto Rico: San Juan.
Texas: Dallas, Houston.
Virgin Islands: Charlotte Amalie.
Virginia: Norfolk.
Washington: Seattle.
Wisconsin: Milwaukee.

Switzerland
Chancery: 2900 Cathedral Avenue, NW 20008; 462-1811.
State Department Desk Officer: 632-2005.
Consulates:
California: Los Angeles, San Francisco.
Colorado: Denver.
District of Columbia: Washington.

Georgia: Atlanta.
Hawaii: Honolulu.
Illinois: Chicago.
Louisiana: New Orleans.
Massachusetts: Boston.
Minnesota: Minneapolis.
Missouri: Kansas City, St. Louis.
New York: New York.
Ohio: Cincinnati, Cleveland, Columbus.
Pennsylvania: Philadelphia, Pittsburgh.
Puerto Rico: San Juan.
South Carolina: Spartanburg.
Texas: Houston.
Utah: Salt Lake City.
Washington: Seattle.

Syria
Chancery: 2215 Wyoming Avenue, NW 20008; 232-6313.
State Department Desk Officer: 632-1019.

Tanzania
Chancery: 2139 R Street, NW 20008; 232-0501.
State Department Desk Officer: 632-3040.

Thailand
Chancery: 2300 Kalorama Road, NW 20008; 667-1446.
State Department Desk Officer: 632-3276.
Consulates:
Alabama: Montgomery.
California: Los Angeles.
Florida: Miami.
Hawaii: Honolulu.
Illinois: Chicago.
Massachusetts: Boston.
Michigan: Detroit.
Missouri: Kansas City.
New York: New York.
Pennsylvania: Philadelphia.
Texas: El Paso.
Virginia: Richmond.

Togo
Chancery: 2208 Massachusetts Avenue, NW 20008; 234-4212.
State Department Desk Officer: 632-0842.

Tonga
State Department Desk Officer: 632-9690.

Trinidad and Tobago
Chancery: 1708 Massachusetts Avenue, NW 20036; 467-6490.
State Department Desk Officer: 632-3449.
Consulate: New York: New York.

Tunisia
Chancery: 2408 Massachusetts Avenue, NW 20008; 234-6644.
State Department Desk Officer: 632-3614.
Consulate: Maryland: Baltimore.

Turkey
Chancery: 1606 23d Street, NW 20008; 667-6400.
State Department Desk Officer: 632-1562.
Consulates:
California: Los Angeles, San Francisco.

District of Columbia: Washington.
Florida: Tampa.
Illinois: Chicago.
Louisiana: New Orleans.
Massachusetts: Boston.
New York: New York.

Uganda
Chancery: 5909 16th Street, NW 20011; 726-7100.
State Department Desk Officer: 632-0857.
Union of Soviet Socialist Republics
Chancery: 1125 16th Street, NW 20036; 628-7551.
State Department Desk Officer: 632-8671.
Consulates:
California: San Francisco.
District of Columbia: Washington.
United Arab Emirates
Chancery: Suite 740, 600 New Hampshire Avenue, NW 20037; 338-6500.
State Department Desk Officer: 632-1334.
Upper Volta
Chancery: 5500 16th Street, NW 20011; 726-0992.
State Department Desk Officer: 632-3066.
Consulate: Louisiana: New Orleans.
Uruguay
Chancery: 1918 F Street, NW 20006; 331-1313.
State Department Desk Officer: 632-1551.
Consulates:
California: San Francisco.
District of Columbia: Washington.
Illinois: Chicago.
Louisiana: New Orleans.
Pennsylvania: Philadelphia.
New York: New York.
Puerto Rico: San Juan.
Vatican City
Apostolic Delegation (to U.S. Catholic Church): 3339 Massachusetts Avenue, NW 20008.
State Department Desk Officer: 632-8210.
Venezuela
Chancery: 2445 Massachusetts Avenue, NW 20008; 265-9600.
State Department Desk Officer: 632-3338.
Consulates:
Alabama: Mobile.
California: Los Angeles, San Francisco.
Florida: Miami.
Georgia: Savannah.
Illinois: Chicago.
Louisiana: New Orleans.
Maryland: Baltimore.
Massachusetts: Boston.
Missouri: St. Louis.
New York: New York.
Oregon: Portland.
Pennsylvania: Philadelphia.
Puerto Rico: Ponce, San Juan.
Texas: Houston.

Vietnam
State Department Desk Officer: 632-3132.
Western Samoa
State Department Desk Officer: 632-9690.
Consulate: California: Los Angeles.
Yemen Arab Republic
Chancery: Suite 860, 600 New Hampshire
Avenue, NW 20037; 965-4760.
State Department Desk Officer: 632-1334.
Consulate: New York: New York.
Yemen, People's Democratic Republic of
State Department Desk Officer: 632-3121.
Yugoslavia
Chancery: 2410 California Street, NW
20008; 462-6566.
State Department Desk Officer: 632-3655.
Consulates:
California: San Francisco.
District of Columbia: Washington.
Illinois: Chicago.
New York: New York.
Ohio: Cleveland.
Pennsylvania: Pittsburgh.
Zaire, Republic of
Chancery: 1800 New Hampshire Avenue,
NW 20009; 234-7690.
State Department Desk Officer: 632-1706.
Zambia, Republic of
Chancery: 2419 Massachusetts Avenue,
NW 20008; 265-9717.
State Department Desk Officer: 632-8851.

° The area code for all telephone numbers listed
here is 202.

INTERNATIONAL ORGANIZATIONS: STATE DEPARTMENT DESK OFFICE TELEPHONE NUMBERS*

East African Community	632-3228
East-West Center	632-0896
Economic and Social Commission for Asia and the Pacific	632-1654
Economic Commission for Africa	632-1654
Economic Commission for Europe (ECE)	632-0315
Economic Commission of Latin America	632-1654
European Atomic Energy Commission (EURATOM)	632-0315
European Coal and Steel Community (ECSC)	632-1708
European Communities	632-1708
European Economic Community	632-1708
European Free Trade Association	632-0457
European Launcher Development Organization (ELDO)	632-0315
European Programs	632-9246
European Space Research Organization (ESRO)	632-0315

U.S. Chambers of Commerce Abroad

Argentina
The American Chamber of Commerce in Argentina, Avenida R. Saenz Peña 567, 1352 Buenos Aires.

Australia
American Chamber of Commerce in Australia, 50 Pitt Street, Sydney, New South Wales 2000.

American Chamber of Commerce in Australia, Guardian Assurance Building, 50 Grenfell Street, Adelaide, S.A. 5000.

American Chamber of Commerce in Australia, 139 Leichhardt Street, Busbane, Old. 4000.

American Chamber of Commerce in Australia, 186 Exhibition Street, Melbourne, Victoria, 3000.

American Chamber of Commerce in Australia, 16 St. George's Terrace, Perth, W.A. 6000.

Austria
American Chamber of Commerce in Austria, Severingasse 1, A-1090, Vienna.

Belgium
American Chamber of Commerce in Belgium, Rue du Commerce 21, 1040 Brussels.

Brazil
American Chamber of Commerce for Brazil—Rio de Janeiro, P.O. Box 916-ZC-00, Rio de Janeiro.

American Chamber of Commerce for Brazil—Sao Paulo, P.O. Box 8109, 01000 Sao Paulo.

American Chamber of Commerce for Brazil—Porto Alegre, Branch Office of Sao Paulo, 90.000, Porto Alegre.

American Chamber of Commerce for Brazil—Recife Branch, Caixa Postal 3351, 30,000, Recife, Pernambuco, Brazil.

American Chamber of Commerce for Brazil, Conselheiro Dantas, 8, Sala 904, Edificio Paraguassu, Salvador, Bahia.

Chile
Chamber of Commerce of the U.S.A. in the Republic of Chile, Casilla 4131, Santiago.

Colombia
Colombian-American Chamber of Commerce, Bogota Hilton Hotel, Apartado Aereo 8008, Bogota.

Colombian-American Chamber of Commerce, Apartado Aereo 5943, Cali.

Costa Rica
American Chamber of Commerce, of Costa Rica, P.O. Box 4946, San Jose.

Dominican Republic
American Chamber of Commerce of the Dominican Republic, Santo Domingo.

Ecuador
Ecuadorian-American Chamber of Commerce, P.O. Box 2432, Quito.

El Salvador
American Chamber of Commerce of El Salvador, Apartado Postal (05) 9, San Salvador, El Salvador.

England
American Chamber of Commerce (United Kingdom), 75 Brook Street, London, WIY 2 EB.

France
American Chamber of Commerce in France, 21 Avenue George V, Paris 75008.

Germany
American Chamber of Commerce in Germany, 1000 Berlin 12, Fasanentrasse 4.

American Chamber of Commerce in Germany, Rossmarkt 12, 6 Frankfurt/Main.

American Chamber of Commerce in Germany, Zweibruekenstrasse 6, 8000 Munich 22.

Greece
American-Hellenic Chamber of Commerce, 17 Valaoritou and Amerikis Streets, Athens 134.

Guatemala
American Chamber of Commerce of Guatemala (Cámara de Comercio Norteamericana de Guatemala), 9a. Calle 5-54, Zona 1, Guatemala City.

Hong Kong
American Chamber of Commerce in Hong Kong, 322 Edinburgh House, Hong Kong.

Indonesia
American Chamber of Commerce in Indonesia, P.O. Box 2086, Jakarta.

Iran
Iran American Chamber of Commerce, Iranians' Bank Building, Takhte Jamshid Avenue, Tehran.

Ireland

The United States Chamber of Commerce in Ireland, 16 Eustace Street, Dublin 2, Ireland.

Italy

American Chamber of Commerce in Italy, Via Agnello 12 20121 Milan.

The American Chamber of Commerce in Italy, Via Lombardia 40, 00187, Rome.

Japan

American Chamber of Commerce in Japan, 701 Tosho Building, 2-2, Marunouchi 3-chome, Chiyoda-ku, Tokyo 100, Japan.

American Chamber of Commerce Okinawa, Manneng Building, 136 Oyama, Ginowan-shi, Okinawa-ken, Japan 904.

Korea

American Chamber of Commerce in Korea, Chosun Hotel, Seoul.

Mexico

American Chamber of Commerce of Mexico, Lucerna No. 78, Mexico 6, D.F.

American Chamber of Commerce of Mexico, Condominio Guadalajara, 16 de Septiembre 730-301, Guadalajara, Jalisco.

American Chamber of Commerce of Mexico, A.C., Condominio Acero Desp. 213, Monterrey, Nuevo Leon.

Morocco

American Chamber of Commerce in Morocco, Hotel El Mansour, 27, Avenue de l'Armee Royale, Casablanca.

Netherlands

American Chamber of Commerce in the Netherlands, Carnegieplein 5, The Hague.

New Zealand

American Chamber of Commerce in New Zealand, P.O. Box 3408, Wellington.

Nicaragua

American Chamber of Commerce of Nicaragua, Apartado 2720, Managua, Nicaragua.

Peru

American Chamber of Commerce of Peru. Juan de Arona 883–8° piso San Isidro, Casilla 2888, Lima.

Philippines

American Chamber of Commerce of the Philippines, Inc., P.O. Box 1578 MCC, Makati, Metro, Manila.

Singapore

American Business Council, Yen San Building, 268 Orchard Road, Singapore 9.

Spain

American Chamber of Commerce in Spain: Avda; Generalisimo Franco, 477, Barcelona-11.

Eurobuilding, Oficina 9A, Padre Damián 23 Madrid-16.

Switzerland

American Chamber of Commerce in Switzerland, Talacker 41, 8001 Zurich.

Thailand

The American Chamber of Commerce in Thailand, P.O. Box 11-1095, Bangkok.

Uruguay

The Chamber of Commerce of the U.S.A. in Uruguay, P.O. Box 389, Montevideo.

Venezuela

Venezuelan-American Chamber of Commerce and Industry, Apartado 5181 Caracas, 101.

Foreign Chambers of Commerce in the United States

African-American Chamber of Commerce, Inc., 65 Liberty Street, NY, 10005.

U.S.-Arab Chamber of Commerce, One World Trade Center, New York, NY, 10048.

American-Arab Association for Commerce & Industry, Inc., 342 Madison Avenue, New York, NY, 10017.

American-Arab Chamber of Commerce, 319 World Trade Building, Houston, TX, 77002.

Mid-American Arab Chamber of Commerce, 135 S. LaSalle Street, Chicago, IL, 60603.

U.S.-Arab Chamber of Commerce (Pacific), Inc., 230 California Street, San Francisco, CA, 94111; 1 World Trade Center, New York, NY, 10048.

Argentine-American Chamber of Commerce, Inc., 11 Broadway, New York, NY, 10004.

United States-Austrian Chamber of Commerce, Inc., 165 W. 46th Street, New York, NY, 10036.

Belgian American Chamber of Commerce in the United States, Inc., 50 Rockefeller Plaza, New York, NY, 10020.

Belgian American Chamber of Commerce (Midwest), % Metron Steel Corporation, 12900 S. Metron Drive, Chicago, IL, 60633.

Brazilian American Chamber of Commerce, Inc., 22 W. 48th Street, New York, NY, 10036.

British-American Chamber of Commerce, 10 E. 40th Street, New York, NY, 10016.

British American Chamber of Commerce, 350 S. Figueroa Street, Los Angeles, CA, 90071.

British-American Chamber of Commerce, 68 Post Street, San Francisco, CA, 94104.

Central American Chamber of Commerce in the U.S., Inc., 65 Liberty Street, New York, NY, 10005.

Chile-American Association, Inc., 220 E. 81st Street, New York, NY, 10028.

The Chamber of Commerce, Industries and Tourism of Chile and California, 303 World Trade Center, San Francisco, CA, 94111.

The Chinese Chamber of Commerce of New York Inc., 180 Park Row, New York, NY, 10038.

Chinese Chamber of Commerce of San Francisco, 730 Sacramento Street, San Francisco, CA, 94108.

Colombian-American Association, Inc., 55 Liberty Street, New York, NY, 10005.

Ecuadorean American Association, Inc., 55 Liberty Street, New York, NY, 10005.

Finnish American Chamber of Commerce, Finland House, 540 Madison Avenue, New York, NY, 10022.

Finnish American Chamber of Commerce of the Midwest, One IBM Plaza, Chicago, IL, 60611.

Finnish-American Chamber of Commerce on the Pacific Coast, Inc., 3600 Wilshire Boulevard, Los Angeles, CA, 90010.

French Chamber of Commerce in the United States, Inc., 1350 Avenue of the Americas, New York, NY, 10019.

German American Chamber of Commerce, Inc., 666 Fifth Avenue, New York, NY, 10019.

German American Chamber of Commerce of Chicago, 77 E. Monroe Street, Chicago, IL, 60603.

German American Chamber of Commerce, 2 Houston Center, Houston, TX, 77002.

German American Chamber of Commerce of Los Angeles, 3250 Wilshire Boulevard, Los Angeles, CA, 90010.

German American Chamber of Commerce, 2 Houston Center, Houston, TX, 77002.

German-American Chamber of Commerce of the Pacific Coast, 465 California Street, San Francisco, CA, 94104.

Hellenic-American Chamber of Commerce, 25 Broadway, New York, NY, 10004.

American Indonesian Chamber of Commerce, Inc., 120 Wall Street, New York, NY, 10005.

Iran American Chamber of Commerce, Inc., 555 Fifth Avenue, New York, NY, 10017.

Ireland-United States Council for Commerce and Industry, 460 Park Avenue, New York, NY, 10022.

American-Israel Chamber of Commerce & Industry, Inc., 500 Fifth Avenue, New York, NY, 10036.

American-Israel Chamber of Commerce & Industry, Inc., Midwest, 180 N. Michigan Avenue, Chicago, IL, 60601.

American-Israel Chamber of Commerce & Industry, Cleveland Chapter, 10800 Brookpark Road, % Foreign City Enterprises, Inc., Cleveland, OH, 44130.

American-Israel Chamber of Commerce & Industry, Inc., 1776 S. Jackson, Denver, CO, 80210.

American-Israel Chamber of Commerce & Industry, Philadelphia Chapter, 1500 Walnut Street, Philadelphia, PA, 19107.

American-Israel Chamber of Commerce & Industry, Pittsburgh Chapter, % Vanguard Imports Company, 2417 Smallman Street, Pittsburgh, PA, 15222.

California-Israel Chamber of Commerce, 6399 Wilshire Boulevard, Los Angeles, CA, 90048.

Florida-Israel Chamber of Commerce, 3950 Biscayne Boulevard, Miami, FL, 33137.

Italy-America Chamber of Commerce, Inc., 350 Fifth Avenue, New York, NY, 10001.

Italian Chamber of Commerce of Chicago, 327 S. LaSalle Street, Chicago, IL, 60604.

Italian-American Chamber of Commerce of the Western United States, World Trade Center, San Francisco, CA, 94111.

Japanese Chamber of Commerce of New York, Inc., 39 Broadway, New York, NY, 10006.

Japanese Chamber of Commerce and Industry of Chicago, 230 N. Michigan Avenue, Chicago, IL, 60601.

Japanese Chamber of Commerce of Northern California, World Trade Center, Ferry Building, San Francisco, CA, 94111.

Japanese Chamber of Commerce of Southern California, 355 N. First Street, Los Angeles, CA, 94111.

U.S./Korea Economic Council, Inc., 88 Morningside Drive, New York, NY, 10027.

Korean-American Midwest Association of Commerce and Industry, % Swift Agricultural Chemicals Corp., 111 W. Jackson Boulevard, Chicago, IL, 60604.

Chamber of Commerce of Latin America in the United States, Inc., One World Trade Center, New York, NY, 10048.

United States Lebanese Chamber of Commerce, Inc., Five World Trade Center. New York, NY, 10048.

Association of Asian-American Chambers of Commerce, P.O. Box 2801, Washington, DC, 20013.

Mexican Chamber of Commerce of the U.S., Inc., Five World Trade Center, New York, NY, 10048.

Mexican American Chamber of Commerce and Industry, 18th Street, Chicago, IL, 60611.

Mexican Chamber of Commerce of Los Angeles, 125 Paseo de la Plaza, Los Angeles, CA, 90012.

United States-Mexico Chamber of Commerce, 1800 "K" Street, NW, Washington,

DC, 20006.

The Netherlands Chamber of Commerce in the U.S., Inc., One Rockefeller Plaza, New York, NY, 10020.

Nigerian American Chamber of Commerce, 65 Liberty Street, New York, NY, 10005.

Norwegian American Chamber of Commerce, Inc., 800 Third Avenue, New York, NY, 10022.

Norwegian American Chamber of Commerce, Inc., Midwest-Chicago Chapter, 360 N. Michigan Avenue, Chicago, IL, 60601.

Norwegian American Chamber of Commerce, 800 Foshay Tower, Minneapolis, MN, 55402.

Norwegian American Chamber of Commerce Inc., World Trade Center, Los Angeles, CA, 90071.

Norwegian American Chamber of Commerce, One Embarcadero Center, San Francisco, CA, 94111.

Norwegian American Chamber of Commerce, 1120-4th Avenue, Seattle, WA, 98101.

Pakistani-American Chamber of Commerce, Inc. (Under reorganization. Telephone contact: 516-488-4100.)

Peruvian-American Association, Inc., 11 Broadway, New York, NY, 10004.

Philippine American Chamber of Commerce, Inc., 565 Fifth Avenue, New York, NY, 10017.

Puerto Rico Chamber of Commerce in the U.S. Inc., 65 Liberty Street, New York, NY, 10005.

Spain-U.S. Chamber of Commerce, Inc., 500 Fifth Avenue, New York, NY, 10036.

Spain-U.S. Chamber of Commerce of The Middle West, 180 N. Michigan Avenue, Chicago, IL, 60601.

Spain-U.S. Chamber of Commerce of the Pacific Coast, Inc., World Trade Center, Los Angeles, CA, 90071.

Cámara Oficial Expañola de Comercio en Puerto Rico, Comercio 452-2°, San Juan, PR, 00902.

Swedish-American Chamber of Commerce, Inc., 1 Dag Hammarskjold Plaza, New York, NY, 10017.

Swedish-American Chamber of Commerce of the Western United States, Inc., World Trade Center, San Francisco, CA, 94111.

Trinidad and Tobago Chamber of Commerce of the United States of America, Inc., 400 Madison Avenue, New York, NY, 10017.

Venezuelan American Association of the United States, Inc., 55 Liberty Street, New York, NY, 10005.

U.S. Customs Information

U.S. CUSTOMS SERVICE

Headquarters: 1301 Constitution Avenue NW, Washington, DC 20229. Telephone information: 202-566-2475.

The major responsibility of the U.S. Customs Service is to administer the Tariff Act of 1930, as amended. Primary duties include the assessment and collection of all duties, taxes, and fees on imported merchandise, the enforcement of customs and related laws, and the administration of certain navigation laws and treaties. As a major enforcement organization, it engages in combating smuggling and frauds on the revenue and enforces the regulations of numerous other federal agencies at ports of entry and along the land and sea borders of the United States.

Under the President's Reorganization Plan No. 1 of 1965, the customs offices in the United States, Puerto Rico, and the Virgin Islands were reorganized into regions, districts, and port levels, headed respectively by regional commissioners of customs, district directors of customs, and port directors of customs. Regions receive primary direction from the Commissioner of Customs in Washington; while the districts and ports arranged under the nine regions derive their primary supervision from the regional commissioners.

Whenever it is suggested that you write to the district director of customs for information or a decision, the district director or port director referred to is the one at the port of entry through which your goods will be entered.

CUSTOMS PORTS OF ENTRY—BY STATE (INCLUDING PUERTO RICO AND THE VIRGIN ISLANDS)

Alabama
  Birmingham
  Mobile
Alaska
  Alcan
  Anchorage
  Fairbanks
  Juneau
  Ketchikan
  Kodiak
  Pelican
  Petersburg
  Sand Point
  Sitka
  Skagway
  Wrangell
Arizona
  Douglas
  Lukeville
  Naco
  Nogales
  Phoenix
  San Luis
  Sasabe
Arkansas
  Little Rock–N.
    Little Rock
California
  Andrade
  Calexico
  Eureka
  Fresno
  **Los Angeles–Long
    Beach†**
  Port San Luis
  San Diego
  **San Francisco–
    Oakland†**
  Tecate
Colorado
  Denver
Connecticut
  Bridgeport
  Hartford
  New Haven
  New London
Delaware
  Wilmington
**District of
Columbia**

District shown in boldface.
° Under jurisdiction of an area director of customs.
† Regional headquarters.
‡ Consolidated as the Columbia River port of entry.
§ Consolidated as the Beaumont, Orange, Port Arthur, Sabine port of entry.
Source: *Exporting to the United States*, U.S. Department of the Treasury.

Washington
Florida
  Apalachicola
  Boca Grande
  Carrabelle
  Fernandina Beach
  Jacksonville
  Key West
  Miami†
  Panama City
  Pensacola
  Port Canaveral
  Port Everglades
  Port St. Joe
  St. Petersburg
  Tampa
  West Palm Beach
Georgia
  Atlanta
  Brunswick
  Savannah
Hawaii
  Honolulu
  Hilo
  Kahului
  Nawiliwili–Port
    Allen
Idaho
  Eastport
  Porthill
Illinois
  Chicago†
  Peoria
Indiana
  Evansville
  Indianapolis
  Lawrenceburg
Kansas
  Wichita
Kentucky
  Louisville
Louisiana
  Baton Rouge
  Lake Charles
  Morgan City
  New Orleans†
Maine
  Bangor
  Bar Harbor
  Bath
  Belfast
  Bridgewater
  Calais
  Eastport
  Fort Fairfield
  Fort Kent
  Houlton
  Jackman
  Jonesport
  Limestone
  Madawaska
  Portland
  Rockland

  Van Buren
  Vanceboro
Maryland
  Annapolis
  Baltimore†
  Cambridge
  Crisfield
Massachusetts
  Boston†
  Fall River
  Gloucester
  Lawrence
  New Bedford
  Plymouth
  Salem
  Springfield
  Worcester
Michigan
  Detroit
  Muskegon
  Port Huron
  Saginaw–Bay **City**
  Sault Ste. Marie
Minnesota
  Baudette
  Duluth and
    Superior, Wis.
  Grand Portage
  International Falls–
    Ranier
  Minneapolis–St.
    Paul
  Noyes
  Pinecreek
  Roseau
  Warroad
Mississippi
  Greenville
  Gulfport
  Pascagoula
  Vicksburg
Missouri
  Kansas City
  St. Joseph
  St. Louis
Montana
  Butte
  Del Bonita
  Great Falls
  Morgan
  Opheim
  Piegan
  Raymond
  Roosville
  Scobey
  Sweetgrass
  Turner
  Whitetail
  Whitlash
Nebraska
  Omaha
Nevada

Las Vegas
Reno
New Hampshire
Portsmouth
New Jersey
Perth Amboy
New Mexico
Albuquerque
Columbus
New York
Albany
Alexandria Bay
Buffalo–Niagara
Falls
Cape Vincent
Champlain-Rouses
Point
Chateaugay
Clayton
Fort Covington
Massena
Morristown
New York
Kennedy Airport
Area*†
Newark Area*†
New York Seaport
Area*†
Ogdensburg
Oswego
Rochester
Sodus Point
Syracuse
Trout River
Utica
Waddington
North Carolina
Beaufort–Morehead
City
Charlotte
Durham
Reidsville
Wilmington
Winston-Salem
North Dakota
Ambrose
Antler
Carbury
Dunseith
Fortuna
Hannah
Hansboro
Maida
Neche
Noonan
Northgate
Pembina
Portal
Sarles
Sherwood
St. John
Walhalla

Westhope
Ohio
Akron
Ashtabula
Cincinnati
Cleveland
Columbus
Conneaut
Dayton
Sandusky
Toledo
Oklahoma
Oklahoma **City**
Tulsa
Oregon
Astoria‡
Coos Bay
Newport
Portland‡
Pennsylvania
Chester
Erie
Harrisburg
Philadelphia
Pittsburgh
Puerto Rico
Aguadilla
Fajardo
Guanica
Humacao
Jobos
Mayaguez
Ponce
San Juan
Rhode Island
Newport
Providence
South Carolina
Charleston
Georgetown
Greenville–
Spartanburg
Tennessee
Chattanooga
Memphis
Nashville
Texas
Beaumont§
Brownsville
Corpus Christi
Dallas/Ft. Worth
Del Rio
Eagle Pass
El Paso
Fabens
Freeport
Galveston
Hidalgo
Houston†
Laredo
Orange§
Port Arthur§

Port Lavaca–Point
  Comfort
Presidio
Progresso
Rio Grande City
Roma
Sabine§
San Antonio
Utah
  Salt Lake City
Vermont
  Alburg
  Beecher Falls
  Burlington
  Derby Line
  Highgate Springs
  Island Pond
  Newport
  North Troy
  Richford
  St. Albans
Virgin Islands
  Charlotte Amalie,
    St. Thomas
  Christiansted
  Coral Bay
  Cruz Bay
  Frederiksted
Virginia
  Alexandria
  Cape Charles City
  Norfolk–Newport
    News
  Reedville
  Richmond–
    Petersburg
Washington
  Aberdeen
  Anacortes
  Bellingham
  Blaine
  Boundary
  Danville
  Everett
  Ferry
  Friday Harbor
  Frontier
  Laurier
  Longview‡
  Lynden
  Metaline Falls
  Neah Bay
  Nighthawk
  Olympia
  Oroville
  Port Angeles
  Port Townsend
  Seattle
  South Bend–
    Raymond
  Spokane
  Sumas
  Tacoma

West Virginia
  Charleston
Wisconsin
  Ashland
  Green Bay
  Manitowoc
  Marinette
  Milwaukee
  Racine
  Sheboygan

CUSTOMS REGIONS AND DISTRICTS

Region I—Boston, MA 02203
  Information number: 617-223-7506
  Districts:
    Portland, ME 04111
    St. Albans, VT 05478
    Boston, MA 02109
    Providence, RI 02903
    Buffalo, NY 14202
    Ogdensburg, NY 13669
    Bridgeport, CT 06609
Region II—New York, NY 10048
  Information number: 212-466-4444
  Districts:
    New York District, which is coextensive
    with the New York Region, has three
    administrative areas: Kennedy Airport
    Area, Newark Area, and New York Sea-
    port Area.
Region III—Baltimore, MD 21202
  Information number: 301-962-3288
  Districts:
    Philadelphia, PA 19106
    Baltimore, MD 21202
    Norfolk, VA 23510
    Washington, DC 20018
Region IV—Miami, FL 33166
  Information number: 305-350-5952
  Districts:
    Wilmington, NC 28401
    San Juan, PR 00903
    Charleston, SC 29402
    Savannah, GA 31401
    Tampa, FL 33601
    Miami, FL 33132
    St. Thomas, VI 00801
Region V—New Orleans, LA 70113
  Information number: 505-589-5952
  Districts:
    Mobile, AL 36601
    New Orleans, LA 70130
Region VI—Houston, TX 77002
  Information number: 713-226-4893
  Districts:
    Port Arthur, TX 77640
    Galveston, TX 77550
    Houston, TX 77052

Laredo, TX 78040
El Paso, TX 79985
Region VII—Los Angeles, CA 90053
Information number: 213-688-5900
Districts:
Nogales, AZ 85621
San Diego, CA 92101
Los Angeles, CA 90731
San Pedro, CA 90731
Region VIII—San Francisco, CA 94102
Information number: 415-556-3500
Districts:
San Francisco, CA 94126
Honolulu, HI 96806
Portland, OR 97209
Seattle, WA 98104
Anchorage, AK 99501
Great Falls, MT 59401
Region IX—Chicago, IL 60603
Information number: 312-353-4733
Districts:
Chicago, IL 60607
Pembina, ND 58271
Minneapolis, MN 55401
Duluth, MN 55802
Milwaukee, WI 53202
Cleveland, OH 44199
St. Louis, MO 63105
Detroit, MI 48226

U.S. CUSTOMS OFFICES ABROAD

England
American Embassy
Room G94
24/32 Grosvenor Square
London, W.1

Canada
U.S. Consulate
Tour du Sud
Complex des Jardins
Montreal 4B 1G1, P.Q.
France
American Embassy Annex
58 Bis, Rue La Boetie
75008, Paris
Germany
American Embassy
Room 2069
Mehlemer Aue
53 Bonn-Bad Godesberg 1
American Consulate General
21 Siesmayerstrasse
6 Frankfurt/M
Hong Kong
American Consulate General
26 Garden Road
Italy
Consular Building
American Embassy
Room 302
Via Veneto 119
00187 Rome
Japan
American Embassy, Room 202
2, Akasaka, Aoi-cho, Minato-ku
Tokyo 107
Mexico
American Embassy
Reforma 305, Room 353
Apartado Postal 88-Bis
Mexico, D. F.
Taiwan
American Embassy
Box 2
APO San Francisco, CA 96263

Source: *Exporting to the United States*, U.S. Department of the Treasury.

Japanese Trading Companies

Exporters and importers generally find it essential to use the services of the Japanese trading companies, which offer a wide range of services including negotiation of overseas deals, transportation, storage, finance, and marketing. The ten largest trading companies are listed below. The small exporter will often do better using smaller trading companies that specialize in one or two types of products. Exporters seeking an appropriate trading company should contact the local office of the Japan Trade Center:

Bank of America Towers
555 S. Flower Street
Los Angeles, CA 90071

1737 Post Street
San Francisco, CA 94115

232 N. Michigan Avenue
Chicago, IL 60601

1221 Avenue of the Americas
New York, NY 10020

One World Trade Center
2100 Stemmous Freeway
Dallas, TX 75207

Melrose Boulevard
1127 Walker Street
Houston, TX 77002

P.O. Box 3356
Marina Station
Mayaguez, PR 00708

TRADING COMPANIES (JAPANESE OFFICES)

Mitsubishi Corporation
6–3 Marunouchi 2-chome
Chiyoda-ku
Tokyo. 210-2121

Mitsui & Co., Ltd.
2–1 Ohte-machi 1-chome
Chiyoda-ku
Tokyo. 285-1111

Marubeni
3–3 Honmachi
Higashi-ku
Osaka. 271-2231

C. Itoh & Co.
4 Nihonbashi-Honcho
2-chome

Chuo-ku
Tokyo. 662-5111
68, 4-chome
Kitakyutaro-machi
Higashi-ku
Osaka. 241-2121

Sumitomo Shoji
Shin-Sumitomo Building
15 5-chome
Kitahama
Higashi-ku
Osaka. 220-6000

2-2 2-1 chome
Hitotsubashi
Chiyoda-ku
Tokyo. 217-5000

Nissho-Iwai
30 Imabashi 3-chome
Higashi-ku
Osaka. 202-1201

4-5 Akasaka 2-chome
Minato-ku
Tokyo. 588-2111

Toyo Menka Kaisha
64 Kawaramachi 2-chome
Higashi-ku
Osaka. 203-1351

1–3 Ohtemachi 1-chome
Chiyoda-ku
Tokyo. 218-8781

Kanamatsu-Gosho
5 Takara-cho 2-chome
Chuo-ku
Tokyo. 562-8111

Itoman & Co. Ltd.
30 Kitakyutaro-machi 4-chome
Higashi-ku
Osaka. 252-1216

Nichimen
2–15 Nakanoshima
Kita-ku
Osaka. 202-2271

1–6 Takara-cho
Chou-ku
Tokyo. 566-2111

MAJOR TRADING COMPANIES (U.S. OFFICES)

Mitsubishi
277 Park Avenue
New York, NY 10017
601 California Street
San Francisco, CA 94108

Mitsui & Co. (USA), Inc.
200 Park Avenue
New York, NY 10017

One California Street
San Francisco, CA 94111

Marubeni Corporation
200 Park Avenue
New York, NY 10017

One Wilshire Building
624 S. Grand Avenue
Los Angeles, CA 90017

C. Itoh & Co. (America), Inc.
270 Park Avenue
New York, NY 10017

One Maritime Plaza
Golden Gateway Center
San Francisco, CA 94111

Sumitomo Shoji America, Inc.
345 Park Avenue
New York, NY 10022

One California Street
San Francisco, CA 94111

Nissho-Iwai American Corp.
1211 Avenue of the Americas
New York, NY 10036

One Wilshire Building
624 S. Grand Avenue
Los Angeles, CA 90017

Toyomenka (America), Inc.
One World Trade Center
New York, NY 10048

445 South Figuerosa Street
Los Angeles, CA 90017

Kanematsu-Gosho (USA), Inc.
One World Trade Center
New York, NY 10048

425 California Street
San Francisco, CA 94104

Itoman US Inc.
1211 Avenue of the Americas
New York, NY 10036

Nichimen Co., Inc.
1185 Avenue of the Americas
New York, NY 10036

Occidental Center
1150 S. Olive Street
Los Angeles, CA 90015

Doing Business with the USSR and Eastern Europe

SOVIET UNION

With the advent of detente in 1972, the Soviet Union, the world's second ranking power, has become a potentially prime U.S. market.

Foreign trade under the Soviet constitution is a state monopoly administered by the Ministry of Foreign Trade. The Foreign Trade Ministry supervises the activities of about 50 specialized All-Union Foreign Trade Organizations (FTO) listed below. Each FTO is responsible for the import or export of a particular group of commodities or services, including the negotiating of contracts on behalf of internal (end user) customers in the USSR. While the FTO conduct commercial negotiations and conclude contracts with foreign firms, actual purchase decisions are made by the end user. FTO negotiations generally proceed on customary commercial principles such as price, quantity, delivery terms, and credit conditions.

Because of the shortage of hard currencies in the USSR and the Eastern European countries, barter deals are common.

Information relating to U.S. export licenses for merchandise shipped to the USSR may be obtained from the Bureau of East-West Trade, Department of Commerce.

The following ten rules are useful guides for U.S. businessmen who are thinking of entering the Soviet market:

1. Do not begin unless you are prepared to invest substantial front-end investment without early return.
2. Do not begin unless you are prepared to negotiate the first transaction for one to three years.
3. Do not begin unless you are prepared to commit substantial amounts of senior executive time.
4. Do not begin unless you are prepared to walk away from a negotiation at any time. If you go to Moscow with the idea that you must come home with a contract in your pocket, the chances are you will make a very bad deal.

5. Do not negotiate concessionary terms in order to establish a position; you will simply lose respect. Each transaction must stand on its own.
6. Do not reject unusual transactions out of hand. Barter, long-term barter, switch transactions, and coproduction agreements can be profitable. However, it is advisable to consult a trading company specializing in barter transactions.
7. Concentrate on personal relationships and the establishment of mutual trust and respect. This, plus quality performance, are the bases for subsequent business.
8. Substantial market research is feasible; good advance work is imperative. Do not make a trip to Moscow without adequate preparation.
9. Negotiate contracts with a maximum degree of specificity. The Soviets have the reputation of living up to the letter of a contract, but of being rather unsympathetic toward items which were inadvertently overlooked.
10. U.S.–USSR trade is not El Dorado. It is not about to soar into the tens of billions. It is a good potential market, but one that takes a great deal of time and effort and should be looked at with cold objectivity.

INITIATING CONTACTS

Businessmen interested in trade with the USSR should contact a Soviet commercial representative in the United States in order to obtain a preliminary indication of interest and to identify key personnel at the appropriate FTO and other organizations in the USSR.

The following Soviet offices in the United States handle commercial matters:

Amtorg Trading Corp.
750 Third Avenue
New York, NY 10017

Soviet Business and Trade Office
1511 K Street NW
Washington, DC 20006

If the preliminary contact indicates that

Source: Department of Commerce Overseas Reports "Trading with the USSR."

there is potential interest, then negotiations may be advanced by writing the appropriate FTO chairman in Moscow. As much specific information as possible about the product should be included. If correspondence proves to be unsatisfactory in initiating a contact and if market estimates justify the expense, a visit to FTO headquarters in Moscow is advised. Personal relationships are particularly important in dealing with Soviet agencies.

The U.S. Embassy in Moscow and the Soviet Embassy in Washington are helpful in arranging an invitation from an FTO and in processing visas. The U.S. Commercial Office in Moscow offers U.S. businessmen demonstration facilities as well as commercial information and services. Another key information and contact center for U.S. businessmen interested in promoting trade with the USSR and Eastern Europe is the U.S. East-West Trade Development Office in Vienna. U.S. firms should also consider arranging for exhibitions at Soviet trade fairs held in Moscow and other major cities. Travel arrangements are usually made by the official Soviet trade agency, Intourist (address below).

Trade missions of U.S. businessmen to the Soviet Union are organized, planned, and led by the U.S. Department of Commerce. These missions are very helpful in introducing U.S. businessmen to the Soviet market as well as to key personnel. For information concerning trade fairs and exhibitions, contact:

Director, Trade Promotion Division
Bureau of East-West Trade
U.S. Department of Commerce
Washington, DC 20230

USEFUL U.S. ADDRESSES

Intourist
630 Fifth Avenue
New York, NY 10020

Embassy of the USSR
1125 Sixteenth Street NW
Washington, DC 20006

Chamber of Commerce
U.S.–USSR Trade and Economics Council, Inc.
280 Park Avenue
New York, NY 10017

USEFUL FOREIGN ADDRESSES

U.S. East-West Trade Development Office
A-1010 Vienna, Friedrick Schmidtplatz, Austria

U.S. Commercial Office
15 Ulitsa Chaikovskogo
Moscow, USSR

U.S. Embassy
19/23 Ulitsa Chaikovskogo
Moscow, USSR

U.S. BANKS WITH OFFICES IN MOSCOW

Bank of America, San Francisco, CA
Citibank, New York, NY
Chase-Manhattan Bank, New York, NY

OTHER EASTERN EUROPEAN COUNTRIES

Commercial transactions with Bulgaria, Czechoslovakia, East Germany, Hungary, Poland, and Romania are similar to those with the USSR. Contracts are negotiated with the appropriate Foreign Trade Organization. For detailed information about trade shows, missions, export licenses, and FTOs, contact the Bureau of East-West Trade, Department of Commerce in Washington, or the Commerce Department Offices at the district level. Another key source of information is the U.S. East-West Trade Development Office in Vienna. Addresses are given above in the Soviet Union section.

BULGARIA

U.S. contacts
Bulgarian Embassy
2100 16th Street NW
Washington, DC 20009

Bulgarian Commercial Counselor
50 E. 42nd Street
New York, NY 10017

Foreign contacts
U.S. Embassy
1 Alexander Stamboliski Boulevard
Sofia, Bulgaria

Bulgarian Chamber of Commerce
11-a Stamboliski Boulevard
Sofia, Bulgaria

CZECHOSLOVAKIA

U.S. contacts
Czechoslovakian Embassy
3900 Linnean Avenue NW
Washington, DC 20008
Office of the Czechoslovakian Commercial Counselor
180 Madison Avenue
New York, NY 10016

Foreign contacts
U.S. Embassy
Trziste 15–12548
Prague, Czechoslovakia

EAST GERMANY
(German Democratic Republic)

U.S. contacts
Embassy of the German Democratic Republic
1717 Massachusetts Avenue NW
Washington, DC 20036

Permanent Mission of German Democratic
Republic to the United Nations
58 Park Avenue
New York, NY 10016

Foreign contacts
U.S. Embassy
Shadowstrasse 3
Berlin, German Democratic Republic

U.S. banks with offices in Berlin
Citibank, New York, NY

HUNGARY

U.S. contacts
Embassy of Hungary to the United States
2437 15th Street NW
Washington, DC 20009

Office of the Commercial Counselor of the
Embassy of Hungary
2401 Calvert Street
Washington, DC 20008

Trade Representation of the Hungarian People's Republic
150 E. 58th Street
New York, NY 10022

Foreign contacts
U.S. Embassy
V. Szabadsag, Ter. 12
Budapest, Hungary

Hungarian Chamber of Commerce
P.O. Box 106
Budapest, Hungary

POLAND

U.S. contacts
Economic Counselor's Office
Embassy of the Polish People's Republic
2640 16th Street NW
Washington, DC 20008

Polish Consulate General
233 Madison Avenue
New York, NY 10016

Polish Commercial Counselor's Office
1 Daghammarskjold Plaza
New York, NY 10017

Office of Polish Commercial Consul
333 E. Ontario Street
Chicago, IL 60611

Polish Chamber of Foreign Trade
44 Montgomery Street
San Francisco, CA 94104

Foreign contacts
US Embassy
Aleje Ujazdowskie 29/31
Warsaw, Poland

U.S. Trade Development Center
Wiejska St. 20
00–49 Warsaw, Poland

Polish Chamber of Foreign Trade
Trebacka 4
Warsaw, Poland

U.S. banks with offices in Warsaw
First National Bank, Chicago

ROMANIA

U.S. contacts
Romanian Embassy
1607 23rd Street NW
Washington, DC 20008

Romanian Office of the Economic Counselor
95 Madison Avenue
New York, NY 10016

Romanian Foreign Trade Promotion Office
100 W. Monroe Street
Chicago, IL 60603

Romanian Foreign Trade Promotion Office
22 Battery Street
San Francisco, CA 94111

Foreign contacts
U.S. Embassy
Strada Tudor Argezhi 9
Bucharest, Romania

U.S. banks with offices in Bucharest
Manufacturer's Hanover Trust, New York, NY

Doing Business in the Near East and North Africa

INTRODUCTION

Since the oil price rise in 1973, the 19 Near East/North African countries* have become increasingly important in terms of the U.S. balance of payments. On the export side, U.S. sales to the area have risen over 240 percent from $3.5 billion in 1973 to $12 billion in 1977. An additional 13 percent rise is projected for 1978, bringing the total U.S. sales to the area to over $13.5 billion. U.S. exports to the region accounted for only 4.9 percent of total U.S. exports in 1973 but had more than doubled to 10.3 percent by 1977.

According to U.S. Department of Commerce trade statistics, many diverse American suppliers find attractive sales opportunities in the Near East and North Africa. Food products, primarily cereals, and special category (military) goods account for approximately 12.5 percent each of U.S. exports to the area. The largest component, however, consists of machinery and transport equipment accounting for over 31 percent and 25 percent of sales, respectively. Machinery sales are led by construction equipment but also include sizable shipments of communications, power generation, agricultural, textile, food processing, heating and cooling, and mechanical handling equipment. Motor vehicles and aircraft make up the bulk of transport equipment exports.

In addition to exports of goods which are reflected in the above statistics, the United States exports a variety of consulting, architectural, engineering and construction services to the area. The American Embassy in Tehran, for example, estimates U.S. invisible earnings from Iran alone at $1 billion annually. The value of U.S. services sold to Saudi Arabia was estimated at $700 million during 1976.

On the import side, the United States is purchasing a growing quantity of Near East/North African petroleum and gas at a higher price. In 1973, U.S. imports from the region accounted for 2.7 percent of our total imports; by 1977 this percentage had climbed to 13.5 percent. In dollars, U.S. purchases from the region totaled $1.8 billion (customs value) in 1973 and $19.9 billion (f.a.s. value) in 1977. Although the figures are not directly comparable, they give an indication of the tremendous increase in U.S. imports over the past several years.

The area's oil exporting countries are using this additional revenue to undertake rapid, large-scale development in their own countries, in neighboring countries and in many other third-world nations. This development and resultant expanded economic activity are creating vast commercial opportunities for U.S. business.

In pursuing these opportunities, American companies face intense competition from Western Europe, Japan and, increasingly, from newcomers like South Korea. However, your venture starts with a built-in advantage since U.S. products and services are held in high regard throughout the region. Even remote hinterland shops display wide varieties of familiar U.S. brands.

Near East/North African consumers are shrewd buyers desiring the best but conscious of price, service, availability of spare parts and delivery time. Personal contact is imperative in cultivating the market, since the customer will rarely buy from a catalog unless assured of the integrity of the firm and its representatives.

This section is designed to provide U.S. business with information on how these immense oil revenues will be spent, the nature of the market, how to do business in the area, and how the Department of Commerce can assist in penetrating the market.

The Commerce Action Group for the Near East (CAGNE) within the Bureau of International Commerce serves as the focal point for the U.S. Department of Commerce response to the dramatically changed economic situation and significant business opportunities in the Near East and North Africa. The group assembles, analyzes, and disseminates to the U.S. business community information

---

* Algeria, Bahrain, Egypt, Iran, Iraq, Israel, Jordan, Kuwait, Lebanon, Libya, Morocco, Oman, Peoples Democratic Republic of Yemen, Qatar, Saudi Arabia, Syria, Tunisia, United Arab Emirates, Yemen Arab Republic.

Source: Excerpted from *A Business Guide to the Near East & North Africa*, Bureau of International Commerce, U.S. Department of Commerce.

on economic conditions and new opportunities in the area, provides counseling for and makes representations on behalf of U.S. exporters, and plans and organizes promotional programs to assist U.S. firms to take advantage of the market boom. CAGNE also coordinates Department of Commerce participation in joint commission activities.

To take advantage of these programs call 202-377-5767 (Near East); 202-377-5737 (North Africa); 202-377-3752 (Iran, Israel, Egypt). For information concerning major projects, call 202-377-4441. The mailing address is Commerce Action Group for the Near East, Bureau of International Commerce, Room 3203, Washington, DC 20230.

Personal assistance from International Trade Specialists is as close as the Department of Commerce district office in your area.

Assistance is also available from specialists in the U.S. Department of State and other U.S. government agencies. Your own bank can also be an excellent starting point; it may have a correspondent relationship with local banks in the Near East and North Africa, as well as relationships with American banks who have on-the-scene experience in many of these countries.

SELLING IN THE NEAR EAST AND NORTH AFRICA

The markets of the Near East and North African region are not homogeneous. A number are rich; others have severe foreign exchange shortages. Some rely on the free market mechanism, while others are dominated by government ownership in almost every sector.

The first step in your program to penetrate the markets in this region should be to locate sales opportunities in the area of public tenders, which Near East and North African governments issue frequently for the operating requirements of their agencies, state monopolies, and government-owned industries. You can locate these opportunities through representatives or agents physically located in the market of your choice. You can also locate opportunities on major projects through the Business Facilitation Staff of the Commerce Action Group for the Near East.

Once a project or sales opportunity has been identified, many firms familiar with the area have found that a "package offer" of equipment, spare parts, and training courses for repairmen, and perhaps even an offer to set up and equip maintenance facilities, will assist in obtaining contracts with both governmental entities and private entrepreneurs. A well-thought-out plan outlining what must be done—from the development of an empty plot of land to initiation of production—is a distinct asset. In other words, the foreign firm that advises what is needed and offers to provide the complete technical package can expect to have a great advantage over foreign firms that offer partial projects.

U.S. business must be prepared to abandon traditional ways of doing business in the developed markets of Western Europe. They must investigate the human and material resources and social and cultural characteristics of the region, and tailor their products and proposals accordingly.

U.S. TRADE WITH NEAR EAST/NORTH AFRICAN COUNTRIES, 1975, 1976, 1977 (in $ millions)

	U.S. Exports, Including Reexports			U.S. General Imports		
	1975	1976	1977	1975	1976	1977
Total for area	10,313.3	11,190.2	12,341.6	7,871.3	13,628.6	19,873.4
Percent of U.S. total	9.4	9.7	10.3	8.2	11.3	13.5
Arab countries of Near East	3,502.9	5,052.0	5,858.8	3,690.7	7,107.7	9,451.5
Bahrain	90.2	279.2	203.3	100.7	29.5	74.4
Iraq	309.7	381.8	210.9	19.1	110.0	381.5
Jordan	195.4	234.0	301.8	0.8	1.4	3.2
Kuwait	366.1	471.5	547.8	111.4	37.6	214.5
Lebanon	402.3	48.5	123.8	33.3	4.6	42.5
Oman	74.7	57.1	56.9	52.7	222.6	424.3
People's Democratic Republic of Yemen	2.8	4.4	30.9	0.6	0.8	2.8
Qatar	50.3	78.7	113.1	56.5	119.0	292.2
Saudi Arabia	1,501.8	2,774.1	3,575.3	2,624.6	5,212.9	6,358.5
Syria	127.8	272.2	133.6	7.0	9.8	16.2
United Arab Emirates	371.5	424.8	515.1	683.8	1,359.2	1,640.8
Yemen Arab Republic	8.3	25.4	46.4	0.2	0.3	0.6
Arab countries of North Africa	1,835.5	1,953.0	2,305.5	2,468.0	4,618.1	7,062.8
Algeria	631.8	487.0	526.5	1,358.6	2,209.4	3,064.5
Libya	231.5	276.6	313.7	1,045.7	2,243.4	3,796.1
Morocco	199.5	297.0	371.6	10.2	16.5	21.0
Tunisia	90.0	82.4	111.3	26.0	56.3	11.2
Egypt	682.7	810.0	982.4	27.5	92.5	170.0
Non-Arab countries of Near East	4,792.9	4,185.2	4,177.3	1,712.6	1,902.8	3,359.1
Iran	3,241.7	2,776.0	2,730.8	1,399.8	1,480.1	2,788.8
Israel	1,551.2	1,409.2	1,446.5	312.8	422.7	570.3

Source: U.S. Department of Commerce, Bureau of Census, Report FT 990.
Compiled by: Commerce Action Group for the Near East, January 31, 1978.

Including Special Category Commodities.
Imports—f.a.s. value.
Exports—f.a.s. value.

DOING BUSINESS IN THE NEAR EAST AND NORTH AFRICA

TRADE POLICIES

Most of the Near East countries can be said to pursue liberal trade policies. **Saudi Arabia, Kuwait,** the **United Arab Emirates, Bahrain, Qatar,** and **Lebanon** have few import restrictions or licensing requirements, and no exchange controls.

Iran's import policy, which had favored capital goods, recently was relaxed to include consumer items as well, although all imports remain subject to government control. Several ministries have a voice in determining which commodities may be imported and the Central Bank controls the foreign exchange transactions. No import licenses or exchange permits are necessary for the majority of Iranian imports.

Imports into **Israel** are largely free from quantitative restrictions. Licensing is required for most imports but for many items is issued automatically. Exchange for licensed goods and goods not subject to licensing is issued automatically. Tariff rates are changed frequently, and the purchaser is ultimately the best source of information about the rate of customs duty on a particular product. U.S. goods are guaranteed most favored nation treatment under a Treaty of Friendship, Commerce and Navigation. Israel is also a member of the General Agreement on Tariffs and Trade (GATT).

Egypt has been moving slowly toward a more liberalized trade policy. While still facing foreign exchange shortages, the Egyptian government has removed customs duties from imported foodstuffs and has implemented a number of measures designed to lift restrictions on private sector imports and exports of a wide range of goods. Egyptian imports require exchange permits.

Although **Iraq** has made recent changes to liberalize its import policy, the policy remains relatively strict, requiring both import licenses and exchange permits. Practically all importing is done by government agencies or government-owned importing companies.

SALES APPROACH

U.S. firms that use aggressive sales methods, use effective local agents, and send senior sales executives to the area frequently can expect to increase sales in spite of strong competition. Attractive financing terms will improve sales prospects, an aspect in which competing nations often have the upper hand. But financing alone will rarely make or break a deal, and where an offer is highly acceptable in every other respect, satisfactory financing can almost always be arranged.

The key to successful sales in the Near East and North Africa is the personal touch. Businessmen in this area are famous for their informal business approach and their hospitality. Few visitors have a business or government office without drinking the always present coffee or tea over which business is discussed and the foundation for a sale laid.

Personal visits and face-to-face salesmanship still are the tried and true method of market promotion in the countries of the Near East and North Africa. While it is true that some sales have been made in the area by firms that have never sent a representative there, the really big sales and continued business come as a result of exploratory and follow-up visits by Americans who realize that this method is the only effective way to meet and beat the intense competition from aggressive European and Japanese businessmen.

Effective local representation is another key for sales penetration in any of the Near East and North African markets. In fact, most of the governments insist that goods imported must be handled by nationals of their own country. Therefore, almost all U.S. companies with significant sales in the area are represented in each country by a distributor or agent and do not try to cover one country with an agent from another.

Branch offices are not used to a great extent, although Beirut in past years was the regional headquarters for over 500 U.S. firms. Due to civil disturbances in Lebanon during 1975 and 1976, many firms left Beirut and established temporary or permanent offices elsewhere in the area. Many firms use Casablanca as a regional base for North and Subsaharan Africa.

While some business can be done on a direct basis without the use of an agent or distributor, such an approach is not generally recommended except in a state-enterprise monopoly system such as Algeria. Knowledge of local trading practices and customs often is essential in making a sale. Also, concluding a transaction or bidding on a project often takes a long time—too long for an official of the home office to spend in the area. Then, too, both local government officials and private businessmen tend to rely on the technical knowledge of local representatives in drawing up specifications for goods. Thus, if the local decision-maker has confidence in a firm's agent, the chances are that sooner or later it will get the business.

Finally, there may be continuing problems with quotations, financing, import regulations, and collections that are best solved by a local representative. If your stakes are sufficiently high—and considering the vastly increased purchasing potential of the oil-producing countries they may well be—you may wish to station an able American representative in a specific country in addition to having good local representation. Many local businessmen in the area expect to see an American representing an American company, especially if it is a large company.

What kind of representative should an American company select—a distributor or an agent? Distributorships are the most common form of representation for machinery, motor vehicles, consumer items, and other products that require regular servicing and the maintenance of stocks of original equipment and spare parts.

Distributors act as principals and buy on a letter-of-credit basis when required by government regulations or foreign suppliers. They also buy on extended credit terms. Most distributorship agreements are made on an exclusive basis for an entire country. Thus, any direct inquiries received from other merchants are referred by the manufacturer to his distributor.

A complaint often heard in the area is that some companies appoint local subagents who, in turn, are responsible to another agency outside the country. Iranians, Saudis, and others feel their national pride affronted by this system, and many capable companies reject such appointments outright. Their stand is difficult to refute, especially if most of a U.S. company's sales in the area are in the slighted country.

Increasing prices to support another agency tier may critically reduce competitiveness. But if subagents are cut in at previous price levels, commission splitting may leave all parties dissatisfied.

While representatives in such countries as Saudi Arabia, Kuwait, and Iran operate in the private business sector, you will find that in seeking a representative in Iraq (and generally Algeria) you must choose one of the public sector import companies to represent your line of products. However, this is not a new situation and should not be a major deterrent, for U.S. firms find they can still make attractive sales. Officials of state trading companies in Algeria and Iraq ask that U.S. businessmen come to visit them to discuss possible sales of all types of industrial equipment, machinery, and consumer durables.

FINANCING

Good banking facilities are prominent throughout the Near East and North Africa including local and foreign banks, and U.S. companies interested in the area can be assured of the availability of a full range of banking services. Branches or correspondents of such U.S. banks as First National City Bank, Bank of America, Continental Illinois, and Chase Manhattan are located in all major trading centers. In the United Arab Emirates, there are over a dozen banking establishments in Abu Dhabi and Dubai, alone. Banking facilities in Egypt have significantly improved recently with the beginning of activities by Chase Manhattan, American Express, and First National of Chicago. In addition to the Central Bank of Iran (Bank Markazi), 29 banks with some 7,000 branches are operating in Iran. Foreign banking in Iran is in the form of minority participation in joint ventures established under the laws of Iran.

While the Near East and North African countries have highly developed commercial banking systems, credit available in the various markets, with the exception of Iran and Israel, tends to be relatively limited and short term. Importers and distributors may give extended credit terms to retailers and end users. Credit also is extended by commercial bank and professional money lenders. Notes payable are commonly used. Discounted short-term notes are rediscounted several times, particularly in bazaars.

Until recently, most business in Saudi Arabia was conducted on a cash basis. For most government purchases, this is still the case. However, such consumer items as automobiles, air conditioners, and home appliances are being financed by Saudi retailers. On a larger scale, heavy machinery dealers are beginning to finance their customers.

Most U.S. exports to Egypt are made against a letter of credit. In Iran, short-term credit is available through 18 private and 9 public banks. Good import financing facilities are available in the United Arab Emirates to serve local and international business.

WHOLESALE AND RETAIL METHODS

The principal retail outlet for light industrial goods throughout most of the Near East and North Africa has long been the bazaar. Almost all cities, towns, and villages have one. Retailing, wholesaling, financing, storage, and light manufacturing all take place there.

Although the bazaar once was the only principal location of business offices in the Near East and North Africa, today many firms have moved their main offices to more modern and spacious quarters. Importers of capital goods, appliances, vehicles, and other products requiring showroom and service facilities generally are located in a modern building either in the center of the city or in a nearby suburb. However, it is still common for importers of competitive products, such as automotive parts, to be located together on one street or in one area.

GOVERNMENT PURCHASES

Frequently the largest buyer in a Near East and North African country is its own government. Requirements often are on an annual basis. Regardless of the country in which a firm bids on tenders, many government orders are likely to be of substantial size and thus compensate for any delays and extra efforts of negotiating a final sale.

Sales to governments may involve dealing directly or through private agents, with state trading companies, government ministries and agencies, or state-owned industrial firms. Local agents for foreign manufacturers should be registered with applicable local government agencies in order to qualify to receive and bid on tenders.

Government procurement procedures center on the issuance of tenders. Prospective suppliers, therefore, should acquaint themselves with tender notices that are published in the local press and familiarize themselves with bidding requirements and government procedures.

The government of Israel seldom issues international tenders, preferring to "shop around." While municipal governments issue tenders, there is usually insufficient time for foreign companies to bid. The Israeli government maintains a Supply Mission, 850 Third Avenue, New York, NY 10020, which makes purchases in the United States. The Histadrut, Israel's General Federation of Labor and the largest employer, makes its purchases in the United States through Solcoor Inc., 415 Madison Avenue, New York, NY 10017.

In bidding on large government projects, it is essential to do as much spadework as possible before the actual tender notice appears. Such contracts rarely are awarded to firms that begin to compete only when tender documents are in hand.

Advance preparation, including time spent in the country, also can prove a valuable hedge against the chance that a final, detailed bid, often produced at great expense, is not the low bid. Where the evaluating authority has developed respect for a firm's technical ability, product quality, and experience, the firm may be able to salvage an otherwise uncompetitive position. Even if the project is awarded to a competitor, the residual goodwill generated by an earnest effort will serve well in future competitions.

The Algerian government closely controls foreign trade and domestic marketing. State enterprises, of which there are about 100, virtually monopolize importing/exporting and are undertaking a wide range of new industrial investments.

Although Iran basically is a free enterprise economy, the government buys many items in addition to its day-to-day operating requirements. The government operates over 200 manufacturing and processing plants in the food, textile, chemical, mining, and other industries. The Foreign Transactions Company, an agency of the Ministry of Economy, buys the operating requirements of some government agencies, while other departments buy their requirements directly.

Three large purchasing entities are in Saudi Arabia—the government, the Arabian American Oil Company (Aramco), and the U.S. Corps of Engineers.

All government purchasing is theoretically controlled by the Ministry of Finance under the Tenders and Bids Regulations. In practice, each ministry and major government agency has the right to carry out its own contracting for purchases of goods and services. While procedures vary, the following generally apply. Each firm interested in supplying services of equipment to a ministry must "prequalify" before it can submit bids. Once a firm has prequalified, the ministry will accept a tender from the firm. However, all bids are not always open to every company; the ministry decides which firms will be invited to tender and issues a short list. This is determined by the firm's technical qualifications and its past performance.

Aramco buys a wide diversity and volume of foreign products as its needs range far beyond those of the normal petroleum producer. In 1976 alone, for example, Aramco spent almost $750 million on American-made goods ranging from gas turbines to potato chips. In addition to its own purchases, Aramco has been designated by the Saudi government to manage some of the most ambitious projects the world has ever tackled, costing well into the billions of dollars.

Many U.S. products—sophisticated and expensive construction machinery, for example—owe their acceptance in the Saudi Arabian market as a whole to the fact that they are used by Aramco. Local purchasers feel that whatever Aramco buys represents the best possible value. A sale to Aramco exercises, in many instances, a strong positive effect on the prospects for sales of that product to the Saudi government and consumer.

U.S. firms enjoy no special privileges in their dealings with Aramco. The company's prequalification procedures are rigid, and decisions to buy are based on a worldwide comparison of price, quality, and availability. U.S. firms should contact Aramco's Houston office, prequalify, and eventually visit the

Dhahran headquarters where many of the final decisions are made. The Houston office is located at Aramco Services, 1100 Milan, Houston, TX 77002 (713-651-5800).

The activities of the U.S. Army Corps of Engineers in Saudi Arabia are unique. Under a long-standing agreement, the corps acts as management consultant to the Saudi Arabian Ministry of Defense and Aviation for all military construction projects within the kingdom. At present the corps handles construction projects totaling some $24 billion. The corps, on behalf of the ministry, identifies projects, prequalifies, and selects firms to design and engineer these facilities. The corps then issues tenders for construction of the projects, selects the best qualified firm, supervises, and then accepts the project on behalf of the Saudi government. The corps is also responsible in many cases for the equipment, such as furniture, laboratory equipment, and communications systems, to be used in the projects.

U.S. firms are at an advantage in tendering for these projects due to their familiarity with corps procedures; however, this does not guarantee that they will be awarded contracts.

The corps has awarded major contracts to qualified West German, South Korean, and other companies on the basis of price, quality, and ability to meet construction deadlines. The corps has relocated its headquarters for support of its Saudi Arabian projects to the United States. The point of contact is U.S. Army Engineer Division/Middle East, P.O. Box 2250, Winchester, VA 22601 (703-667-2250).

BUSINESS TRAVEL

The best time to visit the Near East and North Africa is between October and May, when the climate generally is mild and pleasant. Many merchants are away during the hot summer months. From May to October skies are cloudless and rain seldom, if ever, falls—most of the area's rainfall occurs from December through February.

The continuing hotel construction boom in the area is resulting in a chain of comfortable, first-class hotels stretching from Casablanca to Tehran. Hilton, Sheraton, and Intercontinental hotels are located throughout most of the area. Hotel reservations are imperative and should be confirmed before leaving the United States, due to heavy travel throughout the area.

Taxi service is available in all the Near East and North African countries. Fares should be agreed upon in advance. If the price seems high, a bit of bargaining might bring it down.

An American sensitive to the customs and attitudes of other people does not need a long list of "dos" and "don'ts" to prepare for a trip to the Near East or North Africa. You will find that businessmen throughout the area are familiar, to a degree at least, with Western ways. You may be surprised at the number of men you meet who are graduates of American universities.

Businessmen like the straightforward approach of the average American. Negotiations generally do not take long to relax from the more formal atmosphere of the first meeting; they often end up doing business on a first-name basis.

Price will be a major subject of discussion with the businessman and government official, but if a product is attractive, the lowest price is not always the deciding factor. There is enormous respect for American quality. Therefore, an American businessman should not automatically become discouraged if it appears at first that his price and financing do not seem to meet those of his European or Japanese competitors.

Knowledge of English is widespread in Near East commercial and government quarters. If the company manager does not speak English, he will have a junior officer present at the interview who does. In French-speaking North Africa, English is less commonly understood. You will need to speak French or hire a local interpreter.

Business cards are an asset. In addition to English, Arabic is preferable for the Arab Near East, Farsi for Iran, Hebrew for Israel, and French for North Africa. They should be printed ahead of time, but in most cases can be printed locally. English-speaking secretarial help may be difficult to find, but the American Embassy's or Consulate's commercial section may be able to provide useful advice.

Preparation for a trip to the area should include contacts with the Commerce Action Group for the Near East and the Commerce district office to gather as much information as possible before leaving the United States. U.S. embassy commercial staffs, who have experienced an extraordinary influx of business visitors seeking assistance since 1974, reiterate the better prepared the business traveler is before arrival in the area, the better the chances of success.

Having focused on your business objectives, you should enter into correspondence with prospective customers or agents before your trip. The business entities in these countries also can be helpful in planning your itinerary, arranging appointments, and facilitating entry into the country.

Logistic arrangements such as hotel reservations, hiring of translators, etc., should always be made well ahead of your scheduled arrival. Travel agents or carriers are able to do this. American embassies and consulates cannot undertake to provide such logistic services. However, you are welcome to write them advising of your intended travel and describing your business objectives, to enable them to respond with some suggestions, if appropriate.

Once you have arrived in the Near East or North Africa, you should make the office of the U.S. commercial officer your first stop in every city where there is one. The officer generally will be able to provide you with certain information and assistance in connection with your business interests.

While the commercial officer may be able to advise you on the appropriate person to contact in the public and private sectors, you will not always be able to readily obtain appointments with top-level officials in ministries or firms. The growing number of projects and trade opportunities is attracting a large influx of business visitors from all industrial countries to the Near East and North Africa. Senior officials of governments and firms generally receive more requests for appointments than they can accommodate, especially at short notice.

HOW THE U.S. GOVERNMENT CAN HELP

DEPARTMENT OF COMMERCE

To facilitate the Department of Commerce's efforts to assist U.S. business in penetrating the lucrative Near East/North African markets, the Commerce Action Group for the Near East (CAGNE) was formed in July 1974. The group assembles, analyzes, and disseminates information on economic conditions and new opportunities in the area, provides counseling for and makes representations on behalf of U.S. exporters and plans and organizes promotional programs to stimulate U.S. firms to take advantage of the market boom.

Much information on specific countries is available—ranging from current economic reports prepared by foreign service officers in the field to product information and marketing guides. You may be especially interested in Commerce's *Overseas Business Reports*, covering marketing and doing business in the countries of the area. Country specialists in the CAGNE can usually answer your questions on import duties or restrictions, outlook for sales of your product, local production, imports and exports, methods of doing business, etc.

Information about projects in the Near East and North Africa is disseminated to the U.S. business community by CAGNE through direct contact with U.S. firms and through *Commerce Business Daily*. CAGNE provides assistance to U.S. companies at each step, from learning about a project at the earliest possible stage of development to making a successful bid.

Companies interested in getting into the Near East or North African market or in introducing new product lines should consider participating in U.S. Department of Commerce-sponsored trade promotion events.

A U.S. Trade Center established in Tehran in November 1973 holds a number of major exhibitions each year in which American manufacturers and suppliers are invited to show their latest products. Some upcoming shows will feature medical equipment, textile machinery, electrical energy systems, and business and data processing equipment. Between major exhibitions, the Trade Center is available to U.S. firms at no charge for sales promotions and meetings. Information on the Trade Center can be obtained from CAGNE or the nearest Commerce district office.

Other Commerce-sponsored activities include specialized trade missions of 5 to 12 U.S. businessmen and a Commerce director, which introduce the U.S. company to the market and its prime customers, including key foreign government officials; and catalog shows that display a number of U.S. product sales catalogs to overseas customers and include a Commerce-provided industry expert to represent the participating firms and answer questions.

To take advantage of any of these CAGNE programs, write to the U.S. Department of Commerce, ITA/CAGNE, Room 3203, Washington, DC 20203, or telephone the following offices at area code 202:

```
North Africa ....................... 377-5737
Arab Near East .................... 377-5767
Iran/Israel/Egypt ................. 377-3752
Business Facilitation Staff ......... 377-4441
Trade Promotion Staff ............. 377-2952
```

Other Commerce services to exporters which are available for most countries throughout the world include the Trade Opportunities Program (TOP) and the Agent/Distributor Service (ADS). Administered by the Overseas Business Opportunities Division, Office of Export Development, Bureau of International Commerce, TOP is a subscription trade lead service that furnishes notices of trade opportunities to U.S. companies registered in the program. Participating U.S. firms are computer matched to the trade leads according to three criteria—type of opportunity, product interest, and country interest. Commercial opportunities processed in this way are not published in the biweekly magazine *Commerce America*.

The ADS will give you the names of three prospects identified by the U.S. Foreign Service who agree to correspond with you. If you are interested in doing business with a specific foreign firm, a background report called a World Traders Data Report (WTDR) can be obtained from the Export Information Division, Office of Export Development, Bureau of International Commerce, U.S. Department of Commerce, Washington, DC 20230.

Additional information on these and other Commerce programs for exporters can be obtained from International Trade Specialists located in the Commerce district offices in 43 cities throughout the country.

DEPARTMENT OF STATE

The Department of State and its embassies and consulates abroad are able to offer advice and assistance to U.S. businessmen.

In the United States, businessmen seeking information on specific countries are invited to draw upon the expertise of the Department of State desk officers for briefings on particular countries. Requests for information or briefings can be funneled through the Regional Economic Office of the Near East and South Asia Bureau (NEA); telephone 202-632-1794; mailing address: Department of State, Washington, DC 20520.

If you intend to pursue your marketing initiatives by traveling abroad, you are invited to contact the U.S. commercial officer attached to the American embassy or consulate in the cities you plan to visit. A listing of Economic/Commercial Offices in the Near East/North African area is contained under the heading of Country Data in this section. No special introduction is needed to call on members of the Economic/Commercial section at foreign service posts. They will be helpful to you because they have the first-hand knowledge of local market conditions, and can provide briefings on economic developments and the business climate. They can discuss with you local opportunities for your product line, suggest suitable agents, and provide tips on business practices prevailing in the country which are particularly useful to new-to-market firms. The commercial officers will gladly help you identify the appropriate local government officials and executives of firms to contact.

OTHER GOVERNMENT ASSISTANCE

The Export-Import Bank of the United States offers a number of export financing programs ranging from the Commercial Bank Exporter Guarantee Program and credit insurance offered by the Foreign Credit Insurance Association to the Cooperative Financing Facility. An Export Finance Counseling Service also is available. Write to the Export-Import Bank, Washington, DC 21568.

If you are concerned that you may not be paid by your customer, you should know about the Foreign Credit Insurance Association (FCIA). The FCIA offers credit insurance policies against such risks. Almost any businessman is eligible. You can get information about FCIA's services and applications for policies from insurance agents, brokers, or firms. FCIA regional offices are located in New York, Atlanta, Chicago, Cleveland, Los Angeles, Milwaukee, Houston, San Francisco, and Washington, DC. General questions also may be directed to the FCIA ombudsman in the New York office. Call 212-432-6383.

COUNTRY DATA

ALGERIA

REPRESENTATION

Embassy of Algeria
2118 Kalorama Road NW
Washington, DC 20008
Telephone: 202-234-7246

American Embassy
4 Chemin Cheikh Bachir
Brahimi B.P. 549
Alger-Gare
Algiers, Algeria
Telephone: 60.1.5/60.12.55
Telex: 52064

American Consulate
14 Square de Banako
Oran, Algeria
Telephone: 35.55.02

SONATRACH, Inc.
(Algerian State Enterprise for Oil, Gas, Petrochemicals, Plastics, Fertilizers)
816 Connecticut Avenue NW
Washington, DC 20006
Telephone: 202-638-7180

CURRENCY: Algerian Dinar (DA).

ENTRY REQUIREMENTS

Algerian visas must be obtained from the embassy in Washington. Can be single or multiple entry. Must be accompanied by self-addressed return envelope, stamped for registered mail. Processing time: generally 24–48 hours.

Vaccinations: Smallpox is required.

BUSINESS CUSTOMS

Work week is Saturday through Wednesday, generally 8:30 A.M. to noon and 2:30 to 6:00 P.M. Private firms and state enterprises open Thursday morning for limited business.

American Embassy hours: 8:30 A.M.–12:30 P.M., 1:30–5:30 P.M. (varies in summer months).

Business cards are recommended. French is the working language; English is rarely understood.

BANKS

Banking is a state monopoly. Several deal in foreign trade and have correspondent relationships with U.S. banks, including:

Banque Nationale d'Algérie, 8 Blvd. Ché Guevara, Algiers
Telephone: 62.7600, Telex: 52788.

Banque Extérieur d'Algérie, 12 Blvd. Colonel Amirouche, Algiers
Telephone: 63.86.92/99, Telex: 52755.

Banque Centrale d'Algérie, 8 Blvd. Zirout Youcef, Algiers
Telephone: 64.74.00/02, Telex: 52709.

Banque Algérienne de Développement, 38 rue Franklin Roosevelt, Algiers
Telephone: 60.13.29, Telex: 52529.

SELECTED GOVERNMENT ENTITIES

Ministry of Agriculture and Agrarian Reform
12 Blvd. Colonel Amirouche, Algiers
Telephone: 63.89.50

Ministry of Commerce
Rue Belouzdad, Belcourt, Algiers
Telephone: 66.33.66

Ministry of Housing and Construction
148 Ave. de l' ALN
Hussein-Dey, Algiers
Telephone: 77.30.67/68
Telex: 52680

Ministry of Heavy Industry
Rue Ahmed Bey de Constantine, Algiers
Telephone: 60.82.88

Ministry of Light Industries
Rue Ahmed Bey de Constantine, Algiers
Telephone: 60.06.66

Ministry of Public Works
135 Rue Didouche Mourad, Algiers
Telephone: 61.16.10

Ministry of Transport
19 Rue Rabah Maidat, Algiers
Telephone: 66.33.41/46
Telex: 52775

SONACOME (Société Nationale de Construction Mécanique) (Mechanical industries)
Route Nationale 1, Bockadem B.P.8, Algiers
Telephones: 60.28.33, 66.95.83
Telex: 52800

SONAREM (Société Nationale de Recherches et d' Exploitation Minières) (Mining and large scale quarrying)
127 Blvd. Salah Bouakouis
B.P. 860 Alger, Algiers
Telephones: 63.15.55/67
Telex: 52910

SONATRACH (Société Nationale de Transport et de Commercialisation des Hydro-carburex) (Hydrocarbons, fertilizers, plastics and petrochemicals)
80 Ave Ahmed Ghermoul, Algiers
Telephone: 66.33.00
Telex: 52916

SONELEC (Société Nationale de Fabrication et de Montage du Materiel Electrique et Electronique) (Electric and electronic equipment)
4–6 Blvd. Mohamed V, Algiers
Telephone: 63.70.82/86
Telex: 52867

BAHRAIN

REPRESENTATION

Embassy of Bahrain
2600 Virginia Avenue NW
Washington, DC 20037
Telephone: 202–965–4930

American Embassy
P.O. Box 431
Manama, Bahrain
Telephone: 714151

CURRENCY: Bahrain Dinar (BD).

ENTRY REQUIREMENTS

Visa may be obtained at the Bahrain airport if the entrant is planning to remain less than 72 hours. Otherwise, to secure a visa, applicants must submit to the Consular Section, Bahrain Permanent Mission, a valid passport, one completed application, one photo, a valid inoculation certificate against cholera, smallpox, and yellow fever, a letter of guaranty from the applicant's firm, and a certified check or money order for $14 payable to the Consulate of Bahrain. Visas are normally issued in three working days.

BUSINESS CUSTOMS

Government offices are open from 7:00 A.M. to 1:00 P.M., Saturday through Thursday. Commercial establishments: Saturday through Thursday, 7:30 A.M. to 12:30 P.M. and 3:30 P.M. to 6:30 P.M. Banks: 7:00 A.M. to 1:00 P.M., Saturday through Wednesday, and 8:00 A.M. to 11:30 A.M. on Thursday. American Embassy hours: Saturday through Thursday, 7:00 A.M. to 3:00 P.M. Friday is the weekly holiday in Bahrain.

BANKS

United States (regular banking services): Chase Manhattan Bank, Citibank, Continental Bank of Illinois. Thirty-four U.S. and foreign banks have off-shore banking units in Bahrain, including Bank of America, American Express, Chemical Bank, Chase Manhattan, and Manufacturers Hanover Trust.

SELECTED GOVERNMENT ENTITIES

Ministry of Finance and Economy
Manama
Telephone: 53361

Ministry of Commerce and Agriculture
Manama
Telephone: 50813

Ministry of Development and Industry
Manama
Telephone: 53361

ARAB REPUBLIC OF EGYPT

REPRESENTATION

Embassy of the Arab Republic of Egypt
2310 Decatur Place NW
Washington, DC 20008
Telephone: 202-232-5400

American Embassy
5 Sharia Latin American
Garden City, Cairo
Arab Republic of Egypt
Telephone: 28219

Commercial and Economic Office
2715 Connecticut Avenue NW
Washington: DC 20008
Telephone: 202-234-1414

Consulate of the Arab Republic of Egypt
1110 Second Avenue
2nd Floor
New York, NY 10022
Telephone: 212-759-7120

Consulate of the Arab Republic of Egypt
3001 Pacific Avenue
San Francisco, CA 94115
Telephone: 415-346-9700

U.S. Consulate General

15 Rue Djabarti
Alexandria
Arab Republic of Egypt
Telephone: 28186

CURRENCY: Egyptian pound (E).

ENTRY REQUIREMENTS

Egyptian visas may be obtained from the Consular Section of the Egyptian Embassy in Washington as well as from the Egyptian Consulates in New York City and San Francisco. To obtain a visa, a valid U.S. passport and a letter stating the purpose of the trip and giving financial guarantees are required. Visas cost $2.80 and are valid for three months and for a stay of one month. Visitors planning to stay more than two days are required to exchange into Egyptian pounds an amount equivalent to 100 pounds sterling. Upon departure, remaining Egyptian currency may be reexchanged for foreign currency after deduction of an amount equivalent to 20 pounds sterling for each night spent in the country.

BUSINESS CUSTOMS

American Embassy is open Monday through Friday, 8:00 A.M. to 5:00 P.M. Banking hours are 8:00 A.M. to 12:30 P.M. Saturday through Thursday, and 10:00 A.M. to noon Sunday. Government offices are open Saturday through Thursday, 8:00 A.M. to 2:00 P.M.

BANKS

Of the four Egyptian banks, the National Bank of Egypt handles almost all foreign transactions. Chase National Bank (Egypt) is a joint venture between the National Bank of Egypt and Chase Manhattan Bank. Misr International Bank is a joint venture between the First National Bank of Chicago, the Bank of Alexandria, Banco di Roma Holdings, and UBAF, Ltd. A third joint venture commercial bank, the Egyptian-American Bank, involves the Bank of Alexandria and the American Express International Bank Corp. Bank of America intends to open a joint venture bank with Egyptian and Arab interests called the Misr-American International Bank. Citibank and Manufacturers Hanover Trust Co. have foreign currency operations in Egypt as well.

SELECTED GOVERNMENT ENTITIES

Ministry of Agriculture
Sharia Wezaret El Zeraa
Dokki, Cairo
Telephone: 703388

General Authority for Investment and Free
  Zones
8 Sharia Adli
P.O. Box 1007, Cairo
Telephone: 902645

Ministry of Electric Power
Medinet Nasr, Cairo
Telephone: 8344351

Ministry of Housing and Reconstruction
  (Includes water and sewage projects)
1, Sharia Ismail Abaza, Cairo
Telephone: 23122

Ministry of Industry
2, Sharia Amrika El Latinia, Cairo
Telephone: 25023

General Organization for Industrialization
  (Approves major industrial purchases, in-
  vestments, and licenses)
6, Sharia Khalil Agha
Garden City, Cairo
Telephone: 20678

Ministry of Petroleum
2, Sharia Amrika El Latinia
Garden City, Cairo
Telephone: 35033

Ministry of Supply
  (Makes major purchases of bulk commodities)
99, Sharia Kasr El Eini, Cairo
Telephone: 33882

IRAN

REPRESENTATION

Embassy of Iran
30005 Massachusetts Avenue NW
Washington, DC 20008
Telephone: 202-797-6500

American Embassy
260 Avenue Takht-e-Jamshid
Tehran, Iran
Telephone: 820091, 825091, 829051

Consular Section
Embassy of Iran
2135 Wisconsin Avenue NW
Washington, DC 20007
Telephone: 202-333-8585

Consulate General of Iran
Standard Oil Building
Suite 7959
200 E. Randolph Street
Chicago, IL 60601
Telephone: 312-861-0990

Consulate General of Iran
630 Fifth Avenue

New York, NY 10020
Telephone: 212-397-1444

Consulate General of Iran
One Embarcadero Center
San Francisco, CA 94111
Telephone: 415-986-3500

Consulate General of Iran
601 Jefferson Street
Houston, TX 77002
Telephone: 713-236-8800

American Consulate
Shahnaz Avenue
Tabriz, Iran
Telephone: 2101, 5487

American Consulate
Trade Center Building
24th of Esfand Square
Esfahan, Iran
Telephone: 32079

American Consulate
Charkhabi Building
Bagh Eram Avenue
Shiraz, Iran
Telephone: 32023, 32024

U.S. Trade Center
61 Boulevard Elizabeth
P.O. Box 50
Tehran, Iran
Telephone: 657350/1
Telex: IR 213-179

ENTRY REQUIREMENTS

Iranian visas may be obtained from consulates in New York, Chicago, San Francisco,
the Iranian Embassy in Washington. Evidence
of current vaccination against smallpox and
cholera must be presented before visa is issued
and upon entry into Iran. Visas normally are
issued for a 12-month period permitting multiple entries, provided the passport is valid for
the 12-month period; each visit may be for a
period of up to three months, and the visa
may be renewed in Iran.

BUSINESS CUSTOMS

As in other Muslim countries, the work
week is Saturday through Thursday. Government offices are generally open to the public
8:00 A.M. to 4:30 P.M., Saturday through
Wednesday. American Embassy hours: Sunday through Thursday, 7:30 A.M. to 4:00 P.M.

BANKS

There are 24 commercial banks in Iran. By
far the largest commercial bank, with over
1,500 branches in Iran and 27 branches

abroad including New York City, is the government-owned Bank Melli Iran. The Central Bank (Bank Markazi Iran) is responsible for the stabilization of the rial, the formulation and implementation of monetary and credit policies, and the modernization of banking procedures. Foreign banking in Iran is in the form of minority participation in joint ventures with local banks. The following U.S. banks are represented in Iran: Chase Manhattan, Citibank, Bank of America, Continental Bank of Chicago, Bankers Trust Co., First National Bank of Chicago, Manufacturers Hanover, Midland Bank Group, and Philadelphia National; the first four are engaged in joint ventures.

SELECTED GOVERNMENT ENTITIES

Ministry of Agriculture and Natural Resources
Elizabeth Boulevard, Tehran

Ministry of Education
Ekbatan Avenue, Tehran

Ministry of Economic Affairs and Finance
Davar Avenue, Tehran

Ministry of Energy
Varzesh Avenue, corner Kazhan Street, Tehran

Ministry of Health
Kourosh Kabir Avenue, Tehran

Ministry of Housing and Urban Planning
Varzesh Avenue, Tehran

Ministry of Industry and Mines
Ark Square and Davar Avenue, Tehran

Ministry of Post, Telephone, and Telegraph
Bism Qasr Avenue, Tehran

Ministry of Roads and Transport
Ark Square, Tehran

National Iranian Oil Company
Corner Takhte-Jamshid and Hafez Avenues, Tehran

IRAQ

REPRESENTATION

Iraqi Interests Section
Indian Embassy
1801 P Street NW
Washington, DC 20008
Telephone: 202-483-5700

U.S. Interests Section
Belgian Embassy
MASBAH 52/5/35
P.O. Box 2447, Alwiyah
Baghdad, Iraq

Telephone: 4613819
Telex: 2287 USINT IK

CURRENCY: Iraqi Dinar (ID).

ENTRY REQUIREMENTS

Iraqi visa restrictions are stringent. Visas will not be issued unless the Iraqi ministry involved (usually the one with which the applicant intends to do business) cables approval of the visit to the Iraqi Interests Section in Washington. No fees are charged to holders of U.S. passports.

BUSINESS CUSTOMS

Iraqi government working hours: Summer (April 1–September 30); Saturday through Wednesday 8 A.M.–2 P.M.; Thursday 8 A.M.–1 P.M.; closed Friday. Winter (October 1–March 31); Saturday 8:30 A.M.–1:30 P.M.; Sunday through Wednesday 8:30 P.M.–2:30 P.M.; closed Friday.

Private business offices and shops: Major business firms follow Iraqi government work hours winter and summer. Other private sector firms work two shifts a day, summer and winter, from 9 A.M. to 2 P.M. and from 4:30 P.M. to 7:30 P.M. Closed Friday.

U.S. interests section: Saturday through Tuesday, 7:30 A.M. to 2:30 P.M.; Wednesday and Thursday, 7:30 A.M. to 1:30 P.M. Closed Friday and on following U.S. holidays: January 1, Washington's Birthday, May 31, July 4, Labor Day, Columbus Day, Veterans' Day, Thanksgiving, December 25.

SELECTED GOVERNMENT ENTITIES

State Organization for Trade and Capital Goods
Khullani Square, Baghdad
Cable: "TRESTO BAGHDAD"

State Organization for Agricultural Development
Saadoon Street, Baghdad
Cable: "YAKTEEN BAGHDAD"

State Organization for Oil Refineries and Gas Industry
P.O. Box 3069
Saadoon Street, Baghdad
Cable: MASAFI BAGHDAD

BANKS

All banks were nationalized in 1964. All commercial banking activities were consolidated in the Rafidain Bank in 1974.

ISRAEL

REPRESENTATION

Embassy of Israel
1621 22nd Street NW
Washington, DC 20008
Telephone: 202-483-4100

American Embassy
71 Hayarkon Street
Tel Aviv, Israel
Telephone: 56171

U.S. Consulate General
18 Agron Road
Jerusalem, Israel
Telephone: 82231

Israel Consulates General:
    Atlanta, Boston, Chicago, Houston, Los
    Angeles, New York City, Philadelphia, and
    San Francisco

Investment Office and Branches:
641 Lexington Avenue
New York, NY 10022
Telephone: 212-486-8530

111 E. Wacker Drive
Chicago, IL 60601
Telephone: 312-644-4149

Israel Trade Center
111 W. 40th Street
New York, NY 10018
Telephone: 212-456-8562

6380 Wilshire Boulevard
Los Angeles, CA 90048
Telephone: 213-658-7924

805 Peachtree Street, NE
Atlanta, GA 30308
Telephone: 404-875-6947

CURRENCY: Israel Pound (IL).

ENTRY REQUIREMENTS

Citizens of many countries, including the United States, do not require transit or visitors' visas. Passports are required. Visitors intending a later visit to Arab countries may request the Israel entry stamp not be placed in their passports.

BUSINESS CUSTOMS

Government offices are generally open for visitors between 9:00 A.M. and 1:00 P.M., on Sunday through Friday. However, actual working hours start earlier and continue longer than visiting hours. If a matter is urgent, the department will normally be ac-commodating. Most commercial establishments are open 8:00 A.M.–1:00 P.M. and 4:00–7:00 P.M. Most offices and stores close somewhat earlier on Friday to prepare for the Sabbath, which lasts from sundown Friday until sundown Saturday. Banks are usually open 8:30 A.M.–12:30 P.M. and 4:00–5:30 P.M., Sunday through Thursday. On Friday and days preceding holidays they are open from 8:30 A.M. until early afternoon. All business activity ceases on Saturday and religious holidays usually start from the midday preceding them. Embassy hours: Monday–Friday, 8:00 A.M.–4:00 P.M.

SELECTED GOVERNMENT MINISTRIES

Ministry of Commerce and Industry
30 Agron Boulevard, Palace Building, Jerusalem

Ministry of Communications
23 Jaffa Road, Jerusalem

Ministry of Agriculture
Helena Hamalka Street, Jerusalem

Ministry of Health
20 Rehov David Hamelech, Jerusalem

BANKS

American-Israel Bank, 11 Rothschild Boulevard, Tel Aviv; Bank of Israel, Ltd., 18 Lincoln Street, Tel Aviv.

There are 23 commercial banks with nearly 800 branches. The three largest are the Bank Leumi Le-Israel, the Israel Discount Bank, Ltd., and Bank Hapoalim. These banks have subsidiaries or branches in the United States as do other Israeli banks.

JORDAN (HASHEMITE KINGDOM OF)

REPRESENTATION

Embassy of Jordan
2319 Wyoming Avenue, NW
Washington, DC 20008
Telephone: 202-265-1606

Consulate General
866 U.N. Plaza
New York, NY 10017
Telephone: 212-752-0135

American Embassy
Jebel Amman
Amman, Jordan
Telephone: 443716

Consulates are also located in Houston, Texas; Chicago, Illinois; Scottsdale, Arizona; and Palm Beach, Florida.

CURRENCY: Jordanian Dinar (JD).

ENTRY REQUIREMENTS

Visas are multiple entry, valid for one year.

BUSINESS CUSTOMS

American Embassy Commercial Office hours: Saturday through Thursday, 9 A.M.–1:30 P.M.

BANKS

Foreign: Arab Bank, British Bank of the Middle East, Ottoman Bank, Cairo Amman Bank, Rafidain Bank S.A.E., Bank al Mashrek, National and Grindlays Banks.

National: Jordan National Bank, Bank of Jordan.

SELECTED GOVERNMENT ENTITIES

Ministry of Industry and Commerce
Amman, Jordan

Ministry of Public Works
Amman, Jordan

Ministry of Supply
Amman, Jordan

STATE OF KUWAIT

REPRESENTATION

Embassy of Kuwait
2940 Tilden Street NW
Washington, DC 20008
Telephone: 202-966-0702

American Embassy
P.O. Box 77
Kuwait, State of Kuwait
Telephone: 424-156/7/8

CURRENCY: Kuwaiti Dinar.

ENTRY REQUIREMENTS

A transit visa valid for a maximum period of 24 hours may be obtained at the airport. The applicant's sponsor must meet the traveler at the airport. Visas valid for a longer stay should be requested at the Kuwait Embassy in Washington, D.C. Petitioner must present a valid passport, visa application, photograph, and a letter from the applicant's firm stating the purpose of the visit and guaranteeing all expenses will be paid. Valid smallpox and cholera immunizations are required. Visa fee

is $4. Normal waiting period for visa is two to three working days.

BUSINESS CUSTOMS

Government offices are open 8:00 A.M.–2:00 P.M., Saturday through Thursday. Commercial establishments open 8:00 A.M.–12:30 P.M. and 4:30–7:30 P.M., Saturday through Wednesday and 8:00 A.M.–noon on Thursday. U.S. embassy is open 8:00 A.M.–1:00 P.M. and 2:00–5:00 P.M., Saturday through Wednesday. Banks usually open 9:00–11:30 A.M. and 4:30–6:00 P.M., Saturday through Wednesday. During the hot summer months many government officials and private businessmen leave the country for several months.

BANKS

All banks in Kuwait must be owned by Kuwaiti citizens. Principal banks are National Bank of Kuwait, Bank of Kuwait and the Middle East, Commercial Bank of Kuwait, Gulf Bank, Al-Ahli Bank, Kuwait Real Estate Bank, Industrial Bank of Kuwait, Credit and Saving Bank, and Central Bank of Kuwait.

SELECTED GOVERNMENT ENTITIES

Ministry of Commerce and Industry
P.O. Box 2944, Safat
Telephone: 422101

Ministry of Oil
P.O. Box 5077, Kuwait
Telephone: 415201

Ministry of Public Works
P.O. Box 8, Safat
Telephone: 435151

Ministry of Planning
P.O. Box 15, Kuwait

LEBANON

Note: Due to the Civil War (1975–76) only partial information on the Lebanese economy is available. Damage from the war is roughly estimated at $2–$3 billion. Productive capacity at the end of 1976 may have been as low as one half of the 1974 level. Security has largely been established through the intervention of the Syrian Army (except in the Israeli border area); the airport and port are now rapidly approaching pre-war traffic levels; many services have been re-established; most banks have reopened; and industrial and agricultural production is being gradually restored. So far only a few of the hundreds of firms with regional offices in Beirut that left the city have returned. The

U.S. Agency for International Development is taking an active role in assisting in the rehabilitation and reconstruction of Lebanon. U.S. exports to Lebanon, which declined from $402 million in 1975 to $49 million in 1976, increased to $124 million in 1977.

REPRESENTATION

Embassy of Lebanon
2560 28th Street NW
Washington, DC 20008
Telephone: 202-332-0300

Consulate General
9 E. 76th Street
New York, NY 10021
Telephone: 212-744-7905

Consulate General
1300 Lafayette East, Suite 101
Detroit, MI 48207
Telephone: 313-963-0233

American Embassy
Corniche at Rue Ain Mreisseh
Beirut, Lebanon
Telephone: 361800

CURRENCY: Lebanese Pound (L£).

ENTRY REQUIREMENT

Visas easily obtained; nominal fee.

BUSINESS CUSTOMS

The normal work week is Monday through Friday. American Embassy hours: Monday through Thursday from 8:00 A.M. to 5:30 P.M., Friday from 8:00 A.M. to 2:00 P.M. Government offices open at 8:00 or 8:30 A.M. to 1:00 P.M. and from 3:00 P.M. to 7:00 P.M. In the summer, most offices close at 1:00 or 2:00 P.M.

SELECTED GOVERNMENT ENTITIES

Ministry of Economy and Trade
Beirut

Ministry of Public Works and Transport
Beirut

Ministry of Water and Electricity Resources
Beirut

BANKS

Beirut was the financial hub of the Near East in banking but many banks have withdrawn their foreign personnel from Beirut temporarily and a number recently decentralized part of their operations to Bahrain.

U.S. banks in Lebanon include Chase Manhattan Bank, Chemical New York Corporation, First National City Bank of New York, Bank of America, Manufacturers Hanover Trust Co., Morgan Guaranty Trust Co., Irving Trust Co., Bankers Trust Co. Many other foreign and local banks are represented.

LIBYA

REPRESENTATION

Embassy of the Socialist People's Libyan Arab Jamakiriya
1118 22nd Street NW
Washington, DC 20037
Telephone: 202-452-1290

American Embassy
Sh. Mohammad-et-Tabat
P.O. Box 289
Tripoli, Libyan Arab Republic
Telephone: 4021/25

CURRENCY: Libyan Dinar (LD).

ENTRY REQUIREMENTS

Libyan visas, valid for 30 days stay in Libya, must be obtained from the Libyan Embassy. Processing time: 24–48 hours. Libyan authorities require that personal data in the passport be translated into Arabic before the embassy will process. Visa requests must be accompanied by a stamped, self-addressed envelope.

Smallpox vaccination is required.

BUSINESS CUSTOMS

Government offices are open Saturday through Thursday, 7:30 A.M. to 2:30 P.M., November through May, and 7:30 A.M. to 2:00 P.M., June through October. Private businesses are open in the late afternoon, 4:00 P.M. to 7:00 P.M. Embassy hours: 8:00 A.M. to 5:30 P.M., Sunday through Thursday, Wednesday 8:00 A.M. to 4:00 P.M., closed Friday and Saturday.

Arabic is the official language; many officials understand and will speak English.

BANKS

All banks are state controlled. They include: Central Bank of Libya, P.O. Box 1103, Tripoli; Masraf al-Wahda, P.O. Box 375, Tripoli; Masraf al-Jumhuriyya, P.O. Box 3224, Tripoli; Masraf at-Tijari al-Watani, P.O. Box 4647, Tripoli; Masraf Sahara, P.O. Box 2151, Benghazi; Masraf al-Umma, P.O. Box 685, Tripoli; National Agricultural Bank, 52 Omar al-Mukhtar Street, Tripoli.

SELECTED
GOVERNMENT ENTITIES

Ministry of Agriculture and Agrarian Reform
Sidi Masri, Tripoli

Ministry of Industry and Minerals
Alfath Road, Tripoli

Ministry of Communications
Ben Ashur Street, Tripoli

Ministry of Petroleum
Sadoon Swehli Street, Tripoli

Ministry of Housing
Shuhada Square, Tripoli

General Corporation for Industrialization,
Sanaa Street, P.O. Box 4388, Tripoli

Posts and Telecommunications Corporation
Algiers Square, Tripoli

MOROCCO

REPRESENTATION

Embassy of Morocco
1601 21st Street NW
Washington, DC 20009
Telephone: 202-462-7979/82

American Embassy
2 Avenue de Marrakech
Rabat, Morocco
Telephone: 30361, 30362

Consulate General
(includes Moroccan National Tourist
Office)
597 Fifth Avenue
New York, NY 10017
Telephone: 212-421-5771

American Consulate General
No. 8 Blvd. Moulay Youssef
B.P. 675
Casablanca, Morocco
Telephone: 60521/23, 60562

American Consulate General
Chemin des Amoureux
Tangier, Morocco
Telephone: 35904

CURRENCY: Moroccan Dirham (DH).

ENTRY REQUIREMENTS

Visas are not required for stay of three
months or less.
Smallpox vaccination required.

BUSINESS CUSTOMS

Work week for government offices: Monday through Thursday, 8:30 A.M. to noon,
2:30 P.M. to 6:00 P.M.; Friday, 8:30 A.M. to
11:00 A.M. and 4:00 P.M. to 6:00 P.M.;
Saturday, 8:30 A.M. to noon. In July and
August, 8:00 A.M. to noon and 4:00 P.M. to
7:00 P.M.

Work week for businesses: Monday
through Friday, 8:30 A.M. to noon and 3:30
P.M. to 7:00 P.M.; Saturday, 8:30 A.M. to
1:00 P.M. In summer some offices work only
from 8:00 A.M. to 1:00 P.M., Monday through
Saturday.

Embassy hours: Monday through Friday,
8:30 A.M. to 12:30 P.M., 2:00 P.M. to 6:00
P.M., with summer variations.

French is the business language; Spanish
is understood in the north; English is rarely
spoken.

The best hours to meet responsible executives are early morning and early afternoon
for businessmen; late morning and late afternoon for government officials.

BANKS

Large number of state and private banks
including the following:

Banque Marocaine de Commerce Extérieur
241 Blvd. Mohammed V, B.P. 425
Casablanca

Crédit Immobilier et Hôtelier,
159 Ave. Hassan II, Casablanca

Banque Nationale pour le Développement
Economique
Place des Alaouites, B.P. 407, Rabat

First National City Bank (Maghreb)
52 Ave. Hassan II, Casablanca

Société de Banque et de Crédit
26 Ave. des Forces Armées Royales
B.P. 972, Casablanca

SELECTED
GOVERNMENT ENTITIES

Ministry of Commerce, Industry, Mines and
    Merchant Marine
Rabat

Office of Industrial Development (ODI)
8, rue Ghandi, Rabat

Ministry of Public Works and Communications
Rabat

Ministry of Agriculture and Agricultural Reform
Avenue Mohamed V, Rabat

Office Cherifien des Phosphates (OCP)
(phosphates)

305 Avenue Mohamed V, Rabat

Bureau de Recherches et de Participation Minières (BRPM) (other minerals)
27, Avenue Moulay Hassan, Rabat

OMAN

REPRESENTATION

Embassy of the Sultanate of Oman
2342 Massachusetts Avenue NW
Washington, DC 20008
Telephone: 202-387-1980

American Embassy
P.O. Box 966
Muscat, Oman
Telephone: 72-2021

Combined Consulate and Permanent Mission
 to the United Nations
605 Third Avenue
Room 3304
New York, NY 10016
Telephone: 202-682-0447

CURRENCY: Omani Rial (RO).

ENTRY REQUIREMENTS

The cost of visa is $8.50. Requirements include: A letter from the firm stating the purpose of the visit, a letter from the local U.S. Chamber of Commerce, and two photographs of the traveler.

BUSINESS CUSTOMS

Government office hours are from 8:00 A.M. to 2:00 P.M., Saturday through Wednesday. In summer months office hours are from 7:00 A.M. to 1:00 P.M. American Embassy hours are Saturday through Wednesday, 7:30 A.M. to 3:30 P.M. Major business hours are 8:30 A.M. to 12:30 P.M. and 4:00 P.M. to 6:00 P.M., Saturday through Wednesday; however, these hours vary widely.

BANKS

U.S.: First National City Bank.
Others: British Bank of the Middle East, Chartered Bank, Ltd., Grindlays Bank, Ltd., Paribas, and Banque de Paris du Pays Bas.

SELECTED
GOVERNMENT ENTITIES

Ministry of Industry and Commerce
P.O. Box 550, Muscat

Ministry of Communications and Transport
P.O. Box 684, Muscat

Ministry of Agriculture, Fisheries, Petroleum
 and Minerals
P.O. Box 551, Muscat

QATAR

REPRESENTATION

Embassy of Qatar
600 New Hampshire Avenue NW
Washington, DC 20037
Telephone: 202-338-0111

American Embassy
P.O. Box 2399
Doha, Qatar
Telephone: 870701

CURRENCY: Qatar Riyal (QR).

ENTRY REQUIREMENTS

All business visa applicants must submit two visa applications and photographs together with a letter from the sponsoring firm which explains the purpose of the travel, states who the visitors will see, and guarantees that all expenses will be covered. Smallpox and cholera vaccination certificates are also required. No visa fee is charged to U.S. citizens. It presently takes approximately two weeks to issue the visa as the embassy must request authorization from the Foreign Ministry of Doha. A transit visa valid for a maximum of 72 hours can still be obtained at the Doha airport if the business traveler is met by a representative of a bona fide Qatari business firm who brings an authorized letter of sponsorship.

BUSINESS CUSTOMS

Government office hours are Saturday through Thursday, 8:00 A.M.–12:30 P.M. Commercial and banking hours are Saturday through Thursday, 8:00 A.M.–12:30 P.M. Some firms reopen in the afternoon 3:30–6:30 P.M. American Embassy hours are Saturday through Wednesday, 7:30 A.M.–3:30 P.M.

BANKS

U.S.: Citibank.
Others: Qatar National Bank, Arab Bank, Banque de Paris du Pays Bas, British Bank of the Middle East, National and Grindlays Bank, Bank Saderat (Iran), Bank of Oman, Chartered Bank, United Bank, Ltd. (Pakistan), Commercial Bank of Qatar.

SELECTED
GOVERNMENT ENTITIES

Ministry of Commerce and Economy
P.O. Box 1968, Doha

Ministry of Finance and Petroleum
P.O. Box 83, Doha

Ministry of Public Works
P.O. Box 38, Doha

SAUDI ARABIA

REPRESENTATION

Saudi Arabian Embassy
1520 18th Street NW
Washington, DC 20036
Telephone: 202-483-2100

Consulate General
633 Third Avenue
New York, NY 10017
Telephone: 212-371-0480

American Embassy
Palestine Road
Jidda, Saudi Arabia
Telephone: 53410, 54110

Downtown Commercial Office
Jidda, Saudi Arabia
Telephone: 51553, 56897

Consulate General
Dhahran, Saudi Arabia
Telephone: 43200

U.S. Liaison Office
Riyadh, Saudi Arabia
Telephone: 20363

CURRENCY: Saudi Riyal (SR).

ENTRY REQUIREMENTS

It is extremely important to have the correct documentation to enter Saudi Arabia. Saudi immigration officials will refuse entry to any person who does not have a correct and valid visa when he arrives at a Saudi airport.

To obtain a Saudi visa, application must be made at either the embassy or consulate. Two photographs must be submitted with the application. Business representatives visiting Saudi Arabia must have either a cable telex or letter of invitation from a Saudi business firm or government agency in hand or on file at the issuing office before a visa can be issued. Visas currently have a validity of one month.

Saudi visa offices are overloaded, and ample time should be allowed to obtain a visa; usual processing time is five to seven days. As Saudi visa requirements change periodically, it is wise to check with the embassy or consulate for current requirements. A valid International Health Certificate with current vaccinations for cholera, smallpox, and yellow fever is required. As there are no immunization facilities at Saudi airports, failure to have a current certificate usually results in the traveler's being denied entry.

Saudi customs regulations prohibit the importation of any form of alcohol, pork products, or pornographic literature. Attempts to smuggle these into the country may result in imprisonment.

Exit visas are required of all travelers and must be obtained prior to departure.

BUSINESS CUSTOMS

Government offices operate Saturday through Wednesday from 8:00 A.M. to 2:00 P.M. The American Embassy is open from 8:00 A.M. to 5:00 P.M., Saturday through Wednesday. Businesses and shops open 8:00 A.M. to 2:00 P.M., close for lunch, reopen 4:30 P.M. until 8:00 P.M., Saturday through Wednesday; open 9:00 A.M. to 1:00 P.M. on Thursday. Banks are open from 8:30 A.M. to 12:00 P.M. Business hours are somewhat limited during the pilgrimage season.

BANKS

United States: Citibank (Jidda and Riyadh).

Other foreign: British Bank of the Middle East, Bank Melli Iran, Saudi Dutch Bank, Al-Jazira Bank (National Bank of Pakistan).

Saudi banks: National Commercial and the Riyadh Bank have a network of branches throughout the Kingdom.

SELECTED GOVERNMENT ENTITIES

Ministry of Commerce
Airport Road, Riyadh
Telephone: 23400
Telex: 20057 TIJARAH SJ

Ministry of Industry and Water
Airport Road, Riyadh
Telephone: 62577

Saudi Arabian Basic Industrial Corporation
Riyadh
Telephone: 20901

Industrial Studies and Development Center
Airport Road, Riyadh
Telephone: 20900

Ministry of Petroleum and Mineral Resources
Airport Road, Riyadh
Telephone: 61133

Ministry of Planning

Riyadh
Telephone: 23800
Telex: PLAN SJ

Saudi Industrial Development Fund
Al Washam Street, Riyadh
Telephone: 33703
Telex: 20065 SIDFUND SJ

SYRIAN ARAB REPUBLIC

REPRESENTATION

Embassy of the Syrian Arab Republic
2215 Wyoming Avenue NW
Washington, DC 20008
Telephone: 202–232–6313

American Embassy
P.O. Box 29
Damascus, Syria
Telephone: 332814

CURRENCY: Syrian Pound (S£)

ENTRY REQUIREMENTS

Visa applications should be made to the
Embassy of the Syrian Arab Republic. A letter stating the purpose of the trip is required.
Fees are $8 for a single-entry visa and $16
for a double-entry visa; both are good for six
months. An additional fee of $2.75 must be
paid if the passport is to be returned by mail.

BUSINESS CUSTOMS

American Embassy hours: Monday through
Friday, 8 A.M. to 5 P.M. Summer hours: Mon-
day through Friday, 7:30 A.M. to 2:30 P.M.;
Saturday, 7:30 A.M. to 12:30 P.M.

Local business hours: Most government
offices are open 8:30 A.M.–2:00 P.M.; private
business is open 8:00 A.M.–1:00 P.M. and
4:00–7:00 P.M. All government offices and
many business firms are closed Thursday afternoon and all day Friday.

SELECTED
GOVERNMENT ENTITIES

Ministry of Economy and Foreign Trade
Damascus

The General Organization of Foreign Trade
  for Machinery and Equipment (AFTOMA-
  CHINE)
P.O. Box 3130, Damascus

The General Organization for Trade and Distribution (GOTA)
P.O. Box 15, Damascus

BANKS

Syrian Commercial Bank, Popular Credit
Bank, Industrial Development Bank.

TUNISIA

REPRESENTATION

Embassy of Tunisia
2408 Massachusetts Avenue NW
Washington, DC 20008
Telephone: 202-234-6644

American Embassy
144 Avenue de la Liberté
Tunis, Tunisia
Telephone: 282.566

Tunisian Investment Promotion Agency
Tunisian National Tourist Office
630 Fifth Avenue, Suite 863
New York, NY 10020
Telephone: 212-582-3760

CURRENCY: Tunisian Dinar (TD).

ENTRY REQUIREMENTS

Visas are not required for stay of four
months or less.
Smallpox vaccination is required.

BUSINESS CUSTOMS

French is the business language; English
is rarely understood. Commercial establishments and government offices are open Monday through Friday, and sometimes Saturday
mornings from 8:30 A.M. to 12:30 P.M. and
2:30 P.M. to 5:30 P.M. Summer hours are
7:00 A.M. to 1:00 P.M. Embassy hours: 8:30
A.M. to 5:30 P.M., Monday–Friday, with special summer hours from mid-June to mid-
September.

BANKS

Several national and foreign banks, including:
Société Tunisienne de Banque
1 Avenue Habib Thameur, Tunis

Banque Franco-Tunisienne
13 rue d'Alger, Tunis

Banque Nationale de Tunisie
19 Avenue de Paris, Tunis

British Bank of the Middle East
70 Avenue Habib Bourguiba, Tunis

Société Marseillasie de Crédit
12 Avenue de France, Tunis

Chase Manhattan, Bankers, Trust and Citibank have opened "off-shore" branches in Tunis.

SELECTED GOVERNMENT ENTITIES

Ministry of Agriculture
Place du Gouvernement
La Kasbah, Tunis

Ministry of National Economy
Place du Gouvernement
La Kasbah, Tunis

Ministry of Transport and Communications
Rue d'Angleterre, Tunis

Agence de Promotion des Investissements (API) (State investment promotion agency)
17, rue Belhassen Ben Chaabane
El Omrane, Tunis

Establissement Tunisien pour les Activites Petrolieres (ETAP) (national oil company)
Tunis

SNIT (Société Nationale Tunisienne Immobiliere de Tunisie) (housing construction)
Immeuble Intilak, Cité Mahrajane
El Menzah, Tunis

UNITED ARAB EMIRATES

REPRESENTATION

Embassy of the United Arab Emirates
600 New Hampshire Avenue NW
Washington, DC 20037
Telephone: 202-338-6500

American Embassy
Box 4009
Arabian Gulf
Abu Dhabi, UAE
Telephone: 61534/5
Telex: 949-2229

CURRENCY: Dirham (D).

ENTRY REQUIREMENTS

Visas must be obtained at the UAE Embassy in Washington. Applicant must present valid passport, three completed application forms, three photos, and a letter from company stating purpose of visit and guaranteeing maintenance. Valid inoculation certificate against smallpox and cholera must be attached. Application must be accompanied by a money order or certified check for $2.75

for a three-month visa. A multiple entry visa is issued for $8.25. Visitors may remain one month each time.

BUSINESS CUSTOMS

Commercial offices are open Saturday through Thursday, 8:00 A.M. to 1:00 P.M. and 4:00 P.M. to 7:00 P.M. Government offices are open 7:00 A.M. to 1:00 P.M. Saturday through Wednesday, and to noon on Thursdays in the summer. In the winter, government offices are open 8:00 A.M. to 2:00 P.M. Saturday through Wednesday, and to noon on Thursdays. Banking hours are 8:00 A.M. to noon, Saturday through Wednesday, and to 11:00 A.M. on Thursday. American Embassy hours: Saturday through Wednesday, 7:30 A.M. to 2:30 P.M., and Thursday, 7:30 A.M. to 12:30 P.M.

BANKS

U.S.: First National City Bank, Commercial Bank (owned partly by Chase Manhattan), First National Bank of Chicago.

Foreign: British Bank of the Middle East, Bank of Oman, Arab Bank, Algemere Nederland Bank.

Local: National Bank of Dubai, Al-Ahli Bank of Dubai, Commercial Bank of Dubai, Abu Dhabi, Dubai Bank, Ltd.

SELECTED GOVERNMENT ENTITIES

Ministry of Planning
P.O. Box 904, Abu Dhabi

Ministry of Commerce and Trade
P.O. Box 901, Abu Dhabi

Ministry of Finance and Industry
P.O. Box 433, Abu Dhabi

Ministry of Petroleum and Mining Resources
P.O. Box 59, Abu Dhabi

YEMEN ARAB REPUBLIC

REPRESENTATION

Embassy of the Yemen Arab Republic
600 New Hamphsire Avenue NW
Washington, DC 20037
Telephone: 202-965-4760

American Embassy
P.O. Box 1088
Sana, Yemen Arab Republic
Telephone: 5826, 2790

Consulate of the Yemen Arab Republic
211 E. 43rd Street
New York, NY 10017
Telephone: 212-986-0990

CURRENCY: Yemen rial (Yrl.).

ENTRY REQUIREMENT

Single entry visa required as well as cholera and smallpox vaccinations.

BUSINESS CUSTOMS

Most government and business offices open 8:00 A.M. to 1:00 P.M., Saturday through Thursday. Stores are generally open in the evenings as well. American Embassy hours: Saturday through Wednesday, 8:00 A.M. to 1:00 P.M.; 2:30 to 5:30 P.M.

BANKS

First National City Bank, P.O. Box 3133, Sana (Telephone: 5796): four other foreign banks. Local bank: Yemen Bank for Reconstruction and Development, Midan Tahrir, Sana.

SELECTED GOVERNMENT ENTITIES

Ministry of Economy
P.O. Box 607, Sana

The Highway Authority
P.O. Box 1185, Sana

Commercial Trading Terms

FOREIGN TRADE TERMS

Since the issuance of *American Foreign Trade Definitions* in 1919, many changes in practice have occurred. The 1919 definitions did much to clarify and simplify foreign trade practice and received wide recognition and use by buyers and sellers throughout the world. At the Twenty-Seventh National Foreign Trade Convention, 1940, further revision and clarification of these definitions were urged as necessary to assist the foreign trader in the handling of his transactions.

The following *Revised American Foreign Trade Definitions—1941* are recommended for general use by both exporters and importers. These revised definitions have no status at law unless there is specific legislation providing for them, or unless they are confirmed by court decisions. Hence, it is suggested that sellers and buyers agree to their acceptance as part of the contract of sale. These revised definitions will then become legally binding upon all parties.

In view of changes in practice and procedure since 1919, certain new responsibilities for sellers and buyers are included in these revised definitions. Also, in many instances, the old responsibilities are more clearly defined than in the 1919 definitions, and the changes should be beneficial to both sellers and buyers. Widespread acceptance will lead to a greater standardization of foreign trade procedure, and to the avoidance of much misunderstanding.

Adoption by exporters and importers of these revised terms will impress on all parties concerned their respective responsibilities and rights.

GENERAL NOTES OF CAUTION

1. As foreign trade definitions have been issued by organizations in various parts of the world, and as the courts of countries have interpreted these definitions in different ways, it is important that sellers and buyers agree that their contracts are subject to the *Revised American Foreign Trade Definitions—1941*

Source: National Foreign Trade Council, Inc., 10 Rockefeller Plaza, New York, NY 10020.

These definitions were adopted on July 30, 1941, by a joint committee representing the Chamber of Commerce of the United States of America, the National Council of American Importers, Inc., and the National Foreign Trade Council, Inc.

and that the various points listed are accepted by both parties.

2. In addition to the foreign trade terms listed herein, there are terms that are at times used, such as Free Harbor, C.I.F. & C. (Cost, Insurance, Freight, and Commission), C.I.F.C. & I. (Cost, Insurance, Freight, Commission, and Interest), C.I.F. Landed (Cost, Insurance, Freight, Landed), and others. None of these should be used unless there has first been a definite understanding as to the exact meaning thereof. It is unwise to attempt to interpret other terms in the light of the terms given herein. Hence, whenever possible, one of the terms defined herein should be used.

3. It is unwise to use abbreviations in quotations or in contracts which might be subject to misunderstanding.

4. When making quotations, the familiar terms "hundredweight" or "ton" should be avoided. A hundredweight can be 100 pounds of the short ton, or 112 pounds of the long ton. A ton can be a short ton of 2,000 pounds, or a metric ton of 2,204.6 pounds, or a long ton of 2,240 pounds. Hence, the type of hundredweight or ton should be clearly stated in quotations and in sales confirmations. Also, all terms referring to quantity, weight, volume, length, or surface should be clearly defined and agreed upon.

5. If inspection or certificate of inspection is required, it should be agreed in advance whether the cost thereof is for account of seller or buyer.

6. Unless otherwise agreed upon, all expenses are for the account of seller up to the point at which the buyer must handle the subsequent movement of goods.

7. There are a number of elements in a contract that do not fall within the scope of these foreign trade definitions. Hence, no mention of these is made herein. Seller and buyer should agree to these separately when negotiating contracts. This particularly applies to so-called customary practices.

DEFINITIONS OF QUOTATIONS

(I) EX (POINT OF ORIGIN)

"EX FACTORY," "EX MILL," "EX MINE," 'EX PLANTATION," 'EX WAREHOUSE," etc. (named point of origin): Under this term, the price quoted applies only at the point of origin, and the seller agrees to place the goods at the disposal of the buyer at the agreed place on the date or within the period fixed.

Under this quotation:
Seller must:

1. Bear all costs and risks of the goods until such time as the buyer is obliged to take delivery thereof.
2. Render the buyer, at the buyer's request and expense, assistance in obtaining the documents issued in the country of origin, or of shipment, or of both, which the buyer may require either for purposes of exportation, or of importation at destination.

Buyer must:

1. Take delivery of the goods as soon as they have been placed at his disposal at the agreed place on the date or within the period fixed.
2. Pay export taxes, or other fees or charges, if any, levied because of exportation.
3. Bear all costs and risks of the goods from the time when he is obligated to take delivery thereof.
4. Pay all costs and charges incurred in obtaining the documents issued in the country of origin, or of shipment, or of both, which may be required for purposes either of exportation or of importation at destination.

(II) F.O.B (FREE ON BOARD)

Note: Seller and buyer should consider not only the definitions but also the "Comments on All F.O.B. Terms" given at end of this section (page 702), in order to understand fully their respective responsibilities and rights under the several classes of F.O.B. terms.

(II-A) "F.O.B. (named inland carrier at named inland point of departure)":° Under this term, the price quoted applies only at inland shipping point, and the seller arranges for loading of the goods on, or in, railway cars, trucks, lighters, barges, aircraft, or other conveyance furnished for transportation.

Under this quotation:
Seller must:

1. Place goods on, or in, conveyance, or deliver to inland carrier for loading.
2. Provide clean bill of lading or other transportation receipt, freight collect.
3. Be responsible for any loss or damage, or both, until goods have been placed in, or on, conveyance at loading point, and

° See Note above and Comments on All F.O.B. Terms (page 702).

clean bill of lading or other transportation receipt has been furnished by the carrier.
4. Render the buyer, at the buyer's request and expense, assistance in obtaining the documents issued in the country of origin, or of shipment, or of both, which the buyer may require for purposes either of exportation, or of importation at destination.

Buyer must:

1. Be responsible for all movement of the goods from inland point of loading, and pay all transportation costs.
2. Pay export taxes, or other fees or charges, if any, levied because of exportation.
3. Be responsible for any loss or damage, or both, incurred after loading at named inland point of departure.
4. Pay all costs and charges incurred in obtaining the documents issued in the country of origin, or of shipment, or of both, which may be required for purposes either of exportation or of importation at destination.

(II-B) "F.O.B. (named inland carrier at named inland point of departure) FREIGHT PREPAID TO (named point of exportation)":° Under this term, the seller quotes a price including transportation charges to the named point of exportation and prepays freight to named point of exportation, without assuming responsibility for the goods after obtaining a clean bill of lading or other transportation receipt at named inland point of departure.

Under this quotation:
Seller must:

1. Assume the seller's obligations as under II-A, except that under 2, he must provide clean bill of lading or other transportation receipt, freight prepaid to named point of exportation.

Buyer must:

1. Assume the same buyer's obligations as under II-A, except that he does not pay freight from loading point to named point of exportation.

(II-C) "F.O.B. (named inland carrier at named inland point of departure) FREIGHT ALLOWED TO (named point)":° Under this term, the seller quotes a price including the transportation charges to the named point, shipping freight collect and deducting the

° See Note above and Comments on All F.O.B. Terms (page 702).

cost of transportation, without assuming responsibility for the goods after obtaining a clean bill of lading or other transportation receipt at named inland point of departure.

Under this quotation:

Seller must:

1. Assume the same seller's obligations as under II-A, but deducts from his invoice the transportation cost to named point.

Buyer must:

1. Assume the same buyer's obligations as under II-A, including payment of freight from inland loading point to named point, for which seller has made deduction.

(II-D) "F.O.B. (named inland carrier at named point of exportation)": Under this term, the seller quotes a price including the costs of transportation of the goods to named point of exportation, bearing any loss or damage, or both, incurred up to that point.

Under this quotation:

Seller must:

1. Place goods on, or in, conveyance, or deliver to inland carrier for loading.
2. Provide clean bill of lading or other transportation receipt, paying all transportation costs from loading point to named point of exportation.
3. Be responsible for any loss or damage, or both, until goods have arrived in, or on, inland conveyance at the named point of exportation.
4. Render the buyer, at the buyer's request and expense, assistance in obtaining the documents issued in the country of origin, or of shipment, or of both, which the buyer may require for purposes either of exportation or of importation at destination.

Buyer must:

1. Be responsible for all movement of the goods from inland conveyance at named point of exportation.
2. Pay export taxes, or other fees or charges, if any, levied because of exportation.
3. Be responsible for any loss or damage, or both, incurred after goods have arrived in, or on, inland conveyance at the named point of exportation.
4. Pay all costs and charges incurred in obtaining the documents issued in the country of origin, or of shipment, or of both, which may be required for purposes either of exportation or of importation at destination.

* See Note and Comments on All F.O.B. Terms (page 702).

(II-E) "F.O.B. VESSEL (named port of shipment)": Under this term, the seller quotes a price covering all expenses up to, and including, delivery of the goods upon the overseas vessel provided by, or for, the buyer at the named port of shipment.

Under this quotation:

Seller must:

1. Pay all charges incurred in placing goods actually on board the vessel designated and provided by, or for, the buyer on the date or within the period fixed.
2. Provide clean ship's receipt or on-board bill of lading.
3. Be responsible for any loss or damage, or both, until goods have been placed on board the vessel on the date or within the period fixed.
4. Render the buyer, at the buyer's request and expense, assistance in obtaining the documents issued in the country of origin, or of shipment, or of both, which the buyer may require for purposes either of exportation or of importation at destination.

Buyer must:

1. Give seller adequate notice of name, sailing date, loading berth of, and delivery time to, the vessel.
2. Bear the additional costs incurred and all risks of the goods from the time when the seller has placed them at his disposal if the vessel named by him fails to arrive or to load within the designated time.
3. Handle all subsequent movement of the goods to destination:
   a. Provide and pay for insurance.
   b. Provide and pay for ocean and other transportation.
4. Pay export taxes, or other fees or charges, if any, levied because of exportation.
5. Be responsible for any loss or damage, or both, after goods have been loaded on board the vessel.
6. Pay all costs and charges incurred in obtaining the documents, other than clean ship's receipt or bill of lading, issued in the country of origin, or of shipment, or of both, which may be required for purposes either of exportation or of importation at destination.

(II-F) "F.O.B. (named inland point in country of importation)": Under this term, the seller quotes a price including the cost of the merchandise and all costs of transportation.

Under this quotation:

Seller must:

* See Note and Comments on All F.O.B. Terms (page 702).

1. Provide and pay for all transportation to the named inland point in the country of importation.
2. Pay export taxes, or other fees or charges, if any, levied because of exportation.
3. Provide and pay for marine insurance.
4. Provide and pay for war risk insurance, unless otherwise agreed upon between the seller and buyer.
5. Be responsible for any loss or damage, or both, until arrival of goods on conveyance at the named inland point in the country of importation.
6. Pay the costs of certificates of origin, consular invoices, or any other documents issued in the country of origin, or of shipment, or of both, which the buyer may require for the importation of goods into the country of destination and, where necessary, for their passage in transit through another country.
7. Pay all costs of landing, including wharfage, landing charges, and taxes, if any.
8. Pay all costs of customs entry in the country of importation.
9. Pay customs duties and all taxes applicable to imports, if any, in the country of importation.

Note: The seller under this quotation must realize that he is accepting important responsibilities, costs, and risks, and should therefore be certain to obtain adequate insurance. On the other hand, the importer or buyer may desire such quotations to relieve him of the risks of the voyage and to assure him of his landed costs at inland point in country of importation. When competition is keen, or the buyer is accustomed to such quotations from other sellers, seller may quote such terms, being careful to protect himself in an appropriate manner.

Buyer must:

1. Take prompt delivery of goods from conveyance upon arrival at destination.
2. Bear any costs and be responsible for all loss or damage, or both, after arrival at destination.

COMMENTS ON ALL F.O.B. TERMS

In connection with F.O.B. terms, the following points of caution are recommended:
1. The method of inland transportation, such as trucks, railroad cars, lighters, barges, or aircraft should be specified.
2. If any switching charges are involved during the inland transportation, it should be agreed, in advance, whether these charges are for account of the seller or the buyer.
3. The term "F.O.B. (named port)," without designating the exact point at which the liability of the seller terminates and the liability of the buyer begins, should be avoided. The use of this term gives rise to disputes as to the liability of the seller or the buyer in the event of loss or damage arising while the goods are in port, and before delivery to or on board the ocean carrier. Misunderstandings may be avoided by naming the specific point of delivery.
4. If lighterage or trucking is required in the transfer of goods from the inland conveyance to ship's side, and there is a cost therefore, it should be understood in advance whether this cost is for account of the seller or the buyer.
5. The seller should be certain to notify the buyer of the minimum quantity required to obtain a carload, a truckload, or a bargeload freight rate.
6. Under F.O.B. terms, excepting "F.O.B. (named inland point in country of importation)," the obligation to obtain ocean freight space, and marine and war risk insurance, rests with the buyer. Despite this obligation on the part of the buyer, in many trades the seller obtains the ocean freight space, and marine and war risk insurance, and provides for shipment on behalf of the buyer. Hence, seller and buyer must have an understanding as to whether the buyer will obtain the ocean freight space, and marine and war risk insurance, as is his obligation, or whether the seller agrees to do this for the buyer.
7. For the seller's protection, he should provide in his contract of sale that marine insurance obtained by the buyer include standard warehouse-to-warehouse coverage.

(III) F.A.S. (FREE ALONG SIDE)

Note: Seller and buyer should consider not only the definitions but also the "Comments" given at the end of this section (page 703), in order to understand fully their respective responsibilities and rights under "F.A.S." terms.

"F.A.S. VESSEL (named port of shipment)": Under this term, the seller quotes a price including delivery of the goods along side overseas vessel and within reach of its loading tackle.

Under this quotation:
Seller must:

1. Place goods along side vessel or on dock designated and provided by, or for, buyer on the date or within the period fixed; pay any heavy lift charges, where necessary, up to this point.
2. Provide clean dock or ship's receipt.
3. Be responsible for any loss or damage, or both, until goods have been delivered along side the vessel or on the dock.

4. Render the buyer, at the buyer's request and expense, assistance in obtaining the documents issued in the country of origin, or of shipment, or of both, which the buyer may require for purposes either of exportation or of importation at destination.

Buyer must:

1. Give seller adequate notice of name, sailing date, loading berth of, and delivery time to, the vessel.
2. Handle all subsequent movement of the goods from along side the vessel:
   a. Arrange and pay for demurrage or storage charges, or both, in warehouse or on wharf, where necessary.
   b. Provide and pay for insurance.
   c. Provide and pay for ocean and other transportation.
3. Pay export taxes, or other fees or charges, if any, levied because of exportation.
4. Be responsible for any loss or damage, or both, while the goods are on a lighter or other conveyance along side vessel within reach of its loading tackle, or on the dock awaiting loading, or until actually loaded on board the vessel, and subsequent thereto.
5. Pay all costs and charges incurred in obtaining the documents, other than clean dock or ship's receipt, issued in the country of origin, or of shipment, or of both, which may be required for purposes either of exportation or of importation at destination.

F.A.S. COMMENTS

1. Under F.A.S. terms, the obligation to obtain ocean freight space, and marine and war risk insurance, rests with the buyer. Despite this obligation on the part of the buyer, in many trades the seller obtains ocean freight space, and marine and war risk insurance, and provides for shipment on behalf of the buyer. In others, the buyer notifies the seller to make delivery along side a vessel designated by the buyer and the buyer provides his own marine and war risk insurance. Hence, seller and buyer must have an understanding as to whether the buyer will obtain the ocean freight space, and marine and war risk insurance, as is his obligation, or whether the seller agrees to do this for the buyer.

2. For the seller's protection, he should provide in his contract of sale that marine insurance obtained by the buyer include standard warehouse-to-warehouse coverage.

(IV) C. & F. (COST AND FREIGHT)

Note: Seller and buyer should consider not only the definitions but also the "C. & F. Comments" and the "C. & F. and C.I.F. Comments" (page 704), in order to understand fully their respective responsibilities and rights under "C. & F." terms.

"C. & F. (named point of destination)": Under this term, the seller quotes a price including the cost of transportation to the named point of destination.

Under this quotation:
Seller must:

1. Provide and pay for transportation to named point of destination.
2. Pay export taxes, or other fees or charges, if any, levied because of exportation.
3. Obtain and dispatch promptly to buyer, or his agent, clean bill of lading to named point of destination.
4. Where received-for-shipment ocean bill of lading may be tendered, be responsible for any loss or damage, or both, until the goods have been delivered into the custody of the ocean carrier.
5. Where on-board ocean bill of lading is required, be responsible for any loss or damage, or both, until the goods have been delivered on board the vessel.
6. Provide, at the buyer's request and expense, certificates of origin, consular invoices, or any other documents issued in the country of origin, or of shipment, or of both, which the buyer may require for importation of goods into country of destination and, where necessary, for their passage in transit through another country.

Buyer must:

1. Accept the documents when presented.
2. Receive goods upon arrival, handle and pay for all subsequent movement of the goods, including taking delivery from vessel in accordance with bill of lading clauses and terms; pay all costs of landing, including any duties, taxes, and other expenses at named point of destination.
3. Provide and pay for insurance.
4. Be responsible for loss of or damage to goods, or both, from time and place at which seller's obligations under 4 or 5 above have ceased.
5. Pay the costs of certificates of origin, consular invoices, or any other documents issued in the country of origin, or of shipment, or of both, which may be required for the importation of goods into the country of destination and, where necessary, for their passage in transit through another country.

C. & F. COMMENTS

1. For the seller's protection, he should

provide in his contract of sale that marine insurance obtained by the buyer include standard warehouse-to-warehouse coverage.

2. The comments listed under the following C.I.F. terms in many cases apply to C. & F. terms as well, and should be read and understood by the C. & F. seller and buyer.

(V) C.I.F. (COST, INSURANCE, FREIGHT)

Note: Seller and buyer should consider not only the definitions but also the "Comments" at the end of this section, in order to understand fully their respective responsibilities and rights under "C.I.F." terms.

"C.I.F. (named point of destination)": Under this term, the seller quotes a price including the cost of the goods, the marine insurance, and all transportation charges to the named point of destination.

Under this quotation:
Seller must:

1. Provide and pay for transportation to named point of destination.
2. Pay export taxes, or other fees or charges, if any, levied because of exportation.
3. Provide and pay for marine insurance.
4. Provide war risk insurance as obtainable in seller's market at time of shipment at buyer's expense, unless seller has agreed that buyer provide for war risk coverage (see Comment 10c, page 705).
5. Obtain and dispatch promptly to buyer, or his agent, clean bill of lading to named point of destination, and also insurance policy or negotiable insurance certificate.
6. Where received-for-shipment ocean bill of lading may be tendered, be responsible for any loss or damage, or both, until the goods have been delivered into the custody of the ocean carrier.
7. Where on-board ocean bill of lading is required, be responsible for any loss or damage, or both, until the goods have been delivered on board the vessel.
8. Provide, at the buyer's request and expense, certificates of origin, consular invoices, or any other documents issued in the country of origin, or of shipment, or both, which the buyer may require for importation of goods into country of destination and, where necessary, for their passage in transit through another country.

Buyer must:

1. Accept the documents when presented.
2. Receive the goods upon arrival, handle and pay for all subsequent movement of the goods, including taking delivery from vessel in accordance with bill of lading clauses and terms; pay all costs of landing, including any duties, taxes, and other expenses at named point of destination.
3. Pay for war risk insurance provided by seller.
4. Be responsible for loss of or damage to goods, or both, from time and place at which seller's obligations under 6 or 7 above have ceased.
5. Pay the cost of certificates of origin, consular invoices, or any other documents issued in the country of origin, or of shipment, or both, which may be required for importation of the goods into the country of destination and, where necessary, for their passage in transit through another country.

C. & F. AND C.I.F. COMMENTS

Under C. & F. and C.I.F. contracts there are the following points on which the seller and the buyer should be in complete agreement at the time that the contract is concluded:

1. It should be agreed upon in advance who is to pay for miscellaneous expenses, such as weighing or inspection charges.

2. The quantity to be shipped on any one vessel should be agreed upon in advance, with a view to the buyer's capacity to take delivery upon arrival and discharge of the vessel, within the free time allowed at the port of importation.

3. Although the terms C. & F. and C.I.F. are generally interpreted to provide that charges for consular invoices and certificates of origin are for the account of the buyer and are charged separately, in many trades these charges are included by the seller in his price. Hence, seller and buyer should agree in advance whether these charges are part of the selling price, or will be invoiced separately.

4. The point of final destination should be definitely known in the event the vessel discharges at a port other than the actual destination of the goods.

5. When ocean freight space is difficult to obtain, or forward freight contracts cannot be made at firm rates, it is advisable that sales contracts, as an exception to regular C. & F. or C.I.F. terms, should provide that shipment within the contract period be subject to ocean freight space being available to the seller, and should also provide that changes in the cost of ocean transportation between the time of sale and the time of shipment be for account of the buyer.

6. Normally, the seller is obligated to prepay the ocean freight. In some instances, shipments are made freight collect and the

amount of the freight is deducted from the invoice rendered by the seller. It is necessary to be in agreement on this in advance, in order to avoid misunderstanding which arises from foreign exchange fluctuations which might affect the actual cost of transportation, and from interest charges which might accrue under letter of credit financing. Hence, the seller should always prepay the ocean freight unless he has a specific agreement with the buyer, in advance, that goods can be shipped freight collect.

7. The buyer should recognize that he does not have the right to insist on inspection of goods prior to accepting the documents. The buyer should not refuse to take delivery of goods on account of delay in the receipt of documents, provided the seller has used due diligence in their dispatch through the regular channels.

8. Sellers and buyers are advised against including in a C.I.F. contract any indefinite clause at variance with the obligations of a C.I.F. contract as specified in these definitions. There have been numerous court decisions in the United States and other countries invalidating C.I.F. contracts because of the inclusion of indefinite clauses.

9. Interest charges should be included in cost computations and should not be charged as a separate item in C.I.F. contracts, unless otherwise agreed upon in advance between the seller and buyer; in which case, however, the term C.I.F. and I. (Cost, Insurance, Freight, and Interest) should be used.

10. In connection with insurance under C.I.F. sales, it is necessary that seller and buyer be definitely in accord upon the following points:

a. The character of the marine insurance should be agreed upon in so far as being W.A. (With Average) or F.P.A. (Free of Particular Average), as well as any other special risks that are covered in specific trades, or against which the buyer may wish individual protection. Among the special risks that should be considered and agreed upon between seller and buyer are theft, pilferage, leakage, breakage, sweat, contact with other cargoes, and other peculiar to any particular trade. It is important that contingent or collect freight and customs duty should be insured to cover Particular Average losses, as well as total loss after arrival and entry but before delivery.

b. The seller is obligated to exercise ordinary care and diligence in selecting an underwriter that is in good financial standing. However, the risk of obtaining settlement of insurance claims rests with the buyer.

c. War risk insurance under this term is to be obtained by the seller at the expense and risk of the buyer. It is important that the

seller be in definite accord with the buyer on this point, particularly as to the cost. It is desirable that the goods be insured against both marine and war risk with the same underwriter, so that there can be no difficulty arising from the determination of the cause of the loss.

d. Seller should make certain that in his marine or war risk insurance, there be included the standard protection against strikes, riots, and civil commotions.

e. Seller and buyer should be in accord as to the insured valuation, bearing in mind that merchandise contributes in General Average on certain bases of valuation which differ in various trades. It is desirable that a competent insurance broker be consulted, in order that full value be covered and trouble avoided.

(VI) EX DOCK

(VI) "EX DOCK (named port of importation)"

Note: Seller and buyer should consider not only the definitions but also the "Ex Dock Comments" at the end of this section (page 706), in order to understand fully their respective responsibilities and rights under "Ex Dock" terms.

Under this term, seller quotes a price including the cost of the goods and all additional costs necessary to place the goods on the dock at the named port of importation, duty paid, if any.

Under this quotation:
Seller must:

1. Provide and pay for transportation to named port of importation.
2. Pay export taxes, or other fees or charges, if any, levied because of exportation.
3. Provide and pay for marine insurance.
4. Provide and pay for war risk insurance, unless otherwise agreed upon between the buyer and seller.
5. Be responsible for any loss or damage, or both, until the expiration of the free time allowed on the dock at the named port of importation.
6. Pay the costs of certificates of origin, consular invoices, legalization of bill of lading, or any other documents issued in the country of origin, or of shipment, or of both, which the buyer may require for the importation of goods into the country of destination and, where necessary, for their passage in transit through another country.
7. Pay all costs of landing, including wharfage, landing charges, and taxes, if any.
8. Pay all costs of customs entry in the country of importation.

9. Pay customs duties and all taxes applicable to imports, if any, in the country of importation, unless otherwise agreed upon.

Buyer must:

1. Take delivery of the goods on the dock at the named port of importation within the free time allowed.
2. Bear the cost and risk of the goods if delivery is not taken within the free time allowed.

Ex Dock Comments

This term is used principally in United States import trade. It has various modifications, such as "Ex Quay," "Ex Pier," etc., but it is seldom, if ever, used in American export practice. Its use in quotations for export is not recommended.

ABBREVIATIONS FOR UNITS OF QUANTITY

Abbreviation	Description
MBALE	1,000 bales
MBBL	1,000 barrels
MBU	1,000 bushels
MCAR	1,000 carats
MCWT	1,000 hundredweight
MLB	1,000 pounds
MLTN	1,000 long tons
MIL	1,000,000
MIL-LB	1,000,000 pounds
MPFG	1,000 proof gallons
MPR	1,000 pair
MSTN	1,000 short tons
MSYD	1,000 square yards
NO	Number

Acronyms and Abbreviations

A.A.R.	Against all risks
AATUF	All African Trade Union Federation
A.B.	Stock company (Swedish)
ACDA	Arms Control and Disarmament Agency
ADB	Asian Development Bank
ADELA	Atlantic Community Development Group for Latin America
ADP	Automatic data processing
ADR	America depository receipt
ADS	Agent Distributor Service
ADTS	Automated Data and Telecommunications Service
AEC	Atomic Energy Commission
AFL-CIO	American Federation of Labor—Congress of Industrial Organizations
A.G.	Incorporated (stock company) (German)
AICPA	American Institute of Certified Public Accountants
AID	Agency for International Development
AIDCA	Agro-Industrial Complex
AMS	Agricultural Marketing Service
Amtrak	National Railroad Passenger Corporation
ANCOM	Andean Common Market
A/P	Authority to purchase or authority to pay
APHIS	Animal and Plant Health Inspection Service
ARC	American Red Cross
ARO	Asian Regional Organization
ARS	Advanced Records Systems; Agricultural Research Service
A/S	Closed corporation or public corporation (Norwegian)
ASA	Association of Southeast Asia
ASCS	Agricultural Stabilization and Conservation Service
ASP	American selling price
ATUC	African Trade Union Federation
AUCCTU	Soviet Union Central Council of Trade
B/E	Bill of exchange
BEWT	Bureau of East West Trade
BIA	Bureau of Indian Affairs
BIC	Bureau of International Commerce
BIS	Bank for International Settlements
B/L	Bill of lading
BLS	Bureau of Labor Statistics
B.M.	Board measure
B.P.B.	Barrels per day
CAB	Civil Aeronautics Board
CACM	Central American Common Market
C.A.D.	Cash against documents
CAEU	Council of Arab Economic Opportunity
CAGNE	Commerce Action Group for the Near East
CAP	Civil Air Patrol
CARICOM	Caribbean Community and Common Market
CARIFTA	Caribbean Free Trade Area
CCC	Commodity Credit Corporation
CD	Certificate of deposit
C. & D.	Collection and delivery
CDC	Commonwealth Development Corporation (United Kingdom)
CEA	Council of Economic Advisors
CENEL	European Standards Coordinating Committee
CENTO	Central Treaty Organization
CETA	Comprehensive Employment and Training Act
C. & F.	Cost and freight
CFA	African Financial Community
C. F. & I.	Cost, freight, and insurance
CFR	Code of Federal Regulations
CFTC	Commodity Futures Trading Commission
C. & I.	Cost and insurance
Cia	Company (Spanish)
C.I.F.	Cost, insurance, freight
C. I. F. & C.	Cost, insurance, freight, and commission (or charges)
C. I. F. C. & I.	Cost, insurance, freight, commission (or charges), and insurance
C.I.F. & E.	Cost, insurance, freight, and exchange
CIPEC	Council of Copper Exporting Countries

CISL	Conferazine Italino Sindicati Lavoratori (Italian Confederation of Trade Unions)
CMEA	Council of Mutual Economic Assistance
COCOM	Coordinating Committee (for export control)
Co. Ltd.	Closed corporation
COMECON	Council for Mutual Economic Assistance (East European)
COPANT	Pan American Standards Commission
C. por A.	Closed corporation (Spanish)
CP	Commercial paper
CPSC	Consumer Products Safety Commission
CRS	Community Relations Service
CSC	Civil Service Commission
CSRS	Cooperative State Research Service
CWT	Hundredweight (100 pounds of the short ton or 112 pounds of the long ton)
CXT	Common external tariff
D/A	Documents against acceptance
DARPA	Defense Advanced Research Projects Agency
DC	Developed country
DCA	Defense Communications Agency
DCAA	Defense Contract Audit Agency
D/D	Days after date
DEA	Drug Enforcement Administration
DEG	German export finance
D.F.	Dead freight
DIBA	Domestic and International Business Administration
DISC	Domestic International Sales Corporation (U.S.)
D.N.	Debit note
DNA	Defense Nuclear Agency
DOD	Department of Defense
DOT	Department of Transportation
D/P	Documents against payment
D/S	Days after sight
DSA	Defense Supply Agency
DSAA	Defense Security Assistance Agency
DSR	Debt service ratio
D/TR	Documents against trust receipt
EC	European Community

ECGD	Export Credit Guarantee Department (United Kingdom)
ECLA	European Committee for Latin America
ECOSOC	Economic and Social Council
ECSC	European Coal and Steel Community
EDA	Economic Development Administration
EEC	European Economic Community
EEE	European Economic Community
EEOC	Equal Employment Opportunity Commission
EFTA	European Free Trade Association
EHS	Environmental Health Services
EIB	European Investment Bank
EMS	Export Marketing Service
E. & O.E.	Errors and omissions excepted
E.O.M.	End of month
EPA	Environmental Protection Agency
EPGA	Emergency Petroleum and Gas Administration
ERDA	Energy Research and Development Administration
ERISA	Employee Retirement Income Security Act of 1974
EROS	Earth Resources Observation Systems
ERS	Economic Research Service
ESA	Employment Standards Administration
ESARS	Employment Service Automated Reporting System
ESF	European Social Fund (U.S.)
ESOP	Employee Stock Ownership Plans
ETC	Export Trade Corporation (U.S.)
Ex	Point of origin
EXIMBANK	Export-Import Bank of the United States
FAA	Federal Aviation Administration
F.A.F.	Fly away field
FAIR	Fair access to insurance requirements
FAO	Food and Agricultural Organization (United Nations)
F.A.Q.	Free at quay
F.A.S.	Free along side

FAS	Foreign Agricultural Service	FRC	Federal Regional Councils
FASB	Financial Accounting Standards Board	FRS	Federal Reserve System
		FSLIC	Federal Savings and Loan Insurance Corporation
FBI	Federal Bureau of Investigation	FSS	Federal Supply Service
FCA	Farm Credit Administration	FTC	Federal Trade Commission (U.S.)
FCC	Federal Communications Commission	FTC	Foreign Trade Commission (Japan)
FCIA	Federal Credit Insurance Association	FTO	Foreign Trade Organization (USSR)
F.C. & S.	Free from capture and seizure	FTS	Federal Telecommunications System
FCS	Farmer Cooperative Service	F/X	Foreign exchange
FDA	Food and Drug Administration	G.A.	General average
		GAO	General Accounting Office
FDIC	Federal Deposit Insurance Corporation	GATT	General Agreement on Trade and Tariffs
FDPC	Federal Data Processing Centers	Gebr.	Brothers (German)
FEA	Federal Energy Administration	G.K.	United partnership (Japanese)
Fed	Federal Reserve System	G.m.b.H.	Limited liability company (German)
FHA	Federal Housing Administration	GNMA	Government National Mortgage Association (known as "Ginnie Mae")
FHLBB	Federal Home Loan Bank Board		
FHWA	Federal Highway Administration	GNP	Gross national product
		GPO	Government Printing Office
F.I.	Free in (expenses for loading into the hold of a ship are for the consignee's account)	GSA	General Services Administration
		G.T.	Gross time
		Handelsges.	Partnerships (German)
FIA	Federal Insurance Administration	H/B	Partnerships (Swedish)
		HEW	Department of Health, Education, and Welfare
FIC	Federal Information Centers	HFA	Housing Finance Agency
FICA	Foreign Insurance Credit Association (U.S.)	HGOC	House Government Operations Committee
FMC	Federal Maritime Commission	Hijo(s)	Son(s) (Spanish)
		Hnos	Brothers (Spanish)
FMCS	Federal Mediation and Conciliation Service	HRA	Health Resources Administration
FMHA	Farmers Home Administration	HUD	Department of Housing and Urban Development
FMO	Export Finance (Dutch)	IADB	Inter-American Defense Board
FNMA	Federal National Mortgage Association (known as "Fannie Mae")	IAEA	International Atomic Energy Administration
F.O.	Free out (expenses covering unloading from hold of a vessel are for consignee's account)	IATA	International Air Transport Association
		IBRD	International Bank for Reconstruction and Development (World Bank)
F.O.B.	Free on board (vessel)	ICAO	International Civil Aviation Organization
F.O.R.	Free on rails		
F.P.A.	Free of particular average	ICATO	International Conference of Arab Trade Unions
F.P.A.A.C.	Free of particular average American conditions		
F.P.A.E.C.	Free of particular average English conditions	ICC	Interstate Commerce Commission; Indian Claims Commission
FPC	Federal Power Commission		
FRA	Federal Railroad Administration	ISIC	International Standard Industrial Classification
FRB	Federal Reserve Board		

IDA	International Development Association	MFN	Most favored nation
IDB	Inter-American Development Bank	M/R	Mate's receipt
IFC	International Finance Corporation	MSC	Military Sealift Command
IFCTU	International Federation of Christian Trade Unions	MTMTS	Military Traffic Management and Terminal Service
ILO	International Labor Organization	M/V	Motor vessel
IMCO	Intergovernmental Maritime Consultative Organization	NAB	National Alliance of Businessmen
IMF	International Monetary Fund	NAE	National Academy of Engineering
Inc.	Incorporated	NARS	National Archives and Records Service
INTERPOL	International Criminal Police Organization	NAS	National Academy of Science
IPC	International Petroleum Company	NASA	National Aeronautics and Space Administration
IRS	Internal Revenue Service	NATO	North Atlantic Treaty Organization
ISO	International Organization for Standardization	NAT-OJT	National On-the-Job Training
ITS	International Trade Secretariat	NBS	National Bureau of Standards
ITU	International Telecommunications Union	NCUA	National Credit Union Association
JEC	Joint Economic Committee	NEA	National Energy Administration; Near East and South Asia Bureau
JETRO	Japan External Trade Organization	NHTSA	National Highway Safety Administration
JOBS	Job Opportunities in the Business Sector	NIER	National Industrial Equipment Reserve
K.B.	Limited partnership (Norwegian or Swedish)	NIH	National Institutes of Health
Kd.	Knock down	NLRB	National Labor Relations Board
K.G.	Limited partnerships (German)	NOAA	National Oceanic and Atmospheric Administration
K.G.K.	Limited partnerships with shares (Japanese)	N.O.E.	Not otherwise enumerated
K.K.	Public corporations (Japanese)	NRC	Nuclear Regulatory Commission
LAFTA	Latin-America Free Trade Association	NRC	National Research Council
L/C	Letter of credit	NSA	National Security Agency
LDC	Less developed country	NSC	National Security Council
LEAA	Law Enforcement Assistance Administration	NSF	National Science Foundation
LMSA	Labor Management Service Administration	n.s.f.	Not sufficient funds
LORAN	Long-range navigation	NTB	Nontariffs barrier
LTD	Limited liability company (British)	NTIS	National Technical Information Center
MA	Maritime Administration	NTSB	National Transportation Safety Board
MAC	Military Airlift Command; Municipal Assistance Corporation (New York City)	N/V	Public corporation (Dutch)
M.E.C.	Marine extension clause	O/A	Open account
MEDLARS	Medical Literature Analysis and Retrieval Systems	OAPEC	Organization of Arab Petroleum Exporting Countries
MESBIC	Minority Enterprise Small Business Investment Companies	OAS	Organization of American States
		OAU	Organization of African Unity
		O.C.P.	Overland common points
		OCR	Office of Coal Research
		O.E.C.D.	Organization for Economic

	Cooperation and Development		ish, Italian, Portuguese)
OEDP	Office of Employment Development Programs	SALT	Strategic Arms Limitation Talks
OEO	Office of Economic Opportunity	SARL	Corporation (French, Italian, Portuguese)
OEP	Office of Emergency Preparedness	SBA	Small Business Administration (U.S.)
OFCC	Office of Federal Contract Compliance	SBIC	Small Business Investment Companies
OFDI	Office of Foreign Direct Investments	S. de R. L.	Limited partnership (Spanish)
OMB	Office of Management and Budget	S. en C.	Limited partnership with shares (French, Spanish, Portuguese)
OMBE	Office of Minority Business Enterprise	S. en N.C.	Closed corporation (Spanish)
OMDP	Office of Manpower Development Programs	S. en N.C.	Partnership (Spanish)
ONR	Office of Naval Research	SCORE	Service Corporation of Retired Executives
OOG	Office of Oil and Gas		
OPEC	Organization of Petroleum Exporting Countries	SCS	Soil Conservation Service
		S/D	Site draft
OPIC	Overseas Private Investment Corporation (United Kingdom)	S/D—BL	Site draft with bill of lading attached
		S/D—D/P	Site draft, documents against payments
ORIT	Inter-American Regional Organization of Workers	SDR	Special drawing rights
O.R.L.	Owner's risk of leakage	SEATO	Southeast Asian Treaty Organization
OSHA	Occupational Safety and Health Administration	SEC	Securities and Exchange Commission
OTP	Office of Telecommunications Policy	SESA	Social and Economic Statistics Administration
OWRR	Office of Water Resources Research	SIC	Standard Industrial Classification
O/Y	Stock company (Finnish)	SITC	Standard International Trade Classification
PAHO	Pan-American Health Organization	S.L. & C.	Shipper's load and count
PBGC	Pension Benefit Guaranty Corporation	S.P.A.	Corporation (Italian)
		S.P.R.L.	Company of persons with limited liability (Belgium)
PEFCO	Private Export Funding Corporation (U.S.)	SRS	Statistical Reporting Service
PEP	Public Employment Program	S.S.	Steamship
		SSA	Social Security Administration
PHS	Public Health Service		
PICA	Private Investment Corporation for Asia	T/A	Trade acceptance
		TOP	Trade Opportunities Program
PMDS	Property Management and Disposal Service	T.T.	Telegraphic transfer
P/N	Promissory note	TUC	Trade Union Congress
Pty. Ltd.	Proprietary Limited (Australian)	TVA	Tennessee Valley Authority
		UAW	United Auto Workers
RCD	Regional Cooperation for Development	UIS	Unemployment Insurance Service
R & D	Research and Development		
REA	Rural Electrification Administration	UMTA	Urban Mass Transportation Administration
REAP	Rural Environmental Assistance Program	UNCTAD	United Nations Commission for Trade and Development
RIS	Regulatory Information System	UNDP	United Nations Development Program
R.R.	Railroad	UNESCO	United Nations Educational, Scientific and Cultural Or-
SA	Corporation (French, Span-		

	ganization	USN	United States Navy
UNICEF	United Nations International Children's Emergency Fund	USTC	United States Tariff Commission
UNIDO	United Nations Industrial Development Organization	USTS	United States Travel Service
UNITAR	United Nations Institute for Training and Research	VA	Veterans Administration
		VAT	Value added tax
UPU	Universal Postal Union	VRA	Voluntary Restraint Arrangement
USA	United States Army	W.A.	With average
USAF	United States Air Force	WFTU	World Federation of Free Trade Unions
USCG·	United States Coast Guard	WHO	World Health Organization
USDA	United States Department of Agriculture	WHTC	Western Hemisphere Trade Corporation (U.S.)
USES	United States Employment Service	WMO	World Meteorological Organization
USIA	United States Information Agency	W/R	Warehouse receipt
		W.R.	War risk
USIS	United States Information Service	WTDR	World Trades Data Report
USMC	United States Marine Corps	Y.K.	Limited Liability Company (Japanese)

Postal Information

First-class mail: Included in this category are typewritten or handwritten messages, bills, statements of account, postal cards, and postcards. Sealed matter that is mailed first class may not be opened for postal inspection.

Second-class mail: Newspapers and magazines published at least four times a year may be mailed as second-class mail provided a permit to do so has been obtained.

Third-class mail: Third-class mail consists of catalogs, booklets, newsletters, and other items such as photographs, merchandise, and some factory and farm products, e.g., cuttings and roots weighing no more than 1 pound. Third-class matter can be shipped as individual pieces or in bulk.

Pieces in a bulk mailing must be identical in size, weight, and number of enclosures, but the textual material need not be identical. Each piece must have a zip code and the entire mailing must be presorted and bound or tied by zip code.

Fourth-class mail (parcel post): This includes parcel post, library, and certain catalog mailings and is primarily used for material weighing between 1 and 70 pounds.

Certified mail: Certified mail service provides a receipt to the sender and a record of delivery at the office of address. No record is kept at the office at which the material is mailed. It will be dispatched and handled in transit as ordinary mail. No insurance coverage is provided. Return receipts and restricted delivery services may be obtained by the payment of additional fees. Any mailable matter of no intrinsic value on which postage at the first-class rate has been paid will be accepted as certified mail.

Registered mail: Registered mail provides added protection for valuable and important mail plus evidence of mailing and delivery and indemnity (insurance) in case of loss or damage. All mailable matter prepaid with postage at the first-class, air mail, or priority rates may be registered.

Special handling: Special handling service is available for third- and fourth-class mail only, including that which is insured or sent COD. It provides preferential handling to the extent practicable in dispatch and transportation, but does not provide special delivery. Special handling parcels are delivered as parcel post is ordinarily delivered —on regular scheduled trips.

Source: **U.S. Postal Service Manual:** Detailed descriptions of the various categories of mail service are available in the Postal Service Manual as well as in various publications which are generally available in local post offices.

Business Telecommunications Systems

TELEPHONE COMPANY SERVICES

The telephone company provides many services to the business community. These include:

Station-to-station: This is the call to make if you want to talk with anyone who answers.

Direct distance dialed: These are calls where the caller dials the number directly and no operator assistance is required.

Operator-assisted: Station-to-station calls requiring operator assistance are charged at a higher rate than those that are completed without an operator's help. Included are calls such as coin phone, collect, credit card, billed to a third number, code billing, time and charges (including hotel guest calls), sequence calls, and calls placed by the operator at customer request.

Person-to-person: Call person-to-person when you wish to talk to a particular person or extension number. Dial "0" and say you want to make a person-to-person call. You can also dial person-to-person calls.

Collect: Station-to-station or person-to-person calls may be made collect if the person or firm receiving the call agrees to pay the charges. Operator assistance is required.

Credit card: Bell System Credit Card holders may place calls and charge them to their credit card number. Credit cards may be obtained free of charge from the local telephone business office. Operator assistance is needed.

Bill to third number: Customers may place calls and transfer the charge to another telephone. This call may be either station-to-station or person-to-person and requires operator assistance.

Time and charges: Customers, when placing calls, may request from the operator the amount of time and the charge for the call. The call may be either station-to-station or person-to-person and operator assistance is required.

Conference arrangements: You can talk with several people in different places at the same time, either station-to-station or person-to-person. Dial the operator and say you want to make a conference call.

A portable conference telephone is also available which amplifies the telephone voice of a distant speaker so that it can be clearly heard by a group. It permits individual members of the audience to speak directly to the distant speaker, ask or answer questions, exchange views, and develop meaningful interaction.

Mobile: You can make local and long-distance calls to automobiles, trucks, aircraft, boats, and ships. Ask the operator for the Mobile, Marine, or High Seas operator.

Overseas calls: These can be either operator assisted or direct dialed. By simply dialing the appropriate area code and telephone number, calls can be placed to Alaska, Hawaii, Canada, Mexico City, certain border points, the Bahamas, the Virgin Islands, and Puerto Rico.

You can also dial your own station calls direct to the countries listed below.

Andorra	Japan
Australia	Liechtenstein
Austria	Luxembourg
Belgium	Monaco
Brazil	Netherlands
Chile	New Zealand
China, Rep. of	Norway
Costa Rica	Peru
Denmark	Philippines
El Salvador	San Marino
France	Singapore
Germany, Fed. Rep.	South Africa
Greece	Spain
Guatemala	Sweden
Hong Kong	Switzerland
Ireland, Rep. of	United Kingdom
Israel	Vatican City
Italy	Venezuela

For station calls to all countries listed, "011" International Dialing procedures are followed; "011" is the simplest and fastest way to call abroad. A directory of country and city routing codes is available from the telephone company.

INTERNATIONAL DIALING INSTRUCTIONS

Station calls: To dial international station calls, dial in sequence:

1. The International Access Code—011.
2. The Country Code—a two- or three-digit number.
3. The City Routing Code—a one- to five-digit number.

Sources: American Telephone and Telegraph, New York Telephone Company, and Western Union.

4. The local telephone number—a two- to nine-digit number.
5. The "#" button—where the telephone is Touch-Tone equipped.

For example: To place a call to Germany (Country Code 49), Frankfurt (Routing Code 611), telephone number 123456, you would dial:

011	+	49	+ 611	+ 123456	+	#

International Access Code	Country Code	Routing Code	Local number	Button, if Touch-Tone equipped

After dialing the entire number, allow at least 45 seconds for the ring to start.

Also, because "0" (operator) is the first digit of the International Access Code (011), remember to dial the second digit (1) within 3 seconds, or you will reach the local operator.

Operator-assisted calls: Dial "0" if you need the operator's services. You do this if you are placing a person-to-person, collect, or credit card call, or if you are charging the call to a third number.

Dial "0" (operator) if you need assistance:

1. To obtain a telephone number you don't know.
2. To obtain City Routing Codes.
3. For help in completing a call.
4. For credit on a call on which you had difficulty, i.e., reached a wrong number.

DIALING NOTES

Signals (ringing, number busy, and others) in other countries often differ from those in the United States. Also, when overseas numbers are shown on letterheads or on business cards, they are usually preceded by a national access digit and the routing code. For example, a typical number may appear this way in a letterhead: (02) 123456. The first digit "0" is a national access digit and is used only when dialing within that foreign country; it should not be used when dialing from the United States. You would dial:

011 + Country Code + 2 + 123456

Wide area telecommunications service (WATS): WATS provides large-volume telephone users with markedly reduced costs. WATS can be purchased to cover various geographic regions or so-called bands.

Inward WATS: Station-to-station long-distance calls may be made, without charge to a caller, from certain locations to businesses that have wide area telecommunications service. To determine whether the party you want offers this service, dial area code 800 + 555-1212. This inward WATS directory assistance number serves the entire United States. There is no charge for the call.

Outward WATS: As many outgoing calls as desired can be placed during the service time purchased by a business for a previously arranged geographic region or band.

Personal signaling service: This service is provided by a small, lightweight portable receiver which alerts you to phone calls from authorized persons. You then call a prearranged number for the message.

Foreign exchange (FX) service: This provides a company with a telephone listing in a distant city's telephone directory. Customers at the distant location call the local number and are directly connected to the home office. Calls to and from the home office are made as local calls.

Special reverse charge call: This operator-assisted call provides a listing in the out-of-town directory in the form of a prefix (such as "Zenith" or "Enterprise") plus a four-digit number. The telephone directory listing requests the customer to call the operator and ask for the listed number. The operator then places the call and charges the home office.

WESTERN UNION BUSINESS SERVICES

Western Union offers a number of services to the business community, many of which include the transmission of printed messages. This service is often less expensive than the telephone services and has the advantage of providing a printed record of the communication. Two automated telewriter services are available: **Telex,** a message-oriented, 66-word-per-minute service, and **TWX,** a message- and data-oriented, 100-word-per-minute service. Both systems can communicate with each other by means of a computer interface. The teletypewriters can be purchased or leased from Western Union as well as from other manufacturers.

The general public may utilize the services of Western Union by dialing a toll-free local number and dictating the message to an operator. Users possessing teletype equipment (Telex or TWX) may communicate directly with the Western Union office or with other teletype stations.

Service includes the following: The **telegram** is now principally used for business purposes. Telephone delivery is guaranteed within 2 hours, and, at the recipient's request, the message will also be mailed. Messenger delivery, available in most places, is guaranteed within 5 hours for an additional fee. Classes of service include telegram and overnight telegram (night letter); the latter is delivered by 2 P.M. the following day.

Personal opinion telegrams are a service by which messages can be sent to the President, Vice President, congressmen, and senators in Washington, DC, or to governors, lieutenant governors, and state representatives and senators at their respective state capitals.

International telegram (cablegram) traffic is accepted by Western Union for domestic transmission to the international carriers who handle transmission to the overseas delivering agency. Classes of service include fast cablegram and letter telegram. **International money order** traffic is, in all but a few cases, turned over by Western Union to American Express for overseas transmission and delivery.

Mailgram service, a joint offering of Western Union and the United States Postal Service, allows messages to be sent electronically to any location in the United States for delivery with the next business day's mail.

The general public can enter a mailgram message either by a toll-free call to Western Union or at one of the company's public offices. All telephone calls are received at one of three Central Telephone Bureaus, where telephone operators record and then forward the messages.

Customers equipped with facsimile and word teleprocessing machines compatible with equipment at a Central Telephone Bureau can send mailgrams by calling and transmitting messages directly to the bureau.

Confirmation service is available for any mailgram message, and is delivered to the sender by either first-class mail or another mailgram transmission. For large users of the mailgram, **business reply mailgram** provides a postage-paid return envelope with the regular mailgram so that the addressee can return it to the sender with an enclosure. Certified return receipt service offers certification of delivery of the message by a standard return receipt.

By inputting mailgram messages on magnetic tape, the high-volume user can have thousands of messages transmitted simultaneously—as a common text to many addresses, as a different text to each address, as a common text with variable inserts, or as a mix of all three. Western Union will provide assistance to the user's data processing operation in preparing the magnetic tape, or the user can have the magnetic tape prepared by a service bureau.

Western union stored electronic mailgram service uses a computer system at McLean, VA, to store address lists, key paragraphs of frequently used texts, and signature elements previously filed by subscribers to the service. Stored mailgram service can be accessed either through a terminal leased to the customer or by a toll-free phone call to a Western Union Central Telephone Bureau. The customer then calls out of the computer any of the coded stored material he wishes to use, adds any new text or other message elements, and the packaged transmission is sent on its way into the mail delivery stream.

Domestic money orders, the original form of electronic funds transfer, are heavily used by businesses and individuals. The traditional basic service is still used; the sender pays the principal sum over the counter at a public office or agency and that sum is payable to a specific addressee at a specific destination office. Western Union notifies the recipient when the money is available and where to call for it.

In addition, Western Union has established a **Money Order Central** with toll-free telephone access, offering a number of variations on funds transfer by telephone. Transfer of money to authorized points in the continental United States, Canada, and Mexico is available to individuals with Master Charge credit cards. They can send up to $300 by calling Money Order Central.

Telephone-to-telephone money order service permits the sender to originate money orders by telephone through Money Order Central at Mount Vernon, IL, without specifying destination. The payee then selects a Western Union office or agency paying location, which calls Money Order Central, verifies the existence of a money order, and receives authorization to make payment. Supplementary messages may be included. This service is by prior arrangement and authorization and is available to business establishments only.

Stored address list services available to Telex and TWX subscribers eliminate hours of repetitive typing and the mailing procedures of addressing, inserting, and stamping. With RediList, stored address lists can be called out by computer and a common text message delivered to each addressee by Telex, TWX, mailgram service, telegram, or any combination of these.

NiteCast prestores address lists, accepts a common text message, stores it until evening hours, and has it printed out in the recipient's Telex or TWX terminal by 8:00 A.M. the next morning. The off-peak transmission permits cost savings.

Additional services designed particularly for Telex/TWX subscribers include:

Datagram links a central operation with its field representatives, installations, or customers. A user calls Western Union toll-free, gives his Datagram identification number, and dictates the message for headquarters. The Central Telephone Bureau operator keyboards the message—either as straight text or as fill-in for a prestored format such as a standard report form or order blank. It is then transmitted to headquarters, where it is printed out on a Telex or TWX machine.

FYI News Service furnishes, either automatically by subscription or on demand by dial-up request, current news summaries on a variety of subjects. Commodity futures and prices, sports, government activities, and special interest items are included in the catalog of available information.

Facsimile service: The Facsimile Transceiver (FAX) both transmits and receives a reproduction of a page. FAX is highly useful for rapid transmission of urgently needed materials or formatted information that would be difficult—if not technically impossible—to explain orally, type, or redraw.

This can include typewritten copy, engineering drawings, photographs, or complicated charts.

Most FAX machines currently in use can transmit the contents of a conventional business-size page ($8\frac{1}{2} \times 11$ inches) in 4–6 minutes. Transceivers that take 1 minute or less are not yet in wide use because the cost for this relatively new technology is still high. Because of cost, this service is at present not recommended for lengthy documents.

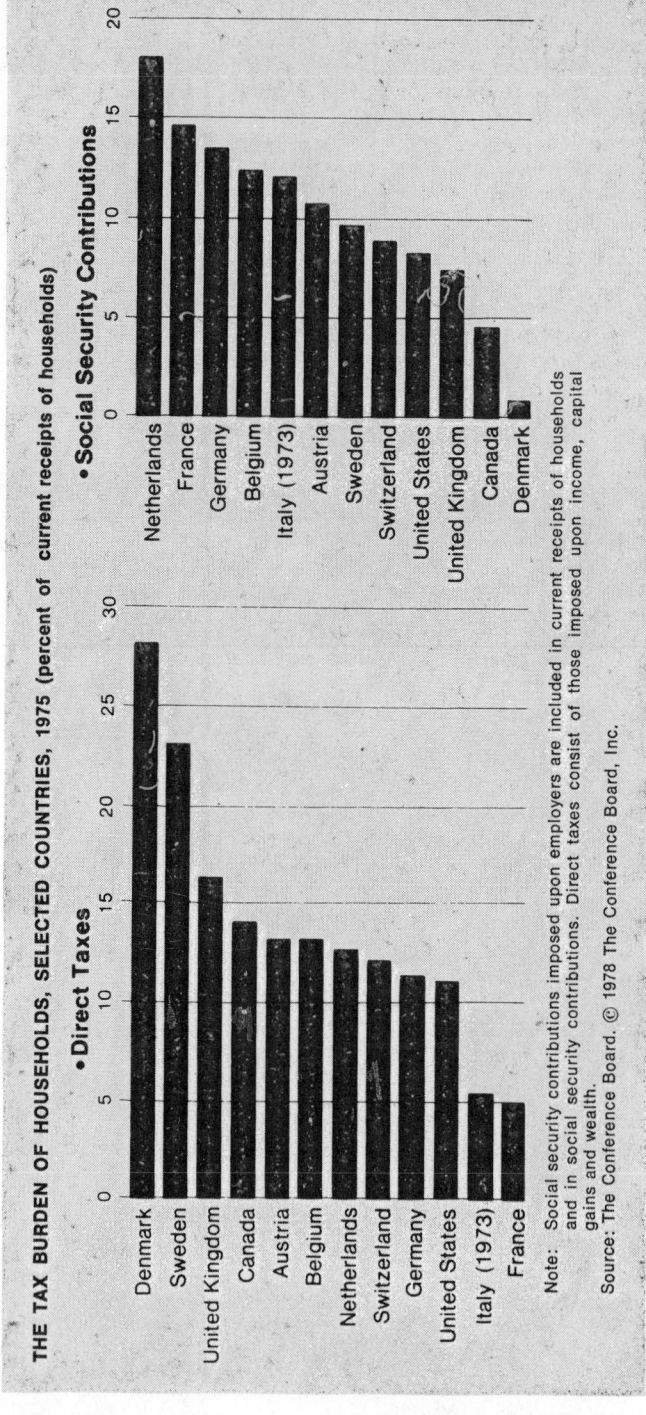

THE TAX BURDEN OF HOUSEHOLDS, SELECTED COUNTRIES, 1975 (percent of current receipts of households)

• Social Security Contributions

• Direct Taxes

Note: Social security contributions imposed upon employers are included in current receipts of households
        and in social security contributions. Direct taxes consist of those imposed upon income, capital
        gains and wealth.

Source: The Conference Board. © 1978 The Conference Board, Inc.

International Trade Shows and Fairs*

Business-sponsored events: U.S. trade centers are available to American firms wishing to display, market, and sell their equipment and services or to hold training programs or seminars. Market counseling and trade center facilities are provided without charge.

Catalog Events (CE): Commerce-organized and managed displays of the catalogs and brochures of U.S. companies in selected foreign markets.

Commercial and Industrial Fairs: Commerce-managed exhibitions in selected overseas markets. Except for "solo" promotions, these events are held in conjunction with established International Trade Fairs or especially important National Trade Fairs.

In-Store Promotions (ISP): Marketing events for U.S.-manufactured consumer goods held by specific retail establishments in selected foreign countries.

Joint Export Establishment Promotion (JEEP): A small trade center exhibition designed for the sole purpose of introducing U.S. companies in the market.

"Solo" Commercial Fair: A commercial fair organized and managed by the U.S. Department of Commerce for the sole purpose of exhibiting U.S.-made products. These events are held in markets where market research indicates favorable opportunities for the sale of U.S.-made products, but where other suitable promotion vehicles are not available.

Target Industries (TIR): Fifteen industry segments that have been selected by the

U.S. Department of Commerce for special trade promotion emphasis.

Seminar Mission (SM): Events with all of the features of specialized trade missions but with the addition of organized formal presentations of papers by the members in each city visited.

Specialized Trade Mission (STM): U.S. government trade mission.

Trade Center Exhibitions: Scheduled exhibitions of U.S.-made products in U.S. trade centers in response to favorable market research.

Trade Missions: Organized trips by groups of U.S. businessmen that feature U.S. government-sponsored business receptions and preplanned appointments. Specialized Trade Missions (STM) are organized, managed, and led by staff officers selected by the U.S. Department of Commerce; missions that are organized, managed, and led by industry groups with U.S. government approval and support are designated (ITM).

(Certain commodities may not be exported from the United States for exhibition or demonstration abroad without specific prior approval from the Office of Export Administration. For information on commodities to be exhibited or demonstrated contact the Exporters' Service Branch or call (202) 377-4811.)

U.S. Trade Centers: Permanent product exhibit facilities in selected overseas locations operated by the U.S. Department of Commerce.

Video/Catalog Exhibitions (VTR/CE): Commerce-organized and managed exhibitions co-sponsored by relevant trade associations featuring new product presentations on video tape along with displays of full line catalogs. These events can be held in many locations at the same time.

---

* Provided by the U.S. Department of Commerce, Domestic and International Business Administration, Bureau of International Commerce, Office of International Marketing. The information contained herein is the best available at the time of publication and is subject to change. For further information call the appropriate number listed in the International Marketing Directory on page 730.

EXHIBITIONS IN 1979

Trade Centers	January	February	March	April	May	June
London (International Marketing Center)	Special promotional activities			International fire, security and safety exhibition and conference [Offsite] 4/23–27	Special promotional activities	Fast food handling and catering equipment [Offsite] 6/18–22
Cologne (International Marketing Center)	Special promotional activities	International Hardware Fair (Building supplies and equipment) [Offsite] Cologne] 2/18–20	DIDACTA (Audio-visual equipment educational aids) [Offsite: Duesseldorf] 3/27–29	Special promotional activities	INTERHOSPITAL '79 (Health care industries equipment) [Offsite: Duesseldorf] 5/27–31	Special promotional activities
Paris (International Marketing Center)	Pleasure boats and equipment 1/11–22 (Paris Boat Show) HYPER '79; Micro-wave equipment (LSE) 1/16–19	Special promotional activities	Special promotional activities	COMPOSANT '79 (Electronic components) [Offsite] 4/2–7	MACROPAK (Packaging equipment) [Offsite: Netherlands] 5/14–19	Business equipment 6/5–8 Sporting goods and recreation equipment [Offsite: Amsterdam]
Milan (International Marketing Center)	Electronica '79 (Electronic production and test equipment and electronic components) 1/23–26 (LSE)	Hi-fi equipment (LSE) Computers and peripheral equipment [Offsite: Rome] 2/6–9	Energy conservation systems and seminar 3/26–30	Special promotional activities	GEC (Printing and graphic arts) [Offsite] 5/19–27	EDP '79 (Computers and peripheral) 6/12–15
Tokyo	Emergency medical equipment 1/29–2/2	Avionics and ground support equipment 2/27–3/3	Printing and graphic arts 3/26–30	Privately sponsored events	Privately sponsored events	Laboratory instruments 6/11–15

Sydney (International Marketing Center)	Special promotional activities	AIMEX (Mining and exploration) [Offsite] 2/12–17	Special promotional activities	Computer and related equipment/business equipment [Offsite; Melbourne] 4/2–6	Special promotional activities	Automotive and test equipment
Sao Paulo	METROLOGY (Measurement, tooling, and light machine tools) 1/15–19	Computer and peripheral equipment 2/12–16	Communications equipment 3/26–30	Privately sponsored events	Privately sponsored events	Equipment for the chemical and petrochemical industry 6/4–8
Singapore (International Marketing Center) ..	Special promotional activities	Agribusiness (AME/FPP) [Offsite: Bangkok] 2/12–16	Special promotional activities	Electronics industry production test equipment 4/23–28	Special promotional activities	Shipbuilding and repair [Offsite] 6/11–16
Taipei	Privately sponsored events	Industrial quality and process control instruments and equipment 2/19–23	Privately sponsored events	Privately sponsored events	Communications instruments and equipment 5/14–18	Pollution control equipment 6/11–15
Mexico City	Privately sponsored events	PETROAVANCE '79 (Petroleum production and handling equipment) 2/6–8	Privately sponsored events	Vehicular and motor maintenance equipment 4/24–27	Privately sponsored events	Metalworking and finishing equipment 6/12–15
Tehran	Electrical energy equipment 1/14–18	Privately sponsored events	EDP/Business equipment 3/4–8	Privately sponsored events	Privately sponsored events	Industrial renovation equipment
Moscow	Industrial packaging equipment 1/15–19	Special promotional activities	New technology in mining 3/12–16	Medical equipment	Materials test equipment 5/14–18	Electrical power systems

EXHIBITIONS IN 1979 (continued)

Trade Centers	July	August	September	October	November	December
London (International Marketing Center)	Special promotional activities	Special promotional activities		Business equipment [Offsite: Birmingham] 10/23–11/1	Electronic components [Offsite] 11/20–23	Computer and peripheral equipment 12/3–5
Cologne (International Marketing Center)	Laser opto-elektronic (Laser/electro-optics) [Offsite: Munich] 7/2–6	Special promotional activities	SYSTEMS '79 (Computers) [Offsite: Munich] 9/17–21 DATA KONTOR (Computers) [Offsite: Sweden] 9/6–9	KUNSTOFFE (Plastics and rubber production equipment) [Offsite: Duesseldorf] 10/10–17 Process control instrumentation [Offsite: Stockholm] 10/18–24	PRODUCTRONICA (Electronics industry production equipment and test equipment [Offsite: Munich] 11/6–10	Process control instrumentation [Offsite] 12/10–15 Industrial assembly/trans. gears/P.V.C. [Offsite] 12/3–8
Paris (International Marketing Center)	Special promotional activities	Special promotional activities	Housewares 9/25–28 EQUIP-AUTO '79 (Automotive and repair equipment)	Hotel, restaurant, and catering equipment 10/14–22 Industrial and commercial security equipment [Offsite: Utrecht] 10/15–19	Special promotional activities	
Milan (International Marketing Center)	Special promotional activities	Special promotional activities	Thessaloniki Fair [Offsite: Greece]	Machine tools [Offsite] 10/10–18 Electronic component/electronic industrial production and test equipment [Offsite: Barcelona]	Special promotional activities	Medical equipment (International medical exhibition) [Offsite: Stockholm] 12/5–8
Tokyo	Privately sponsored events	Privately sponsored events	Privately sponsored events	Privately sponsored events	Rehabilitation equipment 11/5–9	Test and measurement equipment 12/3–7

Sydney (International Marketing Center)	International engineering exhibition [Offsite: Melbourne] 7/23–28	Printing and graphic arts	Special promotional activities	Educational training aids	Special promotional activities	Special promotional activities
Sao Paulo	Privately sponsored events	Laboratory and scientific instruments 8/20–24	Energy systems 9/17–21	Privately sponsored events	Privately sponsored events	Ceramic industries equipment 12/3–7
Singapore (International Marketing Center)	Computers and peripheral equipment 7/30–8/3	Industrial process control instruments and equipment	Special promotional activities	Special promotional activities	Printing and packaging equipment [Offsite] 11/5–9	Special promotional activities
Taipei	Electrical energy systems 7/23–27	Privately sponsored events	Plant operations equipment (Security, materials handling, and maintenance) 9/10–14	Privately sponsored events	Privately sponsored events	Metalworking and machine tools [Offsite]
Mexico City	Communications equipment 7/9–13	Privately sponsored events	Furniture production equipment	Privately sponsored events	Computers '80	Privately sponsored events
Tehran	Privately sponsored events	Privately sponsored events	Tehran International Fair [Offsite]	Privately sponsored events	Privately sponsored events	Privately sponsored events
Moscow	Special promotional activities	Special promotional activities	Recycling of materials	Printing and graphic arts	Chemical analytical equipment	Special promotional activities

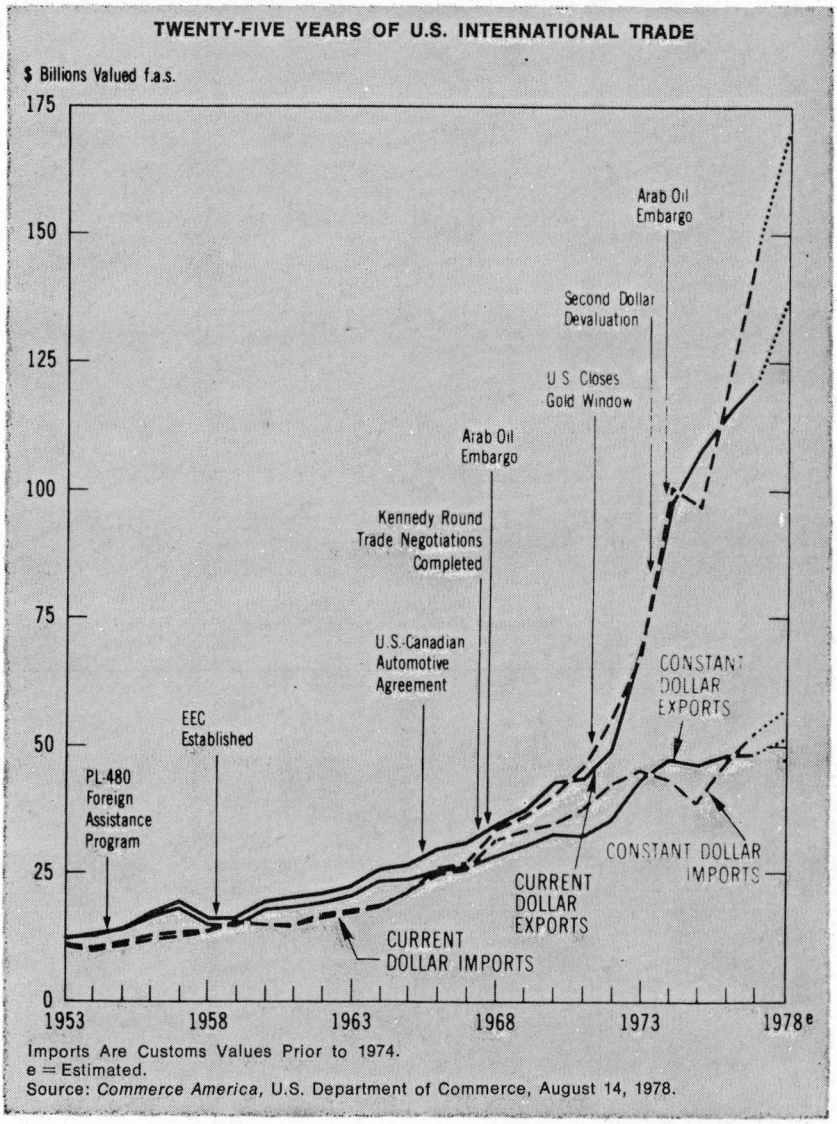

TWENTY-FIVE YEARS OF U.S. INTERNATIONAL TRADE

$ Billions Valued f.a.s.

PL-480
Foreign
Assistance
Program

EEC
Established

U.S.-Canadian
Automotive
Agreement

Kennedy Round
Trade Negotiations
Completed

Arab Oil
Embargo

U S Closes
Gold Window

Second Dollar
Devaluation

Arab Oil
Embargo

CONSTANT
DOLLAR
EXPORTS

CONSTANT DOLLAR
IMPORTS

CURRENT
DOLLAR
EXPORTS

CURRENT
DOLLAR IMPORTS

Imports Are Customs Values Prior to 1974.
e = Estimated.
Source: *Commerce America*, U.S. Department of Commerce, August 14, 1978.

COMMERCIAL AND INDUSTRIAL FAIRS 1979

January	Caracas	Petroleum on-shore/off-shore explorations, drilling, production, and pipeline equipment (Solo) 1/23–27
March	Cairo	International Fair
	Leipzig	Leipzig Spring Fair (Industrial equipment)
	Seoul	Metal working and finishing equipment 3/26–30
April	Casablanca	International Fair 4/27–5/13
May	Budapest	Budapest Spring Fair (Electronic equipment)
June	Paris	Air Show (Avionics/aviation ground support) 6/9–17
	Tel Aviv	Technology '79
	Drahan	Building and construction equipment
	Poznan	Technical Fair (General industrial equipment)
	Caracas	Agricultural machinery and equipment 6/5–9
	Moscow	Land reclamation
July	Damascus	International Fair
August	Caracas	Heavy equipment (Construction, mining, materials handling) (Solo) 8/7–11
September	Zagreb	Fall Fair (General industrial equipment)
	Brno	Engineering Fair (Laboratory instruments) 9/14–22
	Caracas	Medical equipment (Solo) 9/11–15
October	Budapest	MIPEL (Industrial electronics)
	Manama	Middle East materials handling
November	Caracas	Pollution control (Solo)

TRADE MISSIONS, TECHNICAL SALES SEMINARS, AND CATALOG EXHIBITIONS 1979

Geographic Region	January	February	March	April	May	June
Western Europe ..	Lasers and electro-optics, Czechoslovakia/Hungary/Poland/Austria (SM)	Packaging equipment and materials, Belgium (CE)		Autoparts/accessories, (AUTOVAK) Netherlands (CE) Housewares/household products, Netherlands (CE)	Water technology, Belgium (CE)	Metalworking/finishing equipment, Belgium (CE)
Southern Europe ...		Commercial and industrial security equipment, Spain/Portugal/Switzerland/Italy (STM) Construction equipment, Syria/Turkey/Greece (STM)		Metallurgical process equipment, Yugoslavia (see CAGNE below) (SM)	Industrial process control instruments and equipment, Yugoslavia (CE)	
Japan/Australia/New Zealand ..		Electronic industry association, Japan (ITM)	Timber industries equipment, Australia/Papau New Guinea/New Zealand (STM) State of Michigan, Australia/New Zealand/Taiwan/Hong Kong (ITM)	Pennsylvania Bureau of International Commerce, Japan/Korea/Taiwan (ITM)	Fishing equipment, New Zealand/Papua New Guinea/Korea (CE)	
Near East (CAGNE) .	Water resources, Oman/United Arab Emirates (STM)	Construction equipment, Syria/Turkey/Greece (STM) Housewares, Iran (VTR/CE) Dallas Chamber of Commerce, Saudi Arabia/Iran (ITM)	Health care industries, Iraq/Saudi Arabia (STM)	Communications equipment, Saudi Arabia/Egypt (STM) South Carolina, Saudi Arabia/Iran/United Arab Emirates (ITM) Electrical energy systems,	Housewares, Qatar/Bahrain/United Arab Emirates (VTR/CE)	Plastic production equipment, Algeria/Morocco/Tunisia (VTR/CE)

Far East	Health care equipment, India (4 stops) (CE); NMTBA (Metalworking equipment), India (ITM); Electric power equipment, Indonesia/Malaysia/Thailand (SM); State of Michigan, Australia/New Zealand/Taiwan/Hong Kong (ITM); Hospital/medical equipment, Korea/Hong Kong/Philippines (SM); Fishing equipment, New Zealand/Papua New Guinea/Korea (CE); Industrial process control, India (4 stops) (CE); Pennsylvania Bureau of International Commerce, Japan/Korea/Taiwan (ITM)
Latin America	Illinois state metalworking, Venezuela/Colombia/Bolivia (ITM); Energy Systems, Guatemala/Nicaragua/Costa Rica (CE); Building and construction equipment and supplies, Guatemala/Honduras/El Salvador (CE); Plastics production equipment, Ecuador/Peru/Chile (STM); Construction mining machinery, Argentina (CE); Illinois State automotive, Panama/Guatemala (ITM)
Africa	Housewares, Liberia/Nigeria (VTR/CE); Energy systems, Cameroon/Ivory Coast/Gabon/Nigeria (SM); Construction and engineering services, Nigeria/Sudan (STM); Food machinery, Cameroon/Ivory Coast/Kenya (VTR/CE); Sahellian agriculture, Senegal/Sudan (SM); Algeria/Morocco/Tunisia (SM)
East-West Trade (BEWT)	Lasers and electro-optics, Czechoslovakia/Hungary/Poland/Austria (SM); Sewing and garment production, Bulgaria/Romania/Czechoslovakia (SM); Printing and graphic arts, Finland/Hungary/Poland (SM); Metallurgical process equipment, Bulgaria/German Democratic Republic/Romania/Yugoslavia (SM); Packaging equipment, Czechoslovakia (VTR/CE); Machine tools, Bulgaria (VTR/CE); Resource recovery, Czechoslovakia/German Democratic Republic/Romania (SM)

TRADE MISSIONS, TECHNICAL SALES SEMINARS, AND CATALOG EXHIBITIONS 1979 (continued)

Geographic Region	July	August	September	October	November	December
Western Europe			Instrumentation, Netherlands (CE)	Computers/E.I.P.T./components, Switzerland (CE)	Furniture, Belgium (CE) Materials handling equipment, Netherlands (CE)	
Southern Europe ...				Medical equipment/laboratory equipment/process control, Spain/Israel (CE)	Electronic Industry production and test equipment, Greece (CE)	
Japan/Australia/ New Zealand				Music Makers USA, Australia (VTR/CE)	Power generation equipment, New Zealand/Australia (SM)	
Near East (CAGNE) .				Communications Equipment, Jordan/Oman/United Arab Emirates (STM) Medical equipment/laboratory equipment/process controls, Israel/Spain (CE)		Avionics, Iran/Saudi Arabia (STM) Franchise operations, Bahrain/Kuwait/Qatar/United Arab Emirates (STM)
Far East		Timber processing equipment, Indonesia/Malaysia (SM)	Pollution control equipment, Korea/Philippines/Malaysia (CE)	Mining earthmoving and materials, India (3 stops) (STM) Energy systems, Phillipines/Hong Kong/Korea (CE)	Farm machinery and equipment, Pakistan (4 stops) (CE) Consumer goods, Taiwan/Hong Kong/Singapore/Fiji (CE)	Metalworking and finishing, India (4 stops) (CE)
Latin America		Textile machinery, Chile/Colombia/Venezuela/Bolivia (CE)	Agriculture machinery and equipment, Nicaragua/Honduras/Panama (STM)	Educational systems, Venezuela/Dominican Republic/Ecuador (SM)	Health care equipment, Ecuador/Chile/Colombia (SM)	Timber and woodworking equipment, Venezuela/Colombia/Chile (STM)

Africa	Railroad equipment, Sudan/Kenya/Tanzania (STM)	Educational supplies and equipment, Nigeria (CE)	Prestressed concrete production machinery and construction equipment, Bolivia/Colombia/Ecuador (CE) Plastic industry equipment, Nigeria/Kenya (CE)	Construction equipment, Ivory Coast/Cameroon/Zaire/Sudan (STM)	Industrial and agricultural chemicals, Ivory Coast/Cameroon/Gabon/Nigeria (STM)
East-West trade (BEWT)			Packaging equipment, Hungary (VTR/CE) Chemical processing, German Democratic Republic (CE)		

INTERNATIONAL MARKETING DIRECTORY

Assistance or information about overseas marketing may be obtained by dialing key people directly: 202–377 plus the given ex- tension. For information related to specific countries contact the Country Marketing Manager:

Africa (sub-Sahara)	4927
Europe	
France and Benelux countries	4504
Germany and Austria	5228
Italy, Greece, and Turkey	3944
Nordic countries	3848
Spain, Portugal, Switzerland, and Yugoslavia	2795
United Kingdom and Canada	4421
Far East	
Australia and New Zealand	3646
East Asia and the Pacific	5401
Japan	2425
South Asia	2522
Latin America	
Brazil, Argentina, Paraguay, and Uruguay	5427
Mexico, Central America, and Panama	2314
Remainder of South America and Caribbean countries	2995
East West Trade	
U.S.S.R. Affairs Division	4655
Eastern European Affairs Division	2645
People's Republic of China Division	3583

EXHIBITION INFORMATION: NONGOVERNMENT SOURCES

A private organization, Successful Meetings, 1422 Chestnut Street, Philadelphia, PA 19102 (215-563-0680), provides a world data bank service of meetings in various areas of business.

Help in planning and exhibiting exhibits is provided by Exhibit Designers and Producer Association, 521 Fifth Avenue, New York, NY 10017 (212-MU7-9071).

FOREIGN BUYER PROGRAM

This program is designed to promote increased foreign business visitors to the United States for the purpose of purchasing American products and services. The Foreign Buyer Program provides substantive assistance to individuals and groups of foreign visitors to ensure the accomplishment of business objectives during their stay in the United States. Facilitative services include identifying U.S. suppliers, services, and technology. This service also includes setting up complete itineraries, business appointments, plant visits, seminars, and other arrangements best suited to the visitors' business objectives and providing the visitors with the names of U.S. firms exhibiting at domestic trade shows which are seeking business partners (agents/distributors, etc.) abroad. Further information may be obtained by calling 202-377-2256.

Source: Foreign Buyer Program, Domestic and International Business Administrator, U.S. Department of Commerce.

FOREIGN BUYER PROGRAM: U.S. TRADE SHOWS

January 6–10: International Western Apparel and Equipment Market
Address: Merchandise Mart, Denver, Colorado
Sponsor: Mountain States Western Apparel Club, 4585 Denver Merchandise Mart, Denver, CO 80216
Contact: Executive Director, 303-573-7440

January 10–15: (NAVA '79) National Audio-Visual Convention and Exhibit
Address: Rivergate, New Orleans, Louisiana
Sponsor: National Audio-Visual Association (NAVA), 3510 Spring Street, Fairfax, VA 22030
Contact: Exhibit Manager, 703-273-7200

January 15–18: National Housewares Exposition (NHMA)
Address: McCormick Place, Chicago, Illinois
Sponsor: National Housewares Manufacturers Association (NHMA), 1130 Merchandise Mart, Chicago, IL 60654
Contact: Managing Director, 312-644-3333

February 8–11: National Sporting Goods Association (NSGA) Show
Address: McCormick Place, Chicago, Illinois
Sponsor: National Sporting Goods Association (NSGA), 717 N. Michigan Avenue, Chicago, IL 60611
Contact: Assistant Executive Director, 312-944-0205

February 25–March 2: INTELCOM '77 (World Communications Exposition)
Address: Convention Center, Dallas, Texas
Sponsor: Horizon House International, 610 Washington Street, Dedham, MA 02026
Contact: Director of Programs, 617-326-8220, Telex: 928-289-MICROSOL

April 1–6: IEEE/PES Conference and Exposition on Overhead and Underground Transmission and Distribution
Address: Georgia World Congress Center, Atlanta, Georgia
Sponsors: Institute of Electrical and Electronic Engineers, New York; Power Engineering Society
Contact: International Coordinator, 404-522-6060

June 4–7: National Computer Conference (NCC-79)
Address: Coliseum, New York, New York
Sponsor: American Federation of Information Processing Societies (AFIPS), 210 Summit Avenue, Montvale, NJ 07645
Show contact and management: Executive Director, 201-391-9810

June 18–22: National Plastics Exposition (NPE '79)
Address: McCormick Place, Chicago, Illinois
Sponsors: The Society of the Plastics Industry, Inc., 355 Lexington Avenue, New York, NY 10017
Contact: 175 W. 93rd Street, New York, NY 10025, 212-865-5087
Show management: Robert T. Kenworthy, Inc., 866 United Nations Place, New York, NY 10025

October 24–27: Fish Expo '79
Address: Coliseum, Seattle, Washington
Producer/sponsor: National Fisherman Exposition, Inc., 21 Elm Street, Camden, ME 04843
Contact: General Manager, 207-236-4342

November 3–6: American Meat Institute—Annual Meeting
Address: McCormick Place, Chicago, Illinois

Sponsor: American Meat Institute, P.O. Box 3556, Washington, DC 20007
Contact: Director of Conventions and Meetings, 703-841-2400

WORLD COMMERCIAL HOLIDAYS: TIPS FOR U.S. BUSINESS TRAVELERS

Business travelers may find office doors locked and their intended contacts unavailable unless they take commercial holidays into consideration when planning itineraries. Commercial holidays in more than 100 countries are listed each year in the December issue of *Commerce America*. State Department Desk officers, listed on p. 647, can also provide this information.

There are hundreds of commercial holidays abroad which U.S. business executives are advised to consider in planning overseas travel. In fact, there are only a few days when there will be no commercial holiday somewhere in the world which will probably close both business and government offices in the celebrating countries.

Many commercial holidays occur on different calendar dates from year to year. Holidays and even weekends often vary from country to country and from region to region. Some holidays do not recur from one year to the next, while other holidays may vary in duration as well as in calendar date.

In cases where holidays fall on Saturday or Sunday, commercial establishments may be closed on the preceding Friday or the following Monday.

For many countries, such as those in the Muslim world, holiday dates can be only approximate because they are based on the lunar calendar. Note that references to the Muslim holidays often vary in spelling and in dates, and that businesses in many Muslim countries are closed on Fridays.

It is suggested that U.S. holidays be taken into account when making appointments with U.S. commercial officers abroad.

Source: *Commerce America.*

Index